WESTERN
CIVILIZATIONS
VOLUME 1

WORLD · POLITICAL

NATIONAL BOUNDARIES

While man's impact is quite evident, and even striking, on many remotely sensed scenes, sometimes, as in the case with most political boundaries, it is invisible. State, provincial, and national boundaries can follow natural features, such as mountain ridges, rivers, or coastlines. Artificial constructs that possess no physical reality—for example, lines of latitude and longitude—can also determine political borders. The world political map (right) represents man's imaginary lines as they slice and divide Earth.

The National Geographic Society recognizes 192 independent states in the world as represented here. Of those nations, 185 are members of the United Nations.

Winkel Tripel Projection

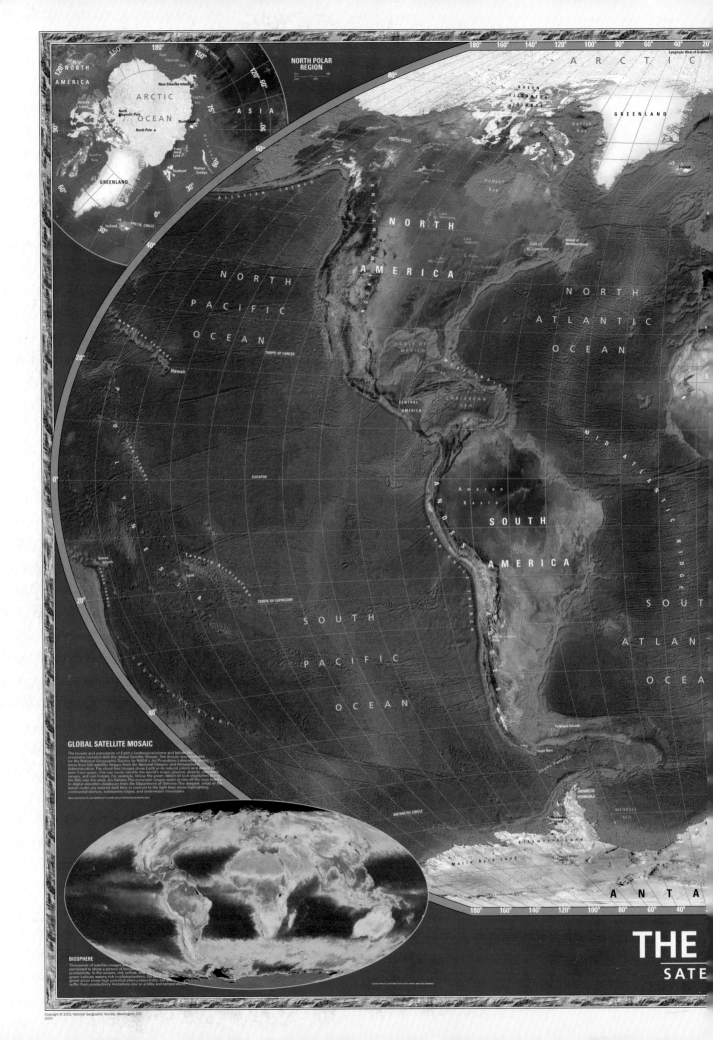

GLOBAL SATELLITE MOSAIC

The beauty and complexity of Earth's landscapes—above and below the oceans—is revealed with the Global Satellite Mosaic. The mosaic was produced for the National Geographic Society by NASA's Jet Propulsion Laboratory using more than 500 satellite images from the National Oceanic and Atmospheric Administration. The cloud-free images show Earth in its natural colors as it would be seen from space. One can easily identify the world's major glaciers, deserts, mountain ranges, and rain forests. For example, follow the green ribbon of lush vegetation along the Nile into the stark, dry Sahara. The mountain ranges seem to rise off the map thanks to digital elevation databases from the Department of Defense. The deepest areas of the ocean realm are colored dark blue in contrast to the light blue areas highlighting continental shelves, submarine ridges, and underwater mountains.

BIOSPHERE

Thousands of satellite images are combined to show a picture of biological productivity. In the oceans, red, yellow, and green indicate waters rich in phytoplankton. On land, green areas show high-potential plant productivity; tan areas suffer from productivity limitations due to aridity and temperature.

THE

SATE

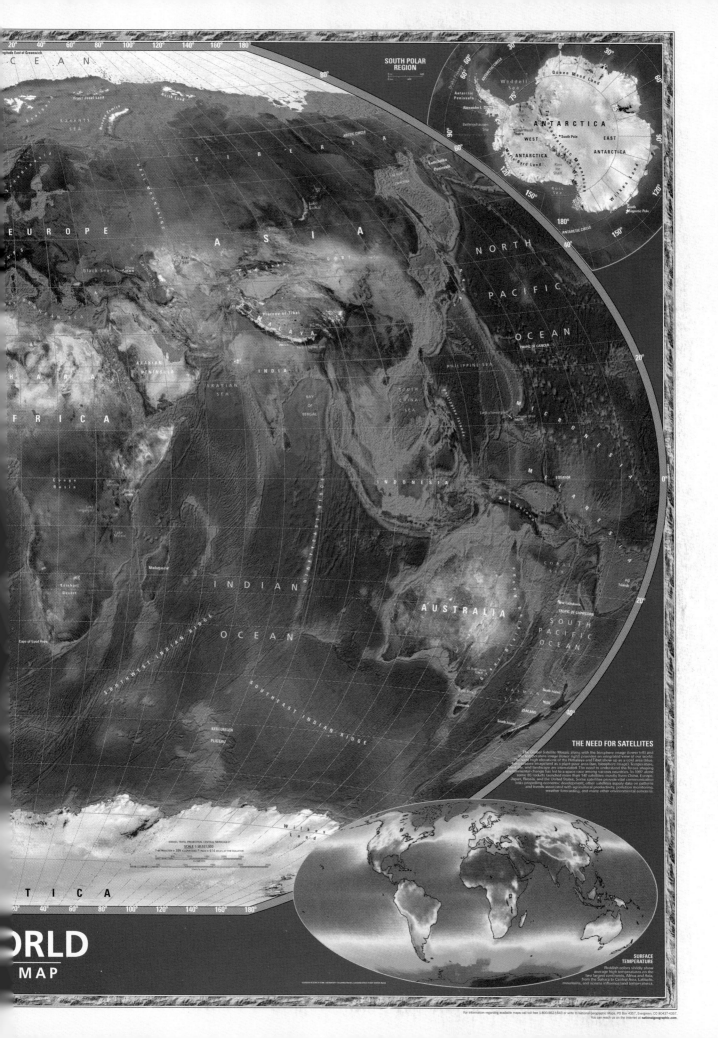

WORLD
MAP

SOUTH POLAR REGION

THE NEED FOR SATELLITES

The Global Satellite Mosaic along with the biosphere image (lower left) and surface temperature image (lower right) provide an integrated view of our world. The very high elevations of the Himalaya and Tibet show up as a cold area (blue atmosphere imagined as a plant-poor area) can, biosphere image). Temperature, land use, and landscape are interrelated. The need to understand the forces shaping environmental change has led to a space race among various countries. In 1997 alone some 80 rockets launched more than 140 satellites—mostly from China, Europe, Japan, Russia, and the United States. Some satellites provide vital communication links propelling economic development; other satellites supply data on patterns and trends associated with agricultural productivity, pollution monitoring, weather forecasting, and many other environmental concerns.

SURFACE TEMPERATURE
Reddish colors vividly show average high temperatures on the two largest continents, Africa and Asia, from the Sahara to Central Asia. Latitude, mountains, and oceans influence land temperatures.

For information regarding available maps call toll free 1-800-962-1643 or write to National Geographic Maps, PO Box 4357, Evergreen, CO 80437-4357.
You can reach us on the internet at nationalgeographic.com

FOURTEENTH EDITION
VOLUME 1

JUDITH G. COFFIN

ROBERT C. STACEY

ROBERT E. LERNER

STANDISH MEACHAM

BASED ON THE ORIGINAL *WESTERN CIVILIZATIONS*
BY EDWARD MCNALL BURNS

W · W · NORTON & COMPANY · NEW YORK · LONDON

WESTERN
CIVILIZATIONS

THEIR HISTORY
& THEIR CULTURE

Copyright © 2002, 1998, 1993, 1988, 1984, 1980, 1973, 1968, 1963, 1958, 1954, 1949, 1947, 1941 by
W. W. Norton & Company, Inc.
Printed in the United States of America

The text of this book is composed in Weiss Roman
with the display set in Bauer Text Initials and Bell Gothic
Composition by TSI
Manufacturing by Courier Corporation, Kendallville
Title page spread photo: ©2001 Paloma Pajares Ayuela, from "Cosmatesque Ornament"
Editor: Jon Durbin
Associate Managing Editor—College: Jane Carter
Director of Manufacturing—College: Roy Tcdoff
Cover & Text Designer: Antonina Krass
Page layout: Carole Desnoes
Copy editor: Barbara Gerr
Project editors: Sarah Caldwell, Lory Frenkel
Photograph editor: Neil Ryder Hoos
Assistant editor: Aaron Javsicas

The Library of Congress has cataloged the one-volume edition as follows:

Coffin, Judith G., 1952–
     Western civilizations, their history and their culture / Judith G. Coffin . . . [et al.].—14th ed.
          p. cm.
     Rev. ed. of: Western civilizations, their history and their culture / Robert E. Lerner. 13th ed. 1998.
     Includes bibliographical references and index.
     ISBN 0-393-97686-6
          1. Civilization, Western. 2. Europe—Civilization. I. Lerner, Robert E. Western civilizations, their
     history and their culture. II. Title.

CB245 .C56 2002
909'.09812—dc21   2001044708
ISBN 0-393-97771-4 (pbk.)

W. W. Norton & Company, Inc., 500 Fifth Avenue, New York, NY 10110
www.wwnorton.com

W. W. Norton & Company Ltd., Castle House, 75/76 Wells Street, London W1T 3QT
1 2 3 4 5 6 7 8 9 0

To our families—Robin, Will, and Anna Stacey, and Willy, Zoe, and Aaron Forbath—for their patience and support. They reminded us that books such as this are worth the work, and also that there are other things in life.

To Robert Lerner, Standish Meacham, Edward McNall Burns, and Marie Burns, our predecessors who successfully guided *Western Civilizations* for thirteen editions, spanning six decades.

ABOUT THE AUTHORS

JUDITH G. COFFIN received her Ph.D. in modern French history from Yale University. She has taught at Harvard University and the University of California, Riverside, and is currently associate professor of history at the University of Texas at Austin, where she won a 1999 University of Texas President's Associates' Award for Teaching Excellence. Her research interests focus on the social and cultural history of gender, mass culture, slavery, race relations, and colonialism. She is the author of *The Politics of Women's Work: The Paris Garment Trades, 1750–1915*.

ROBERT C. STACEY is professor and chair of the history department and a member of the Jewish Studies faculty at the University of Washington in Seattle. A long-time teacher of western civilization and medieval European history, he has received Distinguished Teaching Awards from both the University of Washington and Yale University, where he taught from 1984 to 1988. He is the author or coauthor of four books, including a textbook, *The Making of England to 1399*. He holds an M.A. from Oxford University and a Ph.D. from Yale.

ROBERT E. LERNER is professor of medieval history at Northwestern University, where he has served as director of the Humanities Program. He has won awards from the National Endowment for the Humanities, the American Council of Learned Studies, the Guggenheim Foundation, and the Rockefeller Foundation. His books include *The Age of Adversity: The Fourteenth Century; The Heresy of Free Spirit in the Middle Ages;* and *The Powers of Prophecy*.

STANDISH MEACHAM is professor emeritus at the University of Texas at Austin. He has received grants from the Guggenheim Foundation, the American Council of Learned Studies, and the American Philosophical Society. His books include *Henry Thornton of Clapman, 1760–1815; Lord Bishop: The Life of Samuel Wilberforce; A Life Apart: The English Working Class, 1890–1914;* and *Toynbee Hall and Social Reform, 1880–1914*.

CONTENTS

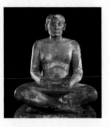

PART II THE GREEK AND
         ROMAN WORLDS

PART III   THE MIDDLE AGES

PART IV FROM MEDIEVAL TO MODERN

PART V   EARLY MODERN EUROPE

Maps

CHRONOLOGIES

DOCUMENTS

PREFACE

SINCE THE 1920s, the western civilization survey course has held a central place in the curricula of American universities and high schools. Yet the concept of "western civilization" can be elusive. As this textbook begins its seventh decade of life, in the hands of a new team of authors, it seems appropriate to define our terms. At the beginning of the twenty-first century, how now do we conceive of our subject?

"Western" civilization was long considered to mean the civilization of western Europe, to which the earlier history of the Ancient Near East was somewhat arbitrarily attached. Western European civilization was thus presented as beginning at Sumer, developing in Egypt, and then flowering in Greece. Rome acquired it from Greece, and in turn passed it on to France, Germany, England, Italy and Spain, whose emigrating colonists transferred it to the Americas, beginning in the sixteenth century. Rather like a train passing through stations, western civilization was thus conceived as picking up "cargo" at each of its stops, but always retaining the same engine and the same baggage cars.

This vision of western civilization is not only selective, it is often tied to a series of contentious assumptions. It casts the worldwide dominance of the European imperial powers between roughly 1800 and 1950 as the culmination of several thousand years of historical development, which it is the obligation of historians to explain. Behind this assumption there frequently lies another: that European global dominance in the nineteenth and twentieth centuries reflected and demonstrated the inherent superiority of western European civilization over the African, Asian, and Native American civilizations the Europeans conquered during the heyday of their imperial expansion.

Historians today are keenly aware of how much such an account leaves out. It slights the use of force and fraud in European expansion. It ignores the sophistication, dynamism, and humanity of the many cultures it sidelines. By neglecting the crucial importance of Byzantium and Islam, it gives a misleadingly narrow account of the development of European civilization. It also misleads us about the western civilizations created in North and South America after the conquest, which were creole, or hybrid, cultures, not simply European cultures transplanted to other shores. This is not to argue that a study of western civilization must give way to a study of world civilization. It is merely to insist that understanding the historical development of western civilization requires us to place it in a much wider context.

In this textbook, we will argue that western civilization is not a single historical culture with uniform and unchanging characteristics. It is not a single train, making stops at selected stations. Rather, there have been a number of western civilizations, whose fundamental characteristics have changed markedly over time. We mean, therefore, for our title, *Western Civilizations*, to be taken seriously. In this book, we will treat "western" as a geographical designator, to refer to the major civilizations that developed in and around the Mediterranean Sea between 3500 B.C.E. ("Before the Common Era," equivalent to the Christian dating system B.C., "Before Christ") and 500 C.E. ("Common Era," equivalent to the Christian dating system A.D., "Anno Domini," "the Year of the Lord"). We will also treat as "western" the civilizations that developed out of the Mediterranean world in the centuries after 500 C.E., as the Greco-Roman world of antiquity divided into Islamic, Byzantine, and Latin Christian realms. The interdependence and mutual influence of these three western civilizations upon each other will be a recurring theme of this book.

From the twelfth century C.E. onward, however, we focus more intensively upon the evolving culture of the European continent. Between 1100 and 1500, Europe's distinctive social, economic, political, and religious characteristics combined to make it the most powerful and expansive of the three civilizations. From the sixteenth century on, Europeans turned these expansionist impulses outward, away from the Mediterranean world and into the Atlantic and Indian Oceans, becoming the first global imperial power in history. Today, we live in the shadow of that world. We need to understand the unpredictable and surprising ways in which that world took shape. To do so, we must pay attention to both the internal conflicts in which expansion was entwined and the political, economic, and cultural transformations that it entailed.

In undertaking to revise this book, we have been constantly reminded of the very high quality of the work upon which we are building. Between 1941 and 1973, Edward McNall Burns constructed a textbook with enduring features—a vigorous narrative style, and a wide-ranging attention to the diverse ways in which humans have organized their lives in response to changing environments, visions, and goals—that were

expertly carried on and updated by Robert Lerner and Standish Meacham. In preparing the fourteenth edition of their work, we have tried to retain the book's traditional strengths by remaining attentive to narrative; by aiming for clarity and accessibility without "talking down" to our audience; and by bringing together "high" politics and culture with the everyday experiences and beliefs of ordinary people.

At the same time, we have made some significant changes in this new edition, devoting, for example, more attention to the world outside northwestern Europe. We have taken a more historical approach to our story, presenting artistic and cultural developments as firmly rooted in the circumstances and conditions of their age, rather than expressions of timeless genius. We have continued to integrate new scholarly work in social and cultural history and the history of gender into our narrative, but we have also substantially increased the attention we pay to economics, religion, and military history. In addition to shortening the text by about 15 percent, we have also changed the book's design, using a two-column layout for the text, adding boxes with primary source documents, redesigning the maps, and increasing the size of the illustrations.

We have substantially revised many of the individual chapters. Parts I and II, which cover the Ancient Near East and the Mediterranean world up to c. 500 C.E., have been completely reconceived and rewritten. In keeping with our emphasis on the historical interactions and interdependence of western civilizations, we no longer present Mesopotamian, Egyptian, Myceneaean, Minoan, Persian, and Hebrew history in separate chapters as if these cultures were isolated from one other. Instead, we take a more directly chronological and comparative approach. Chapter 1 traces human history in the Mediterranean and Near Eastern world from its Stone Age origins up to c. 2000 B.C.E. Chapter 2 considers the impact of the developing empires of the ancient Near East upon Mesopotamia, Egypt, and the Aegean Sea region between roughly 2000 B.C.E. and 1200 B.C.E. Chapter 3 examines the early Iron Age, from roughly 1200 B.C.E. to 500 B.C.E., emphasizing the religious imperialism of the era and the impact of that imperialism upon the development of Hebrew monotheism.

In Part II, Chapter 4 deals with Greece from roughly 1200 B.C.E. until 400 B.C.E., while Chapter 5 treats the extension of Greek cultural influence throughout the Mediterranean world between c. 400 B.C.E. and the mid-second century B.C.E. In both these chapters, we have tried to pay particular attention to the political, social and economic context for the important cultural and intellectual developments of these eras. Chapter 6 deals with republican and imperial Rome from its origins until the mid-third century C.E. Readers will find here a new discussion of the early history of Rome, and a significantly revised presentation of Roman religion. Chapter 7 traces the impact of Romanization and Christianization upon the late antique world, paralleling the discussion of Hellenization in Chapter 5 and complicating conventional ideas about the "fall" of Rome.

Part III, "The Middle Ages," has also been reorganized and revised. Chapter 8, "Rome's Three Heirs," discusses Byzantium, the Islamic world, and Europe up to the year 1000, emphasizing that all three civilizations drew heavily upon Greek and Roman traditions. The section on early medieval Europe has been rewritten. Coverage of Byzantine and Islamic history after 1000 has been expanded and moved to Chapter 9, with significantly increased attention to the Byzantine revival, the crusades, and the economic relations between the three civilizations. Chapter 11 contains a revised section on medieval Russia and its connections with Byzantium. Throughout Part III, long-time users will also note smaller revisions and alterations in emphasis where the authors determined that new work has significantly altered earlier views.

Part IV, "From Medieval to Modern," now begins with a new chapter (12) on "Commerce, Conquest, and Colonization, 1300–1600." This chapter starts with the Mongol conquests of central Asia, then discusses the rise of the Ottoman Empire and the growth of European colonial enterprises in the Mediterranean and along the Atlantic coast of Africa. It concludes with the sixteenth century expansion of European commerce and military conquest into the Indian Ocean and across the Atlantic in the Americas. Chapter 13 offers a revised discussion of Machiavelli, and carries further the previous emphasis on the medieval roots of the Renaissance. Chapter 14 now focuses exclusively on the reformations of the sixteenth century. Coverage of the European voyages of discovery, previously found here, has been moved to Chapter 12 on "Commerce, Conquest, and Colonization." We have also tried to sharpen the focus of Chapter 15, linking the cultural developments of the era more directly with the tensions in European life that arose out of the religious conflicts of the sixteenth and seventeenth centuries.

In Part V, the most important changes are two new chapters (18 and 19) on the Scientific Revolution and Enlightenment. Both chapters are concerned with the context in which new ideas were forged and with how those ideas came to matter for a range of people, from philosophers, rulers, and bureaucrats to explorers, artists, and artisans. Chapter 19 highlights the international setting of Enlightenment thought. Here and throughout, we have expanded the treatment of gender. That has meant adding more material concerning women but also, more importantly, showing the ways in which family, sexuality, models of femininity, and the rights and duties of men and women became central to politics and culture at different historical moments.

In Part VI, Chapter 20 contains a new section on slavery and anti-slavery movements, including the Haitian Revolution. Chapters 21 and 22 set the industrial revolution in its international economic context. In Chapters 23 and 24, we have tried to clarify the many meanings and uses of nationalism.

In Part VII, we have added an entirely new chapter (25) on nineteenth-century imperialism. It begins with the relationship between the "new imperialism" and earlier moments of expansion, in keeping with the book's overall theme of outward expansion and inner conflict. It analyzes the forces that drove European imperialism in different regions and the resistance those forces encountered, resistance that shaped colonial culture and European rule. Next, the thirteenth edition's two chapters on the late nineteenth century have been condensed into one, focusing on the key events of late-nineteenth-century politics and culture. Those cuts allowed us to expand our treatment of war, spending more time on the battlefield as well as on the home front. The chapters on World Wars I and II (27 and 29) include more military history and more discussion of the world arena in which political and military battles were fought.

In Chapter 28 we have revised the treatments of Nazism and Stalinism, and added a new section on mass culture, tying it to mass politics and underscoring its democratic as well as authoritarian potential. Chapter 29 includes a short discussion of the Pacific war, and a new section, with documents, on the Holocaust.

In Part VIII, "The West and the World," Chapter 30 includes more analysis of developments in Eastern Europe. The section on culture is more attentive to the "Americanization" of popular culture in particular. Chapter 31 includes a new section on changes in consumption, youth culture, and new social movements. In Chapter 32, we have expanded the analysis of decolonization, especially the collapse of the British and French empires.

Innovative Pedagogical Program

Western Civilizations, Fourteenth Edition is designed for maximum readability. The crisp, clear, and concise narrative is also accompanied by a highly useful pedagogical program designed to help students study while engaging them in the subject matter. Highlights of this innovative program include:

- **In-Text Documents.** Designed to add depth to the more focused narrative of *Western Civilizations*, each chapter contains five primary sources, two of which are paired together to convey a sense of historical complexity and diversity.

- **Map Program with Enhanced Captions:** Over one hundred beautiful maps appear throughout the text, each accompanied by an enhanced map caption designed to engage the reader analytically, while conveying the key role that geography plays in the development of history and the societies of the world.

- **In-Chapter Chronologies.** Several brief chronologies built around particular events, topics, or periods appear throughout each chapter and are designed to provide road maps through the narrative detail.

- **Focus Question System.** Ensures that readers remain alert to key concepts and questions on every page of the text. Focus questions guide students' reading in three ways: (1) a focus question box appears at the beginning of the chapter to serve as a preview of the chapter's contents; (2) relevant questions reappear at the start of the section where they are discussed; and (3) running heads on the right hand pages keep these questions in view throughout the chapter.

- **Pull-Quotes.** Lifted directly from the narrative, pull-quotes appear throughout each chapter and are designed to highlight key thoughts and keen insights, while keeping students focused on larger concepts and ideas.

Outstanding Ancillaries for Both Instructors and Students

Western Civilizations Online Tutor
www.wwnorton.com/wciv
by Steven Kreiss, Wake Technical College
This online resource for students—designed specifically for use with *Western Civilizations*—provides free access to online review and research materials. Included are online quizzes, Norton iMaps, world history excursion exercises, electronic versions of the Global Connections/Disconnections feature boxes, images from the text, audio and video clips, and Norton e-Reserves.

Norton Media Library with PowerPoint Slides
This CD-ROM contains a presentation program designed to assist instructors who want to make multimedia presentations in lecture. The easy-to-use program includes all the maps in the text, dynamic Norton iMaps, various images from the book.

Instructor's Manual and Test-Item File
by Maarten Ultee, University of Alabama, Tuscaloosa
The Instructor's Manual includes lecture outlines, ideas for launching lectures, sample lecture topics, classroom exercises, suggested films and readings, and recommended web links. The Test-Item File contains multiple-choice, short-answer, and essay questions for each chapter of the text.

Study Guide
by Stephen Wessley, York College of Pennsylvania
This valuable guide contains chapter objectives, chapter outlines, chronologies, key terms, multiple-choice questions, map exercises and a highly useful collection of primary sources tied directly to *Western Civilizations, Fourteenth Edition*.

Acknowledgments:

The final version of the manuscript was greatly influenced by the thoughts and ideas of a select group of instructors to whom we are greatly indebted and wish to express our sincere thanks:
- James Brophy, University of Delaware;
- Lawrence Duggan, University of Delaware;
- Janusz Duzinkiewicz, Purdue University, North Central Campus;
- Stephen Epstein, University of Colorado at Boulder;
- William Jordan, Princeton University;
- Stephen Kreiss, Wake Technical College;
- Harry Liebersohn, University of Illinois, Urbana-Champaign;
- Thomas Max Safley, University of Pennsylvania;
- Jeffrey Merrick, University of Wisconsin-Milwaukee;
- Ian Morris, Stanford University;

- Cat Nilan;
- John Robertson, Central Michigan University;
- Evan A. Thomas, Grandview College;
- and Maarten Ultee, University of Alabama, Tuscaloosa.

We want to thank Steve Forman and Jon Durbin at W. W. Norton for their faith in this project, and Jon Durbin, Aaron Javsicas, and Sarah Caldwell for their help in seeing it through to completion. Without these friends and supporters, we could not have done it. We also want to thank Toni Krass for creating a beautiful new design, Carol Desnoes for her eye-catching page layout, and Neil Hoos for finding the images for the covers.

We are grateful for the helpful criticisms and suggestions of a large number of scholars, some of whom reviewed the thirteenth edition, and others who reviewed earlier drafts of this one.

Robert Stacey has been principally responsible for revising Chapters 1–17. He owes special thanks to Carol Thomas and Joel Walker of the University of Washington for advice on early Greek and late antique matters respectively; to Daniel Waugh (University of Washington) for his searching criticisms of Mongol, Ottoman, and early Russian matters; and to Lawrence Duggan (University of Delaware) for his help with the Renaissance chapter and for many valuable discussions on the Reformation over many years. His greatest debt, however, is to Dr. Jason Hawke, now of the University of Iowa, without whose assistance in both research and writing the revisions to Chapters 1 through 6 could not have been accomplished.

Judith Coffin is principally responsible for the revisions to Chapters 18–32. Many of her colleagues have supplied advice and expertise, but she is especially grateful to Caroline Castiglione, David Crew, Paul Hagenloh, Standish Meacham, John Merriman, Gail Minault, Joan Neuberger, Paula Sanders, Daniel Sherman, James Sidbury, Robert Stephens, Michael Stoff, and Charters Wynn. James Brophy of the University of Delaware deserves special thanks for rewriting the chapters on the late nineteenth century. Cori Crider, Patrick Timmons, Marion Barber and, especially, Justin Glasson, were terrific research assistants. Her greatest debt is to Geoffrey Clayton, whose research, writing, and energy were critical in nearly every chapter.

WESTERN
CIVILIZATIONS

VOLUME 1

PART I
THE ANCIENT NEAR EAST

THE HUMAN HISTORY of the Mediterranean world begins only about 40,000 years ago, with the completed evolution of homo sapiens sapiens, the fully modern human species to which we all belong. Civilization is an even more recent development. To the peoples of the ancient world, civilization — government, literature, science, and art — was necessarily a product of civic life. But cities only became possible as a result of the agricultural and technological discoveries that emerged between the end of the last Ice Age, about 13,000 years ago, and the appearance, in Mesopotamia, of the first true cities approximately 5,000 years ago. The story of western civilizations is thus a short one. In geologic time, it is but a momentary blip on a radar screen.

From their origins between the Tigris and Euphrates Rivers in modern-day Iraq, cities grew up throughout the Near Eastern world. Independent cities gave way to empires that rose and fell in turn. Around 1200 B.C.E. the imperial system of the entire Mediterranean world collapsed in cataclysm, to be replaced, by the middle of the first millennium B.C.E., by new empires that were larger, better armed, and more aggressively imperialistic than any of their predecessors.

At the same time, dramatic developments were occurring in religious and cultural life. The pyramids of Egypt, the Epic of Gilgamesh, the works of Homer, and the religious traditions of Zoroastrianism and Judaism had all taken shape by the time our period closes around 500 B.C.E. Upon these foundations, all the subsequent civilizations of the western, Mediterranean world have continued to rest.

	POLITICS	SOCIETY AND CULTURE	ECONOMY	INTERNATIONAL RELATIONS
B.C.E. 40,000		Paleolithic Era (40,000–11,000 B.C.E.)		
		End of the Ice Age, beginning of the Neolithic Era (11,000 B.C.E.)		
		Settled agriculture in Fertile Crescent (8500–7000 B.C.E.)	Grain storage begins (9500 B.C.E.)	
8000		Stone walls and tower of Jericho (8000 B.C.E.)	Emergence of pottery in Jericho (8000–7000 B.C.E.)	
			Domestication of animals, raising of crops (7000 B.C.E.)	
6000	Ubaid culture governed by priestly class (5900 B.C.E.)		Ubaid culture builds irrigation channels of stone (5900 B.C.E.)	Ubaid culture (Mesopotamia) (5900 B.C.E.)
		Agriculture established in Egypt and the Balkans (5000 B.C.E.)	Long-distance trade emerges (5000 B.C.E.)	
		Increased trade engenders social stratification (5000 B.C.E.)		
		First-known settlement in Egypt (4750 B.C.E.)		
4000		Uruk Period (4300–2900 B.C.E.)		
		End of the Stone Age (4000 B.C.E.)	Copper tools appear (4000 B.C.E.)	
		Cities form in fertile Mesopotamia (3500–3000 B.C.E.)	Building of the White Temple at Uruk (3500–3300 B.C.E.)	
			Pottery-throwing wheels (3500 B.C.E.)	
			Ubaid/Sumerians begin inscribing symbols on tablets (3300 B.C.E.)	
			Wheeled chariots (3200 B.C.E.)	
			Egyptians build fortifications, temples, settlements (3200 B.C.E.)	
			Appearance of cuneiform script (3100 B.C.E.)	Sumerian civilization (3100 B.C.E.)
3000	The Archaic Period in Egypt (3000–2715 B.C.E.)	Beginning of the Bronze Age (3000 B.C.E.)	Discovery of bronze (3000 B.C.E.)	
		Egyptians develop hieroglyphs and hieratic script (3000 B.C.E.)		
	Emergence of lugal leadership in Mesopotamia (2900–2500 B.C.E.)			
	Early Dynastic Period (I & II) (2900–2500 B.C.E.)			
	The Old Kingdom in Egypt (2715–2170 B.C.E.)	Great Pyramids of Giza (2640–2510 B.C.E.)		
	The Third through Sixth Dynasties in Egypt (2715–2205 B.C.E.)	Royal Tombs of Ur (2550–2450 B.C.E.)		
	Early Dynastic (III) (2500–2350 B.C.E.)	Epic of Gilgamesh (2500 B.C.E.)		Elamite (present-day Iran) culture (2500 B.C.E.)
	The Akkadian Period (2350–2160 B.C.E.)			Sargon of Akkad conquers Mesopotamia (2360 B.C.E.)
	Sargon organizes Mesopotamia (2350 B.C.E.)			
	Unity of Egypt dissolves (2150 B.C.E.)			Gutians conquer Sumer and Akkad (2160 B.C.E.)
	Ur Dynasty III (2100–2000 B.C.E.)			

Politics	Society and Culture	Economy	International Relations	
				B.C.E. 2000
The Middle Kingdom in Egypt (2000–1683 B.C.E.)	Indo-European linguistic forms appear (2000 B.C.E.)	Horses introduced to Near East (2000–1700 B.C.E.)		
The "Palace Age" in Minoan culture (1900–1700 B.C.E.)		Major expansion of trade (1900–1700 B.C.E.)	Minoan civilization flourishes in Crete (1900–1500 B.C.E.)	
Hammurabi unifies Sumero-Akkadian area (1792–1750 B.C.E.)	Code of Hammurabi (1750 B.C.E.)	Minoan trade with Egypt, Anatolia, and Cyprus (1700 B.C.E.)		
			The Hyksos overrun Egypt (1650–1550 B.C.E.)	
			Hittites capture Babylon (1595 B.C.E.)	
The New Kingdom (1550–1075 B.C.E.)	Appearance of Linear B in Mycenaean Greece (1500 B.C.E.)	Trade surges with new internationalism (1500 B.C.E.)	The Mitannians adopt cavalry and chariot technology (1500 B.C.E.)	**1500**
			Mycenaean civilization established (1500 B.C.E.)	
Thutmosis III and Hatshepsut take the throne (1479 B.C.E.)			Age of internationalism begins (1500 B.C.E.)	
			Hittite empire (1450 B.C.E.)	
			Mycenaeans subjugate Crete (1400 B.C.E.)	
Reign of Amenhotep III, the Magnificent (1387–1350 B.C.E.)			Complex societies developed at Mycenae, Thebes, Athens, etc. (1400–1200 B.C.E.)	
Middle Assyrian Period (1362–859 B.C.E.)				
Amenhotep IV, later Akhenaton, takes the throne (1350 B.C.E.)	Rise of Amon as Egyptian national god (1350 B.C.E.)			
			Treaty between Egypt and Hittite Empire (1286 B.C.E.)	
			Rise of Phoenicians (Canaanites) (1200 B.C.E.)	
			Mycenaean civilization implodes (1200 B.C.E.)	
			Sea Peoples ravage Near East (1200–1179 B.C.E.)	
			Ramses III defeats Sea Peoples (1179 B.C.E.)	
Saul becomes first Hebrew king (1025 B.C.E.)		Philistines introduce vine and olive tree to the Levant (1050 B.C.E.)	Philistine preeminence in the Levant (1050 B.C.E.)	
Reign of King David (1000–973 B.C.E.)			Egypt collapses (1000 B.C.E.)	**1000**
Hebrew kingdom splits upon death of King Solomon (c. 933 B.C.E.)				
Neo-Assyrian Empire (883–859 B.C.E.)			Phoenicians establish Carthage (800 B.C.E.)	
Reign of Sargon II (722–705 B.C.E.)		Assyrians master iron-smelting (700 B.C.E.)	Assyrian Empire expands (800–700 B.C.E.)	**700**
	Zoroaster, founder of Zoroastrianism (600 B.C.E.)		Hebrew captivity in Babylon begins (587 B.C.E.)	
Reign of Darius I of Persia (521–486 B.C.E.)			Athens defeats Darius I at Battle of Marathon (490 B.C.E.)	
			Alexander the Great invades Persia (334 B.C.E.)	

Chapter ONE

The Origins of Western Civilizations in the Ancient Near East

CATHERINE MORLAND, the heroine of Jane Austen's novel *Northanger Abbey*, complained that history "tells me nothing that does not either vex or weary me. The quarrels of popes and kings, with wars or pestilences in every page; the men all so good for nothing, and hardly any women at all, it is very tiresome." Although Jane Austen's heroine said this around 1800, she might have lodged the same complaint until quite recently, for until deep into the twentieth century most historians considered history to be little more than "past politics"—and a dry chronicle of past politics at that. The content of historical study was restricted primarily to battles and treaties, the personalities and politics of statesmen, the laws and decrees of rulers. But important as such data are, they by no means constitute the whole substance of history. Especially within the last few decades historians have come to recognize that history comprises a record of past human activities in every sphere—not just political developments, but also social, economic, and intellectual ones. Women as well as men, the ruled as well as the rulers, the poor as well as the rich are part of history. So too are the social and economic institutions that women and men have created and that in turn have shaped their lives: family and social class; manorialism and city life; capitalism and industrialism. Ideas and attitudes, too, not just of intellectuals, but also of people whose lives may have been virtually untouched by "great books," are all part of the historian's concern. And most important, history includes an inquiry into the causes of events and patterns of human organization and ideas—a search for the forces that impelled humanity toward its great undertakings, and the reasons for its successes and failures.

As historians have extended the scope of their work, they have also equipped themselves with new methods and tools, the better to practice their craft. No longer do historians merely pore over the same old chronicles and documents to ask whether Charles the Fat was at Ingelheim or Lustnau on July 1, 887. To evaluate quantitative data, they learn the methods of the statistician. To interpret the effect of a rise in the cost of living, they study economics. To deduce marriage patterns or evaluate the effect on an entire population of wars and plagues, they master the

FOCUS QUESTIONS

• Why do we know so little about early nomadic life?

• What changes allowed the transition from nomadic to sedentary societies?

• How did irrigation and temple building figure in early Mesopotamian civilization?

• Why did a common religion not create peace among the Sumerians?

• How was the Nile River central to the development of Egyptian civilization?

skills of the demographer. To explore the phenomena of cave dwelling or modern urbanization, they become archaeologists, studying fossil remains, fragments of pots, or modern city landscapes. To understand the motives of the men and women who have acted in the past, they draw on the insights of social psychologists and cultural anthropologists. To illuminate the lives and thoughts of those who have left few or no written records, they look for other cultural remains such as folk songs, folk tales, and funerary monuments.

Of course with all their ingenuity historians cannot create evidence. An almost infinite number of past events are not retrievable because they transpired without leaving any traces; many others are at best known imperfectly. Thus some of the most fundamental questions about "how things were" in the past either can never be answered or can be answered only on the grounds of highly qualified inferences. Questions regarding motives and causes may not have definite answers for other reasons. Since individual humans often hardly understand their own motives, it is presumptuous to think that anyone can ever be entirely certain about establishing the motives of others. As for the causes of collective developments such as wars, economic growth trends, or changes in artistic styles, these are surely too complex to be reduced to a science. Nonetheless, the more evidence we have, the closer we come to providing valid reconstructions and explanations of what happened in the past. Moreover, the difficulties inherent in assembling and interpreting all sorts of data for the purposes of historical analysis should not be regarded with despair but looked on as stimulating intellectual challenges.

Should we go to the past to celebrate one or another lost age or seek to learn how we got to be the way we are now? Obviously neither one of these extremes is satisfactory, for nostalgia almost invariably leads to distortion, and at any rate is useless, whereas extreme "present-mindedness" also leads to distortion, and at any rate is foolish in its assumption that everything we do now is better than whatever people did before. It seems best, then, to avoid either revering the past or condescending to it. Instead, many historians seek to understand how people of a given era strove to solve their problems and live their lives fruitfully in terms appropriate to their particular environments and stages of development. Other historians look for change over time without postulating a march of progress to a current best of all possible worlds. Such historians believe (and let us hope they may be right) that identifying patterns and mechanisms of change will allow a better

understanding of the present and a greater possibility of plotting prudent strategies for coping with the future.

THE STONE AGE BACKGROUND

Why do we know so little about early nomadic life?

"Prehistory," the era before the appearance of written records around 3000 B.C.E. (Before the Common Era), is a period of much greater duration than human history. Humanlike ancestors first appeared in eastern Africa roughly four million years ago, and tool-making hominids (species belonging to the genus *Homo*, to which we as *Homo sapiens sapiens* belong) approximately two million years ago. The materials these early hominids employed were made principally out of stone, and from their use of stone tool technologies all human cultures down to the fourth millennium B.C.E. are referred to as belonging to the "Stone Age."

UPPER PALEOLITHIC ERA

The Stone Age is divided into various stages. Dominating the period is the Paleolithic ("Old Stone" Age), which most anthropologists would extend down to roughly 11,000 B.C.E. Within this vast expanse of time, however, scholars also speak of an Upper Paleolithic Era beginning around 40,000 B.C.E. Around this benchmark date archaeologists discern some stunning departures in human behavior, which may be associated with the appearance of anatomically modern humans in the Near East, North Africa, and Europe (though the correspondence here, if any, is highly controversial).

Among these Upper Paleolithic departures is the appearance of sophisticated figurative artwork (such as the cave paintings from Spain and southern France), which may have served religious or magical purposes for the people who created it. Archaeological finds also reveal the diffusion of microlith technologies, that is, the replacement of rather clumsy and cumbersome stone tools with smaller, more effective and increasingly fine implements (fishhooks, arrowheads, sewing needles, and so forth), usually made of stone but also of other materials such as animal bone. The development of such technologies reflects an increasing capacity to

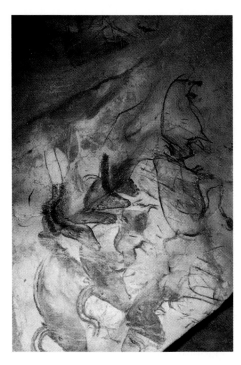
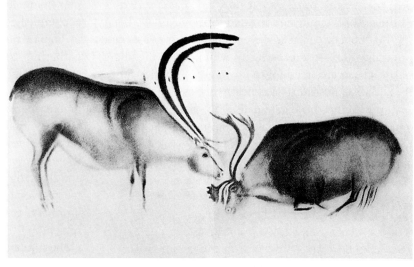

Cave Paintings from Southern France. On the left, one of the many cave paintings discovered in 1994. On the right, a stylized depiction of reindeer by an inspired artist "of the French school" who worked about fifteen thousand years ago.

work with perishable materials (wood, antlers, and so on) that are only rarely preserved for archaeologists.

As fundamental as some of these changes were, the basic pattern of human life seems to have remained largely unchanged in the Upper Paleolithic Era. Virtually all human societies before 11,000 B.C.E. were nomadic; small bands of people, probably never exceeding more than a few dozen individuals, moved incessantly from place to place, hunting and gathering their food. Because they depended entirely on what the local environment provided for their survival, they could not stay in any one location for long. As a result, such societies leave no continuous archaeological record whereby we might trace the development of their culture. Our knowledge of these early human societies is therefore very limited.

The social, economic and political consequences of Paleolithic nomadism were profound. Because humans had no domestic animals to transport their goods, they could have no significant material possessions—wealth—aside from basic tools they could easily carry on their persons. Without the ability to accumulate goods over time, disparities in individual wealth, with their attendant distinctions of rank and status, were unlikely to develop. Such societies may well have been highly organized—it is a gross error to presume that early societies were necessarily primitive—but hierarchical structures of leadership were uncommon, and possibly unknown. When conflicts arose within a group, the usual solution was probably to divide and

separate—a process that might also have been necessary simply to keep the total numbers in the band commensurate with what the natural resources of the local area could support.

We do not know how labor was divided between the members of these Paleolithic bands. Although scholars once assumed that men did the hunting and women the gathering, such gendered presumptions do not reflect the complex realities of modern nomadism, and they may not be applicable to the Paleolithic period either. It is more likely that all members of a Paleolithic band (except for the very young and the very

Bison Carved from a Reindeer Horn. Perhaps the most graceful of all known European prehistoric carvings, this bison was carved from a piece of antler between fifteen thousand and twelve thousand years ago. Whatever its use might have been no one quite knows.

old) engaged to some extent in all the basic activities of the group. Acquiring food and tools must have been the first concern of nearly every member of the group. Specialization—the process by which some members of the group are freed up to engage in activities other than food acquisition—was nearly impossible. Specialization requires the accumulation of storable surpluses, and this was something Paleolithic nomads lacked the technology to accomplish.

THE NEOLITHIC REVOLUTION

What changes allowed the transition from nomadic to sedentary societies?

Significant changes in the patterns of human existence began to take shape only around 11,000 B.C.E., the dawn of the Neolithic or "New Stone" Age. These breakthroughs included the development of managed food production, the beginnings of semipermanent and permanent settlements, and the rapid intensification of trade, both local and long distance. For the first time, it became possible for individuals and communities to accumulate and store wealth on a large scale. The results were far reaching. Communities became more stable, and human societies more complex. Specialization developed, along with distinctions of status and rank. The "revolution" represented by the innovations of the Neolithic Era was a necessary step before cities in the truest sense could appear toward the end of the fourth millennium B.C.E.

THE ORIGINS OF FOOD PRODUCTION

During the Upper Paleolithic "Ice Age" (c. 40,000–11,000 B.C.E.), daytime temperatures in Mediterranean Europe and Asia averaged about 60°F (16°C) in the summer and about 30°F (−1°C) in the winter. Accordingly, cold-loving game species such as reindeer, elk, wild boar, bison, and mountain goats roamed the hills and valleys. But as the last glaciers receded northward such species retreated with them. Some humans may have moved north with the game, but others stayed behind, creating an extremely different sort of world.

Specifically, within about three thousand to four thousand years after the end of the Ice Age, the peoples living at the eastern end of the Mediterranean Sea accomplished one of the most momentous revolutions in human history: a switch from subsistence by food gathering to producing food for themselves. Substantial numbers of humans now began to domesticate animals and raise crops, thereby making possible greater permanence and stability in their settlement patterns. Stable settlements ultimately paved the way for other developments we associate with civilization: the emergence of cities, the development of writing, and the growth of scholarship. Although a process that takes several thousand years may seem less than "revolutionary" to our current sensibilities, it is important to remember that humans in a few small areas of the globe fundamentally altered, in a relatively short time, a pattern of survival that had existed for millions of years.

The story is roughly as follows. Around 11,000 B.C.E. most of the larger game herds had left southwestern Asia, part of the region (together with Egypt) known as the Near East. Yet people in territories that today lie in Turkey, Syria, Israel, and western Iran were not starving because the warmer and wetter climate created a nurturing environment for plentiful fields of wild grain. Because of the abundant natural food resources of the region (and its related agricultural productivity in later historical times), this arc through western Asia is often referred to as the Fertile Crescent. For at least part of the year, a society of humans could now count on plant resources plentiful enough to sustain a seasonal or permanent settlement. The shift from a nomadic to a sedentary existence had begun.

The emergence of semipermanent and permanent settlements, combined with attendant increases in overall food supply, had profound effects on human life. Most important, it produced a rapid increase in human numbers. By around 8000 B.C.E., however, the human population was beginning to exceed the natural carrying capacity of the land. To support this growing population, humans now had to take steps to increase the food-growing capacity of the land. This marked the beginnings of deliberately managed agriculture.

But the systematic and managed production of plant food also required a crucial intermediary step: storage. Even when plentiful, grain does not grow during the winter. By around 9500 B.C.E., however, peoples along the eastern coast of the Mediterranean (known as Natufians to prehistorians) had learned how to preserve their grain by digging storage pits. This strengthened their sedentary way of life: no longer were they forced to move away from their settled communities

WHAT CHANGES ALLOWED THE TRANSITION FROM NOMADIC TO SEDENTARY SOCIETIES?

THE NEOLITHIC REVOLUTION   11

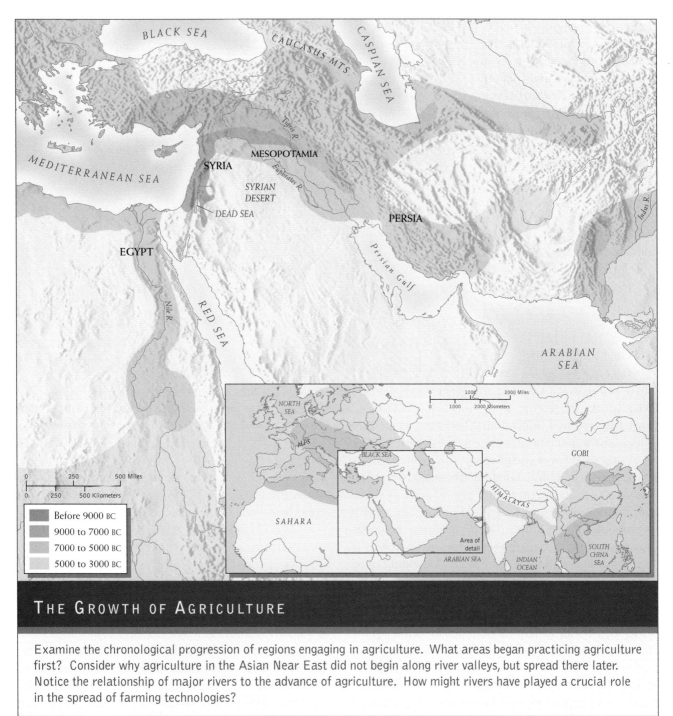

THE GROWTH OF AGRICULTURE

Examine the chronological progression of regions engaging in agriculture. What areas began practicing agriculture first? Consider why agriculture in the Asian Near East did not begin along river valleys, but spread there later. Notice the relationship of major rivers to the advance of agriculture. How might rivers have played a crucial role in the spread of farming technologies?

during the parts of the year when grain was not ready for harvesting. This in turn encouraged some Natufians to build more permanent, circular dwellings on stone foundations, although others continued to live in caves and other natural rock shelters.

Storage did more than simply reinforce a reluctance to move away from "home": after constructing their storage pits, the Natufians (and other early Neolithic peoples) probably also began to notice how grain

began sprouting and rooting in or near the pits at the start of the spring rains. Once the importance of this observation impressed itself on the inhabitants of a sedentary community, they could begin to store grain not only for future consumption, but also to provide seed with which to produce more grain in the following year. This revelation had three important effects. First, humans could deliberately plant crops in a more concentrated fashion, thus producing the higher yields necessary to support a higher population (with the effect of growing the population even faster). Second, should nature fail to produce its usual abundance in a given year, both the grain and the seed needed to avert famine and the dissolution of the community would be at hand. Third, with intensification and storage, humans now had the surpluses they needed to support domestic animals, which they could now afford to feed all year.

The earliest archaeological evidence for fully sedentary agriculture comes from several areas in the Fertile Crescent between roughly 8500 and 7000 B.C.E. By 6000 B.C.E. much of the Near East (especially within the Fertile Crescent) had adopted agriculture as its primary mode of survival. In all these areas agriculture

Stone Foundation of a Sedentary Dwelling. Once people in western Asia became agriculturalists, they began to build homes for year-round habitation. This stone foundation for a prehistoric house was found at the site of the village of Jarmo (in Iraq) and dates from about 6000 B.C.E.

was supplemented by domestic livestock, which by 7000 B.C.E. included cattle and pigs as well as sheep and goats. Animal protein was, of course, an ancient feature of human diet. Domestication, however, brought a host of benefits, guaranteeing not only a more reliable supply of meat, but also providing milk, leather, wool, bone, and horn for handicrafts.

Exactly how the shift to agriculture and the domestication of animals became so widespread so quickly is a matter of debate. It may be that similar demographic and environmental conditions around the region created a spontaneous shift to agriculture in several places at once. Some scholars have argued that large-scale migrations of populations with knowledge of agricultural methods spread the new technology. Still others believe that the spread was due to a slow but steady wave of new agriculturally based communities, founded beyond the "mother" settlements when the higher carrying capacity of the land, improved through agricultural technologies, still proved inadequate to growing populations. Other scholars see the role of trade networks as crucial to the diffusion of ideas about agriculture across the region. As is so often the case when dealing with such profound and fundamental change in human history, no single explanation suffices. All of these factors

must have played a role in the spread of agriculture across the Fertile Crescent and beyond, to Egypt and even the Balkans, by 5000 B.C.E.

THE GREAT VILLAGES OF THE NEAR EAST

The next steps in the Near East's accelerating evolution toward civilization were the emergence of villages and the concurrent rise of handicrafts, long-distance trade, and warfare, all made possible by the development of some degree of specialization. Villages constituted the most advanced form of human organization in western Asia from about 6500 to about 3500 or 3000 B.C.E., when some villages began to evolve into cities. A typical Near Eastern village numbered around one thousand inhabitants, but numbers could vary greatly. At first almost all of the able-bodied men and women engaged in field work, and all the women additionally in cloth production, but gradually there came to be full-time specialists in handicrafts, as well as a few full-time traders.

One of the first examples of the transition from preagricultural communities to fully agricultural and

WHAT CHANGES ALLOWED THE TRANSITION FROM NOMADIC TO SEDENTARY SOCIETIES?

THE NEOLITHIC REVOLUTION   13

completely sedentary settlements comes from Jericho in what is today northern Israel. The first continuous sequence of settlements at Jericho is associated with the preagricultural Natufians and typifies the trends we have already noted. Jericho emerged as a seasonal settlement around 9000 B.C.E., probably due to its abundant freshwater springs. Around 8000 B.C.E., however, the inhabitants of Jericho undertook a spectacular building program. Many new dwellings were built on stone foundations, and a massive, skillfully dressed stone wall was constructed around the entire settlement. Built into this perimeter wall was a circular tower, the excavated remains of which still reach to a height of thirty feet.

The precise function of this wall is impossible to know, but most likely it was intended as some sort of defense, perhaps as much against nature as human threats (Jericho lies several hundred feet below sea level and is thus vulnerable to flash floods and mudslides). The "watchtower" is even more puzzling and illustrates how difficult it is to interpret archaeological remains in the absence of written documents. Was the tower meant as a lookout post against foreign enemies and marauders, or did its ambitious height extend toward the heavens for some religious purpose? Whatever the case, the wall and its tower encircled and served an impressive population: the early site of Jericho covered 8 acres (almost 3.25 hectares) and supported a population of two to three thousand people. This population was sustained by the intense cultivation of recently domesticated strains of wheat and barley, irrigated by water from the nearby springs.

Starting in the eighth millennium B.C.E., Jericho's inhabitants also produced some of the earliest known pottery. The importance of this breakthrough, both for ancient culture and modern scholarship, cannot be overstated. For the settlers at Jericho, the invention of pottery enabled them to store more goods than ever before. Liquids in particular could now be preserved as an important part of the community's surplus. Pottery also made possible long-distance trade in such desirable commodities as beer, wine, and various oils. Pottery now provides archaeologists with a more precise means for dating prehistoric sites. Although individual ceramic objects are extremely fragile, fragments (shards) of broken pottery are virtually indestructible. Because styles of pottery changed very rapidly in the ancient world, archaeologists have been able to use pottery shards to create a more accurate (but still relative and rough) chronology for the world before recorded history.

Early Village Pottery. A shallow bowl from a western Asian village site dating from about 5000 B.C.E.

No less impressive than Jericho is Çatal Hüyük in the south central part of the Anatolian Plateau in modern Turkey. A somewhat later site than Jericho, Çatal Hüyük had its preeminence from 6500–5500 B.C.E. The agricultural technology of the inhabitants was quite advanced. They produced a wide range of vegetable foods, from peas and lentils to cereal crops. They also cultivated fruits and nuts. Meat and dairy products were also an important part of their diet; among much else, Çatal Hüyük provides us with our earliest indisputable evidence of domesticated cattle herds. But although their diets were relatively healthy, the people's life expectancies were short. Men died on average around the age of thirty-four, and women around the age of thirty.

Agricultural surpluses had important social consequences. Unlike hunter-gatherer societies, settled communities engaged in agriculture accumulated surpluses and stored commodities. This in turn allowed differences to arise in the amount of surplus wealth that individuals in a community could acquire and stockpile for themselves. Moreover, once humans became accustomed to sedentary agriculture, they found it much more difficult to split off from the community, even when the consequences of social and economic differentiation became oppressive. With agriculture, significant social and economic distinctions emerged within human societies for the first time.

At Jericho and Çatal Hüyük villagers speculated on

the supernatural powers they believed ruled their world, and how they might relate to those powers. This too was an immensely important step in the evolution of human culture. Further, the fact that humans believed these forces required special services and gifts in the form of ritual and sacrifice allowed for the emergence over time of a "priestly class," individuals uniquely qualified to commune with the supernatural forces that governed the life of the community. Such religious leadership was a natural bridge to more obviously "political" forms of authority: leading war bands, constructing defenses, and extracting resources from those subject to their authority. Through their command of the community's religious, military, and economic resources, village elites began to establish themselves as a self-justifying ruling class.

Trade was another important development in these early Neolithic villages. By 5000 B.C.E. a series of important long-distance trade networks had arisen across the Near East; local trade routes were undoubtedly even older, but are impossible to trace. Exotic goods were frequent objects of exchange: obsidian from Çatal Hüyük was an important commodity, as were precious stones such as turquoise, lapis lazuli, and jadeite. Marine shells were also prized across the region. Long-distance trade accelerated the exchange of commodities and ideas throughout the Fertile Crescent. At the same time, however, it also increased the degree of social stratification within these village communities. Long-distance trade was generally controlled by local elites, whose status was enhanced by their special access to high-prestige luxury goods. As a result, a self-perpetuating cycle developed. Trade encouraged the further stratification of society; elites, anxious to enhance their power and status, encouraged further trade as a way of acquiring even more economic and social power. Elites sought to control overland and overseas trade more effectively, and to organize the production of marketable goods within their own communities. As a result, control over specialist artisans emerged as an important feature of elite social status in these Neolithic village communities.

As this last example may suggest, what underlay all these social and economic changes was the economic specialization that agricultural surpluses made possible. In hunter-gatherer societies, every member of the community participated in the basic business of food

CHRONOLOGY

FROM PREHISTORY TO HISTORY

Appearance of figurative artwork	40,000 B.C.E.
Origin of food production	11,000 B.C.E.
Beginnings of sedentary agricultural societies	7000 B.C.E.
Emergence of villages	6500–3000 B.C.E.
Development of writing	3300–2500 B.C.E.
Emergence of cities	3100 B.C.E.

acquisition. In an organized agricultural community, however, certain people could devote at least a portion of their labor to pursuits other than agriculture: the making of pottery or cloth, the manufacture of weapons and tools, the design and construction of fortifications, the conduct of long-distance trade. Surpluses and specialization also permitted the emergence of social elites, who by organizing and exploiting the labor and production of others, were able to turn ruling into yet another specialist occupation. As villages grew larger and more sophisticated, the amount of specialization increased, until a significant fraction of the population could become full-time nonagriculturalists. This was the essential first step in the development of true urban-based civilizations.

What underlay all these social and economic changes was the economic specialization that agricultural surpluses made possible.

MESOPOTAMIA: THE EMERGENCE OF THE FIRST CITIES AND PRIMARY CIVILIZATIONS

How did irrigation and temple building figure in early Mesopotamian civilization?

Surprisingly, the initial transition from prehistory to history, and the shift from village to city, did not take place in the Fertile Crescent. Rather, the first true cities

HOW DID IRRIGATION AND TEMPLE BUILDING FIGURE IN EARLY MESOPOTAMIAN CIVILIZATION?

MESOPOTAMIA   15

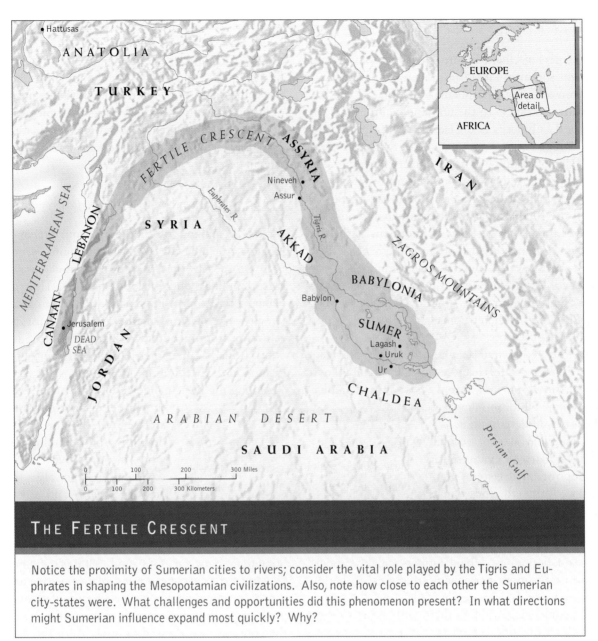

THE FERTILE CRESCENT

Notice the proximity of Sumerian cities to rivers; consider the vital role played by the Tigris and Euphrates in shaping the Mesopotamian civilizations. Also, note how close to each other the Sumerian city-states were. What challenges and opportunities did this phenomenon present? In what directions might Sumerian influence expand most quickly? Why?

developed in one of the most inhospitable environments imaginable—an area known later to the Greeks as Mesopotamia, "the land between the rivers." Corresponding roughly to the area of modern Iraq, Mesopotamia does not enjoy much rainfall, and summer temperatures routinely exceed 110°F. The soils of the region are sandy and infertile unless they are irrigated. And the two rivers that supply this flat and largely featureless plain with water—the Tigris and the Euphrates—are notorious for their violence and unpredictability. Both rivers are prone to flooding, and the Tigris could in ancient times jump its banks and

change course from one year to the next. Nevertheless, it was in this most uninviting of environments where the first true cities emerged. The civilization and people that arose in southern Mesopotamia are called Sumerian, and the area they inhabited known as Sumer. By 3100 B.C.E., the Sumerians had created one of the world's first primary civilizations, that is, a culture that "invented" the city without having adapted it from a previously established civilization. In order to understand how the Sumerians forged their civilization, we must therefore examine the roots of urban development in southern Mesopotamia.

UBAID CULTURE

The founders of Ubaid culture (so called from its best-described site at al-Ubaid in modern Iraq) appear to have moved into Mesopotamia around 5900 B.C.E. What attracted them to the unfriendly confines of the Tigris and Euphrates is unclear. Growing population densities may have forced them out of the Fertile Crescent. Or they could have been refugees from the catastrophic flooding that occurred around the Black Sea at this time, when the land bridge that had previously divided the Mediterranean Sea from what is now the Black Sea (but what was then an enormous freshwater lake) burst, inundating lakeshore settlements with a cascade of seawater. But whatever compelled the Ubaid peoples to move into Mesopotamia, it appears they brought their village culture with them. They were not hunter-gatherer nomads who had fallen into difficult circumstances.

The most consistent features of Ubaid life were ever-intensifying efforts to control their natural environment through irrigation and a pronounced emphasis on temple building. Almost as soon as we find farming settlements in what would become Sumer, we discover evidence for fairly sophisticated systems of irrigation. Although these may have begun as simple channels and collection pools to harness the excess waters from the periodic flooding of the Tigris and Euphrates, Ubaid farmers quickly undertook to create more permanent structures. Irrigation canals and ponds were excavated: soon thereafter, Ubaid peoples began lining them with stone so they would last from one season to the next. They also constructed dikes and levees to control the seasonal flooding of the rivers, and to direct the flow of water into the canals they had built for irrigation. Despite the hostile environment, Ubaid agricultural communities were soon producing surpluses sufficient to support specialists in weaving, pottery making, metalwork, trade, and construction—the typical attributes of a Neolithic village.

The inhabitants of these settlements also established central structures that served religious functions. Starting out as simple and fairly humble shrines, the edifices they erected soon evolved into impressive temples built of dried mud brick: the scarcity of stone in the region compelled them to save that material for tools. Each larger settlement had such a building,

Despite the hostile environment, Ubaid agricultural communities were soon producing surpluses sufficient to support specialists.

which became progressively larger with successive rebuildings. From these temples, a priestly class served both as the officiants of religious life in the settlements and as managers of the economic resources of the community. In this latter role, they organized not only the construction of ever-larger temples, but also developed and maintained the complex irrigation systems that made village life possible in the Mesopotamian desert.

URUK PERIOD (4300–2900 B.C.E.)

By the beginning of the fourth millennium B.C.E., Ubaid settlements were coalescing into larger and more prosperous sites, with ever more elaborate temples, buildings and village planning. This period, named after its most impressive site, the great Sumerian city-state of Uruk (modern Warka), witnessed the transition from Neolithic Ubaid villages to Sumerian cities. It marks, therefore, the true beginnings of civilization in the Mediterranean world.

Among the principal developments of the period is the further elaboration of temple architecture. This trend reflects not only the centrality of religion in the lives of these communities, but also the increasing wealth and control of the priestly class over communal life. The White Temple at Uruk provides a stunning example of this general trend. Sometime between 3500 and 3300 B.C.E., builders constructed a massive sloping platform that towered nearly forty feet above the surrounding flatlands. The platform, with its four corners at the cardinal points of the compass, was dressed in brick. Atop the platform stood another structure, the shrine or temple proper, also dressed in brick but painted a brilliant white. Per-

CHRONOLOGY

ORIGINS OF MESOPOTAMIAN SOCIETY

Ubaid Period	5900–4300 B.C.E.
Uruk Period	4300–2900 B.C.E.
Early Dynastic Period	2900–2500 B.C.E.
Akkadian Period	2350–2160 B.C.E.
Ur Dynasty	2100–2000 B.C.E.

HOW DID IRRIGATION AND TEMPLE BUILDING FIGURE IN EARLY MESOPOTAMIAN CIVILIZATION?

MESOPOTAMIA 17

haps dedicated to the sky god known in later Sumerian sources as An, the temple betrays an ambition to serve the gods with increasing monumentality, and—it has been suggested—to provide them with "mountaintop" homes in a part of the world conspicuous for its absence of mountains.

Such temples (which grew up across Sumer) reflect the increasingly urbanized character of Sumerian life. Throughout the region, smaller, satellite villages were falling under the control of the greater sites. Uruk, for example, organized under its management the various settlements and their separate irrigation systems extending for six miles in every direction. The larger villages were also growing rapidly, their teeming economic activity almost certainly attracting immigrants. Uruk and other principal centers were now characterized by densely packed dwellings accessed by winding streets. By the end of the Uruk Period Sumer also shared a common language, a fact made clear thanks to the invention that moves the Sumerians fully into the light of history: writing.

THE DEVELOPMENT OF WRITING

Like many of the breakthroughs we have considered in this chapter, the invention of writing did not occur overnight. For millennia, the villagers of the Near East had been using clay tokens to represent various commodities, perhaps to help them keep track of inventories and to facilitate the burgeoning trade of the region. Such tokens were cumbersome, however, especially for long-distance trade: imagine having to carry a different clay token to represent each piece of obsidian you carried as well as the obsidian itself! Merchants therefore began to create single tokens specifying both the nature and the number of their trade goods. Ultimately, the practice developed of placing all the tokens from a single transaction inside a hollow clay ball, and inscribing, on the outside of the ball, the shapes of all the tokens it contained. This helped not only to ensure accuracy of exchange, but probably also discouraged dishonest middlemen from skimming off the top of their cargos.

In its earliest phases, writing thus evolved as a means of record keeping in connection with economic pursuits. This origin meant it was natural and well suited for keeping track of the growing wealth of the Uruk Period protocities. By 3300 B.C.E., the priestly class (or those working for them) realized that they could dispense with the clumsy token-and-ball system and replace it with flat clay tablets, on which they could note the desired information by inscribing the appropriate symbols. For some time, this system remained purely pictographic: the symbols

Cuneiform Writing. On the left, a Sumerian clay tablet from about 3000 B.C.E. Here standardized pictures are beginning to represent abstractions. On the right, carvings on limestone from about 2600 B.C.E. The evolution of standardized cuneiform writing is now complete: the inscription proclaims that a king of Ur has built a temple.

marked into the clay represented physical objects, and often in some crude way resembled the objects in question. Over the course of time, however, the same symbol might be used to evoke not only a physical object, but an idea associated with that object. The symbol for a bowl of food, *ninda* (a noun) might thus be used to express a more abstract notion such as bread or sustenance—an idea not otherwise easily represented by a quick sketch into soft clay. Each symbol also came to be associated with a particular phonetic sound. The next stage in the evolution of writing was then to use a particular symbol not to evoke the thing it represented, but the sound with which it was associated. Thus any time a Sumerian scribe needed to employ the sound *ninda*, even as part of another word or name, he would use the symbol for a bowl of food. Later, special marks were added so that the reader could discern whether the writer intended the object itself or the *phonogram* (the sound represented by the symbol).

By 3100 B.C.E. scribes had largely abandoned writing with pointed sticks. Instead, they now used a more durable reed stylus to make symbols in clay, a stylus which left an impression shaped like a wedge (the Latin word for which is *cuneus*). We refer to the script rendered with this new writing implement as *cuneiform*. Cuneiform symbols could be impressed more quickly and efficiently into the soft clay, and the reeds themselves were less likely to break than were sticks. However, the new stylus made it more difficult to draw pictograms that accurately reflected the original shape (such as a bowl of food) they were meant to represent. As a result, the symbols of the language became more and more abstracted, until they barely resembled the original pictograms at all.

Symbols ultimately were invented for every possible vowel-consonant combination in the Sumerian language, and the symbols therefore ran into the hundreds. Understandably, it took many years to learn to read and write cuneiform, and only a small minority of the population ever did so. Those who did, however, became important and influential people in Sumerian society. For the entirety of the third millennium, it was largely the sons of the elite who attended the "Houses of the Tablet," as the scribal schools were called. But despite the wide variety of symbols and the complicated nature of the script, cuneiform proved remarkably durable. For over fifteen hundred years after its development, it remained the principal writing system of the Asian Near East, even in societies that no longer spoke the Sumerian language.

THE SUMERIANS ENTER HISTORY

Why did a common religion not create peace among the Sumerians?

After about 2500 B.C.E., the Sumerians used writing for a wide variety of economic, political, and religious purposes. Tens of thousands of these records survive, mostly in the form of clay tablets. These records make it possible for us to know a great deal more about the Sumerians than we do about any other human society of the time. We can begin to understand their political relationships, their feelings about their gods, and the social and economic structure of their society. The Sumerians are, in this sense, the first historical—as opposed to prehistorical—society.

The great centers of Sumerian culture—Uruk, Ur, Lagash, Eridu, Kish, and others—shared a common culture and a common language. The Sumerian language, however, appears not to be related to any other known language in the world. Attempts to relate it to the languages of the Asian subcontinent or those of western Asia have failed. This has led to bitter scholarly arguments over whether the Sumerians—a label applied to them by their neighbors—moved into southern Mesopotamia from elsewhere, or whether their unique culture (language included) developed out of Ubaid culture. The continuity of cult activity supports the latter view, as does the lack of any significant evidence for invasion; but ultimately, the question is unanswerable given the current state of knowledge on the subject.

Like language, religion was another shared element of Sumerian culture. The primacy accorded to temple building and the preeminence of the ruling priestly class continued down to the end of the Uruk period (c. 2900 B.C.E.). This common religion did not produce peace between the Sumerian cities, however. Although all Sumerian communities recognized the totality of the Sumerian pantheon (some fifteen hundred gods), the citizens of each city-state saw their city as the estate of one particular god, and sought through their endeavors to glorify their patron deity. The result was intense competition, which could easily escalate into open warfare.

A significant proportion of the cultivable land of each city belonged outright to the temple of the pa-

WHY DID A COMMON RELIGION NOT CREATE PEACE AMONG THE SUMERIANS?

THE SUMERIANS ENTER HISTORY 19

tron god, and much of the economic produce of the city was brought into the great temple-warehouse complexes. There the priests and their officials would determine the redistribution of the city's food and other goods. Each Sumerian city had a ruling aristocracy, from which the priests and important officials of the temples no doubt came; but it was the priests who stood at the top of these highly theocratic societies. In this early period of Sumerian civilization perhaps as much as half the population consisted of commoners, free persons who held small parcels of land sufficient to sustain themselves and make any required payments to the temple complex. The temples also had large numbers of legally free dependents engaged in activities ranging from the artisan workshops of the city's god (making pottery, working as smiths) to undertaking agricultural labor on temple lands. But the elites held the lion's share of nontemple land and exercised political and economic power. Commoners had few if any political rights, and their social and economic position seems to have eroded over time.

There were also large numbers of slaves in Sumerian society. The high degree of urbanization in many ancient civilizations required the production of surpluses substantial enough to support sizable numbers of priests, aristocrats, poets, artists and the like. Often such surpluses were produced through the labor of unfree persons. In Sumer, as elsewhere in the ancient world, slaves were often prisoners of war. If the slave came originally from another Sumerian city, there were strict limits on the master's power over him or her, and he or she had to be released after three years. Non-Sumerians could be held indefinitely, although there were means by which slaves might buy their freedom. Despite these safeguards, slaves in Sumer were still the chattel property of their owners. They could be beaten, punished, branded like animals, or bought and sold on their owner's whim. Although ancient slavery may not have been quite so horrible as more modern examples (such as that practiced in the New World), it was still a highly undesirable thing to be a slave.

Although the Sumerians shared a common language and religion, individual city-states were fiercely independent and frequently hostile to one another. Because the great centers identified themselves with particular gods, and the populations of those cities conceived of their activities as being dedicated to their patron deity, intense jealousy and competition among the Sumerian city-states resulted. The members of a Sumerian city would have considered any political submission or military defeat a disgrace and a failure; they had disappointed their patron deity and allowed him or her to be humiliated by the members of a community serving another god. Thus there was little possibility of greater political unification in Sumer once the pattern of domination by twelve great cities became set. Of course the tension between the Sumerian city-states also had an economic dimension: water rights and access to both arable land and trade routes were at stake. But the organization of Sumerian society meant that conflicts over economic resources by definition inevitably involved a religious dimension. To allow another god's city to encroach on the estate of your own patron deity was unthinkable. The Sumerians shared a common culture, but a common government was impossible.

Commoners had few if any political rights, and their social and economic position seems to have eroded over time.

THE EARLY DYNASTIC PERIOD, PHASES I AND II (2900–2500 B.C.E.)

As we have seen, Mesopotamian society was dominated by the religious elite from the Ubaid period until the early part of the third millennium. Religion remained central to Sumerian thought and experience throughout the history of this people. However, the intense competition and rivalry between the Sumerian city-states allowed for the emergence of a new type of leadership that would compete for preeminence with the priesthood within Sumerian cities: war leadership and, as it evolved, something we might recognize as kingship. This has led historians to term this phase of Sumerian civilization the Early Dynastic Period.

Around 2900 B.C.E. conflicts between the great centers of Sumerian civilization intensified. As each city-state grew larger (with anywhere from ten thousand to fifty thousand inhabitants), it invariably found its frontiers colliding with those of other cities and, with its population still expanding, was more desperate than ever to secure the necessary resources to survive. In the harsh deserts of southern Mesopotamia, threats to irrigation rights and access to cultivable land were life-and-death matters. Warfare now became a regular feature of Sumerian life, and those individuals who could most successfully lead armies into battle and defend the interests of the city and its god acquired tremendous prestige and power. A variety of titles denoted authority in Sumerian society: *en* ("lord"), *ensi* ("governor"), and *lugal* (literally, "big man"). The last of these, *lugal*, became the favorite choice of those men who managed to put themselves in positions of authority by way of their martial ability.

Within Sumerian society the *lugal* soon eclipsed the power of the temple priesthood, but we should not think of his role as secular. Far from it: the *lugal* led the armies of the city's god into battle, and once the position of *lugal* became institutional, hereditary, and supreme, these men were careful to surround their power with the approval and holiness of the city's patron deity. Sumerian kingship was no more "secular" than the temple—with all of its political and economic pursuits—was purely "religious." Rather than a struggle between "religious" and "secular" authority, what developed was a certain tension between the power of the temple and the power of the palace, with the officials of each believing they should hold chief importance in the lives of the community. In practice, however, the power of the *lugal* grew throughout the Early Dynastic Period, as demonstrated by two important documents, the Sumerian King List and the Epic of Gilgamesh.

The Sumerian King List was originally composed toward the end of the third millennium, perhaps c. 2125 B.C.E.; but it draws on earlier sources and is clearly an attempt, probably by the priests at the important city of Eridu, to identify the origins of kingship and the individuals who had exercised such authority in the past. It is characteristic of the King List, as with much Near Eastern literature, that its authors attempted to recapture and rationalize a long-lost and mythical past, ascribing impossibly long reigns (tens of thousands of years, in some cases) to their ancient kings. The King List does, however, preserve some historically credible information. It begins with a story about a Great Flood, just possibly a memory of the great inundations that resulted around 5500 B.C.E. when the land bridge between the Mediterranean and the Black Sea collapsed. The King List's primary concern, however, is to demonstrate the continuity of Sumerian kingship as an institution handed down from heaven. As a result, the King List creates the impression that Sumer was more politically unified than it actually was: no Sumerian *lugal* extended his domain over a city other than his own until

at least 2600 B.C.E., although the King List would have its readers believe otherwise. Nonetheless, its concern to demonstrate the continuity and power of *lugal*-ship is itself telling; by the later third millennium, when the King List was composed, real power was perceived as residing with the *lugal*, not with the heads of the temple priesthood.

The Epic of Gilgamesh is a very different kind of source. It is a literary document, the first of its kind in world history, that recounts the exploits of a legendary king of Uruk named Gilgamesh. The epic enjoyed tremendous popularity and staying power throughout the Near East, being translated and copied for well over two thousand years after the original Sumerian version was composed. Scholars have reconstructed a significant proportion of the tale from the various fragments— some lengthy, some meager— discovered over the course of the last century. Although the composite nature of the epic as it exists today means that we may not have a "version" of the Gilgamesh story exactly like that read in ancient Sumer, most experts agree that the epic as we have it largely reflects Sumerian society and culture around the middle of the third millennium B.C.E.

The character Gilgamesh was a powerful *lugal* who had won his reputation through military conquest and general heroism, particularly against barbarians. (One occupational hazard of city-dwellers was that their collections of "fixed assets" made them attractive and tempting targets not only for other cities, but for nomads.) Through the fame and prestige he acquired, he became so powerful that he could surmount many of the conventions of his day. We hear at the start of the epic how the people complained about their king, even though they still revered him: he kept their sons away at war for too long; he showed no respect for the nobles, carousing with their wives and daughters as he pleased; he disappointed them by his sacrilegious conduct. They prayed to the gods for relief, and ultimately a wild man named Enkidu was fashioned by the deities to challenge Gilgamesh.

The confrontation between Gilgamesh and Enkidu is rich with historically useful information. Gilgamesh is a creature of the city, but his challenger is of the wilderness, barely more than a beast himself until he is "civilized" by a sexual tryst with a temple prostitute— an urban, specialist profession to say the least. After his contact with her, Enkidu is unable to return to the sim-

> The King List's primary concern is to demonstrate the continuity of Sumerian kingship as an institution handed down from heaven.

WHY DID A COMMON RELIGION NOT CREATE PEACE AMONG THE SUMERIANS?

THE SUMERIANS ENTER HISTORY   21

ple life, and the animals of the wilderness no longer speak to him; in Sumerian terms, his urbanization had literally made a man out of him.

This episode reflects the dichotomy the Sumerians perceived between city and wilderness, between what was "civilized" and what was not. We recognize in Enkidu the hunter-gatherer who was doubtless far more intimate with nature than were the Sumerians after centuries of civic life; but such "naturalness" was not a quality the Sumerians admired. The epic does not intend to provoke sympathy for Enkidu's loss of innocence; instead, that loss allows him to fulfill his destiny—to become human so he can first fight and then befriend the king of Uruk. Such disdain on the part of the urbanized and civilized toward those who were uncivilized is voiced in almost every ancient civilization. Even Aristotle's famous dictum that "Man is a political animal" means, in essence, that humans are creatures who must live in cities; otherwise, they cannot be fully human.

The episode following the friendship forged between Gilgamesh and Enkidu illustrates the hostility and fear Sumerians felt toward the wilderness. The two men set off into the forest to do battle with a terrifying nature demigod named Humbaba, who nearly bests the heroes. In the end, however, they prevail, another triumph of civilized humanity over a natural world that would destroy humanity and its creations if it gained the upper hand. Given the harsh climate and unpredictable environment in which the Sumerians lived, their adversarial relationship with the natural world is understandable. Battling uncooperative rivers, searing heat, salinization of the soil, and the raids of less civilized folk, the Sumerians developed a pessimistic attitude toward their natural environment that is mirrored not only in their general view of life, but also in their view of the gods.

SUMERIAN RELIGION

One of the Sumerian creation stories held that people had been created when the powerful god Enlil used the wind to separate the male heaven from the female earth, and then fashioned a pickax with which he broke open the earth. Through this fissure, humankind—already created inside the earth—was able to emerge and populate the surface of the world. The Sumerians thus believed that humanity itself had been

wrested from the inhospitable earth and created for one purpose, to serve the gods. Every aspect of Sumerian society and culture was thus imbued with religiosity. Their art, architecture, and literature all reflected the Sumerians' concern with fulfilling their duties. Throughout the third millennium, much of any Sumerian city's economy continued to be centered on the chief temple and administered by the huge hierarchy of priests and priestesses, entertainers and seers, eunuchs and temple slaves who kept the temples teeming with sacred activity. However much a powerful *lugal* might distance himself from the temple priesthood, it was axiomatic that his authority was also divinely inspired and bestowed, his kingship a gift from heaven.

We should not assume, though, that relations between humans and gods were warm. Gods were on the one hand to be exalted; massive temples called ziggurats, made of dried mud brick and reaching into the sky, evolved out of the increasingly elaborate shrines of the Uruk Period. The great ziggurat to a city's patron deity would have been the central architectural feature of the community—a *lugal's* palace might rival it in splendor, but for sheer awe-inspiring conspicuousness, the ziggurat was unmatched.

> The Sumerians thus believed that humanity itself had been wrested from the inhospitable earth and created for one purpose, to serve the gods.

That such effort and expense continued to be poured into honoring the gods tells us that however much a king might have eclipsed the temple priesthood, the latter was by no means weak. The gods remained a critically important part of the lives of Sumerians, who went to great pains to honor their gods dutifully with temples, festivals, and sacrifices.

Affection for the gods, however, was not the primary motivation. Fear and suspicion characterized the Sumerian attitude toward divinity. They expected the gods to be cruel, mean-spirited, and capricious, attending to their own whims with little care for the effect those whims might have on humanity, whether positive or negative. Like most ancient peoples, the Sumerians sought primarily to appease their gods through the proper performance of rituals and sacrifices, in hopes the gods would remain favorable to the city and its inhabitants. A benign detachment toward humanity was what most Sumerians sought from their gods. To ask for more could be dangerous. Appeals to the gods for help were a last resort in desperate circumstances, for inviting the gods to involve themselves directly in human life could have unforeseen and often unpleasant consequences.

Sumerian Ziggurat. This edifice, built in Ur around 2100 B.C.E., is the best-preserved surviving ziggurat. As can be seen from the diagram of its original form at left, a shrine, reached by climbing four stories and passing through a massive portal, was the goal of the worshiper's ascent and the most sacred part of the temple.

The Sumerian view of an afterlife was similarly grim. Whatever devotion one might pay to the gods in this world, it was only in this world that one might enjoy the benefits. The Sumerians, despite their complex pantheon and sophisticated theology, never developed a refined sense of an afterlife. They expected neither eternal punishment nor reward. Instead, the dead simply crossed a man-eating river into the "Land of No Return," a gloomy place which enjoyed no light. Relatives might bury the dead with basic articles such as food and clothing, and diversions such as musical instruments and games, in the hope of making the glum, unhappy underworld a bit more bearable for the departed. In many ways, the afterlife was thus a continuation of the anxious, pessimistic existence of this world, only worse.

With such pessimism came a degree of quiet resignation toward the unpleasantness and ultimate futility of life. When his friend Enkidu is killed by the goddess Inanna (whom both Gilgamesh and Enkidu have mocked), Gilgamesh's horror at Enkidu's death propels him to seek immortality for himself. Against the advice of other characters, he continues his quest until he learns of a plant of eternal life at the bottom of a

Sumerian Praying Figures. These statues dating from about 2700 B.C.E. show Sumerians praying for the gods to bring them prosperity.

THE FLOOD: TWO ACCOUNTS

The Epic of Gilgamesh preserves a traditional account of a destructive flood sent by the gods to punish humanity. As we have seen, the tale of Gilgamesh originated in the early third millennium B.C.E., meaning that it predates biblical accounts by at least fifteen hundred years, if not more. The stunning similarity between the versions of Gilgamesh and the Book of Genesis is evidence of the strong cultural influence exerted by older Near Eastern civilizations on the early Hebrews.

THE EPIC OF GILGAMESH

[Utnapishtim said to Gilgamesh]: "High up the constant Euphrates there rests a place you call Shurrupak, where gods and goddesses recline. Then came the flood, sent by gods' intent. . . . [The god] Ea [gave] me this advice: 'Arise and hear my words: abandon your home and build a boat. Reject the stinking stench of wealth. . . . Take the seed of all you need aboard with you and carefully weigh anchor after securing a roof that will let in no water.' . . . By week's end I engineered designs for an acre's worth of floor upon the ark we built . . . 120 cubits measured its deck. . . . Pitch for the hull I poured into the kiln. . . . My clan brought on the food they'd eat and all the things we thought we'd need. At last it was my turn just then to shepherd beasts and birds and babies wet and loud. . . . The sky screamed and storms wrecked the earth. . . . Flood ended. . . . I released the watch-bird, to soar in search of land. The bird came back within a day exhausted, unrelieved from lack of rest. I then released a swallow, to soar in search of land, [which also returned]. I then released a raven, to soar in seach of land. The bird took flight above more shallow seas, found food and found release and found no need to fly back to me. . . . [I] offered sacrifice [spreading] the scents that gods favored. When [the god] Enlil saw the boat, he released his calm reason and released the Igigi, monsters of blood. 'What force dares defy my anger? How dare a man still be alive?' . . . Then with these words Ea himself said to Enlil: 'How dare you drown so many little people without consulting me? Why not just kill the one who offended you, drown only the guilty?' . . . [Enlil] gently raised me from the slime, placed my wife beside my kneeling form, and blessed us both at once with hands upon our bowed heads."

Danny P. Jackson, trans. *The Epic of Gilgamesh*, Tablet XI, Columns I–IV. (Wauconda, Ill.: Bolchazy-Carducci Publishers, 1997), pp. 78–82.

BOOK OF GENESIS

The Lord saw that the wickedness of humankind was great in the earth and . . . said "I will blot out from the earth the human beings I have created . . . for I am sorry I have made them." But Noah found favor in the sight of the Lord. . . . God saw that the earth was corrupt and . . . said to Noah, "I have determined to make an end to all flesh. . . . Make yourself an ark of cypress wood; make rooms in the ark, and cover it inside and out with pitch. . . . Make a roof for the ark, and put the door of the ark in its side. . . . For my part I am going to bring a flood on the earth, to destroy from under heaven all flesh. . . . But I will establish a covenant with you; and you shall come into the ark, you, your sons, your wife, and your sons' wives with you. And of every living thing you shall bring two of every kind into the ark, to keep them alive with you. . . . Also take with you every kind of food that is eaten." . . . All the fountains of the great deep burst forth, and the windows of the heavens were opened. . . . The waters gradually receded from the earth. . . . At the end of forty days, Noah opened a window of the ark . . . and sent out the raven, and it went to and fro until the waters were dried up from the earth. Then he sent out the dove from him, to see if the waters had subsided from the

face of the ground, but the dove found no place to set its foot, and it returned. . . . He waited another seven days, and again sent out the dove [which] came back to him . . . and there in its beak was a freshly plucked olive leaf; so Noah knew the waters had subsided from the earth. Then he . . . sent out the dove, and it did not return to him anymore. . . . Noah built an altar to the Lord . . . and offered burnt offerings. And when the Lord smelled the pleasing odor, the Lord said in his heart, "I will never again curse the ground because of humankind . . . nor will I ever again destroy every living creature as I have done.". . . God blessed Noah and his sons.

Genesis 6:5–9:1, *The New Oxford Annotated Bible.* (Oxford: Oxford University Press, 1994).

deep pool. Gilgamesh swims to the bottom and retrieves it, only to have it stolen from him as he surfaces by a serpent, who then disappears below with Gilgamesh's only chance for immortality. In the end, Gilgamesh, the great king of Uruk, ponders the futility of all human endeavor. Reflecting on the impermanence of his own deeds, even of Uruk's walls, he asks, "Why do I bother working for nothing? Who even notices what I do?"

SCIENCE, TECHNOLOGY, AND TRADE

Despite their doubt and gloominess, the Sumerians were not paralyzed by their uncertainties. Indeed, their general suspicion of the gods and their adversarial relationship with the environment seem to have inculcated in the Sumerians a high degree of self-reliance, and a number of indispensable inventions—beyond writing—are the result of Sumerian ingenuity.

The Sumerians were first-rate metallurgists, despite the fact that their land had no natural mineral resources. By the end of the Neolithic Age, a number of cultures throughout the Near East had learned how to produce copper weapons and tools. Mesopotamia itself had no copper, but by the Uruk Period (4300–2900 B.C.E.), trade routes were bringing raw copper into Sumer, where the Sumerians processed it and hammered it into weapons and tools. Shortly before 3000 B.C.E., perhaps starting in eastern Anatolia, people discovered that copper could be alloyed with arsenic (or later, tin) to produce bronze. Bronze is almost as malleable as copper, but pours more easily

Sumerian War Chariots. The earliest known representation of the wheel, dating from about 2600 B.C.E., shows how wheels were carpentered together from slabs of wood. (For a later Mesopotamian wheel with spokes, see the illustration on p. 59.) We can also observe that at the dawn of recorded history, military aims stimulated technological innovation, as they have ever since.

WHY DID A COMMON RELIGION NOT CREATE PEACE AMONG THE SUMERIANS?

THE SUMERIANS ENTER HISTORY   25

into molds and, when cooled, maintains its rigidity and shape better than copper. Because of the widespread use of bronze in which the Sumerians and the neighboring cultures engaged, we refer to a Bronze Age beginning around 3000 B.C.E.

Alongside writing, the invention of the wheel stands at the top of any list of fundamental advancements in human technology. The Sumerians were using potters' wheels by the middle of the fourth millennium B.C.E., allowing for the production of high-quality clay vessels in greater quantity than ever before. By around 3200 B.C.E., the Sumerians were also using two-wheeled chariots and four-wheeled carts drawn by donkeys. (Horses were unknown in western Asia until they were introduced by eastern invaders sometime between 2000 and 1700 B.C.E.). The chariots and carts were mounted on wheels that were solid, not spoked: two or three slabs of wood were shaped into a circle and fastened together with studs or braces. Wheeled chariots were used mainly in warfare; surviving illustrations from about 2600 B.C.E. depict them trampling the enemy. Wheeled carts were an even more important advance, however, because they dramatically increased the productivity of the Sumerian work force.

The use of the wheel in pottery may have suggested its application for transport, but such a connection is far from inevitable. The Egyptians were using the potter's wheel by at least 2700 B.C.E., but they did not use the wheel for transport until a millennium later, and even then they probably learned of it from Mesopotamia. In the Western Hemisphere, wheeled transport was unknown (except for children's toys) until the sixteenth century C.E. We should not underestimate, therefore, either the importance or the uniqueness of Sumerian wheel technology.

The Sumerians were also pioneers in the study of mathematics. Their mathematical interests may have been encouraged by the nature of Sumerian agriculture: to construct their elaborate systems of irrigation canals, dikes, and reservoirs, they had to develop sophisticated measuring and surveying techniques, as well as the art of map making. Agricultural concerns probably also lay behind the lunar calendar they invented, which consisted of twelve months, six lasting thirty days, and six lasting twenty-nine days. Since this produced a year of only 354 days, the Sumerians eventually discovered that they had to add a month to their calendars every few years in order to predict the recurrence of the seasons with sufficient accuracy. But the Sumerian practice of dividing time into multiples of sixty has lasted to the present day, not only in our notions of the thirty-day month (which corresponds approximately with the phases of the moon), but also in our division of the hour into sixty minutes, and the minute into sixty seconds. Mathematics also contributed to Sumerian architecture, allowing the people to build domes and arches thousands of years before the Romans would rediscover them.

An assortment of other breakthroughs are also credited to the Sumerians. They developed the bronze plow, complete with attachments for depositing seed as the ground was broken, a labor-saving device that increased the efficiency and productivity of Sumerian agriculture. Sumerians developed the first sailboats, crucial for their quest to exploit overseas trade along the shores of the Persian Gulf and beyond. They used the raw materials of other lands to manufacture textiles, paints, perfumes, and medicines. Indeed, by the

A Sumerian Plow with a Seed Drill. Such plows were still being used in the seventh century B.C.E., when this black stone tablet was engraved.

middle of the third millennium, the Sumerians had invented something like a science of pharmacology, producing drugs to cure ailments they had once ascribed to divine displeasure or possession.

The Sumerians' ability to engage in these activities depended, however, on the acquisition of raw materials through trade, for their homeland was almost completely devoid of natural resources. The Sumerians therefore pioneered trade routes up and down the Tigris and Euphrates and into the hilly flanks of Mesopotamia, following the tributaries of these great rivers. They blazed trails across the deserts toward the west, where they interacted with and influenced the Egyptians. By sea, they traded with the peoples of the Persian Gulf and, directly or indirectly, with the civilizations of the Indus Valley. Like the Neolithic traders who conveyed goods from village to village, the Sumerians carried their ideas with them along with their merchandise: their literature, their art, their use of writing, and the whole cultural complex that arose from their urban way of life. From its Sumerian roots, the idea of civilization thus spread throughout the ancient Near Eastern world.

THE DYNAMISM OF THE EARLY DYNASTIC PERIOD, PHASE III (2500–2350 B.C.E.)

Contemporary records from the final phase of the Early Dynastic Period allow us to describe it in more detail than earlier epochs of Sumerian history. Competition among the Sumerian city-states for prestige, power, and resources now reached a fever pitch. Inter-city warfare intensified, as did attempts by ambitious *lugals* to magnify the standing of themselves and their cities. At the same time, the tensions that had once existed between temple aristocracy and royal power were lessening, leaving *lugals* freer to exercise their authority than they had been in earlier ages. *Lugals* now included the priesthood more extensively than ever before in the process of choosing and legitimating successors, while the priestly aristocracy gave greater religious function and sanctification to the kingship.

The coalescence of a more politically and religiously unified elite, however, meant that the wider population had even less of a voice than before. More and more

Objects from the Royal Tombs at Ur. On the right, a queen's headdress, made of gold leaf, lapis lazuli, and carnelian. On the left, a helmet made of an alloy of gold and silver. Its cloth lining would have been attached through the holes visible around the edges of the helmet.

WHY DID A COMMON RELIGION NOT CREATE PEACE AMONG THE SUMERIANS?

THE SUMERIANS ENTER HISTORY   27

commoners fell into debt slavery as their economic, social, and political standing declined. Once useful allies to both royal and priestly authority, the commoners no longer had any political value to either side, now that kings and priests no longer vied with one another for supremacy. So diminished had their lot become that by the close of Early Dynastic (ED) III, a *lugal* of Lagash named Urukagina set down rules to try to protect the downtrodden commoners.

Such attempts at reform were ineffective. The final phase of the Early Dynastic period witnessed a tremendous concentration of wealth and power at the top of Sumerian society. The royal tombs of Ur, dating from 2550 B.C.E. to 2450 B.C.E., provide a breathtaking demonstration of this phenomenon. Within these tombs are found the fruits of virtually every Sumerian cultural advance. Striking architectural features surrounded astonishing displays of wealth, including trade goods, ceremonial chariots, oxen, and most surprising of all, the bodies of scores of members of the royal household, from ladies-in-waiting to guards to entertainers. The presence of so many people in the royal tombs has inspired heated debate as to whether the Sumerians practiced human sacrifice. The excavator of the tombs believed that they had willingly gone to their deaths by drinking poison, a self-sacrifice so they could remain with their masters. At present, however, the question remains unresolved.

The wealth displayed in these tombs—both human and material—indicates the growing stature of the royalty, and points also to a shift in Sumerian ideas about the afterlife. It appears that at least a few members of Sumerian society—namely the kings and their supporters—now believed they would enjoy a different, better kind of afterlife, and that their tombs were stocked specifically for this purpose. Could this have been an idea the Sumerians borrowed from the pharaohs of Egypt? At present, we can only speculate. Such practices do give us some sense, however, of just how lofty the power of the *lugal* had become, and of the divide that had by now opened up between leaders and followers in Sumerian society.

The relatively rich documentary evidence from this period concerns itself largely with the military exploits of these powerful kings. We learn of a cycle of brutal warfare among the leading city-states, as the *lugal* of each sought to establish his supremacy over the others. In and of itself, this was nothing new; the great *lugals*

of earlier ages had also claimed dominion on the basis of military victories over both barbarian and rival Sumerian armies. During ED I the king of Kish had established such dominion, and later strongmen of Sumer—regardless of their actual seat of power—would arrogate to themselves the title of "king of Kish." In ED III, however, the pattern intensified as the struggle to maintain access to resources and trade routes became ever more desperate.

An emerging secondary civilization to the east of Sumer—the Elamites of present-day southwest Iran—also played a pivotal if indirect role in the story of ED III. Under the influence of their Sumerian neighbors, the Elamites had become increasingly urbanized and specialized, and therefore more dangerous. Indeed, the final phase of the Early Dynastic period sees increasing aggression on the part of the Elamites toward Sumer. Most exposed to the danger were the eastern Sumerian city-states of Umma and Lagash. But both communities were galvanized by the threat, and produced dynamic leaders in response to it.

Sumerians shared a common culture and religion, but this did not deter them from brutalizing one another pitilessly.

By defeating the Elamites, the armies of Umma and Lagash became the most powerful in Sumer, and the *lugals* of these two cities vied for the title of "king of Kish". Around 2450 B.C.E., the *lugal* Eannatum of Lagash expelled the Elamites and even claimed to have conquered Elam, thus safeguarding Sumer for the foreseeable future. He then turned his attention on Umma, Lagash's nearby rival, only eighteen miles away. After humbling his powerful neighbor, Eannatum extended his dominion over the rest of Sumer, declaring himself not only king of Kish but also "He Who Subjects All the Lands."

Eannatum is a particularly interesting figure because we have contemporary documentation for his actions and claims, found on the Stele of the Vultures, a limestone slab that survives in fragments. On the stele (inscribed stone monument), Eannatum describes in both words and pictures his victory over Umma and the peace terms he imposed on the city. The document thus records in vivid detail the issues between the cities, and testifies to the vicious nature of the resulting warfare. One register on the stele portrays Eannatum in military dress leading well-armed troops in formation, trampling the bodies of his foes. Another scene, from which the stone takes it name, shows vultures carrying away the severed heads and limbs of Eannatum's defeated enemies. Sumerians shared a common culture and religion, but this did not deter them from brutalizing one another pitilessly.

Umma would have its revenge roughly a century later, when it came under the rule of the forceful Lugalzagesi. This man had usurped the throne of Umma, and had incorporated his new title into his name as a way of legitimating his position. Like Eannatum, he led the battle-hardened armies of his home city to victory over the rival states of Sumer, and by 2360 B.C.E. could lay claim to the title of King of Kish. Although he claimed to have conquered "from the Lower Sea to the Upper Sea" (by which he meant from the Persian Gulf to the Mediterranean), the truth was rather different. Like most Sumerian strongmen before him, he had defeated his enemies in war and forced them to acknowledge his supremacy by paying him tribute. He did not claim direct sovereignty over them, however, probably because he could not imagine doing so.

One of the fundamental strengths of Sumerian civilization—the self-reliant and independent dynamism of the powerful city-states—would prove to be one of its basic shortcomings by the twenty-fourth century B.C.E. The interwoven nature of Sumerian politics and religion meant that to destroy another Sumerian city or completely subject it to the will of another necessarily humiliated the patron god of that city. As the Sumerians recognized a pantheon in common, they seem to have been uneasy about denigrating any god so blatantly. Their ingrained competition and will to self-determination prompted the Sumerians to innovate technologically, but it also precluded any meaningful attempt at greater political unification or integration. Left to its own devices, Sumer would probably have remained a collection of independent city-states, each one forced periodically to acknowledge the domination of one of its rivals.

Naram-Sin. A bronze head thought to depict Sargon's grandson and successor.

> The Sumerians' ingrained competition prompted them to innovate technologically, but it also precluded any meaningful attempt at greater political unification.

fluenced by them. The Akkadians preserved their own language, however, a member of the Semitic family of tongues (which includes such languages as Assyrian, Aramaic, Hebrew, Arabic, and Ethiopic; we will have occasion to consider Semitic speakers more fully in the next chapter). As an "outsider," Sargon seems not to have been bound by the traditional assumptions and conventions of Mesopotamian warfare. Instead, he launched a systematic program of conquest, beginning around 2360 B.C.E. while Lugalzagesi was still establishing his own sway over Sumer itself. Within a decade, Sargon had subjected all of the areas around Sumer, completely surrounding the region. Unlike Lugalzagesi, Sargon did in fact campaign from the Upper to the Lower Sea, gaining control of vital trade routes. Around 2350 B.C.E., he defeated Lugalzagesi of Umma. Only when it was too late did the Sumerians realize that Sargon now had their land by the throat.

After ruthlessly organizing all of Mesopotamia under his centralized rule, Sargon founded a new capital which he called Akkad, just north of Kish. From there he appointed mostly Akkadian-speaking governors to

THE AKKADIAN PERIOD (2350–2160 B.C.E.)

But Sumer was not left to its own devices. The impulse toward unification came from within Sumerian civilization, but the energy that made unification possible came from an "outsider," Sargon of Akkad. Sargon was not Sumerian but rather Akkadian. The Akkadians were the predominant people of central Mesopotamia to the north of Sumer, and by the 2400s had been greatly in-

WHY DID A COMMON RELIGION NOT CREATE PEACE AMONG THE SUMERIANS?

THE SUMERIANS ENTER HISTORY   29

rule the cities of Sumer, pull down fortifications, collect taxes, and do the will of the new king. Sargon had, for the first time in history, supplanted the city with a much larger political unit as the basis for organization: a kingdom or empire. Sargon supported his empire (arguably the first true empire in human history) by managing and exploiting the network of trade routes that crisscrossed the Near East. As a result, his economic influence stretched from Ethiopia to the Indus Valley. Sargon made his capital the most splendid city in the world, and he exercised unprecedented power for fifty-six years.

Sargon was eventually succeeded by his talented grandson, Naram-Sin, who reigned, like his grandfather, for over a half century. Naram-Sin extended the Akkadian conquests, and consolidated caravan and overseas trade routes. An energetic promoter of culture and a patron of the arts, Naram-Sin encouraged literary and artistic endeavors throughout his realm. By dint of conquest and the quickened pace of commerce, he also helped to stimulate the growth of cities throughout the Near East. Like many conquerors in the ancient world, Sargon and Naram-Sin were products of urban life who found it easier to rule cities and to rule from them. Cities also facilitated trade, making it more convenient and more profitable. For all these reasons, these Akkadian rulers saw the proliferation of urban settlements as advantageous.

> Although the Akkadians worshiped their own Akkadian deities, they were careful to respect and revere the gods and practices of the Sumerians.

Although the Akkadians' emphasis on political centralization and imperial organization represented a clear break with the Sumerian past, culturally the Sumerians and Akkadians differed little from one another. By the twenty-third century B.C.E. most people in central and southern Mesopotamia would have been able to converse in either language. Much of Akkadian literature and art was at its root Sumerian, translated and slightly transformed to appeal to Akkadian tastes. And although the Akkadians worshiped their own Akkadian deities, they were careful to respect and revere the gods and practices of the Sumerians. Scholars speak of a Sumero-Akkadian cultural synthesis, and indeed after the reign of Sargon the two civilizations were virtually indistinguishable except for their different languages. Despite its new imperial trappings, the urban model Sargon and Naram-Sin helped to promote was still essentially the urban model of the Sumerians.

A SUMERIAN "RENAISSANCE": UR DYNASTY III (2100–2000 B.C.E.)

Court intrigue and a series of weak successors followed the long reign of Naram-Sin. By around 2160, most of Sumer and Akkad were under the rule of an invading

A Sumerian Banquet. This fine inlay, made of shell and lapis lazuli, shows animals and foodstuffs (lower two levels) being carried to a banquet (top level), perhaps held to celebrate the military victory illustrated on the opposite side.

hill people from the Iranian Plateau, the Gutians. When Sumerian civilization later recovered and re-asserted itself, Sumerians and Akkadians alike would view this period as a "Dark Age," a shameful period of foreign domination. But although the Gutians may have been uncivilized when they arrived, they quickly adapted themselves to Sumero-Akkadian culture. So thoroughly did they assimilate that they have left no archaeological remains to distinguish them from the Sumerians and the Akkadians whom they conquered. For all of its drawbacks, urban life as it had developed in Mesopotamia was simply too attractive for most invaders to resist.

After the Gutian interlude, Sumer became once again a constellation of rival, independent city-states. Around 2100 B.C.E., however, a new dynasty from Ur, the so-called Ur Dynasty III, established itself under the rule of its first king, Ur-Nammu, and his son Shulgi. Ur-Nammu was responsible for the construction of the great ziggurat at Ur, which towered seventy feet above the surrounding plain, and for many other architectural marvels. Shulgi promulgated something like a law code, which called (among much else) for fair weights and measures, the protection of widows and orphans, and checks on the power of the mighty. In a striking departure from previous practice, he also tried to limit the application of the death penalty, reserving death or mutilation for serious crimes only. Together, Ur-Nammu and Shulgi modeled their kingship on that of Sargon and Naram-Sin, pursuing military conquests, the centralization of Sumerian government, commercial expansion and consolidation, and the patronage of art and literature. Together, the Akkadian rulers and Ur Dynasty III thus established a pattern of rule that would influence the region for centuries to come.

Although the rulers of Ur Dynasty III issued their official documents in Sumerian and consciously asserted "Sumerian" culture, Mesopotamia was now a much different place from what it had been even in ED

III. The influence of Semitic speakers on the political and religious affairs of Ur Dynasty III was significant, just as it was in Sumerian culture generally. This Semitic influence became increasingly important as time wore on. As we will learn in the next chapter, the growing influence of one particular Semitic people, the Amorites, would prove instrumental in the overthrow of Ur Dynasty III (the last Sumerian rulers of Mesopotamia) and the establishment of a new era in Near Eastern history.

EARLY EGYPT

How was the Nile River central to the development of Egyptian civilization?

The other primary civilization of the Mediterranean world arose in Egypt, roughly contemporaneous with the Sumerians. Unlike the inhabitants of Mesopotamia, however, the Egyptians did not have to wrest their survival from an unwilling and unpredictable environment. Instead, their land was constantly nourished by the predictable annual summer flooding of the Nile River. The rich black soil the river left behind made the Nile valley and delta the richest agricultural region in the entire Mediterranean world. Much of the distinctiveness of Egyptian civilization rests upon this fundamental ecological fact.

Ancient Egypt was a narrow, elongated land, snaking north from the First Cataract (a series of rocks and rapids in the river at the ancient city of Elephantine) along both banks of the Nile toward the Mediterranean Sea for a distance of almost seven hundred miles (1200 km). Outside this narrow band of territory—which ranged in breadth from a few hundred yards to no more than fourteen miles (23 km)—lay an uninhabitable desert, where rain almost never falls. This contrast between the fertile, "Black Land" along the Nile and the dessicated "Red Land" beyond deeply influenced the way the Egyptians viewed their world. Egypt itself they saw as the center of the cosmos. The lands beyond Egypt, however, they regarded as lying utterly beyond the boundaries of civilized life.

As a land, a nation, and a civilization, Egypt has enjoyed remarkable continuity. The roots of Egyptian culture extend into prehistory, and Egypt continued to thrive as an independent and distinct culture until its

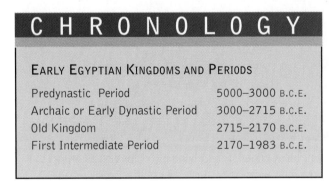

CHRONOLOGY	
EARLY EGYPTIAN KINGDOMS AND PERIODS	
Predynastic Period	5000–3000 B.C.E.
Archaic or Early Dynastic Period	3000–2715 B.C.E.
Old Kingdom	2715–2170 B.C.E.
First Intermediate Period	2170–1983 B.C.E.

HOW WAS THE NILE RIVER CENTRAL TO THE DEVELOPMENT OF EGYPTIAN CIVILIZATION?

EARLY EGYPT   31

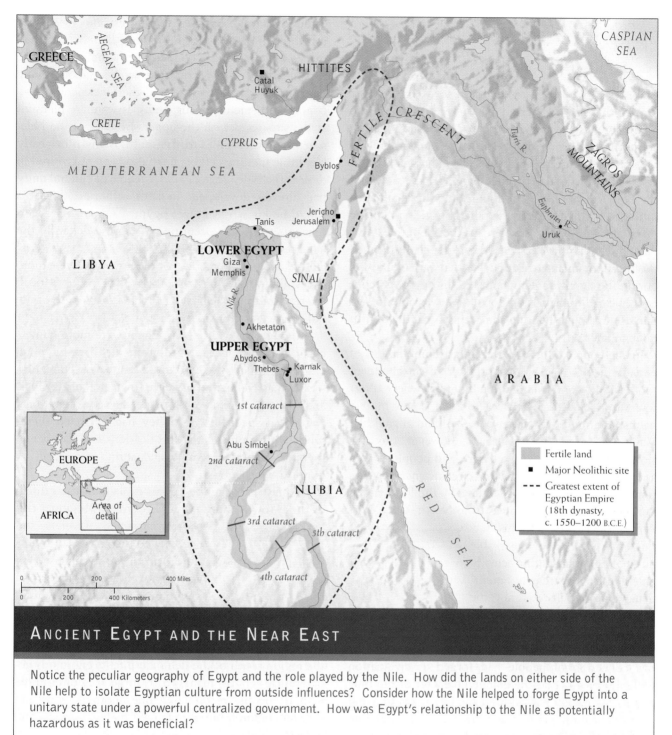

ANCIENT EGYPT AND THE NEAR EAST

Notice the peculiar geography of Egypt and the role played by the Nile. How did the lands on either side of the Nile help to isolate Egyptian culture from outside influences? Consider how the Nile helped to forge Egypt into a unitary state under a powerful centralized government. How was Egypt's relationship to the Nile as potentially hazardous as it was beneficial?

assimilation into the Roman Empire after 30 B.C.E. To speak of ancient Egypt therefore requires us to survey over three thousand years of history and development. For convenience, historians divide this history into "Kingdoms" and "Periods," as shown in the accompanying box. Generally, the "Kingdoms" were phases of strength, prosperity, and unity; during the Intermediate Periods Egypt suffered from a variety of woes, out of which a unified Egypt would then reemerge. The final two phases (the Late and Hellenistic Periods) were characterized by foreign domination by Assyrians, Persians, and lastly Greeks.

PREDYNASTIC EGYPT
(C. 5000–3000 B.C.E.)

Prehistoric Egypt is often referred to as Predynastic Egypt, that is, the period prior to the rise of the pharaohs. Using archaeology to glean information about this age is notoriously difficult. Many predynastic settlements are now buried under innumerable layers of silt, or were destroyed long ago by the waters of the Nile. Furthermore, for a long time the abundance of the Nile Valley discouraged the transition to village life that took place elsewhere in the Neolithic Near East. In the Fertile Crescent, rising population forced the Mesopotamians to adopt a settled agricultural life during the eighth millennium B.C.E. In Egypt, by contrast, a steadily increasing population was able to sustain itself through hunting and gathering until the fifth millennium B.C.E.

Egypt's population rose through a combination of natural increase—itself the product of an abundant food supply—and immigration from elsewhere. Prior to around 10,000 B.C.E., the region that is now the Sahara supported a rich variety of plant and animal life. With the retreat of the glaciers, however, the area slowly began to turn into a desert, and people as well as animals looked for better circumstances. Many found their way to the Nile Valley. By the Predynastic Period a multitude of peoples from North Africa, East Africa, and western Asia had settled in Egypt. The remarkable unity of Egyptian culture actually emerged from extremely heterogeneous roots. It was not the product of any particular ethnic or racial group.

Until recently historians believed that this multifarious collection of people had forged a "civilization without cities"—that the unique character of the Nile and its hydrology had allowed the Egyptians to avoid full urbanization, yet to enjoy the fruits of civilization. Further archaeological research has modified this assessment. The first known permanent settlement in Egypt dates to approximately 4750 B.C.E. and was situated near the modern town of Merimde Beni Salama, at the southwestern edge of the Nile Delta. It was a thriving farming community that may have numbered as many as sixteen thousand residents (although this number, based as it is on burial remains that are difficult to interpret, is open to contention). Thereafter, the Egyptian economy rapidly became more sophisticated. By around 3500 B.C.E., the residents of Ma'adi, just three miles away from Merimde Beni Salama, had extensive commercial contacts with the Levant (the east coast of the Mediterranean Sea: modern-day Lebanon, Syria, and Israel) and the Sinai peninsula—copper implements, beads, and glassware are plentiful at the site—and with the upper stretches of the Nile, several hundred miles to the south. Many other early Neolithic farming centers have also been discovered in or near the Nile Delta, where a degree of cultural unity had already developed. In later centuries, this area would be known as Lower Egypt. Comparable developments were also occuring outside the delta. By the late Predynastic Period (3500–3000 B.C.E.) the material culture and burial practices of the Egyptians were more or less uniform from the southern edge of the delta all the way south to the First Cataract, a vast length of the Nile known as Upper Egypt.

Although towns in Lower Egypt were more numerous, it was in Upper Egypt that the first true Egyptian cities developed. By 3200 B.C.E., important communities such as Nekhen, the South Town at Naqada, This, and Abydos all exhibited high degrees of occupational and social specialization. They had encircled themselves with sophisticated fortifications and had begun to build elaborate temple and shrine complexes to honor the local gods.

This last fact may be key to explaining the growth of these towns into cities. Their role as regional cult centers attracted travelers and encouraged the growth of industries. And travel in Upper Egypt was relatively easy: almost all Egyptians lived within sight of the Nile, with the great river serving as a highway binding the nation together. It was due to the Nile, therefore, that the region south of the delta, despite its enormous geographical length, managed to forge a cultural unity, with its people recognizing one another's gods and sharing common burial practices, material goods, and industries.

The Nile fed Egypt and united it. The river served as a conduit for people, goods, and ideas. It also provided a way for centralizing rulers to project their power quickly and effectively up and down its course. By the close of the Predynastic Period the cities of Upper Egypt had banded together in a confederacy under the leadership of This (the Thinite Confederacy). The pressure exerted by this confederacy in turn forced the towns of Lower Egypt to adopt their own form of

> The Nile fed Egypt and united it. The river served as a conduit for people, goods, and ideas.

HOW WAS THE NILE RIVER CENTRAL TO THE DEVELOPMENT OF EGYPTIAN CIVILIZATION?

EARLY EGYPT   33

Narmer Palette.
Dating from about 3100 B.C.E., this stone carving shows Narmer subduing an enemy from the north with a mace. The falcon probably represents the god Horus, who looks with approval on the birth of Egyptian unification in violence.

loose political organization. By the close of the fourth millennium, the rivalry between these competing regions had thus given rise to the two nascent kingdoms of Upper and Lower Egypt.

THE UNIFICATION OF EGYPT: THE ARCHAIC PERIOD (3000–2715 B.C.E.)

With the rise of powerful rulers who sought to unify these two Egyptian kingdoms, we enter the dynastic phase of Egyptian history. The numbering system for the pharaonic dynasties was developed (or at least enshrined in writing) by a third-century B.C.E. Egyptian priest named Manetho. By and large, Manetho's categorizations have withstood the scrutiny of modern historians and archaeologists. Recent research has led to the necessity of recognizing a "Dynasty 0," an assortment of early kings instrumental in the unification of all Egypt. These rulers, known almost exclusively from archaeological evidence, remain shadowy figures at best. Among their number was an Upper Egyptian strongman known as "King Scorpion" from a mace head that details—in pictures—his assertion of authority over most of Egypt. One of his successors, King Narmer, appears to have been responsible for the final political unification of Upper and Lower Egypt, and might possibly be identified with the legendary king Menes or Min whom later Egyptians credited with this feat.

Following the political unification of the land, the basic features of pharaonic rule took shape, more or less along lines that would persist through all of Egyptian history. From very early on, the pharaoh was identified closely with divinity. By the first and second dynasties he was regarded as an earthly manifestation of a god. Egyptian rulers thus enjoyed a sacred nature quite different from the early Sumerian *lugal*, merely a mortal who enjoyed divine favor. We do not know how the early pharaohs established their claims to divinity. We do know that the cities of Upper Egypt were closely associated with particular patron deities. It seems probable, therefore, that local potentates in the Late Predynastic Period were already asserting their own special relationship with their city's patron god. As political power extended beyond the confines of a single city and its surrounding territory, rulers may have found it necessary to extend such claims in order to legitimate their rule. No longer was it enough merely to be the human representative of a single city's god; to exercise authority over other cities with their other gods, one now had to claim to be a god oneself.

This is speculation. We do know, however, that legitimating their rule over all of Egypt was a difficult task for the earliest pharaohs. Local loyalties remained strong, and for centuries Lower Egyptians saw themselves as distinct in some respects from their cousins to the south. Efforts to create symbols of Egyptian unity began very early, however. Crowns and other regalia were already known in the middle of the fourth millennium B.C.E. The pharaohs' claims to divinity should probably be seen in the same light. By the end of the Archaic Period, pharaohs were viewed specifically as manifestations of the sky god Horus (identified as Ra in Lower Egypt), an important deity represented by a falcon and worshiped with particular fervor around the area of This and Abydos (the probable source of Egypt's political consolidation under Dynasty 0). Whatever their personal names, pharaohs from Narmer on therefore took a "Horus name" also, to emphasize their identification with the god. By the end of Dynasty 2, pharaoh was not just the ruler of Egypt; in a sense he *was* Egypt, a symbol of the land, its people, and their connection to the divine with which all could identify. By the Old Kingdom, pharaoh was seen as a discreet and vital part of the cosmic order, the guarantor of the presence of *ma'at* (see below).

EGYPTIAN RELIGION AND WORLD VIEW

As we have seen, the Egyptians saw themselves as utterly set apart from all other civilizations. One was

The gods Isis, Osiris, and Horus.

either an Egyptian or a barbarian, and the lines between the two were absolute. Within Egypt, however, what mattered was one's "Egyptian-ness"; aside from gender, all other distinctions paled in comparison to this fundamental distinction between Egyptians and outsiders. The confidence of the Egyptians in their own superiority stemmed from their self-conscious awareness of the uniqueness of their country, nurtured by the Nile and guarded by the brutal deserts and vast seas that surrounded it. For Egyptians, it was simply self-evident that their country was the center of the world.

Although the Egyptians subscribed to a variety of creation myths about the world, they did not concern themselves greatly with how humanity came to exist. They were in this respect quite different from the Hebrews, whose creation myths were otherwise quite similar to those of the Egyptians. Instead, what mattered to the Egyptians was the means by which life itself was created and re-created. In other words, how did the cycle of life come to be? For Egyptians, this was the essential problem. Once the cycle of life had been established, it could duplicate itself endlessly. This cyclical conception gave a certain repetitive, predictable, and ultimately static cast to the way Egyp-

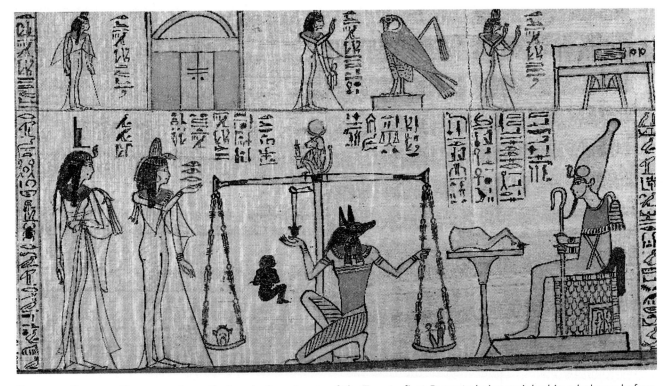

Funerary Papyrus. The scene shows the heart of a princess of the Twenty-first Dynasty being weighed in a balance before the god Osiris. On the other side of the balance are the symbols for life and truth.

THE EGYPTIAN BOOK OF THE DEAD

Though various versions of the Egytian Book of the Dead are known, the best preserved and lengthiest is that of the Papyrus of Ani, produced sometime in the fifteenth century B.C.E. to aid an important official of the priesthoods of Abydos and Thebes and his ka's quest to become assimilated to Osiris and gain immortality. Though this version dates to the New Kingdom, most of its formulas and incantations are believed to be ancient, dating back at least to the Old Kingdom. (Note: Italicized words indicate attempts to translate variations of the root of ma'at).

Says Thoth the righteous judge of the cycle of the great gods. . . . Verily I am justifying the name of Osiris the royal scribe Hunefer. His heart has come forth upon the scale, he has not been found an evil doer. Osiris: hear ye this decision. In very *truth* is weighed the heart of Osiris, his soul is standing as a witness for him; his sentence is just upon the great scales. Any wickedness has not been found in him; he has not wasted food offerings in the temples; he has not done harm in deed; he has not let his mouth go with evil things while he was upon the earth. Says the circle of the great gods to Thoth [dwelling] in Hermopolis: It is decreed that which comes forth from my mouth. *True* and righteous is Osiris, the scribe Ani triumphant. He has not sinned, he has not done evil in respect of us. Do not let Amemet prevail over him. Let there be given to him cakes, and a coming forth in the presence of Osiris, and a field abiding in Sekhet-hetepu ("Fields of Peace") like the followers of Horus. Says Horus the son of Isis: I have come to thee Un-Nefer, I have brought to thee Osiris Ani. His heart is *right* coming forth from the balance, it has not sinned aganst any god or any goddess. Thoth has weighed it according to the decree uttered to him by the cycle of the gods; it is very true and *righteous*. Grant that cakes and beer may be given to him, and a coming forth before Osiris; may he be like the followers of Horus forever!

Based on E. A. Wallis Budge, trans. *The Egyptian Book of the Dead: (The Papyrus of Ani)*. (New York: Dover Publications, 1967), pp. 16–18.

tians perceived the cosmos. Many phenomena were seen as cyclical events, not surprising given the dependence of these people on the annual cycles of the Nile.

At the heart of Egyptian religion lay the myth of the gods Osiris and Isis, brother and sister, husband and wife, and among the "original" nine gods in Egyptian belief. Osiris was the first to hold kingship on earth, but his brother Seth wanted the throne for himself. Seth betrayed and killed Osiris, sealing him in a coffin. Through great effort, Isis retrieved the corpse, but Seth seized it once again. In no mood to take any more chances, he now hacked his brother into pieces and spread his remains throughout Egypt (thus all of Egypt could claim Osiris, and shrines to him were prevalent throughout the land). Still undeterred, Isis sought the help of Anubis, the god of mummification, and together they managed to reassemble Osiris. Isis then revived Osiris long enough to conceive a child by him, the god Horus. With the help of his mother's magic, Horus withstood the assaults of Seth and his henchmen; the image of the wounded Horus was part and parcel of many healing spells and incantations in Egyptian medicine. Horus and Seth then competed over the vacant throne of Osiris, until finally Horus prevailed and avenged his father.

This mythology was very important to the Egyptians. It served as the subject for theatrical re-enactments, and the symbolism contained in the story says much about Egyptian beliefs. The tale of Osiris is a myth about life arising out of death, but it is not a resurrection story: Osiris was revivified only temporarily. The notion of new life arising from the dead probably stretched back to the earliest farming settlements of Egypt, where already bodies were being interred with extensive grave goods and special care. The promise of the continuation of life—rhythmic, cyclical, inevitable—as embodied by Osiris made him an important agricultural deity to the Egyptians.

THE EGYPTIAN DEATH CULT

Osiris was also, however, a central deity in the death cult of the Egyptians. Unlike the Sumerians, the Egyptians did not have a bleak view of death and the underworld. Death was an unpleasant rite of passage, a necessity to be endured on the way to an afterlife that was more or less like one's earthly existence, only better. But the passage was not automatic and was full of dangers. After death, the deceased's *ka*, or otherworldly existence, would have to roam the underworld, the Duat, searching for the House of Judgment, where Osiris and forty-two other judges would decide its fate. Demons and evil spirits might try to frustrate the *ka*'s quest to reach the House of Judgment, and the journey might take some time. If successful and judged worthy, however, the deceased would then enjoy immortality as an aspect of Osiris. For this reason, the dead were often referred to as "Osiris (name of the deceased)."

Because of their beliefs about death, the Egyptians developed an elaborate ritual and cult for dealing with it. It was first of all crucial that the corpse be preserved: this is why the Egyptians developed their sophisticated techniques of embalming and mummification. The body was desiccated, all its vital organs removed (except for the heart, which played a key role in the final judgment), and the body treated with chemicals to help preserve it. A funerary portrait mask was placed on the mummy before burial, so that the corpse would still be recognizable in death despite being wrapped in hundreds of yards of linen. To sustain the deceased on his or her journey through the underworld, food, clothing, utensils, and other items of vital importance would be placed in the grave along with the body.

"Coffin texts" or "Books of the Dead" also accompanied the corpse. These writings contained much that the deceased would need on his or her journey through the Duat: magic spells, ritual incantations, and the like. Not only would this knowledge help the dead navigate the perils on the way to Osiris, but would also help them prepare their hearts for the final test. Before Osiris and the other judges, the deceased performed a "negative confession," a formulaic denial of a litany of offenses. Then the god Anubis weighed the heart of the deceased in front of the judges, placing it in the scales with the feather of the goddess Ma'at. Only if the heart and the feather were in perfect balance did the dead person achieve immortality as an aspect of the god. In the third millennium this privilege was reserved for the royal family alone, but by the Middle Kingdom participation in these death rituals had become accessible to most Egyptians.

The careful detail with which Egyptians confronted death has often led to the erroneous assumption that theirs was a "death culture," completely obsessed with the problem of death. In fact, Egyptian practices and beliefs were mostly life affirming, and the role of Osiris (also, remember, a god of returning life) and the underworld were viewed not with horror, but with hope. Egyptian confidence in the cyclical nature of the cosmos and the resilient power of life is also evidenced by their interpretation of the solar cycle. Each morning the sky, personified as the goddess Nut, literally "gave birth" to the sun (often identified with the god Ra). The sun made his way westward across the celestial waters of the sky in his day boat (toward the direction of Duat, the land of death; Osiris was often called "He Who Rules the West," that is, the land of the dead). The sun's journey in his day boat was observable, a peaceful and orderly course across the sky. His trip through the Duat in his night boat could only be imagined, and the Egyptians believed that a giant serpent tried to block the sun on his journey through the underworld. In the deepest part of the night, the sun reached the mummified body of Osiris and the two gods became one, giving the sun the power to continue his journey until his mother Nut could once again give birth to him. Life always triumphed.

Binding together this great cycle of life, death, and the return of life was *ma'at*. Like many words in the Egyptian language, it has no exact English equivalent. Our concepts of harmony, order, justice, and truth

HOW WAS THE NILE RIVER CENTRAL TO THE DEVELOPMENT OF EGYPTIAN CIVILIZATION?

EARLY EGYPT   37

would all fit comfortably within *ma'at*, though none of these words captures its entire sense. Both the abstract notion and its personification as a female deity named Ma'at were what kept the universe running in its serene, repetitive, predictable fashion. Thus, unlike the Sumerians, the Egyptians of the Archaic Period and Old Kingdom were a supremely confident and optimistic people. They believed that they lived at the center of the created universe, a paradise where stability and peace were guaranteed by *ma'at* and their connection to it through the earthly manifestation of a god who ruled them, their pharaoh. For most of the third millennium, thanks to a long period of successful Nile floods and Egypt's geographical isolation from the outside world, the Egyptians were able to maintain their belief in this perfectly ordered paradise, in which they perceived that little if anything ever changed.

LANGUAGE AND WRITING

Among the many facets of Egyptian culture which have fascinated and mystified later observers is their system of pictographic writing. Called *hieroglyphs* ("sacred carvings") by the Greeks, these strange and elaborate symbols remained completely impenetrable and therefore all the more mysterious until the nineteenth century, when a French scholar named Champollion deciphered them with the help of the newly discovered Rosetta Stone. This document contains three versions of the same text, written in ancient Greek, demotic (the script of a later version of the Egyptian language), and hieroglyphics. Because he could read the text in Greek and demotic, Champollion was able to unravel the hieroglyphic text as well. From this beginning, generations of scholars have added to and refined our knowledge of ancient Egyptian society and language.

The development of writing in Egypt dates to the later phases of the Predynastic Period, and its pictographic nature may betray an influence from Mesopotamia. If so, this would represent by far the most significant cultural exchange between the two regions. Unlike Sumerian cuneiform, however, Egyptian hieroglyphics did not evolve toward a system of phonograms. Rather, the Egyptians developed a simpler, faster, cursive script for representing hieroglyphics, a system of writing called *hieratic*, which they employed for the everyday business of government and commerce.

Little early hieratic writing remains, due largely to the perishable nature of the medium on which it was usually written: papyrus. Produced by hammering, drying, and processing river reeds, papyrus was lighter, easier to write on, and more transportable than the clay tablets used by the Sumerians. When sewn together into scrolls, papyrus also made it possible to record and store large quantities of information in a very small space. Production of this versatile writing material remained one of Egypt's most important industries throughout ancient times, and papyrus became a valuable export item. Even in the sandy and arid conditions of Egypt, however, papyrus is fragile and subject to decay. In wetter climates, it almost never survives for archaeologists to unearth. The vast majority of papyrus documents have therefore been lost, a fact which significantly affects our understanding of Old Kingdom Egypt, when so many records were kept on papyrus.

The language of the ancient Egyptians has long been a matter of debate. Early Egyptian exhibits features that tie it both to the Semitic languages of the Near East and to a number of African language groups, all of which belong to a linguistic "superfamily" known as Afro-Asiatic. Some historical linguists have postulated that early Egyptian might represent the survival of a "root" language from which the other languages of the Afro-Asiatic group evolved. Given the movements of people in and out of and through the Nile Valley in the prehistoric period, this theory is a distinct possibility. But whatever its origins, the Egyptian language has enjoyed a long history. The language of the Old Kingdom survived and evolved over thousands of years, becoming the tongue known as Coptic in classical antiquity; it is still used today in the liturgy of the Coptic Christian Church.

> The development of writing in Egypt dates to the later phases of the Predynastic Period, and its pictographic nature may betray an influence from Mesopotamia.

THE OLD KINGDOM (2715–2170 B.C.E.)

Because so few of the routine business documents of the Old Kingdom survive, writing a history of this period is a difficult venture. Although funerary texts from the tombs of the elite allow us to say something about the achievements of particular individuals and to gain an impression of everyday life, we know little about

An Egyptian Scribe, c. 2400 B.C.E.

the lives of the great majority of ordinary Egyptian people. Further complicating our problem is the attitude of the Old Kingdom Egyptians themselves. Because of their belief in *ma'at* and the unchanging, cyclical nature of the universe, Old Kingdom Egyptians had little interest in history and historical events as we think of them. For all these reasons, it is unlikely we will ever be able to reconstruct their history in any detailed way.

Nevertheless, rich documentation about individuals, practices, and beliefs is available to us through the texts and art of this period. One feature that emerges clearly by the Third Dynasty (c. 2715–2640 B.C.E.) is the degree to which the pharaohs had successfully centralized their power and administration. There are few signs in this period of the earlier divisions between Upper and Lower Egypt. Instead, the pharaohs used centrally appointed local governors (known to the Greeks as *nomarchs*) to control

> Because of their belief in *ma'at* and the unchanging, cyclical nature of the universe, Old Kingdom Egyptians had little interest in history and historical events as we think of them.

their kingdom and extract resources from it. During most of the Old Kingdom period, these governors remained closely bound to the central government. Pharaohs moved the nomarchs and other important officials around the kingdom, lest they be tempted to build up a local power base or conceive of their administrative districts (*nomes*) as personal possessions to be passed down to their descendants. Only in times of pharaonic weakness were these officials allowed to establish local roots in the territories they administered.

Nomarchs were part of an extensive pharaonic bureaucracy. Scribal literacy was widespread in Old Kingdom Egypt, because writing was critical to the management and exploitation of Egypt's vast wealth. Precisely because pharaoh was Egypt, he could call on the resources of the land for his glorification and exaltation; by doing so, he glorified and exalted Egypt. Managing and organizing enormous resources of labor as well as mineral, industrial and agricultural wealth—to say nothing of extensive trade within and beyond Egypt—necessitated a highly skilled and effective administration. Because these literate bureaucrats were absolutely essential to government at the national and local level in Egypt, they enjoyed power, influence, and status. A Middle Kingdom document called "The Satire of the Trades" reminded the scribe in training how much his long and difficult education would benefit him in the end, and how much better his life would be in comparison with the practitioners of other trades. Even a child just beginning his scribal education was considered worthy of great respect.

IMHOTEP AND THE "STEP PYRAMID"

At the dawn of the Old Kingdom, we meet one of the greatest administrative officials in the history of Egypt: Imhotep. Imhotep rose through the ranks of the pharaoh's administration to become a sort of vizier, a right-hand man to Djoser, an early pharaoh of the Third Dynasty. Imhotep's learning and education spanned a variety of disciplines: medicine, astronomy, theology, mathematics, but above all architecture. It was Imhotep, sometime in the twenty-seventh century B.C.E., who decided that pharaoh needed a great monument to his person, power, and position in Egyptian society, and so designed the "Step Pyramid," the first great monument in world history built entirely

HOW WAS THE NILE RIVER CENTRAL TO THE DEVELOPMENT OF EGYPTIAN CIVILIZATION?

EARLY EGYPT   39

of dressed stone. It was not only to be the final resting place of Djoser, but a symbol and expression of his transcendent power as pharaoh.

Built west of the capital at Memphis at the site of modern Saqqara, the Step Pyramid consists of a series of platforms of decreasing size that towers over the desert to a height of 200 feet (63 meters). The design of the monument itself was based on an older form of burial monument, the *mastaba*, a low rectangular building built entirely of brick with a flat top and sloping sides. Imhotep probably began with the mastaba pattern in mind, but he radically altered it by stacking one smaller mastaba on top of another, and constructing each entirely of limestone. Surrounding this impressive monument was a huge temple and mortuary complex, perhaps modeled after Djoser's palace in the capital. These buildings served two purposes. Djoser's *ka* would have what it needed to rule in the afterlife, and the many buildings with their immovable doors and labyrinthine passageways would (it was hoped) frustrate tomb robbers, a chronic problem as pharaonic burials became richer.

Imhotep may have intended his pyramidal design to evoke the descending rays of the life-giving sun; or perhaps the pyramid was meant as the means for the pharaoh's ka to ascend into the sky and incorporate itself with the sun on its journey west after death. But whatever the theological import of the design, no one could miss the pharaonic power that lay behind its construction. Imhotep had set a precedent to which pharaohs throughout the Old Kingdom would aspire. Ultimately, the competition to build ever larger and more elaborate pyramids would ruin them.

Top: **Step pyramid of King Djoser,** c. 2680 B.C.E.
Bottom: **Pyramids at Giza,** with the Great Pyramid of Khufu (Cheops) on the left, c. 2590 B.C.E.

THE INSTRUCTION OF PTAH-HOTEP

Egyptian literature often took the form of "instructions" to important personages, meant to inculcate behaviors and ideals that would lead to success. This document, authored around 2450 B.C.E. by the vizier of a Fifth Dynasty pharaoh, sought to instruct the vizier's son and eventual successor as to the proper conduct of a high-born Egyptian official. Note the emphasis placed on ma'at *in this Old Kingdom document.*

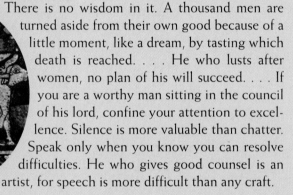

Be not arrogant because of your knowledge, and be not puffed up because you are a learned man. Take counsel with the ignorant as with the learned, for the limits of art cannot be reached, and no artist is perfect in his skills. Good speech is more hidden than the precious greenstone, and yet it is found among slave girls at the millstones. . . . If you are a leader commanding the conduct of many seek out every good aim, so that your policy may be without error. A great thing is *ma'at*, enduring and surviving; it has not been upset since the time of Osiris. He who departs from its laws is punished. It is the right path for him who knows nothing. Wrongdoing has never brought its venture safe to port. Evil may win riches, but it is the strength of *ma'at* that endures long, and a man can say, "I learned it from my father.". . . If you wish to prolong friendship in a house which you enter as master, brother or friend, or any place that you enter, beware of approaching the women. No place in which that is done prospers. There is no wisdom in it. A thousand men are turned aside from their own good because of a little moment, like a dream, by tasting which death is reached. . . . He who lusts after women, no plan of his will succeed. . . . If you are a worthy man sitting in the council of his lord, confine your attention to excellence. Silence is more valuable than chatter. Speak only when you know you can resolve difficulties. He who gives good counsel is an artist, for speech is more difficult than any craft.

Nels M. Bailkey, ed. *Readings in Ancient History: Thought and Experience from Gilgamesh to St. Augustine,* 5th ed. (Boston: Houghton Mifflin, 1995), pp. 39–42.

FOURTH DYNASTY (2640–2510 B.C.E.)

Old Kingdom Egypt reached its height in the Fourth Dynasty (2640–2510 B.C.E.), the period during which the great pyramids of Giza were built. These were true pyramids and have become timeless symbols of Egyptian civilization. Impressive as they are today, they were even more so in ancient times. The Great Pyramid, built for the pharaoh Khufu (or Cheops in the Greek tradition), was originally 481 feet high and 756 feet along each side of its base, consisting of over 2.3 million limestone blocks and enclosing a volume of about 85 million cubic feet. With the exception of a few airways, passages, and burial chambers, the structure is completely solid. The entire pyramid was encased in gleaming white limestone and topped by a massive capstone gilded in gold, as were the two massive but slightly smaller pyramids at the site built for Khufu's successors Khafre (Chephren) and Menkaure (Mycerinus). In the Middle Ages, the builders and

HOW WAS THE NILE RIVER CENTRAL TO THE DEVELOPMENT OF EGYPTIAN CIVILIZATION?

EARLY EGYPT 41

Pharaoh Menkaure and His Queen. Left: A sculpture from the Fourth Dynasty, c. 2500 B.C.E.—an example of the impassive, stately style. Right: A comparison of their profiles leaves little doubt that they were brother and sister as well as husband and wife.

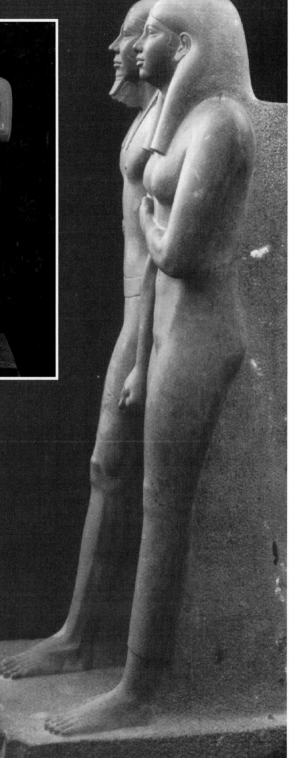

rulers of the great Muslim capital of Cairo stripped the casing stones from these pyramids and used them to construct and fortify their new city. The gold capstones had probably disappeared already. But in antiquity these pyramids, with their gleaming limestone facing, would have glistened brilliantly in the bright Egyptian sunshine, making them visible for miles in all directions.

The Greek historian Herodotus, who toured Egypt more than two thousand years after the pyramids were built, claimed that it took one hundred thousand laborers twenty years to build the Great Pyramid. This is probably an exaggeration. Then as now, Egyptian guides enjoyed telling visitors tall tales. The impression these monuments made on him, however, may be judged by the fact that Herodotus believed what his Egyptian guides were telling him. Once thought to have been the work of slaves, the pyramids were in fact raised by tens of thousands of peasant workers, who labored most intensively on the pyramids while their fields were under water. These workers probably participated willingly in the building projects, which glorified the living god who ruled them and served as their link to *ma'at*.

The monuments of the Third and Fourth Dynasty pharaohs testify to the tremendous administrative and religious power they wielded. The pharaohs were at once the head of state—indeed, the state itself—and the link between their people and the cosmos. With such authority at their disposal, and assisted by an extensive and efficient bureaucracy, the governments of these pharaohs raised Egypt to new heights. They exploited natural resources as never before and ensured an era of prosperity and internal peace, thus demonstrating their importance as the living, divine link to *ma'at*. These powerful pharaohs also extended Egyptian power south beyond the First Cataract into Nubia, with its rich deposits of gold.

FIFTH AND SIXTH DYNASTIES (2510–2205 B.C.E.)

For reasons that are not entirely clear, the Fifth and Sixth Dynasties (2510–2205 B.C.E.) witness the slow erosion of pharaonic power. Although pyramid construction continued, the monuments of this period were less impressive in terms of architecture, craftsmanship, and size. During these two dynasties, a series of developments undermined the power of pharaoh. The priesthood of Ra at Heliopolis asserted itself and its influence against certain weaker pharaohs. Ultimately, these priests demoted pharaoh from being an incarnation of Horus/Ra to being merely the god's son. Also, whether through the actions of ambitious officials, the laziness of certain pharaohs, or both, the nomarchs began to evolve into precisely the type of hereditary nobility that the vigorous Third and Fourth Dynasty kings did not allow. These men had become so powerful and influential that a pharaoh of the Sixth Dynasty, Pepy I, even married the daughters of nomarchs and produced successors by these marriages.

Scholars are uncertain as to how these local officials and powerful priests wrested control and prestige from the pharaonic center. It may be that the extraordinarily costly building efforts of the Fourth Dynasty had overstrained the economy, leading to shortages in labor and material vital to other sectors of Egyptian society and commerce. Other evidence points to changing climatic conditions that may have resulted in increasingly poor or even failed inundations. Egyptians could guard against the worst consequences of this in the short term, but prolonged periods of failure would ultimately spell disaster, as stores of food would be consumed and famine occurred. A relief sculpture from the Seventh Dynasty shows a line of wailing Egyptians, their eyes protruding from their faces and their ribs clearly visible under their skin. Such haunting images are evocative of the type of famine and suffering that can ravage northeastern Africa even today.

In such straitened and desperate circumstances, peo-

ple could and did resort to banditry and violence to survive. Furthermore, perhaps in response to Egyptian aggression, small states began to form in Nubia; with better organization and equipment, the Nubians became a greater menace than ever before and may have restricted Egyptian access to precious metal deposits in and around the First Cataract, with predictable effects on the economy.

With Egypt suffering these woes, the rightful claim of pharaoh to be a link to *ma'at* diminished accordingly. From the Fifth Dynasty on, therefore, local governors and religious authorities took it upon themselves to provide what measure of stability and order they could. Their power, authority, and prestige increased at the expense of the pharaonic government. A significant turning point was the astonishing reign of the long-lived but otherwise weak Sixth Dynasty pharaoh, Pepy II. Pharaoh for ninety-six years, Pepy II came to the throne at the age of six. During his minority, priests and nomarchs took advantage of his youth to increase their prerogatives greatly. Though Pepy II was competent enough once he came of age, the damage had been done. Furthermore, his advanced age at death meant he had outlived all the clear successors to his authority, and the ensuing confusion provided even greater scope for the growing independence of local power.

SEVENTH AND EIGHTH DYNASTIES

The Seventh and Eighth Dynasties represent the close of the Old Kingdom. These pharaohs are very obscure; many attempted to rule from Memphis, but insofar as we know anything about them, they were clearly powerless in the face of the nomarchs of Upper Egypt, each virtually independent. By the middle of the twenty-second century, Egypt had ceased to exist as a united country. Instead, it descended into a period of anarchy known as the First Intermediate Period. A century and a half would pass before one man could again legitimately call himself pharaoh of all Egypt. But although unity returned after the upheavals of the First Intermediate Period, the confidence and optimism of Old Kingdom Egypt did not return with it.

SOCIETY IN OLD KINGDOM EGYPT

The social pyramid of Old Kingdom Egypt was extremely steep. At its apex was of course the pharaoh and the royal family. During the Third and Fourth Dynasties their status, prestige, and power were so great as to set them quite apart from any other Egyptians. There was a class of nobles, but until the Fifth Dynasty the nobility's social and political position was clearly subordinate; their role was to serve as priests and officials of pharaoh's government. Because of the vaunted position of scribes, these were usually recruited and trained from among the sons of the greater families. The economic and social standing of the Egyptian elites allowed them scope for significant luxury. They owned extensive estates with exotic goods and fine furniture. They kept dogs and monkeys as pets, and hunted and fished for sport.

Beneath the tiny minority represented by royalty and nobility was everyone else. Most Egyptians were poor, living in crowded conditions in simple mud-brick dwellings. During the period of prosperity, however, skilled artisans—jewelers, goldsmiths, and the like—could elevate themselves and enjoy more comfortable surroundings, though we should not think of them as anything like a "middle class." Potters, weavers, masons, bricklayers, brewers, merchants, and schoolteachers also enjoyed some measure of respect and prestige, as well as a higher standard of living than most. Among the peasants of Egypt, however, a significant majority would have been unskilled laborers, who provided the brute force necessary for agriculture and construction. Beneath them were slaves, typically captives from foreign wars rather than native Egyptians. But despite the theocratic nature of pharaonic rule and the enormous demands the pharaohs placed on Egypt's wealth, Egyptian society does not appear to have been particularly oppressive. Even slaves had certain legal rights, including the ability to own, dispose of, and bequeath personal property.

WOMEN IN THE OLD KINGDOM

Egyptian women also enjoyed an unusually high degree of legal status and protection by the standards of the ancient world. They were not allowed to undergo scribal training or serve as important officials, but short personal notes between women of social standing suggest at least some degree of female literacy. In times of crisis, as in the case of Queen Nitocris at the close of the Sixth Dynasty, a woman of the royal family might assume pharaonic authority (although usually she would be careful to represent herself in rather mannish fashion). Egyptian women had standing before the courts as their own persons; they could initiate complaints (including suing for divorce), defend themselves, bear witness, and possess property on their own,

without the male guardian or representative that was typically required of women in other ancient societies.

None of this should obscure the fact that Egypt was, at its heart, a rigidly patriarchal society. Aside from the role of priestess, women were barred from state office. Although most Egyptians practiced monogamy, important and powerful men could and did keep harems of lesser wives, concubines, and female slaves. Furthermore, any Egyptian man could practice sexual freedom, married or not, with legal impunity; a wife who did so was subject to severe legal punishments. Gender divisions may have been less clearly defined among the peasantry. Peasant women often worked in the fields during the harvest and carried out a number of menial but vital but labor tasks. As usual in the ancient world, however, we can only glimpse the lives of Egyptian peasants through the eyes of their social superiors.

SCIENCE AND TECHNOLOGY

Their monumental architecture notwithstanding, the Egyptians lagged behind the Sumerians and Akkadians in science and mathematics, as they did in technology generally. Only in the calculation of time did the Egyptians make notable advances. Their astronomy was largely devoted to the observation of the sun for obvious religious and agricultural reasons, and the solar calendar they developed was far more accurate and sophisticated than the Mesopotamian lunar calendar. The Sumerians have bequeathed to us their means of dividing and measuring the day, but the Egyptian calendar, adopted for Rome by Julius Caesar, is the direct ancestor of our modern western calendar. Otherwise, education was mostly restricted to reading and writing, making the ingenious polymath Imhotep all the more impressive and unusual. Although the Egyptians did devise effective irrigation and water-control systems, they did not adopt such labor-saving devices as the wheel until much later than the Sumerians, perhaps because the available pool of peasant labor seemed virtually inexhaustible in densely populated Egypt.

CONCLUSION

Starting around 11,000 B.C.E.—the dawn of the Neolithic, or New Stone Age—human beings in the eastern Mediterranean world began to make a slow transition from nomadic, hunter-gatherer societies into settled agricultural and pastoral communities. With the ability to produce and store surpluses, larger villages and cities began to emerge, allowing both a greater degree of functional specialization and a wider differentiation in wealth and status between individuals and families. In Mesopotamia, where the first cities emerged during the fourth millennium B.C.E., cities served also as religious centers, with elaborate temple complexes and shrines to the city's gods. By around 2500 B.C.E., a sophisticated form of writing, known as cuneiform, had emerged as an important tool in trade and in the management of these temple complexes.

The third millennium B.C.E. saw the emergence of larger city-states with more intense warfare between them. The Mesopotamian city-states were now led by kings who claimed divine sanction for their rule, and whose power and wealth set them further and further apart from their subjects. Around 2300 B.C.E., Sumerian political life was transformed by the emergence of a new, Semitic-speaking people, the Akkadians, whose conquests resulted in the creation of the first true empire in world history. This empire would become the model future rulers of Mesopotamia would aspire to emulate.

In Egypt, the other major center of Near Eastern civilization during these centuries, political consolidation occurred at the beginning of the third millennium, a process assisted by the unique importance of the Nile River system. But Egypt during these centuries was not an empire maintained through conquest. Instead, it was a highly unified society, capable of mobilizing resources on a massive scale to support enormous building projects glorifying the pharaohs, who were conceived by Egyptians to be god-kings. Unlike the Sumerians, the Egyptians did not have to struggle to wrest a precarious living from a forbidding environment. So long as the annual flooding of the Nile occurred, Egyptians could feed themselves easily, with a relative minimum of social tension. This fact lent an air of confidence and ease to Egyptian art that is wholly lacking in Mesopotamian art.

There are many similarities between these two primary civilizations. During the third millennium, both underwent a process of political consolidation, an elaboration of religious life, and a melding of religious and political leadership. Both engaged in massive building projects; both mobilized resources on an enormous scale for temples, monuments, and irrigation projects. At the same time, however, each of these two civilizations developed an inward focus, verging on

parochialism. Although they had some trade relations with each other, and some technology transfers took place, there were no signficant political or cultural interactions between them. For all intents and purposes, they inhabited separate worlds. This relative isolation was about to change, however. The second millennium would see the emergence of large-scale, land-based empires in the Near Eastern world that would transform life in both Egypt and Sumer. These are the developments we will examine in Chapter Two.

SELECTED READINGS

Aldred, Cyril. *The Egyptians*, 3d ed. London, 1998. An indispensable, lively overview of Egyptian culture and history by one of the great masters of Egyptology.

Baines, J., and J. Málek. *Atlas of Ancient Egypt*, rev. ed. New York, 2000. A reliable, well-illustrated survey, with excellent maps.

Bottéro, Jean, Clarisse Herrenschmidt, and Jean-Pierre Vernant. *Ancestor of the West: Writing, Reasoning, and Religion in Mesopotamia, Elam, and Greece*. Chicago, 2000. A stimulating assessment of the impact of writing on the world views of the Sumerians, the Akkadians, the Elamites, the Hebrews, and the Greeks.

Butzer, Karl W. *Early Hydraulic Civilization in Egypt: A Study in Cultural Ecology*. Chicago, 1976. A lucid examination of the Nile's impact on early Egyptian history.

Crawford, Harriet. *Sumer and the Sumerians*. New York, 1991. A solid and reliable survey, up to date on both history and archaeology.

George, Andrew, trans. *The Epic of Gilgamesh: A New Translation. The Babylonian Epic Poem and Other Texts in Akkadian and Sumerian*. New York and London, 1999. The newest and most reliable translation, which carefully distinguishes the chronological "layers" of this famous text; also includes a great many related texts.

Hallo, W. W., and W. K. Simpson. *The Ancient Near East: A History*, rev. ed. New York, 1998. A reliable but somewhat dull survey; a good place to look things up.

Hoffman, Michael A. *Egypt before the Pharaohs: The Prehistorical Foundations of Egyptian Civilization*. New York, 1979. An outstanding guide to the predynastic period of Egyptian history, accessible to students but useful to scholars.

Hornung, Erik. *History of Ancient Egypt: An Introduction*. Ithaca, N.Y., 1999. Concise and authoritative.

James, T. G. H. *An Introduction to Ancient Egypt*. London, 1979. Informative survey with an emphasis on material culture.

Kemp, Barry J. *Ancient Egypt: Anatomy of a Civilization*. London, 1989. An imaginative and probing examination of Egyptian social and intellectual history.

Lichteim, Miriam. *Ancient Egyptian Literature: A Book of Readings.*

3 vols., Berkeley, 1973–1980. A wide-ranging compilation used by students and scholars alike.

Mertz, Barbara. *Red Land, Black Land: Daily Life in Ancient Egypt,* rev. ed. New York, 1990. A reliable guide that emphasizes the role of the Nile and the forbidding natural environment of Egypt.

Neugebauer, Otto. *The Exact Sciences in Antiquity,* 2d ed. New York, 1969. Includes, among much else, the standard account of Mesopotamian mathematical accomplishments.

Postgate, J. N. *Early Mesopotamia: Society and Economy at the Dawn of History.* London, 1992. An excellent, up-to-date, but challenging survey that reaches up to the middle of the second millennium B.C.E.

Redford, Donald B. ed. *The Oxford Encyclopedia of Ancient Egypt.* 3 vols. New York, 2001. An exhaustive reference work, intended for both specialists and beginners.

Roaf, Michael. *Cultural Atlas of Mesopotamia and the Ancient Near East.* New York, 1990. An informative, authoritative, and lavishly illustrated guide, with excellent maps.

Robins, Gay. *The Art of Ancient Egypt.* London, 1997. An excellent, up-to-date survey, likely to become the standard account.

Shafer, Byron E., ed. *Religion in Ancient Egypt: Gods, Myths, and Personal Practice.* London, 1991. A scholarly examination of Egyptian belief and ritual, with contributions from some of the leading modern authorities. Excellent bibliographies.

Shaw, Ian, ed. *The Oxford History of Ancient Egypt.* Oxford, 2000. The best survey of Egyptian history from the Stone Age to the early fourth century of the Common Era, with chapters written by the leading international specialists and excellent, chapter-by-chapter bibliographical essays.

Simpson, William Kelly, ed. *The Literature of Ancient Egypt: An Anthology of Stories, Instructions, and Poetry,* rev. ed. New Haven, 1973. Lichteim is fuller, but Simpson's collection is more widely available, including in paperback.

Spencer, A. J. *Early Egypt: The Rise of Civilisation in the Nile Valley.* London, 1993. More up to date than Hoffman, but less accessible to beginners.

CHAPTER TWO

THE GROWTH OF
EMPIRES IN
THE ANCIENT
NEAR EAST

IN THE SECOND MILLENNIUM B.C.E., the civilizations of the ancient Near East were transformed by the arrival of new population groups and by the emergence of extensive empires built up through systematic military conquest. The growth of these new empires was accompanied by widespread cultural assimilation, deepening economic integration, and the emergence of an international diplomatic system that encompassed almost the entire eastern Mediterranean world.

These migrations and conquests left a great deal of destruction and upheaval in their wake; indeed, Sumerian civilization ceased to exist as a living culture in the early part of the second millennium. However, the new inhabitants of the Asiatic Near East typically assimilated themselves to the older traditions of the area, forging new societies that drew heavily on the cultural legacy of the Sumero-Akkadian past. Even the peoples who moved into the remote limits of the Near East, such as Anatolia (roughly the area of modern-day Turkey), adopted much of the practice and heritage of the region's older civilizations.

Egypt too was transformed by the dynamic changes of the second millennium. During the weakness and division of the First Intermediate Period, foreigners from western Asia and Nubia penetrated the "center of the cosmos" in large numbers. Some came as immigrants; others were brought to Egypt as mercenaries to protect the land from invaders. This strategy was largely successful. Even in the wake of the Old Kingdom's collapse, Egypt did not suffer large-scale armed invasion. But when Egypt recovered its strength in the early second millennium, the confidence in *ma'at* had been shattered. Their optimism dampened, Egyptians became far more suspicious and took a much greater interest in what happened beyond their frontiers. This concern only deepened after the middle of the millennium, in the aftermath of Egypt's subjugation by a foreign army called the Hyksos.

The Late Bronze Age (1500–1200 B.C.E.) was a period of intensifying diplomacy, trade, and internationalism. Once the movements of people died down after the midpoint of the millennium, a balance of power developed between the Egyptians of the New Kingdom and the Hittite Empire of Anatolia. Between them was a

FOCUS QUESTIONS

- What are the origins of Indo-European languages?

- How did Hammurabi bind his empire together?

- How did trade help spread urbanism in the kingdoms of the north?

- What distinctions characterize New Kingdom Egyptians?

- What factors facilitated the creation of the Late Bronze Age international system?

- How did Minoan culture affect Mycenaean culture?

constellation of smaller but astonishingly prosperous and powerful states, fully engaged in the burgeoning trade and cosmopolitan culture of the age. Through their endeavors they influenced societies beyond the Near East, spreading the urban idea and its trappings to the eastern Mediterranean—the islands of Cyprus (ancient Alashiya) and Crete, and through these areas to the mainland of Greece. By the thirteenth century, nations from the southern Balkans to the western fringes of Iran were influencing each other in meaningful ways, resulting in a wide-ranging cultural synthesis. By 1250 B.C.E., the politics and economies of these early states depended in great measure on each other.

This international system proved more fragile than its participants had imagined. Around 1200 B.C.E., a new wave of invasions emanating from the Aegean Sea brought political and economic collapse from Greece to Egypt, and led to the destruction of nearly every great empire of the Late Bronze Age. But although this integrated world collapsed, the cultural and commercial impact of these societies on one another would continue to resonate in the centuries that followed, laying the groundwork for the Greek civilization of the archaic and classical age.

The first truly consequential invasions of Sumer had come near the end of the third millennium B.C.E. at the hands of Sargon and his Akkadians.

MIGRATION AND LANGUAGE

What are the origins of Indo-European languages?

The second millennium B.C.E. began with the migration of two new groups of peoples into the Near Eastern world: Semitic-speaking peoples such as the Amorites and the Assyrians; and Indo-European-speaking peoples such as the Hittites and the early Greeks. The interactions between these two groups of peoples would help to determine the history of the ancient Near East for the next one thousand years.

SEMITIC-SPEAKERS

The first truly consequential invasions of Sumer had come near the end of the third millennium B.C.E. at the hands of Sargon and his Akkadians. Although Sumerians and Akkadians created a new culture not far removed from Sumerian forms, Sargon's imperial ventures began the infiltration of Sumerian civilization by Semitic-speakers closely related to the Akkadians. This paved the way for the further influence of Semitic speakers, until finally Sumerian civilization was completely eclipsed.

The various Semitic speakers of the Near East were a diverse group. On the one hand were the Akkadians, extensively assimilated into Sumerian civilization. There were also the Amorites, nomads who ultimately came to dominate Mesopotamia, urbanizing in the process but retaining much that reflected their rough-and-tumble roots. In northern Mesopotamia were the Assyrians, early caravaners who pioneered trade routes into Anatolia during the early second millennium. Deeply influenced by Sumero-Akkadian culture, the Assyrians would go on to found an important, independent, and long-lasting civilization in their own right. The Phoenicians and their Bronze Age ancestors on the Syro-Palestine coast were the greatest seafarers and merchants of Mediterranean antiquity; their inland cousins, the Canaanites, were warlike seminomads who were one of the great national enemies of another Semitic people very much like themselves, the Hebrews.

As we saw in Chapter One, the rulers of Ur Dynasty III tried to reassert the primacy of Sumerian civilization in the face of the increasing influence of Semitic languages. The dynamic king Shulgi died around 2047 B.C.E., and was succeeded by two competent sons who both died young. As a result the throne fell to Shulgi's grandson, Ibbi-Sin, a hapless individual most charitably described as in over his head. Something of a "mama's boy," he portrayed himself as a beardless youth well into middle age, and the only attested name for his mother from his royal records is "Mommy." He surrounded himself with flatterers and other courtiers, and the imperial bureaucracy bloated under his rule.

His archives trace the anatomy of a dying empire. One by one, the royal archives trail off in the cities under Ur's dominion. Slowly but surely, Ibbi-Sin lost control of his empire, and ultimately turned to his field marshal, a man of Amorite descent named Ishbi-Irra. Ishbi-Irra was shrewd and ruthless, time and again letting affairs reach an impasse and then applying his considerable military talents only at the last moment in exchange for more power and prerogatives for himself. Thanks to Ishbi-Irra, Ibbi-Sin remained on the throne

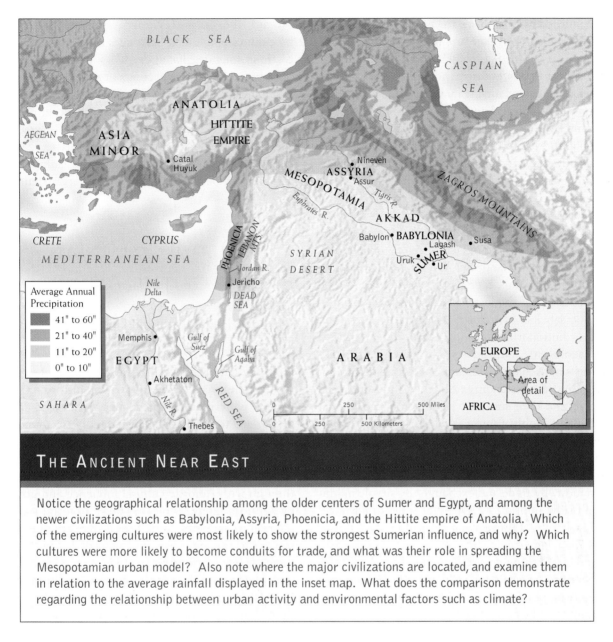

THE ANCIENT NEAR EAST

Notice the geographical relationship among the older centers of Sumer and Egypt, and among the newer civilizations such as Babylonia, Assyria, Phoenicia, and the Hittite empire of Anatolia. Which of the emerging cultures were most likely to show the strongest Sumerian influence, and why? Which cultures were more likely to become conduits for trade, and what was their role in spreading the Mesopotamian urban model? Also note where the major civilizations are located, and examine them in relation to the average rainfall displayed in the inset map. What does the comparison demonstrate regarding the relationship between urban activity and environmental factors such as climate?

for twenty-four years until an Elamite army sacked Ur. Only after the Elamites had carried Ibbi-Sin into captivity did Ishbi-Irra spring heroically into action, driving off the remaining invaders and claiming the kingship for himself. For the inhabitants of Mesopotamia, the memory of Ibbi-Sin resonated for centuries as the epitome of criminal stupidity and hopeless incompetence.

Ishbi-Irra was unable to reassert power over the whole of the shattered empire of Ur Dynasty III. The various cities of the realm had broken free for good, many of them now under the rule of ambitious and powerful Amorite chiefs. For the first two centuries of the second millenium, the geopolitical history of

Mesopotamia exhibits a pattern of warfare among a constellation of petty Amorite kingdoms based on the great urban centers of the Sumero-Akkadian past. Not until the eighteenth century B.C.E. would one of these Amorite-descended kings, the remarkable Hammurabi of Babylon, create a new unity in the region.

THE INDO-EUROPEANS

In 1786 Sir William Jones, a British judge serving in Calcutta, India, made a discovery that transformed knowledge about the world of prehistory and began the formal discipline of historical linguistics. Trained in "Oriental studies" before his legal education, Sir

William turned his spare time toward the study of Sanskrit, the ancient language from which the predominant languages of the South Asian subcontinent derive. In the course of his endeavor to master Sanskrit, he found that Sanskrit shared features of grammar and vocabulary with Latin and ancient Greek to an extent inexplicable by sheer coincidence. His interest piqued, Sir William examined the early Germanic tongue called Gothic, the ancient Celtic languages of Europe, and Old Persian. They likewise exhibited similar structure and shared extensive vocabularies with Sanskrit. He concluded that all of these languages must have come from a common source, probably long extinct by the time of Sanskrit and ancient Greek, and not preserved as any known language. Within another generation, the ancient language whose existence Jones had hypothesized, and the later languages derived from it, would be labeled as Indo-European, reflecting their wide distribution from India to Ireland.

Archaeologists, anthropologists, linguists, and ancient historians have done much since Jones to increase our understanding of the Indo-European languages and their speakers. But much of our knowledge remains highly controversial. Was there an original form of the language, Proto-Indo-European (PIE), spoken by a single population at some point in time? If so, when and where? How did Indo-European spread? By conquest? By trade and exchange? By simple migration and slow infiltration? Or by a "wave-of-advance" model, whereby PIE-speaking agriculturalists slowly spread their language(s) by seeking out new land to farm and establishing new settlements? Can their diffusion be traced archaeologically, by the presence of characteristic pottery types and burial practices, or are such things not be correlated at all with the patterns of linguistic change? We have no definitive answers to any of these questions.

It is certain, however, that Indo-European linguistic forms began to appear in the Near East and eastern Mediterranean shortly after 2000 B.C.E., when speakers of early forms of Persian and Sanskrit made their way into and through the Iranian Plateau, and the Hittites arrived in their historical homeland in central Anatolia. Around this same time, another group of Indo-European-speaking people began to move into the Aegean basin, combining the basic structure and much of their vocabulary with indigenous linguistic elements to produce an early form of Greek.

The impact that Semitic- and Indo-European-speaking peoples had on the history of the ancient world was tremendous. Indeed, from the second millennium onward, the story of Western antiquity is dominated by cultures employing languages from one or the other of these linguistic families. We should bear in mind, however, that these newcomers did not, at most times and in most places, constitute apocalyptic waves of destroyers who wiped the slate clean. However rude they may have been when they first came into contact with the older civilizations of the Near East, they generally accommodated themselves quickly, spreading and developing the pattern of urban life and organization.

THE OLD BABYLONIAN EMPIRE OF THE AMORITES

How did Hammurabi bind his empire together?

From the fall of Ibbi-Sin to the beginning of the eighteenth century B.C.E., Mesopotamian history resumed a familiar pattern under a new guise. Once again a cycle of warfare took place over water rights, arable land, trade routes, power, and prestige. Instead of being waged by independent Sumerian city-states, however, these wars were fought among small kingdoms shot through with Amorite cultural influence and governed by Amorite kings. Typically, these Amorite states are referred to as "petty," and indeed they are in comparison with the empires that preceded and followed them. A few of their kings made important contributions to the unfolding of the Western tradition, such as Lipit-Ishtar, king of Isin in the nineteenth century B.C.E. His "law code" advanced the notion of using precedent set in past cases to create general rules for future judicial problems. As we will see, this development had a profound influence on a later Amorite king of the region, Hammurabi.

THE RISE OF HAMMURABI OF BABYLON

In 1792 B.C.E. a young man named Hammurabi ascended the throne of Babylon, a weak kingdom in the middle of Mesopotamia based in an insignificant city of the same name. When Hammurabi came to power, Babylon was both fragile and precariously wedged between a number of other, more powerful Amorite kingdoms. Babylon's site on the Tigris and Euphrates was potentially of great economic and military significance; but it was also dangerous, because Babylon sat

Mesopotamian Royal Head. A diorite head of a Mesopotamian king, conventionally identified as Hammurabi. Such headdresses were worn by the rulers of Mesopotamian cities between roughly 2100 and 1700 B.C.E. Hammurabi is shown wearing such a headdress on p. 52, but there is nothing else to identify this bust with Hammurabi.

perilously amid mighty antagonists who were often tempted to "play through" the city on their way to other conquests.

Hammurabi may have been the first sovereign in world history to understand that power need not be based on brute force. He recognized that the application of intellect, political strategy, and ruthless cunning might accomplish what his army could not. A rich archive of tablets found at the city of Mari (which eventually fell under Hammurabi's rule) testifies to the cleverness and talent of this remarkable king.

The Babylonian king used writing as a weapon, but did so with such subtlety that his targets only noticed

> Hammurabi may have been the first sovereign in world history to understand that power need not be based on brute force.

much too late. He did not try to confront his mightier neighbors directly. Rather, with letters and embassies, double-dealing diplomacy, and general deceit, he induced his stronger counterparts to embroil themselves ever deeper in armed conflict with each other. While the other Amorite kingdoms exhausted themselves in costly and pointless wars, Hammurabi fanned their hatred for one another, skillfully and privately portraying himself as a friend to all sides. His role as a potential ally resulted often in his neighboring rulers' dispatching resources—material and military—to Hammurabi, in hopes that he might help them. Quietly he consolidated his kingdom, augmenting his own strength; when the time was right he fell on his depleted and weary neighbors. In so doing, he transformed his petty Amorite state into what historians describe as the Old Babylonian Empire.

Mesopotamia under Hammurabi's rule achieved an unprecedented degree of political integration. His realm ultimately stretched from the Persian Gulf into Assyria. The southern half of the region, formerly known as Sumer and Akkad, would for the rest of antiquity be known as Babylonia. Hammurabi introduced an innovation that affected religion and politics together. He elevated the otherwise little-known patron deity of Babylon, Marduk, to be the ruler-god of his entire empire. Although the king was careful to observe long-standing, traditional religious scruples by continuing to pay homage to the ancient gods of Sumer and Akkad, Marduk now sat atop the official pantheon. People could continue to worship the ancient patron deities of their cities if they wished; but all now owed allegiance to Marduk.

RELIGION AND LAW

The notion that political rule was tied to divine action and approval was nothing new, of course. Its foundations were readily discernible in the practices and beliefs of the Sumerians. What Hammurabi did was to utilize the rule of his god over a diverse people as a means of uniting them politically and conferring legitimacy on his rule over them all as king of Babylon, the city of Marduk. The precedent established by Hammurabi would become a hallmark of many Near Eastern civilizations thereafter. A number of peoples—among them the Assyrians and Hebrews—would launch wars of aggression in the name of their foremost god.

Code of Hammurabi. The entire code of Hammurabi survives on an eight-foot column made of basalt. The top quarter of the column depicts the Babylonian king paying homage to the seated god of justice. Directly below one can make out the cuneiform inscriptions that are the law code's text.

Close associations continued to exist between political power and religious practice. The annual new year celebration of the Amorite Babylonians consisted of mock battles reenacting the victory of Marduk over the Sumerian god of chaos. It was because of this confrontation that Marduk had been able to claim his place astride heaven and earth as the chief god. Marduk's imposition of orderliness helped the predictability and controllability of the environment, the Babylonians believed, and thus helped fertility. Indeed, during the same new year festivities, as priests chanted the mythological stories recounting Marduk's ascent, the king would retire with a sacred prostitute inside the temple, and the two would have ritual sexual intercourse as a magical aid to the fertility of nature. The Babylonian king's importance was far from only political.

Babylonians believed strongly in the connections between ritual intercourse and fertility. Temple prostitutes were highly respected, recruited from among both men and women. The Babylonians attached no stigma, as nearly as we can tell, to the practice of both heterosexual and homosexual relations with the sacred prostitutes. Temple prostitutes were of course busiest during times of high religious festivals, when people from around the empire came to worship Marduk. The Babylonians believed that sexual intercourse between worshipers and the temple prostitutes helped to inspire a mysterious and holy experience in the former.

Hammurabi did not rely entirely on religion to bind his empire together. Building on the precedents of centuries and rulers past, Hammurabi issued a collection of laws that more properly approached what we might consider a "code." Known from an impressive eight-foot stele (inscribed stone monument) discovered in southwestern Iran and now in the Louvre, the so-called Code of Hammurabi addressed a wide range of legal concerns. The code was not an attempt to prescribe remedies for all conceivable infractions that might occur in Babylonian society. Rather, the code represented actual rulings handed down by the king in particular cases. Hammurabi's innovation was to have his decisions published throughout his realm, expecting that they would serve as the foundation of future judicial decisions by his local governors and judges.

OLD BABYLONIAN SOCIETY

How did trade help spread urbanism in the kingdoms of the north?

Aside from the interesting cross-cultural influences embodied in the provisions of Hammurabi's code, as a source it reveals much about the structure of Amorite Babylonian society. Overall, the more complicated social arrangements of Sumerian civilization had been succeeded by a simpler but more oppressive system. An upper class of nobles—palace officials, temple priests, high-ranking military officers, and wealthy merchants—controlled large estates and staggering wealth. Beneath this small stratum was an enormous class of legally free individuals who in economic and political terms might best be described as "dependents" of the palace or the temple, or who leased land from the estates of the powerful. Among these dependents were laborers and artisans, small-time merchants,

THE CODE OF HAMMURABI

The laws of Hammurabi, published on the authority of the king and set up throughout the Babylonian empire, exhibit the influences both of the urban society on which they were imposed and the rough justice of Amorite tradition. While Hammurabi built on older, urban legal traditions, he sought to extend the authority of his law into more realms of life and provide sterner punishments for its violation. This sampling of his provisions illustrates the severity of his system for criminals, while providing protections in unusual circumstances.

If a man accuses a man, and charges him with murder, but cannot convict him, the accuser shall be put to death.

If a man steals an ox or sheep, ass or pig, or boat—if it belonged to the god or palace, he shall pay thirty fold; if it belonged to a common man, he shall restore ten fold. If the thief has nothing wherewith to pay, he shall be put to death.

If a fire breaks out in a man's house and a man who goes to extinguish it . . . takes the household property of the owner of the house, that man shall be thrown into the fire.

If a man aids a male or a female slave of the palace, or a male or female slave of a common man, to escape from the city, he shall be put to death.

If a man who is a tenant has paid the full amount of money for his rent for the year to the owner of the house, and he (the owner) says to him before "his days are full," "Vacate," the owner of the house, because he made the tenant move out of the house before "his days were full" shall lose the money which the tenant paid him.

If an agent should be careless and not take a receipt for the money which he has given to the merchant, the money not receipted for shall not be placed to his account.

If the wife of a man be taken in lying with another man, they shall bind them and throw them into the water.

If a woman hates her husband and says, "Thou shalt not have me," her past shall be inquired into for any deficiency of hers; and if she has been careful and without past sin and her husband has been going out and greatly belittling her, that woman has no blame. She shall take her dowry and go to her father's house.

If a man destroys the eye of another man, they shall destroy his eye. If a man knocks out the tooth of a man of his own rank, they shall knock out his tooth . . . if the tooth of a common man, he shall pay one-third mana of silver.

Sara Robbins, ed. *Law: A Treasury of Art and Literature.* (New York: Beaux Arts Editions), 1990, pp. 20–22 (slightly revised).

small-scale farmers, and the minor political and religious officials of the state.

At the bottom of Babylonian society were the slaves. Far more numerous in Babylonian than Sumerian culture, slaves at this time were also treated much more harshly. They were also readily identifiable as a separate group within Sumerian society. Both nobles and dependents wore long hair and beards, but slaves were shaven and branded. Babylonians acquired slaves by a number of means, including active importation through trade, a marked departure from Sumerian practice. Like previous Mesopotamian societies, the Babylonians also took prisoners of wars as slaves, and through debt and as punishment for certain offenses free citizens could fall into slavery. Restrictions were many, and treatment was harsh: slaves could accumulate property and borrow as a means of gaining freedom, but we have no way of knowing how often this occurred in practice.

Class had a significant influence on relationships in Babylonian society. As Hammurabi's code reveals, offenses committed against nobles carried far more severe penalties than did the same crime committed against a dependent or slave (although nobles were also punished more severely than were commoners for crimes they committed against other nobles). Marriage arrangements and customs also reflected class differences, with bride price and dowry depending on the status of the parties involved.

Hammurabi's code also provides evidence as to the status and treatment of women in Babylonian society. Women did enjoy certain protections under the law, especially with regard to the ability to divorce abusive, neglectful, or indigent husbands. Furthermore, a husband who chose to divorce a wife "without cause" was obligated to provide financial support for his wife and their children. It is important to bear in mind, however, that Babylonian law essentially regarded wives as the property of their husbands, and a wife who went around her city bad-mouthing or rumor-mongering about her spouse was subject to drowning; she would suffer the same fate, along with her lover, were she caught in the act of adultery. Husbands, however, enjoyed the legal right to significant sexual promiscuity.

Women and Textiles. Women were the predominant producers of textiles throughout the ancient Near Eastern world. Even upper-class women spun thread and wove cloth for their households. Here, a servant fans an elegant lady spinning thread with a spindle.

HAMMURABI'S LEGACY

Hammurabi died around 1750 B.C.E. Although some contraction of the Old Babylonian empire followed under his successors, Hammurabi's efforts in establishing legal norms and consistent administration throughout his realm paid dividends. The Old Babylonian empire was no house of cards, dependent on the dynamism of talented kings to maintain viability. His administrative reforms, combined with his innovations in state religious worship around Marduk, created a durable and important state in Mesopotamia. For another two centuries the Old Babylonian empire played a significant role in the Near East, until invaders from the north sacked the capital and occupied it. Babylon itself remained the region's most famous city through the second and first millennia B.C.E.

Hammurabi's legacy extended well beyond the borders of his own kingdom. His success, and the flair and aplomb with which he achieved it, were instrumental in shaping the conception of kingship in the ancient Near East. After Hammurabi, religion would play an increasingly important role in the policies of Near

HOW DID TRADE HELP SPREAD URBANISM IN THE KINGDOMS OF THE NORTH?

OLD BABYLONIAN SOCIETY   55

Eastern kings. Hammurabi had also demonstrated the effectiveness and importance of writing as a political tool. Diplomacy, the keeping of extensive archives, international relations—all became characteristic concerns of subsequent Near Eastern rulers. So too did the claim of kings to be the protectors of the weak and the arbiters of justice within their realms. In this last accomplishment Hammurabi built on a long-standing tendency among Mesopotamian kings. His greatness, however, transformed law giving into an imperative for any ambitious ruler of a Near Eastern kingdom.

THE KINGDOMS OF THE NORTH

Beyond the northern reaches of Hammurabi's dominion important changes were taking shape during the first few centuries of the second millennium B.C.E. Through trade, the urban model had spread far and wide, making considerable inroads into Anatolia. At the same time, newcomers made their presence felt in dramatic ways, reshaping the face of the Near East and its history. They would establish powerful kingdoms and play an important role in the transmission of Near Eastern social and cultural patterns across the sea to the Aegean islands and the Greek mainland.

THE ASSYRIANS

The northern part of Mesopotamia was Assyria, homeland to another group of Semitic-speakers who played an influential role throughout Near Eastern history. The greatest phase of Assyrian civilization belonged to the first millennium B.C.E., and we will encounter these people in more detail in Chapter Three. But the Assyrians also played an important role in the second-millennium empires whose growth we are considering here.

The Assyrians were principally responsible for extending urbanism to the northwest, particularly into Anatolia. In antiquity, this mountainous region possessed astonishing natural wealth and played a vital role in the economic and political history of several empires well into the modern period. This bounty went untapped by the civilizations we have so far examined. It was the Assyrians who blazed economic trails into the region and accelerated the pace of urban life and society in Anatolia, especially in the central region known in classical times as Cappadocia.

The Assyrians were principally responsible for extending urbanism to the northwest, particularly into Anatolia.

Before 1900 B.C.E., the Assyrians began to organize extensive trade networks between Mesopotamia and Anatolia, as well as within Anatolia itself. Either because of their primary interest in commerce or the impracticality of conquest, the Assyrians did not seek military gains in the region. They were content to enter into understandings with the local Cappadocian rulers, who reigned from strongholds not dissimilar to the great villages of the late Neolithic. Assyrian merchants relied on the military protection of these local potentates, while they organized the trade that made the rulers of Cappadocia and other parts of Anatolia rich. The great Assyrian families organized themselves into boards of trade, determining prices, assigning trade routes and sharing out profits among themselves. Although they usually lived in the outlying districts of the great centers of Anatolian trade, Assyrians had a profound impact on Hattic (or "Cappadocian") culture. Assyrians served as advisors to kings, filling important posts and marrying into the important families of Hattic towns. In the process, they carried Mesopotamian civilization and its trappings into the region and into the districts lying between Assyria and Anatolia proper, such as northern Syria.

Mesopotamian civilization remained in many ways true to its Sumerian roots. Cuneiform remained the basic script in which many peoples of the Near East, including the Assyrians, wrote their language. Also, although Sumerian as a living, spoken language died out early in the second millenium, its legacy as a language of literature and education continued. Gilgamesh may have started as a Sumerian hero, but his fame and legend remained popular throughout Near Eastern history. Much like Latin during the Middle Ages, Sumerian was deemed a language worthy of study by educated people for many centuries after it had passed from daily usage. Therefore, the civilized tradition of Anatolia and the northern reaches of Syria was imbued with a substrate of the most revered traditions of the ancient Mesopotamian past. New peoples might move into the region, but they would accommodate themselves to the pattern of urban life established in Sumer centuries previously, absorb its heritage, and consider themselves fully a part of the Near Eastern synthesis, culturally as well as politically.

After 1800 B.C.E. the pace of direct commercial and cultural interaction between Assyria and Anatolia slackened. By the second quarter of the eighteenth century, the Assyrians had to dedicate their energies to fending off the ambitious Hammurabi to their south. At the same time, invaders were infiltrating Anatolia and northern Syria, disrupting the trade networks for a time as they overwhelmed the states of the Hattic peoples.

HURRIANS, HITTITES, AND KASSITES

In the wake of this Assyrian-assisted urbanization, new kingdoms and new population groups emerged throughout Anatolia, northern Syria, and Mesopotamia. One of these new kingdoms was established by the Hurrians. The Hurrians spoke a distinct language, neither Semitic nor Indo-European. Their exact origin and time of arrival are mysterious, but they probably entered eastern Anatolia and northern Syria from the north around the middle of the third millennium. By 1800 B.C.E. or so they had established a patchwork of Hurrian kingdoms that endured for two and a half centuries.

The Hurrians played a critical role in the transmission of Mesopotamian culture to the Hittites, an Indo-European-speaking people who penetrated Anatolia sometime around the turn of the second millennium. Hittite is but one of several closely related Indo-European languages whose speakers migrated and settled throughout Anatolia around this time, but over the course of several centuries the Hittites imposed themselves and their language on the peoples of the region as a ruling minority class. They established themselves within the growing cities of central Anatolia, particularly in Cappadocia, and remained politically independent of one another until about 1700 B.C.E. At that time the ruler of one of these city-states integrated the Hittites into a larger kingdom. About fifty years later, a ruler of this larger kingdom organized his warrior nobility into a more efficient military machine, expanded the frontiers of the kingdom, and captured a strategic mountain stronghold that dominated the area, named Hattusas. To reflect this new capital, the king changed his name to Hattusilis; he was the founder of the Hittite Old Kingdom.

Hittite culture was intensely militaristic. Partly as a result, the Hittites fielded some of the greatest armies of the Bronze Age. A great part of any Hittite king's energies was necessarily devoted to warfare and to maintaining control over his fractious and ambitious warrior nobility. Alongside this military tradition, the Hittites adopted enthusiastically the practices of those

they conquered. At some point, the Hittites adapted cuneiform to represent their own language. They seem to have begun fairly early the practice of writing down their laws, which reflect the influence of urban life on a previously nomadic culture.

Under Hattusilis I, the Hittites extended their power throughout the Anatolian plateau. Like the Assyrians, the Hittites were anxious to control trade routes throughout the region. Unlike the Assyrians, however, the Hittites also aimed at military conquest. For both reasons, the Hittites were particularly concerned to control the overland trade routes for copper and arsenic, the latter being one of the metals that can be alloyed with copper to produce bronze, the basic material of tools and weapons in the second millennium B.C.E. Combining plunder with trade, Hattusilis transformed his Hittite kingdom into an economic and military power.

Hattusilis's grandson and successor, Mursilis I (c. 1620–1590 B.C.E.) proved even more dynamic and ambitious. He sought to control the region of the upper Euphrates and to subjugate some of the small but powerful Hurrian kingdoms of northern Syria. In a brilliant campaign he drove southeastward into Mesopotamia, collecting booty and tribute until he found himself before the fabled gates of Babylon. Babylon was still the center of an Amorite kingdom, now ruled by a distant descendant of Hammurabi. Mursilis I captured and sacked Babylon in 1595 B.C.E., collecting for himself the accumulated riches of centuries. He then withdrew and abandoned the ruined city to its fate.

> The Hurrians played a critical role in the transmission of Mesopotamian culture to the West by preserving many of the literary and cultural ideas of the region.

What followed was something of a "dark age" in the history of the Near East, largely because our sources for the period are very poor. The next hundred years after the sack of Babylon seem to have been characterized by upheaval. A group known as the Kassites moved into the devastated city and seized control of the Old Babylonian Kingdom. The origins and language of the Kassites are highly debatable. Some scholars have claimed that certain Kassite names bear Indo-European traits, but the arguments are inconclusive. Like many invaders of Mesopotamia before them, the Kassites adapted themselves speedily to the older civilization they found there. Though they arrived as invaders, the Kassites ultimately presided over a largely peaceful and prosperous Babylonian realm for the next five hundred years.

The Hittites, however, brought no stability to the region. Mursilis achieved too much too soon; his growing

HOW DID TRADE HELP SPREAD URBANISM IN THE KINGDOMS OF THE NORTH?

OLD BABYLONIAN SOCIETY   57

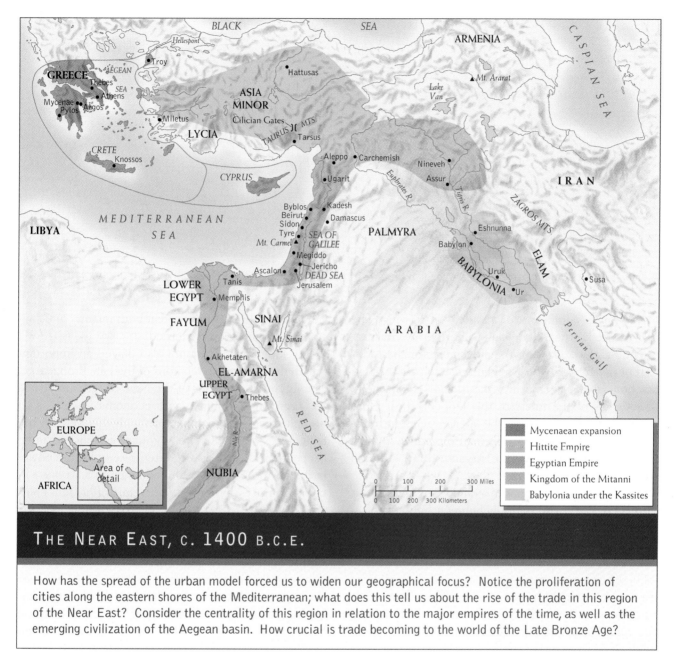

THE NEAR EAST, C. 1400 B.C.E.

How has the spread of the urban model forced us to widen our geographical focus? Notice the proliferation of cities along the eastern shores of the Mediterranean; what does this tell us about the rise of the trade in this region of the Near East? Consider the centrality of this region in relation to the major empires of the time, as well as the emerging civilization of the Aegean basin. How crucial is trade becoming to the world of the Late Bronze Age?

strength alarmed the warrior nobility, not yet ready to cede so much prestige and authority to a centralized kingship. Mursilis may have been impelled to abandon Babylon so quickly because of trouble at home; shortly after his arrival back in his capital Hattusas, he fell victim to a palace conspiracy. After his assassination, Hittite power ebbed for the next century or so.

Mursilis left tremendous destruction in his wake. The Hurrians, who had the bad luck to lie between Mursilis and his ambitions, were overrun by the Hittite king, and the Hurrian kingdom was destroyed. When our sources once again become clearer after 1500

B.C.E., a new group had made their presence felt in northern Syria: the Mitannians.

THE KINGDOM OF MITANNI

Like the Hittites, the Mitannians were an Indo-European minority who imposed themselves on a native people as a ruling class. This warrior aristocracy penetrated northern Syria and assumed control of the Hurrian centers that Mursilis had undermined, knitting these petty Hurrian states into a single kingdom, the kingdom of Mitanni.

A Near Eastern War Chariot, here used for lion hunting by the Assyrian king Assurnasirpal II (883–859 B.C.E.).

Mitanni is significant for a variety of reasons. The appearance of the Mitannians in northern Syria may provide a clue regarding the movements of the Indo-European-speakers who would ultimately pass through the Iranian plateau and into the Indian subcontinent. The names of the rulers of this kingdom bear close similarity to those used by the later invaders of India, and they recognized gods familiar from northern India in later times: Mitrasil (the Aryan Mitra), Arunasil (Varuna), and Indar (Indra).

The Mitannians introduced a number of innovations into Near Eastern warfare, including a lighter, horse-drawn chariot, which they used to carry archers around the field and strike terror into their enemies. They were also masters of horse training and cavalry tactics. For a time, these inventions and skills allowed them to keep the Hittites in check to their west, while to their east they reduced the powerful Assyrians to the status of a vassal kingdom. But when the opponents of Mitanni began employing chariots themselves

and using scale armor to protect both infantry and cavalry, the balance quickly turned.

The kingdom of Mitanni also played an important role in the diplomatic relations of the Late Bronze Age. The Egyptian pharaohs of the New Kingdom pursued an aggressive military and economic policy that brought them into competition with the New Hittite Kingdom. As a result, the Egyptians established an alliance with Mitanni as a counterpoise to Hittite power in the north. As a sign of this alli-ance, at least one Mitannian princess entered the harem of Pharaoh Thutmosis IV (1401–1391 B.C.E.). Weakened by a dynastic dispute in the middle of the fourteenth century, however, Mitanni finally collapsed in the face of renewed Hittite aggression. The Hittites allowed a rump kingdom of Mitanni to survive as a buffer state between themselves and Assyria. But the removal of the powerful Hurrian kingdom meant that the Egyptians and Hittites now embroiled themselves directly in military conflict, with enormous consequences for both.

CHRONOLOGY

TRANSFORMATIONS IN THE ANCIENT NEAR EAST

Semitic peoples invade Sumer	2000 B.C.E.
Indo-European peoples arrive in the Near East	2000 B.C.E.
Rise of Old Babylonian Empire	1800 B.C.E.
Assyrians organize trade networks	1900 B.C.E.
Creation of Hurrian, Hittite, Kassite, and Mittani kingdoms	1800–1400 B.C.E.

EGYPT IN THE SECOND MILLENNIUM B.C.E.

What distinctions characterize New Kingdom Egyptians?

Once the kingdom of Mitanni had been reduced by the Hittites, the way was open for the Egyptians and Hittites to compete directly for control of the Near East.

Compared with our description of Egypt in Chapter One, the notion of an imperialistic Egypt may seem odd. To explain this development, we must therefore shift our gaze away from the Asiatic Near East in the Late Bronze Age and return to Egypt at the end of the First Intermediate Period (2170–1983 B.C.E.).

MIDDLE KINGDOM EGYPT (1983–1795 B.C.E.)

The First Intermediate period was a time of political disunity and intense suffering for many Egyptians. The central authority of Memphis collapsed, and eventually a familiar pattern of Egyptian history reemerged: the consolidation of a northern center of power, opposed by a separate regime consolidating its power in the south. Based in the city of Herakleopolis in the north, men claiming to be pharaohs extended their sway over the northernmost part of Upper Egypt, but their control over Lower Egypt was tenuous at best. The delta region fell victim to incursions from Asiatic nomads from time to time, but curiously no native Lower Egyptian dynasty ever tried to assert itself in the power vacuum.

In the south, a competing dynasty arose around the city of Thebes, which refused to recognize the northern rulers as legitimate pharaohs. Likewise, the northerners at Herakleopolis scoffed at "the southern nomes" or "the head of the south." The close of the twenty-first century and the beginning of the twentieth century B.C.E. witnessed increasing warfare between the two dynasties until the Theban Mentuhotep II conquered the north and established himself as pharaoh of a united Egypt.

Mentuhotep is an intriguing figure. Although he clearly considered himself Egyptian, the location of

Thebes in the deep south and the infiltration of Nubians during the First Intermediate gave the Eleventh Dynasty a slightly different cast and outlook, more akin in some respects to the cultures of sub-Saharan Africa than to the Old Kingdom. Mentuhotep's dynasty also exhibits a matriarchal element that may be linked with Nubian practice. After they became firmly established, however, Mentuhotep and his successors took pains to present themselves as traditional Egyptian rulers, and strove to be just as culturally "Egyptian" as their Old Kingdom counterparts.

With the reestablishment of unified government, now centered in the south at Thebes, Egypt entered the period of the Middle Kingdom. Soon after Mentuhotep II's death, a usurper, the vizier Amenemhet, established himself and his descendants as Egypt's brilliant Twelfth Dynasty. Amenemhet retained Thebes as a center of power but also built a new capital just south of Memphis (the name of which, Itj-towy, means "Amenemhet takes possession of the Two Lands"). Dynasty 12 remained in power for nearly two hundred years, producing a succession of remarkable pharaohs.

Under this dynasty, the Egyptians now began to exploit more thoroughly the potential for trade to the south. They mounted expeditions to the land of Punt (probably the coast of Somalia) and secured their border with Nubia. By the middle of the nineteenth century B.C.E., Nubia was firmly under Egypt's control, and the small states and principalities of Palestine and Syria were under heavy Egyptian political and economic influence. But despite Egypt's renewed strength, the Egyptians did not incorporate the lands to the northeast into their realm. Instead, Amenemhet I constructed the "Walls of the Prince" in Sinai to guard against incursions from Egypt's Asian neighbors.

The great fortifications built along Egypt's frontiers during Dynasty 12 demonstrate the great resourcefulness of these pharaohs, but they also betray a marked shift in the Egyptian outlook on the world. Long gone was the placid serenity epitomized by *ma'at*. Middle Kingdom Egyptians viewed the world beyond their borders with suspicion and fear. Egypt was not as yet an imperial power; pharaohs in the Middle Kingdom did not integrate their conquests into their kingdom in any meaningful way. But unlike their Old Kingdom counterparts, the Egyptians of the Middle Kingdom were now taking a direct interest in events beyond Egypt itself.

Pharaoh's position had also changed. None of the Middle Kingdom pharaohs portrayed themselves with the serene confidence of Old Kingdom depic-

CHRONOLOGY

EGYPTIAN PERIODS AND KINGDOMS IN THE SECOND MILLENNIUM

Middle Kingdom	1983–1795 B.C.E.
Second Intermediate Period	1795–1550 B.C.E.
New Kingdom	1550–1075 B.C.E.
Third Intermediate Period	1075–656 B.C.E.
Late Period	656–332 B.C.E.
Hellenistic Period	332–30 B.C.E.

Sesostris III (1870–1831 B.C.E.). This powerful Twelfth-Dynasty pharaoh led military campaigns into Nubia, constructed massive, garrisoned fortresses along the Nile, and dug new waterways near Aswan. More than one hundred portrait busts of Sesostris survive, all with similar features. The overhanging brow, deep-set eyes, and drawn-down mouth are all intended to communicate the enormous burden of responsibility the pharaoh bore as the ruler of all Egypt.

tions. Pharaoh continued to enjoy a special position as god-king, but his authority did not derive from a vaunted, remote position as such. Rather, in the Middle Kingdom pharaohs represented themselves as—and were expected to be—good shepherds, tenders of their Egyptian flock. *Ma'at* could not help them in these duties; only by diligently protecting Egypt from a hostile outside world could pharaohs provide the peace, prosperity, and security desired by their subjects. Portraits of the great pharaohs of Dynasty 12 poignantly reflect the concern and anxiety with which they lived.

Egyptians had lost that vision of the Old Kingdom wherein the land was a perfect and inviolable paradise. The literature of the Middle Kingdom demonstrates the change in attitude. Among the most popular literary forms were "Instructions" to various kings, such as the *Instruction of King Merykare* or the *Instruction of*

Amenemhet. This literature is characterized by cynicism and resignation. A pharaoh must trust no one: not a brother, not a friend, not intimate companions. He must crush the ambitions of local nobles with ruthless ferocity, and he must always be on the lookout for potential trouble. In return for his exertions on behalf of his people, he should expect neither gratitude nor reward; he should expect only that each new year will bring new dangers and more pressing challenges.

Egyptian chauvinism nevertheless remained. Even at the zenith of Middle Kingdom power under Sesostris III, the Egyptians continued to produce execration texts, loaded with curses against foreign peoples and their rulers. Literary texts show the same attitudes. In the popular *Story of Sinuhe*, the title character of the tale—a royal courtier—is gripped by an irrational terror at the death of Amenemhet I and flees the country. He sojourns in Palestine, where he is rescued by Semitic nomads. Living as an exile among them, he rises to become a tribal leader. At the end of his life, however, hoping for a proper Egyptian burial, he returns to Egypt, where the pharaoh Sesostris I receives him and honors him. The story underscores that it was better to live and die as a subject of pharaoh in Egypt than to be a prince among "vile Asiatics"; at the same time, the *Story of Sinuhe* rhapsodizes on the theme of pharaoh's power, wisdom, and forgiveness.

Though the attitude of Middle Kingdom Egyptians may strike us as somewhat overwrought, their feelings of insecurity were justified. The Egyptians recognized that they had been slowly drawn into a much wider world, a world that underwent a series of upheavals during the course of the early second millennium. The first pharaohs of Dynasty 13 (c. 1786–1633 B.C.E.) were greatly alarmed by the growing power of Hammurabi and his imperial ambitions. Precisely because Egypt remained a highly distinct culture unto itself, the wider world beyond the frontiers of the Two Lands appeared all the more alien, frightening, and potentially dangerous to the Egyptians.

THE SECOND INTERMEDIATE PERIOD AND REUNIFICATION

Just how dangerous this world was became clear in the middle of the seventeenth century B.C.E., when a new group of invaders overran the country. Known as the Hyksos (a Greek version of the Egyptian *beka khaswt*, or "rulers of foreign lands"), these invaders—whose exact origins are unknown, but who may have been Amorites—carved out a kingdom in the eastern delta and projected their authority over most of Egypt.

The period of Hyksos domination lasted about a century and came to be regarded as the great shame of Egyptian national history. Never before had all Egypt fallen under the domination of foreigners. About the Hyksos themselves, however, we know little; and much of what we do know derives from later, highly propagandistic Egyptian accounts of them. Clearly, however, they took over the machinery of pharaonic government in the north, and took steps to legitimate their rule. Some Hyksos rulers even incorporated the name of Ra into their names, despite later Egyptian references to them as "those who ruled without Ra." But the Hyksos also retained much of their foreign material culture, while maintaining close economic and diplomatic ties with the Aegean world, Syria and Palestine. In southern Egypt, Hyksos control was less complete. A native regime maintained a tenuous independence in Thebes, although they too sometimes had to acknowledge the suzerainty of the foreigners in the north.

Despite later Egyptian characterizations of them, the Hyksos established themselves and Egypt as the most significant power in the Near East, especially after the eclipse of Hittite power following Mursilis's assassination. The Second Intermediate Period (1795–1550 B.C.E.) was a not a time of total anarchy and profound weakness for Egypt, as the First Intermediate had been. Nevertheless, the confusion created by the Hyksos conquest allowed the Nubians to break free and found an independent kingdom called Kush (a much greater threat to the native dynasty in the south than to the Hyksos in the north). Under pressure from all sides, the southern pharaohs began to play on nationalist sentiment, launching "wars of liberation" against the "hated" Hyksos in the north. The strategy succeeded. By the end of the sixteenth century B.C.E., the southern pharaoh Ahmose had driven out the invaders, establishing a new dynasty and a new era in Egyptian history.

THE NEW KINGDOM (1550–1075 B.C.E.)

During the Late Bronze Age, Egyptian civilization reached the zenith of its magnificence and power. This phase is termed the New Kingdom by historians, who date it from the foundation of the Eighteenth Dynasty by the pharaoh Ahmose around 1550 B.C.E. The New Kingdom is in many ways a radical departure in Egyptian history and culture, though many of the basic religious, economic, and political forms remained, and art and literature continued much in the tradition established in Egypt's "classical" period. However, the dynamism of the New Kingdom—particularly its focus on imperialism and militarism—changed the very fabric of Egyptian life.

PHARAONIC RULE IN DYNASTY 18

Easy characterizations of Dynasty 18 are impossible. The pharaohs of this regime ruled Egypt for more than two and a half centuries, and some striking developments, uncharacteristic even within Egyptian society, took place during the period. The dynasty was forged in battle, with Ahmose winning fame as the man who finally expelled the Hyksos from the country. During his reign and that of his successors, we witness the rise of a new type of nobility in the context of Egyptian society, an aristocracy of military commanders and leaders. These officers gained wealth through the spoils of pharaoh's wars—including slaves to work the crown lands granted them as rewards for their successful military service.

The earliest pharaohs of Dynasty 18 were not so outwardly aggressive or imperialistic as some of their successors, but certain exigencies necessitated conquest. After the reunification of Egypt proper, Ahmose and his immediate heirs directed their efforts to the south, toward Nubia. By the dawn of the fifteenth century, the entire Near East had more or less evolved a gold standard for commerce and finance, and if Egypt was to maintain its stature it needed to control the rich Nubian gold mines. Under Thutmosis I (c. 1504–1491 B.C.E.), the Egyptians also penetrated to the northeast, driving deep into Syria and Palestine. This great pharaoh claimed to rule the land from beyond the Fourth Cataract in the south to the banks of the Euphrates in the north; no pharaoh had ever held sway over so much territory. Nor was his success merely fleeting: the Egyptians would sustain a serious military presence in the Asiatic Near East for the remainder of the New Kingdom; more than a century after Thutmosis, pharaohs undertook massive temple- and statuary-building projects deep into the Sudan.

> During the Late Bronze Age, Egyptian civilization reached the zenith of its magnificence and power.

New Kingdom Egyptians embodied a new spirit and attitude, at once removed and yet also in touch with the brilliance of the Old Kingdom. The pharaohs of the Eighteenth Dynasty deliberately and consciously cultivated the heritage of Egypt's glorious past, encouraging the revival of certain artistic forms as well as the recording and archiving of historical records and literary monuments. Taking pride in the cultural and historical strength of Egyptian civilization, New Kingdom Egyptians resuscitated that sense of self-confident superiority that the Middle Kingdom, for all its achievements, had lacked.

The new Egyptian outlook also owed much to its Middle Kingdom predecessor. New Kingdom pharaohs —with one notable exception we shall soon meet—had no conception of Egypt as an isolated Nile kingdom detached from its surroundings. They understood, as did the pharaohs of the Twelfth Dynasty, that Egypt's success and survival depended in great measure on its involvement beyond its borders. Egyptian prosperity and security were ensured through active acquisition of resources— by trade and selective conquest —and by maintaining political and diplomatic contacts.

A major distinction characterized the New Kingdom, however. Whereas there was a certain defensiveness and paranoid concern during the Middle Kingdom, New Kingdom pharaohs pursued an ambitious strategy of defense through offense. The embarrassment of the Hyksos domination translated itself into a steely determination to prevent such an episode from occurring ever again. This was to be accomplished not by preparing for the day when more invaders might arrive, but by actively projecting Egyptian strength into regions from which danger might come. The Egyptians had also learned something about battle tactics from the Hyksos, employing the horse-drawn battle chariots the Hyksos had used against them to devastating effect against their new enemies.

The peak of military activity came during the fifteenth century, in the wake of what could have been a crisis for Dynasty 18. Thutmosis II died young (probably in 1479 B.C.E.), leaving a youth as his heir, the future Thutmosis III. In the course of Egyptian history, such incidents often led to instability and even changes of dynasty. On this occasion, however, family politics and a remarkable personality served as a force for cohesion and continuity. It was pharaonic practice

in the New Kingdom (and perhaps earlier) that pharaoh—himself a manifestation of a god—could marry as his official "queen" only someone worthy of such a union. Put in baldest terms, this meant the daughter of a god, that is to say of the previous pharaoh, and thus a sister of the new pharaoh. Such brother-sister unions do not appear to have been the routine way to produce heirs: pharaoh also had a vast harem of subsidiary wives and concubines with whom to procreate. Such was the case with Thutmosis II, whose queen was his sister Hatshepsut, while his son and heir had been born to him by another wife.

QUEEN HATSHEPSUT

On the death of Thutmosis II, Hatshepsut assumed pharaonic authority along with her stepson-nephew Thutmosis III. She was not simply a regent, someone entrusted to rule until such time as a young monarch reaches his or her majority. While Thutmosis III was still a youth, Hatshepsut effectively pulled the strings of government. For her part, she was careful to mask her femininity from the majority of Egyptians. Her inscriptions typically utilize masculine pronouns, and many of her monumental statues portray her with the long, narrow beard of her male counterparts. Egyptian women had always enjoyed a relatively high status compared with that of women in other Near Eastern cultures, and a few had even ruled as queens. The Theban origin of this dynasty, with its strong Nubian attributes, may also have allowed for a certain matriarchal element and the accession of a woman as pharaoh, at least within court circles. However, in an increasingly militaristic society, Hatshepsut deemed it necessary, at the very least, not to flaunt the fact of her being a woman to her subjects.

Her dynamism and statecraft proved crucial to the continued vitality of the dynasty and of Egypt. As co-ruler with Thutmosis III, she reigned for twenty-two years, and several military campaigns are recorded under her leadership. She is best remembered for the spectacular mortuary temple she built for herself, which seems to have been the signature moment in a process by which the mortuary temple and the funerary-cult temple to the pharaoh became separate. (The famous "Valley of the Kings" near ancient Thebes was established in the New Kingdom, a remote location where—it was hoped—the locations of pharaonic tombs would remain secret and thus safe from robbery.

> Whereas there was a certain defensiveness and paranoid concern during the Middle Kingdom, New Kingdom pharaohs pursued an ambitious strategy of defense through offense.

Hatshepsut as Pharaoh, c. 1460 B.C.E. Notice her masculine figure and ceremonial beard.

Meanwhile, the actual cult rituals practiced in reverence to the pharaoh took place elsewhere.)

THUTMOSIS III

Thutmosis III enjoyed the tutelage and protection of his stepmother, who seems not to have begrudged him his position or to have schemed against him in any way. Once he reached adulthood, however, he began to chafe at sharing rule with her, and after a revolt in Palestine against Egyptian rule, she disappears from our records around 1458 B.C.E. From that date, Thutmosis III commenced the thirty-two years of his sole rule. Eventually he defaced many of Hatshepsut's monuments and removed her name from as many of her inscriptions as he could find, creating the impression that he had always ruled alone.

Despite his ingratitude, Thutmosis III was a great pharaoh. Launching a total of seventeen campaigns, he penetrated deep into Palestine, capturing the strategic town of Megiddo (Armageddon). He followed up this famous victory by seizing many of the vital port towns

of the Syrian coast. Thutmosis's son, Amenhotep II (c. 1428–1397 B.C.E.), continued his father's conquests. He campaigned deep into Syria, crossing the Orontes River and capturing several important cities. His campaigns netted him seven Syrian princes, six of whom he sacrificed by hanging them upside down at Thebes (the seventh was similarly displayed at Napata, deep in the Sudan), and capturing some seventy-one thousand prisoners of war.

The Asian campaigns of Thutmosis III and Amenhotep II were intended not only to augment Egyptian strength, but also to undermine the economic and military might of the Hurrian kingdom of Mitanni. In this they were entirely successful, but to ironic effect. Mitanni was now so weakened that the Hittites were able to reassert themselves and their ambitions in Syria and Mesopotamia. The Assyrians also broke free of their vassalage to Mitanni, ultimately proving a far more aggressive foe to Egypt than the Mitanni had been. At the time, however, the long-term consequences of Mitanni's demise were not apparent, and the Eighteenth Dynasty basked in the glow of its military accomplishments.

In addition to the tremendous power and wealth Thutmosis III and Amenhotep II accrued, these rulers also established an Egyptian reputation for determination and ruthlessness. Amenhotep III (c. 1387–1350 B.C.E.), known as "the Magnificent," found therefore that he did not have to pursue military conquests equal to his grandfather's or his great-grandfather's. By and large, his task was to administer effectively the domains already gained for Egypt, and to exploit the economic and diplomatic advantages already won. This Amenhotep III did with skill and aplomb. The pharaoh received tribute from far and wide, including a land called Keftiu (usually identified with the Biblical Caphtor, and most likely the island of Crete). He concluded treaties with Mitanni and received at least two Mitannian princesses into his harem. So long as Amenhotep III remained vigilant with regard to his conquests and tended to his diplomatic interests, he had no need to do more than enjoy the benefits of his predecessors' endeavors.

RELIGIOUS CHANGE AND RELIGIOUS CHALLENGE

Another effect of the great conquests of Dynasty 18 was the mind-boggling amount of spoil brought back to Egypt. The wealth plundered from Nubia and the

Asian Near East seems to have left the pharaohs with a literal embarrassment of riches. Much of this wealth went to the personal glorification of the pharaoh, through grand temples, tombs, and other monuments, to say nothing of the ubiquitous royal stelae that provide us with so much historical information. Another significant portion of the booty went to the increasingly important officer class, the military aristocracy that made such conquests possible. But vast quantities of wealth still remained, and much of this went to propitiate the gods with thank offerings for Egypt's bountiful success. Temples throughout Egypt enjoyed the profits of conquest, and as the temples became wealthy, so too did the priests who administered those temples.

THE TEMPLE OF AMON

No temple complex made out quite so well as that dedicated to Amon in Thebes. Thebes was the hometown of the Eighteenth Dynasty, and the city's patron deity remained an important part of the dynasty's nomenclature, propaganda, worship, and general self-representation. The association between the pharaohs of this dynasty and Amon may have been crucial to their success within Egypt. Amon had grown in stature and popularity throughout the Middle Kingdom, and

increasingly the person of Amon was incorporated with that of the sun god Ra (thus the common New Kingdom formulation Amon-Ra). The Amon-Ra godhead became something of a national god, around whom Dynasties 17 and 18 had rallied as they reconquered and reunified Egypt.

The name *Amon* means "hidden": Amon was the unknowable god of the Old Kingdom, a powerful, transcendent, yet elusive deity. The theology of this god was most highly developed by the priests of the temples of Luxor and Karnak just outside Thebes, dedicated to Amon around the beginning of the New Kingdom. The priests had worked out a system that took advantage of Amon's invisible but mighty essence to elevate him above the other gods. All other gods became manifestations of Amon (thus facilitating identifi-

Tomb of Tutankhamon. Inside this solid gold coffin weighing twenty-five hundred pounds was the mummified body of "King Tut."

The Temple at Karnak. Most of this building has collapsed or been carried away, but the huge columns give an idea of the massiveness of Egyptian temples.

cations such as Amon-Ra). One Egyptian papyrus from the Nineteenth Dynasty states, "All the gods are three: Amon, Ra, and Ptah, without seconds; his identity is hidden as Amon, Ra is his face, Ptah his body." In other words, all gods were really just these three gods, and these three in turn were merely manifestations of a single godhead. This trinitarian conception of the Egyptian godhead represents the closest approach to monotheism yet seen in the ancient world and would remain an important part of Egyptian religious thought until Egypt became predominantly Christian in the second century C.E. As Egypt was an early center of Christian theological development, the impact of this ancient "trinity" on later Christian doctrines may have been substantial.

The favor shown to the priesthood of Amon at Thebes, coupled with the tremendous wealth deposited there, made the priests of Amon a formidable political and economic force. Indeed, by the end of Amenhotep the Magnificent's reign, the priesthood of Amon enjoyed political clout surpassing even that of the officer class, and the priests themselves had become influential persons within the court of pharaoh.

THE REIGN OF AKHENATEN

All these factors came to a fateful intersection in one of history's most intriguing figures. On the death of Amenhotep III in the middle of the fourteenth century, his son succeeded him as Amenhotep IV. Amenhotep IV showed early on a preference toward sun-god worship, as distinct from veneration of Amon: his earliest inscriptions exalt Ra not as an aspect of Amon, but as his own discrete divinity, visibly manifest in the light of the sun's rays. In his dedications to Ra the king laid aside the traditional depiction of a falcon (or a falcon-headed man), and replaced it with the *Aten*, the sun disk itself, its rays of light reaching toward earth. Before long, the new pharaoh had changed his name from Amenhotep ("Amon is pleased") to Akhenaten ("He is effective for the Aten"). As Akhenaten, he built a new capital halfway between Memphis in the north and Thebes in the south, calling it Akhetaten ("The place where the Aten becomes effective"), the modern site of el-Amarna. The short-lived but characteristic culture of Akhenaten's reign is therefore designated the Amarna Period.

Akhenaten introduced a variety of innovations into Egyptian religion and culture. The worship of Aten was more stringently monotheistic than the evolving, trinitarian view of Amon had been. Whereas Theban

Amon theology recognized other gods as aspects of Amon, Akhenaten recognized only the life-giving power of light, embodied by the Aten. Unlike the ancient deities of Egyptian religion, Aten could not be captured or represented in art. The image of the Aten, a dominant feature of Amarna period art, is therefore an elaboration of the Egyptian hieroglyph for light.

Life and its affirmation seem to be central aspects of Akhenaten's religious revolution. The Aten was often depicted with hands at the end of each ray of light, holding in them the *ankh*, the Egyptian hieroglyph for "life." Akhenaten also had himself portrayed in curious fashion, although it is unclear whether the uniqueness of this representation was due to ideology or to features of his own anatomy. In a complete departure from the confident virility of his ancestors, Akhenaten is always shown with an elongated head and limbs, an exaggerated nose and exceptionally full lips. His eyes are catlike, and the pronounced protrusion in his belly is somewhat reminiscent of female fertility figurines. The overall effect is of a certain androgyny, the significance of which is unclear. Akhenaten was clearly a family man and had himself pictured as the most human of pharaohs, enjoying the company of his beautiful queen Nefertiti as they played with their children. Indeed, a palpable sense of humanity—an almost "common" touch compared with other pharaonic art—pervades the Amarna examples.

Beyond these observations, Akhenaten's theology is difficult to comprehend. It was clearly monotheistic, and the conception of Aten may have had an influence

Akhenaten, His Wife Nefertiti, and Their Children. The Aten is depicted here as a sundisk, raining down power on the royal family.

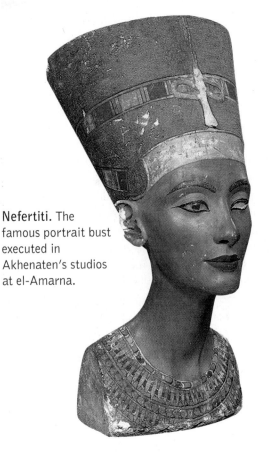

Nefertiti. The famous portrait bust executed in Akhenaten's studios at el-Amarna.

strenuous resistance to the pharaoh's religious innovations. To make matters worse, Akhenaten seems also to have been largely uninterested in military affairs. His exertions on behalf of his new god may even have encouraged him to neglect Egypt's interests abroad. The revolts that inevitably followed cost pharaoh the support of his officer class. Akhenaten's revolution failed.

His failure was the harbinger of the Eighteenth Dynasty's decline. He was ultimately succeeded by Tutankhaten, who changed his name to Tutankhamon (the famous "King Tut") to reflect his rejection of Akhenaten's heresies and the restoration of the god Amon and his priesthood. Akhetaten was abandoned as a capital and its memory cursed; its neglect thereafter is largely responsible for its high state of preservation today. Akhenaten, meanwhile, was remembered only as "Akhetaten's heretic." His monuments were destroyed throughout the land. But the damage had been done. Egypt's position in the wider world had eroded at an astonishing rate since the outset of Akhenaten's reign, and his heir was a sickly teenager. On the early death of the boy king, confusion ensued until an important military commander named Horemheb assumed the throne in 1319 B.C.E. Horemheb maintained stability for nearly three decades but had no heir. He passed his position to another general, who founded the next dynasty and restored Egypt to glory in the Near East.

well beyond New Kingdom Egypt. Great controversy still exists regarding Akhenaten's motives. Some believe him to be the world's first truly revolutionary intellectual, who applied imaginative force and exceptional insight to break the bonds of tradition and head in new directions. Others see him as a reactionary, troubled by the absorption of Ra into Amon, who chose to reassert the worship of the sun. Still further, one might argue for the evidence that he was a cagey politician who sought to undermine the disturbing influence of Amon's priests by shoving that god aside in favor of a new religious regime.

These various explanations are by no means mutually exclusive. As we have seen, politics and religion were inextricably intertwined in the ancient Near East, as they would be in Greece and Rome also. Akhenaten's religious revolution was by definition also a political coup of sorts, and he expended tremendous energy in trying to achieve it. Most of his fellow Egyptians were unimpressed, however, and did not follow pharaoh in his religious experiment. However bewildering and complex traditional Egyptian religion may seem to us, the average Egyptian apparently preferred it to a remote and impersonal god, however benevolent. The powerful priesthood of Amon also put up

Throne of "King Tut." Dating from about 1360 B.C.E., this relief in gold and silver is part of the back of the young pharaoh's throne. The relaxed lounging position of the pharaoh's right arm is typical of the stylistic informality of the period.

AKHENATEN, THE HEBREWS, AND MONOTHEISM

One of the great literary monuments of Akhenaten's religious revolution was his "Hymn to the Aten," extolling the life-affirming virtues of the god he sought to place atop the Egyptian religious system. Although Akhenaten's experiment failed in Egypt, it may have played a significant role in shaping the religious traditions of other societies throughout the Levant, including the ancient Hebrews.

HYMN TO THE ATEN

You appear beautifully on the horizon of the heavens, living Aten, the beginning of life! When you arise on the eastern horizon, you have filled every land with your beauty. You are gracious, great, glistening, and high over every land; your rays encompass the lands to the limit of all that you have made. . . . When you set in the western horizon, the land is in darkness, in the manner of death. They sleep in a room, with heads wrapped up, nor sees one eye the other. All their goods which are under their heads might be stolen, but they would not perceive it. . . .

Creator of seed in women, you who makes fluid into man, who maintains the son in the womb of his mother, who soothes him with that which stills his weeping, you nurse even in the womb, who gives breath to sustain all that he has made! . . . How manifold it is, that which you have made! They are hidden from the face of man. O sole god, like whom there is no other! You created the world according to your desire, while you were alone: all men, cattle, and wild beasts, whatever is on earth, going upon its feet, and what is on high, flying with its wings. . . .

The world came into being by your hand, according to how you have made them. When you have risen they live, when you set they die. You are lifetime itself, for one lives only through you.

Based on James B. Pritchard, ed. *Ancient Near Eastern Texts Relating to the Bible*, 3rd rev. ed. with supplement. (Princeton, N.J.: Princeton University Press, 1969), pp. 370–371.

PSALM 104

Bless the Lord, O my soul. . . . You are clothed with honor and majesty, wrapped in light as with a garment. You stretch out the heavens like a tent. . . . You set the earth on its foundations, so that it shall never be shaken. You cover it with the deep as with a garment; the waters stood above the mountains. At your rebuke they flee. . . . You cause the grass to grow for the cattle, and plants for people to use, to bring forth food from the earth, and wine to gladden the human heart. You make darkness, and it is night, when all the animals of the forest come creeping out. The young lions roar for their prey, seeking their food from God.

O Lord, how manifold are your works! In wisdom you have made them all; the earth is full of your creatures. . . . These all look to you to give them food in due season; when you give them to them, they gather it up; when you open your hand, they are filled with good things. When you hide your face, they are dismayed; when you take away your breath they die.

The New Oxford Annotated Bible. (Oxford: Oxford University Press, 1994).

THE INTERNATIONAL "SYSTEM" OF THE LATE BRONZE AGE

What factors facilitated the creation of the Late Bronze Age international system?

The fates of many nations after 1500 B.C.E., including Egypt, are intelligible only within the wider context of international relations. From the middle of the second millennium on, the destinies of the various Near Eastern kingdoms became increasingly interwoven, and an international system developed that stretched throughout the eastern and central Mediterranean.

The Late Bronze Age was an age of superpowers. As we have seen, the great pharaohs of the Eighteenth Dynasty had transformed Egypt into a conquering state, feared and respected throughout the Near East. But the pressure they applied to the kingdom of Mitanni allowed for the emergence of a revived Hittite empire after 1450 B.C.E. It was the Hittites who dealt Mitanni the most crushing blows, succeeding once again to the mantle of northern power in the region. The Assyrians also revived, and the Kassite kingdom of Babylonia remained a significant force in the economic and military relationships of the age. Between these imperial powers arose numerous smaller but important states, concentrated along the coasts and river valleys of Syria, but extending to Cyprus and the Aegean Sea.

INTERNATIONAL DIPLOMACY

Though warfare remained a characteristic feature of ancient international relations, the great states of the Late Bronze Age developed something of an equilibrium, a balance of power that helped to stabilize trade and diplomacy as the period progressed. Internationalism had existed in some form since the age of Hammurabi, who, as we have seen, employed diplomacy and intrigue to tip the scales in his own favor. But by the fourteenth century, an international standard had developed, within which many nations and their leaders came to understand the value of peace over war. This is not to say that war never occurred in the pursuit of political or economic advantage. However, many people at the time seem to have understood that security and stability helped trade to flourish, whereas war could prove disruptive and—in the long run—unprofitable.

The archives discovered by modern archaeologists at Akhenaten's accursed capital (present-day el-Amarna) provide us with a clear picture of this international diplomatic standard. Flurries of correspondence took place between the leaders of nations, sometimes over great matters, but often not. Maintaining lines of communication seems to have been an important end in and of itself. The most powerful kings developed a language of diplomatic rank, addressing one another as "brother," while the princes of lesser states showed their deference and respect to pharaoh, the Hittite king, or other powerful sovereigns by calling them "father." Breach of this protocol was cause for diplomatic offense. When an Assyrian king of the thirteenth century arrogated to himself the privilege of addressing the Hittite ruler Hattusilis III as "brother," he received a stern rebuke: "What is this you keep saying about 'brotherhood'? You and I were born of the same mother? Far from it; even as my father and grandfather were not in the habit of writing about 'brotherhood' to the King of Assyria, so stop writing to me about brotherhood and Great Kingship!"

Rulers of the period also exchanged lavish gifts and entered into marriage alliances with one another. After Akhenaten's death, his supporters even tried to gain the Hittite crown prince for the late pharaoh's daughter to shore up their failing power. Under more routine circumstances, groups of professional envoys journeyed back and forth between the centers of Near Eastern power, conveying valuable treasures as gifts and handling politically sensitive missions. In the case of Egypt, such emissaries were also often merchants, sent not only to handle matters of diplomacy but also to explore the possibility of trade opportunities for pharaoh.

INTERNATIONAL TRADE

Trade became an increasingly important aspect of international relations during the Late Bronze Age. Seaborne trade flourished up and down the coast of the eastern Mediterranean, allowing smaller, seaside centers such as Ugarit and Byblos to become powerful merchant city-states. The great coastal cities of the eastern Mediterranean became wealthy entrepots for the exchange of a bewildering variety of goods. A single merchant vessel's cargo might contain scores of distinct items originating anywhere from the interior of Africa to the Baltic Sea. At the same time, the great states of the region continued to exploit their control

WHAT FACTORS FACILITATED THE CREATION OF THE LATE BRONZE AGE INTERNATIONAL SYSTEM?

THE INTERNATIONAL "SYSTEM" OF THE LATE BRONZE AGE   69

of overland trade routes, relying more than ever on moving goods to an international market. Trade was rapidly becoming the lifeline of all these Late Bronze Age empires.

Busy and lucrative trade routes also served as a conduit for artistic motifs, literary and religious ideas, architectural forms, and ideas in tool making and weapon smithing. Whereas in the past such influences spread slowly and unintentionally, the societies of the Late Bronze Age were now developing a very self-conscious cosmopolitanism. Egyptians delighted in Canaanite glass; Bronze Age Greeks prized Egyptian amulets; and the merchants of Ugarit admired and desired Greek pottery and wool. Examples of such active longing for the products of other cultures could be endlessly multiplied.

In the great merchant towns such as Ugarit, this cosmopolitanism could have further repercussions. Ugarit was a meeting place of cultures, languages, and beliefs—not surprising, as the town had several "quarters," areas in which alien merchants and artisans plied their trades, worshiped their own gods, and took advantage of Ugarit's teeming commercial activity. Of course Ugaritic—a Semitic dialect and precursor to

later Phoenician—was spoken, as were Hurrian and Hittite, Assyrian, various dialects native to Cyprus and Crete, Egyptian, and probably the several Indo-European languages of western Anatolia. The swirl of commerce and the multiplicity of languages may have impelled the citizens of Ugarit to develop a simpler form of writing than the Sumero-Akkadian cuneiform system still current throughout the Near East. An Ugaritic alphabet appears at the end of the Bronze Age, a system of about thirty symbols representing consonants. Vowels had to be inferred, potentially sacrificing some clarity between reader and audience; but the elegant, less cumbersome alphabetic system was more easily mastered and more efficient for recording the heady pace of trade in the city's harbors.

The search for more markets, greater resources, and new trade routes heightened economic competition but promoted greater understanding between cultures. After a great battle between Egypt and the Hittites near Kadesh (c. 1286 B.C.E.), the magnificent Dynasty 19 pharaoh Ramses II realized that more was to be gained through peaceful relations with his northern neighbors than through pointless warfare. The treaty he established with the Hittites served as a pillar of

The Temple of Ramses II at Abu-Simbel. Each of these colossal figures stands sixty-six feet high. The smaller figures at Ramses' feet represent his wives and relatives. Ramses II lived to be more than ninety years old and fathered at least one hundred children.

geopolitical stability in the region and allowed even further economic integration to develop during the thirteenth century B.C.E. Greater integration also meant greater mutual dependence. If one economy suffered in this international system, the effects of that decline were sure to be felt elsewhere.

EXPANSION OF THE NEAR EASTERN SYNTHESIS

Heightened economic activity and the expansion of markets also introduced the Near Eastern synthesis to peoples beyond the Near Eastern heartland. In many cases, these new peoples adapted their societies to accommodate Near Eastern political and economic forms so as to trade more easily. The further the Near Eastern model of civilization spread from its roots in Mesopotamia and Egypt, however, the more superficial and potentially fragile it became. Furthermore, the new markets of the Late Bronze Age included societies whose own degree of "civilization," however enthusiastic they may have been, was questionable. Their rough, warlike spirit made them valuable mercenaries, especially for smaller states lacking the manpower resources to field large standing armies of their own. But these new trading partners and mercenaries could prove unreliable and may ultimately have helped to destroy the Near Eastern synthesis. We turn our attention now to their story.

AEGEAN CIVILIZATION: MINOANS AND MYCENAEANS

How did Minoan culture affect Mycenaean culture?

The ancient Greeks treasured many legends about a heroic and distant past, a golden age when great men mingled with the gods, and powerful kingdoms—larger and stronger than any known to the later world of classical Greece—contended for power and glory. For a very long time, scholars dismissed this picture of a "prehistoric" component of the Greek experience. Tales of the Trojan War, Theseus and the Minotaur, or

Mycenaean Death Mask, c. 1550–1500 B.C.E. When Schliemann discovered this gold mask in the shaft graves at Mycenae, he immediately declared it to be the mask of Agamemnon. Although certainly royal, the mask itself is too early to have been Agamemnon's.

the great adventure of Odysseus were regarded as myths—products of Greek imagination not at all reflective of any historical truth. For these scholars, Greek history began in 776 B.C.E., the date of the first recorded Olympic Games. The Bronze Age, it was believed, simply did not matter to the later, glorious history of classical Greece.

In the late nineteenth century, an amateur archaeologist named Heinrich Schliemann believed differently. He believed the epic poems of Homer, the *Iliad* and the *Odyssey*, were not merely stories. Using Homer as his guide, he discovered the site of the great city of Troy near the coast of northwest Anatolia. He then went on to discover a number of once-powerful citadels on the mainland of Greece, including Mycenae, the home of the legendary, powerful, and mythical king Agamemnon. Though Schliemann's work met with considerable skepticism, and many of his secondary conclusions have been demonstrated to be erroneous, his discoveries ultimately forced a reevaluation of Greek civilization and its roots. It is now no longer possible to dismiss Bronze Age Greece (or, as it is more

CHRONOLOGY

CIVILIZATIONS OF THE LATE BRONZE AGE NEAR EAST	
New Kingdom Egypt	1550–1075 B.C.E.
Near Eastern international "system"	1550–1200 B.C.E.
Minoan civilization	1900–1500 B.C.E.
Mycenaean civilization	1600–1200 B.C.E.

often termed, Mycenaean Greece, after the mighty kingdom of Greek myth based at the site of Mycenae) as if it had nothing to do with the classical Greek civilization that succeeded it.

Schliemann's work stimulated further exploration, and at the turn of the twentieth century Sir Arthur Evans complicated our understanding even further. Excavating on the island of Crete, Evans found a great palace at Knossos that predated any of the major centers on the Greek mainland. A wealthy and magnificent culture had clearly thrived here in the Bronze Age, which Evans dubbed "Minoan" after King Minos, the powerful king whom the later Greeks believed had once ruled far and wide from Crete, dominating the Aegean Sea.

Both of these Aegean cultures, the Mycenaean and the Minoan, played an important role in the history of the Bronze Age Near East. Because of the nature of the evidence, there is much about them that remains mysterious. But their importance can no longer be denied.

THE MINOAN THALASSOCRACY

Thucydides, a fifth-century B.C.E. Athenian historian, wrote that King Minos had ruled a "thalassocracy," that is, a sea empire. Always careful about substantiating his claims—at least by ancient standards—Thucydides had deduced this statement from a variety of sources, including legend and the presence of many ancient towns around the Aegean basin named Minoa. Until the work of Arthur Evans, Thucydides' claim seemed mere fancy; afterward, more careful consideration became necessary.

Minoan civilization flourished from c. 1900 B.C.E. until the middle of the second millennium B.C.E., making it contemporary with Middle Kingdom Egypt, Hammurabi, and the Hittite Old Kingdom. It had a

much deeper prehistory and may have been a descendant of the Neolithic culture known as Cycladic that prevailed in the Aegean. The peoples of the Cycladic Aegean traded far and wide in a variety of goods, especially the volcanic glass obsidian, a highly prized commodity. The Minoans inherited the tradition of maritime commerce pioneered by these Stone Age inhabitants of the region.

As early as the middle of the third millennium we can see the outlines of a developing civilization on Crete. By 1900 B.C.E. this culture had developed a high degree of material and architectural sophistication; as a result, the period of Minoan civilization from 1900 to 1700 B.C.E. is sometimes referred to as the "Palace Age." Like its Near Eastern counterparts, the Minoan palace sat at the center of a redistributive economy, drawing in the resources under its control and then parceling them out as the palace bureaucracy saw fit. Several impressive complexes are to be found on Crete from this period, including the brilliant palace at Knossos, comprising several acres, hundreds of rooms, and winding hallways. It was obvious at once to excavators that such structures could have served as the inspiration for the famous story of the Labyrinth, in which the Greek hero Theseus slew the terrible Minotaur. The exact political relationship between these centers is unclear, but many scholars believe that by 1700 B.C.E. Knossos must have exerted some influence over the better part of the island.

Wall Painting from Thera. The volcanic eruption on the island of Thera preserved many splendid paintings. Here an elegant priestess is burning incense.

Scenes from the Bull Ring: Minoan Mural, c. 1500 B.C.E. Evident are the youth, skill, and agility of the Minoan athletes, the center one a male, the other two female. The body and horns of the bull are exaggerated, as are the slenderness of the athletes and their full-face eyes in profile heads. There is probably also some exaggeration in content: modern experts in bullfighting insist that it is impossible to somersault over the back of a charging bull.

The secret to Minoan success was certainly the control of overseas trade. An important site on the island of Santorini (ancient Thera), buried by a massive volcanic eruption in the middle of the second millennium, preserves evidence of the far-flung commercial and cultural influence of the Minoans. A thriving, cosmopolitan trading city existed there, exchanging a range of exotic goods. By 1700 B.C.E., the Minoans were trading regularly with Egypt, southwest Anatolia, and Cyprus. Through Cyprus, they also had indirect contacts with the Levant.

Wealth allowed the Minoans to build their magnificent palaces, palaces noteworthy for their lack of fortifications. Coupled with the playful, idyllic scenes depicted in surviving Minoan frescoes (frescoes are paintings executed in fresh plaster), the apparent serenity of the Minoans once led scholars to believe that they were a peace-loving people, interested only in the even-handed exchange of goods. Evidence of Minoan devotion to an obscure mother goddess, often portrayed with serpents in her hands as she tamed a wild beast at either side, was also seen as evidence of the peaceful nature of Minoan life, and as evidence for a strong matriarchal element in Minoan culture.

Such romanticism now appears misplaced. Crete's relative geographical isolation may have lessened the need for strong landward defenses; but the Minoans'

extensive trade networks and widespread cultural influence strongly suggest that they possessed a powerful navy, capable of stopping a hostile force before it reached Cretan shores. Evidence for a bull cult—a cult typically associated with patriarchal societies in the Near East—abounds within Minoan civilization, and there are strong arguments for human sacrifice as a regular part of Minoan religious life. Women were certainly important in Minoan culture, not least as producers of the famous Minoan textiles. But it seems unlikely, given current knowledge, that the Minoans were in any sense a matriarchal society.

Much about the Minoans remains unknown. They had a

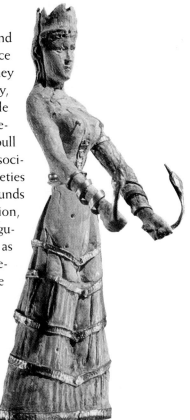

Minoan Snake Goddess. A statuette in ivory and gold discovered near the palace of Knossos and dating from 1550 B.C.E.

Cretan Labyrinth Coin. According to legend, King Minos of Crete built a labyrinth to pen in the Minotaur, part man, part bull. This coin from about 300 B.C.E. shows the labyrinth as the emblem of Knossos.

written language, that Sir Arthur Evans dubbed Linear A to distinguish it from another script, similar but clearly distinct and far better represented, which he discovered and called Linear B. But although we can determine that the tongue enshrined in Linear A is non-Indo-European, the scanty Minoan records preserved in Linear A remain untranslatable. Scholars must rely instead on the distribution of pottery and other archaeological objects to determine how and when Minoan culture spread to the other islands and shores of the Aegean Sea.

One focus of Minoan commercial activity was clearly the mainland of Greece. The presence of a wide variety of objects there, including pottery, metalwork, and textiles, suggests the export of Minoan technologies, and perhaps even Minoan craftworkers, from Crete to the mainland. But the exact nature of the relationship between Minoan Crete and Mycenaean Greece remains controversial. There is no question that before 1600 B.C.E., the Minoans enjoyed a much higher level of sophistication than their mainland counterparts. As a result, they may have been able to dominate the inhabitants of Greece's rocky landscape, at least commercially and perhaps politically. The myth of Theseus and the Labyrinth claims that the hero went to Crete to free Athens from the heavy tribute laid on the city by King Minos. Might this story

perhaps preserve a memory of a time when Crete dominated the Greeks of the mainland?

Close contacts between the Minoans and the mainland led to a variety of developments in Mycenaean Greece. The quality of material culture improved, and the mainland was drawn more tightly into the network of international commercial and diplomatic relationships that characterized the Near East during these centuries. The inhabitants of the mainland learned how to build great fortified palaces, hybrids of the Minoan palaces and the imposing strongholds of the Hittites. The mainland Greeks also became prized throughout the Near East as valuable and dangerous mercenaries. They learned to write from the Minoans, taking Linear A and modifying it to suit their own language better. The resulting script is the one Sir Arthur Evans called Linear B—a script that captures the earliest written form of Greek.

THE MYCENAEANS

When Linear B was finally deciphered in the 1950s, it turned the world of Greek scholarship decisively toward a reckoning with the Bronze Age past. Until then, scholars could continue to wonder whether the impressive sites unearthed by Schliemann, Evans, and others had anything at all to do with the story of classical Greek civilization. That Linear B represented an ancient but unmistakably Greek dialect proved conclusively that Greek history stretched well back into the Bronze Age. But what role did the Mycenaean Greeks play in that story?

The question of the arrival of "Greeks" (or more accurately, peoples speaking a form of very primitive Greek) in the Aegean basin is a vexatious and contentious one. Greece was inhabited as early 6000 B.C.E., and a few scholars contend that these Neolithic villagers were already Indo-European-speakers and thus in some sense Greek. This, however, is a minority view. The ancient Greeks clearly believed that they

Linear B Tablet from Knossos.

were distinct from an earlier group, the Pelasgians, whose language was very different from their own. This belief has subsequently been confirmed by historical linguists who have pointed out the non-Indo-European endings on many Greek place names. Because geographical and topographical names tend to be preserved, even when one culture conquers another (witness the profusion of Native American place-names used in the United States), these endings must suggest that the Greeks dominated and absorbed an earlier, non-Indo-European-speaking people.

The arrival of early Greek speakers may coincide with the destruction of several important sites in Greece around the turn of the second millennium B.C.E. New or modified architectural types and the presence of a new pottery culture around this time may also testify to an invasion or immigration. But another significant displacement of peoples and material goods took place around 1600 B.C.E. Which one of these events represents "the coming of the Greeks"? The answer, as the eminent Mycenaean scholar John Chadwick has suggested, may be as simple as this: the Greeks were always in the process of "becoming" in the Middle and Late Bronze Age. Several groups of early Greek-speakers may have infiltrated the region over a period of several centuries, intermingling with and largely assimilating the native population in a process that may have continued over several further centuries.

Mycenaean civilization was the culmination of this process in Bronze Age Greece. By 1500 B.C.E., powerful citadels dotted the Greek landscape. The rulers of these early palaces were clearly warriors, who touted their martial prowess on their gravestones and had themselves buried with their implements of war. These early rulers no doubt based their authority on their ability to lead men successfully into battle and to reward their followers with plunder. The most effective leaders managed to gain control of strategic sites from which they could exploit the major passages through Greece while never straying too far from the sea, where they engaged in both trade and piracy. The line between trade and piracy was a fine one in the ancient world, and would remain so until the nineteenth century of the common era. Like many other maritime peoples, ancient and modern, the Mycenaeans raided where they could, and traded where they could not raid.

Over time, and perhaps under the influence of Mi-

The line between trade and piracy was a fine one in the ancient world, and would remain so until the nineteenth century of the common era.

noan culture, the Mycenaean palace citadels developed into far more complex societies. By the thirteenth century B.C.E., the most powerful sites had carved out territorial kingdoms more extensive than anything the Greek world would see again for almost a millennium. The citadel served as a nerve center for the kingdom, functioning both as a place of government and as a warehouse for the storage of economic surpluses. The evidence of the Linear B tablets—of which there are thousands—suggests that the kings of the Mycenaean centers had gained control over a redistributive economy not unlike those we have seen operating in the Near East, Anatolia, and Crete. By the fourteenth and thirteenth centuries, a variety of such sites—Mycenae, Thebes, Athens, Iolkos, Pylos, and the Menelaion near the later site of Sparta—were flourishing. Some of these Mycenaean kingdoms had as many as a hundred thousand inhabitants, dwarfing the typical Greek urban centers of the Classical Period.

The Linear B tablets also reveal that the model of the Near Eastern palace center was not ideally suited to the Greek landscape. Archaeologists have pieced together evidence that reveals a high degree of inefficiency in a kingdom such as Pylos, and significant confusion as to who owed what to whom—between landowners, between farmer and palace, between palace and shrine, and so forth. In war also, Mycenaean imitation of Near Eastern examples had its limits. Although Mycenaean kings may have cherished the war chariot in imitation of their Near Eastern contemporaries, such chariots were highly impractical in Greece's rocky terrain.

Despite these and other differences between them, the Mycenaean Greeks played a very important role in the closing stages of the Near Eastern Bronze Age. We have already noted their commercial importance. They were no less important as soldiers. By c. 1400 B.C.E., they had subjugated the island of Crete, taking over Knossos and using it as a Mycenaean center; if the "Keftiu" mentioned by Amenhotep III is indeed Crete, it was most likely he treated with its Mycenaean conquerors. Their later, urban refinements notwithstanding, the Mycenaeans remained true to their martial roots and enjoyed great prestige in the Near East as warriors. At least one Mycenaean king exercised enough influence in western Anatolia to be addressed by a Hittite king as "my brother." Their combined activities as traders and raiders made it

MYCENAEAN GREECE

Note the mountainous landscape of Greece and how the peculiar shape of the region creates thousands of miles of coastline; consider that Greece is almost devoid of major rivers but that few places are far from the sight of the open sea. Notice that a map of "Greece" in antiquity always includes the western coast of Asia Minor as well as the islands of the Aegean. How would this dry, mountainous country surrounded by the sea potentially affect the nature of Greek civilization and its economic interests? Would the Near Eastern model be a good "fit" for Greece?

possible for the Mycenaeans to import food and other goods at levels far beyond what their land itself could support—with fateful consequences, as we shall see.

All of these features make the Mycenaeans more a part of the Near Eastern than the Greek story. The political and commercial arrangements of the Mycenaean world—a powerful palace, headed by a king who was also a war leader, a warrior aristocracy, a bureaucracy of local officials, state-mandated land holdings, a redistributive economy, large territorial kingdoms—distinguished the Mycenaeans fundamentally from the Greeks of the Classical Age. At the same time, however, we can trace certain fundamental features of later Greek civilization back to the Myce-

THE MYCENAEANS AND THE NEAR EAST: THE "TAWAGALAWAS LETTER"

Around 1260 B.C.E., the Hittite king Hattusilis III sent the following missive to the "King of Ahhiyawa," taken by most scholars to be the Hittite equivalent of one early Greek label for themselves, "Akhaiwoi," the Achaeans of Homer. In the letter we see the respect Hattusilis accorded this Greek king, as well as the adventures of one Greek warrior upsetting economic and political arrangements in the western Anatolian city of Millawanda (classical Miletus).

I have to complain of the insolent and treacherous conduct of one Tawagalawas. We came into contact in the land of Lukka [Lycia, in western Anatolia], and he offered to become a vassal of the Hittite Empire. I agreed, and sent an officer of most exalted rank to conduct him to my presence: he had the audacity to complain that the officer's rank was not exalted enough; he insulted my ambassador in public, and demanded that he be declared vassal-king there and then without the formality of interview. Very well: I order him, if he desires to become a vassal of mine, to make sure that no troops of his are found in Ijalanda when I arrive there. And what do I find when I arrive in Ijalanda?— the troops of Tawagalawas, fighting on the side of my enemies. I defeat them, take many prisoners . . . scrupulously leaving the fortress of Atrija intact out of respect for my treaty with you. Now a Hittite subject, Pijamaradus by name, steals my 7,000 prisoners, and makes off to your city of Millawanda. I command him to return to me: he disobeys. I write to you: you send a surly message unaccompanied by gift or greeting, to say that you have ordered your representative in Millawanda, a certain Atpas, to deliver Pijamaradus up. Nothing happens, so I go fetch him. I enter your city of Millawanda, for I have something to say to Pijamaradus, and it would be well that your subjects there should hear me say it. But my visit is not a success. I ask for Tawagalawas: he is not at home. I should like to see Pijamaradus: he has gone to sea. You refer me to your representative Atpas: I find that both he and his brother are married to daughters of Pijamaradus; they are not likely to give me satisfaction or to give you an unbiased account of these transactions. . . . Are you aware, and is it with your blessing, that Pijamaradus is going round saying that he intends to leave his wife and family, and incidentally my 7,000 prisoners, under your protections while he makes continual inroads on my dominion? . . . Do not let him use Ahhiyawa as a base for operations against me. You and I are friends. There has been no quarrel between us since we came to terms in the matter of Wilusa [very possibly the Greek Ilios, the territory of Troy]: the trouble there was my fault, and I promise it will not happen again. As for my military occupation of Millawanda, please regard it as a friendly visit. . . . [as for the problems between us], I suggest that the fault may not lie with ourselves but with our messengers; let us bring them to trial, cut off their heads, mutilate their bodies, and live henceforth in perfect friendship.

Denys Page, *History and the Homeric Iliad.* (Berkeley: University of California Press, 1959), pp. 11–12.

naeans, including the Greek language, as well as institutional and cultural continuities. The Linear B tablets speak of a group with considerable economic and political rights, the *damos*; this group would seem to be the precursor of the later *demos*, which later sought full political empowerment in many Greek cities. The tablets also preserve the names of several Greek gods familiar from the classical period, such as Zeus, Poseidon, Dionysos, and (possibly) Demeter; others, however, are absent, or their identities obscured behind completely different names. Finally, of whatever dubious use legends may be to the modern historian, for the classical Greeks the myths of their distant and heroic past were more than history—they were truth. The men and women who populated those stories were the same ones who built the massive stone walls that were still visible in the sixth, fifth and fourth centuries B.C.E., which the classical Greeks imagined to have been built by gods or monsters. However little the Greeks knew of their Mycenaean ancestors, the force on the Greek imagination of what they thought they knew about them was considerable.

Mycenaean civilization ended under a cloud of mystery on which the Linear B records, largely annual accounting books, shed very little light. Over the course of the thirteenth century B.C.E., some Mycenaean centers suffered violent destruction, whereas others prospered. This suggests a cycle of warfare within Greece that had the potential to destroy the entire culture. Mycenaean Knossos was already shattered before 1350 B.C.E.; Thebes followed shortly after 1300 B.C.E.; Pylos, around 1230 B.C.E.; Mycenae itself went through a period of conflagration and rebuilding until it succumbed in the twelfth century B.C.E.. And Troy, not perhaps properly Mycenaean but clearly a part of that world through trade and warfare, suffered its legendary destructions between roughly 1270 and 1180 B.C.E.

The Mycenaean world seems to have collapsed under its own weight around the end of the thirteenth century B.C.E. What triggered this collapse is impossible to say: natural disasters, drought, famine, disease, and social unrest have all been posited as causes. None of the theories can be proven or disproved in the current state of our knowledge. But the consequences of the Mycenaean collapse are clearer. Because it was such an integrated part of an intricate and fragile network of trade, military, and political relationships, the Mycenaean world could not implode without the reverberations of its collapse being felt across the entire Near East.

THE SEA PEOPLES AND THE END OF THE BRONZE AGE

Around the same time the Mycenaean world was in its death throes, a wave of destruction swept from north to south across the western portion of the Near East. The nature of this devastation is obscure, because it was the handiwork of a people so thorough that they utterly destroyed everything in their path until they reached Egypt. Were it not for the narrow victory of the Dynasty 20 pharaoh Ramses III in about 1179 B.C.E., we might know nothing at all of the invaders who so suddenly unraveled the Near Eastern synthesis.

In the commemorative inscription of his victory set up at Medinet Habu, Ramses III referred to the invaders as the "Sea Peoples" and named several of the groups within this coalition. The names he presented were familiar to the Egyptians. The Egyptians had employed many of them as mercenaries or had confronted them as mercenaries in the pay of other leaders. Ramses' description of these Sea Peoples marks certain of them out as clearly Aegean, from their battle gear and dress. Most notable of these were the Peleset, who, after their defeat by Egypt, withdrew to populate the coast of the region named after them, Palestine.

The arc of annihilation started in the north and may have helped to trigger the final collapse of Mycenaean Greece. Disruption of the northern trade networks must have had a profound effect on the Mycenaean kingdoms, which would have suddenly been faced with an apocalyptic combination of overpopulation, drastic food shortages, and incessant warfare. A wave of desperate refugees must have fled the Aegean basin. The undermining of commerce in the north would also have devastated the economy of the Hittites and the very underpinnings of their power. The Hittite New Kingdom collapsed with astonishing rapidity. We catch only a few glimpses in our sources of a desperate Hittite king fighting to save Hattusas against a myriad of enemies.

Down the coast of the Mediterranean we find other clues. The king of Ugarit had prepared a letter for his "brother," the king of Alashiya on Cyprus. Apparently, the invasions that overwhelmed him were as unexpected as they were terrifying. Taken completely off guard, Ugarit's ruler hoped to beseech his counterpart for immediate help. In a poignant note, however, we have his letter only because the clay tablet on which it was written was baked hard in the fire that destroyed the palace. The letter was never sent, and the Sea Peoples moved on.

On their arrival in Egypt, the picture of the Sea Peoples sharpens. These were not mindless marauders: they came with their families, their oxcarts, and their possessions. The Sea Peoples wanted land and food, but their search for it created more chaos and even more displacement. The invasion of the Sea Peoples began as a movement out of the Aegean; but it metastasized across the Near East, losing some groups who settled in the newly conquered lands. They gained desperate adherents longing to find a new place to settle, their previous homes and ways of life having been destroyed by the very force with which they now joined. Ramses III defeated them, killing many, driving others off. But the damage had been done; the world was a very different place by 1170 B.C.E. than it had been a generation or two before.

CONCLUSION

The eruption of the Sea Peoples destroyed much of civilization as the Mediterranean world had known it. The destruction was not total. Cities and kingdoms did not go away, and trade did not vanish. But the aftermath was nonetheless striking. The Hittite empire was gone, replaced by a bewildering variety of neo-Hittite principalities, possessed of little economic or military strength; they did not last long, for the most part. The great cosmopolitan cities of the eastern Mediterranean coast lay in ruins, and new groups—sometimes contingents of the Sea Peoples—populated the seaboard. Mycenaean Greece was no more. Depopulated by as much as 90 percent over the next century, the Greek mainland slipped into a "dark age," more or less isolated culturally and economically from the Near East for the next two and a half centuries. The Greeks would have to reinvent urbanism on terms more amenable to their unique environment.

Even where the Sea Peoples were defeated, they made their presence felt. Ramses III won the battle, but when the dust had settled his major trading partners had all been destroyed. Egypt went into a long decline; within a hundred years an Egyptian official would complain of his ill treatment at the hands of peoples who once feared Egypt (see p. 76). Assyria likewise suffered from the effects of the invasions. The next few centuries saw the Assyrians fighting for their very survival. To the south, the peaceful and prosperous rule of the Kassites also collapsed, along with Babylon's economy.

In the centuries immediately after the Sea Peoples, no great empires arose in the Near East. Economic and diplomatic internationalism, carefully elaborated over half a millennium, had disappeared. In the wake of all the destruction, however, new traditions and new cultural experiments began to emerge. With the international standard gone, new arrangements could now take its place. Fresh political and religious configurations could and did take shape, and a new metallurgical technology—based on iron—began to supplant the use of bronze. Out of the ashes of the Late Bronze Age, a more enduring, more integrated cultural synthesis arose, the culture of the Iron Age Near East.

SELECTED READINGS

Many of the works and source collections cited in the Selected Readings to Chapter 1 will also be of value for this chapter.

Aldred, Cyril. *Akhenaten.* London, 1988. An excellent overview of the reign, motivations, and cultural legacy of this enigmatic pharaoh. Compare with Redford's quite different account (below).

Beal, Richard H. *The Organization of the Hittite Military.* Heidelberg, 1992. A useful survey of the Hittite military that provides insight into the militaristic nature of Hittite society as a whole.

Bourriau, Janine. *Pharaohs and Mortals: Egyptian Art in the Middle Kingdom.* Cambridge, 1988. An enlightening examination of the material culture of the Middle Kingdom as a reflection of changing attitudes within Egyptian society and the world beyond Egypt.

Bryce, Trevor. *The Kingdom of the Hittites.* Oxford, 1998. The newest scholarly synthesis, with an emphasis on political and military history.

Budge, E. A. Wallis, ed. *The Egyptian Book of the Dead (The Papyrus of Ani): Egyptian Text, Transliteration and Translation.* New York, 1967. A reprinting of the original 1895 British Museum publication. An important if sometimes confusing text for understanding Egyptian funerary cult and belief.

Chadwick, John. *The Mycenaean World.* Cambridge, 1976. A fine, accessible introduction by the pioneering scholar who helped to decipher Linear B.

Dickinson, O. T. P. K. *The Aegean Bronze Age.* Cambridge, 1994. An excellent compendium of archaeological evidence and scholarly argument concerning the Minoan, Mycenaean and other cultures of the Bronze Age Aegean basin.

Drews, Robert. *The End of the Bronze Age: Changes in Warfare and the Catastrophe ca. 1200 B.C.* Princeton, 1993. A comprehensive but stimulating survey of the explanations that have been offered for the sudden collapse of Bronze Age civilization throughout the Near East, with excellent bibliographies.

———. *The Coming of the Greeks: Indo-European Conquests in the Aegean and the Near East.* Princeton, 1988. A courageous, lucidly written attempt to reconstruct the arrival of "Greeks" in the Aegean basin.

Gurney, O. R. *The Hittites,* rev. ed. London, 1990. Although a bit dated, Gurney's introduction remains an accessible starting point for discussion of the Hittites.

James, T. G. H., ed. *The Hekanakhte Papers and Other Early Middle Kingdom Documents.* New York, 1962. An extraordinary collection of domestic letters from an Egyptian father to his family, full of intimate details of family life.

Kemp, Barry. *Ancient Egypt: Anatomy of a Civilization.* London, 1989. A brilliant book, with an excellent treatment of el-Amarna.

Kitchen, K. A. *Pharaoh Triumphant: The Life and Times of Rameses II, King of Egypt.* Warminster, 1983. An elegant account of the long-lived pharaoh who reestablished Egypt as a superpower.

Kozloff, Arielle P., and Betsy M. Bryan, with Lawrence M. Berman. *Egypt's Dazzling Sun: Amenhotep III and His World.* Cleveland, 1992. A museum exhibition catalogue from an exhibit of treasures from the reign of this important New Kingdom pharaoh.

Lichteim, Miriam. *Ancient Egyptian Autobiographies, Chiefly of the Middle Kingdom.* Freiburg, 1988. A fine edition of some remarkable source material.

Macqueen, J. G. *The Hittites and their Contemporaries in Asia Minor.* London, 1986. A stimulating overview of Hittite culture that emphasizes the important intermediary role played by the Hittites in the ancient Near Eastern world.

McDowell, A. G. *Village Life in Ancient Egypt: Laundry Lists and Love Songs.* Oxford, 1999. A fascinating collection of translated texts recovered from an Egyptian peasant village, dating from 1539 to 1075 B.C.E.

Parkinson, Richard, ed. *Voices from Ancient Egypt.* London, 1991. Particularly strong on Middle Kingdom literature.

Potts, D. T. *The Archaeology of Elam.* Cambridge, 2000. A scholarly, demanding, but rewarding study of the territory that would later become Persia.

Redford, Donald. *Akhenaten: The Heretic King.* Princeton, 1984. Another influential treatment, quite different from Aldred (see above).

Renfrew, Colin. *Archaeology and Language: The Puzzle of Indo-European Origins.* Cambridge, 1987. A masterful but controversial work by one of the most creative archaeologists of the twentieth century.

Saggs, H. W. *The Greatness That Was Babylon: A Survey of the Ancient Civilizations of the Tigris-Euphrates Valley,* rev. ed. London, 1988. A useful and reliable introduction and reference work.

———. *Civilization before Greece and Rome.* New Haven, 1991. An excellent survey, focused mainly on the second millennium B.C.E.

Sandars, Nancy K. *The Sea Peoples: Warriors of the Ancient Mediterranean,* rev. ed. London, 1985. The essential starting point for all students interested in the subject.

Wilhelm, Gernot. *The Hurrians.* Trans. Jennifer Barnes. Warminster, 1989. A valuable introductory survey of this elusive but influential people that sets their history firmly in the context of the ancient Near East.

Wood, Michael. *In Search of the Trojan War.* New York, 1985. Aimed at a general audience, this carefully researched and engagingly written book is an excellent introduction to the late Bronze Age context of the Trojan War.

CHAPTER THREE

GODS AND EMPIRES:
THE IRON AGE
NEAR EAST

THE SECOND-MILLENNIUM synthesis lay in tatters after 1200 B.C.E. For the peoples who lived through the invasions and the resulting chaos, the destruction the Sea Peoples left in their wake must have seemed a catastrophe. Certainly that is how it has appeared to modern scholars. Centuries-old centers of political, economic, and military power—not to mention great cultural achievement—had been wiped out. Mycenaean Greece, the Hittite kingdom, Kassite Babylonia, many of the great commercial kingdoms of the Eastern Mediterranean—by 1100 B.C.E. only the tattered remnants of these civilizations survived. Even those who weathered the storm were profoundly transformed by it. The Assyrians survived but would spend the next several centuries fighting for their lives, ultimately emerging as the most nakedly militaristic empire of the ancient world. Egypt endured also, but would not be a dominant power in the Mediterranean world again until the third century B.C.E., when descendants of one of Alexander the Great's generals returned it to prominence. Around the turn of the first millennium B.C.E., we thus enter a new world, organized along profoundly different lines from the great empires of the Near Eastern past.

At the heart of the great second-millennium empires of the Hittites and the Assyrians, for example, lay a very old model of organization—the Mesopotamian city-state. Even the Mycenaean Greeks drew heavily on this model. With the exception of Egypt, no Bronze Age empire came close to being an integrated, territorial state. The empires of the Bronze Age were ultimately collections of cities ruled by kings who claimed to rule through divine favor. Even in Egypt, where the accidents of geography encouraged greater territorial integration, the organization of political power and its religious trappings had remained surprisingly stable—almost static— through nearly two thousand years of Egyptian civilization. The only substantive attempt to reorganize political and religious governance in Egypt—the "revolution" initiated by Akhenaten—ended in utter failure.

The stagnation of the Late Bronze Age produced a precarious balance of power in the Mediterranean world. In an age of economic prosperity and military security,

- Why did Phoenician cities prosper during the Iron Age?

- How did David consolidate the Hebrew Kingdom?

- What were the bases for the structure of Assyrian government?

- Around what central ideas was Zoroastrianism formed?

- What developments marked the Hebrew transition from polytheism to monotheism?

few people at the time realized how fragile their world had become. By the turn of the first millennium B.C.E., however, that older world was gone. In the new age that was dawning, iron would slowly replace bronze as a primary ingredient for tools and weapons. New, larger, and more brutal empires would emerge, and new ideas about gods and their relationship to humanity would begin to displace older ones. In the Iron Age Near East, two of the world's most enduring religious traditions—Judaism and Zoroastrianism—were born, altering peoples' conceptions of religion, politics, ethics, and the relationship between humanity and the natural world. The Iron Age was a fateful historical crossroads for Western civilizations, as elements both old and new combined to reconfigure the ancient Near Eastern world.

> The Iron Age was a fateful historical crossroads for Western civilizations, as elements both old and new combined to reconfigure the ancient Near Eastern world.

THE SMALL-SCALE STATES OF THE EARLY IRON AGE

Why did Phoenician cities prosper during the Iron Age?

With the destruction of the superpower balance of the Late Bronze Age, the geopolitical map of the Near East changed significantly. In Anatolia, a patchwork of small, largely Indo-European realms emerged from the collapse of the Hittite empire, including Lydia, Phrygia, and the kingdom of Urartu. Similar developments were taking place in the Levant, the eastern Mediterranean coastal area that today comprises Israel, Lebanon, and parts of Syria. For centuries, this area had been under either Egyptian or Hittite control. With the collapse of both these empires, the resulting power vacuum in the region allowed new civilizations and petty states to emerge. As political and military powers, the small-scale states of the Early Iron Age were at best second rate. However, they had a profound impact on the intellectual and religious development of Western civilizations.

THE PHOENICIANS

The coastal cities of present-day Lebanon were well positioned to recover from the onslaught of the Sea Peoples. Invasion and commercial disruption could not change basic facts of geography and climate. Although the Sea Peoples had destroyed the great city-state of Ugarit, the population centers of the coast survived and emerged from the chaos as some of the most famous cities of the ancient Mediterranean. Deep gorges divide the coast into naturally isolated and sheltered deep-water harbors, and many of the cities that flourished there during the Iron Age centered on the offshore islands opposite these great harbors. These cities thus enjoyed not only natural defenses from landward aggressors but still profited from the trade and commerce their ports attracted.

The group that succeeded to Ugaritic commercial success was the Phoenicians, related to the inhabitants of Ugarit by culture and language. The Phoenicians spoke a Semitic language closely related to Ugaritic, Hebrew, Amorite and other West Semitic dialects. They recognized themselves culturally and linguistically as Canaanites, "Phoenician" being the Greek designation for these residents of modern-day Lebanon and Israel. In political terms, however, the Phoenicians exhibited a familiar pattern of Near Eastern urbanism, almost a throwback to the days before the great empires of the Late Bronze Age. Phoenician cities were all independent of each other, and a Phoenician's first loyalty and identification would have been with his or her city, not to an abstract notion of being Canaanite or Phoenician. In the homeland of Phoenicia, the independent cities lived under hereditary royal governments, but in the overseas colonies a new type of

CHRONOLOGY	
DEVELOPMENT OF IRON AGE EMPIRES	
Phoenicians gain independence from Egypt	1200 B.C.E.
Philistine military dominance	1100–1000 B.C.E.
Consolidation of the kingdom of Israel	1000–973 B.C.E.
Revival of Assyrian power	883 B.C.E.
Persian defeat and annexation of Babylon	539 B.C.E.

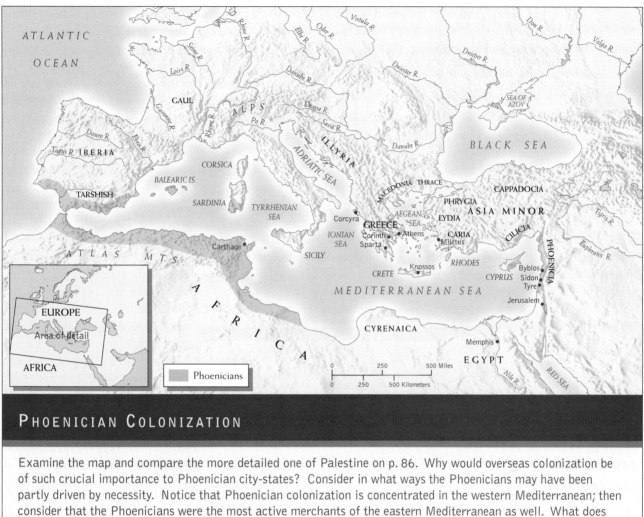

PHOENICIAN COLONIZATION

Examine the map and compare the more detailed one of Palestine on p. 86. Why would overseas colonization be of such crucial importance to Phoenician city-states? Consider in what ways the Phoenicians may have been partly driven by necessity. Notice that Phoenician colonization is concentrated in the western Mediterranean; then consider that the Phoenicians were the most active merchants of the eastern Mediterranean as well. What does their westward colonization imply about the Phoenicians' aims and the level of civilization in the West as compared with the East?

government ultimately emerged, perhaps spurred by the commercial interests of competing families. Aristocratic governments, wherein a sharing of power among a handful of elite families replaced royal authority, soon became the prevailing pattern in the overseas colonies.

Phoenicians had been active at the end of the Late Bronze Age, but most of their cities had lain under the control of the Egyptian Eighteenth and Nineteenth Dynasties. The erosion of Egyptian imperial power after 1200 B.C.E. gave rise to the possibility of independence once order was reestablished. The Phoenicians seized the opportunity, capitalizing on their natural commercial advantages and their reputation as great merchants going back to the Late Bronze Age. One Phoenician city, Gubla (the Greek name for

which was Byblos), had been a teeming center of trade under Egyptian rule, particularly as an entrepot for papyrus, the highly prized Egyptian writing material. So closely connected was Byblos with the trade in this commodity that the Greeks used their name for the city as the root of their word *biblion,* "book." All of the centers of Phoenician trade dealt in coveted luxury goods and building materials. The seabeds off the coast yielded the purple-reddish dye from the murex snail (hence the Greek name Phoenician, which essentially means "purple people"), and the finished textiles of Phoenician industry commanded a high price everywhere Phoenician merchants went. Also sought by trading partners were the Phoenicians' resources of tall timber (especially cedar), and the famous Canaanite glass that had also been traded in the Late Bronze

Age. Through their import and export activities, the Phoenicians developed expert industries in metalworking, ivory carving, and shipbuilding.

PHOENICIAN CITIES

Tucked as they were along a mountainous coast, Phoenician cities oriented themselves toward the sea. Throughout the first millennium, Phoenicians were famous as merchants and seafarers. They were also aggressive colonists; confronted by the dual pressure of commercial competition with each other and the limited carrying capacity of their surroundings, Phoenicians planted trading colonies across the Mediterranean. These colonies had a variety of purposes. First, they served as an outlet for excess population in the home city. Second, they were valuable trading partners for the cities of the Phoenician coast, providing access to new sources of raw materials and wealth. Third, the colonies acted as friendly ports for Phoenician merchant ventures and as bases from which to monopolize seaborne trade. By the end of the tenth century, Phoenicians were active from one end of the Mediterranean to the other. They probably sailed beyond as well. Evidence suggests that Phoenicians ventured as far away as Cornwall in Britain (a good source of tin), and the Greek historian Herodotus relates a credible story of how Phoenician merchant-explorers circumnavigated Africa. At the end of the ninth century, colonists from Tyre established Carthage in what is modern-day Tunisia. Carthage would ultimately rise to become the preeminent power in the western Mediterranean, bringing it into conflict with Rome centuries later.

CULTURAL INFLUENCES

The widespread colonial and mercantile efforts of the Phoenicians meant that they influenced cultures across the Mediterranean. Among their early overseas trading partners were the Greeks, and some scholars have made persuasive arguments that the Phoenicians played an important role in reintroducing urban life into the Greek world, as well as bringing a number of Near Eastern artistic and literary influences. Although the extent and nature of these borrowings are debatable, there is little question about the fundamental legacy of the Phoenicians to world history, via the Greeks: the alphabet.

As we have seen, a "cuneiform alphabet" had already evolved at Ugarit by the end of the Bronze Age. The Phoenicians of the early twelfth and eleventh centuries further refined the system of writing to twenty-two characters, all representing consonants; vowel sounds had to be inferred from context, as is the case with modern Arabic and Hebrew. The Phoenicians had thus developed an even simpler, more efficient way of writing, which probably helped facilitate trade and the accounting of it. Precisely why they chose to share their invention with the previously illiterate Greeks of the eleventh and tenth centuries is uncertain; but it may have been to encourage the type of trading and record-keeping practices of the Phoenicians among their new partners. Whatever the case, the Greeks remained very much aware of their debt to the Phoenicians, a debt that is clear from the Hellenized letter names (alpha, beta, gamma, delta . . .) of their Phoenician antecedents (aleph, bayt, gimel, dalet . . .). The Greeks believed that Cadmus, the legendary hero who "invented" their alphabet, was a Phoenician who settled in Greece. Though we may doubt the details of the story, it betrays a consciousness on the part of the Greeks of this early borrowing.

> One of history's great ironies is that the Phoenicians, inventors of such an important and indispensable tool for record keeping, have left very little history of their own.

One of history's great ironies is that the Phoenicians, inventors of such an important and indispensable tool for record keeping, have left very little history of their own. We know the Phoenicians largely through the accounts of other groups with whom they interacted—the Greeks, the Persians, and the Hebrews, the last of whom also referred to the Phoenicians as Canaanites. We can also infer a great deal from the rich documentary evidence from Ugarit, because the Phoenicians appear to have preserved many Ugaritic religious practices and beliefs.

Phoenician ritual exhibited a number of common Near Eastern features, and had a significant impact—both positive and negative—on other belief systems of the region. Death and fertility were preoccupations, and like the Babylonians many Phoenicians experienced the divine through temple prostitution. The chief god of the Phoenician pantheon was El. This primitive regional name for a divinity later manifested itself in Hebrew names and constructions (e.g., Israel, Gabriel, Michael, Samuel, and so on) as well. More crucial to the daily lives of Phoenicians however was the god Ba'al, who presented himself through various manifestations but was the primary

A Canaanite Deity. Thought to be an image of Baal, a god of storms and fertility, this statuette was discovered in a thirteenth-century B.C.E. temple in northern Palestine.

god of storms (important for the return of vegetation). His queen-consort was Ashtart, akin to the Mesopotamian Ishtar and better known by her Greek name (Astarte) and her biblical name (Ashtoreth). The goddess of war, sexual love and fertility, she enjoyed great veneration among the Phoenicians as well as many of their neighbors.

The cult practices of the Phoenicians, or Canaanites, were highly influential throughout the Levant. Worshiping at both elaborate temples and simple stone altars, the Phoenicians offered incense, various fruits, and wines to please the gods. Animal sacrifice, in which part of the animal would be burned on an altar, was a regular part of Phoenician worship. In times of crisis, the Phoenicians also practiced human sacrifice. Unlike most earlier Near East peoples, however, the Phoenicians were reluctant to represent their deities in corporeal form. Instead they used symbols such as cult stones and vacant thrones to represent their gods. Although stylized metal pendants depicting Ashtart as a fertility goddess or statues portraying Ba'al as a calf or a bull were known, these were symbols rather than portraits.

Phoenician ritual practice and Phoenician ideas about the unrepresentable qualities of the gods would exercise a profound influence on the neighboring Hebrews.

THE PHILISTINES

South along the Levantine coast from Phoenicia lay the Philistines. Few cultures have enjoyed historical reputations so bad as theirs. Regarded as villains of the Hebrew scriptural tradition, the uncouth, aggressive, and faithless Philistines have even suffered the ignominy of having their name used as an adjective in modern time to designate boorish, uncultured, and ignorant people. Their infamy stems from their unique position in the Levant at the beginning of the Iron Age, where as descendants of the Peleset—one of the Sea Peoples defeated by Ramses III—they settled, urbanized, and quickly gained the upper hand over their pastoralist neighbors in the region. One of those people was the Hebrews, for whom the Philistines were the great national enemy.

The Philistines retained a separate identity from the other peoples of the region for several generations; with each new archaeological discovery this identity becomes more and more rooted in an Aegean past. Although we know little about the Philistine language—few written materials survive, and they gradually adopted a Canaanite dialect—their material culture, behavior and organization all exhibit close affinities with the Mycenaean world. Scientific study of fossilized pollen and vegetation remains indicates that the Philistines also introduced the vine and the olive tree to the Levant from the Aegean basin. With the profits of their oil industry, they were able to create powerful armies that dominated the region in the twelfth and eleventh centuries B.C.E. They even established a monopoly over metalsmithing in the southern Levant, making it virtually impossible for their enemies to forge their own weapons.

Once they had settled themselves in the aftermath of the raid on Egypt, the Philistines established five great strongholds, the so-called Pentapolis. Less cities than citadels, the great Philistine centers—Gaza, Ashkelon and Ashdod on the coast, Ekron and Gath inland—exhibit striking similarities to the fortified palace centers of the Late Mycenaean world, and appear to have served many of the same functions. From the great citadels, each of the Philistine cities sought to dominate the surrounding countryside, organize agricultural production and control major trade routes, as well as provide strategic points from which

THE HEBREW KINGDOM, c. 900 B.C.E.

Notice the scale of the map and consider the comparatively small orbit of this world. Why did the Philistines and Phoenicians present such a perceived cultural challenge to the Hebrews? What advantages did the Philistines and Phoenicians possess, geographically and otherwise? What political and religious consequences might have resulted from the division of the kingdom of Israel after the death of King Solomon, especially the position of Jerusalem and the Temple in the south?

at an early date and have left behind virtually no written records. We know the Philistines primarily through the eyes of their enemies, the Hebrews, who at first feared them and later held them in contempt. Like other Near Eastern cultures, the Hebrew historical tradition was notorious for slandering its enemies, declaring, for example, that the Moabites and Ammonites were the descendants of Lot's incestuous union with his daughters, and decrying both Philistine and Canaanite cultural practices as "evil in the sight of the Lord." We should not be misled by such invective. The brutish arrogance of Goliath or the sexual treachery of Delilah, the two most infamous Philistines in the Hebrew Bible, is no basis for sweeping conclusions about the character of Philistine society. Unfortunately, however, we have little else on which to base our evaluations.

The Hebrews had good reason to fear the Philistines. By the end of the Late Bronze Age, these Aegean warriors were highly effective mercenaries; once they had established themselves in the Levant, they quickly turned toward the conquest and exploitation of their weaker, less organized neighbors. A Philistine prince of Ashkelon extended his control over the Phoenician city of Byblos for a short time, and felt confident in snubbing even Egyptian emissaries and court officials. If the Philistines could dominate the urbanized, wealthy, resourceful Phoenicians and hold their own against the Egyptians, however briefly, we can well imagine the challenges they presented to weaker, tribal societies such as the early Hebrews.

The picture we may glean from Hebrew texts such as the Books of Judges and Samuel makes the situation clear: at one point the southern tribes of Judah explain to Samson, the judge of the tribe of Dan, "You know the Philistines rule over us." Philistine pressure on the central Hebrew hill country of Ephraim was constant, threatening the holy sanctuary at Shiloh, the original resting place of the sacred Ark of the Covenant, which contained the original tablets of the law given by the Hebrew god Yahweh to Moses on Mount Sinai. In Hebrew tradition, the desperate tribes of Israel carried the Ark before them against the Philistines, only to lose it in battle and witness the destruction of Shiloh. The Philistines established garrisons throughout the land of the Hebrews and denied them access to metallurgical technology. Meanwhile, they exacted tribute and, according to the biblical account, engaged in the typical abuses of an occupying people.

to mount raids against neighbors while presenting virtually impregnable defenses against would-be attackers. An independent lord ruled over each Philistine citadel, and no doubt tensions and rivalries existed among them. But much like the heroes of Greek epic, the Philistines of the Bible could set aside their differences to confederate for the purpose of waging war.

Otherwise, it is difficult to know the Philistines on their own terms. Their history as an independent culture was brief. They abandoned their own language

THE REPORT OF WENAMUN

Around 1085 B.C.E. an official of the Theban temple to Amun-Re named Wenamun was sent to Lebanon to collect timber for a new ceremonial barge for the god. Egypt's power had declined, however, and the Philistine ruler of Byblos was not inclined to provide, unrewarded, the timber that Wenamun expected from him.

Wenamun of the Temple of Amun . . . [departed] to fetch timber for the great noble [river] bark of Amun-Re, King of Gods. . . . [Reaching the realm] of the prince of Byblos, [he] . . . sent to me saying: 'Leave my harbor!" I sent to him saying: "Where shall I go? If you have a ship to carry me, let me be taken back to Egypt!" I spent twenty-nine days in his harbor and he . . . [sent] to me daily to say: "Leave my harbor!". . . [Finally] I had found a ship headed for Egypt. I had loaded all my belongings into it and was watching for the darkness. . . . Then the harbor master came to me, saying: "Wait until morning, says the prince!"

When morning came, [the prince] sent for me. . . . I said to him: "Blessings of Amun!" He said to me: "How long is it . . . since you came from the place where Amun is?" I said to him: "Five whole months until now!" He said to me: ". . . where is the dispatch of Amun, which should be in your hand? Where is the letter of the High Priest of Amun, which should also be in your hand? . . . On what business have you come?" I said to him: "I have come in quest of timber for the great noble bark of Amun-Re, King of Gods. What your father did, what the father of your father did, you too will do it." . . . He said to me: "True they did it. If you pay me for doing it, I will do it. My relations carried out this business after Pharaoh had sent six ships laden with the goods of Egypt, and they had been unloaded into [my] storehouses. You, what have you brought for me?"

He said to me . . . "I am not your servant, nor am I the servant of him who sent you!" . . . I said to him: "Wrong! . . . There is no ship on the river that does not belong to Amun. His is the sea and his the Lebanon of which you say, 'It is mine.' . . . You too, you are the servant of Amun."

From Miriam Lichtheim, ed., *Ancient Egyptian Literature: Three Volumes*, Vol. 2, (Berkeley: University of California Press, 1976), pp. 224-229.

✤ THE HEBREWS

How did David consolidate the Hebrew Kingdom?

We will have occasion at the end of this chapter to discuss the central feature of Hebrew cultural experience, the development of their monotheistic conception of divinity. In this section, we will focus our attention on the political development of Hebrew society within the Iron Age Levant. However, in any discussion of Hebrew society, religious conceptions and practices can never be far from the surface. Like all ancient cultures, the Hebrews initially made little distinction between politics and religion. What set them apart, however, was their unusual theology and the impact it had on their development as a people. Were it not for the resilience of their religious tradition, and the fundamental impact it has had on the subsequent development of Western civilizations, we would have little reason to discuss the early Hebrews at length. As it is, however, the Hebrews were one of the most important cultures in world history.

ORIGINS

We are blessed as historians by one of the unique achievements of the Hebrews: the Hebrew Bible, known to Christians as the Old Testament. The Bible is an unparalleled historical resource, full of extraordinary detail about cultural practices and historical events, as well as being a guide to the intellectual unfolding of the most important religious tradition of the Western world. It is not, however, a history as modern people would conceive of it. The Bible is a composite work, assembled over many centuries, mostly by unknown authors. Although it contains some ostensibly historical accounts, it is essentially a story of the relationship between a transcendent, unchanging, creator god and those whom he chose to be his special people; of the covenant that was forged between them; and of the trials by which that relationship was repeatedly tested and reaffirmed.

Most scholars regard with particular suspicion the historical accounts contained in the first five books of the Bible (these books are known to Christians as the Pentateuch, and to Jews as the Torah). Aside from the chronological difficulties posed by a series of impossibly long-lived patriarchs (Methusaleh, for example, is said to have lived for more than nine hundred years), much of this historical material appears to have been borrowed from other Near Eastern cultures. The creation and flood stories have Sumerian parallels; the laws and practices of the patriarchs have clear Hurrian antecedents; the tale of Moses' childhood is virtually a replica of Sargon's legend; and the story of the exodus from Egypt is fraught with problems from a historical standpoint. Although the Book of Joshua claims that the Hebrews who returned from Egypt conquered and expelled the Canaanites, many scholars now believe, on the basis of strong archaeological and linguistic evidence, that the Hebrews were essentially inland Canaanites who may have merged with scattered Hebrew refugees from Egypt in the aftermath of the Sea

> We are blessed as historians by one of the unique achievements of the Hebrews: the Hebrew Bible, known to Christians as the Old Testament.

Peoples, but who for the most part had been continuously resident in Canaan for centuries. Important religious and cultural developments clearly occurred among the Hebrews of the second millennium B.C.E., but the first five books of the Bible have the look and feel of retrospective extrapolation and justification, not secure historical record.

Once we move into the so-called historical books of the Bible, the information becomes more credible. In the Book of Judges, the Hebrews appear as a semi-nomadic people just beginning to settle down into seasonal occupation around the springs and valleys that provided sustenance in an otherwise arid landscape. The Hebrews had also organized themselves into twelve "tribes"—extended clan units in which families owed each other mutual aid and protection in times of war, cattle raiding, and judicial dispute. Each tribe was ruled over by a "judge" who exercised the typical functions of authority in a clan-based society: war leadership, high priesthood, and dispute settlement. By the middle of the twelfth century, these tribes had established some kind of rough territorial "turf," those in the south calling themselves Judah, and those in the north Israel.

HEBREWS AND PHILISTINES

These collective labels should not mislead us. Although they create an impression of greater cohesion, in fact the Hebrew tribes had few mechanisms for concerted action. The inherent weakness of their organization was laid bare by contact with the Philistines, who quickly conquered so much of the Levantine coastal region around 1050 B.C.E. that it became known as Palestine, meaning "the Philistine country." Faced with the threat of extinction, the Hebrews now put up desperate resistance from their bases in the hilly interior of the country. By the end of the eleventh century, however, the future of the Hebrews as a people was not promising. To their north, they felt the economic, religious and sometimes military pressure of the Phoenicians, with their dynamic and eclectic culture; to their west and south, they confronted the military might of the Philistines.

To meet the Philistine threat, a tighter, "national" form of government was needed. Accordingly, around 1025 B.C.E., Samuel, a tribal judge and holy man with the force of personality to gain adherence from all the

Hebrew tribes, selected for them a king who would make them, "like other nations," a united people. King Saul, however, quickly provoked the resentment of Samuel, who withdrew his support from the embattled king. Saul also proved an indifferent general. Although he succeeded in stopping Philistine penetration into the hill country, he was unable to oust the Philistines from the valleys or coastal plains. So Samuel threw his support behind a young warrior, David, a member of Saul's court who now schemed actively to draw popular support away from Saul. Waging his own military campaigns, David achieved one triumph over the Philistines after another. In contrast, the armies of Saul met frequent reverses, which the Biblical authors portrayed as divine retribution for Saul's own inadequacies. David, however, was not exactly a national patriot. When Saul finally drove him from his court, David first became an outlaw on the fringes of Hebrew and Philistine society before ultimately becoming a mercenary in Philistine service. It was as a Philistine mercenary that David fought against Saul in the climactic battle in which Saul was killed. Soon thereafter, David himself became king, first over Judah, his home territory, and later over Saul's home kingdom of Israel also.

> It was as a Philistine mercenary that David fought against Saul in the climactic battle in which Saul was killed.

CONSOLIDATION OF THE HEBREW KINGDOM

With David's ascension to the throne around 1000 B.C.E., the most glorious period in the political history of the ancient Hebrew kingdom began. David took advantage of a number of new developments and trends to extend his rule and the power of his kingdom. Egypt went into sharp decline at the very end of the eleventh century, and this may have had a significant impact upon the Philistine economy, disrupting Philistine society. At the same time, years of battle against the Philistines had hardened the Hebrew warriors and accustomed them to Philistine tactics. Through a combination of cunning, opportunism, and inspired leadership, David reduced the Philistines to an inconsequential strip of coastal land in the south. He also defeated the Moabites and Ammonites, extending his control east of the River Jordan and the Dead Sea. By David's death in 973 B.C.E., the united kingdom of Israel stretched from the middle Euphrates in the north to the Gulf of Aqaba in the south,

from the Mediterranean coast in the west into the Syrian deserts beyond the River Jordan. Israel was now a serious force in the politics of the Near East, its status increased by the temporary weakness of its imperial neighbors Egypt and Assyria.

Within his kingdom, David incorporated the native Canaanites to such a degree that during the next few generations they lost their separate identity and became fully merged with the Hebrew people. As this process of amalgamation progressed, the Hebrews increasingly put aside pastoralism and took up either farming or urban occupations. As David's power and prestige grew, he was able to impose on his subjects a highly unpopular system of taxation and forced labor. His goal was to build a glorious political and religious capital at Jerusalem, a Canaanite settlement that he transformed into the central city of his kingdom. It was a shrewd choice. As a newly conquered city, Jerusalem had no previous affiliation with any of Israel's twelve tribes, and so stood outside the ancient rivalries between them. Geographically, Jerusalem lay between the southern tribes of Judah (of which David was a member) and the northern tribes of Israel (from which Saul had come). David took steps to exalt the city as a religious center. He reorganized the priesthood of Yahweh; and by making Jerusalem the resting place of the sacred Ark of the Covenant, which contained the tablets of the religious law given by Yahweh to Moses on Mount Sinai, David made his new city the central place for the kingdom's unifying national cult of Yahweh. By so doing, he hoped to forge a new national identity, focused on the House of David, that would transcend the old divisions between Israel and Judah.

CHRONOLOGY

THE TRANSFORMATION OF HEBREW SOCIETY

Early efforts to form national government	1025 B.C.E.
David crowned king of Israel	1000 B.C.E.
Split between Israel and Judah	924 B.C.E.
Fall of Judah and start of Babylonian Captivity	586 B.C.E.

TWO ACCOUNTS OF SAUL'S ANOINTING

When the judge Samuel anointed Saul as the first king of the Hebrews, he opened a new chapter in the political history of Israel. Saul's kingship was not a success, however, and Samuel ultimately declared against him, throwing his support behind Saul's rival (and son-in-law) David. These two quite different accounts of Saul's elevation by Samuel may reflect the tensions that later arose between the supporters of Saul and of David. The first account also suggests the ambivalence some Hebrew scribes and prophets felt about having a human king at all.

1 SAMUEL 8:4–22, 10:20–25

All the elders of Israel gathered together and [said to Samuel]: "You are old and your sons do not follow in your ways; appoint for us, then, a king to govern us, like other nations." But the thing displeased Samuel [who] prayed to the Lord, and the Lord said to Samuel, "Listen to the voice of the people in all that they say to you; for they have not rejected you, but they have rejected me from being king over them. Just as they have done to me, from the day I brought them up out of Egypt to this day, forsaking me and serving other gods, so they are also doing to you. Now then, listen to their voice; only—you shall solemnly warn them, and show them the ways of the king who shall reign over them." So Samuel reported all the words of the Lord to the people who were asking for a king. "These will be the ways of the king who will reign over you: he will take sons and appoint them to his chariots . . . he will take your daughters to be perfumers and cooks and bakers . . . he will take one-tenth of your grain and your vineyards and give it to his officers and courtiers . . . and one-tenth of your flocks, and you shall be his slaves. But the people refused to listen, and Samuel said to the people, "Each of you return to his home."

Then Samuel brought all the tribes of Israel near, and the tribe of Benjamin was chosen by lot. He brought the tribe of Benjamin near by its families . . . and Saul the son of Kisk was chosen by lot. But when they sought him, he could not be found. So they inquired again of the Lord . . . and the Lord said, "See, he has hidden himself among the baggage." Then they ran and brought him from there. When he took his stand among the people, he was head and shoulders taller than any of them. Samuel said, "Do you see the one whom the Lord has chosen? There is no one like him among the people." And the people all shouted, "Long live the king!" Samuel told the people the rights and duties of the kingship; and he wrote them in a book and laid it up before the Lord.

1 SAMUEL 9:1—10:1

There was a man of Benjamin whose name was Kish . . . [who] had a son whose name was Saul, a handsome young man . . . he stood head and shoulders above everyone else. Now the donkeys of Kish had strayed. So Kish said to his son Saul, "Take one of the boys with you; go and look for the donkeys." . . . As they were entering [a] town, they saw Samuel coming out toward them on his way up to the shrine. Now the day before Saul came, the Lord revealed to Samuel, "Tomorrow about this time I will send you a man from the land of Benjamin, and you shall anoint him to be ruler over my people Israel. He shall save my people from the hand of the Philistines; for I have seen the suffering of my people, because their outcry has come to me." . . . Saul approached Samuel inside the gate and said, "Tell me please, where is the house of the seer?" Samuel answered Saul, "I am the seer, go up before me to the shrine. . . . As for your donkeys that were lost three days ago, give no further thought to them, for they have been found. And on whom is all Israel's desire fixed, if not on you and your ancestral house?" Saul answered, "I am only a Benjaminite, from the least of the

tribes of Israel, and my family is the humblest of all the families of the tribe of Benjamin. Why then have you spoken of me this way?" . . . As they were going down to the outskirts of town, Samuel said to Saul, "Tell the boy to go on before us . . . that I may make known to you the word of God." Samuel took a vial of oil and poured it on [Saul's] head and kissed him; he said: "The Lord has anointed you ruler over his people Israel. You shall reign over the people of the Lord and you will save them from the hand of their enemies all around."

The New Oxford Annotated Bible. (Oxford: Oxford University Press, 1994), slightly adapted.

THE LEGEND OF KING DAVID

David was clearly a historical figure, and his successes are beyond doubt. But the legend of King David sits oddly nonetheless with the rest of the Hebrew Bible. David's exploits have the ring of another tradition, a heroizing element more in keeping with Greek epics such as the *Iliad* and *Odyssey*. David is presented as an adventurer, a singer of songs and a doer of deeds, who leaves a parade of lovers and a trail of decapitated victims in his wake. His individual military exploits are those of a Greek hero; while his relationship with Jonathan, the son of Saul, resembles the intimate friendship between Achilles and Patroclus in the *Iliad*. David is more Ajax than Ezra, more Agamemnon than Moses; and at its end, his life takes a turn typical of Greek tragedy, when his power and pride lead him to flout the laws of God against adultery and murder, and inevitable retribution falls on him and his house.

What, precisely, we ought to make of such parallels is unclear. Clearly, however, David's age was characterized by extensive cross-cultural influences. We know, for example, that the Philistines dominated the Hebrews during the early part of King David's life both militarily and culturally. The Philistines, with their epic traditions imported from the Aegean basin, may have had a profound impact on the way David was remembered among the Hebrews, as a figure more in keeping with early Greek than with Hebrew ideals. Nor should we discount the possibility that David himself modeled his own conduct in part on Aegean ideals of heroism he learned from his Philistine overlords. How much of what the Bible tells us about

David is historical, and how much is literary and legendary, we have no way to determine. The earliest accounts of David's reign were not written down until at least the reign of his son Solomon; in their present form, these accounts may be as late as the fifth century B.C.E., five hundred years after David's death.

However much his life may be legendary, David succeeded in fashioning a patchwork of seminomadic tribes into a nation with a distinct religious identity. In creating a unified, centralized, vigorous nation, David transformed the Hebrews into the most fearsome power in the Levant. By instituting taxes, conscription, and custom duties on trade, David took full advantage of the region's limited natural resources. Furthermore, the Davidic episode founded the idea of Israel as a unified nation, a manifest fulfillment of the relationship the Hebrews believed they enjoyed with their god, Yahweh. This notion was to prove a powerful resource for the survival of Hebrew culture and identity when political and military events later turned against this people.

THE REIGN OF KING SOLOMON

Continuing his father's policies but on a much grander scale, King Solomon built a great temple complex at Jerusalem, wherein he housed the sacred Ark of the Covenant. Solomon's support of the Yahweh cult played particularly well with the writers of Hebrew scripture. His exaltation of Yahweh and the establishment of an official cult and a temple produced, in their eyes, a golden age for the Hebrews.

Despite his proverbial wisdom, however, Solomon

was a ruthless and often brutal ruler whose promotion of the Yahweh cult coincided with a program of despotic rule and royal self-aggrandizement. Solomon kept an enormous harem of some three hundred wives and seven hundred concubines, many of them drawn from subject or allied peoples. His palace complex—of which the temple was a part—allowed him to rule in the grand style of ancient Near Eastern potentates, and he instituted a variety of oppressive taxation and administrative schemes to finance his expensive tastes and programs. The king also profited from his kingdom's widening commercial contacts. With the help of Hiram, the Phoenician king of Tyre, Solomon constructed a commercial fleet based at the head of the Gulf of Aqaba. These ships plied the waters of the Red Sea and beyond, trading among other commodities the gold and copper mined by Solomon's slaves in the southern Negev. By the middle of the tenth century, widespread domestication of the camel had made long-distance caravans a regular feature of the Near Eastern landscape. Solomon imposed customs duties on the lucrative trade passing through his country, and wealth poured into Israel as never before.

> Their centuries-long fight for existence ultimately had a profound effect on the Assyrian world view.

But it was not enough. Solomon maintained a large standing army made up of conscripts from his own people, equipped with chariot and cavalry squadrons, and powered by horses purchased abroad. To undertake his ambitious building program, Solomon required many of his people, particularly from the agricultural north, to serve as forced labor four months out of every year. This level of oppression was too much for many Israelites. The north seethed with rebellion against the royal capital, and after Solomon's death, his son and successor was faced with revolt. Before long the united monarchy had split in two, the House of David ruling a southern kingdom still centered on Jerusalem (Judah), the ten northern tribes banding together into the kingdom of Israel with its capital at Shechem.

THE NORTHERN AND SOUTHERN KINGDOMS

The split not only weakened the Hebrews politically, but also had serious consequences religiously. The first king of the northern state of Israel, Jeroboam I, sought to establish worship and ritual independent from the temple in Jerusalem. He revived two ancient sanctuaries at Dan and Bethel and appealed to the popular but theologically taboo symbolism of Canaanite worship. Jeroboam and his successors hoped to stop the pilgrimages and dedications by the citizens of Israel at the temple in Judah, which drained the resources of the more populous northern kingdom. Jeroboam and his successors thus incurred the wrath of the temple-centered and pro-Judean scriptural tradition, but archaeology as well as the biblical account itself demonstrate that the cult of Yahweh was far from a monopoly in either the north or south. Foreign ritual and worship, particularly of the Canaanite deities Ba'al and Ashtart, remained a prominent feature of Hebrew religious life for several more centuries.

Although the two Hebrew kingdoms maintained an independent existence for several centuries—the north until 722 B.C.E., the south until 586 B.C.E.—the changing situation of the Near East made their divided state ever more vulnerable. Within a few generations of Solomon's death, the Hebrews and other nations of the Near East would find themselves menaced by the revived Mesopotamia-based empire of the Assyrians.

THE ASSYRIAN EMPIRE

What were the bases for the structure of the Assyrian government?

We have already encountered the Assyrians, a Semitic-speaking group with a rich past, centered in northern Mesopotamia. In Chapter Two, we learned how the Assyrians took advantage of their unique position along the upper Tigris and middle Euphrates to establish a network of caravan and trade routes. The Assyrians were also a crucial conduit for the spread of Mesopotamian urban society and organization into the Anatolian plateau. Although they were eclipsed temporarily by the rise of the Old Babylonian Empire, the Assyrians possessed a remarkably resilient identity and culture, which survived the power struggle between the Hittites and Egyptians and the catastrophe of the Sea Peoples. Their centuries-long fight for existence ultimately had a profound effect on the Assyrian world view; in the ninth century, they would extend their

WHAT WERE THE BASES FOR THE STRUCTURE OF THE ASSYRIAN GOVERNMENT?

THE ASSYRIAN EMPIRE   93

CHRONOLOGY

EVOLUTION OF ASSYRIA IN THE IRON AGE

Assyria begins to reestablish its influence	1362–883 B.C.E.
Assurnasirpal II founds neo-Assyrian empire	883–859 B.C.E.
Birth of the Sargonid dynasty	722 B.C.E.
Destruction of the Assyrian state	612–605 B.C.E.

power and influence by means of a terrible, brutal, long-lasting, and systematic victimization of their neighbors. Its terrors notwithstanding, their aggression helped to shape the religious and political traditions of their neighbors, spreading Near Eastern culture to the Aegean basin, synthesizing a new type of imperial organization, and imparting important lessons about what did and did not make for successful governance of a far-flung, international empire.

THE MIDDLE ASSYRIAN PERIOD (1362–859 B.C.E.)

The decline of the kingdom of Mitanni in the fourteenth century gave the Assyrians the opportunity to reestablish themselves as a great kingdom. As Hittite pressure from the west eroded the strength of the Hurro-Mitanni realm, Assyria extended its own influence and commercial control along its frontier with the kingdom of Mitanni, ultimately causing the collapse of what had become a Hittite puppet state. The first to take the title "king of Assyria" was a governor of the city of Assur (sometimes spelled Ashur), and thus the governor on earth of the city's patron deity of the same name. This man, Assur-uballit I (r. 1362–1327 B.C.E.), established the Assyrian kingship and sought to extend his power over northern Mesopotamia. He also fought against the Kassite kings of Babylonia. Assur-uballit and his successors possessed a very self-conscious sense of their history and identity. They regarded Babylonia as ancestral to their own culture and considered the Kassites interlopers. Assur-uballit's immediate successors evoked the distant, northern Mesopotamian past by arrogating to themselves the names of such Amorite kings as Shamshi-Adad. But despite their claim to be the heirs of Mesopotamian

culture, Assur-uballit and his immediate successors practiced great restraint in their policies, doing little to upset the delicate balance of the region.

With the accession of Tukulti-Ninurta I in 1244 B.C.E., the restraint was dropped. Tukulti-Ninurta was a conqueror of the first order, remembered in the Book of Genesis as Nimrud and in Greek tradition as Ninos. Tukulti-Ninurta sacked Babylon, carrying its Kassite king and the statues of the city's patron deity, Marduk, into captivity and claiming the prestigious kingship of Babylon for himself. To maintain his tenuous grip over Babylonia, however, Tukulti-Ninurta was forced to engage in constant campaigning; but endless warfare and his sacrilegious treatment of the Babylonian god alienated his own subjects, who murdered him in about 1208 B.C.E.

A century of Assyrian decline followed as its neighbors sought both vengeance and control over the vital trade routes that crisscrossed Assyrian territory. For nearly a century, the Assyrians once again fought for their survival. More than once, the Assyrians were almost destroyed; but the constant cycle of desperate fighting forged them into a highly militaristic people. A brief resurgence occurred during the reign of Tiglath-Pileser I (1115–1077 B.C.E.), who took the battle-hardened armies of Assyria on westward campaigns until his power reached the shores of the Mediterranean. But the Assyrians soon found themselves overextended and vulnerable to encroachments by other nations following Tiglath-Pileser's death.

The survivalist character of the Assyrian experience continued until the close of the Middle Assyrian period, when a brutal but brilliant ruler, Assurnasirpal II (883–859 B.C.E.), revived Assyrian strength and founded the neo-Assyrian empire. Under his ruthless leadership, the Assyrians conducted aggressive military campaigns on an annual basis. The targets of Assyrian might had to pay tribute or face the full onslaught of the Assyrian military machine, which under Assurnasirpal acquired a deserved reputation for savagery and viciousness. The great Near Eastern scholar A. H. Olmstead referred to Assurnasirpal's policy as one of "calculated frightfulness," a refined name for a strategy of military terror and the extraction of protection money through plunder.

THE NEO-ASSYRIAN EMPIRE

The conquests of Assurnasirpal and his son, Shalmeneser III, inspired stiff resistance to Assyrian expansion. The northern kingdom of Israel, along with a

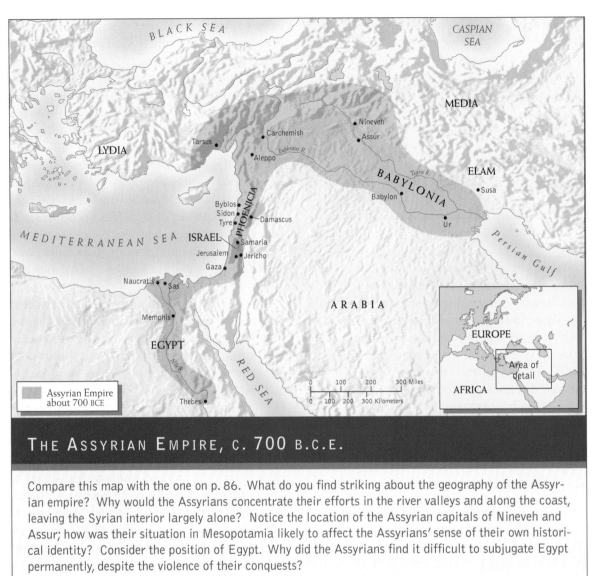

THE ASSYRIAN EMPIRE, C. 700 B.C.E.

Compare this map with the one on p. 86. What do you find striking about the geography of the Assyrian empire? Why would the Assyrians concentrate their efforts in the river valleys and along the coast, leaving the Syrian interior largely alone? Notice the location of the Assyrian capitals of Nineveh and Assur; how was their situation in Mesopotamia likely to affect the Assyrians' sense of their own historical identity? Consider the position of Egypt. Why did the Assyrians find it difficult to subjugate Egypt permanently, despite the violence of their conquests?

variety of other states in the region of Syria-Palestine, formed an alliance to stop Shalmeneser III (853–827 B.C.E.). Shalmeneser had directed his father's terrifying military might against the west, dealing hammer blow after hammer blow to the petty states there. Ultimately the hostile coalition fought him to a standstill in the 850s; he had to settle for smaller victories against the Armenians to his northwest and the Medes to his northeast, until the "Great Revolt" of Assyrian elites ended his reign and nullified his western gains. In the aftermath of Assyrian aggression, new kingdoms such as Urartu to the north and the invigorated Medes to the northeast managed to hold their own and even extend suzerainty beyond their frontiers. The Aramaeans of Syria took advantage of Assyrian weakness to become the new bullies of the Levant, and Assyria found itself stalemated by the newfound strength of its opponents.

The respite proved brief for the Near East. A usurper who took the name Tiglath-Pileser III seized the Assyrian throne in 744 B.C.E. and immediately prepared a great western campaign. In his first year he demanded tribute from various western kingdoms that had not paid up for generations; many predictably refused, to their cost. The course of Tiglath-Pileser III's punitive western campaign was breathtaking. He destroyed the powerful Anatolian kingdom of Urartu, brought recalcirant Assyrian governors to heel, and

> The course of Tiglath-Pileser III's punitive western campaign was breathtaking.

WHAT WERE THE BASES FOR THE STRUCTURE OF THE ASSYRIAN GOVERNMENT?

THE ASSYRIAN EMPIRE   95

annexed the great Syrian principality of Carchemish—an important commercial center—along with several Phoenician cities. Menahem, the usurper king of Israel, paid tribute and hoped to enlist Assyrian support for his dynasty. When that support failed and an anti-Assyrian party came to power, Tiglath-Pileser pitilessly crushed the kingdom, destroying fortifications, detaching key regions from Israel, and reducing it to the status of a vassal state.

When Tiglath-Pileser III died in 727 B.C.E., the various states of western Asia apparently anticipated that the familiar pattern of Assyrian dynastic instability would repeat itself. Many of the newer acquisitions rebelled, only to find that Tiglath-Pileser's son, Shalmeneser V, proved a worthy successor, energetically crushing the rebellions. Though he died in battle, he was quickly and seamlessly replaced by one of his military commanders, Sargon II (722–705 B.C.E.). Typical of Assyrian historical consciousness, Sargon was thinking of Sargon of Akkad as the "first" Sargon; he was laying claim to be the successor to a great Near Eastern empire nearly fifteen hun-

dred years in the past. The dynasty founded by Sargon II is called the Sargonid, and its century of rule proved the most magnificent and impressive in all of Assyrian history.

The Sargonids extended the frontiers of the Assyrian empire from the foothills of western Iran to the shores of the Mediterranean. Briefly, they even subjugated parts of Egypt. Sargon himself put an end to the kingdom of Israel on taking the throne, and scared the southern kingdom of Judah into remaining a loyal and quiet vassal. The ancient Elamite kingdom fell during the Sargonid period, and by the seventh century B.C.E. Assyria was the unrivaled power of the ancient Near East.

GOVERNMENT AND ADMINISTRATION

The neo-Assyrian empire was an armed state, based on the ability of its army to spread terror and oppress both enemies and subjects alike. At the head of the Assyrian government was the king, the earthly representative of the god Assur. As well as being its military leader, the king was also the empire's chief religious figure; when the army was not in the field the king's time was taken up with elaborate sacrifices and rituals to appease the "great god" Assur. Divination and the consultation of oracles were central features of Assyrian religion. The Assyrian king, as chief priest, had to be able to discern the will of Assur through the portents of nature.

The survivalist character of the Middle Assyrian period had encouraged the Assyrians to develop a very strong hereditary principle within their kingship. The crown prince underwent a thorough education and training for his future duties as king, and as he grew older assumed increasingly important functions of government at his father's side. Potential rivals within the royal family had to acknowledge and swear loyalty to the crown prince while the king lived. Although the position of women generally in Assyria did not differ much from that in other Mesopotamian societies, the prestige

Assyrian Winged Human-Headed Bull. This relief was found in the palace of King Sargon II (722–705 B.C.E.). It measures sixteen feet wide by sixteen feet high and weighs approximately forty tons.

and power of the queen were considerable. She enjoyed special deference as the wife of the king and mother of the crown prince, and if the king died while the crown prince was still young, the queen ruled as regent for her son until he came of age.

Around the central royal government was an extensive bureaucracy of governors, high priests and military commanders, professions by no means mutually exclusive in the Assyrian context. These administrators also formed the highest class in Assyrian society, exercising local authority on behalf of the king. As a people who ruled principally through military prowess, the Assyrians appreciated the importance of transportation and lines of communication. They constructed an extensive network of roads that would serve as the basis for travel and communication across the Near East for centuries. The Assyrians also deployed a system of messengers and spies to report to the royal court on the activities of subjects and provincial governors.

Provincial governors collected tribute, recruited for the army, maintained Assyrian control, and administered the king's law. Not surprisingly, the law of the Assyrians bore close resemblance to the code of Hammurabi, though many of its penalties were more severe. The Assyrians reserved the harshest punishments for practices deemed as detrimental to reproduction, and the penalties for homosexuality and abortion were barbaric and grisly. Assyrian law also demonstrates the subordinate position of women to men: only the husband had the power of divorce within his discretion, and for certain offenses he could inflict on his wife a variety of penalties, from corporal punishment through mutilation or even death.

THE ASSYRIAN MILITARY-RELIGIOUS ETHOS

Assyrian religious, political, and military ideas took shape in the centuries during which Assyria fought defensive wars to secure its survival. When the Assyrians gained the upper hand, however, this ethos became the foundation for their empire's relentless conquests.

The two fundamental characteristics of this Assyrian military-religious ethos were holy war and the exaction of tribute through terror. The Assyrians were convinced that their god Assur demanded that his worship be extended through military conquest. Even more than to the king, therefore, the Assyrian army belonged to Assur; and all who did not accept Assur's supremacy were, by that fact alone, enemies of Assur's people, the Assyrians. Ritual humiliation of a defeated

city's gods was therefore a regular feature of Assyrian conquests. Frequently the conquered gods would be carried off to the Assyrian capital, where they would live as hostages at the "court" of Assur. Meanwhile, an image of Assur himself (usually represented as a sun disk with the bust of an archer) would be installed in the defeated city, which the conquered people would now be required to worship. Worship of Assur did not necessarily mean that conquered peoples abandoned their previous gods altogether. But in Assyrian eyes, there was no question that Assur should be the supreme deity for all the peoples of their empire. As time went on, other gods gradually lost their defining characteristics, looking more and more like smaller versions of Assur, who became increasingly remote and aloof, the god of a state religion whom everyone in the Assyrian empire was expected to serve.

Tribute for the Assyrians initially meant the taking of

Assyrian Atrocities. These Judean captives are being impaled on stakes after their city has fallen to the Assyrian king Sennacherib (704–681 B.C.E.). This carving comes from the walls of Sennacherib's palace at Nineveh.

WHAT WERE THE BASES FOR THE STRUCTURE OF THE ASSYRIAN GOVERNMENT?

THE ASSYRIAN EMPIRE   97

Assyrian Relief Sculptures. These panels, representative of Assyrian "frightfulness," depict the emperor Assurbanipal on the hunt.

plunder. Rather than defeat their foes once and impose formal tribute thereafter, the Assyrians raided even their vanquished foes each year, extracting tribute by force. This strategy succeeded in terrifying Assyria's subjects and keeping the Assyrian military machine primed for battle. But it also entailed difficulties. Perpetual reconquests did little to inspire loyalty among subject peoples, who eventually reached a point of desperation at which they had little to lose through rebellion. Moreover, these annual Assyrian invasions not only sharpened the Assyrian army but also the forces of subjects, and by the end of the ninth century other nations of the region had become accomplished at the Assyrians' own game. It was not until Tiglath-Pileser III that the Assyrians abandoned the policy of collecting tribute by force each year, settling instead for more orthodox forms of payment.

Assyrian warfare was also notoriously savage. Ancient warfare was never pretty: mutilations of prisoners, decapitations, rape, and the mass deportations and/or enslavement of civilian populations were commonplace. The Assyrians, however, relished and celebrated such barbarities as did no other ancient empire. Their artwork and inscriptions revel in the butchering and torture of their enemies. Smiling Assyrian archers are shown shooting fleeing enemies in the back, while

> Rather than defeat their foes once and impose formal tribute thereafter, the Assyrians raided even their vanquished foes each year, extracting tribute by force.

remorseless soldiers fling the citizens of a captured Judean town from the walls, impaling them on stakes below. The most extreme barbarities were reserved for rebellious subjects whose rebellion was an offence not only against Assyria, but also against Assur.

The army itself had developed by the ninth century into a devastating force. Like many ancient societies, the Assyrians had originally employed a seasonal peasant army of part-time soldiers. But from the reign of Assurnasirpal II onward, the Assyrians recruited a massive standing army of over one hundred thousand soldiers. Furthermore, the Assyrians mastered large-scale iron-smelting techniques, and by the ninth century equipped their fighting men with high-quality steel weapons that overwhelmed opponents still reliant on bronze.

Assyrian strategy and tactics were the most highly sophisticated the world had yet seen, in great part due to the organization of the army. The core of the Assyrian army was heavily armed and armored shock troops, equipped with a variety of thrusting weapons and bearing tall shields for protection. These Assyrian storm troopers were the main force for crushing enemy infantry in the field and for routing the inhabitants of an enemy city once inside. To harass enemy infantry and break up their formations, the Assyrians deployed light skirmishers with slings and javelins. The Assyrians also combined archery and chariotry as never before. With a swift and efficient two-wheeled design, Assyrian chariots sped about the battlefield, carrying one to two archers and another couple of shield bearers. Thus chariots became highly mobile firing platforms, and from them the expert Assyrian archers could wreak havoc. Finally, the Assyrians during the course of their ascendancy managed to develop a true cavalry force, with individual warriors mounted on armored steeds and wielding bows and arrows or heavy lances.

In the open field the combined arms tactics of Assyrian warfare were too much for their opponents. The obvious answer was not to face the Assyrians in a stand-up fight, because the art of siege warfare was not highly evolved by the early first millennium. The warlike Assyrians trained a corps of combat engineers, however, highly skilled in sapping walls, building catapults, siege engines, battering rams, and battle towers. Thus the walls of most cities provided little refuge from Assyrian military onslaught. After a city fell, an even more extraordinary series of atrocities usually followed: in addition to the usual dismemberments and mutilations, captives might also be burned or skinned alive.

THE END OF ASSYRIA AND ITS LEGACY

The successors of Sargon II continued Assyrian military policies while at the same time devoting great energies to what we might broadly consider "culture." Sargon's immediate successor Sennacherib (704–681 B.C.E.) rebuilt the ancient Assyrian city of Nineveh, fortifying it with a double wall nine miles around. He constructed an enormous palace raised on a giant platform decorated with marble, ivory, and exotic woods. He also ordered the construction of a massive irrigation system, including an aqueduct that carried fresh water to the city from thirty miles away.

Sennacherib's son Esarhaddon (681–669 B.C.E.) sought to ease the tensions between Assyria and the city of Babylon, which had been brutally punished by his father. Esarhaddon also attempted to mollify the hard feelings caused by Assyria's religious imperialism, allowing for the conditional return of cult objects to conquered peoples. Esarhaddon rebuilt and glorified Babylon, and was a patron of the sciences and arts. None of this, however, changed the fact that he was at heart an Assyrian king. In 671 B.C.E. he invaded Egypt, chasing the Nubian pharaoh Taharqa from the throne. The expedition was largely punitive, Esarhaddon having tired of Taharqa's constant meddling with Assyria's vassal states. But Egypt was too far away for the Assyrians to maintain firm control, and Taharqa returned to power on Esarhaddon's departure. The conquest of Egypt was left to the next Assyrian king, Esarhaddon's son Assurbanipal.

Assurbanipal (669–627 B.C.E.) was perhaps the greatest of all the Assyrian kings. He maintained a strong military presence throughout the empire, and for a time ruled the entire Delta region of Egypt. After the Assyrian adventure in Egypt ultimately ended in failure, he turned his attention to a series of internal reforms, seeking ways to govern his empire other than through the traditional weapons of military terror and religious imperialism. Assur remained central—anything else would have been sacrilege. But following in his father's footsteps, Assurbanipal was something of an "enlightened" Assyrian king, hoping to knit the empire into something more permanent and stable than an armed camp in a perpetual state of warfare with its subjects and neighbors.

The study of the ancient Near East owes a tremendous debt to Assurbanipal. Like all Assyrian kings, he had a conscious sense of the rich traditions of Mesopotamian culture and history, and laid claim to these to justify Assyrian rule over the whole of the region. Assurbanipal went even further, however; at the great Assyrian capital of Nineveh, Assurbanipal ordered the construction of a magnificent library, where copies of all the great works of literature of the Mesopotamian past would be copied into Assyrian cuneiform and preserved. It also served as an important archive for the correspondence and official acts of the king. When the Englishman Austen Henry Layard and his assistant Hormuzd Rassam discovered Nineveh in the nineteenth century, they also unearthed this unexpected treasure trove of historical documentation. All modern editions of the Epic of Gilgamesh depend on the Assyrian versions from Nineveh.

> Assurbanipal was something of an "enlightened" Assyrian king, hoping to knit the empire into something more permanent and stable than an armed camp in a perpetual state of warfare with its subjects and neighbors.

When Assurbanipal died in 627 B.C.E., the Assyrian empire appeared to be at its zenith. Its borders were secure, the realm was largely at peace with its neighbors, and the most recent kings had adorned Assyrian

THE SENJIRLI STELE OF KING ESARHADDON

Set up in northern Syria by the Assyrian king Esarhaddon, this inscribed stone monument is one of the most important records of his reign. Accompanying the text (which proclaims his victories over Egypt and the Phoenician coast of Syria) was a depiction of Esarhaddon holding a cup in his right hand and a mace in his left. His left hand also grasped reins fastened to shackles holding a captured prince of Egypt and a Syrian ruler, both of whom begged for mercy. The inscription demonstrates Assyrian kingship's bombastic propaganda, its conscious connection to the Sumero-Akkadian past, and the cruelty which characterized Assyrian conquests. (Assur, Anu, Ba'al, Ea, and Ishtar were all gods or goddesses.)

To Assur, father of the gods, lover of my priesthood, Anu mighty and pre-eminent, who called me by name, Ba'al, the exalted lord, establisher of my dynasty, Ea, the wise, all-knowing . . . Ishtar, lady of battle and combat, who goes at my side . . . all of them who determine my destiny, who grant to the king, their favorite, power and might. . . . the king, the offering of whose sacrifices the great gods love . . . their unsparing weapons they have presented him as a royal gift . . . [he] who has brought all the lands in submission at his feet, who has imposed tribute and tax upon them; conqueror of his foes, destroyer of his enemies, the king, who as to his walk is a storm, and as to his deeds, a raging wolf; . . . the onset of his battle is powerful, he is a consuming flame, a fire that does not sink: son of Sennacherib, king of the universe, king of Assyria, grandson of Sargon, king of the universe, king of Assyria, viceroy of Babylon, king of Sumer and Akkad. . . . I am powerful,

I am all powerful, I am a hero, I am gigantic, I am colossal, I am honored, I am magnified, I am without an equal among all kings, the chosen one of Assur . . . the great lord [who] in order to show to the peoples the immensity of my mighty deeds, made powerful my kingship over the four regions of the world and made my name great. . . . Of Tirhakah, king of Egypt and Kush, the accursed . . . without cessation I slew multitudes of his men, and him I smote five times with the point of my javelin, with wounds, no recovery. Memphis, his royal city, in half a day . . . I besieged, I captured, I destroyed, I devastated, I burned with fire . . . . The root of Kush I tore up out of Egypt and not one therein escaped to submit to me.

Daniel David Luckenbill, ed. *Ancient Records of Assyria and Babylonia*, Vol. 2. (Chicago: University of Chicago Press, 1926–1927), pp. 224–227.

---

capitals with culture and magnificent artwork that captured all the heritage of the ancient Near East. The end of Assyria is therefore all the more dramatic for its suddenness. Within fifteen years of the mighty Assurbanipal's reign, Nineveh lay in ruins; a few years later, the Assyrian state was no more, obliterated from the face

of the earth with the same speed and violence by which it had established itself.

Despite the best efforts of Esarhaddon and Assurbanipal at reform, centuries of savagery had left deep scars on the psyche of the region, and hatred of the Assyrians was widespread by the end of the seventh

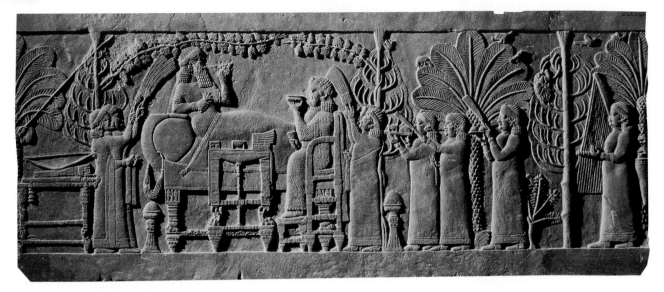

Assurbanipal Feasting with His Wife in a Garden. The head of his defeated enemy, the king of Elam, can be seen hanging from the pine tree on the left.

century. After the death of Assurbanipal, a coalition formed between the Indo-European-speaking Medes of northwestern Iran and the Chaldeans, a Semitic-speaking people who once controlled the southern half of Babylonia. In 626 B.C.E., the Assyrian governor of

Reconstruction of the Ishtar Gate. Visitors to the Near Eastern Museum in Berlin can see this impressive reconstruction of the gate built in Babylon by King Nebuchadnezzar around 575 B.C.E. rising to a height of fifty feet. About half of the reconstruction is original.

southern Babylonia, a Chaldean named Nabopolasser, revolted and enlisted the support of the powerful Median king Cyaxares. In one of history's many ironies, Cyaxares had grown mighty largely because the Assyrians had dismantled his principal rival for power, the ancient state of Elam.

The allies launched an attack on Nineveh in 612 B.C.E., taking the city and setting ablaze its great temples and palaces. By 605 B.C.E., the Chaldeans (also described as neo-Babylonians) had destroyed the last remnants of Assyrian culture and power on the upper Euphrates. The Medes retired to the Iranian Plateau and extended their suzerainty there; the Chaldeans inherited much of Assyria's power in Mesopotamia and the Levant. The Chaldeans proved little better than the hated Assyrians, however, earning the enmity of their subjects by exercising the same type of cruelty that had made the Assyrians infamous. They even continued the very practice that they themselves had found so detestable in the

Assyrians, the mass deportation of conquered foes. Whenever the Assyrians had wanted to hedge against future rebellion, they would remove thousands—sometimes tens of thousands—of the conquered inhabitants, sending them far away from their homelands and the places and symbols of their national cult. The Chaldeans were no different, the most famous example being when their ruthless king Nebuchadnezzar captured Jerusalem in 587/586 B.C.E., destroyed the Temple, and removed tens of thousands of Hebrews to Babylon, an exile known in Jewish history as the "Babylonian Captivity."

The Persians

Around what central ideas was Zoroastrianism formed?

Although they had succeeded to Assyrian power, a Chaldean empire based on plunder and fear would prove no more tenable than an Assyrian one. Furthermore, the Chaldeans possessed nothing like the great war machine of the Assyrian empire, nor did they exhibit the fervor of the Assyrian military-religious ethos. But in the power vacuum that existed after the fall of Assyria, the power of the Chaldeans went largely unchallenged. The other great powers of the Near East at the beginning of the sixth century were too distant or otherwise occupied to challenge Chaldean dominance. The Indo-European-speaking Lydians, one of the successor states to Hittite power, had carved out a wealthy kingdom in western Anatolia, but they tended to orient themselves west toward the Aegean and the Greeks. The Medes, meanwhile, sought to secure dominance over the various, closely related groups of the Iranian Plateau, effectively keeping themselves out of Mesopotamian and Levantine politics. One of the collection of tribes subject to the Medes, the Persians established themselves in the former area of the Elamites and would prove to be the deciding factor in breaking this stalemate and reuniting the ancient Near East.

THE ORIGINS OF THE PERSIAN EMPIRE

Almost nothing is known of the Persians before the middle of the sixth century B.C.E., except that they lived on the eastern shore of the Persian Gulf, spoke an Indo-European language, and were subject to the Medes. Out of this obscurity the Persians emerged suddenly into the spotlight of history under an extraordinary prince named Cyrus, who succeeded to the rule of a southern Persian tribe in 559 B.C.E. Shortly thereafter Cyrus made himself ruler of all the Persians, and around 549 B.C.E. he threw off the lordship of the Medes, taking over their domination of lands that stretched from the Persian Gulf to the Halys River in Asia Minor.

By occupying part of Asia Minor, Cyrus became a neighbor of the kingdom of Lydia, which then comprised the western half of Asia Minor up to the Halys. The Lydians by this time had attained great prosperity as a result of gold prospecting and acting as intermediaries for overland commerce between Mesopotamia and the Aegean Sea. They dominated the wealthy Greek cities of the western Anatolian coast and sat atop an abundance of natural resources themselves. In connection with their commercial and industrial enterprises the Lydians invented the use of metallic coinage as a medium of exchange for goods and services. When Cyrus reached their border, the reigning king of the Lydians was Croesus, a great admirer of the culture of the Greeks he ruled, and so rich that the expression "rich as Croesus" remains embedded in our language. Distrusting his new neighbor, Croesus decided in 546 B.C.E. to wage a preventive war in order to preserve his kingdom from conquest. According to Herodotus, Croesus consulted the oracle at Delphi in Greece whether he should attack immediately, and gained the reply that if he crossed the Halys he would destroy a great nation. He did, but the nation he de-

An Early Lydian Coin. Probably struck during the reign of Croesus.

THE RECEPTION OF PERSIAN RULE

After the centuries of Assyrian and Chaldean oppression, many peoples of the Near East viewed the Persians as liberators. So grateful were the Hebrews to Cyrus for allowing the Hebrews in exile to return from Babylon and rebuild the temple, that to many he seemed the messiah promised by the prophets, the one who would spread the cult of Yahweh among all nations. This selection from the Hebrew prophet Isaiah provides some sense of the initial glee with which the peoples of the Near East received Persian rule in the middle of the sixth century B.C.E.

Thus says the Lord to his anointed, to Cyrus, whose right hand I have grasped to subdue nations before him and strip kings of their robes, to open doors before him—and the gates shall not be closed: I will go before you and level the mountains. . . . I will give you the treasures of darkness and riches hidden in secret places, so that you may know that it is I, the Lord, the God of Israel, who calls you by your name. For the sake of my servant Jacob, and Israel my chosen, I call you by your name, I surname you, though you do not know me. . . . I have aroused Cyrus in righteousness, and I will make all his paths straight; he shall build my city and set my exiles free, not for price or reward says the Lord of hosts. Thus says the Lord: The wealth of Egypt and the merchandise of Kush, and Sabeans, tall of stature, shall come over to you and be yours, they shall follow you, they shall come over in chains and bow down to you. They will make supplication to you, saying "God is with you alone, and there is no other; there is no god besides him." . . . Israel is saved by the Lord with everlasting salvation.

Isaiah 45:1–4, 13–17, *The New Oxford Annotated Bible.* (Oxford: Oxford University Press, 1994).

stroyed was his own, as Cyrus defeated his forces and annexed his prosperous realm as a province of the Persian state.

Cyrus invaded Mesopotamia in 539 B.C.E., striking so quickly that he took Babylon without a fight. Once he was in Babylon the entire Chaldean Empire was his. Cyrus allowed the Hebrews captive in Babylon since the time of Nebuchadnezzar to return to Palestine and set up a semi-independent vassal state. Cyrus allowed other conquered peoples considerable self-determination as well, especially in terms of cult practices, making Persian rule a welcome change from that of the Assyrians and Chaldeans. Cyrus fell in bat-tle in 529 from wounds he suffered while campaigning against barbarian tribes near the Aral Sea, to the north of his realms. He left behind the largest empire the world had yet seen. After his death, the trend of Persian expansion continued as his son and successor Cambyses conquered Egypt in 525 B.C.E.

THE CONSOLIDATION OF THE PERSIAN NEAR EAST

Cambyses was a brilliant general, a worthy successor to his father's military greatness. Difficulties abounded

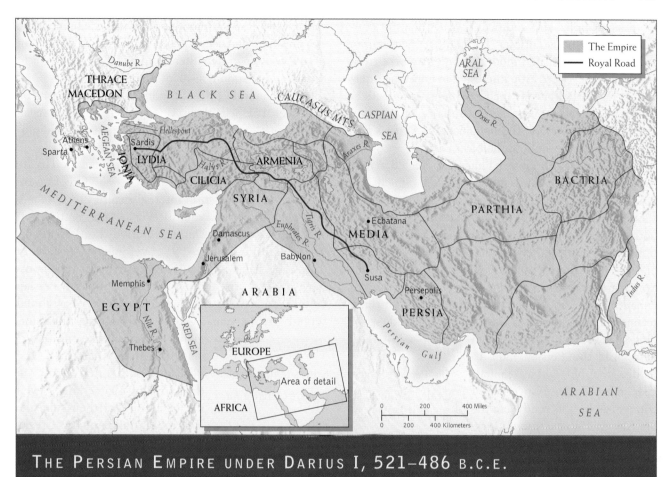

THE PERSIAN EMPIRE UNDER DARIUS I, 521–486 B.C.E.

What accounts for the enormous extent of the Persian empire in comparison to earlier imperial realms? Why is the "royal road" especially noted on this map? Consider the location of the Persian heartland and the four administrative centers of Persepolis, Susa, Ecbatana, and Sardis. What purpose did such multiple "capitals" serve? Examine the northwest frontiers of the empire. Why would the Persians have an interest in continuing to expand in this direction?

during his reign, however, as both contemporaries and centuries of historians have argued over whether the young king was insane. In any event, he died young and without a son, throwing open the question of succession and leaving the Persian Empire a cumbersome and poorly organized collection of rapid conquests.

After a short period of civil war, the aristocratic inner circle that had served both Cyrus and his son settled on a collateral member of the royal family as the new king. Cambyses' successor, Darius I, ruled Persia from 521 to 486 B.C.E. and concentrated on consolidating his predecessors' military gains by improving the administration of the Persian state. Darius divided the empire into provinces called satrapies, each administered by a satrap. The satraps enjoyed extensive powers and considerable political latitude, but they owed fixed tributes and absolute loyalty to the central government, as did vassal states such as the technically autonomous Jewish kingdom.

Adhering to the tolerant policy of Cyrus, Darius allowed the various non-Persian peoples of the Persian Empire to retain most of their local institutions while enforcing a standardized currency and system of weights and measures. In Egypt, Darius's satrap restored ancient

> Darius divided the empire into provinces called satrapies, each administered by a satrap.

Egyptian temples and codified Egyptian laws in consultation with native priests. Throughout their empire the Persians established modest tribute payments; but otherwise, they were little interested in imposing onerous taxes, martial law, or their own religious practices on their subject peoples. After centuries of Assyrian and Chaldean tyranny, the light hand of Persian rule was welcomed throughout the Near East.

Darius was also a great builder. He erected a new royal residence and ceremonial capital, which the Greeks called Persepolis ("Persia City"). He ordered a canal dug from the Nile to the Red Sea to facilitate trade with the Egyptian interior, and installed irrigation systems on the Persian plateau and on the fringe of the Syrian desert to increase agricultural production. Darius also expanded the Assyrian road system to enhance trade and communications in his far-flung realms. The most famous was the "Royal Road" spanning sixteen hundred miles from Susa near the Persian Gulf to Sardis (the old Lydian capital) near the Aegean. Government couriers along this road were the first postal system, passing messages and goods in relay stages from one "post" to another. Each post was a day's horseback ride from the next: a fresh horse and rider would be ready at each post to carry what had been brought by the "postman" before him. The extensive spy network of the "great king" of Persia utilized this network to keep the crown informed of developments throughout the massive empire. The "intelligence service" founded by Darius was famed throughout Persian history as "the eyes and ears of the king."

An extraordinarily gifted administrator, Darius made an enormous mistake in military strategy when he attempted to extend Persian hegemony into Greece. After Cyrus' conquest of Lydia had made Persia the ruler of Greek-speaking cities on the western coast of Asia Minor, these cities disdained Persian toleration and yearned for the idealized freedom of other Greek city-states. Consequently, between 499 and 494 B.C.E. the Greeks on the Asian mainland waged a war for independence and briefly gained the support of troops from Athens, who joined the Asian Greeks in burning the important Persian regional administrative center at Sardis. After quelling the uprising in Asia, Darius sent a force across the Aegean to punish Athens and serve notice of his dominion to all European Greeks. At the battle of Marathon in 490, the Athenians dealt Darius the only major setback of his reign. In 480 his son and

successor, Xerxes, attempted to avenge the humiliation by crushing Greece with a tremendous army, but heroic resistance by Athens and Sparta forced him to retreat and abandon his plans a year later. At that point the Persians realized that the limits of their expansion had been reached; they concentrated on their Asian possessions and settled for using money and diplomacy to meddle in Greek affairs.

In fact, from 479 B.C.E. until Alexander the Great's invasion of Asia Minor in 334 B.C.E., the Greeks were usually too embroiled in internal rivalries to pose any challenge to Persia. From the Persian perspective that was fortunate, for during this period the Persian empire was often beset by governmental instability caused by palace intrigues and provincial rebellions. Nevertheless, the cosmopolitan nature of Persian culture and the general toleration they exhibited served the Persians well in maintaining their immense realm. Unlike the Assyrians or the Chaldeans, the Persians could often count on the loyalty—sometimes even the affection—of their subjects. The recalcitrance of the Greeks should not blind us to the fact that the Persians successfully maintained a culturally and linguistically diverse empire for over two centuries and would have done so longer were it not for Alexander the Great's invasion in the later fourth century. The Persians established an imperial model based on the accommodation of local institutions and practices, steady and consistent administration through a trained bureaucracy, and rapid communications between center and periphery. It was a model from which both the Macedonians and the Romans would learn much in later centuries.

> The Persians successfully maintained a culturally and linguistically diverse empire for over two centuries.

ZOROASTRIANISM

Even more enduring than Persia's political legacy was its religious one, embodied in Zoroastrianism. This important world religion, along with Buddhism and Judaism, was one of the three major universal and personal religions known to the world before Christianity and Islam. The religion's founder was Zoroaster (the Greek form of the Persian name Zarathustra). Zoroaster, a Persian who lived shortly before 600 B.C.E., was the first real theologian in history, devising a fully developed system of religious belief. He seems to have conceived it as his mission to purify the traditional customs of the Persian tribes—to eradicate polytheism, animal sacrifice, and magic—and to establish worship on a more coherent and ethical plane.

Zoroastrianism was a universal religion insofar as Zoroaster taught that there was one supreme god in the universe, whom he called Ahura-Mazda, the "wise lord." Ahura-Mazda embodied the principles of light, truth, and righteousness; there was nothing wrathful or evil about him, and his light shone everywhere, not just on one tribe. Because sin and sorrow were inexplicable by reference to Ahura-Mazda, Zoroaster posited the existence of a counter-deity, Ahriman, treacherous and malignant, presiding over the forces of darkness and evil. Apparently in Zoroaster's own view Ahura-Mazda was vastly stronger than Ahriman, whom Ahura-Mazda allowed to exist almost by absentmindedness. Later, the priests of Zoroastrianism, the magi, emphasized the dualistic aspect of the founder's thought by insisting that Ahura-Mazda and Ahriman were evenly matched, engaged in a desperate struggle for supremacy. According to them, only on the last great day would "light" decisively triumph over "darkness," when Ahura-Mazda would overpower Ahriman and cast him into the abyss.

Zoroastrianism was a personal religion, making private, spiritual demands as opposed to public, cultic, and ritual ones. As a result, Zoroastrianism was quite different from traditional Near Eastern beliefs, in which politics and religion were necessarily indistinguishable. The fervor of the Persian dynasty for Zoroaster's teachings nevertheless made Zoroastrianism important to the conduct of Persian government, and helps to explain the general eclecticism and tolerance of Persian rule. Ahura-Mazda patronized neither tribes nor states but only individuals who served his cause of truth and justice. Humans possessed free will and could choose to sin or not to sin. Zoroastrianism urged people not to sin but to be truthful, to love and help one another to the best of their powers, to aid the poor, and to practice generous hospitality. Those who did so would be rewarded in an afterlife, for the religion posited the resurrection of the dead on "judgment day" and their consignment to a realm either of bliss or flames. In the scriptures of the Zoroastrian faith, known as the Avesta (a work compiled by accretion over the course of many centuries), the rewards for righteousness are explicit.

This recital of Zoroastrianism's tenets reveals numerous similarities to Judaism and Christianity. Zoroastrianism's ethical content resembles the teachings of the Hebrew prophets, and its heaven and hell resemble aspects of the afterlife teaching of Christianity. Even the existence of authoritative scriptures is reminiscent of the weight accorded by Jews (and later by Christians) to the Bible. As with so many other cultural phenomena in the Ancient Near East, central aspects of different religious and intellectual traditions took shape in a Near Eastern world characterized by cross-cultural influence. Cyrus and Darius—both convinced Zoroastrians—cast a considerable shadow across the cultural atmosphere of their times. Furthermore, entirely aside from likely Zoroastrian influence on Judaism and later Christian beliefs, the Persian faith exerted some influence on western Asia's later Greek conquerors, encouraging them to think of religion in ever more universalistic and personal terms.

Universalism also characterized Persia's cultural contribution to the unfolding story of Western civilizations. Unlike the Assyrians, the Chaldeans, or even the Egyptians, all of whom tried to impose their own customs on conquered peoples (when they did not simply enslave them), the Persians adopted a tolerant "one-world" policy. They conceived themselves to be the guiding force over an assemblage of nations. Whereas Mesopotamian potentates characteristically called themselves "true king," Persian rulers took the title "king of kings," implying that they recognized the continued existence of various peoples with native rulers under the canopy of Persian overlordship. The greatest Persian monarchs, such as Cyrus and Darius, also sought to learn whatever they could from the peoples they conquered. Among much else, they adopted metallic coinage from the Lydians, and learned to chart the night skies from Babylonian astronomers.

Persian eclecticism can also be observed in architecture. The Persians copied the terraced building style that had been standard in Babylonia, and they also imitated the winged bulls, the brilliantly colored glazed bricks, and other decorative motifs of Mesopotamian architecture. Yet in place of the Mesopotamian arch and vault they adopted the column and the colonnade from Egypt. Interior arrangements and the use of palm and lotus designs at the base of columns also show Egyptian influence. The fluting of columns and the scrolls beneath the capitals were not Egyptian, however, but Greek, adopted from the Greek cities of Asia Minor. But despite such evidence of cultural borrowing, relations between Persia

Zoroastrianism's tenets reveal numerous similarities to Judaism and Christianity.

Persian Gold Drinking Cup. Persian fondness for lions probably derived from the art of the Assyrians.

and Greece were hostile. As we will see in the next chapter, the Greeks and Persians held profoundly different values; this clash led to generations of warfare between these two great cultures.

THE DEVELOPMENT OF HEBREW MONOTHEISM

What developments marked the Hebrew transition from polytheism to monotheism?

Of all the cultural developments that took place in the Iron Age Near East, none was of greater significance to the civilizations of the West than was monotheism—the belief that there is but a single god, the creator and ruler of all things. This development is traditionally, and rightly, associated with the Hebrews. But even the Hebrews were not always monotheists. Those who argued for the exclusive worship of Yahweh—a group whom we shall refer to as the Yahwists—were often a minority within Hebrew society, albeit a vocal and as-

sertive one. That the Hebrews came ultimately to recognize Yahweh as the only divine being in the universe, and to root their identity as a people in such an exclusive religious outlook, is a development that can be explained only against the backdrop of the tumultuous and confusing world in which Hebrew society itself arose.

FROM MONOLATRY TO MONOTHEISM

The emergence of Hebrew monotheism took place in a world conditioned by polytheism. For those who later advocated the exclusive worship of Yahweh, the early history of the Hebrews was full of embarrassments. At every turn, the Hebrews of the twelfth through tenth centuries B.C.E. can be found worshiping gods other than Yahweh, and especially those of their Canaanite neighbors. Even Yahweh himself, in commanding that his people should "have no other gods before me," seemed implicitly to acknowledge that there were indeed other gods whom his people worshiped. In the Book of Judges, Yahweh is represented as more or less an equal of the Moabite god Chemosh. An older, polytheistic strain is visible also in Hebrew nature spirits such as Azazel, and in the popularity of the Canaanite god El, whose name is an important element in many Hebrew word constructions (for example, Bethel). Even Solomon included symbols of Ba'al and altars to Ashtart in the temple complex he built for Yahweh at Jerusalem. Such toleration of non-Yahwist cult practices continued among later Hebrew kings also, despite the protests of religious purists advocating the exclusive worship of Yahweh.

Despite lingering polytheism, however, by the beginning of the first millennium Hebrew religion had clearly moved into a new stage of national *monolatry*—the exclusive worship of one god, without denying utterly the existence of others. Precisely how this came about is unclear. Although Moses is often credited with the beginnings of the ascendancy of the cult of Yahweh, he is a figure too legendary and too distant to be fully understood. There is better evidence to suggest that the promotion of the Yahweh cult took place under the auspices of the Levites, a tribe whose unique claims to priestly authority made them a religious elite within Hebrew society. Advocating both the ritual and the prophetic elements of Yahweh worship, the Levites sought to enhance their

WHAT DEVELOPMENTS MARKED THE HEBREW TRANSITION FROM POLYTHEISM TO MONOTHEISM?

THE DEVELOPMENT OF HEBREW MONOTHEISM   107

own power and prestige by exalting Yahweh above the other gods traditionally revered in Hebrew and Canaanite society.

The Levites also enjoyed a higher degree of literacy than most of their fellow Hebrews. As a tool for shaping the traditions and consciousness of a society, the power of the written word is formidable. This was especially so in the ancient world, where writing enjoyed a sort of magical aura, and the authority surrounding texts was literally awe-inspiring. In an age of constant threats to Hebrew religious and political sovereignty, the literacy of the Levites thus helped to preserve and promote Yahweh worship. So too, of course, did the House of David, which by promoting the Yahweh cult and centralizing it in Jerusalem, helped to link the political and the religious identity of the Hebrews to the worship of Yahweh as the supreme (if not yet the only) god of the universe.

Nevertheless, the worship of other gods persisted, and there was a swell of popularity for Canaanite fertility cults in the eighth and seventh centuries, perhaps in reaction to the austere morality demanded and imposed by the Yahwists. Religious figures as late as Jeremiah (c. 637–587 B.C.E.) continued to rail against "foreign" cults, and to warn of the disastrous consequences that would arise if Yahweh's people did not remain faithful to Yahweh alone. Despite his supremacy over all other gods, however, Yahweh remained a somewhat limited god in the eighth and seventh centuries B.C.E., even in the eyes of the Yahwists. He was conceived as possessing a physical body and was sometimes capricious or irascible. Nor was Yahweh omnipotent, for his power was largely limited to the territory occupied by the Hebrews.

Despite these polytheistic holdovers, some of the Hebrews' most important contributions to subsequent Western religious thought had emerged by the middle of the eighth century B.C.E. One was their unique *transcendent theology.* In the eyes of his priests and prophets, Yahweh was not part of nature but entirely outside of it. He could therefore be understood in purely intellectual or abstract terms, entirely apart from the operations of the natural world he had created. Complementing this principle of divine transcendence was the belief that Yahweh had appointed humans to be the rulers of nature by divine mandate. The famous line from Genesis, in which Yahweh or-

ders Adam and Eve to "be fruitful and multiply, and replenish the earth and subdue it, and have dominion over . . . every living thing," stands in striking contrast with Babylonian creation accounts, in which humans are created merely to serve the gods, "so that the gods might be at ease." Finally, although not fully developed, universalizing ethical considerations are also present in Hebrew religious thought during this period. According to the Babylonian flood story, a particularly petulant god decided to destroy humans on the grounds that their noise deprived him of sleep. In Genesis, by contrast, Yahweh sends a flood in response to human wickedness, but saves Noah and his family because "Noah was a just man."

The Hebrews honored Yahweh during the period of monolatry by subscribing to moral precepts, rituals, and taboos. The exact form of the Ten Commandments (as they became known from the seventh century B.C.E. onward, and as they appear in Exodus 20:3–17) may not have existed before the Babylonian captivity. But the Hebrews certainly observed some set of commandments, including ethical injunctions against murder, adultery, bearing false witness, and "coveting anything that is thy neighbor's." In addition they observed ritualistic demands, such as refraining from labor on the seventh day and not boiling a kid in its mother's milk. But the moral standards enjoined by Yahweh upon the Hebrew community were not necessarily binding when dealing with outsiders. Lending at interest, for example, was not acceptable between Hebrews, but was quite acceptable between a Hebrew and a non-Hebrew. Such distinctions applied also to more serious issues, such as the killing of civilians in battle. When the Hebrews conquered territories in Canaan, they took "all the spoil of the cities, and every man they smote with the sword . . . until they had destroyed them, neither left they any to breathe." Rather than having any doubts about such a brutal policy, the Yahwists believed it had been ordered by their Lord himself—indeed, that Yahweh had inspired the Canaanites to offer resistance so that there would be reason to slaughter them: "For it was of the Lord to harden their hearts, that they should come against Israel in battle, that He might destroy them utterly" (Joshua 11:20).

With the fragmentation of the united Hebrew kingdom after Solomon's death, however, important

> Some of the Hebrews' most important contributions to Western thought emerged by the middle of the eighth century B.C.E.

regional distinctions also arose within the Yahweh cult. The rulers of the northern kingdom discouraged their citizens from participating in cultic activities at Jerusalem, thereby earning the scorn of the Jerusalem-based Yahwists who shaped the biblical tradition. Disunity and the loss of Hebrew identity was accelerated by the appearance of the Assyrians, who under Sargon II absorbed the northern kingdom as a province and deported nearly twenty-eight thousand Hebrews to the interior of the Assyrian empire—the famous Ten Lost Tribes of Israel. The southern kingdom of Judah survived, but found it expedient to become an Assyrian vassal state. As we have seen, however, political collaboration with the Assyrians also meant acceptance of the Assyrian god Assur.

The Assyrian threat was the whetstone on which the Yahwist prophets sharpened their demands not for monolatry but for an exclusive monotheism. Prophets were political as much as religious figures, and most understood that military resistance to the Assyrians was futile. If the Hebrews were to survive as a people, then they had to exalt the one thing that separated them from everyone else in the region: the worship of Yahweh. The prophets' insistence, during the eighth and seventh centuries B.C.E., that Yahweh alone should be worshiped and that no other gods existed, was thus an aggressive reaction to the equally aggressive promotion of Assur by the Assyrians. Nor could there be any room for compromise in the Yahwists' demand for a thoroughgoing and exclusive monotheism. Only by worshiping Yahweh alone could the Hebrews combat the insinuating effects of Assyrian religious imperialism.

Although the word *prophet* has come to mean someone who predicts the future, its original meaning is closer to "preacher"—more exactly someone who has an urgent message to proclaim, because he or she believes that his or her message derives from divine inspiration. The foremost Hebrew prophets were Amos and Hosea, who preached in the kingdom of Israel before its fall to the Assyrians in 772 B.C.E.; Isaiah and Jeremiah, who prophesied in Judah before its fall in 586 B.C.E.; and Ezekiel and the second Isaiah (the Book of Isaiah was written by at least two and possibly three different authors), who prophesied "by the waters of Babylon" during the exile. Despite some differences in emphasis, the prophets' messages were

> The Assyrian threat was the whetstone on which the Yahwist prophets sharpened their demands not for monolatry but for an exclusive monotheism.

sufficiently similar to each other to warrant treating them as if they formed a single coherent body of religious thought.

Three doctrines made up the core of the prophets' teachings: (1) absolute monotheism—Yahweh is the ruler of the universe; he even makes use of nations other than the Hebrews to accomplish his purposes; the gods of others are false gods; (2) Yahweh is exclusively a god of righteousness; he wills only the good, and evil in the world comes from humanity, not from him; (3) since Yahweh is righteous, he demands ethical behavior from his Hebrew people above all else; he cares less for ritual and sacrifice than that his followers should "seek justice, relieve the oppressed, protect the fatherless, and plead for the widow." The eighth-century B.C.E. prophet Amos summed up "the prophetic revolution" and marked one of the epoch-making moments in human cultural development when he expressed Yahweh's resounding warning in words that have echoed down to our own day (Amos 5:21–24):

> I hate, I despise your feasts, and I take no delight in
>   your solemn assemblies.
> Even though you offer me your burnt offerings and
>   cereal offerings,
> I will not accept them, and the peace offerings of your
>   fatted beasts I will not look upon.
> Take away from me the noise of your songs; to the
>   melody of your harps I will not listen.
> But let justice roll down like waters, and righteousness
>   like an ever-flowing stream.

THE COALESCENCE OF JUDAISM

Through their insistence that Yahwist monotheism was the cornerstone of the Hebrews' identity as a people, the Yahwists made it possible for the Hebrews to survive under Assyrian domination. As the Assyrian threat receded in the late seventh century B.C.E., the Yahwists triumphed religiously and politically. The new king of Judah, Josiah (621–609 B.C.E.), was a committed monotheist who employed prominent prophets at his court, including Jeremiah. With Assyrian power crumbling, Josiah found himself in a position where he could pursue a purification of cult practices. His efforts centered on redrafting and revising the "Law of Moses" and expelling corrupt priests

WHAT DEVELOPMENTS MARKED THE HEBREW TRANSITION FROM POLYTHEISM TO MONOTHEISM?

THE DEVELOPMENT OF HEBREW MONOTHEISM   109

and "foreign" practices from holy places of worship. It was during his reign that the Book of Deuteronomy was discovered, purporting to be another book authored by Moses. As Deuteronomy is by far the most stridently monotheistic book of the Torah, it seems likely that it was authored during (or perhaps slightly before) the reign of Josiah to lend the weight and credibility of Moses' great name to the religious and political program Josiah pursued.

To the dismay of the Yahwists, Josiah died in battle while trying to prevent an Egyptian force from aiding the last remnants of Assyrian power. With his death, the monotheists fell hard from power. Jeremiah was placed under house arrest, denied the right to speak in public, and finally carried off into Egypt where he was murdered. All the while, he continued to denounce the corruption of the Hebrews, suggesting that they would fall before the Chaldeans just as they had before the Assyrians, in punishment for their disobedience to Yahweh.

Within a generation of King Josiah's death, Jeremiah's predictions were fulfilled. The Chaldeans under Nebuchadnezzar conquered Jerusalem, destroyed the Temple, and carried thousands of Hebrews off to Babylon. The Babylonian Captivity brought many challenges for the Hebrews living there, paramount among them being the maintenance of their religious and ethnic identity. The leading voices in defining that identity continued to be the patriotic Yahwists, the same people who would later spearhead the return to Palestine after Cyrus' capture of Babylon. Among the Yahwists, the prophetic tradition thus continued, even in a foreign land. The prophet Ezekiel stressed that salvation could be found only through religious purity, which meant ignoring all foreign gods and acknowledging Yahweh alone. States and empires and thrones did not matter in the long run, Ezekiel said. In this he made explicit the passing observations of predecessors such as Nahum and Jeremiah, who had also commented on the transitory nature of human power and existence. What mattered for the Hebrews living in exile was the creature God had created in his image—man—and the relationship between that Creator God, his chosen people, and his creation.

The disassociation of political identity from religious practice that triumphed during the Babylonian Captivity was an intensification of intellectual currents already discernible in the earlier prophetic tradi-

tion. The period of captivity was nevertheless decisive for the emergence of Judaism as a universalizing religion. In Babylon, Judaism became something more than simply the national cult of the Hebrews. No longer was Yahweh's worship tied to any particular political entity or dynasty, for after 586 B.C.E. neither a Hebrew state nor a Hebrew ruling dynasty existed. Nor was his worship tied to any specific place. In Babylon and in the Holy Land, Judaism survived despite the destruction of the Temple and the removal of the Jewish people from their land. In the ancient world, this was an unparalleled achievement. No other ancient people is known to have survived so long an exile from its central holy place.

Within a generation of King Josiah's death, Jermiah's prophecies were fulfilled.

After 538 B.C.E., when Cyrus permitted the Hebrews of Babylon to return to the Holy Land and rebuild the temple, Jerusalem became once again central holy place of Jewish religious life. But the new developments that had arisen within Judaism during the Captivity would prove to be lasting ones, despite the religious conflicts that soon erupted between the returning exiles and those Hebrews who had managed to remain in the Holy Land, and so were untouched by the changes that had taken place within Judaism during the exile. These conflicts are a measure of the extent to which Judaism itself had been transformed in Babylon.

Increasingly, Jewish religious teachings would be presented in ethical and behavioral terms, as obligations owed by all human beings toward their creator, independent of place or political identity. Ritual requirements and religious taboos, by contrast, would remain the exclusive obligation of Jews, for whom they symbolized the special covenant that bound Yahweh to his people; and these would be rigorously reinforced by the late-fifth-century ruler Nehemiah. But the notion of a creator god who existed outside time, nature, place, and kingship became ever more powerful in Second Temple Judaism, and would be taken up later by Christianity and Islam. So too would the Hebrew claim that Yahweh was a jealous god, who would not permit his followers to worship any other divinity in any form. In the context of the ancient world, both remained peculiar ideas, which would not be fully absorbed for a millennium. But despite its peculiarity, the transcendental monotheism developed by the Hebrews would ultimately become a fundamental feature of the religious outlook of all Western civilizations.

CONCLUSION

Between 1200 and 1000 B.C.E., the devastation wrought by the Sea Peoples, combined with the declining power of Egypt, cleared the way for a number of new, small groups to emerge in the Near and Middle East. These included the Phoenicians, the Philistines, the Hebrews, and the Lydians. These small groups began and developed many of the crucial cultural and economic developments of the early Iron Age, including alphabetic writing, coinage, exclusive monotheism, and mercantile colonization. But the dominant states of the early Iron Age Mediterranean world continued to be the great land empires centered in Asia Minor: first Assyria, then Chaldean Babylonia, and finally Persia. On the surface, it may appear therefore as if nothing very dramatic had changed since the middle of the second millennium B.C.E. But such geographic continuities can be deceiving. The empires of the early Iron Age were quite different from the collections of quasi-independent city-states that had dominated Asia Minor a thousand years before. These new empires were much more highly unified than the earlier empires had been. They had capital cities, centrally managed systems of communication, sophisticated administrative structures, and imperial ideologies that justified their aggressive imperialism as a religious obligation imposed upon them by a single, all-powerful god. They commanded armies of unprecedented size, and they demanded from their subjects a degree of obedience impossible for any previous rulers to imagine. They were not all-powerful. As the Assyrian case reveals, a coalition of small states could still, on occasion, defeat them. But they were larger, more powerful, and more thoroughgoing in their claims to political and religious obedience than any previous western empires.

At the same time that these great land empires were declaring themselves to be the chosen instruments of their god's divine will, we also mark the emergence of more personalized monotheistic traditions in the early Iron Age. Cult and sacrifice were important religious obligations in both Zoroastrianism and Judaism, as they were to all ancient religions. Zoroastrianism in particular was fully compatible with an imperialist ideology. It was, indeed, the driving spiritual force that lay behind the expansion of the Persian empire. Judaism, by contrast, was forged in the struggle to resist the religious imperialism of Assyria and Chaldean Babylonia. But both Zoroastrianism and Judaism added an important new emphasis on personal ethical conduct as a fundamental element in religious life, and both pioneered the development of authoritative, written scriptures as a foundation for their religious teachings. These developments would exercise an enormous influence on Western religious life, and would provide the models on which Christianity and Islam would ultimately erect their own imperial traditions.

SELECTED READINGS

Aubet, Maria Eugenia. *Phoenicia and the West: Politics, Colonies, and Trade.* Trans. Mary Turton. Cambridge, 1993. An intelligent and thought-provoking examination of Phoenician civilization and its influence.

Boardman, John. *Assyrian and Babylonian Empires and Other States of the Near East from the Eighth to the Sixth Centuries B.C.* New York, 1991. Scholarly and authoritative.

———. *Persia and the West.* London, 2000. A great book by a distinguished classical scholar, with a particular focus on art and architecture as projections of Persian imperial ideologies.

Boyce, Mary. *Textual Sources for the Study of Zoroastrianism.* Totowa, N.J., 1984. An invaluable collection.

Brinkman, J. A. *Prelude to Empire: Babylonian Society and Politics, 747–626 B.C.* Philadelphia, 1984. A stimulating examination of the city and culture of Assyrian Babylon as a prelude to the later emergence of the neo-Babylonian (Chaldean) empire.

The Cambridge History of Iran, vols. 1–3. Cambridge, 1969–1983. The authoritative work, with chapters by expert contributors.

Curtis, John. *Ancient Persia.* Cambridge, Mass., 1990. Concise, solid, reliable.

Dothan, Trude, and Moshe Dothan. *People of the Sea: The Search for the Philistines.* New York, 1992. A wide-ranging examination of Philistine culture and its links to the late Bronze Age civilizations of the Aegean basin.

Finkelstein, Israel, and Nadav Na'aman, eds. *From Nomadism to Monarchy: Archaeological and Historical Aspects of Early Israel.* Jerusalem, 1994. A collection of scholarly articles on the Hebrews' transformation from pastoralists to a sedentary society focused on Yahweh worship.

Hallo, W. W., and K. L. Younger, eds. *The Context of Scripture: Canonical Compositions from the Biblical World.* 2 vols. Leiden, 1997. A fine collection of Egyptian, Sumerian, Babylonian, and Hittite texts (v. 1) and inscriptions (v. 2), with valuable introductions and notes.

Kamm, Antony. *The Israelites: An Introduction.* New York, 1999. A concise, accessible introduction covering the period up to 70 C.E. that balances biblical, archaeological, and historical sources.

Knapp, A. Bernard. *The History and Culture of Ancient Western Asia and Egypt.* Chicago, 1988. Although this book surveys the entire ancient period of ancient Near Eastern history, it is strongest on the period after 1200 B.C.E.

Kuhrt, Amélie. *The Ancient Near East, c. 3000–330 B.C.* 2 vols. London, 1995. An outstanding survey, intended for students, that includes Egypt and Israel as well as Mesopotamia, Babylonia, Assyria, and Persia. Excellent bibliographies.

Luckenbill, Daniel David, ed. and trans. *Ancient Records of Assyria and Babylonia.* 2 vols. Chicago, 1926–1927. Still one of the best and most readily accessible collections of primary sources on Assyrian attitudes and policies in war, religion, and politics.

Malandra, William W., ed. and trans. *An Introduction to Ancient Iranian Religion: Readings from the Avesta and Achaemenid Inscriptions.* Minneapolis, 1983. A helpful introduction to Zoroastrianism through the most important primary sources.

Mathews, Victor H., and D. C. Benjamin. *Social World of Ancient Israel, 1250–587 B.C.E.* Peabody, Mass., 1993. An examination of ancient Hebrew society from a variety of sources and perspectives.

Metzger, Bruce M., and Michael D. Coogan, eds. *The Oxford Companion to the Bible.* New York, 1993. An outstanding reference work, with contributions by leading authorities.

Niditch, Susan. *Ancient Israelite Religion.* New York, 1997. A short, suggestive introduction designed for students, emphasizing the diversity of Hebrew religious practice while remaining close to the biblical sources.

Redford, Donald B. *Egypt, Canaan, and Israel in Ancient Times.* Princeton, 1992. An up-to-date overview of the interactions between these peoples from around 1200 B.C.E. up to the beginning of the Common Era.

Saggs, H. W. F. *The Might That Was Assyria.* London, 1984. A lively narrative history of the Assyrian empire, with an analysis of the institutions that underlay its strength.

Tubb, Jonathan N., and Rupert L. Chapman. *Archaeology and the Bible.* London, 1990. A good starting point for students that illustrates clearly the difficulties in linking archaeological evidence to biblical accounts of early Hebrew history and society.

PART II
THE GREEK AND ROMAN WORLDS

THE CLASSICAL CIVILIZATIONS of Greece and Rome dominated the Mediterranean world from the sixth century B.C.E. until the sixth century C.E. Both drew heavily upon the traditions and achievements of the ancient Near East, but each represented a distinct departure from this earlier world. Together, however, Greece and Rome constituted the seedbed out of which all subsequent western civilizations would develop.

Beginning in the eighth century B.C.E., Greek civilization took shape in the warring, particularistic, and fiercely independent city-states that grew up around the Aegean and the Adriatic Seas. But it was not until the end of the fourth century B.C.E., when the conquests of Alexander the Great created an empire that stretched from Greece through Persia to India and Egypt, that Greek civilization became the common cultural currency of the Mediterranean and Near Eastern worlds.

In central Italy, the city of Rome was slowly extending its dominion over the Italian peninsula. In the last two centuries B.C.E., Rome extended its rule throughout the entire Mediterranean world and into western Europe. By the end of the first century C.E., Rome had built an empire larger even than Alexander's. In an extraordinary triumph of organization, discipline, and cultural adaptability, the Romans maintained that empire, substantially intact, for the next four hundred years.

	POLITICS	SOCIETY AND CULTURE	ECONOMY	INTERNATIONAL RELATIONS
B.C.E. 1150		The Dark Age of Greece (1150–800 B.C.E.)	Greek trade increases in Aegean Sea (1000–800 B.C.E.)	
	Birth of the Greek polis (800 B.C.E.)	Introduction of Phoenician alphabet into Greece (800 B.C.E.)		Carthage founded (800 B.C.E.)
		Archaic Greece (800–480 B.C.E.)		
		Homer's *Iliad* and *Odyssey* are written down (800 B.C.E.)		
		First Greek colonies appear (800–600 B.C.E.)		
		First Olympic games (776 B.C.E.)		Rome founded (753 B.C.E.)
	Spartans enslave Messenians (700–680 B.C.E.)			
	Kylon sent into exile for tyranny (632 B.C.E.)			
600	Hoplite tactics become military standard (600 B.C.E.)		Solon encourages cash-crop farming and urban industries (600–550 B.C.E.)	Miletus becomes colonial power (600–400 B.C.E.)
	Tarquin the Proud gains kingship over Rome (543 B.C.E.)			
500	Roman Republic (500-527 B.C.E.)		Athens becomes principal exporter of olive oil, wine, and pottery (500 B.C.E.)	
	Xerxes succeeds Darius the Great (486 B.C.E.)	Sophocles, author of *Oedipus*, (496–406 B.C.E.)		The Ionian Revolution (499–494 B.C.E.)
	Plebian rebellion leads to Law of the Twelve Tables (480 B.C.E.)	Emergence of Greek sculpture (490–480 B.C.E.)		Persians sack Eritrea (490 B.C.E.)
		Golden Age of Greek civilization (480–323 B.C.E.)		Hellenic League formed (480 B.C.E.)
		Socrates (469–399 B.C.E.)		Persian army defeated at battle of Salamis (480 B.C.E.)
	Pericles elected strategos of Athens (462–461 B.C.E.)	Thucydides (460–400 B.C.E.)		
		Sophists emerge (450 B.C.E.)		Athens gains control of Delian League (450s B.C.E.)
		Parthenon built in Athens (447–438 B.C.E.)		Peloponnesian War (431–404 B.C.E.)
		Plato, author of the *Republic*, (429–349 B.C.E.)		
		Aristotle, author of *Nicomachean Ethics*, (384–322 B.C.E.)		Corinthian War (394–387 B.C.E.)
	Reign of Philip II (359–336 B.C.E.)	Greek migrations into western Asia (325–225 B.C.E.)	Alexander's conquests open commercial routes between Greece and Asia (323 B.C.E.)	Philip II defeats Greek alliance and forms League of Corinth (338 B.C.E.)
	Reign of Alexander III, the Great (336–323 B.C.E.)	Euclid, *Elements of Geometry* (300 B.C.E.)		Reign of Alexander the Great (336–323 B.C.E.)
300				Ptolemy establishes dynasty in Egypt (332 B.C.E.)
				Alexander defeats the Persian army (331 B.C.E.)
			First standard coinage in Rome (269 B.C.E.)	Seleucus establishes dynasty in Persia (281 B.C.E.)
				Punic Wars (264–146 B.C.E.)
	Roman slave revolts (146–130 B.C.E.)			Carthage razed (146 B.C.E.)
100		Cicero (106–43 B.C.E.)	Roman commerce relies on one million slaves (100 B.C.E.)	
	Spartacus's revolt (73–71 B.C.E.)	Virgil, author of the *Aeneid*, (70–19 B.C.E.)		
		Horace (65–8 B.C.E.)		
	Caesar defeats Pompey (48 B.C.E.)	Livy, author of *History of Rome*, (59 B.C.E.–17 C.E.)		
	Octavian becomes emperor (27 B.C.E.)	Ovid, author of *Metamorphoses*, (43 B.C.E.–17 C.E.)		
	The Principate of early Roman empire (27 B.C.E.–180 C.E.)			

Politics	Society and Culture	Economy	International Relations	
				C.E. 10
	Saul of Tarsus, or Paul the Apostle (10–67 C.E.)			
	Christians begin arriving in Rome (40 C.E.)		Claudius enters Britain (48 C.E.)	
	Gospel of Mark is written (70 C.E.)		Romans destroy the Temple of Jerusalem (70 C.E.)	
Pax Romana (96–180 C.E.)		Romans excel in engineering aqueducts and roads and develop new tax system under Trajan (98–117 C.E.)		100
			Romans destroy the city of Jerusalem (135 C.E.)	
The Third-Century Crisis in Roman empire (180–284 C.E.)				
	Growth of monasticism emerges (200s C.E.)	One-third of population of Roman empire dies as a result of disease, low birth rate, and war (180–284 C.E.)		
	Neoplatonism (200–300 C.E.)		Goths defeat Romans and cross the Danube (251 C.E.)	
The Dominate or later Roman empire (284–610 C.E.)		Currency is stabilized and new coinage introduced under Diocletian (284–305 C.E.)		
Diocletian, soldier-emperor (284–305 C.E.)				
	The Great Persecution of Christians (303–313 C.E.)			300
Reign of Constantine over Western Roman empire (312–324 C.E.)	Conversion of Constantine to Christianity (312 C.E.)			
Reign of Constantine over Roman empire from Constantinople (324–337 C.E.)			Council of Nicea condemns Arianism (325 C.E.)	
	Saint Jerome (340–420 C.E.)		Visigoths defeat Romans (378 C.E.)	
	Saint Ambrose (340–397 C.E.)			
	Saint Augustine, author of *Confessions* and *On the City of God*, (354–430 C.E.)		Visigoths sack Rome (410 C.E.)	400
	Christianity becomes official Roman religion (392 C.E.)			
	Saint Benedict (480–547 C.E.)			
			Vandals sack Rome from the sea (455 C.E.)	
Justinian rules as emperor in East (r. 527–565 C.E.)			Justinian recaptures Italy from Ostrogoths (536 C.E.)	
Corpus Juris Civilus (532 C.E.)	Papacy of St. Gregory the Great (590–604 C.E.)		The Lombards seize northern parts of Italy (568 C.E.)	
Tenure of Pope Gregory I (Saint Gregory the Great) (590–604 C.E.)				

CHAPTER FOUR

THE GREEK
EXPERIMENT

THE IMAGE THAT COMES MOST OFTEN to mind when Americans or Europeans think of the ancient world is the Acropolis of Athens, its gleaming temples and shrines still impressive despite their age and ruined condition. The rationality, harmony, and repose of this symbol of Greek culture seem to many to bespeak something quintessentially "Western": the triumph of reason and freedom over the "superstition" and "despotism" of "Eastern" cultures such as Assyria or Persia.

Such easy and self-congratulatory contrasts tell us more about ourselves than they do about the ancient Greeks. Greek civilization developed under the heavy influence of the Near East from the Mycenaean period onward. The cross-cultural dialogue between the Greeks and their eastern neighbors has continued until the present day. The achievements of classical Greek civilization would have been impossible without the debt Greece owed to Phoenician, Assyrian, and Egyptian ideas and inventions.

Yet the florescence of Greek civilization during the first millennium B.C.E. is nonetheless a watershed in the development of Western civilizations. Building on their historical experiences after the Bronze Age collapse, the Greeks of the Iron Age came to cherish assumptions and values that differed greatly from those of their Near Eastern neighbors. Human dignity, individual liberty, participatory government, artistic innovation, scientific investigation, constitutional experimentation, confidence in the creative powers of the human mind—the Greeks espoused all of these values, although, as ever in human affairs, practice often fell short of their ideals.

What we mean by such terms as democracy, equality, justice, and freedom differs from what the Greeks would have meant by them. But there is nonetheless an intelligibility for the modern West in the institutions and beliefs of this tenacious, quarrelsome, and energetic people, whose small-scale societies started a cultural revolution and created a civilization distinctly different from any other before it. The democracies of the modern Western world are not the only heirs of this Greek experiment, but they are unimaginable without it.

• What cultural changes marked the end of the "Dark Age" of Greece?

• How did the emergence of hoplite tactics affect Greek political norms?

• What characteristics defined the Athenian, Spartan, and Milesian poleis?

• How were the Greek armies able to defeat the much larger Persian forces?

• How was the fabric of society changed during the golden age of classical Greece?

• How did the Peloponnesian War influence Greek philosophy?

THE DARK AGE OF GREECE (1150–800 B.C.E.)

What cultural changes marked the end of the "Dark Age" of Greece?

By the end of the twelfth century the last remnants of Mycenaean civilization had vanished, and Greece entered on an undocumented Dark Age. Mainland Greece witnessed depopulation of up to 90 percent in the one hundred fifty years following 1200 B.C.E. Except at Athens, the great citadels were destroyed in the conflagrations at the end of the Bronze Age; and even in Athens, the population steadily declined. At Pylos, which in the thirteenth century B.C.E. had numbered one hundred thousand inhabitants, only scattered communities survived by the year 1000, containing at most one hundred households. Linguistic patterns suggest that many of the inhabitants of the mainland fled to the highlands of southern Greece and across the sea to Cyprus and the coast of Anatolia. In Greek legend and historical tradition, this flight was precipitated by the arrival of a related sub-group of Greeks from the north called Dorians. Many scholars now doubt the veracity of this tradition, seeing the Dorians at most as opportunists who migrated south when the palace centers collapsed. What is clear, however, is that tensions between the speakers of the Doric dialect and the "older," Attic-speaking peoples of Greece such as the Athenians would continue right on up until the end of the classical period of Greek history.

Depopulation at the beginning of the Dark Age had severe effects on social organization, economy, and material culture in Greece. Settlements shrank in size and moved inland, away from vulnerable locations near the sea. Their residents were mainly pastoralists, producing little of the fine material culture of Mycenaean times. Dark Age pottery was

> Pottery and burial remains suggest a world that remained static and backward, cut off from the centers of Near Eastern civilization, in which even Greek communities had little economic contact with each other.

The Parthenon. The largest and most famous of Athenian temples, the Parthenon is considered the classic example of Doric architecture. Its columns were made more graceful by tapering them in a slight curve toward the top. Its friezes and pediments were decorated with lifelike sculptures of prancing horses, fighting giants, and confident deities.

WHAT CULTURAL CHANGES MARKED THE END OF THE "DARK AGE" OF GREECE?

THE DARK AGE OF GREECE (1150–800 B.C.E.)   119

functional and inelegant, but it did change in design over time, allowing archaeologists to construct at least a rough chronology of an illiterate people. Pottery and burial relics suggest a world that remained static and backward, cut off from the centers of Near Eastern civilization, in which even Greek communities had little economic contact with each other.

In the first centuries of the Dark Age, these small communities exhibited little social or political differentiation. Some villages may have had chiefs, but even a chief's home and material possessions differed little from those of his neighbors. Each household (*oikos*, from which the word "economy" is derived) was largely self-sufficient and substantially autonomous, with a fundamental social, political, and economic equality among the patriarchal heads of these households. This Dark Age background, with its presumptions of political and economic equality, had a profound effect on the later political assumptions of the classical Greeks.

In a world where survival was often precarious, the Greeks took a dim view of the gods. Religion and ritual remained interwoven in the fabric of Greek society, but the Greeks were very suspicious of their gods and did not necessarily see them as positive forces. The gods were capricious, possessing all the failings of any human being while wielding superhuman power and delighting in interfering in human affairs. For the Greeks, the gods were to be appeased and propitiated, but never trusted fully. Greeks relied far more on the power of the individual human spirit than on divine intervention, although the Greeks developed the idea of *hubris* (excessive pride) to discourage men from becoming too enamored of their own accomplishments. Being overly proud attracted the attention of the gods and threatened them, and they punished the hubristic man with relish. These notions were well developed in later, historical times, but have their roots in the Dark Age past.

HOMER AND THE HEROIC TRADITION

By the year 1000 B.C.E., the complete isolation of Greece was ending, and Greek society was becoming gradually more complex. In 1980, at Lefkandi on the island of Euboea, archaeologists unearthed an enormous house, apparently built as a tomb for one important individual, his stunning material possessions, and the other human members of his household. Dating to c. 1000 B.C.E., this tomb proves that the inhabitants of Euboea were once again trading for long-distance and luxury commodities, and that an economic and political elite had now reemerged.

Pottery also became more sophisticated from about the turn of the millennium. The production of finely made pottery with intricate geometric designs—soon to be prized across the eastern and central Mediterranean—must reflect an upswing in the material culture and prosperity of the Greek mainland. The villages that would ultimately become Corinth dominated this new pottery trade in its early years, but potters at other locales such as Athens would soon challenge Corinthian preeminence. The resulting competition fueled not only artistic but economic and political rivalries as well.

As trade became an increasingly important feature of the Dark Age Greek economy, wealth increased and social stratification became more pronounced. Because wealth acquired through trade did not derive directly from the local Greek community, it did not carry with it the same social obligations of gift giving and exchange that accompanied more traditional sources of wealth. Successful traders could therefore hoard their wealth or employ it to augment their own political and social standing. A small group of aristocrats thus began to emerge, who justified their preeminence as a reflection of their own superior qualities—the "best men." The late Dark Age remained a rough and tumble world, however. Although wealth might be acquired by trade, it was also to be had through warfare and plunder. Nor was wealth alone sufficient to establish one's aristocratic standing. A great man had also to be a singer of songs, a doer of deeds, a winner of battles, and above all favored by the gods. In short, he had to be a hero.

We know much about the heroic ideal of late Dark Age Greece through the *Iliad* and the *Odyssey*, epic poems ascribed to the authorship of Homer. Though these astonishing epics—among the finest examples of literature in the Western tradition—were not written down until after 800 B.C.E. and the introduction of the Phoenician alphabet, they were rooted in a much older oral tradition. The Greeks were aware of a deeper past—they could see the ruins of the Mycenaeans all around them. Homer's poems are set at the end of the

> Because wealth acquired through trade was not obligated to the rest of the community through ties of reciprocity and exchange, successful traders could hoard their wealth or employ it to augment their own political and social standing.

GREEK GUEST FRIENDSHIP AND HEROIC IDEALS

Before the reemergence of true state mechanisms in Greece, relations among communities depended largely on the personal and heritable connections made between the leading families of different villages and peoples. Often founded upon the exchange of gifts or hospitality, the bonds of guest friendship imposed serious obligations on those involved in such relationships. Honoring them was part and parcel of the heroic ideal, as this encounter in Homer's Iliad *between the Greek hero Diomedes and the Lycian Glaukos, fighting for Troy, illustrates. Hospitality remained an important value of Greek society throughout its ancient history.*

Glaukos son of Hippolochus and Tydeus' son Diomedes met in the no man's land between both armies: burning for battle, closing, squaring off and the lord of the war cry Diomedes opened up, "Who are you, my fine friend?—another born to die? I've never noticed you on the lines where we win glory, not till now. But here you come, charging out, in front of all the rest with such bravado—daring to face the flying shadow of my spear. Pity the ones whose sons stand up to me in war!"

The noble son of Hippolochus answered staunchly, "High-hearted son of Tydeus, why ask about my birth? . . . If you'd like to hear it, here's my story. . . . Brave Bellerophon [threatened by a jealous king] went off to Lycia, safe in the escort of the gods, and once he reached the highlands cut by the rushing Xanthus, the king of Lycia gave him a royal welcome . . . when the king could see the man's power at last, a true son of the gods, he pressed him hard to stay, he offered his own daughter's hand in marriage . . . his wife bore good Bellerophon three children: Isander,

Hippolochus, and Laodamia. . . . Hippolochus fathered me, I'm proud to say, and sent me off to Troy. . . . There you have my lineage. That is the blood I claim, my royal birth."

When he heard that, Diomedes' spirits lifted . . . and with winning words he called out to Glaukos, the young captain, "Splendid—you are my friend, my guest from the days of our grandfathers long ago! Noble Oeneus hosted your brave Bellerophon once . . . and they gave each other handsome gifts of friendship. . . . So now I am your host and friend in the heart of Argos, you are mine in Lycia when I visit your country. Come let us keep clear of each other's spears. . . . Plenty of Trojans for me to kill . . . and plenty of Argives [people of Argos] too—kill them if you can." Both agreed. Both fighters sprang from their chariots, clasped each other's hands and traded pacts of friendship.

Homer, *Iliad*, 6. 138–279. Translated by Robert Fagles. (New York: Penguin Classics, 1990), pp. 199–203.

Bronze Age, but over generations of retelling, only Bronze Age curiosities remained, while the social and political relationships portrayed in the poems changed to reflect the assumptions of each new generation. In other words, the great events and many of the material objects of Homeric epic are relics of the Bronze Age, but the society described in the epics is by and large the society of late Dark Age Greece.

WHAT CULTURAL CHANGES MARKED THE END OF THE "DARK AGE" OF GREECE?

THE DARK AGE OF GREECE (1150–800 B.C.E.)   121

Homer depicts a world in which competition and relative status are of paramount concern to the warrior elite. The aristocracy of one community would have had more in common with the aristocracy of another than with the commoners of their own village. Through the exchange of expensive gifts and hospitality, aristocrats created important ties of guest friendship with one another. In a stateless society, such ties often substituted for diplomacy among widely scattered communities. Competition between aristocratic households was constant, however, and ultimately gave rise to hero cults. An important family would claim that an impressive nearby Mycenaean tomb was that of their own famous ancestor and practice dutiful sacrifice and other observances at the tomb to strengthen the claim. This devotion could extend to their followers and dependents; sometimes an entire community could identify itself with such a famous local hero. The heroic ideal thus became a deeply ingrained feature of Greek society, which Homer's epics would preserve and propagate throughout the classical period and beyond.

FOREIGN CONTACTS AND THE RISE OF THE POLIS

The ninth century B.C.E. saw dramatic changes throughout the Aegean basin. Greeks had reestablished economic contact with the Phoenicians by the end of the eleventh century. During the ninth century, however, these contacts intensified. Most crucially, the Greeks adopted the Phoenician alphabet, improving it by converting unneeded consonantal symbols to represent vowels. A "vocalized" alphabet was thus created, capturing in script the sound of speech. The rolling melody and power of Homeric epic could now not only be heard but recorded and read. The Phoenicians also introduced many artistic and literary traditions of the Near East into Greece, which the Greeks incorporated and reshaped to their own purposes. Some famous Greek legends and myths may even have arisen to explain the strange and fascinating narrative scenes that appeared on pots imported into Greece from Phoenicia.

Phoenicians also pointed the way for a new activity among the Greeks—seafaring. Until the tenth century, most Greeks who engaged in trade were passive, al-

lowing the Phoenicians to come to them. By the end of the Dark Age, however, some Greeks had managed to copy Phoenician designs for merchant vessels, setting out on trading ventures of their own and engaging in piracy. The importance of these new activities and the wider awareness of the world the Greeks gained from them are reflected in the *Odyssey*. Greek commercial activity increased throughout the Aegean world during the tenth and ninth centuries B.C.E. Significant movements of Greeks among the homeland, the islands, and Anatolia also took place, foreshadowing the colonial explosion that issued from the Aegean in the eighth and seventh centuries.

These economic and cultural developments were accompanied by dramatic growth in the Greek population. Around Athens, the population may have quadrupled during the ninth and early eighth centuries. Such rapid population growth placed increased demands upon the resources of Greece, a mountainous country not blessed with copious amounts of good land. As smaller villages grew into towns, their territory and their requirements expanded, bringing increasing contact and rivalry with other settlements. The alternatives were conflict or cooperation, and there is evidence for both at the end of the Dark Age.

Warfare and conquest created obvious difficulties, but cooperation presented challenges also. While many religious rituals and customary practices were similar across different communities, they were not necessarily compatible with each other. Each local community had its own religious cults and its own aristocratic luminaries; each treasured its traditional

> These economic and cultural developments were accompanied by dramatic growth in the Greek population.

CHRONOLOGY

GREECE EMERGES FROM THE DARK AGE

Adoption and refinement of Phoenician alphabet	1000–900 B.C.E.
Sharp increase in Greek population	900–700 B.C.E.
Increase in commercial shipping throughout Aegean	1000–800 B.C.E.
Rise of the polis as major political unit	800 B.C.E.

autonomy and independence. As the population grew, some degree of economic, political, and social cooperation became necessary. But the heroic values of the Dark Age Greek world did not make such cooperation easy.

The Greek answer to these questions was the *polis*. The Greek polis was a unique blend of state and local practice. Many Greeks considered the polis not so much a state as a collectivity: ancient sources refer to "the Athenians," "the Spartans," or "the Thebans" more often than to *poleis* (the plural of *polis*) as such. Poleis differed widely, therefore, in size, institutions, importance, and means of livelihood. Structurally, however, each polis was organized around a political and social urban center known as the *asty*, the location of most markets and important meetings, where the basic business of the polis was conducted. Surrounding the asty was the *khora*, the "land." The khora of a larger polis might support several towns of significance besides the asty, as well as numerous villages. The vast majority of citizens were thus farmers, who came to the asty to participate in the affairs of their polis, but who did not reside in the urban center.

Synoikismos (the "bringing together of dwellings") was how Greeks described the process of early polis formation. Synoikismos—or synoecism—could be accomplished through conquest or absorption, and/or through the slow process of neighboring communities' working together and accommodating one another. What spurred synoecism is a matter of debate. The Greeks may have borrowed a Near Eastern (and particularly Phoenician) practice of orienting an urban center around a temple precinct; certainly the heightened frequency of temple building around and after 800 B.C.E. lends support to this theory. On the other hand, temple building and glorification of the gods may more often have been the result of polis formation rather than its cause, as elites competed with each other to exalt their polis and bring glory on themselves. The question remains troublesome and may not have a single answer. The developed polis typically did have a central temple site that served as the focus for the civic religion. But this site was not necessarily located within the city's walls. Athens, for example, had its temple to Athena and associated altars and temples to other gods located on the Acropolis, in the heart of the asty. Argos, by contrast, considered its principal shrine to be the massive temple to Hera located several miles away from any sizable settlement. As was typical of Greek life generally, there was probably no standard pattern by which the early Greek poleis took shape.

Athena. A relief dating from about 450 B.C.E., discovered in the ruins of ancient Athens. The mourning goddess is contemplating a list of citizens who died fighting for her city.

ARCHAIC GREECE (800–480 B.C.E.)

How did the emergence of hoplite tactics affect Greek political norms?

With the emergence of the polis and the return of writing and literacy, the Archaic Age begins. The name is misleading, coined at a time when modern research focused on the Classical Age (480–323 B.C.E.), to which the "archaic" period seemed a rude but necessary prelude. As our understanding of Greece has increased, so too has our appreciation of Archaic Greek culture. After languishing in obscurity for nearly four centuries, Greek civilization burst forth with a dynamism and energy that is breathtaking for all of its achievements,

HOW DID THE EMERGENCE OF HOPLITE TACTICS AFFECT GREEK POLITICAL NORMS?

ARCHAIC GREECE (800–480 B.C.E.)   123

and remarkable for its willingness to try new avenues in religion, society, and politics. Aptly, this period has been called the "Age of Experiment."

COLONIZATION AND PANHELLENISM

In the eighth and seventh centuries the physical and economic frontiers of the Greek world expanded considerably, as smaller-scale trading ventures and migrations across the Aegean developed into a full-fledged colonization effort. A colony was an independent foundation with emotional and sentimental ties to its mother city, but no political obligations. By the end of the sixth century, Greeks had founded several hundred new colonies from the Black Sea to the western Mediterranean, permanently altering the cultural geography of the Mediterranean world. The western shores of Anatolia would remain a stronghold of Greek culture until the end of the Middle Ages; so many Greeks settled in southern Italy and Sicily that the Romans called the region Magna Graecia, "Greater Greece." By the fourth century B.C.E., more Greeks lived in Magna

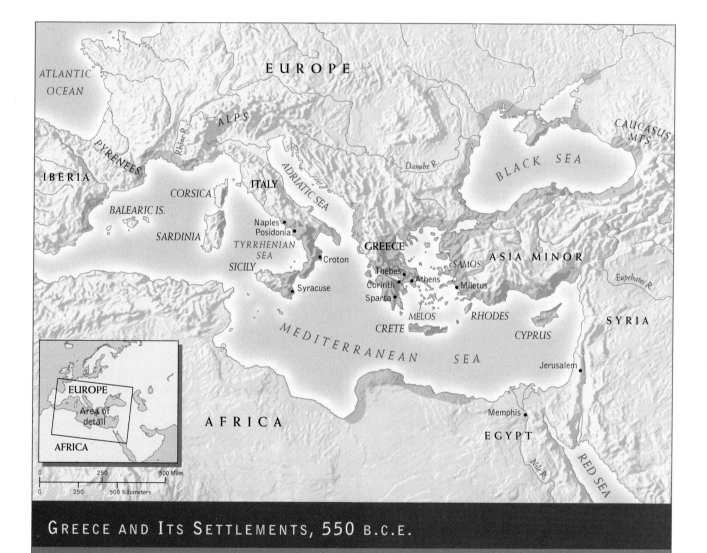

GREECE AND ITS SETTLEMENTS, 550 B.C.E.

Note the direction of Greek settlement, and compare this map with the one on p. 83. How did Greek colonization complement Phoenician expansion, and how did the position of some Greek colonies set up the potential for competition with Phoenician foundations in the West? Notice the major Greek settlements in southern Italy and Sicily. Why would the Greeks play an important role in the development of early Roman culture, and why did the Romans call the area to their south "Greater Greece"? How did small, land-starved communities in the Aegean homeland help to fuel the spread of Greek colonies in the Archaic Age?

Graecia than in Greece itself; and Greek colonies could be found even further westward, in North Africa and along the southern coast of France.

Motives for the colonization effort varied. Some of the emergent poleis, especially Corinth, had been blessed by geography but cursed by the agricultural poverty of its khora. Trade became especially important for Corinthian livelihood and survival, and so the ruling aristocratic clan of eighth-century Corinth undertook an ambitious colonization scheme, planting colonies up the coast of the Adriatic and in Sicily. Meanwhile, some Euboean poleis with older commercial traditions than most Greek cities also forged westward, founding colonies in southern Italy and nearby islands. Other poleis, confronted by population pressures and political turmoil, used colonization as an outlet for excess population and/or troublemakers.

Colonial expansion had important effects on the culture and outlook of the Greek mainland. Most obviously, it intensified Greek contacts with other cultures. The Greeks now encountered Egyptian art and culture firsthand, with profound effects upon archaic Greek art. At the same time, however, this intensified contact with cultures different from their own sharpened the Greeks' awareness of their own common identity and peculiarity as Hellenes (the Greeks' name for themselves). Whereas Dark Age Greeks noted differences among themselves, their contact with outsiders during the Archaic Period gave them a greater appreciation of what it meant to be Greek.

Such self-conscious "Hellenism" did not necessarily result in greater political cooperation among the fiercely independent poleis. Like the Sumerians, the Greeks were particularists, who had little use for permanent political associations larger than the individual polis. Apart from their political differences, they were also divided by linguistic distinctions. Athens, the Aegean Islands, and most of the Greek cities along the Anatolian coast spoke an Ionian dialect of Greek; Sparta, Corinth, Crete, and the southwestern coast of Anatolia spoke Dorian.

Hellenism did, however, encourage the growth and recognition of Panhellenic cult sites, such as the Oracle of Delphi. From all over the Greek world, people went to Delphi to ask questions of the priestess of Apollo (the Pythia), who sat over a vent in the earth munching on eucalyptus leaves. Her answer to a particular question would be unintelligible, spoken in an ecstatic state, but there were priests at hand to "translate" her answer into perfect verse. The fame of the Delphic oracle even spread to cultures beyond the frontiers of Hellenism.

Such oracular pronouncements played a large part in the historical thinking of the Greeks, who believed that divine will and intervention continued to be interwoven with human affairs. The answers of the Delphic priests were sufficiently vague that the oracle could rarely be proven wrong in hindsight.

Hellenism also encouraged the growth of Panhellenic festivals, in which the Greeks honored the gods through athletic competition. The competitive spirit was a constant feature of Greek culture, an important value outweighed perhaps only by victory—athletic, political, or military. The Greeks celebrated four great festivals, held in a quadrennial cycle. Of these, the Olympic Games were the most important, a festival to the king of the gods, Zeus, near the giant temple to him at Olympia. (Greek historians even dated events by "olympiads," four-year periods that began with the supposed date of the first games in 776 B.C.E.). The Greeks took great pride in these games. Only Greeks were permitted to participate in them; all wars among Greeks ceased while the competitions took place; a victory in the games could catapult the victor into a position of social and even political power within his polis. Although they did little to stop contentiousness and rivalry between the poleis, such Panhellenic events strengthened their cultural identification with each other.

HOPLITE WARFARE

Changes in warfare represent another hallmark of the Archaic Period. Through the late Dark and early Archaic ages, the military power of a Greek community resided with the elite, who had the time, material resources, and training (as well as the social impulse) to become "Homeric" warrior heroes. Common foot soldiers played a secondary role as followers and supporters of the aristocratic warriors who dueled in single combat. This monopoly on military prowess gave the aristocracy tremendous political and social leverage within the nascent poleis, which emerged with distinctly elite "constitutions," wherein aristocrats dominated magisterial offices and priesthoods as well as economic life. There was little the nonelite could do about it. Even a sizeable and angry rabble was still no match against a highly skilled, well-armed aristocratic warrior.

The introduction of hoplite tactics brought aristocratic military dominance to an end. Hoplites were foot soldiers armed with spears or short swords and protected by a large round shield (a *hopla*), a breast-

HOW DID THE EMERGENCE OF HOPLITE TACTICS AFFECT GREEK POLITICAL NORMS?

ARCHAIC GREECE (800–480 B.C.E.) 125

plate, a helmet, and sometimes wrist guards and leg guards (greaves). In battle, hoplites stood shoulder to shoulder in a close formation called a phalanx, several rows across and several lines deep, with each hoplite carrying his shield on the left arm to protect the unshielded right side of the man standing next to him. In the right hand each hoplite carried a thrusting weapon such as a spear or short sword, so that an approaching phalanx presented a nearly impenetrable wall of armor and weaponry to its opponents. If a man in the front rank fell, the one behind him stepped up to take his place; indeed, behind the front line was literally the weight of the entire phalanx, each soldier aiding the assault by leaning with his shield into the man in front of him. The tight formation and heavy armor (as much as seventy pounds including the shield) required but one skill: the ability to stay together. As long as the phalanx remained intact, it was a nearly unbeatable formation.

Where, when, and how hoplite tactics first came to Greece remains a mystery. They are first mentioned in the early seventh century B.C.E. when Pheidon, the king of Argos, employed a hoplite army to inflict crushing defeats on the surprised warrior champions of neighboring poleis. Pheidon (or one of his predecessors) may have learned these tactics from the Assyri-

> By the end of the seventh century, hoplite tactics were a standard element in Greek warfare.

ans. The armor and large shield are reminiscent of Assyrian heavy infantry, and certainly the Assyrians had used tight infantry formations to great effect. But wherever they came from, once hoplite tactics were introduced into Greece, all the poleis rushed to adopt them. By the end of the seventh century, hoplite tactics (with their accompanying requirements for training in close-order drill) were a standard element in Greek warfare.

The result was a social and political revolution. Since every polis needed a hoplite force to protect its independence, those farmers who could afford the requisite armor soon became a recognizable political and social force within the archaic polis—a "hoplite class." But the sacrifices demanded by hoplite warfare were great, and the men who had now become indispensable to the polis's survival quickly grew restless without a share in its political decisions. Scholars once believed their disquiet was sufficient by itself to force a series of concessions by the aristocrats, including access to political decision making and the writing down of laws to guarantee "equal" justice. But while the hoplite class was indisputably an essential element in the growth of democracy in some poleis, the real impetus toward change and the rallying point for angry hoplites may in fact have come from disgruntled aristocrats.

Hoplite Infantry Advancing into Combat. This Corinthian vase, dating to around 650 B.C.E., is the earliest known depiction of hoplites.

ARISTOCRATIC CULTURE AND THE RISE OF TYRANNY

For the better part of the seventh and sixth centuries, aristocrats dominated the Greek poleis. But these aristocrats were not a monolithic, cohesive group. Struggles for influence between competing aristocratic families were commonplace; often enough, new laws and the dispatching of colonial expeditions were weapons by which aristocratic families sought to hamstring their enemies. Despite the aristocracy's internecine rivalries, however, serving as the magistrate of a polis was an unsalaried duty, which only the wealthy could afford. The aristocrats of a polis might not have a unified agenda, but they still held all of its official power.

The Greek aristocrats of the Archaic Age pursued not only wealth, power, and glory, but also a distinct culture and defining lifestyle. Holding office and participating in politics was part of this lifestyle; but so too was the symposium, an intimate gathering at which elite men would enjoy prodigious quantities of wine, the recitation of poetry (ranging from epics to bawdy drinking songs), dancing competitions, and female courtesans who provided musical accompaniment as well as sexual ser-

> The Greek aristocrats of the Archaic Age pursued not only wealth, power, and glory, but also a distinct culture and defining lifestyle.

vices. Respectable women were by definition excluded from such meetings, as they were excluded from all other aspects of political life. The symposium was thus far more than a social occasion. It was an essential feature of aristocratic male life within the polis.

Homosexuality was another important aspect of aristocratic culture in the archaic period. Appropriate aristocratic homosexual behavior was regulated by social custom. Typically, a man in his late twenties to late thirties and on the rise in political life took as a lover and protégé an aristocratic youth in his early to mid-teens. The two formed a close and intimate bond of friendship, in which sexual intercourse played an important role. The close personal bond between the man and the boy was believed to benefit the younger partner, as he learned the workings of government and society, and through his older lover made important political and social connections that would benefit him later in life. Indeed, Plato would argue that true love could only exist between two such male lovers, because only within such a relationship could a man find a partner worthy of his affections.

A whole complex of values, ideas, practices, and assumptions thus informed aristocratic identity in the Archaic Period. As a result, it was impossible for those outside this elite world to participate fully in the political, economic, social, and cultural life of the polis. By the middle of the Archaic Age, however, the circle of the aristocratic elite was narrowing even further. A small number of aristocrats now dominated the higher magistracies, putting them in a position to control a wide swath of civic life at the expense of their one-time rivals. As the circle of aristocrats exercising real power narrowed, a significant number of elites were left on the outside of their own culture, looking in. For these men, the remedy to their problem was often close at hand—the hoplites, who had concerns and complaints of their own.

As the circles of political power narrowed during the seventh century, violence between aristocratic groups increased, ultimately giving rise to the emergence of tyranny as an alternative form of government. The word *tyrannos* was not originally Greek, but borrowed from Lydia, signifying someone who seized power and ruled outside the traditional constitutional framework. A tyrant in archaic Greece was thus not necessarily an abusive ruler. In fact, the fundamental features of Greek democracy—especially in Athens—could never

A bearded Greek male and his young lover. This illustration is from a red figure cup, c. 480 B.C.E.

HOW DID THE EMERGENCE OF HOPLITE TACTICS AFFECT GREEK POLITICAL NORMS?

ARCHAIC GREECE (800–480 B.C.E.)   127

Music and Poetry in Everyday Greek Life. The Greeks proudly used pottery design to depict their daily activities. Here a musician entertains a boy while a poet writes verses for another boy. The homoerotic implications of such scenes were intentional.

have succeeded without an episode of tyranny. Later Greek thinkers were fascinated and horrified by the unrestrained power of archaic tyrants, and Aristotle would condemn tyranny as a perversion of the "pure" form of monarchy, hereditary kingship. For many people in the Archaic Period, however, the tyrant led the way to greater political enfranchisement.

The Greek tyrant was usually an aristocrat who had tired of his exclusion from the elite or had become frustrated with the petty rows of aristocratic factions within the polis. Would-be tyrants appealed instead to the hoplite class, whose armed might could propel them to a position of sole power. To stay in power, however, the tyrant had then to redress the grievances of his hoplite supporters. In doing so, tyrants broadened rights of political participation, or gave hoplites new economic and judicial guarantees, while at the same time striving to retain the reins of power in their own hands. This was an inherently unstable state of affairs. As a result, on the Greek mainland tyranny rarely lasted more than two generations. Once the original tyrant and his heirs had fulfilled the wishes of the hop-

lites, the continuance of tyranny became an obstacle to even greater power for the people, the *demos*. After a second generation in power, tyrannical dynasties usually found the hoplite army more inclined to withdraw its support than lend it. Structurally, therefore, tyranny was often a way station on the road from aristocracy to democracy.

LYRIC POETRY

Characteristic of archaic Greek culture is lyric poetry, a new departure in literature that took place in the seventh century and continued as a strong tradition thereafter. The first monuments of Greek literature are the imposing epics of Homer, magnificent in scope and brimming with the heroic themes of Greek society. Hesiod (c. 700 B.C.E.), Homer's immediate successor in the epic tradition, composed shorter yet still impressive poems imbued with traditional outlooks. Hesiod's *Theogony* described the origins of the gods and the created cosmos. His *Works and Days*, a personal diatribe against his scheming brother and the elite of his home-

THRASYBOULOS ON HOW TO BE A TYRANT

The fifth-century historian Herodotus relates how Periander, tyrant of Corinth from 627 to 587 B.C.E., sought advice from his older contemporary, Thrasyboulos of Miletus, on how best to secure tyrannical power. The excerpt below describes Thrasyboulos' response to Periander's emissary, and the Corinthian's response to his strange reply. Although Herodotus' negative attitude toward tyranny is typical of later classical thought, Periander and his father before him had in fact been instrumental in breaking a narrow aristocratic regime and increasing Corinth's commercial prosperity.

At the beginning Periander was gentler than his father [Cypselus] had been. But afterwards, when he had dealt with Thrasyboulos, prince of Miletus, he became yet bloodier than Cypselus. . . . Thrasyboulos had led out Periander's messenger, outside the city, and with him entered a sown field; then he walked through the corn, questioning, and again questioning the herald, about his coming from Corinth. And ever and again as he saw one of the ears growing above the rest he would strike it down, and what he struck down he threw away, until by this means he had destroyed all the fairest and strongest of the corn. So he passed through the whole place and, having added no suggestions, sent the herald away. When the herald came back to Corinth, Periander was anxious to know what suggestion Thrasyboulos had made. But the man said that Thrasyboulos had made no suggestion at all, and indeed he wondered what sort of man this was he had been sent to, a madman and a destroyer of his own property. . . . But Periander understood the act of Thrasyboulos and grasped in his mind that what he was telling him was that he should murder the most eminent of the citizens. And so from this time forth he displayed every form of wickedness toward his fellow countrymen. Whatever Cypselus had spared of death and banishment, Periander completed.

Herodotus, v. 92. Translated by David Grene. (Chicago and London: University of Chicago Press, 1987), pp. 397–398 (somewhat revised).

---

town, quickly expands to such topics as the rewards of hard work, the place of justice in the polis, and the importance of treating one's neighbors well.

The next generations of poets were less ambitious in scope, but their work often has a greater appeal because of its highly personal nature. The poets of the lyric tradition avoided conventional motifs and concentrated on themes of more interest to themselves, often naming their authorship within the lines of the poem. In many instances, they flouted typical mores and values. Archilochus of Paros (c. 680–640 B.C.E.), commemorated his service as a mercenary by writing, "Some barbarian waves my shield, as I had to abandon it/ . . . but I escaped, so it matters not/ . . . I can get another just as good." So much for heroism and standing firm in battle! Archilochus happily threw away his equipment and fled to save himself. Archilochus also gave vent to his personal anger with a faithless lover and the best friend she ran off with, comparing her with a fig tree that feeds every raven and wishing that he would be taken as a slave to the wild country of Thrace.

Among the most famous and accomplished of the lyric poets was Sappho (c. 620–550 B.C.E.). Living in the polis of Mytilene on the island of Lesbos, Sappho witnessed political upheaval and factional strife in her homeland. She left the invective to an associate named Alcaeus, choosing for herself to write beautiful and poignant poetry on themes of romantic longing and sexual lust, sometimes about men, but more often about other women. Of a female lover she wrote, "Like the very gods in my sight is he who / sits where he can look in your eyes, who listens / close to you, to hear the soft voice, its sweetness murmur in love and / laughter, all for him. . . . Let me only glance where you are, the voice dies, I can say nothing, / but my lips are stricken to silence, under/neath my skin the tenuous flame suffuses . . ." She opened another poem with the following lines: "Some there are who say that the fairest thing seen / on the black earth is an array of horsemen; / some, men marching; some would say ships; but I say she whom one loves best is the loveliest."

Though some lyric poets did extol martial virtues and praise heroism, they did so in a new context, that of the collective hero, the hoplite phalanx. At Sparta, the poets Alcman and Tyrtaeus sang of the glory of those who fought for the polis, not those who fought for their own personal gain. Aside from these occasional civic-minded themes, the intimacy of lyric reveals to us something quite new in the history of the West: the individual who expresses his or her feelings, even when these are at odds with the dominant culture of the time.

THE ARCHAIC POLIS IN ACTION

What characteristics defined the Athenian, Spartan, and Milesian poleis?

Although some developments and trends were common across the Greek world, every Greek polis had a very conscious sense of its own history and culture. The variety of experience in the Archaic Age encouraged this outlook, and we will now examine the historical development of three different Greek poleis. Even these present a paradox, at once exemplary and excep-

tional: they illustrate the infinite possibilities for the expression of the Greek polis and stand as paradigms for the courses Greek political development might take, yet are also unique. We know a great deal about certain poleis, especially Athens. The vast majority of Greek poleis, however, remain quite obscure to us, and are likely to remain so.

ATHENS

The Athenians believed that they and their city had survived continuously since the Bronze Age, and that they were themselves an indigenous people. The patterns of linguistic distribution would indicate otherwise, but the Athenians promoted their Bronze Age origins as integral to their identity and their sense of self-importance within the larger Greek world. But although Attica (the area in which Athens was located) was one of the wealthiest and most populous regions in mainland Greece at the end of the Dark Age, Athens itself was not of any great significance. For much of the early Archaic Period, Corinth was the leading commercial city of Greece; Sparta was the preeminent military power; and the islands of the Aegean along with the central coast of Anatolia were the leading cultural centers.

Athens emerged from the Dark Age with a distinctly agricultural economy. Whatever gains the aristocracy had made from trade had been reinvested in the land, and by the early Archaic Age the Athenian elite believed commerce to be a disreputable means of earning a living. Nevertheless, their city's orientation toward the Aegean, the excellent harbors along the Attic coast, and the potential of the land were all inescapable legacies for Athens, which would become famous as a mercantile and seafaring polis.

The landed aristocracy of Athens was in an unassailable position of power until the sixth century. The central props of their power were the elected magistracies, which they monopolized, and the council of state, which was composed of former magistrates. By the early seventh century, aristocratic officials called *archons* wielded executive power in Athens; ultimately nine archons in all presided over the civil, military, judicial, and religious functions of the polis. The archons served a term of one year, after which they became lifetime members of the Areopagus Council, where much of the real power in Athens resided. Indeed, the Areopagus elected the archons, thus controlling its own future membership. The Areopagus served as a kind of "high court" for Athenian society, with tremendous influence over the judicial procedures of Athens.

Over the course of the seventh century, deep economic and social divisions developed in Athenian society, as a significant proportion of the population fell into debt slavery (the practice of securing a loan with one's person as collateral and, when unable to pay up, becoming indentured to the creditor). Add to this economic and social injustice a serious political rivalry between aristocratic political factions, and Athens by the last third of the seventh century was in upheaval. In 632 B.C.E. a prominent aristocrat named Kylon attempted to establish a tyranny, only to surrender under a pledge of safe conduct. Kylon's political rivals violated their promise of immunity, however, slaughtering his supporters and driving Kylon himself into exile. Hard feelings would endure for a generation.

It was a generation of momentous change, however. The endless cycle of revenge killing that followed Kylon's failed coup inspired the first attempt at written law in Athens. In 621 B.C.E., an aristocrat named Drakon was charged with "setting the laws," and his most famous dealt with the problem of homicide. His attempt at stabilizing Athens failed, and the work of reform was left to another, some three decades later when Athens was on the brink of civil war. Hoping to avoid this unthinkable state of affairs, aristocrats and hoplites alike settled on Solon as a compromise candidate for archon in 594 B.C.E. Solon was born an aristocrat but had made his name and fortune as a merchant; this led everyone in Athenian society to trust Solon, as he was not beholden to any single interest. The centerpiece of Solon's year as archon was a series of political and economic reforms essential to the later development of Athenian democracy.

Solon addressed a number of issues. He forbade the practice of debt slavery, and set up a fund to buy back Athenian debt slaves sold abroad. He encouraged the Athenians to cultivate olives and grapes, thus spurring cash-crop farming and the urban industries (such as pottery, oil production, and shipbuilding) necessary to making Athens a commercial power. Solon set up courts in which a broader range of citizens served as jurors, and to which any Athenian might appeal if he disliked a decision of the Areopagus. Crowning his program was a new political and social system that determined the level of political power and access of any Athenian citizen. Solon based eligibility for political office on property qualifications, thus making it possible for someone not born an aristocrat to gain access to power through the accumulation of wealth. He established the *boule*, whose membership was drawn from a wider circle of the population and which served as a kind of steering committee for the policies and actions of the Athenian state. He also gave the citizen assembly, the *ekklesia*, a more prominent role in the political workings of the state. This was a significant step, since all free-born Athenian men over the age of eighteen would participate in that organ of government.

Despite the moderation of his reforms, Solon disappointed many Athenians. The aristocracy felt he had

Harmodius and Aristegiton were lovers who slew Peisistratos' son Hipparchus, and so helped bring the Peisistratid tyranny over Athens to an end. Athenians celebrated them as liberators. This statue is a Roman copy of an original carved around 500 B.C.E.

Ostracism. The system took its name from the potsherds (in Greek, *ostraka*) on which the names of unpopular citizens were scratched. Many of the "ballots" have survived. Here we see "Aristeides," "Kimon," and "Themistokles."

gone too far, the demos, not nearly far enough. Those in power resisted implementing Solon's laws, and three factions based on regional and economic rivalries within Attica vied for dominance. The aristocrat Peisistratos exploited this state of affairs and established himself as tyrant in 546 B.C.E. Peisistratos offered few original measures; he mainly insisted on observing Solon's laws, and allowed the organs of government to function as Solon intended. Behind it all, however, was the quiet but very present intimidation that Peisistratos practiced through the hiring of foreign mercenaries and the ruthlessness with which he crushed any dissent to his regime. By enforcing Solon's wishes, Peisistratos made the demos powerful, so much so that the later Athenian democracy tried to distance itself from him by heroizing the aristocrats who murdered one of Peisistratos' sons and successors and drove the other into exile.

In the aftermath of the Peisistratid overthrow in 510 B.C.E., there was a brief aristocratic counterrevolutionary regime supported by the Spartans. However, two generations of increasing access to power meant that the Athenian demos had no interest in returning to an elite oligarchy. For the first time in history, the populace at large spontaneously rose up and overthrew the government, preferring different leadership. They rallied behind Cleisthenes, also an aristocrat but a man who had served the Peisistratid government ably and who championed the cause of the demos after the fall of tyranny. Once voted in as archon in 508/507 B.C.E., Cleisthenes reformed the voting practices of the Athenians, reorganizing the countryside and the population into ten voting "tribes" that helped suppress natural economic and regional tension within Attica. He made the boule a more representative body and extended the machinery of democratic government to the local level throughout Attica. Cleisthenes also introduced the practice of ostracism, whereby the Athenians could decide each year whether they wanted to banish someone for ten years, and if so, whom. Cleisthenes believed that with this power, the demos could protect itself from the potential return of a tyrant and quell factional strife if it seemed civil war might result.

Over the course of the archaic period, men such as Solon, Peisistratos, and Cleisthenes helped transform the Athenian polis into one of the most powerful in all of Greece. By the end of the sixth century, Athens was the principal exporter of olive oils, wines, and pottery in the Greek world, surpassing even "wealthy Corinth." The history of Athenian political development culminated, in the age of Cleisthenes, in a far more democratic temper than any other Greek polis possessed. The Athenians of the fifth century came to view themselves as the guardian of all that was good in Greek culture, including their own, more inclusive brand of democracy.

CHRONOLOGY

THE CHANGING LANDSCAPE OF ARCHAIC GREECE

Panhellenic colonial expansion by Greek poleis	800–400 B.C.E.
Hoplite tactics become standard in Greek warfare	725–650 B.C.E.
Emergence of tyrannical governments	700–600 B.C.E.
Militarization of Sparta	600 B.C.E.
Solon's reforms	594 B.C.E.
Cleisthenes' reforms	508 B.C.E.

SPARTA

Located in the southern part of the Peloponnesus (the large peninsula that forms southern Greece), the Spartans represented for all of Greece everything that Athens was not. Athens was cultured, sophisticated, cosmopolitan; Sparta was basic, earthy, and traditional. Depending on one's point of view, either set of adjectives might serve as admiration or criticism.

Sparta underwent a synoikismos (see p. 118) when four villages (and ultimately a fifth) combined to form the polis of Sparta. Perhaps as a result of the unification process, Sparta retained a highly peculiar institution, a dual monarchy. Sparta had two royal families, with two lines of succession. Although seniority or capacity usually determined which of two ruling kings had more influence, neither was technically superior to the other, a situation that led to political intrigue within Sparta.

Greek historians believed—as did the Spartans—that a figure from the Heroic Age named Lycurgus had given Sparta its unique constitution and social system. "Lycurgus" was probably a person to whom the Spartans gave credit for achievements and developments spanning hundreds of years across the Dark and early Archaic Age. The Spartans believed Lycurgus promulgated the "Great Rhetra," a "document" that remained unwritten at a time when many Greek poleis were writing down their laws. The Great Rhetra, orally preserved (and no doubt altered as circumstances demanded) represented for the Spartans the constitutional wisdom of Lycurgus.

The "reforms of Lycurgus" militarized Sparta. By the end of the seventh century, everything in Sparta was oriented to the maintenance of Greece's most feared and respected hoplite army, a force so superior that the Spartans confidently left their city unfortified. The Spartan system made every full citizen, called a Spartiate (or, alternatively, an "equal"), a professional soldier of the phalanx. Whereas Athenian government was democratized to reflect the interests and outlook of her people, in Sparta the citizenry was in essence "aristocratized," making every citizen-soldier a warrior-champion of the hoplite phalanx.

The Spartan system depended on the conquest of Messenia, an agriculturally wealthy region west of Sparta. In the early seventh century, the Spartans subjugated the region and enslaved the population. These

helots (as the enslaved Messenians were now called) remained to work the land, which was now parceled out among the Spartiates. The result was that Spartiates did not have to engage in manual labor of any kind, freeing all their time for their military training.

Sparta was a society organized for war. At birth, every child was examined by the five *ephors*, Spartan officials who served as guardians of the Great Rhetra. They determined whether a child was healthy enough to bother raising; if not, the infant was exposed in the mountains. If deemed worthy of upbringing, a child was placed at age seven in the state-run Spartan educational system, the *agoge*. Boys and girls trained together until age twelve, participating in exercise, gymnastics, and other physical drills and competitions. At that age, boys went to live in the barracks, where their military training would commence in earnest, while girls continued an education in letters until they married (marriageable age being the onset of puberty). Barracks training was rigorous, designed to accustom the young Spartan male to physical hardships. At age eighteen, the young man would try to gain membership into a *syssition*, a communal mess tent as well as a kind of fighting brotherhood. Failure to gain admission to a syssition meant that the young man would not become a full Spartiate, falling to a lower status and losing his citizen rights.

> Failure to gain admission to a syssition meant that the young man would not become a full Spartiate, falling to a lower status and losing his citizen rights.

Assuming the young man's career continued as anticipated, he remained in the barracks until he was thirty, although he could marry at twenty-one. By the time he could take up residence in his own home, he had thus spent eighteen years in the barracks. The homoerotic culture of the Spartan military—along with the limited opportunities for procreation afforded to a young married couple—may have been a significant contributing factor to the falling number of Spartiates over the course of sixth and fifth centuries. A Spartiate remained on active military duty until he was sixty years old, although after the age of forty-five he was unlikely to see phalanx combat.

All Spartiate males were members of the assembly, the *apella*, which voted yes or no on matters put to it by superior organs of government. The upper levels of government included the kings and the council of elders. Any Spartiate at the age of sixty could stand for election to this council, which included twenty-eight seats at large and two for the kings. The apella elected members to the council of elders for life, and the council served as the main policy maker of the polis. In addition, the five ephors ruled on whether certain proposals or courses of action were in keeping with the Great Rhetra. An ephor could even depose a king from command of the army while on campaign. The ephors, who usually served a term of one year, wielded tremendous power, further augmented by their supervision of the Spartan secret service, the *krypteia*. The ephors recruited agents for the krypteia from among the most promising young Spartiates. Although these agents spied on citizens suspected of unusual activities, their main job was to infiltrate the helot populations, identify potential troublemakers, and eliminate them.

Spartan policy often hinged on the precarious relationship between the helots and the Spartiates. The helots outnumbered the Spartiates ten to one, and Messenia routinely seethed with revolt. The Spartans took the helots on campaign with them as shield bearers, spear bearers, and baggage handlers. Remarkably, we know of no helot revolt on campaign. At home, however, the helots were prone to rebellion, one reason the Spartans disliked committing their army for long periods of time far from home, fearing that the prolonged absence of the fighting men might encourage an uprising. Every year the Spartans ritually declared war on the helots, as a reminder that they would not tolerate any attempt to break free. Although the existence of the helots made the might of Sparta possible, Sparta's reliance on a hostile population of slaves also proved a serious weakness.

Spartiates themselves could not engage in trades or commerce, and Lycurgus prohibited the use of coinage, instead prescribing the use of iron spits for currency, which were both cumbersome and worthless outside of Sparta. Lycurgus believed that the use of money and the ability to accumulate wealth would create serious economic and political divisions among Spartiates and distract them from the pursuit of martial virtue. Therefore economic activity in the Spartan state fell to the *perioikoi*, "those dwelling round about." The perioikoi were subjects of the Spartan state not reduced to helot status. The perioikoi enjoyed certain rights and protections within Spartan society and grew wealthy handling its business concerns. They were forever excluded from the exercise of any political rights within the Spartan state, however, and Sparta conducted their foreign

> Spartiates themselves could not engage in trades or commerce, and Lycurgus prohibited the use of coinage, instead prescribing the use of iron spits for currency, which were both cumbersome and worthless outside of Sparta.

policy for them. Spartiates who lost their rights of full participation also became perioikoi.

From the Archaic Period on, the Spartans professed little use for innovation or change. They styled themselves the protectors of the "traditional constitutions" of Greece, by which they meant older, aristocratic regimes. The Spartans often tried to prevent the establishment of tyrannies or overthrew them in neighboring states. In the late sixth century, the Spartan king Cleomenes even supported the aristocratic counterrevolution in Athens. Sparta's defense of tradition and its military-social system made it an object of admiration throughout the Greek world, though few Greeks had any desire to live that way themselves. And in certain respects, it was a system that was inherently flawed. There were many ways to fall from the status of Spartiate—such as criminal behavior or other unseemly conduct—but there was only one way to become one: by birth. As a result, the number of full Spartiates declined from perhaps as many as ten thousand in the sixth century to only a few thousand by the beginning of the fourth.

MILETUS

Across the Aegean from the Greek "homeland" lay the Greek poleis of Anatolia (an area also known as Asia Minor). During the archaic period, the city of Miletus was the foremost commercial, cultural, and military power of Ionia, a narrow coastal strip dominating the central part of the west coast of Anatolia. Miletus had long been a part of the Greek world. Archaeological evidence supports what the Milesians themselves claimed, that they had ties to both Minoan and Mycenaean civilization. But there must also have been a substantial influence from the indigenous peoples of the area, whom later Greek tradition claimed had been conquered by Ionian-speaking settlers from Athens.

Despite its diversity, Miletus' population was ultimately subsumed under a single, strongly Hellenic identity, but Near Eastern influences continued to shape Milesian culture. Ionia was the birthplace of Greek epic, and the proximity of Miletus to the Near East has occasioned scholarly debate over the extent to which Asian models influenced Greek epic. Certainly there was influence in other creative endeavors. Fantastic animals, a long-standing theme of Near Eastern decorative art, were frequently represented on Milesian pottery during the seventh and sixth centuries. The close though often difficult relationship between the Ionians of the coast and the interior kingdom of Lydia also led to extensive cross-cultural exchange. Through the Ionians, the Lydian invention of coinage was introduced to the Greek world, while the Ionians played a crucial role in hellenizing the interior of Asia Minor. Under the pressure of the Lydians—who sought the fabulous ports of the Aegean coast for themselves—the major cities of Ionia banded together to form the Ionian League, a political and religious confederation of independent poleis pledged to support one another in time of need. It was the first such organization known in the Greek world.

Milesians stood at the vanguard of the colonial movement, especially in and around the Black Sea. Miletus was also active in the Egyptian markets; the main Greek trading posts in Egypt were Milesian foundations. Their colonial efforts, combined with their advantageous position for trade with the rest of Asia Minor, brought Miletus great wealth. Miletus reached the peak of its power in the early sixth century, when its tyrant Thrasyboulos successfully warded off Lydian aggression and (probably) constructed a fleet to protect Milesian shipping interests. After his death, however, continuing Lydian pressure combined with competition from the Ionian island of Samos led to Miletus' slow decline over the course of the sixth century.

Miletus also became the center for Greek speculative thinking and philosophy. Beginning in the sixth century B.C.E., a series of thinkers known to historians as the "Pre-Socratics" (because they came before the great philosopher Socrates) raised serious questions about the relationship between the natural world (the *kosmos*), the gods, and humans. Oftentimes, their explanations moved divine agency to the margins or removed it altogether—and for that, everyday Greeks looked upon them with suspicion. The so-called Milesian School consisted of three successive thinkers. The first, Thales, was an accomplished astronomer, also concerned with questions about nature and the "first principle," a substance from which all other matter had been created. His intellectual successors, Anaximander and Anaximenes, posited theories about the heavens

and the first principle, and explored the problem of change, including the differentiation of animal species. All three built on older traditions of Near Eastern learning, such as Babylonian astronomy; but in typically Greek fashion, they turned those ideas on their heads. Calculating and observing the movements of the heavens, the thinkers of the Milesian School sought physical explanations for what they saw, refusing to presume that the heavenly bodies were gods. By making the observations of humans, not the will of the gods, the starting point for their thinking, the Milesian school began to formulate rational theories to explain the physical universe they observed.

> By making the observations of humans, not the will of the gods, the starting point for their thinking, the Milesian school began to formulate rational theories to explain the physical universe they observed.

Stimulated by the cosmopolitanism of their city, Milesian philosophers also began to rethink their place in the human world, inaugurating what has sometimes been called "the Ionian revolution in thought." Hecataeus of Miletus, the first Greek to attempt a map of the known world, wrote after extensive travels during which he studied other cultures and their gods: "Hecataeus of Miletus says this: the sayings of the Greeks are many and foolish." Xenophanes of Colophon observed that the Thracians (a barbarian people living to the north of the Greeks) believed the gods had blue eyes and red hair, whereas the Ethiopians portrayed their gods as dark skinned and curly haired. Xenophanes concluded from this that if oxen could speak and make objects, they would pray and fashion idols to gods who looked like oxen. For Xenophanes, men made gods in their image, not the other way around. Such relativism was new, but it would become a distinctive strand in the diversity of later Greek philosophy.

This fissure between religious belief and philosophical speculation was a crucial development in the history of Western thought. It was less complete, however, than is often imagined. Philosophy was a game for a few, not for the average Greek; and as philosophers turned their attention to humanity's relationship to the gods, citizens in even the most progressive of poleis were unnerved. The gods were too central a part of daily life for the average Greek not to feel threatened by such impious philosophizing.

The struggle between religion and philosophy would finally be fought out not in Miletus, but in Athens more than a hundred years after Xenophanes' bold proclamation. The Ionian revolution in thought

HOW WERE THE GREEK ARMIES ABLE TO DEFEAT THE MUCH LARGER PERSIAN FORCES?

THE PERSIAN WARS   135

slowed when Cyrus conquered Lydia in 546 and inherited Lydia's suzerainty over the Greek city-states of Asia Minor, including Miletus. Milesian independence was always in jeopardy under Persian rule. Although often autonomous, the city remained under the constant threat of Persian intervention. Ultimately, Miletus would trigger the greatest cultural clash the Greek world had yet known—war with the mighty Persian empire.

THE PERSIAN WARS

How were the Greek armies able to defeat the much larger Persian forces?

The Archaic Period of Greek history closed with dramatic struggles against Persia. When hostilities erupted between the Greeks and Persia, the latter was the mightiest state the world had ever seen, capable of mustering over a million armed men. The Greeks, in contrast, remained a collection of poleis, fiercely suspicious of one another and competitive to the bitter end. An exceptionally large polis, such as Athens or Sparta, might put ten thousand hoplites in the field; but the vast majority of Greek states could provide only a few hundred each. For two decades the threat of Persian conquest loomed on the Greek horizon. When finally the immediate danger to Greek freedom receded, the experience of war had changed the Greek world immeasurably.

THE IONIAN REVOLT (499–494 B.C.E.)

Our main source for the Persian Wars is Herodotus, the "father of history." His account reflects many of the intellectual currents of mid-fifth-century Athens, where he lived and worked. His account is idiosyncratic, anecdotal, sometimes dubious, but always entertaining. Though he was from Halicarnassus in Asia Minor, he was a keen judge of his Athenian audience, and so emphasized the role Athens itself played in the wars. With a kind of geographical and cultural determinism, he ascribed the war between Persia and Greece to the rekindling of an ancient hatred between Europe and Asia. But his own narrative shows that the immediate political cause of the war was a political conflict in Miletus.

By 501 B.C.E., Aristagoras—the Persians' puppet tyrant of Miletus—grew concerned that his days as a favorite of Darius the Great were numbered. To protect his political future, he turned from puppet to patriot, rousing the Milesians and the rest of Ionia to revolt against Persian rule. Because they had little hope of winning on their own, Aristagoras tried to enlist military support from the Greek mainland. The Spartans showed initial interest but opted out when Aristagoras showed them the Persian Empire on Hecataeus' map. He then approached Athens and the city of Eretria on Euboea, playing to their sympathies as fellow Ionians. The Athenians voted twenty ships and crews, the Eretrians five. With the help of this small expeditionary force, the Ionians managed to take the old Lydian capital of Sardis (now a Persian administrative center) by surprise. The Athenians and Eretrians burned the city and then sailed home, leaving the Ionians to their own devices. After five years of brave struggle, the rebels were finally overwhelmed by the vastly superior might of Persia in 494 B.C.E.

Darius realized, however, that so long as his Greek subjects in Asia Minor could cast a hopeful eye to their cousins across the Aegean, they would long for freedom. Darius therefore set out on a punitive expedition to teach Athens and Eretria a lesson. The king sent a force of twenty thousand soldiers under two of his finest generals on an island-hopping campaign across the Aegean. Landing on Euboea in the summer of 490, Persian forces captured Eretria, sacked and burned it, and then crossed the narrow strait to Attica, landing in the plain of Marathon.

MARATHON AND ITS AFTERMATH

Recognizing the danger they now faced, the Athenians sought help from the Spartans, who responded that they were unable to assist due to an ongoing religious festival. Only the small, nearby polis of Plataea offered the Athenians aid. The Athenians would have to engage the mighty Persians on their own.

Heavily outnumbered and without effective cavalry to counter the Persians, the Athenian phalanx took a position between two hills blocking the main road to the asty. After a standoff of several days, the Athenian general Miltiades received word that the Persians were watering their horses, and that the Persian infantry, numerically superior but poorly equipped compared with Athens' ten thousand hoplites, was vulnerable. Miltiades led a charge that smashed the Persian force and resulted in catastrophic losses for the Persians. Herodotus records that sixty-four hundred Persians fell,

Bust of Themistocles. His leadership enabled Athens to defeat Persia and become the primary naval power in the Aegean Sea.

compared with only 192 Athenians. The Persians withdrew.

The Athenians had defeated the world's greatest empire, and they had done it without Spartan help. It was a tremendous boost to Athenian confidence, and many exulted in their victory, a victory of the demos. The Athenian politician Themistocles believed, however, that Greece had not seen the last of the Persians, who would inevitably return in much greater force. Several years after Marathon, the Athenians discovered a rich silver vein in the Attic countryside. Themistocles persuaded them not to divide the windfall among themselves (the customary practice), but to build a fleet of two hundred triremes, state-of-the-art warships. Athens transformed itself into the preeminent naval power of the Greek world, just in time to confront a new Persian onslaught.

XERXES' EXPEDITION

Darius died in 486 B.C.E. and was succeeded by his son Xerxes. Xerxes spent the first several years of his reign quelling a revolt in Egypt, but he never forgot his father's desire to punish the Athenians. Indeed, Xerxes decided to go Darius one better. He planned an all-out, overland invasion of Greece to conquer the entire country. By the spring of 480, his grand army (probably numbering some three hundred fifty thousand troops) set out from Sardis, crossing the narrow strait separating Europe from Asia on pontoon bridges. Unlike his father, who had dispatched talented generals against Athens, Xerxes led this campaign himself.

Before his arrival in Greece, Xerxes had already received the submission of several important sites in northern and central Greece, including Thebes and Delphi. Athens, Sparta, and others refused to bow, however, and formed the Hellenic League to defeat the Persian menace. Under the military leadership of Sparta, the outnumbered Greek allies resolved to face Xerxes at the pass of Thermopylae in August of 480. For three days the Greeks held off the Persian multitude, while an allied Greek fleet engaged a Persian flotilla at nearby Artemisium. The Spartan-led defense at Thermopylae failed, but the naval engagement—though technically a draw—proved significant. The sacrifice at Thermopylae allowed the fleet, under Themistocles' guidance, to inflict heavy losses on the Persians and then withdraw safely to the south.

After the defeat at Thermopylae the road to Athens lay open. Realizing they could not defend their city, Themistocles persuaded his fellow Athenians to abandon the city and their possessions. They evacuated noncombatants to other locales and removed the core of Athenian military strength, including the fleet, to the island of Salamis off the coast of Attica. In early September, the Athenians watched the Persians put Athens to the torch, and Themistocles struggled to keep the allied fleet together as the Persians feigned an advance toward Corinth and Sparta.

Time, however, was on Themistocles' side. The massive size of his army meant Xerxes was dependent on his fleet for supplies. Bad weather made sailing the Aegean in autumn a risky business; the Persians were now desperate to force a decisive battle before the season turned against them. In late September, the numerically superior Persian fleet, believing the Greeks were about to flee Salamis, sailed into the Bay of Eleusis, only to find that Themistocles had the Greek fleet ready for combat. The Greeks smashed the Persian

HOW WAS THE FABRIC OF SOCIETY CHANGED DURING THE GOLDEN AGE OF CLASSICAL GREECE?

THE GOLDEN AGE OF CLASSICAL GREECE   137

Greek Forces Defeat Persians. This detail from a fifth-century B.C.E. attic bowl depicts an Athenian soldier standing over a defeated Persian soldier from Xerxes' army.

fleet while Xerxes watched the disaster from a throne above the bay. The Persian king left behind a substantial army, but he himself withdrew to his empire; the battle of Salamis had effectively ended his campaign. The following year, the Greeks prevailed on land at the battle of Plataea, driving the Persians completely from mainland Greece. Against all odds, the small, fractious, outnumbered Greek poleis had defeated the mightiest empire of the Mediterranean world. It was a turning point in the history of Greece, ushering in the Classical (or "Golden") Age.

THE GOLDEN AGE OF CLASSICAL GREECE

How was the fabric of society changed during the golden age of classical Greece?

In the fifty years following the battle of Salamis, Athens enjoyed a meteoric rise in power and prestige, becoming the premier naval power of the eastern Mediterranean and a rival even to Sparta. When Spartan leadership failed after the war, those poleis who wished to continue the fight against the Persians formed an alliance on the island of Delos under the military leadership of Athens—the Delian League. Each member state contributed ships or money to the cause, and all vowed to fight until the Persians ceased to be a threat. As the leader of the league, Athens controlled the funds and resources of the alliance, a fact that allowed the Athenians to make their polis—in the words of their brilliant political leader Pericles—"the school of Hellas." The fifth century witnessed the greatest achievements of Greek culture and the fruition of the Athenian democracy. But both were fueled by the increasingly awkward relationship Athens enjoyed with its allies, who by the 430s had begun to look more like Athenian subjects than free allies.

PERICLEAN ATHENS

The reforms of Cleisthenes made possible further experiments in Greek democracy, including the election of major officers of the polis by lot. Only one major position was left open to traditional voting: the office of *strategos*, or general. A man could be elected strategos (unlike all other positions) year after year, and so this office became the focus for Athens' most talented and ambitious public figures. Themistocles had been a strategos, as had Cimon, who led the Delian League to stunning victories over Persia in the 470s and 460s. But Cimon also turned the league against members who tried to opt out, suppressing their "revolts" by force of arms, and turning the league more and more into an instrument of Athenian policy.

Cimon's military successes made him the most powerful politician in Athens. By the 460s, however, the political mood in Athens was changing, and new voices were calling for a greater role in government. Athens' power was a result not so much of its hoplite phalanx (mediocre by Greek standards) as its fleet. The enormous navy of triremes required nearly forty thousand rowers drawn from those Athenians too poor to afford hoplite equipment, the lowest of the four classes established by Solon. Since the beginning of the sixth century, these men had enjoyed very limited political power. For all of his magnanimity and generosity, Cimon was too conservative to consider shifting the balance of political power in the direction of the poorer mass of Athenian citizens, the *thetes*.

An unlikely champion emerged for their cause, an aristocrat from one of Athens' most prestigious noble

Bust of Pericles. A Roman copy, in marble, of a Greek original, made in bronze during Pericles' own lifetime. Like the tyrant Peisistratos, Pericles is said to have had a deformed head. Pericles wore a helmet to conceal this potentially provocative resemblance.

families—Pericles. A political rival of Cimon's, Pericles used a platform of greater enfranchisement of the thetes and an anti-Spartan foreign policy to defeat Cimon. Pericles was elected strategos for 462–461, and secured the ostracism of Cimon from Athens. He then pushed through reforms to make Athens more fully democratic. He gave every member of the assembly (that is, any Athenian citizen) the right to propose and amend legislation, not just vote yes or no. This shifted power away from the Areopagus—still made up of ex-archons and therefore wealthier citizens—and from the more deliberative boule. He also made it easier for any citizen to participate in the assembly and the great appeals courts of Athens by paying an average day's wage for attendance. This allowed Athens' poorer citizens to take part without losing income. They now became a significant force in politics, loyal to the man who had made it possible.

Along with these and other important political measures, Pericles glorified Athens' democracy with an am-

bitious scheme of public building and lavish festivals to honor the gods, especially Athena. He was a great patron of the arts, sciences, and literature, attracting the best minds of the day to Athens. As a result of his populist political stance and his ability to inspire a sense of Athenian superiority, Pericles enjoyed an unprecedented run of success in politics. He was returned as strategos every year for three decades, and his guidance and vision have prompted historians to apply his name to this phase of Athenian history. Despite Pericles' often poor decisions regarding foreign policy, there is no question that Periclean Athens represents a dramatic and brilliant moment in the history of Western civilizations.

LITERATURE AND DRAMA

Although Athens was not the only city to produce great works of literature during the "golden age," our knowledge of classical Greek literature is dominated by the poetry and drama (both tragic and comedic) produced in fifth-century Athens. Epic and lyric poetry were already established Greek literary forms when the fifth century began. Drama, however, appears to have been an innovation that developed out of the choruses that chanted poetic odes to the god Dionysius at the great spring festival devoted to him. It was probably the tyrant Peisistratos who first organized the Great Dionysia, and Cleisthenes who converted it into a festival at which tragic dramas were presented. From the beginning, therefore, Athenian drama was closely connected to the political and religious life of the state, which sponsored it. Credit for transforming the Dionysian odes into a genuine drama with characters and a chorus belongs, however, to the great tragedian Aeschylus (525–456 B.C.E.), who by introducing a second (and later a third) character into the performance, made it possible to present conversation, and hence human conflict, on the stage for the first time. Staging remained very simple, however: two or three actors (all male) wearing masks, with a chorus of twelve to fifteen members chanting commentary on the action. Dialogue was in verse, and movements were slow, solemn, and formal, punctuated by music and dance; but the emotional impact of tragic drama could be overwhelming.

Efforts to define and explain the nature of tragedy began with Aristotle, who declared that the purpose of tragedy was to inspire pity and fear in the audience, and so to purge these emotions through a catharsis. Although enormously influential, this formulation is

HOW WAS THE FABRIC OF SOCIETY CHANGED DURING THE GOLDEN AGE OF CLASSICAL GREECE?

THE GOLDEN AGE OF CLASSICAL GREECE   139

probably too limiting to be helpful. The fundamental themes of tragedy—justice, law, and the conflicting demands of piety and obligation that drive a heroic man or woman to destruction—were derived from Homer. Although most tragedies told well-known tales from a legendary past—Agememnon's sacrifice of his daughter, his murder by his wife Clytemnestra, and the vengeance taken by his son Orestes; or the Oedipus story, about a king who unwittingly slays his father and marries his mother—tragedy could also have a decidedly contemporary aspect. In his *Persians*, Aeschylus told of the great Athenian victory at Salamis (in which Aeschylus himself may have participated) through the eyes of the Persian king Xerxes, who thus became its tragic hero. Sophocles' (496–406 B.C.E.) great masterpiece, *Oedipus at Colonus*, was presented in the midst of Athens' ultimately disastrous war with Sparta; Eu-

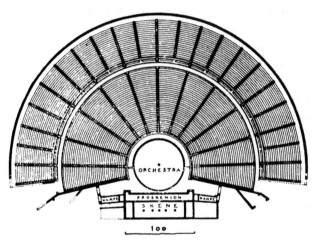

ripides' (485–406 B.C.E.) *Trojan Women* was presented in 415, the year of the expedition to Syracuse (see p. 141), and the turning point in the Athenians' march toward defeat. Tragedy dealt in absolutes, most memorably perhaps in Sophocles' *Antigone*, the story of a clash between justice and law, and the competing obligations of familial piety and civic necessity; but its context was inevitably the history of Athens in the period of its own greatest achievements and failures.

Comedy was even more directly a genre of direct political commentary. Comedy was crude, parodic, and outspoken, full of slapstick, absurdity, and vulgarity. Its themes were (in the scholar Peter Levi's words) "sex, life on the farm, the good old days, the nightmare of politics, the oddities of religion, the strange manners of the town." Aristophanes (c. 448–382 B.C.E.), the greatest of the Athenian comedic playwrights, ridiculed everything that offended or amused him: the philosophy of Socrates, the tragedies of Euripides, and especially the imperialistic warmongering of contemporary politicians such as Cleon. Some of his jokes were simply crude, as when he had Socrates explain thunder as "the farting of the clouds." In his timeless masterwork, *Lysistrata*, women of enemy cities bring an end to a stupid war by refusing to have sex with their husbands until a peace agreement is signed. Above all else, Aristophanes was a social critic, who routinely savaged the powerful political figures whom he believed (with justice) were leading Athens to its doom. He was repeatedly dragged into court to defend him-

Greek Theater in Epidauros. Greek dramas were invariably presented in the open air. The construction of this theater, which takes advantage of the slope of the hill, and the arrangement of the stage are of particular interest. The plan for the theater is shown above.

self against the politicians whom he had attacked. But despite their anger, the politicians never dared to shut down the comedic theater for long. It was too much a part of the spirit of democratic Athens.

Periclean Athens also proved fertile ground for the development of Greek prose. Through the sixth century, Greeks typically expressed philosophical or political ideas through poetry. In the fifth century, however, perhaps reflecting the increasing functional literacy of the Athenians, prose emerged as a distinct literary form. Herodotus found a ready market for his "inquiries" (*historiai*) in Athens. His younger contemporary Thucydides (c. 460–c. 400 B.C.E.) wrote a masterful history of the great war between Athens and Sparta at the end of the fifth century. Between them, these two historians developed a new approach to history, emphasizing among other things the reliability of their sources and looking for credible cause-and-effect relationships in historical events. The development and elaboration of prose would make possible in the fourth century even further literary achievements, such as the great philosophical treatises of Plato and Aristotle and the stirring political and legal speeches of the great Attic orators we will meet in the next chapter.

ART AND ARCHITECTURE

The Greeks of the golden age showed a similar range of genius in the visual arts as they did in their drama. Their comic gift—exuberance, cheerful sensuality, and coarse wit—can be seen especially in their pottery. In "black figure" vases and jugs done throughout the Greek world in the sixth and fifth centuries B.C.E., the characters often look like grinning rascals up to some sort of mischief, usually sexual. More dignified were the marble statuary and sculptured reliefs the Greeks made for temples and public places. Here too Athens was preeminent. Athenian sculptors took human greatness as their theme, depicting the beauty of the human form in statuary that was simultaneously naturalistic and idealizing.

Perhaps the most striking development in fifth-century sculpture was the relatively sudden appearance of the well-proportioned, naturalistic nude. This happened first in Athens in the years around 490 to 480 B.C.E., not coincidentally the time of the Greek victory over Persia. Nothing like it had ever been seen, and it is difficult not to conclude that the triumph of Greek ideals of human dignity and freedom in the Persian War had something to do with it. Convinced that all Persians bowed down to their rulers like slaves,

Greek Sculptor at Work. The Greeks were not prudish.

whereas they themselves enjoyed political and social equality, the Greeks expressed their idea of human greatness by commemorating the dignity of the unadorned human body in stone.

The Athenians also made exceptional contributions to architecture. The "classic" Greek temple was not an Athenian invention; it emerged gradually throughout the Greek world during the sixth century. All Greek temples sought to create an impression of harmony and repose; but of all the Greek temples ever built, the Parthenon of Athens, constructed between 447 and 438 B.C.E., and decorated with statuary and reliefs by the sculptor Phidias, is generally considered the finest. It was a stunning achievement, expensive and difficult, urged on the Athenians by their visionary leader Pericles. Once completed, the Parthenon became a symbol of the Athenians' devotion to their patron goddess and a triumphant celebration of their power and confidence.

WOMEN AND MEN IN THE DAILY LIFE OF ATHENS

Toward the end of his stirring Funeral Oration, Pericles briefly addressed the married women in his audience and urged them to do three things: to rear more children for the sake of Athens; to show no more weakness than was "natural to their sex," and to avoid gossip. His remarks reveal widely held male attitudes toward women in classical Greece.

HOW WAS THE FABRIC OF SOCIETY CHANGED DURING THE GOLDEN AGE OF CLASSICAL GREECE?

THE GOLDEN AGE OF CLASSICAL GREECE   141

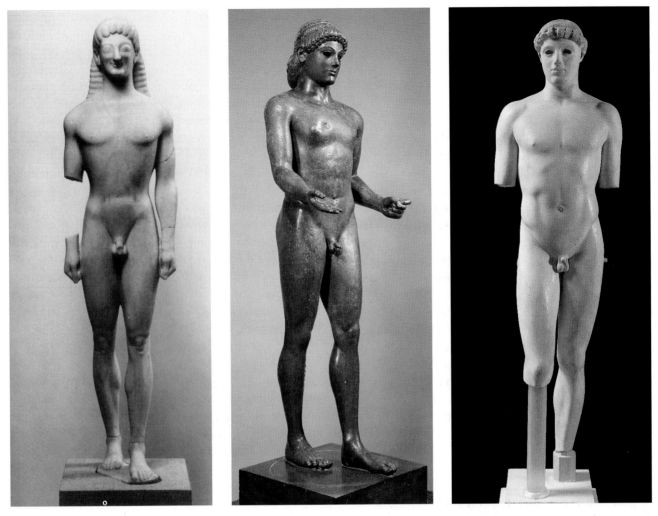

Apollo of Tenea; Apollo of Piombino; "The Critian Boy." These three statues, dating from about 560, 500, and 480 B.C.E. respectively, display the progressive "unfreezing" of Greek statuary art. The first stiff and symmetrical statue is imitative of Egyptian sculpture (see statue of the pharaoh Menkaure, p. 41). Roughly half a century later it is succeeded by a figure that begins to display motion, as if awakening from a sleep of centuries in a fairy tale. The last figure introduces genuine naturalism in its delicate twists and depiction of the subject's weight resting on one leg.

Rather than leading to greater equality among the sexes, the growth of Greek democracy had the opposite result. In the aristocratic society of the Dark Age women were sometimes portrayed as possessing extraordinary traits of beauty, wisdom, or courage. The Trojan War was allegedly fought over Helen, the wise Andromache offered shrewd military advice to her husband, and Penelope exhibited heroic courage and fidelity waiting for Odysseus to return. Such women, while still clearly subordinate, did not exist entirely in the shadows.

But as aristocratic ideals gave way to more democratic ones throughout Greece, life in the shadows increasingly became women's lot. In Athens, an emphasis on the infantry and its spirit of equality encouraged training together and developing close relationships, often of a homosexual nature and perhaps reflective of the older, heroic ideal of the aristocratic age. In addition, the ostentation of individual aristocratic women was discouraged, and the rearing of children to supply the infantry became an imperative. Public spaces were located in towns for "male activities" such as athletics and political gatherings, and private spaces were delimited for female activities such as child rearing and weaving. "Respectable" women lived in seclusion.

Girls could be married at age fourteen—as soon as they were biologically ready for childbearing—to husbands twice their age (younger men were supposed to dedicate themselves more fully to war). A girl's father arranged her marriage without concern for his daugh-

Flute Player. An Athenian marble relief dating from about 470 B.C.E. The relaxed pose (reclining position, crossed legs) and naturalistic representation of the naked female form were unprecedented in human art before the classical age of the Greeks.

ter's preferences and provided her with a dowry that her husband was expected to use for her support. Legally, wives became the property of their husbands. Shortly after a wife entered her new home, a regular schedule of childbearing began. Typically the interval between births was between two and four years, meaning that the average young wife would have borne between four and six children before she died, usually around the age of thirty-five.

Women seldom went out of doors, because it was thought immodest for them to be seen by other men except at public festivals. At home, women were expected to prepare and weave cloth. Since the ideology of democratic Athens opposed excessive displays of wealth or leisure, women were not supposed to sit around idly; but since "women's work" was basically menial, men looked down on women for engaging in it. Available evidence suggests that husbands customarily had little emotional attachment to their wives, regarding them as natural inferiors. In a revealing passage Herodotus says of a certain Lydian king, "this

Candaules fell in love with his own wife, a fancy that had strange consequences. . . ." Athenian men of the fifth and fourth centuries B.C.E. tended to idealize male homosexual relationships, since men were considered superior to women. Athenian men did seek heterosexual physical pleasure also, but for sexual gratification a man could rely on household slaves or prostitutes. As an Athenian orator remarked, "prostitutes we have for pleasure, concubines for daily physical attendance, wives to bear us legitimate children and be our faithful housekeepers."

Athenian society was as dependent on slavery as the Spartans were on their helots. None of the extraordinary Athenian accomplishments in politics, thought, or art would have been possible had slaves not done the heavy labor while free men debated in assemblies or discussed the true and the beautiful at symposia. There is, indeed, a direct relationship between the rise of democratic government in Greece, especially in Athens, and the increasing prevalence of slavery in Greek society. The Athenian ideal of dividing and rotating governmental duties among all free men depended on the assumption that slaves would be widely available to work in fields, businesses, and homes while free men engaged in politics. In fact, the Athenian democratic system began to function fully only with the expansion of Athenian mining and commerce around 500 B.C.E. Whereas previously the supply of slaves had been limited to war captives, their new wealth now enabled the Athenians to buy slaves from the north and east in vastly larger numbers.

Although widespread, Athenian slavery was small in scale. The only exception was in the state-owned silver mines, where large numbers of slaves toiled in miserable conditions. Otherwise, slaves were distributed in small numbers among Athenian families, rather than working in large teams on plantations or in industries. Typically every family would own a slave or two to perform its hardest and most menial work, tilling the soil or doing the laundry. In such circumstances slaves seldom suffered cruel treatment, although their masters were free to inflict beatings. The very notion that slaves were not entirely human, made it easier for Athenian free men to assume that nature had chosen some for servile labor, and others, like themselves, for political life.

For the male citizen or resident alien, however, daily life in Periclean Athens had numerous attractions. Male citizens enjoyed considerable social and economic equality. Small-scale farming and commerce were the norms, and what little industry existed—pottery and

Women Processing in the Panathenaea, c. 447–438 B.C.E. This image shows a portion of a sculptural frieze from the Parthenon in Athens. Every four years, this annual religious procession in honor of Athena would be celebrated in a particularly elaborate manner. This procession was one of the few public occasions on which respectable Athenian women were permitted to appear in public.

armaments manufacture—was also limited in scale, being carried on in shops owned by individual artisans who produced their own wares. Factories employing large numbers of workers were rare but on the rise: one of the largest in fifth-century Athens, a shield factory, was staffed by 120 workers and owned by a resident alien. Some citizens were of course richer than others, but the richest were required to donate some of their wealth to support public festivals or equip the navy. Athens in the fifth century was an exciting, bustling, cosmopolitan center of commerce and culture.

LEAGUE BUILDING AND THE PELOPONNESIAN WAR

How did the Peloponnesian War influence Greek philosophy?

Athenians saw themselves as the freest of men, but their freedom rested on the servitude of others. Slaves performed much of the labor at home, while Athens' allies in the Delian League provided the resources that underlay Athenian greatness. During the 450s, the Athenians gained sole control over league policy and

the management of its funds, both of which the Athenian assembly determined under the guidance of Pericles. Without the surplus wealth flowing into Athens from the League, none of the projects which Pericles undertook—pay for political participation, the glorification of the Athenian democracy through great buildings (also, incidentally, an employment program for poorer citizens), the patronage of Athenian drama— would have been possible. All of this made Athens powerful and its democracy vibrant, and kept Pericles popular and in power. But Athens' democratic achievements rested upon her control over an alliance she had transformed into an empire.

Since the 470s, Athens had faced attempts by its allies to break away, and it had crushed those efforts ruthlessly. Through the 450s, such revolts were rare. But in the early 440s, Pericles determined on a more aggressive policy toward Sparta, by then Athens' only real rival for supremacy in the Greek world. To give himself a freer hand, he concluded a formal peace with Persia. After this peace, the purpose of the Delian League evaporated, and Athens had no justification for compelling its allies to remain within it. Many remained loyal nonetheless, paying their contributions and enjoying the economic benefits of warm relations with Athens. Others, however, did not, and Athens found itself increasingly forcing its allies back into line, often installing Athenian garrisons and planting

GREECE DURING THE PELOPONNESIAN WAR

Consider that Macedonia and Thessaly were still rather backward by Greek standards, and then examine the pattern of Athenian and Spartan alliances. Why would Pericles have urged his fellow Athenians to abandon the land to Sparta and concentrate their own military efforts on the sea? How did the strength of Athens' navy present special problems for the Spartans? Consider that Athens relied for a great proportion of its grain supply on shipments from the Black Sea. How did the geography of the northeastern Aegean make Athens particularly vulnerable? What political consequences might there have been in Athens due to the great reliance placed on the lower-income rowers in the war fleet?

Athenian colonists—who retained their Athenian citizenship—to ensure future loyalty.

In the context of Greek culture, such behavior was disturbing. The Athenians had anchored the Delian League to preserve Greek independence against the Persians. Now many Greeks accused Athens of having become a tyrannical empire itself. Foremost among the accusers were the Corinthians, whose own economic standing was seriously threatened by Athenian dominance of the Aegean. The Corinthians were close allies of the Spartans, the central power of what historians call the "Peloponnesian League" (the Greeks called it simply "the Spartans and their allies"). When war finally erupted between Athens and Sparta, the great historian Thucydides ascribed it to the growing power of Athens, and the fear and envy this inspired in Sparta. No modern historian has improved upon Thucydides' formulation. For the Athenian democracy and its leader, there could be no question of relinquishing their empire, the cornerstone of their cultural and political ascendancy. By the 430s, however, Athens could not preserve that empire without threatening the interests of Sparta and her allies.

THE PELOPONNESIAN WAR ERUPTS

After a series of provocations, the Athenians and Spartans found themselves at war with one another in 431 B.C.E. Athens could not defeat Sparta on land; but neither Sparta nor her allies had a fleet capable of facing the Athenians on the seas. Pericles therefore developed a bold strategy: to pull the entire population of Attica within the walls of Athens and its harbor, abandoning the countryside to Sparta. In the meantime, the superior Athenian fleet would supply Athens from the sea and ravage the coasts of Spartan territory. As with many of history's pivotal contests, both sides believed a conclusion would come quickly. Instead, the war dragged on for twenty-seven years.

The Spartans plundered the farms and pastures of Attica, frustrated that the Athenians would not send their hoplites out for a decisive battle. Meanwhile, the Athenians inflicted significant destruction on Spartan territory in a series of lightning raids, while at the same time successfully encouraging revolt among the helots. Time appeared to be on Athens' side, but in 429 B.C.E. the crowded conditions of the besieged city gave rise to an epidemic that claimed over a third of the Athenian population, including Pericles. Events after his death revealed that Pericles was the only man capable of managing the democratic political forces he had unleashed. His successors were mostly demogogues, ambitious men who played to the worst instincts of the demos in order to gain power for themselves. The most successful of these was a warmonger named Cleon, a particular target of Aristophanes' invective, who refused a Spartan offer of peace in 425 B.C.E. and continued the war until his own death in battle four years later.

A short-lived truce ensued, authored by an able Athenian leader named Nicias. But the Athenian demos was not in the mood for peace for very long, and ultimately fell under the spell of a charming but unscrupulous aristocrat named Alcibiades. A flamboyant adventurer and ne'er-do-well, Alcibiades convinced the Athenians in 415 B.C.E. to reopen hostilities with an ill-advised attack on the distant city of Syracuse in Sicily. Because of his own personal political problems, he did not lead the expedition; instead, the task fell to Nicias and Demosthenes, an accomplished general who, like Nicias, had opposed the venture. The expedition immediately ran into trouble and ultimately failed, with thousands of Athenians killed or falling into slavery.

News of the Syracusan disaster shattered the Athenian demos. Recriminations began immediately. Many politicians were driven from the polis, and in 411 B.C.E. the demos suffered a momentary but monumental lack of self-confidence. While many of the rowers in the fleet were away, the Athenians essentially voted the democracy out of existence, replacing it with a narrow oligarchy of four hundred citizens. The Athenian fleet, stationed in Samos, replied by reestablishing a democratic government in exile under the leadership of none other than Alcibiades. The oligarchy proved to be short lived, and democracy was restored to Athens by 409. But the fact that the war could force such desperation did not bode well for the future.

THE END OF THE WAR

The Spartans too despaired of bringing the war to an end. Despite Athens' problems, its fleet was still invincible. Sparta, a nation with no seafaring tradition to speak of and, thanks to its social system, notoriously short on cash, turned to the one power ready and willing to stir up trouble in the Greek world. The Persians supplied the gold and expertise necessary for the Spartans to take to the sea and try to beat the Athenians at their own game. By 407, a talented and ambitious Spartan commander, Lysander, was harrying the Athenians throughout the eastern Aegean.

Perhaps the most disturbing development of the closing years of the war was the self-destructive passion with which the Athenians now began to turn against each other. To take but one example: in 406, the Athenians won a key victory in the Aegean at Arginusae. After the engagement, a storm came up, preventing the Athenian commanders from rescuing those

> Time appeared to be on Athens' side, but in 429 B.C.E. the crowded conditions of the besieged city gave rise to an epidemic that claimed over a third of the Athenian population, including Pericles.

A Modern Replica of an Athenian Trireme. These versatile warships were powered by both oars and sail.

sailors whose ships had been wrecked in the course of battle. When the sailors drowned, a firestorm of protest erupted in Athens, fanned by demagogues who secured through show trials the execution of those generals foolish enough to return to Athens. One of them was Pericles, the son of Pericles, who thus became a victim of the democracy his father had brought into being. Through such measures, the Athenians managed either to kill or drive into exile their most experienced and able commanders.

The result, in hindsight at least, was predictable. Lysander destroyed the poorly led Athenian fleet in 404 B.C.E. Without their fleet the Athenians could neither feed themselves nor defend their city. Lysander sailed around the Aegean unopposed, installing pro-Spartan oligarchies among the former allies of Athens. Finally, he besieged Athens itself. Facing the inevitable, the Athenians surrendered. Corinth and Thebes called for Athens' utter destruction. The Spartans declined, to their credit, but imposed harsh terms on the Athenians: the dismantling of their walls, the scrapping of their fleet, and the acceptance of an oligarchic government of thirty Athenians.

The war's postscript was grim, even for the victors. In Athens, the so-called Thirty Tyrants confiscated property and murdered over fifteen hundred of their political opponents in the roughly eighteen months of their rule. Their excesses drove committed demo-crats to desperate resistance; a bloodbath was averted only through the reasoned intervention of the Spartan king Pausanias. By the end of 401, Athens was once again a democracy, but more moderate in its behavior than during the war—although, as we will see, it still had one last act of brutality and shortsightedness to perform.

The Spartans now succeeded to the Athenians' unenviable role as the protector of the Greeks against the Persians. It was a thankless job, made worse by the losses Sparta itself had suffered during the war, and by the fact that the Spartans were far more heavy-handed in their control of the Aegean than the Athenians had been. The Spartans now found themselves in a position they had avoided throughout their history, as their far-flung imperial interests sapped their manpower and undermined their control over the helots. They also faced a reinvigorated Persian empire, which had benefited from the Greeks' fratricidal struggles. Within a decade of the Peloponnesian War's end, Sparta found itself opposed by four poleis whose ancient hatreds for each other were legendary—Athens, Argos, Thebes, and Corinth. Their cooperation speaks volumes about how unpopular Spartan preeminence had become in just a few short years.

For the Greeks, the Peloponnesian War was a disaster. From the long perspective of historical distance, we may view it as demonstrating the limitations of the

CHRONOLOGY

EVOLUTION OF PHILOSOPHICAL THOUGHT IN ARCHAIC GREECE

Emergence of the "Milesian School" (pre-Socratics)	600–500 B.C.E.
Pythagoreans emerge in southern Italy	530 B.C.E.
Rise of the Sophists	450 B.C.E.
Death of Socrates	399 B.C.E.

polis system. The competitive ethos that characterized the Greek poleis had proved to be their tragic flaw. To the Greeks themselves, however, the war offered no such clear lessons. Instead, it brought demoralization and a questioning of all the old certainties. Democracies had collapsed, empires had crumbled, and aristocracies such as Sparta had proven themselves incapable of rising to the challenges they now confronted. Even the gods seemed to be in disarray. These were the circumstances in which the great Athenian philosopher Socrates (469–399 B.C.E.) attempted to refound ethical and political life on new and more certain foundations. To understand his accomplishments, however, we must trace briefly the history of philosophical speculation in the half century before his birth.

The competitive ethos that characterized the Greek poleis proved to be their tragic flaw.

THE PYTHAGOREANS AND THE SOPHISTS

After the Persian conquest of Asia Minor, many of the Milesian philosophers fled to Sicily and southern Italy. Philosophical speculation thus continued in the Greek "far west," but it was now tinged with a pessimism and religious coloration that reflected Greek distress over the loss of freedom. Typifying this reaction was Pythagoras, a thinker who migrated around 530 B.C.E. from the island of Samos to southern Italy, where he founded a sect—half philosophical, half mystical—in the city of Croton. Pythagoras and his followers regarded the speculative life as the highest good, but they believed that in order to pursue it, one must be purified of desires of the flesh. They believed that the essence of things was not matter but number, and so they concentrated on the study of mathematics and musical theory, discovering harmonies and dividing numbers into categories such as odd and even. Pythagoreans also proved an old Babylonian assumption, preserved for us as the "Pythagorean theorem"— that the square of the hypotenuse of any right-angled triangle is equal to the sum of the squares of the other two sides. Thus, even though the Pythagoreans turned away from the material world, they still exhibited the characteristic Greek quest for regularity and predictability in that world.

Victory in the Persian War enabled the Greeks to overcome the failure of nerve exemplified by the Pythagoreans. Above all in Athens, the increasing power of the individual citizen motivated inquiry into how the individual might best act in the here and now. Around 450 B.C.E., to fulfill the demand to cultivate such worldly wisdom, teachers emerged who were called "Sophists," a term simply meaning "those who are wise." Unlike the Milesians or the Pythagoreans, the Sophists were professional teachers, the first in the history of the West who made a living from selling their knowledge. Because they were later opposed by Socrates and Plato, the term "Sophist" became one of abuse, meaning someone who deviously employs false reasoning, and their entire movement acquired a poor reputation. But modern research has shown that the Sophists were often impressive thinkers and educators.

The Sophists were not a coherent philosophical school. But their work displayed certain common threads, as shown by that of Protagoras, active in Athens from about 445 to 420 B.C.E. and the most prototypic of the intellectually ambitious Sophists. His famous dictum, "man is the measure of all things," meant that goodness, truth, and justice are relative to the needs and interests of human beings. In religious matters Protagoras was agnostic, declaring that he did not know whether the gods existed or what they did, "for there are many hindrances to such knowledge—the obscurity of the subject and the brevity of life." Since he knew nothing of the gods, he concluded that there could be no absolute truths or eternal standards of right. If sense perception was the only source of knowledge, there could be only particular truths valid for the individual knower.

Such teachings struck many Athenians as corrosive of social cohesion. Sophists were courageous in calling

TWO VIEWS OF SOPHISM

SOCRATES AS A SOPHIST

The image of Socrates held by most people is of the sage thinker who challenged the prevailing prejudices of his day and opposed the Sophists. During his own time, however, he was not so universally admired. In his comedy The Clouds, *Aristophanes' protagonist Strepsiades—ruined by the wastefulness of his son—goes to Socrates and his "Thought Shop" so that Socrates can make him and his son Pheidippides orators capable of winning lawsuits and thus enriching himself. Aristophanes implies throughout that Socrates is essentially just another Sophist, a man who teaches word games and logic tricks for hire.*

STREPSIADES: See that he [Pheidippides] learns your two Arguments, whatever you call them—oh yes, Right and Wrong—the one that takes a bad case and defeats Right with it. If he can't manage both, then at least Wrong—that will do—but that he must have.

SOCRATES: Well, I'll go and send the Arguments here in person, and they'll teach him themselves.

STREPSIADES: Don't forget, he's got to be able to argue against any kind of justified claim at all.

RIGHT: This way, Let the audience see you. . . .

WRONG: Sure, go wherever you like. The more of an audience we have, the more soundly I'll trounce you.

RIGHT: What sort of trick will you use?

WRONG: Oh, just a few new ideas.

RIGHT: Yes, they're in fashion now, aren't they, [to the audience] thanks to you idiots. . . . [to Pheiddipides] You don't want to be the sort of chap who's always in the agora telling stories about other people's sex lives, or in the courts arguing about some petty, filthy, little dispute. . . .

WRONG: People here at the Thought Shop call me Wrong, because I was the one who invented ways of proving anything wrong, laws, prosecutors, anything. Isn't that worth millions—to have a really bad case and yet win? . . . Suppose you fall in love with a married woman—have a bit of fun—and get caught in the act. As you are now, without a tongue in your head, you're done for. But if you come and learn from me, then you can do whatever you like and get away with it . . . and supposing you do get caught with someone's wife, you can say to him. . . . "What have I done wrong? Look at Zeus; wasn't he always a slave of his sexual passions? And do you expect a mere mortal like me to do any better than a god?" . . .

STREPSIADES [to Socrates]: I wonder if you'd accept a token of my appreciation? But my son, has he learned that Argument we were listening to a moment ago?

SOCRATES: Yes, he has.

STREPSIADES: Holy Fraud, how wonderful!

SOCRATES: Yes, you'll now be able to win any case at all.

STREPSIADES: Even if the witnesses were actually there when I was borrowing the money?

SOCRATES: Even if there were a thousand of them.

Aristophanes, *The Clouds*, based on the translation by Alan H. Sommerstein. (New York: Penguin, 1973), pp. 148–150, 154, 159–160.

SOPHISTRY IN ACTION: THE MELIAN DIALOGUE

During the truce authored by the Athenian statesman Nicias in 421 B.C.E., both Athens and Sparta continued to pursue a "dirty war," living by the letter of their agreement but not its spirit, while preparing for the inevitable reopening of the conflict. The Aegean island of Melos—originally a Spartan colony—had so far maintained a policy of neutrality between Athens and Sparta. In 416, however, the Athenians insisted on their submission, and the Athenian envoys justified their position with a chillingly logical argument that "might makes right."

ATHENIANS: For ourselves, we will not trouble you with specious pretenses—either of how we have a right to our empire because we overthrew the Mede, or are now attacking you because of wrong that you have done us—and make a long speech which would not be believed; and in return we hope that you, instead of thinking to influence us by saying that you did not join the Spartans, although their colonists, or that you have done us no wrong, will aim at what is feasible, holding in view the real sentiments of us both; since you know as well as we do that right, as the world goes, is only in question between equals in power, while the strong do what they can and the weak suffer what they must. . . . We would desire to exercise empire over you without trouble, and see you preserved for the good of us both.

MELIANS: And how, pray, could it turn out as good for us to serve as for you to rule?

ATHENIANS: Because you would have the advantage of submitting before suffering the worst, and we should gain by not destroying you.

MELIANS: So you would not consent to our being neutral, friends instead of enemies, but allies of neither side?

ATHENIANS: ' No; for your hostility cannot so much hurt us as your friendship will be an argument to our subjects of our weakness, and your enmity of our power.

MELIANS: Is that your subjects' idea of equity, to put those who have nothing to do with you in the same category with peoples that are most of them your own colonists, and some conquered rebels?

ATHENIANS: As far as right goes they think one has as much of it as the other, and that if they maintain their independence it is because they are strong, and that if we do not molest them it is because we are afraid; so that besides extending our empire we should gain in security by your subjection. . . .

MELIANS: What is this but to make greater the enemies that you have already, and to force others to become so who would otherwise have never thought of it? . . . we know that the fortune of war is sometimes more impartial than the disproportion of numbers might lead one to suppose; to submit is to give ourselves over to despair, while action still preserves for us a hope that we may stand. . . .

ATHENIANS: Hope . . . may be indulged in by those who have abundant resources, if not without loss, at all events without ruin; but its nature is to be extravagant, and those who go so far as to stake their all upon the venture see it in its true colors only when they are ruined. . . . Let not this be the case with you, who are weak and hang on a single turn of the scale; nor be like the vulgar, who, when abandoning such security as human means may still afford, when visible hopes fail them in extremity, turn to the invisible, to prophecies and oracles, and other such inventions that delude men with hopes to their destruction. . . . When we come to your notion about the Spartans, which leads you to believe that shame will make them help you, here we bless your simplicity but do not envy your folly. . . . You do not adopt the view that expediency goes with security, while justice and honor cannot be followed without danger; and danger the Spartans generally court as little as possible. . . . Is it likely that while we are masters of the sea they will cross over to an island?

MELIANS: Should the Spartans miscarry in this, they would fall upon your land, and upon those left of your allies . . . and instead of places which are not yours, you will have to fight for your own country and your own confederacy.

ATHENIANS: Some diversion of the kind you speak of you may one day experience, only to learn, as others have done, that the Athenians never once yet withdrew from a siege for fear of any. . . . Think over the matter, therefore, and reflect once and again that it is for your country that you are consulting, and that upon this one deliberation depends its prosperity or ruin.

Thucydides, Book 5. *The Landmark Thucydides*, edited by Robert Strassler. (New York: Landmark Press, 1995), pp. 352–356.

Socrates. According to Plato, Socrates looked like a goatman but spoke like a god.

THE LIFE AND THOUGHT OF SOCRATES

Socrates drew on sufficient income so that he never had to teach for a living. Having twice fought in the Athenian infantry, he was an ardent patriot who believed Athens was being corrupted by the shameful doctrines of the Sophists. Yet far from being an unthinking cherisher of slogans, he wished to submit every slogan to rigorous questioning in order to erect the life of the Athenian state on the firm basis of ethical certainties. It is bitterly ironic that such a dedicated idealist should have been put to death by his own countrymen. Shortly after the end of the Peloponnesian War, in 399 B.C.E., while Athens was recovering from the shock of defeat and violent internal upheavals, a democratic faction determined that Socrates was a threat to the state. A jury court agreed, condemning him to death on a charge of impiety and "corrupting the youth." Although his friends made arrangements for him to flee, Socrates decided to accept the popular judgment and abide by the laws of his polis. He died by calmly taking a cup of poison.

Because Socrates wrote nothing himself, it is difficult to determine exactly what he taught. Contemporary reports, however, especially by his student Plato, make a few points clear. First, Socrates wished to subject all inherited assumptions to reexamination. In his view the complacent people who thought they knew everything really knew nothing. Styling himself a "gadfly," he continually engaged such people in conversation and managed to show them by "Socratic" questioning that all their supposed certainties were nothing more than unthinking prejudices resting on false assumptions. According to Plato, an oracle once said that Socrates was the wisest person in the world and Socrates agreed: everyone else thought he knew something, but he was wiser because he knew he knew nothing. Second, he wished to base his philosophical speculations on sound definitions of words. Third, he wished to advance to a new system of truth by examining ethics rather than by studying the physical world. He shunned discussions of why things exist, why they grow, and why they perish, urging people instead to reflect on principles of conduct both for their own sake and for that of society. One should think of the meaning of one's life and actions at all times, for according to one of his most memorable

assumptions into doubt and encouraging Athenians to examine each new situation on its own terms and merits; everyday life became for the first time the subject of systematic discussion. Yet the relativism of Sophists such as Protagoras could easily degenerate into the doctrine that the wise man is the one who knows best how to manipulate others and gratify his own desires, and so could be used to rationalize monstrous acts of brutality. To some critics, such ideas were antidemocratic; to others, they smacked of atheism and anarchy. If there was no final truth, and if goodness and justice were merely relative to the whims of the individual, then religion, morality, the state, and society itself could not be maintained. This conviction led to the growth of a new philosophical movement grounded on the theory that truth is real and that absolute standards do exist. The initiator of this new trend was Socrates.

> Sophists were courageous in calling assumptions into doubt and encouraging Athenians to examine each new situation on its own terms and merits; everyday life became for the first time the subject of systematic discussion.

sayings, "the unexamined life is not worth living."

So far, Socrates might seem rather like a Sophist; indeed, he felt compelled at his trial to insist that he was not. Together with the Sophists, he was a "philosopher of the marketplace" who held tradition and cliché up to doubt, and like them he treated daily affairs in order to help people improve their lives. The overwhelming difference between Socrates and the Sophists lay in Socrates' belief in certainties—even if he avoided saying what they were—and in the standard of absolute good rather than expediency he applied to all aspects of life. To reestablish the polis, however, it would be necessary to go further and construct a system that offered a positive framework of truth and reality. This was the task that would be attempted in the next century

Socrates Gaining Wisdom from the Wise Woman Diotima. In Plato's *Symposium* Socrates learns the philosophical meaning of love from Diotima, an ethereal female being, wiser than he. In this sculptural representation of the scene the winged figure between Diotima and Socrates is probably a personification of love itself.

by Socrates' most brilliant student, Plato, in the wake of the disasters of the Peleponnesian War. In so doing, he would lay the groundwork for all Western philosophical thinking up to the present day.

CONCLUSION

Ever since the Renaissance, Western Europeans have liked to think of themselves as the heirs of the classical Greeks, and to imagine the Greeks as mirror images of themselves. Such uncritical admiration is misleading, both about the Greeks and ourselves. Despite the religious skepticism of a few intellectuals, the Greeks were neither secularists nor rationalists. Although they invented the concept of democracy, only a small percentage even of the male population of Athens was ever permitted to play a role in political affairs. The Spartans kept the mass of their population in serflike subjection, and the Athenians took slavery for granted, subjecting slaves who toiled in the mines to the most brutal treatment. Women throughout the

Greek world were exploited by what today would be called a "patriarchy"—a repressive system managed by fathers and husbands. Greek statecraft was characterized by imperialism and aggressive war. The Greeks made no great advances in economic enterprise, and they scorned commerce. Finally, not even the Athenians could be described as tolerant. Socrates was not the only man put to death merely for expressing his opinions.

And yet the profound significance of the Greek experiment for the history of the civilizations of the West is undeniable. This significance can be seen with particular clarity if we compare Greek cultural traits with those of Mesopotamia and ancient Egypt. Mesopotamian and Egyptian civilizations were dominated by autocracy, supernaturalism, and the subjection of the individual to the group. The typical political regime of the ancient Near Eastern world was that of an absolute monarch supported by a powerful priesthood. Culture served mainly as an instrument to enhance the prestige of rulers and priests, and economic life tended to be controlled by powerfully organized governmental and religious bodies.

In contrast, the civilization of Greece, notably in its Athenian form, was founded upon ideals of freedom, competition, individual achievement, and human glory. The Greek word for freedom—*eleutheria*—cannot be translated into any ancient Near Eastern language, not even Hebrew. The culture of the Greeks was the first in the West to be based on the primacy of the human intellect; there was no subject they feared to investigate. As Herodotus has a Greek (in this case a Spartan) say to a Persian, "You understand how to be a slave, but you know nothing of freedom. . . . If you had but tasted it you would counsel us to fight for it not only with spears but with axes."

Another way of appreciating the enduring importance of Greek civilization to the Western world is to recall some of the words that come to us from this civilization: politics, democracy, philosophy, metaphysics, history, tragedy. These are all ways of thinking and acting that have helped enrich human life immeasurably and that had hardly been known before the Greeks invented them. To a startling degree the Western concept of "humanity" itself—the exalted role within nature of the human race in general and the individual human in particular—comes to us from the Greeks. For the Greeks, the aim of existence was the fullest development of one's human potential: the work of becoming a person, called in Greek *paideia*, meant that every free man was supposed to be the sculptor of his or her own statue. When the Romans took up this ideal from the Greeks, they called it *humanitas*, from which we derive the English word "humanity." The Romans admitted their indebtedness when they remarked that "Greece was where humanity was invented." It is hard to doubt that they were right.

SELECTED READINGS

Penguin Classics and the Loeb Classical Library both offer reliable translations of Greek literary, philosophical, and historical texts.

Andrewes, Antony. *The Greek Tyrants.* London, 1974. Originally published in 1956, this work remains the standard treatment of its subject.

Boardman, John, Jaspar Griffin, and Oswyn Murray, eds. *Greece and the Hellenistic World.* Oxford, 1988. A reprint of the Greek and Hellenistic chapters from *The Oxford History of the Classical World,* originally published in 1986. Excellent, stimulating surveys, accessible to a general audience but provocative to specialists.

Brunschwig, Jacques, and Geoffrey E. R. Lloyd. *Greek Thought: A Guide to Classical Knowledge.* Trans. Catherine Porter. Cambridge, Mass., 2000. An outstanding, up-to-date work of reference.

Buckley, Terry, ed. *Aspects of Greek History, 750–323 B.C.: A Source-Based Approach.* London, 1999. An outstanding new collection of source materials.

Burkert, Walter. *Greek Religion.* Cambridge, Mass., 1985. Detailed and challenging, but fundamental for understanding the subject.

Cartledge, Paul A. *Sparta and Laconia: A Regional History, 1300–362 B.C.* London, 1979. The standard survey of Spartan history by the leading English-speaking authority.

Coldstream, J. N. *Geometric Greece.* New York, 1977. A thoroughgoing and illuminating discussion of Greek material culture in the late Dark Age.

Connor, W. Robert. *The New Politicians of Fifth-Century Athens.* Indianapolis, 1992. A ground-breaking discussion of how a new breed of politicians redefined Athenian democracy.

Donlan, Walter. *The Aristocratic Ideal and Selected Papers.* Wauconda, Ill., 1999. A reprint of Donlan's 1980 work, supplemented with a number of his scholarly articles, all emphasizing the central role played by elite status, power, and identity in Archaic Greece.

Dover, Kenneth J. *Greek Homosexuality.* Cambridge, Mass., 1978. The standard account of an important subject.

Fantham, Elaine, Helene Foley, Natalie Kampen, Sarah B. Pomeroy, and H. A. Shapiro. *Women in the Classical World: Image and Text.* Oxford, 1994. Wide-ranging analysis drawing on both visual and written sources, covering both the Greek and the Roman periods.

Finley, Moses I. *The World of Odysseus.* New York, 1979. A revised edition of the author's classic 1954 study, which forever changed the study of Dark Age Greece by demonstrating the historical nature of Homeric society.

Fornara, Charles W., and Loren J. Samons II. *Athens from Cleisthenes to Pericles.* Berkeley, 1991. An excellent narrative history of Athenian politics during the first half of the fifth century B.C.E.

Freeman, Charles. *The Greek Achievement: The Foundation of the Western World.* New York, 1999. An admiring survey written for a general audience.

Garlan, Yvon. *Slavery in Ancient Greece.* Ithaca, N.Y., 1988. Now the standard account.

Hanson, Victor Davis. *The Other Greeks: The Family Farm and the Agrarian Roots of Western Civilization.* New York, 1995. Occasionally polemical and idiosyncratic, but convincing in its emphasis on small-holding farmers as the backbone of Greek urban society.

Hodkinson, Stephen. *Property and Wealth in Classical Sparta.* London, 2001. A revisionist account that shows the Spartan economy to be much more like the economies of other Greek poleis than is often assumed.

Horden, Peregrine and Nicholas Purcell. *The Corrupting Sea: A Study of Mediterranean History.* Oxford, 2000. An immense and learned survey of the ecological history of the Mediterranean world from prehistory to the end of the Middle Ages.

Jones, Nicholas F. *Ancient Greece: State and Society.* Upper Saddle River, N.J., 1997. A concise survey from the Minoans up to the end of the classical period that emphasizes the connections between the social order and politics.

Levi, Peter. *Atlas of the Greek World.* New York, 1984. Excellent maps and illustrations supplement an outstanding text.

Morris, Ian, and Barry Powell, eds. *A New Companion to Homer.* Leiden, 1997. A collection of thirty specialist but accessible scholarly articles, encompassing the most recent research on Homer and Dark Age Greece.

Pomeroy, Sarah B., Stanley M. Burstein, Walter Donlan, and Jennifer Tolbert Roberts. *Ancient Greece: A Political, Social, and Cultural History.* Oxford, 1999. An outstanding new textbook: clear, lively, and up to date, with good bibliographies.

Price, Simon. *Religions of the Ancient Greeks.* Cambridge, 1999. Concise and authoritative, this survey extends from the archaic period up to the fifth century C.E.

Rowlandson, Jane, R. S. Bagnall, Alan Bowman, and Willy Clarysse, eds. *Women and Society in Greek and Roman Egypt: A Sourcebook.* Cambridge, 1999. A wide-ranging collection of sources from an extraordinarily well-documented area of the ancient world.

Snodgrass, Anthony. *The Dark Age of Greece: An Archaeological Survey of the Eleventh to the Eighth Centuries [B.C.E.].* Edinburgh, 1971. Still a valuable starting point.

———. *Archaic Greece: The Age of Experiment.* Berkeley, 1980. A seminal work that thoroughly revised earlier views of the period.

Strassler, Robert B., ed. *The Landmark Thucydides.* New York, 1996. A reprinting of the classic Richard Crawley translation, with maps, commentary, notes, and appendices by leading scholars.

Tandy, David W. *Warriors into Traders: The Power of the Market in Early Greece.* Berkeley, 1997. A revisionist examination of the impact of economic change on the cultural and political outlook of Greeks in the eighth and seventh centuries B.C.E.

Thomas, Carol G. and Craig Conant. *Citadel to City-State: The Transformation of Greece, 1200–700 B.C.E.* Bloomington, 1999. A lucid and accessible study that examines developments at a number of representative Dark Age sites.

CHAPTER FIVE

CHAPTER CONTENTS

THE EXPANSION OF GREECE

THE SUPREME TRAGEDY OF THE GREEKS was their failure to solve the problem of internecine political conflict. The fifth century in Greece had ended with a debilitating and destructive war of attrition between Athens and Sparta. The fourth century continued along much the same path, as the major poleis—Sparta, then Thebes, then Athens again—jockeyed for dominance within the Greek world. But the independent temper of Greek political life could not suffer such dominance for long; and so as each great polis appeared on the brink of realizing its goals, a coalition of age-old enemies would form to defeat it. Despite mounting calls for the Greeks to set aside their local differences and unite in a common cause, they could not escape their heritage of particularism.

Alongside the political difficulties, there were continuing social and economic problems. These stemmed from ideologically driven civil wars within the poleis as well as from the endemic warfare between them. Faith in the old ideals of equality decayed as a vast gulf opened up between the rich and the poor. Increasingly, the wealthy withdrew from politics altogether, while the number of free citizens declined as poverty-stricken freemen and freewomen descended into slavery. The result was despair and cynicism.

The age did not lack for creative energy. Philosophy, science, and literature blossomed in the fourth century, as men of talent shunned the vagaries of public life and devoted themselves instead to the life of the mind. As the polis system decayed, serious thinkers turned their attention to what the polis was, how and why it functioned, and how it might be improved. But even the greatest of these thinkers remained enclosed within the parochial world of the polis.

The unhappy equilibrium of the Greek world was shattered in the last half of the fourth century by the sudden emergence of the kingdom of Macedonia. The extraordinary conquests of Philip of Macedon unified Greece. Those of his son Alexander the Great extended Greek culture by force of arms from Egypt to Persia

FOCUS QUESTIONS

• What conditions led to the growing number of mercenaries in the fourth century B.C.E.?

• In his *Republic,* what prescriptions does Plato offer for the achievement of an ideal state?

• How did Philip II of Macedon strengthen his kingdom?

• What characteristics defined the three major Hellenistic kingdoms?

• Why was prosperity not more widespread in the Hellenistic economy?

• What was the relationship between Epicureanism and Stoicism?

• Why did Hellenistic architecture become grander?

• Why did science and medicine flourish in this period?

to the frontiers of India. Alexander's empire did not last. But the cosmopolitan, Greeklike (hence, *Hellenistic*, as opposed to *Hellenic*) culture to which it gave rise became the most powerful and pervasive cultural influence the Near Eastern world would know until the rise of Islam almost a thousand years later.

FAILURES OF THE FOURTH-CENTURY POLIS

What conditions led to the growing number of mercenaries in the fourth century B.C.E.?

There is little in the early fourth century B.C.E. to suggest that the greatest age of Greek cultural influence still lay ahead. The Peloponnesian War had left Sparta as the preeminent power in the Greek world, but the Spartans showed little talent for the position their unexpected victory had thrust upon them. At home, Spartan politicians remained deeply divided over the wisdom of committing Spartan force beyond their frontiers; while abroad, the Spartans showed even less restraint than had the Athenians in strong-arming their subject-allies. By 394, a significant portion of Greece had aligned itself against Sparta in the so-called Corinthian War (394–387 B.C.E.). The Spartans, for their part, could bring matters to a resolution only by forcing a peace on their fellow Greeks brokered from the outside—essentially composed and guaranteed by the Persians who had encouraged the conflict in the first place. This pattern was repeated time and again over the next fifty years, during which the advantage shifted steadily toward Persia.

THE STRUGGLE FOR HEGEMONY

The Spartans learned little from the resistance of their allies, hardly noticing that in the Corinthian War Athens had allied herself with one of Sparta's oldest allies (Corinth) and with one of her own ancient enemies (Thebes). After the Corinthian War, the Spartans did, however, occupy Thebes, placing a garrison there for four years. This was a grave and quite unjustified affront to the freedom of another great polis. After the Thebans regained their autonomy, they elected as their leader Epaminondas, a fierce patriot and a military genius. For decades, Greeks had been experimenting with the basic form of the hoplite phalanx, adding light skirmishers and archers to enhance its effectiveness. Epaminondas now went further. In imitation of the Spartan system, he formed an elite hoplite unit known as the "Theban Sacred Band," made up of one hundred fifty homosexual couples. Epaminondas also developed lighter-armed troops. By the early 370s he was ready for a trial of strength with the Spartans.

The Theban and Spartan armies met at Leuctra in the Theban territory of Boeotia in 371. Epaminondas eschewed convention, placing his very best troops (the Sacred Band) not on the right-hand side of his formation, but on the left. He stacked the left-hand side of his phalanx fifty rows deep, a surprise he disguised with a flurry of arrow and javelin attacks. When the two sides met, the weight of the Theban left smashed the Spartan right, and with its best troops overrun, the Spartan phalanx collapsed. A Spartan king was left dead on the field, and Epaminondas followed his victory by marching through Messenia and freeing the helots. Spartan power—and in a sense Spartan society—was at an end. Overnight, Epaminondas had reduced Sparta to a merely local force.

As Theban power grew, so did the suspicions of others. Although in 371 Athens had supported Thebes, when the Thebans and Spartans squared off again in 362 at Mantinea in the northern Peloponnesus, the Athenians allied themselves with the Spartans. Although the Theban army carried the day, Epaminondas fell in battle, and the Theban hegemony died with him. Athens attempted to fill the vacuum by establishing a naval confederacy, organized more equitably than the Delian League. But the Athenians quickly reverted to abusing their allies, and the naval confederacy dissolved in rebellions. Greece thus remained a constellation of petty warring states, all greatly weakened by their struggles with each other over the course of a century.

Within the poleis themselves there was also great turmoil. Although Athens was spared the political revolutions many other cities had suffered (mostly because the Thirty Tyrants had discredited the cause of "oligarchy" there), strife between democrats and oligarchs continued throughout the Greek world. Argos suffered through civil war and brutal reprisals, as did many of the states of the Aegean islands and Thessaly,

> The Spartans learned little from the resistance of their allies.

IN HIS *REPUBLIC*, WHAT DOES PLATO PRESCRIBE FOR THE ACHIEVEMENT OF AN IDEAL STATE?

THE CULTURAL AND INTELLECTUAL RESPONSE   157

in northern Greece. An abortive coup attempt was even uncovered at Sparta, plotted by a disenfranchised Spartiate who had hoped to rally the disaffected elements of Spartan society.

SOCIAL AND ECONOMIC CRISES

The incessant warfare, combined with internal political struggles, profoundly affected society and economy throughout the Greek world. Even wealthy cities like Athens and Sparta had exhausted themselves through their war efforts. Many personal fortunes had been lost, and many ordinary people had been driven from their homes or reduced to slavery. Country towns had been ravaged, some repeatedly, as had farmlands throughout Greece. The destruction of orchards and vineyards was particularly devastating, because of the long time it takes to nourish olive trees and grape vines to a productive state; but even arable land was now less productive than it had been earlier. As a result, standards of living declined significantly during the fourth century. Although prices rose in general around 50 percent (and some staples tripled and quadrupled in cost), wages remained more or less the same. Taxes increased, and in Athens the wealthy were required to employ their personal wealth to underwrite the construction of public theaters and buildings, the maintenance of warships, and the presentation of festivals. Even so, state treasuries were never again as flush as they had been in the fifth century, and the kind of ambitious public spending undertaken by the tyrants or Pericles was unknown in the fourth-century polis.

Unemployment was widespread, and so many Greek men turned to the one profession where work was almost always available—mercenary service. The Greek states of Sicily and Italy hired mercenaries from the mainland, as did Sparta to supplement her own campaigns in Asia Minor. A pretender to the Persian throne even hired a mostly Greek mercenary army in an attempt to overthrow his older brother, the reigning king. These Greeks fought their way into the heart of the Persian empire, and when the pretender fell in battle, the ten thousand Greek mercenaries fought their way back out. It was a stunning demonstration of what even a smallish Greek army might accomplish on Persian soil. Long-term mercenary service abroad was disruptive to the household-based culture of many Greek poleis, and when mercenaries could not find work abroad, they were likely to terrorize the local Greek countryside. Such depredations only added to the disastrous cycle of destruction, inflation, and overpopulation caused by land failure.

THE CULTURAL AND INTELLECTUAL RESPONSE

In his *Republic,* what does Plato prescribe for the achievement of an ideal state?

The breakdown of polis society during the fourth century had a profound impact on philosophy, the arts, and political thought. These developments laid the groundwork for the even more stunningly creative departures of the Hellenistic era. In the past, scholars have sometimes described these fourth-century cultural developments as if they represented a decline from the great artistic and intellectual achievements of the fifth century B.C.E. But such a sweeping verdict on fourth-century B.C.E. culture is unjustified. It diminishes not only the continuities between fifth- and fourth-century Greek culture, but also the originality and creativity of these new, fourth-century developments.

ART AND LITERATURE

Sculptors, for example, were already attempting to achieve a heightened sense of realism, especially in portraiture, when the fourth century B.C.E. began. Realism had been a hallmark of fifth-century art, but in the fourth century artists tried increasingly to render objects as they actually looked, rather than portraying them in an idealized, dignified form. Artists also paid

CHRONOLOGY

DECLINE OF THE GREEK POLIS

Sparta becomes leading Greek polis	404 B.C.E.
Prices rise by 50 percent throughout Greece	400–350 B.C.E.
Corinthian War	394–387 B.C.E.
Epaminondas defeats Spartans at Leuctra	371 B.C.E.

Left: **Hellenistic Aphrodite.** This figure, dating from the fourth century B.C.E., displays the Hellenistic fascination with ungainly, "unnatural" postures.
Right: **French Bather.** This statuette done by Edgar Degas around 1890 shows some evident continuities between Hellenistic and modern art.

more attention to life and movement, particularly in the flow and fold of the drapery that clothed human figures. All these sculptural trends would continue and intensify in the breathtaking and evocative works of the Hellenistic period.

Drama changed even more dramatically during the fourth century than did sculpture, although here the verdict of "decline" may have more justification. No fourth-century authors emerged to match the great tragedians of the Athenian golden age. Even fourth-century audiences seem to have preferred the fifth-century tragedies of Sophocles, Aeschylus, and Euripedes to the works of their own fourth-century contemporaries. Nor did the comic genius of Aristophanes have any true fourth-century successors. Even in his own lifetime, however, Aristophanes' biting, satirical style was beginning to give way to a milder, less provocative drama that bears some resemblance to modern television comedies. It was this new style that laid the groundwork for the "New Comedy" of the fourth and third centuries B.C.E.

Perhaps the most striking development in fourth-century drama is the flight from social and political commentary. The new comedies of the fourth century offer none of the scathing indictments of society in general and of prominent individuals in particular that Aristophanes had pioneered. Fourth-century audiences looked to drama and literature for diversion and escape; they no longer cared for brutal critiques of their society. Comedic humor was now based on mistaken identities, tangled familial relationships, comic misunderstandings, and breaches of etiquette. Hellenistic novels (a new literary genre that emerges by the end of the fourth century) are broadly similar in tone to the new comedies. Lovers face extraordinary obstacles, but their affairs almost always end happily, with the lovers themselves reunited after perilous adventures and a long separation.

The most famous comic poet of the age was Menander (342 B.C.E.?–292 B.C.E.), most of whose work survives only in fragments. To some modern critics, his comedies can seem contrived and artificial. To his contemporaries, however, and also to the Romans (who based their own comedic tradition on the works of

IN HIS *REPUBLIC*, WHAT DOES PLATO PRESCRIBE FOR THE ACHIEVEMENT OF AN IDEAL STATE?

THE CULTURAL AND INTELLECTUAL RESPONSE   159

Menander and his contemporaries), these frothy, light-hearted comedies of daily life had great appeal.

PHILOSOPHY AND POLITICAL THOUGHT IN THE AGE OF PLATO AND ARISTOTLE

The intellectual shift begun by Socrates was carried on brilliantly by his most talented student, Plato. Born in Athens to an aristocratic family around 429 B.C.E., Plato joined Socrates' circle as a young man and soon saw his mentor condemned to death. This experience made such an indelible impression on Plato that from then until his own death around 349 B.C.E. he shunned direct political involvement, seeking instead to vindicate Socrates by constructing a philosophical system based on Socratic precepts. Plato taught this system in Athens in an informal school (no buildings, tuition, or set curriculum) called the Academy, and also by writing a series of *dialogues* (treatises expressed in dramatic form) in which Socrates was the main speaker. The Platonic dialogues, among which some of the most important are the *Phaedo*, the *Symposium*, and the *Republic*, are enduring works of literature as well as the earliest surviving complete works of philosophy.

Plato was influenced by the two worlds in which he lived. As a young man, he had watched his teacher engage the relativism of the Sophists, and in his adult life he lived in a world of few apparent absolute truths and a remarkable amount of rapid and disturbing change. Plato understood that in order to combat skepticism and refute the Sophists he needed to provide a secure foundation for ethics. This he did by means of his doctrine of Ideas. He conceded that relativity and change are characteristics of the world we perceive with our senses, but he denied that this world is the entire universe. A higher, spiritual realm exists, composed of eternal forms or Ideas that only the mind can grasp. The Ideas are not mere abstractions but have a real existence. Each is the pattern of some class of objects, or relationships between objects, on earth. Thus there are Ideas of chair, tree, shape, color, proportion, beauty, and justice. Highest is the Idea of the Good, the cause and guiding principle of the universe. The things we perceive through our senses are merely imperfect copies of the supreme realities, the Ideas, and relate to them as shadows relate to material objects. By understanding and contemplating the Good, one might achieve the ultimate goal of fulfillment through virtue.

Understanding that a virtuous life would be difficult to attain in a society full of turbulence, Plato addressed himself to politics in his most famous dialogue, the *Republic*, the first systematic treatment of political philosophy ever written. Because Plato sought social harmony and order rather than liberty or equality, he argued for an elitist state in which most of the people—the farmers, artisans, and traders—would be governed by intellectually superior "guardians." The guardian class itself would be divided. All guardians would serve first as soldiers, living together without private property, but then those found to be the wisest would receive more education and ultimately become Plato's famous "philosopher-kings." In Plato's view neither wealth nor hereditary title equipped one properly to rule but only the greatest intelligence, enhanced by the best possible education. Once philosophers were in power they would always choose the wisest to succeed them and see to it that everyone in the state was subordinated to the Idea of the Good. Later commentators have usually

> Plato was influenced by the two worlds in which he lived.

Plato.

found this ideal of rule by the wisest to be seductive, but they ask of Plato, "Who will guard the guardians?" Plato's system presumed that properly educated rulers would never be corrupted by power or wealth—a proposition that has yet to be sustained in practice.

ARISTOTELIAN THOUGHT

Such practical considerations were typical of the thought of Plato's own greatest student, Aristotle (384–322 B.C.E.). Aristotle was the son of a physician and learned from his father the importance of carefully observing natural phenomena. He accepted Plato's assumption that there are some things only the mind can grasp, but his own philosophical system was based on his confidence that the human mind could understand the universe through the rational ordering of sense experience. In contrast to Plato, who taught that everything we see and touch is but an untrustworthy reflection of some intangible truth, Aristotle believed in the objective reality of material objects and taught that systematic investigation of tangible things, combined with rational inquiry into how they function, could yield full comprehension of the natural order and of human beings' place within it.

Aristotle surveyed a wide variety of subjects in numerous separate but interrelated treatises on logic, metaphysics, ethics, poetics, and politics. He was the earliest formal logician known to human history, and probably the greatest. He established rules for the syllogism, a form of reasoning in which certain premises inevitably lead to a valid conclusion, and he established precise categories underpinning all philosophical and scientific analysis, such as substance, quantity, relation, and place. Aristotle's central belief was that all things in the universe consist of the imprint of form on matter. This was a compromise between Platonism, which tended to ignore matter, and the purest materialism, which saw no patterns in the universe other than the accidents of matter impinging on matter. For Aristotle, forms are the purposeful forces that shape the world of matter; thus the presence of the form of humanity molds and directs the human embryo until it ultimately becomes a human being. Since everything has a purposeful form, the universe for Aristotle is teleological—that is, every item and every class of items is inherently aiming toward its own particular end. Aristotle's universe is therefore in a constant state of motion, as everything within it moves toward its ultimate perfected form (known in Greek as its *telos*).

Aristotle's moral philosophy was expressed most

Aristotle.

fully in his *Nicomachean Ethics*, although important aspects of his ideas are also contained in his *Politics*. Aristotle taught that the highest good consists in the harmonious functioning of the individual human mind and body. Humans differ from the animals by virtue of their rational capacities, and so they find happiness by exercising these appropriately. For most people this will mean exercising reason in practical affairs. Good conduct is virtuous conduct, and virtue resides in aiming for the golden mean: courage rather than rashness or cowardice, temperance rather than excessive indulgence or ascetic denial. Better even than the practical life, however, is the contemplative life, for such a life allows those few men equipped by nature for it to exercise their rational capacities to the utmost. Aristotle believed therefore that philosophers were the happiest of men, but he understood that even they could not engage in contemplation without interruption. As a practical person, moreover, he deemed it necessary for them to intersperse their speculative activities with practical life in the real world. Whereas Plato conceived of politics as a means to an end, the orderly pursuit of the supernatural Good, Aristotle thought of politics as an end in itself, the collective exercise of the good life. But Aristotle also took it for granted that some people—"barbarians"—were not fully human and so were meant by nature to be slaves. He also excluded women from the life of the polis, and so from a full measure of humanity, since they could not share in the life of the state in which human rational faculties enjoyed their fullest exercise. All male citizens, on the other hand, were meant to share in it, for, as Aristotle proposed, "man is by nature a political animal" (or, to be more faithful to the Greek, "a creature of the polis"). This view did not mean that the best form of government was democracy, however; Aristotle saw that as a "debased" form of government. What he preferred was the polity, in which monarchical, aristocratic, and democratic elements were combined by means of checks and balances. Such a government would allow free men to realize their rational potential, showing themselves to be located in nature's hierarchy above the animals and right below the gods.

For all of their brilliance and originality, Plato and Aristotle could not "think outside the box" of their fourth-century world. Their answer to society's ills was not to restructure Greek political life, but to improve the life of the individual polis. Indeed, both men indicated that poleis such as Athens or Thebes were already too large to function as an ideal polis. Both imagined the perfect society as one made up of a few thousand households, largely engaged in agriculture and living in a face-to-face, participatory society. Although Greek civilization had begun in such a world, the realities of fourth-century political life were very different. The fact that Plato and Aristotle considered the problem at all is testament to their recognition that something was "wrong" with the polis; but for both men, the answer was a reorganization of the existing polity, not something new in its place.

XENOPHON AND ISOCRATES

Another product of the Socratic intellectual tradition was Xenophon, a contemporary of Plato. Xenophon had served in the mercenary army that fought its way out of Persia, and also fought for the Spartan king Agesilaus in Asia Minor. Disillusioned with what his fellow Athenians had done to his teacher Socrates, Xenophon lived most of his life as a comfortable exile in Spartan territory. There, Xenophon composed histories (including the tale of the ten thousand Greeks who fought their way out of Persia), biographies, his memories of Socrates, and treatises on ideal kingship, the Spartan constitution, household management (the

Oikonomikos, the root of our word *economics*), and on the raising of hunting dogs. Like most Greeks, Xenophon assumed that good government was to be sought through exemplars and moral paragons. This led him to embellish or omit facts that did not contribute toward moral uplift. Still, he was aware that the world had changed for the worse, a point driven home to him as he watched Epaminondas cripple the state Xenophon so admired, Sparta. So contemptuous was he of the Theban leader that in his "continuation" of Thucydides' history, Xenophon refused to record Epaminondas' name.

The Athenian orator Isocrates (436–338 B.C.E.) was also well aware that something had gone horribly awry. Again, his solution was not an overhaul of the Greek polis or the creation of greater forms of political organization. What he proposed was a great invasion of Persia led by a man of vision and ability, someone who could unite the Greek world behind his cause. Isocrates cast about most of his life for such a man, favoring at one point Agesilaus of Sparta, at other times powerful tyrants from the western and northern parts of the Greek world. Toward the end of his life, he began to think the man for the job was a man whom most Athenians considered no Greek at all: Philip II, the king of Macedon. Isocrates issued an open letter to Philip, detailing the ills of the Greek world, and declaring that masterful action was needed to rescue Greece from its endless cycle of self-destruction.

THE RISE OF MACEDON AND THE CONQUESTS OF ALEXANDER

How did Philip II of Macedon strengthen his kingdom?

By the middle of the fourth century, the Greeks had become so embroiled in political and socioeconomic turmoil that they at first barely noticed the growing power of Macedon, a kingdom on the northern fringes of the Greek world. There was little reason for them to do so; until the fourth century, Macedon had been a weak kingdom, ruled by a royal house barely strong enough to control its own nobility, and beset by intrigue and murderous ambition from within. As recently as the 360s, Macedon had teetered on collapse, surrounded by barbarian neighbors who nearly overran the kingdom. Most Greeks viewed the Macedonians as barbarians, despite the efforts of a few Macedonian kings to add a bit of Hellenic culture to their court (one late fifth-century king had successfully invited Euripides and Sophocles to Macedon; Socrates had refused a similar request). Therefore, when a young and energetic Macedonian king named Philip II consolidated the southern Balkans under his rule, many Greek patriots saw it as a development no less troubling than the approach of the Persian "barbarians" in the fifth century.

THE REIGN OF PHILIP II (359–336 B.C.E.)

Philip came to the throne of Macedon after his older brother died fighting a barbarian invasion, leaving as his heir a small boy. Philip had himself made regent for the boy, but soon dispensed with that fiction and took the throne himself. By 356, he certainly considered himself king. That same year a son was born to him; Philip named the child Alexander, and marked him out as his successor.

Once he assumed the kingship, Philip's first problem was to stabilize his northern borders. Through a combination of warfare and diplomacy, Philip subdued the tribes of the southern Balkans and incorporated their territory into Macedonia. Philip's success had much to do with his reorganization of the Macedonian army. As a young boy, Philip had been a hostage at the court of Epaminondas; the observant youth may have learned something from watching the Theban general. In any event, Philip turned the Macedonian phalanx from an ill-organized peasant army into a highly drilled, well-

Philip II of Macedon. This tiny ivory head was discovered in the tomb of Philip of Macedon. The damaged right eye strongly suggests that it is a portrait of Philip himself, whose eye was damaged by a catapult bolt.

armed fighting machine. The mineral resources Philip captured early in his reign made him wealthy enough to establish what was in essence a professional army—just one of his gold mines produced as much in one year as the Delian League collected annually at its height. Philip also organized an elite cavalry squad—the Companions—who fought with and beside the king. These elite horsemen were drawn from the nobility; Philip hoped to inspire a greater esprit de corps

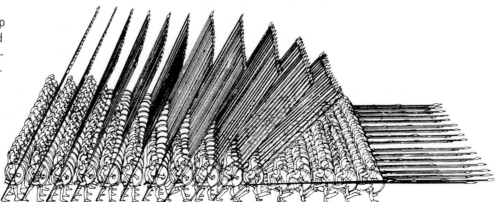

Macedonian Phalanx. Philip of Macedon's infantry—and Alexander the Great's thereafter—was armed with two-handed pikes and massed in squares sixteen rows deep and wide. Members of the phalanx were trained to wheel in step in any direction or to double their front by filing off in rows of eight.

TWO VIEWS OF PHILIP

Philip II of Macedon provoked strong reactions among the Athenians, through whose eyes we must evaluate him due to the nature of our sources. As these passages illustrate, we could interpret his actions very differently, depending on whether we see in him a savior of Greece or a would-be barbarian conqueror.

ISOCRATES, TO PHILIP

As I kept going over these questions [of war and peace] in my own thoughts, I found that . . . the greatest states of Hellas should resolve to put an end to their mutual quarrels and carry the war beyond our borders into Asia. . . . I am going to advise you to champion the cause of concord among the Hellenes and of a campaign against the barbarian. . . . I affirm that, without neglecting any of your own interests you ought to reconcile Argos and Lacedaemon [Sparta] and Thebes and Athens; for if you can bring these cities together, you will not find it hard to unite the others as well. . . .
If you can persuade four cities only to take a sane view of things, you will deliver the others also from many evils. . . . No quarrel should ever have arisen between you and any one of them. But unfortunately we are all prone by nature to do wrong more often than right. . . . For the future you must be on your guard to prevent a like occurrence, and must consider what service you can render them which will make it manifest that you have acted in a manner worthy both of yourself and what these cities have done. . . . It is a good thing to have the appearance of conferring benefits upon the greatest states of Hellas and at the same time to profit yourself no less than them. . . . You see how utterly wretched these states have become because of their warfare . . . and now perhaps someone will venture to object to what I have proposed, saying that I am trying to persuade you to set yourself to an impossible task. . . . While I grant that no one else in the world could reconcile these cities, yet nothing of the sort is difficult for you; for I see that you have carried through to a successful end many undertakings which the rest of the world looked upon as hopeless and unthinkable.

George Norlin, trans. *Isocrates.* Vol. 1. (Cambridge, Mass.: Harvard University Press, 1928), pp. 251, 255, 263–271.

DEMOSTHENES, SECOND AND THIRD OLYNTHIACS

I do not choose, Athenians, to enumerate the resources of Philip and by such arguments to call on you to rise to the occasion. Because it seems to me that any dissertation on that topic is a tribute to his enterprise, but a record of our failure. For the higher he has raised himself above his proper level, the more he wins the admiration of the world; but the more you have failed to improve your opportunities, the greater is the discredit you have incurred. . . . Now to call a man perjured and faithless, without drawing attention to his acts, might justly be termed mere abuse. . . . I have two reasons for thinking the whole story worth telling: Philip shall appear as worthless as he really is, and those who stand against his apparent invincibility shall see that he has exhausted all the acts of chicanery on which his greatness was founded at the first, and that his career has now reached the extreme limit. . . . He has hoodwinked everyone that has had any dealings with him; he has played upon the folly of each party in turn and exploited their ignorance of his own character. This is how he has gained his power. . . . Never was there a crisis that demanded more careful handling than the present. . . . Quite apart from the disgrace that we should incur if we shirk our responsibilities [to out threatened allies], I see not a little danger . . . if there is nothing to hinder Philip, when he has crushed his present foe, from turning his arms against Attica.

J. H. Vince, ed. and trans. *Demosthenes*, Vol. 1. (Cambridge, Mass.: Harvard University Press, 1930), pp. 23–27, 43,47.

among them as well as a deeper loyalty to the royal house. Philip recruited future Companions (and gained valuable hostages) by bringing the most promising sons of the nobility to his capital at Pella, where they trained as pages with the crown prince, Alexander. Through a series of dynastic marriages, Philip also managed to gain the good will and alliance of many neighboring kingdoms.

His expansion and consolidation in the north, largely completed by 352 B.C.E., brought him into increasing conflict with Athenian commercial interests. Philip was slowly transforming Thessaly into a northern puppet state, and by the early 340s Thebes found its influence in the north all but gone. The growing power of Macedon alarmed some in the Greek world, most notably an Athenian orator named Demosthenes. Whereas some Greeks, like Isocrates, saw in Philip a potential answer to Greece's woes, Demosthenes and others believed that Philip was a half-barbarian aggressor whose ultimate aim was to end the independence of the poleis and subject Greece to his rule. There is no doubt of the threat that Philip now posed; nevertheless, Demosthenes and other Athenians seemed to have misunderstood Philip's ultimate policy aims. Athenian vanity simply could not accept that they were not Philip's final target.

There is no question that Philip was an aggressor, but his expansion in the north was designed to secure his frontiers and the resources necessary to support his real goal: an invasion of Asia Minor that would allow him to tap that land's fabulous wealth. From 348 on, he was keen to conciliate the major Greek poleis, especially Athens. At one point, he even asked for an alliance wherein the Athenians would provide the war fleet for his proposed invasion of the Persian Empire; in return he would support their claim to hegemony over Greece. The Athenians took Demosthenes' advice and refused to cooperate with Philip. This miscalculation would prove disastrous for Athens.

Although Demosthenes saw Philip's actions in the north as easing his entry into Greece, Philip was actually trying to prepare his exit from it. He wanted a secure and peaceful Greece behind him when he took on the might of Persia. But his inability to reach any understanding with Athens, despite strenuous diplomatic effort on Philip's part, ultimately led to war between the Macedonians on one side and Athens, Thebes, and a number of smaller poleis on the other (Sparta remained aloof). At the battle of Chaeronea in 338 B.C.E., the Macedonians won a narrow victory over the Athenians and their allies. In the aftermath, Philip called delegates from around mainland Greece to Corinth, where he established a new league. By and large, he left the independence of the major Greek poleis unaffected. The main purpose of the "League of Corinth" was to provide forces for the invasion of Asia Minor by electing Philip as their military commander. But the league also played some role in maintaining peace between the rival Greek poleis.

Philip's dream of invading Persian territory was never realized. At a festival in Macedon in 336 B.C.E., a disgruntled lover charged into the arena and assassinated Philip. The kingship now fell to the twenty-year-old young man who had led his father's cavalry at Chaeronea, Alexander III. To the Greeks he would be

CHRONOLOGY

MACEDONIAN CONQUEST

Philip II crowns himself king of Macedon	356 B.C.E.
Defeat of Athens and formation of the "League of Corinth"	338 B.C.E.
Alexander defeats the Persian army	331 B.C.E.
Death of Alexander	323 B.C.E.

known as Alexander Poliorcetes, the "Sacker of Cities." To the Romans, far more impressed by conquerors than were the Greeks, he was Alexander the Great.

THE CONQUESTS AND REIGN OF ALEXANDER (336–323 B.C.E.)

Alexander is a difficult figure for historians to understand, not least because in his own lifetime romantic legend had already built up around him and his achievements. Scholars have seen in Alexander a visionary, a genius, and a butcher; what he did was nothing less than transform the world, translating Greek culture from its parochial, small-scale homeland into a world culture, spreading it as far as the modern states of Afghanistan and Pakistan.

Alexander's military victories are well known. After first quelling revolts in Greece that erupted immediately on his father's death, by 334 he was ready to invade the Persian empire, then under the rule of Darius III. Persia had experienced internal weakness for over a decade. Darius III had been placed on the throne by a scheming vizier who sought to control the young nobleman, only to find that his puppet had designs of his own. Darius killed the kingmaker, and then ruled capably during the few years of peace he enjoyed until Alexander's appearance in Asia.

The Macedonian king won a series of startling victories, starting in northwest Asia Minor. At one point, Darius offered to cede his western possessions to

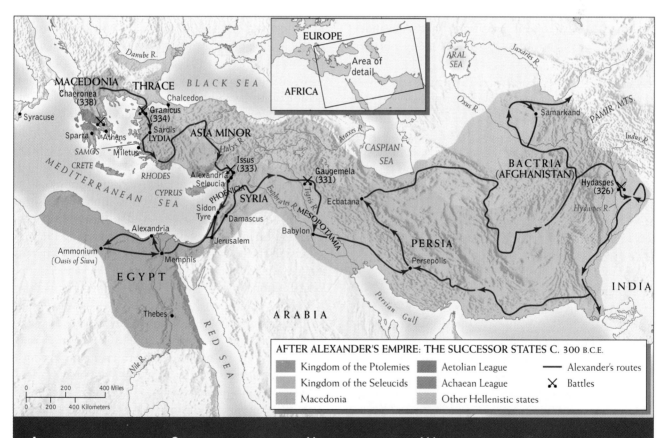

ALEXANDER THE GREAT AND THE HELLENISTIC WORLD

Why did Alexander continue eastward even after defeating Darius III at Gaugamela? Consider the vastness of his empire compared with the Aegean basin; how would the acquisition of so much territory profoundly reshape the Greek world? Note the position of the three successor kingdoms and how each one was based on one of three major axes of civilizations we have studied so far: Egyptian, Asian Near Eastern, and Aegean. What might the division of Alexander's empire along such "traditional" lines say about the durability of his empire even if he had lived?

Alexander in exchange for his family (whom Alexander had captured in battle) and a peace treaty. Alexander's field marshal, Parmenio, advised "I would accept it, if I were you." Alexander replied, "And I would too, if I were Parmenio." Within three years of his initial invasion, Alexander had subdued Anatolia, the Syria-Palestine coast, and had detached Egypt from the Persian empire. During his time in Egypt, Alexander appears to have reflected on what he had already achieved, and to have become increasingly convinced of his superhuman qualities. Indeed, to many Alexander had already achieved more than one might have expected out of the squabbling, petty gods of Mount Olympus, who seemed to grow smaller by comparison as Alexander and his talented staff of officers achieved ever more.

In September of 331 B.C.E., Darius mustered the remaining strength of his empire to face Alexander's Graeco-Macedonian army in what is today northern Iraq. At the battle of Gaugamela, Alexander destroyed the Persian army. Darius himself fled to the hills, where he was captured and slain by a chieftain hoping to ingratiate himself to Alexander. But as the new king of Persia, Alexander executed the chieftain for having killed his predecessor. The next spring, Alexander destroyed the Persian capital of Persepolis, lest it serve as a rallying point for Persian resistance.

Over the next few years, Alexander campaigned in the mountains of Bactria (modern Afghanistan), the hardest fighting of the campaign. He ultimately succeeded in conquering much of the region, but his grasp there was tenuous. Among the Bactrians he found the woman he would take as his queen, Roxane. From there he moved down the Indus Valley, meeting stiff resistance. At the mouth of the Indus, his soldiers mutinied and refused to press on. Alexander reluctantly led them back toward Babylon, arriving there by the end of 324 B.C.E.

What Alexander planned to do with his new empire is difficult to say. Some scholars see him merely as a pirate, bent on conquest and plunder in a self-serving quest for glory worthy of the Homeric heroes from whom he claimed descent. Others counter by pointing to his systematic foundation of Greek-style poleis along his campaign route. These new cities served not only as garrisons to control the local populations but also as foci of Greek culture. There is also the bizarre mass marriage he forced on his officers, compelling them to put aside their wives and take Persian noblewomen as brides. Once seen as a reflection of Alexander's supposed visionary desire to eliminate ethnic distinctions within his empire, this act is now viewed as an attempt to breed a new nobility, loyal not to Macedonian or Persian concerns but to him and his successors alone. Alexander took no realistic steps to create an administration for his new realm, although he did move various officers and groups of veterans about in an attempt to reshuffle certain responsibilities. Our sources hint at plans for further conquests, perhaps Arabia, perhaps toward Italy and Sicily in the west. Given what we know about Alexander, it is hard to imagine him ever being satisfied with what he had.

We will never know for certain. In late May 323, Alexander fell ill with malarial symptoms and, ignoring the advice of his doctors, continued to play the part of the Homeric king, drinking mightily and exerting himself incautiously. Alexander had often been wounded

> Given what we know now about Alexander, it is hard to imagine him ever being satisfied with what he had.

Marble Head of Alexander. Alexander the Great was reputed to have been very handsome, but all surviving representations doubtless make him more handsome still. This one dates from about 180 B.C.E. and is typical in showing Alexander with "lion's-mane hair."

in battle during the course of his career, and no doubt his body was the worse for wear. His condition declined until on June 10, 323 B.C.E., Alexander died, not yet thirty-three years old. His friends and officers had gathered around his deathbed, and asked to whom he wished to leave his empire. One source states that, just as he went unconscious, a wry smile adorned Alexander's face as he whispered "To the strongest." This might mean any of several talented and ambitious generals around him, who were second only to Alexander himself in prestige and martial skill.

THE HELLENISTIC KINGDOMS

What characteristics defined the three major Hellenistic kingdoms?

After Alexander's death, epic struggles unfolded among the men and women who wanted to keep the realm together, those who wished to mark out their own kingdoms, and among the latter, those who wanted the biggest possible share. The wars and intrigues that took place in the two generations after the death of the great conqueror are too involved to describe in detail. By 275 B.C.E., however, three separate axes of military and political power had emerged, each with a distinctive outlook despite their common background and their Graeco-Macedonian ruling class. One of the striking features of the period is the return to something old, especially in the Near East and Egypt, where the successors of Alexander the Great established sprawling cities and revived the concept of the god-king.

PTOLEMAIC EGYPT

Following Alexander's death in Babylon, his inner circle met to decide the fate of his empire. For the moment, the empire remained united, but Ptolemy asked to be made governor of Egypt. The rest of Alexander's generals seem to have been glad to let Ptolemy have the hot, sweltering land of Egypt, but Ptolemy himself recognized the country's vast potential and its virtual invulnerability to attack. As soon as he arrived, Ptolemy set about making Egypt an independent kingdom under his rule. The dynasty he established would rule Egypt for the next three hundred years (332–30 B.C.E.). The male heirs of the line all took the name Ptolemy, hence Ptolemaic Egypt.

Ruling from Alexandria, the great coastal city founded by Alexander, the Ptolemies acted as Macedonian kings for the Greek and Macedonian subjects living in the thriving capital. Outside of Alexandria, however, they played the role of pharaohs, surrounding themselves with the trappings and symbols of Egypt's pharaonic heritage. The Ptolemies were by no means a political failure. The third century in particular was a time of prosperity and internal peace for Ptolemaic Egypt. But even in antiquity, people recognized the divide between the Macedonian kings and the ancient land they ruled. Geographers described Alexandria as "by" Egypt, not "of" it. No matter how well they aped the Egyptian rulers of the past, the Macedonian ruling class largely disdained their subjects. Until the last Ptolemaic ruler, Cleopatra VII, no Ptolemaic ruler even bothered to learn Egyptian.

For the Ptolemies as for the ancient pharaohs, all of Egypt was basically crown land, to be exploited for the benefit of the royal house. Alongside this Egyptian tradition, however, was the Macedonian idea that conquered land—land "won by the spear"—was plunder, to be used for personal enrichment and glorification. The Ptolemies attempted to squeeze every last drop of wealth from the Egyptian countryside. Most of this wealth ended up in Alexandria. The Ptolemies had little interest in improving the lot of the Egyptian peasantry; in the ancient world it was often assumed that what kept the poor complacent and dutiful was their desperate poverty. The Ptolemies, however, overdid it, and from the end of the third century they faced regular and dangerous revolts from the native peasantry.

Nevertheless, Ptolemaic Egypt proved the most durable of the Hellenistic kingdoms, and the dynasty used the wealth of the country to patronize science and the arts. Early in the dynasty the museum and library of Alexandria were established, and the city became a center of scholarship that attracted the greatest minds of the Hellenistic world, displacing even Athens, which had retained some importance as a sort of "university" town. Many breakthroughs in astronomy, applied sciences, and physics took place in Alexandria, and the study of medicine advanced

Until the last Ptolemaic ruler, Cleopatra VII, no Ptolemaic ruler even bothered to learn Egyptian.

greatly under Ptolemaic rule. Freed from the taboos of their homeland, Greek medical researchers in Egypt were permitted to perform autopsies on the bodies of dead criminals, making it possible for anatomy to become a scientific discipline in its own right. The Ptolemies were not selfless patrons. They were largely interested in the glory and prestige their patronage brought them, rather than the practical benefits that might arise from the research they sponsored. But whatever its motives, Alexandrine scholarship left a permanent mark on the Mediterranean world.

SELEUCID ASIA

The vast Asian possessions of Alexander the Great eventually fell to another Macedonian, Seleucus, by 281 B.C.E. Seleucus had not been a senior officer during Alexander's lifetime, but he had navigated the turmoil after Alexander's death successfully, exploiting the fears and suspicions among Alexander's more prominent successors.

Ruling such an expansive realm proved as much curse as blessing. The Persian dynasty founded by Seleucus, the Seleucids, struggled with the problem of secession throughout its history. Their hold on the easternmost provinces was especially tenuous—even during Alexander's lifetime that had been the case—as Seleucus recognized. He therefore ceded much of the Indus Valley to the great Indian warrior-king Chandragupta in exchange for peace and a squad of war elephants. By the middle of the third century, the Seleucids had also lost control of Bactria, where a series of Indo-Greek states were emerging with a unique cultural complex of their own. (One Bactrian Greek king, Menander, is remembered in Buddhist tradition and may have had Buddhist sympathies himself.) By the 260s, they had also lost control of the western half of Asia Minor. The Seleucid heartland now became Syria–Palestine, Mesopotamia, and the western half of Persia: still a great, wealthy kingdom, but far less than what Alexander had left.

Like the Ptolemies, the Seleucids offered two faces to their subjects, one rooted in ancient Near Eastern tradition for their Persian and Mesopotamian subjects, another decidedly more Greek for the heavily Hellenized populations of the coast. Seleucus' son, Antiochus I, proclaimed in terms reminiscent of a Sargon or a Hammurabi, "I am Antiochus, the Great King, the legitimate king . . . king of Babylon, king of all countries." Throughout their empire, the Seleucids encouraged the recognition of their divine status and the

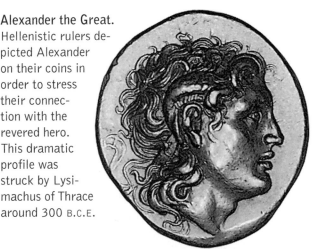

Alexander the Great. Hellenistic rulers depicted Alexander on their coins in order to stress their connection with the revered hero. This dramatic profile was struck by Lysimachus of Thrace around 300 B.C.E.

Antiochus I, "Soter." A Hellenistic ruler of Syria (281–261 B.C.E.), whose chosen title of *soter* meant "savior." The faraway stare connotes supernatural inspiration.

divine honors owed to them. In the great urban centers of Seleucid Asia, shrines and temples were built for the cult of the living ruler.

Seleucid rulers continued the tradition of Alexander, planting new cities throughout their empire, cities that were fundamentally Greek in their assumptions but in many cases grew to be thriving commercial and industrial cities, such as Antioch. These cities attracted a great deal of professional and mercantile talent eastward, encouraging trade and manufactures that the Seleucids were expert at exploiting. While they controlled the land and agricultural production through the traditional Persian system of noble-held lands in return for loyalty and services to the king, the Seleucids employed a wide variety of taxes, tariffs, and levies to tap into the growing commercial wealth of their realm. Although their bureaucracy was less organized than that of the Ptolemies, in an empire of as many as 30 million inhabitants even haphazard tax col-

THE GREEK INFLUENCE ON ISRAEL

Greek culture was a powerfully intoxicating force throughout the Hellenistic world, even in a comparative cultural back-water like Israel. In the second century B.C.E., the Hellenized ways of the Jewish upper classes in Jerusalem finally occasioned a revolt by a native Hebrew dynasty known as the Maccabees, who decried the "debaucheries" Greek culture had introduced into Jewish life. In the passage that follows, note that even the high priest of the Temple bears the Greek name Jason.

In those days [the reign of Antiochus IV Epiphanes, 175–164 B.C.E.] certain renegades came out from Israel and misled many, saying, "Let us go and make a covenant with the Gentiles [Greeks] around us, for since we separated from them many disasters have come upon us." . . . Some of the people went to the king, who authorized them to observe the ordinances of the Gentiles. So they built a gymnasium in Jerusalem, according to Gentile custom, and removed the marks of circumcision, and abandoned the holy covenant. They joined with the Gentiles and sold themselves to do evil. . . . When Antiochus succeeded to the kingdom, Jason the brother of Onias obtained the high priesthood by corruption. . . . He at once shifted his compatriots over to the Greek way of life. . . . Despising the sanctuary and neglecting the sacrifices, they hurried to take part in the unlawful proceedings in the wrestling arena after the signal for the discus-throwing, disdaining the honors prized by their ancestors and putting the highest value upon Greek forms of prestige. . . . When the quadrennial games were being held at Tyre and the king was present, Jason sent envoys . . . to carry three hundred silver drachmas for the sacrifice to Heracles. . . . Harsh and utterly grievous was the onslaught of evil. For the Temple was filled with debauchery and reveling by the Gentiles, who dallied with prostitutes and had intercourse with women within the sacred precincts. . . . The altar was covered with abominable offerings that were forbidden by the laws.

1 Maccabees 2; 2 Maccabees 4–6. *The New Oxford Annotated Bible.* (Oxford: Oxford University Press, 1994).

---

lection could reap huge rewards. Like their Persian predecessors, however, the Seleucids did not reinvest their gains into what we would call capital improvements. Instead, they hoarded their wealth in great state treasuries. All the same, they had more than enough cash to provide for the smooth operation of their government and to defend their borders through the third century, a period of regular warfare with the Ptolemies. It was not until the second century, when Antiochus III lost a costly war with the Romans, that he had to plunder temples and private wealth in order to pay off his war indemnity.

ANTIGONID MACEDON AND GREECE

The Macedonian homeland did not possess the vast wealth of the new kingdoms carved from Alexander's conquests. It also remained highly unstable from the time of Alexander's death until 276 B.C.E., when a general named Antigonus was finally able to establish his rule over the area. Macedon drew its strength from considerable natural resources and its influence over Aegean trade, as well as its de facto overlordship of the Greek homeland. Furthermore, the Macedonians could still field the finest army of any of the successor states, and the Antigonid kings of Macedon held what many of the monarchs of the Hellenistic world desired, the kingship of the land once ruled by Philip and Alexander.

Antigonus was influenced by the Stoic outlook (see below) and viewed kingship as something of a noble servitude, an office to be suffered rather than enjoyed. This outlook, combined with his circumscribed resources, convinced him not to compete with the Seleucids and Ptolemies for dominance. Instead, Antigonid policy was to keep these other two powers at war and away from the Macedonian sphere of influence. Antigonus and his successors thus pursued a policy more reminiscent of Philip than of Alexander. They secured the northern frontiers, maintained a strong, standing military, and kept the fractious Greeks to the south at heel.

The Greeks, however, were restive under the Antigonids, and two emergent forces within the Greek world served as rallying points for cries of freedom and war against the "barbarian." These two forces, the Aetolian League and Achaean League, were a departure in Greek political organization. Unlike the defensive alliances of the classical period, these two leagues represented a real political unification, with some centralization of governmental functions. Under the Achaean League, for example, citizens of the member poleis participated in councils of state that dealt with foreign policy and military affairs, trials for treason, and the annual election of a league general (also the chief executive officer) and his second in command. New members were admitted on an equal footing with existing members, and all citizens of the various poleis enjoyed joint citizenship throughout the league. The same laws, weights and measures, coinage, and judicial procedures also applied throughout this federal system. So impressive was the degree of cooperation and unification that James Madison, John Jay, and Alexander Hamilton employed the Achaean League as one of their models in advocating federalism in the United States.

> Antigonus was influenced by the Stoic outlook and viewed kingship as something of a noble servitude, an office to be suffered rather than enjoyed.

THE GROWTH OF TRADE AND URBANIZATION

Why was prosperity not more widespread in the Hellenistic economy?

In regard to economics, the Hellenistic world was generally prosperous, owing to the growth of long-distance trade, finance, and cities. The growth of trade may be explained by several factors, first among which was the opening up of a vast trading area as the result of Alexander's conquests. Long before the time of Alexander, Greeks had been energetic long-distance traders, but they were hampered in trading with Persian realms and with areas east of Persia because Persian emperors and satraps preferred to act in their own economic interests rather than in Greek ones. But when Greek rulers became ensconced throughout Egypt and western Asia after 323 B.C.E., and when Greek-speaking communities dotted the terrain from Alexandria in Egypt, to another Alexandria in northern Syria, to yet another Alexandria at the head of the Persian Gulf, steady trading connections were facilitated from the eastern Mediterranean to central Asia. Moreover, with bases in Egypt, Asia Minor, Persia, and Bactria, Greek traders could fan out farther, venturing into sub-Saharan Africa, Russia, and India. Second, Alexander unwittingly stimulated a growth of intensive investment when he placed in circulation hoards of Persian gold and silver in the form of coins, jewelry, and luxury utensils. And third, manufacturing industries aimed at providing items for trade were now more consciously promoted by autocratic rulers as a means of increasing their revenues.

New trading ventures were particularly vigorous and lucrative in Ptolemaic Egypt and the area of western Asia ruled over by the Seleucid monarchs, the heartland of which was Syria. Every facility was provided by the Ptolemies and the Seleucids for the encouragement of trade. Harbors were improved, warships were sent out to police the seas, and roads and canals were built. Moreover, the Ptolemies employed geographers to discover new routes to distant lands and thereby open up valuable markets. As a result of such methods Egypt developed a flourishing commerce in the widest variety of products. Into the port of Alexandria came spices from Arabia, gold from Ethiopia and India, tin from Britain, elephants and ivory from Nubia, silver from Spain, fine carpets from Asia Minor, and even silk from China. Profits for the government and for some of the merchants were often as high as 20 or 30 percent.

Cities grew enormously during the Hellenistic Age, for a combination of reasons. Entirely aside from economic motives, Greek rulers imported Greek officials and especially Greek soldiers to maintain their control over non-Greek populations. Often this policy resulted in the creation of urban settlements from nothing. Alexander the Great himself had founded some seventy cities as outposts of Greek domination, and in the next two centuries his successors founded about two hundred more. Yet urbanization also increased because of the expansion of commerce and industry and the proliferation of governmental bureaus responsible for economic supervision. Hence the growth of populations in some urban centers was explosive. The population of Antioch in Syria quadrupled during a single century. Seleucia on the Tigris grew from nothing to a metropolis of several hundred thousand in less than two centuries. The largest and most famous of all the Hellenistic cities was Alexandria in Egypt, with about five hundred thousand inhabitants. Before imperial Rome, no other city in ancient times surpassed it in size or magnificence. Its streets were well paved and laid out in regular order. It had splendid public buildings and parks, a museum, and a library of half a million scrolls. The masses of its people, however, had no share in the brilliant and luxurious life around them, although it was paid for in part out of the fruits of their labor.

Although the Hellenistic economy was basically a dynamic one, throughout the Hellenistic period agriculture remained the major occupation and the primary source of wealth. (Only within the last century did trade and industry replace agriculture as the major source of wealth in western Europe and North America.) Furthermore, although industry advanced in Hellenistic Egypt and parts of western Asia, nowhere did a true "industrial revolution" based on any technological breakthrough occur. Rather, all industry was based on manual labor rather than being power driven.

Despite the overall growth and prosperity of the Hellenistic economy, prosperity was by no means en-

joyed by everyone. Quite to the contrary: for some people sudden wealth was followed by sudden penury, and for others poverty was a constant. Individual merchants and speculators were those most subject to drastic fluctuations in their fortunes, owing to the natural precariousness of mercantile endeavors. A trader who did very well selling a luxury cloth might decide to invest heavily in it, only to find that tastes had changed, or that a ship he had dispatched to convey his wares had sunk. Merchants were also particularly exposed to what economists now recognize as the "boom and bust" syndrome. A merchant, thinking he would make a fortune during an upward price spiral, might go into debt in order to take advantage of the upward trend, only to find that supply in the commodity he traded suddenly exceeded demand, leaving him nothing with which to pay back his creditors. Among those whose poverty remained unchanged were small-scale farmers who grew crops for sale in regional markets. (In Greece they may have become poorer because Greece suffered during the Hellenistic era from a negative balance of payments, having little to offer for long-distance trade except objects of art.) Those who emigrated to cities in most cases probably did not improve their economic status, and many of them became subject to badly overcrowded living conditions. All told, therefore, it seems clear that the economic landscape of the Hellenistic world was one of contrasting extremes, an image worth remembering as we move to a consideration of Hellenistic thought and culture.

Although the Hellenistic economy was basically a dynamic one, throughout the Hellenistic period agriculture remained the major occupation and the primary source of wealth.

HELLENISTIC CULTURE: PHILOSOPHY AND RELIGION

What was the relationship between Epicureanism and Stoicism?

Hellenistic philosophy exhibited two trends that ran almost parallel throughout the civilization. The major trend, exemplified by Epicureanism and Stoicism, showed a fundamental regard for reason as the key to the solution of human problems. This trend was a manifestation of Greek influence, although philosophy and science, as combined by Aristotle, had now come to a parting of the ways. The minor trend, exemplified by the Skeptics and various cults, tended to reject reason, to deny the possibility of attaining truth, and in some cases to turn toward mysticism and reliance on faith. Despite the differences in their teachings, the philosophers and religious enthusiasts of the Hellenistic age generally agreed on one thing: the necessity of finding some release from the trials of human existence, for with the decline of free civic life as a means for the expression of human idealism, alternatives needed to be found to make life seem meaningful, or at least endurable.

EPICUREANISM AND STOICISM

Epicureanism and Stoicism both originated about 300 B.C.E. The founders were, respectively, Epicurus (c. 342–270 B.C.E.) and Zeno (fl. after 300 B.C.E.), both residents of Athens. The two philosophies had several features in common. Both were individualistic, concerned not with the welfare of society but with the good of the individual. Both were materialistic, denying the existence of any spiritual substances; even divine beings and the soul were declared to be formed of matter. Moreover, Stoicism and Epicureanism alike contained elements of universalism. Both taught that people are the same the world over and recognized no distinctions between Greeks and non-Greeks.

But in most ways the two systems were quite different. The Stoics believed that the cosmos is an ordered whole in which all contradictions are resolved for ultimate good. Evil is, therefore, relative; the particular misfortunes that befall human beings are but necessary incidents to the final perfection of the universe. Everything that happens is rigidly determined in accordance with rational purpose. No individual is master of his or her fate; human destiny is a link in an unbroken chain. People are free only in the sense that they can accept their fate or rebel against it. But whether they accept or rebel, they cannot overcome it. Their supreme duty is to submit to the order of the universe in the knowledge that this order is good. Through such an act of resignation the highest happiness will be attained, which consists of tranquility of mind. Those who are most truly happy are thus the ones who by the assertion of their rational natures have accomplished a perfect adjustment of their lives to the cosmic purpose and purged their souls of all bitterness and whining protest against evil turns of fortune.

The Stoics' ethical and social theory grew from their general philosophy. Believing that the highest good is serenity of mind, they emphasized duty and self-discipline as cardinal virtues. Recognizing the prevalence of particular evils, they taught tolerance for and forgiveness of each other. They also urged participation in public affairs as a duty for those of rational mind. They condemned slavery and war, although they took no real actions against these evils since they believed that the results that might arise from violent measures of social change would be worse than the diseases they were meant to cure. With appropriate qualifications, the Stoic philosophy was one of the noblest products of the Hellenistic Age in teaching egalitarianism, pacifism, and humanitarianism.

The Epicureans based their philosophy on the materialistic "atomism" of an earlier Greek thinker named Democritus, who lived in the latter part of the fifth century B.C.E. According to this theory the ultimate constituents of the universe are atoms, infinite in number, indestructible, and indivisible. Every individual object or organism in the universe is the product of a fortuitous concourse of atoms. Taking this as given, Epicurus and his followers proposed that since there is no ultimate purpose in the universe, the highest good is pleasure—the moderate satisfaction of bodily appetites, the mental pleasure of contemplating excellence and satisfactions previously enjoyed, and above all, serenity of soul. The last end can be best achieved through the elimination of fear, especially fear of the supernatural, since that is the greatest source of mental pain. The individual must understand that the soul is material and therefore cannot survive the body, that the universe operates of itself, and that no gods intervene in human affairs. The Epicureans thus came by a different route to the same general conclusion as the Stoics—nothing is better than tranquility of mind.

The practical moral teachings and the politics of the Epicureans rested on utilitarianism. In contrast to the Stoics, they did not insist on virtue as an end in itself but taught that the only reason why one should be good is to increase one's own happiness. In like manner, they denied that there is any such thing as absolute justice; laws and institutions are just only insofar

> With appropriate qualifications, the Stoic philosophy was one of the noblest products of the Hellenistic Age in teaching egalitarianism, pacifism, and humanitarianism.

as they contribute to the welfare of the individual. Certain rules have been found necessary in every society for the maintenance of order. These rules should be obeyed solely because it is to each individual's advantage to do so. Epicurus considered the state as a mere convenience and taught that the wise man should take no active part in politics. He did not propose that civilization should be abandoned; yet his conception of the happiest life was essentially passive and defeatist. Epicurus taught that the thinking person will recognize that evils in the world cannot be eradicated by human effort; the individual will therefore withdraw to study philosophy and enjoy the fellowship of a few congenial friends.

SKEPTICISM

A more radically defeatist philosophy was that propounded by the Skeptics. Skepticism reached the zenith of its popularity about 200 B.C.E. under the influence of Carneades. The chief source of its inspiration was the teaching that all knowledge is derived from sense perception and therefore must be limited and relative. From this the Skeptics deduced that people cannot prove anything. Since the impressions of our senses deceive us, no truth can be certain. All we can say is that things appear to be such and such; we do not know what they really are. We have no definite knowledge of the supernatural, of the meaning of life, or even of right and wrong. It follows that the sensible course to pursue is suspension of judgment; this alone can lead to happiness. If we will abandon the fruitless quest for absolute truth and cease worrying about good and evil, we will attain peace of mind, which is the highest satisfaction that life affords. The Skeptics were even less concerned than the Epicureans with political and social problems. Their ideal was one of escape from a world neither reformable nor understandable.

RELIGION

Hellenistic religion similarly tended to offer vehicles of escape from collective political commitments. Although Greek religion in the age of the city-states had emphasized the worship of gods associated with given cities to advance the fortunes of those cities, such civic-oriented worship was now losing its vitality. Its

According to the philosophy of Skepticism, people have no definite knowledge of the supernatural, of the meaning of life, or even of right and wrong.

place was taken for many of society's leaders by the philosophies of Stoicism, Epicureanism, and Skepticism. Most ordinary people, on the other hand, tended to embrace emotional personal religions offering elaborate ritual in this world and salvation in the next. In Greek-speaking communities, cults that stressed extreme ascetic atonement for sin, ecstatic mystical union with divinity, and otherworldly salvation attracted ever more followers. Among these mystery cults, so called because their membership was secret and their rites held in private, one of the most popular was the Orphic cult, based on the myth of the death and resurrection of the god Dionysius. Even today the word *dionysian* connotes dedication to ecstatic religious practices bordering on the orgiastic. In Persian communities Zoroastrianism became ever more extreme in its dualism, with Zoroastrian magi insisting that everything material was evil and demanding that believers practice austerities in order to ready their immaterial souls for ethereal joy in the afterlife. Finally, among Greeks and non-Greeks alike, an offshoot of Zoroastrianism known as Mithraism gained ever more popularity.

Exactly when Mithraism became an independent religion is unknown, but it was certainly not later than the fourth century B.C.E. The cult gained its name from Mithras, at first a minor deity in Zoroastrianism. Mithras gradually became recognized by many as the god most deserving of worship, probably because of his emotional appeal. He was believed to have lived an earthly existence involving great suffering and sacrifice. He performed miracles, giving bread and wine to humanity and ending a drought and also a disastrous flood. He proclaimed Sunday as the most sacred day of the week since the sun was the giver of light. He declared the twenty-fifth of December as the most sacred day of the year because, as the approximate date of the winter solstice, it was the "birthday" of the sun, when its life-giving powers began to increase for the benefit of humankind. Drawing its converts mostly from the lower classes of Hellenistic society, Mithraism offered them an elaborate ritual, contempt for life in this world, and a clearly defined doctrine of redemption through Mithras, a personal savior. Not surprisingly it outlasted the Hellenistic period, becoming after about 100 C.E. one of the most popular religions in the Roman Empire and exerting some influence on Christianity.

HELLENISTIC CULTURE: LITERATURE AND ART

Why did Hellenistic architecture become grander?

Both the literature and the art of the Hellenistic Age were characterized by a tendency to take aspects of earlier Greek accomplishments to extremes. It is difficult to be certain of the reasons for this tendency, but apparently writers and artists wished to demonstrate their purely formal skills in order to please their autocratic patrons. The greater uncertainties of existence in Hellenistic times may also have led consumers of art to seek gratification from more dramatic and less subtle forms of artistic expression. Whatever the case, rather than being an integral expression of civic activities, art during this period became more of a commodity. Artistic works became more numerous and more widely available: we know the names of at least eleven hundred Hellenistic authors. Many of these works are mediocre, but some are enduring masterpieces of art and literature.

PASTORAL LITERATURE

The most prominent Hellenistic verse form was the pastoral, a new genre depicting a make-believe world of shepherds and wood nymphs. The inventor of the genre was a Greek named Theocritus, who lived and wrote around 270 B.C.E. in the big-city environment of Alexandria. Theocritus was a merchant of escapism. In the midst of urban bustle, faced with despotic rulers, and within sight of overcrowded, slumlike conditions, he celebrated the charms of hazy country values and idealized the "simple pleasures" of rustic folk. One of his pastorals might start like this: "Begin my country song, sweet muses, begin, I am Thrysis from Etna, this is Thrysis's lovely voice." To many the falseness of such verse is alienating; how could shepherds talk this way? But other readers enjoy the poetic lushness. In creating the pastoral, Theocritus founded an enduring tradition that outlasted the Hellenistic world to be taken up by such masters as Virgil and Milton and that provided a wealth of themes for the visual arts. Even composers of modern concert music, such as Claude Debussy in his *Prelude to "The Afternoon of a Faun,"* owe a debt to the escapist poet from Alexandria.

PROSE

The field of Hellenistic prose literature was dominated by historians and biographers. By far the most profound of the writers of history was the mainland Greek Polybius, who lived during the second century B.C.E. According to Polybius, historical development proceeds in cycles, nations passing so inevitably through stages of growth and decay that it is possible to predict exactly where a nation is heading if one knows what has happened to it in the past. From the standpoint of historical method, Polybius deserves to be ranked second only to Thucydides among all the historians of ancient times, and he even surpassed Thucydides in his grasp of the importance of social and economic forces. Although most biographies of the time were light and gossipy, their popularity bears eloquent testimony to the literary tastes of the Hellenistic period.

Cupid and Psyche. Hellenistic tastes often inclined toward "dainty" representations of eroticism. Cupid's right hand conveys a studied sensuality held in check only by his fig leaf.

ARCHITECTURE

Consonant with the despotic style of rule, the main traits of Hellenistic architecture were grandeur and ornamentation. In place of the balance and restraint that had distinguished Greek architecture of the fifth and early fourth centuries B.C.E., Hellenistic public building drew on Greek elements but moved toward standards set by Persian monarchs and Egyptian pharaohs. Two examples (both of which unfortunately no longer survive) were the great lighthouse of Alex-

ESCAPE TO THE COUNTRYSIDE

The bewildering urban centers and social upheaval wrought by the Hellenistic Age encouraged some people to retreat into an imaginary world of simple country pleasures expressed in poetry and literature. Theocritus (born around 300 B.C.E. in Syracuse) was one of the poets who crafted such Arcadian fantasies of the simple life for an anxious urban audience looking for escape.

I finished my song, and with an ingenious laugh he gave me the (shepherd's) crook, a token of what we had shared. Then taking the road to the left which leads to Pyxa he parted from us. Eucritus and I turned off, with young Amyntas, for Phrasidemus's farm. There, happy in our welcome, we flung ourselves down on couches of fragrant reeds and freshcut vineleaves. Above our heads a grove of elms and poplars stirred gently. We could hear the noise of water, a lively stream running from the cave of the Nymphs. Sunburnt cicadas, perched in the shadowy thickets, kept up their rasping chatter; a distant tree-frog muttered harshly as it picked its way among thorns; larks and linnets were singing, a dove made moan, and brown bees loitered, flitting about the springs. The tall air smelt of summer, it smelt of ripeness. We lay stretched out in plenty, pears at our feet, apples at our sides and plumtrees reaching down, branches pulled earthward by the weight of the fruit. The seal broken from the wine jars was four years old. Nymphs of Castalia, haunters of steep Parnassus, tell me, was Heracles given such wine to drink by ancient Chiron in Pholus's rocky cave? . . . May I set the winnowing fan in another year's heaped grain while the laughing goddess clutches her poppies and sheaves.

Robert Wells, trans. *The Idylls of Theocritus.* (Manchester and New York: Carcanet, 1988), pp. 86–87.

---

andria, which rose to a height of nearly four hundred feet with three diminishing stories and eight columns to support the light at the top, and the citadel of Alexandria, dedicated to the god Serapis and built of stone covered with blue-tinted plaster, and said by a contemporary to have "risen into mid-air." In Pergamon in Asia Minor an enormous altar to Zeus (transported in modern times to Berlin) and an enormous open-air theater looked out over a high hill. In Ephesus, not far away, the streets were paved with marble. The "signature" of Hellenistic architecture of whatever dimension was the Corinthian column, a form of column more ornate than the Doric and Ionic alternatives that had predominated in earlier Greek building.

SCULPTURE

In the final analysis, probably the most influential of all products of Hellenistic culture were works of sculpture. Whereas earlier Greek sculpture had sought to idealize humanity and to express Greek ideals of modesty by understated restraint, Hellenistic sculpture emphasized extreme naturalism and unashamed extravagance. In practice this meant that sculptors went to great lengths

The Marble Streets of Ephesus. Taken from the Persians by Alexander in 334 B.C.E., this cosmopolitan city on the west coast of Asia Minor was noted for its splendor.

Old Market Woman, second century B.C.E. Sculptures of this period often showed ordinary people engaged in ordinary activities. This realistic marble sculpture is of an old, tired woman who is carrying a basket of fruits and vegetables and chickens to market.

to recreate facial furrows, muscular distensions, and complex folds of drapery. Awkward human postures were considered to offer the greatest challenges to the artist in stone, to the degree that sculptors might prefer to show people stretching themselves or balancing on one leg in ways that hardly ever occur in real life. Since most Hellenistic sculpture was executed for wealthy private patrons, it is clear that the goal was to create something unique in terms of its conception and craftsmanship—something a collector could show off as the only one of its type. Not surprisingly, therefore, complexity came to be admired for its own sake, and extreme naturalism sometimes teetered on the brink of dis-

The Corinthian Order of Architecture. This characteristically Hellenistic style for constructing columns was much more ornate than its classical predecessors.

torted stylization. Yet when moderns see such works they frequently experience a shock of recognition, for the bizarre and exaggerated postures of Hellenistic sculptures exerted an enormous influence on Michelangelo and his followers, and later inspired some of the most "modern" sculptors of the nineteenth and twentieth centuries. Three of the most famous examples of Hellenistic sculpture, which reveal different aspects of Hellenistic aesthetic ideals, may be cited here: the *Dying Gaul*, done in Pergamon around 220 B.C.E., shows consummate skill in portraying a twisted human body; the *Winged Victory of Samothrace* of about 200 B.C.E. displays flowing drapery as if it were not stone but real cloth; and the *Laocoön* group, of the first century B.C.E., offers one of the most intensely emotional as well as complex compositions known in the entire history of sculptural art.

Dying Gaul Seen from Front and Back. A famous example of Hellenistic realism and pathos, this statue was executed around 220 B.C.E. in the court of Perga-mon in Asia Minor. (The original is lost; shown here is a faithful Roman copy.) The sculptor clearly wished to exhibit skill in depicting an unusual human pos-ture and succeeded remarkably in evok-ing the thin line that separates human dignity from unappeasable loneliness and physical suffering.

Laocoön. In sharp contrast to the serenity of the *Winged Victory* is this famous sculpture group from the first century B.C.E., depicting the death of Laocoön. According to legend, Laocoön warned the Trojans not to touch the wooden horse sent by the Greeks and was punished by Poseidon, who sent two serpents to kill him and his sons. The intense emotionalism of this work later had a great influence on western European art from Michelangelo onward.

The Winged Victory of Samoth-race. In this figure, done around 200 B.C.E., a Hellenistic sculptor preserved some of the calmness and devotion to grace and propor-tion characteristic of Hellenic art in the golden age.

SCIENCE AND MEDICINE

Why did science and medicine flourish in this period?

The most brilliant age in the history of science prior to the seventeenth century C.E. was the Hellenistic period. There are two major reasons for the impressive development of science in the centuries after Alexander's conquest of the Persian empire. One was the enormous stimulus given to intellectual inquiry by the fusion of Mesopotamian and Egyptian science with the learning and the curiosity of the Greeks. The other was that many Hellenistic rulers were generous patrons of scientific research, subsidizing scientists who belonged to their retinues just as they subsidized sculptors. It was once thought that the motives for such patronage were practical—that rulers believed the progress of science would enhance the growth of industry in their territories and would also improve their own material comforts. Yet students of Hellenistic civilization now doubt that any ruler was hoping for an "industrial revolution" in the sense of applying technology to save human labor, for labor was cheap and autocratic princes were completely indifferent to the sufferings of the laboring classes. As for the supposed connection between science and the enhancement of material comfort, Hellenistic rulers had adequate numbers of slaves to fan them and were not inclined to introduce mechanical devices that would have lessened the public grandeur of being tended by deferential subordinates. To be sure, practical aims motivated the patronage of science in some areas, above all in medicine and anything that might relate to military technology. Yet it has become clear that the autocrats who financed the scientific endeavors did so primarily for motives of prestige: sometimes a scientist might fashion a splendid gadget for a ruler that he could show off to visitors as he would show off his sculptures; and even if not, purely theoretical achievements were so much admired among the Greek-speaking leisured classes that a Hellenistic prince who subsidized a theoretical breakthrough would share the prestige for it in the way the mayor of an American city might bask in prestige today if his or her city's football team were to win the Super Bowl.

The most influential Hellenistic mathematician was Euclid, the master of geometry.

SCIENCE

The major Hellenistic sciences were astronomy, mathematics, geography, medicine, and physics. The most renowned of the earlier Hellenistic astronomers was Aristarchus of Samos (310–230 B.C.E.), sometimes called the "Hellenistic Copernicus." His primary accomplishment was his deduction that the earth and the other planets revolve around the sun. This view was not accepted by his successors because it conflicted with the teachings of Aristotle and with the conviction of the Greeks that humanity, and therefore the earth, must be at the center of the universe. Later the fame of Aristarchus was overshadowed by that of Ptolemy of Alexandria (second century C.E.). Although Ptolemy made few original discoveries, he systematized the work of others. His principal writing, the *Almagest*, based on the geocentric theory (the view that all heavenly bodies revolve around the earth), was handed down to medieval Europe as the classic summary of ancient astronomy.

Closely allied with astronomy were mathematics and geography. The most influential Hellenistic mathematician was Euclid, the master of geometry. Until the middle of the nineteenth century his *Elements of Geometry* (written around 300 B.C.E. as a synthesis of the work of others) remained the accepted basis for the study of that branch of mathematics. The most original of the Hellenistic mathematicians was probably Hipparchus (second century B.C.E.), who laid the foundations of both plane and spherical trigonometry. Hellenistic geography owed most of its development to Eratosthenes (c. 276–c. 196 B.C.E.), astronomer and librarian of Alexandria. By means of sundials placed some hundreds of miles apart, he calculated the circumference of the earth with an error of less than two hundred miles. Eratosthenes was also the first to suggest the possibility of reaching eastern Asia by sailing west. One of his successors divided the earth into the five climatic zones that are still recognized, and explained the ebb and flow of the tides as due to the influence of the moon.

MEDICINE

Other Hellenistic advances in science were in the field of medicine. Especially significant was the work of Herophilus of Chalcedon (c. 335–c. 280 B.C.E.), who conducted his research in Alexandria at about the beginning of the third century B.C.E. Herophilus was the greatest anatomist of antiquity and probably the first to practice human dissection. Among his achievements were a detailed description of the brain, with an insistence (against Aristotle) that the brain is the seat of human intelligence; the discovery of the significance of the pulse, and its use in diagnosing illness; and the discovery that the arteries contain blood alone (not a mixture of blood and air as Aristotle had taught), and that their function is to carry blood from the heart to all parts of the body. About the middle of the third century, Erasistratus of Alexandria gained much of his knowledge of bodily functions from vivisection. He discovered the valves of the heart and distinguished between motor and sensory nerves. In addition, he rejected Hippocrates' theory that the body consists of four "humors" and consequently criticized excessive bloodletting as a method of cure. Unfortunately the humoral theory and an emphasis on bloodletting were revived by Galen, the great encyclopedist of medicine who lived in the Roman empire in the second century C.E.

Prior to the third century B.C.E., physics had been a branch of philosophy. It was made a separate, experimental science by Archimedes of Syracuse (c. 287–212 B.C.E.), who discovered the law of floating bodies, or specific gravity, and formulated with scientific exactness the principles of the lever, the pulley, and the screw. Among his memorable inventions were the compound pulley and the screw propeller for ships. Although he has been considered the greatest technical genius of antiquity, in fact he placed no emphasis on his mechanical contraptions and preferred to devote his time instead to pure scientific research. Tradition

relates that he discovered "Archimedes' principle" (specific gravity) while pondering possible theories in his bath: when he reached his stunning insight he dashed out naked into the street crying "Eureka" ("I have found it").

CONCLUSION

The supremacy of the great Hellenistic kingdoms and the rise of new forms of political organization in the Greek world outside of monarchy might lead one to ask, What became of the polis, the foundation of Greek culture? Although the great decisions and events of history took place away from the traditional polis, some poleis—such as Rhodes and to a lesser extent Athens—continued to thrive as centers of trade. It is also important to remember that the great empires of the ancient Mediterranean were not so much modern-looking territorial concepts as they were collections of cities, and for the most part the Greco-Macedonian rulers of the Hellenistic era continued to carry the cultural and political baggage of the polis world.

Nevertheless, the Hellenistic polis—even when it had not grossly outgrown its heritage and become a sprawling megalopolis such as Alexandria or Antioch—was in many ways a fundamentally different place than its classical precursor. As we have already seen, the changes afoot in the fourth century were disrupting the traditional bonds of Greek social and political life. What Alexander achieved, apart from the conquest of western and central Asia, was a chance at escape for many of the Greeks in the fourth-century homeland. Alexander had created, perhaps unwittingly, a cosmopolitan world full of economic opportunity for a Greek-speaker, a common Greek-based culture that engulfed the eastern Mediterranean and western Asia, and a sense of "Greekness" that transcended political and geographical boundaries. Into this vast, exciting world, Greeks poured en masse, and the population of the Greek mainland declined by as much as one half in the century between 325 and 225 B.C.E. Many Greeks sought fortunes—financial and otherwise—in a "Greek" world of massive empires and bustling cosmopolitan cities simply unimaginable even in classical Athens.

> Although the great decisions and events of history took place away from the traditional polis, some poleis—such as Rhodes and to a lesser extent Athens—continued to thrive as centers of trade.

CHRONOLOGY

SCIENTIFIC LUMINARIES OF THE HELLENISTIC WORLD

Herophilus of Chalcedon	c. 335–c. 280 B.C.E.
Euclid	330?–270? B.C.E.
Aristarchus of Samos	310–230 B.C.E.
Archimedes of Syracuse	c. 287–212 B.C.E.
Eratosthenes	c. 276–c. 196 B.C.E.

Such a transformation had serious effects on Greek culture and the polis. We need only think of the small-scale Dark Age communities and archaic poleis from which Greek cultural expression grew. In these societies everybody knew virtually everyone else, and innumerable social and political ties bound the citizens. Greek traditions of participation in government had led to a greater share in the franchise than any other culture had achieved in antiquity. Every citizen of the Greek world, to a lesser or greater extent, had some share, some stake in his society, its institutions, its gods, its army, and its cultural life.

If we transport the ingrained outlook inherited by the Greeks from this earlier pattern of life into the swirling cosmopolitanism of the Hellenistic city, we can well imagine the effects on the individual. All of those things that defined one's life as a person and a citizen were by and large gone. The intimate connection with the political life of the state, often even at the local level, had vanished. In place of the nexus of social and familial relationships prevalent in the Greek mainland, an average Greek in one of the Hellenistic kingdoms might have only his immediate family to rely on, if even that. What resulted was a traumatic separation between traditional values and assumptions and the social and political realities of the day.

> Above all, the fact that Hellenistic science was the most advanced in the Western world until the seventeenth century demonstrates the intellectual creativity that marked the Hellenistic world.

Judged from the vantage point of classical Greece, Hellenistic civilization may at first seem no more than a degenerate phase of Greek civilization. The autocratic governments of the Hellenistic Age appear repugnant in contrast to Athenian democracy, and the Hellenistic penchant for extravagance may appear debased in contrast to the earlier Greek taste for chaste beauty. Even the best Hellenistic literary works lack the inspired majesty of the great Greek tragedies, and none of the Hellenistic philosophers matched the profundity of Plato and Aristotle. Yet Hellenistic civilization had its own achievements also, that the classical age could not match. Most Hellenistic cities offered a greater range of public facilities, such as museums and libraries, than earlier Greek cities did, and we have seen that numerous Hellenistic thinkers, writers, and artists left to posterity important new ideas, impressive new genres, and imaginative new styles. Above all, the fact that Hellenistic science was the most advanced in the Western world until the seventeenth century demonstrates the intellectual creativity that marked the Hellenistic world.

Probably the most important contribution of the Hellenistic era to subsequent historical development was the role it played as intermediary between Greece and Rome. In some cases the Hellenistic contribution was simply that of preservation. For example, most of the familiarity the ancient Romans had with classical Greek thought came to them by way of copies of Greek philosophical and literary texts preserved in Hellenistic libraries. In other areas, however, transfer involved transmutation. Hellenistic art, for example, evolved from earlier Greek art into something related but quite different, and it was this "Greek-like" art that exerted the greatest influence on the tastes and artistic accomplishments of the Romans. A similar case might be made for drama.

In conclusion, two particularly remarkable aspects of Hellenistic culture deserve special comment—Hellenistic cosmopolitanism and Hellenistic "modernity." Not only does the word "cosmopolitan" itself come from Greek cosmopolis, meaning "universal city," but it was the Greeks of the Hellenistic period who came the closest among Westerners to turning this ideal of cosmopolitanism into reality. Specifically, around 250 B.C.E. a leisure-class Greek could have traveled from Sicily to the borders of India, always meeting people who "spoke his language," both literally and in terms of shared ideals. Moreover, this same Greek would not have been a nationalist in the sense of professing any deep loyalty to a city-state or kingdom. Rather, he would have considered himself a "citizen of the world." Hellenistic cosmopolitanism was partly a product of the cosmopolitanism of Persia, and it helped in turn to create the cosmopolitanism of Rome, but in contrast to both it was not imperial—that is, it was entirely divorced from constraints imposed by a supranational state—although it was achieved through Greek exploitation of subject peoples. Finally, although cosmopolitanism is surely not an obvious condition of the present, other aspects of Hellenistic civilization must seem very familiar to observers today. Authoritarian governments, ruler worship, economic instability, extreme skepticism existing side by side with intense religiosity, rational science existing side by side with irrational superstition, flamboyant art and ostentatious art collecting: all these traits might make the thoughtful student of history wonder whether the Hellenistic Age is not one of the most relevant in the entire human record for comparison with our own.

SELECTED READINGS

Penguin Classics and the Loeb Classical Library both offer reliable translations of scores of literary and historical texts from this period. Particularly important are historical works by Arrian (*Anabasis of Alexander*) and Plutarch (*Lives*).

Adcock, F. E. *The Greek and Macedonian Art of War.* Berkeley, 1957. Still a valuable introduction to the guiding principles and assumptions of Greek and Macedonian warfare.

Austin, M. M. *The Hellenistic World from Alexander to the Roman Conquest: A Selection of Ancient Sources in Translation.* Cambridge, 1981.

Bagnall, R. S., and P. Derow. *Greek Historical Documents: The Hellenistic Period.* Chico, Calif., 1981.

Bosworth, A. B. *Conquest and Empire: The Reign of Alexander the Great.* Cambridge, 1988. A political and military analysis of Alexander's career that successfully strips away the romance, maintaining a clear vision of the ruthlessness and human cost of his conquests.

Borza, Eugene N. *In the Shadow of Olympus: The Emergence of Macedon.* Princeton, 1990. The standard account of the rise of Macedon up to the accession of Philip II.

Burstein, Stanley M., ed. and trans. *The Hellenistic Age from the Battle of Ipsos to the Death of Kleopatria VII.* Cambridge, 1985. An excellent collection, with sources not found elsewhere.

Cartledge, Paul A. *Agesilaus and the Crisis of Sparta.* Baltimore, 1987. A thorough but readable analysis of the social and political challenges besetting Sparta in the fourth century B.C.E.

Ellis, J. R. *Philip II and Macedonian Imperialism.* London, 1976. A densely written examination of Philip's actions that tries to strip away the biases of Athenian sources.

Green, Peter. *Alexander to Actium: The Historical Evolution of the Hellenistic Age.* Berkeley, 1990. An outstanding, comprehensive and wide-ranging history of the period; balanced and sensible.

———. *Alexander of Macedon, 356–323 B.C.* Berkeley, 1991. Revised edition of the author's 1972 biography; entertainingly written, and rich in detail and insight.

Hammond, Nicholas G. L. *The Genius of Alexander the Great.* Chapel Hill, 1998. A clear, authoritative, admiring account, distilling a lifetime of research on the subject.

Hansen, Mogens H. *The Athenian Democracy in the Age of Demosthenes.* Oxford, 1991. An intelligent examination of the political institutions of Athens in the fourth century B.C.E.

Ober, Josiah. *Mass and Elite in Democratic Athens: Rhetoric, Ideology, and the Power of the People.* Princeton, 1989. An excellent study of the ideology of democracy in Athens in the fourth century B.C.E. that borrows intelligently from modern social scientific insights.

Pollitt, Jerome J. *Art in the Hellenistic Age.* New York, 1986. The standard account, written from the perspective of cultural history as well as art history.

Sherwin-White, Susan, and Amélie Kuhrt. *From Samarkhand to Sardis: A New Approach to the Seleucid Empire.* London, 1993. A stimulating examination of the relationship between rulers and ruled in the vast expanses of the Seleucid empire.

Strauss, Barry. *Athens after the Peloponnesian War: Class, Faction, and Policy. 403–386 B.C.* London, 1986. A narrowly focused but highly informative analysis of the consequences of the Peloponnesian War for Athenian society.

Tritle, Lawrence A. ed. *The Greek World in the Fourth Century: From the Fall of the Athenian Empire to the Successors of Alexander.* New York, 1997. A wide-ranging collection of scholarly essays.

CHAPTER SIX

ROMAN CIVILIZATION

WHILE THE GREEKS STRUGGLED against the Persians and then each other, a new civilization was emerging on the banks of the Tiber River in central Italy. By the end of the fourth century B.C.E. Rome was already the dominant power on the Italian peninsula. For five centuries thereafter Rome's power steadily increased. By the first century C.E., it ruled most of the Hellenistic world as well as most of western Europe. These conquests, together with Rome's destruction of the powerful North African city of Carthage, united the entire Mediterranean world and made the Mediterranean itself a "Roman lake." Rome's empire brought Greek institutions and ideas not only to the western half of the Mediterranean world, but also to Britain, France, Spain, and Romania. Rome was thus the builder of a great historical bridge that connected Europe to the cultural and political heritage of the ancient Near East. Without Rome, European civilization as we know it would not exist.

Rome was deeply influenced by Greek culture, but Rome was also a distinctive civilization in its own right. On the one hand, the Romans were much more tradition minded than were the Greeks. Rome revered its old agricultural traditions, its household gods, and its sternly military values. But as their empire grew, the Romans also came to see themselves as having a divinely ordained mission to civilize their world by teaching it the arts of law and government that were Rome's own peculiar genius. Virgil (70–19 B.C.E.), the great epic poet of Rome, expressed this self-conscious sense of Rome's historical mission in the *Aeneid*, which tells one of the several competing legends Romans treasured about the founding of their city. Here, Anchises of Troy speaks prophetically to his son Aeneas, who (in Virgil's account) would go on to become one of the founders of the city of Rome. Speaking about the Romans, Anchises tells his son of his people's future:

FOCUS QUESTIONS

• How did the Etruscans and Greeks influence early Roman society?

• In what ways did the early Roman Republic become more democratic?

• What economic and social changes resulted from Roman territorial expansion?

• What issues caused the social struggles of the Late Republic?

• How did Roman interaction with the Hellenistic world accelerate social changes?

• How did Rome control its far-flung territories?

• What role did upper-class women play in Roman society?

• What factors brought the Roman empire to the brink of ruin?

• Did Rome fall? Why or why not?

"Others will cast more tenderly in bronze
Their breathing figures, I can well believe,
And bring more lifelike portraits out of marble;
Argue more eloquently, use the pointer
To trace the paths of heaven accurately
And accurately foretell the rising stars.
Roman, remember by your strength to rule
Earth's peoples—for your arts are to be these:
To pacify, to impose the rule of law,
To spare the conquered, battle down the proud."

Virgil, *Aeneid*, Book VI, lines 848–857, trans. Robert Fitzgerald (New York: Random House, 1982) p. 190.

Not all the peoples whom Rome conquered welcomed the experience. But all were transformed by it.

EARLY ITALY AND THE ROMAN MONARCHY

How did the Etruscans and Greeks influence early Roman society?

The particular geography of the Italian peninsula had a decisive influence upon the course of Rome's development. Aside from excellent marble and small quantities of lead, tin, copper, iron (on the island of Elba), and silver, Italy has no mineral resources to speak of. Despite its extensive coastline, Italy has only a few good harbors, and most of these face toward the west, away from Greece and the Near East. Ancient Italy did have sizable forests and a considerably greater amount of fertile land than did Greece. But Italy was also more exposed to invasion. The Alps posed no effective barrier to the influx of peoples from central Europe, and the low-lying Italian coastline invited conquest by sea. The Romans were absorbed in military pursuits almost from the moment of their settlement on Italian soil because they were continuously forced to defend their own conquests against other invaders.

The particular geography of the Italian peninsula had a decisive influence upon the course of Rome's development.

THE ETRUSCANS

The dominant early settlers on the Italian peninsula were a non-Indo-European-speaking people known as the Etruscans. Our knowledge of the Etruscans is severely limited by the fact that their language, although written in a Greek alphabet, has not yet been fully deciphered. It appears, however, that Etruscan settlements go back to the late Bronze Age, and that they were in early and frequent contact with both Greece and Assyria. By the sixth century B.C.E., the Etruscans had established a confederation of cities that stretched over most of northern and central Italy. They were skilled metalworkers, artists, and architects, from whom the later Romans took their knowledge of the arch and the vault, among much else. In addition to their alphabet, the Etruscans also shared with the Greeks a religion based on the worship of gods in human (rather than animal or metereological) form.

In contrast with Greek practice, Etruscan women enjoyed a comparatively elevated place in society. Etruscan women participated in public life and sporting events; they attended dramatic performances and athletic competitions (which, because the participants were usually nude, were forbidden to Greek women); and they danced in ways that shocked both Greeks and Romans. Etruscan wives ate meals with their husbands, reclining together on the same banqueting couch; and after death, they were buried together in the same mortuary vaults. Some Etruscan families even traced their descent through the female line.

Early Roman society was deeply influenced by Etruscan example. Not only the Roman arch and vault, but also the cruel sport of gladiatorial combat and the practice of foretelling the future by studying the entrails of animals or the flight of birds went back to Etruscan beginnings. The Roman practice of centering urban life around massive stone temples with their attendant cults was probably adopted from an Etruscan example. Even the two most famous myths the Romans told about the founding of Rome itself they probably drew from the Etruscans: that involving Aeneas of Troy (noted above in connection with Virgil's *Aeneid*), and that involving the infant twins Romulus and Remus, who were raised by a female wolf after being abandoned by their parents.

The Romans also borrowed heavily from the Greek settlers of Italy. Large numbers of colonists from mainland Greece began to arrive in southern Italy and Sicily during the eighth century B.C.E. By the end of the seventh century B.C.E., Greek civilization in Magna Graecia (as southern Italy and Sicily were

HOW DID THE ETRUSCANS AND GREEKS INFLUENCE EARLY ROMAN SOCIETY?

EARLY ITALY AND THE ROMAN MONARCHY   185

Etruscan Sarcophagus.

known) was as advanced as it was in Greece itself. Such famous Greeks as Pythagorus, Archimedes, and even Plato for a time lived in Greek Italy, which also became a key battlefield in the Peleponnesian War between Athens and Sparta. From the Greeks, the Romans derived their alphabet, many of their religious concepts (it is difficult to disentangle Etruscan from Greek influence here), and much of their art and mythology. The high culture of Rome was thoroughly and pervasively Greek in inspiration and imitation.

THE RISE OF ROME

As for the Romans themselves, they descended from a cluster of peoples of the Indo-European language group who entered Italy by way of the Alps between 2000 and 1000 B.C.E. Recent archaeological research places the founding of the city of Rome by Latin-speaking people, thereafter known as Romans, quite near the traditional date of 753 B.C.E. Rome's strategic location along the Tiber brought it many advantages. Trading ships—but not large war fleets—could navigate the Tiber far up its course. Rome could thus serve as a port without being threatened by attack from the sea. Rome's famous hills increased the defensibility of the site. Rome also sat astride the first good ford

across the Tiber River, making it a major land and river cross-roads. Rome therefore became an important and comparatively wealthy city in the region of Latium, sitting as it did along the frontier between that area and Etruria, the Etruscans' homeland.

The topography of Latium—a broad, flat plain with few natural obstacles—also influenced the way Rome dealt with neighboring communities. At an early date, the Romans established with the other Latin communities a series of common "rights," including *commercium* (all contracts between Latins were enforceable throughout Latium), *connubium* (Latins could intermarry with legal recognition in the community of both husband and wife), and *migratio* (a Latin of one town could migrate to another and, if he remained there for a year, transfer his citizenship). Together, these privileges were known as the "Latin Right," and stand in sharp contrast to the rigid particularism and jealous suspicion that divided the cities of Sumer or Greece.

Romulus and Remus. A sixth-century B.C.E. Etruscan bronze statue known as the "Capitoline Wolf." Although the present statues of the twins were added during the fifteenth century C.E., there were probably comparable figures of Romulus and Remus in the same basic posture in the original statue.

The willingness of the Romans to extend the Latin Right to "outsiders" was a key fact in the success of their later expansion.

According to Roman legend, the government was initially a monarchy in which a patriarchal king exercised jurisdiction over his subjects comparable to what a male family head would exercise over the members of his household. A senate, or council of elders (*senex* is Latin for "old man"), was composed of the heads of the various clans that formed the community, but its function in this early period is unclear. It was probably an advisory body to Rome's kings.

The monarchy, however, did not last. Legend has it that in 534 B.C.E. an Etruscan tyrant, Tarquin the Proud, gained control of the kingship in Rome. This period of Etruscan overlordship was crucial in transforming Rome from a prosperous village into a true urban center, as Tarquin used Rome's strategic location to dominate Latium and the agriculturally wealthy district of Campania further south. But Tarquin lorded it over the Romans with extreme cruelty. The final indignity came in 510 B.C.E., when Tarquin's son raped a virtuous Roman wife, Lucretia. When Lucretia committed suicide rather than living on "in dishonor," the Romans rose up in revolt, overthrowing not only the Etruscan tyranny but the entire form of monarchical government itself.

The story of Lucretia is probably patriotic myth, but there was a change in government in Rome around 500 B.C.E. (whether gradual or sudden is unknown) that ended the kingship and replaced it with a republic. Thereafter, the Romans would cultivate the conviction that kingship itself was inherently dangerous; and they would come to hold the name of king (in Latin *rex*) in the same fear and contempt with which the Greeks ul-

> The history of the early Roman Republic was one of almost constant warfare.

timately held the name "tyrant." Whatever the truth of Lucretia's story, it does therefore tell us something important about early Roman attitudes toward government and the family.

THE EARLY REPUBLIC

In what ways did the early Roman Republic become more democratic?

The history of the early Roman Republic was one of almost constant warfare. At first the Romans were on the defensive because rival cities took advantage of the confusion accompanying the change of regime to invade Roman territory. After Rome managed to ward off these attacks, the city began to shift to the offensive. As time went on the Romans steadily conquered all the Etruscan territories and then took over the Greek cities of southern Italy, thus intensifying Roman contacts with Greek culture. The Romans did not usually impose heavy burdens on the cities they conquered. More often, they demanded instead that their defeated foes contribute soldiers to the Roman army. To many conquered cities, Rome also extended the Latin Right, giving them a further stake in Rome's continued political and military success. Thus Rome gained for itself nearly inexhaustible reserves of fighting men. By the middle of the third century B.C.E., Rome's army may have numbered as many as three hundred thousand men—a huge force by the standards of the ancient or the medieval worlds.

This long series of conflicts reinforced both the agrarian and the military character of the Roman nation. The acquisition of new lands made it possible for needy Roman citizens to maintain themselves as farmers in the new Roman colonies. By accommodating its increasing population in this way, Rome was thus able to remain a staunchly agricultural civilization for a surprisingly long time. As a result, it developed an interest in shipping and commerce fairly late, compared to the Greeks or Phoenicians. Continual warfare also confirmed among the Romans a steely military ideal. Many of the most familiar Roman legends of martial heroism date from the early Republican period. The brave Horatio, for example, with the help of two friends, held a key bridge against an entire army; the retired soldier Cincinnatus (with whom George Wash-

CHRONOLOGY

PERIODS OF ROMAN CIVILIZATION, 753 B.C.E.–610 C.E.

The rise of Rome	c. 753 B.C.E.
Roman Republic	c. 500–27 B.C.E.
Principate	27 B.C.E.–180 C.E.
Third-Century Crisis	180 C.E.–284 C.E.
Later Empire, or "Dominate"	284–610 C.E.

THE RAPE OF LUCRETIA

The Roman historian Livy compiled his history of Rome in the last half of the first century B.C.E., and most of what survives of his treatise involves the early history of Rome. The events he described surrounding Rome's beginnings are of dubious authenticity in historical terms, but nevertheless help to illustrate the archetypes and values that Romans had long held paramount in their society. The tale of Lucretia, her violation by an Etruscan prince, and the resulting revolution (traditionally dated to 509 B.C.E.) provide one such example.

The young princes spent most of their leisure enjoying themselves in entertainments on the most lavish scale. They were drinking one day in the quarters of Sextus Tarquinius—Collatinus was also present—when someone chanced to mention the subject of wives. Each of them extravagantly praised his own, until Collatinus cried, "Stop! What need is there of words, when in a few hours we can prove beyond doubt the incomparable superiority of my Lucretia? We are all young and strong: why shouldn't we ride to Rome and see with our own eyes what kind of women our wives are?". . .

They reached the city as dusk was falling; and there the wives of the royal princes were found enjoying themselves with a group of young friends at a dinner-party, in the greatest luxury. The riders then went on to Collatia, where they found Lucretia very differently employed: it was already late at night, but there, in the hall of her house, surrounded by her busy maid-servants, she was still hard at work by lamplight upon her spinning. Which wife had won the contest in womanly virtue was no longer in doubt. . . .

A few days later Sextus, without Collatinus's knowledge, returned where he was hospitably welcomed in Lucretia's house. . . . He waited till the house was asleep, and then, when all was quiet, he drew his sword and made his way to Lucretia's room. . . . Sextus urged his love, threatened . . . but not even the fear of death could bend her will. "If death will not move you," Sextus cried, "dishonor shall. I will kill you first, then cut the throat of a slave and lay his naked body by your side." . . . Even the most resolute chastity could not have stood against this dreadful threat. Lucretia yielded. Sextus enjoyed her and rode away, proud of his success.

[After Lucretia told her father and husband what had happened], she said, "What is due to [Sextus] is for you to decide. As for me I am innocent of fault, but I will take my punishment. Never shall Lucretia provide a precedent for unchaste women to escape what they deserve." With these words she drew a knife from under her robe, drove it into her heart and fell forward, dead.

Her father and husband were overwhelmed with grief. While they stood weeping helplessly, Brutus [her father] drew the bloody knife from Lucretia's body, and holding it before him cried: "By this girl's blood—none more chaste till a tyrant wronged her—and by the gods, I swear that with sword and fire, and whatever else can lend strength to my arm, I will pursue Lucius Tarquinius the Proud, his wicked wife, and all his children, and never again will I let them or any other man be King in Rome!"

Livy i.57–59. Based on A. de Selincourt, trans. *Livy: The Early History of Rome.* (New York: Penguin, 1960), pp. 97–99.

ROMAN EXPANSION TO 265 B.C.E.

Controlled by Rome in 485 B.C.E.
To 387 B.C.E.
To 334 B.C.E.
To 300 B.C.E.
To 290 B.C.E.
To 265 B.C.E.

ROMAN EXPANSION IN ITALY, 485–265 B.C.E.

Note the pattern of Roman expansion in central Italy, and that Latium (the area in red) was conquered early by the Romans. How did this early conquest help knit the Latins closely to the Romans? Why did the Romans conquer the Etruscans last, though they were just across the Tiber River? How did the Tiber River help the Romans solidify their control of central Italy? Consider whose interests Rome threatened after 265 B.C.E. by transforming itself into the dominant power of the Italian peninsula, and why.

IN WHAT WAYS DID THE EARLY ROMAN REPUBLIC BECOME MORE DEMOCRATIC?

THE EARLY REPUBLIC   189

ington would be frequently compared) left his farm at a moment's notice to fight for Rome on the battlefield.

THE GOVERNMENT OF THE EARLY REPUBLIC

Meanwhile, Rome underwent a very slow political evolution. Even the replacement of the monarchy was about as conservative a political change as it is possible for any political change to be. Its chief effect was to substitute for the king two elected officials called *consuls*, and to exalt the position of the Senate by granting it control over the public funds. Although the consuls were chosen by the *comitia centuriata* (literally, the Roman "people-in-arms"), this body differed greatly from the citizen assembly of ancient Athens because it met in groups. Each group in the Roman assembly had one vote, and since groups consisting of the wealthiest citizens voted first, a majority could be reached even before the votes of the poorer groups were cast. Consequently the consuls, who served annually, were usually senators who acted as the agents of aristocratic interests. Each consul was supposed to possess the full executive and judicial authority that had previously been wielded by the king, limited by the right each possessed to veto the action of the other. If a conflict arose between them, the Senate might be called on to decide; or in time of grave emergency, a dictator might be appointed for a term of not greater than six months.

After the establishment of the Republic the political dominance of the early aristocracy, known as the *patricians*, began to be challenged by the *plebeians*, who made up nearly 98 percent of the citizen population but who initially had no access to political power. The plebeians were a diverse group. Some had grown wealthy through trade or agriculture, but most were small-holding, prosperous farmers, merchants, or the urban poor. The grievances of the plebeians were numerous. Forced to serve in the army in time of war, they were nevertheless excluded from holding office. They frequently felt themselves the victims of discriminatory decisions in judicial trials. They did not even know what legal rights they were supposed to enjoy, for the laws were unwritten, and the patricians alone had the power to interpret them. Worst was the oppression that could stem from debt because a debtor could be sold into slavery outside Rome by his creditor.

These grievances prompted a plebeian rebellion in the early fifth century B.C.E. that forced the patricians

to agree to the election of new officers known as *tribunes* who could protect the plebeians by vetoing unlawful patrician acts. This victory was followed by a successful demand for codification of the laws about 450 B.C.E. The result was the issuance of the famous Law of the Twelve Tables, so called because it was written on tablets ("tables") of wood. Although this law was later revered by the Romans as a kind of charter of the people's liberties, it was really nothing of the sort, for it mostly perpetuated ancient custom without even abolishing enslavement for debt. Nevertheless, at least there was now a clear definition of law. Roughly a generation later the plebeians won eligibility to positions as lesser magistrates, and about 367 B.C.E. the first plebeian consul was elected. Gradually, plebians also gained access to the Senate. The final plebeian victory came in 287 B.C.E. with the passage of a law stipulating that measures enacted by the *concilium plebis* (a more democratically organized assembly composed only of plebeians) would be binding on the Roman government whether the Senate approved them or not. It is from this citizen assembly that English derives its modern word *plebiscite*.

These reforms had several important consequences, although they took a very long time to manifest themselves, owing to the conservative outlook of the Romans and the constitutional safeguards of the Republic. Because successful plebeians could now work their way into the upper reaches of Roman society and compete for its honors, the Roman aristocracy gradually shifted (at least to some degree) from one of birth to one of wealth. At the same time, however, the social and economic standing of the poorer citizens was slowly being eroded. In an attempt to prevent

CHRONOLOGY

THE RISE OF ROME, 750–FIRST CENTURY B.C.E.

Legendary founding of the city of Rome	753 B.C.E.
Establishment of the Latin Right	493 B.C.E.
Roman Republic established	c. 500 B.C.E.
Plebeian rebellions	fifth century B.C.E.
Law of the Twelve Tables	c. 450 B.C.E.
Concillium plebis gains power	287 B.C.E.
Equestrian order established	third century B.C.E.

wealth from becoming too much of a factor in Roman political life, laws were passed barring senators from engaging directly in commerce. But this restriction only fueled the rise of the important "equestrian" order, men who had the wealth and influence of senators, but who chose a life of business rather than one in politics. Nor were the equestrians and the senators wholly distinct from each other. Often, some members of important families would stay "aloof" from politics by becoming equestrians, while underwriting the political careers of their brothers and cousins, who served as "silent partners" in the family's business concerns. Meanwhile, those few families who managed to win election generation after generation became increasingly prestigious and disproportionately influential. As a result, by the first century B.C.E. even powerful and aristocratic Romans were coming to feel excluded from real political influence within their city, styling themselves as the champions of a downtrodden public interest while pursuing their own private political agendas.

Scholars continue to debate how "democratic" Rome was in the fourth, third, and second centuries B.C.E. A republic differs from a monarchy insofar as supreme power resides in a body of citizens and is exercised by officers in some way responsible to those citizens. But a republic is not necessarily democratic, for it can devise systems for reserving power to an oligarchy or privileged group. The Roman constitution ensured oligarchical rule by the balance it struck between competing governmental institutions: the assembly, the Senate,

For the Greek historian Polybius, the Roman constitution was an ideal balance of monarchical, oligarchic, and democratic principles. It was, in his view, a perfect Aristotelian polity.

and officeholders such as consuls, tribunes, judges, and administrators. In this system no single individual or family clique could become overwhelmingly strong, nor could direct expressions of the popular will unduly affect Roman policy. For the Greek historian Polybius, the Roman constitution was thus an ideal balance of monarchical, oligarchic, and democratic principles. It was, in his view, a perfect Aristotelian polity.

CULTURE, RELIGION, AND MORALITY

Political changes in early republican Rome moved glacially. So too did intellectual and cultural ones. Although writing had been adopted as early as the sixth century B.C.E., the Romans made little use of it except for laws, treaties, and funerary inscriptions. Education was largely limited to instruction imparted by fathers to sons in manly sports, practical arts, and military virtues; as a result, literary culture long remained a minor part of Roman life, even among the aristocracy. War and agriculture continued to be the chief occupations for the bulk of the population. A few artisans could be found in the cities, and a minor development of trade had occurred. But the fact that the Republic had no standard system of coinage until 269 B.C.E. reflects the comparative insignificance of Roman commerce at this time.

During the period of the early Republic, religion assumed the character it retained through the greater part of Roman history. In several ways this religion resembled that of the Greeks—not surprising, since it was directly influenced by Roman knowledge of Greek beliefs. Thus major Roman deities performed the same functions as their Greek equivalents: Jupiter corresponded to Zeus as god of the skies, Neptune to Poseidon as god of the waves, Venus to Aphrodite as goddess of love. Like the Greeks, the Romans had no dogmas or sacraments, nor did they place great emphasis on rewards and punishments after death. But there were also significant differences between the two religions. One was that Romans literally revered their ancestors; their "household gods" included deceased members of a lineage who were worshiped in order to ensure a family's continued prosperity. Another difference was that Roman religion was even more closely tied up with political life. Since the Romans believed that their state could flourish only with divine support, they appointed committees of priests virtually as branches of government to tend to the cult of various gods, preside over public rites, and serve as guardians of sacred traditions. These priests were not full-time professionals, but rather prominent oligarchs who rotated in and out of priestly offices in addition to serving as leaders of the Roman state. This dual role made Roman religion an even more integral part of the fabric of public and political life.

The Romans looked to their gods to bestow on their households and their city the blessings of prosperity, victory, and fertility. Roman morality emphasized patriotism, duty, masculine self-control, and respect for authority and tradition. Its chief virtues were bravery, honor, self-discipline, and loyalty to country and family. A Roman's primary duty was to honor his ancestors

WHAT ECONOMIC AND SOCIAL CHANGES RESULTED FROM ROMAN TERRITORIAL EXPANSION?

THE FATEFUL WARS WITH CARTHAGE   191

Junius Brutus. A Roman noble of the first century B.C.E., Brutus is shown here holding the busts of two of his ancestors. Honoring one's ancestors was an important part of Roman social and religious life, especially among the aristocracy.

by his conduct, but the greatest honor attached to those who sacrificed themselves for Rome. For the good of the Republic, therefore, citizens had to be ready to sacrifice not only their own lives but, if necessary, those of their family and friends. The cold-bloodedness of certain consuls who put their sons to death for breaches of military discipline was to the Romans a matter of deep admiration bordering on awe.

THE FATEFUL WARS WITH CARTHAGE

What economic and social changes resulted from Roman territorial expansion?

By 265 B.C.E. the Romans had reduced the last vestiges of Etruscan resistance and thereby controlled three quarters of the Italian peninsula. Confident of their strength over Italy, the Romans were now free to engage in overseas ventures. Scholars disagree as to whether the Romans continually extended their rule as a matter of deliberate policy, or whether their conquests grew more accidentally, by a series of reactions to changes in the status quo that could be interpreted as a threat to Rome's security. Probably the truth lies between these extremes. Whatever the case, beginning in 264 B.C.E., a year after its final victory over the Etruscans, Rome became embroiled in a series of wars with overseas nations that decidedly altered the course of its history.

By far the most crucial was the struggle with Carthage, a great maritime empire that stretched along the northern coast of Africa from modern-day Tunisia to the Straits of Gibraltar, and that controlled parts of Sicily, Sardinia, and Corsica. Carthage had been founded about 800 B.C.E. as a Phoenician colony. In the sixth century it developed into a rich and powerful independent state. The prosperity of its upper classes was founded upon commerce and the exploitation of North African natural resources.

Carthaginian government was oligarchic. The real rulers were thirty merchant princes who constituted an inner council of the Senate. Carthaginian religion and culture remained true in many ways to its Canaanite roots, but by the third century B.C.E. its civilization had gained a material prosperity that would have baffled their Phoenician forebears. In naval might, commercial prowess, and control of crucial material resources, Carthage was far the superior of Rome.

The protracted struggles between Rome and Carthage are known collectively as the Punic Wars because the Romans called the Carthaginians Poeni, that is, "Phoenicians." The First Punic War began in 264 B.C.E., apparently because of Rome's genuine fear of potential Carthaginian expansion. Carthage already controlled most of Sicily and now was threatening to gain control of Messina, directly across from the Italian mainland. Unwilling to allow Carthage to become a menacing next-door neighbor, a Roman consul brought an army over the straits to defend Messina, against the objections of many prominent senators who wanted to avoid embroilment with the Carthaginians. Carthage took massive measures to counterattack and twenty-three years of bitter fighting ensued. Finally, by a peace agreement in 241, Carthage was forced to cede all of Sicily to Rome and to pay a large indemnity. As a result Sicily became Rome's first overseas province. Shortly after the war, a faction of Roman senators sought to renegotiate the terms, seizing Corsica and Sardinia in the process; hard feelings on the Carthaginian side understandably ran deep.

Because the Romans had fought so hard to defeat Carthage, they became determined not to let their enemy become dominant in other Mediterranean areas. Accordingly, in 218 the Romans interpreted Carthage's attempt to expand its rule in Spain as a threat to Roman interests and responded with a declaration of war. The renewed struggle, known as the Second Punic War, raged for sixteen years. At first Rome was entirely thrown off guard by the brilliant exploits of the famous Carthaginian commander Hannibal. Already commanding an army in Spain, Hannibal in a truly remarkable military feat brought this force, including war elephants, through southern France and then over the Alps into Italy. With Carthaginian troops on Italian soil, Rome escaped defeat by the narrowest of margins. Only "delaying tactics" ultimately saved the day, for time was on the side of those who could keep an invader short of supplies and worn down by harassment. No less decisive, however, was Hannibal's failure to win Rome's Latin allies over to his side. Rome's generous treatment had made them loyal and unshakable in their support of Rome. Deep reserves of Roman manpower and the discipline of Rome and her closest allies ultimately overcame Hannibal's military genius. From 212 B.C.E. onward, the Romans increasingly put the Carthaginians on the defensive, in Spain as well as in Italy and Sicily. The

Hannibal. A coin from Carthage representing Hannibal as a victorious general, with an elephant on the reverse.

architect of the Spanish offensive, Publius Cornelius Scipio, drove into North Africa and defeated Hannibal at Zama, near Carthage, in 202 B.C.E. His victory ended the Second Punic War, and Scipio was honored with the additional name "Africanus," as conqueror of Africa.

Carthage was now more completely humbled than before, being compelled to abandon all its possessions except the city of Carthage itself and its surrounding territory in Africa, and to pay an indemnity three times greater than that paid at the end of the First Punic War. Yet Roman suspicion of Carthage remained obsessive. About the middle of the second century B.C.E. Carthage had recovered some of its former prosperity—and this was enough to provoke the displeasure of the Romans. Nothing now would satisfy the most influential Roman senators but the total demolition of the Carthaginian state. In 150 B.C.E. the Roman war hawk

WHAT ECONOMIC AND SOCIAL CHANGES RESULTED FROM ROMAN TERRITORIAL EXPANSION?

THE FATEFUL WARS WITH CARTHAGE   193

Cato the Censor ended every speech he made in the Senate with the same words: "Carthage must be destroyed." The Senate agreed, and in the following year seized on a minor pretext to demand that the Carthaginians abandon their city and settle at least ten miles from the coast. Since this demand amounted to a death sentence for a nation dependent on commerce, it was refused—as the Romans probably realized it would be. The result was the Third Punic War, fought between 149 and 146 B.C.E. The final Roman assault was carried into the city of Carthage, and a frightful butchery took place. When the victorious Roman general—Scipio Aemilianus, the grandson of Africanus—saw Carthage going up in flames he said, "It is a glorious moment, but I have a strange feeling that some day the same fate will befall my own homeland." With the might of the Carthaginians completely broken, the fifty-five thousand that remained alive were sold into slavery, their once magnificent city was razed, and the site was accursed in Roman imagination. (The legend of the Romans sowing the land with salt was clearly an exaggeration, because a generation later a Roman politician proposed founding a Roman colony on the site.)

TERRITORIAL EXPANSION

The wars with Carthage had momentous effects on Rome's development. Most obvious was an enormous increase in Roman territory. The Roman victories over Carthage led to the creation of new overseas provinces in Sicily, North Africa, and Spain. This not only brought Rome great new wealth—above all Sicilian and African grain and Spanish silver—but was the beginning of a policy of westward expansion that proved to be one of the great formative influences on the history of Europe.

The wars also brought Rome into conflict with eastern Mediterranean powers and thereby paved the way for still further conquests. During the Second Punic War, Philip V of Macedon had entered into an alliance with Carthage and was said to have designs on Egypt. Declaring a disinterested intention to forestall Philip's moves, Rome sent an army to the east. The result was the conquest of Greece and Asia Minor and the reduction of Egypt to a Roman sphere of influence. By 146 B.C.E., Greece and Macedon had become Roman provinces, Seleucid Asia had been deprived of most of its territories, and Ptolemaic Egypt was largely a pawn of Roman commercial and naval interests.

The wars with Carthage had momentous effects on Rome's development.

ECONOMIC AND SOCIAL CHANGE

As Roman tentacles stretched out over the Mediterranean, a host of fundamental economic and social changes ensued. One was a huge increase in slavery due to the capture and sale of prisoners of war. We have seen that fifty-five thousand Carthaginians were enslaved in 146 B.C.E.; not long before, one hundred fifty thousand Greeks had met the same fate. By the end of the second century about a million slaves toiled in Italy, mainly in the fields, making Rome one of the most slave-based economies known to history. Concomitant with this development was the decline of the small farmer as a result of the establishment of the plantation system based on slave labor and the influx of cheap grain from the provinces. Small farmers, in turn, took refuge in the cities, above all the city of Rome itself, creating a large new urban element; this dynamic was itself exacerbated by the great wealth empire brought to the aristocracy, who sought to reinvest their gains in land. Since many small farmers now served several years in the army away from home—whether in distant Spain or the Greek East—their farms declined, and the temptation to sell at above-market prices to a land-hungry elite was too much for their struggling families to resist. Inevitably this trend, along with the incorporation of overseas areas long oriented to trade, and the need for an administrative apparatus, expanded and strengthened the numbers and the political clout of the equestrians who, in addition to their private business activities, also held gov-

CHRONOLOGY

PUNIC WARS, 264–146 B.C.E.

First Punic War begins	264 B.C.E.
First Punic War ends	241 B.C.E.
Second Punic War begins	218 B.C.E.
Second Punic War ends	201 B.C.E.
Third Punic War begins	149 B.C.E.
Third Punic War ends	146 B.C.E.
City of Carthage destroyed	146 B.C.E.

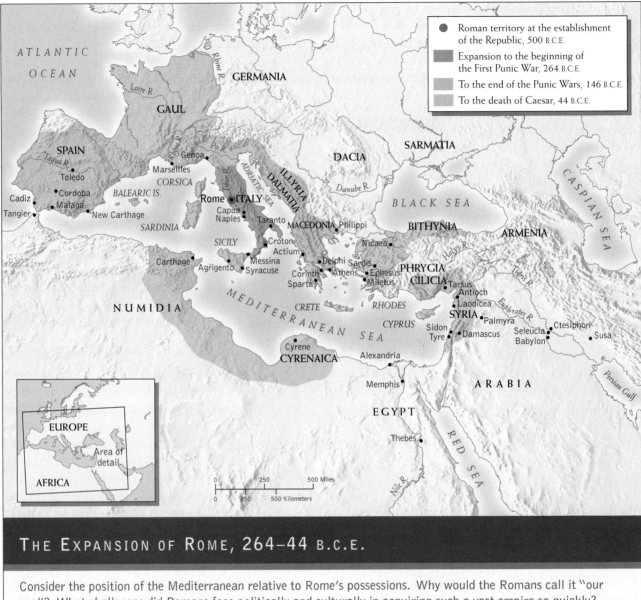

ATLANTIC
OCEAN

GERMANIA

GAUL

SARMATIA

SPAIN

DACIA

BLACK SEA

CASPIAN SEA

Genoa
Marseilles
CORSICA
Rome · ITALY
ADRIATIC SEA
ILLYRIA
DALMATIA
Danube R.
Capua
Naples
Taranto
MACEDONIA   Philippi
BITHYNIA
ARMENIA
Toledo
Cadiz
Cordoba
Malaga
Tangier
New Carthage
BALEARIC IS.
SARDINIA
SICILY
Croton
Actium
Messina
Agrigento   Syracuse
Nicaea
Delphi   Sardis
Corinth   Athens   Ephesus
Sparta   Miletus
PHRYGIA
CILICIA
Tarsus
Antioch
Laodicea
SYRIA   Palmyra
Ctesiphon
Carthage

NUMIDIA

MEDITERRANEAN SEA

CRETE

RHODES

CYPRUS

Sidon
Tyre   Damascus
Seleucia
Babylon
Susa

Cyrene
CYRENAICA

Alexandria

ARABIA

Memphis

EGYPT

Thebes

RED SEA

Nile R.

EUROPE
Area of
detail
AFRICA

Loire R.
Rhine R.
Rhone R.
Po R.
Tiber R.
Tagus R.
Halys R.
Tigris R.
Euphrates R.
Persian Gulf

0   250   500 Miles
0   250   500 Kilometers

● Roman territory at the establishment
of the Republic, 500 B.C.E.

■ Expansion to the beginning of
the First Punic War, 264 B.C.E.

■ To the end of the Punic Wars, 146 B.C.E.

■ To the death of Caesar, 44 B.C.E.

THE EXPANSION OF ROME, 264–44 B.C.E.

Consider the position of the Mediterranean relative to Rome's possessions. Why would the Romans call it "our sea"? What challenges did Romans face politically and culturally in acquiring such a vast empire so quickly? Note the distribution of major cities on this map; how was the disparity between East and West in terms of urban development likely to affect Roman approaches to rule? What particular problems did Julius Caesar create by extending Roman rule into Gaul, well away from the Mediterranean basin?

ernment contracts to operate mines, build roads, or collect taxes. Yet the cities were also full of impoverished drifters because Rome never made a transition to industrialism; with slaves to do all the hard work, a great disincentive existed for the technological initiative that might have led to industrialism, and without large-scale manufacture the urban population remained underemployed. Thus a traveler to Italy around 150 B.C.E. would have found a countryside full

of slaves and cities full of disgruntled ex-farmers, living from hand to mouth.

FAMILY LIFE AND THE STATUS OF WOMEN

Yet another change that accompanied the acquisition of new territories was a change in the nature of family

WHAT ISSUES CAUSED THE SOCIAL STRUGGLES OF THE LATE REPUBLIC?

THE SOCIAL STRUGGLES OF THE LATE REPUBLIC   195

life and the status of women. In earlier times the Roman family was based on the husband's legal and financial authority, which gave him nearly absolute powers. The wife was subordinated and served as custodian of the home while the husband managed outside affairs and expected to be treated with reverence. In the second century B.C.E., however, two legal innovations greatly altered this pattern. One was the introduction of "free marriage," whereby the wife's share of her father's property remained her own instead of passing to her husband, and then reverted to her father or her father's heirs on her death. Together with "free marriage" came new rules for divorce, whereby either side, instead of just the man, could initiate proceedings. Apparently the motive of these changes was to prevent the transfer of property from one family to another, which would diminish the size of the large estates created with the influx of slaves. Yet both changes resulted in giving wives greater legal independence. In addition, the slave system itself gave wealthier women greater practical independence, for slaves could now take over tasks of child rearing and household maintenance. Upper-class Roman women began to spend more time away from the home and to engage in a range of social, intellectual, and artistic activities.

Cultivated upper-class life for both men and women had been made possible by a final change attendant on Roman expansion, the introduction of Greek ideas and customs. These flowed more easily to Rome with the conquest of the Hellenistic East and were adopted once upper-class Romans began to become really wealthy as a result of their conquests. In particular, children were given much more education, theater and literature increasingly were in fashion, and the creature comforts that Hellenistic Greeks had begun to prize in Syria and Egypt became equally prized in turn by the Roman conquerors of the Mediterranean world. Some conservative Roman males viewed such changes with repugnance. For them the "good old Roman ways" with emphasis on family life based on fatherly authority and sober military discipline were giving way to the collapse of the family and the debilitating lures of soft living. But whether they liked it or not, Rome had now become irreversibly transformed from a republic of farmers into a complex society with vast gaps between rich and poor and new habits, at least among the well-to-do, of greater personal autonomy.

> Rome had now become irreversibly transformed from a republic of farmers into a complex society with vast gaps between the rich and poor and new habits of greater personal autonomy.

THE SOCIAL STRUGGLES OF THE LATE REPUBLIC

What issues caused the social struggles of the Late Republic?

The period from the end of the Third Punic War in 146 to about 30 B.C.E. was one of enormous turbulence. Social conflicts, assassinations, struggles between rival dictators, wars, and insurrections were common occurrences of the time. Slave uprisings were also part of the general disorder. Some seventy thousand slaves defeated a Roman army in Sicily in 134 B.C.E. before this revolt was put down by further Roman reinforcements, with slaves again ravaging Sicily in 104. But the most threatening slave revolt of all was led by a slave named Spartacus from 73 to 71. Spartacus, who was being trained to become a gladiator (which meant certain death in the arena), escaped with a band of fugitives to Mount Vesuvius near Naples, there attracting a huge host of other fugitive slaves. For two years the escapees under his leadership held off Roman armies and overran much of southern Italy until they were finally defeated and Spartacus was slain in battle. Six thousand of those captured were left crucified along the length of a road from Capua to Rome (about one hundred fifty miles) to provide a terrible warning.

THE GRACCHI

Meanwhile, an extended conflict among elements of the Roman governing class began in 133 B.C.E. with the attempts at social and economic reform instituted by the two Gracchus brothers. Though of aristocratic lineage themselves, they proposed to alleviate social and economic stress by granting government lands to the landless. Although they and their senatorial allies stood to gain from the electoral loyalty of the many clients who would have received this land, Tiberius Gracchus also seems to have been motivated by genuine concern for the welfare of Rome's farmers and the attendant manpower shortage in the army. A man had to meet certain property qualifications to serve in the Roman army, and at a time when Rome's military commitments were expanding, the available pool of citizen soldiers was contracting. In 133 B.C.E. Tiberius Gracchus, as tribune, proposed a law that restricted the current renters or holders of state lands to a maximum of three hundred acres per citizen plus one hundred fifty acres for each child in the family. The excess was to be given to the poor in small plots. Conservative aristocrats bitterly opposed this proposal and engineered its veto by Octavius, Tiberius' fellow tribune. Tiberius removed Octavius from office, a highly irregular action, and when his own term expired attempted to stand for reelection. Both of these moves seemed to threaten a dictatorship and offered the conservative senators an excuse for resistance. Armed with clubs, they went on a rampage during the elections and murdered Tiberius and many of his followers.

Nine years later, Tiberius' younger brother, Gaius Gracchus, renewed the struggle. Though Tiberius' land law had finally been enacted by the Senate, Gaius believed that the campaign had to go further. Elected tribune in 123 B.C.E., and reelected in 122, he enacted several laws for the benefit of the less privileged. One provided for stabilizing the price of grain in Rome. For this purpose public granaries were built along the Tiber. Another exercised controls on governors suspected of exploiting the provinces for their own advantage, and gave the equestrian order a judicial role in checking the administrative abuses of the senatorial class. In an attempt to gain further support, he suggested the extension of full Roman citizenship to vast numbers of Italian allies, a move that would have completely altered the political landscape of Rome. These and similar measures provoked so much anger among the vested interests that they resolved to eliminate their enemy. The Roman Senate proclaimed Gaius Gracchus an outlaw and authorized the consuls to take all necessary steps for the defense of the Republic. In the ensuing conflict Gaius was killed, and about three thousand of his followers lost their lives in vengeful purges.

ARISTOCRATIC REACTION

After the downfall of the Gracchi, two military leaders who had won fame in foreign wars successively made themselves rulers of the state. The first was Marius, who was elevated to the consulship by the plebeian party in 107 B.C.E. and reelected six times. Unfortunately, Marius was no statesman and accomplished nothing for his followers beyond demonstrating the ease with which a general with an army behind him could override opposition. Partly for party political motives, partly to meet the shortfall in manpower, Marius scrapped the property qualification for the army altogether. Thereafter, Rome's soldiers would come increasingly from the ranks of the urban poor and the landless country dwellers. The result was that gradually, Roman armies became more loyal to the individual interests of their commanders than they were to the Republic itself, because the political success of their generals could best guarantee rewards for the impoverished soldiers of the army.

Following Marius' death in 86 B.C.E., conservatives took a turn at governing through the army. Their champion was Sulla, another victorious commander. Appointed dictator in 82 B.C.E. for an unlimited term, Sulla ruthlessly proceeded to exterminate his opponents. He extended the powers of the Senate (whose ranks, depleted by civil war, he packed with men loyal to himself), and curtailed the authority of the tribunes. After three years of rule Sulla decided his job was done and retired to a life of luxury on his country estate.

POMPEY AND JULIUS CAESAR

Sulla's actions did not stand unchallenged after he relinquished his office, for the effect of his decrees was to give control to a selfish aristocracy. Several new leaders now emerged to espouse the cause of the people. The most prominent were Pompey (106–48 B.C.E.) and Julius Caesar (100–44 B.C.E.). For a time they cooperated in a plot to gain control of the government, but later they became rivals and sought to outdo each other in bidding for popular support. Both of them were men who, despite their successes, failed to gain complete acceptance from the established elite, but who in any event would have found the "rules" too much of an obstacle to their personal talents and ambitions. Pompey won fame as the conqueror of Syria and Palestine, while Caesar devoted his energies to a series of brilliant forays against the Gauls, adding to the Roman state the territory of modern Belgium, Germany west of the Rhine, and France. In 52 B.C.E., after protracted mob disorders in Rome, the Senate turned to Pompey and engineered his election as sole consul. Caesar, stationed in Gaul, was branded an enemy of the state, and Pompey conspired with the senatorial faction to deprive him of political power. The result was a deadly war between the two men. In 49 B.C.E. Caesar crossed the Rubicon River into Italy (ever since an image for a fateful decision) and marched on Rome. Pompey fled to the east in the hope of gathering an

THE INFLUENCE OF GREEK LUXURY

Lucius Licinius Lucullus (106?–57 B.C.E.) was a partisan of the dictator Sulla and a member of Rome's highest aristocracy. He commanded Roman forces admirably in the East, but his demands for discipline from the army and his intolerance of corruption among the equestrians and senatorial governors made him powerful enemies. His conquests made him quite wealthy and, once he tired of trying to preserve his political career against his foes, he retired from public life. This passage from Plutarch's biography of him demonstrates the effects Eastern luxury could have on the Roman elite, the staggering wealth they could acquire, and their enjoyment of it especially once they abandoned the public career for one of private pleasure.

And indeed, Lucullus' life, like the Old Comedy, presents us at the commencement with acts of policy and of war, at the end offering nothing but good eating and drinking, feastings, and revelings, and mere play. For I give no higher name to his sumptuous buildings, porticos, and baths, still less to his paintings and sculptures, and all his industry about these curiosities, which he collected with vast expense, lavishly bestowing all the wealth and treasure he got in the war upon them, insomuch that even now, with all the advance of luxury, the Lucullean gardens are counted the noblest the emperor has. Tubero the Stoic, when he saw his buildings at Naples, where he suspended the hills upon vast tunnels, brought in the sea for moats and fish-ponds round his house, and built pleasure-houses in the waters, called him Xerxes in a toga. He had also fine seats in Tusculum, belvederes, and large open balconies for men's apartments, and porticos to walk in, where Pompey, coming to see him, blamed him for making a house which would be pleasant in summer, but uninhabitable in winter; whom Lucullus answered with a smile, "You think me, then, less provident than cranes and storks, not to change my home with the season." . . . Lucullus's daily entertainments were ostentatiously extravagant, not only with purple coverlets, and plate adorned with precious stones, and dancings, and interludes, but with the greatest diversity of dishes and the most elaborate cookery, for the vulgar to admire and envy. . . . Cato [the Younger] was his friend and connection, but, nevertheless, so hated his life and habits that when a young man made a long and tedious speech in praise of frugality and temperance, Cato got up and said, "How long do you mean to go on making money like Crassus, living like Lucullus, and talking like Cato?"

Plutarch, *Life of Lucullus*. Based on John Dryden, trans. *Plutarch's Lives*. (New York: Modern Library, 1992), pp. 621–622.

army large enough to regain control of Italy. In 48 B.C.E. the forces of the rivals met at Pharsalus in Greece. Pompey was defeated and soon afterward murdered by supporters of Caesar.

Caesar then intervened in Egyptian politics at the court of Cleopatra (whom he left pregnant). Then he conducted another military campaign in Asia Minor in which victory was so swift that he could report,

Julius Caesar.

"I came, I saw, I conquered" (*Veni, vidi, vici*). After that Caesar returned to Rome. No one now dared challenge his power. With the aid of his veterans he cowed the Senate into granting his every desire. In 46 B.C.E. he became dictator for ten years, and two years later for life. In addition, he assumed nearly every other title that could augment his power. He obtained from the Senate full authority to make war and peace and to control the revenues of the state. For all practical purposes he was above the law, and rumors spread that he intended to make himself king. Such fears led to his assassination on the Ides of March (the 15th) in 44 B.C.E. by a group of conspirators under the leadership of Brutus and Cassius, who hoped to return Rome to republican government.

Although Caesar was once revered by historians as a superhuman hero, he is now often dismissed as insignificant. Both extremes of interpretation should be avoided. Certainly he did not "save Rome," nor was he the greatest statesman of all time. He treated the Republic with contempt and made the problem of governing more difficult for those who came after him. Yet some of the measures he took as dictator did have lasting effects. With the aid of a Greek astronomer he revised the calendar so as to make a 365-day year (with an extra day added every fourth year). This "Julian" calendar—adjusted by Pope Gregory XIII in 1582—is still with us. Appropriately, the seventh month is named after Julius as "July." By conferring citizenship on thousands of Spaniards and Gauls, Caesar took an important step toward eliminating the distinction between Italians and provincials. He also helped relieve economic inequities by settling many of his veterans and some of the urban poor on unused lands. Vastly more important than these reforms, however, was Caesar's farsighted resolve, made before he seized power, to invest his efforts in the West. Whereas Pompey, and before him Alexander, went to the East to gain fame

Ides of March Coin. This coin was struck by Brutus to commemorate the assassination of Julius Caesar. Brutus is depicted on the obverse; on the reverse is a liberty cap between two daggers and the Latin abbreviation for the Ides of March.

HOW DID ROMAN INTERACTION WITH THE HELLENISTIC WORLD ACCELERATE SOCIAL CHANGES?

LATE REPUBLICAN CULTURE AND SOCIETY   199

and fortune, Caesar was the first great leader to recognize the potential significance of northwestern Europe. By incorporating Gaul into the Roman world he brought Rome great agricultural wealth and helped bring urban life and culture to what was then the wild West. Western European civilization, later to be anchored in just those regions that Caesar conquered, might not have been the same without him.

LATE REPUBLICAN CULTURE AND SOCIETY

How did Roman interaction with the Hellenistic world accelerate social changes?

Between the end of the Punic Wars and the death of Julius Caesar, Rome came ever more under the influence of Hellenistic civilization. The result was a flowering of intellectual activity and the adoption of Hellenistic schools of thought, especially Epicureanism and Stoicism, by the upper classes of the western half of the empire.

EPICUREANISM AND STOICISM

The most renowned of the Roman exponents of Epicureanism was Lucretius (98–55 B.C.E.), the author of a book-length philosophical poem, *On the Nature of Things.* In writing this work Lucretius wished to explain the universe in such a way as to remove fear of the supernatural, which he regarded as the chief obstacle to peace of mind. Worlds and all things in them, he taught, are the result of fortuitous combinations of atoms. Though he admitted the existence of the gods, he conceived of them as living in eternal peace, neither creating nor governing the universe. Everything is a product of mechanical evolution, including human beings and their habits and beliefs. Since mind is indissolubly linked with matter, death means utter extinction; consequently, no part of the human personality can survive to be rewarded or punished in an afterlife. Lucretius' conception of the good life was simple: what one needs, he asserted, is not enjoyment but "peace and a pure heart." Whether one agrees with Lucretius' philosophy or not, there is no doubt that he was an extraordinarily fine poet. In fact his musical cadences, sustained majesty of expression, and infectious enthusiasm earn him a rank among the greatest poets who ever lived.

Stoicism was introduced into Rome about 140 B.C.E. and soon came to include among its converts numerous influential leaders of public life. The greatest of these was Cicero (106–43 B.C.E.), the "father of Roman eloquence." Although Cicero adopted doctrines from a number of philosophers, including both Plato and Aristotle, he derived more of his ideas from the Stoics than from any other source. Cicero's ethical philosophy was based on the Stoic premises that virtue is sufficient for happiness and that tranquillity of mind is the highest good. He conceived of the ideal human being as one who has been guided by reason to an indifference toward sorrow and pain. Cicero diverged from the Greek Stoics in his greater approval of the active, political life. To this degree he still spoke for the older Roman tradition of service to the state. Cicero never claimed to be an original philosopher; rather his goal was to bring the best of Greek philosophy to the West. In this he was remarkably successful, for he wrote in a rich and elegant Latin prose style that has never been surpassed. Cicero's prose immediately became a standard for composition and has remained so until the present century. Thus even though not a truly great thinker, Cicero was the most influential Latin transmitter of ancient thought to the medieval and modern western European worlds.

Lucretius and Cicero were the two leading exponents of Greek thought but not the only fine writers of the later Roman Republic. It now became the fashion among the upper classes to learn Greek and to strive to reproduce in Latin some of the more popular forms of Greek literature. Some results of enduring literary merit were the ribald comedies of Plautus (257?–184 B.C.E.), the passionate love poems of Catullus (84?–54? B.C.E.), and the crisp military memoirs of Julius Caesar.

> It now became the fashion among the upper classes to learn Greek and to strive to reproduce in Latin some of the more popular forms of Greek literature.

SOCIAL CHANGE DURING THE LATE REPUBLIC

In addition to its intellectual effects, Roman interaction with the Hellenistic world accelerated the process of social change, foremost of which was the cleavage between classes. The Italian people, numbering about 8 million on the death of Caesar, had come to be divided into four main social orders: the senatorial aristocracy, the equestrians, the common citizens, and the slaves. The senatorial aristocrats numbered three hundred citizens and their families (although the political maneuvers of the civil wars tended to bloat the Senate well beyond this number). Most of the aristocrats gained their living as officeholders and as owners of great landed estates. By the first century B.C.E., the equestrians had become the chief offenders in the exploitation of the poor and the provincials. As moneylenders they often charged exorbitant interest rates, and as tax farmers they squeezed the provinces for profit, often colluding with the senatorial governors in unconscionable corruption and abuse. By far the largest number of the citizens were mere commoners. Most of these were independent farmers, a few were industrial workers, and some were indigent city dwellers who lived by intermittent employment and public relief. When Julius Caesar became dictator, 320,000 citizens were receiving free grain from the state.

Roman slaves were scarcely considered people at all but instruments of production like cattle. Notwithstanding the fact that some of them were cultivated foreigners taken as prisoners of war, the standard policy of their owners was to get as much work out of them as possible during their prime until they died of exhaustion or were released to fend for themselves. The ready availability and cheapness of slaves, a consequence of Rome's conquests, made Roman slavery a far more impersonal and brutal operation than it had been among other ancient civilizations. Although domestic slaves might from time to time have been treated decently, and some slave artisans in the city of Rome were relatively free to run their own businesses, the general lot of the slave was horrendous. Slaves grew much of the food supply and did much of the work in the urban shops as well. Slaves were also employed in numerous nonproductive activities. A lucrative form of investment for the business classes was ownership of slaves trained as gladiators who could be slaughtered by each other or by wild animals for amusement. The growth of luxury also required the employment of thousands of slaves in domestic service. The man of great wealth insisted on having his doorkeepers, his litter-bearers, his couriers, his valets, and his tutors for his children. Some great households had special servants with no other duties than to rub the master down after his bath or to care for his sandals. All such servants would have been slaves.

This extreme reliance on slave labor, combined with the relative cheapness of slaves, encouraged among the Romans a mindset that scorned the application of mechanical knowledge to improve industrial or agricultural productivity. Water mills and a crude steam engine, among many other labor-saving innovations, were known to the Romans during the course of their history, but they showed little interest in them. There was no need for labor-saving devices when the supply of cheap human labor seemed inexhaustible.

The religious beliefs of the Romans were altered in various ways in the last two centuries of the Republic—again mainly because of Rome's interaction with the Hellenistic world. Most pronounced was the spread of Eastern mystery cults, which satisfied the craving for a more emotional religion than traditional Roman worship and offered the reward of immortality to the wretched of the earth. From Egypt came the cult of Osiris (or Serapis, as the god was now more commonly called), while from Asia Minor was introduced the worship of the Great Mother, with her eunuch priests and ritualistic orgies. Most popular of all at the end of the period was the Persian cult of Mithraism (see Chapter Five), which offered awe-inspiring underground rites and a doctrine of the afterlife of the soul.

CHRONOLOGY

STRUGGLES OF THE LATE REPUBLIC, 146–27 B.C.E.

Third Punic War	149–146 B.C.E.
Slave revolts in Sicily	134–104 B.C.E.
Gracchian reforms	133–122 B.C.E.
Rule of Marius	107–86 B.C.E.
Sulla becomes dictator	82 B.C.E.
Slave revolt led by Spartacus	73–71 B.C.E.
Pompey becomes sole consul	52 B.C.E.
Caesar becomes sole consul	48 B.C.E.
Caesar becomes dictator	46 B.C.E.
Caesar assassinated	44 B.C.E.
Rule of Octavian, Mark Antony, and Lepidus	42–31 B.C.E.
Octavian becomes sole consul	31 B.C.E.
Octavian becomes emperor	27 B.C.E.

Roman Mystery Rites. The "Villa of the Mysteries" in Pompeii preserves an astonishing cycle of wall paintings done around 50 B.C.E. The exact meaning is debatable, but the most persuasive interpretation is that it shows a succession of cult rites. Here a young woman is being whipped, probably an initiation ceremony, while a cult member performs a solemn dance in the nude.

THE PRINCIPATE OR EARLY EMPIRE (27 B.C.E.–180 C.E.)

How did Rome control its far-flung territories?

In his will, Julius Caesar had adopted posthumously as his sole heir his grandnephew Octavian (63 B.C.E.–14 C.E.), then a young man of eighteen acting in his uncle's service in Illyria across the Adriatic Sea. On learning of Caesar's death, Octavian hastened to Rome to see if he could claim his inheritance. He soon found that he had to join forces with two of Caesar's powerful

friends, Mark Antony and Lepidus. The following year the three formed an alliance to crush the political faction responsible for Caesar's murder, who had justified their actions as necessary to defend the Republic against a tyrant. The methods employed were not to the new leaders' credit. Prominent members of the opposition were hunted down and slain and their property confiscated. The most noted of the victims was Cicero, brutally slain by Mark Antony's thugs; though he had taken no part in the conspiracy against Caesar's life, Cicero had actively sought to undermine Antony during his term as consul and have him branded a public enemy. Caesar's real murderers, Brutus and Cassius, escaped and organized an army, but they were defeated by Antony and Octavian near Philippi in 42 B.C.E.

With the "republican" opposition effectively crushed, tensions mounted between the members of the alliance, inspired primarily by Antony's jealousy of Octavian. The subsequent struggle became a contest between East and West. Antony went to the East and made an alliance with Cleopatra, hoping to use the resources of the Egyptian kingdom in the power struggle with Octavian. Octavian, as the junior partner, established himself in Italy and the West. It was a risky move: Octavian had to deal with the problems of resettling veterans while maintaining his position in the roiling political environment in Rome. But Italy provided him with manpower and the opportunity to style himself as the protector of Rome and its heritage against Antony, whom he skillfully portrayed as in the clutches of a foreign, female potentate who intended to become queen over Rome. As in the earlier contest between Caesar and Pompey the victory again went to the West. In the naval battle of Actium (31 B.C.E.) Octavian's forces defeated those of Antony and Cleopatra, both of whom soon afterward committed suicide. Egypt's independent existence came to an end, and Rome reigned supreme throughout the Mediterranean world.

THE GOVERNMENT OF ROME UNDER AUGUSTUS

The victory at Actium ushered in a new period in Roman history, the most glorious and the most prosperous that Rome ever experienced. When Octavian returned to Rome he announced the restoration of complete peace. First he ruled for four years as consul, but in 27 B.C.E. he accepted from the Senate the honorific titles of *emperor* and *augustus*, a step that historians count as the beginning of the Roman empire. This periodization is somewhat arbitrary because Octavian was as strong before his title change as after; moreover, *emperor* at the time meant only "victorious general"; *augustus* signified "venerable" or "worthy of honor." But gradually, after his successors took the title of emperor as well, it became the primary designation for the ruler of the Roman state. Actually the title by which Octavian preferred to have his authority designated was the more modest *princeps*, or "first citizen." For this reason the period of his rule and that of his successors is properly called the Principate (or, alternatively, the early empire), to distinguish it from the periods of the Republic (sixth century–27 B.C.E.),

Octavian. When Octavian gained sole rule he became known as Augustus. Many statues of him survive, all of them idealized.

the "Third-Century Crisis" (180 C.E.–284 C.E.), and the later Empire or "Dominate" (284–610 C.E.).

Octavian, or Augustus as he was now called, was determined not to seem a dictator. In theory the Senate and the citizens were the supreme sovereigns, as they had always been. Hence most of the republican institutions were left in place even though their functioning had clearly become a charade. Augustus himself, in practical control of the army, freely determined all governmental policy. Fortunately he was a very gifted statesman. Among the measures he instituted were the establishment of a new coinage system for use throughout the Roman empire; the introduction within Rome itself of a range of public services, including police and fire fighting; and more self-government for cities and provinces than they had enjoyed before. He also abolished the old system of farming out the collection of financial dues. Whereas previously tax collectors were remunerated solely by being allowed to keep a percentage of their intake, a system that led inevitably to graft and extortion, Augustus now appointed his own representatives as tax collectors, paid them regular salaries, and kept them under strict supervision. Above all, Augustus instituted a program of incentives for colonization of the provinces in order to shift the excess free population out of Italy and thereby remove a major source of social tensions and political upheaval. All told, such measures did enhance local peace.

> Augustus instituted a program of incentives for colonization of the provinces in order to shift the excess free population out of Italy and thereby remove a major source of social tensions and political upheaval.

THE GROWTH OF THE ROMAN EMPIRE

From the time of Augustus until that of Trajan, the Roman empire continued to expand. Augustus gained more land for Rome than did any other Roman ruler. His generals advanced into central Europe, conquering the modern-day territories of Switzerland, Austria, and Bulgaria. Only in what is today central Germany did Roman troops meet defeat, a setback that convinced Augustus to hold the Roman borders at the Rhine and Danube. Subsequently, in 43 C.E., the Emperor Claudius began the conquest of Britain, and at the beginning of the next century Trajan pushed beyond the Danube to add Dacia (now Romania) to the empire's realms. Trajan also conquered territories in Mesopotamia, but in so doing aroused the enmity of the Persians. His successor Hadrian halted the conquests, and embarked on a defensive policy epitomized by the construction of

> Augustus' system of governance was so ingenious that even after his death Rome enjoyed nearly two centuries of peace, prosperity, and stability.

Hadrian's Wall in northern Britain. The Roman empire had now reached its territorial limits; in the third century these limits would begin to recede.

When Augustus died in 14 C.E. after four decades of rule, his remarkable experiments in statesmanship might have died with him. His system was so ingenious, however, that Rome enjoyed nearly two centuries of peace, prosperity, and stability as a result of his reforms. Aside from one brief period of civil war in 68 C.E., the transition of power was generally peaceful and the growing imperial bureaucracy managed affairs competently even when individual emperors proved to be vicious. Several talented men succeeded Augustus, but few of them had his panache for disguising the true power of the princeps. Many of his successors had difficult relationships with the Senate, and because members of the senatorial elite were almost invariably the historians of the time, several imperial reputations have suffered unfairly. Tiberius (14–37 C.E.) and Claudius (41–54 C.E.) were both skilled administrators, but their tensions with the Senate led them at times to extreme measures that angered the elite. Nero (54–68 C.E.) and Domitian (81–96 C.E.), both reviled by the senatorial aristocracy, were universally popular among the masses at Rome and in the provinces; indeed, Domitian's reforms of provincial government and his murderous disregard for senatorial privilege explains both the aristocracy's hostility and his subjects' adoration. The height of the Augustan system, however, came between 96 and 180 C.E., under the "Five Good Emperors." All five were capable administrators, and all proved worthy successors of Augustus, respecting the Senate and preserving republican forms while running an essentially autocratic government. Until 180, none had a son who survived him, and so each adopted a man deemed worthy of succeeding him; they thus avoided the difficulties of dynastic politics, one of the great horrors of first-century imperial life in the eyes of senatorial historians.

Rome's successful governance of such a vast empire from the time of Augustus to that of Marcus Aurelius (d. 180 C.E.) was certainly one of its greatest accom-

TWO VIEWS OF AUGUSTUS' RULE

AUGUSTUS SPEAKS FOR HIMSELF

The emperor Augustus was a master propagandist with an unrivaled capacity to present his own actions in the best possible light. This document was written by Augustus himself and was to be carved on two bronze pillars set up before his tomb, to tell the world what Augustus wanted remembered about his deeds.

Below is a copy of the accomplishments of the deified Augustus by which he brought the whole world under the empire of the Roman people, and of the moneys expended by him on the state and the Roman people. . . .

1. At the age of nineteen, on my own initiative and at my own expense, I raised an army by means of which I liberated the Republic, which was oppressed by the tyranny of a faction.

2. Those who assassinated my father I drove into exile, avenging their crime by due process of law.

3. I waged many wars throughout the whole world by land and by sea, both civil and foreign, . . .

5. The dictatorship offered to me . . . by the people and by the senate . . . I refused to accept. . . . The consulship, too, which was offered to me . . . as an annual office for life, I refused to accept.

6. [T]hough the Roman senate and people together agreed that I should be elected sole guardian of the laws and morals with supreme authority, I refused to accept any office offered me which was contrary to the traditions of our ancestors.

7. I have been ranking senator for forty years, . . . I have been *pontifex maximus*, augur, member of the college of fifteen for performing sacrifices, member of the college of seven for conducting religious banquets, member of the Arval Brotherhood, one of the Titii sodales, and a fetial [all priestly offices under the Republic].

9. The senate decreed that vows for my health should be offered up every fifth year by the consuls and priests. . . . the whole citizen body, with one accord, . . . prayed continuously for my health at all the shrines.

17. Four times I came to the assistance of the treasury with my own money. . . . providing bonuses for soldiers who had completed twenty or more years of service.

20. I repaired the Capitol and the theater of Pompey with enormous expenditures on both works, without having my name inscribed on them. I repaired . . . the aqueducts which were falling into ruin in many places . . . I repaired eighty-two temples . . . I reconstructed the Flaminian Way. . . .

34. [H]aving attained supreme power by universal consent, I transferred the state from my own power to the control of the Roman senate and people. . . . After that time I excelled all in authority, but I possessed no more power than the others who were my colleagues in each magistracy.

35. At the time I wrote this document I was in my seventy-sixth year.

"Res Gestae Divi Augusti," in *Roman Civilization, Sourcebook II: The Empire,* ed. Naphtali Lewis and Meyer Reinhold (New York: Harper and Row, 1966), pp. 9–19.

THE HISTORIAN TACITUS WEIGHS UP AUGUSTUS' REIGN

Writing in the first decades of the second century C.E., the senatorial historian Tacitus began his chronicle of imperial rule, the Annals, *with the death of Augustus in* 14 *C.E. Tacitus placed the two contrasting evaluations that follow in the mouths of Augustus' contemporaries. Tacitus used this literary device often; but despite the appearance of even-handedness he thus creates, Tacitus' own views are rarely in doubt.*

Intelligent people praised or criticized Augustus in varying terms. One opinion was as follows. Filial duty and a national emergency, in which there was no place for law-abiding conduct, had driven him to civil war—and this can be neither initiated nor maintained by decent methods. He had made many concessions to Antony and to Lepidus for the sake of vengeance on his father's murderers. When Lepidus grew old and lazy, and Antony's self-indulgence got the better of him, the only possible cure for the distracted country had been government by one man. However, Augustus had put the State in order not by making himself king or dictator but by creating the Principate. The empire's frontiers were on the ocean, or on distant rivers. Armies, provinces, fleets, the whole system was interrelated. Roman citizens were protected by the law. Provincials were decently treated. Rome itself had been lavishly beautified. Force had been sparingly used—merely to preserve peace for the majority.

The opposite view went like this. Filial duty and national crisis had been merely pretexts. In actual fact, the motive of Octavian, the future Augustus, was lust for power. Inspired by that, he had mobilized ex-army settlers by gifts of money, raised an army—while he was only a half-grown boy without any official status—won over a consul's brigade by bribery, pretended to support Sextus Pompeius [the son of Pompey], and by senatorial decree usurped the status and rank of a praetor. Soon both consuls . . . had met their deaths—by enemy action; or perhaps in the one case by the deliberate poisoning of his wound, and in the other at the hand of his own troops, instigated by Octavian. In any case, it was he who took over both their armies. Then he had forced the reluctant Senate to make him consul. But the forces given him to deal with Antony he used against the State. His judicial murders and land distributions were distasteful even to those who carried them out. True, Cassius and Brutus died because he had inherited a feud against them; nevertheless, personal enmities ought to be sacrificed to the public interest. Next he had cheated Sextus Pompeius by a spurious peace treaty, Lepidus by spurious friendship. Then Antony, enticed by treaties and his marriage with Octavian's sister, had paid the penalty of that delusive relationship with his life. After that, there had certainly been peace, but it was a bloodstained peace. . . . And gossip did not spare his personal affairs—how he had abducted [Livia] the wife of Tiberius Claudius Nero, and asked the priests the farcical question whether it was in order for her to marry while pregnant. Then there was the debauchery of his friend Publius Vedius Pollio. But Livia was a real catastrophe, to the nation, as a mother and to the house of the Caesars as a stepmother.

Tacitus, *Annals* i.9–10. Based on Michael Grant, trans. *Tacitus: The Annals of Imperial Rome.* (New York: Penguin, 1989), pp. 37–39.

plishments. During these two centuries, Rome had few external enemies. The Mediterranean was now under the control of a single military power and experienced the passage of centuries without a single naval battle; while on land, Roman officials ruled from the borders of Scotland to those of Persia. A contemporary orator justly boasted that "the whole civilized world lays down the arms which were its ancient burden, as if on holiday . . . all places are full of gymnasia, fountains, monumental approaches, temples, workshops, schools; one can say that the civilized world, which had been sick from the beginning . . . has been brought by right knowledge to a state of health."

ROMANIZATION AND ASSIMILATION

This "Roman Peace" (*Pax Romana*) was not universal. In Britain, the Roman army massacred tens of thousands of Britons in the aftermath of Queen Boudicca's revolt. In Judea, perhaps the most restive of all the Roman

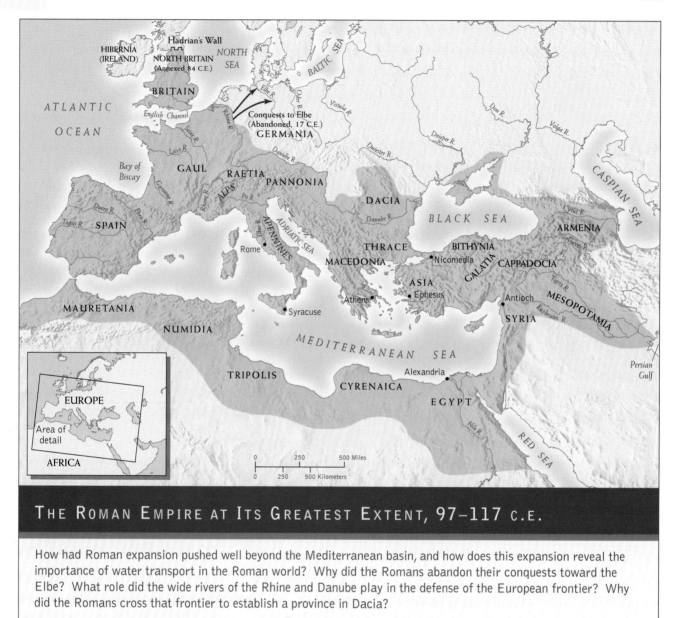

THE ROMAN EMPIRE AT ITS GREATEST EXTENT, 97–117 C.E.

How had Roman expansion pushed well beyond the Mediterranean basin, and how does this expansion reveal the importance of water transport in the Roman world? Why did the Romans abandon their conquests toward the Elbe? What role did the wide rivers of the Rhine and Danube play in the defense of the European frontier? Why did the Romans cross that frontier to establish a province in Dacia?

provinces, a Roman army destroyed the Temple at Jerusalem in 70 C.E. in the wake of one rebellion, and in 135 C.E. destroyed the entire city of Jerusalem in the wake of another, massacring its inhabitants and scattering the survivors throughout the empire. Upwards of half a million people may have been killed in Judea during these years, and an equal number enslaved. Jerusalem, meanwhile, was refounded by the Emperor Hadrian as a pagan capital named Aelia Capitolina. For the next five hundred years, Jews would be forbidden to live there.

> Rome controlled its far-flung territories by assimilating their residents into the common cultural and political life of Rome itself.

Such rebellions were not the norm, however, even in Palestine. Although the Roman empire rested on the backs of its armies, the empire was not really a military occupation. Rome controlled its far-flung territories by assimilating their residents into the common cultural and political life of Rome itself. Local gods became Roman gods and were adopted into the Roman pantheon of divinities. Cities were constructed, and the amenities of urban life introduced: baths, temples, amphitheaters, aqueducts, and paved roads. Rights of citizenship were extended, and able provincials could rise far in Roman service. Some, like Trajan and Hadrian, even rose to become emperors.

Even the frontier areas of the empire need to be understood in this light. Although for convenience' sake historians speak of the empire's "borders," in fact these borders were highly fluid and permeable. We ought, more properly, to speak not of "borders" but of "frontiers," and to see these frontiers as zones of particularly intensive cultural interaction between provincial Romans and the non-Roman peoples who lived beyond them. Roman influence thus reached far beyond the frontier areas, across the Rhine and the Danube into the heartland of Germany and the Gothic lands to the east. When, in the third century, frontier garrisons were withdrawn in order to take part in civil wars within the empire itself, many of these Romanized Germans and Goths moved into the empire, sometimes as plunderers, but often as settlers and aspiring Romans.

Culture and Life in the Period of the Principate

What role did upper-class women play in Roman society?

The intellectual and artistic achievements of the Principate outshone those of all other ages in the history of Rome. Three eminent exponents of Stoicism lived in Rome in the two centuries that followed the rule of Augustus: Seneca (4 B.C.E.–65 C.E.), wealthy adviser for a time to Nero; the slave Epictetus (60?–120 C.E.); and the emperor Marcus Aurelius (121–180 C.E.). All of them agreed that inner serenity is the ultimate human goal, that true happiness can be found only in surrender to the benevolent order of the universe. They preached the ideal of virtue for virtue's sake, deplored the sinfulness of human nature, and urged obedience to conscience. Seneca and Epictetus both expressed deep mystical yearnings as part of their philosophy, making it almost a religion. They worshiped the cosmos as divine, governed by an all-powerful Providence that ordained all that happened for ultimate good. The last of the Roman Stoics, Marcus Aurelius, was more fatalistic and less hopeful. Although he did not reject the concept of an ordered and rational universe, he did not believe that immortality would balance suffering on earth and was inclined to think of humans as creatures buffeted by evil fortune for which no distant perfection of the whole could fully compensate. He urged, nevertheless, that people should continue to live nobly, that they should not abandon themselves to either gross indulgence or angry protest, but that they should derive what contentment they could from dignified resignation to suffering and tranquil submission to death.

The Forum. The civic center of imperial Rome consisted of avenues, public squares, triumphal arches, temples, and government buildings. The arch of Titus, erected to celebrate Rome's final victory over Hebrew rebels, is in the background at the far right. Roman streets and buildings were arranged in rectilinear patterns to emphasize a sense of order and to facilitate triumphal processions.

Marcus Aurelius. This equestrian statue is one of the few surviving from the ancient world: the Christians destroyed most Roman equestrian statues because they found them idolatrous, but they spared this one because they mistakenly believed that it represented Constantine, the first Christian Roman emperor. The statue stood outdoors in Rome from the second century until 1980, when it was taken into storage to protect it from air pollution.

LITERATURE OF THE GOLDEN AND SILVER AGES

Roman literature of the Principate is conventionally divided into two periods: works of the *golden age*, written during the reign of Augustus, and works of the *silver age*, written during the first and early second centuries C.E. Most of the literature of the golden age was vigorous, affirmative, and uplifting, and—it should be noted—much of it served the political and social propaganda programs of Augustus' government. The poetry of the greatest of all Roman poets, Virgil (70–19 B.C.E.), was prototypic. In a set of pastoral poems, the *Eclogues*, Virgil expressed an idealized vision of human life led in harmony with nature. The *Eclogues* also implicitly extolled Augustus as the bringer of peace and abundance. Virgil's masterpiece, the *Aeneid*, is an epic poem about a Trojan hero, Aeneas (whom the family of Caesar and Augustus claimed as an ancestor), who was reputed to have traveled to Italy and to have played a role in the formation of the Roman people (see p. 183). Written in elevated, yet sinewy and stirring metrical verse ("Arms and the man, I sing. . . ."), the *Aeneid* tells of the founding of a great state by means of warfare and toil and foretells Rome's glorious future.

Other major golden age writers were Horace (65–8 B.C.E.), Livy (59 B.C.E.–17 C.E.), and Ovid (43 B.C.E.–17 C.E.). Of these, Horace was the most philosophical. His *Odes* drew from the practical teachings of both the Epicureans and the Stoics, combining Epicurean justification of pleasure with Stoic passivity in the face of trouble. The chief claim to fame of Livy, a narrative historian, rests on his skill as a prose stylist. His *History of Rome*, starting "from the founding of the city," is often factually unreliable but replete with dramatic and picturesque narrative designed to appeal to patriotic emotions. Ovid was the least typical of the Latin golden age writers insofar as his outlook tended to be more satiric than heroically affirmative. His main poetic accomplishment was a highly sophisticated retelling of Greek myths in a long poem of fifteen books, the *Metamorphoses*, full of wit and eroticism. Whereas the emperor Augustus delighted in the *Aeneid*, he found the mocking and dissolute tone of Ovid's verses to be so repellent that he banished Ovid from his court. Augustus was trying to present himself as a stern moralist, whereas Ovid's verses treated such subjects as how to attract women at the race track and his adulterous affair with the wife of a Roman senator.

The literature of the silver age was typically less calm and balanced than that of the golden age. Its ef-

A SCATHING CRITIQUE OF ROMAN SOCIETY

Roman society, even at its height under the "Five Good Emperors," was not without its critics. Among the most incisive and resonant indictments were those of Juvenal, whose Satires *attacked everything from the general erosion of public morality to the effete tastes of the elite. His language is often bitter, and he did not shy away from lacing his intelligent and perceptive verses with a vulgarity still shocking across the centuries. Like those of Aristophanes, many of his references are highly topical, and their exact meaning is lost to us. No doubt his audience understood the allusions, making his public excoriations all the more personal and pointed. Contrast this portrayal of contemporary women with the model of the virtuous Lucretia.*

What conscience has Venus drunk? Our inebriated beauties can't tell head from tail at those midnight oyster suppers when the best wine's laced with perfume, and tossed down neat from a foaming conch-shell, while the dizzy ceiling spins round, and the tables dance, and each light shows double. Why, you may ask yourself, does the notorious Maura sniff at the air in that knowing, derisive way as she and her dear friend Tullia pass by the ancient altar of Chastity? And what is Tullia whispering to her? Here, at night, they stagger out of their litters and relieve themselves, pissing in long hard bursts all over the goddess's statue. Then, while the Moon looks down on their motions, they take turns to ride each other, and finally go home. So you, next morning, on your way to some great house, will splash through your wife's piddle. Notorious, too, are the ritual mysteries of the Good Goddess, when flute-music stirs the loins, and frenzied women, devotees of Priapus, sweep along in procession, howling, tossing their hair, wine-flown, horn-crazy, burning with the desire to get themselves laid. . . . So the ladies, with a display of talent to match their birth, win all the prizes. No make-believe here, no pretense, each act is performed in earnest, and guaranteed to warm the age-chilled balls of a Nestor or a Priam.

Juvenal, *Sixth Satire* 301–326. Based on Peter Green, trans. *Juvenal: The Sixteen Satires*. (New York: Penguin, 1974), pp. 138–139.

fects derived more often from self-conscious artifice. The tales of Petronius and Apuleius describe the more exotic and sometimes sordid aspects of Roman life. The aim of the authors is less to instruct or uplift than to tell an entertaining story or turn a witty phrase. An entirely different viewpoint is presented in the works of the other most important writers of this age: Juvenal the satirist (60?–140 C.E.) and Tacitus the historian (55?–117? C.E.). Juvenal wrote with savage indignation about what he took to be the moral degeneracy of his contemporaries. His taste for bitingly compressed rhetorical phrases has made him a favorite source for quotation. A similar attitude toward Roman society characterized the writing of Tacitus, who described the events of his age not with a view to dispassionate analysis but largely for the purpose of moral indictment. His description of the customs of the ancient Germans in his *Germania* heightened the contrast

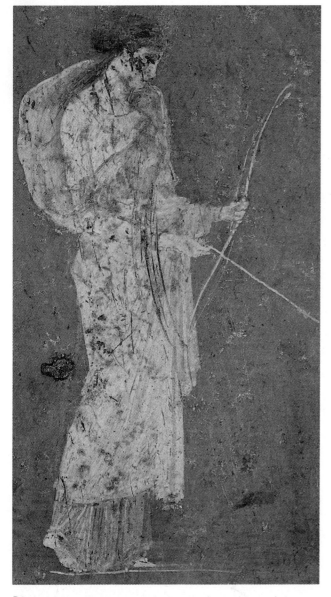

Diana. A Roman painting depicting the goddess of the hunt. Roman art was often gentle and impressionistic, far from the military grandeur most often associated today with the Romans.

passed for an art of Rome was really an importation from the Hellenistic East. Conquering armies brought back to Italy wagonloads of statues, reliefs, and marble columns as part of the plunder from Greece and Asia Minor. These became the property of the wealthy and were used to embellish their sumptuous mansions. As demand increased, hundreds of copies were made, with the result that by the end of the Republic Rome came to have a profusion of objects of art that had no more roots in the culture than the Picassos hanging on the walls of modern corporate offices.

The aura of national glory that surrounded the Principate, however, stimulated the growth of an art that was more indigenous; again Augustus led the way, encouraging and patronizing art that glorified the virtues of Rome, of which he saw himself as restorer. This art was more varied than is often assumed, running from the grandest public architecture to the most delicate wall paintings. In architecture Romans experimented with the dome and pioneered in the building of amphitheaters, public baths, and race courses. Public buildings were customarily of massive proportions and solid construction. Among the largest and most noted were the Pantheon, with its dome having a diameter of 142 feet, and the Colosseum, which could accommodate fifty thousand spectators at gladiatorial combats. Roman sculpture stayed close to the Greek, preferring ideals that were ever more naturalistic. This was particularly apparent on coins, since new coins with images of the current emperor were issued every year. Rather than being prettified, the rulers were usually depicted just as they looked: often one can trace on an annual basis a ruler's receding hairline or advancing double chin. But painting was the Romans' most original art. Wealthy Romans loved intense colors and surrounded themselves with wall paintings and mosaics—pictures produced by fitting together small pieces of colored glass or stone. These created a gamut of effects from fantastic seascapes to dreamy landscapes to introspective portraiture.

Closely related to achievements in architecture were Roman triumphs in engineering (although the Romans accomplished little in science). The imperial Romans built marvelous roads and bridges, many of which still survive. In the time of Trajan (98–117 C.E.) eleven aqueducts brought water into Rome from the nearby hills and provided the city with 300 million gallons daily for drinking and bathing as well as for flushing a well-designed sewage system. Water was cleverly funneled into the homes of the rich for their private gardens, fountains, and pools. The emperor Nero built a famous

between the manly virtues of an unspoiled race and the effeminate vices of the decadent Romans. Whatever his failings as a historian, he was a master of ironic wit and brilliant aphorism. Referring to Roman conquests, he makes a barbarian chieftain say, "They create a wilderness and call it peace."

ART AND ARCHITECTURE

Roman art first assumed its distinctive character during the period of the Principate. Before this time what

The Pantheon in Rome. Built by the Emperor Hadrian, it boasted the largest dome without interior supports of the ancient world. The dome forms a perfect sphere, exactly as high as it is wide.

"Golden House" in the center of Rome with pipes fitted for sprinkling his guests with perfume, baths supplied with medicinal waters, and a pond "like a sea." In addition, a spherical ceiling in the banquet hall revolved day and night like the heavens, all contributing to Nero's deserved reputation as a voluptuary. (Supposedly, when Nero moved in he was heard to say, "At last I can live like a human being.")

ARISTOCRATIC WOMEN UNDER THE PRINCIPATE

One of the most striking aspects of Roman society under the Principate was the important role played by upper-class women.

Roman Aqueduct at Segovia, Spain. Aqueducts conveyed water from mountains to the larger cities.

The Colosseum. Built by the Roman emperors between 75 and 80 C.E. as a place of entertainment, it was the scene of gladiatorial combats. The most common form of Greek secular architecture was the theater (see p. 135), but the most common Roman form was the amphitheater.

We have seen that under the Republic wealthier women were less confined to domesticity and obscurity than their counterparts in Athens, and this custom became even more pronounced in the early Empire. It is true that Roman women were assigned the names of their fathers with feminine endings—for example, Julia from Julius, Claudia from Claudius, Marcia from Marcus. Yet unlike women in most modern societies, they did not change their names when they were married. This was a reflection of the fact that wealthier Roman women had a status quite independent from that of their husbands. With numerous slaves to take care of their households and wealth of their own to draw on, upper-class Roman women customarily were educated in the liberal arts and were free to engage in intellectual and artistic pursuits. Some wrote poetry, others studied philosophy, and others presided over literary salons. Aristocratic Roman women often had their portraits painted or chiseled in stone, revealing their cultivation of physical elegance. The busts of several emperors' wives or daughters even appeared on the Roman coinage, partly because the emperors wished to proclaim the greatness of their families, and partly because some of these women really did play an influential role (albeit an informal one) in affairs of state. Of course, women wielded none of the power of men, yet by the standards of the ancient world they were relatively liberated. In less elevated circumstances, Roman women played an important role in the teeming shops and industries of the great cities, the wives of small-time shopkeepers more closely approximating partners than anything else.

GLADIATORIAL COMBATS

For most modern sensibilities, the most repellent aspect of Roman culture during the period of the Principate was cruelty. Whereas the Greeks entertained themselves with theater, the Romans more and more preferred "circuses," which were really exhibitions of human slaughter. During the Principate the spectacles became bloodier than ever. The Romans could no longer obtain a sufficient thrill from mere exhibitions of athletic prowess: pugilists were now required to have their hands wrapped with thongs of leather loaded with iron or lead. The most popular amusement of all was watching the gladiatorial combats in amphitheaters built for thousands of spectators. Fights between gladiators were nothing new, but they were now presented on a much more elaborate scale. Not only common people attended them, but also wealthy aristocrats, and frequently the head of the government himself. The gladiators fought to the accompaniment of savage cries and curses from the audience. When one went down with a disabling wound, the crowd was asked to decide whether his life should be spared or whether the weapon of his opponent should be plunged into his heart. One contest after another, often featuring the sacrifice of men to wild animals, was staged in the course of a single exhibition. Should the arena become too sodden with blood, it was covered over with a fresh layer of sand, and the revolting performance went on. Most of the gladiators were condemned criminals or slaves, but some were volunteers, even from the respectable classes. Commodus, the troubled and ineffectual son of Marcus Aurelius, entered the arena several times for the sake of the plaudits of the mob, and fancied himself a modern-day Hercules.

> The taste for blood and savagery may have been but one expression of a deeper psychological trend which sought not only outlets for its anxiety, but answers for it.

NEW RELIGIONS

The taste for blood and savagery may have been but one expression of a deeper psychological trend which sought not only outlets for its anxiety, but answers for it. The age of the Principate was characterized by an even deeper interest in salvationist religions than had prevailed under the Republic. Mithraism now gained adherents by the thousands, absorbing many of the followers of the cults of the Great Mother and of Serapis. About 40 C.E. the first Christians appeared in Rome. The new sect grew steadily and eventually displaced Mithraism as the most popular of the salvationist faiths, owing in part to its inclusion of women, at first on terms more or less equal to men.

THE ECONOMY OF THE PRINCIPATE

The establishment of stable government by Augustus ushered in a period of prosperity for Italy that lasted for more than two centuries. Trade was now extended to all parts of the known world, even to Arabia, India, and China. Manufacturing increased, especially in the production of pottery, textiles, and articles of metal and glass. In spite of all this, the economic order was far from healthy. Prosperity was not evenly distributed. Since the stigma attached to manual labor persisted as strongly as ever, production was bound to decline as the supply of slaves diminished. Perhaps worse was the fact that Italy had a decidedly unfavorable balance of trade. The meager industrial development was by no means sufficient to provide enough articles of export to meet the demand for luxuries imported from the provinces and from the outside world. As a consequence, Italy was gradually drained of its supply of precious metals. By the third century, the western Roman economy was beginning to collapse.

ROMAN LAW

There is general agreement that one of the most important legacies the Romans left to succeeding cultures was their system of law. The Roman legal system's gradual evolution began roughly with the publication of the Twelve Tables about 450 B.C.E. In the later centuries of the Republic, the Law of the Twelve Tables was transformed by the growth of new precedents and principles. These emanated from different sources: from changes in custom, from the teachings of the Stoics, from the decisions of judges, but especially from the edicts of the *praetors*, magistrates who had authority to define and interpret the law in particular suits and issue instructions to judges.

Roman law attained its highest stage of development under the Principate. This resulted in part from the extension of the law over a wider field of jurisdiction, over the lives and properties of aliens in strange environments as well as over the citizens of Italy. But the major reason was the fact that Augustus and his successors gave to certain eminent jurists the right to deliver opinions on the legal issues of cases under trial in the courts. The most prominent of the men thus designated from time to time were Gaius, Ulpian, Papinian, and Paulus. Although most of them held high judicial office, they had gained their reputations primarily as lawyers and writers on legal subjects. The responses of these jurists came to embody a science and philosophy of law unlike anything that had gone before, and were accepted as the basis of Roman jurisprudence.

The Roman law as it was developed under the influence of the jurists comprised three great branches or divisions: the civil law, the law of peoples, and the natural law. The civil law was the law of Rome and its citizens. As such it existed in both written and unwritten forms. It included the statutes of the Senate, the decrees of the emperor, the edicts of magistrates, and also certain ancient customs operating with the force of law. The law of peoples was the law held to be common to all people regardless of nationality, a sort of rudimentary "international law." This law authorized slavery and private ownership of property and defined the principles of purchase and sale, partnership, and contract. It was not superior to the civil law but supplemented it as especially applicable to the alien inhabitants of the Empire.

This development of the concept of abstract justice as a legal principle was one of the noblest achievements of the Roman civilization.

The most interesting and in many ways the most important branch of Roman law was the natural law, a product not of judicial practice, but of philosophy. The Stoics had developed the idea of a rational order of nature that is the embodiment of justice and right. They had affirmed that all men are by nature equal, and that they are entitled to certain basic rights that governments have no authority to transgress. The father of the law of nature as a legal principle, however, was not one of the Hellenistic Stoics, but Cicero. "True law," he declared, "is right reason consonant with nature, diffused among all men, constant, eternal. To make enactments infringing this law, religion forbids, neither may it be repealed even in part, nor have we power through Senate or people to free ourselves from it." This law existed prior to the state itself, and any ruler who defied it automatically became a tyrant. Most of the great jurists subscribed to conceptions of the law of nature very similar to those of the philosophers. Although the jurists did not regard this law as an automatic limitation upon the civil law, they

thought of it as an ideal to which the statutes and decrees of men ought to conform. This development of the concept of abstract justice as a legal principle was one of the noblest achievements of the Roman civilization.

THE CRISIS OF THE THIRD CENTURY (180–284 C.E.)

What factors brought the Roman empire to the brink of ruin?

With the death of Marcus Aurelius in 180 C.E. the period of beneficent imperial rule came to an end. One reason for the success of the "Five Good Emperors" was that the first four designated particularly promising young men, rather than sons or close relatives, for the succession. But Marcus Aurelius broke this pattern with unfortunate results. Although he was one of the most philosophic and thoughtful rulers who ever reigned, he was not wise enough to recognize that his son Commodus was a self-indulgent adolescent who lacked the discipline or the capacity to rule effectively. To some degree, Marcus Aurelius had his hands tied; it is likely that any attempt to make someone other than his natural son his heir would have met with stiff resistance from the army. Although history has been unkind to Commodus—not without reason—he did put an end to costly wars that profited Rome nothing, an eminently sensible step but one that made him unpopular with both the army and the Senate. He vacillated between trying to accommodate the Senate and terrifying its membership. When a policy proved unpopular among the senators, Commodus would attempt to placate them by executing one or more of his advisors. As a result, few talented people wanted to work for him. He treated the Senate with contempt, and he scorned the traditional expectations for aristocratic conduct, indulging his taste for perversities both public and private, and even appearing as a gladiator in the Colosseum. His erratic and frequently violent behavior resulted in a conspiracy originating inside his own palace: his wrestling coach finally strangled him in

Commodus. The self-deluded ruler encouraged artists to portray him as the equal of the superhuman Hercules.

brother and coemperor Gela. So desperate was Caracalla to raise revenues and pay bonuses to his increasingly covetous armies (especially to appease them after his assassination of his more popular brother), that he made everyone in the empire a Roman citizen. This was hardly an act of enlightenment, but rather was aimed at increasing the tax base of the Roman state. In the process, he cheapened Roman citizenship, once the prized glue that held the far-flung empire together. His successors in the Severan dynasty proved no better. Elagabalus tried to introduce an eastern sun cult as the official religion of Rome, and he flouted sexual and moral convention on the very floor of the Senate.

If not for a series of remarkable imperial women fighting to keep the dynasty and empire together, the results might have been disastrous. First Julia Domna, the wife of Septimius Severus, helped to manage the empire for her son Caracalla, and seems to have acted as the one restraint on his vicious personality; she took her own life when he fell victim to an assassin in 217 C.E. Her sister, Julia Maesa, was the grandmother of both Elagabalus and his successor, Severus Alexander. Her political influence was considerable (although probably somewhat exaggerated by the author Herodian), and she proved instrumental in Elagabalus's downfall when his abuses endangered the state. Finally, her daughter Julia Mamaea, mother of Severus Alexander, enjoyed unusual prominence and popularity during the reign of her young son (222–235 C.E.), and exercised an almost regentlike authority within his government. But they could not stem the tide started by the dynasty's founder, Septimius. The growing

192 C.E. Matters thereafter became worse. With no obvious successor to Commodus, the armies of the provinces raised their own candidates and civil war ensued. A provincial general, Septimius Severus (193–211 C.E.), emerged victorious, making it clear that provincial armies could now interfere in imperial politics at will.

THE SEVERAN DYNASTY

Severus and some of his successors aggravated the problem by eliminating even the theoretical rights of the Senate and ruling as military dictators. Severus dispensed with showing any deference at all to the Senate, and on his deathbed advised his two sons, "Enrich the soldiers, boys, and scorn the rest." His son Caracalla was little more than a thug who murdered his

Coin Depicting Emperor's Wife. This Roman coin, dating from about 200 C.E., bears the image of Julia Domna, wife of the emperor Septimius Severus.

prominence of the army made it increasingly uncontrollable. Once the role of brute force was openly revealed, any aspiring general could try his luck at seizing power. Severus Alexander and Julia Mamaea were murdered in 235 C.E. when the army turned against them. Fifty years of endemic civil war followed. From 235 to 284 C.E. there were no fewer than twenty-six "barracks emperors," of whom only one managed to escape a violent death.

THE HEIGHT OF THE THIRD-CENTURY CRISIS

The half century between 235 and 284 was certainly the worst for Rome since its rise to world power. In addition to political chaos, a number of other factors combined to bring the empire to the brink of ruin. The civil war had disastrous economic effects. Not only did constant warfare interfere with agriculture and trade, but the rivalry of aspirants to rule led them to drain the wealth of their territories in order to gain favor with their armies. Following the maxim of "enriching the soldiers and scorning the rest," they raised funds by debasing the coinage and by nearly confiscatory taxation of civilians. Landlords, small tenants, and manufacturers thus had little motive to produce at a time when production was most necessary. In human terms the poorest, as is usual in times of economic contraction, suffered the most. Often they were driven to the most abject destitution. In the wake of war and hunger, disease became rampant. Already during the reign of Marcus Aurelius a terrible plague had swept through the empire, decimating the army and the population at large. In the middle of the third century pestilence returned and struck at the population with its fearful scythe for fifteen years.

The resulting strain on human resources came at a time when Rome could least afford it, for still another threat to the empire in the middle of the third century was the advance of Rome's external enemies. With Roman ranks thinned by disease and Roman armies fighting each other, Germans in the West and Persians in the East broke through the old Roman defense lines. In 251 C.E. the Goths defeated and slew the emperor Decius, crossed the Danube, and marauded at will in the Balkans. An even more humiliating disaster came in 260 C.E. when the emperor Valerian was captured in battle by the Persians and made to kneel as a footstool for their ruler. When he died his body was stuffed and hung on exhibition. For a time, the western provinces

The Emperor Philip the Arab. An artistic legacy of the Roman "age of anxiety."

broke free as an independent empire in their own right, despairing of Rome's ability to help them, let alone actually provide lasting solutions. Clearly the days of Augustus were far in the past.

NEOPLATONISM

Understandably, the culture of the third century was marked by pervasive anxiety. One can even see expressions of worry in the surviving statuary, as in the bust of the Emperor Philip (244–249 C.E.), who appears almost to realize that he will soon be killed in battle. In response, the Neoplatonic philosophy of withdrawal from the world came to the fore. Neoplatonism (meaning "new Platonism") drew the spiritualist tendency of Plato's thought to extremes.

The first of its basic teachings was emanationism: everything that exists proceeds from the divine in a continuing stream of emanations. The initial stage in the process is the emanation of the world soul. From this come the divine Ideas or spiritual patterns, and then the souls of particular things. The final emanation is matter. But matter has no form or quality of its own; it is simply the residue that is left after the spiritual rays from the divine have burned themselves out. It follows that matter is to be despised as the symbol of evil and darkness.

Neoplatonism's second major doctrine was mysticism. The human soul was originally a part of God, but it has become separated from its divine source through its union with matter. The highest goal of life should be mystic reunion with the divine, which can be accomplished through contemplation and through emancipation of the soul from bondage to matter. Human beings should be ashamed of the fact that they possess a physical body and should seek to subjugate it in every way possible. Asceticism was therefore the third main teaching of this philosophy.

The real founder of Neoplatonism was Plotinus, who was born in Egypt about 204 C.E. In the later years of his life he taught in Rome and won many followers among the upper classes before he died in 270. His principal successors diluted the philosophy with more and more bizarre superstitions. In spite of its antirational viewpoint and its utter indifference to the state, Neoplatonism became so popular in Rome in the third and fourth centuries C.E. that it almost completely supplanted Stoicism. No fact could have expressed more eloquently the turn of Rome away from the realities of the here and now. At the same time, people turned increasingly to religions of redemption, of which Christianity was but one. The internal organization of the Christian churches gave them particular appeal and aided the spread of this particular cult, as we will see in the following chapter.

ROMAN RULE IN THE WEST: A BALANCE SHEET

Did Rome fall? Why or why not?

As Rome was not built in a day, so it was not lost in one. As we will see in the next chapter, strong rule returned in 284 C.E. Thereafter the Roman empire endured in the West for two hundred years more and in the East for a millennium. But the restored Roman state differed greatly from the old one—so much so that it is proper to end the story of characteristically Roman civilization here and review the reasons for Rome's transformation into a distinctly different type of society, one that we will examine in detail in the next chapter.

EXPLAINING THE "FALL" OF ROME

More has been written on the fall of Rome than on the death of any other civilization. The theories offered to account for the decline have been many and varied. Perhaps the strangest recent one is that Rome fell from the effects of lead ingested from cooking utensils, but if this were true we would have to ask why Rome did so well for so long. Moralists have found the explanation for Rome's fall in the descriptions of lechery and gluttony presented in the writings of such authors as Juvenal and Petronius. Such an approach, however, overlooks the facts that much of this evidence is patently overdrawn, and that nearly all of it comes from the period of the early Principate: in the later centuries, when the empire was more obviously collapsing, morality became more austere through the influence of ascetic religions. One of the simplest explanations is that Rome fell only because of the severity of German attacks. But barbarians had always stood ready to attack Rome throughout its long history: German pressures did increase at certain times but German invasions would never have succeeded had they not come at moments when Rome was already weakened internally. Indeed, from the fourth century C.E. onward, increasing numbers of Germanic tribes were less interested in destroying Rome than in becoming a part of it. It was often the case that Roman bigotry, maladministration and abuse had more to do with violent outbursts from the Germans than any propensity for rape and pillage on the part of the "barbarians" themselves.

> More has been written on the fall of Rome than on the death of any other civilization.

POLITICAL FAILURES

It is best then to concentrate on Rome's most serious internal problems. Some of these were political. The most obvious political failing of the Roman constitution under the Principate was the lack of a clear law of succession. Especially when a ruler died suddenly, there was no certainty about who was to follow him. In modern America the deaths of a Lincoln or Kennedy might shock the nation, but people at least knew what would happen next; in imperial Rome no one knew and civil war increasingly became the result. For all of Augustus' achievements, this was his system's greatest failure. Indeed, by disguising the reality of autocratic rule behind republican forms, there was little any emperor could do to provide for an orderly succession to an imperial position that did not officially exist. So long as prosperity and deference for the institutions of ancient Rome remained, transitions might be effected more or less smoothly. But from 235 to 284 C.E. warfare and instability fed on each other. Civil war was also nurtured by the lack of constitutional means for reform. If regimes became unpopular, as most did after 180 C.E., the only means to alter them was to overthrow them. But resorting to violence always bred more violence, especially as the soldiery became the arbiter of success or failure of an imperial regime.

ECONOMIC CRISIS

The Roman empire also had its share of economic problems, though the lessons to be drawn from this remain unclear. Rome's worst economic problems derived from its slave system and from labor shortages. Roman civilization was based on cities, and Roman cities existed largely by virtue of an agricultural surplus produced by slaves. Slaves were worked so hard that they did not normally reproduce to fill their own ranks. Until the time of Trajan (98–117 C.E.), Roman conquests provided fresh supplies of slaves to keep the system going, but thereafter the economy began to run out of human fuel. Landlords could no longer be so profligate of human life, barracks slavery came to an end, and the countryside produced less of a surplus to feed the towns. The fact that no technological advance took up the slack may also be attributed to slavery. Later in Western history agricultural surpluses were produced by technological revolutions, but Roman landlords were indifferent to technology because interest in it was thought to be demeaning. As long as slaves were present to do the work, Romans had no interest in labor-saving devices, and attention to any sort of machinery was deemed a sign of slavishness. Landlords proved their nobility by their interest in "higher things," but while they were contemplating

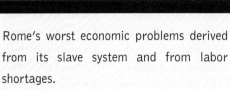

Rome's worst economic problems derived from its slave system and from labor shortages.

these heights their agricultural surpluses gradually became depleted.

Labor shortages also aggravated Rome's economic problems, especially in the west. The end of foreign conquests and the decline of slavery meant a pressing need for people to stay on the farm, but barbarian pressures also meant a steady need for men to serve in the army. The plagues of the second and third centuries sharply reduced the population just at the worst time. It has been estimated that between the reign of Marcus Aurelius and the restoration of strong rule in 284 C.E. disease, warfare and a declining birthrate combined to reduce the population of the Roman empire by one third. The result was that there were neither sufficient farmers to work the land nor enough soldiers to fight Rome's enemies.

Despite all of this, it is important to remember that Rome was scarcely poverty stricken. Wealth still poured into Roman society, but in the western provinces especially it tended to concentrate itself in the hands of a very few families. These families gradually accrued to themselves such extensive privileges (to say nothing of their ability to hire, when necessary, private means of force) that they rarely contributed anything to the coffers of the Roman state. The burden for the upkeep of cities thus fell increasingly on a local elite that could not shoulder it; as these men were reduced to poverty or fled the cities altogether, the urban basis of classical Roman civilization and its commonly shared civic ideals was further undermined. Regional differences were also growing more pronounced, leading to a series of secessionist movements among the western provinces. Enormous dedication and exertion on the part of its citizenry might just possibly have saved the empire, but too few citizens were now willing to work hard for the public good. Ultimately, the decline of Rome was accompanied by lack of interest, and the Roman world slowly came to an end not so much with a bang as with a whimper.

Ultimately, the decline of Rome was accompanied by lack of interest, and the Roman world slowly came to an end not so much with a bang as with a whimper.

ROMAN ACHIEVEMENTS

Focusing our attention on the dynamics of Rome's decline in the West should not cause us to overlook the many ways in which Roman society was a towering success. No state has ever encompassed so much territory, with such a large percentage of the world's population under its dominion, for so long a span of time. Roman rule maintained its vitality in the West from the Second Punic War to the end of the fourth century C.E. In the East, the Roman empire survived until 1453. Part of that success resulted from the Roman government's ability to create and maintain systems of communication, trade, and travel as no other state had done before, and as none would do again until modern times. Underlying these successes was the fundamental strength of the Roman economy. While much is made of the collapse of the Roman economy in the third century and its runaway inflation, the Romans had maintained a relatively stable currency and a prosperous international trade for four previous centuries without any of the mechanisms or safeguards of a modern market economy. This too remains an unparalleled achievement.

Most fundamentally, however, the Roman empire's survival was a political achievement. The Roman political system was inclusive to a degree no modern empire has ever matched. Through their willingness to extend the franchise to non-Romans, to allow even provincials to become senators and ultimately emperors, Rome gave a share of power to its population that no Near Eastern or Greek empire could have ever imagined. Although the Persians were tolerant of foreign cultic practice, and the Athenians generous with political rights among their own citizenry, extending real political power to "outsiders" was out of the question. For the Romans, extension of the franchise was key to their success, from the mechanism of the Latin Right in early Italy to the granting of citizenship to all the inhabitants of their empire under Caracalla. As a prominent historian of Rome once remarked, if the British empire had been as willing to extend its franchise as the Romans were to extend theirs, the American Revolution might never have occurred.

> No state has ever encompassed so much territory, with such a large percentage of the world's population under its dominion, for so long a span of time.

tiquity; and second, because Rome seems to bear such a close kinship to the modern temper. The resemblances between Roman history and the history of Great Britain or the United States in the nineteenth and twentieth centuries have often been noted. Like America's, the Roman economy evolved from a simple agrarianism to a complex urban system with problems of unemployment, gross disparities of wealth, and financial crises. Like the British empire, the Roman empire was founded on conquest. And like both the British and the American empires, the Roman empire justified its conquests by celebrating the peace those conquests allegedly brought to the world.

Ultimately, however, such parallels are superficial. Rome was an ancient, not a modern, society that differed profoundly from any of the societies of the modern Western world. As noted already, the Romans disdained industrial activities. Neither did they have any idea of the modern national state; ultimately their empire was a collection of cities, not an integrated territorial body politic. The Romans never developed an adequate representative government, and they never solved the problem of succession to imperial power. Nor were Roman social relations in any way comparable with those of more recent centuries. The Roman economy rested on slavery to a degree unmatched in any modern society. Technology was primitive; social stratification was extreme; and gender relations were profoundly unequal. Roman religion rested on the assumption that religious practice and political life were inseparable from one another, and Roman emperors were worshiped (especially in the East) as living gods.

Nevertheless, the civilization of Rome exerted a great influence on later cultures. Roman architectural forms survive to this day in the design of many of our government buildings, and Roman styles of dress continue to be worn by the clergy of the various Christian churches. Through the sixth-century code of the emperor Justinian (see Chapter 7), Roman law was handed down to the Middle Ages and on into modern times. American judges still cite legal maxims coined by Gaius or Ulpian; and third-century legal precedents continue to be valid in the legal systems of nearly all continental European countries and the American state of Louisiana. Roman sculpture provided the model on which virtually all modern sculpture rests, and Roman authors set the standards for prose composition in

CONCLUSION

It is tempting to believe that we today have many similarities to the Romans: first of all, because Rome is nearer to us in time than the other civilizations of an-

Europe and America until the end of the nineteenth century. Even the organization of the Catholic Church was adapted from the structure of the Roman state; today the pope bears the title of supreme pontiff (*pontifex maximus*), once born by the emperor in his role as head of the Roman civic religion.

But perhaps the most important of all Rome's contributions to the future was its role in transmitting Greek civilization throughout the length and breadth of its empire. When, finally, the united Roman empire did collapse, three different successor civilizations would emerge to occupy Rome's former territories: Byzantium, Islam, and western Europe. Each of these civilizations would be characterized by a distinctive religious tradition, and each would adopt and adapt different aspects of its Roman inheritance. What these three western civilizations shared, however, was a common cultural inheritance derived from Greece by way of Rome—an inheritance of urbanism, cosmopolitanism, imperialism, and learning that would forever mark the West as a unique experiment in human history.

This cultural inheritance would be Rome's epitaph; and in the mid-third century C.E., it must have seemed that an epitaph for the Roman empire was the only thing needed to bring the Roman empire to an end. In fact, the Roman empire did not collapse. It went on to enjoy another several centuries of life. Rome did not fall in the third century, or the fourth century, or even the fifth. But it was transformed, and in this transformed state the Roman inheritance would pass to the Western civilizations of the Middle Ages. It is to those transformations that we now turn.

SELECTED READINGS

Translations of Roman authors are available in the appropriate volumes of the Penguin Classics series and in the Loeb Classical Library.

Badian, Ernst. *Foreign Clientelae (264–70 B.C.).* Oxford, 1958. A seminal work demonstrating how the Roman aristocracy extended traditional bonds of personal obligation into conquered territories as a way to enhance their own power in Rome.

Beard, Mary, John North, and Simon Price. *Religions of Rome, Volume I: A History.* Cambridge, 1998. An authoritative account, full of new ideas.

———. *Religions of Rome, Volume II: A Sourcebook.* Cambridge, 1998. A definitive source collection that supplements *Volume I: A History.*

Boardman, John, Jasper Griffin, and Oswyn Murray. *The Oxford History of the Roman World.* Oxford, 1990. Reprint of relevant portions of the excellent *Oxford History of the Classical World* (1986). Stimulating, accessible topical chapters by British specialists.

Brunt, P. A. *Social Conflicts in the Roman Republic.* New York, 1971. An outstanding overview of the social and economic developments that undermined the republic.

Cornell, T. J. *The Beginnings of Rome: Italy and Rome from the Bronze Age to the Punic Wars (c. 1000–264 B.C.).* London, 1995. An expert, ambitious survey of the archaeological and historical evidence for early Rome.

Crawford, Michael. *The Roman Republic.* 2d ed. Cambridge, Mass., 1993. A lively, fast-paced survey of Republican Rome. An excellent place to start.

Gardner, Jane F. *Women in Roman Law and Society.* Bloomington, 1986. A monograph focused on Roman women's control over property.

Garnsey, Peter, and Richard Saller. *The Roman Empire: Economy, Society, and Culture.* Berkeley, 1987. A straightforward short survey.

Gruen, Erich S. *The Last Generation of the Roman Republic.* Berkeley, 1974. An important but controversial account of the personalities and dynamics that brought an end to the Roman Republic.

———. *The Hellenistic World and the Coming of Rome.* 2 vols. Berkeley, 1984. A massive survey, focused on the unpredictable rise of Rome to a position of dominance within the Mediterranean world.

Hallett, Judith. *Fathers and Daughters in Republican Rome: Women and the Elite Family.* Princeton, N.J., 1984. A detailed examination of the important role played by aristocratic women in shaping political relationships in the family-dominated world of Roman government.

Harris, William V. *War and Imperialism in Republican Rome, 327–70 B.C.* Oxford, 1979. A challenging study arguing that Rome's need for military conquest and imperial expansion was deeply embedded in the political and social fabric of Roman life.

Lancel, Serge. *Carthage: A History.* Trans. by Antonia Nevill. Oxford, 1995. An up-to-date account of Rome's great rival for control of the Mediterranean world.

Lewis, Naphtali, and M. Reinhold. *Roman Civilization: Selected Readings.* 2 volumes. New York, 1951–1955. The standard collection, especially for political and economic subjects. Volume I covers the Republic; Volume II, the empire.

MacMullen, Ramsay. *Roman Social Relations, 50 B.C.–A.D. 284.* New Haven, 1981. An excellent overview of the social structure of Rome from the end of the Republic to the end of the Principate.

Meier, Christian. *Caesar: A Biography.* New York, 1982. An entertaining but reliable biography of Julius Caesar, enlivened by sympathetic portraits of his foes as well as his friends.

Millar, Fergus G. B. *The Emperor in the Roman World, 31 B.C.–A.D. 337.* London, 1977. A classic work that showed (among much else) the importance of emperor worship to the religious outlook of the Roman empire.

————. *The Roman Near East, 31 B.C.–A.D. 337.* Cambridge, Mass., 1993. An exhaustive examination of Roman strategies of control and attitudes toward ethnicity under the Principate.

————. *The Crowd in Rome in the Late Republic.* Ann Arbor, 1999. A revisionist account that emphasizes the reality of Roman democracy in the late Republic, against those who would see the period's politics as entirely under the control of aristocratic families.

Ward, Allen M., Fritz Heichelheim, and Cedric A. Yeo. *A History of the Roman People,* 3d ed. Upper Saddle River, N.J., 1999. An informative, well-organized textbook covering Roman history from its beginnings to the end of the sixth century C.E.

Wells, Colin. *The Roman Empire,* 2d ed. Cambridge, Mass., 1992. An easily readable survey from the reign of Augustus to the mid-third century C.E., particularly useful for its treatment of the relationship between the Roman central government and its Italian provinces.

CHRISTIANITY
AND THE
TRANSFORMATION
OF THE
ROMAN WORLD

THE ROMAN EMPIRE DECLINED after 180 C.E., but it did not collapse. In 284 C.E. the vigorous soldier-emperor Diocletian began a reorganization of the empire that gave it a new lease on life. Throughout the fourth century the Roman state continued to encompass the entire Mediterranean world. In the fifth century the western half of the empire did fall to foreign invasions, but many Roman institutions continued, and in the sixth century the empire reconquered a good part of the western Mediterranean shoreline. Only in the seventh century did it become fully evident that divisions between the eastern and western halves of the Roman empire would be permanent, and that the two regions would thereafter develop in fundamentally different ways. With this division, the world of classical antiquity came to an end.

Historians used to underestimate the longevity of Roman institutions and begin their discussions of medieval history in the third, fourth, or fifth century C.E. Since historical periodization is always approximate and depends largely on which aspects of development a historian wishes to emphasize, this approach cannot be dismissed. Certainly the transition from the ancient to the medieval world was gradual, with some "medieval" ways emerging in the West as early as the third century C.E. But it is now more customary to conceive of ancient history as continuing after 284 C.E. and lasting until the Roman empire lost control over the Mediterranean in the seventh century. The period from 284 to about 610 C.E., although transitional (as, of course, all ages are), has certain themes of its own and is best described as neither Roman nor medieval but as the age of late antiquity.

The major cultural trend of late antiquity was the spread and triumph of Christianity throughout the Roman world. At first Christianity was just one of many otherworldly religions that appealed to increasing numbers of people during the later empire. But in the fourth century it was adopted as the Roman state religion and thereafter became one of the greatest shaping forces in the development of Western civilizations.

FOCUS QUESTIONS

- How did Diocletian transform the Roman empire?

- What caused the substantial growth of Christianity in the third century?

- What major changes did Christianity undergo during the fourth century?

- How did the Germanic tribes triumph over the western Roman empire?

- What was Augustine's conception of history?

- How was classical culture Christianized?

- What did Justinian's plan to reunite the Roman empire fail?

Outside Palestine, Christianity found its first adherents in the cities of the Roman empire, and spread only gradually from these urban centers into the surrounding countryside. Its extension, first from city to city, and then from city to countryside, was a vital element in an ongoing process of cultural assimilation that characterized the late antique Roman world. As cultural developments traveled from one part of the empire to another, however, they also became less sophisticated and less rooted in the local areas (such as Palestine) where they had originated. The result was an increasing cultural diffusion that brought with it a "watering down" of the high culture of the classical era—a process we shall call "vulgarization."

At the same time, cultural influences from outside the Mediterranean world were also having a growing impact, especially on the western parts of the empire. This process the Romans themselves called "barbarization," from the Greek word *barbaros*, meaning "foreigner." Barbarian culture was not necessarily primitive, but it was nonurban and non-Greek—and in the eyes of Mediterranean elites, these facts alone were enough to stigmatize it. But "barbarian" influence grew steadily nonetheless, first within the army, and then throughout society. None of these processes were cataclysmic; but by the end of the sixth century C.E., Christianization, vulgarization, and barbarization had combined to bring the ancient Mediterranean world to an end.

THE REORGANIZED EMPIRE

How did Diocletian transform the Roman empire?

The chaos of the mid-third century C.E. might well have destroyed the Roman empire. That it did not is largely due to the energetic work of a remarkable soldier named Diocletian, who ruled as emperor from 284 to 305 C.E. Well aware of the problems that had undone his predecessors, Diocletian embarked on a number of fundamental political and economic reforms. Recognizing that the dominance of the army in the life of the state had hitherto been too great, he introduced measures to separate military from civilian administrative chains of command. Aware that new pressures, both external and internal, had made it nearly impossible for one man to govern the entire Roman empire, he divided his realm in half, granting the western part to

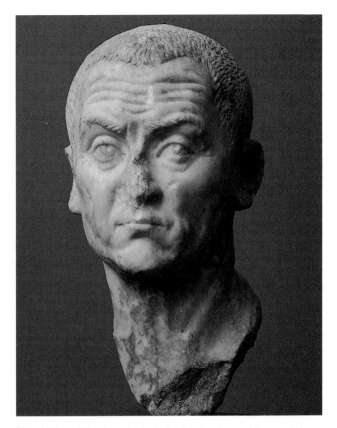

Diocletian. His short hair is in the Roman military style.

a trusted colleague, Maximian, who recognized Diocletian as the senior ruler. The two then chose lieutenants, called caesars, to govern large subsections of their territories. This system (known as the Tetrarchy, "the rule of the four") was also meant to provide for an orderly succession, for the caesars were supposed to inherit the major rule of either East or West and then appoint new caesars in their stead.

THE REIGN OF DIOCLETIAN

In the economic sphere Diocletian stabilized the badly debased currency, introduced a new system of taxation, and issued legislation designed to keep agricultural workers and town dwellers at their jobs so that the basic work necessary to support the empire would continue to be done. To check inflation, he attempted (without much success) to fix prices and wages; to unite the empire, he sought to enforce observance of the rituals of the Roman imperial cult on dissident groups, such as Christians, who refused to participate in them. The result, between 303 and 313 C.E., was "the Great Persecution," in which hundreds of Christians perished throughout the empire.

Although Diocletian succeeded in restoring an empire that had been on the verge of expiring, he also transformed the empire by "orientalizing" it in three primary and lasting ways. Most literally, Diocletian began a geographical orientalization of the empire by shifting its administrative weight toward the East. Between 284 and 303 C.E. Diocletian ruled his empire not from Rome, but from Nicomedia, a city in modern-day Turkey, in a tacit recognition of the fact that the wealthier and more vital part of the empire now lay in the East. Second, as befitting one who turned his back on Rome, Diocletian adopted the titles and ceremonies of a Near Eastern potentate. Abandoning Augustus' policy of appearing to be a constitutional ruler, Diocletian presented himself as an undisguised autocrat. He took the title not of *princeps*, or "first citizen," but of *dominus*, or "lord." He wore a diadem and a purple gown of silk interwoven with gold, and he introduced Persian-style ceremony into his court. Those who gained an audience had to prostrate themselves before him; a privileged few were allowed to kiss his robe.

Diocletian's Palace in Split. An artistic reconstruction.

The third aspect of orientalization in Diocletian's policy was his growing reliance on an imperial bureaucracy. By separating civilian from military commands and legislating on a wide variety of economic and social matters, Diocletian created the need for many new officials. Not surprisingly, by the end of his reign subjects were complaining that "there were more tax collectors than taxpayers." These officials did keep the empire going, but the new bureaucracy was prone to graft and corruption; worse, the growing number of bureaucrats called for reservoirs of manpower and wealth at a time when the Roman empire no longer had large supplies of either. Taken together, the various aspects of Diocletian's easternizing made him seem more like a Hellenistic sacral monarch than a Roman ruler: it was almost as if the defeat of Antony and Cleopatra at Actium was now being avenged.

Diocletian's rigid regime left little room for spontaneity or individual freedom. The results can be seen most clearly in the architecture and art of the age. Dio-

Porphyry Sculptures of Diocletian and His Colleagues in Rule. Every effort is made to make the two senior rulers and their two junior colleagues look identical by means of stylization. Note also the emphasis on military strength.

Colossal Head of Constantine. In this head of Constantine the eyes are enlarged as if to emphasize the ruler's spiritual vision. The head is approximately seven times larger than life and weighs about nine tons.

cletian himself preferred a colossal, bombastic style of building that was meant to emphasize his own power. The baths he constructed in Rome, when he finally arrived there in 303 C.E., were the largest yet known, encompassing about thirty acres. When he retired in 305 Diocletian built a palace for himself in what is now Split (Croatia) that was laid out along a rectilinear grid like an army camp. A plan of this palace shows clearly how Diocletian favored regimentation in everything.

Roman portrait statuary, which had hitherto featured striking naturalism and individuality, also became impersonal and unexpressive during this period. Human faces were impassive and symmetrical rather than reflecting a free play of emotions. Porphyry, a particularly hard and dark stone that had to be imported from Egypt—another sign of easternization—often replaced marble for imperial busts. Sculpted in porphyry, groups of statues of Diocletian, Maximian, and their two caesars show the new hardness and symmetry at their fullest, for the figures were made to look so similar that they are indistinguishable from each other.

THE REIGN OF CONSTANTINE

In 305 C.E. Diocletian decided to abdicate to raise cabbages—an unprecedented move for a late Roman ruler. At the same time he obliged his colleague Maximian to retire as well, and their two caesars moved peacefully up the ladder of succession. But the concord did not last. Civil war broke out among Diocletian's successors and continued until Constantine, the son of one of the original caesars, emerged victorious. From 312 until 324 Constantine ruled only in the West, but from 324 until his death in 337 C.E. he did away with power sharing and ruled over a reunited empire. Except for the fact that he favored Christianity, an epoch-making decision to be examined in the next section, Constantine continued to govern along the lines laid down by Diocletian. Bureaucracy proliferated and the state became so vigilant in keeping town dwellers and agricultural laborers at their posts that society began to harden into a caste system. In keeping with Constantine's grandiose conception of himself, he built a new capital in 330 C.E. and named it Constantinople. This new capital was the most visible manifestation yet of the continued shift in the "weight" of Roman civilization toward the East. Situated on the border of Europe and Asia, Constantinople had commanding advantages as a center for Eastern-oriented communications, trade, and defense. Surrounded on three sides by water and protected on land by walls, it was to prove nearly impregnable and would remain the center of "Roman" government for the next one thousand years.

Constantine also made succession to the imperial throne hereditary. By so doing he brought Rome back to the principle of dynastic monarchy that it had thrown off about eight hundred years earlier. But Constantine, who treated the empire as if it were his private property, did not pass on united rule to one son. Instead he divided his realm among three of them. Not surprisingly, his three sons started fighting each other after their father's death, a conflict exacerbated by religious differences. Warfare and dynastic squabbles continued on and off for most of the fourth century C.E., as did periodic challenges from aspiring usurpers of the imperial throne. But these disturbances were never so serious as the civil wars of the third century, and from time to time one or another contestant was able to reunite the empire for a period of years. The last to do so was Theodosius I (379–395 C.E.), who butchered thousands of innocent citizens of Thessalonica in retribution for the death of one of his officers, but whose energies in preserving the empire by holding off Ger-

WHAT CAUSED THE SUBSTANTIAL GROWTH OF CHRISTIANITY IN THE THIRD CENTURY?

THE EMERGENCE AND TRIUMPH OF CHRISTIANITY   227

manic barbarians still gave him some claim to his title "the Great."

The period between Constantine and Theodosius saw the hardening of earlier tendencies. With Constantinople now the leading city of the empire, the center of commerce and administration was located clearly in the East. Regionalism too grew more pronounced: the Latin-speaking West was losing a sense of rapport and contact with the Greek-speaking East, and in both West and East local differences were becoming accentuated. In economic life the hallmark of the age was the growing gap between rich and poor. In the West large landowners were able to consolidate their holdings, and in the East some individuals became prosperous by rising through the bureaucracy and enriching themselves with graft, or by trading in luxury goods. But the taxation system initiated by Diocletian and maintained throughout the fourth century C.E. weighed heavily on the poor, forcing them to carry the burden of supporting the bureaucracy, the army, and the lavish imperial court or courts. The poor, moreover, had no chance to escape their poverty, for legislation demanded that they and their heirs stay at their unrewarding and heavily taxed jobs. Most people in the fourth century thus lived in desperate and unrelenting poverty against a backdrop of ostentatious wealth. The Roman empire may have been restored in the years from 284 to 395 C.E., but it was nonetheless a fertile breeding ground for a new religion of otherwordly salvation.

> The Roman empire may been restored in the years from 284 to 395 C.E., but it was nonetheless a fertile breeding ground for a new religion of otherworldly salvation.

THE EMERGENCE AND TRIUMPH OF CHRISTIANITY

What caused the substantial growth of Christianity in the third century?

Christian beginnings of course go back several centuries before Constantine to the time of Jesus. Christianity was formed primarily by Jesus and Saint Paul and gained converts steadily thereafter. But the new religion became widespread only during the chaos of the third century C.E. and triumphed in the Roman empire only in the fourth century, after it became the favored religion of Constantine and his family. At the time of its humble beginnings no one could have predicted that Christianity would become the official religion of the Roman empire by the year 392 C.E.

THE CAREER OF JESUS

Jesus of Nazareth was born in Judea sometime near the beginning of the Common (or Christian) Era. He was not born exactly in the "year one"—we owe this mistake in our dating system to a sixth-century monk. When Jesus was born, the Roman conquest of Judea was not even a generation old. The atmosphere of the region was charged with religious division and political discontent. Banditry, sometimes tinged by nationalism, was commonplace in the countryside; in the cities and villages, the talk was of rebellion, and the hope for a messiah who would expel the idolatrous Romans from the holy land of Israel. Most extreme of those who sought hope in politics were the Zealots, who sought to overthrow the Romans by force of arms. Their activities eventually led to two disastrous revolts. The first, in 69–70 C.E., brought about the destruction of the Temple at Jerusalem; the second, in 132–135 C.E., caused the expulsion of the entire Jewish population of the city. Thereafter, Jews were forbidden to live there, and the shattered city itself was refounded as a pagan city, Aelia Capitolina.

For the career of Jesus, however, the religious divisions within Judaism matter most. In the centuries following the rebuilding of the Temple, Judaism had become an uncompromisingly monotheistic religion, built on the covenantal relationship between Yahweh and his chosen people, the Jews. Within Second Temple Judaism, however, important differences in the interpretation of that covenant soon emerged. By the fourth century B.C.E., the first five books of the Bible had assumed their present form. These books contain the written Torah—the laws and commandments binding on Jews as a result of their covenant with Yahweh. The guardians of these written traditions were the Temple priesthood and their aristocratic allies, a group known together as the Sadducees. As one would expect in the ancient world, the alliance between religious and political authorities in Judea was close. Before the Roman conquest, the high priest of the

Temple at Jerusalem had been appointed by the Hasmonean Jewish monarchs, who had secured their independence from the Seleucid rulers of Syria in the second century B.C.E. After the Roman conquest, however, the high priest was appointed by Rome. As a result, the Sadducees were inevitably tinged by suspicions of collaborationism, despite the central role they played in the religious observances of the Temple cult.

Their main rivals for the religious allegiance of the people were the Pharisees, a group of teachers and preachers of religious law who were in many ways the heirs of the prophetic tradition of the First Temple period. In contrast to the Sadducees, who considered most of the proscriptions of religious law to pertain only to the priesthood, the Pharisees insisted that all 613 of Yahweh's commandments were binding on all Jews. As interpreters of religious law, their authority rested on their claim that at Sinai, Yahweh had given Moses both a written and an oral Torah. The written Torah was contained in the Bible; but the oral Torah, which explained how the written Torah was to be applied to daily life, has been handed down by the spoken word, from teachers to students, across the generations from Moses to the present day. In addition to their rigorous legalism, the Pharisees also believed in a life after death characterized by individual rewards and punishments. They actively sought out converts through preaching; and they looked forward to the imminent arrival of the messiah whom God had promised to his people. In all these respects they differed from the more conservative and more traditional Sadducees. Even more radical, however, were various splinter groups such as the Essenes, a quasi-monastic group that hoped for spiritual deliverance through asceticism, repentance, and mystical union with God.

Although some scholars see Essene influence behind the career of Jesus of Nazareth, it seems clear that in most respects Jesus stood squarely within the Pharisaic tradition. As historians, we are handicapped, of course, in saying anything about Jesus' life by the fact that virtually the only sources of information about him are the Gospels, the first four books of the Christian New Testament, the earliest of which (the Gospel of Mark) was written some thirty years after Jesus' death. Inevitably, these sources are full of inaccuracies, in part because they were not eyewitness accounts, but primarily because they were never meant to be strictly factual reports—rather, they were intended as proclamations of supernatural faith. So far as we can know, however, when Jesus was about thirty years old he was acclaimed by a preacher of moral reform, John the Baptist, as one "mightier than I, whose shoes I am not worthy to stoop down and unloose." For about three years thereafter Jesus' career was a continuous course of preaching, healing the sick, "casting out demons," and teaching humility by precepts, parables, and his own example.

Believing he had a mission to save humanity from sin, Jesus denounced greed and licentiousness and urged love of God and neighbor. Additionally, it seems reasonably clear that he taught the following: (1) the fatherhood of God and the brotherhood of humanity; (2) the Golden Rule ("do unto others as you would have others do unto you"); (3) forgiveness and love of one's enemies; (4) repayment of evil with good; (5) shunning of hypocrisy; (6) opposition to literalism in the application of Jewish religious law; (7) the imminent approach of the kingdom of God; and (8) the resurrection of the dead and the establishment of the kingdom of heaven. In so doing, Jesus crossed swords with both the Sadducees and many rival Pharisees. To the Pharisees, Jesus' willingness to bend religious law (for example, the prohibition against working on the Sabbath) in the name of ethical precepts threatened to undermine the obligatory nature of the law altogether; to the Sadducees, the turning point came at Passover, when Jesus entered Jerusalem in an openly messianic manner, and then proceeded to drive the merchants and moneychangers physically out of the Temple precincts, declaring that "It is written: my house shall be called a house of prayer, but you have made it a den of thieves."

The city's religious leaders quickly arrested him, tried him in their highest court for blasphemy, condemned him, and handed him over to Pontius Pilate, the Roman governor, for sentencing. As with any Roman governor, Pilate's principal interest lay in preserving peace during a volatile religious festival in a restive part of the empire. No doubt he was also anxious to maintain good relations with the religious authorities in Jerusalem, his capital city. He therefore condemned the troublemaker to death by crucifixion, a standard Roman criminal penalty for those judged guilty of sedition against Rome.

The crucifixion of Jesus marked a decisive moment in Christian history. At first Jesus' death was viewed by his followers as the end of their hopes. Yet after a few days their despair began to dissipate, for rumors began to spread that the Master was alive and had been seen by some of his disciples. In short order Jesus' followers became convinced that not only had Jesus risen from the dead but that he had walked on earth thereafter for

WHAT CAUSED THE SUBSTANTIAL GROWTH OF CHRISTIANITY IN THE THIRD CENTURY?

THE EMERGENCE AND TRIUMPH OF CHRISTIANITY 229

forty days; hence, he truly was a divine being. With their courage restored, they fanned out to preach the good news of Jesus' divinity and to testify in the name of their martyred leader. Soon belief in Jesus' godliness and resurrection became articles of faith for thousands: Jesus was the "Christ" (Greek for the "anointed one"), the divine Son of God who was sent to earth to suffer and die for the sins of humanity, and who, after three days in the tomb, had risen from the dead and ascended into heaven, whence he would come again to judge the world at the end of time.

THE PROPAGATION OF EARLY CHRISTIANITY

Christianity was broadened and invested with a more elaborate theology by Jesus' followers, above all by the Apostle Paul, originally known as Saul of Tarsus (c. 10–c. 67 C.E.). Paul was not a native of Palestine but a Jew born in the city of Tarsus in southeastern Asia Minor. A staunch Pharisee, Saul was initially a persecutor of Christians, but after a blinding conversion experience, he adopted Christianity, changed his name, and devoted his limitless energy to propagating the new faith throughout the Near East. It would be almost impossible to overestimate the significance of his work. Denying that Jesus was sent merely as the redeemer of the Jews, Paul proclaimed Christianity to be a universal religion with a mission to the entire world. Furthermore, he placed major emphasis on the idea of Jesus as the Christ, as the anointed God-man whose death on the cross was an atonement for the sins of humanity. Declaring himself to be the Apostle to the Gentiles (non–Jews), Paul rejected the binding nature of Jewish religious law, declaring it to be irrelevant to salvation. Sinners by nature, human beings could be saved only by faith and by the grace of God "through the redemption that is in Christ Jesus." It follows, according to Paul, that salvation is almost entirely dependent on the will of God, for "has the potter no power over the clay, to make out of the same lump one vessel for beauty, and another for menial use?" (Romans 9:21). God has mercy "on whomever he wills, and he hardens the heart of whomever he wills" (Romans 9:18).

Despite the new faith's Jewish origins, Christianity drew relatively few converts from among the Jews of the Roman world. Most of the new converts were Gentiles, drawn perhaps from the groups of "god-fearers" who tended to gather around the Jewish communities scattered across the Roman world. But Christianity only began to attract substantial numbers of adherents in the third-century "age of anxiety." During a time of extreme political turbulence and economic hardship, people began to treat life on earth as an illusion and to place their hopes in a world beyond this one. The human body and the material world were more and more regarded as either evil or basically unreal. As the philosopher Plotinus wrote, "When I come to myself, I wonder how it is that I have a body. . . . by what deterioration did this happen?" Plotinus devised a philosophical system to answer this question, but his system was far too abstruse to have much meaning for large numbers of people. Instead, several religions that emphasized the dominance of spiritual forces in this world and the absolute preeminence of otherworldly salvation gained hold as never before.

At first Christianity was just one of these religions; Mithraism and the cult of Serapis were others. It is natural to ask, therefore, why Christianity gained converts in the third century at the expense of its rivals. A number of answers may be posited. Perhaps most strikingly, Christian preachers were unusually effective in "casting out demons." In a world that believed firmly in the ubiquity of demonic possession, this was no small recommendation for a new faith, and helped it to overcome the instinctive Roman hostility to religious novelties. More important ultimately, however, were the new religion's view of salvation, its social dimensions, and its organizational structure.

Although other religions also promised an afterlife, Christianity's doctrine on this subject was the most far reaching. In an age of fears, Christian warnings that nonbelievers would "liquefy in fierce fires" for eternity while believers would enjoy eternal blessedness understandably made many converts. Christians also drew converts from all classes. From its origins, Christianity had been a religion of the humble—carpenters, fishermen, and tentmakers—that promised the exaltation of the lowly. As the religion grew it gained a few wealthy patrons, but it continued to find its greatest strength among the lower and middle classes, who comprised the greatest numbers in the Roman empire. It may also have had a particular appeal to women, perhaps because it accorded women some role in worship at first

> Christianity was broadened and invested with a more elaborate theology by Jesus' followers, above all by the Apostle Paul (c. 10–c. 67 C.E.).

Altar of Mithras. Dating from the third century C.E., this altar used for Mithraic services in an underground chamber in the heart of Rome depicts Mithras slaying a bull. A century later, when Christianity triumphed in the Roman empire, a Christian church was built over the Mithraic sanctuary.

and an equal hope for salvation. This fact gave it an advantage over Mithraism, which excluded women from its cult entirely. In addition to all these considerations, a final reason for Christianity's success lay in its organization. Unlike the rival mystery religions, by the third century it had developed an organized hierarchy of priests to direct the life of the faith. More than that, Christian congregations were tightly knit communities that provided services to their members—such as nursing, support of the unprotected, and burial—that went beyond strictly religious concerns. Those who became Christians found human contacts and a sense of mission while the rest of the world seemed to be collapsing about them.

Christians were never so brutally persecuted by the

> Despite all that has been said, the triumph of Christianity in the Roman empire was by no means inevitable.

Roman state as used to be thought. In fact the attitude of Rome was usually one of indifference: Christians were customarily tolerated unless local magistrates chose to prosecute them for refusing to worship the official state gods. From time to time there were more concerted persecutions, but these were too intermittent and short lived to do irreparable damage; on the contrary, they served to give Christianity some helpful publicity. To this degree the blood of martyrs really was the seed of the church, but only because the blood did not flow too freely. One last great persecution took place toward the end of the reign of Diocletian and was continued by one of his immediate successors, a particularly bitter enemy of Christianity named Galerius. But by then the religion had gained too many converts to be wiped out by persecution, a fact that Galerius finally recognized by issuing an edict of toleration just before his death in 311 C.E..

Despite all that has been said, the triumph of Christianity in the Roman empire was by no means inevitable. Although exact statistics are impossible to come by, estimates of the number of Christians in the empire around 300 C.E. range from 1 percent to 5 percent of the total population. Even in the relatively more Christianized eastern part of the empire, Christians in the year 300 did not number more than 10 percent of the population, and were probably closer to 5 percent. It was only the conversion of the emperor Constantine in 312 C.E. that ensured the success of the new faith. Exactly why Constantine became a Christian will never be known; legend has it that he thought he saw a cross in the sky while preparing for battle and then switched allegiance to the new faith, hoping that it would yield him victory in a contest for political supremacy. As Constantine did in fact gain military victories and ultimately rose to become sole emperor, his commitment to Christianity became ever more pronounced. By the time of his death in 337 he had showered favors on the Christian clergy and patronized the building of churches throughout the empire. This was the turning point, for although Constantine did not yet prohibit paganism, his sons and emperors after them were raised as Christians and were ever less inclined to tolerate competing faiths. A brief exception was the reign from 360 to 363 C.E. of Julian "the Apostate," an emperor who attempted to launch a pagan revival. But after Julian was killed in battle with the Persians, his pro-pagan edicts were revoked, and by

PROSECUTING CHRISTIANS

THE LETTERS OF PLINY THE ELDER AND THE EMPEROR TRAJAN

Until the third century, the Roman imperial government rarely initiated the persecution of Christians. Local administrators, such as the elder Pliny, were anxious to follow proper legal procedures in dealing with the new sect, which they regarded as absurd but not particularly dangerous. But neither Pliny nor the emperor Trajan (98–117 C.E.) wanted to see the Roman state actively seek out Christians for punishment.

LETTER 97: PLINY TO TRAJAN

It is a rule, Sir, which I inviolably observe, to refer myself to you in all my doubts; for who is more capable of removing my scruples, or informing my ignorance? Having never been present at any trials concerning those who profess Christianity, I am unacquainted not only with the nature of their crimes, or the measure of their punishment, but how far it is proper to enter into an examination concerning them. . . .

The method I have observed towards those who have been brought before me as Christians, is this: I interrogated them whether they were Christians; if they confessed I repeated the question twice again, adding threats at the same time; when, if they still persevered, I ordered them to be immediately punished: for I was persuaded, whatever the nature of their opinions might be, a contumacious and inflexible obstinacy certainly deserved correction. . . .

But this crime spreading (as is usually the case) while it was actually under prosecution, several instances of the same nature occurred. An information was presented to me without any name subscribed, containing a charge against several persons, who upon examination denied they were Christians, or had ever been so.

They repeated after me an invocation to the gods, and offered religious rites with wine and frankincense before your statue (which for the purpose I had ordered to be brought together with those of the gods); and even reviled the name of Christ: whereas there is no forcing, it is said, those who are really Christians, into a compliance with any of these articles: I thought proper therefore to discharge them. . . .

I judged it . . . necessary to endeavor to extort the real truth [about Christian rites and beliefs] by putting two female slaves to the torture, who were said to administer in their religious functions: but I could discover nothing more than an absurd and excessive superstition. I thought proper therefore to adjourn all further proceedings in this affair, in order to consult with you. . . . For this contagious superstition is not confined to the cities only, but has spread its infection among the country villages. Nevertheless, it still seems possible to remedy this evil and restrain its progress. The temples, at least, which were once almost deserted, begin now to be frequented; and the sacred solemnities, after a long intermission, are again revived. . . . From hence it is easy to imagine, what numbers might be reclaimed from this error, if a pardon were granted to those who shall repent.

The method you have pursued, my dear Pliny, in the proceedings against those Christians which were brought before you, is extremely proper; as it is not possible to lay down any fixed plan by which to act in all cases of this nature. But I would not have you officiously enter into any enquiries concerning them. If indeed they should be brought before you, and the crime is proved, they must be punished; with the restriction, however, that where the party denies himself to be a Christian, and shall make it evident that he is not, by invoking our gods, let him (notwithstanding any former suspicion) be pardoned upon his repentence. Information without the accuser's name subscribed ought not to be received in prosecutions of any sort, as it is introducing a very dangerous precedent, and by no means agreeable to the equity of my government.

W. Melmoth, trans. *The Letters of Pliny the Consul, Vol. 2* (London: J. Dodsley, 1770), pp. 671–677. Reprinted in *Western Societies: A Documentary History*, Vol. 1, edited by Brian Tierney and Joan Scott (New York: Knopf, 1984), pp. 166–168.

---

the end of the century Theodosius the Great had completed Constantine's work by prohibiting pagan worship of any sort, public or private. Meanwhile most citizens of the Roman empire had converted to Christianity because of the environment of official support.

THE NEW CONTOURS OF FOURTH-CENTURY CHRISTIANITY

What major changes did Christianity undergo during the fourth century?

Once the new faith became dominant within the Roman empire it underwent some major changes in forms of thought, organization, and conduct. These changes all bore relationships to earlier tendencies, but the triumph of the faith greatly accelerated certain trends and altered the course of others. The result was that in many respects the Christianity of the late fourth century was a very different religion from that persecuted by Diocletian and Galerius.

DOCTRINAL QUARRELS

One consequence of Christianity's triumph was the flaring up of bitter doctrinal disputes. These brought great turmoil to the church but resulted in the hammering out of dogma and discipline. Before the conversion of Constantine there had of course been disagreements among Christians about doctrinal matters, but as long as Christianity was a minority religion it managed to control its internal divisions in order to present a united front against hostile outsiders. As soon as the new faith emerged victorious, however, sharp splits developed within its own ranks. These were due partly to the fact that there had always been a tension between the intellectual and emotional tendencies within the religion that could now come more fully into the open, and partly to the fact that different regions of the empire tried to preserve a sense of their separate identities by preferring different theological formulas.

The first of the bitter disputes was between the Arians and Athanasians over the nature of the Trinity. The Arians—not to be confused with Aryans (a racial term)—were followers of a priest named Arius. Under the influence of Greek philosophy they rejected the idea that Christ could be equal with God. Instead they maintained that the Son was created by the Father in time, and therefore was not coeternal with Him or formed of the same substance. The followers of Saint Athanasius held that even though Christ was the Son he was fully God: that Father, Son, and Holy Spirit were all absolutely equal and composed of an identical substance. After protracted struggles Athanasius' side won out and the Athanasian doctrine became the Christian doctrine of the Trinity, as it remains today.

The struggle between the Arians and Athanasians was followed by numerous other doctrinal quarrels during the next few centuries. The issues at stake were generally too abstruse to warrant explaining here, but the results were momentous. One was that the dogmas of the Catholic faith gradually became fixed. Granted, this was a slow development and many basic tenets of Catholicism were defined much later (for example, the theory of the Mass was not formally promulgated until

WHAT MAJOR CHANGES DID CHRISTIANITY UNDERGO DURING THE FOURTH CENTURY?

THE NEW CONTOURS OF FOURTH-CENTURY CHRISTIANITY   233

Jesus. Conception from a sixth-century mosaic in Ravenna.

1215; the doctrine of the Immaculate Conception of the Virgin Mary until 1854; and that of the bodily assumption of the Virgin into heaven until 1950). Nonetheless, the faith was beginning to take on a sharply defined form unprecedented in the history of earlier religions. Above all, this meant that anyone who differed from a certain formulation would be excluded from the community and often persecuted as a heretic. In the subsequent history of Christianity this concern for doctrinal uniformity was to result in both strengths and weaknesses for the church.

A second result of the doctrinal quarrels was that they aggravated regional hostilities. In the fourth century differences among Christians increased alienation between West and East and also worsened hostilities among regions within the East. Although the Roman empire was evolving toward regionalism for many different reasons, including economic and administrative

ones, and although regionalism was partly a cause of religious differences, the sharper and more frequent doctrinal quarrels became, the more they intensified regional antagonisms.

Finally, the doctrinal quarrels provoked the increasing involvement of the Roman state in the governance of the church. Because Constantine had hoped that Christianity would be a unifying rather than a divisive force in the empire, he was horrified by the Arian conflict and intervened in it by calling the Council of Nicea (325 C.E.), which condemned Arius. It is noteworthy that this council—the first general council of the church—was convened by a Roman emperor and that Constantine presided over it, assuming a role as Christ's representative on earth that would also be claimed by his successor emperors, especially in the East. There were two major reasons for this. First, religious disputes were more prevalent in the East than in the West, and quarreling parties often appealed to the emperor for support. Second, the weight of imperial government was generally heavier in the East, and after 476 C.E. there were no Roman emperors in the West at all. When Eastern emperors were not appealed to by quarreling parties they interfered in religious disputes themselves, as Constantine had done before them, in order to preserve unity. The result was that in the East the emperor assumed great religious authority and control, whereas in the West the future of relations between the state and the Church was more open.

GROWTH OF ECCLESIASTICAL ORGANIZATION

This fourth-century consolidation of religious with imperial authority was mirrored in the church's own internal organization. We have seen that some distinction between clergy and laity was recognized very early in the history of Christianity. The next step was the development of a hierarchical organization within the ranks of the clergy. Christian organization was centered in cities, and one bishop in each important city had become the authority to which all the clergy in the surrounding vicinity answered even before Constantine converted to Christianity. But as the number of congregations multiplied and as the influence of the church increased due to the adoption of Christianity as the official religion of Rome, distinctions of rank among the bishops themselves also began to appear. Those who had their headquarters in the larger cities came to be called metropolitans (today known in the West as archbishops), with authority over the clergy of an entire province. In the fourth century the still higher rank of patriarch was established to designate those bishops who ruled over the oldest and largest of Christian communities—such cities as Rome, Jerusalem, Constantinople, Antioch, and Alexandria, and their surrounding districts. Thus the Christian clergy by 400 C.E. had come to embrace a definite hierarchy of patriarchs, metropolitans, bishops, and priests.

The climax of all this development would be the growth of the primacy of the bishop of Rome, or the rise of the papacy. For several reasons the bishop of Rome claimed a preeminence over the other patriarchs of the Church. The city in which he ruled was venerated by the faithful as a scene of the missionary activities and eventual martyrdom of the Apostles Peter and Paul. The tradition was widely accepted that Peter had founded the bishopric of Rome, and that therefore all of his successors were heirs of his authority and prestige. This tradition was supplemented by the theory that Peter had been commissioned by Christ as his vicar on earth and had been given the keys of the kingdom of heaven with power to punish people for their sins and even to absolve them of guilt (Matthew 16:18–19). This theory, known as the doctrine of the Petrine Succession, has been used by popes ever since as a basis for their claims to authority over the Church. The bishops of Rome had an advantage also in the fact that after the transfer of the imperial capital to Constantinople, there was seldom an emperor with effective sovereignty in the West. Finally, in 445 C.E. the emperor Valentinian III issued a decree commanding all Western bishops to submit to the jurisdiction of the pope. It must not be supposed, however, that the church was by any means yet under a monarchical form of government. The patriarchs in the East regarded the extreme assertions of papal claims as brazen effrontery, and even many bishops in the West continued to ignore them.

The growth of ecclesiastical organization helped the church to conquer the Roman world in the fourth century and to minister to the needs of the faithful thereafter. The existence of an episcopal administrative structure was particularly influential in the West as the Roman empire decayed and finally collapsed in the fifth century C.E.. Since every city had a bishop trained to some degree in the arts of administration, the church in the West took over many of the functions of government and helped to preserve order amid the deepening chaos. But the new emphasis on administration also had its detrimental effects: as the church developed its own rationalized administrative structure, it inevitably became more worldly and distant in spirit from the simple faith of Jesus and the apostles.

> The growth of eccelesiastical organization helped the church to conquer the Roman world in the fourth century.

THE SPREAD OF MONASTICISM

The clearest reaction to this trend was expressed in the spread of monasticism. Today we are accustomed to thinking of monks as groups of priests who live communally in order to dedicate themselves primarily to lives of contemplation and prayer. In their origins, however, monks were not priests but laymen who al-

WHAT MAJOR CHANGES DID CHRISTIANITY UNDERGO DURING THE FOURTH CENTURY?

THE NEW CONTOURS OF FOURTH-CENTURY CHRISTIANITY   235

most always lived alone and who sought extremes of self-denial rather than ordered lives of spirituality. Monasticism began to emerge in the third century as a response to the anxieties of that age, but it became a dominant movement within Christianity only in the fourth century. Two obvious reasons for this fact stand out. First of all, the choice of extreme hermitlike asceticism was a substitute for martyrdom. With the conversion of Constantine and the abandonment of persecution, most chances of winning a crown of glory in heaven by undergoing death for the faith were eliminated. But the desire to prove one's religious ardor by self-abasement and suffering was still present. Second, as the fourth century progressed, the priesthood became more and more immersed in worldly concerns. Those who wished to avoid secular temptations fled to the deserts and woods to practice an asceticism that priests and bishops were forgetting. (Monks customarily became priests only later in history, during the late Middle Ages.) In this way even while Christianity was accommodating itself to practical needs, monasticism satisfied the inclinations of ascetic extremists.

Monasticism first emerged in the East, where for about one hundred years after Constantine's conversion it spread like a mania. Hermit monks of Egypt and Syria vied with each other in their pursuit of the most inhuman and humiliating excesses. Some grazed in the fields after the manner of cows, others penned themselves into small cages, and others hung heavy weights around their necks. A monk named Cyriacus stood for hours on one leg like a crane until he could bear it no more. The most extravagant of these monastic ascetics was Saint Simeon Stylites, who performed self-punishing exercises—such as touching his feet with his head 1,244 times in

succession—on top of a high pillar for thirty-seven years, while crowds gathered below to worship "the worms that dropped from his body."

In time such ascetic hysteria subsided, and it became recognized that monasticism would be more enduring if monks lived in a community and did not concentrate on self-torture. The most successful architect of communal monasticism in the East was Saint Basil (c. 330–379), who started his monastic career as a hermit and ascetic extremist but came to prefer communal and more moderate forms of life. Basil expressed this preference in writings for monks that laid down the basic guidelines for Eastern monasticism

St. Simeon Stylites on his Pillar. The devil is shown as a huge snake. Admirers who wished to speak to the saint would climb the ladder shown on the left. This gold plaque dates from the sixth century.

down to the present. Rather than encouraging extremes of self-torture, Basil encouraged monks to discipline themselves by useful labor. Although his teachings were still extremely severe by modern standards, he prohibited monks from engaging in prolonged fasts or lacerating their flesh. Instead he urged them to submit to obligations of poverty and humility, and to spend many hours of the day in silent religious meditation. With the triumph of Saint Basil's ideas, Eastern monasticism became more organized and subdued, but even so Basilian monks preferred to live as far away from the "world" as they could and never had the same civilizing influence on the world outside the cloister as did their brothers in western Europe.

Monasticism did not at first spread quickly in the West because the appeal of asceticism was much weaker there. This situation changed only in the sixth century when Saint Benedict (c. 480–c. 547) drafted his famous Latin rule, which ultimately became the guide for nearly all Western monks. Modern scholarship has shown that Benedict copied much of his rule from an earlier and much harsher Latin text known as the "Rule of the Master." Benedict, however, produced a document notable for its brevity, flexibility, and moderation. The Benedictine rule imposed obligations similar to those laid down by Saint Basil: poverty, sexual chastity, obedience, labor, and religious devotion. Yet Benedict prescribed less austerity than Basil did: the monks were granted a sufficiency of simple food, clothing, and sleep; they were even allowed to drink a small amount of wine, although meat was granted only to the sick. The abbot's authority was absolute, and he was allowed to flog monks for disobedience. Yet Benedict urged him to try "to be loved rather than feared," and ordained that the abbot gather advice before making decisions "because the Lord often reveals to a younger member what is best." For such reasons the Benedictine monastery became a home of religious enrichment rather than a school for punishment.

We will continue the story of Benedictine monasticism in later chapters, but here we may point out in advance some of its greatest contributions to the development of Western European civilization. One was that Benedictine monks were committed from an early date to missionary work: they were primarily responsible for the conversion of England and later most of Germany. Such activities not only helped to spread the faith but also created a sense of cultural unity throughout western Europe. Another positive contribution lay in the attitude of the Benedictines toward work.

Whereas the highest goal for ancient philosophers and aristocrats was to have enough leisure time for unimpeded contemplation, Saint Benedict wanted his monks always to keep busy, for he believed that "idleness is an enemy of the soul." Therefore he prescribed that they should be occupied at certain times in manual labor, a prescription that would have horrified most thinkers of earlier times. Accordingly, early Benedictines worked hard themselves and spread the idea of the dignity of labor to others. With Benedictine support, this idea would become one of the most distinctive traits of Western culture. We read of Benedictines who gladly milked cows, threshed, plowed, and hammered: in so doing they increased the prosperity of their own monasteries and provided good examples for others. Benedictine monasteries became particularly successful in farming and later in the management of agricultural estates. Thus they often helped to advance the level of the western European economy and sometimes even to provide wealth that could be drawn on by emerging western European states.

CHANGING ATTITUDES TOWARD WOMEN AND MARRIAGE

Returning to our original subject—the changes that took place in Christian institutions and attitudes during the fourth century—a final fateful trend was the development of a negative attitude toward women. Compared with most other religions, Christianity was favorable to women. Female souls were regarded as equal to male souls in the eyes of God, and human nature was deemed to be complete only in both sexes. Saint Paul even went so far as to say that after baptism "there is neither male nor female" (Galatians 3:28), a spiritual egalitarianism that meant that women's salvation was no less important than men's. But Christians from earliest times shared the view of their contemporaries that in everyday life and in marriage women were to be strictly subject to men. Not only did early Christians believe that women should be excluded from positions of leadership or decision making, meaning that they should be "silent in Church" (1 Corinthians 14:34–35) and could never be priests, but they shared the standard classical view that women were more "fleshly" than men and therefore should be subjected to men as the flesh is subjected to the spirit (Ephesians 5:21–33).

With the growth of the ascetic movement in the third and fourth centuries, the denigration of women

WHAT MAJOR CHANGES DID CHRISTIANITY UNDERGO DURING THE FOURTH CENTURY?

THE NEW CONTOURS OF FOURTH-CENTURY CHRISTIANITY   237

An Early Christian Woman. A wall painting from the catacomb of Priscilla, Rome, third century C.E.

as dangerously "fleshly" creatures became more and more pronounced. Since sexual abstinence lay at the heart of asceticism, the most perfect men were expected to shun women. Monks, of course, shunned women the most. This was a primary reason why they fled to deserts and forests. One Eastern ascetic was struck by the need for virginity in the midst of his marriage ceremony, ran off to a hermit's cell, and blocked the entrance; another monk who was forced to carry his aged mother across a stream swaddled her up as thoroughly as he could so that he would not catch any "fire" and no thoughts of other women would attack him. With monks taking such an uncompromising attitude, the call for continence was extended to the priesthood. Originally priests could be married, just as several of Jesus' apostles had been (1 Corinthians 9:5). But in the course of the fourth century the doctrine spread that priests could not be married after ordina-

tion, and that those already married were obliged to live continently with their wives afterward.

Once virginity was accepted as the highest standard, marriage could be only second best. Saint Jerome expressed this view most earthily when he said that virginity was wheat, marriage barley, and fornication cow dung: since people should not eat cow dung he would permit them barley. The major purposes of marriage were to keep men from "burning" and to propagate the species. (Jerome went so far as to praise marriage above all because it brought more virgins into the world!) Thus Christianity reinforced the ancient view that woman's major earthly purpose was to serve as mother. Men and women were warned not to take pleasure even in marital intercourse but to indulge in it only for the purpose of procreation. Since they could not become priests and only a very few could become nuns (female monasticism was regarded as a very expensive luxury in the premodern world), almost all women were expected to become submissive wives and mothers. As wives they were not expected to have their own careers and were not meant to be educated or even literate. Hence even though they had full hopes for salvation, they were treated as inferiors in the everyday affairs of the world, a treatment that would endure until modern times.

CHRONOLOGY

THE GROWTH OF CHRISTIANITY, FIRST–FOURTH CENTURIES C.E.

Birth of Jesus	beginning of the Common Era
The apostles propagate Christianity	first century C.E.
Destruction of the Temple at Jerusalem	69–70 C.E.
Expulsion of the Jews from Jerusalem	132–135 C.E.
Emperor Constantine converts to Christianity	312–325 C.E.
Council of Nicea	325 C.E.
Christianity becomes official religion of Roman empire	392 C.E.
Era of "doctrinal quarrels"	fourth century C.E.
Growth of ecclesiastical organization	fourth–sixth centuries C.E.

CHANGING ATTITUDES TOWARD THE CELIBACY OF BISHOPS

Bishops had emerged as key figures in the organization of the early Christian church by the end of the first century C.E. By the mid-second century, a hierarchical structure of bishops, priests, deacons, and lesser officials was already in place. Until the fourth century, most of these officials were married, as were most socially respectable Roman men. By the end of the fourth century, however, efforts were being made, especially in the western parts of the empire, to require bishops and even priests to be celibate. This shift reflects an increasing admiration for asceticism as a mark of holiness that we find throughout the fourth-century world among both Christians and non-Christians, as shown in the following excerpt from an early third-century church manual and a papal letter.

THE DIDASCALIA

The shepherd who is appointed bishop and head among the presbyterate [that is, the priesthood] in the church in every congregation: "It is required of him that he shall be blameless, in nothing reproachable" [1 Timothy 3:2; Titus 1:7], one remote from all evil, a man not less than fifty years of age, who is now removed from the conduct of youth and from the lusts of the adversary, and from the slander and blasphemy of false brethren. . . . But if it is possible, let him be instructed and able to teach; but if he does not know letters, he shall be capable and skilful in the word; and let him be advanced in years.

And let him be vigilant and chaste and stable and orderly; and let him not be violent, and let him not be one who exceeds in wine; and let him not be malicious; but let him be quiet and not be contentious; and let him not be money-loving. And let him not be youthful in mind, lest he be lifted up and fall into the judgment of Satan, for everyone that exalts himself is humbled.

But it is required that the bishop shall be "a man that has taken one wife, and who has managed his house well" [1 Timothy 3:2, 4]. And thus let him be proved when he receives the imposition of hands to sit in the position of the episcopacy: whether he is chaste, and whether his wife also is a believer and chaste; and whether he has brought up his children in the fear of God, and admonished and taught them; and whether his household fear and reverence him and all of them obey him. For if his household in the flesh stands against him and does not obey him, how shall they who are without his house become his, and be subject to him?

Didascalia Apostolum Corpus Scriptorum Christianorum Orientalium, ed. Arthur Vööbus. (Louvain: Peeters, 1979). Reprinted in *After the New Testament: A Reader in Early Christianity*, ed. Bart D. Ehrman (Oxford and New York: Oxford University Press, 1999), pp. 333–334.

LETTER OF POPE DAMASUS I (366–384)
ON PRIESTLY CELIBACY

This is what has been decided, about bishops in the first place, but also about priests and deacons, whose duty it is to take part in the divine sacrifice [of the Eucharist] and whose hands confer the grace of baptism and make present the body of Christ. It is not only us but divine Scripture that binds them to be perfectly chaste. . . . How could a bishop or priest dare to preach continence to a widow or virgin, or urge anyone to keep his bed pure, if he himself were more concerned to have children for this world than for God? Why did Paul say, "You are not in the flesh but in the spirit" and "Let those who have wives live as though they had none"? Would he, who so exhorted the people, complaisantly allow carnal activity to priests? — he who also said, "Make no provision for the flesh, to gratify its desires" and "I wish that all were as I myself am." One who is in the service of Christ, who sits in the chair of the master, can he not observe the rule of service. . . . Even idolaters, in order to celebrate their impious cult and sacrifice to demons, imposed continence on themselves as regards women and abstained from certain foods so as to remain pure. And you ask me if the priest of the living God, who is to offer spiritual sacrifices, should live always in a state of purity or if, wholly involved in the flesh he should give himself to the cares of the flesh. . . . Intercourse is defilement. . . . that is why the mystery of God may not be entrusted to men of that sort, defiled and faithless. . . . They doubtless know that "flesh and blood cannot inherit the kingdom of God, nor does the corrupt inherit the incorruptible"; shall a priest or deacon dare then to lower himself to act as the animals do?

Brian Tierney and Joan Scott, eds. *Western Societies: A Documentary History,* Vol. 1 (New York: Knopf, 1984), p. 174.

THE GERMANIC INVASIONS AND THE FALL OF THE ROMAN EMPIRE IN THE WEST

How did the Germanic tribes triumph over the western Roman empire?

While Christianity was conquering the Roman empire from within, another force, the Germanic barbarians, was threatening it from without. The Germans, who had already almost brought Rome to its knees in the third century, were held off from the time of Diocletian until shortly before the reign of Theodosius the Great. But thereafter they demolished western Roman resistance and, by the end of the fifth century, succeeded in conquering all of the Roman West. Germanic kingdoms then became the new form of government in territories once ruled over by Caesar and Augustus.

GERMANIC-ROMAN RELATIONS

It was once customary to think that the Germans were fierce and thoroughly uncouth savages who wantonly destroyed the western Roman empire out of sheer hatred for civilization. But that is a misunderstanding. The Germans were barbarians in Roman eyes because they did not live in cities and were illiterate, but they were not therefore savages. On the contrary, they often practiced settled agriculture—although they preferred hunting and grazing—and were adept in making iron tools and weapons as well as lavish jewelry. Physically they looked enough like Romans to intermarry without causing much comment, and their Indo-European language was related to Latin and Greek. Prolonged interaction with the Romans had a decisive civilizing influence on the Germans before they started their final conquests. Germans and Romans had shared common frontiers along the Rhine and the Danube for centuries, and had developed steady trading relations with each other. Even during times of war Romans were often allied with some German tribes while they fought others. By the fourth century, moreover, German tribes often served as auxiliaries of depleted Roman armies and were sometimes allowed to settle on borderlands of the empire where Roman farmers had given up trying to cultivate the land. Finally, many German tribes had been converted to Christianity in the fourth century, although the Christianity they accepted was of the heretical Arian version. All these interactions made the "barbarians" very familiar with Roman civilization and substantially favorable to it.

The Germans began their final push not to destroy Rome but to find more and better land. The first breakthrough occurred in 378 C.E. when the Visigoths, who had recently settled on some Roman lands in the Danube region, revolted against mistreatment by Roman officials and then defeated a punitive Roman army in the battle of Adrianople. The Visigoths did not immediately follow up this victory because Theodosius the Great cleverly bought them off and made them allies of the empire. But when Theodosius died in 395 C.E. he divided his realm between his two sons, neither of whom was as competent as he, and both halves of the empire were weakened by political intrigues. The Visigoths under their leader Alaric took advantage of this situation to wander through Roman realms almost at will, looking for the best land and provisions. In 410 they sacked Rome itself—a great shock to some contemporaries—and in the following years marched into southern Gaul. Meanwhile, in December of 406, a group of allied Germanic tribes led by the Vandals crossed the frozen Rhine and capitalized on Roman preoccupation with the Visigoths by streaming through Gaul into Spain. Later they were able to cross the straits of Gibraltar into northwest Africa, then one of the richest agricultural regions of the empire. From Africa they took control of the central Mediterranean, even sacking Rome from the sea in 455. By 476 C.E. the ineffectual western Roman emperor, a mere boy derisively nicknamed Augustulus ("little Augustus"), was easily deposed by a leader of a mixed band of Germans and Huns who then assumed the title of king of Rome. Accordingly, 476 is conventionally given as the date for the end of the western Roman empire. But it must be remembered that a Roman emperor, who maintained some claims to authority in the West, continued to rule in Constantinople.

THE SUCCESS AND IMPACT OF GERMAN INVASIONS

Two questions that historians of the German invasions customarily ask are, How did the Germans manage to triumph so easily? and Why was it that they were particularly successful in the West rather than the East? The ease of the German victories appears particularly striking when we recognize that the German armies were remarkably small: the Visigoths who won at Adrianople numbered no more than ten thousand men, and the total number of the Vandal "hordes" (including women and children) was about eighty thousand—about the same population as an average-sized American suburb. But the Roman armies themselves were depleted because of declining population and the need for manpower in other occupations, above all in the new bureaucracies. More than that, German armies often won by default (Adrianople was one of the few pitched battles in the history of their advance) because the Romans were no longer zealous about defending themselves. Germans were seldom regarded with horror—many German soldiers had even risen to positions of leadership within Roman ranks—and the coercive regime begun by Diocletian was not deemed worth fighting for by a great many of the empire's citizens, including its most prominent aristocrats.

The reasons that the Germans fared best in the West are complex—some having to do with personalities and mistakes of the moment, and others with geographical considerations. But the primary explanation why the eastern Roman empire survived while the western did not is that the East was simply richer. By the fifth century most western Roman cities had shrunk in terms of both population and space to a small fraction of their earlier size, and they were often little more than empty administrative shells or fortifications. The economy of the West was becoming more

CHRONOLOGY

GERMANIC INVASIONS OF THE ROMAN EMPIRE, FIFTH CENTURY C.E.

Visigoth victory at the battle of Adrianople	378 C.E.
Vandals invade Gaul, Spain, and North Africa	406 C.E.
Visigoths sack Rome	410 C.E.
Vandals sack Rome	455 C.E.
Germanic tribes depose last western Roman emperor	476 C.E.
Anglo-Saxon tribes invade England	c. 500 C.E.

HOW DID THE GERMANIC TRIBES TRIUMPH OVER THE WESTERN ROMAN EMPIRE?

THE GERMANIC INVASIONS AND THE FALL OF THE ROMAN EMPIRE   241

THE BARBARIAN INVASIONS OF THE ROMAN EMPIRE

Consider the extent of Christianity in relation to the territory of the Roman Empire. What might this suggest about the identification of imperial government with the church? What does the situation in Britain suggest about the nature and depth of Roman Christianity there? Notice the routes taken by the majority of the barbarian invaders. Why did so many bypass the wealthier, urbanized East in favor of targeting the West?

and more strictly agricultural, and agricultural produce served only to feed farm laborers and keep rich landlords in luxuries. In the East, on the other hand, cities like Constantinople, Antioch, and Alexandria remained teeming metropolises because of their trade and industry. Because the eastern part of the empire had greater reserves of wealth to tax, it was more vig-

orous. It could also afford to buy off the barbarians with tribute money, which it did with increasing regularity. So Constantinople was able to stay afloat while Rome floundered and sank.

A map of western Europe around the year 500 C.E. reveals the following major political divisions. Germanic tribes of Anglo-Saxons, who had crossed the

English Channel in the middle of the fifth century, were extending their rule on the island of Britain. In the northern part of Gaul, around Paris and east to the Rhine, the growing kingdom of the Franks was ruled by a crafty warrior named Clovis. South of the Franks stood the Visigoths, who ruled the southern half of Gaul and most of Spain. South of them were the Vandals, who ruled throughout previously Roman northwest Africa. In Italy the Ostrogoths, eastern relatives of the Visigoths, held sway under their impressive and highly Romanized king Theodoric; around the headwaters of the Rhone, the Burgundians ruled another wealthy and highly Romanized region of the western empire. Of these new barbarian realms, however, only that of the Franks would survive beyond the early eighth century as a unified kingdom; most of the rest would disappear within a century of their foundation.

The effects of the Germanic conquests in the West were not catastrophic. The greatest difference between the Germans and the Romans had been that the former did not live in cities, but since the western Roman cities were already in a state of decline, the invasions only accelerated a process of urban decay that was already well advanced. On the land Germans replaced Roman landlords without interrupting basic Roman agricultural patterns. Moreover, since the Germans were never very numerous, they usually took over no more than a part of Roman lands. Germans also tried to avail themselves of Roman administrative machinery, but administrations tended to decline gradually because of the decrease in wealth and literacy. The German invasions fractured the political unity of the empire, but they did not bring an end to Roman culture, or to the influence of Rome on the new immigrants. As Theodoric, the Ostrogothic conqueror of Italy, was fond of remarking: "An able Goth wishes to be like a Roman; but only a poor Roman would want to be like a Goth."

THE SHAPING OF WESTERN CHRISTIAN THOUGHT

What was Augustine's conception of history?

As the western Roman empire declined during the fourth and fifth centuries, a few Western Christian thinkers formulated an approach to the world and to God that was to guide the thought of the West for roughly the next eight hundred years. This concurrence of political decline and theological advance was not coincidental. With the empire falling and being replaced by barbarian kingdoms, it seemed clearer than ever to thinking Christians both that the classical inheritance had to be reexamined and that God had not intended the world to be anything more than a transitory testing place. The consequences of these assumptions accordingly became urgent questions. Between about 380 and 525 C.E., answers were worked out by Western Christian thinkers whose accomplishments were intimately interrelated. The towering figure among them was Saint Augustine, but others had great influence as well.

THE FIRST THREE GREAT FATHERS OF THE WESTERN LATIN CHURCH

Three contemporaries who knew and influenced each other—Saint Jerome (c. 340–420), Saint Ambrose (c. 340–397), and Saint Augustine (354–430)—count as three of the four greatest "Fathers" of the western, Latin Church. (The fourth, Saint Gregory the Great, came later and will be discussed in the next chapter.) Saint Jerome's greatest single contribution was his translation of the Bible from Hebrew and Greek into Latin. His version, known as the Vulgate (or "common" version), became the standard Latin Bible used throughout the Middle Ages; with minor variations it continued to be used long afterward by the Roman Catholic Church. Fortunately Jerome was one of the best writers of his day, and he endowed his translation with vigorous, often colloquial prose and, occasionally, fine poetry. Since the Vulgate was the most widely read work in Latin for centuries, Jerome's writing had as much influence on Latin style and thought as the King James Bible has had on English literature. Jerome, who was the least original thinker of the great Latin Fathers, also influenced western Christian thought by his contentious but eloquent formulations of contemporary views. Among the most important of these were the beliefs that much of the Bible was to be understood allegorically rather than literally, that classical learning could be valid for Christians if it was thoroughly subordinated to Christian aims, and that the most perfect Christians were rigorous ascetics. In keeping with the last position Jerome avidly supported monasticism. He also taught that women should not take baths so that they would not see their own bodies naked.

ROMANIZED BARBARIANS AND BARBARIANIZED ROMANS

These two letters from Sidonius Apollinaris (c. 430–c. 480) illustrate the ways in which cultural assimilation in the late-fifth-century western empire was rapidly blurring the boundaries between "Roman" and "barbarian." Sidonius himself was the descendant of an illustrious Roman provincial family in Gaul. He was one of the admired Latin stylists of his day, in both poetry and prose. Although he eventually became a bishop and was regarded locally as a saint after his death, his letter collection (from which these extracts are taken) tells us much more about the late Roman literary culture of Visigothic southern Gaul than it does about his Christianity. Arbogastes was the Frankish governor of Treves; Syagrius was from an ancient Gaulish Roman family.

LETTER 4:17: SIDONIUS TO HIS FRIEND ARBOGASTES

My honored Lord, your friend Eminentius has handed me a letter written by your own hand, a really literary letter, replete with the grace of a three-fold charm. The first of its merits is certainly the affection which prompted such condescension to my lowly condition, for if not a stranger I am in these days a man who courts obscurity; the second virtue is your modesty. . . . In the third place comes your urbanity which leads you to make a most amusing profession of clumsiness when as a matter of fact you have drunk deep from the spring of Roman eloquence and, dwelling by the Moselle, you speak the true Latin of the Tiber: you are intimate with the barbarians but are innocent of barbarisms, and are equal in tongue, as also in strength of arm, to the leaders of old, I mean those who were wont to handle the pen no less than the sword.

Thus the splendor of the Roman speech, if it still exists anywhere, has survived in you, though it has long been wiped out from the Belgian and Rhenic lands: with you and your eloquence surviving, even though Roman law has ceased at our border, the Roman speech does not falter. For this reason . . . I rejoice greatly that at any rate in your illustrious breast there have remained traces of our vanishing culture. If you extend these by constant reading you will discover for yourself as each day passes that the educated are no less superior to the unlettered than men are to beasts.

LETTER 5:5 SIDONIUS TO HIS FRIEND SYAGRIUS

You are the great-grandson of a consul, and in the male line too—although that has little to do with the case before us; I say, then, you are descended from a poet, to whom his literary glory would have brought statues had not his magisterial glories done so . . . and the culture of his successors has not declined one whit from his standard, particularly in this respect. I am therefore inexpressibly amazed that you have quickly acquired a knowledge of the German tongue with such ease.

And yet I remember that your boyhood had a good schooling in liberal studies and I know for certain that you often declaimed with spirit and eloquence before your professor of oratory. This being so, I should like you to tell me how you managed to absorb so swiftly into your inner being the exact sounds of an alien race, so that now after reading Virgil under the schoolmaster's cane and toiling and working the rich fluency of [Cicero] . . . you burst forth before my eyes like a young falcon from an old nest.

You have no idea what amusement it gives me, and others too, when I hear that in your presence the barbarian is afraid to perpetrate a barbarism in his own language. The bent elders of the Germans are astounded at you when you translate letters, and they adopt you as umpire and aribitrator in their mutual dealings. . . . And although these people are stiff and uncouth in body and mind alike, they welcome in you, and learn from you, their native speech combined with Roman wisdom.

Only one thing remains, most clever of men: continue with undiminished zeal, even in your hours of ease, to devote some attention to reading; and, like the man of refinement that you are, observe a just balance between the two languages: retain your grasp of Latin, lest you be laughed at, and practice the other, in order to have the laugh of them. Farewell.

W. B. Anderson, ed. *Sidonius, Poems and Letters*, Vol. 2 (Cambridge, Mass.: Harvard University Press, 1980), pp. 127–129, 181–183.

Unlike Jerome, who was primarily a scholar, Saint Ambrose was most active in the concerns of the world. As archbishop of Milan, the aristocratic Ambrose was the most influential church official in the West—more so even than the pope. Guided by practical concerns, he wrote an ethical work, *On the Duties of Ministers,* which followed closely Cicero's *On Duties* in title and form, and also drew heavily on Cicero's Stoic ethics. But Ambrose differed from Cicero and most of traditional classical thought on two major points. One was that the beginning and end of human conduct should be reverence for God rather than any self-concern or interest in social advancement. The other—Ambrose's most original contribution—was that God helps some Christians but not others in this pursuit by the gift of grace, a point that was to be greatly refined and amplified by Saint Augustine. Ambrose put his concern for proper conduct into action by his most famous act, his confrontation with the emperor Theodosius the Great over the massacre of innocent civilians. Ambrose argued that by violating divine commandments Theodosius had made himself subject to church discipline. Remarkably the archbishop succeeded in forcing the emperor to do penance. This famous incident symbolized the church's claim to preeminence in the sphere of morality, and epitomized the western church's developing sense of autonomy on religious matters, even when faced with the power of an emperor.

THE THOUGHT AND WRITINGS OF SAINT AUGUSTINE

Saint Ambrose's disciple, Saint Augustine, was the greatest of all the Latin Fathers; indeed he was one of the most powerful Christian intellects of all time. Augustine's influence on subsequent medieval thought was incalculable. Even after the Middle Ages his theology had a profound influence on the development of Protestantism; in the twentieth century many leading Christian thinkers called themselves neo-Augustinians. Augustine's Christianity may have been so searching because he began his career by searching for it. Although his mother was a Christian, he hesitated until the age of thirty-three to be baptized, passing from one system of thought to another without being able to find intellectual or spiritual satisfaction in any. Only increasing doubts about all other alternatives, the appeals of Saint Ambrose's teachings, and a mystical experience movingly described in his autobiographical *Confessions* led Augustine to embrace the faith wholeheartedly in 387. Thereafter he advanced rapidly in ecclesiastical positions, becoming bishop of the North African city of Hippo in 395. Although he led a most active life in this office, he still found time to write more than a hundred profound, complex, and powerful treatises in which he set forth his convictions concerning the most fundamental problems of Christian thought and action.

Saint Augustine's theology revolved around the principles of the profound sinfulness of humanity and divine omnipotence. Ever since Adam and Eve turned away from God in the Garden of Eden humans have remained basically sinful. One of Augustine's most vivid illustrations of human depravity appears in the *Confessions,* where he tells how he and some other boys once stole pears from a neighbor's garden, not because they were hungry or because the pears were beautiful, but simply for the sake of the evil itself. God would be purely just if He condemned all human beings to hell,

"The City of the Earth." A medieval illustration for Augustine's *On the City of God* showing Cain slaying Abel and Romulus slaying Remus. Its message is that all human society on earth is a product of sin.

the central guide to doing good was the doctrine of "charity," which meant leading a life devoted to loving God and loving one's neighbor for the sake of God, rather than a life of "cupidity," of loving earthly things for their own sake. Put in other terms, Augustine taught that humans should behave on earth as if they were travelers or "pilgrims," keeping their eyes at all times on their heavenly home and avoiding all materialistic concerns.

Augustine built an interpretation of history on this view in one of his major works, *On the City of God*. In this treatise, he argued that the entire human race from the Creation until the Last Judgment was and will be composed of two warring societies, those who "live according to man" and love themselves, and those who "live according to God." The former belong to the "City of Earth" and will be damned, whereas the blessed few who compose the "City of God" will on Judgment Day put on the garment of immortality. As for when the Last Judgment would come, Augustine argued vehemently that no human could know its exact date; nonetheless since the Judgment might come at any time, all mortals should devote their utmost efforts to preparing for it by leading lives of righteousness.

but since He is also merciful He has elected to save a few. Ultimately human will has nothing to do with this choice: although one has the power to choose between good and evil, one does not have the power to decide whether or not to be saved. God alone, from eternity, predestined a portion of the human race to salavation and sentenced the rest to be damned. In other words, God fixed for all time the number of human inhabitants of heaven. If this seems unfair, Augustine's answer is, first, that strict "fairness" would confine all to perdition; and second, that the basis for God's choice is a mystery shrouded in His omnipotence—far beyond the realm of human comprehension.

Even though it might seem to us that the practical consequences of this rigorous doctrine of predestination would be lethargy and fatalism, neither Augustine nor his later followers saw it that way at all. Humans themselves must do good, and if they are "chosen" they usually will do good; since no one knows who is chosen and who is not, all should try to do good in the hope that they are among the chosen. For Augustine

Although Saint Augustine formulated major new aspects of Christian theology, he believed that he was doing no more than drawing out truths found in the Bible. Indeed, he was convinced that the Bible alone contained all the wisdom worth knowing. But he also believed that much of the Bible was expressed obscurely, and that it was therefore necessary to have a certain amount of education in order to understand it thoroughly. This conviction led him to a modified acceptance of classical learning. The ancient world had already worked out an educational system based on the "liberal arts," or those subjects necessary for the worldly success and intellectual growth of free men. Augustine argued that privileged Christians could learn the fundamentals of these subjects, but only in a limited way and for a completely different end—study of the Bible. Since in his day nonreligious schools existed that taught these subjects, he permitted a Christian elite to attend them; later, when such schools died out, their place was taken by schools in monasteries and cathedrals. Thus Augustine's teaching laid the groundwork for some continuity of educational practice as well as for the theory behind the preservation of some classical treatises. But we must qualify this by remarking that Augustine intended liberal education only for an elite; all others were simply to be catechized, or drilled, in the faith. He also thought it far worse that anyone should become engaged in classical thought for its own sake than that someone might not know any classical thought at all. The true wisdom of mortals, he insisted, was piety.

BOETHIUS LINKS CLASSICAL AND MEDIEVAL THOUGHT

Augustine had many followers, of whom the most interesting and influential was Boethius, a Roman aristocrat who lived from about 480 to 524. Until recently, it was not customary to say that Boethius was a follower of Saint Augustine because some of Boethius' works do not make explicit mention of Christianity. Indeed, since Boethius was indisputably interested in ancient philosophy, wrote in a polished, almost Ciceronian style, and came from a noble Roman family, it has been customary to view him as the "last of the Romans." But in fact he intended the classics to serve Christian purposes, just as Augustine had prescribed, and his own teachings were basically Augustinian.

Because Boethius lived a century after Augustine he could see far more clearly that the ancient world was coming to an end. Therefore he made it his first goal to preserve as much of the best ancient learning as possible by a series of handbooks, translations, and commentaries. Accepting a contemporary division of the liberal arts into seven subjects—grammar, rhetoric, logic, arithmetic, geometry, astronomy, and music—he wrote handbooks on two: arithmetic and music. These summaries were meant to convey all the basic aspects of the subject matter that a Christian might need to know. Had Boethius lived longer he probably would have written similar treatments of the other liberal arts, but as it was he concentrated his efforts on his favorite subject: logic. In order to preserve the best of classical logic, he translated from Greek into Latin some of Aristotle's logical treatises as well as an introductory work on logic by Porphyry (another ancient philosopher). He also wrote his own explanatory commentaries on these works in order to help beginners. Since

Boethius. A twelfth-century artist's conception of Boethius as a musician, a reputation he earned because of his treatise on music.

Latin writers had never been interested in logic, even in the most flourishing periods of Roman culture, Boethius' translations and commentaries became a crucial link between the thought of the Greeks and that of the Middle Ages. Boethius' works helped to endow the Latin language with a logical vocabulary, and when interest in logic was revived in the twelfth-century West it rested first on a Boethian basis.

Although Boethius was an exponent of Aristotle's logic, his world view was not Aristotelian but Augustinian. This can be seen both in his several orthodox treatises on Christian theology and above all in his masterpiece, *The Consolation of Philosophy*. Boethius wrote the *Consolation* at the end of his life, after he had been condemned to death for treason by Theodoric the Ostrogoth, whom he had served as an official. (Historians are unsure about the justice of the charges.) In it Boethius asks the age-old question of what is human frain from looking at her he was forced to die and was condemned to hell himself. In other words, Orpheus was too worldly and material; he should not have loved a woman but should have sought God. True Christians, on the other hand, know that "happy is he who can look into the shining spring of good [i.e., the divine vision]; happy is he who can break the heavy chains of earth."

THE CHRISTIANIZATION OF CLASSICAL CULTURE IN THE WEST

How was classical culture Christianized?

As we have seen, none of the Christian intellectuals of late antiquity was prepared to throw out altogether the classical tradition of literature and philosophy they had inherited. For all of them, however, this tradition posed severe challenges. It was, in the first place, thoroughly pagan, and paganism remained a significant threat to Christianity until well into the fifth century. It was also associated with syncretism—that is to say, with the easy acceptance of both Christian and pagan beliefs simultaneously, which had been so marked a feature of aristocratic culture during the fourth century Constantinian Revolution. There was no denying the seductive lure of classical literature and philosophy, however. Jerome worried openly that on Judgment Day, God would find him less a follower of Christ than of Cicero; and Augustine spent years fighting to free himself from the attractions of pagan philosophical systems such as the Neoplatonism of Porphyry and Plotinus (see Chapter 6), or the dualistic doctrines of Manicheanism, which explained why there was evil in the world by positing the existence of two competing gods.

Moreover, these Christian thinkers were working within a world that still celebrated philosophers as purveyors of wisdom about the good life. Christian intellectuals—indeed, the Christian clergy generally—wanted desperately to be regarded as philosophers, so as to replace the doctrines of pagan philosophy with the doctrine of Christ. To do this, however, force alone

happiness and concludes that it is not found in earthly rewards such as riches or fame but only in the "highest good," which is God. Human life, then, should be spent in pursuit of God. Since Boethius speaks in the *Consolation* as a philosopher rather than a theologian, he does not refer to Christian revelation or to the role of divine grace in salvation. But his basically Augustinian message is unmistakable. *The Consolation of Philosophy* became one of the most popular books of the Middle Ages because it was extremely well written, because it showed how classical expression and some classical ideas could be appropriated and subordinated into a clearly Christian framework, and most of all, because it seemed to offer a real meaning to life. In times when all earthly things really did seem crude or fleeting it was genuinely consoling to be told eloquently and "philosophically" that life has purpose if led for the sake of God.

At a climactic moment in the *Consolation* Boethius retold in verse the myth of Orpheus in a way that might stand for the common position of the four writers just discussed: that is, how Christian thinkers were willing to accept and maintain some continuity with the classical tradition. But Boethius also made new sense of the story. According to Boethius, Orpheus' wife, Eurydice, symbolized hell; since Orpheus could not re-

> None of the Christian intellectuals of late antiquity was prepared to throw out altogether the classical tradition of literature and philosophy they had inherited.

would not be sufficient. What was needed was a way of Christianizing the classical inheritance, and conveying it to the Christian masses in an intellectually satisfying way. The political collapse of the western empire, and the growing barbarization of western Roman culture, further emphasized the urgency of the task. It was, therefore, to the preservation and reinterpretation of classical Latin culture for a mixed audience of vulgar Romans and aspiring barbarians that the Christian intellectuals of the fourth, fifth, and sixth centuries devoted themselves.

This process took two forms. The first was a gradual winnowing out of the classical texts that had been produced in Greece and Rome between the fifth century B.C.E. and the second century C.E. Much of this winnowing had been accomplished already. By and large, Roman readers of the third and fourth centuries had little taste for the scientific and mathematical works of the classical Greeks. They preferred bestiaries, with their entertaining tales of hyenas that changed their sex yearly, and of weasels who conceived through the ear. Nor did they have much interest in the philosophical works of Plato and Aristotle, or the literary works of the classical Greek dramatists. They preferred Neoplatonism, a quasi-mystical set of doctrines that posited a divine principle of some sort as lying behind the created world, and that saw creation and existence as part of a continuing process by which the material world emanated from this divinity, and gradually returned to it. In literature, their tastes ran toward comedies and novels, of which Petronius' *Satyricon* is a ribald, but not atypical, example.

The second form of Christianizing classical culture was to arrive at an understanding of the purposes of classical culture for a Christian audience. The Christian thinker Tertullian had raised this question in the second century C.E. by asking, "What has Athens (the symbol of classical learning) to do with Jerusalem (the symbol of Christian salvation)?" Tertullian's answer had been "Nothing"; but this answer was not suitable to the changed circumstances of the Christian church from the fourth century on. Jerome and Augustine were more positive; but on the whole, the early monastic movement sided with Tertullian. Despite the later role Benedictine monasteries would play in the preservation of classical literary texts, Saint Benedict himself was no admirer of classical culture. Quite to the contrary, he wanted his monks to serve only Christ—not literature or philosophy. But unlike some of his monastic contemporaries, he did assume that monks would have to read well enough to say their prayers and to read the

Bible. This meant that some teaching in the monasteries would be necessary, not least because boys were often given over from birth to the monastic profession, and would have no other way to learn their letters. For Benedict, however, preserving classical learning was no part of a monastery's proper duties.

CASSIODORUS AND THE BENEDICTINE TRADITION OF LEARNING

The impetus for the development of Benedictine monasticism's tradition of learning came not from Benedict himself, but from Cassiodorus (c. 490–c. 583), an official at the Ostrogothic court under Theodoric. Early in his career, Cassiodorus wrote a *History of the Goths* for his barbarian overlord. Cassiodorus showed the Goths to themselves in a Roman mirror, as a people whose history was a part of the history of Rome. He also composed (and eventually published) several volumes of his official correspondence, reflecting his training in the classical rhetorical tradition. During the last forty years of his life, however, Cassiodorus turned his attention to religion, composing commentaries on the Psalms and founding an important monastery at Vivarium in southern Italy. It was for his monks that Cassiodorus composed his most influential work, the *Institutes.* Inspired by Saint Augustine, Cassiodorus believed that study of classical literature was the essential preliminary to a proper understanding of the Bible and the church fathers. His *Institutes* were therefore a reading list at heart, comprising first the essential works of classical, pagan literature a monk should know before he moved on to the more difficult and demanding study of theology and the Bible. Through this work, Cassiodorus created a classical literary canon that would influence Christian educational practice until the end of the Middle Ages.

To provide his monks with books, Cassiodorus also encouraged the copying of manuscripts, arguing that such copying was in itself "manual labor" of the sort that Saint Benedict had demanded, and that it might even be more appropriate for monks than hard work in the fields. As Benedictines began to subscribe to these ideas, Benedictine monasteries emerged as the most important centers for the preservation and study of classical literature in the Latin-speaking West. They would have no serious rivals until the twelfth century. Hardly any of the works of classical Latin literature, including such "licentious" writings as the poems of Catullus and Ovid, would survive today had they not been copied and preserved during the early Middle

Cassiodorus. This frontispiece of a Bible executed around 700 C.E. in an English Benedictine monastery depicts Cassiodorus as a copyist and preserver of books. (Since books were exceedingly rare until the invention of printing in the fifteenth century, they customarily were stored in cupboards, lying flat.)

not only of aristocratic Christian bishops, but also of their barbarian overlords.

Boethius, whom we discussed earlier, and Cassiodorus both worked at the court of the most thoroughly Romanized ruler in the sixth-century barbarian world. Yet all their efforts to extend, preserve, and Christianize the classical cultural tradition bespeak their awareness that this world was passing away. Theodoric himself ruled Italy from 493 to 526 as the designated representative of the emperor at Constantinople. He was a great admirer of Roman civilization who tried to preserve it as best he could. He fostered agriculture and commerce, repaired public buildings and roads, patronized learning, and maintained a policy of religious toleration. In short, he provided Italy with a more enlightened government than it had known for several centuries. But none of this was sufficient to erase the palpable sense of distrust that in Theodoric's final years tore his kingdom apart. The problem was that for all their *romanitas* ("Romanness"), Theodoric and the Goths were Arian heretics, whereas the local bishops and landowners of Italy were orthodox Trinitarian Christians—and this fact made the Italian aristocrats the faithful subjects not of Theodoric, but of his imperial sponsor in Constantinople. When, in 523, the emperor issued an edict, valid also in Italy, forbidding Jews, pagans, and heretics (by whom he probably meant Arians) to hold public office, the storm broke. Although Cassiodorus remained loyal to Theodoric, Boethius was imprisoned, accused of conspiring to re-

Ages by Benedictine monks following the example of Cassiodorus.

Others too were active in trying to preserve and Christianize what remained of the classical literary tradition. At the request of Pope Symmachus (498–514), Priscian (c. 500) composed what would become the standard treatise of the Middle Ages on Latin grammar. At the request of another pope, the sixth-century scholar Dionysius Exiguus undertook to collect and codify the laws of the Roman church; yet another pope, Agapetus (535–536), assembled the greatest Christian library in Rome—a library from which his relative, Pope Gregory the Great (590–604), would draw most of his knowledge of Saint Augustine. To some degree, of course, all such efforts were aimed at an educated, aristocratic elite that was fast disappearing from the sixth-century Latin West. But this fact should not obscure the extent to which this Christianized classical culture was slowly becoming the common possession

Theodoric the Ostrogoth. The barbarian ruler is shown here in Roman dress, with an ornate Roman hairstyle and a Roman symbol of victory in his hand. The inscription reads REX THEODERICVS PIVS PRINCIS, Latin for "King Theodoric, pious prince."

turn Italy to direct imperial rule. Theodoric's last years were marked by his continuing persecution of Trinitarian Christians. When he died in 526, he left no son to succeed him; religious tensions continued to tear his kingdom apart. Ten years later, Theodoric's fears would be confirmed when a new emperor, Justinian, attempted to reconstitute the Roman empire of Augustus by reconquering Italy from the Ostrogoths.

EASTERN ROME AND THE WESTERN EMPIRE

Why did Justinian's plan to reunite the Roman empire fail?

Boethius' execution by Theodoric in 524 was in many ways an important historical turning point. For one, Boethius was both the last noteworthy philosopher and last writer of cultivated Latin prose the West was to have for many hundreds of years. Then too Boethius was a layman, and for hundreds of years afterward almost all western European writers would be priests or monks. Boethius' execution was symptomatic in the political sphere as well because it was the harbinger of the collapse of the Ostrogothic kingdom in Italy. Whether or not he was justly condemned, Boethius' execution showed that Arian and Catholic Christians could not live in harmony anywhere in the barbarianized western empire. Soon afterward, the Ostrogoths were overthrown by the eastern Roman empire. That event in turn was to be a major factor in the ultimate divorce between East and West and the consequent final disintegration of the old Roman world.

JUSTINIAN'S REVIVAL OF THE ROMAN EMPIRE

The conquest of the Ostrogoths was part of a larger plan for Roman revival conceived and directed by the eastern Roman emperor Justinian (527–565). Eastern Rome, with its capital at Constantinople, had faced many external pressures from barbarians and internal religious dissensions since the time of Theodosius. But throughout the fifth century it had managed to weather these crises, and by the time of Justinian's accession had regained much of its strength. Although the eastern Roman empire—which then encompassed the modern-day territories of Greece, Turkey, most of the Middle East, and Egypt—was largely Greek- and Syriac-speaking, Justinian himself came from a western province (modern-day Serbia) and spoke Latin. Not surprisingly, therefore, he concentrated his interests on the West. He saw himself as the heir of imperial Rome, whose ancient power and western territory he was resolved to restore. Aided by his astute and determined wife Theodora, who, unlike earlier imperial Roman consorts, played an influential role in his reign, Justinian took great strides toward this goal. But ultimately his policy of recovering the West proved unrealistic.

THE CODIFICATION OF ROMAN LAW

One of Justinian's most impressive and lasting accomplishments was his codification of Roman law. This project was part of his attempt to emphasize continuities with earlier imperial Rome and was also meant to enhance his own prestige and absolute power. Codification of the law was necessary because between the third and sixth centuries the volume of statutes had continued to grow, with the result that the vast body of enactments contained many contradictory or obsolete elements. Moreover, conditions had changed so radically that many of the old legal principles could no longer be applied. When Justinian came to the throne in 527, he immediately decided on a revision and codification of the existing law to bring it into harmony with the new conditions and to establish it as an authoritative basis for his rule. To carry out this work he appointed a commission of lawyers under the supervision of his minister, Tribonian. Within two years the commission published the first result of its labors. This was the Code, a systematic revision of all of the statutory laws that had been issued from the reign of Hadrian to the reign of Justinian. The Code was later supplemented by the Novels, which contained the legislation of Justinian and his immediate successors. By 532 the commission had completed the Digest, a summary of all of the writings of the great jurists. The final product of the work of revision was the Institutes, a textbook of the legal principles reflected in both the Digest and the Code.

> One of Justinian's most impressive and lasting accomplishments was his codification of Roman law.

Justinian and Theodora. Sixth-century mosaics from the Church of San Vitale, Ravenna. The emperor and empress are conceived here to have supernatural, almost priestly powers: they are advancing toward the altar, bringing the communion dish and chalice respectively. Both rulers are set off from their retinues by their haloes. The observant viewer is also meant to note the representation of the "three wise kings from the East" at the hem of Theodora's gown: just as the "three magi" once had supernatural knowledge of Christ, so now do their counterparts, Justinian and Theodora.

All four volumes together constitute the *Corpus Juris Civilis*, or the "body of civil law."

Justinian's *Corpus* was a brilliant achievement in its own terms: the Digest alone has been justly called "the most remarkable and important lawbook that the world has ever seen." In addition, the *Corpus* had an enormous influence on subsequent legal and governmental history. Revived and restudied in western Europe from the eleventh century on, Justinian's *Corpus* became the basis of all the law and jurisprudence of European states, exclusive of England (which followed its own "common law"). The nineteenth-century Napoleonic Code, which provided the basis for the laws of modern European countries and also those of Latin America, is fundamentally the Institutes of Justinian in modern dress.

> Justinian's *Corpus Juris Civilis* was a brilliant achievement in its own terms.

Only a few of the more specific influences of Justinian's legal work can be enumerated here. One is that in its basic governmental theory the *Corpus* was a bastion of absolutism. Starting from the maxim that "what pleases the prince has the force of law," it granted unlimited powers to the imperial sovereign and therefore was adopted with alacrity by later European monarchs and autocrats. But the *Corpus* also provided some theoretical support for constitutionalism because it maintained that the sovereign originally obtained his powers from the people rather than from God. Since government came from the people it could in theory be given back to them. Perhaps most important and influential was the *Corpus'* view of the state as an abstract public and secular entity. In the Middle Ages rival views of the state as the private property of the ruler or as a supernatural creation meant to control sin often predominated. The modern conception of the state as a public entity concerned not with an afterlife but with everyday affairs gained strength toward the end of the Middle Ages in part because of the revival of assumptions found in Justinian's legal compilations.

JUSTINIAN'S MILITARY CONQUESTS

Justinian aimed to be a full Roman emperor in geographical practice as well as in legal theory. To this end he sent out armies to reconquer the West. At first they succeeded easily. In 533 Justinian's brilliant general Belisarius conquered the Vandal kingdom in Northwest Africa, and in 536 Belisarius seemed to have won all of Italy, where he was welcomed by the Trinitarian subjects of the Ostrogoths. But the first victories of the

Italian campaign were illusory. After their initial defeats the Ostrogoths put up stubborn resistance; the war dragged on for decades until the exhausted eastern Romans finally reduced the last Gothic outposts in 563. Shortly before he died, Justinian became master of all Italy as well as northwest Africa and the coastal parts of Spain that his troops had also managed to recapture. The Mediterranean was once more a "Roman" lake. But the cost of the endeavor was enormous and would soon call into question the very existence of the eastern Roman empire.

Justinian's Western campaigns were ill advised for two major reasons. One was that his realm really could not afford them. Belisarius seldom had enough troops to do his job properly: he began his Italian campaign with only eight thousand men. Later, when Justinian did grant his generals enough troops, it was only at the cost of oppressive taxation. But additional troops would probably have been insufficient to hold the new lines in the West because the empire

Hen and Chicks. North Italian small figures from the sixth century made from silver overlaid with gold. The purpose of this luxurious and seemingly humorous work dating from a time of economic decline and grave political crisis is unknown; there are as many theories offered for it as there are chicks.

THE MEDITERRANEAN WORLD UNDER JUSTINIAN, 527–565

Note the extent of the Mediterranean world under Justinian. What areas had been permanently lost to imperial control? Consider that the territories in North Africa, Spain, and Italy were added during Justinian's reign; also note the position of the Byzantine capital, Constantinople. In what direction—east or west—were imperial interests most likely to be focused under normal circumstances? How permanent were Justinian's conquests to be, and what burdens did they place on imperial resources?

had greater interests, as well as enemies, to the East. While the eastern Roman empire was exhausting itself in Italy, the Persians were gathering strength. Justinian's successors had to pull away from the West in order to meet the threat of a revived Persia. Even so, by the beginning of the seventh century it seemed as if the Persians would be able to march all the way to the waters that faced Constantinople. Only a heroic reorganization of the empire after 610 avoided that fate, but this reorganization helped withdraw eastern Rome from the West and helped the West begin to lead a life of its own.

Justinian's wars left most of Italy in a shambles. The protracted fighting had wrought much devastation. Around Rome aqueducts were cut and parts of the countryside returned to marshes not drained until the twentieth century. In 568, only three years after Justinian's death, another, much more primitive Germanic tribe, the Lombards, invaded Italy and took much of it away from the eastern Romans. They met little resistance because the latter were now paying more attention to the East, but the Lombards were still too weak to conquer the whole Italian peninsula. Instead, Italy became divided between Lombard, Eastern Roman, and papal territories. The actors would change, but this division between northern, central and southern

CHRONOLOGY

THE ROMAN REVIVAL OF JUSTINIAN, 527–568 C.E.

Reign of Justinian	527–565 C.E.
Publication of the *Corpus Juris Civilis*	529–532 C.E.
Justinian conquers the Vandal kingdom of northwest Africa	533 C.E.
Justinian reconquers Italian peninsula	536 C.E.
Justinian Defeats last Gothic outposts	563 C.E.
Justinian rules over Mediterranean world	563–565 C.E.
Death of Justinian	565 C.E.
Germanic Lombards conquer Italian peninsula	568 C.E.

Italy would continue to characterize Italian political life until the nineteenth century.

Eastern Roman control over North Africa lasted only a few generations longer than it did in Italy. Weakened by religious dissension and heavy taxation, this area fell during the seventh century to the invading armies of Islam, along with Egypt and the rest of Roman Africa. At this time, Christianity in north Africa largely disappeared.

Further north, the Visigothic kingdom of Spain continued to control the interior portions of the country, despite Justinian's conquest of the Mediterranean coast. After the Roman armies departed, the Visigoths resumed such control as they had ever exercised over these coastal regions. But tensions between the Arian Visigoths and their Trinitarian subjects continued until 582, when the Visigothic king Reccared finally converted to orthodox Christianity. By then, however, a pattern of hostility between the Visigothic kings, their bishops, and the Romanized population of the Mediterranean coast had been established that would last until the end of the Visigothic kingdom. Despite the Visigothic kings' efforts to pattern their rule on Byzantine example, their kingdom quickly collapsed in the early eighth century when Muslim armies crossed the Strait of Gibraltar. By the end of the century, the Christian rulers of Spain controlled only the northern-most parts of Iberian peninsula, along with the area around Barcelona. For the next three hundred years, Spain would be an important part of the Muslim world.

CONCLUSION

From its earliest days, Roman culture had been characterized by its remarkable capacity to assimilate the disparate cultures of the lands Rome conquered. In this process, both Rome and its empire were steadily transformed. The pace of these transformations accelerated markedly, however, from the mid-third century on—so much so that historians now commonly refer to the period from the mid-third century to the early seventh century as "Late Antiquity" to distinguish it from the classical Roman world that preceded it. During these centuries, larger numbers of immigrants entered the Roman empire than ever before, drawn by a combination of land hunger, opportunity, and the desire to participate in the material and cultural benefits of Roman life. In the western empire especially, the number of these new immigrants became so large during the late fourth and fifth centuries that the frontier areas of the empire ceased to be distinguishable from the more "Romanized" areas of the interior.

At the same time, two internal cultural processes were transforming what it meant to be Roman. The learned culture of the Greek and Roman world was being steadily extended to larger numbers of people; but in the process, learned culture itself was increasingly vulgarized. And finally, the empire itself became Christian, first by persuasion, as Constantine and his successors made it attractive for individuals to convert to the new religion, and later by coercion, as Christianity became the official religion of the entire Roman empire. As a result, a new fusion of Christian culture and late Roman governance began to evolve, not only around the imperial court at Constantinople, but also in the provinces.

What did not change, however, was the Mediterranean focus of this evolving Late Antique world. Despite the emergence of new political units in the western Roman empire, Roman civilization in the fifth and sixth centuries remained firmly centered upon the Mediterranean Sea. That too was soon to change. The seventh century would witness the final fracturing of this unified Mediterranean world, and the emergence in its place of three quite different Western civilizations: Byzantium, Western Europe, and Islam. This development marks the end of the classical world and the beginning of the Middle Ages. It is to this development that we now turn.

SELECTED READINGS

Saint Augustine. *The City of God.* Trans. by Henry Bettenson. Baltimore, 1972.

———. *Confessions.* Trans. by Henry M. Chadwick. Oxford, 1991.

———. *The Enchiridion on Faith, Hope and Love.* Ed. by H. Paolucci. Chicago, 1961.

———. *On Christian Doctrine.* Trans. by D. W. Robertson, Jr. New York, 1958.

Boethius. *The Consolation of Philosophy.* Trans. by R. Green. Indianapolis, 1962.

Brown, Peter. *Augustine of Hippo.* Berkeley, 1967. A great biography, by the greatest living scholar of late antiquity.

———. *The World of Late Antiquity.* New York, 1971. Still the best short survey of the period, with excellent illustrations.

———. *The Body and Society: Men, Women and Sexual Renunciation in Early Christianity.* New York, 1988. A revealing study of one of the fundamental transformations Christianity brought to the late antique world.

———. *Power and Persuasion in Late Antiquity: Toward a Christian Empire.* Madison, 1992. An important revisionist account of the impact of Christianization on the political culture of the later Roman empire.

———. *The Rise of Western Christendom: Triumph and Diversity, 200–1000.* Oxford, 1996. Evocatively written picture of the diverse forms Christianity took as it spread east and north from the Mediterranean world.

Bowersock, G. W., Peter Brown, and Oleg Grabar. *Late Antiquity: A Guide to the Postclassical World.* Cambridge, Mass., 1999. An authoritative compilation. The first half is devoted to essays on the cultural features of the period; the second half is organized as an encyclopedia.

Cameron, Averil. *The Later Roman Empire,* A.D. 284–430. London, 1993. Now the standard account of its period, with an emphasis on imperial politics.

———. *The Mediterranean World in Late Antiquity,* A.D. 395–600. London, 1993. Masterful, with excellent, succinct bibliographical essays.

Cassiodorus. *An Introduction to Divine and Human Readings.* Trans. by L. W. Jones. New York, 1946.

Chadwick, Henry M. *Boethius.* Oxford, 1981. The best intellectual biography of this important thinker.

———. *Augustine.* Oxford, 1986. The best short introduction to Augustine's thought.

Clark, Gillian. *Women in Late Antiquity.* Oxford, 1993. A clear, compact account of an important subject.

Ehrman, Bart D., ed. *After the New Testament: A Reader in Early Christianity.* Oxford, 1999.

Eusebius. *The History of the Church.* Trans. by G. A. Williamson. Baltimore, 1965.

———. *Eusebius' Life of Constantine.* Trans. by Averil Cameron and Stuart Hall. Oxford, 1999.

Fowden, Garth. *Empire to Commonwealth: Consequences of Monotheism in Late Antiquity.* Princeton, 1993. Argues for connections between the universalism of monotheisms and empires during this period.

Jones, A. H. M. *The Later Roman Empire,* 284–602: *A Social, Economic, and Administrative Survey.* 2 volumes. London, 1964. An immense, detailed analysis, difficult to read but packed with information.

Lane Fox, Robin. *Pagans and Christians.* New York, 1987. A subtle, perceptive, lengthy, but highly readable exploration of the pagan world within which Christianity grew up.

Lawrence, Clifford Hugh. *Medieval Monasticism,* 3d ed. London, 2000. Concise, intelligent, perceptive survey of monasticism from its beginnings to the end of the Middle Ages.

MacMullen, Ramsay. *Corruption and the Decline of Rome.* New Haven, 1988. Argues for the corrosive effects on the empire of Roman efforts to privatize governmental responsibilities.

Markus, R. A. *The End of Ancient Christianity.* New York, 1990. An expert synthetic study of Christianity in the Western Roman empire between 350 and 600 C.E.

Moorhead, John. *Justinian.* New York, 1994. An up-to-date survey of the emperor and his times.

Pelikan, Jaroslav. *The Christian Tradition, Volume I: The Emergence of the Catholic Tradition.* Chicago, 1971. A history of Christian doctrine that is one of the tours de force of twentieth-century scholarship. Synthetic, clear, and objective.

Procopius. *The Secret History.* Trans. by G. A. Williamson. Baltimore, 1966.

O'Donnell, James J. *Cassiodorus.* Berkeley, 1979. Difficult but rewarding.

Shanks, Hershel, ed. *Christianity and Rabbinic Judaism: A Parallel History of Their Origins and Early Development.* Washington, D.C., 1992. Accessible chapters, written by top authorities, that cover the period from the first to the sixth centuries C.E.

Wallace-Hadrill, John Michael. *The Barbarian West,* 3d ed. London, 1966. Still the most interesting and suggestive analysis of the Romano-Germanic world created by the invasions of the fifth century C.E.

Whittaker, C. R. *Frontiers of the Roman Empire: A Social and Economic Study.* Baltimore, 1994. A convincing picture of the frontiers of the Roman empire as zones of intensive cultural interaction.

Williams, Stephen. *Diocletian and the Roman Recovery.* New York, 1997. A recent account that modifies, but does not replace, A. H. M. Jones (see above).

Wolfram, Herwig. *The Roman Empire and Its Germanic Peoples.* Berkeley, 1997. The best recent survey of its subject.

PART III
THE MIDDLE AGES

THE TERM "MIDDLE AGES" was coined by Europeans in the seventeenth century to express their view that a long and dismal period of interruption extended between the glorious accomplishments of Greece and Rome and their own "modern age." Because the term became so widespread, it is now an ineradicable part of our historical vocabulary; but no serious scholar today uses it with the sense of contempt it once invoked. To the contrary, most scholars would now argue that it was during the Middle Ages—roughly the years between 600 and 1500—that the cultural, political, and religious foundations of all three western civilizations were established. Whether we speak of Byzantium, the Islamic world, or Europe, the Middle Ages were a formative and creative period in the history of western civilizations.

Only with respect to Europe, however, do the years between 600 and 1500 constitute a true "middle age." For the Islamic world, these centuries witnessed the birth, expansion, and maturation of a new civilization that drew heavily upon its classical past, but fused that past with a sweeping new religious vision. For Byzantium, the so-called Middle Ages ended in 1453 with the conquest of the Byzantine empire by the Ottoman Turks. Even for Europe, the metaphor of a middle age is to some extent misleading. Like Islamic civilization, European civilization began to take shape from the seventh century on, but it was not until the twelfth century that a truly distinctive European tradition with respect to politics, religion, and art emerged.

	POLITICS	SOCIETY AND CULTURE	ECONOMY	INTERNATIONAL RELATIONS
570	Muhammad, founder of Islam, born (570) Pope Gregory I (Saint Gregory the Great) (590–604) Umayyad family governs Islamic world (661–750)	Growth of monasteries (600–700) The Hijrah (622)	Economic unity of Mediterranean world ends (650)	Arabs, under Abu-Bakr, rout Byzantium army in Syria (636) Arabs take Antioch, Damascus, and Jerusalem (637) Attempts by Muslims to take Constantinople (677, 717) Arabs take Visigothic Spain (717)
700	Abbasid family governs Islamic world (750–1258) Charlemagne crowned Holy Roman Emperor (800) Capetian dynasty (987–1328)	Iconoclast Contoversy begins (717) Islamic civilization's "middle period" (900–1250) Rise of Romanesque architecture (900s)	Agricultural revolution (700–1300) Invention of iron horseshoe (900) Rus establish principality near Kiev (900s)	Rus sack Constantinople (860) Otto I defeats Hungarians at Lechfield (955)
1000	Split between Roman and Byzantium Churches (1054) Saxon civil war begins (1073) Investiture Conflict (1075) Concordat of Worms distinguishes temporal power of kings from spiritual power of clergy (1122) Reign of Frederick I, Barbarossa, as Holy Roman emperor (1152–1190)	European population triples (1000–1300) *Song of Roland* (1050) Taking of monastic orders increases tenfold (1066–1200) Cisterian order flourishes (1090–1153) Catharism in southern France (1150–1300) Rise of chivalry (1150) Troubadour poets travel Europe (1150–1300) Chretien de Troyes, author of Arthurian legends (1165–1190) Rome decrees all cathedrals must support one schoolteacher (1179) Saint Francis of Assisi (1182–1226)	Invention of tandem harness for plowing (1050) Water mill becomes widely used in Europe (1050) Manorial lords begin trading serfs' freedom for cash (1100s)	Battle of Hastings, England falls to the Normans (1066) Battle of Manzikert, Turks take Anatolia (1071) The First Crusade (1095–1099)
1200	Magna Carta (1215) Fourth Lateran Council (1215) Emergence of English Parliament (1272–1307) Formation of French Estates General (1285–1314)	Theater appears outside of church (1200) *The Cid* and Norse sagas are written down (1200s) Saint Thomas Aquinas, author of *Summa Theologica*, (1225–1274) Dante Alighieri, author of *The Divine Comedy*, (1265–1321) Giotto of Florence, painter (1267–1337) William of Ockham, founder of nominalism (1285–1349)		Crusaders sack Constantinople (1204) England ousted from Normandy, Anjou, and Brittany (1204) Mongols conquer eastern Slavic region (1200s) Mongols take Kiev (1240) Mongols dispose of Abbasid caliphate (1258) Jews expelled from southern Italy, England, and France (1288–1306)

POLITICS	SOCIETY AND CULTURE	ECONOMY	INTERNATIONAL RELATIONS	
		Development of mechanical clocks and compasses (1300) Explorers reach Azores and Cape Verde (1300s)		1300
Babylonian Captivity of the Church (1305–1378)	Giovanni Boccaccio (1313–1375) Over a tenth of Europe dies during the Great Famine (1316–1322) John Wyclif, Oxford theologian (1330–1384) Geoffrey Chaucer (1340–1400) Onset of the Black Death, from which over half of Europe dies (1347)	Severe flooding ruins crops, breeds pestilence (1315) Heavy cannons first employed (1330)	Hundred Year's War (1337–1453)	
Jaquerie rebellion in France (1358) The Great Schism, ended by Council of Constance (1378–1417) Florentine Ciompi uprising (1378) English Peasants' Revolt (1381)	Jan van Eyck (1380–1441) University of Heidelberg founded (1385)	Medici family, originators of modern banking, flourishes (1397–1494)	Poland and Lithuania united (1386)	1400
The Italian territorial papacy (1417–1517)			Rise of Grand Duchy of Moscow (1400s)	
Edward, duke of York dethrones Henry VI after War of the Roses (1461) Reign of Ivan III, the Great, tsar of all Russias (1462–1505) Ferdinand of Aragon marries Isabella of Castille, forming modern Spain (1469)		Invention of movable type (1450) Explorers round the Cape of Good Hope (1487) West Indies reached (1492) India reached by sea (1498)	Turks conquer Constantinople (1453) England loses Bordeaux (1453) French monarchy absorbs Burgundy (1477) Christian monarchs expel Muslims and Jews from Spain (1492)	

ROME'S THREE HEIRS: THE BYZANTINE, ISLAMIC, AND EARLY MEDIEVAL WORLDS

A NEW PERIOD in the history of Western civilizations began in the seventh century. In the year 600, it was still possible for the rulers of the Roman empire living in Constantinople to imagine their empire as uniting the entire Mediterranean world. By the end of the seventh century, however, three different successor civilizations to the Greco-Roman world of antiquity had emerged: the Byzantine, the Islamic, and the western European, each with its own language and distinctive ways of life. The history of Western civilizations from the seventh to the eleventh centuries is largely a story of the rivalries and interactions among these three emerging worlds, each of which preserved and extended different aspects of the late-antique inheritance they shared.

Like the provinces of the eastern Roman empire over which it ruled, Byzantine civilization after 610 was Greek-speaking. It combined the bureaucratic and imperial traditions of late Roman governance with an intense pursuit of the Christian faith. This fusion had been pioneered in the fourth century by Constantine and his successors, and was continuously elaborated in the eastern Roman empire thereafter. Islamic civilization, in contrast, was Arabic-speaking. It was the most cosmopolitan and wide ranging (both geographically and culturally) of the three successor civilizations. The Islamic world was the heir both to the Roman ideal of an expansive empire itself, and to Roman ideals of cultural and religious assimilation as essential attributes of imperial rule. By combining the philosophical and scientific interests of the Hellenistic world with the literary and artistic culture of Persia, Islam created the most dynamic cultural amalgam of the early Middle Ages.

Western Christian civilization in the early Middle Ages was rooted in Latin, but with important cultural influences from Germanic, Celtic, and Latin-derived vernacular languages. In contrast to Byzantium and Islam, it owed relatively little to Roman ideals of empire, except briefly under the Carolingians. It was, however, profoundly influenced by Roman ideals of law and local government, which carried with them a continuing influence from the republican traditions of ancient Rome. For western Europe in the early Middle Ages, law and Latin Christianity represented

FOCUS QUESTIONS

- How did the Byzantine state survive for nearly a millennium?

- How was Islam able to spread so rapidly?

- What forces combined to undermine the political unity of the Islamic empire?

- What caused economic and social change in seventh-century western Europe?

- How did Charlemagne redefine the relationship between Christianity and kingship?

the pinnacles of Roman cultural achievement. They were, indeed, the very essence of what it meant to be Roman; and to be Roman remained an almost universal aspiration in the early medieval West. If we measure civilizations by their highest philosophical and literary accomplishments, western Europe in the early Middle Ages was a laggard in comparison with Byzantium and Islam. It was also the least economically advanced of these three successor states, and faced the greatest organizational weaknesses in both government and religion. By the end of the eleventh century, however, Latin Christian civilization was no longer on the defensive against its rivals in military, economic, or religious terms. Rather, it stood on the verge of an extraordinary period of expansion and conquest that would bring it ultimately to a dominant position in world affairs during the early modern and modern eras.

THE BYZANTINE EMPIRE AND ITS CULTURE

How did the Byzantine state survive for nearly a millennium?

It is impossible to date the beginning of Byzantine history with any precision because the Byzantine empire was the uninterrupted successor of the Roman state. For this reason different historians prefer different beginnings. Some argue that "Byzantine" characteristics had already emerged in Roman history as a result of the easternizing policy of Diocletian; others assert that Byzantine history began when Constantine moved his capital from Rome to Constantinople, the city that subsequently became the center of the Byzantine world. (The old name for the site on which Constantinople was built was "Byzantium," from which we get the adjective "byzantine"; it would be more accurate but cumbersome to say constantinopolitine.) Diocletian and Constantine, however, continued to rule a united Roman empire. As we have seen, as late as the sixth century, after the western part of the empire had fallen to the Germans, the eastern Roman emperor Justinian thought of himself as an

Justinian's reign was clearly an important turning point in the direction of Byzantine civilization because it saw the crystallization of new forms of thought and art that can be considered more "Byzantine" than "Roman."

heir to Augustus and fought hard to win back the West. Justinian's reign was clearly an important turning point in the direction of Byzantine civilization because it saw the crystallization of new forms of thought and art that can be considered more "Byzantine" than "Roman." But this still remains a matter of subjective emphasis: some scholars emphasize these newer forms, whereas others respond that Justinian continued to speak Latin and dreamed of restoring old Rome. Only after 610 did a new dynasty emerge that came from the East, spoke Greek, and maintained a fully Eastern or "Byzantine" orientation. Hence, although good arguments can be made for beginning Byzantine history with Diocletian, Constantine, or Justinian, we will begin here with the accession in 610 of the Emperor Heraclius.

It is also convenient to begin in 610 because from then until 1071 the main lines of Byzantine military and political history were determined by resistance against successive waves of invasion from the East. When Heraclius came to the throne the very existence of the Byzantine empire was being challenged by the Persians, who had conquered almost all of the empire's Asian territories. As a symbol of their triumph the Persians in 614 even carried off from Jerusalem the relic believed to be part of the original cross on which Jesus had been crucified. This relic had been discovered by Helena, the mother of the emperor Constantine, in one of the earliest archaeological "digs" in the Holy Land, and had become a potent symbol of the Christian legitimacy of the eastern Roman emperors. By enormous effort Heraclius rallied Byzantine strength and turned the tide, routing the Persians, recapturing Jerusalem, and retrieving the cross in 627. Persia was then reduced to subordination and Heraclius reigned in glory until 641. But in his last years new armies began to invade Byzantine territory, swarming out of hitherto placid Arabia. Inspired by the new religion of Islam and profiting from Byzantine exhaustion after the struggle with Persia, the Arabs made astonishingly rapid gains. By 650 they had taken most of the Byzantine territories that the Persians had occupied briefly in the early seventh century, including Jerusalem, which became a holy site for Muslims no less than for Christians and Jews. Arab armies also conquered Persia itself, and rapidly made their way westward across North Africa,

HOW DID THE BYZANTINE STATE SURVIVE FOR NEARLY A MILLENNIUM?

THE BYZANTINE EMPIRE AND ITS CULTURE   263

Greek Fire.

where Byzantine control had long been resented. Having become a Mediterranean power, the Arabs also took to the sea. In 677 they tried to conquer Constantinople with a fleet. Failing that, they attempted to take the city again in 717 by means of a concerted land and sea operation.

The Arab threat to Constantinople in 717 marked a new low in Byzantine fortunes, but the threat was countered by the emperor Leo the Isaurian (717–741) with as much resolution as Heraclius had shown in meeting the Persian threat a century before. With the help of a secret incendiary device known as "Greek fire" (a mixture of sulphur, naphtha, and quicklime aimed at the enemy from the prows of ships) and great military ability, Leo was able to defeat the Arab forces on sea and land. Leo's relief of Constantinople in 717 was one of the most significant battles in European history. Had the Islamic armies taken Constantinople there would have been little to stop them from sweeping through the rest of Europe. Over the next few decades, however, the Byzantines reconquered most of Asia Minor, which became the heartland of their empire for the next three hundred years. A stalemate with the Islamic forces prevailed until the Byzantines were able to take the offensive against a decaying Islamic power in the second half of the tenth century. In that period—the greatest in Byzantine history—Byzantine

troops reconquered most of Syria. But in the eleventh century a different Islamic people, the Seljuk Turks, canceled out all the prior Byzantine gains. In 1071 the Seljuks annihilated a Byzantine army at Manzikert in Asia Minor, a stunning victory that allowed them to overrun the remaining Byzantine eastern provinces. Constantinople was now thrown back on itself more or less as it had been in the days of Heraclius and Leo. By

CHRONOLOGY

THE BYZANTINE EMPIRE, 610–1095 C.E.

Ascension of the emperor Heraclius	610
Arabs seize most of Byzantine territory	c. 650
Constantinople nearly falls to the Arabs	717
Byzantines reconquer most of Asia Minor	717–750
Stalemate between Arabs and Byzantines	750–950
Byzantines reconquer most of Syria	c. 950–1000
Seljuk Turks overrun eastern Byzantine provinces	1071
First Crusade	1095

and large, it would remain on the defensive for the next four hundred years until the last remnants of the Byzantine empire fell to the Ottoman Turks in 1453. Turks continue to rule in Constantinople—which they renamed Istanbul—to the present day.

SOURCES OF STABILITY

That Constantinople was finally taken was no surprise. What is a cause for wonder is that the Byzantine state survived for so many centuries in the face of so many different hostile forces. This wonder becomes all the greater when we recognize that the internal political history of the empire was exceedingly tumultuous. Because Byzantine power was so completely focused upon the imperial court at Constantinople, and because rulers followed their late Roman predecessors in claiming the powers of divinely appointed absolute monarchs, there was no way of opposing them other than by intrigue and violence. Hence Byzantine history was marked by repeated palace revolts; mutilations, murders, and blindings were almost commonplace. Byzantine politics became so famous for their behind-the-scenes complexity that we still use the word "byzantine" to refer to highly complex and devious backstage machinations. Fortunately for the empire, some very able rulers did emerge from time to time to wield their unrestrained powers with efficiency. Even more fortunately, a bureaucratic machinery continued to function during times of palace upheaval.

Efficient bureaucratic government indeed was one of the major elements of Byzantine success and longevity. The Byzantines could count on having an adequate labor supply for their bureaucracy because Byzantine civilization preserved and encouraged the practice of education for the laity. This was one of the major differences between the Byzantine East and the early Latin West: from about 600 to about 1200 lay literacy in Western Christendom was very limited, whereas in the Byzantine East widespread lay literacy was the basis of governmental accomplishment. Literate Byzantine bureaucrats supervised education and religion and presided over all forms of economic endeavor. Imperial officials in Constantinople regulated prices and wages, maintained systems of licensing, controlled exports, and enforced the observance of the Sabbath. Even chariot racing fell under strict governmental supervision, with the populace of Constantinople being assigned by governmental command to root for particular teams. Bureaucratic methods also helped regulate the army and navy, the courts, and the diplomatic ser-

The Emperor John I (969–976) Being Crowned by Christ. Byzantine rulers characteristically used coins as objects of propaganda designed to show that their powers came to them supernaturally.

vice, endowing these agencies with organizational strengths incomparable for their age.

Another explanation for Byzantine endurance was the comparatively sound economic base of the state until the eleventh century. As the historian Sir Steven Runciman has said, "if Byzantium owed her strength and security to the efficiency of her Services, it was her trade that enabled her to pay for them." Commerce and cities continued to flourish in the Byzantine East, as they had done in the late-antique period. Above all, in the ninth and tenth centuries Constantinople was a vital trade emporium for Far Eastern luxury goods and Western raw materials. The empire also nurtured and protected its own industries, most notably that of silk making, and it was renowned until the eleventh century for its stable gold and silver coinage. Constantinople, which at times may have had a population of close to a million, was not its only great urban center. During certain periods Antioch, and up until the end of Byzantine history the bustling cities of Thessalonica and Trebizond, were also large and prosperous.

Historians emphasize Byzantine trade and industry because these were so advanced for the time and provided most of the surplus wealth that supported the state. But agriculture was really at the heart of the Byzantine economy as it was of all premodern ones. The story of Byzantine agricultural history consists mainly of the struggle by independent peasant farmers to stay free of the encroachments of large estates owned by wealthy aristocrats and monasteries. Until the eleventh century the free peasantry managed to

HOW DID THE BYZANTINE STATE SURVIVE FOR NEARLY A MILLENNIUM?

THE BYZANTINE EMPIRE AND ITS CULTURE   265

maintain its existence with the help of state legislation, but after 1025 the aristocracy gained power in the government and began to transform the peasants into impoverished tenants. This had many unfortunate results, not the least of which was that the peasants became less interested in resisting the enemy. The defeat at Manzikert in 1071 was in part the result of the government's short-sighted acquiescence to aristocratic ambitions.

BYZANTINE RELIGION

So far we have spoken about military campaigns, government, and economics as if they were at the center of Byzantine survival. Seen from hindsight they were, but what the Byzantines themselves cared about most was the religious orthodoxy of their empire. Remarkable as it might seem, Byzantines battled over abstruse religious questions as vehemently as we today might argue about politics and sports—indeed they struggled more vehemently, because they were often willing to fight and even die over words in a religious creed. The intense preoccupation with questions of doctrine is well illustrated by the report of an early Byzantine writer who said that when he asked a baker for the price of bread, the answer came back, "the Father is greater than the Son," and when he asked whether his bath was ready, was told that "the Son proceeds from nothing." Such zealotry could cause great harm during times of religious dissension, but it also endowed the Byzantine state with a powerful sense of confidence and mission during times of religious concord.

Byzantine religious dissensions were greatly complicated by the fact that the emperors took an active role in them. Because the emperors carried great power in the life of the church—emperors were sometimes deemed by churchmen to be "similar to God"—they exerted great influence in religious debates. Nonetheless, especially in the face of provincial separatism, rulers could never force all their subjects to believe the same doctrines they themselves did. Even Byzantine governmental authority did not stretch that far. Only after the loss of many eastern provinces and the refinement of doctrinal formulae did religious peace seem near in the eighth century. But then it was shattered for still another century by what is known as the Iconoclastic Controversy.

The Iconoclasts were those who wished to prohibit the worship of icons—that is, images of Christ and the saints. Since the Iconoclastic movement was initiated by the Emperor Leo the Isaurian, and subsequently directed with even greater energy by his son Constantine V (740–775), historians have discerned in it different motives. One was certainly theological. The worship of images seemed to the Iconoclasts to smack of paganism. They believed that nothing made by human beings should be worshiped by them, that Christ was so divine that he could not be conceived of in terms of human art, and that the prohibition of worshiping "graven images" in the Ten Commandments (Exodus 20:4) placed the matter beyond dispute.

In addition to these theological points, there were probably other considerations. Since Leo the Isaurian was the emperor who saved Constantinople from the onslaught of Islam, and since Muslims zealously shunned images on the grounds that they were "the work of Satan" (Qur'ān, V. 92), Leo's Iconoclastic policy may have been an attempt to answer one of Islam's greatest criticisms of Christianity and thereby deprive Islam of some of its appeal. There may also have been certain internal political and financial motives. By proclaiming a radical new religious movement the emperors may have wished to reassert their control over the church and combat the growing strength of monasteries. As events turned out, the monasteries did rally behind the cause of images, and as a result, they were bitterly persecuted by Constantine V, who took the opportunity to confiscate much monastic wealth.

The Iconoclastic Controversy was resolved in the ninth century by a return to the status quo, namely the worship of images, but the century of turmoil over the issue had some profound results. One was the destruction by imperial order of a large amount of religious art. Pre-eighth-century Byzantine religious art that survives today comes mostly from places such as Italy or Palestine, which were beyond the easy reach of the Iconoclastic emperors. A second consequence of the controversy was the opening of a serious religious breach between East and West. The pope, who until the eighth century had usually been a close ally of the Byzantines, strongly opposed Iconoclasm. This was not least because Iconoclasm tended to question the cult of saints, and the claims of papal primacy were based on an assumed descent from Saint Peter. Papal opposition to Iconoclasm during the eighth century led to worsening relations between East and West that

> What the Byzantines themselves cared most about was the religious orthodoxy of their empire.

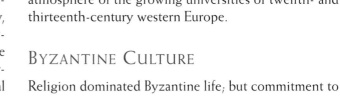

culminated with the crowning of the Frankish leader Charlemagne as the new Roman emperor in the West on Christmas Day 800.

The ultimate defeat of Iconoclasm led to the reassertion of some major traits of Byzantine religiosity, which from the ninth century until the end of Byzantine history remained predominant. One of these traits was a renewed emphasis on the traditional, Orthodox faith of the empire as the key to its political unity and military success. Religious tradition became the touchstone of doctrinal correctness and political legitimacy. As one opponent of Iconoclasm said, "If an angel or an emperor announces to you a gospel other than the one you have received, close your ears." This view strengthened Byzantine religion by ending controversy and heresy, and it helped the religion gain new adherents in the ninth and tenth centuries. But it also reinforced the hegemony of Constantinople's own religious traditions within the empire, thus marginalizing even further the differing religious traditions of Syrian and Armenian Christianity. The fear of heresy also tended to inhibit free speculation, not just in religion but also in related intellectual matters. Although the Byzantine emperors founded and supported a uni-

versity in Constantinople, they never permitted it to exercise any significant degree of intellectual freedom, in marked contrast with the freewheeling intellectual atmosphere of the growing universities of twelfth- and thirteenth-century western Europe.

BYZANTINE CULTURE

Religion dominated Byzantine life; but commitment to Christianity by no means inhibited the Byzantines from revering and preserving their ancient Greek heritage. Byzantine schools based their instruction on classical Greek literature, and especially Homer, to an astonishing degree. Educated people around the Byzantine court could quote but a single line of Homer, and expect that their audience would know immediately the entire passage from which it came. In the English-speaking world, only the King James Bible has ever achieved a degree of cultural saturation comparable with Homer in Byzantium. Like the seventeenth-century Bible, Homer for the Byzantines was simultaneously a literary model, an instructional textbook, and a guide to personal morality and wisdom.

Byzantine scholars also studied intensively the philosophy of Plato and the historical prose of Thucydides. Aristotle's works were also known but were regarded with less interest. By and large, the Greek scientific and mathematical tradition was neglected by the Byzantines, and even philosophy was considerably restricted. Justinian, for example, shut down the Athenian philosophical academies that had existed since Plato's day, declaring that everything worth knowing was already known. Inventiveness was prized in Byzantine culture, but original discoveries and interpretations were not the goal toward which Byzantine intellectual life was directed. Preservation rather than innovation was the hallmark of Byzantine classicism. Nevertheless, such dedicated classicism enriched Byzantine intellectual and literary life and helped preserve the Greek classics for later ages. The bulk of classical Greek

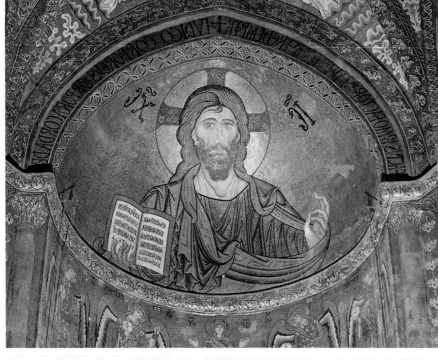

Christ as Ruler of the Universe. A twelfth-century Byzantine mosaic from the Cathedral of Cefalù in Sicily. Although the Byzantines did not rule in Sicily in the twelfth century, the Norman rulers employed Byzantine workmen. Note the use of Greek—the Byzantine language—on the left-hand Bible page and Latin—the Norman language—on the right.

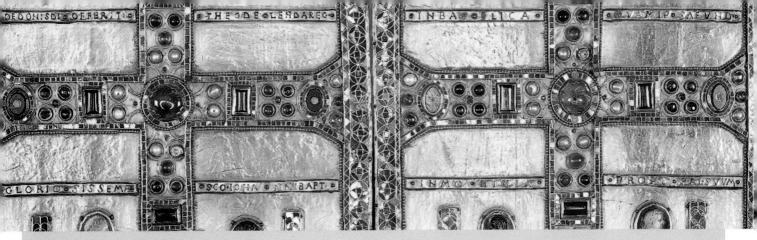

BYZANTINE CLASSICISM

This poem, by an eleventh-century Byzantine scholar, illustrates the sense of continuity learned Byzantines felt between their own Christian world and the world of the ancient Greek philosophers and authors.

May Christ Save Plato and Plutarch from Eternal Damnation

If perchance you wish to exempt certain pagans from punishment, my Christ,
May you spare for my sake Plato and Plutarch,
For both were very close to your laws in both teaching and way of life.
Even if they were unaware that you as God reign over all,
In this matter only your charity is needed,
Through which you are willing to save all men while asking nothing in return.

Deno John Geanokoplos, ed. and trans. *Byzantium: Church, Society, and Civilization Seen through Contemporary Eyes.* (Chicago: University of Chicago Press, 1984), p. 395.

literature that we have today survives only because it was copied by Byzantine scribes.

Byzantine classicism was a product of an educational system for the laity that extended to women as well as to men. Given attitudes and practices in the contemporary Christian West and in Islam, Byzantine commitment to female education was truly unusual. Girls from aristocratic or prosperous families did not go to schools but were relatively well educated at home by private tutors. In the Byzantine world of the ninth, tenth, and eleventh centuries, learned women were praised for being able to discourse like Plato or Pythagoras. The most famous of these Byzantine female intellectuals was the princess Anna Comnena, who described the deeds of her father Alexius in an urbane biography in which she copiously cited Homer and Euripides. But in addition to such literary figures

> Given attitudes and practices in the contemporary Christian West and in Islam, Byzantine commitment to female education was truly unusual.

there were also female physicians in the Byzantine empire, a fact of note given their scarcity in Western society until recent times.

Byzantine achievements in the realms of architecture and art are more familiar. The finest example of Byzantine architecture was the church of Santa Sophia (Holy Wisdom) in Constantinople, constructed at enormous cost by the emperor Justinian in the sixth century. Although built before the date taken here as the beginning of Byzantine history, it was typically Byzantine in both its style and subsequent influence. It was designed by architects of Hellenic descent, but was vastly different from any Greek temple. Its purpose was not to express pride in human accomplishment, but rather to symbolize the inward and spiritual character of the Christian religion. For this reason the architects gave little attention to the

The interior of Justinian's church of Santa Sophia in modern Istanbul, looking from east to west and showing the great dome. Since 1453 the church has been in use as a mosque, as shown in this 1852 drawing.

external appearance of the building. Nothing but plain brick covered with plaster was used for the exterior walls; there were no marble facings, graceful columns, or sculptured friezes. The interior, however, was decorated with richly colored mosaics, gold leaf, colored marble columns, and bits of tinted glass set on edge to refract the rays of sunlight after the fashion of sparkling gems. To emphasize a sense of the miraculous, the building was constructed in such a way that light appeared not to come from the outside at all, but to be generated within.

The structural design of Santa Sophia was something altogether new in the history of architecture. Its central feature was the application of the dome principle to a building of square shape. The church was designed in the form of a cross with a magnificent dome over its central square. The main problem was how to fit the circumference of the dome to the square area it was supposed to cover. The solution was to have four great arches spring from pillars at the four corners of the square. The rim of the dome was then made to rest on the keystones of the arches, with the curved triangular spaces between the arches filled in with masonry.

Santa Sophia. The greatest monument of Byzantine architecture. The four minarets were added after the fall of the Byzantine Empire, when the Turks turned the church into a mosque.

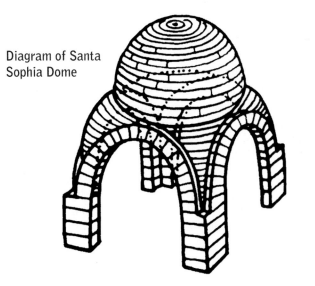

Diagram of Santa
Sophia Dome

The result was an architectural framework of marvelous strength, which at the same time made possible a style of imposing grandeur and even some delicacy of treatment. The great dome of Santa Sophia has a diameter of 107 feet and rises to a height of nearly 180 feet from the floor. So many windows are placed around its rim that the dome appears to have no support at all but to be suspended in midair.

BYZANTIUM AND THE WESTERN CHRISTIAN WORLD

After the skirmishes of the Iconoclastic period relations between eastern and western Christians remained tense, partly because Constantinople resented Western claims (initiated by Charlemagne in 800) to rule a rival Roman empire, but most of all because religious differences between the two continued to grow. From the Byzantine point of view westerners were uncouth and ignorant, incapable of understanding the Greek language, in which all serious theologians worked; whereas to western European eyes, the Byzantines were arrogant, effeminate, and prone to heresy. In 1054, papal claims to primacy over the eastern church provoked a religious schism that has never healed. Thereafter the Crusades drove home the dividing wedge.

After the sack of Constantinople in 1204 by crusaders, Byzantine hatred of westerners became intense. "Between us and them," one Byzantine wrote, "there is now a deep chasm: we do not have a single thought in common." Westerners called easterners "the dregs of the dregs . . . unworthy of the sun's light." Easterners

called westerners the children of darkness, alluding to the fact that the sun sets in the west. The beneficiaries of this hatred were the Turks, who conquered Constantinople in 1453, and soon thereafter conquered most of southeastern Europe up to Vienna.

In view of this long history of hostility (which we will discuss more fully in the next chapter), it is best to end our treatment of Byzantine civilization here by recalling how much the modern Western world owes to it. In simple physical terms the Byzantine empire acted as a bulwark against Islam from the seventh to the eleventh centuries, thus helping to preserve an independent and Christian West. Western Europeans also owe an enormous cultural debt to Byzantine scholars, who preserved much of the classical Greek literary tradition during centuries when these texts were entirely unknown outside the Byzantine empire itself. Byzantine art has also exerted a great and continuing influence on the art of western Europe. Saint Mark's Basilica in Venice was built in close imitation of the Byzantine style, and the art of such great Western painters as Giotto and El Greco owes much in different ways to Byzantine influences. Nor should we stop at listing influences because the great surviving monuments of Byzantine culture retain their imposing appeal in and of themselves. Travelers who view Byzantine mosaics in such cities as Ravenna and Palermo are continually awestruck; others who make their way to Istanbul still find Santa Sophia to be a marvel. In such jeweled beauty, then, the light from the Byzantine East, which once glowed so brightly, continues to shimmer.

THE GROWTH OF ISLAM

How was Islam able to spread so rapidly?

In contrast to Byzantine history, which has no clearly datable beginning but a definite end in 1453, the history of Islamic civilization has a clear point of origin, beginning with the career of Muhammad in the seventh century, but no end. Believers in Islam, known as Muslims, currently comprise about one-seventh of the global population: in their greatest concentrations they extend from Africa through the Middle East and the states of the former Soviet Union to South Asia and Indonesia. All Muslims subscribe both to a common religion and a common way of life, for Islam has always demanded from its followers not just adherence to common forms of worship but also adherence to certain social and cultural norms. Indeed, more than Judaism or Christianity, Islam has been a great experiment in trying to build a worldwide society based on the fullest harmony between religious requirements and precepts for everyday existence. In this section we will trace the early history of the Islamic experiment, with primary emphasis on its orientation toward the West. Nonetheless we must remember that Islam expanded in many directions and that it ultimately had as much influence on the history of Africa and South Asia as it did on that of Europe or western Asia.

> We must remember that Islam expanded in many directions and that it ultimately had as much influence on the history of Africa and South Asia as it did on that of Europe or western Asia.

THE RISE OF ISLAM

Islam was born in Arabia, a desert land so backward before the founding of Islam that the two dominant neighboring empires, the Roman and the Persian, had not even bothered to conquer it. Most Arabs were Bedouins, wandering camel herders who lived off the milk of their animals and the produce, such as dates, that was grown in desert oases. In the second half of the sixth century Arabia saw a quickening of economic life owing to a shift in long-distance trade routes. The protracted wars between the Byzantine and Persian empires made Arabia a safer transit route than other alternatives for caravans going between Africa and Asia. Some towns grew to direct and take advantage of this growth of trade. The most prominent of these was Mecca, which not only lay on the junction of major trade routes, but also had long been a local religious center. In Mecca was located the Kabah, a pilgrimage shrine that served as a central place of worship for many different Arabian clans and tribes. (Within the Kabah was the Black Stone, a meteorite worshiped as a miraculous relic by adherents of many different divinities.) The men who controlled this shrine and also directed the economic life of the Meccan area belonged to the tribe of Quraish, an aristocracy of traders and entrepreneurs who provided the area with whatever little government it knew.

Muhammad, the founder of Islam, was born in Mecca to a family of Quraish about 570. Orphaned early in life, he entered the service of a rich widow whom he later married, thereby attaining financial security. Until middle age he lived as a prosperous trader little different from his fellow townsmen, but around 610 he underwent a religious experience that changed the course of his life and ultimately that of a good part of the world. Although most Arabs until then had been polytheists who recognized at most the vague superiority of a more powerful god they called Allah, Muhammad in 610 heard a voice from heaven tell him that there was no god but Allah alone. In other words, as the result of a conversion experi-

The Kabah. It contains the black stone which was supposed to have been miraculously sent down from heaven, and rests in the courtyard of the great mosque in Mecca.

ence he became an uncompromising monotheist. Thereafter he received further messages that became the basis for a new religion and that commanded him to accept the calling of "Prophet" to proclaim the monotheistic faith to the Quraish. At first he was not very successful in gaining converts beyond a limited circle, perhaps because the leading Quraish tribesmen believed that establishment of a new religion would deprive the Kabah, and therewith Mecca, of its central place in local worship. The town of Yathrib to the north, however, had no such concerns, and its representatives invited Muhammad to emigrate there so that he could serve as a neutral arbiter of local rivalries. In 622 Muhammad and his followers accepted the invitation. Because their migration—called in Arabic the Hijrah (or Hegira)—saw the beginning of an advance in Muhammad's fortunes, Muslims regard it as marking the beginning of their era: as Christians begin their era with the birth of Christ, so Muslims begin their dating system with the Hijrah of 622.

Muhammad changed the name of Yathrib to Medina (the "city of the Prophet") and quickly established himself as ruler of the town. In the course of doing this he consciously began to organize his converts into a political as well as a religious community. But he still needed to find some means of support for his original Meccan followers, and he also desired to wreak vengeance on the Quraish for not heeding his calls for conversion. Accordingly, he started leading his followers in raids on Quraish caravans traveling beyond Mecca. The Quraish endeavored to defend themselves, but after a few years Muhammad's band, fired by religious enthusiasm, succeeded in defeating them. In 630, after several desert battles, Muhammad entered Mecca in triumph. The Quraish thereupon submitted to the new faith and the Kabah was not only preserved but made the main shrine of Islam, as it remains today. With the taking of Mecca other tribes throughout Arabia in turn accepted the new faith. Thus, although Muhammad died in 632, he lived long enough to see the religion he had founded become a success.

THE RELIGIOUS TEACHINGS OF ISLAM

The doctrines of Islam are straightforward. The word *islam* itself means "submission," and the faith of Islam calls for absolute submission to God. Although the Arabic name for the one God is Allah, it is mistaken to believe that Muslims worship a god like Zeus or Jupiter who is merely the first among many: Allah for Muslims means the Creator, God Almighty—the same omnipotent deity worshiped by Christians and Jews. Instead of saying, then, that Muslims believe "there is no god but Allah," it is more correct to say they believe that "there is no divinity but God." In keeping with this, Muslims believe that Muhammad himself was God's last and greatest prophet, but not that he was God himself. In addition to strict monotheism Muhammad taught above all that men and women must surrender themselves entirely to God because divine judgment is imminent. Mortals must make a fundamental choice about whether to begin a new life of divine service: if they decide in favor of this, God will guide them to blessedness, but if they do not, God will turn away from them and they will become irredeemably wicked. On Judgment Day the pious will be granted eternal life in a paradise of delights, but the damned will be sent to a realm of eternal fire and torture. The practical steps the believer can take are found in the Qur'ān, the compilation of the revelations sent by God to Muhammad, and hence the definitive Islamic scripture. These steps include thorough dedication to moral rectitude and compassion, and fidelity to set religious observances—a regimen of prayers and fasts, pilgrimage to Mecca, and frequent recitation of parts of the Qur'ān.

The fact that much in the religion of Islam resembles Judaism and Christianity is not coincidental; Muhammad was definitely influenced by the two earlier religions. (There were many Jews in Mecca and Medina; Christian thought was also known to Muhammad, although more indirectly.) Islam most resembles Judaism and Christianity in its strict monotheism, its emphasis on personal morality and compassion, and its reliance on written, revealed scripture. Muhammad proclaimed the Qur'ān as the ultimate source of religious authority but accepted both the Hebrew Bible and the Christian New Testament as divinely inspired. From Christianity Muhammad seems to have derived his doctrines of the Last Judgment and the resurrection of the body with subsequent rewards and punishments, and his belief in angels (he reported that God's first message to him had been sent by the angel Gabriel). But although Muhammad accepted Jesus Christ as one of the greatest of a long line of prophets, he did not believe in Christ's divinity and

> The fact that much in the religion of Islam resembles Judaism and Christianity is not coincidental; Muhammad was definitely influenced by the two earlier religions.

Exterior and Interior of the Dome of the Rock, Jerusalem. According to Muslim tradition, Muhammad made a miraculous journey to Jerusalem before his death and left a footprint in a rock. The mosque that was erected over the site in the seventh century is, after the Kabah, Islam's second-holiest shrine.

laid claim to no miracles himself other than the writing of the Qur'ān. He also preached a religion without sacraments or priests. Every Muslim believer has direct responsibility for living the life of the faith without intermediaries; instead of priests there are only religious scholars who comment on problems of Islamic faith and law, and who may act as judges in disputes. Muslims are expected to pray together in mosques, but there is no such thing as a Muslim mass. The absence of clergy makes Islam more like Judaism, a similarity that is enhanced by Islamic stress on the inextricable connection among the religious, social, and political life of the divinely inspired community. But unlike Judaism, Islam played a unique role in uniting the world as it started to spread far beyond the confines of Arabia.

THE ISLAMIC CONQUESTS

This move toward world influence began immediately on Muhammad's death. Since he had made no provision for the future, and since the Arabs had no clear concept of political succession, it was unclear whether Muhammad's community would survive at all. But his closest followers, led by his father-in-law, Abu-Bakr, and a zealous early convert named Umar, quickly took the initiative by naming Abu-Bakr *caliph*, meaning "deputy of the Prophet," and so the supreme religious and political leader of all Muslims. Immediately after becoming caliph Abu-Bakr began a military campaign to subdue various Arab tribes that had followed Muhammad but were not willing to accept his successor's authority. In the course of this successful military action Abu-Bakr's forces began to spill northward over the borders of Arabia. Probably to their surprise they found that they met minimal resistance from Byzantine and Persian forces.

Abu-Bakr died two years after his accession but was succeeded as caliph by Umar, who continued to direct the Arabian invasions of the neighboring empires. In the following years Arab triumphs were virtually uninterrupted. In 636 the Arabs routed a Byzantine army in

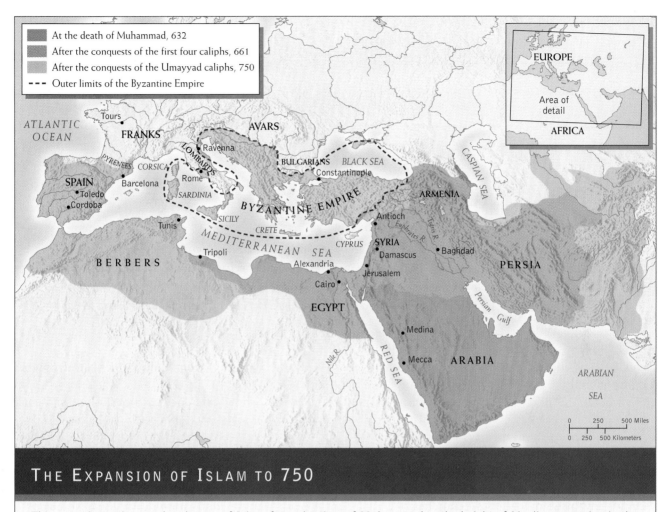

Legend:
- At the death of Muhammad, 632
- After the conquests of the first four caliphs, 661
- After the conquests of the Umayyad caliphs, 750
- - - - Outer limits of the Byzantine Empire

THE EXPANSION OF ISLAM TO 750

This map shows the steady advance of Islam from the time of Muhammad to the height of Muslim expansion in the middle of the eighth century. Note the rapid expansion in the generation after Muhammad's death. What about Islam's organization and fervor helped contribute to the spread of Muslim armies? What does the rapid advance suggest about the preparedness of their initial foes, such as Byzantium and Persia? Why were these foes not better able to resist? Why was the capture of Constantinople so crucial to successive Muslim rulers even after Islam had spread well beyond the eastern Mediterranean?

Syria and then quickly swept over the entire area, occupying the leading cities of Antioch, Damascus, and Jerusalem. In 637 they destroyed the main army of the Persians and marched into the Persian capital of Ctesiphon. Once the Persian administrative center was taken, the highly centralized Persian empire offered little resistance. By 651 the Arabian conquest of the entire Persian realm was complete. The Islamic forces now turned west toward North Africa, capturing Byzantine Egypt by 646 and extending their control throughout the rest of North Africa during the following decades. Attempts in 677 and 717 to capture Constantinople failed; but in 711 the Arabs crossed from North Africa into Visigothic Spain and quickly took

almost all of that area too. Thus within less than a century the forces of Islam had conquered all of ancient Persia and much of the late Roman world.

How can we explain this prodigious expansion? The best approach is to see first what impelled the conquerors and then to see what circumstances helped to ease their way. Contrary to widespread belief, the early spread of Islam was not achieved through a religious crusade. At first the Arabs were not at all interested in converting other peoples: instead, they hoped that conquered populations would not convert so that they could maintain their own identity as a community of rulers and tax gatherers. But although their motives for expansion were not religious, religious enthusiasm

THE "PACT OF UMAR"

When the caliph Umar (d. 644) conquered the city of Jerusalem, he issued a charter of protection to the people of the city, defining the relationship that should exist in the future between the Muslim conquerors and their Christian subjects. In its surviving form, the "Pact of Umar" contains provisions that were probably not in Umar's original document. Nonetheless, the "Pact" does describe accurately the rules that governed Christians and Jews living under Muslin rule during the early middle ages.

This letter is addressed to Allah's servant Umar, the Commander of the Faithful, by the Christians of such-and-such city. When you advanced against us, we asked you for a guarantee of protection for our persons, our offspring, our property, and the people of our sect, and we have taken upon ourselves the following obligations toward you, namely:

We shall not build in our cities or in the vicinity any new monasteries, churches, hermitages, or monks' cells. We shall not restore . . . any of them that have fallen into ruin or which are located in the Muslims' quarters.

We shall keep our gates wide open for passersby and travelers. We shall provide three days' food and lodging to any Muslims who pass our way. . . .

We shall not teach our children the Koran.

We shall not hold public religious ceremonies. We shall not seek to proselytize anyone. We shall not pre-vent any of our kin from embracing Islam if they so desire.

We shall show deference to the Muslims and shall rise from our seats when they wish to sit down.

We shall not attempt to resemble the Muslims in any way. . . .

We shall not ride on saddles.

We shall not wear swords or bear weapons of any kind, or ever carry them with us. . . .

We shall not display our crosses or our books anywhere in the Muslims' thorough-fares or in their marketplaces. We shall only beat our clappers in our churches very quietly. We shall not raise our voices when reciting the service in our churches, nor when in the presence of Muslims. Neither shall we raise our voices in our funeral processions. . . .

We shall not build our homes higher than theirs. . . .

Norman A. Stillman, ed. and trans. *The Jews of Arab Lands: A History and Source Book.* (Philadelphia: Jewish Publication Society, 1979), pp. 157–58.

played a crucial role in making the hitherto unruly Arabs take orders from the caliph and in instilling a sense that they were carrying out the will of God. What really moved the Arabs out of the desert was the search for richer territory and booty, and what kept them moving ever farther was the ease of acquiring new wealth as they progressed.

The Arabs' inspiration by Islam also coincided with a period of weakness in their principal enemies. The Byzantines and Persians had become so exhausted by their long wars with each other and with the "barbarians" that they could hardly rally for a new effort. Moreover, many of the local populations of Egypt, North Africa, and Asia Minor were already fed up with the financial demands made by their bureaucratic empires. To them, Islamic conquest brought deliverance not only from oppressive taxation, but also from the persecuting religious orthodoxy of Constantinople, which had sought systematically to suppress "heretical" Christian groups in all these areas. Because the Arabs did not demand conversion and exacted fewer taxes than the Byzantines and the Persians, they were often preferred to the old rulers. One Christian writer in Syria went so far as to say, "the God of vengeance delivered us out of the hands of the Romans [that is, the Byzantine empire] by means of the Arabs." For all these reasons Islam quickly spread over the territory between Egypt and Iran, and has been rooted there ever since.

THE SHIITE-SUNNI SCHISM

While the Arabs were extending their conquests they ran into their first serious political divisions. In 644 the caliph Umar died; he was replaced by Uthman, a weak ruler who had the added drawback for many of belonging to the Umayyad family, a wealthy clan from Mecca that had not at first accepted Muhammad's call. Those dissatisfied with Uthman rallied around the Prophet's cousin and son-in-law Ali, whose blood, background, and warrior spirit made him seem a more appropriate leader of the cause. When Uthman was murdered in 656 by mutineers, Ali's partisans raised him up as caliph. But Uthman's powerful family and supporters were unwilling to accept Ali. In subsequent disturbances Ali was murdered and Uthman's party emerged triumphant. In 661 a member of the Umayyad family took over as caliph, and that house ruled the Islamic world until 750. Even then, however, Ali's followers did not accept defeat. As time went on they hardened into a minority religious party known as Shiites (*shi'a* is Arabic for "party" or "faction"); this group insisted that only descendants of Ali could be caliphs or have any authority over the Muslim community. Those who stood instead for the actual historical development of the caliphate and became committed to its customs were called Sunnites (*sunna* is Arabic for "religious custom"). The cleft between the two parties has been a lasting one in Islamic history. Often persecuted, Shiites developed great militancy and a deep sense of being the only true preservers of the faith. From time to time they were able to seize power in one or another area, but they never succeeded in converting the majority of Muslims. Today they rule in Iran and are very numerous in Iraq but make up only about one tenth of the worldwide population of Islam.

UMAYYADS AND ABBASIDS

The triumph of the Umayyads in 661 began a more settled period in the history of the caliphate that would last until the tenth century. During these centuries there were two major governing orientations: the westward-looking one represented by the Umayyads, and the eastward-looking orientation of their successors, the Abbasids. The Umayyad capital was Damascus in the old Byzantine territory of Syria, and in many ways the Umayyad caliphate functioned as a Byzantine successor state, continuing even to employ formerly Byzantine bureaucrats. The Umayyads concentrated their energies on dominating the Mediterranean and conquering Constantinople. When their most massive attack on the Byzantine capital failed in 717, Umayyad strength was seriously weakened; it was only a matter of time before a new orientation would develop.

This new perspective came with the takeover by a new family, the Abbasids, in 750. Their rule stressed Persian more than Byzantine elements. Characteristic of this change was a shift in capitals, for the second Abbasid caliph built his new capital of Baghdad in Iraq, near the ruins of the old Persian capital, and even appropriated stones from the ruins. The Abbasids developed their own Muslim administration and imitated Persian absolutism. Abbasid caliphs ruthlessly cut down their enemies, surrounded themselves with elaborate court ceremonies, and lavishly patronized sophisticated literature. This is the world described in the *Arabian Nights*, a collection of stories of dazzling splendor written in Baghdad under the Abbasids. The dominating presence in those stories, Harun al-Rashid, reigned as caliph from 786 to 809 and behaved as extravagantly as he was described, tossing coins in the streets, passing out sumptuous gifts to his favorites and severe punishments to his enemies.

In Spain, however, an Umayyad dynasty continued to rule. Not wishing to be outdone by their Abbasid rivals, the Umayyad rulers of Spain were equally lavish in their literary and cultural patronage. One Umayyad

For some peoples, Islamic conquest brought deliverance not only from oppressive taxation, but also from the persecuting religious orthodoxy of Constantinople.

Carolingian Trade Routes. This sixth or seventh century statue of the Buddha, originally made in northern India, was bought to Helgö, an island off the North Sea coast of Germany, probably in the late eighth century. It was originally one of a pair; its mate is now in a private collection in Kashmir. This object illustrates the enormous geographical extent of Carolingian trade connections.

For the Christians of Byzantium and western Europe, the Abbasid caliphate was significant not only for its cultural achievements, but also because its eastern orientation took a certain amount of military pressure off the Mediterranean West. The Byzantine state, accordingly, was able to recover somewhat after a century of military pressure from the Umayyads. Farther west, the Franks of Gaul also benefited from the advent of the Abbasids. Because an Umayyad dynasty continued to control Spain, the great Frankish ruler Charlemagne (800–814) maintained diplomatic and trade relations with the Abbasid caliphate of Harun al-Rashid against their common Umayyad enemy. The most famous symbol of this connection was the elephant that Harun al-Rashid sent to Charlemagne. More important, however, was the flow of silver that found its way from the Abbasid empire north through Russia and the Baltic and into the Rhineland in exchange for Frankish exports of furs, slaves, wax, honey, and leather. Jewels, silks, spices, and other luxury goods from India and the Far East also flowed north and west into the Frankish world through the Abbasid empire. These trading links with the Abbasid world helped to fund the extraordinary cultural achievements of the Carolingian Renaissance which we will describe in the next section of this chapter.

ruler of the ninth-century went to enormous lengths to recruit to his court a famous Persian musician, astronomer, and geographer, who became a kind of arbiter of elegance to Spanish high society, introducing to the eager Umayyad court a new eastern hairstyle, a taste for asparagus, and a fashion for wearing underarm deodorant. But the rival Muslim rulers also competed with each other in intellectual pursuits. The caliph Al-Hakem II of Cordoba (961–976), for example, amassed a library of more than four hundred thousand volumes—the catalogue of titles alone ran to forty-four volumes—at a time when, in western Europe, a monastery with one hundred books qualified as a center of learning.

C H R O N O L O G Y

THE SPREAD OF ISLAM, 622–750 C.E.

Expulsion of Muhammad from Mecca (Hijrah)	622
Muhammad returns to Mecca	630
Muhammad dies	632
Abu-Bakr becomes caliph	632
Umar becomes caliph	634
Arabs occupy Antioch, Damascus, Jerusalem	636
Arabs occupy Persian capital	637
Arabs invade Egypt	646
Arabs conquer Persian empire	651
Shiite-Sunni schism	661
Arabs conquer North Africa	646–711
Umayyad reign	661–750
Arabs invade Spain	711
Beginning of Abbasid reign	750

WHAT FORCES COMBINED TO UNDERMINE THE POLITICAL UNITY OF THE ISLAMIC EMPIRE?

THE CHANGING ISLAMIC WORLD   277

THE CHANGING ISLAMIC WORLD

What forces combined to undermine the political unity of the Islamic empire?

During the ninth and tenth centuries, however, the power of the Abbasid dynasty rapidly declined. An extended period of decentralization followed that was mirrored during the eleventh century in Umayyad Spain. The major cause for the Abbasid collapse was the gradual impoverishment of the economic base— the agricultural wealth of the Tigris-Euphrates basin— resulting from ecological crises and a devastating revolt by the enslaved African work force that farmed the southern Iraqi marshlands. Tax revenues from the Abbasid empire were also declining, as provincial rulers in North Africa, Egypt, and Syria retained larger and larger portions of these revenues for themselves. As their revenues declined, the Abbasids found themselves unable to support either their large civil service or the new-style mercenary army they had built up. This new army was manned largely by slaves whose loyalties lay not with the caliphate itself, but with the individual caliphs who employed them. To defend its interests, the army soon became a dominant force in making and murdering caliphs. Massively expensive building projects, including the refoundation of the Abbasid capital of Baghdad, further exacerbated the fiscal, military, and political crisis.

Behind the Abbasid crisis lay two fundamental developments of great significance for the future of the Islamic world: the growth of regionalism and the increasing religious divisions between Sunnis and Shiites and among the Shiites themselves. In 909 regional and religious hostilities came together when a local Shiite dynasty known as the Fatimids seized control of the Abbasid province of North Africa. In 969, the Fatimids succeeded in conquering Egypt also. Meanwhile, another Shiite group, rivals of both the Fatimids and the Abbasids, attacked Baghdad in 927 and Mecca in 930, seizing the sacred Black Stone, the Kabah. Thereafter, the effective power of the Abbasids over their empire collapsed entirely. Although an Abbasid caliphate continued to exist in Baghdad until 1258, when invading Mongol armies finally disposed of its last remnants, in practice the Abbasid empire had disappeared by the 930s. In its place a new order began to emerge in the eastern Muslim world that was centered around the rise of an independent Egyptian kingdom and a new Muslim state based in Persia.

In Spain, Umayyad weakness was more directly a consequence of political failures and succession disputes than of economic collapse. Muslim Spain in the ninth and tenth centuries was an enormously wealthy agricultural and commercial region. But from the mid-ninth century on, renewed military pressure from the reviving Christian kingdoms of northern and eastern Spain exacerbated the internal political difficulties of the Umayyad caliphate. In the opening years of the eleventh century, the united Umayyad caliphate in Spain finally dissolved, to be replaced by a host of local, small-scale *taifa* kingdoms, some of which were now paying tribute to the Christian rulers of the north. In 1085, the great city of Toledo fell to the Christian king Alfonso of León. Alarmed, a new group of North African Islamic purists known as the Almoravids invaded Muslim Spain, checking the Christian advance and amalgamating Islamic Spain with their North African empire. Another such group, the Almohades, repeated this pattern during the twelfth century. But neither the Almoravids nor the Almohades succeeded in reuniting the warring petty kingdoms of Islamic Spain. One by one, these local kingdoms gradually fell victim to the advancing forces of the Christian kings of Spain. Although the last Muslim kingdom, the principality of Granada, would not fall to the Christians until 1492, the Christian reconquest of Spain was essentially complete by the middle of the thirteenth century.

Extravagance and incompetence by the Muslim rulers of eleventh-century Spain certainly played a role in the Umayyad caliphate's collapse. But there were larger factors at work in breaking up the unity of the Islamic world that transcended the failures of particular caliphs. Although Islamic society was religiously tolerant, at least with respect to Jews and Christians (who, as "dhimmis," "peoples of the book," were permitted to retain their religions by paying a special tax to their Muslim rulers; pagans, however, were forced to convert to Islam), ethnic tensions within the Islamic world were rampant and grew more divisive as the early idealism of the initial conquests faded with time. These ethnic tensions among Arabs, Turks, Berbers, sub-Saharan Africans, and Persians additionally complicated the deep regional divisions that had characterized this area of the world for centuries before the Islamic conquests began. Adding further to the political instability of the Muslim world was the uncompromising monotheism and religious egalitarianism of Islam itself. Muslim rulers (such as some of the Abbasids) who took on Persian styles of semidivine rulership were frequently murdered as blasphemers. Tensions between the universality of Islamic belief and the realities of regional particularism, ethnic hostility, and religious conflict between Sunnis and Shiites thus combined to undermine the political unity of the Islamic empire.

MUSLIM SOCIETY AND CULTURE, 900–1250

The political decentralization of the Muslim world did not automatically bring cultural decay, however. In fact, Islamic civilization prospered greatly in the "middle period," above all from about 900 to about 1250. During these centuries Islamic rule expanded into modern-day Turkey and India despite the collapse of the caliphates. Islamic history is certainly not a story of steady decline from the time of Harun al-Rashid. On the contrary, Islam's most creative cultural period was only beginning as the ninth century came to an end.

Islamic culture and society were extraordinarily cosmopolitan and dynamic from their earliest days. Muhammad himself was not a desert Arab but a town-dwelling trader imbued with advanced ideals. Subsequently, Muslim culture became highly cosmopolitan for several reasons: it inherited the sophistication of Byzantium and Persia; it remained centered at the crossroads of long-distance trade between the Far East and West; and the prosperous town life in most Muslim territories counterbalanced agriculture. The importance of trade meant much geographical mobility. Muhammad's teachings furthermore encouraged social mobility because the Qur'ān stressed the equality of all Muslims. The result was that at the courts of Baghdad and Córdoba, and later at those of the Muslim states that succeeded them, careers were open to those with talent. Since literacy was remarkably widespread—a rough estimate for around the year 1000 is that 20 percent of all Muslim males could read the Arabic of the Qur'ān—many could rise through education. Offices were seldom regarded as hereditary, and "new men" could arrive at the top by enterprise and skill.

There was one major exception to this rule of Muslim egalitarianism: the treatment of women. Perhaps because social status was so fluid, successful men were extremely anxious to preserve and enhance their posi-

tions and their "honor." They could accomplish this by maintaining or expanding their worldly possessions, which included women. For a man's females to be most "valuable" to his status, their inviolability had to be assured. The Qur'ān allowed a man to marry four wives, so women were at a premium, and married ones were segregated from other men. A wealthy man would also have a number of female servants and concubines, whom he kept in a part of his residence called the harem, where they were guarded by eunuchs, that is, castrated men. Within these enclaves women vied with each other for preeminence and engaged in intrigues to advance the fortunes of their children. Although large harems could be kept only by the wealthy, the system was imitated as far as possible by all classes. Based on the principle that women were chattel property, these practices did much to debase women and to emphasize attitudes of domination in sexual life. Although male homosexual relations were tolerated in upper-class society, these relationships too were based on patterns of domination, usually of a powerful adult over an adolescent boy, much as they had been in the ancient Greek world.

Two major avenues were open to men wishing to devote themselves to Islamic religious life. One was that of the *ulama*, learned men whose job was to study and offer advice on all aspects of religion and religious law. Not surprisingly these men usually stood for tradition and rigorous maintenance of the faith; often they exerted great influence on the conduct of public life. Complementary to them were the *sufis*, religious mystics who might be equated with Christian monks were it not for the fact that they were not committed to celibacy and seldom withdrew from the life of the community. Sufis stressed contemplation and ecstasy as the *ulama* stressed religious law; they had no common program and in practice behaved very differently. Some Sufis were "whirling dervishes," so known in the West because of their dances; others were *faqirs*, associated in the West with snake charming in marketplaces; and others were quiet, meditative men who practiced no exotic rites. Sufis were usually organized into "brotherhoods" that did much to convert outlying areas such as Africa and India. Throughout the Islamic world Sufism provided a channel for the most intense religious impulses. The ability of the *ulama* and the Sufis to coexist is testimony to the cultural pluralism of the Islamic world. But the absence of any avenues for religious women comparable with the convents of the Christian world is a reminder of the limits imposed by gender on that pluralism.

WHAT FORCES COMBINED TO UNDERMINE THE POLITICAL UNITY OF THE ISLAMIC EMPIRE?

THE CHANGING ISLAMIC WORLD 279

MUSLIM PHILOSOPHY, SCIENCE, AND MEDICINE

More remarkable still is the fact that the *ulama* and the Sufis often coexisted with representatives of yet another world view, students and practitioners of philosophy and science. Islamic philosophers were called *faylasufs* in Arabic because they were dedicated to the cultivation of what the Greeks had called *philosophia*. Islamic philosophy was based on the study of earlier Greek thought, above all the Aristotelian and Neoplatonic strains. Around the time when the philosophical schools were closed in Athens by order of the emperor Justinian, Greek philosophers migrated east, and the works of Aristotle and others were translated into Syriac, a Semitic dialect. From that point of transmission Greek philosophy gradually entered the life of Islam and became cultivated by the class of faylasufs, who believed that the universe is rational and that a philosophical approach to life was the highest God-given calling. The faylasufs' profound knowledge of Aristotle can be seen, for example, in the fact that Avicenna (d. 1037), one of the greatest faylasufs, read practically all of Aristotle's works in the remote town of Bukhara before he reached the age of eighteen.

The most serious problem faced by the faylasufs was that of reconciling Greek philosophy with Islamic religion. The faylasufs followed their Greek sources in believing—in opposition to Islamic doctrine—that the world is eternal and that there is no immortality for the individual soul. Different faylasufs reacted to this problem in different ways. Of the three greatest, Al-Farabi (d. 950), who lived mainly in Baghdad, was least concerned by it; he taught that an enlightened elite could philosophize without being distracted by the common religious beliefs of the masses. Even so, he never attacked those beliefs, considering them necessary to hold society together.

Unlike Al-Farabi, Avicenna (980–1037), who was active farther east, taught a less rationalistic philosophy that came close in many points to Sufi mysticism. (A later story held that Avicenna said of a Sufi, "All I know, he sees," while the Sufi replied, "All I see, he knows.") Finally, Averroës (1126–1198) of Córdoba, Spain, was a thoroughgoing Aristotelian who led two lives, one in private as an extreme rationalist and the other in public as a believer in the official faith, indeed even as an official censor. Averroës was the last really important Islamic philosopher: after him rationalism either blended into Sufism, the direction pointed to by Avicenna, or became too constrained by religious orthodoxy to lead an independent existence. But in its heyday between about 850 and 1200, Islamic philosophy was far more advanced and sophisticated than anything found in either the Byzantine or Western Christian realms.

Before their decline Islamic faylasufs were as distinguished in studying natural science as they were in philosophical speculation. Usually the same men were both philosophers and scientists, because although they could not make a living by commenting on Aristotle (there were no universities in which to teach), they could rise to positions of wealth and power by practicing astrology and medicine. As it was throughout the ancient and medieval world, astrology among the Muslims was an "applied science" intimately related to accurate astronomical observation. After an Islamic astrologer carefully studied and foretold the courses of the heavenly bodies, he would endeavor to apply his knowledge to the course of human events, particularly the fortunes of wealthy patrons. To account for heavenly motion, some Muslims considered the possibilities that the earth rotates on its axis and revolves around the sun, but these theories were not accepted because they did not fit in with ancient preconceptions such as the assumption of circular planetary orbits. It was therefore not in these suggestions that Muslim astrologers later influenced the West, but rather in their extremely advanced observations and predictive tables that often went beyond the most careful work of the Greeks.

Islamic accomplishments in medicine were equally remarkable. Faylasufs serving as physicians appropriated the knowledge contained in the medical writings of the Hellenistic age but were rarely content with that. Avicenna discovered the contagious nature of tuberculosis, described pleurisy and several varieties of nervous ailments, and pointed out that disease can be spread through contamination of water and soil. His chief medical writing, the *Canon of Medicine*, was accepted in Europe as authoritative until late in the seventeenth century. Avicenna's older contemporary Rhazes (865–925) was the greatest clinical physician of the medieval world. His major achievement was the discovery of the difference between measles and smallpox. Other Islamic physicians discovered the value of

> The most serious problem faced by the faylasufs was that of reconciling Greek philosophy with Islamic religion.

cauterization and of styptic agents, diagnosed cancer of the stomach, prescribed antidotes for cases of poisoning, and made notable progress in treating diseases of the eyes. In addition, they recognized the infectious character of bubonic plague, pointing out that it could be transmitted by clothes. Finally, the Muslims excelled in the organization of hospitals and in the control of medical practice. At least thirty-four great hospitals were located in the principal cities of Persia, Syria, and Egypt, and appear to have been organized in a strikingly modern fashion. Each had wards for particular cases, a dispensary for giving out medicine, and a library. The chief physicians and surgeons lectured to the students and graduates, examined them, and issued licenses to practice. Even the owners of leeches (used for bloodletting, a standard medical practice of the day) had to submit them for inspection at regular intervals.

Other great Islamic scientific achievements came in optics, chemistry, and mathematics. Islamic physicists founded the science of optics and drew a number of significant conclusions regarding the theory of magnifying lenses and the velocity, transmission, and refraction of light. Islamic chemistry was an outgrowth of alchemy, an invention of the Hellenistic Greeks, the system of belief that was based on the principle that all metals were the same in essence, and that baser metals could therefore be transmuted into gold if only the right instrument, the philosopher's stone, could be found. But the efforts of scientists in this field were by no means confined to this fruitless quest; some even denied the whole theory of transmutation of metals. As a result of experiments by Muslim scientists, various new substances and compounds were discovered, among them carbonate of soda, alum, borax, nitrate of silver, saltpeter, and nitric and sulphuric acids. In addition, Islamic scientists were the first to describe the chemical processes of distillation, filtration, and sublimation. In mathematics Islam's greatest accomplishment was to unite the geometry of the Greeks with the number science of the Hindus. Borrowing what Westerners know as "Arabic numerals," including the zero, from the Hindus, Islamic mathematicians developed an arithmetic based on the decimal system and made advances in algebra (itself an Arabic word). Building on Greek geometry with reference to heavenly motions, they also made great progress in spherical trigonometry. Thus they brought together and advanced all the areas of mathematical knowledge that would later be developed in the Christian West.

> Islam brought together and advanced all the areas of mathematical knowledge that would later be developed in the Christian West.

LITERATURE AND ART

In addition to its philosophers and scientists, medieval Islamic culture was distinguished by its poets. Even before their conversion to Islam, Arabs had excelled in writing poetry. Afterward, literary accomplishment quickly became recognized as a way to distinguish oneself at the Umayyad and Abbasid courts. Probably the greatest of Islamic poets were the Persians (who wrote in their own language more often than in Arabic), of whom the best known in the West is Umar Khayyam (d. 1123), whose *Rubaiyat* was turned into a popular English poem by the Victorian Edward Fitzgerald. Although Fitzgerald's translation distorts much, the hedonism of Umar's poem ("a jug of wine, a loaf of bread—and thou") faithfully reflects a common theme in much Islamic and Jewish poetry of the period. Similarly sensuous lyric poetry was cultivated in the courts of Muslim Spain. Such poetry too was by no means inhibited, as can be seen from lines like "such was my kissing, such my sucking of his mouth / that he was almost made toothless." As these lines will suggest, much of this work was frankly homosexual, a fact which seems to have occasioned no concern amongst the elite court circles within which this poetry was composed and performed.

Jews too participated in this new literary world, especially in Spain, where they wrote sensuous and playful poems, in both Hebrew and Arabic verse, praising wine, sexuality, and song. Muslim Spain also saw a great flowering of Jewish religious culture. The greatest of the Jewish scholars who flourished during this period was Moses Maimonides (1135–1204), a physician as well as a profound religious thinker, who is sometimes called "the second Moses" for his work in synthesizing the teachings of Jewish law in his famous *Mishneh Torah*. Scores of other Jewish scholars—grammarians, biblical commentators, and legal authorities—preceded Maimonides. But few followed him, at least in Spain. Maimonides himself was driven into exile by the Almohades, first to North Africa and ultimately to Egypt, where he became physician to the Muslim ruler of Cairo. His story is a reminder of the reactionary religious winds blowing through the Islamic world during the twelfth century, and that

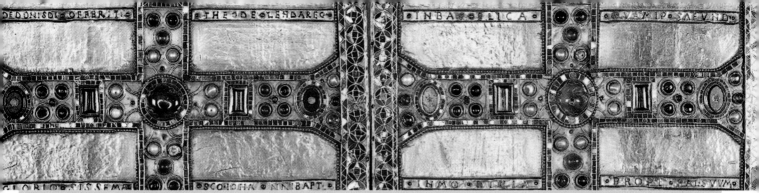

A HEBREW POEM IN PRAISE OF WINE, BY SAMUEL THE NAGID

In the courts of tenth- and eleventh-century Muslim Spain, Jewish poets and courtiers began to write a new style of Hebrew verse, closely modeled on contemporary Arabic examples. Samuel the Nagid was perhaps the most remarkable of this group of poets. He became the military leader of the Muslim kingdom of Granada as well as the head of the Jewish community there. In addition to his three volumes of poetry, he also wrote treatises on Hebrew grammar and on Jewish religious law.

Your debt to God is righteously to live,
   And His to you, your recompense to give.
Do not wear out your days in serving God;
   Some time devote to Him, some to yourself.
To Him give half your day, to work the rest;
   But give the jug no rest throughout the night.

Put out your lamps! Use crystal cups for light.
   Away with singers! Bottles are better than lutes.
No song, nor wine, nor friend beneath the sward—
   These three, O fools, are all of life's reward.

Raymond P. Scheindlin, ed. and trans. *Wine, Women, and Death: Medieval Hebrew Poems on the Good Life.* (Philadelphia: The Jewish Publication Society, 1986), p. 47.

---

would ultimately bring this Islamic cultural efflorescence to an end, first in Spain but ultimately throughout the Islamic Mediterranean world.

In their artistic endeavors Muslims were highly eclectic. Their main sources of inspiration came from the art of Byzantium and Persia. The former contributed many of the structural features of Islamic architecture, especially the dome, the column, and the arch. Persian influence was probably responsible for the intricate, nonnaturalistic designs that were used as decorative motifs in practically all of the arts. From both Persia and Byzantium came the tendency to subordinate form to rich and sensuous color. Architecture was the most important of the Islamic arts; the development of both painting and sculpture was inhibited by religious prejudice against representation of the human form. By no means were all of the examples of this architecture mosques; many were palaces, schools, libraries, private dwellings, and hospitals. Among the principal elements of Islamic architecture were bulbous domes, minarets, horseshoe arches, and twisted columns, together with the use of tracery in stone, alternating stripes of black and white, mosaics, and Arabic script as decorative devices. As in the Byzantine style, comparatively little attention was given to exterior ornamentation. The so-called minor arts of the Muslims included the weaving of gorgeous pile carpets and rugs, magnificent leather tooling, and the making of brocaded silks and tapestries, inlaid metalwork, enameled glassware, and painted pottery. Most of the products of these arts were embellished with complicated patterns of interlacing geometric designs, plants and fruits and flowers, Arabic script, and fantastic animal figures. In general, art laid particular emphasis on pure visual design. Separated from any role in religious teaching, it became highly abstract and nonrepresenta-

The Great Mosque of Córdoba, in Spain, was built in stages between 784 and 990. Its striped, horseshoe-shaped arches are characteristic features of Islamic architecture at this time. A Christian cathedral, visible in the right-hand background, was later constructed within a small portion of this enormous building.

tional. For these reasons Islamic art often seems more "modern" than any other art of premodern times.

TRADE AND INDUSTRY

The economic life of the Islamic world varied greatly according to time and place, but underdevelopment was certainly not one of its primary characteristics. On the contrary, in the central areas of Islamic civilization from the first Arab conquests until about the fourteenth century, mercantile life was extraordinarily advanced. The principal reason for this was that the Arabs inherited in Syria and Persia an area that was already marked by an enterprising urban culture and that lay at the crossroads of the Mediterranean world, linking together the major trade routes between Africa, Europe, India, and China. Islamic traders built venturesomely on these earlier foundations. Muslim

merchants penetrated into southern Russia and equatorial Africa; caravans of thousands of camels traveled to the gates of India and China. Ships from the Muslim world established new routes across the Indian Ocean, the Persian Gulf, and the Caspian Sea. For periods of time Islamic ships also dominated parts of the Mediterranean. Indeed, one reason for the eventual decline of medieval Islamic civilization was that Western Christians took hold of the Mediterranean in the tenth and eleventh centuries and seized control of the Indian Ocean in the sixteenth century.

The great Islamic expansion of commerce would scarcely have been possible without a corresponding development of industry. It was the ability of the people of one region to turn their natural resources into finished products for sale to other regions that provided a basis for a large part of the trade. Nearly every one of the great cities specialized in some particular

WHAT CAUSED ECONOMIC AND SOCIAL CHANGE IN SEVENTH-CENTURY WESTERN EUROPE?

WESTERN CHRISTIAN CIVILIZATION IN THE EARLY MIDDLE AGES   283

variety of manufacture. Mosul, in Syria, was a center of the manufacture of cotton cloth; Baghdad specialized in glassware, jewelry, pottery, and silks; Damascus was famous for its fine steel and for its "damask," or woven-figured silk; Morocco was noted for the manufacture of leather; and Toledo, in Spain, for its excellent swords. The products of these cities did not exhaust the list of manufactures. Drugs, perfumes, carpets, tapestries, brocades, woolens, satins, metal items, and a host of other products were turned out by the craftsmen of many cities. From the Chinese the Muslims learned the art of papermaking, and the products of that industry were in great demand, not only within the empire itself but in Europe as well.

> Islamic civilization so overshadowed that of the Christian West until the twelfth century that there can be no comparison. When the West did move forward it was able to do so partly because of what it learned from Islam.

CONTRIBUTIONS OF EARLY ISLAMIC CIVILIZATIONS

In all the areas we have reviewed, Islamic civilization so overshadowed that of the Christian West until the twelfth century that there can be no comparison. When the West did move forward it was able to do so partly because of what it learned from Islam. In the economic sphere westerners absorbed many accomplishments of Islamic technology, such as irrigation techniques, the raising of new crops, papermaking, and the distilling of alcohol. Islamic economic influence is also reflected in the large number of common English words that were originally of Arabic or Persian origin. Among these are traffic, tariff, magazine, alcohol, muslin, orange, lemon, alfalfa, saffron, sugar, syrup, and musk. The word "admiral" also comes from Arabic—in this case deriving from the title of *emir*.

Western Europe was equally indebted to Islam in intellectual and scientific life. Here too, borrowed words tell some of the story: algebra, cipher, zero, nadir, amalgam, alembic, alchemy, alkali, soda, almanac, and names of many stars such as Aldebaran and Betelgeuse all derive from Arabic originals. Islamic civilization preserved and expanded Greek philosophical and scientific knowledge when such knowledge was almost entirely forgotten in the West. All the important Greek scientific works surviving from ancient times were translated into Arabic; during the twelfth and thirteenth centuries, most were in turn translated from Arabic into Latin through the combined efforts of

Muslim, Jewish, and western Christian scholars. Above all, the preservation and interpretation of the works of Aristotle was one of Islam's most enduring accomplishments. About two-thirds of Aristotle's works were reacquired in the West by means of Latin translations from Arabic texts. Aristotle's ideas were also interpreted with Islamic help, above all that of Averroës, whose prestige was so great that he was simply called "the Commentator" by medieval Western writers. Arabic numerals, adopted from India by Muslim mathematicians, are another tremendously important intellectual legacy, as anyone will discover by trying to balance a checkbook with Roman ones.

Aside from these specific contributions, the civilization of Islam arguably had its greatest influence on the West merely by standing as a powerful rival and spur to the imagination. Byzantine civilization was at once too closely related to the Christian West and, from the eleventh century on, too weak to serve this function. Westerners in the high and late Middle Ages usually looked down on the Byzantine Greeks, but they respected and feared the Muslims. And they were right to do so, for Islamic civilization at its zenith (to use another Arabic word) was surely one of the world's greatest. Though loosely organized, it brought Arabs, Persians, Turks, Africans, and Indians together into a common cultural and religious world, creating a diverse society and a splendid legacy of original discoveries and achievements.

WESTERN CHRISTIAN CIVILIZATION IN THE EARLY MIDDLE AGES

What caused economic and social change in seventh-century western Europe?

In western Europe also, the seventh century marked the transition between the late antique and the early medieval worlds. At the end of the sixth century, the Frankish chronicler Gregory of Tours still saw himself as living in a discernibly Roman world of cities, trade, taxation, and local administration. Gregory was proud of his family's status as Roman senators, and took it for granted that he and his male relatives should be bishops who ruled, by right of birth and status, over their episcopal cities and the surrounding countryside. Like others of his class, Gregory still spoke and wrote Latin—a quite different Latin, to be sure, from the polished prose of Cicero six hundred years before, but a Latin that was nonetheless the same language, and that had certainly changed less since Cicero's day than English has changed since the time of Chaucer. Gregory was of course aware that the western Roman empire was now in the hands of Frankish, Visigothic, Ostrogothic, and Lombard kings. But he saw those kings as Romans nonetheless, because they ruled in accordance with Roman models and, in the case of the Franks, because they ruled with the approval of the Roman emperor in Constantinople. It was also a source of satisfaction to Gregory that in recent years, all these barbarian kings had converted to orthodox, Catholic Christianity. This too, for Gregory, reinforced their *romanitas* ("Roman-ness"), and thus lent legitimacy, both earthly and heavenly, to their rule.

> This awareness of a break with the Roman past developed during the seventh century. It was the consequence of profound economic, religious, and cultural changes; and it marks the beginning of a new era in the history of western European civilization.

Two hundred years later, however, when Charlemagne, the greatest of all the Frankish rulers, was crowned as the new Roman emperor in the West, the sense of direct continuity that Gregory of Tours had had with the Roman world was gone. When Charlemagne set out to reform the cultural, religious, and political life of his empire, his goal was to revive a Roman empire from which he and his contemporaries now saw themselves as estranged. Charlemagne sought a *renovatio Romanorum imperii*—a renewal of the empire of the Romans—thus conceding in his very motto that he sought to revive an empire that had fallen. Somewhere between Gregory of Tours and Charlemagne a rupture occurred in western Europeans' relationship to their Roman past. Cultured Europeans ceased to see themselves as living in a continuing Roman empire and began instead to dream of reconstructing that empire. This awareness of a break with the Roman past developed during the seventh century. It was the consequence of profound economic, religious, and cultural changes; and it marks the beginning of a new era in the history of western European civilization.

ECONOMIC DISINTEGRATION AND POLITICAL INSTABILITY

As we have seen, the economy of the western Roman empire was becoming increasingly regionalized from the third century C.E. onward. The Mediterranean world, however, remained a reasonably well-integrated economic unit until the late sixth century. In the year 550, a gold coinage still circulated in both the eastern and the western Roman empire; a luxury trade in silks, spices, swords, and jewelry continued to move west; and slaves, wine, grain, and leatherwork still moved east from North Africa, Gaul, and Spain toward Constantinople, Egypt, and Syria. By 650, however, the economic unity of the Mediterranean world had broken down. This breakdown resulted partly from the destructiveness of Justinian's efforts to reconquer the western empire. Partly it was a consequence of ruinous Byzantine taxation of agricultural land, especially in Egypt and North Africa, where the resentments of overtaxed peasant farmers prepared the way for the Islamic conquests. Piracy by Muslim raiders also played a role in undermining the economy of the seventh-century Mediterranean world—although Muslims quickly became important maritime traders, and in the long run Muslim conquests did more to reconstruct than to destroy the patterns of Mediterranean commerce.

For western Europe, however, the most important causes of these seventh-century economic changes were internal. The cities of Italy, Gaul, and Spain continued to decline. Although bishops still ruled from cities, and so continued to provide a market for certain kinds of luxury goods, the kings and nobles of western Europe were moving to the countryside during the seventh century, living as much as possible from the produce of their own estates rather than purchasing their supplies in the marketplace. At the same time, agricultural land was passing out of cultivation, especially on the larger estates, whose owners were finding it too costly to maintain the gangs of field slaves that had been the backbone of late Roman commercial agriculture. As trade declined, so too did the revenues lords took from tolls. The late Roman system of land taxes was also collapsing, not least because free-born Franks and Goths were claiming exemptions from it, leaving only the Roman population and the servile peasantry

WHAT CAUSED ECONOMIC AND SOCIAL CHANGE IN SEVENTH-CENTURY WESTERN EUROPE?

WESTERN CHRISTIAN CIVILIZATION IN THE EARLY MIDDLE AGES   285

Book Cover. The cover of a gospel book encrusted with jewels and ivory cameos presented by Pope Gregory the Great to a Lombard queen around the year 600.

to pay these taxes. The coinage systems of western Europe were also breaking down. From the 630s on, the Islamic conquests seriously reduced the supply of gold available in western Europe; but gold coins were already too valuable to be useful in local marketing anyway. From the 660s on, western European rulers shifted from a gold to a silver coinage. Europe would remain a silver-based economy for the next one thousand years.

During the seventh century, western Europe thus became a basically two-tier economy. Gold, silver, and luxury goods circulated among the wealthy, but the peasantry relied mainly on barter and various currency substitutes to facilitate their transactions. Lords collected rents from their peasants in foodstuffs but found it difficult to convert these payments of grain, wine, and meat into the weapons, jewelry, and silks that brought prestige in seventh-century aristocratic society. In a world in which the power of lords depended on their ability to give such high-prestige gifts to their military followers, the inability to convert peasant renders into cash was a serious handicap. It meant that for great men to give weapons and jewelry to their followers, they first had to acquire these items either through traders and artisans, or else through plunder and tribute. Either way, the processes by which such gifts were acquired were likely to be destabilizing.

Some rulers attempted to solve this problem by establishing and controlling special ports, known as *emporia*, where foreign merchants and craft workers would gather at specific seasons of the year to exchange their goods. Emporia offered a degree of security to merchants and provided the rulers who controlled them with an important source of power and influence. Control over these emporia was therefore a frequent source of conflict. Far more disruptive, however, were the incessant wars and raids fought among the various kings and lords of seventh-century Europe. The causes of these wars were almost infinitely various, but behind them lay the fundamental importance of plunder and tribute to the dynamics of power in the early medieval world.

The successful rulers of the seventh, eighth, and ninth centuries tended to be those whose territories adjoined wealthy but poorly defended territories that could be easily and profitably attacked. Such "soft frontiers" provided rulers with land and wealth they could distribute to their followers. Successes of this sort would bring more followers to a lord's service; so long as more conquests then followed, the process of amassing power and wealth would continue. But power acquired through plunder and conquest was inherently unstable. A few defeats might speedily reverse the entire process.

Another factor contributing to the instability of power in this world was the difficulty all the royal dynasties of the early middle ages experienced in trying to regulate the succession to their thrones. The kings who established themselves during the invasion period of the fifth and sixth centuries did not come from the traditional royal families of their peoples. Moreover, the barbarian armies who took over the western Roman empire during these years were rarely if ever composed of a single people anyway. They were usually made up of many different peoples, including a sizable number of disaffected Romans. Such unity as they possessed was largely the creation of the charismatic warrior-kings who led them, and this charisma was not easily passed on by inheritance.

Of all the barbarian groups that established kingdoms in the western empire during the fifth and sixth centuries, only the Franks succeeded in establishing a single royal dynasty from which the future kings of the Franks would be drawn for the next two hundred fifty years. This dynasty was established by Clovis (d. 511), the great warrior-king of the Franks, who by converting to orthodox, Catholic Christianity also established an alliance between his dynasty and the powerful Roman bishops of Gaul. But the dynasty itself came to be known as the Merovingians, after Clovis' legendary grandfather Merovech, who was a sea dragon. We need not take this claim seriously; but it is, at the very least, a telling indication of how short was Clovis' known genealogy, that no one could be quite sure who his grandfather actually was.

Even in Gaul, however, the Merovingians were not the only noble family with a plausible claim to be kings; and in Visigothic Spain, Anglo-Saxon England, and Lombard Italy, the numbers of such rival royal families were even greater. Nor was the right of succession limited to the eldest male claimant of each competing royal family. Early medieval Europe was a world in which all the sons of a king (and frequently all his cousins and nephews too) could stake a plausible claim to the throne. In Visigothic Spain, the bloody succession disputes that resulted when a reigning king died so horrified the resident Roman population that they spoke of this inability to regulate the succession as a kind of a sickness: the *morbus Gothorum*, the "sickness of the Goths." In Gaul, the Franks were more successful in restricting claims to kingship to descendants of the Merovingian dynasty; but the Merovingians' custom of dividing the kingdom up into its constituent, regional parts, and installing a different king over each part, guaranteed plenty of civil strife in Merovingian Gaul also.

MONASTICISM AND CONVERSION

The brutal conflicts between these rival Merovingian kings, together with the blackening of their reputations by their Carolingian rivals and successors, can easily obscure the real strength and sophistication of Merovingian governance. Many elements of late Roman local administration survived throughout the Merovingian period. Literacy remained an important element in Merovingian administration, providing a foundation on which the Carolingians would build. Even the cultural

renaissance associated with the reign of Charlemagne really began in the late seventh century, with the production of deluxe biblical and other manuscripts at Merovingian monasteries such as Luxeuil.

Monasteries grew remarkably under the Merovingians, especially during the seventh century, reflecting the great wealth of the country. Of the approximately five hundred fifty monasteries that existed in Gaul by the year 700, more than three hundred had been established in the preceding century. The Frankish bishoprics also prospered greatly under the Merovingians, amassing approximately three quarters of their total landed possessions by the end of the seventh century. This massive redistribution of wealth reflected a fundamental shift in the economic gravity of the Frankish kingdom. In the year 600, the wealth of Gaul was still concentrated in the south, where it had been throughout the late Roman period. By the year 750, however, the economic center of the kingdom lay north of the Loire, in the territories that extended from the Rhineland westward to the North Sea. It was here that most of the new monastic foundations of seventh-century Gaul were established.

Behind this shift in wealth from south to north lay a long and successful effort to bring under cultivation the rich, heavy soils of northern France. This effort was assisted by the development of heavy-wheeled plows capable of cutting and turning grassland sod and heavy clay, and by increasingly efficient devices for harnessing animals (particularly oxen, but sometimes horses) to pull these plows. Gradually warming weather improved the fertility of these wet, northern soils, lengthening the growing season and so making possible more efficient crop-rotation systems. The population began to expand as food became more plentiful. Northern France remained a land of scattered settlements separated by heavy forest, but it was a much more densely populated region by 750 than it had been in 600. All these developments would continue during the Carolingian period and beyond. But although the Carolingians would enjoy the fruits of this gradually increasing northern agricultural prosperity, the developments that made it possible began during the seventh century under their Merovingian predecessors.

THE SPREAD OF MONASTICISM

Momentous developments also took place in religious life during the seventh century, especially in the monasteries. Throughout Christian Europe, the seventh century witnessed a rapid increase in the founda-

WHAT CAUSED ECONOMIC AND SOCIAL CHANGE IN SEVENTH-CENTURY WESTERN EUROPE?

WESTERN CHRISTIAN CIVILIZATION IN THE EARLY MIDDLE AGES   287

tion of monastic houses. Monasteries had existed in Gaul, Italy, and Spain since the fourth century, but most were located in the highly Romanized cities of southern Spain, Gaul, and northern Italy. In Gaul, where the Merovingian kings were Catholic, kings had begun to forge ties with monasteries during the sixth century. In Spain, Italy, and England, whose rulers had previously been Arian heretics (Spain and Italy) or pagans (England), ties between monasticism and monarchy arose only in the seventh century, after the royal dynasties of these areas had converted to Catholic Christianity. Even in Gaul, however, relations between the Merovingian kings and the Frankish monasteries became markedly closer from the late sixth century on, as the royal dynasty and the principal noble families embarked on a massive campaign of new monastic foundations that permanently altered the spiritual geography of western Europe.

Most of the new monastic foundations of the seventh century were deliberately located in rural areas, where they played an important role in the continuing struggle to Christianize the countryside. Often they were granted special privileges known as immunities, which by freeing them from the control of local bishops cemented their dependence on their founders. Frequently these new foundations were either double monasteries (in which a house of religious men was joined to a house of religious women), or convents, established for women only. Either way, they were usually ruled over by abbesses drawn from among the women of the royal family: dowager queens, royal princesses, or sometimes even a reigning queen herself.

Monastic life had great appeal to the royal and noble women of the early Middle Ages. It provided them with a socially sanctioned arena within which they could exercise a degree of power over their lives denied them outside the cloister. It gave them an honorable position in society from which they could influence the affairs of their families, while protecting them from abduction, rape, or forced marriages arranged to promote their families' diplomatic or dynastic interests. And it also guaranteed them salvation, at a time when salvation outside the cloister seemed a perilously uncertain prospect. But convents and double monasteries served the interests of the male members of these royal dynasties also—one reason, of course, why they founded and supported them. Convents provided a

dignified place of retirement for inconvenient but potentially powerful women, such as dowager queens. The prayers of holy women were regarded as particularly effective in securing divine support for the kingdom. And by limiting the number of royal women who could reproduce, convents also helped to reduce the number of potential claimants to the throne. Establishing royal women in convents was thus an important way of controlling the succession disputes that so regularly tore these early medieval kingdoms apart.

Many of these new monastic establishments also played an important role in the new round of missionary activity that characterized the seventh-century world. The most famous example of such monastic missionary activity is the conversion of Anglo-Saxon England. In northern England, the work of Christianization began in the late sixth century, led by missionary monks from Ireland. The decisive moment came in 597, however, when a group of forty Benedictine monks, sent by Pope Gregory I (590–604) and led by Saint Augustine of Canterbury (not to be confused with Saint Augustine of Hippo), brought the traditions of Roman Christianity to the kingdom of Kent in southeastern England. Despite some initial setbacks, by the end of the seventh century all of England had been brought firmly within the boundaries of the Roman, Christian world, and English monks had begun their own missionary campaigns in Frisia and Saxony. Frankish missionaries were also active in these areas, as they were in the Low Countries and the Basque lands of the southwest also. But it was the particular loyalty the English monks felt toward the papacy that was to have the most momentous consequences, not only for the papacy, but also for Gaul.

> Many of the new monastic establishments also played an important role in the new round of missionary activity that characterized the seventh-century world.

THE REIGN OF POPE GREGORY I

The architect of this new alliance between the Roman papacy and Benedictine monasticism was Pope Gregory I, known as Saint Gregory the Great. Until his time the Roman popes were generally subordinate to the emperors in Constantinople and to the greater religious prestige of the Christian East. Byzantine power in Italy was declining, however, and although Gregory worked hard to prevent a breach with Constantinople, he also sought to create a more autonomous, Western-oriented Latin Church. As a theologian—the fourth great "Latin father" of the church—he built on the work of Saint

Jerome, Saint Ambrose, and especially Saint Augustine of Hippo, in articulating a theology with distinctively Western elements. Among these were an emphasis on the necessity of penance for the forgiveness of sins, and the concept of purgatory as a place where the soul was purified before it was admitted into heaven. (Western belief in purgatory was thereafter to become one of the major differences in the teachings of the eastern and western churches.) Gregory emphasized the importance of pastoral care by bishops toward the laity, writing an influential book on the subject in a deliberately simplified Latin prose style that made it one of the most accessible and influential books of the early Middle Ages. A powerful liturgical chant with unaccompanied vocal music in Latin has become known as "Gregorian chant," although Gregory's role in creating this music is conjectural and debatable. All these innovations helped to make the Christian West religiously and culturally more independent of the Greek-speaking East than it had ever been before.

Gregory was also a statesman and ruler in the model of his Roman forebears. Within Italy he ensured the survival of the papacy against the barbarian Lombards by clever diplomacy and expert management of the papacy's estates and revenues. He maintained good relations with Byzantium while asserting his authority as pope over the other bishops of the Western church. Above all, he patronized the order of Benedictine monks. Gregory's patronage helped the Rule of Saint Benedict become the predominant monastic rule in the

West; through his encouragement, Benedictine monks emerged as the most important missionary group of the early Middle Ages. Among these Benedictine missionaries, Englishmen such as Saint Boniface and Saint Willibrord deserve pride of place. Their missionary work in Frisia and Germany brought both regions into the western Catholic Church, and laid the groundwork for an alliance between the papacy and the Frankish monarchy that would transform early medieval Europe. Gregory did not live to see this alliance, but his policy of invigorating the Western church contributed greatly to bringing it about.

THE RISE OF THE CAROLINGIANS

How did Charlemagne redefine the relationship between Christianity and kingship?

In Gaul, the weaknesses of the Merovingian dynasty were steadly becoming more apparent as the seventh century drew to a close. Tensions among noble families in the Merovingian heartland of Neustria and those in the border region of Austrasia were increasing. The Austrasian nobles had profited from their steady push into the "soft frontier" areas east of the Rhine, acquiring wealth and military power in the process. The Merovingians, based in Neustria, had no such easy conquests at their disposal. Moreover, a considerable portion of the land they did hold had been given to the church in the course of the seventh century. A succession of short-lived Merovingian kings complicated matters further, producing a series of civil wars between Austrasians and Neustrians. Briefly, in 687, the leader of the Austrasian nobility, Pepin of Heristal, succeeded in forcing his way into office as "mayor of the palace," seeking thereby to control both Austrasia and Neustria. But not until 717, when Pepin's illegitimate son Charles Martel ("the Hammer") finally triumphed over his opponents in both territories, was Pepin's family secure in its control over the Merovingian court. Thereafter, however, the Merovingian kings were largely figureheads in a kingdom ruled by Charles Martel and his sons.

Charles Martel is sometimes considered the second founder (after Clovis) of the Frankish state. His claim to this title is twofold. First, in 733 or 734 (the tradi-

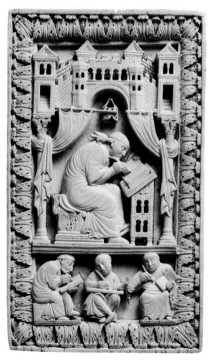

Pope Gregory the Great. In this tenth-century German ivory panel the pope is receiving inspiration from the Holy Spirit in the form of a dove.

HOW DID CHARLEMAGNE REDEFINE THE RELATIONSHIP BETWEEN CHRISTIANITY AND KINGSHIP?

THE RISE OF THE CAROLINGIANS   289

tional date of 732 is erroneous), he turned back a Muslim force from Spain at the battle of Tours (not Poitiers), some one hundred fifty miles from the Merovingian capital of Paris. Although the Muslim contingent was a raiding party rather than a full-scale army, the incursion was nonetheless the high-water mark of Umayyad progress toward northwestern Europe, and Charles's victory won him great prestige. Equally important, Charles began to develop an alliance with the English Benedictine missionaries who were attempting to convert Frisia and central Germany to Christianity. Charles's family had long been active in the drive to conquer and settle these areas, and he understood clearly how missionary work and Frankish expansion could go hand in hand. Charles readily assisted Saint Boniface and his followers in their conversion efforts. In return, the English Benedictines brought Martel and his descendants into contact with the papacy and assisted him in his efforts to reform (and so control) the Frankish church.

Charles Martel died in 741. Although Charles never sought to become king himself, during the last years of his life he was so clearly the effective ruler of Gaul that he did not even bother to arrange for a new king to be selected when, in 737, the reigning Merovingian king died. In 743, however, Martel's sons, Carloman and Pepin, bowed to the forces of legitimism, and a new Merovingian king took the throne. By 750, however, Carloman had withdrawn from public life to a monastery, and Pepin had decided to seize the throne for himself. To effect such a change in dynasties, Pepin needed the support of the Frankish church. It was highly unlikely, however, that the bishops of Merovingian Gaul would support such a usurpation without papal approval. This did not deter Pepin. Through his family's support for Saint Boniface, Pepin was already well regarded in Rome. And the papacy, locked in a bitter fight with the Byzantine emperors over Iconoclasm and with the Lombard kings for control over central Italy, proved only too happy to cooperate in Pepin's elevation, hoping that a powerful new Frankish ruler would take over from the Byzantines the responsibility for protecting papal interests in Italy against the Lombards.

In 751 Saint Boniface, acting as papal emissary, anointed Pepin as king of the Franks. The idea of anointing a newly created king with holy oil was bor-

rowed from the Bible, in which the Hebrew prophet Samuel had anointed Saul as the first king of Israel. The power of these Old Testament associations would grow under Pepin's son Charles the Great (who thus became David) and his grandson Louis the Pious (who became Solomon). In 751, however, they mainly underscored the novelty and uncertainty of the process by which the last Merovingian king was deposed and sent to a monastery, and a new king, who had not a drop of Merovingian blood, was raised to the Frankish throne for the first time in almost three centuries. In 756, Pepin repaid his debt to the pope by launching a military expedition against the Lombards in Italy; but when the expedition went badly, Pepin abandoned it and returned home. Pepin's coronation symbolized the integration of the new Frankish monarchy into the papal-Benedictine orbit. For the moment, however, Pepin had his hands full simply trying to control his new kingdom.

THE REIGN OF CHARLEMAGNE

The real consolidation of this new pattern of papal-Frankish-Benedictine relations took place during the reign of Pepin's son, Charlemagne, from whom the new dynasty takes its name of Carolingian (from "Carolus," the Latin form of "Charles"). When Charlemagne came to the throne in 768, it seemed possible that the Frankish kingdom would break up into its hostile regional parts of Austrasia, Neustria, and Aquitaine. But in an astonishing series of military campaigns, Charlemagne united the Franks by leading them on a series of conquests that annexed the Lombard kingdom of Italy, the greater part of Germany including Saxony, por-

> Charlemagne's conquest of Saxony forged the connection between conquest and conversion, which would characterize western Christian thinking for the next one thousand years.

tions of central Europe, and Catalunya. These conquests set a seal of divine approval on the new Carolingian dynasty. They also provided the plunder, booty, and new lands that enabled Charlemagne to promote his Frankish followers to dizzying heights of wealth and grandeur. Many of the peoples whom Charlemagne conquered were already Christians. In Saxony, however, Charlemagne's armies campaigned for twenty years before finally subduing the pagan Saxons and forcing their conversion to Christianity. Germany was hus forcibly integrated into the Frankish realm. Equally momentous was the connection Charlemagne's conquest of Saxony forged between conquest and conversion, which would characterize western Christian thinking for the next one thousand years.

To rule the vast empire he had conquered, Charlemagne appointed Frankish aristocrats called counts (in Latin, *comites*, meaning "followers") to supervise local administration within their territories. Among the counts' many duties were the administration of justice and the raising of armies. Charlemagne also established a network of other local administrators to supervise courts, collect tolls, administer crown lands, and extract taxation. Charlemagne also created a new coinage system, based on a division of the silver pound into two hundred forty pennies, which would last in France until the French Revolution and in Great Britain until the 1970s, when it was finally replaced by a decimal-based currency. As we have seen, much of the silver for this new coinage originated in the Abbasid empire. Scandinavian traders carried it north through Russia and the Baltic Sea, and then into the Rhineland, where they exchanged it for furs, cloth, and slaves captured in Charlemagne's wars against the Saxons, which they then transported to Baghdad.

Like Carolingian administration generally, this new monetary system depended on the regular use of writ-

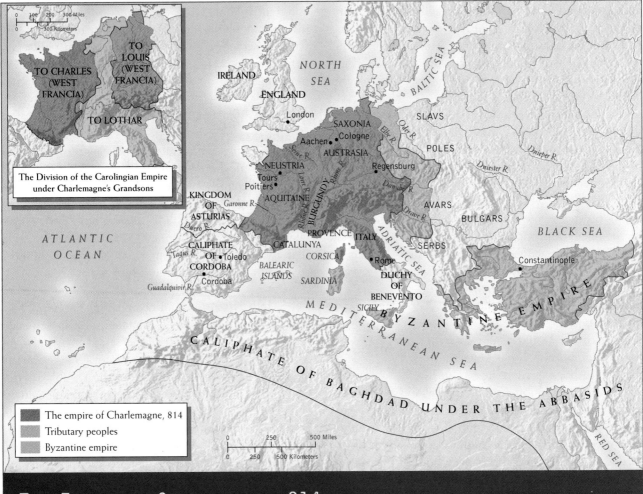

The Division of the Carolingian Empire under Charlemagne's Grandsons

■ The empire of Charlemagne, 814
■ Tributary peoples
■ Byzantine empire

THE EMPIRE OF CHARLEMAGNE, 814

Note the extent of Charlemagne's empire in 814. Could he legitimately claim to be renewing the Roman Empire? How did his possession of Rome strengthen such a claim, and how might it complicate the strong alliance between his house and the papal court? What economic and religious benefits did Charlemagne's exploitation of his large, eastern, "soft frontier" on a national level bring to his reign? Note the inset in the upper left: what does this map suggest about the power of tradition and custom in a world as supposedly "sophisticated" as the one wrought by Charlemagne?

HOW DID CHARLEMAGNE REDEFINE THE RELATIONSHIP BETWEEN CHRISTIANITY AND KINGSHIP?

THE RISE OF THE CAROLINGIANS   291

Charlemagne. A silver penny struck between 804 and 814 in Mainz (as indicated by the letter M at the bottom) showing Charlemagne in a highly stylized fasion as emperor with Roman military cloak and laurel. The inscription reads KAROLVS IMP AVG (Charles, Emperor, Augustus). Charlemagne's portrait is closely modeled upon the imperial portraits on Hellenistic and Roman coins.

ten records and instructions. But Charlemagne did not rely on the written word alone to make his will felt. Periodically he sent special representatives from his court (known as *missi*) on tours through the countryside to relay his instructions personally and check up on local administrators. Charlemagne himself also journeyed regularly around his kingdom from his capital city at Aachen, leading armies, supervising administrators, and listening to the complaints of his subjects. Charlemagne's governmental system was far from perfect. Local officials abused their positions; nobles sought to turn free peasants into unfree serfs; justice in local courts was more often denied than done. But Charlemagne's system produced nonetheless the best government Europe had seen since the Romans, and it became the model on which Western rulers would base their own administrations for the next three hundred years.

CHRISTIANITY AND KINGSHIP

Throughout his reign, Charlemagne took seriously his responsibilities as a Christian king. As his empire expanded, however, he came to see himself not only as the ruler of the Franks, but as the leader of a unified Christian society, Christendom, which he was obliged to defend both militarily and spiritually against its enemies. The Carolingian world did not make the distinc-

tions between the religious and the political realms that would characterize European life from the twelfth century on, any more than did Byzantium or Islam. Especially among churchmen, kingship in early medieval Europe was regarded as a sacred office created by God to protect the church, defend the Christian people, and promote their salvation. Religious reforms were therefore no less central to proper kingship than were justice and defense. In some ways, indeed, a king's responsibilities for his kingdom's religious life were even more important than his other responsibilities: for surely no kingdom could prosper if the lives of its subjects were displeasing to God.

These ideas about the spiritual responsibilities of kingship were not new in the late eighth century, but they took on a new importance as a result of the extraordinary power Charlemagne wielded over his empire. Like other early medieval kings, Charlemagne appointed and deposed bishops and abbots, just as he did his counts and other officials. But he also changed the liturgy of the Frankish church, reformed rules of worship in Frankish monasteries, declared changes in basic statements of Christian belief, prohibited pagan observances, enforced tithes on the Frankish peasantry (a tithe was a tenth of peasant's produce, owed to the church), and imposed basic Christian observances, including baptism, on the conquered peoples of Saxony. To Charlemagne, such measures were clearly required if God's new Israel, the Franks, were to avoid the fate that befell biblical Israel whenever its people turned away from their obedience to God.

As the dominant political power in central Italy, Charlemagne was also the protector of the papacy. Although carefully acknowledging the pope's role as the spiritual leader of western Christianity, Charlemagne dealt with the pope much as he did with the other bishops of the Frankish empire. He supervised and approved papal elections, while protecting the pope against his enemies. In 796, just after the election of Pope Leo III, Charlemagne explained the relationship between his authority and that of the pope in the following words: "It is for us," wrote Charlemagne to Leo, "in accordance with the help of divine goodness, outwardly to defend by force of arms the Holy Church of Christ in all places from the incursions of pagans and the ravages of infidels, and inwardly to fortify her with our confession of the Catholic faith. It is for you, most holy father . . . to aid our armies, to the end that with you as intercessor and with God as guide and giver, our Christian people may in all places have the victory over the enemies of its holy name, and that the name of Our Lord Jesus Christ may be renowned throughout all the world."

THE CAROLINGIAN RENAISSANCE

Similar ideals lay behind the Carolingian Renaissance, a cultural and intellectual flowering that took place around the Carolingian royal court. Like their biblical exemplars, the Hebrew kings David and Solomon, Charlemagne and Louis the Pious took seriously their role as patrons of poetry and learning. In so doing, they created an ideal of the court as an intellectual and culture center that would profoundly influence Western European cultural life until the end of the nineteenth century. What lay behind the Carolingians' support for scholarship, however, was their conviction that classical learning was the foundation on which Christian wisdom rested, and that such wisdom was essential to the salvation of God's people. Supporting scholarship was therefore a paramount obligation for a Christian king.

To promote classical learning and Christian wisdom, Charlemagne recruited scholars from throughout Europe to his court, including the English Benedictine monk Alcuin, whose command of classical Latin grammar established him as the intellectual leader of Charlemagne's court school. Carolingian scholars produced a good deal of original Latin poetry and an impressive number of theological and pastoral tracts. Under Alcuin, however, their primary efforts were devoted to collating, correcting and recopying classical Latin texts, including, most important, the text of the Latin Bible, which had become corrupted by generations of copyists' mistakes. To detect and correct these errors, Alcuin and his associates gathered as many different versions of the biblical text as they could find and compared them word by word. After determining the correct version among all the variants, they made a new, corrected copy and destroyed the other versions. They also developed a new style of hand-writing, with simplified letter forms and spaces inserted between words, that further reduced the likelihood that subsequent copyists would misread the corrected texts. Although modified again by Italian Renaissance scholars in the fifteenth century, this new style of handwriting, known as Carolingian miniscule, is the foundation for the typefaces in which almost all European books, including this one, are still printed.

CHARLEMAGNE AND THE REVIVAL OF THE WESTERN ROMAN EMPIRE

The climax of Charlemagne's career came in Rome on Christmas Day 800, when he was crowned as the new Roman emperor in the West by Pope Leo III. Centuries later, popes would cite their role in this event as precedent for the political superiority they claimed over the Holy Roman emperor (a title that became common only in the twelfth century, but that can be used for convenience to designate the Western emperors from Charlemagne on). In the year 800, however, Pope Leo was entirely under Charlemagne's thumb. Although Charlemagne said later that he would never have gone to church that day had he known Leo's plans to crown him, it is highly unlikely Pope Leo would have mounted such a coronation ceremony with-

Carolingian Handwriting. Even the untrained reader has little difficulty in reading this excerpt from a Carolingian manuscript. For example, the first two words in the heading read "Incipit Liber," and the two words below them "Haec Hannibal."

CHARLEMAGNE ON THE IMPORTANCE OF MONKS STUDYING CLASSICAL LITERATURE

To Charlemagne and his contemporaries, a Christian king bore total responsibility for the salvation of his people. To this end, Charlemagne believed it essential to encourage the study of both classical and Christian literature within his kingdom. Copies of this letter were probably sent to most of the monasteries in the Frankish kingdom.

We, Charles, by the grace of God king of the Franks and Lombards and patrician of the Romans, to Abbot Baugulf and all your congregation. . . . Be it known to your devotion . . . that we, along with our faithful advisers, have deemed it useful that the bishoprics and monasteries, which through the favor of Christ have been entrusted to us to govern should, in addition to the way of life prescribed by their rule and their practice of holy religion, devote their efforts to the study of literature and to the teaching of it . . . so . . . that those who seek to please God by living aright may not fail to please him also by rightness in their speaking. . . . For . . . letters have often been sent to us in these last years from certain monasteries . . . and we found that in most of these writings their sentiments were sound but their speech uncouth. . . . And so . . . we began to fear that their lack of knowledge of writing might be matched by a more serious lack of wisdom in the understanding of holy scripture. We all know well that, dangerous as are the errors of words, yet much more dangerous are the errors of doctrine. Wherefore we urge you, not merely to avoid the neglect of the study of literature, but . . . to strive to learn it, so that you may be able more easily and more rightly to penetrate the mysteries of the holy scriptures. For since there are figures of speech, metaphors and the like to be found on the sacred pages, there can be no doubt that each man who reads them will understand their spiritual meaning more quickly if he is first of all given full instruction in the study of literature. . . . For we want you, as befits the soldiers of the Church, to be inwardly devout and outwardly learned, pure in good living and scholarly in speech; so that whoever comes to see you in the name of God and for the inspiration of your holy converse, just as he is strengthened by the sight of you, so he may be instructed also by your wisdom, both in reading and chanting, and return rejoicing, giving thanks to Almighty God.

H. R. Loyn and J. Percival, eds. *The Reign of Charlemagne.* Documents of Medieval History 2. (London: Edward Arnold, 1975), pp. 63–64.

out Charlemagne's knowledge or consent, not least because it was certain to anger the Byzantines, with whom Charlemagne already had strained relations. Nor did the imperial title add much to Charlemagne's position as king of the Franks. Why, then, did he accept it, and in 813 transfer it to his son, Louis the Pious?

Historians do not know. What is clear, however, is the symbolic significance of the action. Until 800 only the Roman emperor who ruled in Constantinople could lay claim to being the direct heir of Caesar Augustus. Although the Byzantines had lost most of their influence in the West, they continued to regard it vaguely as an outlying province of their empire. Charlemagne's assumption of the imperial title was a clear slap in the face to the Byzantines, who were already suspicious of Charlemagne's relationship with Byzantium's enemy Harun al-Rashid, the Abbasid caliph in Baghdad. In the West, however, it was a declaration of self-confidence and independence that was never forgotten. With only occasional interruptions, western Europeans would continue to crown Roman emperors until the nineteenth century, when Napoleon retired the title. Whatever his specific motives may have been, Charlemagne's revival of the western Roman empire proved to be a major step in the developing self-consciousness of western European civilization.

THE COLLAPSE OF THE CAROLINGIAN EMPIRE

When Charlemagne died in 814, his empire descended intact to his only surviving son, Louis the Pious. Under Louis, however, the empire rapidly began to disintegrate. When Louis died in 843, the empire was divided between his three sons. Western Francia, which became France, went to Charles the Bald; Eastern Francia, which became Germany, went to Louis the German; and the so-called Middle Kingdom, stretching from the Rhineland to Rome, went to Lothair, along with the imperial title. When Lothair's line died out in 856, a civil war erupted between the East Franks and the West Franks for control over Lothair's former

---

CHRONOLOGY

THE RISE OF THE CAROLINGIAN EMPIRE, 717–814 C.E.

Charles Martel becomes mayor of the palace	717
The Carolingians (Charles, Pepin, and Carloman) share power with the Merovingian kings	717–751
Pepin becomes king of the Franks	751
Charlemagne succeeds Pepin	768
Charlemagne is crowned Holy Roman emperor	800
Louis the Pious becomes emperor	813
Charlemagne dies	814

---

territories and the imperial mantle. Lotharingia (or, in French, Alsace-Lorraine) would remain a flashpoint for hostilities between France and Germany until the end of the Second World War.

The collapse of the Carolingian empire is often blamed on Louis the Pious' incapacity as a ruler, but this is much too simple. Louis was not an incompetent ruler, but he faced an almost impossible task in trying to hold together the empire his father had created. Charlemagne's empire had been built on successful conquest. By 814, however, Charlemagne had pushed the borders of his empire as far as they could reasonably go. To the west, he now faced the Umayyad rulers of Spain; to the north, the Vikings; in the east, his armies were too preoccupied with settling the German territories they had already conquered to push far into the Slavic lands that lay beyond them. The pressures that had driven the Frankish conquests, however—the need for booty, land, and plunder with which to reward and promote one's followers—had become even more pronounced as a result of Charlemagne's successes. Under Charlemagne, the number of counts in the Frankish empire had tripled, from approximately one hundred to three hundred. Louis the Pious could not possibly turn three hundred counts into nine hundred. The resources to do so simply did not exist.

Frustrated by their emperor's inability to reward them, Frankish nobles turned on each other. Civil wars erupted among Louis' quarrelsome and difficult sons; regional hostilities between Austrasians, Neustrians, and Aquitanians flared up again. As central imperial authority broke down, free peasants, a critical group in the eighth-century Carolingian world, found themselves increasingly under the thumb of powerful local nobles who treated them as if they were unfree serfs, bound to the soil and forbidden to leave it. At the same time, internal troubles in the Abbasid empire caused a breakdown in the foreign trade routes through which Viking traders brought Abbasid silver into Carolingian domains. The Vikings then turned to destructive raiding along the coasts and up the river systems. Under these combined pressures the Carolingian empire fell apart completely, and a new political map of Europe began to emerge.

THE LEGACY OF THE CAROLINGIANS

Just the Carolingian period was crucial for marking the beginnings of a common North Atlantic, western European civilization, so the tenth century was crucial for marking the beginnings of the major modern Euro-

HOW DID CHARLEMAGNE REDEFINE THE RELATIONSHIP BETWEEN CHRISTIANITY AND KINGSHIP?

THE RISE OF THE CAROLINGIANS   295

Viking Dragon Head.
Wooden carvings like these
on the stemposts of Viking
ships were calculated to inspire terror.

pean political entities. England, which never had been part of Charlemagne's empire, and which hitherto had been divided among smaller warring Anglo-Saxon states, became unified in the late ninth and the tenth century owing to the work of King Alfred the Great (871–899) and his successors. Alfred and his heirs re-organized the army, infused new vigor into local gov-ernment, founded new towns, and codified English laws. In addition, Alfred established a court school and fostered an interest in Anglo-Saxon writing and other elements of a national culture. In all these re-spects, Alfred modeled himself closely on Carolingian example. His success in defending his own West Saxon kingdom from Viking attacks, combined with the destruction of every other competing Anglo-Saxon royal dynasty by the Vikings, allowed Alfred and his successors to claim for themselves the mantle of a single, united English monarchy. The increasing prosperity of the country, largely a product of the wool trade, also brought increasing power to the monarchy. By the year 1000, Anglo-Saxon England had become the most administratively sophisticated state in western Christian Europe.

On the Continent, the most powerful monarchs of the tenth century were the dukes of Saxony, who be-came kings of Germany (East Francia) in 917, after the Carolingian line of kings expired. Like the West Saxon kings of England, the Saxon kings of Germany mod-eled their kingship closely on Carolingian example. They drew, however, on different aspects of their com-mon Carolingian inheritance. Tenth-century England became a highly effective administrative monarchy, with a centralized monetary and judicial system and extensive control over towns and trade. In Germany, by contrast, royal power in the tenth century rested much more on the profits of successful conquest than it did on the profits of trade and administration. In the eighth century, the Carolingians had built their power on successful conquests in Saxony. In the tenth cen-tury, the Ottonian kings of Germany, based in Saxony, built their authority on successful conquests into the Slavic lands that lay on their "soft" eastern frontier. They were also careful to nurture their image as Chris-tian kings on the Carolingian model. In 955, Otto I de-feated the pagan Hungarians in a decisive battle while carrying a sacred lance that had once belonged to Charlemagne. This victory established Otto as the dominant power in central Europe and as a man wor-thy to inherit Charlemagne's imperial throne. In 962 Otto went to Rome to be crowned western emperor by the pope, a thoroughly dissolute young man named John XII, who hoped to use Otto in his own factional squabbles in Rome. Otto, however, refused to go home when Pope John had no further use for him. Scandal-ized by John's behavior as pope, Otto instead deposed John, and selected a new pope to replace him.

By becoming emperor, Otto hoped to strengthen his control over the church in Germany and to claim a va-riety of dormant but potentially lucrative imperial rights in northern Italy and Burgundy, parts of the "Middle Kingdom" once held by the emperor Lothair. Protecting the papacy was, of course, Otto's responsi-bility as a Carolingian-style emperor, but Otto also needed papal support to achieve these other, more concrete, objectives. In Italy, however, Otto quickly discovered that unless he was prepared to remain there full time, he could not even control the papacy, much less the rapidly growing and highly independent towns of northern Italy. If he remained in Italy too long, how-ever, his authority in Saxony would break down, as local lords began to lead and profit from the continu-ing conquests in the Slavic east. Balancing their local concerns in Saxony with their imperial concerns in Italy presented a dilemma neither Otto I nor his son (Otto II, 973–983) nor his grandson (Otto III, 983–1002) were able to solve. The result was a gradu-ally increasing alienation of the Saxon nobility from their emperor. This alienation accelerated dramatically

The Crown of the Tenth-Century Holy Roman Emperors.

after 1024, when the German throne passed to a new dynasty, the Salians, centered not in Saxony but in Franconia. It was not until the 1070s that the Salian king Henry IV finally attempted to reassert his control over the formerly royal lands in Saxony and the Slavic east. When he did so, he touched off a civil war between himself and the Saxon nobility that was to have momentous repercussions not only for Germany, but for the entirety of western Europe. The consequences of this great Saxon war are discussed more fully in Chapter Ten.

Aspects of the Carolingian inheritance also survived in the tenth-century Mediterranean world. In Catalunya, counts descended from Carolingian appointees continued to administer public, territorial law through a system of public courts throughout the tenth century. Free peasants prospered as they settled new lands. Classical and Christian learning flourished in reformed Benedictine abbeys and cathedrals. The counts drew their revenues from public fiscal lands and from tolls on a rapidly expanding trade; and the city of Barcelona grew rapidly as both a long-distance and a regional market under the protection of the Catalunyan counts. In Aquitaine also, the counts of Poitiers and Toulouse continued to rest their authority on Carolingian foun-

dations until the eleventh century, when in both Aquitaine and Catalunya these Carolingian traditions of public authority finally collapsed.

The tenth century also witnessed a remarkable growth of towns and cities in western Europe, particularly in areas where rulers patterned themselves on Carolingian example. In Anglo-Saxon England, the West Saxon kings established new towns and encouraged existing ones. They tightly regulated coinage and encouraged the growth of marketing, not least by insisting that the taxation they collected be paid in coin. By 1066, when England fell to the invading Normans, at least 10 percent of the English population lived in towns, making it the most highly urbanized country in eleventh-century Europe. Cities also grew rapidly in the Low Countries and the Rhineland, fueled by long-distance trade (especially in wool and wool cloth) and by the discovery of silver deposits in the mountains of Saxony. In Catalunya, the growth of Barcelona was beginning to transform the political and social life of the country; while in Aquitaine, both Poitiers and Toulouse prospered from their location along the overland trade route that connected Mediterranean with Atlantic Europe.

In tenth- and eleventh-century Italy, urban growth occurred in the absence of an effective Carolingian-style ruler. Instead, the prosperity of tenth-century Italian cities depended on the success of the Byzantine emperors in suppressing Muslim piracy in the eastern Mediterranean. The most prosperous cities in tenth-century Italy lay in the Byzantine-controlled areas of the peninsula: Venice in the north, Amalfi, Naples, and Palermo in the south. Their prosperity rested upon their role in the carrying trade that brought silks, spices, and other luxury goods from the Byzantine and Muslim worlds into western Europe. In the eleventh century, however, Norman invasions of southern Italy disrupted this trade, as Turkish invasions of Asia Minor turned Byzantine attentions eastward. By the end of the eleventh century, it would be the north Italian cities whose navies would control the eastern Mediterranean, and which would profit from their role as middlemen in the lucrative traffic between Byzantium, the Muslim world, and western Europe.

On the Carolingian heartland, however, these developments had little influence. Here, Carolingian-style kingship disintegrated during the tenth century under the combined weight of Viking raids, economic collapse, and the growing power of local lords. In some areas, a few Carolingian institutions, such as public courts and a centrally minted coinage, survived in

HOW DID CHARLEMAGNE REDEFINE THE RELATIONSHIP BETWEEN CHRISTIANITY AND KINGSHIP?

THE RISE OF THE CAROLINGIANS   297

EUROPE IN THE ELEVENTH CENTURY

This map shows the alignment of geopolitical power that had emerged by 1050, a few generations after the final collapse of Carolingian rule. What states appeared to be the most dominant ones in this world? What recent successes could a resurgent Byzantium claim? What advantages did the German rulers of the empire possess in terms of resources and their strategic position in northern and central Italy? Note the position of Kievan Russia. In what ways was its development affected by the West, and in what respects was it isolated from the Western experience? What disadvantages or challenges did these various powers face?

the hands of counts and dukes who utilized them in building up new, essentially autonomous territorial principalities in Anjou, Normandy, Flanders, and Aquitaine. Elsewhere in France, even this modicum of continuity with the Carolingian world disappeared. France still had a king who continued to be recognized as the ruler of the western part of Charlemagne's former territories. After 987, however, the kings of France were no longer Carolingians. Instead, a new dynasty, the Capetians, had taken the throne, after having established their reputation as Counts of Paris by defending that city against the Vikings. But it would be another century before the Capetian kings of France could begin to reverse the trends that had destroyed their predecessors, and begin again to rebuild monarchical power in France upon new foundations.

CONCLUSION

This spectacle of Carolingian collapse may suggest that little had changed in western Europe between 750 and 1000. Any such impression would, however, be seriously misleading. It is certainly true that compared with Byzantium or the Muslim world, western Europe remained an intellectual and cultural backwater, more so perhaps by the year 1000 than it had been two centuries before. Politically, no western European ruler in the year 1000 could approach the power of the Byzantine emperor or the Umayyad caliph of Córdoba. Economically also, western Europe was a dependency of Byzantium and Islam, importing finished and luxury goods, and exporting furs, leather, and slaves. Beneath the surface, however, western European society was becoming steadily more formidable. Urbanization was proceeding rapidly on the margins of the collapsing Carolingian world. Long-distance trade was also growing. Italian traders were active in Constantinople, and Muslim traders were common in the south Italian ports. Anglo-Saxon merchants were regular visitors to Italy, the Low Countries and the Rhineland. Jewish merchants in the Rhineland were carrying on an active trade with the Jewish communities of Muslim Egypt, while Viking traders had reopened the trade routes from the Baltic through Russia to the Black Sea and were busily founding cities from Novgorod to Dublin.

Western Europe's borders were also expanding. By the year 1000, its boundaries extended from the Baltic to the Mediterranean Sea, and from the Pyrenees to Poland. Within this vast territory, moreover, every ruler was, or would soon be, Christian. The Christian church was as yet highly localized, but the emergence of new confederations of reformed Benedictine monasteries under papal protection (to be discussed in more detail in Chapter Ten) was beginning to point the way toward a more unified and centralized Latin Christian church. Political omens were less promising. But out of the chaos of tenth-century western Europe, effective territorial principalities and kingdoms were beginning to emerge. During the early Middle Ages, Europe had become a society mobilized for war to a degree unmatched in either Byzantium or Islam. This was, to be sure, a mixed blessing. In the centuries to come, however, the militarization of western European society was to prove a decisive factor in the steadily shifting balance of power between Europe, Byzantium and the Muslim world.

SELECTED READINGS

Arberry, Arthur John. *The Koran Interpreted.* 2 volumes. London, 1955.

Bede. *A History of the English Church and People.* Trans. by Leo Sherley-Price. Baltimore, 1955. A fascinating account by the greatest historian of eighth-century Europe.

Brand, Charles M., ed. *Icon and Minaret: Sources of Byzantine and Islamic Civilization.* Englewood Cliffs, N.J., 1969.

Campbell, James, ed. *The Anglo-Saxons.* Oxford, 1982. The best and most interesting treatment of its subject, splendidly illustrated.

Collins, Roger. *Early Medieval Europe, 300–1000.* 2d ed. New York, 1999. Dry and detailed, but a useful textbook nonetheless.

———. *Early Medieval Spain: Unity in Diversity 400–1000.* New York, 1983. An excellent introduction, written for students, that gives equal attention to Visigothic and Umayyad Spain.

Donner, Fred. *The Early Islamic Conquests.* Princeton, 1981. A scholarly but readable narrative and analysis.

Einhard and Notker the Stammerer. *Two Lives of Charlemagne.* Trans. by Lewis Thorpe. Baltimore, 1969. Lively and entertaining.

Fletcher, Richard A. *The Barbarian Conversion: From Paganism to Christianity.* Berkeley, 1999. Slow paced but informative, perceptive, and enjoyable to read.

———. *Moorish Spain.* Berkeley, 1993. The best short survey in English.

Geanakoplos, Deno John, ed. *Byzantium: Church, Society and Civilization Seen through Contemporary Eyes.* Chicago, 1984. An outstanding source book, with a great deal of fresh material.

Geary, Patrick J. *Before France and Germany: The Origins and Transformation of the Merovingian World.* New York, 1988. Accessible introduction to recent scholarship, much of it otherwise unavailable in English.

Gibb, H. A. R. *Arabic Literature: An Introduction,* 2d ed. Oxford, 1974. An excellent survey.

Godman, Peter, and Roger Collins. *Charlemagne's Heir: New Perspectives on the Reign of Louis the Pious (814–840).* Oxford, 1990. A massive collection of revisionist essays by almost all of the top scholars in the field.

Gregory of Tours. *History of the Franks.* Trans. by Lewis Thorpe.

Baltimore, 1974. Difficult to follow, but by far the most revealing single source on Merovingian kingship.

Herrin, Judith. *The Formation of Christendom*. Princeton, 1987. A synthetic history of the Christian civilizations of Byzantium and western Europe from 500 to 800 C.E., written by a prominent Byzantinist.

Hodges, Richard. *Dark Age Economics: The Origins of Towns and Trade*, A.D. 600–1000. London, 1982. Emphasizes the importance of trade connections between early medieval Europe and the Islamic world.

Hodges, Richard, and David Whitehouse. *Mohammed, Charlemagne and the Origins of Europe*. London, 1983. An analysis and recasting of the "Pirenne thesis," which claimed (wrongly, as this book shows) that the advent of Islam disrupted the economic unity of the Mediterranean world.

Hourani, Albert. *A History of the Arab Peoples*. New York, 1992. A sympathetic, clear, and intelligent survey written for non-specialists.

Hussey, Joan M. *The Byzantine World*. 4th ed. London, 1970. A useful short introduction that combines narrative with topical chapters.

———. *The Orthodox Church in the Byzantine Empire*. Oxford, 1986. A broad but deep and sophisticated survey.

Kazhdan, Alexander P., ed. *The Oxford Dictionary of Byzantium*. 3 volumes. Oxford, 1991. An authoritative reference work.

Kennedy, Hugh. *The Early Abbasid Caliphate: A Political History*. Totowa, N.J., 1981. A standard account.

———. *The Prophet and the Age of the Caliphates*. London, 1986. A lucid introduction to the political history of Islam from the sixth through the eleventh centuries.

Krautheimer, Richard. *Early Christian and Byzantine Architecture*. 4th ed. New York, 1986. A classic work by one of the greatest Byzantine art historians of the twentieth century.

Leyser, Karl. *Rule and Conflict in an Early Medieval Society: Ottonian Saxony*. Oxford, 1979. A concise, challenging, brilliant account of the dynamics of rule in tenth-century Saxony, that pays special attention to the importance of royal women.

Loyn, Henry R., and John Percival, eds. and trans. *The Reign of Charlemagne*. London, 1975. An excellent collection of sources; not easy to find, but worth the trouble.

Mango, Cyril. *Art of the Byzantine Empire*, 312–1453. Englewood Cliffs, N.J., 1972. A standard survey.

———. *Byzantium: The Empire of New Rome*. London, 1980. A traditional but still valuable picture of Byzantine civilization.

McKitterick, Rosamond. *The Frankish Kingdoms Under the Carolingians*, 751–987. New York, 1983. An authoritative account of politics and intellectual developments.

———, ed. *The Uses of Literacy in Early Medieval Europe*. New York, 1990. A superb collection of essays representing some of the freshest recent thinking on this subject.

McNamara, Jo Ann, and John E. Halborg, eds. *Sainted Women of the Dark Ages*. Durham., N.C., 1992. Translated saints' lives from Merovingian and Carolingian Europe.

Obolensky, Dmitri. *Byzantium and the Slavs*. Crestwood, N.Y., 1994. The classic survey of the Byzantine empire's relations with the Balkans.

Ostrogorsky, George. *History of the Byzantine State*, rev. ed. New Brunswick, N.J., 1969. A classic political history.

Pelikan, Jaroslav. *The Christian Tradition, Volume II: The Spirit of Eastern Christendom*. Chicago, 1974. An outstanding synthetic treatment of the doctrines of Byzantine Christianity.

Peters, F. E. *Aristotle and the Arabs*. New York, 1968. Well written and engaging.

Reuter, Timothy. *Germany in the Early Middle Ages*, 800–1056. New York, 1991. The best and most up-to-date survey in English.

Saint Boniface. *Letters of Saint Boniface*. Trans. by Ephraim Emerton. New York, 1972.

Sawyer, Peter, ed. *The Oxford Illustrated History of the Vikings*. Oxford, 1997. The best one-volume account, lavishly illustrated.

Stillman, Norman A. *The Jews of Arab Lands: A History and Source Book*. Philadelphia, 1979. An essential resource.

Todd, Malcolm. *The Early Germans*. Oxford, 1992. A reliable survey, particularly strong in its use of archaeological evidence.

Treadgold, Warren. *A History of the Byzantine State and Society*. Stanford, 1997. A massive, encyclopedic narrative of the political, economic, and military history of Byzantium from 284 until 1461.

Wallace-Hadrill, John Michael. *The Barbarian West*, 400–1000. 3d ed. London, 1967. More a set of interpretive essays than a conventional textbook, this book remains the most stimulating introduction to its subject.

———. *Early Germanic Kingship in England and on the Continent*. Oxford, 1971. A remarkably interesting analysis of changing ideas about the nature and responsibilities of kingship in early medieval Europe, emphasizing the links between Anglo-Saxon and Carolingian theories of kingship.

———. *The Frankish Church*. Oxford, 1983. A masterful account that links together the Merovingian and the Carolingian churches.

Watt, W. Montgomery. *Islamic Philosophy and Theology*, 2d ed. Edinburgh, 1985. The standard English account.

Wemple, Suzanne Fonay. *Women in Frankish Society: Marriage and the Cloister*, 500–900. Philadelphia, 1981. An influential account of changing attitudes toward marriage among the early Franks.

Whittow, Mark. *The Making of Orthodox Byzantium*, 600–1025. London, 1996. Emphasizes the centrality of orthodoxy in shaping Byzantine history. Particularly good on Byzantine relations with the peoples outside the empire.

Wood, Ian. *The Merovingian Kingdoms*, 450–751. New York, 1994. Full of the latest thinking, but detailed and difficult for beginners.

THE EXPANSION OF
EUROPE: ECONOMY,
SOCIETY, AND
POLITICS IN THE
HIGH MIDDLE AGES,
1000–1300

BETWEEN 1000 AND 1300, the balance of power between western Europe, Byzantium, and the Islamic world shifted profoundly. In the year 1000, Europe remained politically fractured and militarily threatened by Viking, Magyar, and Muslim attacks. Although towns in western Europe were beginning to grow, none could compare in size or sophistication with the ancient Mediterranean cities of Byzantium and the Islamic world. Economically, western Europe continued to depend on Byzantine and Islamic traders for its cotton, silk, spices, and precious metals. With respect to literature and learning, the imbalances were even greater. Europeans knew only a small portion of the cultural and intellectual riches Byzantium and Islam had inherited from the classical world. Outside Sicily, Venice, and the Muslim-controlled areas of Spain, western Europeans knew no Arabic and virtually no Greek. Even Latin, the language of western learning for more than a thousand years, was increasingly a foreign tongue. King Alfred (871–899) complained that in his day hardly anyone in England knew enough Latin to perform correctly the services of the Christian church. A century later, Latin learning in England and Germany was somewhat better. In France and Italy it was probably worse.

By the year 1300, however, Europe was the dominant military, economic, and political power among the three western successor civilizations to Greece and Rome. Hungary, Poland, and Bohemia were now thoroughly integrated parts of a Catholic, European world. Combining conquest with conversion, European Christians had forcefully pushed their borders eastward into Prussia, Lithuania, Livonia, and the Balkans. They had conquered Spain from the Muslims and Constantinople from the Byzantines. They had also established (and in 1300, just lost) a Latin kingdom in the Middle East, with its capital at Jerusalem. European navies controlled the Mediterranean Sea and had outposts on the Black Sea and the Caspian Sea, allowing

FOCUS QUESTIONS

• What impact did the first agricultural revolution have on the lives of Europeans?

• What were the major causes of urban growth during the High Middle Ages?

• How did the First Crusade alter the balance of power between Europe and Byzantium?

• What was the relationship between chivalry and the cult of "courtly love"?

• How did government and politics change in the High Middle Ages?

• What was the relationship between feudalism and the rise of national monarchies?

European traders to dominate the long-distance trade routes that brought eastern luxury goods into western Europe. European missionaries and traders were beginning to follow these trade routes back through Central Asia, opening up connections with Mongolia and China; to the west, Italian merchants had initiated a seaborne trade route through the Strait of Gibraltar, thus connecting the Mediterranean and the north Atlantic world.

This expansion of European commerce, both local and long distance, was accompanied by significant urbanization. By 1300, Europe could claim at least a dozen cities with populations between fifty thousand and one hundred thousand people, with hundreds of smaller towns and cities scattered across the landscape. The growth of cities mirrored the general growth in the European poulation which, on a rough estimate, tripled between 1000 and 1300. The economy grew even more rapidly, however, leading to increased per capita wealth and a rising standard of living. By no means, however, were these economic gains distributed equally among the entire population. Governments grew more powerful, and social stratification increased. New wealth increased the demand for luxury goods among social elites, but it also freed up huge sums of money for investment in agriculture, commerce, and construction. It fueled remarkable new religious, cultural, and intellectual developments, which will be discussed in the next chapter.

Not all of this growth proved sustainable. By 1300, living standards for many Europeans were falling as western Europe began to approach the demographic limits of its natural resources. More powerful governments kept better internal peace, but they also claimed a larger proportion of their subjects' wealth, which they used to support bigger armies and grander campaigns of conquest and domination. In the fourteenth century, famine, war, and plague reduced the European population by at least a third, fundamentally transforming the economic, political, and social order of the High Middle Ages. Despite these setbacks, however, the predominance western Europe established over Byzantium and the Islamic world during the High Middle Ages would endure, providing the foundation on which the European world empires of the modern era would be built.

THE FIRST AGRICULTURAL REVOLUTION

What impact did the first agricultural revolution have on the lives of Europeans?

Like all premodern economies, the western European economy in the Middle Ages rested on agriculture. Change in agricultural practices tends to be slow; even so, it may seem absurd to speak of agricultural changes that took place across six hundred years as constituting a "revolution." In western Europe, however, the agricultural changes that took place between 700 and 1300 were so sweeping, and their consequences so profound, that comparisons with the more famous agricultural revolution of the early eighteenth century seem justified. Technological innovations, combined with an improved climate, new crop rotation systems, and increased investment in tools, livestock, and mills, increased the productivity of European agriculture dramatically. As agricultural productivity increased, so too did the marketing of agricultural surpluses, leading to increased specialization of production with resulting efficiencies of scale. Without these changes, western Europe could never have supported the tripling of its overall population, or the massive investments in buildings, ships, books, armies, and art that shaped the high medieval world.

> The agricultural changes that took place in western Europe between 700 and 1300 were so sweeping, and their consequences so profound, that comparisons with the more famous agricultural revolution of the early eighteenth century seem justified.

TECHNOLOGICAL ADVANCES

The basic technological advances that made possible the increasing productivity of high medieval agriculture were developed in the early Middle Ages. The heavy-wheeled plow, fitted with an iron-tipped coulter and dragged by a team of oxen, could cut and turn the rich, wet soil of northern Europe to a depth impossible for the Mediterranean scratch plow to reach, thus aerating the soil and providing excellent drainage for water-logged territories. The new plow also saved labor, allowing more frequent plowing and better control of weeds. Related improvements in collars and harnesses increased the efficiency of plow oxen, and made

WHAT IMPACT DID THE FIRST AGRICULTURAL REVOLUTION HAVE ON THE LIVES OF EUROPEANS?

THE FIRST AGRICULTURAL REVOLUTION 303

Light Plow and Heavy Plow. Note that the peasant using the light plow (above) had to press his foot on it to give it added weight. The major innovation of the heavy plow (often wheeled, as shown below) was the long moldboard, which turned over the ground after the plowshare cut into it. The picture below depicts a second crucial medieval invention as well—the padded horse collar, which allowed horses to throw their full weight into pulling.

it possible for the first time for horses to pull heavy loads without choking themselves. Oxen remained the most commonly used plow animals in Europe until at least the fourteenth century. They were cheaper, more powerful, and less prone to disease than were horses, and when they died they could be eaten. Horses, however, were faster and more efficient cart animals, especially after the development of iron horseshoes (around 900) and tandem harnessing (around 1050),

which allowed horses to pull behind each other. As marketing of agricultural produce increased during the twelfth and thirteenth centuries, so too, therefore, did the prevalence of horses in the European countryside.

Other labor-saving devices further increased the productivity of high medieval agriculture. Despite the advent of the heavy-wheeled plow, most of the work of raising crops continued to be done by individual peasant farmers using hand tools. As iron became more

Medieval Windmill. The peasant on the left is bringing his grain in a sack to be ground into flour. Note that the mill is built on a pivot so that it can rotate in the direction of any prevailing wind.

common during the High Middle Ages, the quality of these hand tools steadily improved. Iron-tipped hoes, forks, and shovels were much more effective than the wooden implements with which most eighth-century farmers had had to make do; the increasing number of iron sickles and scythes permitted speedier and more efficient harvesting of hay and grain, especially by women, whose field labor was critically important, particularly during harvesttime. Wheelbarrows were another homely but important technological innovation. So too was the harrow, a tool drawn over the field after the plow to level the earth and mix in the seed. Technology also had an impact on cooking techniques, and hence on nutrition. Iron pots allowed food to be boiled rather than just warmed, reducing the chances of contamination; communal ovens preserved a larger share of the nutrients in food than did boiling.

Mills represented another major technological innovation in food processing. The Romans had known about water mills but hardly used them, relying instead upon human- and animal-powered wheels to grind grain into flour. Starting around 1050, however, there was a veritable craze in northern Europe for building water mills of steadily increasing efficiency. One French area saw a growth from fourteen water mills in the eleventh century to sixty in the twelfth; in another part of France about forty mills were built between 850 and 1080, forty more between 1080 and 1125, and 245 between 1126 and 1175. Once Europeans had mas-

tered the complex technology of building water mills, they turned their attention to windmills, which proliferated rapidly from the 1170s on, especially in flat lands such as Holland that had no swiftly flowing streams. Although the major use of mills was to grind grain, they could be adapted to drive saws, process cloth, press oil, provide power for iron forges, and crush pulp for manufacturing paper. The importance of such mills cannot be overstated. They would remain the world's only source of mechanical power for manufacturing until the nineteenth-century invention of the steam engine.

With the exception of the windmill and tandem harnessing, most of the technological innovations that lay behind the medieval agricultural revolution were already known to the Carolingians. Only from the mid-eleventh century, however, did these innovations become sufficiently widespread as to have a decisive effect on European agricultural production. Various explanations for this delay have been offered. Climatic change must have played some role; but although the warming climate benefited northern Europe by drying the soil and lengthening the growing season, it hurt Mediterranean agriculture in equal measure. Greater physical security also played a role. Viking, Magyar, and Muslim attacks were decreasing, and more powerful governments kept better domestic peace than they had been able to do a century before. The fundamental change, however, lay in the growing confidence of en-

WHAT IMPACT DID THE FIRST AGRICULTURAL REVOLUTION HAVE ON THE LIVES OF EUROPEANS?

THE FIRST AGRICULTURAL REVOLUTION   305

trepreneurial peasants and lords that if they invested labor and money in agricultural improvements, they would profit from the resulting surpluses. More than anything else, it was the expanding demand for agricultural produce that encouraged peasants and landlords to make productive investments in the land. Behind the growing demand for foodstuffs lay the two fundamental economic factors that drove the high medieval economy forward: a rapidly increasing European population, and an increasingly efficient market for goods.

MANORIALISM, SERFDOM, AND AGRICULTURAL PRODUCTIVITY

In England, northern France, and western Germany, increasing use of the heavy-wheeled plow between 800 and 1050 coincided with a fundamental change in patterns of peasant settlement. During the early

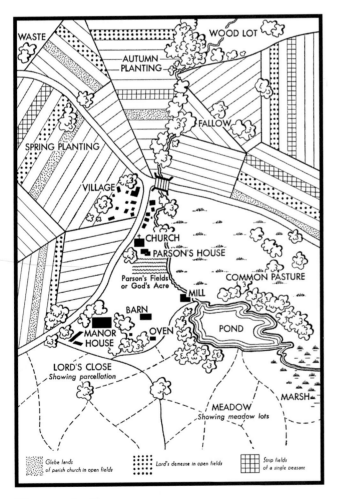

Diagram of a Manor.

Middle Ages, most free peasant farmers lived on individual plots of land that they farmed with their own resources, and for which they paid their landlord some kind of customary rent. Starting in the ninth century, however, many of these individual peasant holdings began to be consolidated into large, common fields that were farmed communally by peasants living in villages. The resulting complex of rents, renders, dues, fines, and fields is sometimes called a "manor."

In some areas, the impetus for these changes in settlement patterns may have come from the peasants themselves. Large fields could be farmed more efficiently than small fields. Investment costs were lower: a single plow and a dozen oxen might suffice for an entire village, obviating the need for every farmer to maintain his own plow and plow beasts. Common fields were potentially more productive also, allowing the villagers to experiment with new crops and new crop-rotation systems and to support larger numbers of animals on common pastures. Peasants living together in a village might be able to support a parish church, a communal oven, a blacksmith, a mill, and a tavern. They could also converse and socialize, celebrate and mourn with their neighbors. In a difficult and demanding natural environment, these were not negligible considerations.

Despite the potential advantages the manorial system offered to peasants, lords played the dominant role in forcing its creation, and it was they who took the greatest benefits from it. It was easier for lords to control and exploit peasants living in villages than peasants living on scattered individual farms. Manorialism also allowed lords to claim a larger share of their peasants' agricultural production. On many manors, the common fields were divided into narrow strips assigned in alternating fashion to individual peasants, for which each peasant landholder paid rent to the lord, but from which each peasant took the profits. In addition to their rents, however, most lords also claimed a third to a half of the total acreage in the common fields as their own demesne (pronounced "demean") land, from which they took all the produce for their own use. To farm this demesne land, manorial lords imposed or increased labor services on peasant farmers, reducing many formerly free peasants to the status of serfs.

Serfs had existed in Europe for centuries, even in areas where the manorial system never took hold. There is no doubt, however, that the development of manorialism considerably increased the incidence of serfdom in northern Europe as compared with Spain,

Sowing Seed. When the peasant sows his seed broadcast, the crows are not far off to help themselves. Here, one is bold enough to peck at the sack while another is momentarily chased off by a dog.

northern Italy, southern France, and central Germany. Unlike free peasants, serfs could not leave their land or their lord without his permission (although in practice, many did so, especially to become town dwellers). Serfs worked for their lords regularly without pay, paid humiliating fines to their lord when they fornicated illicitly, married, or died, and were subject to the jurisdiction of their lord's manorial court. Like slaves, their servile status was heritable; but unlike slaves, their obligations to their lord were fixed by custom, and they were not supposed to be sold apart from the lands they held.

NEW CROP ROTATION SYSTEMS

From the standpoint of agrarian productivity, the greatest advantage of the manorial system was the fact that it made possible the adoption of new, more efficient crop-rotation systems. For centuries, farmers had known that if they sowed the same crop on the same land year after year, they would eventually exhaust the soil. The traditional solution to this difficulty was to divide one's land, planting half in the fall to harvest in the spring, and leaving the other half to lie fallow. In the dry, thin soils of the Mediterranean, this remained the most common cropping pattern throughout the Middle Ages. In the wet, fertile soils of northern Europe, however, farmers slowly discovered that a three-field crop-rotation system could pro-

duce a sustainable increase in overall agricultural production. Under this system, one third of the land would lie fallow, often being used for pasturage, so that the animals' droppings would fertilize the soil; one third would be planted with winter wheat or rye, which was sown in the fall and harvested in the early summer; and one third would be planted with another crop (usually oats or barley, but sometimes legumes or fodder crops such as alfalfa, clover, or vetch) that could be sewn in the spring and harvested in the fall. The fields were then rotated over a three-year cycle.

This system immediately increased, from 50 percent to 67 percent, the amount of land under cultivation in any given year. No less important, it also produced higher yields per acre of wheat and rye, particularly if legumes or fodder crops (which replace the nitrogen that wheat and rye leach out of the soil) were a regular part of the crop-rotation pattern. With two separate growing seasons, the system provided some insurance against loss from natural disasters. It also produced new types of food. Oats could be consumed by both humans and horses, while legumes provided a source of protein to balance the major intake of cereal carbohydrates from bread and beer, the two main staples of the peasant diet. Additional fodder made it possible to support more and healthier animals, increasing the efficiency of plow beasts, diversifying the economy of the manor, and providing an additional source of protein in the human diet through meat and milk. The new crop-rotation system also helped to spread labor more evenly over the course of the year, allowing more careful attention to weed control, liming, and fertilizing of the common fields.

With all these advantages, it may seem surprising that the three-field system was not adopted more widely and more quickly than it was on the great manors of northern Europe. Some of the resistance was cultural. Northern Europeans thought of oats and legumes primarily as food for animals, to be

> The new crop-rotation system immediately increased, from 50 percent to 67 percent, the amount of land under cultivation in any given year.

WHAT IMPACT DID THE FIRST AGRICULTURAL REVOLUTION HAVE ON THE LIVES OF EUROPEANS?

THE FIRST AGRICULTURAL REVOLUTION   307

Medieval Peasants Slaughtering a Pig. Deep in winter, probably around Christmas, it is finally time to slaughter the household pig. But nothing can be wasted, so even the blood is caught in a pan to make blood pudding.

eaten by humans only when nothing else was available. Some of the obstacles were economic. Because wheat was the most important "cash crop" in northern European agriculture, both lords and peasants tended to favor wheat cultivation, even on lands better suited to growing barley, oats, or legumes. But some of the resistance to the new crop-rotation systems may also have been political, the mute protest of servile peasants who stood to gain little personally from improving the productivity of their lords' lands. It may be significant, therefore, that in England, where peasant servility on the great estates lasted into the fifteenth century, the new crop-rotation patterns seem to have been adopted most enthusiastically on the medium-sized (twenty- to fifty-acre) farms owned by free peasant proprietors and lesser knights, and not on manors, which depended heavily on the unpaid labor of unfree peasants.

SERFDOM AND THE LIMITS OF MANORIALISM

It is important to remember that "classic" manorialism of the high medieval type, with servile peasants laboring on lordly demesne lands, was never the predomi-

nant form for European agriculture. By and large, the manorial system was limited to England, northern France, and western Germany. Even in these areas, moreover, it was beginning to break down by the end of the twelfth century, as lords began to commute labor services into cash payments, to free their serfs (again in return for cash payments), and to live from rents rather than from the direct agricultural revenues of their estates.

The reasons for the decline of serfdom during the thirteenth century are complex and did not affect all areas of Europe equally. As the European economy became increasingly monetarized, many lords simply found it more convenient to collect their revenues directly from their peasants in cash, rather than taking the risks associated with marketing agricultural produce directly. This strategy also had its dangers, however. In the inflationary circumstances of the thirteenth century, lords who could not increase the rents their peasants paid them suffered marked declines in their real incomes, sending many knights and lesser lords into economic crisis. In England and Catalunya, by contrast, which had two of the most thoroughly commercialized agricultural economies in medieval Europe, serfdom lasted longer than almost anywhere else in western Europe. In Austria and Poland, which were far less monetized, serfdom also actually increased during the thirteenth century, as it did in northern Spain also. There is thus no simple correlation between commercialization and the decline of serfdom. In most of Europe, however, the generalization holds: serfs and free peasants became increasingly indistinguishable during the thirteenth century as lords enfranchised serfs in return for cash. Even in France, however, some servile obligations would continue to exist as nagging indignities right down to the French Revolution in 1789. And in central and eastern Europe and Russia, serfdom underwent a resurgence during the later Middle Ages that would carry it into the eighteenth and nineteenth centuries.

TRANSFORMATIONS OF THE FIRST AGRICULTURAL REVOLUTION

Between 1050 and 1300, the growing European population made use of improved technology and new crop-rotation systems to produce a remarkable intensification of European agriculture. Crop yields on existing lands increased, and new lands were opened up to cultivation. Forests were cleared, wetlands drained, and wastelands turned into arable or pasture, sometimes through the self-directed efforts of peasant communities, sometimes at the command of entrepreneurial lords. New lands were opened up between existing settlements, and new peasant communities were established in the "frontier" areas of eastern Germany, Holland, northern England, and Castile. As agricultural production increased, it also became more specialized. No longer was it necessary or even desirable for individual peasant communities to produce for themselves the wide variety of crops and goods they needed to consume over the course of a year. As towns grew and local and regional markets expanded, it became possible for individual manors and even entire regions to produce only those crops best suited to their own soil and climate. Gascony became a region of vineyards, Sicily a region of grainfields, northern England a region of sheep. Further increases in productivity resulted as European agriculturalists benefited from the resulting efficiencies of specialization and scale.

THE GROWTH OF TOWNS AND COMMERCE

What were the major causes of urban growth during the High Middle Ages?

This agricultural revolution was the foundation on which the commercial revolution of the High Middle Ages rested. Here too, the groundwork for new developments had been laid in the ninth and tenth centuries. By the year 1000, silver from the Harz Mountains in Saxony was already fueling a triangular trade among England, Flanders, and the expanding cities of the Rhineland that brought raw wool from England to Flanders and wool cloth from Flanders to the Rhineland, whose merchants then distributed it as far away as Italy and Byzantium. Millions of silver pennies were in circulation around the North Sea, where an integrated system of exchange among English, Scandinavian, and Rhenish currencies had developed. English merchants were active in Constantinople and northern Spain, exchanging northern silver for Byzantine silks, Islamic spices, and African gold. Scandinavian merchants and warriors ranged even more widely, establishing cities in Ireland, principalities in Normandy and southern Italy, and trading outposts

such as Novgorod and Kiev along the Russian trade routes that ran from the Baltic to the Black Sea (and thence to Constantinople) and to the Caspian Sea (and on into the Abbasid empire).

COMMERCE

During the eleventh and twelfth centuries, however, the greatest developments in long-distance commerce took place in the burgeoning cities of northern Italy. A series of victories by Venetian, Pisan, and Genoese naval forces gave these cities control over the carrying trade between Constantinople, Alexandria, and the West. The growing prosperity of western European nobles and churchmen created an expanding market for eastern luxury goods, while the improved domestic security of high medieval Europe made it possible for merchants to provide such goods with at least a modicum of security and safety. In the twelfth century, an organized system of fairs emerged in the central French region of Champagne, where Flemish mer-

Medieval Tollbooth. Whoever made use of a medieval road for transporting merchandise had to pay tolls to finance its upkeep.

WHAT WERE THE MAJOR CAUSES OF URBAN GROWTH DURING THE HIGH MIDDLE AGES?

THE GROWTH OF TOWNS AND COMMERCE 309

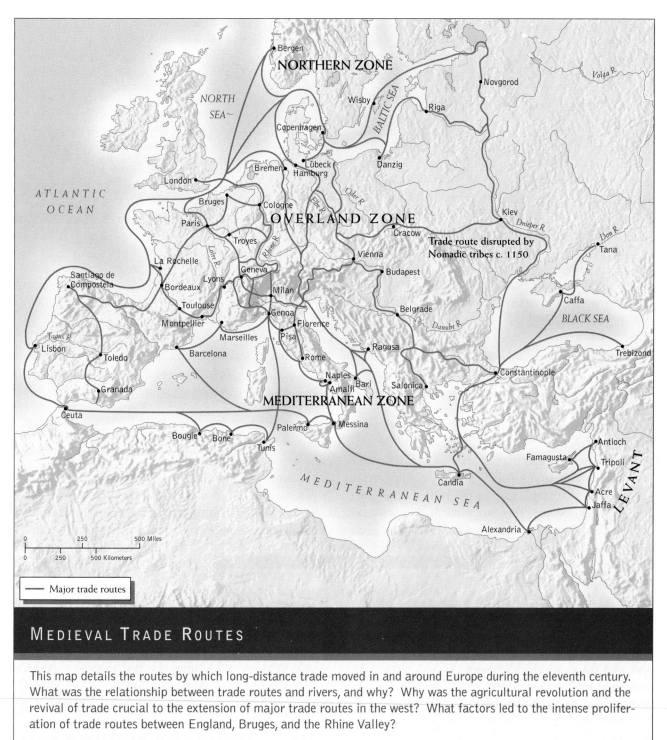

MEDIEVAL TRADE ROUTES

This map details the routes by which long-distance trade moved in and around Europe during the eleventh century. What was the relationship between trade routes and rivers, and why? Why was the agricultural revolution and the revival of trade crucial to the extension of major trade routes in the west? What factors led to the intense proliferation of trade routes between England, Bruges, and the Rhine Valley?

chants sold cloth to Italians, and Italian merchants sold Muslim spices and Byzantine silks to Flemings, French, and Germans. By 1300, however, these fairs were beginning to decline as Italian merchants succeeded in opening up a direct route by sea between Italy and the Atlantic ports of northern Europe. It now became practical to import raw wool directly from England to northern Italy, where towns like Florence could produce and finish wool cloth themselves. As the Italian cloth industry grew, the Flemish cloth industry declined, yet another sign of the increasing extent to which Europe was becoming a unified economy.

Long-distance trade was a risky enterprise. Fortunes could be lost as easily as they could be made. Piracy

View of Paris. The city looked this way at the end of the Middle Ages, around 1480. Note the prominence of the Cathedral of Notre Dame in the center and the large number of other church spires; note, too, how closely all the buildings are packed behind the walls.

was commonplace, and the Mediterranean Sea was notoriously dangerous to sailors and their ships. Merchants were often disdained by the landed aristocracy because they could claim no ancient lineages and because they were too obviously concerned with pecuniary gain. Their courage, however, was undeniable; even in battle, the citizen armies of Milan or Florence often got the better of their aristocratic opponents. Above all, however, Italian success in opening up the new trade routes of the High Middle Ages depended on the willingness of both merchants and nobles to invest substantial sums of money in ships, cargoes, and pack animals. To facilitate such investment, Italian merchants developed new forms of commercial partnership contracts, new methods of accounting (including double-entry bookkeeping), and new credit mechanisms, some of which they borrowed from Byzantine and Muslim examples. Some of these new credit arrangements ran afoul of the western Christian church, which condemned almost all forms of moneylending as usury. But the demand for capital to fuel the new commercial economy was irresistable, and slowly attitudes began to

> Italian success in opening up the new trade routes of the High Middle Ages depended on the willingness of both merchants and nobles to invest substantial sums of money in ships, cargoes, and pack animals.

change. Although the medieval church never formally abandoned its prohibition of moneylending, it did come to approve making profits on commercial risks, which was often close to the same thing. From the thirteenth century on, leading churchmen also began to speak more favorably of merchants. Saint Bonaventura, a thirteenth-century Italian Franciscan, argued, for example, that in Old Testament times, God had shown special favor to shepherds such as King David; in New Testament times, he had favored fishermen such as Saint Peter; but in modern times, God's favor now went out to merchants such as Saint Francis of Assisi.

It would be misleading, however, to think of the commercial revolution or the urban revolution of the High Middle Ages as principally the result of long-distance trade. Some towns did receive great stimulus from such trade, and the growth of such major cities as Venice (about one hundred thousand people in 1300) and Genoa (eighty thousand) would have been impossible without it. But the prosperity of most towns, including such enormous cities as Paris (with a population of two hundred thousand people in 1300), Florence (one hun-

WHAT WERE THE MAJOR CAUSES OF URBAN GROWTH DURING THE HIGH MIDDLE AGES?

THE GROWTH OF TOWNS AND COMMERCE   311

dred thousand), Milan (eighty thousand to one hundred thousand), and London (sixty thousand to eighty thousand), depended primarily on the wealth of their surrounding hinterlands, from which they drew their food supplies, their raw materials, and the bulk of their population. The quickening of economic life in general was the major cause of urban growth during the High Middle Ages. Long-distance trade was but one aspect of this larger economic and commercial transformation of European life.

TOWNS

Towns, both large and small, existed in a symbiotic relationship with the countryside around them, providing markets and manufactured goods while living off the rural food surplus and expanding through the constant immigration of free peasants and escaped serfs in search of a better life. (Escaped serfs were guaranteed their freedom if they stayed in a town a year and a day.) Once towns started to flourish, many of them began to specialize in certain enterprises. Paris and Bologna gained considerable wealth by becoming the homes of leading universities; Venice, Genoa, Cologne, and London became centers of long-distance trade; Milan, Florence, Ghent, and Bruges specialized in manufactures. The most important urban industries were those devoted to the making and finishing of wool (and in Venice, cotton) cloth. Some cloth manufacturers developed techniques of large-scale production and investment that are ancestors of the modern factory system and industrial capitalism. Nonetheless, large industrial enterprises of this sort were not typical of medieval economic life as a whole. Most urban manufacturing continued to be done by individual artisans in small, privately owned workshops whose production was regulated by professional associations known as "guilds."

Usually only master artisans, who were experts at their trade and ran their own shops, were allowed to be fully fledged, voting members of a craft guild. As a result, guilds generally promoted the interests of their richest and most successful members by trying to preserve monopolies and limit competition. To these ends, terms of employment were strictly regulated. If an apprentice or a journeyman (from the French *journée*, meaning "day," or by extension "day's work": that is, someone who had completed his apprenticeship but still worked

for a master craftsman) wished to become a master, he often had to produce a "masterpiece" for judging by the masters of the guild. If the market was judged too weak to support additional master craftsmen, even a masterpiece would not secure a craftsman the coveted right to set up his own shop; yet without such status, some towns even forbade journeymen to marry. Craft guilds also controlled prices and wages, prohibited after-hours work, and formulated detailed regulations governing methods of production and the quality of materials to be used by their members. They also served important social functions as religious associations, benevolent societies, and drinking clubs, looking after their members in times of trouble and supporting his dependents when a master craftsman died.

Merchants established guilds also, which in some towns became so powerful that membership in a merchant guild became a prerequisite for service in town government. Like the more numerous but less powerful craft guilds, merchant guilds sought to maintain a monopoly of the local market for their members by restricting competition and enforcing uniform pricing. Often they also controlled admissions to citizenship in the city. By their nature, guilds were exclusionary organizations. Because they were explicitly Christian, they were almost invariably closed to Jews and Muslims. They also significantly restricted the economic opportunities available to ordinary wage earners, and especially to women. Women were not automatically excluded from most guilds, and a few craft guilds were specifically female. Despite the important role women played as urban wage earners, however, the male-dominated guilds ensured that women would have no influence over the terms and conditions under which they worked, or the wages they would be paid for their labor.

> Guilds generally promoted the interests of their richest and most successful members by trying to preserve monopolies and limit competition.

To modern eyes, most medieval towns and cities would still have seemed half rural even in 1300. Streets were often unpaved, houses had gardens for raising vegetables, and farm animals were everywhere. In the early twelfth century, the heir to the throne of France was killed when his horse tripped over a pig running loose in the streets of Paris. Sanitary conditions were poor and the air must often have reeked of excrement, both animal and human. One fourteenth-century Londoner channeled his sewage for months into the basement of his neighbor's house; only when the basement filled and the sewage began to flood the public street was his offense detected. In such a world, disease ran rampant, especially in the overcrowded neighborhoods where the poorest urban dwellers lived. At every level of urban society, however, fertility rates were low and infant mortality high. Most cities sustained their population only through continuing immigration from the countryside. Fire was an omnipresent danger, and economic tensions and family rivalries could lead to bloody riots. Yet for all this, urban folk took great pride in their new cities and ways of life. A famous paean to London, for example, written by a twelfth-century denizen of the city, boasted of its prosperity, piety, and perfect climate (!), and claimed that except for frequent fires, London's only nuisance was "the immoderate drinking of fools." His pride was echoed in scores of other European cities as their citizens increasingly asserted their distinctive local identities and their communal privileges as merchants, artisans, and self-governing corporations.

A City on Fire. Once a fire began to spread in a medieval city, women, children, and priests were swiftly evacuated and servants of the rich would start carrying out their masters' possessions. Here the Swiss city of Bern is shown in flames: although a "bucket brigade" tried desperately to extinguish the fire with water taken from the town moat, chronicles report that the city was leveled by flames in less than half an hour.

BYZANTIUM, ISLAM, AND THE CRUSADES

How did the First Crusade alter the balance of power between Europe and Byzantium?

As the power of the Abbasid caliphate declined during the ninth and tenth centuries, the Byzantine empire expanded in its military, religious, and cultural aspects. In the mid-ninth century, Byzantium's position was still precarious. A Muslim fleet had recently captured Sicily and Crete; pagan Slav immigration into the Balkans was rapidly undermining Byzantine control of that region; Muslim pressure on the eastern borders of the empire continued unabated, although the borders themselves remained pretty much where they had been since the early eighth century; and a new enemy had emerged in the Viking raiders and traders (known locally as the Rus, for their reddish complexions) who had established themselves along the Russian river systems (in particular, the Volga and the Dnieper) that fed into the Black and the Caspian Sea. The Rus's most important trading connections were with the Abbasids, with whom they exchanged slaves, honey, wax, and furs for Abbasid silver, Indian spices, and Chinese silks. But the Rus knew their way to Constantinople also. In 860, when the Byzantine emperor and his army were busy on the eastern frontier with the Muslims, a Rus fleet sailed into the Black Sea and sacked Constantinople itself.

THE BYZANTINE REVIVAL

By 1025, however, Byzantium's position had been transformed. After several centuries of missionary inactivity, ninth-century Byzantine missionaries, most famously Saints Cyril and Methodius, converted the Balkan Slavs to Orthodox Christianity, devising for them a written language known as Old Church Slavonic and creating the Cyrillic alphabet which is

HOW DID THE FIRST CRUSADE ALTER THE BALANCE OF POWER BETWEEN EUROPE AND BYZANTIUM?

BYZANTIUM, ISLAM, AND THE CRUSADES   313

THE BYZANTINE EMPIRE, C. 1025

What challenges faced the Byzantine Empire in the eleventh century? Note the land controlled by the Muslims and the emerging power of Kievan Russia. How was the long-standing influence of the Muslims in the Near East likely to affect the character of Byzantine culture? How did the domain of Kievan Russia potentially create additional economic and military pressure on Byzantium, directly as well as indirectly?

still used today in Bulgaria, Serbia, and Russia. Military conquest quickly followed. By 1025, when Emperor Basil II ("the Bulgar-slayer") died, the Byzantines had firmly annexed Greece, Bulgaria, and modern-day Serbia to their empire. They had also established a military and commercial alliance with the western Rus kingdom centered around Kiev, decisively reorienting the Rus toward Constantinople and away from Islam. In 911, seven hundred Rus served with the Byzantine fleet in an attack on Muslim Crete. In 945 a commercial treaty was established. In 957, a Kievan Christian princess named Olga was lavishly entertained on a state visit to Constantinople. And in 989, the emperor Basil II turned to Vladimir, prince of Kiev, for the troops he needed to win a civil war against his imperial rival, Bardas Phokas, a member of the increasingly powerful nobility from the eastern borders of the empire. In return for Vladimir's help, Basil gave his sister, Anna, in marriage to Vladimir, and Vladimir, along with his people, accepted baptism into the Orthodox church. Russia has remained an Orthodox bastion until the present day.

Between the 930s and the 970s, the Byzantines also launched a series of successful campaigns along their eastern and southeastern frontiers with the Abbasids, reconquering territories that had not been in Byzantine hands since the seventh century. Paradoxically, however, the consequences of these campaigns ultimately undermined the survival of the Byzantine empire itself by fueling the forces of regional separatism. As ever in Byzantium, a good part of the difficulty was religious. Although most of the peoples of the reconquered territories had remained Christian through three centuries of Islamic rule, the Armenians and the Syrians in particular had their own distinctive Christian traditions that were at odds, both doctrinally and linguistically, with the Greek-speaking church at Constantinople. For an empire that had defined itself for centuries on the basis of its orthodoxy (the word itself means "correct belief"), incorporating such "heretics" threatened the foundations on which the unity of the empire rested.

Even more important, however, the eastern conquests greatly increased the power of the local noble families who led them and profited from them, creating for the first time a center of power within the empire that lay outside the imperial capital at Constantinople. Tensions and rivalries between these eastern noble families and the imperial officials at the capital disturbed Byzantine politics for most of the tenth century. After an attempted coup by the head of one such family, the emperor Basil II (976–1025) savagely suppressed the leading eastern magnate families, building up his own imperial lands in the east and promoting new families, among them the Comneni. He also reoriented Byzantine military power westward toward Bulgaria, which he conquered with the assistance

Venetian Coin. The patron saint of Venice, Saint Mark, grants a banner symbolizing worldly rule to the Venetian doge. The Venetians consciously imitated Byzantine coinage (see p. 264) as part of a successful effort to replace the Byzantine Empire as the dominant trading power in the Mediterranean basin.

of a naval force supplied by the Venetians. But this check on the eastern magnates' ambitions proved only temporary. After Basil's death, the imperial throne passed to a series of aged and incompetent relations. In the resulting power vacuum, noble military families came more and more to dominate the countryside; while at court, tax revenues decreased as imperial expenditures rose. To pay the bills, the emperors debased the Byzantine gold coinage, reducing its value by 50 percent between 1040 and 1080 and undermining Byzantine commerce precisely when Venice, Genoa, and Pisa were consolidating their control over the eastern Mediterranean trade routes. By 1081, when the eastern magnate families triumphed by placing Alexius Comnenus on the imperial throne, the Byzantine empire had been crippled as a Mediterranean power.

THE INVASION OF THE TURKS

By the late eleventh century, Byzantium faced new threats from several quarters. Viking adventurers from Normandy, already established in Sicily and southern Italy, were beginning to eye Constantinople itself as a target for conquest. Venice, Genoa, and Pisa had emerged as the dominant naval powers in the eastern Mediterranean and had to a considerable extent taken over the lucrative trade between Islamic North Africa (including Egypt) and the west. The growing power of

ADVICE TO THE BYZANTINE EMPEROR, ELEVENTH CENTURY

This anonymous work was addressed to one of the eleventh-century Byzantine emperors. It reflects the author's concern with the indolence of the emperor and the growing power of the nobility on the eastern frontiers of the empire. The problems the author addresses here would culminate in 1081 with the ascension of one of these eastern nobles, Alexius Comnenus, to the imperial throne.

Holy Lord, God has elevated you to the imperial authority and has made you by his grace, as you are called, a god on earth, to do and to act as you will. Let then your acts and your deeds be full of understanding and truth, and may justice dwell in your heart. Look, therefore, and act toward all—toward those who are in a position of authority and toward all others—with an equal eye. And do not evilly coerce some while bestowing benefits on others. . . . But let there be equality for all. . . .

The emperor is the model and example for all, and all men look up to him and imitate his conduct. And if his ways are good, men are eager to follow them quickly; but if they are bad and worthy of blame, men will do the same. Therefore, I beg you, take hold of and adopt the four virtues: courage (I mean that of the soul), and justice, temperance, and wisdom. . . .

I know, Your Majesty, that by nature man is desirous of relaxation. But there has come into fashion a custom not helpful but rather damaging; that the emperor not go abroad into the countries under his rule, both in the East and in the West, but that he spend his time in Constantinople, as if in prison there. If someone had indeed restricted you to a single city, in that case you would have to make an effort to leave that area. But the fact is that you have done this to yourself. What, then, is to be said? Go out into the countries under your rule and into your provinces and see for yourself what injustices the poor suffer and what the tax collectors, whom you dispatch, are doing. Ascertain whether the poor have been wronged, and correct all wrong things. Thus both the provinces of the Byzantines and the lands of the peoples under your rule will know that they have an emperor and lord who rules them. Then you yourself will know the strength of each province and fortress and land, how each is situated, and what damage it suffers and what benefits accrue to it. Then there will arise no rebellion or revolt against your agents, but all the areas under your rule will be at peace.

I realize that your ministers . . . will admonish you that this advice is not sound; they will tell you that, as you advance through your countries and provinces with your army and imperial entourage, you will oppress them. They may even say that, if you leave Byzantium, another will seize the imperial throne in your place. When I have thought of this, I have laughed. For the one left by you in the palace, charged with the direction of affairs . . . will, if he is energetic and adequate, be entirely effective, and he will be ever vigilant and will do whatever should be done.

Deno John Geanakoplos, ed. and trans. *Byzantium: Church, Society and Civilization Seen through Contemporary Eyes.* (Chicago: University of Chicago Press, 1984), pp. 20–21.

CHRONOLOGY

BYZANTINE EMPIRE, 1025–1204

Annexation of Greece, Bulgaria, and Serbia	1025
Successful campaigns against the	
Abassid rulers	930–970
Russia converts to orthodoxy	911–989
Turkish invasions (defeat of Manzikert)	1071
Reign of Alexius Comnenus	1081–1118
First Crusade	1095–1099
Fourth Crusade, Capture of	
Constantinople	1204

Fatimid Egypt was beginning to roll back Byzantine gains along the empire's southeastern frontier with Syria. But most disastrously of all, a new Sunni Muslim power, the Seljuk Turks, had emerged in central Asia and had begun to move into Asia Minor, the very heartland of the Byzantine empire. When the Turks captured Armenia, the emperor tried to eject them; but the eastern noble families refused their support, and in the decisive battle of Manzikert (1071), the imperial army was annihilated. The way now lay open for the Turks to seize all of Anatolia; at a blow, the wealthiest and most productive part of the Byzantine empire now fell into Turkish hands. In the same year, another Turkish band captured Jerusalem from the Shi'ite Fatimids, restoring the Holy City to Sunni control. Within five years, almost all of Syria and Asia Minor lay in Turkish hands. In the west, a rebellion by the Balkan Slavs also erupted around this time, further reducing the already severely depleted treasury of the Byzantine empire.

By the 1090s, however, Alexius Comnenus had rebuilt the treasury, repulsed an attempted Norman invasion from southern Italy, restored Byzantine control over the Balkans, and was beginning to plan a campaign against the Turks. For more than a century, the Byzantine army had utilized western mercenaries in its armies. During the eleventh century, however, western knights had emerged as the most effective heavily armored cavalry troops in the world. Alexius had confronted such knights in 1085, when he repelled a Norman invasion of Greece. He was anxious to make use of them, however, against the mounted but lightly armored Turks. To recruit a force of heavy cavalry, Alexius sent a request to Pope Urban II, hoping for a contingent of a few thousand troops with which he might be able to roll back Turkish gains in Anatolia. Within a year, however, the pope had set in motion a vast crusading army of one hundred thousand Westerners to retake the Holy City of Jerusalem for Christendom.

THE FIRST CRUSADE

The reasons that Urban's summons met with such a massive response are complex. Urban himself probably saw the crusade as a means for achieving at least four ends. One was to bring the Orthodox church back into communion with the papacy. Relations between the two churches had been ruptured in 1054, when a papal emissary and the Orthodox patriarch of Constantinople had each excommunicated the other. In 1095, Alexius himself had hinted that some accommodation might be possible between the churches. If Urban could succeed in uniting the two churches, he would gain a great victory for the Gregorian program of papal monarchy, one of whose goals was to establish the primacy of the papacy over all other bishops and churches. A second motive was to embarrass Urban's greatest enemy, the German emperor Henry IV. Henry and the papacy had been at war for more than twenty years over their respective claims to supremacy within Christendom. By calling a mighty crusade to retake Jerusalem, Urban probably hoped to establish his own claims as pope to be the rightful leader of western Christian society. Third, by sending off a large contingent of fighters, Urban hoped to achieve peace at home. Earlier in the century, a number of French bishops and abbots had supported a "peace movement" that prohibited attacks on noncombatants (the "Peace of God") and prohibited fighting on certain holy days (the "Truce of God"). At the 1095 ecclesiastical council at Clermont where he announced the First Crusade, Urban also promulgated the first full papal approval of this peace movement. In effect, Urban told the assembled knights that if they wished to fight, they could do so justly for a Christian cause overseas. Finally, the goal of Jerusalem itself genuinely inspired Urban. Jerusalem was regarded by medieval geographers as the center of the earth as well as being the most sacred shrine of the Christian religion because it was Jesus' homeland. To the untutored knights of western Europe, as perhaps to Urban himself (whose family came from the knighthood of southern France), it seemed only right that Christian knights should assist their Lord Christ to recover his own land from the Muslims who had seized it from him.

THE SPURIOUS LETTER OF ALEXIUS COMNENUS TO COUNT ROBERT, SEEKING HIS AID AGAINST THE TURKS

This letter to Count Robert of Flanders is a forgery from around the time of the First Crusade. It reflects the kind of propaganda that helped to spur enthusiasm for the crusade against the Turks. With its focus on the sexual sins of the Turks and the riches to be had in Constantinople, the letter offers quite different reasons for going on crusade from those advanced by Pope Urban II at Clermont. There is no evidence that any of the charges against the Turks contained in this letter were true.

O incomparable Count, great defender of the faith, it is my desire to bring to your attention the extent to which the most holy empire of the Christian Greeks is fiercely beset every day by the Patzinaks and Turks . . . and how massacres and unspeakable murders and outrages against Christians are perpetrated. . . .

For they circumcise Christian boys and youths over the baptismal fonts of Christian [churches] and spill the blood of circumcision right into the baptismal fonts and compel them to urinate over them, afterward leading them violently around the church and forcing them to blaspheme the name of the Holy Trinity. Those who are unwilling they torture in various ways and finally murder. When they capture noble women and their daughters, they abuse them sexually in turns, like animals. Some, while they are wickedly defiling the maidens, place the mothers facing, constraining them to sing evil and lewd songs while they work their evil. . . .

But what next? We pass on to worse yet. They have degraded by sodomizing them men of every age and rank—boys, adolescents, young men, old men, nobles, servants, and, what is worse and more wicked, clerics and monks, and even—alas and for shame! Something which from the beginning of time has never been spoken or heard of—bishops! They have already killed one bishop with this nefarious sin.

They have polluted and ruined the holy places in innumerable ways and threaten even worse things. In the face of all this, who would not weep—Who would not be moved? Who would not shudder? Who would not pray? Nearly the entire territory from Jerusalem to Greece, and all of Greece with its upper regions . . . have all been invaded by them, and hardly anything remains except Constantinople, which they threaten soon to take from us unless we are speedily relieved by the help of God and the faithful Latin Christians. . . .

For the sake of the name of God and the piety of all those who uphold the Christian faith, we therefore implore you to lead here to help us and all Greek Christians every faithful soldier of Christ you can obtain in your lands, great, small or middling, that they might struggle for the salvation of their souls to free the kingdom of the Greeks, just as in past years they have liberated, to some extent, Galicia and other western kingdoms from the yoke of the unbelievers. For although I am emperor, no remedy remains to me . . . and I am reduced to waiting in a single city for the imminent arrival of the Turks. And since I prefer to be subject to you, the Latins, rather than have Constantinople taken by the Turks, you should fight courageously and with all your strength so that you might receive in bliss a glorious and indescribable reward in heaven.

[The letter then goes on to describe the many Christian relics in Constantinople, and the wealth of the city, urging Robert to prevent all this from falling into the hands of the Turks.]

Act therefore while you have time, lest you lose the kingdom of the Christians and, what is worse, the sepulcher of the Lord, and so that you may earn a reward rather than a punishment hereafter. Amen.

John E. Boswell, ed. and trans. *Christianity, Social Tolerance and Homosexuality.* (Chicago: University of Chicago Press, 1980,) pp. 367–369.

The response to Urban's call exceeded all expectations. Within a year of the pope's summons, an army of a hundred thousand men, women, and children, drawn from all over western Europe, was on the march toward Constantinople, where they intended to gather before departing for Jerusalem. As with any large enterprise, the participants' motives for joining the crusade varied. Some hoped to win lands or establish principalities for themselves in the east. Others were drawn simply by the prospect of adventure. Many were dependents of greater men, accompanying their lords because it was their duty to do so. A few may have been motivated by obscure prophecies and apocalyptic fervor. Most probably had no idea how long a journey would be involved, or even what direction they would be traveling.

But the dominant motive for going on the First Crusade was religious. Except for a few of the greatest lords—and they mostly Normans from southern Italy—the prospect of winning new lands in the east was both unlikely and undesired. Indeed, one of the greatest challenges facing the Latin (Crusader) kingdom of Jerusalem after 1099 was precisely the fact that crusaders so rarely wanted to stay on in the east. After fulfilling their vows, the vast majority of crusaders went home. The risks of dying on such a journey were high; the costs of embarking on it were enormous. Crusading knights needed a minimum of two years' revenues in hand to finance their journey. To raise such sums, most were forced to mortgage lands and borrow heavily from family, friends, monasteries, and merchants. They then had to find some way to pay back these loans if and when they returned home. On any rational judgment of financial advantage, the crusade was a fool's errand. But it did offer solace to the Christian soul. For centuries pilgrimages had been the most popular type of Christian penance, and the pilgrimage to Jerusalem was considered to be the most sacred and efficacious one of all. Urban II made this point explicit at Clermont, promising that crusaders would be freed from all other penances imposed by the church. Some crusade preachers went even further by promising what became known as a plenary indulgence: that crusaders would be entirely freed from otherworldly punishments in purgatory for all the sins they had committed up to that point in their lives, and that the souls of those who died on crusade would go straight to heaven. The plenary indulgence was a

The dominant motive for going on the First Crusade was religious.

truly extraordinary offer, and crowds flocked to take advantage of it.

Crusade preaching emphasized the vengeance that Christ's soldiers should exact on his enemies in the East. But to some crusaders, it seemed absurd to wait until they arrived in Jerusalem to undertake this aspect of their obligations. Muslims might hold Jesus' property at Jerusalem, but Christian theology held Jews responsible for the death of Jesus himself. During the course of the eleventh century, Jewish communities had grown up in most of the larger cities of the Rhineland and in many of the smaller towns and cities of northern France. Assaults by bands of crusaders against Jewish communities began in northern France in the spring of 1096 and quickly spread to the Rhineland as the crusaders moved east. Hundreds of Jews were killed in Mainz, Worms, Speyer, and Cologne, and hundreds more were forcibly baptized as the price for escaping death at the hands of crusading knights. Despite the efforts of church authorities to prevent them, attacks on Jews would remain a regular and predictable feature of Christian crusading until the thirteenth century.

Surprised by the nature and scale of the western response to his appeal, Alexius Comnenus did his best to move the crusaders quickly through Constantinople and into Asia Minor. Differences in outlook between the western crusaders and the Byzantine emperor quickly became apparent, however. Alexius had little interest in an expedition to Jerusalem, but insisted that the crusaders promise to restore to the empire any territory they captured from the Muslims. To the crusaders, this seemed like treachery—an impression that heightened into certainty when supplies they expected from Constantinople on their journey failed to materialize. From Alexius' standpoint, the crusader army was a threat, not least because it contained within it several of the Norman leaders who had attempted to conquer his empire only ten years earlier. The crusaders, however, saw themselves as on a mission from God. They did not understand the Byzantine emperor's willingness to make alliances with some Muslim rulers against other Muslim rulers, and they speedily concluded that the Byzantines were in fact working to undermine the crusading effort, perhaps even supporting the Muslims against them. Such suspicions were unfounded, but they contributed to a growing western conviction that the Byzantine empire itself was an obstacle to the successful recovery of Jerusalem for Christendom.

HOW DID THE FIRST CRUSADE ALTER THE BALANCE OF POWER BETWEEN EUROPE AND BYZANTIUM?

BYZANTIUM, ISLAM, AND THE CRUSADES   319

THE ROUTES OF THE CRUSADERS, 1096–1204

What factors led to the First Crusade? What was the object of the first three crusades? Why did the Fourth Crusade go no farther than Constantinople? What do the Crusades reveal about the differences in outlook between Eastern and Western Christians? Why was the First Crusade a military success, whereas the others met with mixed results at best?

Against great odds the First Crusade succeeded. In 1098 the crusaders captured Antioch and with it most of Syria. At the end of 1099, they took Jerusalem, mercilessly slaughtering Muslim, Jewish, and Christian inhabitants alike. Their success stemmed mainly from the fact that the crusaders' Muslim opponents were at that moment internally divided. The Fatimids had recaptured Jerusalem from the Turks just months before the crusaders arrived, and the Turks themselves were at war with each other. But western military tactics, in particular the dominance in the open field of the heav-

ily armored knights, also played an important role in the crusaders' success.

Equally critical was the naval support the First Crusade received from Genoa and Pisa, which hoped that a successful crusade would allow them to control the Indian spice trade that passed through the Red Sea and on to Alexandria in Egypt. Venice, which had its own connections to this trade through Constantinople, remained largely neutral during the First Crusade, but moved quickly to establish itself in the new crusader kingdom after 1099. In this respect, the

First Crusade contributed to the further decline of Byzantine commerce, which was already suffering both from Italian competition in the Mediterranean and from the disruptive impact of the Turkish invasions on the trade routes that had previously connected Constantinople with Baghdad and the Central Asian silk route to China. All these trends were underway before the First Crusade began, but the establishment of the Latin kingdom accelerated them. To that extent, the First Crusade contributed significantly to the changing balance of power between Byzantium and the West.

> The First Crusade contributed significantly to the changing balance of power between Byzantium and the West, but had much less of an impact on the balance of power between Islam and the West.

THE LATER CRUSADES

The First Crusade had much less of an impact on the balance of power between Islam and the West. The crusader kingdom was never more than an underpopulated, narrow strip of colonies along the coastline of Syria and Palestine. So long as the crusaders did not control the Red Sea, the main routes of Islamic commerce with India and the Far East were unaffected by the change in Jerusalem's religious allegiance. Nor, for that matter, did the crusaders in any way wish to interfere with the overland caravan routes that led through their new territories. For the Muslims, the loss of Jerusalem was a religious affront much more than an economic one, and it was for religious reasons that they began to plan its recovery. By 1144, most of the crusader principalities in Syria had been recaptured. When Christian warriors led by the king of France and the emperor of Germany came east in the Second Crusade to recoup the losses, they were too internally divided to win any victories. Not long afterward, Syria and Egypt were united under the great Muslim leader Saladin, who finally recaptured Jerusalem in 1187. In response, the Third Crusade was launched, led by the German emperor Frederick Barbarossa, the French king Philip Augustus, and the English king Richard the Lionheart. This campaign also failed. Barbarossa drowned in Asia Minor on the way to Jerusalem, and Philip Augustus soon went home. Richard the Lionheart's heroic efforts enabled the Latin kingdom to survive for another century; but even he could not recapture Jerusalem.

The dream, however, did not die. When Innocent III became pope in 1198, his main ambition was to win back Jerusalem. He summoned the Fourth Crusade to that end, but it proved a disaster. Civil war in Germany, combined with war between England and France, severely reduced the number of knights willing to participate; and when the Venetians, who had contracted to transport the crusader army to the Holy Land, discovered that only half the predicted crusaders would arrive and that they would therefore not be properly paid, they diverted the crusade toward a successful attack on Constantinople itself in 1204. The result was an enormous commercial windfall for Venice, but the effective destruction of the Byzantine empire, which for the next sixty years was divided into Latin-ruled and Greek-ruled provinces. In 1261 the Venetians' rivals, the Genoese, helped a new imperial claimant, Michael VIII Palaeologus, to recover the Byzantine throne and, with it, control over Constantinople. But the Byzantine empire was now reduced to little more than the city itself, leaving both Asia Minor and the Balkans open to their eventual conquest by the Ottoman Turks.

Despite the debacle of the Fourth Crusade, western efforts to recover Jerusalem continued throughout the thirteenth century. Only in 1229, however, when the western Roman emperor Frederick II negotiated a treaty with the Egyptian sultan that returned Jerusalem to Christian control for a period of ten years, did any

---

CHRONOLOGY

THE CRUSADES

First Crusade (recapture of Jerusalem)	1095–1099
Second Crusade (defeated by Seljuk Turks)	1145–1149
Third Crusade (Frederick Barbarossa and Richard "the Lionheart")	1187–1192
Fourth Crusade (sack of Constantinople)	1201-1204
Fifth Crusade (capture of Damietta)	1217–1221
Peace treaty regains Jerusalem	1228–1229
Sixth Crusade (defeat of Louis IX of France)	1248–1254
Seventh Crusade (death of Louis IX of France)	1270

PREPARING TO DEPART ON CRUSADE

Before crusaders departed for the Holy Land, they were obliged to remedy all injustices they might have committed, and to put their affairs in order. This was a religious requirement for anyone setting out on a penitential pilgrimage, but it was also a practical recognition that many crusaders would die on their journey. The human emotions that accompanied such departures are clearly expressed in Jean de Joinville's account of his preparations to depart with King Louis IX of France on the Sixth Crusade (1248–1254).

At Easter, in the year of our Lord 1248, I summoned my men, and all who held fiefs from me, to Joinville. On Easter Eve, when all the people I had summoned had arrived, my son, Jean . . . was born to me by my first wife. . . . We feasted and danced the whole of that week. . . .

On the Friday I said to them: "My friends, I'm soon going overseas and I don't know whether I shall ever return. So will any of you who have a claim to make against me come forward. If I have done you any wrong I will make it good, to each of you in turn, as I have been used to do in the case of those who had any demand to make of me or my people." I dealt with each claim in the way the men on my lands considered right; and in order not to influence their decision I withdrew from the discussion, and afterwards agreed without demur to whatever they recommended.

Since I did not wish to take away with me a single penny to which I had no right, I went to Metz in Lorraine, and mortgaged the greater part of my land. I can assure you that, on the day I left our country to go to the Holy Land, I had in my possession, since my lady mother was still alive, an income of no more than a thousand *livres* from my estates. All the same I went, and took with me nine knights, and two knights-banneret besides myself. I bring these things to your notice so that you may understand that if God, who has never failed me, had not come to my help, I should scarcely have been able to hold out for so long a time as the six years that I remained in the Holy Land. . . .

On the day I left Joinville I sent for the Abbot of Cheminon, who was said to be the wisest and worthiest monk of the Cistercian Order. . . . This same abbot . . . gave me my pilgrim's staff and wallet. I left Joinville immediately after—never to enter my castle again until my return from oversea— on foot, with my legs bare, and in my shirt. Thus attired I went to Blécourt and Saint-Urbain, and to other places where there are holy relics. And all the way . . . I never once let my eyes turn back towards Joinville, for fear my heart might be filled with longing at the thought of my lovely castle and the two children I had left behind.

M. R. B. Shaw, ed. and trans. *Chronicles of the Crusades.* (Baltimore: Penguin Classics, 1963), pp. 192, 195.

western leader attempt to achieve this objective directly. Instead, thirteenth-century crusades were directed mainly toward Egypt (1217–1219, 1248–1254), and, in 1270, Tunis. The crusaders' strategic goal was to cut the economic lifelines that supported Muslim control of the Holy Land. In explaining these later crusades, however, it becomes increasingly difficult to disentangle crusade-motivated calculations toward recapturing Jerusalem (which was, in any event, a shattered city with no walls and a tiny population) from the aspirations of Italian merchants to control the Far Eastern trade that ran through Egypt, and the gold trade from sub-Saharan Africa that ran through Tunis. The great mercantile city of the thirteenth century Latin kingdom was Acre, not Jerusalem. Its fall in 1291 marked the end of any further western expeditions (though not of plans for such expeditions) to recover the Holy Land from Islam.

THE CONSEQUENCES OF THE CRUSADES

For Byzantium, the impact of the crusading movement was disastrous. The crusades coincided with, and to some extent caused, a decisive shift in the balance of economic and military power between Western Europe and the faltering Byzantine empire. On the Islamic world, by contrast, the impact of the crusades was much more modest. Trade between Islam and the West continued despite periodic interruptions caused by crusader attacks on Syria, Egypt, and North Africa. The greatest economic gains went to the Italian maritime republics of Venice and Genoa; but Islamic merchants too came to depend increasingly upon western markets for their goods. Both sides also gained in military terms: westerners learned new technques of fortification, and Muslims learned new methods of siege warfare and new respect for the uses of heavy cavalry. Finally, the crusades also helped to crystallize both Christian and Islamic doctrines of holy war against the infidel. Neither Christian holy war nor Muslim *jihad* drew much doctrinally from the other. The collision between them, however, deepened the mutual hostility that already separated the Islamic world and Christian Europe.

The impact of the crusades on western Europe is more difficult to assess. From one standpoint, the crusades were an ultimately unsuccessful chapter in a generally successful story of western expansionism during the High Middle Ages. In the Middle East, however, as they did in Greenland and North America, western Europeans overreached themselves. They could not maintain the colonies they established, and they were ultimately forced to withdraw. Nor did the crusades "open up" Europeans to a wider world of which they had previously known nothing. That wider world already existed in 1095, and Europeans were already part of it. The economic and cultural horizons of Europeans certainly broadened during the twelfth and thirteenth centuries. But the driving force here was the expansion of the European economy, along with the entrepreneurial enterprise of western merchants. To these developments, the crusades had only a peripheral relevance. Trade with the Islamic world, and beyond it with India and the Far East, did bring enormous prosperity to the Italian maritime republics, especially Genoa and Venice. But these trading links had existed before the crusades and continued after they ended. It is arguable, indeed, that crusading diminished, rather than increased, the economic and cultural exchange between western Europe and the Islamic world that might otherwise have taken place.

It would be wrong, however, to end our discussion of the crusades on such a minor note. A drive by western merchants, backed by western military force, to control the trade in spices, silks, and gold by "cutting out the Islamic middleman" is clearly visible in thirteenth-century crusading. This impulse would continue, and would eventually lead to the creation of worldwide European mercantile and colonial empires from the sixteenth century on. Nor should we ignore or diminish the lasting influence of the crusading ideal on Europeans' image of themselves. Crusading had dramatic successes in Spain, where between 1100 and 1250 the kings of Castile and Portugal and the crown of Aragon led the reconquest of the Iberian peninsula from Islam. In Iberia particularly, crusading retained its ideological significance until the end of the sixteenth century, providing an important motivation behind the Portuguese and Spanish voyages of discovery during the fifteenth century, and the conquest of the Americas during the sixteenth century. Crusading would also continue to color European relations with Islam, and

> It is arguable that crusading diminished, rather than increased, the economic and cultural exchange between western Europe and the Islamic world that might otherwise have taken place.

WHAT WAS THE RELATIONSHIP BETWEEN CHIVALRY AND THE CULT OF "COURTLY LOVE"?

SOCIAL MOBILITY AND SOCIAL INEQUALITY IN HIGH MEDIEVAL EUROPE   323

especially with the Ottoman Turks, whose conquests would eventually lead them to the gates of Vienna and the borders of Italy. Even Napoleon, the last of the western Roman emperors, was not immune to the crusading ideal. He too would lead a successful, but short-lived, reconquest of Jerusalem.

SOCIAL MOBILITY AND SOCIAL INEQUALITY IN HIGH MEDIEVAL EUROPE

What was the relationship between chivalry and the cult of "courtly love"?

The increasing wealth of high medieval Europe also transformed the social structure of European society. In the tenth century, it was still possible to describe European society as being divided among "those who worked, those who prayed, and those who fought." By 1300, however, such functional descriptions no longer bore even a tangential relationship to reality. New commercial and professional elites had emerged in the burgeoning cities of western Europe. By 1300, the wealthiest members of European society were merchants and bankers, not nobles. The greatest noble families affected a disdain for commerce, but nobles too found themselves drawn increasingly into the world of trade, despite their contempt for such "calculators." Nobles still fought, of course; but so too did knights, urban crossbowmen, peasant longbowmen, citizen militias, and peasant levies. Even work had become more complex. By 1300, more than half the peasants in England farmed plots of land too small to support their families. They survived, and sometimes even prospered, on a shifting combination of farming, wage labor, hunting, gathering, and charity. Such lines as existed between town and countryside were easily crossed. Rural people moved to towns and townspeople moved back to the countryside with regularity and ease. Schools of all sorts had emerged, and the products of those schools—lawyers, doctors, estate administrators, clerks, and government

> In the tenth century, it was still possible to describe European society as being divided among "those who worked, those who prayed, and those who fought." By 1300, such functional descriptions no longer bore even a tangential relationship to reality.

officials—comprised a new and growing professional class that further complicated efforts to describe European society in terms of "three orders" of workers, prayers, and fighters.

Increasing wealth made European society more complex. Society also became more fluid. The image of "fortune's wheel," whose ceaseless turning raised the unimportant to greatness while reducing the great to poverty, was a favorite image during the High Middle Ages, and for good reason. A shipwreck, a stolen cargo, a bad investment, or a political miscalculation could ruin even the wealthiest and most powerful families. At the same time, however, poor people with ability and luck could sometimes rise to extraordinary heights. Careers in the church were particularly open to men of talent. Robert Grosseteste, the son of an English peasant family, rose to become bishop of Lincoln and one of the greatest intellectuals of the thirteenth century. Royal service was another route to social advancement. William the Marshal, the fourth son of a minor English baronial family, made a name for himself on the twelfth-century knightly tournament circuit. Recruited into the household of King Henry II of England, Marshal rose to become (through marriage) one of the greatest earls in the land and, at his death, regent of England for the child king Henry III. But fortune's wheel also brought men down. William Cade, the wealthiest Flemish wool merchant of the twelfth century, had his entire fortune confiscated by King Henry II. Dante Alighieri, a rising man in the government of his native city of Florence, in 1301 was exiled from Florence for life. He wrote his greatest poetry in exile, "tasting the bitter crumbs of other men's bread."

NOBLES AND KNIGHTS

New wealth brought social mobility, but it also created a more highly stratified society. We have noted already the hierarchies of status and wealth that characterized the guild system. With the rise of serfdom, new distinctions between free and unfree families also emerged within peasant society. Nowhere, however, is the growing stratification of European society more evident than among the nobility. In the Carolingian period, the nobility comprised a relatively small number of ancient families of approximately equal social rank who married endogamously (that is, among themselves). During the tenth and eleventh centuries, however, new families began to establish themselves as territorial lords, rivaling and sometimes surpassing the old Carolingian noble families in power and wealth. Some of these new families were descended from Carolingian officeholders who had taken advantage of the Carolingians' collapse to establish their independence. Others were simply freebooters whose power rested on their control over castles, knights, and manors. Until the twelfth century, the old Carolingian noble families attempted to

Aristocratic Table Manners. There are knives but no forks or napkins on the table. The large stars mark these nobles as members of a chivalric order.

resist the claims of these new families to noble rank and status. By the end of the thirteenth century, however, a new nobility had emerged in western Europe that included these new families of counts, castle holders, and knights, but that also made a series of careful distinctions in rank among dukes, counts, castellans (castle holders), and knights.

Knights were not necessarily nobles in the eleventh century. Knighthood was instead a social "order" consisting of men of widely varying social rank. Some eleventh-century knights were the sons of great nobles, but others were little more than peasants mounted on horseback and armed with a sword. Some knights were "lords," living from the payments of dependent peasants attached to manors. But most knights were landless hirelings, living in the households of greater men (mostly rural, but some urban) who relied on them to prosecute their quarrels and intimidate their enemies. As a specialized warrior group, knights associated with the nobility. A degree of social prestige rubbed off on them from this fact. But the key developments that raised the knights into the ranks of the nobility took place during the twelfth and thirteenth centuries and were directly connected with the growing wealth of medieval European society. As the costs of knightly equipment rose, the number of men who could afford the heavier horses, stronger swords, and improved armor that mid-thirteenth-century knights required declined dramatically. The style of domestic life expected of knights also became more elaborate and expensive. In 1100, a knight could get by with a woolen surcoat,

two horses, and a groom. By 1250, a knight required a string of horses, silk clothing, and a retinue of servants, squires, and grooms. To support such an extravagant lifestyle, a knight needed either a sizable annual fee from his lord or else large estates, a minimum of twelve hundred acres. At four pence per acre in rent, twelve hundred acres would produce an annual income of twenty pounds per year, the minimum income considered necessary in thirteenth-century England to sustain a man as a knight. By way of comparison, a common laborer, working for wages of around two pence per day, might hope to earn one to two pounds per year.

CHIVALRY AND COURTLY LOVE

As the costs of knighthood increased, so too did its social prestige. From the mid-twelfth century on, the kings and nobles of Europe began to embrace and encourage the knightly code of values known as "chivalry," which stressed bravery, loyalty, generosity, skill with weapons, and proper manners as constituent elements in true nobility. Chivalry literally means "horsemanship," and mounted combat (whether on the battlefield or in tournaments) would for long remain the defining element in the European nobility's image of itself. First and foremost, however, chivalry was a social ideology that appealed to the knights and nobles of western Europe because it gave them a way of distinguishing themselves from all those other groups in high medieval society—merchants, lawyers, artisans, and prosperous free farmers—who were their ri-

WHAT WAS THE RELATIONSHIP BETWEEN CHIVALRY AND THE CULT OF "COURTLY LOVE"?

SOCIAL MOBILITY AND SOCIAL INEQUALITY IN HIGH MEDIEVAL EUROPE   325

vals in wealth and sometimes in political influence. Although traditionally the nobility had stressed descent from noble ancestors as the key element in social rank, in the socially mobile world of the High Middle Ages many families who lived nobly did not in fact have prestigious ancestors, whereas other families who did have such ancestors no longer had the wealth to maintain an appropriately noble style of life. Of what, then, did nobility consist? Was noble status a matter of birth, or was it a result of an individual's own achievements? The amalgamation between knighthood and nobility fostered by chivalry offered something to both sides. To the old noble families, it assured them that virtue inhered in their blood, and that chivalric values were most often to be found in those born to noble parents. To the knights, however, as to the merchants and lawyers who sometimes adopted its language and customs, chivalry offered a way of legitimizing the social positions they had attained through their own loyalty, bravery, and skill.

Chivalry began as the value system of a socially diverse knightly order. By the end of the thirteenth century, however, it had become the ideology of a social class, functioning to demarcate those who were (or aspired to be) noble from those who were (or did) not. These lines of social demarcation were particularly clear on the battlefield, where the chivalric code pertained exclusively to knights. Chivalry obliged a knight to treat a knightly opponent with courtesy and respect, capturing him for ransom rather than killing him, and trusting in his prisoner's word (his *parole*) that his ransom would be paid. No such compunctions applied, however, to common soldiers, urban militias, and archers. Under the laws of chivalric war, they could be slaughtered at will by the knights, without any prospect of being captured for ransom.

Closely linked to the ideology of chivalry was the so-called cult of courtly love, which made noble women into objects of veneration for their knightly admirers. Here too, there was an important element of social class. Courtly love was "refined" love, the "courteous" love appropriate to a royal or noble court. But the exponents of courtly love distinguished sharply between noble women, who alone were capable of "refined" love (and who should therefore be wooed and won through proper manners, poetry, and valiant deeds) and peasant women, on whom such "courtliness" would be wasted. Noble women were to be courted; but peasant women could be taken by force, if they would not yield willingly to the desires of a nobleman.

To what extent did the new doctrines of courtly love (which will be discussed in more detail in the next chapter) actually affect the attitudes of noblemen toward noblewomen? The question remains controversial for two reasons. One is that most of our evidence about courtly love comes from literature, and historians differ as to how accurately literature actually reflects life. The other is that putting women on a pedestal is itself another, albeit gentler, way of constraining women's choices. There can be no question, however, that the material quality of noble life improved for both men and women during the High Middle Ages. Wooden castles gave way to stone during the twelfth century. By 1300, most castles were equipped with chimneys and mantled fireplaces, which meant that instead of having one large fire in a central great hall, individual rooms could be heated and individuals gained some privacy. Some thirteenth-century castles even had glass windows, making their private rooms both warmer and lighter. Nor is there any doubt that there was a revolution in some verbalized attitudes toward the female sex. Until the twelfth century, aside from a few female saints, women were virtually ignored in literature. The typical French epic, such as *The Song of Roland*, told of bloody, warlike deeds that either made no mention of women at all, or portrayed them only in passing as subservient wives and mothers. But within a few decades after 1100, noblewomen were suddenly turned into objects of elaborate veneration by lyric poets and writers of romances.

Although the literature of courtly love was extremely idealistic and somewhat artificial, it surely expressed the values of a gentler noble culture wherein upper-class women were in practice more respected than before. Moreover, certain royal women in the twelfth and thirteenth centuries actually did rule their states on various occasions when their husbands or sons were unable to do so or dead. From 1109 until her death in 1126, Queen Urraca ruled the combined kingdom of León-Castile in Spain. The indomitable Eleanor of Aquitaine (1122?–1204), wife of Henry II, played a crucial role in the government of England when her son Richard I (the Lionheart) went on crusade from 1190 to 1194. The strong-willed Blanche of Castile ruled France extremely well twice in the thirteenth century, once during the minority of her son Louis IX and again when he was off crusading. Queens are not, of course, typical women, and from a modern perspective, high medieval noblewomen were still very constrained. But from the point of view of the past, the High Middle Ages was a time of progress for the women of the upper classes. The most striking symbol of this change comes from the history of the game of chess. Before the twelfth century chess was played in the Islamic world, but there the equivalent of the queen was a male figure, the king's chief minister, who could move only diagonally, one square at a time. In twelfth-century Europe, however, this piece was turned into a queen, and sometime before the end of the Middle Ages she began to move all over the board.

POLITICS AND GOVERNMENT

How did government and politics change in the High Middle Ages?

The profound social and economic changes of the High Middle Ages also gave rise to new forms of government and political life. In the early Middle Ages, monarchy was virtually the only form of government western Europeans knew. Towns were small and usually ruled by their bishops or kings. Kingdoms too were small and were thought of as pertaining to a particular people such as the Lombards, the Visigoths, the West Saxons, or the Salian Franks. During the eighth and ninth centuries, most of these ethnic kingdoms disappeared as larger, more powerful, territorially based kingdoms emerged in England and in the Carolingian empire. In England, the West Saxon monarchy survived the ninth-century Viking invasions to become the sole rulers of a united English kingdom. In Germany also, a single royal dynasty, the Ottonians, emerged during the tenth century as the undisputed kings of the East Frankish realm. In France, Catalunya, and northern Italy, however, the Carolingians' collapse came near to erasing monarchical power altogether. In the resulting power vacuum, two new structures of political authority slowly emerged in the heartland of the former Carolingian empire: feudal principalities and self-governing cities.

URBAN GOVERNMENT

Early medieval kings were well aware of the value of towns, and where strong monarchies survived (as, for

> During the eighth and ninth centuries, most of these ethnic kingdoms disappeared as larger, more powerful, territorially based kingdoms emerged in England and the Carolingian empire.

example, in England and Germany), tenth-century kings were active founders of new towns and cities. In Flanders, Catalunya, and northern Italy, however, where kingship collapsed during the late ninth and tenth centuries, self-governing cities developed during the tenth and eleventh centuries without any close monarchical control. We have spoken already of the general economic factors that led to the growth of cities during the High Middle Ages: the increasing agricultural wealth of the countryside, growing population, and developing networks of local and long-distance trade. These factors brought large numbers of immigrants into the cities. They also attracted the local nobility, many of whom became involved in the burgeoning economic and political life of the city, especially as cities began to extend their control over the surrounding countryside. In northern Italy especially, nobles moved to the cities, where they lived in fortified urban towers surrounded by their knightly retainers, their servants, and their urban supporters just as they would have done in a castle in the countryside. Their presence lent a distinctly aristocratic cast to political life in the towns, but it also introduced a violent culture of honor and vendetta into urban life. Attempts to control noble violence in Italian cities led, in the thirteenth century, to efforts in some towns (such as Florence) to ban nobles from holding governmental office altogether. But the destabilizing effects of such feuds continued, ultimately undermining traditions of urban republican government and paving the way for the emergence, during the later Middle Ages, of such great princely families as the Visconti of Milan and the Medici of Florence, whose dynastic rule made a mockery of the democratic forms of urban political life.

Considering how large the great cities of western Europe became during the twelfth and thirteenth centuries, it is astonishing to realize how informal, even ad hoc, their governmental arrangements were. Where kings or powerful feudal lords continued to rule, towns and cities often received special charters of liberty that defined their jurisdictional rights and established the basic structures of urban self-government. In northern Europe, these usually involved a mayor and a council elected from among the leading citizens of the town. Elsewhere, for example in Rome, powerful rulers such as the pope resisted all efforts to establish independent city governments. In northern Italy, however, only a few powerful lords—mostly bishops—remained to sup-

WHAT WAS THE RELATIONSHIP BETWEEN FEUDALISM AND THE RISE OF NATIONAL MONARCHIES?

FEUDALISM AND THE EMERGENCE OF NATIONAL MONARCHIES   327

port or to resist demands for urban self-government. Urban dwellers in Italy therefore had to work out their governmental arrangements for themselves.

In the twelfth century, many north Italian cities entrusted their governments formally to "consuls," drawn from among the leading magnates of the city. Often, however, an informal association of citizens known as "the commune" undertook a wide variety of governmental functions side by side with the consuls. In the later twelfth century, as consular governments collapsed under the demands of war, the communes emerged as the only effective government many cities had. Even the communes, however, were distinctly oligarchical in character. As social stratification increased during the thirteenth century, many cities found themselves split between a ruling class of "magnates" and a popular party that felt itself excluded from the interlocking structures of power that controlled city government and the guilds. These tensions were heightened by magnates who sought to mobilize the *populares* against their own factional enemies. To control the resulting violence, cities sometimes turned to an outsider, known as a *podestá*, usually a noble with legal training, who ruled as a virtual dictator for a strictly limited term of office. Others cities adopted the model of Venice and became more formally oligarchical, casting off even the pretense of being a popular republic. By 1300, however, even cities that remained republics in principle were becoming increasingly oligarchical in practice. Terms of office were getting longer; the jurisdictional claims of urban governments were expanding; and traditions of dynastic succession to office were beginning that would lead to the urban principalities of the later Middle Ages.

FEUDALISM AND THE EMERGENCE OF NATIONAL MONARCHIES

What was the relationship between feudalism and the rise of national monarchies?

In theory, of course, Europe remained a continent of kingdoms even during the tenth and eleventh centuries, when monarchical power in France and Italy was at its lowest ebb. In France, the Capetian dynasty succeeded the Carolingians without interruption in 987, keeping alive the memory that all France had once owed allegiance to a single king. In northern Italy, a number of local rulers vied with each other to claim the Carolingians' fallen mantle of royalty for themselves until their claims were finally trumped, after 962, by the newly crowned Ottonian emperors of Germany. In practice, however, neither the Ottonians in Italy nor the Capetians in France were able to control the territories over which they claimed to rule. By the year 1000, effective political and military power in France lay in the hands of lesser men—dukes, counts, castellans, and knights—whose power rested on their capacity to channel the increasing wealth of the countryside into their own hands. The symbol of their authority was the castle, often little more than a wooden tower set on a hill with a wooden palisade around it. But when manned by a sufficient force of mounted knights, even a wooden castle could be a formidable fortification, certainly sufficient to overawe the peasant farmers of an area, and frequently capable of withstanding the attacks of rival lords. From their castles, these counts, castellans, and knights constructed "lordships": self-contained territories within which they exercised not only the property rights of landlords over peasants, but also the public rights to mint money, judge legal cases, raise troops, wage war, collect taxes, and impose tolls. By the year 1000, France had thus become a patchwork kingdom composed of essentially independent territorial principalities ruled by counts or dukes, which were in turn divided into smaller lordships ruled by castellans and knights.

THE PROBLEM OF FEUDALISM

This highly decentralized political system, in which "public" powers of minting, justice, taxation and defense were vested in the hands of private lords, is conventionally referred to as *feudalism*. As a term, "feudalism" is in many ways unsatisfactory, not least because it has been used by historians to mean so many different things. Marxist historians use it to describe an economic system—in Marxist terms, a "mode of production"—in which wealth is overwhelmingly agricultural and cities have not yet formed. Social historians see "feudal society" as characterized by an aristocratic social order bound together by mutual ties of land holding and supported by the labor of serfs attached to manors. Legal historians speak of feudalism as a system of land tenure in which lesser men held land from greater men in return for services of various kinds, whereas military historians see feudalism as a method of raising troops, a system whereby kings, dukes, and counts granted land to lesser lords in return for specified quotas of knightly military service. Reflecting on this plethora of meanings, some recent historians have suggested we should abandon the term "feudalism" altogether, arguing that because economic, social, and political relations differed so greatly from one area of medieval Europe to another it is misleading to speak of feudalism as any kind of "system" at all.

> Some recent historians have suggested we should abandon the term "feudalism" altogether.

If, however, we define feudalism as a political system in which public powers are exercised by private lords, then there is general agreement that feudalism took shape first and most fully in tenth- and eleventh-century France, after the Carolingian empire had disintegrated. As we have seen, this was also the era during which manorialism was expanding, with a consequent loss of freedom for many peasant families. It is the coincidence of rapid political decentralization with the growth of manorialism that gives northern European feudalism during the tenth and eleventh centuries its particular character. From France, the language and customs of feudalism spread to other areas of Europe, changing as they were adapted to the particular social, economic, and political circumstances of different regions and countries. Finally, in the twelfth and thirteenth centuries, feudalism developed into an ideology justifying a hierarchical legal and political order that subordinated knights to counts and counts to kings. In this modified form, feudalism gave rise to powerful feudal monarchies and helped to lay the groundwork for the emergence of European nation-states.

What then was feudalism? At its simplest level, a "fee" or "fief" (rhymes with "reef"; in Latin, *feudum*) was a kind of contract, in which someone granted something of value—often land, but sometimes revenues from tolls or mills, or an annual grant of money—to someone else in return for service of some kind. Frequently there was a degree of inequality in such contracts, particularly if land was involved, because land was regarded as the most valuable gift one person could give to another. In a gift-giving society, such inequalities had direct implications for the social status of the two parties involved in the exchange. When a man accepted land from another in return for promises of service, a degree of subordination by the recipient toward the giver was usually implied. In some areas, the recipient of a fief might therefore become the "vassal" (from a Celtic word meaning "boy") of the gift giver, who thereby became his "lord"; and their new relationship might be solemnized by an act of "homage," whereby the vassal became "the man" (in French, *l'homme*) of his lord in return for his fief. Elsewhere, however, fiefs existed without vassalage, and vassalage existed without homage. The terms themselves matter less than the relationship that arose when one individual held land from another in return for service. It was this relationship that lay at the heart of feudalism as it emerged in the chaos of tenth-century France.

In a world in which central governmental authority had collapsed, these essentially personal relationships of service in return for land holding became an important element in ordering social and political relations between counts, castellans, and knights. At the same time, however, these relationships were entirely unsystematic. Even in France, where feudalism pervaded aristocratic life, many castellans and knights held their lands freely, owing no service whatsoever to the count or duke within whose territories their lands lay. Nor were feudal relationships necessarily hierarchical. Counts sometimes held lands from knights; knights frequently held lands from each other, and many landholders held fiefs from a number of different lords. Feudalism in the tenth and eleventh centuries created no "feudal pyramids," in which knights held from counts, and counts held from kings in an orderly, hierarchical system of land holding and loyalty. Feudalism of this sort emerged only in the twelfth and thirteenth centuries, when powerful kings began to insist that feudalism *should* be structured in such an orderly way, with kings at the apex of a political and social pyramid.

THE NORMAN CONQUEST OF ENGLAND

Feudalism first emerged as an ordered, hierarchical system of landholding and military service in England, in the peculiar circumstances resulting from the Norman Conquest of 1066. During the tenth and eleventh centuries, England was the wealthiest, most highly centralized, and administratively sophisticated kingdom in western Europe. In 1066, however, Duke William of Normandy, the descendant of Vikings (known as "Northmen," hence "Normans") who had settled this northwestern corner of France during the tenth cen-

WHAT WAS THE RELATIONSHIP BETWEEN FEUDALISM AND THE RISE OF NATIONAL MONARCHIES?

FEUDALISM AND THE EMERGENCE OF NATIONAL MONARCHIES   329

The Bayeux Tapestry. Embroidered shortly after the Battle of Hastings, the Bayeux Tapestry is a 231-foot document of the battle and the events leading up to it. Here the Saxons have sighted a shooting star (Halley's comet, actually) and, taking it for an omen, report it to King Harold.

tury, laid claim to the English crown and crossed the Channel to conquer what he had claimed. Fortunately for him the newly installed English king, Harold, had just warded off a Viking attack in the north and thus could not offer resistance at full strength. At the battle of Hastings Harold and his English troops fought bravely, but ultimately could not withstand the onslaught of the fresher Norman troops. As the day waned Harold fell, mortally wounded by a random arrow; his forces dispersed, and the Normans took the field—and with it, the kingdom of England. Duke William now became King William the Conqueror and set about to exploit his new prize.

William rewarded his Norman followers with extensive grants of English land. As the kingdom's conqueror, however, William could claim with some justice that all the land of England belonged ultimately to him, and therefore that all the land in England must be held from him in return for feudal service of some sort. For the new Norman lords, the feudal service they owed their new king was mainly military. Even the bishops and abbots of England were assigned fixed knight-service quotas for the lands they held. The Norman lords were already accustomed to feudalism in Normandy. In England, however, feudalism after 1066 was much more highly centralized than it had ever been in Normandy, because in England William could

draw on the administrative authority of the English state to enforce his claims to be the feudal lord of the entire country.

As king of England, William also exercised a variety of public rights that did not derive from feudalism at all. In England, only the king could coin money, and only the king's money was allowed to circulate. Like their Anglo-Saxon predecessors, William and his sons also collected a national land tax, supervised justice in public courts, and had the sole authority to summon the population of England to arms. The Norman kings also retained the Anglo-Saxon officer of local government known as the sheriff to help them administer and enforce their rights. William was also able to insist that all the landholders in England owed loyalty ultimately to the king—even if they did not hold a scrap of land directly from him. William's kingship thus represented a powerful fusion of Carolingian-style traditions of public power with the new feudal structures of power and land holding that had grown up in northern France in the tenth and eleventh centuries.

FEUDAL MONARCHY IN ENGLAND

The history of English government in the two centuries after William is primarily a story of kings tightening up the feudal system to their advantage until they superseded it and created a strong national monarchy. The first to take steps in this direction was the Conqueror's energetic son Henry I (1100–1135). One of his most important accomplishments was to start a process of specialization at the royal court whereby certain officials began to take full professional responsibility for supervising financial accounts; these officials became known as clerks of the Exchequer. Another accomplishment was to institute a system of traveling circuit judges to administer justice as direct royal representatives in various parts of the realm.

THE REIGN OF HENRY II

After an intervening period of civil war Henry I was succeeded by his grandson Henry II (1154–1189), who was very much in his grandfather's activist mold.

Martyrdom of Thomas Becket. From a thirteenth-century English psalter. One of the knights has struck Becket so mightily that he has broken his sword.

Henry II's reign was certainly one of the most momentous in all of English history. One reason was that it saw a great struggle between the king and the flamboyant archbishop of Canterbury, Thomas Becket, over the status of church courts and church law. In Henry's time priests and other clerics were tried for any crimes in church courts under the rules of canon law. Punishment in these courts was notoriously lax. Even murderers were seldom sentenced to more than penance and loss of their clerical status. Also, decisions handed down in English church courts could be appealed to the papal curia (court) in Rome. Henry, who wished to have royal law prevail as far as possible and maintain judicial standards for all subjects in his realm, tried to limit these practices by the Constitutions of Clarendon of 1164. On the matter of clerics accused of crimes he was willing to compromise by allowing them to be judged in church courts but then have them sentenced in royal courts. Becket, however, resisted all attempts at change with great determination. The quarrel between king and archbishop was made more bitter by the fact that the two had earlier been close friends. It reached a tragic climax when Becket was murdered in Canterbury Cathedral by four of Henry's knights, after the king, in an outburst of anger, had rebuked them for doing nothing to rid him of his antagonist. The crime so shocked the English public that Becket was quickly revered as a martyr and became the most famous English saint. Even King Henry was compelled to appear as a penitent, barefoot and dressed only in a shirt, before Becket's tomb to ask the saint's forgiveness for the rash words that had provoked his murder. He was also forced to surrender several of the claims, including the right to try criminal clerics in royal courts, that had provoked his dispute with Becket.

Despite this setback, Henry II made enormous governmental gains in other areas, so much so that some historians maintain that he was the greatest king that England has ever known. His most important contributions were judicial. He greatly expanded the use of the itinerant judges instituted by Henry I and began the practice of commanding sheriffs to bring before these judges groups of men who were familiar with local conditions. These men were required to report under oath every case of murder, arson, robbery, or other major crimes known to them to have occurred since the judges' last visit. This was the origin of the grand jury. Henry also for the first time allowed parties in civil disputes regular access to royal justice through standardized procedures. In the most prevalent type of case, someone who claimed to have been recently dis-

WHAT WAS THE RELATIONSHIP BETWEEN FEUDALISM AND THE RISE OF NATIONAL MONARCHIES?

FEUDALISM AND THE EMERGENCE OF NATIONAL MONARCHIES   331

possessed of his land could obtain a writ from the crown, which would order the sheriff to bring twelve men who were assumed to know the facts before a judge. The twelve were then asked under oath if the plaintiff's claim was true, and the judge rendered his decision in accordance with their answers. Out of such practices grew the institution of the trial jury, although the trial jury was not used in criminal cases until the thirteenth century.

Henry II's legal innovations benefited both the crown and the country in several ways. Most obviously, they made justice more uniform and equitable throughout the realm. They also thereby made royal justice sought after and popular. Particularly in disputes over land—the most important and frequent disputes of the day—the weaker party was no longer automatically at the mercy of a strong-arming neighbor. Even free peasants could sometimes win a legal case against their lords. Only serfs remained entirely at the mercy of their lords, and even they were protected by the criminal jurisdiction of the royal courts. The widespread use of juries in Henry's reign brought more and more people into actual participation in royal government, strengthening their sense of attachment to it. Since these people served without pay, Henry brilliantly managed to expand the competence and popularity of his government at very little cost.

The most concrete proof of Henry II's success is that after his death his government worked so well that it more or less ran on its own. Henry's son, the swashbuckling Richard I, the "Lionheart," ruled for ten years, from 1189 to 1199, but in that time he stayed in England for only six months because he was otherwise engaged in crusading or defending his possessions on the Continent. Throughout the time of Richard's absence governmental administration actually became more efficient, owing to the work of capable ministers. The country also raised two huge sums for Richard by taxation: one to pay for his crusade to the Holy Land and the other to pay his ransom when he was captured by an enemy on his return. But later when a new king needed still more money, most Englishmen were disinclined to pay it.

THE REIGN OF JOHN AND THE MAGNA CARTA

The new king was Richard's brother John (1199–1216), who has the reputation of being a villain but was also a victim of circumstances. Ever since the time of William the Conqueror, the Norman kings had continued to rule their French homeland of Normandy as well as England. When Henry II married Eleanor of Aquitaine, however, her vast estates brought more than half of modern-day France under the control of the English crown. When King Philip Augustus came to the French throne in 1181, he was determined to recover these territories for France. Against Richard, who was the ablest military leader of his day, Philip suffered a series of reverses. Against John, Philip had much greater success. In 1204, he succeeded in ousting John from Normandy, Anjou, and Brittany, leaving only Aquitaine still in English hands.

John devoted the rest of his reign to raising the money he would need to recover his lost French territories. To do so, he pressed his feudal rights to their limits, forcing massive fines from his nobility and imposing heavy taxes upon the country. When John's 1214 military expedition to France met with another crushing defeat at the hands of Philip Augustus, the exasperated magnates of England rebelled. In 1215 they forced John to renounce his extortionate fiscal practices in a great charter of liberties known to posterity as Magna Carta. Because John had relied so heavily on his feudal powers, most of Magna Carta's provisions dealt directly with such matters, insisting that the king must in future respect the traditional rights of his vassals. But it did also enunciate in writing some important general principles: that taxation could not be raised by the crown without consent given by the barons in a common council, and that no free man could be punished by the crown except by the judgment of his equals and by the law of the land. It is in these respects that Magna Carta has sometimes been compared, a bit misleadingly, to the American Bill of Rights. Above all, however, Magna Carta was important as an expression of the principle of limited government and of the idea that the king is bound by the law.

> Magna Carta was important as an expression of the principle of limited government and of the idea that the king is bound by the law.

As the American medievalist J. R. Strayer has said, "Magna Carta made arbitrary government difficult, but it did not make centralized government impossible." In the century following its issuance, the progress of centralized government continued apace. In the reign of John's son, Henry III (1216–1272), the barons vied with the king for control of the government but did so on the assumption that centralized government itself was a good thing. Throughout Henry's reign, adminis-

Legend (top left)

Angevin Empire under Henry II, about 1180

French Royal Domain, 1180

Boundary of France, 1180

✕ Battle sites

Inset (top right)

France at the Death of Philip Augustus 1223

Royal domain

Under English rule

ATLANTIC OCEAN

Campostela

Bay of Biscay

ENGLAND

Paris

FRANCE

LÉON

Main map labels

SCOTLAND
Bannockburn ✕
Edinburgh

IRELAND

Dublin

Carlisle
Durham

York
Stamford Bridge

WALES
Bosworth Field ✕
ENGLAND
Hereford
Gloucester
Ely
Cambridge
Oxford
London
Runnymede
Winchester
Southampton
Hastings ✕
Canterbury

ATLANTIC OCEAN

English Channel

Calais
Bruges
Antwerp
Ypres
Lille
Brussels
FLANDERS
Agincourt ✕
Bouvines
Arras
Scheldt R.
Meuse R.
Rhine R.
HOLY

Bayeux
Rouen
Amiens
Beauvais
VERMANDOIS
Verdun
ROMAN
Caen
NORMANDY
Mont-St. Michel
St. Denis
Rheims
LORRAINE
BRITTANY
MAINE
Chartres
Brétigny
Paris
CHAMPAGNE
Marne R.
Moselle R.
ISLE DE FRANCE
EMPIRE
ANJOU
Troyes
Nantes
Loire R.
BURGUNDY
TOURAINE
Poitiers
Bourges
Autun
POITOU
Dijon
Saône R.
Bay of Biscay
AQUITAINE
Geneva
Lyon
Angoulême
Bordeaux
Rhône R.
Garonne R.
Perigueux
GASCONY
PROVENCE
Albi
Avignon
TOULOUSE
Montpellier
Aigues-Mortes
Marseilles
NAVARRE
LANGUEDOC
Narbonne
ARAGON
MEDITERRANEAN SEA
CORSICA
CATALUNYA

Inset (bottom left)

EUROPE
Area of detail
AFRICA

FRANCE AND ENGLAND, 1180–1223

Consider the vast geographical expanse of the Angevin empire in 1180. What were the primary requirements for holding this empire together? What advantages did the kings of France enjoy in their struggles with the Angevins? What did it mean to be "French" in such a world? Would the wars between the Angevins and the Capetians have encouraged the emergence of national identities within their kingdoms?

WHAT WAS THE RELATIONSHIP BETWEEN FEUDALISM AND THE RISE OF NATIONAL MONARCHIES?

FEUDALISM AND THE EMERGENCE OF NATIONAL MONARCHIES   333

trators continued to perfect more efficient legal and administrative institutions, including a system of central and local courts, and a taxation system that assessed both nobles and commoners in proportion to their wealth.

The last and most famous branch of the medieval English governmental system was Parliament. This gradually emerged as a separate branch of government in the decades before and after 1300, above all owing to the wishes of Henry III's son, Edward I (1272–1307). Although Parliament later became a check against royal absolutism, in its origins Parliament was very much a royal institution, summoned because kings found it useful to consult with their nobles, knights, and burgesses in a single assembly. Edward I called Parliaments frequently to raise money to finance his wars in Wales, Scotland, and France. Magna Carta had demanded that no taxation be imposed without the common consent of the realm. Parliament provided an efficient way to secure such consent, as well as to inform those present (principally the nobility, but frequently including knightly representatives from the counties and the major towns) why such taxation was necessary. Edward also used Parliaments to take advice about pressing concerns; to hear judicial cases involving great men; and to review local administration, hear complaints from the countryside, and promulgate new laws in response to those complaints. Parliaments were thus political institutions no less than financial and judicial ones. They played an essential role in English government from the fourteenth century on.

Edward I's reign also saw the development of a strongly nationalistic monarchy. As a political concept, "Englishness" dates back to King Alfred. Under Edward I, however, Englishness was emerging as not only a political but also a social and cultural force. Edward himself spurred the development of such nationalistic feelings by his aggressive wars of conquest in Wales and Scotland. He also played on such feelings in rallying support for his defensive wars in France against King Philip IV. During the unpopular reign of his father, Henry III, popular and baronial resentments against the "insufferable French" helped provoke a rebellion against the king himself, who was accused of favoring too much his foreign, French relatives. Edward I, however, was able to harness this sense of English national identity and use it to support his own wars of conquest in Wales and Scotland. By the end of his reign, patience was growing thin with the king's arbitrary and imperious style of kingship, and a reaction would follow against the incompetent rule of his son,

CHRONOLOGY

NOTEWORTHY NORMAN AND ANGEVIN KINGS, 1066–1327

William I (the Conqueror)	1066–1087
Henry I	1100–1135
Henry II	1154–1189
Richard I (the Lionheart)	1189–1199
John	1199–1216
Henry III	1216–1272
Edward I	1272–1307
Edward II	1307–1327

Edward II. But the link Edward I forged between English nationalism and foreign conquests would endure for centuries to come.

FEUDAL MONARCHY IN FRANCE

While the process of governmental centralization was making impressive strides in England, it developed more slowly in France. But by around 1300 it had come close to reaching the same point of completion. French governmental unification proceeded more slowly because France in the eleventh century was more decentralized than England and faced greater problems. The last of the weak Carolingian monarchs was replaced in 987 by Hugh Capet, the count of Paris, but the new Capetian dynasty—which was to rule without interruption until 1328—was at first no stronger than the old Carolingian one. Even through most of the twelfth century the kings of France ruled directly only in a small area around Paris known as the Île-de-France, roughly the size of Vermont. Beyond that territory the kings had shadowy claims to being the feudal overlords of numerous counts and dukes throughout much of the area of modern France, but for practical purposes those counts and dukes were almost entirely independent. Thus, whereas William the Conqueror inherited in England a country that had long been unified, the French kings of the High Middle Ages had to unify their country from scratch, with only a vague reminiscence of Carolingian unity to build on.

In many respects, however, luck was on their side. First of all, they were fortunate for hundreds of years in having direct male heirs to succeed them. Consequently, there were no deadly quarrels over the right of succession. In the second place, most of the French kings lived to an advanced age, the average period of rule being about thirty years. That meant that sons were already mature men when they came to the throne and therefore few regencies to squander the royal power during the minority of a prince. More than that, the kings of France were always highly visible, if sometimes not very imposing, when there were power struggles elsewhere, so people in neighboring areas became accustomed to thinking of the kingship as a force for stability in an unstable world. A third favorable circumstance for the French kings was the growth of agricultural prosperity and trade in their home region; this provided them with important sources of revenue. A fourth fortuitous development was that the kings were able to gain the support of the popes because the latter usually needed allies in their incessant struggles with the German emperors. The popes lent the French kings prestige, as they earlier had done for the Carolingians, and they also allowed them much direct power over the local church, thereby bringing the kings further income and influence from patronage. A fifth factor in the French kings' favor was the growth in the twelfth and thirteenth centuries of the University of Paris as the leading European center of studies, and the prestige this lent to the monarchy. Finally, and by no means least of all, great credit must be given to the shrewdness and vigor of several of the French kings themselves.

THE CAPETIAN KINGS

The first noteworthy Capetian king was Louis VI, "the Fat" (1108–1137). Although accomplishing nothing startling, Louis at least managed to pacify his home base, the Île-de-France, by driving out or subduing its turbulent "robber barons." Once this was accomplished, agriculture and trade could prosper and the intellectual life of Paris could start to flourish. But the really startling additions to the realm were made by Louis's grandson Philip Augustus (1180–1223). Philip was wily enough to know how to take advantage of his feudal rights over the counts and dukes of France, including King John of England, who was forced to acknowledge Philip's feudal supremacy over Normandy, Anjou, Brittany, and Aquitaine in 1199. Philip was also decisive enough to defend his gains in battle—at least against King John, who was known to his detractors as "soft sword." Most impressive of all, Philip worked out an excellent formula for governing his new acquisitions. Since these increased his original

King Philip the Fair of France. An author is presenting a copy of his book to the mighty king, enthroned on a pedestal.

lands close to fourfold, and since each new area had its own highly distinct local customs, it would have been hopeless to try to enforce strict governmental standardization by means of what was then a very rudimentary administrative system. Instead, Philip allowed his new provinces to maintain most of their indigenous governmental practices but superimposed on them new royal officials known as *baillis*. These officials were entirely loyal to Philip because they never came from the regions in which they served and were paid impressive salaries for the day. They had full judicial, administrative, and military authority in their bailiwicks: on royal orders they tolerated regional diversities but guided them to the king's advantage. Thus there were no revolts in the conquered territories and royal power was enhanced. This pattern of

WHAT WAS THE RELATIONSHIP BETWEEN FEUDALISM AND THE RISE OF NATIONAL MONARCHIES?

FEUDALISM AND THE EMERGENCE OF NATIONAL MONARCHIES   335

CHRONOLOGY

NOTEWORTHY CAPETIAN KINGS, 987–1328	
Hugh Capet	987–996
Louis VI	1108–1137
Philip Augustus	1180–1223
Louis VIII	1223–1226
Louis IX	1226–1270
Philip IV	1285–1314

local diversity balanced against bureaucratic central-ization was to remain the basic pattern of French gov-ernment. Thus Philip Augustus can be seen as an important founder of the modern French state.

In the brief reign of Philip's son, Louis VIII (1223–1226), almost all of southern France was added to the crown in the name of intervention against religious heresy. Once incorporated, this territory was gov-erned largely on the same principles laid down by Philip. The next king, Louis IX (1226–1270), was so pious that he was later canonized by the church and is commonly referred to as Saint Louis. He ruled strongly and justly (except for great intolerance of Jews and heretics), and brought France a long, golden period of internal peace. Because he was so well loved, the monarchy lived off his prestige for many years afterward.

That prestige, however, came close to being squan-dered by Saint Louis's ruthless grandson Philip IV, "the Fair" (1285–1314). Philip fought many battles at once, seeking to round out French territories in the northeast and southwest and to gain full control over the French church instead of sharing it with the pope in Rome. All these activities forced him to accelerate the process of governmental centralization, especially with the aim of trying to raise money. Thus his reign saw the quick for-mulation of many administrative institutions that came close to completing the development of medieval French government, as the contemporary reign of Ed-ward I did in England. Philip's reign also saw the call-ing of assemblies that were roughly equivalent to the English Parliaments, but these—later called Estates-General—never played a central role in the French governmental system. Philip the Fair was successful in most of his ventures; above all, as we will later see, in reducing the pope to the level of a virtual French fig-urehead. After his death there would be an antimonar-

chical reaction, as there was at the same time in Eng-land, but by his reign France was unquestionably the strongest power in Europe.

ENGLAND AND FRANCE: COMPARISONS AND CONTRASTS

Although England and France followed certain similar processes of monarchical centralization and nation building, they were also marked by basic differences that are worth describing because they typified differ-ences in development for centuries after. England, a far smaller country than France, was much better unified. Aside from Wales and Scotland, no regions in Britain had such different languages or traditions that they thought of themselves as separate territories. Conse-quently, no aristocrats could move toward separatism by drawing on regional resentments. This meant that England never really had to face the threat of internal division and could develop strong institutions of united national government such as Parliament. It also meant that the English kings, starting primarily with

Images of Aristocracy. This early fifteenth-century illustration, from the *Très Riches Heures* commissioned by Jean, Duke of Berry, depicts the leisurely elegance that became such an important feature of medieval aristocratic life.

Henry II, could rely on numerous local dignitaries, above all, the knights, to do much work of local government without pay. The obvious advantage was that local government was cheap, but the hidden implication of the system was that government also had to be popular, or else much of the voluntary work would grind to a halt. This doubtless was the main reason that English kings went out of their way to seek formal consent for their actions. When they did not they could barely rule, so wise kings learned the lesson and as time went on England became more and more clearly a limited monarchy. The French kings, in contrast, ruled a richer and larger country, which gave them—at least in times of peace—sufficient wealth to pay for a more bureaucratic, salaried administration at both the central and local levels. French kings relied less, therefore, on the direct consent of the people over whom they ruled. At the same time, however, they were continually faced with serious threats of regional separatism. Different regions continued to cherish their own traditions and often veered toward separatism in league with the upper aristocracy. So French kings often had to struggle with attempts at regional breakaways and take various measures to subdue their aristocrats. Up to around 1700 the monarchy had to fight a steady battle against regionalism, but it had the resources to win consistently and thereby managed to grow from strength to strength.

GERMANY

Germany in the High Middle Ages followed a very different pattern. In the year 1050, Germany appeared to be the strongest monarchy in western Europe. Although the country was divided into a number of quasi-autonomous duchies, the German emperors had constructed a powerful monarchy on Carolingian-style foundations: a close alliance with the church, a tradition of sacral kingship, and profitable conquests in the Slavic lands to the east. To rule their wide territories—which included Switzerland, eastern France, and most of the Low Countries, as well as claims to northern Italy—the emperors relied heavily on cooperation with the church. The leading royal administrators were archbishops and bishops whom the German emperors appointed and installed in their sacred offices, just as their Carolingian predecessors had done. Even the pope was frequently an imperial appointee. Often, these leading churchmen were members of the imperial family itself, who could counterbalance the strength of the regional dukes. Germany was not so administratively sophisticated as was eleventh-century England, but there was no question about the effectiveness of monarchical authority. It simply rested on other foundations.

THE CONFLICT WITH THE PAPACY

In 1056, however, the emperor Henry III died, leaving as his heir a small boy, the future Henry IV. From this point on, the strength of the monarchy began to unravel. Henry III had installed a new group of reforming clergy at the papal court, whose policies will be discussed more fully in the next chapter. Conflicts between the regents for the boy king Henry IV and the papal reformers began almost immediately. Conflicts also erupted between the regents (who came from central and southern Germany) and the nobility of Saxony. When Henry IV began to rule on his own, the Saxon conflicts escalated. In 1073, these hostilities erupted into a disastrous and destructive civil war.

Just as the Saxon war ended, however, a new conflict broke out with the papal reformers at Rome. For reasons that will be discussed in the next chapter, the newly elected pope Gregory VII (1073–1085) became convinced that to reform the spiritual life of the church, it was necessary first to free the church from the control of laymen, including the emperor. Henry refused to accept Gregory's attempts to prohibit him from selecting and installing in office his own bishops and abbots, and began to plot to remove Gregory from the papacy. Gregory, in turn, allied himself with the Saxon nobility, reigniting the civil war from which Germany had not yet recovered. This time, the war went against Henry, and the dissident nobles, supported by Gregory, began to plot Henry's own deposition. There then followed one of the most dramatic scenes of the Middle Ages. In the depths of winter in 1077 Henry hurried across the Alps to abase himself before Pope Gregory in the north Italian castle of Canossa. As Gregory described the scene in a letter to the German princes, "There on three successive days, standing before the castle gate, laying aside all royal insignia, barefooted and in coarse attire, Henry ceased not with many tears to beseech the apostolic help and comfort." No German ruler, much less a Roman emperor, had ever been so humiliated. The memory would remain etched in German historical consciousness for centuries to come.

The events at Canossa forestalled Henry's deposition, but they did not resolve the war. The struggle between pope and emperor continued until 1122, when

WHAT WAS THE RELATIONSHIP BETWEEN FEUDALISM AND THE RISE OF NATIONAL MONARCHIES?

FEUDALISM AND THE EMERGENCE OF NATIONAL MONARCHIES   337

THE HOLY ROMAN EMPIRE, C. 1200

How does the political geography of Germany present challenges to feudal organization? Why would the German king (and often emperor) rely heavily on the power of church officials as a counterweight to the dukes? Note the position of the papal states and the German dominance of northern Italy. Why was a single heir to the German and Sicilian thrones such a threat to the papacy? Were the fears of successive popes well founded? Why or why not?

Henry's son Henry V finally reached a compromise with the papacy. By then, however, the German nobility had won far more practical independence from the crown than they had had before. After fifty years of nearly constant war, they had also become far more militarized and dangerous. In 1125, when Henry V died childless, they gained further authority by making good on their claims to elect a new ruler regardless of hereditary succession—a principle that would thereafter often lead them to choose the weakest successors or to embroil the country in civil war. The pope's right to crown any new Roman emperor gave him a stake in the selection process also. For obvious reasons, the papacy feared an overly powerful German monarch. Although the popes valued the German emperors as counterweights to the Normans in southern Italy, they feared them in equal measure. Should the German emperors succeed in ruling northern and central Italy directly, the papacy—on whose spiritual independence the salvation of all Christians depended—risked becoming their puppet. This fear propelled the next century of papal-imperial conflict.

FREDERICK BARBAROSSA AND HENRY VI

A major attempt to stem the tide running against the German monarchy was made by Frederick I (1152–1190), who came from the family of Staufen (or Hohenstaufen, meaning "high Staufen"). Frederick, called "Barbarossa" ("red beard"), reasserted the independent dignity of the empire by calling his realm the "Holy Roman Empire," on the theory that it was a universal empire descending from Rome and blessed by God. To make good this claim, Frederick added his own laws directly to those of the sixth-century Roman emperor Justinian and tried to enforce Roman law throughout his empire. At the same time, however, he also tried to rule in cooperation with the German princes, supporting their efforts to bring their own territorial nobles to heel, and trusting that the princes would in turn support his attempts to reassert imperial control over the wealthy but increasingly independent cities of northern Italy.

By and large, Frederick made this system work, but at the cost of a lengthy war in Italy and destructive conflict with the papacy. Led by Milan and supported by the papacy, the north Italian cities formed an urban coalition, the Lombard League, to resist Frederick's claims to rule in Italy. Meanwhile, the princes in Germany were continuing to gather strength, especially by colonizing the rich agricultural lands east of the Elbe. Ultimately, however, Frederick achieved a compromise with both the Lombard League and the papacy, which guaranteed the political independence of the towns in return for large cash payments they would make to the emperor. His 1184 imperial court at Mainz was one of the most splendid occasions of the twelfth century. He secured the princes' approval for his son Henry to succeed him as king and emperor, and he arranged a marriage between Henry and the sister of the Norman king of Sicily. Finally, in 1189, he departed on the Third Crusade and died on his way to the Holy Land.

Barbarossa's careful planning bore fruit in the reign of his son Henry VI. Henry succeeded to his father's throne without difficulty. He enjoyed a huge income from the north Italian towns, and when his wife's brother died suddenly without heirs, he became the king of Sicily also. This was the nightmare the papacy had always feared, for now a single, enormously powerful ruler controlled both northern and southern Italy, leaving the papal lands in central Italy surrounded on all sides. Fortunately for the papacy, however, Henry VI died in 1197 at the age of thirty-two, leaving as his heir a three-year-old son, the future Frederick II. The new pope, Innocent III (1198–1216), threw all his energy into an attempt to break the links that Barbarossa and Henry VI had forged among Germany, northern Italy, and the kingdom of Sicily. When a civil war erupted in Germany over the succession to the throne, Innocent threw his support back and forth between the two main claimants, hoping to secure some kind of promise from the successful claimant that would return Sicily to the papacy, which claimed to have granted it to the Normans as a fief. When Otto IV, the non-Staufen claimant to the throne, finally appeared to have won a decisive victory, Innocent played his last card. He sent the sixteen-year-old Frederick II north with a small army, never imagining that so small a force, led by so young a man, could ever triumph. Otto, however, threw in his lot with his cousin, King John of England; and when Otto's forces were routed at the battle of Bouvines by King Philip Augustus of France, Frederick II wound up as the new, and undisputed, king of Germany.

FREDERICK II

Frederick II (1216–1250) was one of the most fascinating of all medieval rulers. Having grown up in Sicily, Frederick spoke Arabic as well as Latin, German, French, and Italian. He was a patron of learning who composed a famous treatise on falconry that holds an

WHAT WAS THE RELATIONSHIP BETWEEN FEUDALISM AND THE RISE OF NATIONAL MONARCHIES?

FEUDALISM AND THE EMERGENCE OF NATIONAL MONARCHIES   339

honored place in the early history of Western observational science. He maintained a menagerie of exotic animals, a troop of Muslim archers, and a harem of veiled and secluded women, all of which traveled with him on his journeys. When Frederick entered a town, the effect was electrifying. But despite this appearance of exoticism, he was also a very conventional medieval ruler who sought to pursue his grandfather's policies of supporting the territorial princes in Germany while enforcing imperial rights in Italy. Much had changed, however, in the two decades of anarchy that had followed the death of the emperor Henry VI. In Germany, the princes had already become so entirely autonomous that there was little Frederick could do except to recognize their privileges. This he proceeded to do; but in exchange, he got them to elect his sons (first Henry, and then Conrad) to succeed him as kings of Germany. Frederick's biggest problems lay in Italy. In northern Italy, the cities of the Lombard League had once again shaken off their obligations to pay taxes to the empire; while in Sicily, the enormously powerful and administratively sophisticated kingdom created by the Normans had fallen into chaos.

Frederick tackled these problems in order. From 1212 until 1220, Frederick was in Germany, solidifying his relationship with the German nobility and recovering as much Staufen land as he could after twenty years of war. From 1220 until 1226 he was in Sicily and northern Italy, reestablishing his authority there. From 1227 until 1229 he was on crusade, where he succeeded in recovering Jerusalem through negotiations with the Muslim ruler of Egypt, with whom Frederick spoke Arabic and shared a love of falconry. From 1230 to 1235 he was again in Sicily, restoring his authority after an abortive papal invasion of the territory. From 1235 to 1237 he was in Germany, arguably the high point of his reign. In 1237, however, he overreached himself by asserting his rights as emperor to rule the north Italian cities directly, bypassing their own governmental structures. The result was another Lombard League, and another lengthy war, which continued until Frederick's death in 1250. The papacy was a key player in this war, going so far as to excommunicate Frederick from the church, and after his death forbidding any of his descendants to ever again occupy the thrones of Germany or Sicily. We will never know whether the papacy could have made this claim effective, for in 1254, Frederick's last surviving legitimate son died. With him went the last prospect for the continuation of effective monarchical rule in Germany. Emperors would continue to be elected, but in prac-

The Emperor Frederick II. He is shown holding a *fleur de lis,* as a symbol of rule, with a falcon, his favorite bird, at his side. Frederick was the author of a notable book on falconry.

tice, monarchical authority in Germany had effectively collapsed. Power in Germany would henceforth be divided among several hundred territorial princes whose rivalries would embroil German politics until the end of the nineteenth century.

THE "FAILURE" OF MEDIEVAL GERMANY?

Since most other areas of Europe were gaining stronger rule in the twelfth and thirteenth centuries, the decline of monarchical authority in Germany during this period is an intriguing historical problem. It is also a problem of fundamental importance, not least because Germany's "belated" emergence as a European nation state under Bismarck (and the exaggerated nationalism that accompanied this emergence) has been frequently cited to explain German involvement in the disastrous world wars of the twentieth century. Such a "long" view has difficulties, however. If we see the nation-state as the proper historical culmination of European political development, then it makes sense to ask, What went wrong

FREDERICK II CHANGES THE HEIGHT OF THE HEAVENS

As a result of the propaganda war that erupted between Frederick II and the papacy during the 1240s, a series of stories began to circulate about Frederick's "exotic" intellectual and scientific interests: that he had ordered infants to be raised in isolation, to discover what language they would naturally speak; that he had had men disemboweled before him, in order to study the processes of digestion; and that he sealed a man up in a cask to die, to prove that the soul perished with the body. None of these stories has any basis in fact, but all illustrate the impact the image of Frederick had on his contemporaries.

The following story concerns Frederick's court astrologer, Michael Scot (d. 1236), an influential scholar who translated a number of Aristotelian and astronomical works and commentaries from Arabic to Latin. It is taken from the chronicle of Salimbene de Adam, a Franciscan supporter of the pope in the struggle against Frederick.

The seventh example [of Frederick's idiosyncracies] was that he once asked Michael Scot to tell him the distance of his palace from heaven. And after Michael gave the answer that seemed correct to him, the Emperor took him away for a few months as if merely on a pleasure trip, commanding his architects and stone masons in the meantime to lower that room of his palace in such a way that no one could detect it. This was done, and when the Emperor returned to his palace with the astrologer, he asked him again how far distant the palace was from heaven. And after he had completed his calcu-lations, Michael Scot answered that either the heavens had risen or the earth had sunk. Then the emperor know that he was a true astrologer.

I have heard and know many other idiosyncrasies of Frederick, but I keep quiet for the sake of brevity, and because reporting so many of the Emperor's foolish notions is tedious to me.

Joseph Baird, Giuseppe Baglivi, and John Robert Kane, eds. and trans. *The Chronicle of Salimbene de Adam*, v. 40 of Medieval and Renaissance Texts and Studies (Series). (Binghamton, N.Y.: Medieval and Renaissance Texts and Studies, 1986), pp. 355–356.

---

with Germany? If, however, the nation-state itself should prove to be a passing historical phase—a view that becomes more plausible as the European Community becomes more and more powerful—then the history of medieval Germany may come to appear not as a story of failure, but rather as a story about the deep regional divisions that have characterized the history of Europe throughout its recorded history, lasting until the present day. As so often in history, what we see depends greatly upon the perspective from which we look.

IBERIA

The Iberian peninsula was even more regionalized than was Germany. In contrast to Germany, however, Spain would emerge from the Middle Ages with the most powerful monarchy in Europe. The key to the strength of the Spanish monarchies of the High Middle Ages lay in their successful reconquest of the peninsula from the Muslims, and in the lands, booty, and plunder these conquests provided. During the High Middle Ages

WHAT WAS THE RELATIONSHIP BETWEEN FEUDALISM AND THE RISE OF NATIONAL MONARCHIES?

FEUDALISM AND THE EMERGENCE OF NATIONAL MONARCHIES   341

THE RECONQUEST OF IBERIA, 900–1250

Note the position of the Christian kingdoms circa 900, and the progress of the reassertion of Christian control over the subsequent few centuries. What factors helped to shelter and sustain the small Christian kingdoms that survived Islam's initial push? Why did Castile become the largest of the Christian kingdoms as the reconquest progressed? Why did the smaller Aragon and Catalunya maintain important positions as wealthy and significant powers? How did the struggles and successes of Christians in Iberia influence the crusader movement?

Iberia contained four major Christian kingdoms: the northern mountain state of Navarre, which would always remain comparatively insignificant; Portugal in the west; the combined kingdom of Aragon and Catalunya in the southeast; and Castile in the center. Throughout the twelfth century, Christian armies steadily advanced, culminating in the year 1212 in a major victory by a combined Aragonese-Castilian army over the Muslims at Las Navas de Tolosa. The rest was mostly mopping up. By the end of the thirteenth century all that remained of earlier Muslim domination was the small state of Granada in the extreme south, and Granada existed mostly because it was willing to pay tribute to the Christians. Castile became by far the largest Spanish kingdom in area, but it was balanced in wealth by the more urban and trade-oriented kingdom of Aragon and Catalunya. Wars between these two rivals weakened both kingdoms during the later Middle Ages; but when the marriage of Ferdinand of Aragon and Isabella of Castile joined these two ancient enemies, a united Spanish monarchy was born. In 1492, the Catholic monarchs (as Ferdinand and Isabella were known) captured Granada, the last remaining Muslim territory in Spain. A few months later, Isabella commissioned an Italian adventurer named Christopher Columbus to sail to India by heading west across the Atlantic Ocean. Columbus failed. But his accidental encounter with the American continents made sixteenth century Spain the most powerful kingdom in Europe.

CONCLUSION

Until the emergence of national monarchies during the High Middle Ages, there had been two basic patterns of government in Europe: city-states and empires. City-states had the advantage of drawing heavily on citizen participation and loyalty and thus were able to make highly efficient use of their human potential. But they were often divided by economic rivalries, and they were not sufficiently large or militarily strong to defend themselves against imperial forces. The empires, on the other hand, could win battles and often had the resources to support an efficient bureaucratic administrative apparatus, but they drew on little voluntary participation and were too far flung or rapacious to inspire any deep loyalties. The new national monarchies were to prove the "golden mean" between these extremes. They were large enough to have adequate military strength, and they developed administrative techniques that would rival and eventually surpass those of the Roman or Byzantine empires. More than that, building at first on the basis of feudalism, they commanded sufficient citizen participation and loyalty to help support them in times of stress when empires would have foundered. By about 1300 the monarchies of England, France, and the Iberian peninsula had gained the primary loyalties of their subjects, superseding loyalties to communities, regions, or to the government of the church. For all these reasons they brought much internal peace and stability to large parts of Europe where there had been little stability before. Thus they contributed greatly to making life fruitful. The medieval national monarchies were also

the ancestors of the modern nation-states—the most effective and equitable governments of our day (the former Soviet Union was more like an empire). In short, they were one of the Middle Ages' most beneficial bequests to modern times.

SELECTED READINGS

Abulafia, David. *Frederick II: A Medieval Emperor,* London and New York, 1988. The only reliable biography of Frederick II; it strips away much of the legend that has hitherto surrounded this monarch.

Abulafia, David, ed. *The New Cambridge Medieval History. Volume 5: c. 1198–c. 1300.* Cambridge, 1999. An up-to-date survey, with contributions by more than thirty specialists. Excellent bibliographies.

Amt, Emily, ed. *Women's Lives in Medieval Europe: A Sourcebook.* New York, 1993. An excellent source collection.

Arnold, Benjamin. *Princes and Territories in Medieval Germany.* Cambridge and New York, 1991. The best English-language survey; it correctly avoids portraying the political history of medieval Germany as a story of failure.

Baldwin, John W. *The Government of Philip Augustus.* Berkeley and Los Angeles, 1986. A landmark scholarly account, detailed but readable.

Bartlett, Robert. *The Making of Europe: Conquest, Colonization and Cultural Change, 950–1350.* Princeton, N.J., 1993. A wide-ranging examination of the economic, social, and religious expansion of Europe, full of stimulating ideas and insights.

———. *England under the Norman and Angevin Kings, 1075–1225.* Oxford and New York, 2000. An outstanding new synthesis, part of the New Oxford History of England series.

Dunbabin, Jean. *France in the Making, 843–1180,* 2d ed. Oxford and New York, 2000. An authoritative survey of the disparate territories that came to make up the medieval French kingdom.

Fuhrmann, Horst. *Germany in the High Middle Ages, c. 1050–1200.* Cambridge, 1986. A useful, short account in English of the history of twelfth-century Germany.

Gillingham, John. *The Angevin Empire,* 2d ed. Oxford and New York, 2001. The best treatment by far of its subject, brief but full of ideas.

Hallam, Elizabeth, and Judith Everard. *Capetian France, 987–1328,* 2d ed. New York, 2001. An excellent textbook; a bit dry, but clear and well organized.

Herlihy, David, ed. *The History of Feudalism.* New York, 1970. Collects the texts on which scholarly discussion continues to focus.

———. *Medieval Households.* Cambridge, Mass., 1985. Covers family history from late antiquity until the end of the Middle Ages.

Holt, Richard. *The Mills of Medieval England.* Oxford and New

York, 1988. An authoritative account by an historian of medieval agricultural technology.

Hyde, J. Kenneth. *Society and Politics in Medieval Italy.* New York, 1973. A survey that sets the political history of the Italian city-states in its social context.

Jones, P. J. *The Italian City-State: From Commune to Signoria.* Oxford and New York, 1997. A fundamental reinterpretation, with important revisions to the standard accounts of Hyde and Waley.

Kaeuper, Richard W. *Chivalry and Violence in Medieval Europe.* Oxford and New York, 1999. A darker view of chivalry than Keen's (see below).

Keen, Maurice. *Chivalry.* New Haven, 1984. Masterful treatment of chivalry from its origins to the sixteenth century, engagingly written.

Lambert of Ardres. *The History of the Counts of Guines and Lords of Ardres.* Translated by Leah Shopkow. Philadelphia, 2000. A tremendously informative and important chronicle of an important Flemish family, now available for the first time in English.

Leyser, Henrietta. *Medieval Women: A Social History of Women in England, 440–1500.* New York, 1995. Although limited to one country, this is the best of the recent surveys treating medieval women.

Lopez, Robert S., and Irving W. Raymond, eds. *Medieval Trade in the Mediterranean World.* New York, 1990. A pathbreaking collection of source material on Italian medieval trade.

Moore, Robert I. *The First European Revolution, c. 970–1215.* Oxford and Cambridge, Mass., 2000. A remarkable description of the ways in which European society was fundamentally reshaped during the eleventh and twelfth centuries.

Mortimer, Richard. *Angevin England, 1154–1258.* Oxford and Cambridge, Mass., 1994. An expert treatment of politics and society, organized topically.

Otto, Bishop of Freising. *The Deeds of Frederick Barbarossa.* Translated by C. C. Mierow. New York, 1953. A contemporary chronicle interesting enough to read from start to finish.

Poly, Jean-Pierre, and Eric Bournazel. *The Feudal Transformation, 900–1200.* Translated by Caroline Higgitt. New York and London, 1991. A synthesis of recent work by French historians, building on the works of Marc Bloch and Georges Duby.

Pounds, N. J. G. *An Economic History of Medieval Europe,* 2d ed. London and New York, 1994. An excellent textbook, the second edition integrates English economic history into its analysis.

Reilly, Bernard F. *The Medieval Spains.* New York, 1993. A succinct account that covers the entire Iberian peninsula from 500 to 1500.

Reynolds, Susan. *Fiefs and Vassals: The Medieval Evidence Reinterpreted.* Oxford and New York, 1994. A detailed revisionist account that sees feudalism as the invention of high and late medieval legal thinkers rather than as a description of tenth and eleventh century realities.

Richard, Jean. *Saint Louis: Crusader King of France.* Cambridge, 1992. An abridged version of Richard's standard biography of King Louis IX, originally published in French.

Southern, Richard W. *The Making of the Middle Ages.* New Haven, 1992. A classic work, first published in 1951 but still fresh and exciting.

Stow, Kenneth R. *Alienated Minority: The Jews of Medieval Latin Europe.* Cambridge, Mass., 1992. An excellent survey of a neglected topic.

Suger, Abbot of Saint Denis. *The Deeds of Louis the Fat.* Translated by R. Cusimano and J. Moorhead. Washington, D. C., 1992. A revealing picture of the challenges that faced the early twelfth-century kings of France as they fought to subdue the local nobility of the Île-de-France.

Waley, Daniel. *The Italian City-Republics.* New York, 1969. A classic introduction to the subject.

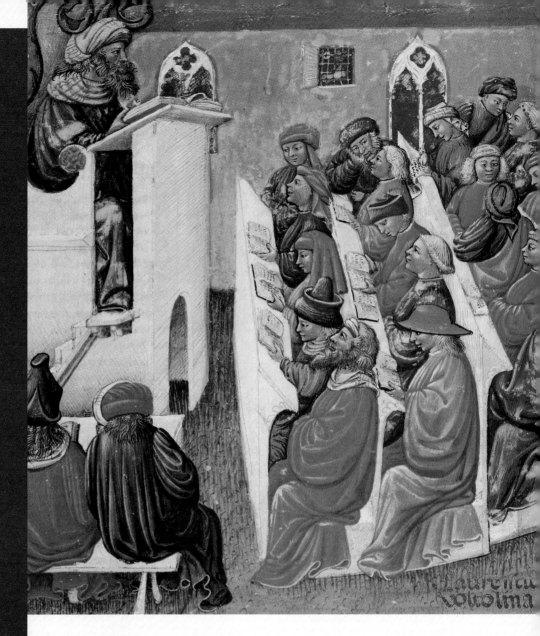

THE HIGH MIDDLE
AGES: RELIGIOUS
AND INTELLECTUAL
DEVELOPMENTS,
1000–1300

THE RELIGIOUS AND INTELLECTUAL CHANGES of the High Middle Ages altered European life profoundly. Indeed, it is not too much to say that the fundamental character of European civilization was permanently transformed by the developments that occurred during these crucial centuries. With respect to religious life, the period witnessed both the emergence of the papacy as the dominant organizational force in western Christianity and a remarkable effort on the part of the church to extend and deepen the influence of Christianity among the laity. Parish churches mushroomed across the landscape, and new monastic and religious orders developed, many of which took as their primary mission the task of ministering to the world outside the monastic cloister. For the first time since the late Roman period, preaching, confession, pilgrimages, and private prayer became central elements in the religious life of European Christians. At the same time, however, these new patterns of Christian piety emphasized the religious and social distinctions between Christians and their non-Christian neighbors. The result was a marked increase in the persecution of minority groups within European society, and the creation of what some historians have called "a persecuting society" in which the identification and oppression of heretics, Jews, gay people, lepers, and Muslims became an essential element in the growing power of both church and state.

The High Middle Ages also witnessed a remarkable revival of intellectual and cultural life. From the mid-twelfth century on, hundreds of new works of classical literature and philosophy, including the entirety of the surviving works of Aristotle, poured into western Europe from the Islamic world and, to a lesser degree, from Byzantium. Even before the stimulus of these new texts, however, European intellectuals had begun to think in new, more rigorous ways about fundamental problems in theology, philosophy, and law. Fueling this intellectual revolution (which is sometimes referred to as the "Renaissance of the Twelfth Century") was the emergence and rapid growth of universities, accompanied by an even more widespread expansion of primary schooling. New literary forms also began to emerge: vernacular lyric poetry, extended allegories, and above all romances. For the first time in centuries it began to be possible to speak of a European reading public.

FOCUS QUESTIONS

- How was the Latin Church reformed?
- How did the Latin Church control popular heresy?
- How did the recovery of classical learning affect medieval intellectual life?
- What constituted the "Renaissance of the Twelfth Century"?

POLITICAL DEVELOPMENTS OF THE HIGH MIDDLE AGES, 1000–c. 1250	
Capetian dynasty in France	987–1328
Norman Conquest of England	1066
First four crusades	1095–1204
Reign of Frederick Barbarossa	1152–1190
Magna Carta	1215
Reconquest of Spain	c. 1000–c. 1250

In education, thought, and the arts, early medieval Europe had been a backwater, especially in comparison with Byzantium and Islam. By 1300, however, Europe had become the intellectual and artistic leader among these three western civilizations. Westerners boasted that learning and the arts had come to them from Egypt, Greece, and Rome; and that although they were pygmies who sat on the shoulders of giants, they nonetheless saw farther and more clearly than had the intellectual giants of antiquity on whose shoulders they sat. Such boasts were largely justified. In the High Middle Ages, Europeans built their intellectual and artistic accomplishments on ancient foundations, but they also began to make major contributions of their own.

In the High Middle Ages, Europeans built their intellectual and artistic accomplishments on ancient foundations, but they also began to make major contributions of their own.

THE REFORM OF THE CHURCH

How was the Latin Church reformed?

The combined effects of Carolingian collapse, Viking, Muslim, and Magyar attacks, and the growing power of local noble families were disastrous for the religious life of ninth- and tenth-century Europe. For several centuries, church reformers had sought to improve the religious lives of the laity by strengthening the control that powerful bishops exercised over the local clergy within their dioceses. By the middle of the tenth century, however, that strategy lay in ruins. Many parish churches had been abandoned or destroyed, while those that survived were often regarded as the personal possession of some powerful local family, whose responsibility for protecting these churches easily became a license to oppress them. In these circumstances, a parish church frequently became simply a manorial appurtenance, like the lord's mill or oven or forge, which his peasants were obliged to use and from which he took the profits. Even bishoprics fell into the hands of noble families, who appointed relatives to them and or sold them as if they were pieces of family property. Monasteries underwent a similar process of "privatization." Some became dumping grounds for aristocratic younger sons who might live in the monastery without ever taking monastic vows. Other monasteries had troops of knights thrust on them. Some even had lay abbots. It was all very distant from what Saint Benedict had outlined in his *Rule for Monasteries*.

In the absence of effective kingship, bishops were helpless against such entrenched local power. Nor could the papacy correct the situation. Indeed, as the bishops of Rome, the popes themselves were among the worst examples of the negative impact too much local influence could have on the spiritual standards of the clergy. Most of the tenth-century popes were incompetent or corrupt, the sons or tools of powerful Roman families who sought to control the papacy in order to rule the city of Rome itself. Some were astonishingly debauched. The worst of them, John XII, became pope in 955 at the age of eighteen through the influence of his family, which had ruled Rome for half a century. Pope John was nearly illiterate and thoroughly licentious. His critics claimed that female pilgrims would not even enter the Lateran Palace for fear that the pope would molest them; and he is reported to have died in the midst of yet another carnal act, either from sheer amorous exertion or else by the sword of a jealous husband who found the pope in bed with his wife. As the guardian of the tombs of Saints Peter and Paul and the spiritual head of western Christendom, the papacy remained a respected institution, even in its tenth-century nadir. But the popes who occupied Saint Peter's chair left a great deal to be desired as moral and spiritual leaders of Western society.

MONASTIC REFORM, 900–1050

The first stirrings of reform emerged in the monasteries of tenth-century Europe, beginning with that of Cluny in Burgundy. Founded in 910 by a pious nobleman, Cluny was a Benedictine house, but with two important constitutional innovations. One was that in order to keep it free from domination by local noble families or the local bishop, Cluny was placed directly under the protection of the papacy. The second was that it undertook the reform or foundation of a large number of "daughter monasteries." Whereas formerly all Benedictine houses had been independent and equal, Cluny established a network of dependent Cluniac houses across Europe, all of which remained subordinate to the mother house at Cluny. By 1049, there were sixty-seven such Cluniac priories (as the daughter monasteries were called), each one performing the same elaborate round of prayer and worship for which Cluny became famous, and each entirely free from the control of local secular or ecclesiastical powers. Under the rule of a series of pious and remarkably long-lived abbots, Cluny became famous for its high spiritual standards and its carefully ordered liturgical life. In the eyes of the Cluniacs, however, their success depended on their absolute freedom from outside interference in their religious life. When Cluny reformed a monastery, therefore, it insisted on two things: first, that the Benedictine vows of poverty, chastity, and obedience be strictly enforced on all monks; and second, that the selection of new abbots and priors be accomplished by a free election of the monks, without any buying or selling of the office (a sin known as "simony," after Simon Magus, a magician in the New Testament who tried to buy the power of the Holy Spirit from Jesus' disciples).

Cluniac influence was strongest in France and Italy, where the virtual absence of effective kingship made royally sponsored monastic reforms impossible. Here, and also in Lotharingia, pious nobles usually took the lead in promoting monastic reforms. In Germany and England, by contrast, monastic reform emerged during the tenth and eleventh centuries as an essential responsibility of a Christian king. Following Cluniac example, these kings insisted on the strict observance of poverty, chastity, and obedience within the monastery, and instituted elaborate rounds of group liturgical prayer. In contrast to Cluny, however, it was the kings themselves who guaranteed the reformed monasteries' freedom from outside interference, and it was they who appointed the abbots, just as they also appointed the bishops of their kingdom.

As a result of these parallel movements for monastic reform, monasticism became the dominant spiritual model for tenth- and eleventh-century Latin Christianity. The peaceful, orderly round of the monks' daily worship was seen as mirroring the perfect harmony of heaven; their prayers were regarded as uniquely effective in preserving a sinful world from the destruction a just God might otherwise wreak on it; and monks themselves were seen as "angelic men," whose personal poverty, chastity, and perfect obedience faithfully reflected the virtues of heaven itself. But monasteries also had an important influence on patterns of piety outside the cloister. For centuries, monasteries had been the repositories and guardians for the relics of departed saints, whose powers were believed to protect the monasteries that housed their earthly bodies. From the tenth century on, however, monasteries increasingly attracted the attentions of pious laypeople, who came seeking miraculous cures from the saint (or saints) whose relics were housed there. The vast majority of such pilgrimages were to local shrines. But regular long-distance pilgrimage routes also began to develop, to such places as Santiago de Compostela in Spain and the Church of Saint Faith in southern France. Traffic also increased to such traditional pilgrimage sites as Rome and Jerusalem. Pilgrimage was one of the important ways in which the new patterns of Christian piety developed in monasteries began to spread to the laity outside the monastic walls.

THE PAPAL REFORM MOVEMENT

From the monasteries, the reform movement began to affect the bishops also. In England, kings appointed a number of reformed monks to bishoprics. In Germany, kings retained nonmonastic bishops but enforced strict requirements of personal holiness on the bishops and abbots whom they appointed to office. With royal encouragement, bishops also began to rebuild and expand their cathedral churches to make them more suitable reflections of divine majesty, in accordance with Cluniac example. The Cluniacs themselves, however, went further, and began to lobby for the reform of the entire church, including bishops, unreformed monasteries, and even the parish clergy. They centered their attacks upon simony—the buying and selling of church offices—but they also demanded that personal poverty and celibacy be enforced on all monks and priests. This last demand was in some ways the most radical. Although a series of

A MIRACLE OF SAINT FAITH

Although pilgrimages and relics cults had been a part of Christian religious practice for centuries, they became much more central elements in popular piety from the tenth century on. To the monasteries that housed miracle-working relics, pilgrims brought money and spiritual prestige, resulting in competition between monastic houses that sometimes led one house to steal the relics of another. But some critics worried that these newly popular pilgrimage shrines were encouraging idolatry. The author of this account, Bernard of Angers, was one such critic, but in this case he was quickly won over by the evidence of Saint Faith's miracles.

The relics of Saint Faith, a fourth-century martyr, were stolen by the monks of Conques (in southern France) during the ninth century, and became famous during the tenth century for their miraculous healing powers. They were housed in the reliquary shown in the accompanying illustration. Bernard's description of his visit to her shrine is a very revealing account of the initially negative impression this ornate reliquary made on him.

It is an ancient custom in all of Auvergne, Rodez, Toulouse and the neighboring regions that the local saint has a statue of gold, silver, or some other metal . . . [that] serves as a reliquary for the head of the saint or for a part of his body. The learned might see in this a superstition and a vestige of the cult of demons, and I myself . . . had the same impression the first time I saw the statue of Saint Gerard . . . resplendent with gold and stones, with an expression so human that the simple people . . . pretend that it winks at pilgrims whose prayers it answers. I admit to my shame that turning to my friend Bernerius and laughing I whispered to him in Latin, "What do you think of the idol? Wouldn't Jupiter or Mars be happy with it?" . . .

Three days later we arrived at St. Faith. . . . We approached [the reliquary] but the crowd was such that we could not prostrate ourselves like so many others already lying on the floor. Unhappy, I remained standing, fixing my view on the image and murmuring this prayer, "St. Faith, you whose relics rest in this sham, come to my assistance on the day of judgment." And this time I looked at my companion . . . because I found it outrageous that all of these rational beings should be praying to a mute and inanimate object. . . .

Later I greatly regretted to have acted so stupidly toward the saint of God. This was because among other miracles Don Adalgerius, at that time dean and later . . . abbot [of Conques] told me a remarkable account of a cleric named Oldaric. One day when the venerable image had to be taken to another place, . . . he restrained the crowd from bringing offerings and he insulted and belittled the image of the saint. . . . The next night, a lady of imposing severity appeared to him: "You," she said, "how dare you insult my image?" Having said this, she flogged her enemy with a staff. . . . He survived only long enough to tell the vision in the morning.

Thus there is no place left for arguing whether the effigy of St. Faith ought to be venerated since it is clear that he who reproached the holy martyr nevertheless retracted his reproach. Nor is it a spurious idol where nefarious rites of sacrifice or of divination are conducted, but rather a pious memorial of a holy virgin, before which great numbers of faithful people decently and eloquently implore her efficacious intercession for their sins.

Bernard of Angers, *The Book of the Miracles of St. Faith*, chapter 28. Slightly modified from *Readings in Medieval History*, 2d edition, edited and translated by Patrick J. Geary. (Petersborough, Ont.: Broadview Press, 1997), p. 317.

The Reliquary of Saint Faith, early tenth century.

fourth- and fifth-century church councils had declared that priests should be celibate, this requirement had been largely ignored thereafter. In the year 1000, the vast majority of the parish priests across Europe were married. Married bishops were rarer, but not unknown. In Brittany, the archbishop of Dol and his wife publicly celebrated the marriage of their daughters, endowing them with lands belonging to the bish-

opric; in Milan, the archbishops flatly rejected reformers' calls for celibacy, declaring that their patron saint, Bishop Ambrose of Milan, had been married, and that he had granted his diocese permission to have a married priesthood forever.

In Rome, however, the papacy remained resolutely unreformed until 1046, when the German emperor Henry III came to Rome, deposed all three of the local Roman nobles who claimed to be pope, and appointed in their place his own relative, a German monastic reformer who took the name Pope Leo IX (1049–1054). Leo and his supporters (mostly German, but some Italian) quickly took control over the papal court and began to promulgate decrees against simony, clerical marriage, and immorality of all sorts throughout the church. To enforce these decrees, Leo and his entourage traveled through France, Italy, Germany, and Hungary, disciplining and deposing clerics who had purchased their positions or who refused to give up their wives (whom the reformers insisted on calling "concubines"). Implicit in Leo's reforming efforts was thus a new vision of the church itself as a hierarchical organization in which priests obeyed bishops and bishops obeyed the pope not only as the spiritual and doctrinal leader of western Christendom, but as the legal and jurisdictional ruler of the entire Christian church.

Leo and the reform popes were able to enforce their decrees only in those areas of Europe where they could count on the support of secular rulers. Among these secular supporters, the most important was of course the emperor Henry III, whose protection insulated the papal reformers from the Roman noble families who would otherwise have deposed them. In 1056, however, Henry III died, leaving a young child as his heir, the future Henry IV. Without their imperial protector, the reformers were now at the mercy of the Roman political factions. When the reigning reform pope died in 1058, the Roman nobles seized their opportunity to install as pope one of their own lackeys. Briefly, it looked as if the entire reform program might be lost. But the reformers rallied outside Rome, and elected their own pope (who took the name Nicholas II). Allying themselves militarily with the Norman rulers of central and southern Italy, they drove the nonreformed pope out of Rome.

In 1059, Pope Nicholas II issued a new decree on papal elections, vesting the right to elect a pope solely with the cardinals, but "saving the rights of the Emperor." The decree is significant for two quite different reasons. First, it represents a milestone in the evolution of the College of Cardinals as a special body within the

Church. Ever since the tenth century a number of bishops and clerics drawn from churches in and near Rome had taken on an important role as advisers and administrative assistants of the popes. This decree was the first time, however, that the cardinals' powers had been clearly recognized. Thereafter the College of Cardinals took on an increasingly well-defined identity, becoming an important force in creating continuity of papal policy, especially when there was a quick succession of pontiffs. The cardinals still elect the pope today.

The decree was also significant, however, because it opened up a breach between the reform party in Rome and the German imperial court. In the circumstances of 1059, the Electoral Decree was intended to justify the reformers' actions of the previous year and to protect future papal elections from the influence of the Roman aristocracy. But although the decree obviously drew on Cluniac ideals about free elections as an essential element in a reformed church, it was not intended to deprive the German emperor of his traditional role as papal protector. The simple fact was, however, that in 1059 there was no emperor who could play this role; and if the alternative was the return of the Roman nobility and the destruction of the entire reform effort, then even an alliance with the brutal and unreliable Normans seemed preferable. Nonetheless, the electoral decree greatly offended the advisors of the young king Henry IV, who saw it as a challenge to the emperors' rights to nominate new popes, and who also bitterly resented the reformers' alliance with the Normans, whose designs on imperial territories in central Italy were well known. The resulting hostility between the young king's regents and the papal court poisoned the atmosphere in which King Henry IV grew to maturity.

THE INVESTITURE CONFLICT

A new and momentous phase in the history of the reform movement began in 1073 with the election of Pope Gregory VII (1073–1085). Gregory was a Roman whose election was violently supported by a mob of Roman citizens. Gregory was already a well-known reformer with long experience at the papal court. It is likely that he would have been elected by the cardinals anyway, even without the interference of the Roman mob. But the circumstances of his election clearly violated the terms of the 1059 Electoral Decree, and this fact weakened Gregory in his first few years as pope. Henry IV was also anxious for a reconciliation with Rome, not least because between 1073 and 1075 he was involved in a major civil war with his own nobility in Saxony. Both Gregory and Henry began, therefore, by treating one another with great deference. Henry blamed the advisors of his youth for the troubles that had arisen between his own court and Rome, and promised to make amends. Gregory, in turn, spoke of pope and emperor as the two eyes of a single, Christian body, and promised to leave the church in Henry's care if he, Gregory, should lead (as he briefly hoped to do) a military expedition eastward against Islam. On the surface, it appeared that the harmonious relations between papacy and empire that had existed under Henry's father had been fully restored.

By the end of 1075, however, relations between the two men were at a breaking point. For the next half century, western Europe would be riven by conflict between the papacy and the empire—a conflict that would permanently alter the relationship between spiritual and temporal authority in western Christendom. Superficially, the issue that divided Gregory and Henry was whether Henry or any other layman could appoint a bishop or abbot and then dress him with the symbols of his spiritual office, a practice known as "lay investiture." In fact, however, the "Investiture Conflict" raised fundamental issues about the nature of Christian kingship, the relationship between political and religious authority, and the control that popes and kings should exercise over the clergy. Not all these issues were fully resolved by 1122, when a compromise known as the Concordat of Worms finally ended the Investiture Conflict. But the conflict was a turning point nonetheless, because it brought to a permanent end the old Carolingian traditions of sacred kingship and established once and for all the independent jurisdictional authority of the church versus all lay rulers.

Gregory was a devoted church reformer whose goals were the traditional ones of ending simony and clerical marriage. Unlike previous papal reformers, however, Gregory became convinced that these goals could not be achieved until the Cluniac goal of ensuring free elections to all church offices had first been realized. Gregory therefore proceeded to prohibit all cler-

> The "Investiture Conflict" raised fundamental issues about the nature of Christian kingship, the relationship between political and religious authority, and the control that popes and kings should exercise over the clergy.

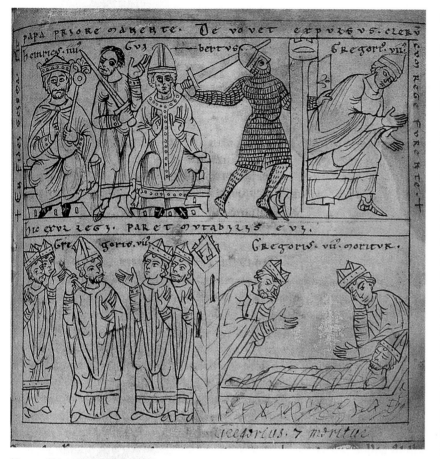

Henry IV and Gregory VII. In the top panel, King Henry appoints Wibert, Archbishop of Milan, to be the new pope, and drives Pope Gregory from Rome. In the lower panel, Pope Gregory is received by the bishops of the Norman kingdom of southern Italy, and then dies in exile. From a twelfth-century German manuscript.

election had violated the terms of the 1059 Electoral Decree, and calling on him to resign. Gregory responded by excommunicating Henry, along with a large number of German and Italian bishops who were supporting Henry.

In itself, the excommunication of a king was not terribly unusual. As we have seen, in the fourth century, Saint Ambrose had even excommunicated the Roman emperor Theodosius the Great. Gregory, however, went much further by equating excommunication with deposition, declaring that since Henry was no longer a faithful son of the church, he was therefore no longer the king of Germany. Gregory now called on Henry's subjects to rebel, prompting the Saxon nobility to renew the civil war that had ended only a few months before. In January 1077, Henry was forced to make a humiliating public submission to Pope Gregory at Canossa in the Italian Alps; but when the pope absolved him of his excommunication, Henry used the opportunity to rally his forces, crush his Saxon opponents, and drive Gregory himself from Rome. In 1085, the aged pope died in exile at Salerno, a virtual prisoner of his Norman allies. His last words were reportedly, "I have loved justice and hated iniquity; that is why I die in exile."

By instinct, Pope Gregory was a radical whose confidence in his own rectitude knew no bounds. Early in his career he had been part of the delegation that provoked the 1054 schism with the Byzantine church by demanding that the patriarch of Constantinople acknowledge the primacy of the papacy. As pope, Gregory was convinced that he spoke with Saint Peter's voice and so could not err. When told that his ideas were novel, he replied "The Lord did not say 'I am custom'; the Lord said 'I am truth.'" When it was suggested to him that his policies had brought war, not peace, he replied by citing Scripture: "Cursed be he that shall withhold his sword from blood." His calls for the people of Germany to rise up against their errant king and his sinful bishops were nothing short of revolutionary. Even his admirers referred to him as a "Holy Satan," recalling the rebellious angel whose pride had caused his downfall.

ics from accepting any church office from a layman, declaring this prohibition to be "a truth . . . necessary for salvation." Henry IV flatly refused to accept this decree, not only because it infringed on his own traditional rights as a Carolingian-style king and emperor, but also because the bishops and abbots of Germany and northern Italy were critically important to his own ability to rule his kingdoms. Henry proceeded, therefore, to appoint and invest a new archbishop in Milan in defiance of Gregory's prohibition. Gregory responded by reminding Henry that he, Gregory, occupied Saint Peter's chair, and that Henry therefore owed to Gregory the same obedience he owed to Saint Peter, who was the gatekeeper to heaven. To drive the point home, Gregory excommunicated a number of Henry's advisors, including several of the north Italian bishops who had participated in the investiture of the new archbishop of Milan. Henry thereupon renounced his obedience to Gregory, reminding the pope that his

Gregory's radical instincts must not obscure, however, his profoundly traditional vision of Christendom. Although the ultimate solution to the Investiture Conflict was to distinguish between "church" and "state" by reserving the symbols of spiritual office to the clergy while permitting laymen to award the symbols of temporal rule, such a distinction was no part of Gregory's own world view. Indeed, it was precisely because neither Henry nor Gregory could conceive of Christendom as anything other than a thoroughly unified religious and political society that the conflict between them was so intractable. Both Henry and Gregory shared the standard Carolingian presumption that it was the responsibility of earthly rulers to lead their subjects to heaven. They disagreed only about whether the supreme ruler within this unified Christian society should be the emperor or the pope. To borrow Gregory's own metaphor, both Gregory and Henry agreed that Christendom was a single body with two eyes. The issue between them was whether pope or emperor should be the lead eye, and so determine the direction in which the Christian body would walk. Neither could imagine a world in which a bishop's spiritual office could be separated from the lands and military forces he controlled, or in which there could be two entirely separate systems of courts, one dealing with religious matters and controlled by the papacy, the other dealing with secular matters and controlled by kings. Without such a division between the spiritual and the temporal, however, the Investiture Conflict was irresolvable. Neither pope nor emperor was powerful enough to defeat the other; and on some level, all Europe was agreed that both spiritual and temporal authorities were necessary. For had not Jesus himself declared that two swords (both of course borne by Peter, as papal champions were quick to point out) were sufficient for the days of trouble that lay ahead?

The consequences of the Investiture Conflict were thus quite different from what Pope Gregory or King Henry had imagined. On the immediate issue of lay investiture, the Concordat of Worms was a compromise. The German emperor was forbidden to invest prelates with the religious symbols of their office, but was allowed to invest them with the symbols of their rights as temporal rulers because the emperor was recognized as their temporal overlord. In practice, the German emperors, like the other kings of western Europe, thus managed to retain a great deal of influence over appointments to bishoprics and abbeys despite allowing the appearance of free elections.

In a larger sense, however, the ultimate consequence of the Investiture Conflict was to create a lasting conceptual distinction between religion and politics in western Europe, and to identify the church with religious authority and the state with political authority. Both ideas had been largely absent from western Europe since the fourth century Constantinian revolution. When the Investiture Conflict began, Henry's principal supporters were his bishops. Gregory's supporters were, for the most part, the Saxon nobility and the other disaffected German princes. In no sense, therefore, did the Investiture Conflict begin as a "church-state" conflict. By 1122, however, that is what it had become. The Concordat of Worms resolved the papal-imperial conflict by distinguishing between the temporal power of kings and the spiritual power of the clergy. It also firmly identified the bishops as a part of a hierarchical clerical order headed by the pope. The boundaries between temporal and spiritual authority would continue to be subject to controversy in medieval Europe. Should kings or clerics judge clergy who committed secular crimes? Who should rule on the validity of marriages when rights to inherit property were at issue? But these were jurisdictional conflicts that sought to define the boundaries between religion and politics. These conflicts did not challenge the fundamental presumption that such a distinction existed. Therefore, these conflicts were resolvable through law—one reason that the elaboration of legal systems, both ecclesiastical and secular, became such a preoccupation for twelfth- and thirteenth-century western Europe. In this respect also, the Investiture Conflict marks a watershed in European history.

> The ultimate consequence of the Investiture Conflict was to create a lasting conceptual distinction between religion and politics in western Europe.

THE CONSOLIDATION OF THE PAPAL MONARCHY

The Concordat of Worms was a compromise, but the Investiture Conflict as a whole was a victory for the papacy. The conflict helped rally the Western clergy behind the pope, strengthening the papacy's claim to jurisdictional supremacy over the entire clerical hierarchy. The dramatic struggle also galvanized the European populace. As one contemporary reported, nothing else was talked about "even in the women's spinning rooms and the artisans' workshops." Pope Gregory and his successors had urged the common people of Europe to reject the authority of simoniac bishops and married priests. Thousands had responded, sometimes with violence. The result was a vastly greater popular interest in religious matters, which the church thereafter would struggle to contain within the bounds of religious orthodoxy.

Like Gregory VII, the popes of the twelfth and thirteenth century were fully committed to establishing the monarchical authority of the papacy over the church. But they were far less impetuous than Gregory had been, choosing instead to pursue their aims by carefully building up the governmental apparatus of the church. The papal writing office (known as the Chancery) was already the most sophisticated in Europe, producing thousands of letters annually on a huge variety of subjects. Specially commissioned papal officials ("legates") were also sent out from Rome to convey and enforce papal commands. Many of these commands arose from the hundreds (and eventually thousands) of legal cases that poured into Rome from litigants seeking justice from the pope. In turn, this growing mass of litigation encouraged the development of an authoritative body of church law by which such cases could be resolved. The key step in this development was taken around 1140 in Bologna by a law teacher named Gratian, whose massive compilation and codification of the decrees of previous popes and church councils (known as the *Decretum* or, more descriptively, as *The Concord of Discordant Canons*) quickly became the standard collection of church ("canon") law.

Gratian's *Decretum* claimed ecclesiastical jurisdiction for all sorts of cases pertaining not only to the clergy but also to the laity, including such matters as marriage, inheritance, and wills. Although all such cases were supposed to be heard first in local church courts, the popes insisted that they alone could issue dispensations from the strict letter of the law and that the papal consistory—the pope and the cardinals—should be the final court of appeals for all canon-law cases. As the power of the papacy and the prestige of the church mounted, cases in canon-law courts and appeals to Rome rapidly increased. By the mid-twelfth century legal expertise had become so important that almost all popes were trained canon lawyers, whereas previously they had usually been monks. Purists decried this de-

> By the mid-twelfth century legal expertise had become so important that almost all popes were trained canon lawyers, whereas previously they had usually been monks.

velopment, but it was an inevitable consequence of the growing power and sophistication of the papal monarchy itself.

THE REIGN OF INNOCENT III

By common consent the most capable and successful of all the high medieval popes was Innocent III (1198–1216). Innocent, who was elected at the age of thirty-seven, was one of the youngest and most vigorous individuals ever to be raised to the papacy; more than that, he was expertly trained in theology and had also studied canon law. His major goal was to unify all Christendom under papal hegemony and thereby to bring about the "right order in the world" so fervently desired by Pope Gregory VII. Unlike Gregory, Innocent never questioned the right of kings and princes to rule directly in the secular sphere. But Innocent believed nonetheless that as pope he was obliged to discipline kings whenever they sinned. Needless to say, this opened a wide arena for papal involvement in temporal affairs. And he was no less insistent on the obligation of every Christian to obey Saint Peter's representative than Gregory VII had been. As Innocent himself remarked, just "as every knee is bowed to Jesus . . . so all men should obey His Vicar [i.e., the pope]."

Innocent sought to implement his goals in many different ways. In order to place papal independence on a solid territorial foundation, Innocent consolidated and

CHRONOLOGY

REFORM OF THE CHURCH, 900–1215

Monastic reform	900–1050
Cluniac priories	910–1050
Papal reform movement	1049–1122
Pope Leo IX	1049–1054
Pope Gregory VII	1073–1085
Investiture Conflict	1075–1122
Concordat of Worms	1122
Consolidation of the Papal monarchy	1100–1216
Concord of Discordant Canons	1140
Reign of Innocent III	1198–1216
Fourth Lateran Council	1215

Pope Innocent III. A thirteenth-century fresco from the lower church of Sacro Speco, Subiaco, in Italy.

expanded the papacy's territories in central Italy. For this reason Innocent is often regarded as the founder of the Papal States, of which Vatican City is the last surviving modern remnant. Innocent's policies in central Italy bear some resemblance to those pursued by the twelfth-century kings of France in the Île-de-France; but he was never able to subject the independent urban communities of central Italy to effective papal control. In other projects he was more completely successful. In Germany, he engineered the triumph of his own candidate for the imperial office, the emperor Frederick II —a triumph his papal successors would live to regret. Innocent disciplined the French king Philip Augustus for his marital misconduct, and forced King John of England to accept Stephen Langton, the pope's own choice, as archbishop of Canterbury. Innocent also compelled John to grant England to the papacy as a fief; and he claimed, with varying degrees of success, a comparable feudal overlordship of Aragon, Sicily, and

Hungary. When southern France was threatened by the spread of the Albigensian heresy (to be discussed later), the pope called a crusade to extinguish it by force. He also levied the first income tax on the clergy to support a crusade to the Holy Land. The crowning achievement of Innocent's pontificate, however, was the summoning of the Fourth Lateran Council to Rome in 1215. This representative assembly of the entire western Church defined central dogmas of the faith and made the leadership of the papacy within Christendom more apparent than ever. The pope was now clearly both disciplining kings and ruling over the church without hindrance.

POPES OF THE THIRTEENTH CENTURY

Innocent's reign was certainly the zenith of the papal monarchy, but it also sowed some of the seeds of future ruin. Innocent himself could administer the Papal

States and seek new sources of income without seeming to compromise the spiritual dignity of his office. But future popes who followed his policies had less of his stature and thus began to appear more like ordinary, acquisitive rulers. Moreover, because the Papal States bordered on the kingdom of Sicily, Innocent's successors quickly came into conflict with the neighboring ruler, who was none other than Innocent's protégé Frederick II. Innocent had raised up Frederick, but he did not suppose that Frederick would later become an inveterate opponent of papal power in Italy.

At first these and other problems were not fully apparent. The popes of the thirteenth century continued to enhance their powers and centralize the government of the church. They gradually asserted the right to name candidates for ecclesiastical positions, both high and low, and they asserted control over the curriculum and doctrine taught at the University of Paris. But they also became involved in a protracted political struggle that led to their own demise as temporal powers. This struggle began with the attempt of the popes to destroy Frederick II. To some degree they were acting in self-defense because Frederick threatened their own rule in central Italy. But in combating him they overemployed their spiritual weapons. Instead of merely excommunicating and deposing Frederick, they also called a crusade against him—the first time a crusade was called on a large scale for blatantly political purposes.

After Frederick's death in 1250 a succession of popes made a still worse mistake by renewing and maintaining their crusade against all of the emperor's heirs, whom they called the "viper brood." In order to implement this crusade they became preoccupied with raising funds, and they sought and won as their military champion a younger son from the French royal house, Charles of Anjou. But Charles helped the popes only for the purely political motive of acquiring the kingdom of Sicily for himself. Charles won Sicily in 1268 by defeating the last of Frederick II's male heirs. But he then taxed the realm so excessively that the Sicilians revolted in the "Sicilian Vespers" of 1282 and offered their crown to the king of Aragon, who had married Frederick II's granddaughter. The king of Aragon accordingly entered the Italian arena and came close to winning Frederick's former kingdom for himself. To prevent such an event Charles of Anjou and the reigning pope prevailed on the king of France—then Philip III (1270–1285)—to embark on a crusade against Aragon. This crusade was a terrible failure, and Philip III died on it. In the wake of these events Philip's son, Philip IV, resolved to alter the traditional French propapal policy. By that time France had become so strong that such a decision was fateful. More than that, by misusing the institution of the crusade and trying to raise increasingly large sums of money to support it, the popes lost much of their spiritual prestige. In 1291 the last crusader outpost in the Holy Land fell without any papal help being offered. Instead, the popes were still trying to salvage their losing crusade against Aragon. Pope Boniface VIII's papal jubilee of 1300, which offered a full crusader's indulgence to anyone who made a pilgrimage to Rome, was a tacit recognition that the Eternal City and not the Holy Land would henceforth be the central goal of Christian pilgrimage.

Charles of Anjou. One of the earliest known medieval statues that may have been done from life.

DECLINE OF THE PAPAL MONARCHY

The temporal might of the papal monarchy finally collapsed in the reign of Boniface VIII (1294–1303). Not all Boniface's troubles were of his own making.

Pope Boniface VIII (1294–1303) commissioned dozens of statues of himself which he distributed throughout the papal states. Despite its idealized features, this statue—from the Museo Civico in Bologna—does also suggest something of the pope's pugnacious obstinacy.

His greatest obstacle was that the national monarchies had gained more of their subjects' loyalties than the papacy could draw on because of the steady growth of royal power and the erosion of papal prestige. Boniface also had the misfortune to succeed a particularly pious, although inept, pope who resigned his office within a year. Since Boniface was entirely lacking in conventional piety or humility, the contrast turned many Christian observers against him. Some even maintained—incorrectly—that Boniface had convinced his predecessor to resign and had murdered him shortly afterward. Boniface ruled assertively and presided over the first papal "jubilee" in Rome in 1300.

This was an apparent, but, as events would show, hollow demonstration of papal might.

Two disputes with the kings of England and France proved to be Boniface's undoing. The first concerned the clerical taxation that had been initiated by Innocent III. Although Innocent had levied this tax to support a crusade and had collected it himself, during the course of the thirteenth century the kings of England and France had begun to levy and collect clerical taxes on the pretext that they would use the funds to help the popes on future crusades to the Holy Land or aid in papal crusades against the Hohenstaufens. Then, at the end of the century, the kings started to levy their own war taxes on the clergy without any pretexts at all. Boniface understandably tried to prohibit this step, but quickly found that he had lost the support of the English and French clergy. Thus when the kings offered resistance, he had to back down.

Boniface's second dispute was with King Philip IV of France, who deliberately challenged the pope by preparing to try a French bishop for treason, in violation of canon-law protections for the clergy. As in the earlier struggle between Gregory VII and Henry IV of Germany, a bitter propaganda war ensued, but now hardly anyone listened to the pope. Instead, Philip pressed absurd charges of heresy against Boniface and sent his minions to arrest the pope to stand trial. At the papal residence of Anagni in 1303 Boniface, who was in his seventies, was captured and mistreated by Philip's forces. Although the pope was finally rescued by the local citizens, the shock of these events was too much for the old man's strength, and he died a month later. But still Philip pressed his advantage. He forced the new pope, Clement V, not only to justify his attack on Boniface, but to thank him publically for his zealous defence of the Catholic faith. Thereafter, any shred of papal independence in regard to the interests of the French monarchy was gone. For the next seventy years, the popes would reside not in Rome, but in Avignon, on the borders of the kingdom of France; and the papacy would come to be regarded as a virtual pawn of French diplomatic interests.

The humiliating defeat of Pope Boniface VIII at the hands of King Philip of France illustrates the enormous gap that had opened up by 1300 between the rhetoric and the reality of papal power. Although Boniface continued to lay claim to a universal spiritual and temporal authority over Christendom, declaring that kings ruled only through the "will and sufferance" of the church, in fact the papal monarchy now exercised its authority only through the will and sufferance of kings. The growth of nationalism, combined with the increasing sophistication of royal justice, royal taxation, and royal propaganda, had shifted the balance of power in Europe decisively toward the state and away from the church. Europeans were not less religious than they had been before, quite the opposite. But from the later thirteenth century on, pious Christians would look increasingly toward the state, and not toward the papacy, to spearhead campaigns of moral and spiritual improvement within their territories. After one hundred fifty years during which the religious nature of royal authority had been steadily undermined, the kings of the later thirteenth century were beginning to restore their sacred luster. This trend would continue throughout the later Middle Ages. It would be shattered, finally, only in the seventeenth century, at the end of a century of religious wars brought on by the Protestant Reformation. Only then would the distinctions between religion and politics established by the Investiture Conflict be fully and firmly established as fundamental principles of European life.

THE OUTBURST OF RELIGIOUS VITALITY

How did the Latin Church control popular heresy?

The papal reform movement spearheaded by Pope Gregory stimulated a European religious revival for two reasons. One was that the campaign to cleanse the Church actually achieved a large measure of success: the laity could now respect the clergy more, and many were inspired to join the clergy themselves. According to a reliable estimate, the number of people who joined monastic orders in England increased tenfold between 1066 and 1200, a statistic that does not include the increase in priests. The other reason that the work of Gregory VII in particular helped inspire a revival was that Gregory explicitly called on the laity to help discipline their priests. In letters of great propagandistic power he denounced the sins of "fornicating priests" (by which he really meant just married ones) and urged the laity to drive them from their pulpits or boycott their services. Not surprisingly, he touched off something close to a vigilante movement in many parts of Europe. This excitement, taken together with the

fact that the papal struggle with Henry IV was really the first European event of universal interest, increased religious commitment immensely. Until about 1050, most western Europeans were Christians in name, but after the Gregorian period Christianity was becoming an ideal and a practice that really began to direct human lives.

CISTERCIANS AND CARTHUSIANS

One of the most visible manifestations of the new piety was the spread of the Cistercian movement in the twelfth century. By around 1100 no form of Benedictine monasticism seemed fully satisfactory to aspirants to holiness who sought great asceticism and, above all, intense "interiority"—unrelenting self-examination and meditative striving toward knowledge of God. The result was the founding of new orders to provide for the fullest expression of monastic idealism. One was the Carthusian order, whose monks were required to live in separate cells, abstain from meat, and fast three days each week on bread, water, and salt. The Carthusians never sought to attract great numbers and therefore remained a small group. But the same was by no means true of the Cistercians. The latter were monks who were first organized around 1100 and who sought to follow the Benedictine rule in the purest and most austere way possible. In order to avoid worldly temptations, they founded new monasteries in forests and wastelands as far away from civilization as possible. They shunned all unnecessary church decoration and ostentatious utensils, abandoned the Cluniac stress on an elaborate liturgy in favor of more contemplation and private prayer, and seriously committed themselves to hard manual labor. Under the charismatic leadership of Saint Bernard of Clairvaux (1090–1153), a spellbinding preacher, brilliant writer, and the most influential European religious personality of his age, the Cistercian order grew exponentially. There were only five houses in 1115 but no less than 343 at the time of Bernard's death in 1153. This growth not only meant that many more men were becoming monks, but also that many pious lay people were donating funds and lands to support the new monasteries.

At the same time that more people were entering or patronizing new monasteries, the very nature of religious belief and devotion was also changing. One of many examples was a shift away from the cult of saints to emphasis on the worship of Jesus and veneration of the Virgin Mary. Older Benedictine monasteries encouraged the veneration of the relics of local saints that

The Mystery of the Mass. In this illustration by the twelfth-century visionary Hildegard of Bingen, the Church (shown as a crowned queen, and associated by Hildegard with the Virgin Mary, the Queen of Heaven) receives the blood of Christ in a communion chalice, while below, the bread and wine of the Mass, which have now become the body and blood of Christ, rest on the altar.

they housed in order to attract pilgrims and donations. But the Cluniac and Cistercian orders were both centralized congregations that allowed only one saintly patron for all their houses: respectively, Saint Peter (to honor the founder of the papacy) and the Virgin. Since these monasteries contained few relics (the Virgin was thought to have been taken bodily into heaven, so there were no bodily relics of her at all) they deemphasized the cult. The veneration of relics was replaced by a concentration on the Eucharist, or sacrament of the Lord's Supper. Of course celebration of the Eucharist had always been an important part of the Christian faith, but only in the twelfth century was it made really central, for only then did theologians fully work out the doctrine of transubstantiation. According to this doctrine, the priest during mass cooperates with God in the performance of a miracle whereby the bread and wine on the altar are changed or "transubstantiated" into the body and blood of Christ. Popular reverence for the Eucharist became so great in the twelfth century that for the first time the practice of elevating the consecrated bread, or host, was initiated so that the whole congregation could see it. The new theology of the Eucharist greatly enhanced the dignity of the priest and also encouraged the faithful to meditate on the sufferings of Christ. As a result many developed an intense sense of identification with Christ and tried to imitate his life in different ways.

THE CULT OF THE VIRGIN MARY

Coming a very close second to the renewed worship of Christ in the twelfth century was veneration of the Virgin Mary. This development was more unprecedented because until then the Virgin had been only negligibly honored in the Western church. Exactly why veneration of the Virgin became so pronounced in the twelfth century is not fully clear, but whatever the explanation, in the twelfth century the cult of Mary blossomed throughout all of western Europe. The Cistercians made her their patron saint, Saint Bernard constantly taught about her life and virtues, and practically all the magnificent new cathedrals of the age were dedicated to her: there was Notre Dame ("Our Lady") of Paris, and also a "Notre Dame" in Chartres, Rheims, Amiens, Rouen, Laon, and many other places. Mary's theological role was that of intercessor with her son for the salvation of human souls. It was held that Mary was the mother of all, an infinite repository of mercy who urged the salvation even of sinners so long as they were loving and ultimately

Mary and Eve. The "correct" medieval theological view of women. On the left (Latin: *sinister*) side of the naked Adam the naked Eve takes the apple of sin from the serpent and feeds it to erring mortals while a skeleton waits to carry them to hell. On Adam's right Mary counteracts Eve by feeding a different "fruit"—the Eucharistic wafer—to the devout.

contrite. Numerous stories circulated about seeming reprobates who were saved because they venerated Mary, who then spoke for them at the hour of death.

The significance of the new cult was manifold. For the first time a woman was given a central and honored place in the Christian religion. Theologians still taught that sin had entered the world through Eve, the first woman; but they now counterbalanced this by explaining how the triumph over sin had come through Mary, who gave birth to Christ, the second Adam. Artists and writers who portrayed Mary were also able to concentrate on femininity and scenes of human tenderness and family life. This contributed greatly to a general softening of artistic and literary style. But perhaps most important of all, the rise of the cult of Mary was closely associated with a general rise of hopefulness and optimism in the twelfth-century West.

HILDEGARD OF BINGEN

Not only did a woman, Mary, gain a particularly prominent role in the religious cult of the twelfth century, but a few living women gained great religious authority. By far the most famous and influential was the German nun and visionary Hildegard of Bingen (1098–1179). Hildegard's descriptions of her religious visions, dictated in freshly original Latin prose, were so compelling that contemporaries had no difficulty in believing that she was directly inspired by God. Consequently when the pope visited Germany he gave her his blessing, and religious and secular leaders sought her advice. Hildegard wrote on a variety of other subjects such as pharmacology and women's medicine. She also composed religious songs whose beauty has been rediscovered in recent times. Visionary though she was, she probably would be surprised to see people today looking for her works in racks of compact discs, where she is often alphabetized as "Bingen" between Beethoven and Brahms.

THE CHALLENGE OF POPULAR HERESY

Sometimes the great religious enthusiasm of the twelfth century went beyond the bounds approved by the church. After Gregory VII had called on the laity to help discipline their clergy it was difficult to control lay enthusiasm. As the twelfth century progressed and the papal monarchy concentrated on strengthening its legal and financial administration, some people began to wonder whether the church, which had once been so inspiring, had not begun to lose sight of its idealistic goals. Another difficulty was that the growing emphasis on the miraculous powers of priests tended to inhibit the religious role of the laity and place it in a distinct position of spiritual inferiority. The result was that in the second half of the twelfth century large-scale movements of popular heresy swept over western Europe for the first time in its history.

The two major twelfth-century heresies were Catharism and Waldensianism. The Cathars, who were strongest in northern Italy and southern France, believed that all matter was created by an evil principle and that holiness required extreme ascetic practices. Some Cathars even argued that there were two gods, one good, the other evil; that the created world was entirely in the power of the evil god; and that spiritual people must seek to escape it. Although such teachings were at variance with Christianity, most Cathar followers believed themselves nonetheless to be Christians.

THE CONVERSION OF PETER WALDO

The founder of the Waldensian heresy was a layman, Peter Waldo, who was moved to take up a life of preaching and poverty after hearing the story of Saint Alexis, who had abandoned his family and his wealth to pursue a religious life. Waldo's story bears remarkable similarities to the story of Saint Francis of Assisi a generation or so later. But whereas Saint Francis succeeded in getting his movement recognized by the church, Waldo and his followers were ultimately declared heretical because they refused to accept the church's authority to prohibit them from preaching. Waldo's story illustrates the new spiritual impulses that were influencing lay people in twelfth-century Europe.

At about this time, in 1173, there was a citizen of Lyons named Peter Waldo, who had made a great deal of money by the evil means of usury. One Sunday he lingered by a crowd that had gathered round a traveling story-teller, and was much struck by his words. He took him home with him, and listened carefully to his story of how St. Alexis had died a holy death in his father's house. Next morning Waldo hastened to the schools of theology to seek advice about his soul. When he had been told of the many ways of coming to God he asked the master whether any of them was more sure and reliable than the rest. The master quoted to him the words of the Lord, "If thou wilt be perfect go sell what thou hast and give it to the poor and thou shalt have treasure in heaven. And come follow me."

Waldo returned to his wife and gave her the choice between having all his movable wealth or his property in land. . . . She was very upset at having to do this and chose the property. From his movable wealth he returned what he had acquired wrongly, conferred a large portion on his two daughters, whom he placed in the order of Fontevrault without his wife's knowledge, and gave a still larger amount to the poor.

At this time a terrible famine was raging through Gaul and Germany. . . . from May 27 until August 1, Waldo generously distributed bread, soup and meat to anyone who came to him. On the Assumption of the Virgin [August 15] he scattered money among the poor in the streets saying, "You cannot serve two masters, God and Mammon." The people around thought he had gone out of his senses. Then he stood up on a piece of high ground and said, "Friends and fellow-citizens, I am not mad as you think. . . . I know that many of you disapprove of my having acted so publicly. I have done so both for my own sake and for yours: for my sake, because anybody who sees me with money in future will be able to say that I am mad; for your sake, so that you may learn to place your hopes in God and not in wealth.". . .

1177   Waldo, the citizen of Lyons whom we have already mentioned, who had vowed to God that he would possess neither gold nor silver, and take no thought for the morrow, began to make converts to his opinions. Following his example they gave all they had to the poor, and willingly devoted themselves to poverty. Gradually, both in public and in private they began to inveigh against both their own sins and those of others. . . .

1178   Pope Alexander III held a council at the Lateran palace. . . . The council condemned heresy and all those who fostered and defended heretics. The pope embraced Waldo, and applauded the vows of voluntary poverty which he had taken, but forbade him and his companion to assume the office of preaching except at the request of the priests. They obeyed this instruction for a time, but later they disobeyed, and affronted many, bringing ruin on themselves.

Robert I. Moore, ed. and trans. *The Birth of Popular Heresy*. (London: Edward Arnold Publishers, 1975), pp. 111–113 (slightly modified).

They were attracted to the heresy mainly because it challenged the authority of insufficiently zealous Catholic priests and provided an outlet for intense lay spirituality. Noblewomen in southern France played a particularly important role in the spread of Catharism, sheltering the sect's wandering preachers and converting their households to the new faith.

More typical of twelfth-century religious dissent was Waldensianism, a movement that originated in the French city of Lyons and spread to much of southern France, northern Italy, and Germany. Waldensians were lay folk who wished to imitate the life of Christ and the apostles to the fullest. They therefore translated and studied the Gospels and dedicated themselves to lives of poverty and preaching. Since the earliest Waldensians did not attack any Catholic doctrines, the church hierarchy did not at first interfere with them. Indeed, the Waldensians may have seen themselves initially as a countermovement to Catharism. But the papacy forbade the Waldensians to preach without authorization and condemned them for heresy when they refused to obey. At that point they became more radical and started to create an alternative church, which they maintained offered the only route to salvation.

When Innocent III became pope in 1198 he was faced with a very serious challenge from growing heresies. His response was characteristically decisive and fateful for the future of the church. Simply stated it was two pronged. On the one hand, Innocent resolved to crush all disobedience to papal authority, but on the other, he decided to patronize whatever idealistic religious groups he could find that were willing to acknowledge obedience. Papal monarchy could thus be protected without frustrating all dynamic spirituality within the church. Innocent not only launched a full-scale crusade against the Cathars, he also encouraged the use against heresy of judicial procedures that included ruthless techniques of religious "inquisition." In 1252 the papacy first approved the use of torture in inquisitorial trials, and burning at the stake became the prevalent punishment for religious disobedience. Neither the crusade nor the inquisitorial procedures were fully successful in uprooting the Catharian heresy in Innocent's own lifetime, but the extension of such measures did result in destroying the heresy by fire and sword after about the middle of the thirteenth century. Waldensians, like Cathars, were hunted down by inquisitors and their numbers reduced, but scattered Waldensian groups did manage to survive until modern times.

Another aspect of Innocent's program was to pronounce formally the new religious doctrines that enhanced the special status of priests and the ecclesiastical hierarchy. Thus at the Fourth Lateran Council of 1215 he reaffirmed the doctrine that the sacraments administered by the church were the indispensable means of procuring God's grace, and that no one could be saved without them. The decrees of the Lateran Council emphasized two sacraments: the Eucharist and penance. The doctrine of transubstantiation was formally defined. All Catholics were required—as they still are—to confess their sins to a priest and then receive the Eucharist at least once a year. The council also promulgated other doctrinal definitions and disciplinary measures that served both to oppose heresy and to assert the unique dignity of the clergy.

FRANCISCANS AND DOMINICANS

As stated above, the other side of Innocent's policy was to support obedient idealistic movements within the church. The most important of these were the new orders of friars—the Dominicans and the Franciscans. Friars resembled monks in vowing to follow a rule, but they differed greatly from monks in their actual conduct. Above all, they did not withdraw from society into monasteries. Assuming that the way of life originally followed by Christ and the apostles was the most holy, they wandered through the countryside and especially the towns, preaching and offering spiritual guidance. They also accepted voluntary poverty and begged for their subsistence. In these respects they resembled the Waldensian heretics, but they professed unquestioning obedience to the pope and sought to fight heresy themselves.

The Dominican order, founded by the Spaniard Saint Dominic (1170–1221) and approved by Innocent III in 1216, was particularly dedicated to the fight against heresy and also to the conversion of Jews and Muslims. At first the Dominicans hoped to achieve these ends by preaching and public debate. Hence they became intellectually oriented. Many members of the order gained teaching positions in the infant European universities and contributed much to the development of philosophy and theology. The most influential thinker of the thirteenth century, Saint Thomas Aquinas, was a Dominican who addressed one of his major theological works to converting the "gentiles" (that is, all non-Christians). The Dominicans always retained their reputation for learning, but they also came to believe that stubborn heretics were best controlled by legal procedures. Accordingly, they became the leading medieval administrators of inquisitorial trials.

In its origins the Franciscan order was quite different from the Dominican, being characterized less by a commitment to doctrine and discipline and more by a sense of emotional fervor. Whereas Saint Dominic and his earliest followers had been ordained priests who were licensed to preach by their office, the founder of the Franciscans, the Italian Saint Francis of Assisi (1182–1226), was a layman who behaved at first remarkably like a social rebel and a heretic. The son of a rich merchant, he became dissatisfied with the materialistic values of his father and determined to become a servant of the poor. Giving away all his property, he threw off his clothes in public, put on the tattered garb of a beggar, and began without official approval to preach salvation in town squares and minister to outcasts in the darkest corners of Italian cities. He rigorously imitated the life of Christ and displayed indifference to doctrine, form, and ceremony, except for reverencing the sacrament of the Eucharist. But he did wish to gain the support of the pope. One day in 1209 he appeared in Rome with a small ragged band to request that Innocent III approve a primitive "rule" that was little more than a collection of Gospel precepts. Some other pope might have rejected the layman Francis as a hopelessly unworldly religious anarchist. But Francis was thoroughly willing to profess obedience, and Innocent had the genius to approve Francis's rule and grant him permission to preach. With papal support, the Franciscan order spread, and though it gradually became more "civilized," conceding the importance of administrative stability and doctrinal training for all its members, it continued to specialize in revivalistic outdoor preaching and in offering a model for "apostolic living" within an orthodox framework. Thus Innocent managed to harness a vital new force that would help maintain a sense of religious enthusiasm within the Church.

Until the end of the thirteenth century both the Franciscans and Dominicans worked closely together with the papal monarchy in a mutually supportive relationship. The popes helped the friars establish themselves throughout Europe and often allowed them to infringe on the duties of parish priests. On their side, the friars combated heresy, helped preach papal crusades, were active in missionary work, and otherwise undertook special missions for the popes. Above all, by the power of their examples and by their vigorous preaching, the friars helped maintain religious intensity throughout the thirteenth century.

The Earliest Known Portrait of St. Francis. Dating from the year 1228, this fresco shows the saint without the "stigmata," the wounds of Christ's crucifixion he was believed to have received miraculously toward the end of his life.

CHRONOLOGY

EUROPEAN RELIGIOUS REVIVAL, 1100–1300

Cistercian order established	1098
Cult of the Virgin Mary	c. 1100
Catharist heresy emerges	c. 1140
Waldensian heresy emerges	c. 1180
New theology of the Eucharist	c. 1150–1215
Franciscan order established	1209
Fourth Lateran Council	1215
Dominican order established	1216

HOW DID THE RECOVERY OF CLASSICAL LEARNING AFFECT MEDIEVAL INTELLECTUAL LIFE?

THE MEDIEVAL INTELLECTUAL REVIVAL   363

The success of the Franciscans and the Dominicans in combating the appeal of heretical movements represented a great victory for the church, but this success was not sufficient to make the church feel secure in its hold on the people of Europe. Quite the opposite: despite its victories over the Cathars and the Waldensians, the church's inquisitorial processes ground on, discovering heretics even where none in fact existed.

JEWS AND CHRISTIANS

The church also became more and more concerned by the threat it believed that Jews posed to the faith of Christians, despite the fact that persecution and ex-

ploitative taxation had made most Jewish communities both smaller and weaker by 1300 than they had been in 1150. Although the church never officially endorsed the wilder flights of popular anti-Semitism, it did little to combat such attitudes either. As a result, by 1300 many ordinary Christians had come to believe that the Jews who lived among them were nothing less than agents of Satan, who routinely crucified Christian children, consumed Christian blood, and profaned the body of Christ in the Eucharist. The failures of organized campaigns to convert Jews to Christianity added to the sense among Christians that there was something demonic about the continuing Jewish presence in Christian society. Fanciful stories of Jewish wealth added an economic element to the developing anti-Semitism of European society, as did the fact that across much of thirteenth-century Europe, many Jews made their living as moneylenders.

Throughout the thirteenth century, the church had cooperated with kings in imposing more and more severe restrictions on Jewish life. Starting in the late 1280s, however, kings began to expel their Jewish subjects from their kingdoms altogether: in 1288 from southern Italy, in 1290 from England, and in 1306 from France. Further expulsions followed during the fourteenth century in the Rhineland, and in 1492 from Spain. By 1500, only Italy and Poland still retained any substantial Jewish populations, where they would survive until the Nazi Holocaust during the Second World War.

Burning of Jews. From a late medieval German manuscript. After the persecutions of the First Crusade, treatment of Jews in western Europe became worse and worse. These Jews were set upon by the populace because they were suspected of poisoning wells.

THE MEDIEVAL INTELLECTUAL REVIVAL

How did the recovery of classical learning affect medieval intellectual life?

The major intellectual accomplishments of the High Middle Ages were of four related but different sorts: the spread of primary education and literacy; the origin and spread of universities; the acquisition of classical and Muslim knowledge; and the actual progress in thought made by westerners. Any one of these accomplishments would have earned the High Middle Ages a signal place in the history of Western learning; taken together they began the era of Western intellectual predominance that became a hallmark of modern times.

Two Medieval Conceptions of Elementary Education. On the left, an illumination from a fourteenth-century manuscript depicts a master of grammar who simultaneously points to the day's lesson and keeps order with a cudgel. Grammar school education is portrayed more gently on the right, a late medieval scene in which a woman personifying the alphabet leads a willing boy into a tower of learning wherein the stories ascend from grammar through logic and rhetoric to the heights of theology.

THE GROWTH OF SCHOOLS

Around 800 Charlemagne ordered that primary schools be established in every bishopric and monastery in his realm. Although it is doubtful that this command was carried out to the letter, many schools were certainly founded during the Carolingian period. But their continued existence was later endangered by the Viking invasions. Primary education in some monasteries and cathedral towns managed to survive, but until around 1050 the extent and quality of basic education in the European West were meager. Thereafter, however, there was a blossoming that paralleled the efflorescence we have seen in other human activities. Even contemporaries were struck by the rapidity with which schools sprang up all over Europe. One French monk writing in 1115 stated that when he was growing up around 1075 there was "such a scarcity of teachers that there were almost none in the villages and hardly any in the cities," but that by his maturity there was "a great number of

schools," and the study of grammar was "flourishing far and wide." Similarly, a Flemish chronicle referred to an extraordinary new passion for the study and practice of rhetoric around 1120. Clearly, the economic revival, the growth of towns, and the emergence of strong government allowed Europeans to dedicate themselves to basic education as never before.

The high medieval educational boom was more than merely a growth of schools, for the nature of the schools changed, and as time went on so did the curriculum and the clientele. The first basic mutation was that monasteries in the twelfth century abandoned their practice of educating outsiders. Earlier, monasteries had taught a few privileged nonmonastic students how to read because there were no other schools for such pupils. But by the twelfth century sufficient alternatives existed. The main centers of European education became the cathedral schools located in the growing towns. The papal monarchy energetically supported this development by ordering in 1179 that all

HOW DID THE RECOVERY OF CLASSICAL LEARNING AFFECT MEDIEVAL INTELLECTUAL LIFE?

THE MEDIEVAL INTELLECTUAL REVIVAL   365

cathedrals should set aside income for one school-teacher, who could then instruct all who wished, rich or poor, without fee. The papacy believed correctly that this measure would enlarge the number of well-trained clerics and potential administrators.

At first the cathedral schools existed almost exclusively for the basic training of priests, with a curriculum designed to teach only such literacy as was necessary for performing the basic services of the church. But soon after 1100 the curriculum was broadened, for the growth of both ecclesiastical and secular governments created a growing demand for trained officials who had to know more than how to read a few prayers. The revived reliance on law especially made it imperative to improve the quality of primary education in order to train future lawyers. Above all, a thorough knowledge of Latin grammar and composition began to be inculcated, often by studying some of the Roman classics such as the works of Cicero and Virgil. The revived interest in these texts, and attempts to imitate them, have led scholars to refer to a "renaissance of the twelfth century."

Until about 1200 the students in the urban schools remained predominantly clerical. Even those who hoped to become lawyers or administrators rather than mere priests usually found it advantageous to take church orders. But afterward more pupils entering schools were not in the clergy and never intended to be. Some were children of the upper classes who began to regard literacy as a badge of status. Others were future notaries (men who drew up official documents), estate officials, or merchants who needed some literacy and/or computational skills to advance their own careers. Customarily, the latter groups would not go to cathedral schools but to alternate ones that were more practically oriented. Such schools grew rapidly in the course of the thirteenth century and became completely independent of ecclesiastical control. Not only were their students recruited from the laity, their teachers were usually laymen as well. As time went on instruction ceased to be in Latin, as had hitherto been the case, and was offered in the European vernacular languages instead. But the schools continued to be restricted to males. Some laywomen did become highly educated, but they were taught at home by private tutors.

The rise of lay education was an enormously important development in western European history for two related reasons. The first was that the church lost its monopoly over education for the first time in almost a millennium. Learning and resultant attitudes could now become more secular, and they did just that increasingly over the course of time. Laymen could not only evaluate and criticize the ideas of priests, they could also pursue entirely secular lines of inquiry. Western culture therefore ultimately became more independent of religion, and of the traditionalism associated with religion, than any other culture in the world. Second, the growth of lay schools, taken together with the growth of church schools that trained the laity, led to an enormous growth of lay literacy: by 1340 roughly 40 percent of the Florentine population could read; by the later fifteenth century about 40 percent of the total population of England was literate as well. (These figures include women, who were usually taught to read by paid tutors or by female family members at home rather than in schools.) When we consider that literacy around 1050 was almost entirely limited to the clergy and that the literate comprised less than 1 percent of the population of western Europe, we can appreciate that an astonishing revolution had taken place. Without it, many of Europe's other accomplishments would have been inconceivable.

The growth of lay and church schools that trained the laity led to an enormous growth of lay literacy.

THE RISE OF UNIVERSITIES

The emergence of universities was part of the same high medieval educational boom. Originally, universities were institutions that offered instruction in advanced studies that could not be pursued in average cathedral schools: advanced liberal arts and the professional studies of law, medicine, and theology. The earliest Italian university was that of Bologna, an institution that took shape during the course of the twelfth century. Although liberal arts were taught at Bologna, the institution's greatest prominence from the time of its twelfth-century origins until the end of the Middle Ages was as Europe's leading center for the study of law. North of the Alps, the earliest and most prestigious university was that of Paris. The University of Paris started out as a cathedral school like many others, but in the twelfth century it began to become a recognized center of northern intellectual life. One reason for this was that scholars there found the necessary conditions of peace and stability provided by the increasingly strong French kingship; another was that

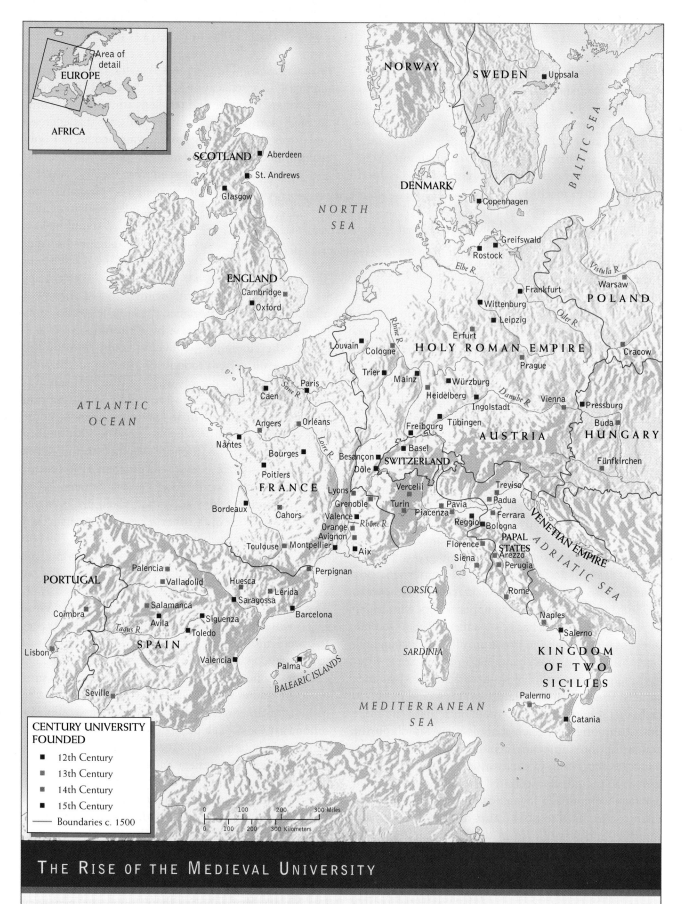

EUROPE

AFRICA

NORWAY

SWEDEN

Uppsala

BALTIC SEA

SCOTLAND
Aberdeen
St. Andrews
Glasgow

DENMARK

Copenhagen

NORTH SEA

Greifswald
Rostock

Elbe R.

Vistula R.

Warsaw

POLAND

ENGLAND
Cambridge
Oxford

Frankfurt
Wittenburg
Leipzig

Erfurt

HOLY ROMAN EMPIRE

Prague

Cracow

Louvain
Cologne

Rhine R.

Trier
Mainz
Würzburg
Heidelberg
Ingolstadt

Vienna
Pressburg

ATLANTIC OCEAN

Paris

Seine R.

Caen

Angers
Orléans

Nantes

Bourges

Poitiers

FRANCE

Bordeaux

Cahors

Freibourg
Tübingen

Danube R.

Buda
HUNGARY

Fünfkirchen

Basel
Besançon
Dôle

SWITZERLAND

Lyons
Grenoble
Valence
Orange
Avignon
Toulouse
Montpellier
Aix

Rhône R.

Turin
Piacenza

Vercelli

Treviso
Padua

Pavia
Ferrara
Reggio
Bologna
Florence
Siena
Arezzo
Perugia

VENETIAN EMPIRE

ADRIATIC SEA

PAPAL STATES

PORTUGAL

Palencia
Valladolid

Huesca
Saragossa
Lérida
Barcelona

Perpignan

CORSICA

Rome

Coimbra

Salamanca
Avila
Toledo

Tagus R.

Siguenza

SPAIN

Lisbon

Valencia

Palma

BALEARIC ISLANDS

SARDINIA

Naples
Salerno

KINGDOM OF TWO SICILIES

Palermo

Seville

MEDITERRANEAN SEA

Catania

CENTURY UNIVERSITY FOUNDED

■ 12th Century
■ 13th Century
■ 14th Century
■ 15th Century
— Boundaries c. 1500

0   100   200   300 Miles
0   100   200   300 Kilometers

THE RISE OF THE MEDIEVAL UNIVERSITY

This map shows the distribution and dates of origin of the major universities of medieval Europe. Why were the twelfth- and thirteenth-century universities founded primarily in France, England, and northern Italy? Notice the number and geographical distribution of universities founded in the fourteenth and fifteenth centuries. How would you explain the pattern of these later foundations?

HOW DID THE RECOVERY OF CLASSICAL LEARNING AFFECT MEDIEVAL INTELLECTUAL LIFE?

THE MEDIEVAL INTELLECTUAL REVIVAL   367

food was plentiful because the area was rich in agricultural produce; third was that the cathedral school of Paris in the first half of the twelfth century boasted the most charismatic and controversial teacher of the day, Peter Abelard (1079–1142). Abelard, whose intellectual accomplishments we will discuss later, attracted students from all over Europe in droves. According to an apocryphal story told at the time, he was such an exciting teacher that when he was forbidden to teach in French lands because of his controversial views, he climbed a tree and students flocked under it to hear him lecture; when he was then forbidden to teach from the air he started lecturing from a boat and students massed to hear him from the banks. As a result of his reputation many other teachers settled in Paris and began to offer much more varied and advanced instruction than anything offered in other French cathedral schools. By 1200 the Paris school was evolving into a university that specialized in liberal arts and theology. Around that time Innocent III, who had studied in Paris himself, called the school "the oven that bakes the bread for the entire world."

It should be emphasized that the institution of the university was really a medieval invention. Of course advanced schools existed in the ancient world, but they did not have fixed curricula or organized faculties, and they did not award degrees. At first, medieval universities themselves were not so much places as groups of scholars. The term "university" originally meant a corporation or guild. In fact, all of the medieval universities were corporations, either of teachers or students, organized like other guilds to protect their interests and rights. But gradually the word "university" came to mean an educational institution with a school of liberal arts and one or more faculties in law, medicine, and theology. After about 1200 Bologna and Paris were regarded as the prototypical universities. During the thirteenth century such famous institutions as Oxford, Cambridge, Montpellier, Salamanca, and Naples were founded or granted formal recognition. In Germany there were no universities until the fourteenth century—a reflection of the disorganized condition of that area—but in 1385 the first university on German soil was founded in Heidelberg, and many others quickly followed.

Every university in medieval Europe was patterned after one or the other of two different models. Throughout Italy, Spain, and southern France the standard was generally the University of Bologna, in which the students themselves constituted the corporation. They hired the teachers, paid their salaries, and fined or discharged them for neglect of duty or inefficient instruction. The universities of northern Europe were modeled after Paris, which was a guild not of students but of teachers. It included four faculties—arts, theology, law, and medicine—each headed by a dean. In the great majority of the northern universities arts and theology were the leading branches of study. Before the end of the thirteenth century separate colleges came to be established within the University of Paris. The original college was nothing more than an endowed home for poor students, but eventually the colleges became centers of instruction as well as residences. Although most of these types of colleges have disappeared from the Continent, the universities of Oxford and Cambridge still retain the pattern of federal organization copied from Paris. The colleges of which they are composed are semi-independent educational units.

Most of our modern degrees as well as our modern university organization derive from the medieval system, but actual courses of study have been greatly altered. No curriculum in the Middle Ages included history or anything like the modern social sciences. The medieval student was assumed to know Latin grammar thoroughly before entrance into a university—this he learned in the primary, or "grammar," schools. On admission—limited to males—he was required to spend about four years studying the basic liberal arts, which meant doing advanced work in Latin grammar and rhetoric and mastering the rules of logic. If he passed his examinations he received the preliminary degree of bachelor of arts (the prototype of our B.A.), which conferred no unusual distinction. To assure himself a place in professional life he then usually had to devote additional years to the pursuit of an advanced degree, such as master of arts (M.A.), or doctor of laws, medicine, or theology. The M.A. degree required three or four years given to the study of mathematics, natural science, and philosophy. This was accomplished by reading and commenting on standard ancient works, such as those of Euclid and especially Aristotle. Abstract analysis was emphasized; laboratory science did not exist. The requirements for the doctor's degrees included more specialized training. Those for the doctorate in theology were particularly arduous: by the end of the Middle Ages the course for the doctorate in theology at the University of Paris had been extended to twelve or thirteen years after the roughly eight years taken for the M.A.! Continuous residence was not required, and accordingly few men became doctors of theology before the age of forty; statutes in fact forbade awarding the degree to anyone under thirty-five. Strictly speaking, doctor's degrees, including even that

A Lecture Class in a Medieval University. Some interesting similarities and contrasts may be observed between this scene and a modern classroom.

in medicine, conferred only the right to teach. But in practice university degrees of all grades were recognized as standards of attainment and became pathways to nonacademic careers.

Student life in medieval universities was often rowdy. Many students were very immature because it was customary to begin university studies between the ages of twelve and fifteen. Moreover, all university students believed that they comprised an independent and privileged community, apart from that of the local townspeople. Since the latter tried to reap financial profits from the students and the students were naturally boisterous, riots and sometimes pitched battles were frequent between "town" and "gown." But actual study was very intense. Because the greatest emphasis was placed on the value of authority and also because

books were prohibitively expensive (they were handwritten on rare parchment), there was an enormous amount of rote memorization. As students advanced in their disciplines they were also expected to develop their own skills in formal, public disputations. Advanced disputations could become extremely complex and abstract; sometimes they might last for days. The most important fact pertaining to medieval university students was that, after about 1250, there were so many of them. The University of Paris in the thirteenth century numbered about seven thousand students, and Oxford somewhere around two thousand in any given year. This means that an appreciable proportion of male Europeans who were more than peasants or artisans were gaining at least some education at the higher levels.

HOW DID THE RECOVERY OF CLASSICAL LEARNING AFFECT MEDIEVAL INTELLECTUAL LIFE?

THE MEDIEVAL INTELLECTUAL REVIVAL   369

THE RECOVERY OF CLASSICAL LEARNING

As the numbers of those educated at all levels vastly increased during the High Middle Ages, so did the quality of learning. This was owing first and foremost to the reacquisition of Greek knowledge and to the absorption of intellectual advances made by the Muslims. Since practically no western Europeans knew Greek or Arabic, works in those languages had to be transmitted by means of Latin translations. But there were very few of these before about 1140: of all the many works of Aristotle only a few logical treatises were available in Latin translations before the middle of the twelfth century. But suddenly an enormous burst of translating activity made almost all of ancient Greek and Arabic scientific knowledge accessible to western Europeans. This activity occurred in Spain and Sicily because Christians there lived in close proximity with Arabic speakers, or Jews who knew Latin and Arabic, either of whom could aid them in their tasks. Greek works were first translated into Latin from earlier Arabic translations; then many were retranslated directly from the Greek by a few westerners who had managed to learn that language, usually by traveling in Greek-speaking territories. The result was that by about 1260 almost the entire Aristotelian corpus that is known today was made available in Latin. So also were basic works of such important Greek scientific thinkers as Euclid, Galen, and Ptolemy. Plato's works were still unknown in Europe, as were the works of the classical Greek poets and dramatists. For the most part, these remained the jealously guarded cultural preserve of Byzantium. But in addition to the thought of the Greeks, Western scholars also became familiar with the accomplishments of the major Islamic philosophers and scientists such as Avicenna and Averroës.

Having acquired the best of Greek and Arabic scientific and speculative thought, the West was able to build on it and make its own advances. This progress came in different ways. In natural science, westerners could build without much difficulty on this new learning, because it seldom conflicted with the principles of Christianity. One of the most advanced thirteenth-century scientists was the Englishman Robert Grosseteste (c. 1168–1253), who was not only a great thinker but was also very active in public life as bishop of Lincoln. Grosseteste became so proficient at Greek that he translated all of Aristotle's *Ethics*. He also made very significant theoretical advances in mathematics, astronomy, and optics. He formulated a sophisticated scientific explanation of the rainbow, and he posited the use of lenses for magnification. Grosseteste's leading disciple was Roger Bacon (c. 1214–1294), who is today more famous than his teacher because he seems to have predicted automobiles and flying machines. Bacon in fact had no real interest in machinery, but he did follow up on Grosseteste's work in optics, discussing, for example, further properties of lenses, the rapid speed of light, and the nature of human vision. Grosseteste, Bacon, and some of their followers at the University of Oxford argued that natural knowledge was more certain when it was based on sensory evidence than when it rested on abstract reason. To this degree they can be seen as early forerunners of modern sci-

> Having acquired the best of Greek and Arabic scientific and speculative thought, the West was able to build on it and make its own advances.

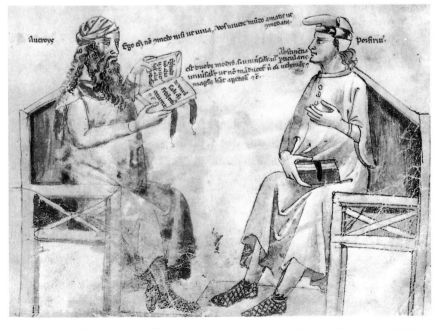

Averroës and Porphyry in Conversation. From a late-thirteenth-century Christian manuscript.

ence. But the important qualification remains that they did not perform any real laboratory experiments.

SCHOLASTICISM

The story of the high medieval encounter between Greek and Arabic philosophy and Christian faith is basically the story of the emergence of Scholasticism. This word can be, and has been, defined in many ways. In its root meaning Scholasticism was simply the method of teaching and learning followed in the medieval schools. That meant that it was highly systematic and also that it was highly respectful of authority. Yet Scholasticism was not only a method of study: it was a world view. As such, it taught that there was a fundamental compatibility between the knowledge humans can obtain naturally—that is, by experience or reason—and the teachings imparted by divine revelation. Since medieval scholars believed that the Greeks were the masters of natural knowledge and that all revelation was in the Bible, Scholasticism consequently was the theory and practice of reconciling classical philosophy with Christian faith.

PETER ABELARD

One of the most important thinkers who paved the way for Scholasticism without yet being fully a Scholastic himself was the stormy Peter Abelard, who was active in and around Paris in the first half of the twelfth century. Probably the first western European who consciously sought to forge a career as an intellectual (rather than being merely a cleric who taught on the side or a schoolteacher who had no goal of adding to knowledge), Abelard was so adept at logic and theology that even as a student he easily outshone the experts of his day who had the misfortune to be his teachers. Others might have been tactful about such superiority, but Abelard gloried in openly humiliating his elders in public debate, thereby making himself many enemies. To complicate matters, in 1118 he seduced a brilliant seventeen-year-old girl, Heloise, who had been taking private lessons with him. When Heloise became pregnant, Abelard married her (against Heloise's own wishes), but the two decided to keep the marriage secret for the sake of his career. This, however, enraged Heloise's uncle because he thought that Abelard was planning to abandon Heloise; therefore he took revenge for his family's honor by having Abelard castrated. Seeking refuge as a monk, Abelard soon witnessed his enemies engineer his first conviction for heresy. Still restless and cantan-

kerous, he found no spiritual solace in monasticism and after quarreling and breaking with the monks of two different communities he returned to life in the world by setting himself up as a teacher in Paris from about 1132 to 1141. This was the peak of his career. But in 1141 he again was charged with heresy, now by the highly influential Saint Bernard, and condemned by a church council. Not long afterward the persecuted thinker abjured, and in 1142 he died in retirement.

Abelard told of many of these trials in a letter called *The Story of My Calamities*, one of the first autobiographical accounts written in the West since Saint Augustine's *Confessions*. On first reading, this work appears atypically modern because the author seems to defy the medieval Christian virtue of humility by constantly boasting about himself. But Abelard did not write about his calamities in order to boast. Rather, his main intention was to moralize about how he had been justly punished for his "lechery" by the loss of those parts which had "offended" and for his intellectual pride by the burning of his writings after his first condemnation. Since Abelard urged intense self-examination and analysis of human motives in an ethical treatise programmatically entitled *Know Thyself*, it seems wisest to conclude that he never intended to recommend egotism but rather was one of several prominent twelfth-century thinkers (ironically including his mortal enemy Saint Bernard) who sought to take stock of the human personality by means of personal introspection.

Abelard's greatest contributions to the development of Scholasticism were made in his *Sic et Non* ("Yes and No") and in a number of original theological works. In the *Sic et Non* Abelard prepared the way for the Scholastic method by gathering a collection of statements from the church fathers that spoke for both sides of one hundred fifty theological questions. It was once thought that the brash Abelard did this in order to embarrass authority, but the contrary is true. What Abelard really hoped to do was begin a process of careful study whereby it could be shown that the Bible was infallible and that other authorities, despite any appearances to the contrary, really agreed with each other. Later Scholastics would follow his method of studying theology by raising fundamental questions and arraying the answers that had been put forth in authoritative texts. Abelard did not propose any solutions of his own in the *Sic et Non*, but he did start to do this in his original theological writings. In these he proposed to treat theology like a science by studying it as comprehensively as possible and by applying to it

HOW DID THE RECOVERY OF CLASSICAL LEARNING AFFECT MEDIEVAL INTELLECTUAL LIFE?

THE MEDIEVAL INTELLECTUAL REVIVAL   371

the tools of logic, of which he was a master. He did not even shrink from applying logic to the mystery of the Trinity (see p. 232), one of the excesses for which he was condemned. Peter Abelard was one of the first to try to harmonize religion with rationalism and was in this capacity a herald of the Scholastic outlook.

THE TRIUMPH OF SCHOLASTICISM

Immediately after Abelard's death two further steps were taken to prepare for mature Scholasticism. One was the writing of the *Book of Sentences* between 1155 and 1157 by Abelard's student Peter Lombard. This raised all the most fundamental theological questions in rigorously consequential order, adduced answers from the Bible and Christian authorities on both sides of each question, and then proposed judgments on every case. By the thirteenth century Peter Lombard's work had become a standard text. Once formal schools of theology were established in the universities, all aspirants to the doctorate were required to study and comment on it; not surprisingly, theologians also followed its organizational procedures in their own writings. Thus the full Scholastic method was born.

> Peter Abelard was one of the first to try to harmonize religion with rationalism and was in this capacity a herald of the Scholastic outlook.

The other basic step in the development of Scholasticism was the reacquisition of classical philosophy that occurred after about 1140. Abelard would probably have been glad to have drawn on the thought of the Greeks, but he could not because few Greek works were yet available in translation. Later theologians, however, could avail themselves fully of the Greeks' knowledge, above all, the works of Aristotle and his Arabic commentators. By around 1250 Aristotle's authority in purely philosophical matters became so great that he was referred to simply as "the Philosopher." Scholastics of the mid-thirteenth century accordingly adhered to Peter Lombard's organizational method, but considered Greek and Arabic philosophical authorities as well as purely Christian theological ones. In doing this they tried to construct systems of understanding the entire universe that most fully harmonized the earlier separate realms of faith and natural knowledge.

THE WRITINGS OF SAINT THOMAS AQUINAS

By far the greatest accomplishments in this endeavor were made by Saint Thomas Aquinas (1225–1274), the leading Scholastic theologian of the University of Paris. As a member of the Dominican order, Saint Thomas was committed to the principle that faith could be defended by reason. More important, he believed that natural knowledge and the study of the created universe were legitimate ways of approaching theological wisdom because "nature" complements "grace." By this he meant to say that because God created the natural world, he can be approached through its terms even though ultimate certainty about the highest truths can only be obtained through the supernatural revelation of the Bible. Imbued with a deep confidence in the value of human reason and human experience, as well as in his own ability to harmonize Greek philosophy with Christian theology, Thomas was the most serene of saints. In a long career of teaching at the University of Paris and elsewhere he indulged in few controversies and worked quietly on his two great Summaries of theology: the *Summa Contra Gentiles* ("Summary against Non-Christians") and the much larger *Summa Theologica* ("Summary of Theology"). In these he hoped to set down all that could be said about the faith on the firmest of foundations.

Most experts think that Saint Thomas came extremely close to fulfilling this extraordinarily ambitious goal. His vast Summaries are awesome for their rigorous orderliness and intellectual penetration. He admits in them that there are certain "mysteries of the faith," such as the doctrines of the Trinity and the Incarnation of God in Christ, that cannot be approached by the unaided human intellect; otherwise, he subjects all theological questions to philosophical inquiry. In this, Thomas relied heavily on the work of Aristotle, but he was by no means merely "Aristotle baptized." Instead, he fully subordinated Aristotelianism to basic Christian principles and thereby created his own original philosophical and theological system. Scholars disagree about how far this system diverges from the earlier Christian thought of Saint Augustine, but there seems little doubt that Aquinas placed a higher value on human reason, on human life in this world, and on the abilities of humans to participate in their own salvation. Not long after his death Thomas was canonized, for his intellectual accomplishments seemed like miracles. His influence lives on today insofar as he helped to inspire confidence in rationalism and human experience. More directly, philosophy in the modern Roman Catholic Church is supposed to be taught according to the Thomistic method, doctrine, and principles.

THE PINNACLE OF WESTERN MEDIEVAL THOUGHT

With the achievements of Saint Thomas Aquinas in the mid-thirteenth century, Western medieval thought reached its pinnacle. Not coincidentally, other aspects of medieval civilization were reaching their pinnacles at the same time. France was enjoying its ripest period of peace and prosperity under the rule of (Saint) Louis IX, the University of Paris was defining its basic organizational forms, and the greatest French Gothic cathedrals were being built. Some ardent admirers of medieval culture have fixed on these accomplishments to call the thirteenth the "greatest of centuries." Such a judgment, of course, is a matter of taste, and many might respond that life was still too harsh and requirements for religious orthodoxy too restrictive to justify this extreme celebration of the lost past. Whatever our individual judgments, it seems wise to end this section by correcting some false impressions about medieval intellectual life.

It is often thought that medieval thinkers were excessively conservative, but in fact the greatest thinkers of the High Middle Ages were astonishingly receptive to new ideas. As committed Christians they could not allow doubts to be cast on the principles of their faith, but otherwise they were glad to incorporate whatever they could from the Greeks and Arabs. Considering that Aristotelian thought differed radically from anything accepted earlier in its emphasis on rationalism and the fundamental goodness and purposefulness of nature, its rapid acceptance by the Scholastics was a philosophical revolution. Another false impression is that Scholastic thinkers were greatly constrained by authority. Certainly they revered authority more than we do today, but such Scholastics as Saint Thomas did not regard the mere citation of texts—except biblical revelation concerning the mysteries of the faith—as being sufficient to clinch an argument. Rather, the authorities were brought forth to outline the possibilities, but reason and experience then demonstrated the truth. Finally, it is often believed that Scholastic thinkers were "antihumanistic," but modern scholars are coming to the opposite conclusion. Scholastics unquestionably gave primacy to

the soul over the body and to otherworldly salvation over life in the here and now. But they also exalted the dignity of human nature because they viewed it as a glorious divine creation, and they believed in the possibility of a working alliance between themselves and God. Moreover, they had extraordinary faith in the powers of human reason—probably more than we do today.

THE BLOSSOMING OF LITERATURE, ART, AND MUSIC

What constituted the "Renaissance of the Twelfth Century"?

The literature of the High Middle Ages was varied, lively, and impressive. The revival of grammatical studies in the cathedral schools and universities led to the production of some excellent Latin poetry. The best examples were secular lyrics, especially those written in the twelfth century by a group of poets known as the Goliards. How these poets got their name is uncertain, but it possibly meant "followers of the devil." That would have been appropriate because the Goliards were riotous poets who wrote parodies of the liturgy and burlesques of the Gospels. Their lyrics celebrated the beauties of the changing seasons, the carefree life of the open road, the pleasures of drinking and sport, and especially the joys of love. The authors of these rollicking and satirical songs were mainly wandering students, although some were men of more advanced years. The names of most are unknown. Their poetry is particularly significant both for its robust vitality and for being the first clear counterstatement to the ascetic ideal of Christianity.

VERNACULAR LITERATURE

In addition to Latin, the vernacular languages of French, German, Spanish, and Italian became increasingly popular as media of literary expression. At first, most of the literature in the vernacular languages was

> With the achievements of Saint Thomas Aquinas in the mid-thirteenth century, Western medieval thought reached its pinnacle.

A GOLIARDIC PARODY OF THE GOSPEL OF MARK, SATIRIZING THE PAPAL COURT

This selection is typical of the parodies of the liturgy and the Bible written by the freewheeling Latin poets of the twelfth century. This particular poem is written in mock biblical verse, and puns on the Christian Gospel of Mark—a mark being a sum of money equal to two thirds of a pound of silver. Like all parodies, it was meant to be humorous, but its accusations—that bribery around the papal court perverted justice—were widespread in twelfth- and thirteenth-century Europe.

Here beginneth the Holy Gospel according to the marks of silver. In those days the Holy Father said unto the Romans: "When the Son of Man shall come unto the seat of our Majesty, first say unto Him: 'Friend, why art Thou come?' but if he continue knocking and give you nothing, then cast Him forth into outer darkness."

And it came to pass that a certain poor priest came to the court of the Lord Pope and cried out, saying, "Do ye at least have pity on me, servants of the Pope, for the hand of poverty hath afflicted me. Verily I am poor and have nothing. I beseech you, therefore, have mercy upon me and pity me." They, however, hearing this were sorely wroth and said unto him, "Friend, may thy poverty go with thee to hell. Get thee behind us, Satan; thou savorest not of money. Amen, Amen we say to thee: thou shalt not enter into the blessings of thy Lord until thou hast given thy last penny."

The poor man went therefore and sold his cloak and his coat and all that he had, and gave unto the cardinals and the treasurers and the papal flunkies. But they said unto him, "And this, what is this among so many?"

And they cast him out utterly, and going forth he wept bitterly and would not be comforted.

After this there came to the court a rich priest, exceedingly wealthy, anointed with grease and great with wealth, who had committed murder for the sake of gain. He first gave unto the treasurer, then he gave unto the flunky, and then he gave unto the cardinals. But they reasoned among themselves, thinking they would receive more. Therefore when the Lord Pope heard that the cardinals and his servants had received many gifts from a priest he was sick, even unto death. But the rich man sent unto him a pallet of gold and silver, and immediately he was made whole.

The Lord Pope called unto him the cardinals and ministers and spake unto them saying: "Beware, brethren, lest any deceive you with vain words. For I have given you an example, so that as I have grasped, so should you grasp also."

Carmina Burana, 21, trans. by Helen Waddell, in *The Wandering Scholars*, 7th ed. (London: Constable, 1934), pp. 150–151, as revised by John E. Boswell.

Charlemagne Weeping for His Knights. A scene from the *Song of Roland*.

written in the form of the heroic epic. Among the leading examples were the French *Song of Roland*, the Norse eddas and sagas, the German *Song of the Nibelungs*, and the Spanish *Poem of the Cid*. Practically all of these works were originally composed between 1050 and 1150, although some (such as the *Cid* and the Norse sagas) were not written down until the thirteenth century. These epics portrayed a virile but unpolished warrior society. Blood flowed freely, skulls were cleaved by battle axes, and heroic warfare, honor, and loyalty were the major themes. If women were mentioned at all, they were subordinate to men. Brides were expected to die for their beloveds, but husbands were free to beat their wives. In one French epic a queen who tried to influence her husband met with a blow to the nose; even though blood flowed she replied, "Many thanks, when it pleases you, you may do it again." Although we find such passages repugnant, the best of the vernacular epics have great literary power despite their unrelentingly masculine focus.

TROUBADOUR POETRY AND COURTLY ROMANCES

In comparison to the epics, an enormous change in both subject matter and style was introduced in twelfth-century France by the troubadour poets and the writers of courtly romances. The troubadours were courtier poets who came from southern France and wrote in a language related to French known as Provençal. The origin of their inspiration is debated, but there can be no doubt that they initiated a movement of profound importance for all subsequent Western literature. Their style was far more finely wrought and sophisticated than that of the epic poets, and the most eloquent of their lyrics, which were meant to be sung to music, originated the theme of romantic love. The troubadours idealized women as marvelous beings who could grant intense spiritual and sensual gratification. Whatever greatness the poets found in themselves they usually attributed to the inspiration they found in love. But they also assumed that their love would lose its magic if it were too easily or frequently gratified. Therefore, they wrote more often of longing than of romantic fulfillment.

In addition to their love lyrics, the troubadours wrote several other kinds of short poems. Some were simply bawdy. In these, love is not mentioned at all, but the poet revels in thoughts of carnality, comparing, for example, riding his horse to "riding" his mistress. Other troubadour poems treat feats of arms, others comment on contemporary political events, and a few even meditate on matters of religion. But whatever the subject matter, the best troubadour poems were always cleverly and innovatively expressed. The literary tradition originated by the southern French troubadours was continued by the trouvères in northern France and by the minnesingers in Germany. Thereafter many of their innovations were developed by later lyric poets in all Western languages. Some of their poetic devices were consciously revived in the twentieth century by such literary modernists as Ezra Pound.

An equally important twelfth-century French innovation was the composition of longer narrative poems known as romances, so called because there were written in vernacular, Romance (that is, deriving from Latin) languages. Romances told engaging stories; they often excelled in portraying character, and their subject matter was usually love and adventure. Some romances elaborated on classical Greek themes, but the most famous and best were "Arthurian." These took their material from the legendary exploits of the

British hero King Arthur and his many chivalrous knights. The first great writer of Arthurian romances was the northern Frenchman Chrétien de Troyes, who was active between about 1165 and 1190. Chrétien did much to help create and shape the new form, and he also introduced innovations in subject matter and attitudes. Whereas the troubadours exalted extramarital love, Chrétien was the first to hold forth the ideal of romantic love within marriage. He also described not only the deeds but the thoughts and emotions of his characters.

A generation later, Chrétien's work was continued by the great German poets Wolfram von Eschenbach and Gottfried von Strassburg, who are recognized as the greatest writers in the German language before the eighteenth century. Wolfram's *Parzival*, a story of love and the search for the Holy Grail, is more subtle, complex, and greater in scope than any other high medieval literary work except Dante's *Divine Comedy.* Like Chrétien, Wolfram believed that true love could be fulfilled only in marriage, and in Parzival, for the first time in Western literature since the Greeks, one can see a full psychological development of the hero. Gottfried von Strassburg's *Tristan* is a more somber work that tells of the tragic, adulterous love between Tristan and Isolde. Indeed, it might almost be regarded as the prototype of modern tragic romanticism. Gottfried was one of the first to develop fully the idea of individual suffering as a literary theme and to point out the in-

distinct line that separates pleasure from pain. For him, to love is to yearn, and suffering and unfulfilled gratification are integral chapters of the book of life. Unlike the troubadours, he could see complete fulfillment of love only in death. *Parzival* and *Tristan* have become most famous today in the form of their operatic reconceptions by the nineteenth-century German composer Richard Wagner.

Not all high medieval narratives were so elevated as the romances in either form or substance. A very different new narrative form was the *fabliau*, or verse fable. Although *fabliaux* derived from the moral animal tales of Aesop, they quickly evolved into short stories that were written less to edify or instruct than to amuse. Often they were very coarse, and sometimes they dealt with sexual relations in a broadly humorous and thoroughly unromantic manner. Many were also strongly anticlerical, making monks and priests the butts of their jokes. Because the *fabliaux* are so "uncourtly" it was once thought that they were written solely for the new urban classes. But there is now little doubt that they were addressed at least equally to the "refined" aristocracy, who liked to have their laughs too. They are significant as expressions of growing worldliness and as the first manifestations of the robust realism that was later to be perfected by Boccaccio and Chaucer.

Completely different in form but similar as an illustration of growing worldliness was the sprawling *Romance of the Rose.* As its title indicates, this was begun as a romance, specifically around 1230 by the courtly Frenchman William de Lorris. But William left his rather flowery, romantic work unfinished, and it was completed around 1270 by another Frenchman, Jean de Meung. The latter changed its nature greatly, inserting long, biting digressions in which he skewered religious hypocrisy. Jean's major theme was the need for procreation. Not love, but the service of "Dame Nature" in sexual fecundity is urged in numerous witty but extremely earthy images and metaphors. At the climax the originally dreamy hero seizes his mistress, who is allegorically depicted as a rose, and rapes her. The work became

Rabbit on the Hunt. Marginal illustrations in medieval manuscripts (this one dates from about 1340) often exhibit ironic humor.

enormously popular, but then as now it provoked strong reactions, including a sweeping condemnation of its treatment of women by the fourteenth-century writer Christine de Pisan.

THE DIVINE COMEDY

In a class by itself as the greatest work of medieval literature is Dante Alighieri's *Divine Comedy*. Dante (1265–1321) was active during the early part of his career in the political affairs of his native city of Florence, and remained throughout his life intensely connected to his native city. Despite his engagement in politics and the fact that he was a layman, he managed to acquire an awesome mastery of the religious, philosophic, and literary knowledge of his time. He not only knew the Bible and the church fathers, but—most unusual for a layman—he also absorbed the most recent Scholastic theology. In addition, he was thoroughly familiar with Virgil, Cicero, Boethius, and numerous other classical writers, and was fully conversant with the poems of the troubadours and the Italian poetry of his own day. In 1301 he was expelled from Florence after a political upheaval and was forced to live the rest of his life in exile. The *Divine Comedy*, his major work, was written during this final period.

> In a class by itself as the greatest work of medieval literature is Dante Alighieri's *Divine Comedy.*

Dante's *Divine Comedy* is a monumental narrative in powerful rhyming Italian verse, which describes the poet's journey through hell, purgatory, and paradise. At the start Dante tells of finding himself in a "dark wood," his metaphor for a deep personal midlife crisis in which he had wandered away from his Christian faith. He is led out of this forest of despair by the Roman poet Virgil, who represents the heights of classical reason and philosophy. Virgil guides Dante on a trip through hell and purgatory; then Dante's deceased beloved, Beatrice, who symbolizes Christian wisdom and blessedness, takes over and guides him through paradise. In the course of this progress from hell to heaven Dante meets both historical personages and his own contemporaries; he is instructed by them and his guides as to why they met their several fates. As the poem progresses Dante grows in wisdom and understanding, until finally he returns with new confidence and certainty to his own lost Christian faith.

Every reader finds a different combination of wonder and satisfaction in Dante's magnificent work. Some—especially those who know Italian—marvel at the vigor and inventiveness of Dante's language and images. Others are awed by his subtle complexity and poetic symmetry; others by his array of learning; others by the vitality of his characters and individual sto-

The Poet Dante Driven into Exile. On the left Dante is expelled from Florence; on the right he begins work on his great poem, the *Divine Comedy*. From a mid-fifteenth-century Florentine manuscript. (The nearly completed dome of Florence's cathedral can be seen at the far left.)

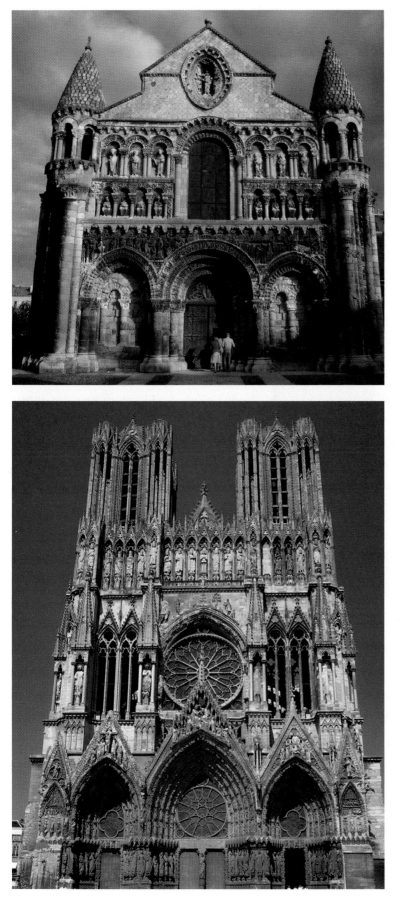

ries; and still others by his soaring imagination. The historian finds it particularly remarkable that Dante could sum up the best of medieval learning in such an artistically satisfying manner. Dante stressed the precedence of salvation, but he viewed earth as existing for human benefit. He allowed humans free will to choose good and avoid evil, and accepted Greek philosophy as authoritative in its own sphere; for example, he called Aristotle "the master of them that know." Above all, his sense of hope and his ultimate faith in humanity—remarkable for a defeated exile—most powerfully expresses the dominant mood of the High Middle Ages and makes Dante one of the two or three most stirringly affirmative writers who ever lived.

ART AND ARCHITECTURE

The closest architectural equivalents of the *Divine Comedy* are the great high medieval Gothic cathedrals, for they too have qualities of vast scope, balance of intricate detail with careful symmetry, soaring height, and affirmative religious grandeur. But before we approach the Gothic style, it is best to introduce it by means of its high medieval predecessor, the style of architecture and art known as the Romanesque. This style had its origins in the tenth century, but became fully formed in the eleventh and the first half of the twelfth centuries, when the religious reform movement sparked the building of many new monasteries and large churches. The Romanesque style aimed to manifest the majesty of God in stone by rigorously subordinating all architectural details to a uniform

Romanesque and Gothic. Top: West front of the Church of Notre Dame la Grande, Poitiers. Constructed between 1135 and 1145, this typical example of Romanesque architecture emphasizes the repetition of rounded arches and horizontal lines. Bottom: Rheims Cathedral. Built between 1220 and 1299, this High Gothic cathedral places great stress on vertical elements. The gabled portals, pointed arches, and multitude of pinnacles all accentuate the height of this structure.

The Upper Chapel of the Sainte-Chapelle, Paris. High Gothic is here carried to its extreme. Slender columns, tracery, and stained-glass windows take the place of walls.

much evocative power and represent the first manifestations of a revived interest in sculpting the human form.

In the course of the twelfth and thirteenth centuries the Romanesque style was supplanted throughout most of Europe by the Gothic. Although trained art historians can see how certain traits of the one style led to the development of the other, the actual appearance of the two styles is distinctively different. In fact, the two seem as different as the epic is different from the romance, an appropriate analogy because the Gothic style emerged in France in the mid-twelfth century exactly when the romance did, and because it was far more sophisticated, graceful, and elegant than its predecessor, in the same way that the romance compared with the epic. The rapid development and acceptance of the Gothic is yet another example of the experimental and dynamic character of twelfth-century culture. When the abbey church of Saint Denis, venerated as the shrine of the French patron saint and burial place of French kings, was torn down in 1144 in order to make room for a much larger one in the strikingly new Gothic style, it was as if the president of the United States were to tear down the White House and replace it with a Mies van der Rohe or Helmut Jahn edifice. Such an act today would be highly improbable, or at least would create an enormous uproar. But in the twelfth century the equivalent actually happened and was taken in stride.

Gothic architecture was one of the most intricate of building styles. Its basic elements were the pointed arch, groined and ribbed vaulting, and the flying buttress. These devices made possible a much lighter and loftier construction than could ever have been achieved with the round arch and the engaged pier of the Romanesque. In fact, the Gothic cathedral could be described as a skeletal framework of stone enclosed by enormous windows. Other features included lofty spires, rose windows, delicate tracery in stone, elaborately sculpted facades, multiple columns, and the more frequent use of gargoyles, or representations of mythical monsters, as decorative devices. Ornamentation was generally concentrated on the exterior. But the inside of the

system. The essential features of the Romanesque style were the rounded arch, massive stone walls, enormous piers (support columns), small windows, and the predominance of horizontal lines. Together, these features gave Romanesque architecture a sense of stability and permanence. Interiors were plain, but sometimes relieved by mosaics or frescoes in bright colors and—a very important innovation for Christian art—the introduction of sculptural decoration, both within and without. For the first time, full-length human figures appeared on facades. These are usually grave and elongated far beyond natural dimensions, but they have

Gothic cathedral was never somber or gloomy. The stained-glass windows served not to exclude the light but to glorify it, to catch the rays of sunlight and suffuse them with a richness and warmth of color that nature itself could hardly duplicate even in its happiest moods.

Many people still think of the Gothic cathedral as the expression of purely ascetic otherworldliness, but this estimation is highly inaccurate. Certainly all churches are dedicated to the glory of God and hope for life everlasting, but Gothic ones sometimes included stained-glass scenes of daily life that had no overt religious significance at all. More important, Gothic sculptures of religious figures such as Jesus, the Virgin, and the saints were becoming far more naturalistic than anything hitherto created in the medieval West. So also was the sculptural representation of plant and animal life, which rose to extraordinary levels of botanical and zoological accuracy. Moreover, Gothic architecture was also an expression of the medieval intellectual genius. Each cathedral, with its many symbolic figures, was a kind of encyclopedia of medieval knowledge carved in stone. Finally, Gothic cathedrals were manifestations of urban pride. Always located in the growing medieval cities, they were meant to be both centers of community life and expressions of a town's greatness. When a new cathedral went up the people of the entire community participated in erecting it, and rightfully regarded it as almost their own property. Many of the Gothic cathedrals were the products of urban rivalries. Each city or town sought to overawe its neighbor with ever bigger or taller buildings, to the degree that ambitions sometimes got out of bounds and many of the cathedrals were left unfinished. But most of the finished ones are still vast enough. Built to last into eternity, they provide the most striking visual manifestation of the soaring exuberance of their age.

DRAMA AND MUSIC

Surveys of high medieval accomplishments should not omit drama and music. Our own modern drama descends at least as much from the medieval form as from the classical one. Throughout the medieval period some Latin classical plays were known in manuscript but were never performed. Instead drama was born all over again within the church. In the early Middle Ages certain passages in the liturgy began to be acted out. Then, in the twelfth century, primarily in Paris, these were superseded by short religious plays in Latin, performed inside a church. Rapidly thereafter, the Latin plays were supplemented or supplanted by ones in the vernacular so that the whole congregation could understand them. Around 1200, these started to be performed outside, in front of the church, so that they would not take time away from the services. As soon as that happened, drama entered the everyday world: nonreligious stories were introduced, character portrayal was expanded, and the way was prepared for the Elizabethans and Shakespeare.

As the drama grew out of developments within the liturgy and then moved far beyond them, so did characteristically Western music. Until the High Middle Ages Western music was homophonic, as is much non-Western music even today. That is, it developed only one melody at a time without any harmonic background. The great high medieval invention was polyphony, the playing or singing of two or more harmonious melodies together. Some experiments along these lines may have been made in the West as early as the tenth century, but the most fundamental breakthrough was achieved at the cathedral of Paris around 1170, when the mass was first sung by two voices weaving together two different melodies in "counterpoint." Roughly concurrently, systems of musical notation were invented and perfected. Because performers no longer had to rely on memory, music could become more complex. All the greatness of Western music followed from these first steps.

CONCLUSION

For almost one hundred years, scholars have spoken of the sweeping intellectual, religious, and cultural changes of the High Middle Ages as constituting the "Renaissance of the Twelfth Century." This categorization still seems apt. Like those of the more famous Italian Renaissance of the fourteenth and fifteenth centuries, the intellectual changes of the High Middle Ages were profoundly influenced by the recovery and intensive study of classical texts. But in both periods, the use made of these classical texts was distinctive and unique. Neither of these movements were mere

> Many people still think of the Gothic cathedral as the expression of purely ascetic otherworldliness, but this estimation is highly inaccurate.

revivals; rather, both were creative adaptations of classical ideas to a new and distinctively Christian culture.

Even more so than the Italian Renaissance, however, the twelfth-century renaissance marks the origin of a set of characteristic attitudes and ideas that have characterized western European civilization ever since. Our modern conceptions of love and friendship; our understanding of human motivation and intention; indeed, our very interest in psychology itself, all derive from twelfth-century developments. So too does our emphasis on the essential interiority of Christian piety; our vision that "true religion" ought to be expressed in practical works of charity in the world; and our presumption that religion and politics are separable spheres of human endeavor and concern. Even our modern impulse to define and persecute minority groups has roots in twelfth- and thirteenth-century efforts to suppress Jews, heretics, and sexual minorities.

Many of the people who made such important contributions to learning, thought, literature, architecture, drama, and music must have intermingled with each other in the Paris of the High Middle Ages. Some of them no doubt prayed together in the cathedral of Notre Dame. The names of the leading scholars are remembered, but the names of most of the others are unknown. Yet taken together they did as much for the civilization of Europe, and created as many enduring monuments, as did their counterparts in ancient Athens. Their names may be forgotten, but their achievements live on still.

SELECTED READINGS

Baldwin, John W. *The Scholastic Culture of the Middle Ages: 1000–1300* Lexington, Mass., 1971. A fine introduction.

Blumenthal, Uta-Renate *The Investiture Controversy.* Philadelphia, 1988. A clear review of a complicated subject.

Boswell, John E. *Christianity, Social Tolerance, and Homosexuality: Gay People in Western Europe from the Beginning of the Christian Era to the Fourteenth Century.* Chicago, 1980. A pioneering account, particularly good on twelfth-century poetry.

Chrétien de Troyes. *Arthurian Romances.* Translated by W. W. Kibler. New York, 1991.

Clanchy, Michael T. *Abelard: A Medieval Life.* Oxford and Cambridge, Mass., 1997. A great biography, which now needs to be supplemented by Mews (see below).

Cobban, Alan B. *The Medieval Universities.* London, 1975. The best short treatment in English.

Colish, Marcia. *Medieval Foundations of the Western Intellectual Tradition, 400–1400.* New Haven, 1997. An encyclopedic and exhaustive work, best used as a reference.

Dante Alighieri. *The Divine Comedy.* Translated by Mark Musa. 3 vols. Baltimore, 1984–1986.

Dronke, Peter. *Women Writers of the Middle Ages.* New York, 1984. A rich literary study.

Gilson, Etienne. *Reason and Revelation in the Middle Ages.* New York, 1938. Somewhat dated, but still a useful introduction for students to the intellectual world of scholasticism.

Goldin, F., ed. *Lyrics of the Troubadours and Trouvères.* Garden City, N.Y., 1973.

Gottfried von Strassburg. *Tristan.* Translated by A. T. Hatto. Baltimore, 1960.

Grundmann, Herbert. *Religious Movements in the Middle Ages.* Notre Dame, Ind., 1995. A classic work, now translated into English, that shows how much of high medieval religious vitality, orthodox and heretical, originated from the search for the "apostolic life."

Knowles, David. *The Evolution of Medieval Thought,* 2d ed. London, 1988. An authoritative survey, thoroughly revised in the second edition.

Lambert, Malcolm. *Medieval Heresy,* 2d ed. Oxford and Cambridge, 1992. The standard synthesis; deeply learned and fully annotated.

Lawrence, Clifford Hugh. *The Friars: The Impact of the Early Mendicant Movement on Western Society.* London and New York, 1994. The best short introduction to the early history of the Franciscans and the Dominicans.

———. *Medieval Monasticism: Forms of Religious Life in Western Europe in the Middle Ages,* 3d ed. London and New York, 2000. This new edition includes material on the friars drawn from his 1994 book.

Leclerq, Jean. *Bernard of Clairvaux and the Cistercian Spirit.* Kalamazoo, Mich., 1976. An empathetic account by the greatest twentieth-century scholar of Cistercianism.

———. *The Love of Learning and the Desire for God,* 3d ed. New York, 1982. A beautiful account of twelfth-century monastic culture, seen from the perspective of Saint Bernard of Clairvaux.

The Letters of Abelard and Heloise. Translated by Betty Radice. London and New York, 1974. Includes Abelard's autobiographical *Story of My Misfortunes.*

Mews, Constant J. *The Lost Love Letters of Heloise and Abelard.* New York, 1999. A recently identified treasure trove of correspondence between the lovers, written before they were detected and separated.

Morris, Colin. *The Papal Monarchy: The Western Church from 1050 to 1250.* Oxford, 1989. An excellent scholarly survey; part of the Oxford History of the Christian Church series.

Newman, Barbara. *Sister of Wisdom: St. Hildegard's Theology of the Feminine.* Berkeley and Los Angeles, 1980. A pioneering work; the 1989 edition includes a discography of Hildegard's music.

———, ed. *Voice of the Living Light: Hildegard of Bingen and Her World.* Berkeley and Los Angeles, 1998. The best introduction to Hildegard's life and work; discusses her roles as abbess, religious thinker, prophet, correspondent, artist, medical writer, composer, dramatist, and poet.

Peters, Edward, ed., *The First Crusade: The Chronicle of Fulcher of Chartres and Other Source Materials*, 2d ed. Philadelphia, 1998. The second edition contains a great deal of new material not available in the first edition.

————. *The Crusades: A Short History*, New Haven, 1987. A reliable account that contains a very useful list of primary sources.

Riley-Smith, Jonathan. *The First Crusade and the Idea of Crusading.* Philadelphia, 1986. A clear and accessible account by an acknowledged expert.

————, ed. *The Oxford Illustrated History of the Crusades*, Oxford and New York, 1995. The most engaging introduction to the subject; first-class text, splendidly illustrated.

Sheingorn, Pamela, trans. *The Book of Sainte Foy.* Philadelphia, 1995.

Smalley, Beryl. *The Study of the Bible in the Middle Ages*, 3d ed. Oxford, 1983. The standard work, gracefully written yet immensely learned.

Southern, Richard W. *Western Society and the Church in the Middle Ages.* Baltimore, 1970. An extremely insightful interpretation of the interplay between society and religion, engagingly written by one of the greatest historians of the twentieth century.

————. *Scholastic Humanism and the Unification of Europe.* Vol. 1: *Foundations.* Oxford and Cambridge, Mass., 1995. A major reinterpretation of scholasticism and humanism by the foremost historian of both traditions.

Swanson, R. N. *The Twelfth-Century Renaissance.* Manchester, Eng., 1999. The most accessible and up-to-date survey of the intellectual developments of the twelfth century.

Tierney, Brian. *The Crisis of Church and State, 1050–1300.* Toronto, 1988. An indispensable collection for both teachers and students.

Wakefield, Walter, and Austin P. Evans, eds. and trans. *Heresies of the High Middle Ages.* New York, 1969, 1991. A comprehensive collection of sources, best used in conjunction with Lambert (see above).

Wilhelm, James J., ed. and trans. *Medieval Song: An Anthology of Hymns and Lyrics.* New York, 1971. An excellent collection of sacred and secular poetry that illustrates the connections between them.

Wolfram von Eschenbach. *Parzival.* Translated by H. M. Mustard and C. E. Passage. New York, 1961.

THE LATER
MIDDLE AGES,
1300–1500

I F THE HIGH MIDDLE AGES were "times of feasts," then the late Middle
Ages were "times of famine." From about 1300 until the middle or latter part of
the fifteenth century calamities struck throughout western Europe with appalling
severity and dismaying persistence. Famine first prevailed because agriculture was
impeded by soil exhaustion, colder weather, and torrential rainfalls. Then, on top of
those "acts of God," came the most terrible natural disaster of all: the dreadful plague
known as the "Black Death," which cut broad swaths of mortality throughout western Europe. As if all that were not enough, incessant warfare continually brought
hardship and desolation. Common people suffered most because they were most exposed to raping, stabbing, looting, and burning by soldiers and organized bands of
freebooters. After an army passed through a region one might see miles of smolder-
ing ruins littered with putrefying corpses; in many places the desolation was so great
that wolves roamed the countryside and even entered the outskirts of the cities. In
short, if the serene Virgin symbolized the High Middle Ages, the grinning death's-
head symbolized the succeeding period. But despite the hardships they faced, Europeans displayed a tenacious perseverance in the face of adversity. Instead of
abandoning themselves to apathy, they resolutely sought to adjust to changed circumstances. Thus civilization did not collapse, but rather a period of creativity and
innovation preserved and extended the most enduring features of high medieval European life.

FOCUS QUESTIONS

• How did famine and plague transform economic life in late medieval Europe?

• What were the causes of the popular rebellions from 1300 to 1450?

• What were the main forms of late medieval popular piety?

• What caused the rise of national monarchies?

• Why was medieval Russia so unlike any other European state?

• What trends led to the rise of vernacular literature?

• How did technological advances affect every-day life?

ECONOMIC DEPRESSION AND THE EMERGENCE OF A NEW EQUILIBRIUM

How did famine and plague transform economic life in late medieval Europe?

By around 1300 the agricultural expansion of the High Middle Ages had reached its limits. Thereafter yields and areas under cultivation began to decline, causing a downturn in the whole European economy that was accelerated by the disruptive effects of war. Accordingly, the first half of the fourteenth century was a time of growing economic depression in both town and countryside. The coming of the Black Death in 1347 made this depression particularly acute because it completely disrupted the affairs of daily life. Recurrences of the plague and protracted warfare continued to depress most of the European economy until deep into the fifteenth century. But between roughly 1350 and 1450 Europeans learned how to adjust to the new economic circumstances and succeeded in placing their economy on a sounder basis. Wages rose while grain prices fell. Although this hurt large-scale grain producers, it benefited smaller farmers (who could more easily diversify their agricultural production) and wage earners. The resulting prosperity was reflected in better diets and housing among European laborers and farmers, and a gradual recovery in overall population. Although the total size of the European economy almost certainly shrank in the century after the Black Death, by 1450 Europe was wealthier per capita than it had been in 1300, and its wealth was more evenly distributed among its people. All told, therefore, Europe emerged in the later fifteenth century with a healthier economy than it had known earlier.

> The first half of the fourteenth century was a time of growing economic depression in both town and countryside.

CLIMATE CHANGE AND AGRICULTURAL FAILURE

The checks on agricultural expansion reached around 1300 were natural ones. There was a limit to the amount of land that could be cleared and a limit to the amount of crops that could be raised without the introduction of scientific farming. In fact, Europeans had gone further in clearing and cultivating than they should have: in the enthusiasm of the high medieval colonization movement, marginal lands had been cleared that were not rich enough to sustain intense cultivation. In addition, even the best plots were becoming overworked. To make matters worse, after around 1300 the weather deteriorated. Whereas western Europe had been favored with a drying and warming trend in the eleventh and twelfth centuries, in the fourteenth century the climate became colder and wetter. Although the average decline in temperature over the course of the century was only about one degree Centigrade, this was sufficient to curtail wine production in many northern areas such as England. Cereal farming too became increasingly impractical in far northern regions because the growing season became too short: in Greenland and parts of Scandinavia, agricultural settlements were abandoned entirely. Increased rainfall also took its toll. Terrible floods deluged all of northwestern Europe in 1315, ruining crops and causing a prolonged, deadly famine that was made worse by epidemic diseases that swept through sheep flocks and cattle herds. For three years peasants were so driven by hunger that they ate their seed grain, ruining their chances for a full recovery in the following season. In desperation they also ate cats, dogs, and rats. Many peasants were so exposed to unsanitary conditions and weakened by malnutrition that they became highly susceptible to disease. The death rate was appalling. In one Flemish city a tenth of the population was buried within a six-month period of 1316 alone. Between 1316 and 1322, 10 percent to 15 percent of the entire European population may have perished in this "Great Famine." Relatively settled farming conditions returned after 1322, but in many parts of Europe heavy rains or other climatic disasters came again. In Italy, floods swept away Florentine bridges in 1333; a tidal wave destroyed the port of Amalfi in 1343. With nature so recurrently capricious, economic life could only suffer.

Although ruinous wars combined with famine to kill off many, Europe remained overpopulated relative to its food supplies until the middle of the fourteenth century. Despite the high mortality rate, this imbalance between population and resources probably worsened after 1300. As cereal production declined, grain prices soared and the poor throughout Europe paid the

HOW DID FAMINE AND PLAGUE TRANSFORM ECONOMIC LIFE IN LATE MEDIEVAL EUROPE?

ECONOMIC DEPRESSION AND THE EMERGENCE OF A NEW EQUILIBRIUM   385

penalty in hunger. Then a disaster struck that was so horrifying that it seemed to many to presage the end of the world.

THE BLACK DEATH

The Black Death was a combined onslaught of bubonic and pneumonic plague that first swept through Europe from 1347 to 1350, returning at periodic intervals for the next three hundred years. This epidemic originated in the Gobi Desert of Mongolia, where the plague bacillus is endemic among the rodents of the area and among the fleas that live on the rodents. Both are capable of carrying the plague; we have no way of knowing which initially carried the disease out of Mongolia during the late 1330s and into China, northern India, and the Crimea. The rapid spread of the disease was an unfortunate consequence of the increasing commercial integration between these areas that the Mongol conquests of the thirteenth century had created. By 1346 the plague had reached the ports along the Black Sea, and from there, in 1347, Genoese galleys brought it, inadvertantly, to Sicily and northern Italy. From Italy it spread throughout western Europe along the trade routes, first striking the seaports, then moving inland.

This calamity was fully comparable—in terms of the death, dislocation, and horror it wrought—with the two world wars of the twentieth century. The clinical effects of the plague were hideous. Once infected with bubonic plague by a flea bite, the diseased person would develop enormous swellings in the groin or armpits, black spots might appear on the arms and legs, diarrhea would ensue, and the victim would die between the fourth and seventh days. If the infection came in the pneumonic form (caused by inhalation) there would be coughing of blood instead of swellings, and death would follow within three days. Some people went to bed healthy and were dead the next morning after a night of agony; ships with dead crews floated aimlessly on the seas. Although the successive epidemics left a few localities unscathed, the overall demographic effects of the plague were devastating. In England, the total population of the country declined by at least 40 percent between 1347 and 1381. The total population of eastern Normandy fell by 30 percent between 1347 and 1357, and again by 30 percent before 1380; in the rural area around Pistoia in Italy a population depletion of about 60 percent occurred between 1340 and 1404. Altogether, the combined effects of famine, war, and, above all, plague reduced the total population of western Europe by at least one half

and perhaps as much as two thirds between 1300 and 1450.

At first, the Black Death caused great hardships for most of the survivors. Since panic-stricken people wished to avoid contagion, many fled from their jobs to seek isolation. Town dwellers fled to the country, and country dwellers fled from each other. Even the pope retreated to the interior of his palace and allowed no one entrance. With large numbers dead and others away from their posts, harvests were left rotting, manufacturing was disrupted, and trade collapsed. Basic commodities became scarcer and prices rose. For these

Bubonic Plague. This representation from a late-fifteenth-century French painting shows a man in the throes of death from the plague. The swelling on his neck is a *bubo,* a form of lymphatic swelling that gave the bubonic plague its name.

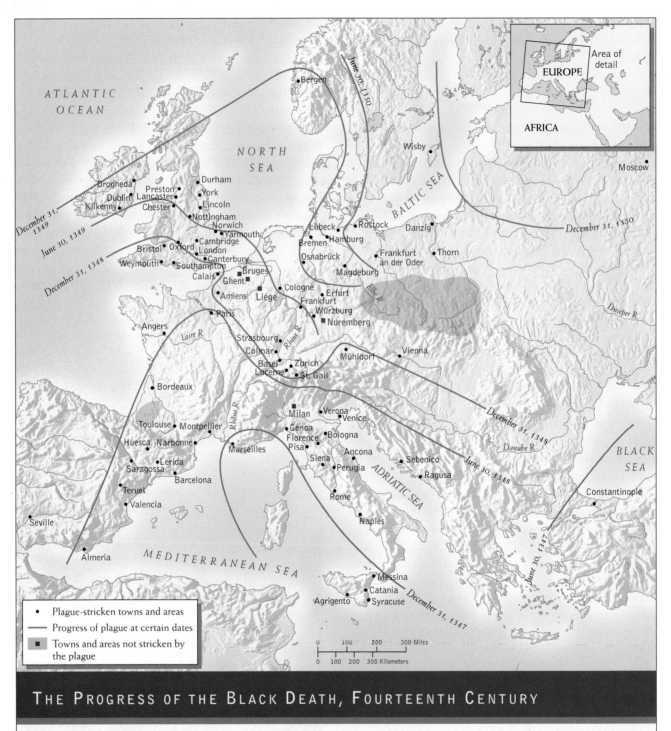

THE PROGRESS OF THE BLACK DEATH, FOURTEENTH CENTURY

Where did the Black Death come from, and where did it enter Europe, generally speaking? Why was the onslaught of the disease so devastating, and what agricultural, economic, and demographic factors helped to make Europeans around 1350 so vulnerable to the disease? Note the rapid spread of the Black Death. Would such a rapid advance have been likely during the early Middle Ages, or even in the ancient world? How did the growth of towns, trade, and travel contribute to the spread of the Black Death?

HOW DID FAMINE AND PLAGUE TRANSFORM ECONOMIC LIFE IN LATE MEDIEVAL EUROPE?

ECONOMIC DEPRESSION AND THE EMERGENCE OF A NEW EQUILIBRIUM   387

reasons the onslaught of the plague greatly intensified Europe's economic crisis.

By 1400, however, the new demographic realities began to turn prices around and alter basic economic patterns. In particular, the prices of staple foodstuffs (for example, grains) began to decline because production gradually returned to normal and there were fewer mouths to feed. Recurrences of the plague or natural disasters sometimes caused prices to fluctuate greatly in certain years, but overall prices of basic commodities throughout most of the fifteenth century went down or remained stable. This trend led to new agricultural specialization. Since cereals were cheaper, people could afford to spend a greater percentage of their income on comparative luxuries such as dairy products, meat, and wine. Hitherto farmers all over Europe had concentrated on growing cereals, but now it was wisest, particularly in areas of poorer soil or unpropitious climate, to shift to specialized production. Depending upon whatever seemed most feasible, land might be used for the raising of livestock for milk, grapes for wine, or malt for beer. Specialized regional economies resulted: parts of England were given over to sheep raising or beer production, parts of France concentrated on wine, and Sweden traded butter for cheap German grain. Most areas of Europe turned to what they could do best, and reciprocal trade of basic commodities over long distances created a sound new commercial equilibrium.

THE IMPACT ON TOWNS

Towns were particularly sensitive barometers of the changing economic climate of the later Middle Ages. After reaching their demographic peak around 1300, many towns were already experiencing declining populations and economic crises even before the Black Death struck. The plague, however, made the existing situation infinitely worse. Overcrowding, combined with the generally unsanitary conditions of medieval urban life, made Europe's cities particularly vulnerable to the plague. In some cities, mortality rates from the plague may have exceeded 60 percent. In northern Italy, southern France, and parts of Spain, however, warfare was even more destructive of urban life than was the plague. Toulouse, for example, weathered the onset of the plague relatively well. Between 1355 and 1385, its population declined only about 15 percent,

from approximately thirty thousand to twenty-six thousand. By 1430, however, after several decades of war, Toulouse's population had dropped to around eight thousand. By 1450, however, as a century of warfare came to an end and visitations of the plague became less frequent and less devastating (presumably because Europeans were beginning to develop some resistance to the plague bacillus), urban life was well on the road to recovery. By 1500, a larger percentage of Europe's people lived in towns, and towns themselves played a larger role in the European economy, than had been the case two centuries before.

Certain urban centers, especially those in northern Germany and northern Italy, profited the most from the new economic circumstances. In Germany a group of cities and towns under the leadership of Lübeck and Bremen allied in the so-called Hanseatic League to control long-distance trade in the Baltic and North seas. Their fleets transported German grain to Scandinavia and brought back dairy products, fish, and furs. The enhanced European per capita ability to buy luxury goods brought new wealth to the northern Italian trading cities of Genoa and, especially, Venice because these cities controlled the importation of spices from the East. Greater expenditures on luxury also aided the economies of Florence, Venice, Milan, and other neighboring cities because those cities concentrated on the manufacture of silks and linens, light woolens, and other fine cloths. Milan, in addition, prospered from its armaments industry, which kept the warring European states supplied with armor and weapons. Because of varying local conditions, some cities and towns, above all those of Flanders, became economically depressed, but altogether European urban centers profited remarkably well from the new economic circumstances and emphasis on specialization.

The changed circumstances also helped stimulate the development of sophisticated business, accounting, and banking techniques. Because sharp fluctuations in prices made investments precarious, new forms of partnerships were created to minimize risks. Insurance contracts were also invented to take some of the risk out of shipping. Europe's most useful accounting invention, double-entry bookkeeping, was first put into use in Italy in the mid-fourteenth century and spread rapidly thereafter north of the Alps. This method allowed for quick discovery of computational errors and easy overview of profits and losses, credits and debits. Large-

> Certain urban centers, especially those in northern Germany and northern Italy, profited the most from the new economic circumstances.

The Banker and His Wife, by Quentin Massys.

THE NEW EQUILIBRIUM

In surveying the two centuries of late medieval economic history, we must emphasize both the role of nature and that of human beings. Bad weather and disease may come at any time, but when humans are already suffering from hunger and conditions of overcrowding, the results of natural disasters will be particularly devastating. That certainly is what happened in the fourteenth century. Nature intervened cruelly in human affairs, but no matter how cruel the immediate effects, the results were ultimately beneficial. By 1450 a far smaller population had a higher average standard of living than the population of 1300. In this result humans too played their part. Because people were determined to make the best of the new circumstances and avoid a recurrence of economic depression, they managed to reorganize their economic life and place it on a sounder footing. The gross European product of about 1450 was probably lower than it was in 1300, but this is not surprising given the much smaller population. In fact, per capita output had risen with per capita income, and the European economy was ready to move on to new conquests.

scale banking had already become common after the middle of the thirteenth century, but the economic crises of the later Middle Ages encouraged banks to alter some of their ways of doing business. Most important was the development of prudent branch-banking techniques, especially by the Florentine house of the Medici. Earlier banks had built branches, but the Medici bankers, who flourished from 1397 to 1494, organized theirs along the lines of a modern holding company. The Medici branches, located in London, Bruges, and Avignon, as well as several Italian cities, were dominated by senior partners from the Medici family who followed common policies. However, each branch was a separate, formal partnership that did not carry any other branch down with it if it collapsed. Other Italian banks experimented with advanced credit techniques. Some even allowed their clients to transfer funds between each other without any real money changing hands. Such "book transfers" were at first executed only by oral command, but around 1400 they started to be carried out by written orders. These were the earliest ancestors of the modern check.

SOCIAL AND EMOTIONAL DISLOCATION

What were the causes of the popular rebellions from 1300 to 1450?

Before the healthy new equilibrium was reached, the economic crises of the later Middle Ages contributed from about 1300 to 1450 to provoking a rash of lower-class rural and urban insurrections more numerous than Europe had ever known before. It was once thought that these were all caused by extreme deprivation, but as we will see, often that was not the case.

WHAT WERE THE CAUSES OF THE POPULAR REBELLIONS FROM 1300 TO 1450?

SOCIAL AND EMOTIONAL DISLOCATION   389

THE JACQUERIE

The one large-scale rural uprising that was most clearly caused by economic hardship was the northern French "Jacquerie" of 1358. This took its name from the proto-typical French peasant, "Jacques Bonhomme," who had suffered more than he could endure. In 1348 and 1349 the Black Death had brought its terror and wreaked havoc with the economy. Then a flare-up of war between England and France had spread great desolation over the countryside. The peasants, as usual in late me-dieval warfare, suffered most from the pillaging and burning carried out by the rapacious soldiers. To make matters even less endurable, after the English deci-sively defeated the French in 1356 at the battle of Poitiers the French king, John II, and numerous aristo-crats had to be ransomed. As always in such cases, the peasants were asked to bear the heaviest share of the burden, but by 1358 they had enough and rose up with astounding ferocity. Without any clear program they burned down castles, murdered their lords, and raped their lords' wives. Undoubtedly their intense economic resentments were the major cause for the uprising, but two qualifications remain in order. The first is that the peasants who participated in the Jacquerie were, comparatively speaking, among the richest in France: apparently those who suffered most abjectly were entirely un-able to organize themselves for revolt. The other qualification is that political factors surely help account for the Jacquerie as well as economic ones. While the king was in captivity in England, groups of townsmen were trying to reform the govern-mental system by limiting monarchical powers, and aristocratic factions were plotting to seize power. Since nobody quite knew which element was going to rule where, the peasants seem to have sensed an op-portunity to take advantage of France's political confu-sion. But in fact the opportunity was not so great as they may have thought: within a month the privileged powers closed ranks, massacred the rebels, and quickly restored order.

> The incidence of the plague did help to increase manumissions of serfs and raise salaries or lower rents of free farm laborers.

THE ENGLISH PEASANTS' REVOLT

The English Peasants' Revolt of 1381—the most seri-ous lower-class rebellion in English history—is fre-quently bracketed with the Jacquerie, but its causes were very different. Instead of being a revolt of desper-ation, it arose from a combination of rising economic expectations combined with political grievances asso-ciated with English defeats in the war with France. By 1381 the effects of the Black Death should have been working in favor of the peasants. Above all, a shortage of labor should have placed their services in demand. In fact, the incidence of the plague did help to increase manumissions (freeings) of serfs and to raise salaries or lower rents of free farm laborers. But aristocratic land-lords fought back to preserve their own incomes. They succeeded in passing legislation that aimed to keep wages at preplague levels and force free laborers to work at the lower rates. Aristocrats also tried to exact all their old dues and unpaid services from the serfs that remained under their control. Because the peas-ants were unwilling to be pushed down into their previous poverty and subservience, a collision was in-evitable.

The spark that ignited the great revolt of 1381 was an attempt to collect a new type of national tax to pay for the failing war with France. Traditionally, English taxes had been assessed village by village in rough proportion to wealth. In 1377 and 1379, however, the government imposed a much less graduated head tax instead of the traditional income tax. These two taxes were collected without resistance, but when agents tried to collect a third, much heavier such tax in 1381, the peasants, artisans, and town dwellers of eastern England rose up to resist. First they burned local records and sacked the dwellings of those they consid-ered their exploiters; then they marched into London, where they executed the lord chancellor and treasurer of Eng-land, whose fiscal mismanagement they blamed for re-cent English defeats in the French war. Recognizing the gravity of the situation, the fourteen-year-old king, Richard II, went out to meet the peasants and won their confidence by promising to abolish serfdom and keep rents low; meanwhile, during negotiations the peasant leader, Wat Tyler, was murdered in a squabble with the king's escort. Lacking leadership, the peasants, who mis-takenly thought they had achieved their aims, rapidly dispersed. But once the boy king was no longer in dan-ger of his life he kept none of his promises. Instead, the scattered peasant forces were quickly hunted down and a few alleged troublemakers were executed without any mass reprisals. The revolt itself therefore did not accom-plish its objectives. It did, however, frighten the English nobility profoundly. No further head taxes were at-

FROISSART ON THE ENGLISH PEASANTS' REVOLT, 1381

Jean Froissart (1337?–1410?) is best known as the author of a lengthy history of the Hundred Years' War. He began his career in the service of the queen of England, but spent much of his later life in the Netherlands and in France. He was not an eyewitness to the events of the Peasants' Revolt, but he had excellent English connections from whom he presumably derived his information. Froissart's perspective is entirely that of the aristocrats whom he served and with whom he associated. This fact makes his modest sympathy for the rebels of 1381 all the more interesting, particularly compared with his earlier, entirely negative portrayal of the 1358 Jacquerie rebels in France.

While these negotiations and discussions were going on, there occurred in England great disasters and uprisings of the common people, on account of which the country was almost ruined beyond recovery. Never was any land or realm in such great danger as England at that time. It was because of the abundance and prosperity in which the common people then lived that this rebellion broke out, just as in earlier days the Jack Goodmans rose in France and committed many excesses, by which the noble land of France suffered grave injury. . . .

It is the custom in England, as in several other countries, for the nobles to have strong powers over their men and to hold them in serfdom: that is, that by right and custom they have to till the lands of the gentry, reap the [grain] . . . , thresh and winnow it; mow the hay . . . , cut logs . . . , and all such forced tasks; all this the men must do by way of serfage to their masters. In England there is a much greater number than elsewhere of such men who are obliged to serve the prelates and the nobles. . . .

These bad people . . . began to rebel because, they said, they were held too much in subjection, and when the world began there had been no serfs and could not be, unless they had rebelled against their Lord, as Lucifer did against God; but they were not of that stature, being neither angels nor spirits, but men formed in the image of their masters, and they were treated as animals. This was a thing they could no longer endure, wishing rather to be all one and the same; and, if they worked for their masters, they wanted to have wages for it. In these machinations they had been greatly encouraged originally by a crack-brained priest of Kent called John Ball . . . who had the habit on Sundays after mass, when everyone was coming out of church, of going to the cloisters or the graveyard, assembling the people round him and preaching thus:

"Good people, things cannot go right in England and never will, until goods are held in common and there are no more serfs and gentlefolk, but we are all one and the same. In what way are those whom we call lords greater masters than ourselves? How have they deserved it? Why do they hold us in bondage? If we all spring from a single father and mother, Adam and Eve, how can they claim or prove that they are lords more than us, except by making us produce and grow the wealth which they spend? They are clad in velvet and camlet lined with squirrel and ermine, while we go dressed in coarse cloth. They have the wines, the spices, and the good bread: we have the rye, the husks and the straw, and we drink water. They have shelter and ease in their fine manors, and we have hardship and toil, the wind and the rain in the fields. And from us must come, from our labor, the things which keep them in luxury. We are called serfs and beaten if we are slow in our service to them, yet we have no sovereign lord we can complain to, none to hear us and do us justice. Let us go to the King—he is young—and show him how we are oppressed, and tell him that we want things to be changed, or else we will change them ourselves. If we go in good earnest and all together, very many people who are called serfs and are held in subjection will follow us to get their freedom. And when the King sees and hears us, he will remedy the evil, either willingly or otherwise."

These were the kind of things which John Ball usually preached in the villages on Sundays . . . and many of the common people agreed with him.

Geoffrey Brereton, ed. and trans. *Froissart: Chronicles.* (London and New York: Penguin Books, 1968), pp. 211–213.

tempted, and enforcement of wage controls on peasant labor came to an end. Within a few decades the natural play of economic forces considerably improved the lot of small- to medium-scale farmers and rural wage laborers, and within a century had brought about the effective disappearance of serfdom in England. The result was a kind of mid-fifteenth-century "golden age" for the English peasantry.

URBAN REBELLIONS

Other rural revolts took place in other parts of Europe, but we may now look at some urban ones. The urban revolts of the later Middle Ages are conventionally viewed as uprisings of exploited workers who were more oppressed than ever because of the effects of economic depression. But this is probably too great a simplification because each case differed and complex forces were always at work. For example, an uprising in the north German town of Brunswick in 1374 was much less a movement of the poor against the rich than a political upheaval in which one political alliance replaced another. A different north German uprising, in Lübeck in 1408, has been aptly described as a "taxpayer's" revolt. This again was less a confrontation of the poor versus the rich than an attempt by a faction that was out of power to initiate less costly government.

The nearest thing to a real proletarian revolt was the uprising in 1378 of the Florentine Ciompi (pronounced "cheeompi"). The *ciompi* were wool combers who had the misfortune to be engaged in an industry that had become particularly depressed. Some of them had lost their jobs; others were frequently cheated or underpaid by the masters of the woolen industry. The latter wielded great political power in Florence, and thus could pass economic legislation in their own favor. This fact in itself meant that if there were to be economic reforms, they would have to go together with political changes. As events turned out, it was a political crisis that called the Ciompi into direct action. In 1378 Florence had become exhausted by three years of war with the papacy. Certain patrician leaders overthrew the old regime in order to alter the war policy and gain their own political advantage. Circumstances led them to seek the support of the lower classes and, once stirred up, the Ciompi became emboldened after a few months to launch their own far more radical rebellion. This rebellion was inspired primarily by economic hardship and grievances, but personal hatreds also played a role. The Ciompi held power for six weeks, during which they tried to institute tax relief, fuller employment, and representation of themselves and other workers' groups in the Florentine government. But they could not maintain their hold on power and a new oligarchical government revoked all their reforms.

If we try to draw any general conclusions about these various uprisings, we can certainly say that few if any of them would have occurred had there not been an economic crisis. But political considerations always had some influence, and the rebels in some uprisings were more prosperous than in others. It is noteworthy that all the genuinely lower-class uprisings of economically desperate groups quickly failed. This was certainly because the upper classes were more accustomed to wielding power and giving orders; even more important, they had access to the money and troops necessary to quell revolts. Sometimes elements within the lower classes might fight among themselves, whereas the privileged always managed to form a united front when faced by a lower-class threat to their domination. In addition, lower-class rebels were usually more intent on redressing immediate grievances than on developing coherent long-term governmental programs; inspiring ideals for cohesive action were generally lacking. The case of the Hussite Revolution in Bohemia—to be treated later—shows that religion in the later Middle Ages was a more effective rallying force for large numbers of people than political, economic, and social demands.

A Party of Late Medieval Aristocrats. Notice the pointed shoes and the women's pointed hats, twice as high as their heads.

ARISTOCRATIC INSECURITIES

Although the upper classes succeeded in overcoming popular uprisings, they perceived the economic and emotional insecurities of the later Middle Ages and the possibility of revolt as constant threats, and became obsessed with maintaining their privileged social status. Late medieval aristocrats were in a precarious economic position because most of their income came from land. In times when grain prices and rents were falling and wages rising, landowners were obviously in economic trouble. Aristocrats also felt threatened by the rapid rise of merchants and financiers who could

make quick killings because of sharp market fluctuations. In practice, really wealthy merchants bought land and were absorbed into the aristocracy, while many land-owning aristocrats were able to stave off economic threats by expert estate management. But most aristocrats still felt more exposed to social and economic insecurities than before. The result was that they tried to set up social and cultural barriers by which to separate themselves from other classes.

Two of the most striking examples of this separation were the aristocratic emphasis on luxury and the formation of exclusive chivalric orders. The later Middle Ages were the period par excellence of aristocratic os-

WHAT WERE THE CAUSES OF THE POPULAR REBELLIONS FROM 1300 TO 1450?

SOCIAL AND EMOTIONAL DISLOCATION   393

The Crucifixion, by Matthias Grünewald from the *Insenheim Altarpiece.*

tentation. While famine or disease raged, aristocrats entertained themselves with lavish banquets and magnificent pageants. At one feast in Flanders in 1468, a table decoration was forty-six feet high. Aristocratic clothing too was extremely ostentatious: men wore long, pointed shoes, and women ornately festooned headdresses. Throughout history rich people have always enjoyed dressing up, but the aristocrats of the later Middle Ages seem to have done so obsessively. They even imposed special sumptuary laws that defined the type of clothing that each rank in society could wear. This aristocratic insistence on maintaining a sharply defined social hierarchy also accounts for the late medieval proliferation of chivalric orders, such as those of the knights of the Garter or the Golden Fleece. By joining together in exclusive orders that prescribed special conduct and boasted special insignia of membership, aristocrats tried to set themselves off from others, in effect, by putting up a sign that read "for members only."

EMOTIONAL EXTREMES

We must not think, however, that late medieval Europeans gave themselves over to riotous living without interruption. In fact, the same people who sought ele-

gant or boisterous diversions just as often went to the other emotional extreme when faced with the psychic stress caused by the troubles of the age, and abandoned themselves to sorrow. Throughout the period grown men and women shed tears in abundance. The queen mother of France wept in public when she first viewed her newborn grandson; the great preacher Vincent Ferrer had to interrupt his sermons on Christ's Passion and the Last Judgment because he and his audience were sobbing too convulsively; and the English king Edward II supposedly wept so much when imprisoned that he gushed forth enough hot water for his own shave. The last story taxes the imagination, but it does illustrate well what contemporaries thought was possible. We know for certain that the church encouraged crying because of the survival of statuettes of weeping Saint Johns, which were obviously designed to call forth tears from their viewers.

People also were encouraged by preachers to brood on the Passion of Christ and on their own mortality. Fearsome crucifixes abounded, and the figure of the Virgin Mary was less a smiling madonna than a sorrowing mother: now she was most frequently depicted

CHRONOLOGY

FAMINE, PLAGUES, REBELLION, AND WARFARE, 1300–1450

"Great Famine"	1315–1322
Black Death	1347–1350
"Jacquerie" rebellion	1358
Ciompi revolt	1378
English peasant rebellion	1381
Hundred Years' War	1337–1453
Venice, Milan, and Florence consolidate their territories	1400–1454

played figures of grinning Death with his scythe, carrying off elegant and healthy men and women, or sadistic devils roasting pain-wracked humans in hell. Because people who painted or brooded on such pictures might the next day indulge in excessive revels, late medieval culture often seems to border on the manic depressive. But apparently such extreme reactions were necessary to help people cope with their fears.

TRIALS FOR THE CHURCH AND HUNGER FOR THE DIVINE

What were the main forms of late medieval popular piety?

The intense concentration on the meaning of death was also a manifestation of a very deep and pervasive religiosity. The religious enthusiasm of the High Middle Ages by no means flagged after 1300; if anything, it became more intense. But religious enthusiasm took on new forms of expression because of the institutional difficulties of the church and the turmoils of the age.

THE LATE MEDIEVAL PAPACY

After the humiliation and death of Pope Boniface VIII in 1303 (see p. 356), the church experienced a period of institutional crisis that was as severe and prolonged as the contemporary economic crisis. We may distinguish three phases: the so-called Babylonian Captivity of the papacy, 1305–1378; the Great Schism, 1378–1417; and the period of the Italian territorial papacy, 1417–1517. During the "Babylonian Captivity" the papacy was located in Avignon instead of Rome and was generally subservient to the interests of the French crown. There were several reasons for this: the most obvious was that since the test of strength between Philip the Fair and Boniface VIII had resulted in a clear victory for the French king, subsequent popes were unwilling to risk French royal ire. In fact, once the popes realized that they could not give orders to the French kings, they found that they could gain certain advantages from currying their favor. One was a safe home in southern France, away from the tumult of Italy. Cen-

A Dead Man Before His Judge. A late medieval reminder of human mortality.

slumping with grief at the foot of the cross, or holding the dead Christ in her lap. The late medieval obsession with mortality can also still be seen in sculptures, frescoes, and book illustrations that reminded viewers of the brevity of life and the torments of hell. The characteristic tombs of the High Middle Ages were surmounted by sculptures that either showed the deceased in some action that had been typical of his or her accomplishments in life, or else in a state of repose that showed death to be nothing more than peaceful sleep. But in the late fourteenth century, tombs appeared that displayed the physical ravages of death in the most gruesome ways imaginable: emaciated corpses were displayed with protruding intestines or covered with snakes or toads. Some tombs bore inscriptions stating that the viewer would soon be "a fetid cadaver, food for worms"; some warned chillingly, "What you are, I was; what I am, you will be." Omnipresent illustrations dis-

Papal Palace at Avignon. This great palace was begun in 1339 and symbolizes the apparent permanence of the papal residence in Avignon.

Europe. The papacy also succeeded in appointing more candidates to vacant church positions than before (in practice often naming candidates proposed by the French and English kings), and they proceeded against heresy with great determination, indeed with ruthlessness. But whatever the popes achieved in power they lost in respect and loyalty. The clergy became alienated as a result of being asked to pay so much money, and many lay people were horrified by the corruption and unbridled luxury displayed at the papal court: there the cardinals lived more splendidly than lords, dining off peacocks, pheasants, grouse, and swans, and drinking from elaborately sculptured

tral Italy and the city of Rome in the fourteenth century had become so politically turbulent and rebellious that the pope could not even count on finding personal safety there, let alone sufficiently peaceful conditions to maintain orderly ecclesiastical administration. But no such danger existed in Avignon. Even though Avignon was not then part of the French kingdom—it was the major city of a small papal territory—French military might was close enough to guarantee the pope much-needed security. Another advantage of papal subservience to French power was help from the French in pursuing mutually advantageous policies in Germany and southern Italy. Perhaps most important was a working agreement whereby the French king would propose his own candidates to become bishops and the pope would then name them in return for sizable monetary payments. Although most of the Avignon popes tried hard to maintain their independence, in practice the balance of power rested clearly with the French king.

At Avignon the popes were more successful than ever in pursuing their policy of centralizing the government of the church. For the first time they worked out a sound system of papal finance, based on the systematization of dues collected from the clergy throughout

fountains that spouted the finest wines. Most of the Avignonese popes themselves were personally upright and abstemious, but one, Clement VI (1342–1352), was worse than his cardinals. Clement was ready to offer any spiritual benefit for money, boasted that he would appoint even a jackass as bishop if political circumstances warranted, and defended his incessant sexual transgressions by insisting that he fornicated on doctors' orders.

As time went on the pressures of informed public opinion forced the popes to promise that they would return to Rome. After one abortive attempt by Urban V in 1367, Pope Gregory XI finally did return to the Holy City in 1377. But he died a year later, and then disaster struck. The college of cardinals, surrounded in Rome by clamoring Italians, yielded to local sentiment by naming an Italian pope who took the title of Urban VI. But most of the cardinals were Frenchmen and quickly regretted their decision, especially because Urban VI immediately began quarreling with them and revealing what were probably paranoid tendencies. Therefore, after only a few months, the cardinals met again, declared the previous election void, and replaced Urban with one of their own number, who called himself Clement VII.

Unfortunately, however, Urban VI did not meekly resign. On the contrary, he named an entirely new Italian college of cardinals and remained entrenched in Rome. Clement VII quickly retreated with his own party to Avignon, and the so-called Great Schism ensued. France and other countries in the French political orbit—such as Scotland, Castile, and Aragon—recognized Clement, while the rest of Europe recognized Urban as the true pope. For three decades Christians looked on helplessly while the rival pontiffs hurled curses at each other and the international monastic orders became divided into Roman and Avignonese camps. The death of one or the other pope did not end the schism; each camp had its own set of cardinals, which promptly named either a French or Italian successor. The desperateness of the situation led a council of prelates from both camps to meet in Pisa in 1409 to depose both popes and name a new one instead. But neither the Italian nor the French pope accepted the council's decision, and both had enough political support to command some obedience. So after 1409 there were three rival claimants hurling curses instead of two.

The Great Schism was finally ended in 1417 by the Council of Constance, the largest ecclesiastical gathering in medieval history. This time the assembled prelates made certain to gain the crucial support of secular powers and also to eliminate all the prior claimants before naming a new pope. After the council's election of Martin V in 1417, European ecclesiastical unity was finally restored. But a struggle over the nature of church government followed immediately. The members of the Council of Constance challenged the prevailing medieval theory of papal monarchy by calling for balanced, "conciliar" government. In two momentous decrees they stated that a general council of prelates was superior in authority to the pope, and that such councils should meet regularly to govern the Church. Not surprisingly, subsequent popes—who had now returned to Rome—sought to nullify these decrees. When a new council met in Basel in 1431, in accordance with the principles laid down at Constance, the reigning pope did all he could to sabotage its activities. Ultimately he was successful: after a protracted struggle the Council of Basel dissolved in 1449 in abject failure, and the attempt to institute constitutional government in the Church was defeated.

But the papacy won this victory over conciliarism only by gaining the support of the rulers of the European states. In separate concordats with kings and princes the popes granted the secular rulers much authority over the various local churches. The popes thus became assured of theoretical supremacy at the cost of surrendering much real power. To compensate for this they concentrated on consolidating their own direct rule in central Italy. Most of the fifteenth-century popes ruled very much like any other princes, leading armies, jockeying for alliances, and building magnificent palaces. Hence, although they did succeed for the first time in creating a viable political state, their reputation for piety remained low.

POPULAR PIETY AND POPULAR HERESY

While the papacy was enduring these vicissitudes, the local clergy throughout Europe was also losing prestige. One reason was that the pope's greater financial demands forced the clergy to demand more from the laity, but such demands were bitterly resented, especially during times of prevailing economic crisis. Then too during outbreaks of plague the clergy sometimes fled their posts just like everyone else, but in so doing they lost whatever claim they had to moral superiority.

Probably the single greatest reason for growing dissatisfaction with the clergy was the increase in lay literacy. The continued proliferation of schools and the decline in the cost of books—a subject we will treat later—made it possible for large numbers of lay people to learn how to read. Once that happened, the laity could start reading parts of the Bible, or, more frequently, popular religious primers. This reading made it clear that their local priests were not living according to the standards set by Jesus and the apostles. In the meantime, the upheavals and horrors of the age drove people to seek religious solace more than ever. Where lay people found the conventional channels of church attendance, confession, and submission to clerical authority insufficient, they sought supplementary or alternate routes to piety. These differed greatly from each other, but they all aimed to satisfy an immense hunger for the divine.

The most widely traveled route was to perform repeated acts of external devotion in the hope that they

> Where lay people found the conventional channels of church attendance, confession, and submission to clerical authority insufficient, they sought supplementary or alternate routes to piety.

THE CONCILIARIST CONTROVERSY

The Great Schism produced a fundamental and far-reaching debate about the nature of authority within the church. Arguments for papal supremacy rested upon the traditional claims that the popes were the successors of Saint Peter, to whom Jesus Christ had delegated his own authority over the church. Arguments for the supremacy of a general council had been advanced around the University of Paris throughout much of the fourteenth century; but it was only in the circumstances of the Schism that these arguments found a wide audience. The documents below trace the history of the controversy, from the declaration of conciliar supremacy at the Council of Constance (Haec Sancta, 1415), to the Council's efforts to guarantee regular meetings of general councils thereafter (Frequens, 1417), to the papal condemnation of appeals to future general councils issued in 1460 (Execrabilis). Note, however, the limitations on Execrabilis. Even this condemnation does not go so far as to actually contradict Haec Sancta. It merely condemns appeals from papal judgment to future general councils that have no specified meeting date. The conciliar ideal was still powerful at the end of the fifteenth century; and in the sixteenth and seventeenth centuries, it would have a profound impact on European political thought about kings.

HAEC SANCTA SYNODUS (1415)

This holy synod of Constance . . . declares that being lawfully assembled in the Holy Spirit, constituting a general council and representing the Catholic Church Militant, it has its power directly from Christ, and that all persons of whatever rank or dignity, even a Pope, are bound to obey it in matters relating to faith and the end of the Schism and the general reformation of the church of God in head and members.

Further, it declares that any person of whatever position, rank, or dignity, even a Pope, who contumaciously refuses to obey the mandates, statutes, ordinances, or regulations enacted or to be enacted by this holy synod, or by any other general council lawfully assembled, relating to the matters aforesaid or to other matters involved with them, shall, unless he repents, be . . . duly punished. . . .

FREQUENS (1417)

The frequent holding of general councils is the best method of cultivating the field of the Lord, for they root out the briars, thorns, and thistles of heresies, errors, and schisms, correct abuses, make crooked things straight, and prepare the Lord's vineyard for fruitfulness and rich fertility. Neglect of general councils sows the seeds of these evils and encourages their growth. This truth is borne in upon us as we recall times past and survey the present.

Therefore by perpetual edict we . . . ordain that henceforth general councils shall be held as follows: the first within the five years immediately following the end of the present council, the second within seven years from the end of the council next after this, and subsequently every ten years forever. . . . Thus there will always be a certain continuity. Either a council will be in session or one will be expected at the end of a fixed period. . . .

Execrabilis (1460)

An execrable abuse, unheard of in earlier times, has sprung up in our period. Some men, imbued with a spirit of rebellion and moved not by a desire for sound decisions but rather by a desire to escape the punishment for sin, suppose that they can appeal from the Pope, Vicar of Jesus Christ; from the Pope, to whom in the person of blessed Peter it was said, "Feed my sheep" and "whatever you bind on earth will be bound in heaven"—from this Pope to a future council. How harmful this is to the Christian republic, as well as how contrary to canon law, anyone who is not ignorant of the law can understand. For . . . who would not consider it ridiculous to appeal to something which does not now exist anywhere nor does anyone know when it will exist? The poor are heavily oppressed by the powerful, offenses remain unpunished, rebellion against the Holy See is encouraged, license for sin is granted, and all ecclesiastical discipline and hierarchical ranking of the Church are turned upside down.

Wishing therefore to expel this deadly poison from the Church of Christ, and concerned with the salvation of the sheep committed to us . . . with the counsel and assent of our venerable brothers, the Cardinals of the Holy Roman Church, together with the counsel and assent of all those prelates who have been trained in canon and civil law who follow our Court, and with our own certain knowledge, we condemn appeals of this kind, reject them as erroneous and abominable, and declare them to be completely null and void. And we lay down that from now on, no one should dare . . . to make such an appeal from our decisions, be they legal or theological, or from any commands at all from us or our successors. . . .

Haec Sancta and *Frequens* from *The Council of Constance*, L. R. Loomis, ed. and trans. (New York: Columbia University Press, 1961), pp. 229, 246–247; *Execrabilis: Defensorum Obedientiae Apostolicae et alia Documenta*, Heiko A. Oberman, Daniel E. Zerfoss, and William J. Courtenay, eds. and trans. (Cambridge, Mass: Harvard Univ. Press, 1968), pp. 224–227, with modifications by R. C. Stacey.

A German Flagellant Procession. These penitents hoped they could ward off the Black Death by their mutually inflicted tortures.

would gain the devotee divine favor on earth and salvation in the hereafter. People flocked to go on pilgrimages as never before and participated regularly in barefoot religious processions: the latter were often held twice a month and occasionally as often as once a week. Men and women also eagerly paid for thousands of masses to be said by full-time "Mass priests" for the souls of their dead relatives, and left legacies for the reading of numerous requiem masses to save their own souls after death. Obsession with repeating prayers reached a peak when some pious individuals tried to compute the number of drops of blood that Christ shed on the cross so that they could say the same number of Our Fathers. The most dramatic form of religious ritual in the later Middle Ages was flagellation. Some women who lived in communal houses beat themselves with the roughest animal hides, chains, and knotted thongs. A young girl who entered such a community in Poland in 1331 suffered extreme internal injuries and became completely disfigured within eleven months. Flailings were not usually performed in public, but during the first onslaught of the Black Death in 1348 and 1349, whole bands of lay people marched through northern Europe chanting and beating each other with metal-tipped scourges in the hope of appeasing the apparent divine wrath.

MYSTICISM

An opposite route to godliness was the inward path of mysticism. Throughout the European continent, but particularly in Germany and England, male and female mystics, both clerical and lay, sought union with God by means of "detachment," contemplation, or spiritual exercises. The most original and eloquent late medieval mystical theorist was Master Eckhart (c. 1260–1327), a German Dominican who taught that there was a power or "spark" deep within every human soul that was really the dwelling place of God. By renouncing all sense of selfhood one could retreat into one's innermost recesses and there find divinity. Eckhart did not recommend ceasing attendance at church—he hardly could have because he preached in churches—but he made it clear that outward rituals were of comparatively little importance in reaching God. He also gave the impression to his lay audiences that they might attain godliness largely on their own volition. Thus ecclesiastical authorities charged him with inciting "ignorant and undisciplined people to wild and dangerous excesses." Although Eckhart pleaded his own doctrinal orthodoxy, some of his teachings were condemned by the papacy.

That Eckhart's critics were not entirely mistaken in their worries is shown by the fact that some lay people in Germany who were influenced by him did fall into the heresy of believing that they could become fully united with God on earth without any priestly intermediaries. But these so-called heretics of the Free Spirit were few in number. Much more numerous were later orthodox mystics, sometimes influenced by Eckhart and sometimes not, who placed greater emphasis on the divine initiative in the meeting of the soul with God and made certain to insist that the ministrations of the church were a necessary contribution to the mystic way. Even they, however, believed that "churches make no man holy, but men make churches holy." Most of the great teachers and practitioners of mysticism in the fourteenth century were clerics, nuns, or hermits, but in the fifteenth century a modified form of mystical belief spread among lay people. This "practical mysticism" did not aim for full ecstatic union with God, but rather for an ongoing sense of some divine presence during the conduct of daily life. The most popular manual that pointed the way to this goal was the *Imitation of Christ*, written around 1427, probably by the north German canon Thomas à Kempis. Because this book was written in a simple but forceful style and taught how to be a pious Christian while still living ac-tively in the world, it was particularly attractive to lay readers. Thus it quickly became translated into the leading European vernaculars. From then until today it has been more widely read by Christians than any other religious work except the Bible. The *Imitation* urges its readers to participate in one religious ceremony—the sacrament of the Eucharist—but otherwise it emphasizes inward piety. According to its teachings, the individual Christian is best able to become the "partner" of Jesus Christ both by receiving communion and by engaging in biblical meditation and leading a simple, moral life.

LOLLARDS AND HUSSITES

A third distinct form of late medieval piety was outright religious protest or heresy. In England and Bohemia especially, heretical movements became serious threats to the church. The initiator of heresy in late medieval England was an Oxford theologian named John Wyclif (c. 1330–1384). Wyclif's rigorous adherence to the theology of Saint Augustine led him to believe that a certain number of humans were predestined to be saved while the rest were irrevocably damned. He thought the predestined would naturally live simply, according to the standards of the New Testament, but in fact he found most members of the church hierarchy indulging in splendid extravagances. Hence he concluded that most church officials were damned. For him the only solution was to have secular rulers appropriate ecclesiastical wealth and reform the church by replacing corrupt priests and bishops with men who would live according to apostolic standards. Wyclif's position was obviously attractive to the aristocracy of England, who may have looked forward to enriching themselves with church spoils and at least saw nothing wrong with using Wyclif as a bulldog to frighten the pope and the local clergy. Thus Wyclif at first received influential aristocratic support. But toward the end of his life he moved from merely calling for reform to attacking some of the most basic institutions of the church, above all the sacrament of the Eucharist. This radicalism frightened off his influential protectors, and Wyclif probably would have been formally condemned for heresy had he lived longer. His death brought no respite for the church, however, because he had attracted numerous lay followers—called Lollards—who zealously continued to propagate some of his most radical ideas. Above all, the Lollards taught that pious Christians should not entrust their salvation to the sacraments of a corrupt church, but should instead study the Bible (which Lollards speedily translated into English) and Lollard religious tracts. Lollardy gained many adherents in the last two decades of the fourteenth century, but after the introduction in England of the death penalty for heresy in 1401 and the failure of a Lollard uprising in 1414, the heretical wave greatly receded. Nonetheless, Lollards survived until the sixteenth century, when they merged into the new religious movements set loose by the Protestant Reformation.

The Hussite declaration of religious independence was a foretaste of what was to come one hundred years later with Protestantism.

Much greater was the influence of Wyclifism in Bohemia. Around 1400, Czech students who had studied in Oxford brought back Wyclif's ideas to the Bohemian capital of Prague. There Wyclifism was enthusiastically adopted by an eloquent preacher named Jan Hus (c. 1373–1415), who had already been inveighing in well-attended sermons against "the world, the flesh, and the devil." Hus employed Wyclifite theories to back up his own calls for an end to ecclesiastical corruption, rallying many Bohemians to the cause of reform in the years between 1408 and 1415. In contrast to the Lollards, however, whose heretical views on the Eucharist cost them much support, Hus emphasized the centrality of the Eucharist to Christian piety by demanding that the laity too should receive not only the consecrated bread of the Mass, but also the consecrated wine, which the late medieval Church reserved solely for priests. This demand, known as Utraquism, gained broad popular support among the Bohemian laity and became a rallying symbol for the Hussite movement. Influential aristocrats supported Hus partly out of national pride, but partly too in the hope that Hus' reforms might allow them to recover the revenues they had lost to the orthodox Catholic clergy over the previous century. Influenced by the politics of the Great Schism, even the king of Bohemia lent Hus his protection. Above all, however, Hus gained a mass following because of his eloquence and concern for social justice. Accordingly, most of Bohemia was behind him when Hus in 1415 agreed to travel to the Council of Constance to defend his views and try to convince the assembled prelates that only thoroughgoing reform could save the Church. But although Hus had been guaranteed his personal safety, this assurance was revoked as soon as he arrived at the Council: rather than being given a fair hearing, the betrayed idealist was tried for heresy and burned.

Hus' supporters in Bohemia were justifiably outraged and quickly raised the banner of open revolt. The aristocracy took advantage of the situation to seize church lands, and poorer priests, artisans, and peasants rallied together in the hope of achieving Hus' goals of religious reform and social justice. Between 1420 and 1424 armies of radical Hussites known as Taborites, led by a brilliant blind general, Jan Zizka, resoundingly defeated several invading forces of well-armed crusading knights from Germany sent against them by the papacy. These victories increased the radicalism of the Taborites, inspiring them to heights of apocalyptic fervor. Finally, in 1434 more conservative, aristocratically dominated Hussites overcame the radicals and negotiated a settlement with the Church that permitted Utraquism in the Bohemian church alongside Catholic orthodoxy. Bohemia did not return fully to the Catholic fold until the seventeenth century. The Hussite declaration of religious independence was both a foretaste of what was to come one hundred years later with Protestantism and the most successful late medieval expression of dissatisfaction with the government of the church.

POLITICAL CRISIS AND RECOVERY

What caused the rise of national monarchies?

The story of late medieval politics at first seems very dreary because throughout most of the period there was incessant strife. Almost everywhere neighbors fought neighbors and states fought states. But closer inspection makes it clear that despite the turmoil there was ultimate improvement in almost all the governments of Europe. In the course of the fifteenth century peace returned to most of the Continent, the national monarchies in particular became stronger, and the period ended on a new note of political as well as economic strength.

ITALY

In southern Italy, the kingdom of Naples remained mired in endemic warfare and maladministration throughout the fourteenth and fifteenth centuries. The fourteenth century was also a time of troubles for the Papal States in central Italy, because forces representing the absent or divided papacy were seldom able to overcome the resistance of refractory towns and rival leaders of marauding military bands. But after the end of the Great Schism in 1417 the popes consolidated their Italian territories and became the effective rulers of most of the middle part of the peninsula. Farther north some of the leading city-states—such as Florence, Venice, Siena, and Genoa—had experienced at least occasional and more often prolonged social warfare during the fourteenth century because of the economic pressures of the age. But sooner or later the most powerful families or interest groups overcame internal resistance. By around 1400 the three leading cities of the north—Venice, Milan, and Florence—had fixed definitively on their own different forms of government: Venice was ruled by a merchant oligarchy, Milan by a dynastic despotism, and Florence by a complex, supposedly republican system that was actually controlled by the rich. (After 1434 the Florentine republic was in practice dominated by the Medici banking family.)

Having settled their internal problems, Venice, Milan, and Florence proceeded from about 1400 to 1454 to expand territorially, conquering almost all the other northern Italian cities and towns except Genoa, which remained prosperous and independent but gained no new territory. Thus, by the middle of the fifteenth century Italy was divided into five major parts: the states of Venice, Milan, and Florence in the north; the Papal States in the middle; and the kingdom of Naples in the south. A treaty of 1454 initiated a half century of peace between these states: whenever one threatened to upset the "balance of power," the others usually allied against it before serious warfare could break out. Accordingly, the last half of the fifteenth century was a fortunate age for Italy. But in 1494 a French invasion initiated a period of renewed warfare in which the French attempt to dominate Italy was successfully countered by Spain.

GERMANY

North of the Alps political turmoil prevailed throughout the fourteenth century and lasted longer into the fifteenth. Probably the worst instability was experienced in Germany. There the virtually independent princes continually warred with the greatly weakened emperors, or else they warred with each other. Between about 1350 and 1450 near anarchy prevailed,

because while the princes were warring and subdividing their inheritances into smaller states, petty powers such as free cities and knights who owned one or two castles were striving to shake off the rule of the princes. Throughout most of the German west these attempts met with enough success to fragment political authority more than ever, but in the east after about 1450 certain stronger German princes managed to assert their authority over divisive forces. After they did so, they started to rule firmly over middle-sized states on the model of the larger national monarchies of England and France. The strongest princes were those in eastern territories such as Bavaria, Austria, and Brandenburg, because there towns were fewer and smaller and the princes had been able to take advantage of imperial weakness to preside over the colonization of large tracts of land. Especially the Habsburg princes of Austria and the Hohenzollern princes of Brandenburg—a territory joined in the sixteenth century with the easternmost lands of Prussia—would be the most influential powers in Germany's future.

FRANCE

France too was torn by strife for much of the period, primarily in the form of the Hundred Years' War between France and England. The Hundred Years' War was actually a series of conflicts that lasted from 1337 to 1453 and whose roots reached back into the 1290s. Of the several different causes for this prolonged struggle, the major one was the longstanding problem of French territory held by the English kings. At the beginning of the fourteenth century the English kings, as vassals of the French crown, still ruled much of the rich southern French lands of Gascony and Aquitaine. The French, who since the reign of Philip Augustus had been expanding and consolidating their rule, obviously hoped to expel the English, making war inevitable. Another cause for strife was that English economic interests in the woolen trade with Flanders led England to support the frequent attempts of Flemish burghers to rebel against French rule. Finally, the war involved a succession dispute over the French crown itself. In 1328, the last of King Philip IV's three sons died without leaving a son to succeed him. A new dynasty, the Valois, thereupon replaced the Capetians on the throne of France. Only by prohibiting inheritance through women, however, could the Valois kings claim to be the closest heirs to the Capetians. Otherwise, the rightful heir to the throne of France was King Edward III of England, whose mother was the daughter

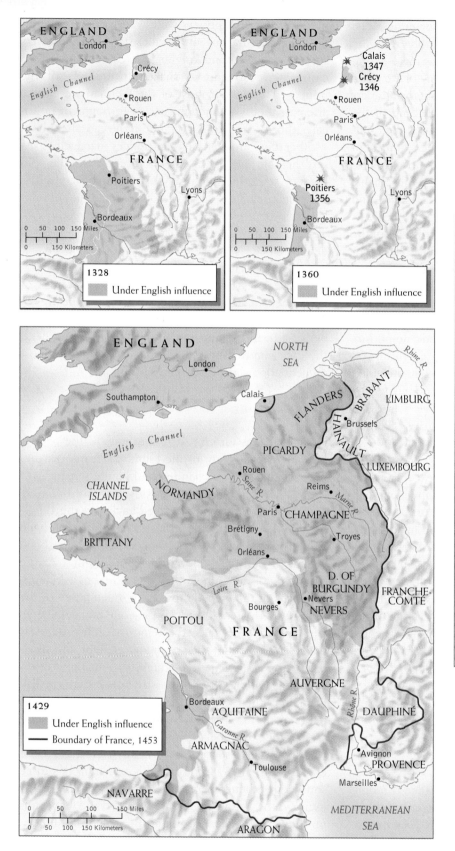

ENGLAND
London
Crécy
English Channel
Rouen
Paris
Orléans
FRANCE
Poitiers
Lyons
Bordeaux

0 50 100 150 Miles
0   150 Kilometers

1328
Under English influence

ENGLAND
London
Calais 1347
Crécy 1346
English Channel
Rouen
Paris
Orléans
FRANCE
Poitiers 1356
Lyons
Bordeaux

0 50 100 150 Miles
0   150 Kilometers

1360
Under English influence

ENGLAND
London
Southampton
NORTH SEA
Calais
Rhine R.
FLANDERS
BRABANT
LIMBURG
HAINAULT
Brussels
PICARDY
English Channel
LUXEMBOURG
CHANNEL ISLANDS
NORMANDY
Rouen
Seine R.
Reims
Marne R.
Paris
CHAMPAGNE
Brétigny
Troyes
BRITTANY
Orléans
Loire R.
D. OF BURGUNDY
Nevers
FRANCHE-COMTÉ
Bourges
NEVERS
POITOU
FRANCE
AUVERGNE
Rhône R.
Bordeaux
AQUITAINE
DAUPHINÉ
Garonne R.
ARMAGNAC
Avignon
PROVENCE
Toulouse
Marseilles
NAVARRE

0 50 100 150 Miles
0 50 100 150 Kilometers

MEDITERRANEAN SEA
ARAGON

1429
Under English influence
— Boundary of France, 1453

FRANCE DURING THE HUNDRED YEARS' WAR

This map shows three snapshots of the political geography of France during the Hundred Years' War between France and England. How did the long-standing lord and vassal relationship between the French and English crowns regarding lands in France help to precipitate the war? How did the change of dynasty in France create additional difficulties for the French war effort? How were the English able to exploit the deep feudal tensions within France to further complicate the situation for the French? How were the French kings ultimately able to strengthen the central, royal government as a result of the war?

of Philip IV of France. In 1328, Edward was only fifteen years of age, and he did not protest the succession of his Valois cousins. In 1337, however, when hostilities erupted between France and England, Edward responded by claiming to be the rightful king of France—a claim that all subsequent English kings would uphold until the eighteenth century.

France should have had no difficulty in defeating England at the start: it was the richest country in Europe and outnumbered England in population by at least three to one. Nonetheless, until the 1430s the English won most of the pitched battles. One reason for this was that the English had learned superior military tactics in their earlier battles with the Welsh and the Scots, and so could use well-disciplined archers to fend off and scatter the heavily armored mounted French knights. In the three greatest battles of the long conflict—Crécy (1346), Poitiers (1356), and Agincourt (1415)—the outnumbered English relied on a tightly disciplined professional army and effective use of the longbow to inflict crushing defeats on the French. Another reason for English success was that the war was always fought on French soil. That being the case, English soldiers were eager to fight because they could look forward to rich plunder, while their own homeland suffered none of the disasters of war. Worst of all for the French was the fact that they often were badly divided. The French crown always had to fear provincial attempts to assert autonomy: during the long period of warfare, many aristocratic provincial leaders took advantage of the confusion to ally with the enemy and seek their own advantage. The most dramatic and fateful instance was the breaking away of Burgundy, whose dukes from 1419 to 1435 allied with the English, an act that called the very existence of an independent French crown into question.

It was in this dark period that the heroic figure of Joan of Arc came forth to rally the French. In 1429 Joan, an illiterate but extremely devout peasant girl, sought out the uncrowned French ruler, Charles VII, to announce that she had been divinely commissioned to drive the English out of France. Charles was persuaded to let her take command of his troops, and her piety and sincerity made such a favorable impression on the soldiers that their morale was raised immensely. Within a few months Joan inflicted several defeats on English forces in central France and had brought Charles to Rheims, where he was crowned

CHRONOLOGY	
HUNDRED YEARS' WAR, 1337–1453	
Valois dynasty begins	1328
Edward III claims French throne	1337
Battle of Crécy	1346
Battle of Poitiers	1356
Battle of Agincourt	1415
French Burgundy allies with English	1419–1435
Joan of Arc commands French troops	1429–1430
Capture of Bordeaux ends war	1453

king. But in May 1430 she was captured by the Burgundians and handed over to the English, who accused her of being a witch and tried her for heresy. Condemned in 1431 after a show trial, she was publicly burned to death in the market square at Rouen. Nonetheless, the French, fired by their initial victories, continued to move on the offensive. When Burgundy withdrew from the English alliance in 1435, and the English king Henry VI proved to be totally incompetent, there followed an uninterrupted series of triumphs for the French side. In 1453 the capture of Bordeaux, the last of the English strongholds in the southwest, finally brought the long war to an end. The English now held no land in France except for the Channel port of Calais, which they ultimately lost in 1558.

More than merely expelling the English from French territory, the Hundred Years' War resulted in greatly strengthening the powers of the French crown. Although several French kings during the long war were ineffective personalities—one, Charles VI (1380–1422), suffered periodic bouts of insanity—the monarchy demonstrated remarkable staying power. And under competent leadership, warfare emergencies allowed the Valois kings to gather new powers, above all, the rights to collect national taxes and maintain a standing army. Hence after Charles VII succeeded in defeating the English, the crown was able to renew the high medieval royal tradition of ruling the country assertively. In the reigns of Charles's successors, Louis XI (1461–1483) and Louis XII (1498–1515), the monarchy became ever stronger. Its greatest single achievement was the destruction of the power of Burgundy in 1477

> More than merely expelling the English from French territory, the Hundred Years' War resulted in greatly strengthening the powers of the French crown.

THE CONDEMNATION OF JOAN OF ARC BY THE UNIVERSITY OF PARIS, 1431

After Joan's capture by the Burgundians, she was handed over to the English, who put her on trial for heresy. Paris was at this date in English hands, so the verdict of the Parisian masters should not be considered unbiased. On the other hand, there is no evidence that it was extracted by force. Learned theologians were not inclined to approve of peasant women who claimed to hear the voices of angels, who dressed in men's clothes, and who led aristocrats into battle. Joan was condemned for heresy and burned at the stake.

You, Joan, have said that, since the age of thirteen, you have experienced revelations and the appearance of angels, of St Catherine and St Margaret, and that you have very often seen them with your bodily eyes, and that they have spoken to you. As for the first point, the clerks of the University of Paris have considered the manner of the said revelations and appearances. . . . Having considered all . . . they have declared that all the things mentioned above are lies, falsenesses, misleading and pernicious things and that such revelations are superstitions, proceeding from wicked and diabolical spirits.

Item: You have said that your king had a sign by which he knew that you were sent by God, for St Michael, accompanied by several angels, some of which having wings, the others crowns, with St Catherine and St Margaret, came to you at the chateau of Chinon. All the company ascended through the floors of the castle until they came to the room of your king, before whom the angel bearing the crown bowed. . . . As for this matter, the clerks say that it is not in the least probable, but it is rather a presumptuous lie, misleading and pernicious, a false statement, derogatory of the dignity of the Church and of the angels. . . .

Item: you have said that, at God's command, you have continually worn men's clothes, and that you have put on a short robe, doublet, shoes attached by points; also that you have had short hair, cut around above the ears, without retaining anything on your person which shows that you are a woman; and that several times you have received the body of Our Lord dressed in this fashion, despite having been admonished to give it up several times, the which you would not do. You have said that you would rather die than abandon the said clothing, if it were not at God's command, and that if you were wearing those clothes and were with the king, and those of your party, it would be one of the greatest benefits for the kingdom of France. You have also said that not for anything would you swear an oath not to wear the said clothing and carry arms any longer. And all these things you say you have done for the good and at the command of God. As for these things, the clerics say that you blaspheme God and hold him in contempt in his sacraments; you transgress Divine Law, Holy Scripture and canon law. You err in the faith. You boast in vanity. You are suspected of idolatry and you have condemned yourself in not wishing to wear clothing suitable to your sex, but you follow the custom of Gentiles and Saracens.

Carolyne Larrington, ed. and trans. *Women and Writing in Medieval Europe.* (New York and London: Routledge, 1995), pp. 183–184.

when the Burgundian duke Charles the Bold fell in battle at the hands of the Swiss, whom Charles had been trying to dominate. Since Charles died without a male heir, Louis XI of France was able to march into Burgundy and reabsorb the breakaway duchy. Later, when Louis XII gained Brittany by marriage, the French kings ruled powerfully over almost all of what is today included in the borders of France.

ENGLAND

Although the Hundred Years' War was fought on French soil rather than English, the war produced great political instability in England also. When English armies in France were successful—as by and large they were during the reigns of Edward III (1327–1377) and Henry V (1413–1422)—the crown rode a crest of popularity and the country prospered from military spoils and the ransoms of captured French prisoners. When the tide of battle turned against the English, however, as it did under Richard II (1377–1399) and Henry VI (1422–1461), the exasperated taxpayers of England held their monarchs responsible for these costly and shameful military failures. Defeat abroad thus quickly undermined a king's political and fiscal support at home, making it politically impossible to withdraw from the French war despite its mounting costs. To make matters worse, England in the later Middle Ages was ruled by an unusually large number of dangerous or incompetent kings. Of the nine English kings who came to the throne between 1307 and 1485, no fewer than five were deposed and murdered by their subjects.

The particular propensity of the English for murdering their monarchs (a subject of comment across Europe) was a consequence of England's peculiar political system. As we have seen, England was the most tightly governed kingdom in Europe, but its political system depended on a monarch's ability to mobilize popular support for his policies through Parliament while maintaining the support of his nobility through successful wars in Wales, Scotland, and France. As a result, incompetent or tyrannical kingship was even more destabilizing and dangerous in England than it was elsewhere in Europe, because of the complexity and power of the English state itself. In France, nobles could endure the insanity of Charles VI because his government was not powerful enough to threaten them. In England, however, the inanity and ultimate insanity of Henry VI (1422–1461) provoked an aristocratic rebellion against him known as the Wars of the Roses, so called (by the nineteenth-century novelist Sir Walter Scott) from the emblems of the two competing factions: the red rose of Henry's family of Lancaster, and the white rose of Henry's cousin, the rival Duke of York. In 1461, after a six-year struggle, Edward, Duke of York finally succeeded in ousting Henry VI and ruled successfully until his death in 1483. But when Edward's brother Richard seized the throne from Edward's own young sons, political stability in England collapsed once again. In 1485, Richard III was in turn defeated and killed in the battle of Bosworth Field by the last surviving Lancastrian claimant, Henry Tudor, who resolved the feud between Lancaster and York by marrying Elizabeth of York. Henry VII systematically elimated rival claimants to the throne, avoided expensive foreign wars, built up a financial surplus through careful management of his estates, and reasserted royal control over the aristocracy. When he died in 1509 the new Tudor dynasty was securely established on the English throne, and English royal power was fully restored. His son Henry VIII (1509–1547) would build on the foundations his father had restored, dissolving the English monasteries and declaring his country religiously independent of Rome.

Despite the turmoil caused by war and rebellion, late medieval English political life had an essential stability. Local institutions continued to function; Parliament became increasingly important as a point of contact between crown, aristocracy, and local communities; and the political community itself became steadily larger as prosperity brought new social groups into prominence. Most important of all, there was never any fundamental challenge to the power of the English state itself. Even aristocratic rebels always sought to control the central government rather than destroy or break away from it. Thus when Henry VII came to the throne, he did not have to win back any English territories as Louis XI of France had to win back Burgundy. More than that, the antagonisms of the Hundred Years' War had the ultimately beneficial effect of strengthening English national identity. From the Norman Conquest until the fourteenth century, French was the preferred language of the English crown and aristocracy, but mounting anti-French sentiment contributed to the triumph of English as the national language by around 1400. The loss of lands in France was also ultimately beneficial. England became an island nation, without significant territorial interests on the European mainland. This fact gave England more diplomatic maneuverability in sixteenth-century European politics and later helped strengthen England's ability to invest its energies in overseas expansion in America and elsewhere.

Ferdinand and Isabella Worshiping the Virgin. A contemporary Spanish painting in which the royal pair are shown with two of their children in the company of saints from the Dominican order.

new country was able to embark on united policies. Isabella and Ferdinand, ruling respectively until 1504 and 1516, subdued their aristocracies, and, in the same year (1492), annexed Granada, the last Muslim state in the peninsula, and expelled all of Spain's Jews. Some historians believe that the expulsion of the Jews was motivated by religious bigotry, others that it was a cruel but dispassionate act of state that aimed to keep Spanish *conversos* (Jews who had previously converted to Christianity) from backsliding. Either way, the forced Jewish exodus led Ferdinand and Isabella to suppose that they had eliminated an internal threat to cohesive nationhood and emboldened them to initiate an ambitious foreign policy: not only did they turn to overseas expansion, most famously in their support of Christopher Columbus, but they also entered decisively into the arena of Italian politics. Enriched by the influx of American gold and silver after the conquest of Mexico and Peru, and nearly invincible on the battlefields, Spain quickly became Europe's most powerful state in the sixteenth century.

SPAIN

While Louis XI of France and Henry VII of England were reasserting royal power in their respective countries, the Spanish monarchs, Ferdinand and Isabella, were doing the same on the Iberian peninsula. The latter area had also seen incessant strife in the Later Middle Ages; Aragon and Castile had often fought each other, and aristocratic factions within those kingdoms had continually fought the crown. But in 1469 Ferdinand, the heir of Aragon, married Isabella, the heiress of Castile, thereby creating a union that laid the basis for modern Spain.

Although Spain did not become a fully united nation until 1716 because Aragon and Castile retained their separate institutions, at least warfare between the two previously independent kingdoms ended, and the

THE TRIUMPH OF NATIONAL MONARCHIES

Ultimately the clearest result of political developments throughout Europe in the late Middle Ages was the preservation of basic high medieval patterns. The areas of Italy and Germany that had been politically divided before 1300 remained politically divided thereafter. The emergence of middle-sized states in both of these areas in the fifteenth century brought more stability than had existed before, but events would show that Italy and Germany would still be the prey of the western powers. The latter were clearly much stronger because they were consolidated around stronger national monarchies. The events of the later Middle Ages put the existence of these monarchies to the test, but after

1450 they emerged stronger than ever. The clearest illustration of their superiority is shown by the history of Italy in the years immediately following 1494. Until then the Italian states appeared to be relatively well governed and prosperous. They experimented with advanced techniques of administration and diplomacy. But when France and Spain invaded the peninsula the Italian states fell over like houses of cards. The national monarchies could simply draw on greater resources and thus inherited the future of Europe.

KIEVAN RUS AND THE RISE OF MUSCOVY

Why was medieval Russia so unlike any other European state?

Just as the later fifteenth century witnessed the consolidation of the power of the western European national monarchies, so too it saw the consolidation of the state that would become the dominant power in the European east—Russia. But Russia was not at all like a Western nation-state; rather, by about 1500 Russia had taken the first decisive steps on its way to becoming Europe's leading Eastern-style empire.

Had it not been for a combination of late medieval circumstances, one or several east Slavic states might well have developed along typical Western lines. As we saw in Chapter Nine, the founders of the first political entity located in the territories of modern-day Russia, Ukraine, and Belarus were themselves Westerners— Swedish Vikings (known as Rus) who in the tenth century established a principality at Kiev along the trade routes that led from Scandinavia to Constantinople. Because the Kievan state they founded lay on the westernmost extremity of the Russian plain (today it is the capital of Ukraine), it was natural for Kiev to maintain diplomatic and trading relations with western Europe as well as with Byzantium. For example, in the eleventh century King Henry I of France was married to a Kievan princess, Anne; their son was consequently given the Kievan name of Philip, a christening that marked the introduction of this hitherto foreign first name into the West. Aside from such direct links with Western cul-

> By about 1500 Russia had taken the first decisive steps on its way to becoming Europe's leading Eastern-style empire.

Signature of Anne of Kiev. The Kievan princess who became queen of France must have learned how to write her name in her native land, for the letters at the bottom of this document dating from 1063 spell out "Queen Anne" in the Russian (Cyrillic) alphabet. Her son Philip, however, could only make his "sign," as indicated at the top.

ture, Kievan government also bore some similarity to Western monarchical patterns inasmuch as the ruling power of the Kievan princes was limited by the institution of the *veche,* or popular assembly.

THE MONGOL INVASIONS

But after 1200 four epoch-making developments conspired to separate Russia from western Europe. The first was the conquest of most of the eastern Slavic states by the Mongols in the thirteenth century. As early as the eleventh century Kiev had been buffeted by the incursions of an Asian tribe known as the Polovtsy, but Kiev and the other loosely federated Russian principalities ultimately managed to hold the Polovtsy at bay. The Mongols, who invaded Russia in 1237, were quite another matter. Commanded by Batu, a grandson of the great Chingiz (Genghis) Khan, the Mongols cut such swaths of devastation as they advanced westward that, according to one contemporary, "no eye remained open to weep for the dead." In 1240 the Mongols overran Kiev, and two years later they created their own state on the lower Volga River—the khanate of the Golden

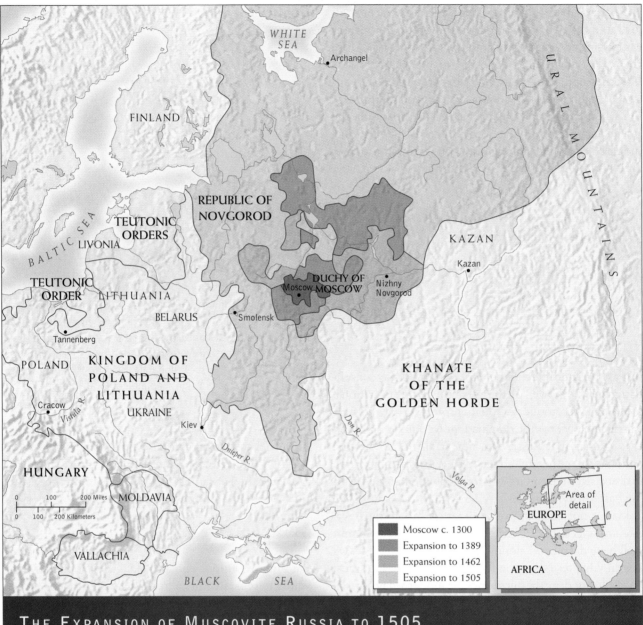

THE EXPANSION OF MUSCOVITE RUSSIA TO 1505

This map shows the expansion of the Grand Duchy of Moscow, the heart of what would soon become the Russian empire. How did the relative isolation of Moscow compared with Kiev allow for the growth of Muscovite power on the one hand, and Moscow's distinctively non-Western culture on the other? Why did the Muscovite Russians identify so closely with the Byzantines, and why did they reserve such pronounced hostility for the West and Latin Christianity? What role did the Kingdom of Poland-Lithuania play in the development of this Russian attitude? How did the natural direction of the expansion of Muscovite power until 1505 help encourage attitudes often at odds with those of western European civilization?

Horde—that exerted suzerainty over almost all of Russia for the following hundred and fifty years. In the thirteenth century, the Mongol rulers of Russia carried out direct censuses, installed their own administrative officials, and required the native Russian princes to travel to Mongolia to secure permission from the great khan to rule their territories. After around 1300, however, the Mongols changed course. Rather than attempting to rule Russia directly, they instead tolerated the existence of several native Slavic states, from which they demanded obedience and regular tribute payments. Kiev, however, never recovered the dominant position it had enjoyed before the Mongol invasions.

THE RISE OF MUSCOVY

The native principality that finally emerged to defeat the Mongols and unify much of Russia was the grand duchy of Moscow. Moscow rose to power in the early fourteenth century as a tribute-collecting center for the Mongol khanate. Moscow's alliance with the Mongols did not necessarily protect it from Mongol attacks: the city was destroyed at the time of the Mongol invasions, and again in 1382. But despite these setbacks, Moscow was able, with Mongol support, to absorb the territory of the grand principality of Vladimir, and so gradually to become the dominant political power in northeastern Russia.

Moscow also had the advantage of being very far away from the Mongol power base on the lower Volga. This remote location made Moscow a particularly valuable ally for the Mongol khanate, while allowing the grand dukes to consolidate their strength without attracting too much attention from the khans. Despite Moscow's remote location (it lay about six hundred miles farther away from France or Italy than did Kiev), the grand duchy maintained some trade contacts with both the Baltic and the Black Sea regions. What really distanced Moscow from western Europe was the enormous religious hostility that existed between the eastern Orthodox churches (of which Moscow was one) and the western church headed by the papacy. As we have seen, the hostility between these two great branches of Christianity had deep historical roots. In the late Middle Ages, however, what particularly excited the religious animosity of Moscow toward western European Christians was the growing strength of the kingdom of Poland and the circumstances that led to the fall of Constantinople to the Ottoman Turks in 1453.

THE RIVALRY WITH POLAND

Throughout most of the Middle Ages the Kingdom of Poland had been a second-rate power, usually on the defensive against German encroachments. But in the fourteenth century that situation changed dramatically, partly because German strength had by then become a ghost of its former self, and above all because

the marriage in 1386 of Poland's reigning queen, Jadwiga, to Jagiello, grand duke of Lithuania, more than doubled Poland's size and enabled it to become a major expansionist state. Even before 1386 the grand duchy of Lithuania had begun to carve out an extensive territory for itself, not just on the shores of the Baltic where the present territory of Lithuania lies, but in Belarus and the Ukraine. Lithuania's expansionist momentum increased after the union with Poland. In 1410 combined Polish-Lithuanian forces in the battle of Tannenberg inflicted a stunning defeat on the German military order of Teutonic knights who ruled neighboring Prussia. In the early fifteenth century, Poland-Lithuania extended its borders so far east that the new power seemed on the verge of conquering all of Russia. Although many of the Lithuanian nobility were eastern Orthodox, Poland subscribed to Roman Catholicism, and the established church in Lithuania was also Roman Catholic. Thus when Moscow took the offensive against Poland-Lithuania in the late fifteenth century, it was able to appeal to religious as well as national sentiments. Prolonged warfare ensued, greatly exacerbating antagonisms toward Poland and toward the Latin Christian tradition it represented in the eyes of Muscovites.

MOSCOW AND BYZANTIUM

The growing alienation between Moscow and western Europe was further increased by events leading up to the fall of Constantinople to the Turks in 1453. Connections between Byzantium and the Rus went back to the tenth century, when missionaries from the Byzantine empire had converted the Kievan Slavs to Orthodox Christianity. Relations between the eastern and western churches had been tense ever since 1054, when the two churches split over papal primacy and the wording of the Nicene Creed. But embittered hatred is the only expression to describe Byzantine attitudes toward Rome after 1204 when the Fourth Crusade sacked Constantinople. Eastern Orthodox Russians sympathized with their Byzantine mentors, and felt all the more that they had extraordinarily good reason to shun the "Roman infection" after the debacle of 1453. This was because in 1438 the Byzantines in Constantinople, sensing correctly that a mighty Turkish onslaught was in the offing, agreed to submit to papal authority and unite with the western church, in the hope that these promises might earn them Western military support for their last stand. But despite this submission, no Western help was forthcoming and Constantinople fell to the Turks in 1453 without a single Roman Catholic knight lifting a hand.

The Orthodox hierarchy of Moscow had refused to follow Byzantium in its religious submission, regarding it as a betrayal of Christian orthodoxy. After Constantinople fell, therefore, the Muscovites concluded that the Turkish victory was a divine punishment for the Byzantines' religious perfidy. The Muscovite state thus became the center of a particularly zealous anti-Roman ideology, as Moscow began to see itself as the divinely appointed successor to Byzantium. The Russian ruler took the title of *tsar*—which simply means "caesar"—and Russians asserted that Moscow was both "a second Jerusalem" and "the third Rome": "Two Romes have fallen," said a Russian spokesman, "the third is still standing, and a fourth there shall not be." This Byzantine-derived ideology underlay both the later growth of Russian imperialism, and the sacred position ascribed to the rulers of the Muscovite (and later Russian) state.

THE REIGN OF IVAN THE GREAT (1462–1505)

Behind such imperial self-confidence lay the steadily growing power of the grand dukes of Moscow. Moscow itself had been effectively independent of the Mongols since the end of the fourteenth century, when a rival Mongol ruler named Timur the Lame (Tamurlane) had destroyed the Mongol khanate of the Golden Horde. But it was Ivan III, customarily known as Ivan the Great, who did the most to transform the grand duchy of Moscow into a true imperial power. Declaring himself to be the White Tsar (and thus the legitimate successor to the Mongol Golden Horde as the emperor of the West), Ivan launched a series of conquests between 1468 and 1485 that annexed, one by one, all the independent Russian principalities that lay between Moscow and the Poland-Lithuania border. After two successive invasions of Lithuania in 1492 and 1501, Ivan also succeeded in bringing parts of Belarus and Ukraine under his control. Battles between Russia and Poland-Lithuania would continue for several centuries thereafter, but by 1505, when Ivan died, he had established Muscovy as a power to be reckoned with on the European scene.

Under Ivan III, Muscovy was evolving in the direction of political autocracy and imperialism. Ivan's assumption of the imperial title meant that he was claiming to be the successor not only of the Mongol khans, but also of the defunct Byzantine emperors, who

themselves had been heirs of the Roman caesars. In 1452, Ivan married the niece of the last Byzantine ruler; later he adopted as his insignia the double-headed eagle and rebuilt Moscow's fortified princely residence, the Kremlin, in magnificent Italian Renaissance style to display his imperial splendor. As tsar, Ivan conceived of himself as the autocratic potentate not just of the Russians of Moscow but of all Russians, and even, potentially, of Belarussians and Ukrainians. In the sixteenth century, Russian expansionism was principally directed toward the south and east, against the small successor states to the Mongol Golden Horde. From the mid-seventeenth century on, however, Muscovite pressure against Ukraine would escalate, leading on to the enormous land empire Peter the Great would construct in the early eighteenth century. We cannot draw a direct line from Ivan III to Peter the Great. But the foundations Ivan laid would be appealed to as justification for Peter's claims to incorporate both Russians and a wide variety of non-Russian peoples into what would become Europe's largest empire.

THOUGHT, LITERATURE, AND ART

What trends led to the rise of vernacular literature?

Although we might guess that the extreme hardships of the later Middle Ages in western Europe should have led to the decline or stagnation of intellectual and artistic endeavors, in fact the period was an extremely fruitful one in the realms of thought, literature, and art.

In this section we will postpone treatment of certain developments most closely related to the early history of the Italian Renaissance, but will discuss some of western Europe's other important late medieval intellectual and artistic accomplishments.

THEOLOGY AND PHILOSOPHY

Theology and philosophy after about 1300 faced a crisis of doubt. This doubt did not concern the existence of God and his supernatural powers, but was rather doubt about human ability to comprehend the supernatural. Saint Thomas Aquinas and other Scholastics in the High Middle Ages had serenely delimited the number of "mysteries of the faith" and believed that everything else, both in heaven and earth, could be thoroughly understood by humans. But the floods, frosts, wars, and plagues of the fourteenth century helped undermine such confidence in the powers of human understanding. Once human beings experienced the universe as arbitrary and unpredictable, fourteenth-century thinkers began to wonder whether there was not far more in heaven and earth than could be understood by their philosophies. The result was a thoroughgoing reevaluation of the prior theological and philosophical outlook.

The leading late medieval abstract thinker was the English Franciscan William of Ockham, who was born around 1285 and died in 1349, apparently of the Black Death. Traditionally, Franciscans had always had greater doubts than Dominicans such as Saint Thomas Aquinas concerning the abilities of human reason to comprehend the supernatural; Ockham, convinced by the events of his age, expressed these doubts most formidably. He denied that the existence of God and numerous other theological matters could be demonstrated apart from scriptural revelation, and he emphasized God's freedom and absolute power to do anything. In the realm of human knowledge per se, Ockham's searching intellect drove him to look for absolute certainties instead of mere theories. In investigating earthly matters he developed the position, known as *nominalism*, that only individual things, not collectivities, are real, and that one thing therefore cannot be understood by means of another: to know a chair one has to see and touch it rather than just know what several other chairs are like. The formal logical system Ockham developed from this fundamental principle became

Theology and philosophy after 1300 faced a crisis of doubt about the human ability to comprehend the supernatural.

the most influential philosophical system of the later Middle Ages.

Ockham's outlook, which gained widespread adherence in late medieval universities, today often seems overly methodological and verging on the arid, but it had several important effects on the development of Western thought. Ockham's concern about what God might do led his followers to raise some of the seemingly absurd questions for which medieval theology has been mocked: for example, asking whether God can undo the past, or whether an infinite number of pure spirits can simultaneously inhabit the same place (the nearest medieval thinkers actually came to asking how many angels can dance on the head of a pin). Nonetheless, Ockham's emphasis on preserving God's autonomy led to a stress on divine omnipotence that became one of the basic presuppositions of sixteenth-century Protestantism. Further, Ockham's determination to find certainties in the realm of human knowledge ultimately helped make it possible to discuss human affairs and natural science without reference to supernatural explanations—one of the most important foundations of the modern scientific method. Finally, Ockham's opposition to studying collectivities and his refusal to apply logic to abstract categories helped encourage empiricism, or the belief that knowledge of the world should rest on sense experience rather than abstract reason. This too is a presupposition for scientific progress: thus it is probably not coincidental that some of Ockham's fourteenth-century followers made significant advances in the study of optics and physics.

VERNACULAR LITERATURE

Ockham's search for reliable truths finds certain parallels in the realm of late medieval literature, although Ockham surely had no direct influence in that field. The major trait of the best late medieval literature was *naturalism*, or the attempt to describe things the way they really are. This was more a development from high medieval precedents—such as the explorations of human conduct pursued by Chrétien de Troyes, Wolfram von Eschenbach, and Dante—than a reaction against them. Furthermore, the steady growth of a lay reading public encouraged authors to avoid theological and philosophical abstractions and seek more to entertain by portraying people realistically with all their strengths and foibles. Another main characteristic of late medieval literature, the predominance of composition in the European vernaculars instead of Latin, also developed out of high medieval precedents but gained great momentum in the later Middle Ages for two reasons. One was that international tensions and hostilities, including the numerous wars of the age and the trials of the universal papacy, led more and more people to identify themselves in national terms, and to regard vernacular tongues as a key element in their national identity. Another even more important was the fact that the continuing spread of education for the laity greatly increased the number of people who could read in a given vernacular language but not in Latin. Hence although much poetry had been composed in the vernacular during the High Middle Ages, in the later Middle Ages use of the vernacular was widely extended to prose. Moreover, countries such as Italy and England, which had just begun to cultivate their own vernacular literatures around 1300, subsequently began to employ their native tongues to impressive literary effect.

BOCCACCIO

The greatest writer of vernacular prose fiction of the later Middle Ages was the Italian Giovanni Boccaccio (1313–1375). Although Boccaccio would have taken an honored place in literary history for some of his lesser works, which included courtly romances, pastoral poems, and learned treatises, by far the most impressive of his writings is the *Decameron*, written between 1348 and 1351. This is a collection of one hundred stories, mostly about love and sex, adventure, and clever trickery, supposedly told by a sophisticated party of seven young ladies and three men who are sojourning in a country villa outside Florence in order to escape the ravages of the Black Death. Boccaccio by no means invented all one hundred plots, but even when he borrowed the outlines of his tales from earlier sources he retold the stories in his own characteristically exuberant, masterful, and extremely witty fashion.

For many reasons, the *Decameron* must be counted as epoch making from a historical point of view. The first is that it was the earliest ambitious and successful work of vernacular creative literature ever written in western Europe in narrative prose. Boccaccio's prose is "modern" in the sense that it is brisk, for unlike the medieval authors of flowery romances, Boccaccio purposely wrote in an unaffected, colloquial style. Simply stated, in the *Decameron* he was less interested in being "elevated" or elegant than in being unpretentiously entertaining. From the point of view of content, Boccaccio wished to portray men and women as they really are rather than as they ought to be. Thus when he wrote about the clergy he showed them to be as susceptible to human appetites and failings as other mortals. His women are not pallid playthings, distant goddesses, or steadfast virgins, but flesh-and-blood creatures with intellects; they interact more comfortably and naturally with men and with each other than any women in Western literature had ever done before. Boccaccio's treatment of sexual relations is often graphic, but never demeaning. In his world the natural desires of both women and men are not meant to be thwarted. For all these reasons the *Decameron* is a robust and delightful appreciation of what it means to be human.

CHAUCER

Similar in many ways to Boccaccio as a creator of robust, naturalistic vernacular literature was the Englishman Geoffrey Chaucer (c. 1340–1400). Chaucer was the first major writer whose English can still be read today with relatively little effort. Remarkably, he was both a founding father of England's mighty literary tradition and one of the four or five greatest contributors to it: most critics rank him just behind Shakespeare and in a class with Milton, Wordsworth, and Dickens.

Chaucer wrote several highly impressive works, but his masterpiece is unquestionably the *Canterbury Tales*, dating from the end of his career. Like the *Decameron*, this is a collection of stories held together by a frame, in Chaucer's case the device of having a group of people tell stories while on a pilgrimage from London to Canterbury. But there are also differences between the *Decameron* and the *Canterbury Tales*. Chaucer's stories are told in sparkling verse instead of prose, and they are recounted by people of all different classes—from a chivalric knight to a dedicated university student to a thieving miller with a wart on his nose. Lively women are also represented, most memorably the gap-toothed, oft-married "Wife of Bath," who knows all "the remedies of love." Each character tells a story that is particularly illustrative of his or her own occupation and outlook on the world. By this device Chaucer was able to create a highly diverse "human comedy." His range is greater than Boccaccio's, and although he is no less witty, frank, and lusty as the Italian, he is sometimes more profound.

CHRISTINE DE PISAN

The later Middle Ages also saw the emergence of professional authors who made their living with their pen.

Christine de Pisan. A leading writer of late-medieval vernacular prose literature, Christine de Pisan (1365–c. 1430) was intent on upholding the dignity of women. She is shown here writing about a gigantic Amazon warrior who could defeat men effortlessly in armed combat.

Significantly, one of the first of these professional *litterati* was a woman, Christine de Pisan. Although she herself was born in Italy, Christine spent her adult life in France, where her husband was a member of the king's household. When he died, the widowed Christine turned to writing to support herself and her children. She wrote in a wide variety of literary genres, including treatises on chivalry and on the art of warfare that she dedicated to her patron, King Charles VI of France. But she also wrote for a larger and more popular audience. Her imaginative tract *The City of Ladies* is an extended defense of the character, nature, and capacities of women against their male detractors, written in the form of an allegory. She also took part in a vigorous pamphlet literature that debated the misogynistic claims made against

> Christine de Pisan was by no means the first female writer of the Middle Ages, but she was the first lay woman to earn a living by her writing.

women in the *Romance of the Rose* (see Chapter 10). This debate continued for several hundred years, and became so famous that it was given a name: the *querelle des femmes,* "the debate over women." Christine was by no means the first female writer of the Middle Ages, but she was the first lay woman to earn a living by her writing.

SCULPTURE AND PAINTING

As naturalism was a dominant trait of late medieval literature, so it was of late medieval art. Already by the thirteenth century Gothic sculptors were paying far more attention than their Romanesque predecessors had to the way plants, animals, and human beings really looked. Whereas earlier medieval art had empha-

The Meeting of Joachim and Anna at the Golden Gate, a fresco by Giotto (c. 1267–1337). Note how the haloes merge: this old and barren couple will soon miraculously have a child, none other than Mary, the mother of Jesus.

to be cultivated in the Middle Ages and long afterward, especially in the form of *frescoes,* or paintings done on wet plaster. But in addition to frescoes, Italian artists in the thirteenth century first started painting pictures on pieces of wood or canvas. These were first done in tempera (pigments mixed with water and natural gums or egg whites), but around 1400 painting in oils was introduced in the European north. These new technical developments created new artistic opportunities. Artists were now able to paint religious scenes on altarpieces for churches and for private devotions practiced by the wealthier laity at home. Artists also painted the first Western portraits, which were meant to gratify the self-esteem of monarchs and aristocrats. The earliest surviving example of a naturalistic, painted portrait is one of a French king, John the Good, executed around 1360. Others followed quickly, so that within a short time the art of portraiture from life was highly developed. Visitors to art museums will notice that some of the most realistic and sensitive portraits of all time date from the fifteenth century.

The most pioneering and important painter of the later Middle Ages was the Florentine Giotto (c. 1267–1337). He did not engage in individual portraiture, but he brought deep humanity to his religious images painted on both walls and movable panels. Giotto was preeminently a naturalist, that is, an imitator of nature. Not only do his human beings and animals look more natural than those of his predecessors, they seem to do more natural things. When Christ enters Jerusalem on Palm Sunday, boys climb trees to get a better view; when St. Francis is laid out in death, one onlooker takes the opportunity to see whether the saint had really received Christ's wounds; and when the Virgin's parents, Joachim and Anna, meet after a long separation, they actually embrace and kiss— perhaps the first deeply tender kiss in Western art. It was certainly not true, as one fanciful storyteller later reported, that an onlooker found a fly Giotto had painted

sized abstract design, the stress was now increasingly on realism: thirteenth-century carvings of leaves and flowers must have been made from direct observation and are clearly recognizable to modern botanists as distinct species. Statues of humans also gradually became more naturally proportioned and realistic in their portrayals of facial expressions and bodily proportions. By around 1290 the concern for realism had become so great that a sculptor working on a tomb portrait of the German emperor Rudolf of Habsburg allegedly made a hurried return trip to view Rudolf in person, because he had heard that a new wrinkle had appeared on the emperor's face.

In the next two centuries the trend toward naturalism continued in sculpture and was extended to manuscript illumination and painting. The latter was in certain basic respects a new art. Ever since the Ice Age, people had painted on walls, but walls of course were not easily movable. The art of wall painting continued so real that he attempted to brush it away with his hand, but Giotto in fact accomplished something more. Specifically, he was the first to conceive of the painted space in fully three-dimensional terms: as one art historian has put it, Giotto's frescoes were the first to "knock a hole into the wall." After Giotto's death a reaction in Italian painting set in. Mid-fourteenth century artists briefly moved away from naturalism and painted stern, forbidding religious figures who seemed to float in space. But by around 1400 artists came back down to earth and started to build on Giotto's influence in ways that led to the great Italian renaissance in painting.

In the north of Europe painting did not advance impressively beyond manuscript illumination until the early fifteenth century, but then it suddenly came very much into its own. The leading northern European

Man with a Red Hat, by Hans Memling (c. 1430–1494).

The Arnolfini Betrothal, by Jan van Eyck. A characteristic synthesis of everyday life and religious devotion. Scenes from Christ's Passion surround the mirror. The artist himself appears reflected in the mirror as if to indicate that he is a witness to the betrothal. In addition, he wrote (above the mirror) "Johannes de eyck fuit hic" (Jan van Eyck was here).

painters were Flemish, first and foremost Jan van Eyck (c. 1380–1441), Roger van der Weyden (c. 1400–1464), and Hans Memling (c. 1430–1494). These three were the greatest early practitioners of painting in oil, a medium that allowed them to engage in brilliant coloring and sharp-focused realism. Van Eyck and van der Weyden excelled most at two things: communicating a sense of deep religious piety and portraying minute details of familiar everyday experience. These may at first seem incompatible, but it should be remembered that contemporary manuals of practical mysticism such as the *Imitation of Christ* also sought to link deep piety with everyday existence. Thus it was by no means blasphemous when a Flemish painter would portray behind a tender Virgin and Child a vista of contemporary life with people going about their usual business and a man even urinating against a wall. This union of the sacred and the profane tended to fall apart in the work of Memling, who excelled in either straightforward religious pictures or secular portraits, but it would return in the work of the greatest painters of the Low Countries, Brueghel and Rembrandt.

ADVANCES IN TECHNOLOGY

How did technological advances affect everyday life?

No account of enduring late medieval accomplishments would be complete without mention of certain epoch-making technological advances. Sadly, but probably not unexpectedly, treatment of this subject has to begin with reference to the invention of artillery and firearms. The prevalence of warfare stimulated the development of new weaponry. Gunpowder itself was a Chinese invention, but it was first put to devastating military uses in the late medieval West. Heavy cannons, which made terrible noises "as though all the dyvels of hell had been in the way," were first employed around 1330. The earliest cannons were so primitive that it often was more dangerous to stand be-

hind than in front of them, but by the middle of the fifteenth century they were greatly improved and began to revolutionize the nature of warfare. In one year, 1453, heavy artillery played a leading role in determining the outcome of two crucial conflicts: the Ottoman Turks used German and Hungarian cannons to breach the defenses of Constantinople—hitherto the most impregnable in Europe—and the French used heavy artillery to take the city of Bordeaux, thereby ending the Hundred Years' War. Cannons thereafter made it difficult for rebellious aristocrats to hole up in their stone castles, and thus they aided in the consolidation of the national monarchies. Placed aboard ships, cannons enabled European vessels to dominate foreign waters in the subsequent age of overseas expansion. Hand-held firearms, also invented in the fourteenth century, were gradually perfected. Shortly after 1500 the most effective new variety of gun, the musket, allowed foot soldiers to end once and for all the earlier military dominance of heavily armored mounted knights. Once lance-bearing cavalries became outmoded and fighting could more easily be carried on by

A Fifteenth-Century Siege with Cannon.

Devil with Eyeglasses. Once spectacles became common even devils in hell sported them.

all, the monarchical states that could turn out the largest armies completely subdued internal resistance and dominated the battlefields of Europe.

Other late medieval technological developments were more life enhancing. Eyeglasses, first invented in the 1280s, were perfected in the fourteenth century. These allowed older people to keep on reading when farsightedness would otherwise have stopped them. For example, the great fourteenth-century scholar Petrarch, who boasted excellent sight in his youth, wore spectacles after his sixtieth year and was thus enabled to complete some of his most important works. Around 1300 the use of the magnetic compass helped ships to sail farther away from land and venture out into the Atlantic. One immediate result was the opening of direct sea commerce between Italy and the north. Subsequently, numerous improvements in ship-building, map making, and navigational devices enabled Europe to start expanding overseas. In the fourteenth century the Azores and Cape Verde Islands were reached; then, after a long pause caused by Europe's plagues and wars, the African Cape of Good Hope was rounded in 1487, the West Indies reached in 1492, India reached by the sea route in 1498, and Brazil sighted in 1500. Partly as a result of technology, the world was thus suddenly made much smaller.

Among the most familiar implements of our modern

Horloge de Sapience (Lady Wisdom with Clocks). This miniature, from a French manuscript of about 1450, reflects the growing fascination with machines of all sorts and clocks in particular.

life that were invented by Europeans in the later Middle Ages were clocks and printed books. Mechanical clocks were invented shortly before 1300 and proliferated in the years immediately thereafter. The earliest clocks were too expensive for private purchase, but towns quickly vied with each other to install the most elaborate clocks in their prominent public buildings. These clocks not only told the time but showed the courses of sun, moon, and planets, and performed mechanical tricks on the striking of the hours. The new invention ultimately had two profound effects. One was the further stimulation of European interest in complex machinery of all sorts. This interest had already been awakened by the high medieval proliferation of mills, but clocks ultimately became even more omnipresent than mills because after about 1650 they became quite cheap and were brought into practically every European home. Household clocks served as models of marvelous machines. Equally if not more significant was the fact that clocks began to rationalize the course of European daily affairs. Until the advent of clocks in the later Middle Ages time was flexible. Men and women had only a rough idea of how late in the day it was and rose and retired more or less with the sun. People who lived in the country in particular performed different jobs at different rates according to the rhythm of the seasons. Even when hours were counted, they were measured at different lengths according to the amount of light in the different seasons of the year. In the fourteenth century, however, clocks first started relentlessly striking equal hours through the day and night. Thus they began to regulate work with new precision. People were expected to start and end work "on time" and many came to believe that "time is money." This emphasis on timekeeping brought new efficiencies but also new tensions: Lewis Carroll's white rabbit, who is always looking at his pocket watch and muttering "how late it's getting," is a telling caricature of time-obsessed Western humanity.

> As soon as books became easily accessible, literacy increased even more and book culture became a basic part of the European way of life.

The invention of printing with movable type was equally momentous. The major stimulus for this invention was the replacement of parchment by paper as Europe's primary writing material between 1200 and 1400. Parchment, made from the skins of sheep or calves, was extremely expensive: since it was possible to get only about four good parchment leaves from one animal, it was necessary to slaughter between two to three hundred sheep or calves to gain enough parchment for a Bible! Paper, made from rags turned into pulp by mills, brought prices down dramatically. Late medieval records show that paper sold at one sixth the price of parchment. Accordingly, it became cheaper to learn how to read and write. With literacy becoming ever more widespread, there was a growing market for still cheaper books, and the invention of printing with movable type around 1450 fully met this demand. By greatly saving labor, the invention made printed books about one fifth as expensive as handwritten ones within about two decades.

As soon as books became easily accessible, literacy increased even more and book culture became a basic part of the European way of life. After about 1500, Europeans could afford to read and buy books of all sorts—not just religious tracts, but instructional manuals, light entertainment, and, by the eighteenth century, newspapers. Printing ensured that ideas would spread quickly and reliably; moreover, revolutionary ideas could no longer be easily extinguished once they were

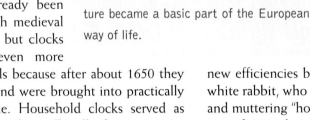

Paper Making at a Paper Mill.

A Printing Press. From a title page of a Parisian printer, 1520.

CONCLUSION

Despite economic dislocation and demographic collapse, the later Middle Ages were one of the most creative and inventive periods in the history of western Europe. Why this was so will always remain something of a mystery, until and unless future scholars should unlock the secrets of human creativity itself. What we can see behind the artistic, philosophical, literary, and technological developments of the period, however, is a consistent drive to understand, control, and replicate the workings of the natural world. This fact may offer some clues toward explaining the sources of these developments.

Perhaps most fundamentally, in the later Middle Ages intellectuals broke with the traditional, Neoplatonic vision of nature as a book in which one could read the mind of God. Instead, they came to see the natural world as operating according to its own laws, which were empirically verifiable but which could tell human beings nothing about the God who lay behind them. The resulting sense of the contingency and independence of the natural world was an essential step toward the emergence of a scientific world view. It also encouraged Europeans to believe that nature itself could be manipulated and directed toward human ends.

Powerful economic and political factors also encouraged the technological inventiveness of the period. Despite the disruptive impact of plague and war, the market for goods was not destroyed. Instead, the resulting labor shortages encouraged European entrepreneurs to experiment with labor-saving technologies and new crops. Incessant warfare in particular encouraged a remarkable burst of military inventiveness. It also enabled more powerful governments to extract a larger percentage of their subjects' wealth through taxation, which they proceeded to invest in ships, cannons, muskets, and the standing armies that the new weaponry made possible. Increasing per capita wealth produced the capital necessary to invest in mills, factories, clocks, books, and compasses. It also made possible a remarkable increase in the educational level of the European population. Between 1300 and 1500 hundreds and perhaps thousands of new grammar schools were established, and scores of new universities emerged, because parents saw such schools as a reliable route to social advancement for their sons. Women were still excluded from the schools, but increasing numbers of girls were being taught at home,

set down in hundreds of copies of books. Thus the greatest religious reformer of the sixteenth century, Martin Luther, gained an immediate following throughout Germany by employing the printing press to run off pamphlets: had printing not been available to him, Luther might have died as Hus did. The spread of books also helped stimulate the growth of cultural nationalism. Before printing, regional dialects in most European countries were often so diverse that people who supposedly spoke the same language often could barely understand each other. Such a situation hindered governmental centralization because a royal servant might be entirely unable to communicate with inhabitants of the provinces. Shortly after the invention of printing, however, each European country began to develop its own linguistic standards, which were disseminated uniformly by books. The "king's English" was what was printed in London and carried to Yorkshire or Wales. Thus communications were enhanced and governments were able to operate ever more efficiently.

making women an extremely important (perhaps even the dominant) part of the "reading public" that was emerging in later medieval Europe.

Finally, it may be that dislocation itself promotes innovation, so long as it does not destroy people's confidence in the ultimate improvability of their lives. Europeans suffered enormously from war, plague, and economic crises during the later Middle Ages. But those who survived seized the opportunities their new world presented to them. The confidence they had developed in the High Middle Ages was not destroyed by the travails of the later Middle Ages. By 1500, most Europeans lived more secure lives than their ancestors had two hundred years before; and they stood on the verge of an extraordinary new period of expansion and conquest that would take European armies, merchants and settlers around the globe.

SELECTED READINGS

Allmand, Christopher T., ed. *Society at War: The Experience of England and France During the Hundred Years' War.* Edinburgh, 1973. An outstanding collection of documents.

———. *The Hundred Years' War: England and France at War, c. 1300–c. 1450.* Cambridge and New York, 1988. Still the best analytic account of the war; after a short narrative, the book is organized topically.

Boccaccio, Giovanni. *The Decameron.* Translated by Mark Musa and P. E. Bondanella. New York, 1977.

Bynum, Caroline Walker. *Holy Feast and Holy Fast: The Religious Significance of Food to Medieval Women.* Berkeley and Los Angeles, 1987. A pathbreaking study of the patterns of female piety in the later middle ages.

Campbell, Bruce M. S. *English Seignorial Agriculture, 1250–1450.* Cambridge and New York, 2000. A definitive, up-to-date, and comprehensive account.

Chaucer, Geoffrey. *The Canterbury Tales.* Translated by Nevill Coghill. New York, 1951. A modern English verse translation, lightly annotated.

Cole, Bruce. *Giotto and Florentine Painting, 1280–1375.* New York, 1976. A clear and stimulating introduction.

Crummey, Robert O. *The Formation of Muscovy, 1304–1613.* New York, 1987. The standard account.

Dobson, R. Barrie. *The Peasants' Revolt of 1381,* 2d ed. London, 1983. A comprehensive source collection, with excellent introductions to the documents and an illuminating discussion of the revolt.

Duffy, Eamon. *The Stripping of the Altars: Traditional Religion in England, 1400–1580.* New Haven, 1992. The fullest study anywhere of the patterns of fifteenth-century piety at the parish level.

Dyer, Christopher. *Standards of Living in the Later Middle Ages: Social Change in England, c. 1200–1520.* Cambridge and New York, 1989. Detailed but highly rewarding.

Froissart, Jean. *Chronicles.* Translated by Geoffrey Brereton. Baltimore, 1968. A selection from the most famous contemporary account of the Hundred Years' War to c. 1400.

Hilton, Rodney H., and Trevor Aston, eds. *The English Rising of 1381.* Cambridge and New York, 1984. An excellent collection of articles that also includes chapters on the *Jacquerie* and the *Ciompi* rebellions.

Horrox, Rosemary, ed. *The Black Death.* New York, 1994. A fine collection of documents reflecting the impact of the Black Death, especially in England.

Hudson, Anne. *The Premature Reformation: Wycliffite Texts and Lollard History.* Oxford and New York, 1988. Despite its misleading title, this is the fullest and best account of Lollardy, written by the premier modern historian of the subject.

Huizinga, Johan. *The Waning of the Middle Ages: A Study of the Forms of Life, Thought, and Art in France and the Netherlands in the Dawn of the Renaissance,* New York, 1924. A classic picture of the "expiring" Middle Ages; a book from whose influence historians are still struggling to escape. Frequently republished, the most recent translation of this work is entitled *The Autumn of the Middle Ages.* Translated by Rodney J. Payton and Ulrich Mammitzsch. Chicago, 1996.

John Hus at the Council of Constance. Translated by M. Spinka, New York, 1965. The translation of a Czech chronicle with an expert introduction and appended documents.

Jordan, William Chester. *The Great Famine: Northern Europe in the Early Fourteenth Century.* Princeton, 1996. An outstanding social and economic study of the disastrous famines that swept northern Europe between 1315 and 1322.

Keen, Maurice, ed. *Medieval Warfare: A History.* Oxford and New York, 1999. The most attractive introduction to this crucially important subject. Lively and well illustrated.

Kempe, Margery. *The Book of Margery Kempe.* Translated by Barry Windeatt. New York, 1985. A fascinating autobiography by an early fifteenth-century Englishwoman who hoped she might be a saint.

Lerner, Robert E. *The Age of Adversity: The Fourteenth Century.* Ithaca, N.Y., 1968. A short, evocative account.

———. *The Heresy of the Free Spirit in the Later Middle Ages,* 2d ed. Notre Dame, Ind., 1991. A revealing study of a heretical movement that terrified contemporaries, yet hardly existed at all.

Lewis, Peter S. *Later Medieval France: The Polity.* London, 1968. Still fresh and suggestive after almost thirty-five years. A masterwork.

McFarlane, K. Bruce. *The Nobility of Later Medieval England.* Oxford, 1980. A pioneering collection of essays by one of the most influential historians of the mid-twentieth century.

Memoirs of a Renaissance Pope: The Commentaries of Pius II, abridged ed. Translated by F. A. Gragg, New York, 1959. Remarkable insights into the mind of a particularly well-educated mid-fifteenth-century pope.

Nicholas, David. *The Transformation of Europe, 1300–1600.* Oxford and New York, 1999. The best textbook presently available.

Oakley, Francis C. *The Western Church in the Later Middle Ages.* Ithaca, N.Y., 1979. The best book by far on the history of conciliarism, the late medieval papacy, Hussitism, and the efforts at institutional reform during this period. On popular piety, see Swanson (below).

Panofsky, Erwin. *Early Netherlandish Painting.* 2 vols. Cambridge, Mass., 1953. A brilliant specialized history by a master art historian.

Pernoud, Régine, ed. *Joan of Arc, by Herself and Her Witnesses.* New York, 1966. A collection of contemporary writings about Joan, including the transcripts of her trial.

Shirley, Janet, trans. *A Parisian Journal, 1405–1449.* Oxford, 1968. A marvelous panorama of Parisian life recorded by an eyewitness.

Swanson, R. N. *Religion and Devotion in Europe, c. 1215–c. 1515.* Cambridge and New York, 1995. An excellent study of late medieval popular piety; an excellent complement to Oakley (see above).

Sumption, Jonathan. *The Hundred Years' War.* Vol. 1, *Trial by Battle;* Vol. 2, *Trial by Fire.* Philadelphia, 1999. The first two volumes of a massive narrative history of the war take the story up to 1369.

Vaughan, Richard. *Valois Burgundy.* London, 1975. A summation of the author's four-volume study of the Burgundian dukes.

Ziegler, Philip. *The Black Death.* New York, 1969. A popular account, but reliable and engrossing.

PART IV
FROM MEDIEVAL TO MODERN

FOR MOST OF THE TWENTIETH CENTURY, historians portrayed the Italian Renaissance and the Protestant Reformation as marking a dramatic break in European history, which brought the Middle Ages to an end and ushered in the modern world. To be sure, the sixteenth and seventeenth centuries saw decisive transformations in European life. For the first time, European sailors, soldiers, and merchants forged worldwide trading networks that brought the mineral and agricultural riches of the western hemisphere into their Atlantic ports. The Protestant Reformation brought an end to the religious unity of Europe, and a century of religious wars served only to cement those divisions. Meanwhile, new trends in cultural and intellectual life, many of which had begun in fourteenth- and fifteenth-century Italy, began to spread widely throughout the rest of Europe.

It is increasingly clear, however, that most of the new developments of the sixteenth and seventeenth centuries had deep roots in the later Middle Ages. The voyages that took sixteenth century Europeans around the globe began in the thirteenth century with the conquest of the "Atlantic Mediterranean." The intensive study of classical Roman and Greek literature that characterized the "humanism" of the Italian Renaissance, developed from the classical revival in the twelfth and thirteenth centuries. Even the theological doctrines of the Protestant reformers had roots in the theological controversies of the later Middle Ages. And all these developments took place in the context of continuing cultural and economic exchange between Europe, the Islamic world, and Byzantium.

	POLITICS	SOCIETY AND CULTURE	ECONOMY	INTERNATIONAL RELATIONS
1200	(Ghengis) Khan rules over Mongol clans (1206–1227)		"Silk Road" connects Europe with India, China, and Indonesia (1200s) Polo brothers travel to China (1200s)	Mongols conquer southern Russia (1237–1240) Mongols annihilate Hungarian army at River Sajo (1241) Mongol forces withdraw from Europe (1241)
1300	Yuan dynasty in China (1279–1368) Rise of Ottoman dynasty (1300) Ming dynasty in China (1368–1644)	Civic humanism begins in Italy (1300s) Francesco Petrarch (1304–1374) Mongols transmit bubonic plague at siege of Caffa (1346) Leonardo Bruni (1370–1444)	Silver shortage begins in Europe (1340s)	Ottomans defeat Serbian empire at battle of Kosovo (1389)
1400		Giovanni Aurispa returns with classical manuscripts (1423) Sandro Botticelli (1445–1510) Neoplatonism in Italy (1450–1600) Leonardo da Vinci (1452–1519) Desiderius Erasmus (1469–1536) Niccolò Machiavelli, author of *The Prince* (1469–1527) Albrecht Dürer (1471–1528) Sir Thomas More (1478–1535) Raphael (1483–1520) The High Renaissance begins (1490) The Catholic Reformation begins (1490)	Portugal establishes Atlantic colonies (late 1400–1460) Dias rounds southern tip of Africa (1488) Portugal founds slave-based plantation in St. Thomas (1490) Columbus lands in West Indies (1492) Disease kills much of Native American population (1492–1538) Vasco da Gama reaches India (1498)	Mehmet II conquers Constantinople (1453)
1500	Reign of Charles V, Holy Roman Emperor (1506–1556)	Roman Inquisition begins (1500) Saint Peter's Basilica erected in Rome (1500–1520) Papacy of Julius II (1503–1513) Saint Francis Xavier, missionary in Asia, (1506–1552) Andrea Palladio (1508–1580) John Calvin (1509–1564) Papacy of Leo X, son of Lorenzo de Medici (1513–1521) Luther posts Ninety-Five Theses (1517) Emergence of Zwinglianism, Anabaptism, and Calvinism (1520–1550) Edict of Worms (1521) Peter Brueghel, painter of *Harvesters* and *Massacre of the Innocents* (1525–1569) Baldassare Castiglione's *The Book of the Courtier* (1528)	Grain prices in Europe increase fivefold (1500–1650) Portuguese ships reach Spice Islands and China (1515)	Cortes conquers Aztec empire (1519–1522) Ottomans conquer Syria, Egypt, and the Balkans (1520–1540) Charles V, Holy Roman Emperor, sacks Rome (1527)

POLITICS	SOCIETY AND CULTURE	ECONOMY	INTERNATIONAL RELATIONS	
	Michel de Montaigne (1533–1592)		Francisco Pizarro topples Incas (1533)	1533
	Henry VIII becomes head of the Church of England (1533–1534)			
	Calvin's *Institutes of the Christian Religion* (1536)			
	St. Ignatius Loyola publishes *The Spiritual Exercises* (1541)	Rapid inflation marks the Price Revolution (1540s)		
	El Greco, painter of *View of Toledo*, (1541–1614)	Silver found in Mexico and Bolivia (1543–1548)		
	Council of Trent (1545)			
Reign of Philip II of Spain (1556–1598)	Edmund Spenser, author of *The Faerie Queen*, (1552–1599)		Peace of Augsburg (1555)	
Reign of Elizabeth I of England (1558–1603)				
	First *Roman Index of Prohibited Books* established (1564)			
	William Shakespeare (1564–1616)		Ottomans defeated by Hapsburgs and Venetians at Lepanto (1571)	
	Papacy of Pius V (1566–1572)		Philip II annexes Portugal (1580)	
	St. Bartholomew's Day massacre (1572)			
English navy defeats the Spanish Armada (1588)		New World silver production peaks at 10 million ounces (1590s)		
Reign of Henry IV, first of the Bourbon dynasty in France (1589–1610)				
Edict of Nantes (1598)				1600
Reign of James I, first of the Stuart dynasty (1603–1625)	John Milton (1608–1674)	Spanish economy collapses when silver imports drop (1620–1640)	Thirty Year's War (1618–1648)	
Cardinal Richelieu, first minister of France (1624–1642)	Blaise Pascal (1623–1662)			
Reign of Charles I of England (1625–1649)			Gustavus Adolphus of Sweden enters Thirty Years' War (1630)	
English Civil War (1642–1649)				
The Fronde, a series of French aristocratic revolts (1648–1653)			Peace of Westphalia (1648)	
Oliver Cromwell rules during the Commonwealth (1649–1658)				
Louis XIV of France comes of age (1651)	Thomas Hobbes' *Leviathan* (1651)			
Charles II and the Restoration (1660–1685)				

CHAPTER TWELVE

COMMERCE, CONQUEST, AND COLONIZATION, 1300–1600

BY 1300, THE GREAT EUROPEAN expansion of the High Middle Ages was coming to an end. In Iberia, there would be no further conquests of Muslim territory until 1492, when Granada fell to King Ferdinand and Queen Isabella. In the east, the Crusader kingdoms of Constantinople and Acre collapsed, in 1261 and 1291 respectively. Only the German drive into eastern Europe continued; but by the mid-fourteenth century, it too had been slowed by the rise of a new Baltic state in Lithuania. Internal expansion was also slowing, as Europe reached the ecological limits of its resources. Thereafter, the pressure on resources was eased only by the dramatic population losses that resulted during the fourteenth century from the combined effects of famine, plague, and war.

But despite these checks, Europeans in the late Middle Ages did not turn inward on themselves. Although land-based conquests slowed, new, sea-based empires emerged in the Mediterranean world during the fourteenth and fifteenth centuries with colonies that extended from the Black Sea to the Canary Islands. New maritime trade routes were opened up through the Strait of Gibraltar, resulting in greater economic integration between the Mediterranean and Atlantic economies and increasing the demand in northwestern Europe for Asian spices and African gold. By the late fifteenth century, Mediterranean mariners and colonists had extended their domination out into the Atlantic, from the Azores in the north to the Canary Islands in the south. Portuguese navigators were also pushing down the west coast of Africa. In 1498 one such expedition would sail all the way around the Cape of Good Hope to India.

The fifteenth-century conquest of the "Atlantic Mediterranean" was the essential preliminary to the dramatic events that began in 1492 with Columbus's attempt to reach China by sailing westward across the Atlantic Ocean and that led, by 1600, to the Spanish and Portuguese conquests of the Americas. Because these events are so familiar, we can easily underestimate their importance. For the native peoples and empires of the Americas, the results of European contact were cataclysmic. By 1600, somewhere between 50 and 90 percent of the indigenous peoples of the

FOCUS QUESTIONS

• How did the Mongols affect trade along the Silk Road?	• How were the Portuguese able to control Indian Ocean trade?
• Why were slaves important to Ottoman society?	• What was the impact of New World silver on the European economy?

Americas had perished from disease, massacre, and enslavement. For Europeans, the results of their conquests were far less fatal, but no less far reaching. By 1300, Europe had eclipsed both Byzantium and the empire of Islam as a Mediterranean power, but outside the Mediterranean and the north Atlantic European power was negligible. By 1600, however, Europe had emerged as the first truly global power in world history, capable of pursuing its imperial ambitions and commercial interests wherever its ships could sail and its guns could reach. European control over the interiors of the African, Asian, and American land masses would not be fully achieved until the end of the nineteenth century, and would last thereafter for less than a century. By 1600, however, European navies ruled the seas and the world's resources were increasingly being channeled through European hands—patterns that have continued until the present day.

THE MONGOLS

How did the Mongols affect trade along the Silk Road?

Trade between the Mediterranean world and the Far East dated back to antiquity, but it was not until the late thirteenth century that Europeans began to establish direct trading connections with India, China, and the "Spice Islands" of the Indonesian archipelago. For Europeans, these connections would prove profoundly important, although less for their economic significance than for their impact upon the European imagination. For the peoples of Asia, however, the appearance of European traders on the "Silk Road" between Central Asia and China was merely a curiosity. The really consequential event was the rise of the Mongol empire that made such connections possible.

> For the peoples of Asia, the appearance of European traders on the "Silk Road" was merely a curiosity. It was the rise of the Mongol empire that made such connections possible.

THE RISE OF THE MONGOL EMPIRE

The Mongols were one of a number of nomadic peoples inhabiting the steppes of central Asia. Although closely connected with various Turkish-speaking peoples with whom they frequently intermarried, the Mongols spoke their own distinctive language and had their own homeland to the north of the Gobi Desert in present-day Mongolia. Sheep provided them with shelter (in the form of wool tents), clothing, milk, and meat. Horses made possible their seasonal movements across the steppes, and also provided them with their national drink, an intoxicating fermented mare's milk called *qumis*. Like many nomadic peoples throughout history, the Mongols were highly accomplished cavalry soldiers who supplemented their own pastoralism and craft production by raiding the sedentary peoples to their south. (It was in part to control such raiding from Mongolia that, many centuries before, the Chinese had built the famous Great Wall.) Primarily, however, China defended itself by attempting to ensure that the Mongols remained internally divided, and so turned their martial energies most often against each other.

In the late twelfth century, however, a Mongol chief named Temüjin began to unite the various Mongol tribes under his rule. By incorporating the army of each defeated tribe into his own army, Temüjin quickly built up a large military force. In 1206, his supremacy was formally acknowledged by all the Mongols, and he took the title Chingiz (Genghis) Khan—"the oceanic (possibly meaning universal) ruler." Chingiz now turned his enormous army against his non-Mongol neighbors. China at this time was divided into three hostile states. In 1209, Chingiz launched an attack on northwestern China; in 1211 he invaded the Chin empire in north China. At first these attacks were probably looting expeditions rather than deliberate attempts at conquest, but by the 1230s a full-scale Mongol conquest of northern and western China was under way, culminating in 1234 with the fall of the Chin. In 1279, Chingiz's grandson Qubilai (Kublai) Khan completed the conquest of southern (Sung) China, thus reuniting China for the first time in centuries. The Yuan dynasty Qubilai established ruled China until 1368, when it was overthrown by a native Chinese dynasty known as the Ming.

Meanwhile, Chingiz turned his forces westward, conquering much of Central Asia and incorporating the important commercial cities of Tashkent, Samarkand, and Bukhara into his expanding empire. When Chingiz died in 1227, he was succeeded by his third son Ögedei, who completed the conquest of the Chin, con-

EUROPE

Moscow
Kiev   Kazan

CUMANS

KHANATE OF THE GOLDEN HORDE

New Sarai

Old Sarai

Lake Baikal

ALTAI MTS.

Karakorum

SEA
OF
JAPAN

JAPAN

BLACK SEA

GEORGIA
CAUCASUS MTS.

SELJUKS Trebizond

Tbilisi

MEDITERRANEAN SEA

Jerusalem

Tabriz

Euphrates R.

Tigris R.

Baghdad   Gurgan

KHWARIZM

CASPIAN SEA

ARAL
SEA

KARA-KHITAI

Lake Balkhash

TIEN SHAN

CHAGATAI EMPIRE

Tashkent

Bukhara

Turfan

GOBI

Huang He

Hangzhou

Kaifeng

EMPIRE OF THE
GREAT KHAN

EAST
CHINA
SEA

MAMELUKS

RED SEA

Persian Gulf

IL-KHAN
EMPIRE

Ormuz

Balkh
Herat

Kabul

HINDU KUSH

SULTANATE
OF DELHI

Delhi

Indus R.

HIMALAYAS

TIBET

Brahmaputra R.

Yangzi R.

SONG EMPIRE
(conquered 1279)

Guangzhou

Nile R.

ARABIA

Ganges R.

INDIA

ARABIAN SEA

BURMA
(MYANMAR)

Mekong R.

ANAM

CHAMPA

SOUTH
CHINA
SEA

Bay
of
Bengal

CEYLON

INDIAN OCEAN

to Java

← Mongol campaigns post-1259

0   500   1000 Miles
0   500   1000 Kilometers

THE MONGOL SUCCESSOR STATES

Consider the breakup of Chingiz Khan's empire after 1259, and the passing similarities its fracture might possess to the disintegration of Alexander's empire, also conquered swiftly and encompassing vast swaths of Europe and Asia. Why did Chingiz Khan's empire splinter? How did the Mongol onslaught against and occupation of major sections of the Arab Muslim world possibly aid the expansion of European civilization and trade into the Mediterranean? At the same time, how did it complicate the situation for the crusader efforts in the Holy Land?

quered the lands between the Oxus River and the Caspian Sea, and then laid plans for a massive invasion toward the west. Between 1237 and 1240, the Mongol horde (so called from the Turkish word *ordu*, meaning "tent" or "encampment") conquered southern Russia, and then launched a two-pronged assault farther west. The smaller of the two Mongol armies swept through Poland toward eastern Germany; the larger army went

southwest toward Hungary. In April 1241 the smaller Mongol force met a hastily assembled army of Germans and Poles at the battle of Liegnitz, where the two sides fought to a bloody standstill. Two days later, the larger Mongol army annihilated the Hungarian army at the River Sajo.

How much farther west the Mongol armies might have pushed will forever remain in doubt, for in

December 1241 the Great Khan Ögedei died, and the Mongol forces withdrew from eastern Europe. It took five years before a new great khan could establish himself, and when he died in 1248, the resulting interregnum lasted for three more years. Mongol conquests continued in Persia, the Middle East, and China, but after 1241 the Mongols never resumed their attacks on Europe. After 1260, when the Mamluk sultanate of Egypt stopped the Mongols' advance toward the southwest, the Mongol empire split into competing and frequently hostile parts. By 1300, the period of Mongol expansion had come to an end.

But the Mongol threat did not suddenly disappear. Descendants of Chingiz Khan continued to rule this enormous land empire (the largest such empire in the history of the world) until the mid-fourteenth century. Later, under the leadership of Timur the Lame (known as Tamerlane to Europeans) it looked briefly as if the Mongol empire might be reunited. But Timur died in

CHRONOLOGY	
RISE OF THE MONGOL EMPIRE, 1206–1260	
Temujin crowned as Chingiz Khan	1206
Mongols conquer northern China	1234
Mongols conquer southern Russia	1237–1240
Mongol forces withdraw from Europe	1241
Mamluk sultanate halts Mongol advance	1260

1405 on his way to invade China; thereafter the various parts of the Mongol empire fell into the hands of local rulers, including (in Asia Minor) the Ottoman Turks. Mongol cultural influence continued, however, and can be seen in the enormously impressive artwork produced during the fifteenth and sixteenth centuries in Persia and in Mughal India.

The Mongols owed their success to the size, speed, and training of their mounted armies; to the intimidating savagery with which they butchered those who resisted them; and to their ability to adapt the administrative traditions of their subjects to their own purposes. Partly because the Mongols themselves put little store even in their own shamanistic religious traditions, they were also unusually tolerant of the religious beliefs of others—a distinct advantage in controlling an empire that comprised a dizzying array of Buddhist, Christian, and Muslim sects. However, little was distinctively "Mongol" about the way they governed their empire. Except in China, where the Yuan dynasty inherited and maintained a complex administrative bureaucracy, the Mongols' rule was relatively unsophisticated, being chiefly directed at securing the steady payment of tribute from their subjects.

The Head of Timur the Lame. A forensic reconstruction based on his exhumed skull.

EUROPE, THE MONGOLS, AND THE FAR EAST

The Mongols had a keen eye for the commercial advantages their empire could offer them. They took steps to control the caravan routes that led from China through Central Asia to the Black Sea. They also encouraged commercial contacts with European traders, especially through the Iranian city of Tabriz, from which both land and sea routes led on to China. Until the Mongol conquests, the "Silk Road" to China

MARCO POLO'S DESCRIPTION OF JAVA

The Venetian merchants Niccolo and Maffeo Polo traveled overland from Constantinople to the court of Qubilai Khan between 1260 and 1269. When they returned a few years later, they brought with them Niccolo's son Marco. A gifted linguist, Marco would remain at the Mongol court until the early 1290s, when he returned to Europe after a journey through Southeast Asia, the Spice Islands, and the Indian Ocean. Marco's account of his Travels would shape European images of the Far East for centuries.

Departing from Ziamba, and steering between south and south-east, fifteen hundred miles, you reach an island of very great size, named Java. According to the reports of some well-informed navigators, it is the greatest in the world, and has a compass above three thousand miles. It is under the dominion of one king only, nor do the inhabitants pay tribute to any other power. They are worshipers of idols.

The country abounds with rich commodities. Pepper, nutmegs, spikenard, galangal, cubebs, cloves and all the other valuable spices and drugs, are the produce of the island; which occasion it to be visited by many ships laden with merchandise, that yields to the owners considerable profit.

The quantity of gold collected there exceeds all calculation and belief. From thence it is that . . . merchants . . . have imported, and to this day import, that metal to a great amount, and from thence also is obtained the greatest part of the spices that are distributed throughout the world. That the Great Khan [Qubilai] has not brought the island under subjection to him, must be attributed to the length of the voyage and the dangers of the navigation.

The Travels of Marco Polo, revised and edited by Manuel Komroff. (New York: Random House), 1926, pp. 267–268.

had been closed to Western merchants and travelers. But almost as soon as the Mongol empire was established, we find Europeans venturing on these routes. The first such travelers were Franciscan missionaries such as William de Rubruck, sent by King Louis IX of France in 1253 as his ambassador to the Mongol court. But Western merchants quickly followed. The most famous of these early merchants were three Venetians: Niccolo, Maffeo, and Marco Polo. Marco Polo's account of his twenty-year sojourn in China in the service of Qubilai Khan, and of his journey home through the Spice Islands, India, and Iran, is one of the most famous travel accounts of all time. Its effect upon the imagination of his contemporaries was enormous. For the next two centuries, most of what Europeans knew about the Far East they learned from Marco Polo's *Travels*. Christopher Columbus's copy of this book still survives.

European connections with the western end of the Silk Road would continue until the mid-fourteenth century. The Genoese were especially active in this trade, not least because their rivals, the Venetians, already dominated the Mediterranean trade with Alexandria and Beirut, through which the bulk of Europe's Far Eastern luxury goods continued to pass. But the Mongols of Iran become progressively more hostile to Westerners as the fourteenth century progressed. By 1344, the Genoese had abandoned Tabriz after attacks on Westerners had made their position there untenable. In 1346, the Mongols of the Golden Horde besieged the Genoese colony at Caffa on the Black Sea. Apart from crippling Genoese commerce in the Black Sea, this siege is memorable chiefly because during it the Black Death was passed from the Mongol army (which had inadvertently brought it from the Gobi Desert, where the disease was endemic) to the Genoese defenders, who returned with it to western Europe, where it proceeded to kill approximately one-third of the entire European population.

The "window of opportunity" that made Marco Polo's travels possible was thus relatively short. By the middle of the fourteenth century, hostilities between the various parts of the Mongol empire were already making travel along the Silk Road perilous. After 1368, when the Mongol (Yuan) dynasty was overthrown, Westerners were excluded from China altogether, and Mongols were restricted to cavalry service in the Ming imperial armies. The overland trade routes from China to the Black Sea continued to operate; Europeans, however, were no longer able to travel along them. But the new, more integrated commercial world the Mongols created had a lasting impact upon Europe, despite the relatively short time during which Europeans themselves were able to participate directly in it. European memories of the Far East would be preserved, and the dream of reestablishing direct connections between Europe and China would survive to influence a new round of European commercial and imperial expansion from the late fifteenth century onward.

THE RISE OF THE OTTOMAN EMPIRE

Why were slaves important to Ottoman society?

Like the Mongols, the Ottoman Turks were initially a nomadic people whose economy continued to depend on raiding even after they had conquered an extensive empire. The peoples who would become the Ottomans were already established in northwestern Anatolia when the Mongols arrived, and were already at least nominally Muslims. But unlike the established Muslim powers in the region, whom the Mongols destroyed, the Ottoman Turks were among the principal beneficiaries of the Mongol conquest. By toppling the Seljuk sultanate and the Abbasid caliphate of Baghdad, the Mongols eliminated the two traditional authorities that had previously kept Turkish border chieftains like the Ottomans in check. Now the Ottomans were free to raid along their soft frontiers with Byzantium unhindered. At the same time, however, they remained far enough away from the centers of Mongol authority to avoid being destroyed themselves.

THE CONQUEST OF CONSTANTINOPLE

By the end of the thirteenth century, the Ottoman dynasty had established itself as the leading family among the Anatolian border lords. By the mid-fourteenth century, it had solidified its preeminence by capturing a number of important cities. These successes brought the Ottomans to the attention of the Byzantine emperor, who in 1345 hired a contingent of Ottomans as mercenaries. Thus introduced into Europe, the Ottomans quickly made themselves at home. By 1370, they had extended their control all the way to the Danube. In 1389 Ottoman forces defeated the powerful Serbian empire at the battle of Kosovo, enabling them to consolidate their control over Greece, Bulgaria, and the Balkans.

In 1396 the Ottomans attacked Constantinople, but were forced to withdraw in order to repel a Western crusading force that had been sent against them. In 1402, they attacked Constantinople again, but once more they were forced to withdraw, this time to confront Timur the Lame's invasion of Anatolia. Ottoman pressure on Constantinople continued after Timur's death in 1405, producing a steady stream of refugees fleeing to Italy, who brought with them the surviving masterworks of classical Greek literature. But it was not until 1451 that a new sultan, Mehmet II, turned his full attention to the conquest of the imperial city. In 1453, after a brilliantly executed siege, Mehmet succeeded in breaching the city's walls. The Byzantine emperor was killed in the assault, and the city itself was thoroughly plundered. The Ottomans then settled down to rule their new imperial capital in a style reminiscent of their Byzantine predecessors.

The Ottoman conquest of Constantinople was an enormous psychological shock to Christian Europe, but its economic impact on western Europe was minor. Ot-

Sultan Mehmet II, "The Conqueror" (1451–1481), by the Ottoman artist Siblizade Ahmed. The sultan's pose and handkerchief are Central Asian conventions in portraiture, but the subdued color and three-quarter profile show the influence of Italian Renaissance portraits. The sultan wears the white turban of a scholar, but also wears the thumb ring of an archer, neatly reflecting his combination of scholarly and military attainments.

between Europe and India, it was their efforts to exclude Muslims from the Indian Ocean spice trade that helped spur the Ottoman conquests of Syria, Egypt, and the Balkans during the 1520s and 1530s. To be sure, these Ottoman conquests had other motives also, including the desire to control the Egyptian grain trade. But by eliminating the merchants who had traditionally dominated the overland spice trade through Beirut and Alexandria, the Ottomans may also have hoped to redirect this trade through Constantinople, and then up the Danube into western Europe.

The effects of the Ottoman conquest of Constantinople on western Europe were modest. Upon the Ottomans themselves, however, their conquest was transformative. Vast new wealth poured into Ottoman society, which the Ottomans further increased by carefully tending to the industrial and commercial interests of their new capital city. Trade routes were redirected to feed the capital, and the Ottomans became a naval power in the eastern Mediterranean and the Black Sea. As a result, Constantinople's population grew from less than one hundred thousand in 1453 to more than five hundred thousand in 1600, making it the largest city in the world outside China.

WAR, SLAVERY, AND SOCIAL ADVANCEMENT

Despite the Ottomans' careful attention to commerce, their empire and its capital city could only be sustained through continuous raiding and conquest. Until the end of the sixteenth century, the Ottoman empire was therefore on an almost constant war footing. The result, however, was a kind of vicious cycle. To continue its conquests, the size of the Ottoman

toman control over the former Byzantine empire did reduce European access to the Black Sea, but the bulk of the Far Eastern luxury trade with Europe had never passed through the Black Sea ports in the first place. Europeans got most of their spices and silks through Venice, which imported them from Alexandria and Beirut. These two cities did not fall to the Ottomans until the 1520s. In no sense, therefore, can the Ottomans be seen as the spur that propelled Portuguese efforts during the late fifteenth century to establish a direct sea route between Europe, India, and the Spice Islands of the Far East. If anything, the opposite is the case. After the Portuguese established a direct sea route

CHRONOLOGY

RISE OF THE OTTOMAN EMPIRE, 1300–1571

Ottomans become leading Anatolian family	1300
Byzantine emperor hires Ottoman mercenaries	1345
Ottomans enter Europe	1350s
Ottomans defeat Serbian empire	1389
Ottomans conquer Constantinople	1453
Ottomans conquer Syria, Egypt, Balkans	1520s
Battle of Lepanto	1571

The Turkish Slave Girl, by the early sixteenth-century Italian artist Parmigianino. This portrait illustrates the expensive clothes and jewels worn by some Ottoman slaves. It also reflects the sensuality and exoticism that many Europeans saw in the Ottoman Turks.

army and administration grew exponentially. But this growth drew more and more manpower from the empire. Because the Ottoman army and administration were largely composed of slaves, the demand for more soldiers and administrators could best be met through further conquests that would capture yet more slaves. Further conquests, however, required a still larger army and an even more extensive bureaucracy; and so the cycle continued.

Slaves were the backbone of the Ottoman army and administration, as they had for long been in Mamluk Egypt also. But slaves were also critical to the lives of the Ottoman upper class. One of the important measures of status in Ottoman society was the number of slaves in one's household. After 1453, new wealth permitted some Ottoman notables to maintain households in which thousands of slaves attended to their masters' whims. In the sixteenth century, the sultan's household alone numbered more than twenty thousand slave attendants, not including his bodyguard and his elite infantry units, both of which were also composed of slaves.

The result was an almost insatiable demand for slaves, especially in Constantinople itself. Many of these slaves were captured in war. Many others were taken from Poland and Ukraine in raids by Crimean slave merchants, who then shipped their captives to the slave markets of Constantinople. But slaves were also recruited (some willingly, some by coercion) from rural areas of the Ottoman empire itself. Because the vast majority of Ottoman slaves were household servants and administrators rather than laborers, some people willingly accepted enslavement, believing that they would be better off as slaves in Constantinople than as impoverished peasants in the countryside. In the Balkans especially, many people were enslaved as children, handed over by their families to pay the infamous "child tax" the Ottomans imposed on rural areas too poor to pay a monetary tribute. Although unquestionably a wrenching experience for families, this practice did open up opportunities for social advancement. Special academies were created at Constantinople to train the most able of these enslaved children to act as administrators and soldiers, and some rose to become powerful figures in the Ottoman empire. Slavery therefore carried relatively little social stigma. Even the sultan himself was most often the son of an enslaved woman.

Because Muslims were not permitted to enslave other Muslims, the vast majority of Ottoman slaves were Christians (although many converted to Islam later in life). But because so many of the elite positions within Ottoman government were held by slaves, the paradoxical result of this reliance on slave administrators was that Muslims, including Turks, were effectively excluded from the main avenues of social and political advancement in Ottoman society. Nor was Ottoman society characterized by a powerful, hereditary nobility of the sort that dominated contemporary European society. As a result, power in the fifteenth- and sixteenth-century Ottoman empire was remarkably, perhaps even uniquely, open to men of ability and talent, provided that such men were slaves and so were not Muslims by birth.

Nor was this pattern of Muslim exclusion limited to government and the army. Commerce and business also remained largely in the hands of non-Muslims, most frequently Greeks, Syrians, and Jews. Jews in particular found in the Ottoman empire a

> Slaves were the backbone of the Ottoman army and administration.

OTTOMAN JANISSARIES

The following account is from a memoir written by a Christian Serb who was captured as a youth by Sultan Mehmet II the Conqueror, converted to Islam, and who then served eight years in the Ottoman janissary corps. In 1463, however, the fortress he was defending for the Sultan was captured by the Hungarians, and the author thereupon returned to Christianity.

Whenever the Turks invade foreign lands and capture their people an imperial scribe follows immediately behind them, and whatever boys there are, he takes them all into the Janissaries and gives five gold pieces for each one and sends them across the sea [to Anatolia]. There are about two thousand of these boys. If, however, the number of them from enemy peoples does not suffice, then he takes from the Christians in every village in his land who have boys, having established what is the most every village can give so that the quota will always be full. And the boys whom he takes in his own land are called *cilik*. Each one of them can leave his property to whomever he wants after his death. And those whom he takes among the enemies are called *pendik*. These latter after their deaths can leave nothing; rather, it goes to the emperor, except that if someone comports himself well and is so deserving that he be freed, he may leave it to whomever he wants. And on the boys who are across the sea the emperor spends nothing; rather, those to whom they are entrusted must maintain them and send them where he orders. Then they take those who are suited for it on ships and there they study and train to skirmish in battle. There the emperor already provides for them and gives them a wage. From there he chooses for his own court those who are trained and then raises their wages.

Konstantin Mihailovic, *Memoirs of a Janissary*, trans. Benjamin Stolz. Michigan Slavic Translations no. 3. (Ann Arbor: Michigan Slavic Publications, 1975), pp. 157–159.

---

welcome refuge from the persecutions and expulsions that had characterized Jewish life in late medieval Europe. After their 1492 expulsion from Spain, more than a hundred thousand Spanish (Sephardic) Jews ultimately immigrated into the Ottoman empire.

RELIGIOUS CONFLICTS

The Ottomans themselves were relentlessly orthodox Sunni Muslims, who lent staunch support to the religious and legal pronouncements of the Islamic scholarly schools. Ottoman emphasis on their religious orthodoxy began in the fourteenth century and increased steadily thereafter. In 1516, the Ottomans captured the cities of Medina and Mecca, thus becoming the defenders of the holy sites. Soon after, they captured Jerusalem and Cairo, putting an end to the Mamluk sultanate of Egypt. In 1538 the Ottoman ruler formally adopted the title of caliph, thereby declaring himself to be the legitimate successor of the Prophet Muhammad.

In keeping with Sunni traditions, the Ottomans were also religiously tolerant toward non-Muslims, especially during the fifteenth and sixteenth centuries.

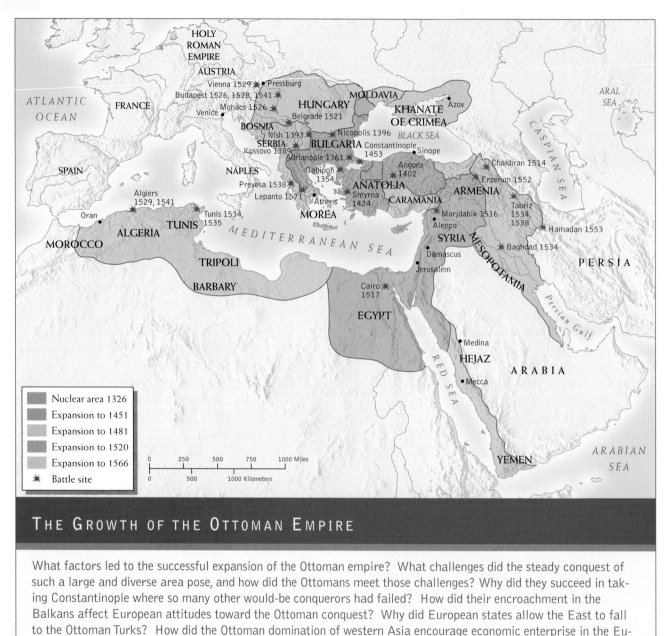

THE GROWTH OF THE OTTOMAN EMPIRE

What factors led to the successful expansion of the Ottoman empire? What challenges did the steady conquest of such a large and diverse area pose, and how did the Ottomans meet those challenges? Why did they succeed in taking Constantinople where so many other would-be conquerors had failed? How did their encroachment in the Balkans affect European attitudes toward the Ottoman conquest? Why did European states allow the East to fall to the Ottoman Turks? How did the Ottoman domination of western Asia encourage economic enterprise in the European states?

They organized the major religious groups of their empire into legally recognized units known as *millets*, permitting them considerable rights of religious self-government. After 1453, however, the Ottomans were particularly careful to protect and promote the authority of the Greek Orthodox patriarch of Constantinople over the Orthodox Christians of their empire. As a result, the Ottomans enjoyed staunch support from their Orthodox Christian subjects during their sixteenth century wars with the Latin Christians of western Europe. Despite the religious diversity of their empire, the Ottomans' principal religious conflicts were therefore not with their own subjects, but with the Shi'ite Muslim dynasty that ruled neighboring Persia. Time and again during the sixteenth century, Ottoman expeditions against western Europe had to be abandoned when hostilities erupted with the Persians.

THE OTTOMANS AND EUROPE

During the sixteenth century, the Habsburg rulers of Spain, Germany, and Austria were similarly distracted by their own conflicts with the Catholic kings of France (with whom the Ottomans made an alliance) and with the Protestant princes of Germany, the Netherlands, and England. As a result, the contest between the Ottoman empire and the Western powers never really lived up to the rhetoric of "holy war" that both sides employed in their propaganda. In 1396, a Western crusader army was annihilated by the Ottomans at the battle of Nicopolis. In the sixteenth and seventeenth centuries, Ottoman armies several times besieged Vienna. But despite these dramatic moments, such conflicts as there were between the Ottomans and the rulers of western Europe were fought out mainly through pirate raids and naval battles in the Mediterranean. The main result of this contest was thus a steady escalation in the scale and cost of navies. In 1571, when a combined Habsburg and Venetian force defeated the Ottoman fleet at Lepanto, more than four hundred ships took part, with both sides deploying naval forces ten times larger than they had possessed half a century before.

Although undeniably a victory for the Habsburgs and their Venetian allies, the battle of Lepanto was far less decisive than is often suggested. The Ottoman

Ottoman Orthodoxy. This Ottoman genealogical chart shows the descent of Sultan Mehmet III (1595–1603) from the Prophet Muhammad (shown veiled).

The Battle of Lepanto. The victory of Spain, Venice, and the papacy over the Ottomans at Lepanto in 1571 became a favorite subject for propagandistic paintings by European artists.

navy was speedily rebuilt; by no means did Lepanto put an end to Ottoman influence over the eastern Mediterranean Sea. Nevertheless, after 1571 both Ottoman and Habsburg interests shifted away from their conflict with each other. The Ottomans embarked upon a long and costly war with Persia, while the Spanish Habsburgs turned their attention toward their new empire in the Atlantic. By the mid-seventeenth century, when a new round of Ottoman-European conflicts began, the strength of the Ottoman empire had been sapped by a series of indolent, pleasure-loving sultans and by the tensions that arose within the Ottoman empire itself as it ceased to expand. The Ottoman empire would last until 1918; but from the mid-seventeenth century on, it was no longer a serious rival to the global hegemony the European powers were beginning to achieve.

MEDITERRANEAN COLONIALISM

How were the Portuguese able to control Indian Ocean trade?

During the fifteenth century, European colonial and commercial ambitions came to be focused more and more on the western Mediterranean and the Atlantic world. Although historians have sometimes argued the contrary, this reorientation was not a result of the rising power of the Ottoman empire. Instead, this westward orientation was the product of two related developments: the growing importance to late medieval Europe of the African gold trade; and the growth of European colonial empires in the western Mediterranean Sea.

SILVER SHORTAGES AND THE SEARCH FOR AFRICAN GOLD

Europeans had been trading for African gold for centuries, mainly through Muslim middlemen who transported this precious metal in caravans from the Niger River area where it was produced to the North African ports of Algiers and Tunis. From the thirteenth century on, Catalan and Genoese merchants both maintained merchant colonies in Tunis, where they traded woolen cloth for North African grain and sub-Saharan gold.

What accelerated the late medieval demand for gold, however, was a serious silver shortage that affected the entire European economy during the fourteenth and fifteenth centuries. Silver production in Europe fell markedly during the 1340s and remained at a low level thereafter, as Europeans reached the limits of their technological capacity to extract silver ore from deep mines. The resulting shortage of coin had a seriously deflationary effect on the European economy. It was not until the 1470s that new mining techniques, combined with discoveries of new silver deposits, began to alleviate this shortage.

This shortfall in silver production was compounded during the fifteenth century by a serious balance-of-payments problem: more European silver was flowing east in the spice trade than could be replaced using existing mining techniques on known silver deposits. Gold currencies represented an obvious alternative for large transactions, and from the thirteenth century on European rulers with access to gold were minting gold coins. But Europe itself had few natural gold reserves. To maintain and expand these gold coinages, new and larger supplies of gold were needed. The most obvious source for this gold was Africa.

MEDITERRANEAN EMPIRES: CATALUNYA, VENICE, AND GENOA

The growing European interest in the African gold trade coincided with the creation of sea-based Mediterranean empires by the Catalans, the Venetians, and the Genoese. During the thirteenth century, the Catalans conquered and colonized a series of western Mediterranean islands, including Majorca, Ibiza, Minorca, Sicily, and Sardinia. Except in Sicily, the pattern of Catalan exploitation was largely the same on all these islands: expropriation or extermination of the native (usually Muslim) population; economic concessions to attract new settlers; and a heavy reliance on slave labor to produce foodstuffs and raw materials for export.

Unlike Catalan colonization efforts, which were mainly carried on by private individuals operating under a crown charter, Venetian colonization was directed by the city's rulers, and was focused mainly on the eastern Mediterranean, where the Venetians dominated the trade in spices and silks. The Genoese, by contrast, had more extensive interests in the western Mediterranean world, where their trade focused on bulk goods such as cloth, hides, grain, timber, and sugar. Genoese colonies tended to be more informal and family based than Venetian or Catalan colonies, constituting more of a network than an extension of a sovereign empire. They were also more closely integrated into the native societies of North Africa, Spain, and the Black Sea than were the Venetian or the Catalan colonies. In particular, the Genoese pioneered the production of sugar and sweet "Madeira" wines in the western Mediterranean, first in Sicily and later in the Atlantic islands off the west coast of Africa. To transport such bulky goods, the Genoese moved away from the oared galleys favored by the Venetians toward larger, fuller-bodied sailing ships that could carry greater volumes of cargo. With further modifications to accommodate the rougher sailing conditions of the Atlantic Ocean, these were the ships that would carry sixteenth-century Europeans around the globe.

FROM THE MEDITERRANEAN TO THE ATLANTIC

Until the late thirteenth century, European maritime commerce had been divided between a Mediterranean and a north Atlantic world. Starting around 1270, however, Italian merchants began to sail through the Strait of Gibraltar and on to the wool-producing regions of England and the Netherlands. This was the essential first step in the extension of Mediterranean patterns of commerce and colonization into the Atlantic Ocean. The second step was the discovery (or possibly rediscovery), during the fourteenth century, of the Atlantic island chains known as the Canaries and the Azores by Genoese sailors. Efforts to colonize the Canary Islands, and to convert and enslave their inhabitants, began almost immediately. But an effective conquest of the Canary Islands did not really begin until the fifteenth century, when it was undertaken by Portugal and completed by Castile. The Canaries, in turn, became the base from which further Portuguese voyages down the west coast of Africa proceeded. They were also the "jumping-off point" from which Christopher Columbus would sail westward across the Atlantic Ocean in hopes of reaching Asia.

Italian merchants sailing through the Strait of Gibraltar was the essential first step in the extension of Mediterranean patterns of commerce and colonization into the Atlantic Ocean.

THE TECHNOLOGY OF SHIPS AND NAVIGATION

The European empires of the fifteenth and sixteenth centuries rested on a mastery of the oceans. This mastery was partly the product of long experience in Atlantic waters. For example, the Portuguese caravel—the workhorse ship of the fifteenth-century voyages to Africa—was based on ship and sail designs that had been in use among Portuguese fishermen since the thirteenth century. Starting in the 1440s, however, Portuguese shipwrights began building larger caravels of about fifty tons displacement, with two masts each carrying a triangular (lateen) sail. Such ships were capable of sailing against the wind much more effectively than were the older, square-rigged vessels. They also required much smaller crews than did the multioared galleys that were still commonly used in the Mediterranean. By the end of the fifteenth century, even larger caravels of around two hundred tons were being constructed, with a third mast and a combination of square and lateen rigging. Columbus's *Niña* was of this design, having been refitted with two square sails in the Canary Islands to enable it to sail more efficiently before the wind during the Atlantic crossing.

Europeans were also making significant advances in navigation during the fifteenth and sixteenth centuries. Quadrants, which calculated latitude in the Northern Hemisphere by the height above the horizon of the North Star, were in widespread use by the 1450s. As sailors approached the equator, however, the quadrant became less and less useful, and they were forced instead to make use of astrolabes, which reckoned latitude by the height of the sun. Like quadrants, astrolabes had been known in western Europe for centuries. In the twelfth century, Abelard and Heloise had even named their son Astrolabe. But it was not until the 1480s that the astrolabe became a really useful instrument for seaborne navigation, with the preparation of standard tables sponsored by the Portuguese crown. Compasses too were also coming into more widespread use during the fifteenth century. Longitude, however, remained impossible to calculate accurately until the eighteenth century, when the invention of the marine chronometer finally made it possible to keep accurate time at sea. In the sixteenth century, Europeans sailing

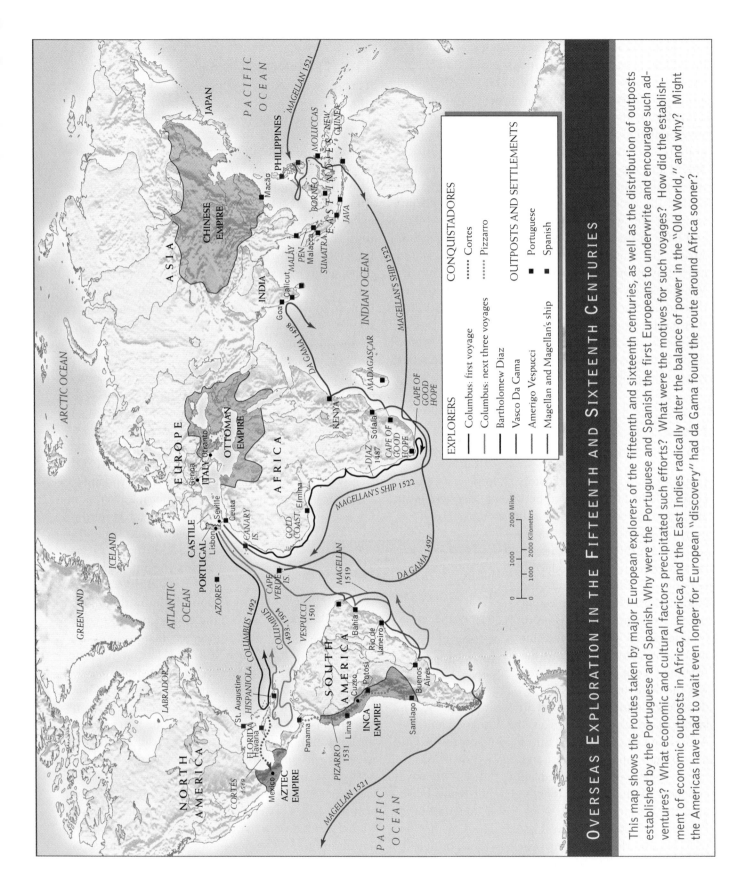

OVERSEAS EXPLORATION IN THE FIFTEENTH AND SIXTEENTH CENTURIES

This map shows the routes taken by major European explorers of the fifteenth and sixteenth centuries, as well as the distribution of outposts established by the Portuguese and Spanish. Why were the Portuguese and Spanish the first Europeans to underwrite and encourage such adventures? What economic and cultural factors precipitated such efforts? What were the motives for such voyages? How did the establishment of economic outposts in Africa, America, and the East Indies radically alter the balance of power in the "Old World," and why? Might the Americas have had to wait even longer for European "discovery" had da Gama found the route around Africa sooner?

east or west across the oceans generally had to rely on their skill at dead reckoning to determine where they were on the globe.

European sailors also benefited from a new interest in maps and navigational charts. Especially important to Atlantic sailors were books known as *rutters* or *routiers.* These contained detailed sailing instructions and descriptions of the coastal landmarks a pilot could expect to encounter on route to a variety of destinations. Mediterranean sailors had had similar books, known as *portolani*, since at least the fourteenth century. In the fifteenth century, however, this tradition was extended to the Atlantic Ocean; by the end of the sixteenth century, rutters spanned the globe.

PORTUGAL, AFRICA, AND THE SEA ROUTE TO INDIA

It was among the Portuguese that these dual interests—in the African gold trade and in Atlantic colonization—first came together. In 1415, a Portuguese expedition captured the north African port of Ceuta. During the 1420s the Portuguese colonized both the island of Madeira and the Canary Islands. During the 1430s, they extended these colonization efforts to the Azores. By the 1440s they had reached the Cape Verde Islands. In 1444 Portuguese explorers first landed in the area between the Senegal and the Gambia river mouths on the African mainland, where they began to collect cargoes of gold and slaves for export back to Portugal. By the 1470s, Portuguese sailors had rounded the African "bulge" and were exploring the Gulf of Guinea. In 1483 they reached the mouth of the Congo River. In 1488 the Portuguese captain Bartholomeu Dias rounded the southern tip of Africa. Blown around it accidentally by a gale, Dias named the point "Cape of Storms," but the king of Portugal took a more optimistic view of Dias's achievement. He renamed it the Cape of Good Hope and began planning a naval expedition to India. Finally in 1497–1498, Vasco de Gama rounded the cape, and then—with the help of a Muslim navigator named Ibn Majid, crossed the Indian Ocean to Calicutt on the southwestern coast of India, opening up for the first time a direct sea route between Europe and the Far Eastern spice trade. Although de Gama lost half his fleet and one-third of his men on his two-year voyage, his cargo of spices was so valuable that his losses were deemed

insignificant. His heroism became legendary, and his story became the basis for the Portuguese national epic, the *Lusiads.*

Now master of the quickest route to riches in the world, the king of Portugal swiftly capitalized on de Gama's accomplishment. After 1500, Portuguese trading fleets sailed regularly to India. In 1509, the Portuguese defeated an Ottoman fleet and then blockaded the mouth of the Red Sea, attempting to cut off one of the traditional routes by which spices had traveled to Alexandria and Beirut. By 1510 Portuguese military forces had established a series of forts along the western Indian coastline, including their headquarters at Goa. In 1511 Portuguese ships seized Malacca, a center of the spice trade on the Malay peninsula. By 1515 they had reached the Spice Islands and the coast of China. So completely did the Portuguese now dominate the spice trade that by the 1520s even the Venetians were forced to buy their pepper in the Portuguese capital of Lisbon.

ARTILLERY AND EMPIRE

Larger, more maneuverable ships and improved navigational aids made it possible for the Portuguese and other European mariners to reach Africa, Asia, and the Americas by sea. But fundamentally, these sixteenth-century European commercial empires were a military achievement. As such, they reflected what Europeans had learned in their wars against each other during the fourteenth and fifteenth centuries. Perhaps the most critical military advance of the late Middle Ages was the increasing sophistication of artillery, a devel-

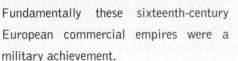

Fundamentally these sixteenth-century European commercial empires were a military achievement.

opment made possible not only by gunpowder, but also by improved metallurgical techniques for casting cannon barrels. By the middle of the fifteenth century, the use of artillery pieces had rendered the stone walls of medieval castles and towns obsolete, a fact brought home in 1453 by the successful French siege of Bordeaux (which brought to an end the Hundred Years' War), and by the Ottoman siege of Constantinople (which brought to an end the Byzantine empire).

One of the reasons the new ship designs (first caravels, and later the even larger galleons) were so important was that their larger size made it possible to mount more effective artillery pieces on them. Increasingly during the sixteenth century, European naval vessels were conceived as floating artillery platforms, with scores of guns mounted in fixed positions along their sides and swivel guns mounted fore and aft. These guns were vastly expensive, as were the ships that carried them; but for those rulers who could afford to possess them, such ships made it possible to project military power around the world. In 1498, Vasco de Gama became the first Portuguese captain to sail into the Indian Ocean; but the Portuguese did not gain control of that ocean until 1509, when they defeated a combined Ottoman and Indian naval force at the battle of Div. Portuguese trading outposts in Africa and Asia were fortifications, built to guard not only against the attacks of native peoples, but also to ward off assaults from other Europeans. Without this essential military component, the European maritime empires of the sixteenth century would not have existed.

> Increasingly, European naval vessels were conceived as floating artillery platforms, with scores of guns mounted along the sides.

PRINCE HENRY THE NAVIGATOR

Because we know that these fifteenth-century Portuguese expeditions down the African coast did ultimately open up a sea route to India and the Far East, it is tempting to presume that this was their goal from the beginning. It was not. The traditional narrative of these events, which presents exploration as their mission, India as their goal, and Prince Henry the Navigator as the guiding genius behind them, no longer commands the confidence of most historians. Only from the 1480s did India clearly become the goal toward which these voyages were directed. Prior to the 1480s, Portuguese involvement in Africa was driven instead by much more traditional goals: crusading ambitions against the Muslims of North Africa; the desire to establish direct links with the sources of African gold production south of the Sahara Desert; the desire to colonize the Atlantic islands; the burgeoning market for slaves in Europe and in the Ottoman empire; and the hope that somewhere in Africa they might find the legendary Prester John, a mythical Christian king whom Europeans believed would be their ally against the Muslims if only they could locate him. In the twelfth and thirteenth centuries, they had sought him in Asia. But from the 1340s on, he was believed to reside in Ethiopia, an expansive term that to most Europeans seems to have meant "somewhere in Africa."

Nor does Prince Henry (whose title, "the Navigator," was not assigned to him until the seventeenth century) seem so central a figure in Portuguese exploration as he was once thought to be. In fact, he directed only eight of the thirty-five Portuguese voyages to Africa between 1419 and his death in 1460; and the stories about his gathering a school of navigators and cartographers on the Atlantic coast of Portugal, about his role in designing improved ships and navigational instruments, and about his encouragement for scientific learning generally, have all been shown to be false. Henry did play an important role in organizing Portuguese

A Turkish Brass Cannon of the Fifteenth Century. This eighteen-ton gun fired balls twenty-five inches in diameter.

THE LEGEND OF PRESTER JOHN

THE TRAVELS OF SIR JOHN MANDEVILLE *is an almost entirely fictional account of the wonders of the East, written by an English expatriate during the first half of the fourteenth century. Despite the fact that "Mandeville" (almost certainly a pseudonym) knew almost nothing about the lands he describes, his book became a primary source for European ideas about South and East Asia. Although Mandeville locates the legendary Prester John in Persia, India, or China (his geography is fuzzy, to say the least), by the fifteenth century Europeans were searching for Prester John in Africa.*

This emperor Prester John has great lands and has many noble cities and good towns in his realm and many great, large islands. For all the country of India is separated into islands by the great floods that come from Paradise, that divide the land into many parts. And also in the sea he has many islands. . . .

This Prester John has under him many kings and many islands and many varied people of various conditions. And this land is full good and rich, but not so rich as is the land of the Great Khan. For the merchants do not come there so commonly to buy merchandise as they do in the land of the Great Khan, for it is too far to travel to. . . .

[Mandeville then goes on to describe the difficulties of reaching Prester John's lands by sea.]

This emperor Prester John always takes as his wife the daughter of the Great Khan, and the Great Khan in the same way takes to wife the daughter of Prester John. For these two are the greatest lords under the heavens.

In the land of Prester John there are many diverse things, and many precious stones so great and so large that men make them into vessels such as platters, dishes, and cups. And there are many other marvels there that it would be too cumbrous and too long to put into the writing of books. But of the principal islands and of his estate and of his law I shall tell you some part.

This emperor Prester John is Christian and a great part of his country is Christian also, although they do not hold to all the articles of our faith as we do. . . .

And he has under him 72 provinces, and in every province there is a king. And these kings have kings under them, and all are tributaries to Prester John.

And he has in his lordships many great marvels. For in his country is the sea that men call the Gravelly Sea, that is all gravel and sand without any drop of water. And it ebbs and flows in great waves as other seas do, and it is never still. . . . And a three-day journey from that sea there are great mountains out of which flows a great flood that comes out of Paradise. And it is full of precious stones without any drop of water. . . .

He dwells usually in the city of Susa [in Persia]. And there is his principal palace, which is so rich and so noble that no one will believe the report unless he has seen it. And above the chief tower of the palace there are two round pommels of gold and in each of them are two great, large rubies that shine full brightly upon the night. And the principal gates of his palace are of a precious stone that men call sardonyxes [a type of onyx], and the frames and the bars are made of ivory. And the windows of the halls and chambers are of crystal. And the tables upon which men eat, some are made of emeralds, some of amethyst, and some of gold full of precious stones. And the legs that hold up the tables are made of the same precious stones. . . .

Mandeville's Travels, edited by M. C. Seymour. (Oxford: Clarendon Press, 1967), pp. 195–199 (language modernized from Middle English by R. C. Stacey).

Prince Henry the Navigator, by a fifteenth-century Portuguese painter. This portrait is taken from a group portrait of the Portuguese royal family. Although thought to depict Henry, the identification is not certain.

The Tower of Belem. The Tower of Belem, a fifteenth-century fort, stands at the beach where Vasco da Gama departed in 1497 to sail beyond the Cape of Good Hope to India.

colonization of Madeira, the Canary Islands and the Azores, and he also pioneered the Portuguese slave trade, first on the Canaries (whose Stone-Age population was almost entirely enslaved) and then along the Sene-Gambian coast of Africa. His main goal, however, was to outflank the cross-Saharan African gold trade by intercepting this trade at its source. To this end, he built a series of forts along the African coastline, most famously at Arguim, to which he hoped to divert the cross-Saharan gold caravans. This was also his main goal in colonizing the Canary Islands, which he saw as a staging ground for expeditions into the African interior. There is no evidence that he ever dreamed of reaching India by sailing around Africa. Indeed, quite the opposite seems to be the case. Portuguese progress toward the Cape of Good Hope proceeded much more rapidly in the years after Henry's death than it had during his lifetime. Henry himself was a crusader against Islam; a prince in search

of a kingdom; a lord seeking resources to support his followers; and an aspiring merchant who hoped to make a killing in the gold trade but found his main profits in slaving. He was, in all these respects, a man of his time, which is to say, of the fifteenth century. He was not the architect, or even the visionary, of Portugal's sixteenth-century maritime empire.

ATLANTIC COLONIZATION AND THE GROWTH OF SLAVERY

The profits Prince Henry had hoped would come from the African gold trade did not materialize during his lifetime. He therefore had to make his expeditions pay by other means. One of those means was the slave trade. Although slavery in most of western Europe had effectively disappeared by the early twelfth century, slavery continued in Iberia (and to a lesser extent in

WHAT WAS THE IMPACT OF NEW WORLD SILVER ON THE EUROPEAN ECONOMY?

EUROPE ENCOUNTERS A NEW WORLD   445

Italy) throughout the high and late Middle Ages. Until the mid-fifteenth century, however, slavery on the Iberian mainland and in Italy remained very small in scale. The major Mediterranean slave markets of the fourteenth and early fifteenth centuries lay in Muslim lands, and especially in the Ottoman empire. Relatively few of the slaves who passed through these markets were Africans. Most were European Christians, predominantly Poles, Ukrainians, Greeks, and Bulgarians. Thus the patterns of slavery were not racialized in the late medieval Mediterranean world, except insofar as "primitive" peoples such as the natives of the Canary Islands or of Sardinia were more likely to be regarded as targets for enslavement.

From the mid-fifteenth century on, however, Lisbon began to emerge as a significant market for enslaved Africans. Something on the order of fifteen to twenty thousand Africans were sold in Lisbon during Prince Henry's lifetime, most of them between 1440 and 1460. In the half century after his death, the numbers grew, amounting to perhaps one hundred fifty thousand African slaves imported into Europe by 1505. For the most part, these slaves were regarded as status symbols—one reason they were so frequently depicted in paintings of the period. Even in the Atlantic colonies—Madeira, the Canaries, and the Azores—the land was worked mainly by European settlers and sharecroppers. Slave labor, if it was employed at all, was generally used only in sugar mills. This meant that on the Azores, which remained a wheat-producing colony, slavery found no real foothold. On Madeira and the Canaries, where sugar became the predominant cash crop during the last quarter of the fifteenth century, some slaves were introduced. But even sugar production did not lead to the widespread introduction of slavery on these islands.

A new style of slave-based sugar plantations began to emerge in Portugal's Atlantic colonies only in the 1460s, starting on the Cape Verde Islands and then extending southward into the Gulf of Guinea. These islands were not populated when the Portuguese began to settle them, and their climate was such as to discourage any large number of Europeans from settling there. They were ideally located, however, to purchase laborers from the slave traders along the nearby West African coast. No comparable system of large-scale, slave-based plantation production had been seen in Europe or Africa since the Roman period. But it was this model of sugar plantations staffed by enslaved Africans that would be exported to the Caribbean islands of the Americas by their Spanish conquerors, with incalculable consequences for Africa, the Americas, and Europe.

EUROPE ENCOUNTERS A NEW WORLD

What was the impact of New World silver on the European economy?

The decision by Spain's rulers to underwrite Columbus's famous voyage was an outgrowth of the progress of these Portuguese ventures. After 1488, when Dias successfully rounded the Cape of Good Hope, it was clear that Portugal would soon dominate the sea lanes leading eastward to Asia. The only alternative for Portugal's Spanish rivals was to finance someone bold enough to try to reach Asia by sailing west. The popular image of Christopher Columbus (1451–1506) as a visionary who struggled to convince hardened ignoramuses that the world was round does not bear up under scrutiny. In fact, the sphericity of the earth had been widely known throughout European society since at least the twelfth century. What made Columbus's scheme seem plausible to King Ferdinand and Queen Isabella was, first, the discovery and colonization of the Canary Islands and the Azores, which had reinforced a view of the Atlantic as being dotted with islands all the way to Japan; and second, the Genoese mariner's own astonishing miscalculation of the actual size of the earth, which convinced him that he could reach Japan and China in about a month's clear sailing westward from the Canary Islands. America was actually rediscovered by Europeans at the end of the fifteenth century as the result of a colossal error in reckoning. Columbus himself never realized his mistake. When he reached the Bahamas and the island of Hispaniola in 1492 after only a month's sailing, he returned to Spain to report that he had indeed reached the outer islands of Asia.

THE DISCOVERY OF A NEW WORLD

Columbus was not the first European to set foot on the American continents. Viking sailors had reached and briefly settled present-day Newfoundland, Labrador, and perhaps New England around the year 1000. But knowledge of these Viking landings had been forgotten or ignored throughout Europe for hundreds of years. In the fifteenth century, even the Scandinavian settlements in Greenland had been abandoned. It would be perverse, therefore, to deny Columbus credit for his accomplishments. Although Columbus himself

The Creator as Architect. This scene from a late-thirteenth-century French Bible shows God working on Creation with a draftsman's compass. Note that the artist understood clearly that the world was round.

The realization that this was indeed a new world was at first a disappointment to the Spanish, for with a major land mass lying between Europe and Asia, Spain could not hope to beat Portugal in the race for Asian spices. Any remaining doubt that not one, but two vast oceans separated Europe from Asia was completely removed in 1513, when Vasco Núñez de Balboa first viewed the Pacific Ocean from the Isthmus of Panama. Not entirely admitting defeat, Ferdinand and Isabella's grandson, the Holy Roman emperor Charles V, accepted Ferdinand Magellan's offer in 1519 to see whether a route to Asia could be found by sailing around South America. But Magellan's voyage demonstrated beyond question that the globe was simply too large for any such plan to be feasible. Of the five ships that left Spain under Magellan's command, only one returned three years later, having been forced to circumnavigate the globe. Out of a crew of 265 sailors, only eighteen survived. Most had died from scurvy or starvation; Magellan himself had been killed in a skirmish with native peoples in the Philippines. This fiasco brought to an end all hope of discovering an easy "southwest passage" to Asia. The dream of a "northwest passage" survived, however, and continued to motivate European explorers of North America until the nineteenth century.

never accepted the reality of what he had discovered, those who followed him soon did, and busily set out to exploit this new world.

Understandably, Columbus brought back no Asian spices from his voyages. He did, however, return with some small samples of gold and a few indigenous people, whose existence gave promise of entire tribes that might be "saved" (by conversion to Christianity) and enslaved by Europeans. This provided sufficient incentive for the Spanish monarchs to finance three more expeditions by Columbus and many more by others. Soon the mainland was discovered as well as further islands, and the conclusion quickly became inescapable that a new world had indeed been found. Awareness of this new world was most widely publicized by the Italian geographer Amerigo Vespucci. Though he may not have deserved this honor, the continents of the Western Hemisphere became known thereafter as "America" after Vespucci's first name.

A Spaniard Kicking an Indian. As this sixteenth-century drawing makes clear, Spanish treatment of the indigenous American population was often brutal.

WHAT WAS THE IMPACT OF NEW WORLD SILVER ON THE EUROPEAN ECONOMY?

EUROPE ENCOUNTERS A NEW WORLD   447

THE SPANISH CONQUEST OF AMERICA

Although the discovery of this new continent was initially a disappointment to the Spanish, it quickly became clear that the New World had great wealth of its own. From the start, Columbus's gold samples, in themselves rather paltry, had nurtured hopes that somewhere in America gold might lie piled in ingots, ready to enrich whatever European adventurer discovered them. Rumor fed rumor, until a few freelance Spanish soldiers really did strike it rich beyond their most avaricious imaginings. Between 1519 and 1521, the *conquistador* (Spanish for "conqueror") Hernando Cortés, with a force of six hundred Europeans but with the assistance of thousands of the Aztecs' unhappy subjects, overthrew the Aztec empire of Mexico and carried off its rulers' fabulous wealth. Then in 1533 another conquistador, Francisco Pizarro, this time with only one hundred eighty men, toppled the highly centralized South American empire of the Incas, and carried off its great stores of gold and silver. Cortés and Pizarro had the advantage of some cannons and a few horses (both unknown to the native peoples of the Americas), but they achieved their victories primarily by sheer audacity, courage, and treachery. They were aided also by the unwillingness of the indigenous peoples whom the Aztecs and the Incas had subjected to fight on behalf of their oppressors. Little did the Spaniards' erstwhile allies know how much worse their new conquerors would soon prove to be.

THE PROFITS OF EMPIRE IN THE NEW WORLD

Cortés and Pizarro were plunderers who captured in one fell swoop hoards of gold and silver that had been accumulated for centuries by the native civilizations of Mexico and Peru. Already, however, a search had begun for the sources of these precious metals. The first gold deposits were discovered in Hispaniola, where surface mines were speedily established utilizing native laborers who died in appalling numbers from disease, brutality, and overwork. Of the approximately one million native people who lived on Hispaniola in 1492, only one hundred thousand survived by 1510.

By 1538, their numbers were down to five hundred. With the loss of so many workers, the Hispaniola mines became uneconomical to operate, and the European colonists turned instead to cattle raising and sugar production. Modelling their sugar cane plantations on those of the Cape Verde Islands and St. Thomas, they imported African slaves to labor in the new industry. Sugar production was by its nature a highly capital-intensive undertaking. The need to import slave labor added further to its costs, guaranteeing that control over the sugar industry would fall into the hands of a few extremely wealthy planters and financiers.

Despite the importance of sugar production on the Caribbean islands and of cattle ranching on the Mexican mainland, it was mining that shaped the Spanish colonies of Central and South America most fundamentally. Gold was the lure that had initially drawn the Spanish conquerors to the New World, but it was silver that became their most lucrative export. Between 1543 and 1548, vast silver deposits were discovered north of Mexico City and at Potosí in Bolivia. Even before the discovery of these deposits, the Spanish crown had taken steps to assume direct governmental control over its Central and South American colonies. It was therefore to the Spanish crown that the profits from these astonishingly productive mines accrued. Potosí quickly became the most important mining town in the world. By 1570, it numbered one hundred twenty thousand inhabitants, despite being located at an altitude of fifteen thousand feet where the temperature never climbs above 59 degrees Fahrenheit. As in Hispaniola, enslaved native laborers died by the tens of thousands in these mines and in the disease-infested boom towns that surrounded them.

New developments in mining techniques (in particular, the mercury-amalgamation process, introduced into Mexico in 1555 and Potosí in 1571) made it possible to produce even greater quantities of silver, at the cost of even greater mortality among the native laborers. Between 1571 and 1586, silver production at Potosí quadrupled, reaching a peak in the 1590s, when ten million ounces of silver per year were arriving in Spain from the Americas. In the 1540s, the corresponding figure was only one and one half million ounces. In the peak years of domestic European silver production, between 1525 and 1535, only about three million ounces of silver per year were being produced, and this figure

> Mining shaped the Spanish colonies of Central and South America most fundamentally.

ENSLAVED NATIVE LABORERS AT POTOSÍ

Since the Spanish crown received one fifth of all the revenues from mines (as well as maintaining a monopoly over the mercury used to refine the silver ore into silver), it had an important stake in ensuring the productivity of the mines. To this end, the Crown granted colonial mine owners the right to conscript native peoples to work in the mines. This account from about 1620 describes the conditions under which these forced native laborers worked. Not surprisingly, mortality rates among such laborers were horrendous.

According to His Majesty's warrant, the mine owners on this massive range [at Potosí] have a right to the conscripted labor of 13,300 Indians in the working and exploitation of the mines, both those which have been discovered, those now discovered, and those which shall be discovered. It is the duty of the *Corregidor* (municipal governor) of Potosí to have them rounded up and to see that they come in from all the provinces between Cuzco . . . and as far as the frontiers of Tarija and Tomina. . . .

The conscripted Indians go up every Monday morning to the . . . foot of the range; the *Corregidor* arrives with all the provincial captains or chiefs who have charge of the Indians assigned him for his miner or smelter; that keeps him busy till 1 P.M., by which time the Indians are already turned over to these mine and smelter owners.

After each has eaten his ration, they climb up the hill, each to his mine, and go in, staying there from that hour until Saturday evening without coming out of the mine; their wives bring them food, but they stay constantly underground, excavating and carrying out the ore from which they get the silver. They all have tallow candles, lighted day and night; that is the light they work with, for as they are underground, they have need for it all the time. . . .

These Indians have different functions in the handling of the silver ore; some break it up with bar or pick, and dig down in, following the vein in the mine; others bring it up; others up above keep separating the good and the poor in piles; others are occupied in taking it down from the range to the mills on herds of llamas; every day they bring up more than 8,000 of these native beasts of burden for this task. These teamsters who carry the metal are not conscripted, but are hired.

Antonio Vázquez de Espinosa, *Compendium and Description of the West Indies,* trans. Charles Upson Clark. (Washington, D.C.: Smithsonian Institution Press, 1968), p. 62.

---

dropped steadily from about 1550 on. Europe's silver shortage came triumphantly to an end during the sixteenth century, but the silver that now circulated there came almost entirely from the New World.

This massive infusion of silver into the European economy exacerbated an inflation that had begun already in the later fifteenth century and had accelerated during the sixteenth century. Initially, this inflation was driven by the renewed growth of the European population, an expanding economy, and a relatively fixed supply of food. From the 1540s on, however, the accelerating inflation was largely the product of the greatly

The Silver Mines of Spanish America. An engraving of 1602. Some of the miners work naked because of the heat.

increased supply of silver that was now entering the European economy. The result was what historians have termed "the Price Revolution." Although the effects of this inflation were felt throughout the European continent, Spain was affected with particular severity. Between 1500 and 1560, Spanish prices doubled; between 1560 and 1600, they doubled again. Such exceptionally high prices in turn undermined the competitiveness of Spanish industries. When the flow of New World silver to Spain slowed dramatically during the 1620s and 1630s, the Spanish economy collapsed.

After 1600, lessening quantities of New World silver entered the European economy, but prices continued to rise until at least mid-century. By 1650, the price of grain within Europe had risen to five or six times its level in 1500, producing social dislocation and widespread misery for many of Europe's poorest inhabitants. In England, the period between about 1590 and 1610 was probably the most desperate the country had experienced for 300 years. As population rose and wages fell, living standards dropped dramatically. If we compute living standards by dividing the price of an average basket of food by the average daily wage of a building laborer, then standards of living were lower in England in 1600 than they had been even in the terrible years of the early fourteenth century. It is no wonder, then, that so many Europeans found emigration to the Americas a tempting prospect. We may wonder, indeed, what might have happened in seventeenth-century Europe had the new world of the Americas not existed as an outlet for Europe's growing population.

CONCLUSION

By 1600, colonization and overseas conquest had produced profoundly important changes within Europe and on the wider world. The emergence during the sixteenth century of Portugal and Spain as Europe's leading long-distance traders permanently moved the center of gravity of European economic power away from Italy and the Mediterranean toward the Atlantic. Deprived of its role as the principal conduit for the spice trade, Venice gradually declined. The Genoese moved increasingly into the world of finance, backing the commercial ventures of others, and particularly of Spain. By contrast, the Atlantic ports of sixteenth-century Spain and Portugal bustled with vessels and shone with wealth. By the mid-seventeenth century, however, economic predominance was passing to the north Atlantic states of England, Holland, and France. Spain and Portugal would retain their American

CHRONOLOGY	
ENCOUNTERING THE NEW WORLD, 1000–1545	
Vikings settle Newfoundland	c. 1000
Columbus reaches Hispaniola	1492
Balboa reaches Pacific Ocean	1513
Magellan's fleet sails around the world	1519–1522
Cortés conquers the Aztecs	1521
Pizarro conquers the Incas	1533
Potosí silver mines opened	1545

colonies until the nineteenth century. But from the seventeenth century on, it would be the Dutch, the French, and especially the English who would establish new European empires in North America, Asia, Africa, and Australia. By and large, these new empires would last until the Second World War.

SELECTED READINGS

Abu-Lughod, Janet L. *Before European Hegemony: The World System A.D. 1250–1350.* Oxford and New York, 1989. A study of the trading links between Europe, the Middle East, India, and China, with special attention to the role of the Mongol empire; extensive bibliography.

Allsen, Thomas T. *Mongol Imperialism: The Policies of the Grand Qan Möngke in China, Russia, and the Islamic Lands, 1251–1259.* Berkeley and Los Angeles, 1987. A pioneering study of how the Mongols ruled their empire.

———. *Commodity and Exchange in the Mongol Empire: A Cultural History of Islamic Textiles.* Cambridge and New York, 1997. A scholarly monograph that emphasizes the sophistication and importance of Mongol involvement in Eurasian trade.

Amitai-Preiss, Reuven, and David O. Morgan, eds. *The Mongol Empire and Its Legacy.* Leiden, 1999. A collection of essays that represents the newest work in Mongol studies.

The Book of Prophecies, Edited by Christopher Columbus. Translated by Blair Sullivan. Edited by Roberto Rusconi. Berkeley and Los Angeles, 1996. After his third voyage, from which Columbus was returned to Spain in chains, he compiled a book of quotations from various sources, selected to emphasize the millenarian implications of his discoveries; a fascinating insight into the mind of the explorer.

Christian, David. *A History of Russia, Central Asia and Mongolia.* Volume 1: *Inner Eurasia from Prehistory to the Mongol Empire.* Oxford, 1998. The first volume of what will surely become the authoritative English-language work on the subject.

Coles, Paul. *The Ottoman Impact on Europe.* London, 1968. An excellent introductory text, still valuable despite its age.

Fernández-Armesto, Felipe. *Before Columbus: Exploration and Colonisation from the Mediterranean to the Atlantic, 1229–1492.* London, 1987. An indispensible study of the medieval background to the sixteenth-century European colonial empires.

———. *Columbus.* Oxford and New York, 1991. An excellent biography that stresses the millenarian ideas that underlay Columbus' thinking. A good book to read after the Phillips' book (see below).

Fleet, Kate. *European and Islamic Trade in the Early Ottoman State: The Merchants of Genoa and Turkey.* Cambridge and New York, 2000. A scholarly monograph that discusses the fifteenth-century rise and decline of Italian (and particularly Genoese) trade with the Ottoman empire.

Flint, Valerie I. J. *The Imaginative Landscape of Christopher Columbus.* Princeton, N.J., 1992. A short, suggestive analysis of the intellectual influences that shaped Columbus's geographical ideas.

The Four Voyages: Christopher Columbus. Translated by J. M. Cohen. New York, 1992. Columbus's own self-serving account of his four voyages to the "Indies."

Goodwin, Jason. *Lords of the Horizons: A History of the Ottoman Empire.* London: Chatto and Windus, 1998. Colorful and engaging popular account; not the most reliable place to look up facts.

Halperin, C. J. *Russia and the Golden Horde: The Mongol Impact on Medieval Russian History.* Bloomington, 1985. The standard authority.

The History and the Life of Chinggis Khan: The Secret History of the Mongols. Translated by Urgunge Onon. Leiden, 1997. A newer version of *The Secret History* (see below), likely to become the standard English version of this important Mongol source.

Inalcik, Halil. *The Ottoman Empire: The Classical Age, 1300–1600.* London, 1973. The standard history by the dean of Turkish historians.

———, ed. *An Economic and Social History of the Ottoman Empire, 1300–1914.* Cambridge, 1994. An important collection of essays, spanning the full range of Ottoman history.

———. *Essays in Ottoman History.* Istanbul, 1998. A collection of Inalcik's own essays; although some are too specialized for students, a number are quite accessible.

Larner, John. *Marco Polo and the Discovery of the World.* New Haven, 1999. A study of the influence of Marco Polo's *Travels* on Europeans by an excellent historian of medieval Italy.

Morgan, David. *The Mongols.* Oxford, 1986. The most accessible introduction to Mongol history and its sources, written by a noted expert on medieval Persia.

Parker, Geoffrey. *The Military Revolution: Military Innovation and the Rise of the West (1500–1800),* 2d ed. Cambridge and New York, 1996. A work of fundamental importance for understanding the global dominance achieved by early modern Europeans.

Phillips, J. R. S. *The Medieval Expansion of Europe,* 2d ed. Oxford, 1998. An outstanding study of the thirteenth- and fourteenth-century background to the fifteenth-century expansion of Europe. Important synthetic treatment of European relations with the Mongols, China, Africa, and North America. The second edition includes a new introduction and a bibliographical essay; the text is the same as in the first edition (1988).

Phillips, William D., Jr., and Carla R. Phillips. *The Worlds of Christopher Columbus.* Cambridge and New York, 1991. The first book to read on Columbus: accessible, engaging, and scholarly. Then read Fernández-Armesto's biography (above).

Ratchnevsky, Paul. *Genghis Khan: His Life and Legacy.* Translated by Thomas Nivison Haining. Oxford, 1991. An English translation and abridgment of a book first published in

German in 1983. The author was one of the greatest Mongol historians of his generation.

Rossabi, M. *Khubilai Khan: His Life and Times.* Berkeley, 1988. The standard English biography.

Russell, Peter. *Prince Henry "The Navigator": A Life.* New Haven, 2000. A masterly biography by a great historian who has spent a lifetime on the subject. The only book one now needs to read on Prince Henry.

Saunders, J. J. *The History of the Mongol Conquests.* London, 1971. Still the standard English-language introduction; somewhat more positive about the Mongols' accomplishments than is Morgan.

Scammell, Geoffrey V. *The First Imperial Age: European Overseas Expansion, 1400–1715.* London, 1989. A useful introductory survey, with a particular focus on English and French colonization.

The Secret History of the Mongols. Translated by F. W. Cleaves. Cambridge, Mass., 1982.

The Secret History of the Mongols and Other Pieces. Translated by Arthur Waley. London, 1963. The later Chinese abridgment of the Mongol original.

The Travels of Marco Polo, trans. R. E. Latham. Baltimore, 1958. The most accessible edition of this remarkably interesting work.

THE
CIVILIZATION OF
THE RENAISSANCE,
C. 1350–1550

THE PREVALENT MODERN NOTION that a "Renaissance period" followed western Europe's Middle Ages was first expressed by numerous Italian writers who lived between 1350 and 1550. According to them, one thousand years of unrelieved darkness had intervened between the Roman era and their own times. During these "Dark Ages" the muses of art and literature had fled Europe before the onslaught of barbarism and ignorance. Almost miraculously, however, in the fourteenth century the muses suddenly returned, and Italians happily collaborated with them to bring forth a glorious "renaissance of the arts."

Ever since this periodization was advanced, historians have taken for granted the existence of some sort of "renaissance" intervening between medieval and modern times. Indeed, from the late eighteenth to the early twentieth centuries many scholars went so far as to argue that the Renaissance was not just an epoch in the history of learning and culture but that a unique "Renaissance spirit" transformed all aspects of European life—political, economic, and religious, as well as intellectual and artistic. Today, however, most experts no longer accept this characterization because they find it impossible to locate any truly distinctive "Renaissance" politics, economics, or religion. Instead, most scholars reserve the term "Renaissance" to describe certain trends in thought, literature, and the arts that emerged in Italy from roughly 1350 to 1550 and then spread to northern Europe during the first half of the sixteenth century. That is the approach that we will follow here: accordingly, when we refer to a "Renaissance" period in this chapter we mean to limit ourselves to an epoch in intellectual and cultural history.

FOCUS QUESTIONS

- What was distinctive about the Renaissance?
- Why did the Renaissance occur in Italy?
- Why did Italian art become fully mature around 1500?
- Why did the Renaissance decline around 1550?
- How did the northern and Italian Renaissances differ from one another?

THE RENAISSANCE AND THE MIDDLE AGES

What was distinctive about the Renaissance?

Granted this restriction, some further qualifications are still necessary. Since the word *renaissance* literally means "rebirth," it is sometimes thought that after about 1350 certain Italians who were newly cognizant of Greek and Roman cultural accomplishments initiated a rebirth of classical culture after a long period during which that culture had been essentially dead. In fact, however, the High Middle Ages witnessed no "death" of classical learning. Saint Thomas Aquinas considered Aristotle to be "the Philosopher"; Dante revered Virgil. Similar examples could be cited almost without limit. It would be equally false to contrast an imaginary "Renaissance paganism" with a medieval "age of faith" because however much most Renaissance personalities loved the classics, none saw their classicism as superseding their Christianity. And finally, all discussions of the Renaissance must be qualified by the fact that there was no single Renaissance position on anything. Renaissance thinkers and artists were enormously diverse in their attitudes, achievements, and approaches. As we assess their accomplishments, we need to beware not to force them into too narrow a mold.

> The High Middle Ages witnessed no "death" of classical learning. Aquinas considered Aristotle to be "the Philosopher" and Dante revered Virgil.

RENAISSANCE CLASSICISM

Nonetheless, in the realms of thought, literature, and the arts, we can certainly find distinguishing traits that make the concept of a "Renaissance" meaningful for intellectual and cultural history. First, regarding knowledge of the classics, there was a significant quantitative difference between the learning of the Middle Ages and that of the Renaissance. Medieval scholars knew many Roman authors, such as Virgil, Ovid, and Cicero, but during the Renaissance the works of others such as Livy, Tacitus, and Lucretius were rediscovered and made familiar. Equally if not more important was the Renaissance recovery of the literature of classical Greece from Byzantium. In the twelfth and thirteenth centuries Greek scientific and philosophical treatises were made available to Westerners in Latin translations through Islam, but none of the great Greek literary masterpieces and practically none of the major works of Plato were yet known. Nor could more than a handful of medieval Westerners read the Greek language. During the Renaissance, on the other hand, large numbers of Western scholars learned Greek and mastered almost the entire Greek literary heritage that is known today.

Second, Renaissance thinkers not only knew many more classical texts than their medieval counterparts, but they used them in new ways. Whereas medieval writers presumed that their ancient sources would complement and confirm their own Christian assumptions, Renaissance writers were more aware of the conceptual and chronological gap that separated their own world from that of their classical sources. At the same time, however, the structural similarities between the ancient city-states and those of Renaissance Italy encouraged Italian thinkers in particular to find in these ancient sources models of thought and action directly applicable to their own day. This firm determination to learn from classical antiquity was even more pronounced in the realms of architecture and art, areas in which classical models contributed most strikingly to the creation of fully distinct "Renaissance" styles.

Third, although Renaissance culture was by no means pagan, it was more worldly and overtly materialistic in its orientation than was the culture of the twelfth and thirteenth centuries. The evolution of the Italian city-states created a supportive environment for attitudes that stressed the importance of the urban political arena and of living well in this world. Such ideals helped to create a culture that was increasingly nonecclesiastical. The relative weakness of the church in Italy also contributed to the more secular culture that emerged there. Italian bishoprics were small, and for the most part poorly endowed. Italian universities were also largely independent of ecclesiastical supervision and control. Even the papacy was severely limited in its ability to intervene in the cultural life of the Italian city-states, not least because the papacy's own role as a political rival in central Italy compromised its moral authority as an arbiter of cultural and religious values. All these factors helped to create a space within which the worldly, materialistic culture of the Renaissance could emerge effectively untrammeled by ecclesiastical opposition.

RENAISSANCE HUMANISM

One word above all comes closest to summing up the most common and basic Renaissance intellectual ideals, namely *humanism*. Renaissance humanism was a program of studies that aimed to replace the thirteenth and fourteenth century scholastic emphasis on logic and metaphysics with the study of language, literature, rhetoric, history, and ethics. The humanists always preferred ancient literature; although some (notably Francesco Petrarch and Leon Batista Alberti) wrote in both Latin and the vernacular, most humanists regarded vernacular literature as at best a diversion for the uneducated. Serious scholarship and literature could only be written in Latin or Greek. That Latin, moreover, had to be the Latin of Cicero and Virgil. Renaissance humanists were self-conscious elitists, who condemned the living Latin of their scholastic contemporaries as a barbarous departure from ancient (and therefore correct) standards of Latin style. Despite their belief that they were thereby reviving the study of the classics, the humanists' position was thus inherently ironic. By insisting on ancient standards of Latin grammar, syntax, and word choice, the humanists of the Renaissance succeeded ultimately in turning Latin into a fossilized language that thereafter ceased to evolve. They thus contributed, quite unwittingly, to the ultimate triumph of the European vernaculars as the primary languages of intellectual and cultural life.

Humanists were convinced that their own educational program—which placed the study of Latin language and literature at the core of the curriculum and then encouraged students to go on to Greek—was the best way to produce virtuous citizens and able public officials. Their elitism was to this extent intensely practical, and directly connected to the political life of the city-states in which they lived. Because women were excluded from Italian political life, the education of women was therefore of little concern to most humanists, although some aristocratic women were given humanist training to make them appear more polished and attractive to men. As more and more fifteenth century city-states fell into the hands of princes, however, the humanist educational curriculum lost its immediate connection to the republican ideals of Italian political life. Nevertheless, humanists never lost their conviction that the study of the "humanities" (as the humanist curriculum came to be known) was the best way to produce leaders for European society. This faith has continued to animate higher education in Europe ever since.

The humanists' faith in the moral value of their curriculum, and in the spiritual and intellectual capacities of properly educated men, led some of them to emphasize the dignity of man as the most excellent of all God's creatures below the angels. Some humanists argued that man was excellent because he alone of earthly creatures could obtain knowledge of God—a standard scholastic position that the humanists were too graceless to acknowledge having borrowed from their opponents. Others saw humanity's excellence as lying in our ability to master our fate and live happily in the world through our own attainments. Either way, many Renaissance humanists, especially in the fifteenth century, had a firm belief in the nobility and possibilities of the human race.

Today, such faith in the nobility of human beings' natural capacities is sometimes referred to as "humanism"—or even "secular humanism." For our purposes, however, it is important to remember that Renaissance humanism was first and foremost an educational program securely rooted in Catholic Christian orthodoxy, and that it gave rise only incidentally to a more general outlook that stressed the potential of human beings to shape and improve their world unaided by divine intervention.

> One word above all comes closest to summing up the Renaissance intellectual ideals, namely *humanism*.

THE RENAISSANCE IN ITALY

Why did the Renaissance occur in Italy?

Although the Renaissance eventually became a Europe-wide intellectual and artistic movement, it developed first and most distinctively in fourteenth- and fifteenth-century Italy. Understanding why this was so is important not only to explaining the origins of this movement, but also to understanding its fundamental characteristics.

THE ORIGINS OF THE ITALIAN RENAISSANCE

The Renaissance originated in Italy for several reasons. The most fundamental reason was that Italy in the later

THE HUMANISTS' EDUCATIONAL PROGRAM

These three selections illustrate the confidence of civic humanists such as Vergerius, Bruni, and Alberti that their elite educational program would be of supreme value to the state as well as to the individual students who pursued it. Not everyone agreed with the humanists' claims, however, and a good deal of self-promotion lies behind them..

VERGERIUS ON LITERAL STUDIES

We call those studies *liberal* which are worthy of a free man; those studies by which we attain and practice virtue and wisdom; that education which calls forth, trains, and develops those highest gifts of body and of mind which ennoble men, and which are rightly judged to rank next in dignity to virtue only. . . . It is, then, of the highest importance that even from infancy this aim, this effort, should constantly be kept alive in growing minds. For . . . we shall not have attained wisdom in our later years unless in our earliest we have sincerely entered on its search. [P. P. Vergerius (1370–1444), *"Concerning Excellent Traits"*]

ALBERTI ON THE IMPORTANCE OF LITERATURE

Letters are indeed so important that without them one would be considered nothing but a rustic, no matter how much a gentlemen [he may be by birth]. I'd much rather see a young nobleman with a book than with a falcon in his hand. . . .

Be diligent, then, you young people, in your studies. Do all you can to learn about the events of the past that are worthy of memory. Try to understand all the useful things that have been passed on to you. Feed your minds on good maxims. Learn the delights of embellishing your souls with good morals. Strive to be kind and considerate [of others] when conducting civil business. Get to know those things human and divine that have been put at your disposal in books for good reason. Nowhere [else] will you find . . . the elegance of a verse of Homer, or Virgil, or of some other excellent poet. You will find no field so delightful or flowering as in one of the orations of Demosthenes, Cicero, Livy, Xenophon, and other such pleasant and perfect orators. No effort is more fully compensated . . . as the constant reading and rereading of good things. From such reading you will rise rich in good maxims and good arguments, strong in your ability to persuade others and get them to listen to you; among the citizens you will willingly be heard, admired, praised, and loved. [Leon Battista Alberti (1404–1472), *"On the Family"*]

BRUNI ON THE HUMANIST CURRICULUM

The foundations of all true learning must be laid in the sound and thorough knowledge of Latin: which implies study marked by a broad spirit, accurate scholarship, and careful attention to details. Unless this solid basis be secured it is useless to attempt to rear an enduring edifice. Without it the great monuments of literature are unintelligible, and the art of composition impossible. To attain this essential knowledge we must never relax our careful attention to the grammar of the language, but perpetually confirm and extend our acquaintance with it until it is thoroughly our own. . . .

But the wider question now confronts us, that of the subject matter of our studies, that which I have already called the realities of fact and principle, as distinct from literary form. . . . First among such studies I place History: a subject which must not on any account be neglected by one who aspires to true cultivation. . . . For the careful study of the past enlarges our foresight in contemporary affairs and affords to citizens and to monarchs lessons . . . in the ordering of public policy. From History, also, we draw our store of examples of moral precepts. . . .

The great Orators of antiquity must by all means be included. Nowhere do we find the virtues more warmly extolled, the vices so fiercely decried. From them we may learn, also, how to express consolation, encouragement, dissuasion or advice. . . .

Familiarity with the great poets of antiquity is essen-tial to any claim to true education. For in their writings we find deep speculations upon Nature, and upon the Causes and Origins of things, which must carry weight with us both from their antiquity and from their authorship. . . .

Proficiency in literary form, not accompanied by broad acquaintance with facts and truths, is a barren attainment; whilst information, however vast, which lacks all grace of expression would seem to be put under a bushel or partly thrown away. . . . Where, however, this double capacity exists—breadth of learning and grace of style—we allow the highest title to distinction and to abiding fame. . . . [Leonardo Bruni (1369–1444), *"Concerning the Study of Literature"*]

Vergerius and Bruni: William Harrison Woodward, ed., *Vittorino da Feltre and Other Humanist Educators.* (London: Cambridge University Press, 1897), pp. 96–110, 124–129, 132–133. Alberti: Eric Cochrane and Julius Kirshner, eds. *University of Chicago Readings in Western Civilization,* Vol. 5: *The Renaissance.* (Chicago: University of Chicago Press, 1986), pp. 81–82.

Middle Ages encompassed the most advanced urban society in all of Europe. Unlike aristocrats north of the Alps, Italian aristocrats customarily lived in urban centers rather than in rural castles and consequently became fully involved in urban public affairs. Moreover, since the Italian aristocracy built its palaces in the cities, the aristocratic class was less sharply set off from the class of rich merchants than in the north. Hence whereas in France or Germany most aristocrats lived on the income from their landed estates while rich town dwellers (*bourgeois*) gained their living from trade, in Italy so many town-dwelling aristocrats engaged in banking or mercantile enterprises and so many rich mercantile families imitated the manners of the aristocracy that by the fourteenth and fifteenth centuries the aristocracy and upper bourgeoisie were becoming virtually indistinguishable. The noted Florentine family of the Medici, for example, emerged as a family of physicians (as the name suggests), made its fortune in banking and commerce, and rose into the aristocracy in the fifteenth century. The results of these developments for the history of education are obvious: not only was there a great demand for education in the skills of reading and counting necessary to become a successful merchant, but the richest and most prominent families sought above all to find teachers who would impart to their offspring the knowledge and skills necessary to argue well in the public arena. Consequently, Italy produced a large number of lay educators, many of whom not only taught students but also demonstrated their learned attainments in the production of political and ethical treatises and works of literature. Italian schools created the best-educated upper-class public in all of Europe, along with a considerable number of wealthy patrons who were ready to invest in the cultivation of new ideas and new forms of literary and artistic expression.

A second reason why late medieval Italy was the birthplace of an intellectual and artistic renaissance lay in the fact that it had a far greater sense of rapport with the classical past than any other territory in western Europe. Given the Italian commitment to an educational curriculum that stressed success in urban politics, the best teachers understandably sought inspiration from ancient Latin and Greek texts because politics and political rhetoric were classical rather than medieval arts. Elsewhere, resort to classical knowledge and classical literary style might have seemed antiquarian and artificial, but in Italy the classical past appeared most "relevant" because ancient Roman monuments were omnipresent throughout the peninsula, and ancient Latin literature referred to cities and sites that Renaissance Italians

Pope Julius II, by Raphael. The acorns at the top of the throne posts are visual puns for the pope's family name, "della Rovere" (of the oak).

recognized as their own. Moreover, Italians became particularly intent on reappropriating their classical heritage in the fourteenth and fifteenth centuries because Italians then were seeking to establish an independent cultural identity in opposition to a scholasticism most closely associated with France. Not only did the removal of the papacy to Avignon for most of the fourteenth century and then the Great Schism from 1378 to 1417 heighten antagonisms between Italy and France, but during the fourteenth century an intellectual reaction against scholasticism on all fronts encouraged Italians to prefer the intellectual alternatives offered by classical literary sources. Once Roman literature and learning became particularly favored in Italy, so too did Roman art and architecture, for Roman models could help Italians create a splendid artistic alternative to French Gothicism just as Roman learning offered an intellectual alternative to French scholasticism.

Finally, the Italian Renaissance could not have occurred without the underpinning of Italian wealth. The Italian economy as a whole was probably more prosperous in the thirteenth century than it was in the fourteenth and fifteenth. But late medieval Italy was

wealthier in comparison with the rest of Europe than it had been before, a fact that meant that Italian writers and artists were more likely to stay at home than to seek employment abroad. Moreover, in late medieval Italy unusually intensive investment in culture arose from an intensification of urban pride and the concentration of per capita wealth. Although these two trends overlapped somewhat, most scholars tend to agree that a phase of predominantly public urban support for culture came first in Italy from roughly 1250 to about 1400 or 1450, depending on place, with the private sector taking over thereafter. In the first phase the richest cities vied with each other in building the most splendid public monuments and in supporting writers whose role was to glorify the urban republics in letters and speeches as full of magniloquent Ciceronian prose as possible. But in the course of the fifteenth century, when most Italian city-states succumbed to the hereditary rule of princely families, patronage was monopolized by the princely aristocracy. It was then that the great princes—the Visconti and Sforza in Milan, the Medici in Florence, the Este in Ferrara, and the Gonzaga in Mantua—patronized art and literature in their courts to glorify themselves, while lesser aristocratic families imitated those princes on a smaller scale. Not least of the great princes in Italy from about 1450 to about 1550 were the popes in Rome, who were dedicated to a policy of basing their strength on temporal control of the Papal States. Hence the most worldly of the Renaissance popes—Alexander VI (1492–1503); Julius II (1503–1513); and Leo X (1513–1521), son of the Florentine ruler Lorenzo de' Medici—obtained the services of the greatest artists of the day and for a few decades made Rome the unrivaled artistic capial of the Western world.

THE ITALIAN RENAISSANCE: LITERATURE AND THOUGHT

In surveying the greatest accomplishments of Italian Renaissance scholars and writers it is natural to begin with the work of Petrarch (Francesco Petrarca, 1304–1374), the most famous of the early Renaissance humanists. Petrarch was a deeply committed Catholic who believed that scholasticism was entirely misguided because it concentrated on abstract speculation rather than on teaching people how to live virtuously and attain salvation. Petrarch thought that the Christian writer must above all cultivate literary eloquence so that he could inspire people to do good. For him the best models of eloquence were to be found in the ancient literary classics, which he thought repaid study doubly inasmuch as they were filled with ethical wisdom. So Petrarch dedicated himself to searching for undiscovered ancient Latin texts and writing his own moral treatises in which he imitated classical style and quoted classical phrases. Thereby he initiated a program of "humanist" studies that was to be influential for centuries to come. Petrarch also has a place in purely literary history because of his poetry. Although he prized his own Latin poetry over the poems he wrote in the Italian vernacular, only the latter have proved enduring. Above all, the Italian sonnets—later called Petrarchan sonnets—that he wrote for his beloved Laura in the chivalrous style of the troubadours were widely imitated in form and content throughout the Renaissance period.

Civic humanists had great success in opening up the field of classical Greek studies.

Because he was a very traditional Christian, Petrarch's ultimate ideal for human conduct was the solitary life of contemplation and asceticism. But from about 1400 to 1450, subsequent Italian thinkers and scholars, located mainly in Florence, developed the alternative of what is customarily called civic humanism. Civic humanists such as the Florentines Leonardo Bruni (c. 1370–1444) and Leon Battista Alberti (1404–1472) agreed with Petrarch on the need for eloquence and the study of classical literature, but they also taught that man's nature equipped him for action, for usefulness to his family and society, and for serving the state—ideally a republican city-state after the classical or contemporary Florentine model. In their view ambition and the quest for glory were noble impulses that ought to be encouraged. They refused to condemn the striving for material possessions, for they argued that the history of human progress is inseparable from mankind's success in gaining mastery over the earth and its resources. Perhaps the most vivid of the civic humanists' writings is Alberti's On the Family (1443), in which he argued that the nuclear family was instituted by nature for the well-being of humanity. Within this framework, however, Alberti consigned women to purely domestic roles, asserting that "man [is] by nature more energetic and industrious," and that woman was created "to increase and continue generations, and to nourish and preserve those already born." Although such dismissals of women's intellectual abilities were fiercely resisted by a few notable women humanists, for the most part Italian Renaissance humanism was characterized by a pervasive denigration of women—a denigration expressed

also in the works of classical literature that the humanists so much admired.

THE EMERGENCE OF TEXTUAL SCHOLARSHIP

In addition to differing with Petrarch in their preference for the active over the solitary or contemplative life, the civic humanists went far beyond him in their study of the ancient literary heritage. Some discovered important new Latin texts, but more important was their success in opening up the field of classical Greek studies. In this they were aided by a number of Byzantine scholars who had migrated to Italy in the first half of the fifteenth century and gave instruction in the Greek language. Italian scholars also traveled to Constantinople and other Eastern cities in search of Greek masterpieces hitherto unknown in the West. In 1423 one Italian, Giovanni Aurispa, alone brought back 238 manuscript books, including works of Sophocles, Euripides, and Thucydides. Soon followed the work of translation into Latin, not word for word, but sense for sense in order to preserve the literary force of the original. In this way most of the Greek classics, particularly the writings of Plato, the dramatists, and the historians, were first made available to western Europe.

Related in his textual interests to the civic humanists, but by no means a full adherent of their movement, was the atypical yet highly influential Renaissance thinker Lorenzo Valla (1407–1457). Born in Rome and active primarily as a secretary in the service of the king of Naples, Valla had no inclination to espouse the ideas of republican political engagement as the Florentine civic humanists did. Instead, he preferred to advertise his skills as an expert in grammar, rhetoric, and the painstaking analysis of Greek and Latin texts by showing how the thorough study of language could discredit old verities. Most decisive in this regard was Valla's brilliant demonstration that the so-called Donation of Constantine was a medieval forgery. Whereas papal propagandists had argued that the papacy possessed rights to temporal rule in western Europe on the grounds of a charter purportedly granted by the emperor Constantine in the fourth century, Valla proved beyond dispute that the document in question was full of nonclassical Latin usages and anachronistic terms. Hence he concluded that the "Donation" was the work of a medieval forger whose "monstrous impudence"

SOME RENAISSANCE ATTITUDES TOWARD WOMEN

Italian society in the fourteenth and fifteenth centuries was characterized by marriage patterns in which men in their late twenties or thirties customarily married women in their mid to late teens. This demographic fact probably contributed to the widely shared belief in this period that wives were essentially children, who could not be trusted with important matters, and who were best trained by being beaten. Renaissance humanism did little to change such attitudes. In some cases, it even reinforced them.

After my wife had been settled in my house a few days, and after her first pangs of longing for her mother and family had begun to fade, I took her by the hand and showed her around the whole house. I explained that the loft was the place for grain and that the stores of wine and wood were kept in the cellar. I showed her where things needed for the table were kept, and so on, through the whole house. At the end there were no household goods of which my wife had not learned both the place and the purpose. . . .

Only my books and records and those of my ancestors did I determine to keep well sealed. . . . These my wife not only could not read, she could not even lay hands on them. I kept my records at all times . . . locked up and arranged in order in my study, almost like sacred and religious objects. I never gave my wife permission to enter that place, with me or alone. . . .

[Husbands] who take counsel with their wives . . . are madmen if they think true prudence or good counsel lies in the female brain. . . . For this very reason I have always tried carefully not to let any secret of mine be known to a woman. I did not doubt that my wife was most loving, and more discreet and modest in her ways than any, but I still considered it safer to have her unable, and not merely unwilling, to harm me. . . . Furthermore, I made it a rule never to speak with her of anything but household matters or questions of conduct, or of the children.

Leon Batista Alberti, "On the Family," in *The Family in Renaissance Florence*, translated and edited by Renée N. Watkins. (Columbia: University of South Carolina Press, 1969), pp. 208–213, as abridged in *Not in God's Image: Women in History from the Greeks to the Victorians*, edited by Julia O'Faolain and Lauro Martines. (New York: Harper & Row, 1973), pp. 187–188.

was exposed by the "stupidity of his language." This demonstration not only discredited a prize specimen of "medieval ignorance," but, more important, introduced the concept of anachronism into all subsequent textual study and historical thought. Valla also employed his skills in linguistic analysis and rhetorical argumentation to challenge a wide variety of philosophical positions, but his ultimate goals were by no means purely destructive,

for he revered the literal teachings of the Epistles of Saint Paul. Accordingly, in his *Notes on the New Testament* he applied his expert knowledge of Greek to elucidating the true meaning of Saint Paul's words, which he believed had been obscured by Saint Jerome's Latin Vulgate translation. This work was to prove an important link between Italian Renaissance scholarship and the subsequent Christian humanism of the north.

RENAISSANCE NEOPLATONISM

From about 1450 until about 1600 dominance in the world of Italian thought was assumed by a school of Neoplatonists, who sought to blend the thought of Plato, Plotinus, and various strands of ancient mysticism with Christianity. Foremost among these were Marsilio Ficino (1433–1499) and Giovanni Pico della Mirandola (1463–1494), both of whom were members of the Platonic Academy founded by Cosimo de' Medici in Florence. The academy was a loosely organized society of scholars who met to hear readings and lectures. Their hero was Plato: sometimes they celebrated Plato's birthday by holding a banquet in his honor, after which everybody gave speeches as if they were characters in a Platonic dialogue. From the standpoint of posterity, Ficino's greatest achievement was the translation of Plato's works into Latin, thereby making them widely available to western Europeans for the first time. Ficino himself, however, regarded his *Hermetic Corpus*, a collection of passages drawn from a variety of ancient mystical writings including the Hebrew Kabbalah, as his greatest contribution to learning. It is debatable whether Ficino's own philosophy should be called humanist because he moved away from ethics to metaphysics and taught that the individual should look primarily to the hereafter. In Ficino's opinion, "the immortal soul is always miserable in its mortal body." The same issue arises with respect to Ficino's disciple Giovanni Pico della Mirandola. Pico was certainly not a civic humanist, since he saw little worth in mundane public affairs. He also fully shared his teacher's penchant for extracting and combining snippets taken out of context from ancient mystical tracts. But he did also believe—and so argued in his famous *Oration on the Dignity of Man*—that there is "nothing more wonderful than man" because he believed that man is endowed with the capacity to achieve union with God if he so wills.

Pico della Mirandola. When the young nobleman Pico arrived in Florence at age nineteen he was said to have been "of beauteous feature and shape." This contemporary portrait may have been done by the great Florentine painter Botticelli.

MACHIAVELLI

Hardly any of the Italian thinkers between Petrarch and Pico were really original: their greatness lay mostly in their manner of expression, their accomplishments in technical scholarship, and their popularization of different themes of ancient thought. The same, however, cannot be said of Renaissance Italy's greatest political philosopher, the Florentine Niccolò Machiavelli (1469–1527). Machiavelli's writings reflect the unstable condition of Italy in his time. At the end of the fifteenth century Italy had become the cockpit of international struggles. Both France and Spain had invaded the peninsula and were competing for the allegiance of the Italian city-states, which in many cases were torn by internal dissension, making them easy prey for foreign conquerors. In 1498 Machiavelli became a prominent official in the government of the Florentine republic, set up four years earlier when the French invasion had led to the expulsion of the Medici. His duties largely involved diplomatic missions to other Italian city-states. While in Rome he became fascinated with the achievements of Cesare Borgia, son of Pope Alexander VI, in cementing a solidified state out of scattered elements. He noted with approval Cesare's combination of ruthlessness with shrewdness and his complete subordination of personal morality to political ends. In 1512 the Medici returned to overthrow the republic of Florence, and Machiavelli was deprived of his position. Disappointed and embittered, he spent the remainder of his life at his country estate, devoting his time primarily to writing.

Machiavelli remains a controversial figure even today. Some modern scholars see him as an amoral theorist of *realpolitik*, disdainful of morality and Christian piety, caring nothing about the proper purposes of political life, but interested solely in the acquisition and exercise of power as an end in itself. Others see him as an Italian patriot, who viewed princely tyranny as the only way to liberate Italy from its foreign conquerors. Still others see him as a follower of Saint Augustine of Hippo, who understood that in a fallen world populated by sinful people, a ruler's good intentions do not guarantee that his policies will have good results. Instead, Machiavelli insisted that a prince's actions must be judged by their consequences and not by their intrinsic moral quality. Human beings, Machiavelli argued, "are ungrateful, fickle, and deceitful, eager to avoid dangers, and avid for gain." This being so, "the necessity of preserving the state will often compel a prince to take actions which are opposed to loyalty, charity, humanity, and religion. . . . So far as he is able, a prince should stick to the path of good but, if the necessity arises, he should know how to follow evil."

The puzzle is heightened by the fact that, on the surface, Machiavelli's two great works of political analysis appear to contradict each other. In his *Discourses on Livy* he praised the ancient Roman republic as a model for his own contemporaries, lauding constitutional government, equality among the citizens of a republic, political independence on the part of city-states, and the subordination of religion to the service of the state. There is little doubt, therefore, that Machiavelli was a committed republican, who believed in the free city-state as the ideal form of human government. But Machiavelli also wrote *The Prince*, "a handbook for tyrants" in the eyes of his critics, and he dedicated this work to Lorenzo, son of Piero de Medici, whose family had overthrown the Florentine republic that Machiavelli himself had served.

Because *The Prince* has been so much more widey read than the *Discourses*, interpretations of Machiavelli's political thought have often mistaken the admiration he expressed in *The Prince* for Cesare Borgia as an endorsement of princely tyranny for its own sake. Machiavelli's real position was quite different. In the political chaos of early sixteenth-century Italy, Machiavelli saw a ruthless prince such as Borgia as the only hope for revitalizing the spirit of independence among his con-

temporaries, and so making them fit, once again, for republican self-rule. However dark his vision of human nature, Machiavelli never ceased to hope that his Italian contemporaries would rise up, expel their French and Spanish conquerors, and restore their ancient traditions of republican liberty and equality. Princes such as Borgia were necessary steps toward that end, but they did not represent, for Machiavelli, the ideal form of government for humankind. In Italy's sunken political situation, however, a princely state such as Borgia's was the best form of government toward which Machiavelli's downtrodden contemporaries could aspire.

THE IDEAL OF THE COURTIER

Far more congenial to contemporary tastes than the shocking political theories of Machiavelli were the guidelines for proper aristocratic conduct offered in *The Book of the Courtier* (1528) by the diplomat and count Baldassare Castiglione. This cleverly written forerunner of modern handbooks of etiquette stands in sharp contrast to the earlier civic humanist treatises of Bruni and Alberti, for whereas they taught the sober "republican" virtues of strenuous service in behalf of city-state and family, Castiglione, writing in an Italy dominated by magnificent princely courts, taught how to attain the elegant and seemingly effortless qualities necessary for acting like a "true gentleman." More than anyone else, Castiglione popularized the ideal of the "Renaissance man": one who is accomplished in many different pursuits and is also brave, witty, and "courteous," meaning civilized and learned. Unlike Alberti, Castiglione said nothing about women's role in "hearth and home," but stressed instead the ways in which court ladies could be "gracious entertainers." Widely read throughout Europe for over a century after its publication, Castiglione's *Courtier* spread Italian ideals of "civility" to princely courts north of the Alps, resulting in the ever-greater patronage of art and literature by the European aristocracy.

Had Castiglione's ideal courtier wished to show off his knowledge of contemporary Italian literature, he would have had many works from which to choose, for sixteenth-century Italians were highly accomplished creators of imaginative prose and verse. Among the many impressive writers who might be mentioned, Machiavelli himself wrote a delightful short story, "Belfagor," and an engagingly bawdy play, *Mandragola;*

> Machiavelli never ceased to hope that his Italian contemporaries would restore their ancient traditions of republican liberty and equality.

MACHIAVELLI'S ITALIAN PATRIOTISM

These passages are from the concluding chapter to Machiavelli's treatise The Prince. *Like the book itself, they are addressed to Lorenzo, the son of Piero de' Medici.*

Reflecting on the matters set forth above and considering within myself whether the times were propitious in Italy at present to honor a new prince and whether there is at hand the matter suitable for a prudent and virtuous leader to mold in a new form, giving honor to himself and benefit to the citizens of the country, I have arrived at the opinion that all circumstances now favor such a prince, and I cannot think of a time more propitious for him than the present. If, as I said, it was necessary in order to make apparent the virtue of Moses, that the people of Israel should be enslaved in Egypt, and that the Persians should be oppressed by the Medes to provide an opportunity to illustrate the greatness and the spirit of Cyrus, and that the Athenians should be scattered in order to show the excellence of Theseus, thus at the present time, in order to reveal the valor of an Italian spirit it was essential that Italy should fall to her present low estate, more enslaved than the Hebrews, more servile than the Persians, more disunited than the Athenians, leaderless and lawless, beaten, despoiled, lacerated, overrun and crushed under every kind of misfortune. . . . So Italy now, left almost lifeless, awaits the coming of one who will heal her wounds, putting an end to the sacking and looting in Lombardy and the spoliation and extortions in the Realm of Naples and Tuscany, and cleanse her sores that have been so long festering. Behold how she prays God to send her some one to redeem her from the cruelty and insolence of the barbarians. See how she is ready and willing to follow any banner so long as there be some one to take it up. Nor has she at present any hope of finding her redeemer save only in your illustrious house [the Medici] which has been so highly exalted both by its own merits and by fortune and which has been favored by God and the church, of which it is now ruler. . . .

This opportunity, therefore, should not be allowed to pass, and Italy, after such a long wait, must be allowed to behold her redeemer. I cannot describe the joy with which he will be received in all these provinces which have suffered so much from the foreign deluge, nor with what thirst for vengeance, nor with what firm devotion, what solemn delight, what tears! What gates could be closed to him, what people could deny him obedience, what envy could withstand him, what Italian could withhold allegiance from him? THIS BARBARIAN OCCUPATION STINKS IN THE NOSTRILS OF ALL OF US. Let your illustrious house then take up this cause with the spirit and the hope with which one undertakes a truly just enterprise. . . .

Niccolò Machiavelli, *The Prince*, translated and edited by Thomas G. Bergin. (Arlington Heights, Ill.: AHM Publishing Corporation, 1947), pp. 75–76, 78.

the great artist Michelangelo wrote many moving sonnets; and Ludovico Ariosto (1474–1533), the most eminent of sixteenth-century Italian epic poets, wrote a lengthy verse narrative called *Orlando Furioso* (*The Madness of Roland*). Although woven substantially from materials taken from the medieval Charlemagne cycle, this work differed radically from any of the medieval epics because it introduced elements of lyrical fantasy and above all because it was totally devoid of heroic idealism. Ariosto wrote to make readers laugh and to charm them with felicitous descriptions of the quiet splendor of nature and the passions of love. His work embodies the disillusionment of the late Renaissance, the loss of hope and faith, and the tendency to seek consolation in the pursuit of pleasure and aesthetic delight.

THE ITALIAN RENAISSANCE: PAINTING, SCULPTURE, AND ARCHITECTURE

Why did Italian art become fully mature around 1500?

Despite numerous intellectual and literary advances, the longest-lived achievements of the Italian Renaissance were made in the realm of art. Of all the arts, painting was undoubtedly supreme. We have already seen the artistic genius of Giotto around 1300, but it was not until the fifteenth century that Italian painting began to come fully of age. One reason for this was that in the early fifteenth century the laws of linear perspective were discovered and first employed to give the fullest sense of three dimensions. Fifteenth-century artists also experimented with effects of light and shade (*chiaroscuro*) and for the first time carefully studied the anatomy and proportions of the human body. By the fifteenth century, too, increasing private wealth and the growth of lay patronage had opened the domain of art to a variety of nonreligious themes and subjects. Even subject matter from biblical history was now frequently infused with nonreligious themes. Artists sought to paint portraits that revealed the hidden mysteries of the soul. Paintings intended to appeal primarily to the intellect were paralleled by others whose main purpose was to delight the eye with gorgeous color and beauty of form. The introduction of

painting in oil, probably from Flanders, also characterized fifteenth-century painting. The use of the new technique doubtless had much to do with the artistic advance of this period. Since oil does not dry so quickly as fresco pigment, the painter could now work more slowly, taking time with the more difficult parts of the picture and making corrections if necessary as he went along.

RENAISSANCE PAINTING IN FLORENCE

The majority of the great painters of the fifteenth century were Florentines. First among them was the precocious Masaccio (1401–1428), known to his contemporaries as "Giotto reborn." Although he died at the

The Impact of Perspective. Masaccio's painting *The Trinity with the Virgin* illustrates the startling sense of depth made possible by the rules of perspective.

The Birth of Venus, by Botticelli. Botticelli was a mystic as well as a lover of beauty, and the painting is most often interpreted as a Neoplatonic allegory.

age of twenty-seven, Masaccio inspired the work of Italian painters for a hundred years. Masaccio's greatness as a painter is based on his success in "imitating nature," which became a primary value in Renaissance painting. To achieve this effect he employed perspective, perhaps most dramatically in his fresco of the Trinity; he also used chiaroscuro with originality, leading to a dramatic and moving outcome.

The best known of the painters who directly followed the tradition represented by Masaccio was the Florentine Sandro Botticelli (1445–1510), who depicted both classical and Christian subjects. Botticelli's work excels in linear rhythms and sensuous depiction of natural detail. He is most famous for paintings that strike the eye as purely pagan because they portray figures from classical mythology without any overt sign of a Christian frame of reference. His *Allegory of Spring* and *Birth of Venus* employ a style greatly indebted to Roman depictions of gods, goddesses, zephyrs, and muses moving gracefully in natural settings. Consequently these works were once understood as the expression of "Renaissance paganism" at its fullest, a celebration of

earthly delights breaking sharply with Christian asceticism. More recently, however, scholars have preferred to view them as allegories fully compatible with Christian teachings. According to this interpretation, Botticelli was addressing himself to learned aristocratic viewers, well versed in the Neoplatonic theories of Ficino that considered ancient gods and goddesses to represent various Christian virtues. Venus, for example, might have stood for a species of chaste love. Although Botticelli's great "classical" works remain cryptic, two points remain certain: any viewer is free to enjoy them on their naturalistic sensuous level, and Botticelli had surely not broken with Christianity, since he painted frescoes for the pope in Rome at just the same time.

LEONARDO DA VINCI

Perhaps the greatest of the Florentine artists was Leonardo da Vinci (1452–1519), one of the most versatile geniuses who ever lived. Leonardo was practically the personification of the "Renaissance man": he was a painter, architect, musician, mathematician,

Ginevra da Benci, by Leonardo da Vinci.

The Virgin of the Rocks, by Leonardo da Vinci. This painting reveals not only Leonardo's interest in human physiognomy, but also his absorption in the atmosphere of natural settings.

The Last Supper, by Leonardo da Vinci.

engineer, and inventor. The illegitimate son of a lawyer and a peasant woman, Leonardo set up an artist's shop in Florence by the time he was twenty-five and gained the patronage of the Medici ruler of the city, Lorenzo the Magnificent. But if Leonardo had any weakness, it was his slowness in working and difficulty in finishing anything. This naturally displeased Lorenzo and other Florentine patrons, who thought an artist was little more than an artisan, commissioned to produce a certain piece of work of a certain size for a certain price on a certain date. Leonardo, however, strongly objected to this view because he considered himself to be no menial craftsman but an inspired creator. Therefore in 1482 he left Florence for the Sforza court of Milan where he was given freer rein in structuring his time and work. He remained there until the French invaded Milan in 1499; after that he wandered about Italy, finally accepting the patronage of the French king, Francis I, under whose auspices Leonardo lived and worked in France until his death.

The paintings of Leonardo da Vinci began what is known as the High Renaissance in Italy. His approach to painting was that it should be the most accurate possible imitation of nature. Leonardo was like a naturalist, basing his work on his own detailed observations of a blade of grass, the wing of a bird, a waterfall. He obtained human corpses for dissection and reconstructed in drawing the minutest features of anatomy, which knowledge he carried over to his paintings. Leonardo worshiped nature, and was convinced of the essential divinity in all living things. It is not surprising, therefore, that he was a vegetarian, and that he went to the marketplace to buy caged birds, which he released to their native habitat.

It is generally agreed that Leonardo's masterpieces are the *Virgin of the Rocks* (which exists in two versions), the *Last Supper,* and his portraits of the Mona Lisa and Ginevra da Benci. *The Virgin of the Rocks* typifies not only his marvelous technical skill but also his passion for science and his belief in the universe as a well-ordered place. The figures are arranged geometrically, with every rock and plant depicted in accurate detail. The *Last Supper,* painted on the walls of

the refectory of Santa Maria delle Grazie in Milan, is a study of psychological reactions. A serene Christ, resigned to his terrible fate, has just announced to his disciples that one of them will betray him. The artist succeeds in portraying the mingled emotions of surprise, horror, and guilt in the faces of the disciples as they gradually perceive the meaning of their master's statement. The third and fourth of Leonardo's major triumphs, the *Mona Lisa* and *Ginevra da Benci,* reflect a similar interest in the varied moods of the human soul.

THE VENETIAN SCHOOL

The beginning of the High Renaissance around 1490 also witnessed the rise of the so-called Venetian school, the major members of which were Giovanni Bellini (c. 1430–1516), Giorgione (1478–1510), and Titian (c. 1490–1576). The work of all these men

Portait of Doge Francesco Venier (1555), by Titian. Titian served as the official painter of the Venetian Republic for sixty years. This superb portrait of Venice's ruler shows Titian's mastery of light and color.

reflected the luxurious life and the pleasure-loving interests of the thriving commercial city of Venice. Most Venetian painters had little of the concern of the Florentine school with philosophical and psychological interests. Their aim was to appeal primarily to the senses rather than to the mind. They delighted in painting idyllic landscapes and gorgeous symphonies of color. For their subject matter they chose not merely the natural beauty of Venetian sunsets and the shimmering silver of lagoons in the moonlight but also the artificial splendor of sparkling jewels, richly colored satins and velvets, and gorgeous palaces. Their portraits were invariably likenesses of the rich and the powerful. In the subordination of form and meaning to color and elegance they mirrored the sumptuous tastes of the wealthy merchants for whom they were created.

PAINTING IN ROME

The remaining great painters of the High Renaissance all accomplished their most important work in the first half of the sixteenth century when Renaissance Italian art reached its peak. Rome was now the major artistic center of the Italian peninsula, although the traditions of the Florentine school still exerted a potent influence.

RAPHAEL

Among the eminent painters of this period at least two must be given more than passing attention. One was Raphael (1483–1520), a native of Urbino, and perhaps the most beloved artist of the entire Renaissance. The lasting appeal of his style is due primarily to his ennobling portrayals of human beings as temperate, wise, and dignified creatures. Although Raphael was influenced by Leonardo and copied many features of his work, he cultivated a much more symbolical or allegorical approach. His *Disputà* symbolized the dialectical relationship between the church in heaven and the church on earth. In a worldly setting against a brilliant sky, theologians debate the meaning of the Eucharist, while in the clouds above, saints and the Trinity repose in the possession of a holy mystery. Raphael's *School of Athens* depicts harmony between the Platonist and Aristotelian philosophies. Plato (painted as a portrait of Leonardo) is shown pointing upward to emphasize the

The Madonna of the Dawn ("Alba Madonna"), by Raphael (1483–1520). Raphael's art was distinguished by warmth, serenity, and tenderness. Here, the artist emphasizes the humility of the Virgin Mary by having her seated on the ground. The fact that the child John the Baptist and the child Christ are holding a cross reminds the viewer of the Crucifixion to come.

spiritual basis of his world of Ideas, while Aristotle stretches a hand forward to exemplify his claim that the created world embodies these same principles in physical form. Raphael is noted also for his portraits and Madonnas. To the latter, especially, he gave a softness and warmth that seemed to endow them with a sweetness and piety quite different from Leonardo's enigmatic and somewhat distant Madonnas.

MICHELANGELO

The last towering figure of the High Renaissance was Michelangelo (1475–1564), a native of Florence. If Leonardo was a naturalist, Michelangelo was an idealist; where the former sought to recapture and interpret fleeting natural phenomena, Michelangelo, who embraced Neoplatonism as a philosophy, was more con-

The School of Athens, by Raphael.

cerned with expressing enduring, abstract truths. Michelangelo was a painter, sculptor, architect, and poet—and he expressed himself in all these forms with a similar power and in a similar manner. At the center of all of his paintings is the male figure, which is always powerful, colossal, magnificent. If humanity, embodied in the male body, lay at the center of Italian Renaissance culture, then Michelangelo, who depicted the male figure without cease, is the supreme Renaissance artist.

Michelangelo's greatest achievements in painting appear in a single location—the Sistine Chapel in Rome—yet they are products of two different periods in the artist's life and consequently exemplify two different artistic styles and outlooks on the human condition. More famous are the sublime frescoes Michelangelo painted on the ceiling of the Sistine Chapel from 1508 to 1512, depicting scenes from the book of Genesis. All the panels in this series, including *God Dividing the Light from Darkness*, *The Creation of Adam*, and *The Flood*, exemplify the young artist's commitment to classical Greek aesthetic principles of harmony, solidity, and dignified restraint. Correspondingly, all exude a sense of sublime affirmation regarding the Creation and the heroic qualities of mankind. But a quarter of a century later, when Michelangelo returned to work in the Sistine Chapel, both his style and mood had changed dramatically. In the enormous *Last Judgment*, a fresco done for the Sistine Chapel's altar wall in 1536, Michelangelo repudiated classical restraint and substituted a style that emphasized tension and distortion in order to communicate the older man's pessimistic conception of a humanity wracked by fear and bowed by guilt.

SCULPTURE

In the realm of sculpture the Italian Renaissance took a great step forward by creating statues that were no longer carved as parts of columns or doorways on church buildings or as effigies on tombs. Instead, Italian sculptors for the first time since antiquity carved

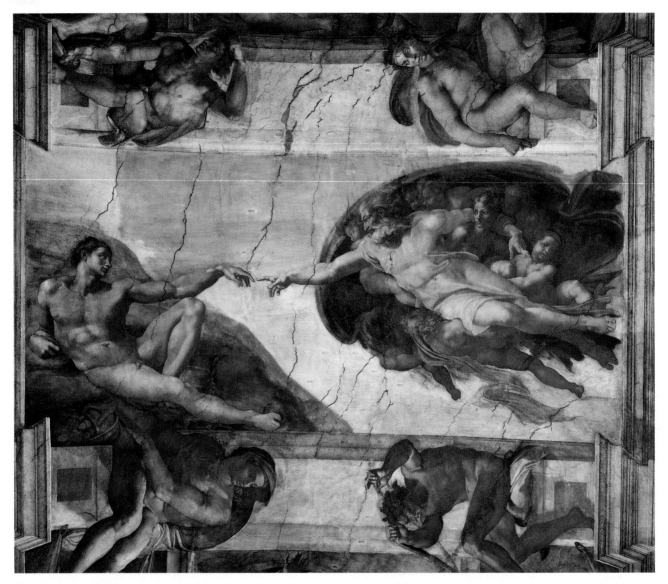

The Creation of Adam, by Michelangelo (1475–1564). One of a series of frescoes on the ceiling of the Sistine Chapel in Rome. Inquiring into the nature of humanity, it represents Renaissance affirmativeness at its height.

free-standing statues "in the round." These freed sculpture from its bondage to architecture and established its status as a separate art frequently devoted to secular purposes.

DONATELLO

The first great master of Renaissance sculpture was Donatello (c. 1386–1466). He emancipated his art from Gothic mannerisms and introduced a new vigorous note of individualism. His bronze statue of David triumphant over the head of the slain Goliath, the first free-standing nude since antiquity, established a precedent of glorifying the life-size nude. Donatello's

David, moreover, was a first step in the direction of imitating classical sculpture, not just in the depiction of a nude body, but also in the subject's posture of resting his weight on one leg. Yet this David is clearly a lithe adolescent rather than a muscular Greek athlete. Later in his career, Donatello more consciously imitated ancient statuary in his commanding portrayal of the proud warrior Gattamelata—the first monumental equestrian statue in bronze executed in the West since the time of the Romans. Here, in addition to drawing very heavily on the legacy of antiquity, the sculptor most clearly expressed his dedication to immortalizing the earthly accomplishments of a contemporary secular hero.

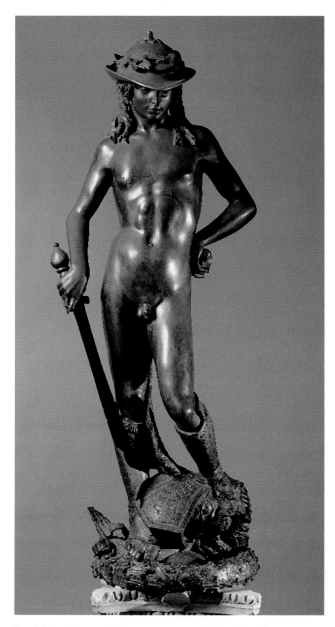

David, by Donatello (c. 1386–1466). The first free-standing nude statue executed in the West since antiquity.

MICHELANGELO

Certainly the greatest sculptor of the Italian Renaissance—indeed, probably the greatest sculptor of all time—was Michelangelo. Believing with Leonardo that the artist was an inspired creator, Michelangelo pursued this belief to the conclusion that sculpture was the most exalted of the arts because it allowed the artist to imitate God most fully in recreating human forms. Furthermore, in Michelangelo's view the most God-like sculptor disdained slavish naturalism, for anyone could make a plaster cast of a human figure,

but only an inspired creative genius could endow his sculpted figures with a sense of life. Accordingly, Michelangelo subordinated naturalism to the force of his imagination and sought restlessly to express his ideals in ever more arresting forms.

Like his painting, Michelangelo's sculpture followed a course from classicism to mannerism, that is, from harmonious modeling to dramatic distortion. The sculptor's most distinguished early work, his *David*, executed in 1501, is surely his most perfect classical statue. Choosing, like Donatello, to depict a male nude, Michelangelo nonetheless conceived of his own

David, by Michelangelo. Over thirteen feet high, this serenely self-confident affirmation of the beauty of the human form was placed prominently by the Florentine government in front of Florence's city hall to proclaim the city's humanistic values.

Descent from the Cross, by Michelangelo. This portrayal of tragedy was made by the sculptor for his own tomb. Note the distortion for effect exemplified by the elongated body and left arm of the figure of Christ. The figure in the rear is Nicodemus, but was probably intended to represent Michelangelo himself.

David as a public expression of Florentine civic ideals, and hence as heroic rather than merely graceful. To this end he worked in marble—the "noblest" sculptural medium—and created a figure twice as large as life. Above all he employed classical style to depict a serenely confident young man at the peak of physical fitness, thereby representing the Florentine republic's own "fortitude" in resisting tyrants and upholding ideals of civic justice. The serenity seen in *David* is no longer prominent in the works of Michelangelo's middle period; rather, in a work such as his *Moses* of about 1515, the sculptor has begun to explore the use of

anatomical distortion to create effects of emotional intensity—in this case, the biblical prophet's righteous rage. While such statues remained awesomely heroic, as Michelangelo's life drew to a close he experimented more and more with exaggerated stylistic mannerisms for the purpose of communicating moods of brooding pensiveness or outright pathos. The culmination of this trend in Michelangelo's statuary is his unfinished but intensely moving *Descent from the Cross,* a depiction of an old man resembling the sculptor himself grieving over the distended, slumping body of the dead Christ.

ARCHITECTURE

To a much greater extent than either sculpture or painting, Renaissance architecture had its roots in the past. The new building style was a compound of elements derived from the Middle Ages and from antiquity. It was not the Gothic, however, a style that had never found a congenial soil in Italy, but the Italian Romanesque that provided the medieval basis for the architecture of the Italian Renaissance. The great architects of the Renaissance generally adopted their building plans from Romanesque churches, some of which they believed, mistakenly, to be Roman rather than medieval. They also copied their decorative devices from the ruins of ancient Rome. The result was an architecture based on the cruciform floor plan of transept and nave and embodying the decorative features of the column and arch, or the column and lintel, the colonnade, and frequently the dome. Horizontal lines predominated. Renaissance architecture also emphasized geometrical proportion because Italian builders, under the influence of Neoplatonism, con-

CHRONOLOGY

LIVES OF ITALIAN RENAISSANCE SCHOLARS AND ARTISTS

Petrarch	1304–1374
Leon Battista Alberti	1404–1472
Giovanni Pico della Mirandola	1463–1494
Niccolò Machiavelli	1469–1527
Leonardo da Vinci	1452–1519
Titian	c. 1490–1576
Raphael	1483–1520
Michelangelo	1475–1564

The Villa Rotonda, by Palladio. A highly influential Renaissance private dwelling near Vicenza.

cluded that certain mathematical ratios reflect the harmony of the universe. A fine example of Renaissance architecture is St. Peter's Basilica in Rome, built under the patronage of popes Julius II and Leo X and designed by some of the most celebrated architects of the time, including Donato Bramante (c. 1444–1514) and Michelangelo. Equally impressive are the artfully proportioned aristocratic country houses designed by the northern Italian architect Andrea Palladio (1508–1580), who created secular miniatures of ancient temples such as the Roman Pantheon to glorify the aristocrats who dwelled within them.

THE WANING OF THE ITALIAN RENAISSANCE

Why did the Renaissance decline around 1550?

Around 1550 the Renaissance in Italy began to decline. The causes of this decline were varied. The French invasion of 1494 and the incessant warfare that ensued was one of the major factors. The French king Charles

VIII viewed Italy as an attractive target for his expansive dynastic ambitions. In 1494 he led an army of thirty thousand well-trained troops across the Alps to press his claims to the Duchy of Milan and the Kingdom of Naples. Florence swiftly capitulated; within less than a year the French had promenaded down the peninsula and conquered Naples. By so doing, however, they aroused the suspicions of the rulers of Spain, who feared an attack on their own territory of Sicily. An alliance among Spain, the Papal States, the Holy Roman empire, Milan, and Venice finally forced Charles to withdraw from Italy. But the respite was brief. Charles's successor, Louis XII, launched a second invasion, and from 1499 until 1529 warfare in Italy was virtually uninterrupted. Alliances and counteralliances followed each other in bewildering succession, but they managed only to prolong the hostilities. The French won a great victory at Marignano in 1515, but they were decisively defeated by the Spanish at Pavia in 1525. The worst disaster came in 1527 when rampaging troops under the command of the Spanish ruler and Holy Roman emperor Charles V sacked the city of Rome, causing enormous destruction. Only in 1529 did Charles V finally manage to gain control over most of the Italian peninsula, putting an end to the fighting for a time. Once triumphant, Charles retained two of the largest portions of Italy for Spain—the Duchy of

THE STATES OF ITALY DURING THE RENAISSANCE, C. 1494

How had the troubles of the papacy in the late fourteenth and early fifteenth centuries helped allow for the growth of aggressive and vibrant states that challenged the papacy within Italy? Why was the kingdom of Naples, despite its more extensive and consolidated territory, at a disadvantage compared with some of its rivals? What event made it possible for the papal states to reassert their influence after 1417? On what economic and political bases did the smaller states of northern Italy grow so powerful? How were these rival states able to maintain equilibrium and prosperity for much of the fifteenth century? How did the Italian "system" leave all of them potentially vulnerable?

Milan and the Kingdom of Naples—and installed favored princes as the rulers of almost all the other Italian political entities except for Venice and the Papal States. These protégés of the Spanish crown continued to preside over their own courts, to patronize the arts, and to adorn their cities with luxurious buildings, but

HOW DID THE NORTHERN AND ITALIAN RENAISSANCES DIFFER FROM ONE ANOTHER?

THE RENAISSANCE IN THE NORTH   475

they were puppets of a foreign power and unable to inspire their retinues with a sense of vigorous cultural independence.

To the Italian political disasters was added a waning of Italian prosperity. Whereas Italy's virtual monopoly of trade with Asia in the fifteenth century had been one of the chief economic supports for Italian Renaissance culture, the gradual shifting of trade routes from the Mediterranean to the Atlantic region, following the overseas discoveries of around 1500, slowly but surely cost Italy its supremacy as the center of world trade. Since the incessant warfare of the sixteenth century also contributed to Italy's economic hardships, as did Spanish financial exactions in Milan and Naples, there was gradually less and less of a surplus to support artistic endeavors.

A final cause of the decline of the Italian Renaissance was the Counter-Reformation. During the sixteenth century the Roman church sought increasingly to exercise firm control over thought and art as part of a campaign to combat worldliness and the spread of Protestantism. In 1542 the Roman Inquisition was established; in 1564 the first Roman Index of Prohibited Books was published. The extent of ecclesiastical interference in cultural life was enormous. For example, Michelangelo's great *Last Judgment* in the Sistine Chapel was criticized by some straitlaced fanatics for looking like a bordello because it showed too many naked bodies. Therefore, Pope Paul IV ordered a second-rate artist to paint in clothing wherever possible. (The unfortunate artist was afterward known as the "underwear maker.") Although this incident may appear merely grotesquely humorous, the determination of ecclesiastical censors to enforce doctrinal uniformity could lead to death, as in the case of the unfortunate Neoplatonic philosopher Giordano Bruno, whose insistence that there may be more than one world (in contravention of the biblical book of Genesis) resulted in his being burned at the stake by the Roman Inquisition in 1600.

The most notorious example of inquisitorial censorship of intellectual speculation was the disciplining of the great scientist Galileo, whose achievements we will discuss in more detail in Chapter 18. In 1616 the Holy Office in Rome condemned the new astronomical theory that the earth moves around the sun as "foolish, absurd, philosophically false, and formally heretical." When Galileo published a brilliant defense of the heliocentric system in 1632 the Inquisition ordered Galileo to recant his "errors" and sentenced him to house arrest for the duration of his life. Galileo was not willing to die for his beliefs, but after he publicly re-tracted his view that the earth revolves around the sun he supposedly whispered, "despite everything, it still moves." Not surprisingly, the great astronomical discoveries of the next generation were made in northern Europe, not in Italy.

Cultural and artistic achievement was by no means extinguished in Italy after the middle of the sixteenth century. On the contrary, impressive new artistic styles were cultivated between about 1540 and 1600 by painters who drew on traits found in the later work of Raphael and Michelangelo. In the seventeenth century came the dazzling Baroque style, which was born in Rome under ecclesiastical auspices. Similarly, Italian music registered enormous accomplishments virtually without interruption from the sixteenth to the twentieth century. But as Renaissance culture spread from Italy to the rest of Europe, the cultural dominance of the Italians began to wane, and the focus of European high culture shifted toward the princely courts of Spain, France, England, Germany, and Poland.

THE RENAISSANCE IN THE NORTH

How did the northern and Italian Renaissances differ from one another?

Throughout the fifteenth century a continuous procession of northern European students went to Italy to study in Italian universities such as Bologna or Padua, and an occasional Italian writer or artist traveled briefly north of the Alps. Such interchanges helped spread ideas, but only after around 1500 did most of northern Europe once again become sufficiently prosperous and politically stable as to provide a truly congenial environment for the widespread cultivation of art and literature. Intellectual interchanges also became much more extensive after 1494, when France and Spain started fighting on Italian battlefields. The result of this development was that more and more northern Europeans began to learn what the Italians had been accomplishing. Leading Italian thinkers and artists, such as Leonardo, also began to enter the retinues of northern kings or aristocrats. Accordingly, the Renaissance became an international movement and continued to be vigorous in the north even as it started to wane on its native ground.

CHRISTIAN HUMANISM AND THE NORTHERN RENAISSANCE

The Renaissance outside Italy was by no means identical to the Renaissance within Italy. Above all, the northern European Renaissance was more explicitly Christian in its outlook and orientation. The main explanation for this difference lies in the different social and cultural traditions that had evolved in Italy and northern Europe during the High Middle Ages. As we have seen, the vigorous urban society of medieval Italy fostered a lay educational system that led, in union with a revival of classicism, to the evolution of new, more secular forms of expression from the thirteenth century on. Northern Europe, in contrast, had a less mercantile and urban-oriented economy than did Italy. City-states on the Italian model did not emerge there. Instead, political power coalesced around the nation-states (or in Germany the princedoms), whose rulers were willing until about 1500 to acknowledge the educational and cultural hegemony of the clergy. This was especially the case with respect to northern universities, which tended to specialize in theological studies and which remained, therefore, under the closer supervision of the church. As a result, the Italian tradition of urban-based lay intellectual and cultural elites simply did not exist in the north. Nor did the northern European universities, dominated as they were by scholasticism, provide a hospitable environment for the new humanist learning emerging out of Italy. Instead, the northern European Renaissance was principally promoted by scholars working outside the university system under the patronage of kings and princes.

The northern Renaissance was the product of the grafting of certain Italian Renaissance ideals onto pre-existing northern traditions. This can be seen very clearly in the case of the most prominent northern Renaissance intellectual movement, Christian humanism. Although agreeing with Italian humanists that medieval scholasticism was too ensnarled in logical hair splitting to have any value for the practical conduct of life, northern Christian humanists more often looked for practical guidance from biblical and religious precepts rather than from Cicero or Virgil. Like their Italian counterparts, they sought wisdom from antiquity, but the antiquity they had in mind was Christian rather than classical—the antiquity, that is, of the

> The northern European Renaissance was more explicitly Christian in its outlook and orientation.

New Testament and the early Christian fathers. Similarly, northern Renaissance artists were moved by the accomplishments of Italian Renaissance masters to turn their backs on medieval Gothic artistic styles and to learn instead how to employ classical techniques. Yet these same artists depicted classical subject matter far less frequently than did the Italians, and virtually never ventured to portray completely undressed human figures.

DESIDERIUS ERASMUS

Any discussion of northern Renaissance accomplishments in the realm of thought and literary expression must begin with the career of Desiderius Erasmus (c. 1469–1536), the "prince of the Christian humanists." The illegitimate son of a priest, Erasmus was born near Rotterdam in Holland, but later, as a result of his wide travels, became in effect a citizen of all northern Europe. Forced into a monastery against his will when he was a teenager, the young Erasmus found there little religion or formal instruction of any kind but plenty of freedom to read what he liked. He devoured all the classics he could get his hands on and the writings of many of the Church fathers. When he was about thirty years of age, he obtained permission to leave the monastery and enroll in the University of Paris, where he completed the requirements for the degree of bachelor of divinity. But Erasmus subsequently rebelled against what he considered the arid learning of Parisian scholasticism. In one of his later writings he reported the following exchange: "Q. Where do you come from? A. The College of Montaigu. Q. Ah, then you must be bowed down with learning. A. No, with lice." Erasmus also never entered into the active duties of a priest, choosing instead to make his living from teaching, writing, and the proceeds of various ecclesiastical offices that required no spiritual duties of him. Ever on the lookout for new patrons, he changed his residence at frequent intervals, traveling often to England, staying once for three years in Italy, and residing in several different cities in Germany and the Netherlands before settling finally toward the end of his life in Basel, Switzerland. By means of a voluminous correspondence that he kept up with learned friends he made wherever he went, Erasmus became the leader of a northern European humanist coterie. And by means of the popularity of

HOW DID THE NORTHERN AND ITALIAN RENAISSANCES DIFFER FROM ONE ANOTHER?

THE RENAISSANCE IN THE NORTH   477

his numerous publications, he became the arbiter of "advanced" northern European cultural tastes during the first quarter of the sixteenth century.

Erasmus' many-sided intellectual activity may best be appraised from two different points of view: the literary and the doctrinal. As a Latin prose stylist, Erasmus was unequaled since the days of Cicero. Extraordinarily learned and witty, he reveled in tailoring his mode of discourse to fit his subject, creating dazzling verbal effects and coining puns that took on added meaning if the reader knew Greek as well as Latin. Above all, Erasmus excelled in the deft use of irony, poking fun at all and sundry, including himself. For example, in his *Colloquies* (from the Latin for "discussions") he had a fictional character lament the evil signs of the times thus: "kings make war, priests strive to line their pockets, theologians invent syllogisms, monks roam outside their cloisters, the commons riot, and Erasmus writes colloquies."

But although Erasmus' urbane Latin style and wit

Erasmus, by Hans Holbein the Younger (1497–1543). This portrait is generally regarded as the most telling visual characterization of "the prince of the Christian humanists."

earned him a wide audience for purely literary reasons, he by no means thought of himself as a mere entertainer. Rather, he intended everything he wrote to propagate in one form or another what he called the "philosophy of Christ." The essence of Erasmus' Christian humanist convictions was his belief that the entire society of his day was caught up in corruption and immorality as a result of having lost sight of the simple teachings of the Gospels. Accordingly, he offered to his contemporaries three different categories of publication: clever satires meant to show people the error of their ways, serious moral treatises meant to offer guidance toward proper Christian behavior, and scholarly editions of basic Christian texts.

In the first category belong the works of Erasmus that are still most widely read today—*The Praise of Folly* (1509), in which he pilloried scholastic pedantry and dogmatism as well as the ignorance and superstitious credulity of the masses; and the *Colloquies* (1518), in which he held up contemporary religious practices for examination in a more serious but still pervasively ironic tone. In such works Erasmus let fictional characters do the talking; hence his own views can be determined only by inference. But in his second mode Erasmus did not hesitate to speak clearly in his own voice. The most prominent treatises in this second genre are the quietly eloquent *Handbook of the Christian Knight* (1503), which urged the laity to pursue lives of serene inward piety, and the *Complaint of Peace* (1517), which pleaded movingly for Christian pacifism. Erasmus' pacifism was one of his most deeply held values, and he returned to it again and again in his published works.

Despite this highly impressive literary production, Erasmus probably considered his textual scholarship his single greatest achievement. Revering the authority of the early Latin fathers Augustine, Jerome, and Ambrose, he brought out reliable editions of all their works. He also applied his extraordinary skills as a student of Latin and Greek to producing a more accurate edition of the New Testament. After reading Lorenzo Valla's *Notes on the New Testament* in 1504, Erasmus became convinced that nothing was more imperative than divesting the New Testament of the myriad errors in transcription and translation that had piled up during the Middle Ages, for no one could be a good Christian without being certain of exactly what Christ's message really was. Hence he spent ten years studying and comparing all the best early Greek biblical manuscripts he could find in order to establish an authoritative text. Finally appearing in 1516, Erasmus'

Greek New Testament, published together with explanatory notes and his own new Latin translation, was one of the most important landmarks of biblical scholarship of all time. In the hands of Martin Luther, it would play a critical role in the early stages of the Protestant Reformation.

SIR THOMAS MORE

One of Erasmus' closest friends, and a close second to him in distinction among the ranks of the Christian humanists, was the Englishman Sir Thomas More (1478–1535). Following a successful career as a lawyer and as speaker of the House of Commons, in 1529 More was appointed lord chancellor of England. He was not long in this position, however, before he incurred the wrath of his royal master, King Henry VIII. More, who was loyal to Catholic universalism, opposed the king's design to establish a national church under subjection to the state. Finally, in 1534, when More refused to take an oath acknowledging Henry as head of the Church of England, he was thrown into the Tower of London, and a year later met his death on the scaffold as a Catholic martyr. Much earlier, however, in 1516, long before More had any inkling of how his life

Sir Thomas More, by Hans Holbein the Younger.

was to end, he published the one work for which he will ever be best remembered, *Utopia*. Creating the subsequently popular genre of "utopian fiction," More's *Utopia* expressed an Erasmian critique of contemporary society. Purporting to describe an ideal community on an imaginary island, the book is really an indictment of the glaring abuses of the time—of poverty undeserved and wealth unearned, of drastic punishments, religious persecution, and the senseless slaughter of war. The inhabitants of Utopia hold all their goods in common, work only six hours a day so that all may have leisure for intellectual pursuits, and practice the natural virtues of wisdom, moderation, fortitude, and justice. Iron is the precious metal "because it is useful," war and monasticism do not exist, and toleration is granted to all who recognize the existence of God and the immortality of the soul. Although More advanced no explicit arguments in his *Utopia* in favor of Christianity, he clearly meant to imply that if the "Utopians" could manage their society so well without the benefit of Christian revelation, Europeans who knew the Gospels ought to be able to do even better.

ULRICH VON HUTTEN

Whereas Erasmus and More were basically conciliatory in their temperaments and preferred to express themselves by means of wry understatements, a third representative of the Christian humanist movement, Erasmus' German disciple Ulrich von Hutten (1488–1523), was of a much more combative disposition. Dedicated to the cause of German cultural nationalism, von Hutten spoke up truculently to defend the "proud and free" German people against foreigners. But his chief claim to fame was his collaboration with another German humanist, Crotus Rubianus, in the authorship of the *Letters of Obscure Men* (1515), one of the most stinging satires in the history of literature. This was written as part of a propaganda war in favor of a scholar named Johann Reuchlin who wished to pursue his study of Hebrew writings, above all, the Talmud. When scholastic theologians and the German inquisitor general tried to have all Hebrew books in Germany destroyed, Reuchlin and his party strongly opposed the move. After a while it became apparent that direct argument was accomplishing nothing, so Reuchlin's supporters resorted to ridicule. Von Hutten and Rubianus published a series of letters, written in intentionally bad Latin, purportedly by some of Reuchlin's scholastic opponents from the University of Cologne. These opponents, given such ridiculous names as

HOW DID THE NORTHERN AND ITALIAN RENAISSANCES DIFFER FROM ONE ANOTHER?

THE RENAISSANCE IN THE NORTH   479

Goatmilker, Baldpate, and Dungspreader, were shown to be learned fools who paraded absurd religious literalism or grotesque erudition. Heinrich Sheep's-mouth, for example, the supposed writer of one of the letters, professed to be worried that he had sinned grievously by eating on Friday an egg that contained the embryo of a chick. The author of another boasted of his "brilliant discovery" that Julius Caesar could not have written Latin histories because he was too busy with his military exploits ever to have learned Latin. Although immediately banned by the church, the letters circulated nonetheless and were widely read, giving ever more currency to the Erasmian proposition that scholastic theology and Catholic religious observances had to be set aside in favor of the most earnest dedication to the simple teachings of the Gospels.

THE DECLINE OF CHRISTIAN HUMANISM

With Erasmus, More, and von Hutten the list of energetic and eloquent Christian humanists is by no means exhausted, for the Englishman John Colet (c. 1467–1519), the Frenchman Jacques Lefèvre d'Étaples (c. 1455–1536), and the Spaniards Cardinal Francisco Ximénez de Cisneros (1436–1517) and Juan Luís Víves (1492–1540) all made signal contributions to the collective enterprise of editing biblical and early Christian texts and expounding Gospel morality. But despite a host of achievements, the Christian humanist movement, which possessed such an extraordinary degree of international solidarity and vigor from about 1500 to 1525, was thrown into disarray by the rise of Protestantism and subsequently lost its momentum. The irony here is obvious, for the Christian humanists' emphasis on the literal truth of the Gospels and their devastating criticisms of clerical corruption and excessive religious ceremonialism certainly helped pave the way for the Protestant Reformation initiated by Martin Luther in 1517. But, as we will see in Chapter 14, very few of the older generation of Christian humanists were willing to go the whole route with Luther in rejecting the most fundamental principles on which Catholicism was based, and the few who did became such ardent Protestants that they lost the sense of quiet irony that earlier had been a hallmark of Christian humanist expression. Most Christian humanists tried to remain within the Catholic fold while still espousing their ideal of non-ritualistic inward piety. But as time went on, the lead-

ers of Catholicism had less and less tolerance for them because lines were hardening in the war with Protestantism. Hence, any internal criticism of Catholic religious practices seemed like giving covert aid to the "enemy." Erasmus himself, who remained a Catholic, died early enough to escape opprobrium, but several of his less fortunate followers lived on to suffer as victims of the Inquisition.

LITERATURE, ART, AND MUSIC IN THE NORTHERN RENAISSANCE

Yet if Christian humanism faded rapidly after about 1525, the northern Renaissance continued to flourish throughout the sixteenth century in literature and art. In France, the highly accomplished poets Pierre de Ronsard (c. 1524–1585) and Joachim du Bellay (c. 1522–1560) wrote elegant sonnets in the style of Petrarch, and in England the poets Sir Philip Sidney (1554–1586) and Edmund Spenser (c. 1552–1599) drew impressively on Italian literary innovations. Indeed, Spenser's *Faerie Queene*, a long chivalric romance written in the manner of Ariosto's *Orlando Furioso*, communicates as well as any Italian work the gorgeous sensuousness typical of Italian Renaissance culture.

RABELAIS

More intrinsically original than any of the aforementioned poets was the French prose satirist François Rabelais (c. 1494–1553), probably the best loved of all the great European creative writers of the sixteenth century. Like Erasmus, whom he greatly admired, Rabelais began his career in the clergy, but soon after taking holy orders he left his cloister to study medicine. Becoming thereafter a practicing physician in Lyons, Rabelais interspersed his professional activities with literary endeavors of one sort or another. He wrote almanacs, satires against quacks and astrologers, and burlesques of popular superstitions. But by far his most enduring literary legacy consists of his five volumes of "chronicles" published under the collective title of *Gargantua and Pantagruel*.

Rabelais' account of the adventures of Gargantua and Pantagruel, originally the names of legendary medieval giants noted for their fabulous size and gross appetites, served as a vehicle for his lusty humor and his penchant for exuberant narrative as well as for the expression of his philosophy of naturalism. To some degree, Rabelais drew on the precedents of Christian humanism. Thus, like Erasmus, he satirized religious ceremonialism, ridiculed scholasticism, scoffed at superstitions, and pilloried every form of bigotry. But unlike Erasmus, who wrote in a highly cultivated classical Latin style comprehensible to only the most learned readers, Rabelais chose to address a far wider audience by writing in an extremely down-to-earth French loaded with the crudest vulgarities. Likewise, Rabelais wanted to avoid seeming in any way "preachy" and therefore eschewed all suggestions of moralism in favor of giving the impression that he wished merely to offer his readers some rollicking good fun. Yet, aside from the critical satire in *Gargantua and Pantagruel*, there runs through all five volumes a common theme of glorifying the human and the natural. For Rabelais, whose robust giants were really life-loving human beings writ very large, every instinct of humanity was healthy, provided it was not directed toward tyranny over others. Thus in his ideal community, the utopian "abbey of Thélème," there was no repressiveness whatsoever, but only a congenial environment for the pursuit of life-affirming, natural human attainments, guided by the single rule of "do what thou wouldst."

ARCHITECTURE

Were we to imagine what Rabelais' fictional abbey of Thélème might have looked like, we would do best to picture it as resembling one of the famous sixteenth-century French Renaissance châteaux built along the River Loire, for the northern European Renaissance had its own distinctive architecture that often corresponded in certain essentials to its literature. Thus, just as Rabelais recounted stories of medieval giants in order to express an affirmation of Renaissance values, so French architects who constructed such splendid Loire châteaux as Amboise, Chenonceaux, and Chambord combined elements of the late medieval French flamboyant Gothic style with an up-to-date emphasis on classical horizontality to produce some of the most impressively distinctive architectural landmarks ever constructed in France. Yet much closer architectural imitation of Italian models occurred in France as well, for just as Ronsard and du Bellay modeled their poetic style very closely on Petrarch, so Pierre Lescot, the French architect who began work on the new royal palace of the Louvre in Paris in 1546, hewed closely to the classicism of Italian Renaissance masters in constructing a facade that emphasized classical pilasters and pediments.

PAINTING

Northern Renaissance painting is another realm in which links between thought and art can be discerned. Certainly the most moving visual embodiments of the ideals of Christian humanism were conceived by the foremost of northern Renaissance artists, the German Albrecht Dürer (1471–1528). From the purely technical and stylistic points of view, Dürer's greatest signifi-

Chambord. Built in the early sixteenth century by an Italian architect in the service of King Francis I of France, this magnificent Loire Valley château combines Gothic and Renaissance architectural traits.

HOW DID THE NORTHERN AND ITALIAN RENAISSANCES DIFFER FROM ONE ANOTHER?

THE RENAISSANCE IN THE NORTH   481

The West Side of the Square Court on the Louvre, by Pierre Lescot. The enlargement of the Louvre, begun by Lescot in 1546, took more than a century to complete. In it, he achieved a synthesis of the traditional château and the Renaissance palace.

cance lies in the fact that, returning to his native Nuremberg after a trip to Venice in 1494, he became the first northerner to master Italian Renaissance techniques of proportion, perspective, and modeling. Dürer also shared with contemporary Italians a fascination with reproducing the manifold works of nature down to the minutest details and a penchant for displaying various postures of the human nude. But whereas Michelangelo portrayed his naked *David* or *Adam* entirely without covering, Dürer's nudes are seldom lacking their fig leaves, in deference to more restrained northern traditions. Moreover, Dürer consistently refrained from abandoning himself to the pure classicism and sumptuousness of much Italian Renaissance art because he was inspired primarily by the more traditionally Christian ideals of Erasmus. Thus Dürer's serenely radiant engraving of Saint Jerome expresses the sense of accomplishment that Erasmus or any other contemporary Christian humanist may have had while working quietly in his study; and his *Four Apostles* intones a solemn hymn to the dignity and penetrating insight of Dürer's favorite New Testament authors, Saints Paul, John, Peter, and Mark.

Dürer would have loved nothing more than to have immortalized Erasmus in a major painted portrait, but circumstances prevented him from doing this because the paths of the two men crossed only once, and after Dürer started sketching his hero on that occasion his work was interrupted by Erasmus' press of business.

Saint Jerome in His Study, by Dürer. Saint Jerome, a hero for both Dürer and Erasmus, represents inspired Christian scholarship. Note how the scene exudes contentment, even down to the sleeping lion, which seems rather like an overgrown tabby cat.

Instead, the accomplishment of capturing Erasmus' pensive spirit in oils was left to another great northern Renaissance artist, the German Hans Holbein the Younger (1497–1543; see p. 477). As good fortune would have it, during a stay in England Holbein also painted an extraordinarily acute portrait of Erasmus' friend and kindred spirit Sir Thomas More, which enables us to see clearly why a contemporary called More "a man of . . . sad gravity; a man for all seasons" (see p. 478). These two portraits in and of themselves point up a major difference between medieval and Renaissance culture. Whereas the Middle Ages produced no convincing naturalistic likenesses of any leading intellectual figures, Renaissance culture's greater commitment to capturing the essence of human individuality created the environment in which Holbein was able to make Erasmus and More come to life.

MUSIC

Music in western Europe in the fifteenth and sixteenth centuries reached such a high point of development that it constitutes, together with painting and sculpture, one of the most brilliant aspects of Renaissance endeavor. The musical theory of the Renaissance was driven largely by the humanist-inspired but largely fruitless effort to recover and imitate classical musical forms and modes. Musical practice, however, showed much more continuity with medieval musical traditions of number and proportion. At the same time, however, a new expressiveness emerges in Renaissance music, along with a new emphasis on coloration and emotional quality. New musical instruments were also developed, including the lute, the viol, the violin, and a variety of woodwind and keyboard instruments including the harpsichord. New musical forms also emerged: madrigals, motets, and, at the end of the sixteenth century, a new Italian form, the opera. As earlier, musical leadership came from men trained in the service of the church. But the distinction between sacred and profane music was becoming less sharp, and most composers did not restrict their activities to a single field. Music was no longer regarded merely as a diversion or an adjunct to worship, but came into its own as a serious independent art.

Different areas of Europe vied with one another for musical leadership. As with the other arts, advances were related to the generous patronage afforded by the prosperous cities of Italy and the northern European princely courts. During the fourteenth century a pre- or early Renaissance musical movement called *ars nova*

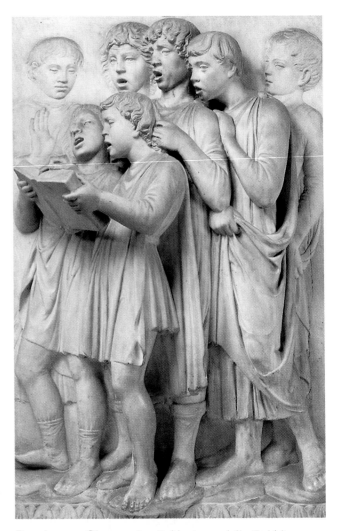

Renaissance Singers. A relief by Luca della Robbia.

("new art") flourished in Italy and France. Its outstanding composers were Francesco Landini (c. 1325–1397) and Guillaume de Machaut (c. 1300–1377). The madrigals, ballads, and other songs composed by the *ars nova* musicians testify to a rich fourteenth-century tradition of secular music, but the greatest achievement of the period was a highly complicated yet delicate contrapuntal style adapted for ecclesiastical motets. Machaut, moreover, was the first known composer to provide a polyphonic version of the major sections of the Mass.

The fifteenth century ushered in a synthesis of French, Flemish, and Italian elements in the ducal court of Burgundy. This music was melodious and gentle, but in the second half of the century it hardened a little as northern Flemish elements gained in importance. As the sixteenth century opened, Franco-Flemish composers appeared in every important court and cathedral all over Europe, gradually establishing regional-national schools, usually in attractive combinations of Flemish with German, Spanish, and Italian musical cultures. The various genres thus created show a close affinity with Renaissance art and poetry. In the second half of the sixteenth century the leaders of the nationalized Franco-Flemish style were the Fleming Roland de Lassus (1532–1594), the most versatile composer of the age, and the Italian Giovanni Pierluigi da Palestrina (c. 1525–1594), who specialized in highly intricate polyphonic choral music written for Catholic church services under the patronage of the popes in Rome. Music also flourished in sixteenth-century England, where the Tudor monarchs Henry VIII and Elizabeth I were active patrons of the arts. Not only did the Italian madrigal, imported toward the end of the sixteenth century, take on remarkable new life in England, but songs and instrumental music of an original cast anticipated future developments on the Continent. In William Byrd (1543–1623) English music produced a master fully the equal of the great Flemish and Italian composers of the Renaissance period. The general level of musical proficiency seems to have been higher in Queen Elizabeth's day than in ours: the singing of part-songs was a popular pastime in homes and at informal social gatherings, and the ability to read a part at sight was expected of the educated elite.

Although accomplishments in counterpoint were already very advanced in the Renaissance period, our modern harmonic system was still in its infancy, and thus there remained much room for experimentation. At the same time we should realize that the music of the Renaissance constitutes not merely a stage in evolution but a magnificent achievement in itself, with

masters who rank among the greatest of all time. The composers Lassus, Palestrina, and Byrd are as truly representative of the artistic triumph of the Renaissance as are the painters Leonardo, Raphael, and Michelangelo. Their heritage, long neglected, has within recent years begun to be appreciated, and is now gaining in popularity as interested groups of musicians devote themselves to its revival.

CONCLUSION

The contrasts between the Italian and the northern Renaissance are real, but they must not be exaggerated. The intellectuals of Renaissance Italy were formed in a more secular and a more urban educational environment than were the northerners, but they were no less fervent in their Christianity. Petrarch's criticism of scholasticism was not that it was too Christian, but rather that it was not Christian enough. Petrarch opposed the emotional aridity and stylistic inelegance of scholasticism because he believed they threatened the salvation of Christians. Much the same point might be made about Lorenzo Valla. His critique of the temporal claims of the papacy sprang not only from the conclusions of his textual scholarship, but also from a firm Christian piety. The Platonic Academy might honor Plato as if he were a saint of the church, but these men approached Plato's works in the same spirit with which thirteenth century scholastic theologians had approached the works of Aristotle. As committed Christians, they were convinced that the conclusions reached by the greatest philosophical minds of classical antiquity must be compatible with Christian truth. It was the task of Christian intellectuals to reveal this compatibility, and by so doing, to strengthen the one true faith.

In considering the contrasts between "civic" and "Christian" humanism, we must keep in mind the enormous diversity of Renaissance thought. Machiavelli is no more "typical" an Italian Renaissance thinker than is Ficino, Alberti, or Bruno. In comparing Italian thinkers with northern thinkers, we must therefore be careful to compare "like" with "like." Too often, scholars overdraw the contrasts between Renaissance thought in Italy and northern Europe by choosing Machiavelli, for example, to represent all of Italian humanism and Erasmus to represent northern humanism. Two more different figures can hardly be imagined; but their differences have much more to do with their contrasting

CHRONOLOGY

LIVES OF NORTHERN RENAISSANCE SCHOLARS AND ARTISTS

Erasmus	c. 1469–1536
Thomas More	1478–1535
Ulrich von Hutten	1488–1523
Edmund Spenser	c. 1552–1599
François Rabelais	c. 1494–1553
Albrecht Dürer	1471–1528
Hans Holbein the Younger	1497–1543

presuppositions about human nature than they do with their "allegiances" to Italian or northern humanism. A very different picture emerges if we compare, for example, John Colet as a representative of northern humanism with Marsilio Ficino as a representative of Italian humanism, or compare Petrarch with Sir Thomas More.

Nor should we overdraw the contrasts between the Renaissance and the High Middle Ages. Both Italian and northern humanists shared an optimistic view of human nature as improvable despite the consequences of Adam and Eve's disobedience; but none were more optimistic on this score than was Saint Thomas Aquinas. Both groups emphasized the importance of personal introspection and self-examination; but none took this injunction more seriously than did the Cistercian thinkers of the twelfth century. And finally, both groups shared a belief that the exhortations of intellectuals would lift everyone's morals and conduct them to new heights of virtue. In this regard, High Renaissance intellectual life has a kind of naïve optimism that contrasts sharply with the darker, more psychologically complex world of the Middle Ages, and with the Reformation era that was about to begin.

SELECTED READINGS

Alberti, Leon Battista. *The Family in Renaissance Florence (Della Famiglia)*. Translated by Renée Neu Watkins. Columbia, S.C., 1969.

Baron, Hans. *The Crisis of the Early Italian Renaissance*. Princeton, 1966. A highly influential account of "civic humanism."

Baxandall, Michael. *Painting and Experience in Fifteenth Century Italy*. Oxford, 1972. A classic study of the perceptual world of the Renaissance.

Brucker, Gene. *Florence, the Golden Age, 1138–1737*. Berkeley and Los Angeles, 1998 The standard account by a master historian.

———. *The Society of Renaissance Florence: A Documentary Study*. New York, 1971. A revealing portrait of Florentine society and social mores through original documents.

Bruni, Leonardo. *The Humanism of Leonardo Bruni: Selected Texts*. Translated by Gordon Griffiths, James Hankins, and David Thompson. Binghamton, N.Y., 1987. Excellent translations, with introductions, to the Latin works of a key Renaissance humanist.

Burke, Peter. *The Renaissance*. New York, 1997. A brief introduction by an influential modern historian.

———. *Culture and Society in Renaissance Italy*, 2d ed. Princeton, N.J., 1999. A revision and restatement of arguments first advanced in 1972.

Burkhardt, Jacob. *The Civilization of the Renaissance in Italy*. Many editions. The nineteenth-century work that first crystallized an image of the Italian Renaissance with which scholars have been wrestling ever since.

Cassirer, Ernst, et al., eds. *The Renaissance Philosophy of Man*. Chicago, 1948. Important original works by Petrarch, Ficino, and Pico della Mirandola, among others.

Castiglione, Baldassare. *The Book of the Courtier*. Many editions. The translations by C. S. Singleton (New York, 1959) and by George Bull (New York, 1967) are both excellent.

Cellini, Benvenuto. *Autobiography*. Translated by George Bull. Baltimore, 1956. The autobiography of a Florentine goldsmith (1500–1571); the source for many of the most famous stories about the artists of the Florentine Renaissance.

Cochrane, Eric, and Julius Kirshner, eds. *The Renaissance*. Chicago, 1986. An outstanding collection, from the University of Chicago Readings in Western Civilization series.

Erasmus, Desiderius. *The Praise of Folly*. Translated by J. Wilson. Ann Arbor, Mich., 1958.

Fox, Alistair. *Thomas More: History and Providence*. Oxford, 1982. A balanced account of a man too easily idealized.

Grafton, Anthony, and Lisa Jardine. *From Humanism to the Humanities: Education and the Liberal Arts in Fifteenth- and Sixteenth-Century Europe*. London, 1986. An influential recent account that presents Renaissance humanism as the elitist cultural program of a self-interested group of pedagogues.

Grendler, Paul, ed. *Encyclopedia of the Renaissance*. New York, 1999. A valuable reference work.

Hale, John R. *The Civilization of Europe in the Renaissance*. New York, 1993. A synthetic volume summarizing the life's work of a major Renaissance historian.

Hankins, James. *Plato in the Italian Renaissance*. Leiden and New York, 1990. A definitive study of the reception and influence of Plato on Renaissance intellectuals.

———, ed. *Renaissance Civic Humanism: Reappraisals and Reflections*. Cambridge and New York, 2000. An excellent collection of scholarly essays reassessing republicanism in the Renaissance.

Jardine, Lisa. *Worldly Goods*. London, 1996. A revisionist account that emphasizes the acquisitive materialism of Italian Renaissance society and culture.

Kanter, Laurence, Hilliard T. Goldfarb, and James Hankins. *Botticelli's Witness: Changing Style in a Changing Florence*. Boston, 1997. This catalogue, for an exhibit of Botticelli's works at the Gardner Museum in Boston, offers an excellent introduction to the painter and his world.

King, Margaret L. *Women of the Renaissance*. Chicago, 1991. Deals with women in all walks of life and in a variety of roles.

Kristeller, Paul. O. *Renaissance Thought: The Classic, Scholastic, and Humanistic Strains*. New York, 1961. Very helpful in defining the main trends of Renaissance thought.

———. *Eight Philosophers of the Italian Renaissance*. Stanford, 1964. An admirably clear and accurate account that fully appreciates the connections between medieval and Renaissance thought.

Lane, Frederic C. *Venice: A Maritime Republic*. Baltimore, 1973. An authoritative account.

Machiavelli, Niccolò. *The Discourses* and *The Prince*. Many editions. These two books must be read together if one is to understand Machiavelli's political ideas properly.

Martines, Lauro. *Power and Imagination: City-States in Renaissance Italy*. New York, 1979. Insightful account of the connections between politics, society, culture, and art.

More, Thomas. *Utopia*. Many editions.

Muir, Edward. *Mad Blood Stirring: Vendetta and Factions in Friuli during the Renaissance*. Baltimore, 1993. A revealing local study of one of the primary challenges to the political and social order of Renaissance cities.

Murray, Linda. *High Renaissance and Mannerism*. London, 1985. The place to start for fifteenth- and sixteenth-century Italian art.

Olson, Roberta, *Italian Renaissance Sculpture*, New York, 1992. The most accessible introduction to the subject.

Perkins, Leeman L. *Music in the Age of the Renaissance*. New York, 1999. A massive new study that nonetheless needs to be read in conjunction with Reese (see below).

Rabelais, François. *Gargantua and Pantagruel*. Translated by J. M. Cohen. Baltimore, 1955. A robust modern translation.

Reese, Gustave. *Music in the Renaissance*, rev. ed. New York, 1959. A great book; still authoritative, despite the more recent work by Perkins (see above), which supplements but does not replace it.

Rice, Eugene F., Jr., and Anthony Grafton. *The Foundations of Early Modern Europe, 1460–1559*, 2d ed. New York, 1994. The best textbook account of its period.

Rocke, Michael. *Forbidden Friendships: Homosexuality and Male Culture in Renaissance Florence*. New York, 1996. A remarkable quantitative study of efforts by the civic authorities of fifteenth-century Florence to suppress same-gender sexual activity among Florentine men; opens up an important subject to detailed examination.

Rowland, Ingrid D. *The Culture of the High Renaissance: Ancients and Moderns in Sixteenth-Century Rome*. Cambridge and New York, 2000. Beautifully written examination of the social, intellectual, and economic foundations of the Renaissance in Rome.

CHAPTER FOURTEEN

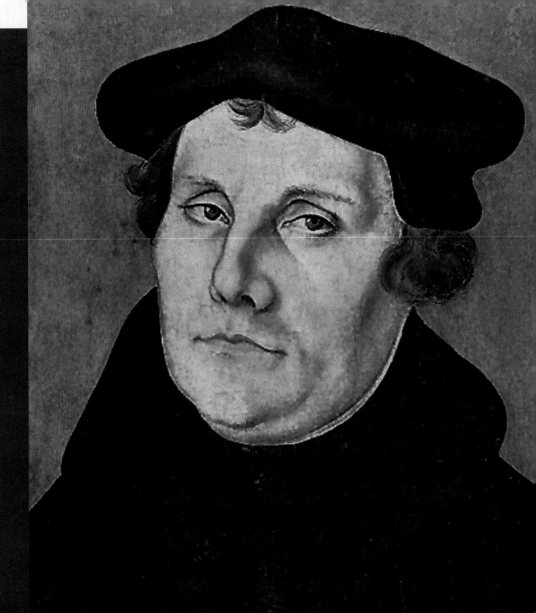

THE PROTESTANT
REFORMATION

AFTER TWO CENTURIES of economic, social, and political turmoil, Europe in the year 1500 was well on the road to recovery. The population was increasing, the economy was expanding, cities were growing, and the national monarchies of France, England, Spain, and Poland were all securely established. Throughout Europe, governments at every level were extending and deepening their control over their subjects' lives. After a late-fourteenth-century hiatus, Europe had also resumed its commercial and colonial expansion. Even Catholic Christianity appeared to be going from strength to strength as the sixteenth century dawned. Although the papacy remained mired in territorial wars in Italy, the church itself had weathered the storms that had beset it during the fifteenth century. The Lollards had been suppressed and the Hussites reincorporated into the church. In the struggle over conciliarism, the Papacy had successfully won the support of all the major European rulers, reducing the conciliarists to academic isolation at the University of Paris. Meanwhile, at the parish level, the devotion of ordinary Christians to their faith had probably never been higher. To be sure, there were also problems. Although the educational standards of the parish clergy were higher than they had ever been, reformers were quick to note that too many priests were still absent, ignorant, or neglectful of their spiritual duties. Monasticism, by and large, seemed to have lost its spiritual fire; while among the populace, religious enthusiasm sometimes led the faithful into gross superstition and doctrinal error. But these were manageable problems. On the whole, the "prospect of Europe" had not looked brighter for several centuries.

No one in 1500 could have predicted that within fifty years Europe's religious unity would be irreparably shattered by a new and powerful Protestant reform movement—or that in the century thereafter an appallingly destructive series of religious wars would shake to their core the foundations of European political life. Remarkably, these extraordinary events began with a single German monk named Martin Luther (1483–1546), whose personal quest for a more certain understanding of sin, grace, and Christian salvation set off a chain reaction throughout Europe, resulting in the secession of millions of Europeans from the Roman Catholic Church and affecting the religious practices of nearly every Christian in Europe, whether

FOCUS QUESTIONS

• What were the theological premises of Lutheranism?

• How did the teachings of Calvin and Luther differ?

• How did notions of family and marriage change during the Reformation?

• What caused the Catholic Reformation?

Catholic or Protestant. The religious movement that Luther touched off was much larger than the man himself; nor should Martin Luther's own spiritual journey be seen as an epitome for all of Protestantism. But that said, there is no doubt that the Reformation movement began with Martin Luther—and so must we if we are to understand the extraordinary upheaval this new religious movement brought about.

THE LUTHERAN UPHEAVAL

What were the theological premises of Lutheranism?

In searching for the causes of the Lutheran revolt in Germany, three main questions arise: (1) why Martin Luther instigated a break with Rome; (2) why large numbers of Germans rallied to his cause; and (3) why a number of German princes decided to put the Lutheran Reformation into effect within their territories. Reduced to the barest essentials, the answers to these questions are that Luther broke with Rome because of his doctrine of justification by faith, that the German masses followed him in a surge of religious nationalism, and that the princes were moved to institute Lutheranism particularly because of their quest for governmental sovereignty. Within a decade preachers, the populace, and many of the German princes would all sing the same stirring Lutheran hymn, "A Mighty Fortress Is Our God," in the same church, but they arrived there by rather different paths.

LUTHER AND LATE MEDIEVAL CATHOLICISM

Many people think that Luther rebelled against Rome because he was disgusted with contemporary religious abuses—superstitions, frauds, and the offer of salvation for money—but that is only part of the story. Certainly abuses in Luther's day were grave and intensely upsetting to religious idealists. In a world beset by disease and disaster, frail mortals clutched at supernatural straws to seek health on earth and salvation in the hereafter. Some superstitious men and women, for ex-

ample, believed that viewing the consecrated host during Mass in the morning would guard them from death throughout the day, and others neglected to swallow the consecrated wafer so that they could use it later as a charm to ward off evil, an application to cure the sick, or a powder to fertilize their crops. Similarly, belief in the miraculous curative powers of saints was hard to distinguish from belief in magic. Every saint had his or her specialty: "for botches and biles, Cosmas and Damian; Saint Clare for the eyes, Saint Apolline for teeth, Saint Job for pox. And for sore breasts, Saint Agatha." Because relics of Christ and the saints were believed to radiate marvelous healing effects, traffic in relics boomed. Luther's patron, the elector Frederick the Wise of Saxony, had a collection in his castle church at Wittenberg of seventeen thousand relics, including a supposed remnant of Moses' burning bush, pieces of the holy cradle, shreds from Christ's swaddling clothes, and thirty-three fragments of the True Cross. In Florence, the Medici family's relic collection was even larger. The authenticity of many of these relics was highly doubtful, but the demand for them seemed to be insatiable.

Superstitions and gross credulity were offensive enough to religious idealists of Luther's stamp, but worse still were the granting of dispensations and the promises of spiritual benefits for money. If a man wished to marry his first cousin, for example, for a fee he could usually receive an official religious dispensation allowing the marriage. Annulments of marriage—divorce being prohibited—similarly came for a price. Most malodorous to many, however, was the sale of indulgences. In Catholic theology, an indulgence is a remission by papal authority of all or part of the temporal punishment due for sin—that is, of the punishment in this life and in purgatory—after the guilt of sin itself is absolved by sacramental confession. As we have seen, the practice of granting indulgences began at the end of the eleventh century as an incentive for encouraging men and women to become crusaders. Once it became accepted that the pope could dispense grace from a "Treasury of Merits" (that is, a storehouse of surplus good works piled up by Christ and the saints), it was taken for granted that the pope could promise people time off in purgatory as well. But indulgences originally granted for extraordinary deeds gradually came to be sold for money; by the fourteenth century, popes started granting indulgences to raise money for

By the fourteenth century, popes started granting indulgences to raise money for any worthy cause whatsoever.

any worthy cause whatsoever, such as the building of cathedrals or hospitals; and finally, in 1476 Pope Sixtus IV (the patron of the Sistine Chapel) took the extreme step of declaring that the benefits of indulgences could be extended to the dead already in purgatory as well as to the living. Money, then, could not only save an individual from works of penance but could save his dearest relatives from eons of agonizing torments after death.

Certainly Luther was horrified by the traffic in relics and the sale of indulgences; indeed, the latter provided the immediate grounds for his revolt against Rome. But it was less the abuses of the late medieval Church than it was medieval Catholic theology itself that Luther ultimately came to reject. To this degree the term "Lutheran Reformation" is misleading, for Luther was no mere "reformer" who wanted to cleanse the current religious system of its impurities. Many Christian humanists of Luther's day were reformers in just that sense, but they shrank from breaking with Rome because they had no objections to the basic principles of medieval Catholicism. Luther, on the other hand, would not have been satisfied with the mere abolition of abuses because it was the entire Catholic "religion of works" that appalled him.

> It was less the abuses of the late medieval Church than it was medieval Catholic theology itself that Luther ultimately came to reject.

Simply stated, Luther preferred a rigorously Augustinian system of theology to a medieval Thomistic one. As we have seen, around the year 400 Saint Augustine of Hippo had formulated an uncompromising doctrine of predestination, maintaining that God alone determined human salvation and that his decisions concerning whom to save and whom to damn were made from eternity, without any regard to merits that given humans might show while sojourning on earth. This extreme view, however, left so little room for human freedom and responsibility that it was modified greatly in the course of the Middle Ages. Above all, during the twelfth and thirteenth centuries theologians such as Peter Lombard and Saint Thomas Aquinas (hence the term "Thomistic") set forth an alternative belief system that rested on two assumptions: (1) since God's saving grace is not irresistible, humans can freely reject God's advances and encompass their own doom; and (2) since the sacramental ministrations of the church communicate ongoing grace, they help human sinners improve their chances of salvation. In Luther's opinion, however, all of this amounted to saying that humans could be saved by the performance of "good works," and it was this theology of works that he became prepared to resist even unto death.

LUTHER'S QUEST FOR RELIGIOUS CERTAINTY

Martin Luther may ultimately have been a source of inspiration for millions, but at first he was a terrible disappointment to his father. The elder Luther, who had risen from Thuringian German peasant stock and gained prosperity by leasing some mines, wanted his son Martin to rise still further. The father therefore sent young Luther to the University of Erfurt to study law, but while there in 1505, Martin shattered his father's ambitions for him by instead becoming a monk of the Augustinian order. In some sense, however, Luther always remained faithful to his father's humble roots. Even after he became famous, Martin Luther always lived simply and expressed himself in the vigorous, earthy vernacular of the German peasantry.

Martin Luther. A portrait by Lucas Cranach.

Like many great figures in the history of religion, Luther arrived at what he conceived to be the truth by a dramatic conversion experience. As a monk, young Martin zealously pursued all the traditional means for achieving his own salvation. Not only did he fast and pray continuously, but he confessed so often that his exhausted confessor would sometimes jokingly say that his sins were actually trifling and that if he really wanted to have a rousing confession he should go out and do something dramatic like committing adultery. Yet, try as he might, Luther could find no spiritual peace because he feared that he could never perform enough good deeds to deserve so great a gift as salvation. But in 1513 he hit upon an insight that granted him relief and changed the course of his life.

Luther's guiding insight pertained to the problem of the justice of God. For years he had worried that God seemed unjust in issuing commandments that he knew human beings could not observe and then in punishing them with eternal damnation for not observing them. But after becoming a professor of biblical theology at the University of Wittenberg (many members of his monastic order were expected to teach), Luther was led by the Bible to a new understanding of the problem. Specifically, while meditating on the words in the Psalms "deliver me in thy justice," it suddenly struck him that God's justice had nothing to do with his disciplinary power but rather with his mercy in saving sinful mortals through faith. As Luther later wrote, "At last, by the mercy of God, I began to understand the justice of God as that by which God makes us just in his mercy and through faith . . . and at this I felt as though I had been born again, and had gone through open gates into paradise." Since the fateful moment of truth came to Luther in the tower room of his monastery, it is customarily called his "tower experience."

After that, everything seemed to fall into place. Lecturing on the Pauline Epistles in Wittenberg in the years immediately following 1513, Luther dwelled on the text of Saint Paul to the Romans (1:17): "the just shall live by faith" to reach his central doctrine of "justification by faith alone." By this he meant that God's justice does not demand endless good works and religious ceremonies, for no one can hope to be saved by his or her own works. Rather, humans are "justified"— that is, granted salvation—by God's saving grace alone, offered as an utterly unmerited gift to those predestined for salvation. Since this grace is manifested in

> Like many great figures in the history of religion, Luther arrived at what he conceived to be the truth by a dramatic conversion experience.

humans through the gift of faith, men and women are justified from the human perspective by faith alone. In Luther's view those who had faith would do good works anyway, but it was the faith that came first. Although the essence of this doctrine was not original but harked back to the predestinarianism of Saint Augustine, it was new for Luther and the early sixteenth century, and if followed to its conclusions could only mean the dismantling of much of the contemporary Catholic religious structure.

THE REFORMATION BEGINS

At first Luther remained merely an academic lecturer, teaching within the realm of theory, but in 1517 he was goaded into attacking some of the actual practices of the church by a provocation that was too much for him to bear. The story of the indulgence campaign of 1517 in Germany is colorful but unsavory. The worldly Albert of Hohenzollern, youngest brother of the elector of Brandenburg, had sunk himself into enormous debt for several discreditable reasons. In 1513 he had to pay large sums for gaining dispensations from the papacy to hold the bishoprics of Magdeburg and Halberstadt concurrently, and for assuming these offices even though at twenty-three he was not old enough to be a bishop at all. Not satisfied, when the see of Mainz fell vacant in the next year, Albert gained election to that too, even though he knew full well that the costs of becoming archbishop of Mainz meant still larger payments to Rome. Obtaining the necessary funds by loans from the German banking firm of the Fuggers, he then struck a bargain with Pope Leo X (1513–1521): Leo proclaimed an indulgence in Albert's ecclesiastical territories on the understanding that half of the income raised would go to Rome for the building of St. Peter's Basilica, with the other half going to Albert so that he could repay the Fuggers. Luther did not know the sordid details of Albert's bargain, but he did know that a Dominican friar named Tetzel soon was hawking indulgences throughout much of northern Germany with Fugger banking agents in his train, and that Tetzel was deliberately giving people the impression that the purchase of an indulgence regardless of contrition in penance was an immediate ticket to heaven for oneself and one's dear departed in purgatory. For Luther this was more than enough because Tetzel's advertising campaign flagrantly violated his own conviction that people are saved by faith, not works. So on October 31, 1517, the earnest theologian offered to his university colleagues a list of ninety-five theses objecting to Catholic indulgence doctrine, an act by which the Protestant Reformation is conventionally thought to have begun.

In circulating his theses within the University of Wittenberg, Luther by no means intended to bring his criticism of Tetzel to the public. Quite to the contrary, he wrote his objections in Latin, not German, and meant them only for academic dispute. But some unknown person translated and published Luther's theses, an event that immediately gained the hitherto obscure monk wide notoriety. Since Tetzel and his allies outside the university did not mean to let the matter rest, Luther was called upon to withdraw his theses or defend himself. At that point, far from backing down, he became ever bolder in his attacks on the government of the church. In 1519 in public disputation before throngs in

> Luther's year of greatest creative activity came in 1520 when he put forth his three theological premises of justification by faith, the primacy of Scripture, and "the priesthood of all believers."

Leipzig, Luther defiantly maintained that the pope and all clerics were merely fallible men and that the highest authority for an individual's conscience was the truth of Scripture. Thereupon Pope Leo X responded by charging the monk with heresy, and after that Luther had no alternative but to break with the Catholic faith entirely.

Luther's year of greatest creative activity came in 1520 when, in the midst of the crisis caused by his defiance, he composed three seminal pamphlets formulating the outlines of what was soon to become the new Lutheran religion. In these writings he put forth his three theological premises: justification by faith, the primacy of Scripture, and "the priesthood of all believers." We have already examined the meaning of the first. By the second he simply meant that the literal meaning of Scripture was always to be preferred to the accretions of tradition, and that all beliefs (such as purgatory) or practices (such as prayers to saints) not explicitly grounded in Scripture were to be rejected. As for "the priesthood of all believers," that meant that the true spiritual estate was the congregation of all the faithful rather than a society of ordained priests.

From these premises a host of practical consequences followed. Since works themselves had no intrinsic value for salvation, Luther discarded such formalized practices as fasts, pilgrimages, and the veneration of relics. He also called for the dissolution of monasteries and convents. Far more fundamentally, he recognized only baptism and the Eucharist as sacraments (in 1520 he also included penance, but he later changed his mind on this), denying that even these had any supernatural effect in bringing down grace from heaven. For Luther, Christ was really present in the consecrated elements of the Lord's Supper, but there was no grace in the sacrament as such; rather, faith was essential to render the Eucharist effective as a means for aiding the believer along the road to eternal life. To make the meaning of the ceremony clear to all, Luther proposed the substitution of German for Latin in church services, and, to emphasize that those who presided in churches had no supernatural authority, he insisted on calling them merely ministers or pastors rather than priests. On the same grounds there was to be no ecclesiastical hierarchy since neither the pope nor anyone else was a custodian of the keys to heaven, and monasticism was to be abolished since it served no purpose whatsoever. Finally, firm in the belief that no

Pope Leo X. Raphael's highly realistic portrait shows the pope with two of his nephews.

Luther and his wife, Katherine von Bora. Portraits done by Cranach for the couple's wedding in 1525.

sacramental distinction existed between clergy and laity, Luther argued that ministers could marry, and in 1525 he took a wife himself.

THE BREAK WITH ROME

Widely disseminated by means of the printing press, Luther's pamphlets of 1520 electrified much of Germany, gaining him broad and enthusiastic popular support. Because this response played a crucial role in determining the future success of the Lutheran movement—emboldening Luther to persevere in his defiance of Rome and soon encouraging some ruling princes to convert to Lutheranism themselves—it is appropriate before continuing to inquire into its causes. Of course, different combinations of motives influenced different people to rally behind Luther, but the uproar in Germany on Luther's behalf was above all a national religious revolt against Rome.

Ever since the High Middle Ages many people throughout Europe had resented the centralization of church government because it meant the interference of a foreign papacy in local ecclesiastical affairs and the siphoning off of large sums of money to the papal court. But certain concrete circumstances made Germany in the early sixteenth century particularly ripe for religious revolt. Perhaps greatest among these was the fact that the papacy of that time had clearly lost the slightest hint of apostolic calling but was demanding as much, if not more, money from German coffers as before. Although great patrons of the arts, successive popes of Luther's day were worldly scoundrels or sybarites. As Luther was growing up, the Borgia pope, Alexander VI (1492–1503), bribed the cardinals to gain the papacy, used the money raised from the jubilee of 1500 to support the military campaigns of his son Cesare, and was so lascivious in office that he was suspected of seeking the sexual favors of his own daughter Lucrezia. Alexander's scandals could hardly have been outdone, but his successor, Julius II (1503–1513), was interested only in enlarging the papal states by military means (a contemporary remarked that he would have gained the greatest glory had he been a secular prince), and Leo X, the pope obliged to deal with Luther's defiance, was a self-indulgent esthete who, in the words of a modern Catholic historian, "would not have been deemed fit to be a doorkeeper in the house of the Lord had he lived in the days of the apostles." Under such circumstances it was bad enough for Germans to know that fees sent to Rome were being used to finance papal politics and the upkeep of luxurious courts, but worse still to pay money in the realization that Germany had no influence in Italian papal affairs, for Germans, unlike the French or Spaniards, were seldom represented in the College of Cardinals and practically never gained employment in the papal bureaucracy.

In this overheated atmosphere, reformist criticisms voiced by both traditional clerical moralists and the new breed of Christian humanists exacerbated resentments. Ever since about 1400 prominent German critics of the papacy had been saying that the entire church needed to be reformed "in head and members," and as the fifteenth century progressed, anonymous prophecies mounted to the effect, for example, that a future heroic emperor would reform the church by removing the papacy from Rome to the Rhineland. Then in the early years of the sixteenth century, Christian human-

Two specimens of Lutheran visual propaganda concerning "true" and "false" spiritual insight. Left: **Luther with Dove and Halo.** While Luther was still a monk (before the end of 1522), the artist Hans Baldung Grien portrayed him as a saint whose insight into Scripture was sent by the Holy Spirit in the form of a dove. Right: **The Pope as a Donkey Playing Bagpipes.** This 1545 woodcut depicts Luther's view that "the pope can interpret Holy Scripture just as well as he can play the bagpipes."

ists began to chime in with their own brand of satirical propaganda. Most eloquent of these humanists, of course, was Erasmus, who lampooned the religious abuses of his day with no mercy for Rome. Thus in *The Praise of Folly*, first published in 1511 and frequently reprinted, Erasmus stated that if popes were ever forced to lead Christlike lives, no one would be more disconsolate than themselves, and in his more daring pamphlet called *Julius Excluded*, published anonymously in Basel in 1517, the clever satirist imagined a dialogue held before the pearly gates in which Pope Julius II was locked out of heaven by Saint Peter because the saint refused to believe that the armored, vainglorious figure who stood before him could possibly be his successor.

In addition to the objective reality of a corrupt Rome and the circulation of anti-Roman propaganda, a final factor that made Germany ready for revolt in Luther's time was the belated growth of universities.

All revolts need to have some general headquarters; universities were the most natural centers for late medieval religious revolts because assembled there were groups of enthusiastic, educated young people accustomed to working together, who could formulate doctrinal positions with assurance, and who could turn out militant manifestos at a moment's notice. There had hardly been any universities on German soil until a spate of new foundations between 1450 and 1517 provided many spawning grounds for cultural nationalism and religious resistance to Rome. Luther's own University of Wittenberg was founded as late as 1502, but soon enough it became the cradle of the Lutheran Reformation, offering immediate support to its embattled hero.

Still, of course, there would have been no Lutheran Reformation without Luther himself, and the daring monk did the most to enflame Germany's dry kindling

Pope Alexander VI: "Appearance and Reality." Even before Luther initiated the German Reformation, anonymous critics of the dissolute Alexander VI surreptitiously spread propaganda showing him to be a devil. By lifting a flap one can see Alexander transformed into a monster who proclaims "I am the pope."

of resentment in his pamphlets of 1520, above all in one entitled *To the Christian Nobility of the German Nation.* Here, in highly intemperate colloquial German, Luther stated that "if the pope's court were reduced ninety-nine percent it would still be large enough to give decisions on matters of faith"; that "the cardinals have sucked Italy dry and now turn to Germany"; and that, given Rome's corruption, "the reign of Antichrist could not be worse." Needless to say, once this savage indictment was lodged, everyone wanted to read it. Whereas the average press run of a printed book before 1520 had been one thousand copies, the first run of *To the Christian Nobility* was four thousand, and these copies were sold out in a few days, with many more thousands following.

THE DIET OF WORMS

Meanwhile, even as Luther's pamphlets were selling so rapidly, his personal drama riveted all onlookers. Late in 1520 the German rebel responded to Pope Leo X's edict ordering his recantation by casting not only the bull but all of church law as well onto a roaring bonfire in front of a huge crowd. With the lines so drawn,

events moved with great swiftness. Since in the eyes of the church Luther was now a stubborn heretic, he was formally "released" to his lay overlord, the elector Frederick the Wise, for proper punishment. Normally this would have meant certain death at the stake, but in this case Frederick was loath to silence the pope's antagonist. Instead, claiming that Luther had not yet received a fair hearing, he brought him early in 1521 to be examined by a "diet" (that is, a formal assembly) of the princes of the Holy Roman empire convening in the city of Worms.

At Worms the initiative lay with the presiding officer, the newly elected Holy Roman emperor, Charles V. Charles was not a German; rather, as a member of the Habsburg family by his paternal descent, he had been born and bred in his ancestral holding of the Netherlands. Since he additionally held Austria, and as grandson of Ferdinand and Isabella by his maternal descent, all of Spain, including extensive Spanish possessions in Italy and America, the emperor had primarily international rather than national interests and surely thought of Catholicism as a sort of glue necessary to hold together all his far-flung territories. Thus from the start Charles had no sympathy for Luther, and

HUMANISM, NATIONALISM, AND THE GERMAN UNIVERSITIES

Conrad Celtis (1459–1508) mastered a humanist curriculum in Italy, then returned to Germany to push forward this new approach to learning in his native land. This oration, delivered in Latin to the faculty of the University of Ingolstadt in 1492, exemplifies the way in which humanism, despite its Italian origins, could fuel anti-Italian feelings of nationalism in German universities.

But I now direct my speech to you, distinguished men and well-born youths, to whom by virtue of the courage of your ancestors and the unconquerable strength of Germany the Italian empire has passed. . . . I urge you to direct your studies to those things first and foremost which will ripen and improve the mind and call you away from the habits of the common herd to devote yourselves to higher pursuits. Keep before your eyes true nobility of spirit, considering that you bring not honor but dishonor to our empire if you neglect the study of literature only to rear horses and dogs and pursue ecclesiastical preferment. . . .

Emulate, noble men, the ancient nobility of Rome, which, after taking over the empire of the Greeks assimilated all their wisdom and eloquence. . . . In the same way you who have taken over the empire of the Italians should cast off repulsive barbarism and seek to acquire Roman culture. Do away with that old disrepute of the Germans in Greek, Latin and Hebrew writers, who ascribe to us drunkenness, cruelty, savagery and every other vice bordering on bestiality and excess. . . .

Assume, O men of Germany, that ancient spirit of yours, with which you so often confounded and terrified the Romans, and turn your eyes to the frontiers of Germany; collect together her torn and broken territories. Let us be ashamed, ashamed I say, to have placed upon our nation the yoke of slavery, and to be paying tributes and taxes to foreign and barbarian kings. O free and powerful people, O noble and valiant race, plainly worthy of the Roman empire, our famous harbor is held by the Pole and the gateway of our ocean by the Dane! In the east also powerful peoples live in slavery, the Bohemians, the Moravians, the Slovaks and the Silesians, who all live as it were separated from the body of our Germany. And I may add the Transylvanian Saxons who also use our racial culture and speak our native language. . . .

But from the south we are oppressed by a sort of distinguished slavery, and under the impulse of greed . . . new commercial ventures are continually established by which our country is drained of its wonderful natural wealth while we pay to others what we need for ourselves. So persistent is fortune or destiny in persecuting and wiping out the Germans, the last survivors of the Roman empire. . . . To such an extent are we corrupted by Italian sensuality and by fierce cruelty in exacting filthy lucre. . . .

And I will assign no other cause for the everflourishing condition of Italy than the fact that her people surpass us in no blessing other than the love of literature and its cultivation. By this they overawe other nations as if by force of arms, and win their admiration for their genius and industry. . . .

Leonard Forster, ed. *Selections from Conrad Celtis.* (Cambridge: Cambridge University Press, 1948), pp. 43–47, 53.

The Emperor Charles V. Two views by the Venetian painter Titian depict the emperor in a grandiose military pose, and as a sage ruler.

since Luther fearlessly refused to back down before the emperor, declaring instead "Here I stand," it soon became clear that Luther would be condemned by the power of state as well as by the church. But just then Frederick the Wise once more intervened, this time by arranging a "kidnapping" whereby Luther was spirited off to the elector's castle of the Wartburg and kept out of harm's way for a year.

Thereafter Luther was never again to be in danger of his life. Although the Diet of Worms did issue an edict shortly after his disappearance proclaiming him an outlaw, the Edict of Worms was never properly enforced because, with Luther in hiding, Charles V soon left Germany to conduct a war with France. In 1522 Luther returned in triumph from the Wartburg to Wittenberg to find that all the changes in ecclesiastical government and ceremonial he had called for had spontaneously been put into practice by his university cohorts. Then, in rapid succession, several German

princes formally converted to Lutheranism, bringing their territories with them. Thus by around 1530 a considerable part of Germany had been brought over to the new faith.

THE GERMAN PRINCES AND THE LUTHERAN REFORMATION

At this point the last of the three major questions regarding the early history of Lutheranism arises: why did German princes, secure in their own powers, heed Luther's call by establishing Lutheran religious practices within their territories? We should by no means underestimate the importance of this question, because no matter how much intense admiration Luther may have gained from the German populace, his cause surely would have failed had it not been for the decisive intervention and support of constituted political authorities. There had been heretics aplenty in Europe before, but most of them had died at the stake, as Luther would have without the intervention of Frederick the Wise. And even if Luther had not been executed, spontaneous popular expressions of support alone would not have succeeded in instituting Lutheranism because they could easily have been put down by the power of the state. In fact, although in the early years of Luther's revolt he was more or less equally popular throughout Germany, only in those territories where rulers formally established Lutheranism (mostly in the north) did the new religion prevail, whereas in the others Luther's sympathizers were forced to flee, face death, or conform to Catholicism. In short, the word of the prince in religious matters was law.

The distinction between populace and princes should not obscure the fact that the motivations of both for turning to Lutheranism were similar, with the emphasis on the princely side being the search for sovereignty. As little as common people liked the idea

of money being pumped off to Rome, princes liked it less: German princes assembled at the Diet of Augsburg in 1500, for example, went so far as to demand the return of some of the ecclesiastical dues sent to Rome on the grounds that Germany was being drained of its coin. Since such demands fell on deaf ears, many princes were quick to perceive that if they adopted Lutheranism, they would not have to send ecclesiastical dues to support unloved foreigners, and much of the savings would directly or indirectly wind up in their own treasuries.

Yet the matter of taxation was only part of the larger issue of the search for absolute governmental sovereignty. Throughout Europe the major political trend in the years around 1500 was toward making the state dominant in all areas of life, religious as well as secular. Hence rulers sought to control the appointments of church officials in their own realms and to limit or curtail the independent jurisdictions of church courts. Because the papacy in this period had to fight off the attacks of internal clerical critics who wanted recogni-

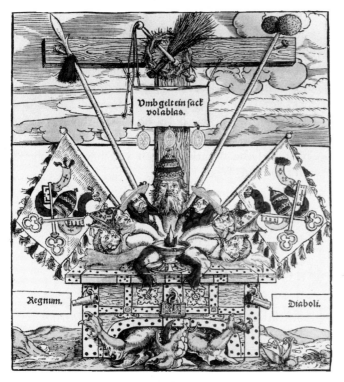

The Seven-Headed Papal Beast. Around 1530 a Lutheran cartoon was circulated in Germany that turned the papacy into the "seven-headed beast" of the Book of Revelation. The papacy's "seven heads" consist of pope, cardinals, bishops, and priests; the sign on the cross reads "for money, a sack full of indulgences"; and a devil is seen emerging from an indulgence treasure chest below.

The Seven-Headed Martin Luther. In response, a German Catholic propagandist showed Luther as Revelation's "beast." In the Catholic conception Luther's seven heads show him by turn to be a hypocrite, a fanatic, and "Barabbas"—the thief who should have been crucified instead of Jesus.

tion of the "conciliarist" principle that general councils of prelates rather than popes should rule the church (see Chapter 11), many popes found it advantageous to sign concordats with the most powerful rulers in the West—primarily the kings of France and Spain—whereby they granted the rulers much of the sovereignty they wanted in return for support against conciliarism. Thus in 1482 Sixtus IV conceded to the Spanish monarchs Ferdinand and Isabella the right to name candidates for all major church offices. In 1487 Innocent VIII consented to the establishment of a Spanish Inquisition controlled by the crown, giving the rulers extraordinary powers in dictating religious policies. And in 1516, by the Concordat of Bologna, Leo X granted the choice of bishops and abbots in France to the French king, Francis I, in return for Francis's support against the conciliarists who had gathered at the Fifth Lateran Council (1512–1517). In Germany, however, primarily because there was no political unity, princes were not strong enough to gain such concessions. Hence what they could not achieve by concordats some decided to wrest by force.

In this determination they were fully abetted by Luther. Certainly as early as 1520 the fiery reformer recognized that he could never hope to institute new religious practices without the strong arm of the princes behind him, so he implicitly encouraged them to expropriate the wealth of the Catholic Church as an incentive for creating a new order. At first the princes bided their time, but when they realized that Luther had enormous public support and that Charles V would not act swiftly to defend the Catholic faith, several moved to introduce Lutheranism into their territories. Motives of personal piety surely played a role in individual cases, but political and economic considerations were more generally decisive. By instituting Lutheranism within their territories, Protestant princes could consolidate their authority by naming pastors, cutting off fees to Rome and curtailing the jurisdiction of church courts. They could also guarantee that the political and religious boundaries of their territories would now coincide. No longer, therefore, would an ecclesiastical prince be able to use his position as a bishop to undermine a rival secular prince's sovereignty over his territory. Given the added fact that under Lutheranism monasteries could be shut down and their wealth simply pocketed by the princes, the practical advantages of establishing the new faith were overwhelming, quite apart from any considerations of religious zeal.

Once safely ensconced in Wittenberg as the protégé of princes, Luther began to express ever more vehemently his own profound conservatism in political and social matters. In a treatise of 1523, *On Temporal Authority*, he insisted that "godly" rulers must be obeyed in all things and that even ungodly ones should never be actively resisted, since tyranny "is not to be resisted but endured." Then, in 1525, when peasants throughout Germany rose up in economic revolt against their landlords—in some places encouraged by the religious radical Thomas Müntzer (c. 1490–1525), who urged the use of fire and sword against "ungodly" powers—Luther responded with intense hostility. In his vituperative pamphlet of 1525, *Against the Thievish, Murderous Hordes of Peasants*, he went so far as to urge all who could to hunt the rebels down like mad dogs, to "strike, strangle, stab secretly or in public, and remember that nothing can be more poisonous than a man in rebellion." Once the princes had ruthlessly put down the Peasants' Revolt of 1525, the firm alliance of Lutheranism with the powers of the state helped ensure social peace. In fact, after the bloody punishment of the peasant rebels there would never again be a mass lower-class uprising in Germany.

As for Luther himself, he concentrated in his last years on debating with younger, more radical religious reformers and on offering spiritual counsel to all who sought it. Never tiring in his amazingly prolific literary activity, he wrote an average of one treatise every two weeks for twenty-five years. To the end Luther was unswerving in his new faith: on his deathbed in 1546 he responded to the question "Will you stand firm in Christ and the doctrine which you have preached?" with a resolute "Yes."

THE SPREAD OF PROTESTANTISM

How did the teachings of Calvin and Luther differ?

Originating as a term applied to Lutherans who "protested" an action of the German Imperial Diet of 1529, the word "Protestant" has come to mean any non-Catholic, non–Eastern Orthodox Christian. In fact, it was soon applied to non-Lutherans after 1529 because the particular form of Protestantism that Luther developed did not prove to be popular much beyond its na-

CHRONOLOGY

ORIGINS OF THE REFORMATION, 1450–1529

Christian humanists call for reforms	fifteenth–sixteenth centuries
Growth of German Universities	1450–1517
Luther posts the Ninety-Five Theses	1517
Luther charged with heresy	1519
Publication of Lutheran theological premises	1520
Diet of Worms declares Luther an outlaw	1521
Peasant Revolt defeated	1525
Luther's break with Zwingli	1529

tive environment of Germany. To be sure, Lutheranism was instituted as the state religion of Denmark, Norway, and Sweden by official decrees of rulers made during the 1520s, and remains the religion of most Scandinavians today. But elsewhere early Protestantism spread in different forms. In England a break with Rome was introduced from above, just as in Germany and Scandinavia, but since Lutheranism appeared too radical for the reigning English monarch, a compromise variety of religious belief and practice, subsequently known as Anglicanism (in America, Episcopalianism), was worked out. At the other extreme, Protestantism spread more spontaneously in several cities of Switzerland where it took on forms that were more radical than Lutheranism.

THE ENGLISH REFORMATION

Although the original blow against the Roman Church in England was struck by the head of the government, King Henry VIII (1509–1547), in breaking with Rome the English monarch had the support of most of his subjects. For this there were at least three reasons. First, in England, as in Germany, many people in the early sixteenth century had come to resent Rome's corruption and the siphoning off of the country's wealth to pay for the worldly pursuits of foreign popes. Second, England had already been the scene of protests against religious abuses voiced by John Wyclif's heretical followers, known as Lollards. The Lollards had indeed been driven underground in the course of the fifteenth century, but numbers of them survived in pockets throughout England, where they promulgated their anticlerical ideas whenever they could. The Lollards enthusiastically welcomed Henry VIII's revolt from Rome when it occurred. Finally, soon after the outbreak of the Reformation in Germany, Lutheran ideas were brought into England by travelers and by the circulation of printed tracts. As early as 1520 a Lutheran group was meeting at the University of Cambridge, and Lutheranism began to gain more and more clandestine strength as the decade progressed.

HENRY VIII AND THE BREAK WITH ROME

Despite all this, England would not have broken with Rome had Henry VIII not commanded it because of his marital difficulties. By 1527 the imperious Henry had been married for eighteen years to Ferdinand and Isabella's daughter, Catherine of Aragon, yet all the offspring of this union had died in infancy, save only Princess Mary. Since Henry needed a male heir to preserve the succession of his Tudor dynasty, and since Catherine was now past childbearing age, Henry had good reasons of state to break his marriage bonds, and in 1527 an immediate incentive arose when he became

Henry VIII, by Hans Holbein the Younger.

infatuated with the dark-eyed lady-in-waiting Anne Boleyn, who would not give in to his advances out of wedlock. The king hence appealed to Rome to allow the severance of his marriage to Catherine so that he could make Anne his queen. Although the law of the Church did not sanction divorce, it did provide that a marriage might be annulled if proof could be given that conditions existing at the time of the wedding had made it unlawful. Accordingly, the king's representatives, recalling that Queen Catherine had previously been married to Henry's older brother, who had died shortly after the ceremony was performed, rested their case on a passage from the Bible that pronounced it "an unclean thing" for a man to take his brother's wife and cursed such a marriage with childlessness (Leviticus 20:31).

Henry's suit put the reigning pope, Clement VII (1523–1534), in a quandary. If he rejected the king's appeal, England would probably be lost to Catholicism, for Henry was indeed firmly convinced that the scriptural curse had blighted his chances of perpetuating his dynasty. On the other hand, if the pope granted the annulment he would provoke the wrath of the Emperor Charles V, Catherine of Aragon's nephew, for Charles was then on a military campaign in Italy and threatening the pope with a loss of his temporal power. There seemed nothing for Clement to do but procrastinate. At first he made a pretense of having the question settled in England, empowering his officials to hold a court of inquiry to determine whether the marriage to Catherine had been legal. Then, after a long delay, he suddenly transferred the case to Rome. Meanwhile Henry had lost patience and resolved to take matters into his own hands. In 1531 the king obliged an assembly of English clergy to recognize him as "the supreme head" of the English Church. Next he induced Parliament to enact a series of laws abolishing all payments to Rome and proclaiming the English church an independent, national unit, subject only to royal authority. With the passage of the parliamentary Act of Supremacy (1534), declaring "the King's highness to be supreme head of the Church of England [having] the authority to redress all errors, heresies, and abuses," the last bonds uniting the English church to Rome had been cut.

Yet these enactments did not yet make England a Protestant country. Quite to the contrary, although the break with Rome was followed by the dissolution of all of England's monasteries, with their lands and wealth being sold to many of the king's loyal supporters, the system of church government by bishops (episco-palianism) was retained, and the English church remained Catholic in doctrine. The Six Articles promulgated by Parliament in 1539 at Henry VIII's behest left no room for doubt as to official orthodoxy: oral confession to priests, masses for the dead, and clerical celibacy were all confirmed; moreover, the Catholic doctrine of the Eucharist was not only confirmed but its denial was made punishable by death.

EDWARD VI

Nonetheless, the influence of Protestantism in England was growing, and during the reign of Henry's son, Edward VI (1547–1553), Protestantism gained the ascendancy. Since the new king (born from Henry's union with his third wife, Jane Seymour) was only nine years old when he inherited the crown, the religious policies of his government were dictated by Thomas Cranmer, archbishop of Canterbury, and the dukes of Somerset and Northumberland, who dominated the regency government. Inasmuch as all three of these men had strong Protestant leanings (as too did the young king himself), the creeds and ceremonies of the Church of England were soon drastically altered. Priests were permitted to marry; English was substituted for Latin in the services; the veneration of images was abolished; and new articles of belief were drawn up repudiating all sacraments except baptism and communion and affirming the Lutheran doctrine of justification by faith alone. Thus when the youthful Edward died in 1553 it seemed as if England had definitely entered the Protestant camp.

MARY TUDOR AND THE RESTORATION OF CATHOLICISM

But Edward's pious Catholic successor, Mary (1553–1558), Henry VIII's daughter by Catherine of Aragon, thought otherwise. Mary associated the revolt against Rome with her mother's humiliations and her own removal from direct succession. On coming to the throne she attempted to return England to Catholicism. Not only did she restore the celebration of the mass and the rule of clerical celibacy, but she prevailed on Parliament to vote a return to papal allegiance.

Yet Mary's policies ended in failure for several reasons. Many of the leading families that had profited from Henry VIII's dissolution of the monasteries had become particularly committed to Protestantism because a restoration of Catholic monasticism would have meant the loss of their newly acquired wealth.

THE SIX ARTICLES

Although Henry VIII withdrew the Church of England from obedience to the papacy, he continued to lean more toward Catholic than Protestant theology. Some of his advisors, most notably Thomas Cromwell, were committed Protestants; and the king allowed his son and heir, Edward VI, to be raised as a Protestant. But after several years of rapid (and mostly Protestant) change in the English church, in 1539 the king reasserted a set of traditional Catholic doctrines in the Six Articles. These would remain binding on the Church of England until the king's death in 1547.

First, that in the most blessed sacrament of the altar, by the strength and efficacy of Christ's mighty word, it being spoken by the priest, is present really, under the form of bread and wine, the natural body and blood of our Savior Jesus Christ, conceived of the Virgin Mary, and that after the consecration there remains no substance of bread or wine, nor any other substance but the substance of Christ, God and man;

Secondly, that communion in both kinds is not necessary for salvation, by the law of God, to all persons, and that it is to be believed and not doubted . . . that in the flesh, under the form of bread, is the very blood, and with the blood, under the form of wine, is the very flesh, as well apart as though they were both together;

Thirdly, that priests, after the order of priesthood received as aforc, may not marry by the law of God;

Fourthly, that vows of chastity or widowhood by man or woman made to God advisedly ought to be observed by the law of God. . . .

Fifthly, that it is right and necessary that private masses be continued and admitted in this the king's English Church and congregation . . . whereby good Christian people . . . do receive both godly and goodly consolations and benefits; and it is agreeable also to God's law;

Sixthly, that oral, private confession is expedient and necessary to be retained and continued, used and frequented in the church of God. . . .

Statutes of the Realm, Vol. 3 (London: Her Majesty's Stationery Office, 1810–1828), p. 739, modernized.

Mary also erred by ordering the burning of Cranmer and a few hundred Protestant extremists. These executions were insufficient to wipe out religious resistance—instead, Protestant propaganda about "Bloody Mary" and the "fires of Smithfield" hardened resistance to Mary's rule, making her seem like a vengeful persecutor. But perhaps the most serious cause of Mary's failure was her marriage to Philip, Charles V's son and heir to the Spanish throne. Although the marriage treaty stipulated that in the event of Mary's death Philip could not succeed her, patriotic Englanders never trusted him. Hence when the queen allowed herself to be drawn by Philip into a war with France on Spain's behalf, in which England lost Calais, its last foothold on the European continent, many English people became highly disaffected. No one knows what might have happened next because death soon after ended Mary's troubled reign.

The Burning of Archbishop Cranmer. In this Protestant conception an ugly Catholic, "Friar John," directs the proceedings, while the martyred Cranmer repeats Christ's words, "Lord, receive my spirit." John Foxe's *Book of Martyrs* (1563), in which this engraving first appeared, was an extraordinarily successful piece of English Protestant propaganda.

THE ELIZABETHAN COMPROMISE

The question of whether England was to be Catholic or Protestant was thereupon settled definitively in favor of Protestantism by Elizabeth I (1558–1603). Daughter of Anne Boleyn and one of the most capable and popular monarchs ever to sit on the English throne, Elizabeth was predisposed in favor of Protestantism by the circumstances of her parents' marriage as well as by her upbringing. But Elizabeth was no zealot, and wisely recognized that supporting radical Protestantism in England posed the danger of provoking bitter sectarian strife. Accordingly, she presided over what is customarily known as "the Elizabethan compromise." By a new Act of Supremacy (1559), Elizabeth repealed all of Mary's Catholic legislation, prohibited the exercise of any authority by foreign religious powers, and made herself "supreme governor" of the English church—a more Protestant title than Henry VIII's "supreme head" insofar as most Protestants be-

As a result of the Elizabethan compromise, the Church of England today is broad enough to include such diverse elements as the "Anglo-Catholics" and the "low-church" Anglicans.

lieved that Christ alone was the head of the Church. At the same time she accepted most of the Protestant ceremonial reforms instituted during the reign of her brother Edward. On the other hand, she retained church government by bishops and left the definitions of some controversial articles of the faith, especially the meaning of the Eucharist, vague enough so that all but the most extreme Catholics and Protestants could accept them. Long after Elizabeth's death this settlement remained in effect. Indeed, as a result of the Elizabethan compromise, the Church of England today is broad enough to include such diverse elements as the "Anglo-Catholics," who differ from Roman Catholics only in rejecting papal supremacy, and the "low-church" Anglicans, who are as thoroughgoing in their Protestant practices as members of most other modern Protestant denominations.

THE REFORMATION IN SWITZERLAND

If the Elizabethan compromise came about through royal decision making, in Switzerland more spontaneous movements to establish Protestantism resulted in the victory of greater radicalism. In the early sixteenth century Switzerland was neither ruled by kings nor dominated by all-powerful territorial princes; instead, prosperous Swiss cities were either independent or on the verge of becoming so. Hence when the leading citizens of a Swiss municipality decided to adopt Protestant reforms no one could stop them, and Protestantism in Switzerland could usually take its own course. Although religious arrangements tended at first to vary in detail from city to city, the three main forms of Protestantism that emerged in Switzerland from about 1520 to 1550 were Zwing-

Church of England
Calvinist and areas of Calvinist influences
Eastern Orthodox
Lutheran
Roman Catholic

RELIGIOUS SITUATION IN EUROPE, C. 1560

This map shows the complicated religious boundaries of Europe in the generation after the protest begun by Martin Luther. Why did the Lutheran movement take such strong hold in Germany and Scandinavia? What political as well as spiritual factors played a role in the success of religious uprising there? What were the central beliefs of John Calvin and similarly inspired religious movements? Why did this movement enjoy the influence it did in Switzerland, Scotland, and along the river valleys of central France? What consequences were there for the Calvinists (Huguenots) in France under a regime that remained Roman Catholic? What relationships can you discern among religious movements and national identities in this map?

lianism, Anabaptism, and, most fateful for Europe's future, Calvinism.

ULRICH ZWINGLI

Zwinglianism, founded by Ulrich Zwingli (1484–1531) in Zürich, was the most moderate form of the three. Although Zwingli was at first a somewhat indifferent Catholic priest, around 1516 he was led by close study of the Bible to conclude that contemporary Catholic theology and religious observances conflicted with the Gospels. But he did not speak out until Luther set the precedent. In 1522, Zwingli started attacking the authority of the Catholic Church in Zürich, and soon all Zürich and much of northern Switzerland had accepted his leadership in instituting reforms that closely resembled those of the Lutherans in Germany. Zwingli differed from Luther, however, concerning the theology of the Eucharist: whereas Luther believed in the real presence of Christ's body, for Zwingli Christ was present merely in spirit. Thus for him the sacrament conferred no grace at all and was to be retained merely as a memorial service. This fundamental disagreement prevented Lutherans and Zwinglians from uniting in a common Protestant front. Fighting independently, Zwingli fell in battle against Catholic forces in 1531, whereupon his successors in Zürich lost their leadership over Swiss Protestantism, and the Zwinglian movement was soon after absorbed by the far more radical Protestantism of John Calvin.

The name Anabaptism means "rebaptism," and stemmed from the Anabaptists' conviction that baptism should be administered only to adults.

ANABAPTISM

Before Calvinism prevailed, however, the phenomenon of Anabaptism briefly flared up in Switzerland and also Germany. The first Anabaptists were members of Zwingli's circle in Zürich, but they quickly broke with him around 1525 on the issues of infant baptism and their conception of an exclusive church of true believers. The name Anabaptism means "rebaptism," and stemmed from the Anabatists' conviction that baptism should be administered only to adults because infants have no understanding of the meaning of the service. Yet this was only one manifestation of the Anabaptists' main belief that men and women were not born into any church. Although Luther and Zwingli alike taught the "priesthood of all believers," they still insisted that everyone, believer or not, should attend services and be part of one and the same officially instituted religious community. But the Anabaptists were separatists, firm in the conviction that joining the true church should be the product of an individual's inspired decision. For them, one had to follow the guidance of one's own "inner light" in opting for church membership, and the rest of the world could go its own way. Since this was a hopelessly apolitical doctrine in an age when almost everyone assumed that church and state were inextricably connected, Anabaptism was bound to be anathema to the established powers, both Protestant and Catholic. Yet in its first few years the movement did gain numerous adherents in Switzerland and Germany, above all because it appealed to sincere religious piety in calling for extreme simplicity of worship, pacifism, and strict biblical morality.

Unhappily for the fortunes of Anabaptism, an unrepresentative group of Anabaptist extremists managed to gain control of the German city of Münster in 1534. These zealots combined sectarianism with millennarianism, or the belief that God wished to institute a completely new order of justice and spirituality throughout the world before the end of time. Determined to help God bring about this goal, the extremists attempted to turn Münster into a new Jerusalem. A former tailor named John of Leyden assumed the title of "King of the New Temple," proclaiming himself the successor of David. Under his leadership Anabaptist religious practices were made obligatory, private property was abolished, the sharing of goods was introduced, and even polygamy was instituted on the grounds of Old Testament precedents. Nonetheless, Münster succumbed to a siege by Catholic forces little more than a year after the Anabaptist takeover, and the new David, together with two of his lieutenants, was put to death by excruciating tortures. Given that Anabaptism had already been proscribed by many governments, this episode thoroughly discredited the movement, and its adherents were subjected to ruthless persecution throughout Germany, Switzerland, and wherever else they could be found. Among the few who survived were some who banded together in the Mennonite sect, named for its founder, the Dutchman Menno Simons (c. 1496–1561). This sect, dedicated to the pacifism and simple "religion of the heart" of original Anabaptism, has continued to exist until the present. Various An-

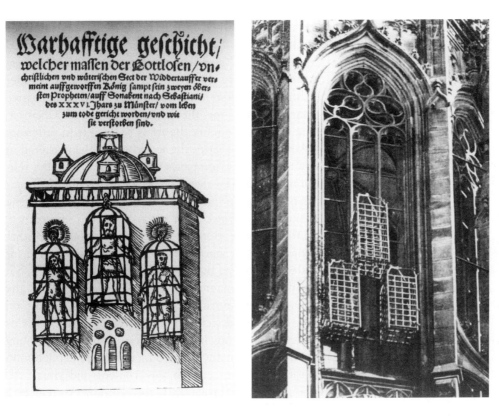

The Anabaptists' Cages, Then and Now. After the three Anabaptist leaders who had reigned in Münster for a year were executed in 1535, their corpses were prominently displayed in cages hung from a tower of the marketplace church. As can be seen from the photo on the right, the bones are now gone but the iron cages remain to this very day as a grisly reminder of the horrors of sixteenth-century religious strife.

abaptist tenets were also revived later by religious groups such as the Quakers and different Baptist and Pentecostal sects.

JOHN CALVIN

A year after events in Münster sealed the fate of Anabaptism, a twenty-six-year-old French Protestant named John Calvin (1509–1564), who had fled to the Swiss city of Basel to escape religious persecution, published the first version of his *Institutes of the Christian Religion,* a work that was soon to prove the most influential systematic formulation of Protestant theology ever written. Born in Noyon in northern France, Calvin originally had been trained for the law and around 1533 was studying the Greek and Latin classics while living off the income from a church benefice. But then, as he later wrote, while he was "obstinately devoted to the superstitions of Popery," a stroke of light made him feel that God was extricating him from "an abyss of filth," and he thereupon opted for becoming a Protestant theologian and propagandist. Though some of these details resemble the early career of Luther, there was one essential differ-

> Calvin's *Institutes of the Christian Religion* became the most theologically authoritative statement of basic Protestant beliefs.

ence: namely, whereas Luther was always a highly volatile personality, Calvin remained a cool legalist through and through. Thus, whereas Luther never wrote systematic theology but only responded to given problems as they arose or as the impulse struck him, Calvin resolved in his *Institutes* to set forth all the principles of Protestantism comprehensively, logically, and consistently. Accordingly, after several revisions and enlargements (the definitive edition appeared in 1559), Calvin's *Institutes of the Christian Religion* became the most theologically authoritative statement of basic Protestant beliefs and the nearest Protestant equivalent of Saint Thomas Aquinas's *Summa Theologica.*

The hallmark of Calvin's rigorous theology in the *Institutes* is that he started with the omnipotence of God and worked downward. For Calvin the entire universe is utterly dependent on the will of the Almighty, who created all things for his greater glory. Because of the original fall from grace, all human beings are sinners by nature, bound hand and foot to an evil inheritance they cannot escape. Nevertheless, the Lord for reasons of his own has predestined some for eternal salvation and damned all the rest to the torments of hell. Nothing that human

John Calvin. A recently discovered anonymous portrait.

Although Calvin always acknowledged a great theological debt to Luther, his religious teachings differed from those of the Wittenberg reformer in several essentials. First of all, Luther's attitude toward proper Christian conduct in the world was much more passive than Calvin's: for the former, the good Christian should merely endure the trials of this life in suffering, whereas for the latter the world was to be mastered in unceasing labor for God's sake. Second, Calvin's religion was more legalistic and more nearly an Old Testament faith than Luther's. This can be illustrated in the attitude of the two men toward Sabbath observance. Luther's conception of Sunday was similar to that which prevails among most Christians today. He insisted, of course, that his followers attend church, but he did not demand that during the remainder of the day they refrain from all pleasure or work. Calvin, on the other hand, revived the Jewish Sabbath with its strict taboos against anything faintly resembling worldliness. Finally, the two men differed explicitly on basic matters of church government and ritual. Although Luther broke with the Catholic system of a gradated ecclesiastical hierarchy, Lutheran district superintendents were not unlike bishops, and Luther also retained a good many features of Catholic worship such as altars and vestments (special clothing for the clergy). In contrast, Calvin rejected everything that smacked to him of "popery." Thus he argued for the elimination of all traces of the hierarchical system, instead having congregational election of ministers and assemblies of ministers and "elders" (laymen responsible for maintaining proper religious conduct among the faithful) governing the entire church. Further, he

beings may do can alter their fate; their souls are stamped with God's blessing or curse before they are born. But this does not mean, in Calvin's opinion, that Christians should be indifferent to their conduct on earth. If they are among the elect, God will implant in them the desire to live rightly. Upright conduct is a sign, though not an infallible one, that whoever practices it has been chosen to sit at the throne of glory. Public profession of faith and participation in the services of the reformed church are also presumptive signs of election to be saved. But most of all, Calvin required an active life of piety and morality as a solemn obligation for members of the Christian commonwealth. For him, good Christians should conceive of themselves as chosen instruments of God with a mission to help in the fulfillment of his purposes on earth, striving not for their souls' salvation but for the glory of God. In other words, Calvin clearly did not encourage his readers to sit with folded hands, serene in the knowledge that their fate was sealed.

Services in a Calvinist Church. "Four bare walls and a sermon."

insisted on the barest simplicity in church services, prohibiting all ritual, vestments, instrumental music, images, and stained-glass windows. When these teachings were put into practice, Calvinist services became little more than "four bare walls and a sermon."

CALVINISM IN GENEVA

Not content with mere theory, Calvin was intent upon putting his teachings into practice. Sensing an opportunity to influence the course of events in the French-speaking Swiss city of Geneva, then in the throes of combined political and religious upheaval, he moved there late in 1536 and began preaching and organizing immediately. In 1538 his activities caused him to be expelled, but in 1541 he returned, with the city eventually coming completely under his sway. Under Calvin's guidance Geneva's government became theocratic. Supreme authority in the city was vested in a "Consistory," made up of twelve lay elders and five ministers. (Although Calvin himself was seldom the presiding officer, he usually dominated the Consistory's decisions until his death in 1564.) In addition to passing on legislation submitted to it by a congregation of ministers, the Consistory had as its main function the supervision of morals. This activity was carried out not merely by the punishment of antisocial conduct but by a persistent snooping into the private life of every individual. Geneva was divided into districts, and a committee of the Consistory could visit any household without warning to check on the habits of its members. Even the mildest forms of self-indulgence were strictly prohibited. Dancing, card playing, attending the theater, working or playing on the Sabbath—all were outlawed as works of the devil. Innkeepers were forbidden to allow anyone to consume food or drink without first saying grace, or to permit any patron to stay up after nine o'clock. Needless to say, penalties were severe. Not only were murder and treason classified as capital crimes, but also adultery, "witchcraft," blasphemy, and heresy. During the first four years after Calvin gained control in Geneva, no fewer than fifty-eight people were executed out of a total population of only sixteen thousand.

As reprehensible as such interference in the private sphere may seem today, in the middle of the sixteenth century Calvin's Geneva appeared as a beacon of thoroughgoing Protestantism to thousands throughout Europe. Calvin's disciple John Knox, for example, who brought Calvinism to Scotland, declared that Geneva under Calvin was "the most perfect school of Christ that ever was on earth since the days of the Apostles." Accordingly, many foreigners flocked to the "perfect school" for refuge or instruction, and usually returned home to become ardent proselytizers of Calvinism. Moreover, since Calvin himself thought of Geneva as a staging point for bringing Calvinism to France and the rest of the world, he encouraged the dispatching of missionaries and propaganda into hostile territories,

Left: **Calvin as seen by His Friends.** An idealized contemporary portrait of Calvin as a pensive scholar.

Right: **Calvin as Seen by His Enemies.** A Catholic caricature in which Calvin's face is a composite made from fish, a toad, and a chicken drumstick.

with the result that from about the middle of the sixteenth century Geneva became the center of a concerted and militant attempt to spread the new faith far and wide. Soon Calvinists became a majority in Scotland, where they were known as Presbyterians; a majority in Holland, where they founded the Dutch Reformed Church; a substantial minority in France, where they were called Huguenots; and a substantial minority in England, where they were called Puritans. In addition, Calvinist preachers zealously made converts in many other parts of Europe, including Hungary, Lithuania and Poland. But just as the Calvinists were fanning out through Europe, the forces of Catholicism were hardening in their determination to head off any further Protestant advances. The result, as we will see in the next chapter, was a bloody series of religious wars that would wrack Europe for the next one hundred years.

THE DOMESTICATION OF THE REFORMATION, 1525–1560

How did notions of family and marriage change during the Reformation?

Protestantism had begun as a revolutionary doctrine whose radical claims for the spiritual equality of all true Christian believers had the potential to undermine the social, religious, political and even gender hierar-chies on which European society rested. Luther himself seems not to have anticipated that his ideas about the priesthood of all believers might have such implications, and he was genuinely shocked and appalled when he realized that the rebellious German peasants and the religious millennarianists at Münster were interpreting his ideas in this way. But Luther was by no means solely responsible for the increasing conservatism of Protestant social ideology after 1525. Outside the ranks of the Anabaptists, none of the early Protestant leaders was a social or political radical. To spread their reform message, moreover, Protestant reformers depended on the support of existing social and political leaders: the princes of course, but no less important, the ruling elites of the German and Swiss towns. As a result, the Reformation movement was speedily "domesticated" in two senses. Not only was the revolutionary potential of Protestantism curbed (Luther rarely spoke about the priesthood of all believers after 1525); but there was also an increasing emphasis within all branches of the burgeoning Protestant movement on the patriarchal family as the central institution of reformed life.

PROTESTANTISM AND THE FAMILY

The domestication of the Reformation in this second sense took place principally in the free towns of Germany and Switzerland ("free" in the sense that they were self-governing, and not controlled by a territorial prince). Here, Protestant attacks on monasticism and clerical celibacy found a receptive audience among townsmen who resented the immunity of monastic houses from taxation, and regarded clerical celibacy as a subterfuge for the seduction of their wives and daughters. The Protestant insistence on the depravity of the human will, and the consequent need for that will to be trained and disciplined by godly authority, also resonated powerfully with guilds and town governments, which were anxious to maintain and increase the control that town elites (mainly merchants and master craftsmen) exercised over the apprentices and journeymen who made up the majority of the town's male population. By eliminating the competing jurisdictional authority of the Catholic Church, Protestantism also allowed town governments to consolidate all authority within the city into their own hands.

Protestantism also offered a powerful reinforcement to the control of individual craftsmen over their wives and children, their servants, and the apprentices who

HOW DID NOTIONS OF FAMILY AND MARRIAGE CHANGE DURING THE REFORMATION?

THE DOMESTICATION OF THE REFORMATION, 1525–1560   509

lived within their households. Protestantism brought a new importance to the family as a "school of godliness" in which an all-powerful father figure was expected to assume responsibility for instructing and disciplining his household in accordance with the precepts of reformed religion. At the same time, Protestantism also introduced a new religious ideal for women. No longer was the celibate nun the exemplar of female holiness; in her place now stood the married and obedient Protestant "goodwife." To this extent, Protestantism resolved the tensions between piety and sexuality that had characterized late medieval Catholicism by declaring firmly in favor of the holiness of marital sexuality.

This did not reflect a newly elevated view of women's spiritual potential, however—quite the contrary. Luther, like his medieval predecessors, continued to regard women as more sexually driven than men and less capable of controlling their sexual desires (although, to be fair, Luther had only a slightly higher view of men's capacity for celibacy). His opposition to convents rested on his belief that, except in extraordinary circumstances, it was impossible for women to remain celibate, so convents simply made illicit sexual behavior inevitable. To control women and prevent sin, it was therefore necessary that all women should be married, preferably at a young age, and so placed under the governance of a godly husband.

For the most part, Protestant town governments were happy to cooperate in shutting down convents. The convent's property went to the town, and most of the nuns were from aristocratic families anyway. But conflicts did arise between Protestant reformers and town fathers over marriage and sexuality, especially over the reformers' insistence that both men and women should marry young as a check on sin. Many German towns were like Augsburg, where men were expected to delay marriage until they had achieved the status of a master craftsmen—a requirement that had become increasingly difficult to enforce as guilds sought to restrict the number of journeymen permitted to become masters. In theory, however, apprentices and journeymen were not supposed to marry. Instead, they were expected to frequent the brothels and taverns, a legally recognized world of non-marital sexuality that town fathers saw as necessary to protect their own wives and daughters from seduction or rape, but that Protestant reformers found morally abhorrent and demanded be abolished.

Towns responded in a variety of ways to these opposing pressures. Some instituted special committees to police public morals, of the sort we have seen already in Calvin's Geneva. Some abandoned Protestantism altogether. Others, like Augsburg, flipflopped back and forth between Protestantism and Catholicism for several decades, before finally settling on one religion or the other. But regardless of a town's final choice of religious allegiance, by the end of the sixteenth century a revolution had taken place with respect to town governments' attitudes toward public morality. In their competition with each other, neither Catholics nor Protestants wished to be seen as "soft on sin." The result, by 1600, was the abolition of publicly recognized brothels throughout Europe, the criminalization of prostitution, and far stricter governmental supervision of many other aspects of private life in both Catholic and Protestant urban communities.

PROTESTANTISM AND CONTROL OVER MARRIAGE

Protestantism also increased parental control over their children's choice of marital partners. The medieval Catholic Church defined marriage as a sacrament that did not require the involvement of a priest. The mutual free consent of the two parties, even if given without witnesses or parental approval, was enough to constitute a legally valid marriage in the eyes of the church; at the same time, however, the church would annul a marriage if either of the parties could prove that he or she had not freely consented to it. Opposition to this doctrine came from many quarters, but especially from parents and other relatives. Because marriage involved rights of inheritance to property, most families regarded it as far too important a matter to be left to the free choice of their children. Instead, parents wanted the power to prevent unsuitable matches, and ideally, to force their children to accept the marriage arrangements that their families might negotiate on their behalf. Protestantism offered an opportunity to achieve such control. Luther had declared marriage to be a purely secular matter, not a sacrament at all, that could be regulated however the governing authorities thought best. Calvin largely followed suit, although Calvinist theocracy drew less of a distinction than did Lutheranism between the powers of church and state. Even Catholicism was eventually forced to give way. Although it never entirely abandoned its insistence that both members of the couple must freely consent to their marriage, by the end of the sixteenth century the

LUTHER ON CELIBACY AND WOMEN

Luther urged the dissolution of monasteries and convents on both theological and practical grounds. In theological terms, he argued that such institutions contributed nothing to the world, aside from (perhaps) the salvation of their inmates. But as the extracts below reveal, he also considered their demands for celibacy to be impossible for most men and women to meet. The result was therefore to increase, rather than decrease, sin.

Listen! In all my days I have not heard the confession of a nun, but in the light of Scripture I shall hit upon how matters fare with her and know I shall not be lying. If a girl is not sustained by great and exceptional grace, she can live without a man as little as she can without eating, drinking, sleeping, and other natural necessities. Nor, on the other hand, can a man dispense with a wife. The reason for this is that procreating children is an urge planted as deeply in human nature as eating and drinking. That is why God has given and put into

the body the organs, arteries, fluxes, and everything that serves it. Therefore what is he doing who would check this process and keep nature from running its desired and intended course? He is attempting to keep nature from being nature, fire from burning, water from wetting, and a man from eating, drinking, and sleeping.

E.M. Plass, ed., *What Luther Says* (St. Louis: Concordia Publishing House, 1959), vol. II, pp. 888–889.

Catholic Church required formal public notice of intent to marry, and insisted on the presence of a priest at the actual wedding ceremony. Both were efforts to prevent elopements, allowing families time to intervene before an unsuitable marriage was concluded. Individual Catholic countries sometimes went even further in trying to reassert parental control over their children's choice of marital partners. In France, for example, although couples might still marry without parental consent, those who did so now forfeited all of their rights to inherit their families' property. In somewhat different ways, however, both Protestantism and Catholicism thus moved to strengthen the control that parents could exercise over their children—and, in the case of Protestantism, that husbands could exercise over their wives.

CATHOLICISM TRANSFORMED

What caused the Catholic Reformation?

The historical novelty of Protestantism in the sixteenth century inevitably tends to cast the spotlight on such religious reformers as Luther and Calvin, but a powerful internal reform movement within the Catholic Church also exercised as profound an effect on the course of European history as did Protestantism. Historians differ about whether to call this movement the "Catholic Reformation" or the "Counter-Reformation." Some prefer the former term because it emphasizes that significant efforts to reform the Catholic Church from within antedated the posting of Luther's theses and that Catholic reform in the sixteenth century was thus not merely a response to Protestantism. Others, however, insist quite properly that most sixteenth-century Catholic reformers were indeed inspired primarily by the urgency of resisting what they regarded as heresy and schism. Fortunately the two interpretations are by no means irreconcilable, for they allude to two complementary phases: a Catholic Reformation that came before Luther and a Counter-Reformation that followed.

> The Council of Trent reaffirmed without exception all the tenets challenged by the Protestant reformers.

THE CATHOLIC REFORMATION

The Catholic Reformation, beginning around 1490, was primarily a movement for moral and institutional reform inspired by principles of Christian humanism and carried on with practically no help from the dissolute Renaissance papacy. In Spain around the turn of the fifteenth century, reform activities directed by Cardinal Francisco Ximénes de Cisneros (1436–1517) with the cooperation of the monarchy led to the imposition of strict rules of behavior for Franciscan friars and the elimination of abuses prevalent among the diocesan clergy. Although Ximénes aimed primarily at strengthening the church in its warfare with the Muslims, his work had some effect in regenerating Spanish Christian spiritual life. Italy had no similarly centralized reform movement, but a number of earnest clerics in the early sixteenth century labored on their own to make the Italian church more worthy of its calling. The task was a difficult one on account of the entrenchment of abuses and the example of profligacy set by the papal court, but despite these obstacles, the Italian reformers did manage to establish some new religious orders dedicated to high ideals of piety and social service. Finally, it cannot be forgotten that such leading Christian humanists as Erasmus and Thomas More were in their own way Catholic reformers, for in criticizing abuses and editing sacred texts, such men helped to enhance spirituality.

Once Protestantism began to sweep over Europe, however, Catholic reform of the earlier variety clearly became inadequate to defend the church, let alone turn the tide of revolt. Thus a second, more aggressive phase of reform under a new style of vigorous papal leadership gained momentum during the middle and the latter half of the sixteenth century. The leading Counter-Reformation popes—Paul III (1534–1549), Paul IV (1555–1559), Saint Pius V (1566–1572), and Sixtus V (1585–1590)—were collectively the most zealous crusaders for reform to preside over the papacy since the High Middle Ages. All led upright personal lives. Indeed, some were so grimly ascetic that contemporaries were unsure whether they were not too holy: as a Spanish councilor wrote in 1567, "We should like it even better if the present Holy Father were no longer with us, however great, inexpressible, unparalleled, and extraordinary His Holiness may be." But in the face of the Protestant onslaught, a pope's reputation for excessive asceticism was vastly preferable to a reputation for profligacy. More than that, becoming fully dedicated to activist revitalization of the church, the Counter-Reformation popes reorganized their finances and filled ecclesiastical offices with bishops and abbots as renowned for austerity as themselves. These appointees in turn set high standards for their own priests and monks.

These papal activities were supplemented by the actions of the Council of Trent, convoked by Paul III in 1545 and meeting at intervals thereafter until 1563. This general council was one of the most important in the history of the church. After early debates about possible grounds for compromise, the Council of Trent reaffirmed without exception all the tenets challenged by the Protestant reformers. Good works were held to be necessary for salvation. The doctrine of the sacraments as indispensable means of grace was upheld. Likewise, transubstantiation, the apostolic succession of the priesthood, the belief in purgatory, the invocation of saints, and the rule of celibacy for the clergy were all confirmed as essential elements in the Catholic system. The Bible and the traditions of apostolic teaching were held to be of equal authority as sources of Christian truth. Papal supremacy over every bishop and priest was expressly maintained, and the supremacy of the pope over any church council was taken for granted. The Council of Trent even reaffirmed the doctrine of indulgences that had touched off the Lutheran revolt, although it did condemn the worst scandals connected with the selling of indulgences.

The legislation of Trent was not confined to matters of doctrine. It also included provisions for the elimination of abuses and for reinforcing the discipline of the

The Inspiration of Saint Jerome, by Guido Reni. In 1546 the Council of Trent declared Saint Jerome's Latin translation of the Bible, known as the Vulgate, to be the official version of the Catholic Church; then, in 1592, Pope Clement VIII chose one edition of the Vulgate to be authoritative above all others. Since Biblical scholars had known since the early sixteenth century that Saint Jerome's translation contained numerous mistakes, Counter-Reformation defenders of the Vulgate insisted that even his mistakes had been divinely inspired and thus were somehow preferable to the original meaning of Scripture. The point is made visually in Guido Reni's painting of 1635.

mained in the faith. A commission was appointed to draw up a list of writings that ought not to be read by faithful Catholics. The publication of this list in 1564 resulted in the formal establishment of the Index of Prohibited Books as a part of the machinery of the church. Later, a permanent agency known as the Congregation of the Index was set up to revise the list from time to time. Altogether more than forty such revisions have been made. The majority of the books condemned have been theological treatises, and probably the effect in retarding the progress of learning has been slight. Nonetheless, the establishment of the Index must be viewed as a symptom of the intolerance that characterized sixteenth-century Christianity, both Catholic and Protestant.

SAINT IGNATIUS LOYOLA AND THE SOCIETY OF JESUS

In addition to the independent activities of popes and the legislation of the Council of Trent, a third main force propelling the Counter-Reformation was the foundation of the Society of Jesus, commonly known as the Jesuit order, by Saint Ignatius Loyola (1491–1556). In the midst of a youthful career as a worldly soldier, the Spanish nobleman Loyola was wounded in battle in 1521 (the same year in which Luther defied Charles V at Worms); while recuperating, he decided to change his ways and become a spiritual soldier of Christ. Shortly afterward he lived as a hermit in a cave near the Spanish town of Manresa for ten months, during which time, instead of reading the Bible as Luther or Calvin might have done, he experienced ecstatic visions and worked out the principles of his subsequent meditational guide, *The Spiritual Exercises.* This manual, completed in 1535 and first published in 1541, offered practical advice on how to master one's will and serve God by a systematic program of meditations on sin and the life of Christ. Soon made a basic handbook for all Jesuits and widely studied by numerous Catholic lay people as well, Loyola's *Spiritual Exercises* had an influence second only to Calvin's *Institutes* among all the religious writings of the sixteenth century.

Nonetheless, Saint Ignatius's founding of the Jesuit order itself was certainly his greatest single accomplishment. Originating as a group of six disciples who gathered around Loyola in Paris in 1534 to serve God in poverty, chastity, and missionary work, Loyola's Society of Jesus was formally constituted as an order of

church over its members. To improve pastoral care of the laity, bishops and priests were forbidden to hold more than one benefice. To address the problem of an ignorant priesthood, it was provided that a theological seminary must be established in every diocese. The council also took steps to suppress a variety of local religious practices and saints cults, replacing them with officially approved and centrally directed observances from Rome. Toward the end of its deliberations the council also decided to censor books, to prevent heretical ideas from corrupting those who still re-

OBEDIENCE AS A JESUIT HALLMARK

The necessity of obedience in the spiritual formation of monks and nuns had been a central theme in Catholic religious thought since the Rule of Saint Benedict. By focusing its demands for obedience specifically on the papacy, however, the Society of Jesus brought a new militancy to this old ideal.

RULES FOR THINKING WITH THE CHURCH

1. Always to be ready to obey with mind and heart, setting aside all judgment of one's own, the true spouse of Jesus Christ, our holy mother, our infallible and orthodox mistress, the Catholic Church, whose authority is exercised over us by the hierarchy.

2. To commend the confession of sins to a priest as it is practised in the Church; the reception of the Holy Eucharist once a year, or better still every week, or at least every month, with the necessary preparation. . . .

4. To have a great esteem for the religious orders, and to give the preference to celibacy or virginity over the married state. . . .

6. To praise relics, the veneration and invocation of Saints: also the stations, and pious pilgrimages, indulgences, jubilees, the custom of lighting candles in the churches, and other such aids to piety and devotion. . . .

9. To uphold especially all the precepts of the Church, and not censure them in any manner; but, on the contrary, to defend them promptly, with reasons drawn from all sources, against those who criticize them.

10. To be eager to commend the decrees, mandates, traditions, rites and customs of the Fathers in the Faith or our superiors. . . .

13. That we may be altogether of the same mind and in conformity with the Church herself, if she shall have defined anything to be black which to our eyes appears to be white, we ought in like manner to pronounce it to be black. For we must undoubtingly believe, that the Spirit of our Lord Jesus Christ, and the Spirit of the Orthodox church His Spouse, by which Spirit we are governed and directed to salvation, is the same. . . .

FROM THE CONSTITUTIONS OF THE JESUIT ORDER

Let us with the utmost pains strain every nerve of our strength to exhibit this virtue of obedience, firstly to the Highest Pontiff, then to the Superiors of the Society; so that in all things . . . we may be most ready to obey his voice, just as if it issued from Christ our Lord . . . leaving any work, even a letter, that we have begun and have not yet finished; by directing to this goal all our strength and intention in the Lord, that holy obedience may be made perfect in us in every respect, in performance, in will, in intellect; by submitting to whatever may be enjoined on us with great readiness, with spiritual joy and perseverance; by persuading ourselves that all things [commanded] are just; by rejecting with a kind of blind obedience all opposing opinion or judgment of our own. . . .

Henry Bettenson, ed. *Documents of the Christian Church,* 2d ed. (Oxford: Oxford University Press, 1967), pp. 259–261.

the church by Pope Paul III in 1540; by the time of its founder's death it already numbered fifteen hundred members. The Society of Jesus was by far the most militant of the religious orders fostered by the Catholic reform movements of the sixteenth century. It was not merely a monastic society but a company of soldiers sworn to defend the faith. Their weapons were not to be bullets and spears but eloquence, persuasion, instruction in correct doctrines, and if necessary, more worldly methods of exerting influence. The organization was patterned after that of a military company, with a general as commander-in-chief and iron discipline enforced for all members. Individuality was suppressed, and a soldierlike obedience to the general was exacted of the rank and file. The Jesuit general, sometimes known as the "black pope" (from the color of the order's habit), was elected for life and was not bound to take advice offered by any other member. But he did have one clear superior, namely the Roman pope himself, for in addition to the three monastic vows of poverty, chastity, and obedience, all senior Jesuits took a "fourth vow" of strict obedience to the Vicar of Christ and were held to be at the pope's disposal at all times.

The activities of the Jesuits consisted primarily of proselytizing Christians and non-Christians, and establishing schools. Originally founded to engage in missionary work abroad, the early Jesuits preached to non-Christians in India, China, and Spanish America. For example, one of Saint Ignatius's closest early associates, Saint Francis Xavier (1506–1552), baptized thousands of native people and covered thousands of miles missionizing in South and East Asia. Yet, although Loyola had not at first conceived of his society as comprising shock troops against Protestantism, that is what it primarily became as the Counter-Reformation mounted in intensity. Through preaching and diplomacy—sometimes at the risk of their lives—Jesuits in the second half of the sixteenth century fanned out through Europe in direct confrontation with Calvinists. In many places the Jesuits succeeded in keeping rulers and their subjects loyal to Catholicism, in others they met martyrdom, and in some others—notably Poland and parts of Germany and France—they succeeded in regaining territory temporarily lost to Protestantism. Wherever they were allowed to settle, the Jesuits set up schools and colleges, for they firmly believed that a vigorous Catholi-

Although Loyola had not at first conceived of his society as comprising shock troops against Protestantism, that is what it primarily became as the Counter Reformation mounted in intensity.

cism depended on widespread literacy and education. Their schools were often so well regarded that, after the fires of religious hatred began to subside, upper-class Protestants sometimes sent their sons to receive a Jesuit education.

COUNTER-REFORMATION CHRISTIANITY

From the foregoing it should be self-evident that there is a "Counter-Reformation heritage" every bit as much as there is a Protestant one. Needless to say, for committed Catholics, the greatest achievement of sixteenth-century Catholic reform was the defense and revitalization of the faith. Without question, Catholicism would not have swept over the globe and reemerged in Europe as the vigorous spiritual force it remains today had it not been for the determined efforts of the sixteenth-century reformers. But other results stemmed from the Counter-Reformation as well. One was the spread of literacy in Catholic countries due to the educational activities of the Jesuits, and another was the growth of intense concern for acts of charity. Since Counter-Reformation Catholicism continued to emphasize good works as well as faith, charitable activities took on an extremely important role in the revitalized religion. Spiritual leaders of the Counter-Reformation such as Saint Francis de Sales (1567–1622) and Saint Vincent de Paul (1581–1660) urged almsgiving in their sermons and writings, and a wave of founding of orphanages and houses for the poor swept over Catholic Europe.

Two other areas in which the Counter-Reformation had less dramatic but still noteworthy effects were in the realm of women's history and intellectual developments. Whereas Protestantism encouraged female literacy so that women could read the Bible, reinvigorated Catholicism pursued a different course. Catholicism did not exalt marriage as a route to holiness for women to the same degree as did Protestantism, but Catholicism did foster a distinctive role for a female religious elite—countenancing the mysticism of Saint Teresa of Avila (1515–1582), and allowing the foundation of new orders of nuns such as the Ursulines and the Sisters of Charity that had no parallel under Protestantism. Both Protestants and Catholics continued to exclude women

CHRONOLOGY

THE COUNTER-REFORMATION, 1534–1564

Counter-Reformation popes	1534–1590
Saint Ignatius Loyola founds the Jesuits	1534
Council of Trent convenes	1545–1563
Index of Prohibited Books	1564

from the ministry or priesthood, but under Catholicism celibate women were permitted to pursue religious lives with at least some degree of independence.

The Counter-Reformation did not perpetuate the tolerant Christianity of Erasmus. Instead, Christian humanists lost favor with Counter-Reformation popes, and all of Erasmus's writings were immediately placed on the Index of Prohibited Books. But sixteenth-century Protestantism was just as intolerant as sixteenth-century Catholicism, and far more hostile to the cause of rationalism. Indeed, because Counter-Reformation theologians returned for guidance to the scholasticism of Saint Thomas Aquinas, they were much more committed to acknowledging the dignity of human reason than were their Protestant counterparts, who emphasized scriptural authority and unquestioning faith. Thus although a hallmark of the subsequent seventeenth-century scientific revolution was the divorce between spirituality of any variety and strict scientific work, it does not seem entirely coincidental that René Descartes, one of the founders of the scientific revolution, who coined the famous phrase "I think, therefore I am," was trained as a youth by the Jesuits.

CONCLUSION: THE HERITAGE OF THE REFORMATION

Inasmuch as Luther's revolt from Rome and the spread of Protestantism occurred after the height of the civilization of the Renaissance and before some particularly fundamental advances in modern European political, economic, and social development, it is tempting to think of historical events unfolding in an inevitably cumulative way, from the Renaissance to the

Reformation to the "Triumph of the Modern World." But history is seldom as neat as that. Although scholars continue to disagree on points of detail, most agree that the Protestant Reformation drew relatively little from the civilization of the Renaissance, that indeed in certain basic respects Protestant principles were completely at odds with the major assumptions of most Renaissance humanists.

In considering the relationship between the Renaissance and the origins of the Protestant Reformation, it would admittedly be false to say that the one had absolutely nothing to do with the other. Certainly, criticisms of religious abuses by Christian humanists helped prepare Germany for the Lutheran revolt. Furthermore, close humanistic textual study of the Bible led to the publication of new, reliable biblical editions used by the Protestant reformers. In this regard a direct line ran from the Italian humanist Lorenzo Valla to Erasmus to Luther, insofar as Valla's *Notes on the New Testament* inspired Erasmus to produce his own Greek edition and accompanying Latin translation of the New Testament in 1516, and that in turn enabled Luther in 1518 to reach some crucial conclusions concerning the literal biblical meaning of penance. For these and related reasons, Luther addressed Erasmus in 1519 as "our ornament and our hope."

But in fact Erasmus quickly showed that he had no sympathy whatsoever with Luther's first principles, and most other Christian humanists shunned Protestantism as soon as it became clear to them what Luther and other Protestant reformers actually were teaching. The reasons for this were that most humanists believed in free will whereas Protestants believed in predestination; that humanists tended to think of human nature as basically good whereas Protestants found it unspeakably corrupt; and that most humanists favored urbanity and tolerance whereas the followers of Luther and Calvin emphasized obedience and conformity.

Although the Protestant Reformation was not the natural outgrowth of the civilization of the Renaissance, it did contribute to certain traits most characteristic of modern European historical development. Foremost among these was the rise of the untrammeled powers of the sovereign state. As we have seen, those German princes who converted to Protestantism were moved to do so primarily by the search for sovereignty. The kings of Denmark, Sweden, and England followed suit for much the same reasons. Since Protestant leaders—Calvin as well as Luther—preached absolute obedience to "godly" rulers, and since the state in Protestant countries assumed direct control of the church, the spread of Protestantism definitely resulted in the growth of state power. But, as we have also seen, the power of the state was growing already, and it continued to grow also in such Catholic countries as France and Spain, where kings had already been granted, by 1500, most of the same rights over the church that were forcibly seized by Lutheran German princes and Henry VIII in the course of their own Reformations.

As for the growth of nationalism, a sense of national pride was already present in sixteenth-century Germany that Luther played on in his appeals of 1520. But Luther himself did much to foster German cultural nationalism by translating the entire Bible into a vigorous German idiom. Up until then Germans from some regions spoke a language so different from that of Germans from other areas that they could not understand each other, but the form of German given currency by Luther's Bible soon became the linguistic standard for the entire nation. Religion did not help to unite the German nation politically because the non-German Charles V opposed Lutheranism, and as a result Germany soon became politically divided into Protestant and Catholic camps. But elsewhere, as in Holland, where Protestants fought successfully against a foreign, Catholic overlord, Protestantism enhanced a sense of national identity. Perhaps the most familiar case of all is that of England, where a sense of nationhood existed before the advent of Protestantism, but where the new faith lent to that nationalism a new confidence that England was indeed a nation peculiarly favored by God.

Finally, we come to the subject of Protestantism's effects on social relationships, specifically those between the sexes. No consensus among historians exists on this subject. What does seem clear, however, is that Protestant men as individuals could be just as ambivalent about women as their medieval Catholic predecessors had been. John Knox, for example, inveighed against the Catholic regent of Scotland, Mary Stuart, in a treatise called *The First Blast of the Trumpet Against the Monstrous Regiment of Women*, yet maintained deeply respectful relationships with women of his own faith. But if we ask how Protestantism as a belief system affected women's lot, the answer appears to be that it enabled women to become just a shade more equal to men, albeit still clearly within a framework of subjection. Above all, since Protestantism, with its stress on the primacy of Scripture and the priesthood of all believers, called on women as well as men to undertake serious Bible study, it sponsored primary schooling for both sexes and thus enhanced female as well as male literacy. But Protestant male leaders still insisted that women were naturally inferior to men and thus should always defer to men in arguments. As Calvin himself said, "let the woman be satisfied with her state of subjection and not take it ill that she is made inferior to the more distinguished sex." Both Luther and Calvin appear to have been happily married, but clearly that meant being happily married on their own terms.

SELECTED READINGS

Bainton, Roland. *Here I Stand: A Life of Martin Luther.* Nashville, Tenn., 1950. The best introductory biography in English; although old, and obviously biased in Luther's favor, it remains absorbing and dramatic.

———. *Erasmus of Christendom.* New York, 1969. Still the best biography in English of the Dutch reformer and intellectual.

Bossy, John. *Christianity in the West, 1400–1700.* Oxford and New York, 1985. A brilliant, challenging picture of the changes that took place in Christian piety and practice as a result of the sixteenth-century reformations.

Bouwsma, William J. *John Calvin: A Sixteenth-Century Portrait.* Oxford and New York, 1988. Still the best biography of the magisterial reformer.

Cameron, Euan. *The European Reformation.* Oxford and New York, 1991. An excellent survey, judicious and fair toward all the competing parties.

Collinson, Patrick. *The Religion of Protestants: The Church in English Society, 1559–1625.* Oxford, 1982. A great book by the best contemporary historian of early English Protestantism.

Dillenberger, John, ed. *Martin Luther: Selections from His Writings.* Garden City, N.Y., 1961. The standard selection, especially good on Luther's theological ideas.

———. *John Calvin: Selections from His Writings.* Garden City, N.Y., 1971. An excellent selection.

Dixon, C. Scott, ed. *The German Reformation: The Essential Readings.* Oxford, 1999. A collection of important recent articles.

Duffy, Eamon. *The Stripping of the Altars: Traditional Religion in England, c. 1400–c. 1550.* By far the best study of the hesitant way in which England eventually became a Protestant country.

Eire, Carlos M. N. *From Madrid to Purgatory: The Art and Craft of Dying in Sixteenth-Century Spain.* Cambridge and New York, 1995. A powerful picture of the religious culture of Spanish Catholicism.

Hillerbrand, Hans J., ed. *The Protestant Reformation.* New York, 1967. Selections are particularly good for illuminating the political consequences of Reformation theological ideas.

Loyola, Ignatius. *Personal Writings.* Translated by Joseph A. Munitiz and Philip Endean. London and New York, 1996. An excellent collection that includes Loyola's autobiography, his spiritual diary, and some of his letters, as well as his *Spiritual Exercises.*

Luebke, David, ed. *The Counter-Reformation: The Essential Readings.* Oxford, 1999. A collection of nine important recent essays.

McGrath, Alister E. *Reformation Thought: An Introduction.* Oxford, 1993. A useful explanation, accessible to non-Christians, of the theological ideas of the major Protestant reformers.

Monter, E. William. *Calvin's Geneva.* New York, 1967. The standard English work.

Mullett, Michael A. *The Catholic Reformation.* London, 2000. A sympathetic survey of Catholicism from the mid-sixteenth to the eighteenth century that presents the mid-sixteenth-century Council of Trent not as a response to Protestantism, but as a continuation of a series of reform efforts dating from the fifteenth century.

Oberman, Heiko A. *Luther: Man Between God and the Devil.* Translated by Eileen Walliser-Schwarzbart. New Haven, 1989. The best recent biography of Luther, stressing his preoccupations with sin, death, and the devil.

O'Malley, John W. *The First Jesuits.* Cambridge, Mass., 1993. A scholarly account of the origins and early years of the Society of Jesus.

Ozment, Steven. *Protestants: The Birth of a Revolution.* New York, 1992. A stirring introduction to the ideas of an influential modern historian of the Protestant Reformation.

Pettegree, Andrew, Alastair Duke, and Gillian Lewis, eds. *Calvinism in Europe, 1540–1620.* Cambridge and New York, 1994. A collection of articles dealing with Calvinism across Europe, mostly from the context of local history.

Pettegree, Andrew, ed. *The Reformation World,* New York, 2000. An exhaustive compendium of articles representing the most recent thinking about the Reformation.

Pelikan, Jaroslav. *Reformation of Church and Dogma, 1300–1700.* Volume 4: *A History of Christian Dogma.* Chicago, 1984. A masterful synthesis of Reformation theology in its late medieval context.

Roper, Lyndal. *The Holy Household: Women and Morals in Reformation Augsburg.* Oxford, 1989. A pathbreaking study of how Protestantism was adopted and adapted by the town councillors of Augsburg, with special attention to its impact on attitudes toward women, the family, and marriage.

Scribner, Robert W. *The German Reformation.* Atlantic Heights, N.J., 1986. A brief survey of work on the social and cultural context for the Reformation. Includes superb bibliographies.

Tracy, James D. *Europe's Reformations, 1450–1650.* Lanham, Md., 1999. An outstanding survey, especially strong on Dutch and Swiss developments, but excellent throughout.

Williams, George H. *The Radical Reformation,* 3d ed. Kirksville, Mo., 1992. Originally published in 1962, this is still the best book on Anabaptism and its offshoots.

RELIGIOUS WARS
AND
STATE BUILDING,
1540–1660

STRANGE AS IT MAY SEEM in retrospect, Martin Luther never intended to fracture the religious unity of Europe. He sincerely believed that once the Bible was available to everyone in an accurate, vernacular translation, then everyone who read the Bible would interpret it in exactly the same way as did he himself. The result, of course, was quite different, as Luther quickly discovered in his bitter disputes with Zwingli and Calvin. Nor did Catholicism crumble in the face of reformed teachings as Luther had believed that it would. Instead, Europe's religious divisions multiplied, speedily crystallizing along political lines. By Luther's death in 1546, a clear pattern had already emerged. With only rare exceptions, Protestantism triumphed in those areas where political authorities supported the reformers. Where rulers remained Catholic, so too did their territories.

This was not the result Martin Luther had intended, but it did faithfully reflect the most basic presumptions of sixteenth-century European life. Anabaptists apart, neither Protestant nor Catholic reformers set out to challenge the standard medieval beliefs about the mutual interdependence of religion and politics—quite the contrary. Sixteenth-century Europeans continued to believe that the proper role of the state was to enforce true religion on its subjects, and sixteenth-century rulers remained convinced that religious pluralism would bring disunion and disloyalty to any state that embraced it. Ultimately, both Catholics and Protestants believed that western Europe had to return to a single religious faith enforced by properly constituted political authorities. What they could not agree on was, "Which faith?" and "Which authorities?"

The result was a brutal series of religious wars between 1540 and 1660 whose reverberations would continue to be felt until the eighteenth century. Vastly expensive and enormously destructive, these wars affected everyone in Europe from peasants to princes. They did not arise solely from conflicts over religion. Regionalism, dynasticism, and nationalism were also potent contributors to the chaos into which Europe now plunged. Together, however, these forces of division and disorder brought into question the very survival of the European political order that had emerged since the thirteenth century. Faced with the prospect of political collapse,

FOCUS QUESTIONS

• Why was the period 1540 to 1660 one of the most turbulent in European history?

• What caused the decline of Spain in the seventeenth century?

• What was Hobbes's solution to the search for authority?

• What was the relationship between the Baroque school and the Counter-Reformation?

Europeans by 1660 were forced to embrace, gradually and grudgingly, a notion that in 1540 had seemed impossible to conceive: that religious toleration, however limited in scope, might be the only way to preserve the political, social, and economic order of the European world.

ECONOMIC, RELIGIOUS, AND POLITICAL TESTS

Why was the period 1540 to 1660 one of the most turbulent in European history?

The troubles that engulfed Europe during the traumatic century between 1540 and 1660 crept up on contemporaries unawares. From the mid-fifteenth century on, most of Europe had enjoyed steady economic growth, and the discovery of the New World seemed the basis of greater prosperity to come. Political trends too seemed auspicious, since most western European governments were becoming ever more efficient and providing more internal peace for their subjects. By the middle of the sixteenth century, however, thunderclouds were gathering that would soon burst into terrible storms.

THE PRICE REVOLUTION

Although the causes of these storms were interrelated, we can examine each separately, starting with the great price inflation. Nothing like the upward price trend that affected western Europe in the second half of the sixteenth century had ever happened before. The cost of a measure of wheat in Flanders, for example, tripled between 1550 and 1600, grain prices in Paris quadrupled, and the overall cost of living in England more than doubled during the same period. The twentieth century would see much more dizzying inflations than this, but since the skyrocketing of prices in the later sixteenth century was a novelty, most historians agree on calling it a "price revolution."

Two developments in particular underlay the soaring prices. The first is demographic. Starting in the later fifteenth century, Europe's population began to mount again after the plague-induced falloff: roughly estimated, there were about 50 million people in Europe around 1450 and 90 million around 1600. Since Europe's food supply remained more or less constant owing to the lack of any noteworthy breakthrough in agricultural technology, food prices were driven sharply higher by greater demand. At the same time, wages stagnated or even declined. As a result, workers around 1600 were paying a higher percentage of their wages to buy food than ever before, even though their basic nutritional levels were declining.

Population trends explain much, but since Europe's population did not increase nearly so rapidly in the second half of the sixteenth century as did prices, other explanations for the great inflation are necessary. Foremost among these is the enormous influx of bullion from Spanish America. Whereas in the five years from 1556 to 1560 roughly 10 million ducats worth of silver passed through the Spanish entry point of Seville, between 1576 and 1580 that figure had doubled, and between 1591 and 1595 it had more than quadrupled. Because most of this silver was used by the Spanish crown to pay its foreign creditors and its armies abroad, or by private individuals to pay for imports from other countries, this Spanish bullion quickly circulated throughout Europe, where much of it was minted into coins. This dramatic increase in the volume of money in circulation further fueled the spiral of rising prices. "I learned a proverb here," said a French traveler in Spain in 1603, "everything costs much here except silver."

Aggressive entrepreneurs and landlords profited most from the changed economic circumstances, while the masses of laboring people were hurt the worst. Merchants in possession of sought-after goods were able to raise prices at will. Landlords profited directly from the rising prices of agricultural produce; or, if they did not farm their own lands, they could always raise rents. But laborers were caught in a squeeze because wages rose far more slowly than prices, owing to the presence of a more than adequate labor supply. Moreover, because the cost of food staples rose at a sharper rate than the cost of most other items of consumption, poor people had to spend an ever greater percentage of their paltry incomes on necessities. When disasters such as wars or poor harvests drove grain prices out of reach, some of the poor literally starved to death. The picture that thus emerges is one of the rich getting richer and the poor getting poorer—splendid feasts enjoyed amid the most appalling suffering.

In addition to these direct economic effects, the price inflation of the later sixteenth century had significant political effects as well because higher prices

WHY WAS THE PERIOD 1540 TO 1660 ONE OF THE MOST TURBULENT IN EUROPEAN HISTORY?

ECONOMIC, RELIGIOUS, AND POLITICAL TESTS   521

placed new pressures on the sovereign states of Europe. The reasons for this were simple. Since the inflation depressed the real value of money, fixed incomes from taxes and tolls in effect yielded less and less. Thus merely to keep their incomes constant governments would have been forced to raise taxes. But to compound this problem, most states needed much more real income than previously because they were undertaking more wars, and warfare, as always, was becoming increasingly expensive. The only recourse, then, was to raise taxes precipitously, but such draconian measures aroused great resentment on the part of their subjects—especially the very poor who were already suffering from the effects of the inflation. Hence governments faced continuous threats of defiance and potential armed resistance.

On the whole, the period from 1600 to 1660 was one of economic stagnation.

After 1600 prices stabilized, as population growth slowed and the flood of silver from America began to abate. On the whole, however, the period from 1600 to 1660 was one of economic stagnation rather than growth, even though a few areas—notably Holland—bucked the trend. The rich were usually able to hold their own, but the poor as a group made no advances, since the relationship of prices to wages remained fixed to their disadvantage. Indeed, if anything, the lot of the poor in many places deteriorated because the mid-seventeenth century saw some particularly

Until religious passions began to cool toward the end of the period, most Catholics and Protestants viewed each other as minions of Satan who could not be allowed to live.

expensive and destructive wars, causing helpless civilians to be plundered by rapacious tax collectors or looting soldiers, or sometimes both. The Black Death also returned, wreaking havoc in London and elsewhere during the 1660s.

RELIGIOUS CONFLICTS

It goes without saying that most people would have been far better off had there been fewer wars during this difficult century, but given prevalent attitudes, newly arisen religious rivalries made wars inevitable. Simply stated, until religious passions began to cool toward the end of the period, most Catholics and Protestants viewed each other as minions of Satan who could not be allowed to live. Worse, sovereign states attempted to enforce religious uniformity on the

grounds that "crown and altar" offered each other mutual support and in the belief that governments would totter where diversity of faith prevailed. Rulers on both sides felt certain that religious minorities, if allowed to survive in their realms, would inevitably engage in sedition; nor were they far wrong, since militant Calvinists and Jesuits were indeed dedicated to subverting constituted powers in areas where their party had not yet triumphed. Thus states tried to extirpate all potential religious resistance, but in the process sometimes provoked civil wars in which each side tended to assume there could be no victory until the other was exterminated. And of course civil wars might become international in scope when one or more foreign powers resolved to aid embattled religious allies elsewhere.

POLITICAL INSTABILITY

Compounding the foregoing problems were the inherent weaknesses of the major European kingdoms. Most of the major states of early modern Europe had built themselves up during the later Middle Ages by absorbing smaller, traditionally autonomous territories, sometimes by conquest, but more often through marriage alliances or inheritance arrangements between their respective ruling families (a policy known as "dynasticism"). At first some degree of provincial autonomy was usually preserved in these newly absorbed territories. But between 1540 and 1660, when governments were making ever greater financial claims on all their subjects or trying to enforce religious uniformity, rulers often rode roughshod over the rights of these traditionally autonomous provinces. The result, once again, was civil war, in which regionalism, economic grievances, and religious animosities were compounded into a volatile and destructive mixture. Nor was that all, since most governments seeking money and/or religious uniformity tried to rule with a firmer hand than before, and thus sometimes provoked armed resistance from subjects seeking to preserve their traditional constitutional liberties. Given this bewildering variety of motives for revolt, it is by no means surprising that the long century between 1540 and 1660 was one of the most turbulent in all of European history.

A CENTURY OF RELIGIOUS WARS

What caused the decline of Spain in the seventeenth century?

The greatest single cause of warfare during this period was religious conflict. The wars themselves divide into four phases: a series of German wars from the 1540s to 1555; the French wars of religion from 1562 until 1598; the Dutch wars with Spain between 1566 and 1609; and the Thirty Years' War in Germany between 1618 and 1648.

THE GERMAN WARS OF RELIGION TO 1555

Wars between Catholics and Protestants in Germany began in the 1540s when the Holy Roman emperor Charles V, a devout Catholic, tried to reestablish Catholic unity in Germany by launching a military campaign against several German princes who had instituted Lutheran worship in their territories. Despite several notable victories, Charles's efforts to defeat the Protestant princes failed. Partly this was because he was simultaneously involved in wars against France, and so could not devote his entire attention to German affairs. Primarily, however, Charles failed because the Catholic princes of Germany feared that if Charles succeeded in defeating the Protestant princes, he might then suppress their own independence also. As a result, the Catholic princes' support for the foreign-born Charles was only lukewarm; at times, they even joined with the Protestant princes in battle against the emperor. Accordingly, religious warfare sputtered on and off until a compromise settlement was reached in the Religious Peace of Augsburg (1555). This rested on the principle of *cuius regio, eius religio* ("as the ruler, so the religion"), which meant that in those principalities where Lutheran princes ruled, Lutheranism would be the sole state religion; where Catholic princes ruled, their territories would be Catholic also. Although the Peace of Augsburg was a historical milestone inasmuch as Catholic rulers for the first time acknowledged the legality of Protestantism, it boded ill for the future in assuming that no sovereign state larger than a free city (for which it made exceptions) could tolerate religious diversity. Moreover, in excluding Calvinism entirely, it ensured that the German Calvinists would become aggressive opponents of the status quo.

The Peace of Augsburg boded ill for the future in assuming that no sovereign state could tolerate religious diversity.

THE FRENCH WARS OF RELIGION

From the 1560s on, Europe's religious wars became far more brutal, partly because the combatants had become more intransigent (Calvinists and Jesuits customarily took the lead on their respective sides), and partly because the later religious wars were aggravated by regional, political, and dynastic hostilities. Since Geneva bordered on France, and since Calvin himself was a Frenchman who longed to convert his mother country, the next act in the tragedy of Europe's confessional warfare was played out on French soil. Calvinist missionaries made considerable headway in France between 1541 (when Calvin took power in Geneva) and the outbreak of religious warfare in 1562. By 1562, Calvinists comprised between 10 and 20 percent of France's population, with their numbers swelling daily. Greatly assisting the Calvinist (Huguenot) cause in France was the conversion of many aristocratic French women to Calvinism because such women often won over their husbands, who in turn maintained large private armies. The foremost example is that of Jeanne d'Albret, queen of the tiny Pyrenean kingdom of Navarre, who brought over to Calvinism her husband, the prominent French aristocrat Antoine de Bourbon, and her brother-in-law, the prince de Condé. Condé took command of the French Huguenot party when civil war broke out in 1562, and was later succeeded in this capacity by Jeanne's son, Henry of Navarre, who came to rule all of France at the end of the century as King Henry IV. But Calvinism in France was also nourished by long-standing regional hosilities within the French kingdom, especially in southern France, where the animosities aroused by the thirteenth-century Albigensian crusade continued to fester.

Until 1562, an uneasy peace continued between the Catholic and the Calvinist forces in France. In 1562, however, the French king died unexpectedly, leaving a young child as his heir. A struggle immediately broke out between the Huguenot Condé and the ultra-Catholic duke of Guise for control of the regency gov-

WHAT CAUSED THE DECLINE OF SPAIN IN THE SEVENTEENTH CENTURY?

A CENTURY OF RELIGIOUS WARS   523

ernment. And since both Catholics and Protestants assumed that France could have only a single *roi, foi,* and *loi* (king, faith, and law), this political struggle immediately took on a religious aspect. Soon all France was aflame. Rampaging mobs, often incited by members of the clergy, ransacked churches and settled local scores. Although the Huguenots were not strong or numerous enough to gain victory, they were too strong to be defeated, especially in their southern French territorial stronghold. Hence, despite intermittent truces, warfare dragged on at great cost of life until 1572, when a truce was arranged by which the Protestant leader, Henry of Navarre, was to marry the Catholic sister of the reigning French king. At this point, however, the cultivated queen mother Catherine de Medici, normally a woman who favored compromise, panicked. Instead of honoring the truce, she plotted with members of the Catholic Guise faction to kill all the Huguenot leaders while they were assembled in Paris for her daugher's wedding to Henry of Navarre. In the early morning of St. Bartholomew's Day (August 24) most of the Huguenot chiefs were murdered in bed and two to three thousand other Protestants were slaughtered in the streets or drowned in the Seine by Catholic mobs. When word of the Parisian massacre spread to the provinces, some ten thousand more Huguenots were killed in a frenzy of blood lust that swept through France. Henry of Navarre escaped, along with his new bride; but after 1572, the conflict entered a new and even more bitter phase.

Only when the politically astute Henry of Navarre succeeded to the French throne as Henry IV (1589–1610), initiating the Bourbon dynasty that would rule until 1792, did the civil war finally come to an end. In 1593 Henry abjured his Protestantism in order to placate France's Catholic majority, declaring as he did so that "Paris is worth a mass." In 1598, however, he offered limited religious freedom to the Huguenots by the Edict of Nantes. Although the Edict recognized Catholicism as the official religion of the kingdom, guaranteeing Catholics the right to practice their religion everywhere in the kingdom, Huguenot nobles were now allowed to hold Protestant services privately in their castles; other Huguenots were allowed to worship at specified places (excluding Paris and all cities where bishops and archbishops resided); and the Huguenot party was permitted to fortify some towns, especially in the south and west, for their own military defense. Huguenots were also guaranteed the right to serve in all public offices, and to enter the universities and hospitals without hindrance.

Although the Edict of Nantes did not countenance absolute freedom of worship, it nevertheless represented a major stride in the direction of toleration. But despite its efforts to create one kingdom with two faiths, the effect of the Edict was to divide the French kingdom into separate religious enclaves. In southern and western France, Huguenots came to have their own law courts, staffed by their own judges. They also received substantial powers of self-government, because it was presumed on all sides that the members of one religious group could not be ruled equitably by the adherents of a competing religion. Because of its regional character, Nantes also represented a concession to the long-standing traditions of provincial autonomy within the kingdom of France. In some ways, indeed, the Huguenot areas became "a state within a state," thus raising again the perpetual fear in Paris that the kingdom of which it was the capital might once again fly apart into its constituent parts, as had happened during the Hundred Years' War. On its own terms, however, the Edict of Nantes was a success. With religious peace established, France quickly began to recover from decades of devastation, even though Henry IV himself was cut down by the dagger of a Catholic fanatic in 1610.

> Although the Edict of Nantes did not countenance absolute freedom of worship, it nevertheless represented a major stride in the direction of toleration.

THE REVOLT OF THE NETHERLANDS

Bitter warfare also broke out between Catholics and Protestants in the Netherlands, where national resentments exacerbated the predictable religious hatreds. For almost a century the Netherlands (or Low Countries), comprising modern-day Holland in the north and Belgium in the south, had been ruled by the Habsburg family of Holy Roman emperors. Particularly the southern part of the Netherlands prospered greatly from trade and manufacture: southern Netherlanders had the greatest per capita wealth of all Europe, and their metropolis of Antwerp was northern Europe's leading commercial and financial center. Moreover, the half-century-long rule of the Habsburg emperor Charles V (1506–1556) had been popular because Charles, who had been born in the Belgian city of Ghent, felt a sense of rapport with his subjects, and allowed them a large degree of local self-government.

Boundary of the Holy Roman Empire

Possessions of Charles V, 1526
(Spanish Habsburgs)

Added by Ferdinand I, 1556
(Austrian Habsburgs)

EUROPE, C. 1560

This map details the political situation in Europe around the year 1560. Despite the fact that the Habsburgs were Catholic, many Catholic nations such as France routinely opposed them; why? How did the rise of nationalism and the emergence of the state further complicate the religious conflicts of the sixteenth century? Note the situation of the Netherlands at this moment in history. Why did the leaders for independence from the Habsburgs convert to Protestantism to achieve their ends? What might this suggest about the use of religion for political ends during the mid-sixteenth century?

WHAT CAUSED THE DECLINE OF SPAIN IN THE SEVENTEENTH CENTURY?

A CENTURY OF RELIGIOUS WARS   525

But around 1560 the good fortune of the Netherlands began to ebb. When Charles V retired to a monastery in 1556 (dying two years later) he ceded all his vast territories outside of the Holy Roman empire and Hungary—not only the Netherlands, but Spain, Spanish America, and close to half of Italy—to his son Philip II (1556–1598). Unlike Charles, Philip had been born in Spain, and thinking of himself as a Spaniard, made Spain his residence and the focus of his policy. Thus he viewed the Netherlands primarily as a potentially rich source of income necessary for pursuing Spanish affairs. But in order to tap the wealth of the Netherlands Philip had to rule it more directly than his father had, and such attempts were naturally resented by the local magnates who until then had dominated the government. To make matters worse, a religious storm also was brewing, for after a treaty of 1559 ended a long war between France and Spain, French Calvinists had begun to stream over the Netherlandish border, making converts wherever they went. Soon there were more Calvinists in Antwerp than in Geneva, a situation that Philip II could not tolerate because he was an ardent Catholic who subscribed wholeheartedly to the goals of the Counter-Reformation. Indeed, as he wrote to Rome on the eve of conflict, "rather than suffer the slightest harm to the true religion and service of God, I would lose all my states and even my life a hundred times over because I am not and will not be the ruler of heretics."

There is much evidence of the complexity of the Netherlandish situation. For example, the leader of resistance to Philip, William "the Silent," was at first not a Calvinist; also, the territories that ultimately succeeded in breaking away from Spanish rule were at first the most Catholic in the Low Countries. William the Silent, a prominent nobleman with large landholdings in the Netherlands, was actually very talkative. He received his nickname from his ability to hide his true religious and political feelings when the need arose. In 1566, while still a Catholic, he and other local nobles not formally committed to Protestantism appealed to Philip to allow toleration for Calvinists. But while Philip momentarily temporized, radical Protestant

Protestants Ransacking a Catholic Church in the Netherlands. The "Protestant fury" of 1566 was responsible for the large-scale destruction of religious art and statuary in the Low Countries, provoking the stern repression of Phillip II.

mobs proved to be their own worst enemy—ransacking Catholic churches throughout the country, methodically desecrating hosts, smashing statuary, and shattering stained-glass windows. Though local troops soon had the situation under control, Philip II nonetheless decided to dispatch an army of ten thousand commanded by the steely Spanish duke of Alva to wipe out Protestantism in the Low Countries forever. Alva's tribunal, the "Council of Blood," soon examined some twelve thousand persons on charges of heresy or sedition, of whom nine thousand were convicted and one thousand executed. William the Silent fled the country, and all hope for a free Netherlands seemed lost.

But the tide turned quickly for two related reasons. First, instead of giving up, William the Silent converted to Protestantism, sought help from Protestants in France, Germany, and England, and organized bands of sea rovers to harass Spanish shipping on the Netherlandish coast. And second, Alva's tyranny helped William's cause, especially when the hated Spanish governor attempted to levy a 10 percent sales tax. With internal disaffection growing, in 1572 William, for tactical military reasons, was able to seize the northern Netherlands even though the north until then had been predominantly Catholic. Thereafter geography played a major role in determining the outcome of the conflict.

Spanish armies repeatedly attempted to win back the north, but they were stopped by a combination of impassable rivers and dikes that could be opened to flood out the invaders. Although William the Silent was assassinated by a Catholic in 1584, his son continued to lead the resistance until the Spanish crown finally agreed by a truce in 1609 to stop fighting and thus implicitly recognized the independence of the northern Dutch Republic. Meanwhile, the pressures of war and persecution had made the whole north Calvinistic, whereas the south—which remained under Spanish control—returned to uniform Catholicism.

ENGLAND AND THE DEFEAT OF THE SPANISH ARMADA

Religious strife could thus take the form of civil war, as in France, or war for national liberation, as in the Netherlands. But it could also take the form of warfare between sovereign states, as in the late-sixteenth-century struggle between England and Spain. After narrowly escaping domination by the Catholic queen Mary and her Spanish husband Philip II, English Protestants rejoiced in the rule of Queen Elizabeth I (1558–1603) and naturally harbored great antipathy toward Philip II and the Counter-Reformation. Furthermore, English economic interests were directly opposed to those of the Spanish. A seafaring and trading people, the English in the later sixteenth century were steadily making inroads into Spanish naval and commercial domination, and were also determined to resist any Spanish attempt to block England's lucrative trade with the Low Countries. But the greatest source of antagonism lay in naval contests in the Atlantic, where English privateers, with the tacit consent of Queen Elizabeth, could not resist raiding silver-laden Spanish treasure ships. Beginning around 1570, and taking as an excuse the Spanish oppression of Protestants in the Netherlands, English admirals or pirates (the terms were really interchangeable) such as Sir Francis Drake and Sir John Hawkins began plundering Spanish vessels on the high seas. In a particularly dramatic sailing exploit lasting from 1577 to 1580, lust for treasure and prevailing winds propelled Drake all the way around the world, to return with stolen Spanish treasure worth twice as much as Queen Elizabeth's annual revenue.

All this would have been sufficient provocation for Philip II to retaliate against England, but because he had his hands full in the Netherlands he resolved to invade the island only after the English openly allied with the Dutch rebels in 1585. And even then Philip did not act without extensive planning and a sense of assurance that nothing could go wrong. Finally, in 1588 he dispatched an enormous fleet, confidently called the "Invincible Armada," to invade insolent Britannia. After an initial standoff in the English Channel, however, the smaller, longer-gunned English warships outmaneuvered the Spanish fleet, while English fireships set some Spanish galleons ablaze and forced the rest to break formation. "Protestant gales" did the rest. After a disastrous circumnavigation of the British Isles and Ireland, the shattered flotilla limped home with almost half its ships lost.

The defeat of the Spanish Armada was one of the most decisive battles of Western history. Had Spain conquered England it is quite likely that the Spanish would have gone on to crush Holland and perhaps even to destroy Protestantism elsewhere in Europe. But, as it was, the Protestant day was saved, and not long afterward Spanish power began to decline, with English and Dutch ships taking ever greater command of the seas. In England, patriotic Protestant fervor became especially intense. Popular even before then, "Good Queen Bess" was virtually revered by her subjects until her death in 1603, and England embarked on its golden "Elizabethan Age" of literary endeavor. War with Spain dragged on inconclusively until 1604, but the fighting never brought England any serious harm and was just lively enough to keep the English people deeply committed to the cause of their queen, their country, and the Protestant religion, which they increasingly saw as identical.

THE THIRTY YEARS' WAR

With the promulgation of the Edict of Nantes in 1598, the peace between England and Spain of 1604, and the truce between Spain and Holland of 1609, religious warfare in northwestern Europe came briefly to an end in the early seventeenth century. But in 1618 a major new war broke out, this time in Germany. Since this struggle raged more or less unceasingly until 1648 it is known as the Thirty Years' War. Far from returning to enduring peace, Spain and France now became engaged in the conflict in Germany and in war with one another. Internal resentments in Spain, France, and England flared up in the decade of the 1640s in concurrent outbreaks of civil war. As an English preacher said in 1643, "these are days of shaking, and this shaking is universal."

WHAT CAUSED THE DECLINE OF SPAIN IN THE SEVENTEENTH CENTURY?

A CENTURY OF RELIGIOUS WARS   527

The Thirty Years' War began in a welter of religious passions as a war between Catholics and Protestants, but it quickly raised basic German constitutional issues and ended as an international struggle in which the initial religious dimension was almost entirely forgotten. Between the Peace of Augsburg in 1555 and the outbreak of war in 1618, Calvinists had replaced Lutherans in a few German territories, but the overall balance between Protestants and Catholics within the Holy Roman Empire had remained undisturbed. In 1618, however, war broke out after Ferdinand, the Catholic Habsburg prince of Poland, Austria, and Hungary, was elected king of the Protestant territory of Bohemia (not a German territory, yet part of the Holy Roman Empire). The staunchly Protestant Bohemian nobility had opposed Ferdinand's election, and when Ferdinand began to suppress Protestantism in Bohemia, they rebelled. German Catholic forces ruthlessly counterattacked, first in Bohemia and then in Germany proper, now led by Ferdinand, who in 1619 became Holy Roman emperor also. Within a decade, a German Catholic league seemed close to extirpating Protestantism throughout Germany.

Ferdinand's success, however, raised once again the prospect that an overly powerful Holy Roman emperor might threaten the political autonomy of the German princes, Catholic and Protestant alike. Thus when the Lutheran king of Sweden, Gustavus Adolphus, the "Lion of the North," marched into Germany in 1630 to champion the Protestant cause, he was welcomed by several German Catholic princes who preferred to see the former religious balance restored rather than risk surrendering their sovereignty to Ferdinand II. To make matters still more ironic, Gustavus' Protestant army was secretly subsidized by Catholic France, whose policy was then dictated by a cardinal of the church, Cardinal Richelieu. This was because Habsburg Spain had been fighting in Germany on the side of Habsburg Austria, and Richelieu was determined to resist any possibility of France being surrounded by a strong Habsburg alliance on the north, east, and south. In any event, the military genius Gustavus Adolphus started routing the Habsburgs, but when he fell in battle in 1632, Cardinal Richelieu had little choice but to send ever greater support to the remaining Swedish troops in Germany, until in 1635 French armies entered the war directly on Sweden's side. From then until 1648 the struggle was really one of France and Sweden against Austria and Spain, with most of Germany a helpless battleground.

The result was that Germany suffered more from warfare in the terrible years between 1618 and 1648 than it ever did before or after until the twentieth century. Several German cities were besieged and sacked nine or ten times over, and soldiers from all nations, who often had to sustain themselves by plunder, gave no quarter to defenseless civilians. With plague and disease adding to the toll of outright butchery, some parts of Germany lost more than half their populations, although others went relatively unscathed. Most horrifying was the loss of life in the final four years, when the carnage continued unabated even while peace negotiators had already arrived at broad areas of agreement and were dickering over subsidiary clauses.

Nor did the Peace of Westphalia, which finally ended the Thirty Years' War in 1648, do much to vindicate anyone's death, even though it did establish some abiding landmarks in European history. Above all, from the international perspective, the Peace of Westphalia marked the emergence of France as the predominant power on the continental European scene, replacing Spain. France would hold this position for the next two centuries. The greatest losers in the conflict (aside, of course, from the German people themselves) were the Austrian Habsburgs, who were forced to surrender all the territory they had gained in Germany and to abandon their hopes of using the office of Holy Roman emperor to dominate central Europe. Otherwise, something very close to the German status quo of 1618 was reestablished, with Protestant principalities in the north balancing Catholic ones in the south, and Germany so hopelessly divided that it could play no united role in European history until the nineteenth century.

> The Thirty Years' War began as a war between Catholics and Protestants and ended as an international struggle in which the religious dimension was almost entirely forgotten.

CHRONOLOGY

RELIGIOUS WARS, 1540s–1648

German wars	1540s–1555
French wars of religion	1562–1598
Dutch wars with Spain	1566–1609
Thirty Years' War	1618–1648

THE DESTRUCTIVENESS OF THE THIRTY YEARS' WAR

Hans Jakob Christoph von Grimmelshausen (1621–1676) lived through the horrors of the Thirty Years' War. His parents were killed, probably when he was thirteen years of age, and he himself was kidnapped the following year. By age fifteen, he was himself a soldier. His comic masterpiece, Simplicissimus, *from which this extract is taken, drew heavily upon these wartime experiences. Although technically "fiction," it portrays with brutal accuracy the cruelty and destructiveness of this war, especially for its peasant victims.*

Although it was not my intention to take the peaceloving reader with these troopers to my dad's house and farm, seeing that matters will go ill therein, yet the course of my history demands that I should leave to kind posterity an account of what manner of cruelties were now and again practised in this our German war: yes, and moreover testify by my own example that such evils must often have been sent to us by the goodness of Almighty God for our profit. For, gentle reader, who would ever have taught me that there was a God in Heaven if these soldiers had not destroyed my dad's house, and by such a deed driven me out among folk who gave me all fitting instruction thereupon? . . .

The first thing these troopers did was, that they stabled their horses: thereafter each fell to his appointed task: which task was neither more nor less than ruin and destruction. For though some began to slaughter and to boil and to roast so that it looked as if there should be a merry banquet forward, yet others there were who did but storm through the house above and below stairs. Others stowed together great parcels of cloth and apparel and all manner of household stuff, as if they would set up a frippery market. All that they had no mind to take with them they cut in pieces. Some thrust their swords through the hay and straw as if they had not enough sheep and swine to slaughter: and some shook the feathers out of the beds and in their stead stuffed in bacon and other dried meat and provisions as if such were better and softer to sleep upon. Others broke the stove and the windows as if they had a never-ending summer to promise. Houseware of copper and tin they beat flat, and packed such vessels, all bent and spoiled, in with the rest. Bedsteads, tables, chairs, and benches they burned, though there lay many cords of dry wood in the yard. Pots and pipkins must all go to pieces, either because they would eat none but roast flesh, or because their purpose was to make there but a single meal.

Our maid was so handled in the stable that she could not come out; which is a shame to tell of. Our man they laid bound upon the ground, thrust a gag into his mouth, and poured a pailful of filthy water into his body: and by this, which they called a Swedish draught, they forced him to lead a party of them to another place where they captured men and beasts, and brought them back to our farm, in which company were my dad, my mother, and our Ursula.

And now they began: first to take the flints out of their pistols and in place of them to jam the peasants' thumbs in and so to torture the poor rogues as if they had been about the burning of witches: for one of them they had taken they thrust into the baking oven and there lit a fire under him, although he had as yet confessed no crime: as for another, they put a cord round his head and so twisted it tight with a piece of wood that the blood gushed from his mouth and nose and ears. In a word each had his own device to torture the peasants, and each peasant his several tortures.

Hans Jakob Christoph von Grimmelshausen, *Simplicissimus*, translated by S. Goodrich (New York: Daedalus, 1995), pp. 1–3, 8–10, 32–35.

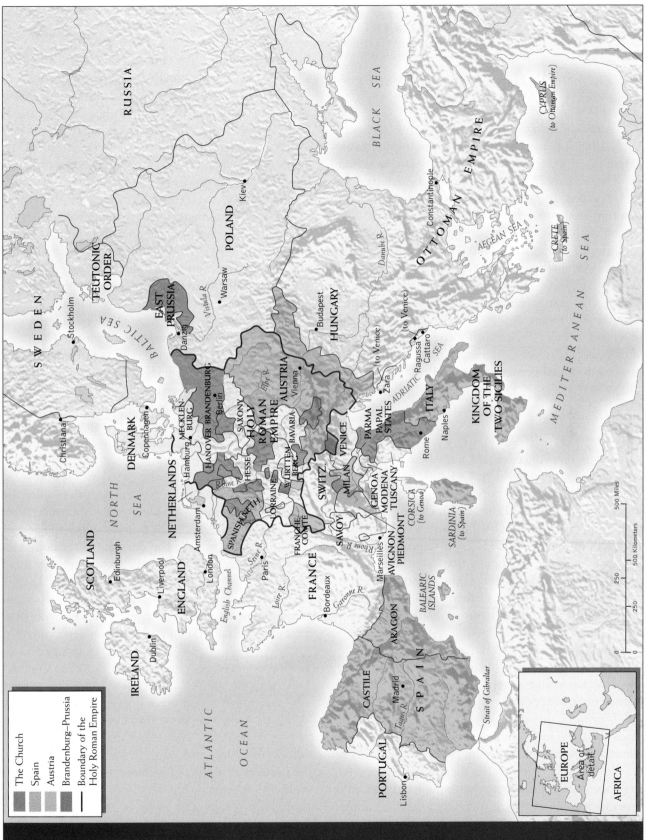

Legend:
- The Church
- Spain
- Austria
- Brandenburg–Prussia
- Boundary of the Holy Roman Empire

RUSSIA

SWEDEN

TEUTONIC ORDER

EAST PRUSSIA

POLAND

Stockholm

Christiana

Vistula R.

Warsaw

Kiev

BLACK SEA

OTTOMAN EMPIRE

Constantinople

CYPRUS (to Ottoman Empire)

AEGEAN SEA

CRETE (to Spain)

BALTIC SEA

Danzig

MECKLEN-BURG

BRANDENBURG

Berlin

Elbe R.

SAXONY

HOLY ROMAN EMPIRE

AUSTRIA

Vienna

Danube R.

Budapest

HUNGARY

(to Venice)

(to Venice)

DENMARK

Copenhagen

Hamburg

HANOVER

HESSE

Rhine

BAVARIA

WÜRTTEM-BERG

Ragussa

Zara

ADRIATIC SEA

Cattaro

MEDITERRANEAN SEA

NORTH SEA

NETHERLANDS

Amsterdam

LORRAINE

SPANISH NETH.

FRANCHE-COMTE

SWITZ.

VENICE

PARMA

PAPAL STATES

ITALY

KINGDOM OF THE TWO SICILIES

MILAN

GENOA

MODENA

TUSCANY

Rome

Naples

SCOTLAND

Edinburgh

Liverpool

ENGLAND

London

English Channel

Seine R.

Paris

SAVOY

PIEDMONT

AVIGNON

Marseilles

Rhône R.

CORSICA (to Genoa)

SARDINIA (to Spain)

IRELAND

Dublin

ATLANTIC OCEAN

Loire R.

FRANCE

Bordeaux

Garonne R.

BALEARIC ISLANDS

ARAGON

CASTILE

Madrid

SPAIN

Tagus R.

Strait of Gibraltar

PORTUGAL

Lisbon

500 Miles

500 Kilometers

250

250

0

EUROPE

Area of detail

AFRICA

EUROPE AT THE END OF THE THIRTY YEARS' WAR

What was at issue in the Thirty Years' War? Why did Catholic France ally with Lutheran Sweden against German and Austrian Catholics? Why did this war, which began as a religious one, soon encompass issues regarding the constitutional government of Germany? How much longer did the Holy Roman empire play an effective role within Europe given the internal upheavals in England, Holland and elsewhere? Why?

DIVERGENT PATHS: SPAIN, FRANCE, AND ENGLAND, 1600–1660

The long century of war between 1540 and 1660 decisively altered the balance of power among the major kingdoms of western Europe. Germany emerged from the Thirty Years' War a devastated and exhausted nation. But after 1600, Spain too was crippled by its unremitting military commitments and exertions. The French monarchy, by contrast, steadily increased its authority over France. By 1660 France had become the most powerful country on the European mainland, decisively eclipsing Spain. In England, meanwhile, a bloody civil war broke out between the king and his critics in Parliament; but after a short-lived experiment in republican rule, England in 1660 returned to its constitutional status as a "mixed" monarchy in which power was shared between king and Parliament.

THE DECLINE OF SPAIN

The story of seventeeth-century Spain's fall from grandeur is almost like a Greek tragedy in its relentless unfolding. Despite the defeat of the "Invincible Armada" in 1588, in 1600 the Spanish empire—comprising all of the Iberian Peninsula (including Portugal, which had been annexed by Phillip II in 1580), half of Italy, half of the Netherlands, all of Central and South America, and the Phillipine Islands in the Pacific Ocean—was still the mightiest power not just in Europe but in the world. Yet a bare half century later this empire on which the sun never set had come close to falling apart

Spain's greatest underlying weakness was economic. At first this may seem like a very odd statement considering that in 1600, as in the three or four previous decades, huge amounts of American silver were being unloaded on the docks of Seville. Yet as contemporaries themselves recognized, "the new world that Spain had conquered was conquering Spain in turn." Lacking either rich agricultural or mineral resources, Spain desperately needed to develop industries and a balanced trading pattern as its rivals England and France were doing. But the dominant Spanish nobility had prized ideals of chivalry over practical business ever since the medieval days when Spanish nobles were engaged in reconquering Christian territory from the Muslims. Thus the Spanish governing class was only too glad to use American silver to buy manufactured goods from other parts of Europe in order to live in splendor and dedicate itself to military exploits. Thus bullion left the country as soon as it entered, virtually no industry was established, and when the influx of silver began to decline after 1600 the Spanish economy remained with nothing except increasing debts.

Nonetheless, the crown, dedicated to supporting the Counter-Reformation and maintaining Spain's international dominance, would not cease fighting abroad. Indeed, the entire Spanish budget remained on such a war footing that even in the relatively peaceful year of 1608 four million out of a total revenue of seven million ducats were paid for military expenditures. Thus when Spain became engaged in fighting France during the Thirty Years' War it overextended itself. The clearest visible sign of this was that in 1643 French troops at Rocroi inflicted a stunning defeat on the famed Spanish infantry, the first time that a Spanish army had been overcome in battle since the reign of Ferdinand and Isabella. Worse still was the fact that by then two territories belonging to Spain's European empire were in open revolt.

In order to understand the causes of these revolts, we must recognize that in the seventeenth century the governing power of Spain lay entirely in Castile. After the marriage of Isabella of Castile and Ferdinand of Aragon in 1469, Castile had emerged as the dominant partner in the Spanish union, becoming even more dominant when it took over Portugal in 1580. In the absence of any great financial hardships, semi-autonomous Catalunya (the most fiercely independent part of Aragon) endured Castilian hegemony. But in 1640, when the strains of warfare induced Castile to limit Catalan liberties in order to raise more money and men for combat, Catalunya revolted and drove out its Castilian governors. Immediately afterward the Portuguese learned of the Catalan uprising and revolted as well, followed by southern Italians who revolted against Castilian viceroys in Naples and Sicily in 1647. At that point only the momentary inability of Spain's greatest external enemies, France and England, to take advantage of its plight saved the Spanish Empire from utter collapse. Nothing if not determined, the Castilian government quickly put down the Italian revolts and by 1652 also brought Catalunya to heel. But Portugal retained its independence, and by the Peace of the Pyre-

The new world that Spain had conquered was conquering Spain in turn.

WHAT CAUSED THE DECLINE OF SPAIN IN THE SEVENTEENTH CENTURY?

A CENTURY OF RELIGIOUS WARS   531

nees, signed with France in 1659, Spain in effect abandoned its ambition of dominating Europe.

THE GROWING POWER OF FRANCE

A comparison of the fortunes of Spain and France in the first half of the seventeenth century is highly instructive. Some striking similarities existed between the two countries, but in the end their differences turned out to be most decisive. Spain and France were of almost identical territorial extent, and both countries had been created by the same process of accretion. Just as the Castilian crown had gained Aragon in the north, Granada in the south, and then Portugal, so the kingdom of France had grown by adding on such diverse territories as Languedoc, Dauphiné, Provence, Burgundy, and Brittany. Since the inhabitants of all these territories cherished traditions of local independence as much as the Catalans or Portuguese, and since the rulers of France, like those of Spain, were determined to govern their provinces ever more firmly—especially when the financial stringencies of the Thirty Years' War made ruthless tax collecting urgently necessary—a direct confrontation between the central government and the provinces in France became inevitable, just as in Spain. But France weathered the storm whereas Spain did not, a result largely attributable to France's greater wealth and the greater prestige of the French crown.

In good times most French people, including those from the outlying provinces, tended to revere their king. Certainly they had excellent reason to do so during the reign of Henry IV. Having established religious peace in 1598 by the Edict of Nantes, the affable Henry, who declared that there should be a chicken in every French family's pot each Sunday, set out to restore the prosperity of a country devastated by four decades of civil war. Fortunately France had enormous economic resiliency, owing primarily to its extremely rich and varied agricultural resources. Unlike Spain, which had to import food, France normally was able to feed itself, and Henry's finance minister, the duke of Sully, quickly saw to it that France could feed itself once more. Among other things, Sully distributed throughout the country free copies of a guide to recommended farming techniques and financed the rebuilding or new construction of roads, bridges, and canals to facilitate the flow of goods. In addition, Henry IV was not content to see France rest its economic development on agricultural wealth alone; instead he ordered the construction of royal factories to manufacture luxury goods such as crystal, glass, and tapestries, and he also supported the growth of silk, linen, and woolen cloth industries in many different parts of the country. Moreover, Henry's patronage allowed the explorer Samuel de Champlain to claim parts of Canada as France's first foothold in the New World. Thus Henry IV's reign certainly must be counted as one of the most benevolent in all French history.

CARDINAL RICHELIEU

Far less benevolent was Henry's de facto successor as ruler of France, Cardinal Richelieu (1585–1642). The cardinal, of course, was never the real king of France—the actual title was held from 1610 to 1643 by Henry IV's ineffectual son Louis XIII. But as first minister from 1624 to his death in 1642 Richelieu governed as he wished, and what he wished most of all was to enhance centralized royal power at home and expand French influence in the larger theater of Europe. Accordingly, when Huguenots rebelled against restrictions placed on them by the Edict of Nantes, Richelieu put them down with an iron fist and amended the Edict in 1629 by depriving them of all their political and military rights. Since his armed campaigns against the Huguenots had been very costly, the cardinal then moved to gain more income for the crown by abolishing the semi-autonomy of Burgundy, Dauphiné, and Provence so that he could introduce direct royal taxation in all three areas. Later, to make sure all taxes levied were efficiently collected, Richelieu instituted a new system of local government by royal officials known as intendants, who were expressly commissioned to ride roughshod over any provincial resistance. By these and related methods Richelieu made French government more centralized than ever and managed to double the crown's income during his rule. But since he also engaged in an ambitious foreign policy directed against the Habsburgs of Austria and Spain, resulting in France's costly involvement in the Thirty Years' War, internal pressures mounted in the years after Richelieu's death.

THE FRONDE

A reaction against French governmental centralization manifested itself in a series of revolts between 1648 and 1653 collectively known as "the slingshot tumults," or in French, the *Fronde*. By this time Louis XIII had been succeeded by his son Louis XIV, but because the latter

CARDINAL RICHELIEU ON THE COMMON PEOPLE OF FRANCE

Armand Jean du Plessis, duke of Richelieu and cardinal of the Roman Catholic church was the effective ruler of France from 1624 until his death in 1642. His Political Testament *was assembled after his death from historical sketches and memoranda of advice he prepared for King Louis XIII, the ineffectual monarch whom he served. Although the book itself was not published until 1688, there is now little doubt that the writings it contains are indeed Richelieu's own thoughts.*

All students of politics agree that when the common people are too well off it is impossible to keep them peaceable. The explanation for this is that they are less well informed than the members of the other orders in the state, who are much more cultivated and enlightened, and so if not preoccupied with the search for the necessities of existence, find it difficult to remain within the limits imposed by both common sense and the law.

It would not be sound to relieve them of all taxation and similar charges, since in such a case they would lose the mark of their subjection and consequently the awareness of their station. Thus being free from paying tribute, they would consider themselves exempted from obedience. One should compare them with mules, which being accustomed to work, suffer more when long idle than when kept busy. But just as this work should be reasonable, with the bur-

dens placed upon these animals proportionate to their strength, so it is likewise with the burdens placed upon the people. If they are not moderate, even when put to good public use, they are certainly unjust. I realize that when a king undertakes a program of public works it is correct to say that what the people gain from it is returned by paying the *taille* [the most important tax paid to the crown by the French peasantry]. In the same fashion it can be maintained that what a king takes from the people returns to them, and that they advance it to him only to draw upon it for the enjoyment of their leisure and their investments, which would be impossible if they did not contribute to the support of the state.

The Political Testament of Cardinal Richelieu, translated by Henry Bertram Hill (Madison: University of Wisconsin Press, 1961), pp. 31–32.

was still a boy, France was governed by a regency consisting of Louis' mother, Anne of Austria, and her paramour Cardinal Mazarin. Considering that both were foreigners (Anne was a Habsburg and Mazarin originally an Italian adventurer named Giulio Mazarini), it is not surprising that many of their subjects, including some extremely powerful nobles, hated them. Popular resentments were greater still because the costs of war and several consecutive years of bad harvests had

brought France temporarily into a grave economic plight. Thus when cliques of nobles expressed their disgust with Mazarin for primarily self-interested reasons, they found much support throughout the country, and uncoordinated revolts against the regency government flared on and off for several years.

France, however, did not come close to falling apart. Above all, the French crown itself, which retained great reservoirs of prestige owing to a well-established

WHAT CAUSED THE DECLINE OF SPAIN IN THE SEVENTEENTH CENTURY?

A CENTURY OF RELIGIOUS WARS   533

national tradition and the undoubted achievements of Henry IV and Richelieu, was by no means under attack. On the contrary, neither the aristocratic leaders of the Fronde nor the commoners from all ranks who joined them in revolt claimed to be resisting the young king but only the alleged corruption and mismanagement of Mazarin. Some of the rebels, it is true, insisted that part of Mazarin's fault lay in his pursuit of Richelieu's centralizing, antiprovincial policy. But since most of the aristocrats who led the Fronde were merely "outs" who wanted to be "in," they often squabbled among themselves—sometimes even arranging agreements of convenience with the regency or striking alliances with France's enemy, Spain, for momentary gain—and proved completely unable to rally any unified support behind a common program. Thus when Louis XIV began to rule in his own name in 1651 and pretexts for revolting against "corrupt ministers" no longer existed, all opposition was soon silenced. As so often happens, the idealists and poor people paid the greatest price for revolt: in 1653 a defeated leader of popular resistance in Bordeaux was broken on the wheel, and not long afterward a massive new round of taxation was proclaimed. Remembering the turbulence of the Fronde for the rest of his life, Louis XIV resolved never to let his aristocracy or his provinces get out of hand again and ruled as the most effective royal absolutist in all of French history.

THE ENGLISH CIVIL WAR

Compared with the civil disturbances of the 1640s in Spain and France, those in England proved the most momentous in their results for the history of limited government. Whereas the revolts against Castile accomplished only the achievement of Portuguese independence and the crippling of an empire that was already in decline, and all that happened in France was a momentary interruption of the steady advance of royal power, in England a king was executed and enduring barriers were erected against royal absolutism.

England around 1600 was caught up in a trend toward the growth of centralized royal authority characteristic of all western Europe. Not only had Henry VIII and Elizabeth I brought the English church fully under royal control, but both monarchs also employed so-called prerogative courts wherein they could proceed against subjects in disregard of traditional English legal safeguards for the rights of the accused. Furthermore, although Parliament met regularly during both reigns, members of Parliament were far less independent than they had been in the fifteenth century: any parliamentary representative who might have stood up to Henry VIII would have lost his head, and almost all parliamentarians admired Elizabeth enough to abide by her policies. Thus when the Stuart dynasty succeeded Elizabeth, the last of the Tudors, it was only natural that the Stuarts would try to increase royal power still more. And indeed they might have succeeded had it not been for their ineptness and an extraordinary combination of forces ranged against them.

JAMES I

Lines of contention were drawn immediately at the accession of Elizabeth's nearest relative, her cousin James VI of Scotland, who in 1603 retained his Scottish crown but also became king of England as James I (1603–1625). Homely but vain, addled but erudite, James fittingly was called by Henry IV of France "the wisest fool in Christendom," and presented the starkest contrast to his predecessor. Whereas Elizabeth knew how to gain her way with Parliament without making a fuss about it, the schoolmasterish foreigner insisted on lecturing parliamentarians that he was semidivine and would brook no resistance: "As it is atheism and blasphemy to dispute what God can do, so it is presumption and high contempt in a subject to dispute what a king can do." Carrying these sentiments further, in a speech to Parliament of 1609 he proclaimed that "kings are not only God's lieutenants on earth . . . but even by God Himself they are called gods."

That such extreme pretensions to divine authority would arouse strong opposition was a result even James should have been able to foresee, for the English ruling groups were still intensely committed to the theory of parliamentary controls on the crown. Yet not just theory was at stake, for the specific policies of the new king antagonized large numbers of his subjects. For example, James insisted on supplementing his income by modes of money raising that had never been sanctioned by Parliament; when the leaders of that body objected, he angrily tore up their protests and dissolved their sessions. Worse, he interfered with the freedom of business by granting monopolies and

> England around 1600 was caught up in a trend toward the growth of centralized royal authority characteristic of all western Europe.

James I. "The wisest fool in Christendom."

Charles I. This portrait by Anthony Van Dyck vividly captures the ill-fated monarch's arrogance.

lucrative privileges to favored companies. And, worst of all in the eyes of most patriotic Englishmen, James quickly put an end to the long war with Spain and refused thereafter to become involved in any foreign military entanglements. Today many of us might think that James's commitment to peace was his greatest virtue; certainly his pacifism was justifiable financially since it spared the crown enormous debts. But in his own age James was hated particularly for his peace policy because it made him seem far too friendly with England's traditional enemy, Spain, and because "appeasement" meant leaving the embattled Protestants of Holland and Germany in the lurch.

Although almost all English people (except for a small minority of clandestine Catholics) objected to James I's pacific foreign policy, those who hated it most were a group destined to play the greatest role in overthrowing the Stuarts, namely, the Puritans. Extreme Calvinist Protestants, the Puritans believed that Elizabeth I's religious compromises had not broken fully enough with the forms and doctrines of Roman Catholicism. Called Puritans from their desire to "purify" the English church of all traces of Catholic ritual and observance, they vehemently opposed the English "episcopal system" of church government by bishops. But James I was as committed to retaining episcopalianism as the Puritans were intent on abolishing it because he viewed royally appointed bishops as one of the pillars of a strong monarchy: "No bishop, no king." Since the Puritans were a powerful influence in the House of Commons and many Puritans were also prosperous merchants who opposed James's monopolistic policies and money-raising expediencies, throughout his reign James remained at loggerheads with an extremely powerful group of his subjects for a combination of religious, constitutional, and economic reasons.

CHARLES I

Nonetheless, James survived to die peacefully in bed in 1625, and had it not been for mistakes made by his son Charles I (1625–1649), England might have gone the way of absolutist France. Charles held even more inflated notions of royal power while lacking altogether the "wise pliancy" that had characterized his father. Consequently, Charles was quickly at odds with the leaders of Parliament. Soon after his accession to the throne Charles became involved in a war with France and needed revenue desperately. When Parliament refused to make more than the customary grants, he resorted to forced loans from his subjects, punishing

WHAT CAUSED THE DECLINE OF SPAIN IN THE SEVENTEENTH CENTURY?

A CENTURY OF RELIGIOUS WARS   535

those who failed to comply by quartering soldiers in their homes or throwing them into prison without a trial. In reaction to these practices, Parliament forced the Petition of Right on the king in 1628. This document declared all taxes not voted by Parliament illegal, condemned the quartering of soldiers in private houses, and prohibited arbitrary imprisonment and the establishment of martial law in time of peace.

Angered rather than chastened by the Petition of Right, Charles I soon resolved to rule entirely without Parliament—and nearly succeeded. From 1629 to 1640 no Parliaments were called. During this "eleven years' tyranny," Charles's government lived off a variety of makeshift dues and levies. For example, the crown sold monopolies at exorbitant rates, revived highly antiquated medieval financial claims, and admonished judges to collect the stiffest of fines. Though technically not illegal, all of these expedients were deeply resented. Most controversial was the collection of "ship money," a levy taken on the pretext of a medieval obligation of English seaboard towns to provide ships (or their worth in money) for the royal navy. Extending the payment of ship money from coastal towns to the whole country, Charles threatened to make it a regular tax in contravention of the Petition of Right, and was upheld in a legal challenge of 1637 brought against him on these grounds by the Puritan squire John Hampden.

By such means the king managed to make ends meet without the aid of taxes granted by Parliament. But he became ever more hated by most of his subjects, above all the Puritans, not just because of his constitutional and financial policies but also because he and his intensely unpopular archbishop of Canterbury, William Laud, seemed to be pursuing a course in religion that came much closer to Catholicism than to Calvinism. It was in Scotland, however, not England, that the storm suddenly broke. Like his father, Charles believed in the adage "no bishop, no king" and hence decided, foolhardily, to introduce church government through bishops into staunchly Presbyterian Scotland. The result was an armed rebellion by the Scots, and the first steps toward civil war in England.

To obtain the funds necessary to put down the Scots, Charles had no other choice but to summon Parliament and soon found himself the target of pent-up resentments. Knowing full well that the king was helpless without money, the leaders of the House of Commons determined to take England's government into their own hands. Accordingly, they not only executed the king's first minister, the earl of Strafford, but

they abolished ship money and the prerogative courts that ever since the reign of Henry VIII had served as instruments of arbitrary rule. Most significant, they enacted a law forbidding the crown to dissolve Parliament and requiring the convening of sessions at least once every three years. After some indecision, early in 1642 Charles replied to these acts with a show of force. He marched with his guard into the House of Commons and attempted to arrest five of its leaders. All of them escaped, but an open conflict between crown and Parliament could no longer be avoided. Both parties collected troops and prepared for an appeal to the sword.

CIVIL WAR AND COMMONWEALTH

These events initiated the English civil war, a conflict at once political and religious, which lasted from 1642 to 1649. Arrayed on the royal side were most of England's most prominent aristocrats and largest landowners, who were almost all loyal to the established Church of England, despite their opposition to some of Charles's own religious innovations. Opposed to them, the followers of Parliament included smaller landholders, tradesmen, and manufacturers, the majority of whom were Puritans. The members of the king's party were commonly known by the aristocratic name of Cavaliers. Their opponents, who cut their hair short in contempt for the fashionable custom of wearing curls, were derisively called Roundheads. At first the royalists, having obvious advantages of military experience, won most of the victories. In 1644, however, the parliamentary army was reorganized, and soon afterward the fortunes of battle shifted. The Cavalier forces were badly beaten, and in 1646 the king was compelled to surrender. Soon thereafter, the episcopate was abolished and a Presbyterian church was established throughout England.

The struggle would now have ended had not a quarrel developed within the parliamentary party. The majority of its members, who had allied with the Presbyterian Scots, were ready to restore Charles to the throne as a limited monarch under an arrangement whereby a uniform Calvinistic Presbyterian faith would be imposed on both Scotland and England as the state religion. But a radical minority of Puritans, commonly known as Independents, distrusted Charles and insisted on religious toleration for themselves and all other non-Presbyterian Protestants. Their leader was Oliver Cromwell (1599–1658), who had risen to command the Roundhead army. Taking advantage of the dissension within the ranks of his opponents, Charles renewed the war in 1648, but after a brief campaign was forced to surrender. Cromwell now resolved to end the life of "that man of blood," and, ejecting all the Presbyterians from Parliament by force of arms, obliged the "Rump" Parliament that remained to vote an end to the monarchy. On January 30, 1649 Charles I was beheaded; a short time later the hereditary House of Lords was abolished, and England became a republic.

But founding a republic was far easier than maintaining one, and the new form of government, officially called a Commonwealth, did not last long. Technically the Rump Parliament continued as the legislative body, but Cromwell, with the army at his command, possessed the real power and soon became exasperated by the attempts of the legislators to perpetuate themselves in office and to profit by confiscating the wealth of their opponents. Accordingly, in 1653 he marched a detachment of troops into the Rump Parliament. Saying "Come, I will put an end to your prating," he ordered the members to disperse. Thereby the Commonwealth ceased to exist and was soon followed by the "Protectorate," a virtual dictatorship established under a constitution drafted by officers of the army. Called the *Instrument of Government*, this text was the nearest approximation to a written constitution England has ever had. Extensive powers were given to Cromwell as "lord protector" for life, and his office was made hereditary. At first a Parliament exercised limited authority in making laws and levying taxes, but in 1655 Cromwell abruptly dismissed its members. Thereafter the government became a thinly disguised autocracy, with Cromwell now wielding a sovereignty more absolute than any Stuart monarch ever dreamed of claiming.

THE RESTORATION OF THE MONARCHY

Given the choice between a Puritan military dictatorship and the old royalist regime, when the occasion arose England unhesitatingly opted for the latter. Years of unpopular Calvinist austerities such as the prohibition of any public recreation on Sundays had discredited the Puritans, making most people long for the milder style of the original Elizabethan church. Thus not long after Cromwell's death in 1658, one of his generals seized power and called for elections for a new Parliament, which met in the spring of 1660 and proclaimed as king Charles I's exiled son, Charles II. With the reign of Charles II (1660–1685) an episcopal Church of England was restored, but the same was not true for unrestrained monarchical power. Rather, stat-

CHRONOLOGY

ORIGINS OF THE ENGLISH CIVIL WAR, 1603–1660

Reign of the Stuarts begins	1603
Reign of Charles I	1625–1649
Rule without Parliament	1629–1640
English civil war	1642–1649
Charles I beheaded	1649
Commonwealth	1649–1652
Protectorate	1653–1658
Restoration of the monarchy	1660

ing with characteristic good humor that he did not wish to "resume his travels," Charles agreed to respect Parliament and observe the Petition of Right. Of greatest constitutional significance was the fact that all the legislation passed by Parliament immediately before the outbreak of the civil war, including the requirement to hold Parliaments at least once every three years, remained as law. Thus in striking contrast to absolutist France, England became a limited monarchy. After one further test in the late seventeenth century, the realm of England would soon live up to the poet Milton's prediction of "a noble and puissant nation rousing herself like a strong man after sleep."

THE PROBLEM OF DOUBT AND THE QUEST FOR CERTAINTY

What was Hobbes's solution to the search for authority?

Between 1540 and 1660, Europeans were forced to confront a world in which all that they had once taken for granted was suddenly cast into doubt. An entirely new world had been discovered in the Americas, populated by millions of people whose very existence compelled Europeans to rethink some of their most basic ideas about humanity and human nature. Equally disorienting, the religious uniformity of Europe, although never absolute, had been shattered to an unprecedented extent by the Reformation and the religious wars that arose from it. In 1540, it was still possible to imagine that these religious divisions might be temporary. By 1660, it was clear they would be permanent. No longer, therefore, could Europeans regard revealed religious faith as an adequate foundation for universal philosophical conclusions, for even Christians now disagreed about the fundamental truths of the faith. Political allegiances were similarly under threat, as intellectuals and common people alike began to assert a right to resist princes with whom they disagreed on matters of religion. Even morality and custom were beginning to seem arbitrary and detached from the natural ordering of the world.

> The religious uniformity of Europe had been shattered to an unprecedented extent by the Reformation and the religious wars that arose from it.

Europeans responded to this pervasive climate of doubt in a variety of ways, ranging from radical skepticism to authoritarian assertions of religious fideism and political absolutism. What united their responses, however, was a sometimes desperate search for new foundations upon which to reconstruct some measure of certainty in the face of Europe's new intellectual, religious, and political challenges.

WITCHCRAFT ACCUSATIONS AND THE POWER OF THE STATE

Adding to the fears of Europeans was their conviction that witchcraft was a mortal and increasing threat to their world. Although most people in the Middle Ages believed that certain persons, usually women, could heal or harm through the practice of magic, it was not until the fifteenth century that learned authorities began to insist that such powers could only derive from some kind of "pact" made by the "witch" with the devil. Once this belief became accepted, judicial officers became much more active in seeking out suspected witches for prosecution. In 1484 Pope Innocent VIII ordered papal inquisitors to use all the means at their disposal to detect and eliminate witchcraft, including torture of suspected witches. Predictably, torture increased the number of accused witches who confessed to their alleged crimes; and as more accused witches confessed, more and more witches were "discovered," accused, and executed, even in areas (such as England) where torture was not employed and where the Inquisition did not operate.

In considering the rash of witchcraft persecution that swept early modern Europe, two facts need to be kept in mind. First of all, the witchcraft trials were by no means limited to Catholic countries. Protestant reformers believed in the insidious powers of Satan just as much as Catholics did. Both Luther and Calvin urged that persons accused as witches be tried more peremptorily and sentenced with less leniency than ordinary criminals, a recommendation their followers were only too happy to follow. Second, it was only when the efforts of religious authorities to detect witchcraft were backed up by the coercive powers of secular governments to execute them that the fear of witchcraft became truly murderous. Between 1580 and about 1660, however, enthusiasm for catching and killing "witches" became something like a mania across much of Europe, claiming tens of thousands of victims, of whom at least three quarters were women. The final death toll will never be known, but in the 1620s there was an average of one hundred burnings a year in the German cities of Würzburg and Bamberg; around the

Supposed Witches Worshiping the Devil in the form of a Billy Goat. In the background other "witches" ride bareback on flying demons. This is one of the earliest visual conceptions of witchcraft, dating from around 1460.

same time it was said that the town square of Wolfen-büttel "looked like a little forest, so crowded were the stakes." After 1660, accusations of witchcraft gradually diminished, but isolated incidents, such as the one at Salem, Massachusetts, continued to crop up for another half century.

This witch mania reflects the fears that early modern Europeans held not only about the devil, but also about the adequacy of traditional remedies (such as prayers, amulets, and holy water) to combat the evils of their world. But it also reflects their growing conviction that only the state, and not the church, had the power to protect them. One of the most striking features of the mania for hunting down "witches" is the extent to which these prosecutions, in both Catholic and Protestant countries, were state-sponsored affairs, carried out by secular authorities claiming to act as the protectors of society against the spiritual and temporal evils that assailed it. Even in Catholic countries, where witchcraft prosecutions were sometimes begun in church courts, these cases would be transferred to the state's courts for final judgment and punishment, because church courts were forbidden to impose capital penalties. In Protestant countries, where church courts had been abolished (only England retained church courts), the entire process of detecting, prosecuting, and punishing suspected witches was carried out under the supervision of the state. In both Catholic and Protestant countries, the result of these witchcraft trials was thus a considerable increase in the scope of the state's powers and responsibilities to regulate the lives of its subjects.

> The result of these witchcraft trials was a considerable increase in the scope of the state's powers and responsibilities to regulate the lives of its subjects.

THE SEARCH FOR AUTHORITY

The crisis of Europe's iron century (as even contemporaries sometimes called it) was fundamentally a crisis of authority. Attempts to reestablish some foundation for agreed authority took many forms. For the French nobleman Michel de Montaigne (1533–1592), who wrote during the height of the French wars of religion, the result was a searching skepticism about the possibilities of any certain knowledge whatsoever. The son of a Catholic father and a Huguenot mother of Jewish ancestry, the well-to-do Montaigne retired from a legal career at the age of thirty-eight to devote himself to a life of leisured reflection. The *Essays* that resulted were a new literary form originally conceived as "experiments" in writing (the French *essai* simply means "trial"). Because they are extraordinarily well written as well as searchingly reflective, Montaigne's *Essays* are among the most enduring classics of French literature and thought.

Although the range of subjects of the *Essays* is wide, two main themes are dominant. One is a pervasive skepticism. Making his motto *Que sais-je?* ("What do I know?"), Montaigne decided that he knew very little for certain. According to him, "it is folly to measure truth and error by our own capacities" because our capacities are severely limited. Thus, as he maintained in one of his most famous essays, "On Cannibals," what may seem indisputably true and proper to one nation may seem absolutely false to another because "everyone gives the title of barbarism to everything that is not of his usage." From this Montaigne's second main principle followed—the need for moderation. Since all people think they know the perfect religion and the perfect government, yet few agree on what that perfection might be, Montaigne concluded that no religion or government is really perfect and consequently no belief is worth fighting for to the death. Instead, people should accept the teachings of religion on faith, and obey the governments constituted to rule over them, without resorting to fanaticism in either sphere.

Although Montaigne can sound surprisingly modern, he was very much a man of the sixteenth century, believing that "reason does nothing but go astray in everything," and that intellectual curiosity "which prompts us to thrust our noses into everything" is a "scourge of the soul." Montaigne was also a fatalist who thought that in a world governed by unpredictable fortune the best human strategy was to face the good and the bad with steadfastness and dignity. Lest people begin to think too highly of their own abilities, he reminded them that "sit we upon the highest throne in the world, yet we do sit upon our own behinds." And he urged a deliberate attitude of detachment toward the struggles of the day: "To compose our character is our duty, not to compose books, and to win, not battles and provinces, but order and tranquillity in our conduct. Our great and glorious masterpiece is to live appropriately. All other things, ruling, hoarding, building, are only little appendages and props, at most." Nonetheless, despite his unheroic and highly personal tone, the wide circulation of Montaigne's *Essays* did

MONTAIGNE ON SKEPTICISM AND FAITH

Michel de Montaigne's Essays *reflect the curious contradictions of his thought, which in turn mirror the tortured combination of uncertainty and faith that characterized the century in which he lived. Although he begins here by asserting the limits on human knowledge, he ends by concluding that these limits impose on human beings an obligation to accept completely every aspect of the church's religious teachings.*

Perhaps it is not without reason that we attribute facility in belief and conviction to simplicity and ignorance; for . . . the more a mind is empty and without counterpoise, the more easily it gives beneath the weight of the first persuasive argument. That is why children, common people, women, and sick people are most subject to being led by the ears. But then, on the other hand, it is foolish presumption to go around disdaining and condemning as false whatever does not seem likely to us; which is an ordinary vice in those who think they have more than common ability. I used to do so once. . . . But reason has taught me that to condemn a thing thus, dogmatically, as false and impossible, is to assume the advantage of knowing the bounds and limits of God's will and of the power of our mother Nature; and that there is no more notable folly in the world than to reduce these things to the measure of our capacity and competence. . . .

It is a dangerous and fateful presumption, besides the absurd temerity that it implies, to disdain what we do not comprehend. For after you have established, according to your fine understanding, the limits of truth and falsehood, and it turns out that you must necessarily believe things even stranger than those you deny, you are obliged from then on to abandon these limits. Now what seems to me to bring as much disorder into our consciences as anything, in these religious troubles that we are in, is this partial surrender of their beliefs by Catholics. It seems to them that they are being very moderate and understanding when they yield to their opponents some of the articles in dispute. But, besides the fact that they do not see what an advantage it is to a man charging you for you to begin to give ground and withdraw, and how much that encourages him to pursue his point, those articles which they select as the most trivial are sometimes very important. We must either submit completely to the authority of our ecclesiastical government, or do without it completely. It is not for us to decide what portion of obedience we owe it.

Montaigne: Selections from the Essays, translated and edited by Donald M. Frame (Arlington Heights, Ill.: AHM Publishing Corporation, 1971), pp. 34–38.

help combat fanaticism and religious intolerance in his own and subsequent ages.

Montaigne sought refuge from the trials of his age in skepticism, distance, and resigned dignity. His contemporary, the French lawyer Jean Bodin (1530–1596), looked instead to resolve the disorders of the day by reestablishing the powers of the state on new and more secure foundations. Like Montaigne, Bodin was particularly troubled by the upheavals caused by the religious wars in France—he had even witnessed the frightful St. Bartholomew's Day Massacre of 1572 in Paris. But instead of shrugging his shoulders about the bloodshed, he resolved to offer a political plan to make sure turbulence would cease. This he did in his monumental *Six Books of the Commonwealth* (1576), the earliest fully developed statement of absolute governmental sovereignty in Western political thought. According to Bodin, the state arises from the needs of collections of families, but once constituted should brook no opposition, for maintaining order is its paramount duty. Whereas previous writers on law and politics had groped toward a theory of governmental sovereignty, Bodin was the first to offer a succinct definition; for him, sovereignty was "the most high, absolute, and perpetual power over all subjects," consisting principally in the power "to give laws to subjects without their consent." Although Bodin acknowledged the theoretical possibility of government by aristocracy or democracy, he assumed that the nation-states of his day would be ruled by monarchs and insisted that such monarchs could in no way be limited, either by legislative or judicial bodies, or even by laws made by their predecessors or themselves. Expressing the sharpest opposition to contemporary Huguenots who were saying (in contravention of the original teachings of Luther and Calvin) that subjects had a right to resist "ungodly princes," Bodin maintained that every subject must trust in the ruler's "mere and frank good will." Even if the ruler proved a tyrant, Bodin insisted that the subject had no warrant to resist, for any resistance would open the door "to a licentious anarchy which is worse than the harshest tyranny in the world."

The case for resisting unrestrained state power was expressed most eloquently by the great English Puritan poet John Milton, who enunciated a stirring defense of freedom of the press in his *Areopagitica* (1644). Similarly bold critics of the unlimited power of monarchs were a party of Milton's Puritan contemporaries known as Levellers, the first exponents of popular democracy in the West since the ancient Greeks. Organizing themselves as a pressure group within Cromwell's army, the Levellers—who derived their name from their advocacy of equal political rights for all classes—agitated in favor of a parliamentary republic based on nearly universal male suffrage. But since Oliver Cromwell, who believed that the only grounds for suffrage was sufficient property, would have none of this, once Cromwell assumed power the Leveller party disintegrated. No widespread extension of the

right to vote in England would occur until the nineteenth century.

Far to the other extreme from the Levellers was the political philosopher Thomas Hobbes (1588–1679), whose reactions to the English civil war led him to become the most forceful advocate of unrestrained state power of all time. Like Bodin, who was moved by the events of St. Bartholomew's Day to formulate a doctrine of political absolutism, Hobbes was moved by the turmoil of the English civil war to do the same in his classic of political theory, *Leviathan* (1651). Yet Hobbes differed from Bodin in several respects. For one, whereas Bodin assumed that the absolute sovereign power would be a royal monarch, Hobbes made no such assumption. Any form of government capable of protecting its subjects' lives and property might act as a sovereign (and hence all-powerful) Leviathan. Then too, whereas Bodin defined his state as "the lawful government of families" and hence did not believe that the state could abridge private property rights because families could not exist without property, Hobbes's state existed to rule over atomistic individuals and thus was licensed to trample over both liberty and property if the government's own survival was at stake.

But the most fundamental difference between Bodin and Hobbes lay in the latter's uncompromisingly pessimistic view of human nature. Hobbes posited that the "state of nature" that existed before civil government came into being was a condition of "war of all against all." Since man naturally behaves as "a wolf" toward other men, human life without government is necessarily "solitary, poor, nasty, brutish, and short." To escape such consequences, people therefore surrendered their liberties to a sovereign ruler in exchange for his agreement to keep the peace. Having granted away their liberties, subjects have no right whatsoever to seek them back, and the sovereign could therefore tyrannize as he likes—free to oppress his charges in any way other than to kill them, an act that would negate the very purpose of his rule, which is to preserve his subjects' lives.

Hobbes's views were vastly unpopular—proponents of constitutional liberties detested his conclusions, and royalists detested his premises. Although he buttressed his conclusions in the (rarely read) third and fourth books of *Leviathan* by citing biblical passages, he developed his arguments in the first two books like a geometric proof, starting with the observable facts of individual sense perception, and then reasoning upwards to the political principles that must flow from these facts. Hobbes was contemptuous of dynastic

DEMOCRACY AND THE ENGLISH CIVIL WAR

The English civil war raised fundamental issues about the political rights and responsibilities of Englishmen. Many of these issues were addressed in a lengthy debate held within the General Council of Cromwell's New Model Army at Putney in October 1647. Interestingly none of the participants in these debates seems to have recognized the implications their arguments might have for the political rights of women. Only King Charles, speaking moments before his execution in 1649, saw the radical implications of the constitutional experiment on which the Parliamentary forces had embarked—but ironically, it was his own radical assertions of monarchical authority that prompted the rebellion that overthrew him.

THE ARMY DEBATES, 1647

Colonel Rainsborough: Really, I think that the poorest man that is in England has a life to live as the greatest man; and therefore truly, sir, I think it's clear, that every man that is to live under a government ought first by his own consent to put himself under that government; and I do think that the poorest man in England is not at all bound in a strict sense to that government that he has not had a voice to put himself under . . . insomuch that I should doubt whether I was an Englishman or not, that should doubt of these things.

General Ireton: Give me leave to tell you, that if you make this the rule, I think you must fly for refuge to an absolute natural right, and you must deny all civil right; and I am sure it will come to that in the consequence. . . . For my part, I think it is no right at all. I think that no person has a right to an interest or share in the disposing of the affairs of the kingdom, and in determining or choosing those that shall determine what laws we shall be ruled by here, no person has a right to this that has not a permanent fixed interest in this kingdom, and those persons together are properly the represented of this kingdom who, taken together, and consequently are to make up the representers of this kingdom. . . .

We talk of birthright. Truly, birthright there is. . . . [M]en may justly have by birthright, by their very being born in England, that we should not seclude them out of England. That we should not refuse to give them air and place and ground, and the freedom of the highways and other things, to live amongst us, not any man that is born here, though he in birth or by his birth there come nothing at all that is part of the permanent interest of this kingdom to him. That I think is due to a man by birth. But that by a man's being born here he shall have a share in that power that shall dispose of the lands here, and of all things here, I do not think it is a sufficient ground.

Divine Right and Democracy: An Anthology of Political Writing in Stuart England, edited by David Wootton (New York: Viking Penguin, 1986), pp. 286–287 (language modernized).

CHARLES I ON THE SCAFFOLD, 1649

I think it is my duty, to God first, and to my country, for to clear myself both as an honest man, a good king, and a good Christian.

I shall begin first with my innocence. In truth I think it not very needful for me to insist long upon this, for all the world knows that I never did begin a war with the two Houses of Parliament; and I call God to witness, to whom I must shortly make an account, that I never did intend to incroach upon their privileges. . . .

As for the people—truly I desire their liberty and freedom as much as anybody whatsoever. But I must tell you that their liberty and freedom consists in having of government those laws by which their lives and goods may be most their own. It is not for having share in government. That is nothing pertaining to them. A subject and a sovereign are clean different things, and therefore, until they do that—I mean that

you do put the people in that liberty as I say—certainly they will never enjoy themselves.

Sirs, it was for this that now I am come here. If I would have given way to an arbitrary way, for to have all laws changed according to the power of the sword, I needed not to have come here. And therefore I tell you (and I pray God it be not laid to your charge) that I am the martyr of the people.

Great Issues in Western Civilization, edited by Brian Tierney, Donald Kagan, and L. Pearce Williams (New York: Random House, 1967), pp. 46–47.

---

claims based on blood lineage, and had seen at first hand that the "divine right of kings" was no deterrent to rebellion and anarchy. He sought therefore to establish a new science of politics that would ground political obligation not on tradition or divine delegation, but instead on empirical observation, reason, and the effective use of force to preserve order. In his attempt to resolve the seventeenth-century crisis of authority, what is most revealing about Hobbes is therefore not his conclusions, but the reasoning by which he arrives at them.

Perhaps the most moving attempt to respond to the problem of doubt in seventeenth-century culture was offered by the French moral and religious philosopher Blaise Pascal (1623–1662). Pascal began his career as a mathematician and scientific rationalist. A modern computer language has been named for him because he constructed the first calculating machine. (He did this when he was nineteen years old.) But at age thirty Pascal abandoned science as the result of a conversion experience and became a firm adherent of Jansenism, a puritanical faction within French Catholicism. From then until his death he worked on a highly ambitious philosophical-religious project meant to persuade

doubters of the truth of Christianity by appealing simultaneously to their intellects and their emotions. Because of his premature death all that came of this effort was his *Pensées* ("Thoughts"), a collection of fragments and short informal pieces about religion written with great literary power. In these he argued that faith alone could show the way to salvation and that "the heart has its reasons of which reason itself knows nothing." Pascal's *Pensées* express the author's own terror, anguish, and awe in the face of evil and eternity, but present that awe itself as evidence for the existence of God. Pascal's hope was that on this foundation, some measure of hopefulness about humanity and its capacity for self-knowledge could be re-erected that would avoid both the dogmatism and the extreme skepticism that were so prominent in seventeenth-century society.

LITERATURE AND THE ARTS

What was the relationship between the Baroque school and the Counter-Reformation?

Doubt and the uncertainty of human knowledge were also primary themes in the profusion of literature and art produced during western Europe's iron century. Of course not every poem, play, or painting of the era expressed the same message. During a hundred twenty years of extraordinary literary and artistic creativity, works of all genres and sentiments were produced, ranging from the frothiest farces to the darkest tragedies, from the serenest still lifes to the most violent scenes of religious martyrdom. The greatest writ-

CHRONOLOGY

THE SEARCH FOR AUTHORITY, 1572–1670

Montaigne's *Essays*	1572–1580
Bodin's *Six Books of the Commonwealth*	1576
Milton's *Areopagatica*	1644
Hobbes's *Leviathan*	1651
Pascal's *Pensées*	1670

WHAT WAS THE RELATIONSHIP BETWEEN THE BAROQUE SCHOOL AND THE COUNTER-REFORMATION?

LITERATURE AND THE ARTS   543

ers and painters of the period all were moved by a realization of the ambiguities and ironies of human existence not unlike that expressed in different ways by Montaigne and Pascal. They all were fully aware of the horrors of war and human suffering so rampant in their day, but they also sought some measure of redemption for human beings caught up in a world that treated them so cruelly. Out of this tragic balance came some of the greatest works in the entire history of European literature and art.

MIGUEL DE CERVANTES (1547–1616)

Cervantes' masterpiece, the satirical romance *Don Quixote*, recounts the adventures of a Spanish gentleman, Don Quixote of La Mancha, who becomes slightly unbalanced by his constant reading of chivalric epics. His mind filled with all kinds of fantastic adventures, he sets out at the age of fifty on the slippery road of knight-errantry, imagining windmills to be glowering giants and flocks of sheep to be armies of infidels whom it is his duty to rout with his spear. In his distorted fancy he mistakes inns for castles and serving girls for courtly ladies on fire with love. Set off in contrast to the "knight-errant" is the figure of his faithful squire, Sancho Panza. The latter represents the ideal of the practical man, with his feet on the ground and content with the modest but substantial pleasures of eating, drinking, and sleeping. Yet Cervantes clearly does not wish to say that the realism of a Sancho Panza is categorically preferable to the "quixotic" idealism of his master. Rather, the two men represent different facets of human nature. Without any doubt, *Don Quixote* is a devastating satire on the anachronistic chivalric mentality that was already hastening Spain's decline. But for all that, the reader's sympathies remain with the protagonist, the man from La Mancha who dares to "dream the impossible dream."

ELIZABETHAN AND JACOBEAN DRAMA

Writing after England's victory over the Spanish Armada, when national pride was at a peak, the dramatists of the so-called English Renaissance exhibited great exuberance without descending into a facile optimism. In fact a strain of reflective seriousness pervades all their best works, and a few, such as the tragedian John Webster (c. 1580–c. 1625), who "saw the skull beneath the skin," were if anything morbid pessimists. Among a bevy of great Elizabethan and Jacobean playwrights, however, the most outstanding were Christopher Marlowe

(1564–1593), Ben Jonson (c. 1572–1637), and William Shakespeare (1564–1616). Of the three, the fiery Marlowe, whose life was cut short in a tavern brawl before he reached the age of thirty, was the most popular in his own day. In plays such as *Tamburlaine* and *Doctor Faustus* Marlowe created larger-than-life heroes who seek and come close to conquering everything in their path and feeling every possible sensation. But they meet unhappy ends because, for Marlowe, there are limits on human striving, and wretchedness as well as greatness lies in the human lot. Thus although Faustus asks a reincarnated Helen of Troy, conjured up by Satan, to make him "immortal with a kiss," he dies and is damned in the end because immortality is not awarded by the devil or to be found in earthly kisses.

In contrast to the heroic tragedies of Marlowe, Ben Jonson wrote corrosive comedies that expose human vices and foibles. In the particularly bleak *Volpone* Jonson shows people behaving like deceitful and lustful animals, but in the later *Alchemist* he balances an attack on quackery and gullibility with admiration for resourceful lower-class characters who cleverly take advantage of their supposed betters.

The greatest of the Elizabethan dramatists, William Shakespeare was born into the family of a tradesman in the provincial town of Stratford-on-Avon. Little is known about his early life. He left his native village, having gained a modest education, when he was about twenty, and went to London where he found employment in the theater. How he eventually became an actor and still later a writer of plays is uncertain, but by the age of twenty-eight he had definitely acquired a reputation as an author sufficient to excite the jealousy of his rivals. Before he retired to his native Stratford about 1610 to spend the rest of his days in ease, he had written or collaborated in writing nearly forty plays, over and above one hundred fifty sonnets, and two long narrative poems.

Since their author's death, Shakespeare's plays have become a kind of secular Bible wherever the English language is spoken. The reasons lie in the author's unrivaled gift of expression, in his scintillating wit, and most of all in his profound analysis of human character seized by passion and tried by fate. Shakespeare's dramas fall thematically into three groups. Those written during the playwright's early years are characterized by a sense of confidence that, despite human foolishness, the world is fundamentally orderly and just. These include a number of the history plays, which recount England's struggles and glories leading up to the triumph of the Tudor dynasty; the lyrical romantic tragedy *Romeo and Juliet*; and a number of comedies including the magical *Midsummer Night's Dream, Twelfth Night, As You Like It*, and *Much Ado about Nothing*. Despite the last-named title, few even of the plays of Shakespeare's early, lightest period are "much ado about nothing." Rather, most explore fundamental problems of psychological identity, honor and ambition, love and friendship. Occasionally they also contain touches of deep seriousness, as in *As You Like It*, when Shakespeare has a character pause to reflect that "all the world's a stage, and all the men and women merely players" who pass through seven "acts" or stages of life.

The plays from Shakespeare's second period are far darker in mood, being characterized by bitterness, pathos, and a troubled searching into the mysteries and meaning of human existence. The series begins with the tragedy of indecisive idealism represented by *Hamlet*, goes on to the cynicism of *Measure for Measure* and *All's Well That Ends Well*, and culminates in the searing tragedies of *Macbeth* and *King Lear*, wherein characters assert that "life's but a walking shadow . . . a tale told by an idiot, full of sound and fury signifying nothing," and that "as flies to wanton boys are we to the gods; they kill us for their sport." Despite their gloom, however, the plays of Shakespeare's second period contain some of the dramatist's greatest flights of poetic grandeur.

Shakespeare ended his dramatic career, however, with a third period characterized by a profound spirit of reconciliation and peace. Of the three plays (all idyllic romances) written during this final period, the last, *The Tempest*, is the widest ranging in its reflections on human nature and the power of art. Ancient animosities are buried and wrongs are righted by a combination of natural and supernatural means, and a wide-eyed, youthful heroine rejoices on first seeing men with the words "O brave new world, that has such people in it!" Here, then, Shakespeare seems to be saying that despite humanity's trials, life is not so bitter after all, and the divine plan of the universe is ultimately benevolent and just.

Though less versatile than Shakespeare, not far behind him in eloquent grandeur stands the Puritan poet John Milton (1608–1674). The leading publicist of Oliver Cromwell's regime, Milton wrote the official defense of the beheading of Charles I as well as a number of treatises justifying Puritan positions in contemporary affairs. But he also loved the Greek and Latin classics at least as much as the Bible, and wrote a perfect pastoral elegy, *Lycidas*, mourning the loss of a dear friend in purely classical terms. Later, when forced into retirement by the accession of Charles II, Milton, though now blind, embarked on writing a classical epic, *Paradise Lost*, out of material found in Genesis concerning the creation of the world and the fall of man. Setting out to "justify the ways of God to man," Milton in *Paradise Lost* first plays "devil's advocate" by creating the compelling character of Satan, who defies God with boldness and subtlety. But Satan is more than counterbalanced in the end by the real "epic hero" of *Paradise Lost*, Adam, who learns to accept the human lot of moral responsibility and suffering, and is last seen leaving Paradise with Eve, the world "all before them."

MANNERISM

The ironies and tensions inherent in human existence were also portrayed with eloquence and profundity by several immortal masters of the visual arts who flour-

Portrait of a Young Man, by Bronzino (1503–1572). Bronzino was a Florentine Mannerist painter who preferred the "objective" representation of oddities. Notice the carefully chiseled grotesques at the bottom and the young man's wandering left eye. The numerous contrasts between light and shade and the large number of vertical surfaces in the background contribute to a sense of surrealism.

WHAT WAS THE RELATIONSHIP BETWEEN THE BAROQUE SCHOOL AND THE COUNTER-REFORMATION?

LITERATURE AND THE ARTS   545

View of Toledo, by El Greco. Light breaks where no sun shines. One of the most awesomely mysterious paintings in the entire Western tradition.

indebted to Michelangelo but went much farther than he did in emphasizing shadowy contrasts, restlessness, and distortion. Of this second group, the two most outstanding were the Venetian Tintoretto (1518–1594) and the Spaniard El Greco (c. 1541–1614). Combining aspects of Michelangelo's style with the traditionally Venetian taste for rich color, Tintoretto produced an enormous number of monumentally large canvases devoted to religious subjects that still inspire awe with their broodingly shimmering light and gripping drama. More emotional still is the work of Tintoretto's disciple, El Greco. Born Domenikos Theotokopoulos on the Greek island of Crete, this extraordinary artist absorbed some of the stylized elongation characteristic of Greco-Byzantine icon painting before traveling to Italy to learn color and drama from Tintoretto. Finally he settled in Spain, where he was called "El Greco"—"the Greek." El Greco's paintings were too strange to be greatly appreciated in his own age, and even now they appear so unbalanced as to seem the work of one almost deranged. Yet such a view slights El Greco's deeply mystical Catholic fervor as well as his technical achievements. Best known today is his transfigured landscape, the *View of Toledo,* with its somber but awesome light breaking where no sun shines. But equally inspiring are his swirling religious scenes and several of his stunning portraits in which gaunt, dignified Spaniards radiate a rare blend of austerity and spiritual insight.

BAROQUE ART AND ARCHITECTURE

The dominant artistic school of southern Europe from about 1600 until the early 1700s was that of the Baroque, a school not only of painting but of sculpture and architecture. The Baroque style retained aspects of the dramatic and the irregular, but it avoided seeming bizarre or overheated and aimed above all to instill a

ished during this tumultuous century. The dominant goal in Italian and Spanish painting during the first half of this period, the years between about 1540 and 1600, was to fascinate the viewer with special effects. This goal, however, was achieved by means of two entirely different styles. (Confusingly, both styles are sometimes referred to as "Mannerism.") The first was based on the style of the Renaissance master Raphael, but moved from that painter's gracefulness to a highly self-conscious elegance bordering on the bizarre and surreal. Representatives of this approach were the Florentines Pontormo (1494–1557) and Bronzino (1503–1572). Their sharp-focused portraits are flat and cold, yet strangely riveting.

The other extreme was theatrical in a more conventional sense—highly dramatic and emotionally compelling. Painters who followed this approach were

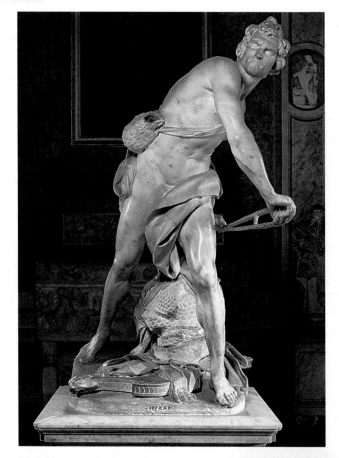

David, by Bernini (1598–1680). Whereas the earlier conceptions of David by the Renaissance sculptors Donatello and Michelangelo were reposeful (see p. 471), the Baroque Sculptor Bernini chose to portray his young hero at the peak of physical exertion.

The Maids of Honor, by Diego Velázquez. The artist himself is at work on a double portrait of the king and queen of Spain (who can be seen in the rear mirror), but reality is more obvious in the foreground in the persons of the delicately impish princess, her two maids, and a misshapen dwarf. The twentieth-century Spanish artist Picasso gained great inspiration from this work.

sense of the affirmative. Originating in Rome as an expression of the ideals of the Counter-Reformation papacy and the Jesuit order, Baroque architecture in particular aimed to gain adherence for a specifically Catholic world view. Similarly, Baroque painting often was done in the service of the Counter-Reformation church, which at its high tide around 1620 seemed everywhere to be on the offensive. When Baroque painters were not celebrating Counter-Reformation ideals, most of them worked in the service of monarchs who sought their own glorification.

The most imaginative and influential figure of the Roman Baroque was the architect and sculptor Gianlorenzo Bernini (1598–1680), a frequent employee of the papacy who created a magnificent celebration of papal grandeur in the sweeping colonnades leading up to St. Peter's Basilica. Breaking with the serene Renaissance classicism of Palladio, Bernini's architecture retained such classical elements as columns and domes, but combined them in ways meant to express both aggressive restlessness and great power. Bernini was also one of the first to experiment with church facades built "in depth"—building frontages not conceived as continuous surfaces but that jutted out at odd angles and

WHAT WAS THE RELATIONSHIP BETWEEN THE BAROQUE SCHOOL AND THE COUNTER-REFORMATION?

LITERATURE AND THE ARTS   547

seemed to invade the open space in front of them. If the purpose of these innovations was to draw the viewer emotionally into the work of art, the same may be said for Bernini's aims in sculpture. Harking back to the restless motion of Hellenistic statuary —particularly the Laocoön group—and building on tendencies already present in the later sculpture of Michelangelo, Bernini's statuary emphasizes drama and incites the viewer to respond to it rather than serenely to observe.

Since most Italian Baroque painters lacked Bernini's artistic genius, to view the very greatest masterpieces of southern European Baroque painting one must look to Spain and the work of Diego

The Harvesters, by Brueghel. Brueghel chose to depict both the hard work and the recreation of the peasantry.

Velázquez (1599–1660). Unlike Bernini, Velázquez, a court painter in Madrid just when Spain hung on the brink of ruin, was not an entirely typical exponent of the Baroque style. Certainly many of his canvases display a characteristically Baroque delight in motion, drama, and power, but Velázquez's best work is characterized by a more restrained thoughtfulness than is usually found in the Baroque. Thus his famous *Surrender of Breda* shows muscular horses and splendid Spanish grandees on the one hand, but un-Baroque sympathy for defeated, disarrayed troops on the other. Velázquez's single greatest painting, *The Maids of Honor,* done around 1656 after Spain's collapse, is one of the most thoughtful and probing artistic examinations of illusion and reality ever executed.

DUTCH PAINTING IN THE GOLDEN AGE

Southern Europe's main northern rival for artistic laurels was the Netherlands, where three extremely dissimilar painters all explored the theme of the greatness and wretchedness of man to the fullest. The earliest, Peter Brueghel (c. 1525–1569), worked in a vein related to earlier Netherlandish realism. But unlike his predecessors, who favored quiet urban scenes,

Brueghel exulted in portraying the busy, elemental life of the peasantry. Most famous in this respect are his rollicking *Peasant Wedding* and *Peasant Wedding Dance,* and his spacious *Harvesters,* in which guzzling and snoring field hands are taking a well-deserved break from their heavy labors under the noon sun. Such vistas give the impression of uninterrupted rhythms of life, but late in his career Brueghel became appalled by the intolerance and bloodshed he witnessed during the Calvinist riots and the Spanish repression in the Netherlands and expressed his criticism in an understated yet searing manner. In *The Blind Leading the Blind,* for example, we see what happens when ignorant fanatics start showing the way to each other. More powerful still is Brueghel's *Massacre of the Innocents,* which from a distance looks like a snug scene of a Flemish village buried in snow. In fact, however, heartless soldiers are methodically breaking into homes and slaughtering babies, the simple peasant folk are fully at their mercy, and the artist—alluding to a Gospel forgotten by warring Catholics and Protestants alike—seems to be saying "as it happened in the time of Christ, so it happens now."

Vastly different from Brueghel was the Netherlandish Baroque painter Peter Paul Rubens (1577–1640). Since the Baroque was an international movement closely linked to the spread of the Counter-

The Massacre of the Innocents, by Brueghel (c. 1525–1569). This painting shows how effectively art can be used as a means of social commentary. Many art historians believe that Brueghel was tacitly depicting the suffering of the Netherlands at the hands of the Spanish in his own day.

The Horrors of War, by Rubens (1577–1640). The war god Mars here casts aside his mistress Venus and threatens humanity with death and destruction. In his old age Rubens took a far more critical view of war than he did for most of his earlier career.

Reformation, it should offer no surprise that Baroque style was extremely well represented in just that part of the Netherlands which, after long warfare, had been retained by Spain. In fact, Rubens of Antwerp was a far more typical Baroque artist than Velázquez of Madrid, painting literally thousands of robust canvases that glorified resurgent Catholicism or exalted second-rate aristocrats by portraying them as epic heroes dressed in bearskins. Even when Rubens's intent was not overtly propagandistic he customarily reveled in the sumptuous extravagance of the Baroque manner, being perhaps most famous today for the pink and rounded flesh of his well-nourished nudes. But unlike a host of lesser Baroque artists, Rubens was not lacking in subtlety and was a man of many moods. His gentle portrait of his son Nicholas catches unaffected childhood in a moment of repose, and though throughout most of his career Rubens had celebrated martial valor, his late *Horrors of War* movingly portrays what he himself called "the grief of unfortunate Europe, which, for so many years now, has suffered plunder, outrage, and misery."

In some ways a blend of Brueghel and Rubens, the greatest of all Netherlandish painters, Rembrandt van Rijn (1606–1669), defies all attempts at facile characterization. Living across the border from the Spanish Netherlands in staunchly Calvinistic Holland, Rembrandt belonged to a society that was too austere to tolerate the unbuckled realism of a Brueghel or the fleshy Baroque pomposity of a Rubens. Yet Rembrandt managed to put both realistic and Baroque traits to new uses. In his early career he gained fame and fortune as a painter of biblical scenes that lacked the Baroque's fleshiness but retained its grandeur in their swirling forms and stunning experiments with light. Rembrandt was also active as a portrait painter who knew how to flatter his subjects by emphasizing their Calvinistic steadfastness, to the great advantage of his purse. But gradually his prosperity faded, apparently in part because he grew tired of flattering and definitely because he made some bad investments. As personal tragedies mounted in the painter's middle and declining years, his art became more pensive and sombre, but it gained

Aristotle Contemplating the Bust of Homer, by Rembrandt (1606–1669). The artist brilliantly captures the philosopher as he appears to be mesmerized by the aura of one of the greatest poets.

in dignity, subtle lyricism, and awesome mystery. Thus his later portraits, including several self-portraits, are imbued with introspective qualities and a suggestion that only half the story is being told. Equally moving are explicitly philosophical paintings such as *Aristotle Contemplating the Bust of Homer,* in which the philosopher seems spellbound by the radiance of the epic poet, and *The Polish Rider,* in which realistic and Baroque elements merge into a higher synthesis portraying a pensive young man setting out fearlessly into a perilous world. Like Shakespeare, Rembrandt knew that life's journey is full of perils, but his most mature paintings suggest that these can be mastered with a courageous awareness of one's human shortcomings.

CONCLUSION

Between 1540 and 1660, Europe was racked by a combination of religious war, political rebellions, and economic crises that undermined confidence in traditional

Self-Portraits. Self-portraits became common during the sixteenth and seventeenth centuries, reflecting the intense introspectiveness of the period. Left: Rembrandt painted more than sixty self-portraits; this one, dating from around 1660, captures the artist's creativity, theatricality (note the costume), and the honesty of his self-examination. Right: Judith Leyster (1609–1660) was a Dutch contemporary of Rembrandt who pursued a successful career as an artist during her early twenties, before she married. Respected in her own day, she was all but forgotten for centuries thereafter.

structures of social, religious, and political authority. The result was fear, skepticism, and a search for new, more certain foundations on which to rebuild the social, political, and religious order of Europe. For artists and intellectuals, the period proved to be one of the most creative epochs in the history of Europe. But for common people, the century was one of extraordinary suffering.

After a hundred years of destructive efforts to restore the religious unity of Europe through war, a de facto religious toleration between states was beginning to emerge by 1660 as the only way to preserve the European political order. Within states, toleration was still very limited when this terrible century ended. But in territories where religious rivalries ran too deep to be overcome, rulers were beginning to discover that loyalty to the state was a value that could override even the religious divisions among their subjects. The end result of this century of crises was thus to strengthen Europeans' confidence in the powers of the state to heal their wounds and right their wrongs, with religion relegated more and more to the private sphere of individual

conscience. In the following centuries, this new confidence in the state as an autonomous moral agent that acts in accordance with its own "reasons of state," and for its own purposes, would prove a powerful challenge to the traditions of limited consensual government that had emerged out of the Middle Ages.

SELECTED READINGS

Bonney, Richard. *The European Dynastic States, 1494–1660.* Oxford and New York, 1991. An excellent recent survey of continental Europe during the "long" sixteenth century.

Briggs, Robin. *Witches and Neighbors: The Social and Cultural Context of European Witchcraft.* New York, 1996. An influential recent account of continental witchcraft.

———. *Early Modern France, 1560–1715,* 2d ed. Oxford and New York, 1997. Updated and authoritative, with new bibliographies.

Cervantes, Miguel de. *Don Quixote.* Translated by Walter Starkie. New York, 1957.

Clarke, Stuart. *Thinking with Demons: The Idea of Witchcraft in Early*

Modern Europe. Oxford and New York, 1999. By placing demonology into the context of sixteenth- and seventeenth-century intellectual history, Clarke makes sense of it in new and exciting ways.

Cochrane, Eric, Charles M. Gray, and Mark A. Kishlansky. *Early Modern Europe: Crisis of Authority*. Chicago, 1987. An outstanding source collection from the University of Chicago Readings in Western Civilization series.

Dunn, Richard S. *The Age of Religious Wars, 1559–1715*, 2d ed. New York, 1979. Still the best textbook on this period.

Guy, John A. *Tudor England*. Oxford and New York, 1988. An excellent textbook account of a highly controversial subject.

Haigh, Christopher. *Elizabeth I*. 1988. A reliable scholarly biography of this much-studied queen, stressing her political acumen.

Held, Julius S., and Donald Posner. *Seventeenth- and Eighteenth-Century Art: Baroque Painting, Sculpture, Architecture*. New York, 1971. The most complete and best-organized introductory review of the subject in English.

Hibbard, Howard. *Bernini*. Baltimore, 1965. The basic study in English of this central figure of Baroque artistic activity.

Hirst, Derek. *England in Conflict, 1603–1660: Kingdom, Community, Commonwealth*. Oxford and New York, 1999. A complete revision of the author's *Authority and Conflict* (1986), this is an up-to-date and balanced account of a period that has been a historical battleground over the past twenty years.

Hobbes, Thomas. *Leviathan*. Edited by C. B. Macpherson. New York, 1968. Macpherson's introduction is dated, but the text is as Hobbes wrote it and contains the entirety of *Leviathan*, not just the first two parts.

Holt, Mack P. *The French Wars of Religion, 1562–1629*. Cambridge and New York, 1995. The most recent and best account.

Kors, Alan Charles, and Edward Peters. *Witchcraft in Europe, 400–1700: A Documentary History*, 2d ed. Philadelphia, 2000. A superb collection of documents, significantly expanded in the second edition, with up-to-date commentary.

Israel, Jonathan I. *The Dutch Republic and the Hispanic World, 1606–1661*. Oxford and New York, 1982. Particularly good on the economic implications of the Dutch revolt.

Kingdon, Robert. *Myths about the St. Bartholomew's Day Massacres, 1572–1576*. Cambridge, Mass., 1988. The most recent detailed account in English of this pivotal moment in the history of France.

Levack, Brian P. *The Witch-Hunt in Early Modern Europe*, 2d ed. London and New York, 1995. The best account of the persecution of suspected witches; coverage extends from Europe in 1450 to America in 1750.

Levin, Carole. *The Heart and Stomach of a King: Elizabeth I and the Politics of Sex and Power*. Philadelphia, 1994. A provocative argument for the importance of Elizabeth's gender if one wishes to understand her reign.

Limm, Peter, ed. *The Thirty Years' War*. London, 1984. An outstanding short survey, followed by a selection of primary source documents.

Lynch, John. *Spain, 1516–1598: From Nation-State to World Empire*. Oxford and Cambridge, Mass., 1991. The best book in English on Spain at the pinnacle of its sixteenth-century power.

MacCaffrey, Wallace. *Elizabeth I*. New York, 1993. An outstanding traditional biography by an excellent scholar.

Martin, Colin, and Geoffrey Parker. *The Spanish Armada*. London, 1988. Incorporates recent discoveries from undersea archaeology with more traditional historical sources.

Martin, John Rupert. *Baroque*. New York, 1977. A thought-provoking, thematic treatment, less a survey than an essay on the painting, sculpture, and architecture of the period.

Mattingly, Garrett. *The Armada*. Boston, 1959. A great narrative history that reads like a novel; for the latest work, however, see Martin and Parker (above).

Montaigne, Michel de. *Essays*. Translated by J. M. Cohen. Baltimore, 1958.

Parker, Geoffrey. *Philip II*. Boston, 1978. A fine biography by an expert in both the Spanish and the Dutch sources.

————, ed. *The Thirty Years' War*, rev. ed. London and New York, 1987. A wide-ranging collection of essays by scholarly experts.

————. *The Dutch Revolt*, 2d ed. Ithaca, N.Y., 1989. The standard survey in English on the revolt of the Netherlands.

Pascal, Blaise. *Pensées* (French-English edition). Edited by H. F. Stewart. London, 1950.

Quint, David. *Montaigne and the Quality of Mercy: Ethical and Political Themes in the "Essais."* Princeton, N.J., 1999. A fine treatment that presents Montaigne's thought as a response to the French wars of religion.

Roberts, Michael. *Gustavus Adolphus and the Rise of Sweden*. London, 1973. Still the authoritative English-language account.

Russell, Conrad. *The Causes of the English Civil War*. Oxford, 1990. A penetrating and provocative analysis by one of the leading "revisionist" historians of the period.

Sprenger, Jakob, and H. Kramer. *Malleus Maleficarum*, 2d ed. Translated by Montague Summers. London, 1948. The *Hammer of Witches* is the most famous of the handbooks written for early modern witch-hunters. Summers' translation is unreliable but has the great merit of existing.

Thomas, Keith. *Religion and the Decline of Magic*. London, 1971. An extremely influential account that sees the rise of witchcraft allegations in England as linked to the particularities of Protestant religious practice.

Tracy, James D. *Holland under Habsburg Rule, 1506–1566: The Formation of a Body Politic*. Berkeley and Los Angeles, 1990. A political history and analysis of the formative years of the Dutch state.

Van Gelderen, Martin. *Political Theory of the Dutch Revolt*. Cambridge, 1995. A fine book on a subject whose importance is too easily overlooked.

PART V
EARLY MODERN EUROPE

SEVENTEENTH- AND EIGHTEENTH-CENTURY European life was shaped by the combined effects of commerce, war, and a steadily growing population. A commercial revolution spurred the development of overseas colonies and trade, while opening up new markets for European industry. Agricultural productivity increased, making it possible for Europe to feed a population that had now reached unprecedented levels. Population growth in turn enabled European governments to wage more frequent wars, and to employ larger and larger armies.

Although monarchs continued to meet with opposition from the various estates within their realms, they increasingly asserted their power as absolute rulers. Warfare remained the chief instrument of European foreign policy; but slowly the notion of a diplomatic and military "balance of power" began to displace the pursuit of unrestrained aggrandizement as the primary goal of European state relations.

Profound changes were also occurring in European intellectual life during these centuries. Using new instruments and applying new mathematical techniques, astronomers proved beyond question that the earth was not the center of the universe. Biologists and physicians pioneered a more sophisticated understanding of the nature and processes by which life was created and sustained, and physicists such as Sir Isaac Newton established for the first time a true science of mechanics. During the eighteenth century, these discoveries gave rise to a new confidence in the capacity of human reason alone to understand nature and so to improve human life—a confidence those who held to it declared to be a sign of Enlightenment.

	POLITICS	SOCIETY AND CULTURE	ECONOMY	INTERNATIONAL RELATIONS
1500		Copernicus's *On the Revolutions of the Heavenly Spheres* (1543) Claudio Monteverdi, father of opera (1567–1643) Johannes Kepler (1571–1630) William Harvey (1578–1657)	Enclosure movement (1500–1700s) Demand for sugar escalates in Europe (late 1500s) Widespread crop failure in France (1597–1694)	Sir Francis Drake leads attack on Spanish fleet at Cadiz (1587)
1600		Literacy increases across Europe (1600–1800) Increased urbanization (1600–1750) Smoking spreads in Europe (early 1600s) Over 80,000 leave England for the New World (1607–1650) Galileo's *The Starry Messenger* (1610)	Mechanically powered saws and calico-printing from the Far East (1600s) Dutch East India Company founded (1602)	A total of 6 million Africans forcibly shipped across the middle passage (1600–1800) English colonists establish Jamestown (1607)
	Jean Baptiste Colbert, French finance minister (1619–1683)	Bacon's *New Instruments* (1620) Galileo charged with heresy (1632) John Locke (1632–1704) Descartes's *Discourse on Method* (1637)		*Mayflower* lands in the New World (1620)
	Reign of Louis XIV, the Sun King, (1643–1715) England promulgates Navigation Acts (1651, 1660) The Restoration and return of Charles II (1660)	Plague outbreaks (1649–1665) Edmond Halley (1656–1742) Founding of the Royal Society of London and the French Academy of Sciences (1660) Daniel Defoe, author of *Robinson Crusoe*, (1660–1731) The "great fire" in London (1666)	French government introduces head tax (c. 1645) Coffee consumption escalates in Europe (1650s) Bank of Sweden founded (1657)	
	Louis XIV revokes the Edict of Nantes (1685)	Johann Sebastian Bach (1685–1750) George Frideric Handel (1685–1759) Newton's *Principia Mathematica* (1687)		Dutch surrender New Amsterdam to England (1667) Austrian Habsburgs repulse Turks' assault on Vienna (1683) Peace of Augsburg (1686) Portugal regains independence from Spain (1688) William of Orange rules England and Holland (1688) War of the League of Augsburg (1688–1697) Battle of the Boyne, English solidify control of Ireland (1690)
	Glorious Revolution in England (1689) Reign of Peter the Great of Russia (1689–1725)	Locke's *Treatise of Civil Government* and *Essay Concerning Human Understanding* (1690)	Bank of England founded (1694)	
1700		Maize and the potato are introduced in Europe (1700s) Proliferation of salons and coffee-houses (1700s) First daily newspaper in England (1702) Rousseau's *Social Contract* (1712–1778)	Fly-shuttle for weaving loom invented (early 1700s) Physiocrats promote concept of *laissez-faire* (1700s) West India replaces the Spice Islands as largest supplier of European sugar (1700s)	War of Spanish Succession (1702–1713) England and Scotland unite to form Great Britain (1707)
	Reign of Charles VI, emperor of Holy Roman Empire (1711–1740) Treaty of Utrecht (1713) Reign of George I, first of Hanoverian dynasty in England (1714–1727) Louis XV (1715–1774) Robert Walpole serves as England's first prime minister (1720–1742)			

POLITICS	SOCIETY AND CULTURE	ECONOMY	INTERNATIONAL RELATIONS	
		German imperial law prohibits journeyman associations (1731) France establishes the Road and Bridge Corps of Engineering (1747)		**1731**
Reign of Frederick the Great, the "enlightened despot" (1740–1786)	Voltaire's *The Philosophical Letters* (1734) Montesquieu's *The Spirit of Laws* (1748) Steady increase in population begins (1750) *The Encyclopedia* published by Diderot and d'Alembert (1751–1772) Wolfgang Amadeus Mozart (1756–1791) Beccaria's *On Crimes and Punishment* (1764)			
Reign of George III of England (1760–1820) Reign of Catherine the Great of Russia (1762–1796) Maria Theresa and Joseph II of Austria rule jointly (1765–1780)		Antislavery movements emerge in Europe (1760s) James Cook explores Pacific (1768–1779) Abbe Raynal's *Philosophical History of Europeans in the Two Indies* (1770)	Seven Years' War/ French and Indian War (1756–1763) Treaty of Paris: France concedes Canada and India to England (1763) French East India Co. dissolves (1769) Russo-Turkish War (1769–1792) American Revolution (1774–1782)	
Reign of Louis XVI of France (1774–1792) The French Revolution breaks out (1789)	Kant's "What Is Enlightenment?" (1784) Wollstonecraft's *A Vindication of the Rights of Woman* (1792) Austen's *Pride and Prejudice* (1813–1817)	Smith's *Inquiry into the Nature and Causes of the Wealth of Nations* (1776)	Russia, Austria, and Prussia fully partition Poland (1795)	**1800**

CHAPTER SIXTEEN

THE ECONOMY AND SOCIETY OF EARLY MODERN EUROPE

BETWEEN 1600 AND 1800, the European economy underwent sweeping transformations. The freebooting overseas expansionism of the sixteenth century brought Europe into the center of a vast system of worldwide trade. In the seventeenth and eighteenth centuries, European governments took deliberate steps to maximize their profits from the new commercial empires they had acquired. Employing an economic theory known as mercantilism, governments attempted to monopolize international trade with their colonies while building up their own domestic industries through protective regulations.

Despite being widely practiced, however, mercantilism was only modestly successful. The true engine of economic development during these centuries was not mercantilism but capitalism, a new economic system that rested on the entrepreneurial ambitions of thousands of individuals willing to invest their own money (capital) in the hope of gain. New institutions developed to facilitate such investment, including banks and joint-stock companies, and these gradually took over the financing of international commercial ventures. As these new financial institutions became larger and more sophisticated, their leaders became influential figures in the halls of government. Trade and governance thus became more and more closely intertwined.

European society changed much more slowly. Europeans remained committed to ideas of social order and hierarchy that had originated in the Middle Ages. Landlords still dominated peasants, and nobles continued to see themselves as entitled, by rank and birth, to rule in consultation with kings. Although vast fortunes were sometimes made in overseas trade, famine, disease, and poverty remained ubiquitous features of seventeenth-century European society. Only in the late eighteenth century, after a series of changes had greatly increased the productivity of European agriculture, did Europe finally break out of the traditional limitations imposed on population growth by epidemic disease and an inadequate food supply. From the mid-eighteenth century onward, however, the European population increased rapidly. Capital cities in particular exploded in size, largely through immigration from the swelling population of the countryside. A new, urban middle class began to emerge with its

FOCUS QUESTIONS

- What factors affected early modern population growth?
- What were the advantages of the putting-out system?

- What factors facilitated the commercial revolution?
- What was the "triangular trade"?
- How did the lives of eastern and western European peasants differ?

own distinctive social, economic, and cultural outlook. For the majority of Europeans, however, the availability of work did not keep pace with the number of laborers looking for employment, and this imbalance was being made worse by the introduction of new, labor-saving technological inventions. As the eighteenth century drew to a close, the tensions and disjunctions between the economy and the social order were approaching a crisis.

LIFE AND DEATH: PATTERNS OF POPULATION

What factors affected early modern population growth?

No facts better illustrate the degree to which the two hundred years of European history between 1600 and 1800 were subject to chance and change than those having to do with life and death—patterns of population—as they imprinted themselves across the early modern period.

FAMINE, DISEASE, AND THE BIRTH RATE

The pattern of life for most Europeans centered on the struggle to stay alive. In most instances their enemy was not an invading army, but famine; it is not surprising that one's well-being was measured simply by one's girth. At least once a decade, climatic conditions—usually a long period of summer rainfall—would produce a devastatingly bad harvest, which in turn would result in widespread malnutrition, often leading to serious illness and death. A family might survive for a time by eating less, but eventually, with its meager stocks exhausted and the cost of grain high, the human costs would mount. In the absence of grain, peasants sometimes ate grass, nuts, and tree bark, but they starved nonetheless.

The patterns of marriages, births, and deaths revealed in local parish registers indicate that the populations of individual communities rose and fell dramatically in rhythm with the fortunes of the harvest. Widespread crop failures occurred at fairly regular intervals—the worst in France, for example, about every thirty years (1597, 1630, 1662, 1694). They helped to cause the series of population crises that are the outstanding feature

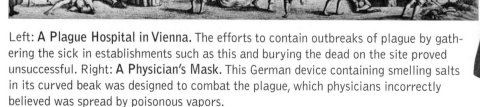

Left: **A Plague Hospital in Vienna.** The efforts to contain outbreaks of plague by gathering the sick in establishments such as this and burying the dead on the site proved unsuccessful. Right: **A Physician's Mask.** This German device containing smelling salts in its curved beak was designed to combat the plague, which physicians incorrectly believed was spread by poisonous vapors.

A DESCRIPTION OF THE IMPOVERISHED PEASANTRY OF RURAL FRANCE

The author of this passage, Marshall Vauban, lived in the region around Vézélay that he is here describing. This account, dated January 1696, must therefore be regarded as that of an eyewitness.

All the so-called *bas peuple* ["little people"] live on nothing but bread of mixed barley and oats, from which they do not even remove the bran, which means that bread can sometimes be lifted by the straw sticking out of it. They also eat poor fruits, mainly wild, and a few vegetables from their gardens, boiled up with a little rape- or nut-oil sometimes, but more often not, or with a pinch of salt. Only the most prosperous eat bread made of rye mixed with barley and wheat. . . .

The general run of people seldom drink [wine], eat meat not three times a year, and use little salt. . . . So it is no cause for surprise if people who are so ill-nourished have so little energy. Add to this what they suffer from exposure: winter and summer, three fourths of them are dressed in nothing but halfrotting tattered linen, and are shod throughout the year with *sabots* [wooden clogs], and no other covering for the foot. If one of them does have shoes he only wears them on saints' days and Sundays: the extreme poverty to which they are reduced, owning as they do not one inch of land, rebounds against the more prosperous town and country bourgeois, and against the nobility and the clergy. . . .

The poor people are ground down in another manner by the loans of grain and money they take from the wealthy in emergencies, by means of which a high rate of usury is enforced, under the guise of presents which must be made after the debts fall due, so as to avoid imprisonment. After the term has been extended by only three or four months, either another present must be produced when the time is up, or they face the *sergent* [bailiff] who is sure to strip the house bare. Many others of these poor people's afflictions remain at my quill's tip so as not to offend anybody.

Since hardship can hardly go much further, its normal effects are a matter of course: firstly, it makes people weak and unhealthy, especially the children, many of whom die for want of good food; secondly, the men become idle and apathetic, being persuaded that only the least and worst part of the fruit of their labors will turn to their own profit; thirdly, there are liars, robbers, men of bad faith, always willing to perjure themselves provided that it pays, and to get drunk as soon as they lay hands on the wherewithal. . . .

Pierre Goubert. *The Ancien Regime: French Society, 1600-1750,* translated by Steve Cox (London: Weidenfeld and Nicolson, 1973), pp. 118–119.

---

of early modern demographic history. Poor harvests and the high grain prices that resulted meant not only undernourishment and possible starvation, but increasing unemployment: with fewer crops to be harvested, more money was spent on food and, consequently, less on manufactured goods. The despair such conditions bred would in turn contribute to a postponement of marriage and of births, and thus to a population decline.

An undernourished population is also particularly susceptible to disease. Bubonic plague ravaged seventeenth-century Europe. Severe outbreaks occurred in Seville in 1649, in Amsterdam in 1664, and in London

"Summer Amusement: Bugg Hunting." In this joking treatment of one of the facts of everyday life, the bedbugs meet sudden death in a full chamber pot.

the following year. By 1700 it had all but vanished; it last appeared in western Europe in a small area of southern France in 1720, though Moscow suffered an outbreak as late as 1771. Epidemics of dysentery, smallpox, and typhus also occurred with savage regularity. As late as 1779, more than one hundred thousand people died of dysentery in the French province of Brittany. Water supplies were contaminated by heedless disposal of human waste and by all manner of garbage and filth. Bathing, feared at one time as a method of spreading disease, was by no means a weekly habit even for the upper classes. Samuel Pepys, a royal official in seventeenth-century London, is typical of the standards of hygiene customary among prosperous urban dwellers. In his diary, Pepys reports that his housemaid regularly picked the lice from his scalp; that he took his first bath only after his wife introduced him to the pleasures of cleanliness; and that he thought nothing of using the fireplace in his bedroom as a toilet when the maid failed to provide him with a chamberpot. Standards of cleanliness among the lower classes were even worse.

The precariousness of life helped encourage most men and women in early-modern Europe to postpone marriage until their mid- to late twenties, by which time they hoped not only to have survived but also to have accumulated sufficient resources to establish a household. Young couples lived on their own, and not, as in societies elsewhere, as part of "extended" families of three generations. Since a son could not inherit until his father died, he was compelled to establish himself independently, and to postpone starting his own family until he had done so. Though historians have failed to find a clear explanation for this pattern of later marriages, it may have resulted from a growing desire on the part of younger men and women for a higher standard of living. Late marriage helped to control the birth rate. Once married, however, a couple generally produced their first child within a year. Although subsequent children appeared with annual or biennial regularity, long periods of breastfeeding, which tends to reduce the mother's fertility, and near poverty went some way toward limiting childbirth.

POPULATION GROWTH

Until the middle of the eighteenth century, populations continued to wax and wane according to the outbreak of warfare, famine, and disease. From about 1750 on, however, there was a steady and significant population increase, with almost all countries experiencing major growth. In Russia, where territorial expansion added further to the increases, the population may have tripled in the second half of the eighteenth century. Gains elsewhere, though not usually so spectacular, were nevertheless significant. The population of Prussia doubled; Hungary's more than tripled; and England's population, which was about 5.5 million in 1700, reached 9 million in 1800. France, already in 1700 the most populous country in Europe (about 20 million), added another 6 million before 1790. Spaniards multiplied from 7.6 million in 1717 to 10.5 million in 1797. Although reasons for the population increase remain something of a mystery, historians believe that it was the cumulative result of a decrease in infant mortality, earlier age at marriage, and a very gradual decline in the death rate, all due in large measure to a gradual increase in the food supply. Partly this increase in the food supply was the result of new agricultural methods and new crops, which we will describe in the following section. Partly it was the result of a change in the weather: it appears that whereas the climate of seventeenth-century Europe was abnormally bad, that of the succeeding hundred years was on the whole favorable. But partly too, Europe's population was better fed because transportation improvements made it possible to distribute existing food supplies more efficiently.

Population increase brought with it new problems and new attitudes. In France, it meant pressure on the land, as more peasants attempted to wring survival from an overpopulated countryside. The consequence was migration from the country to the city. The decline in the death rate among infants—along with an apparent increase in illegitimacy at the end of the eighteenth century—created a growing population of unwanted babies among the poor. Some desperate women resorted to infanticide, though since children murdered at birth died without benefit of baptism, the crime was regarded with particular horror. More often, babies were abandoned at the doors of foundling hospitals. In Paris during the 1780s from seven to eight thousand children were abandoned yearly out of a total of thirty thousand new births. As a British benefactor of several such institutions, Jonas Hanway, remarked in 1766, "it is much less difficult to the human heart and the dictates of self-preservation to drop a child than to kill it." But the distinction between child abandonment and infanticide was less absolute in practice than Hanway's statement might lead us to presume. Mortality rates in the foundling hospitals were horrendous, running as high as 80 or even 90 percent.

URBANISM

Although the vast majority of the population lived in small rural communities, towns and cities were coming to play an increasingly important role in the life of early modern Europe. We must speak of the "rise" of towns and cities with caution, however, since the pace of urbanization varied greatly across the Continent. Russia remained almost entirely rural: only 2.5 percent of its population lived in towns in 1630, and that percentage had risen by only 0.5 percent by 1774. In Holland, on the other hand, 59 percent of the population was urban in 1627 and 65 percent in 1795.

The total number of urban dwellers did not vary markedly after the end of the sixteenth century, when approximately two hundred cities in Europe had a population of over ten thousand. What did change between 1600 and 1800 was, first, the way in which those cities were distributed across the map, concentrated increasingly in the north and west; and second, the growing proportion of very large cities to the whole. Patterns of trade and commerce had much to do with these shifts. Cities such as Hamburg in Germany, Liverpool in England, Toulon in France, and Cadíz in Spain grew by about 250 percent between 1600 and 1750. Amsterdam, the hub of early modern international commerce, increased from 30,000 in 1530 to 115,000 in 1630 and 200,000 by 1800. Naples, the busy Mediterranean port, went from a population of 300,000 in 1600 to nearly half a million by the late eighteenth century. Where goods were traded, processed, and manufactured, fleets built and provisioned, people flocked to work. An eighteenth-century commentator noted that the laborers in Paris were "almost all foreigners"—that is, men and women born outside the city: carpenters from Savoy, water carriers from Auvergne, porters from Lyons, stonecutters from Normandy, wigmakers from Gascony, shoemakers from Lorraine.

The most spectacular urban population growth occurred, however, in the administrative capitals of the increasingly centralized nations of Europe. By the middle of the eighteenth century, Madrid, Berlin, and St. Petersburg all had populations of over 100,000. London grew from 674,000 in 1700 to 860,000 a century later. Paris, a city of approximately 180,000 in 1600, increased to over half a million by 1800. Berlin grew from a population of 6,500 in 1661, to 60,000 in 1721, to 140,000 in 1783. Its increase was due in part to the fact that successive Prussian rulers undertook to improve its position as a trade center by the construction of canals that linked it with Breslau and Hamburg. Its population rose as well, however, because of the marked increase in Prussian army and bureaucratic personnel based in the capital city. Of the 140,000 citizens of Berlin in 1783, approximately 65,000 were state employees or members of their families.

THE DYNAMICS OF AGRICULTURE AND INDUSTRY

What were the advantages of the putting-out system?

The dramatic shifts in population we have been tracing were in some cases the cause, in others the effect, of equally important changes occurring in agriculture and industry. Throughout most of the two-hundred-year period under review, agricultural production was generally carried on according to traditional techniques that kept the volume of production low. By the end of the eighteenth century, however, agricultural productivity in some areas was increasing rapidly as tradition gave way to innovation. This in turn made it possible to feed a population which was larger, by 1800, than any that had ever lived in Europe before.

ENCLOSING THE COMMON FIELDS

One of the obstacles to more efficient agricultural practices was the medieval tradition of open, or "common-field" farming. Under this system, the holdings of individual peasants and their lords were scattered throughout the village's fields, usually (at least in the north) in long, narrow strips. The fields themselves were farmed communally, with livestock grazing together on common pastureland. This system "spread the risk" of localized crop failures, and guaranteed that the most productive lands would not be monopolized by a few peasant families. But it also acted as a serious check on agricultural experimentation and on the introduction of new crops, since it required the agreement of the entire village community before any such innovations could be introduced.

Once landlords, particularly in England and Holland, began to compete for markets as capitalist agricultural entrepreneurs, however, they looked for ways to overcome these inefficiencies, so as to improve the yield on their lands. The most drastic of these methods was the enclosure of open fields to allow for more systematic and therefore more productive farming. "Enclosure" was the term for land reorganization within a traditional village community. The earliest enclosures in England took place in the fifteenth and sixteenth centuries. Because of the great profits from wool, some landlords converted common pastures that hitherto had supported peasant livestock into their own preserves for sheep raising, thus threatening the livelihood of entire peasant communities. The really dramatic enclosure movement in England took place during the eighteenth century, however, when many landlords took steps to abolish the common-field system altogether on their estates, shifting instead toward a system of "scientific farming." Key to this new system was a reduction in the amount of land (traditionally a

third, or in some cases even a half) that lay fallow in any given year. By introducing new farming methods and new crops, "scientific farmers" discovered that they could keep a much higher percentage of their arable land under continuous cultivation. The most important new crops with which landowners experimented were clover, alfalfa, and turnips, which helped to restore the fertility of soil whose nitrogen content had been depleted by grain growing.

Clover, alfalfa, and turnips not only helped landlords do away with fallow lands; they also provided excellent winter food for animals, thereby aiding the production of more and better livestock. More livestock also meant more manure. Accordingly, intensive manuring became another way in which scientific farmers could eliminate the need for fallow land. Other improvements in farming methods introduced in the period were more intensive hoeing and weeding (made possible by the surplus of cheap labor in the countryside), and the use of the seed drill for planting grain. The seed drill in particular eliminated the old wasteful method of broadcast sowing grain by hand, much of it remaining on top of the soil to be eaten by birds.

The enclosure of open fields allowed for more systematic and therefore more productive farming.

All these improvements were most easily accomplished on enclosed fields under the direct management of a single, "improving" landlord. The impact of such improvements on agricultural productivity could be enormous. For villagers, however, the social and economic costs of enclosure were high. Common land afforded the poor not only a place to tether a cow, to fish, or to gather firewood, but to breathe at least a bit of the air of social freedom. Enclosure cost villagers their modest liberties, as well as the traditional right to help determine how the community's subsistence economy was to be managed. Cottagers (very small landholders) and squatters, who had over generations established a customary right to the use of common lands, were reduced to the rank of landless laborers.

Enclosure was more easily accomplished in those countries—England most notably—where there was a system of absolute property rights and wage labor. Where the tradition of "common" rights to grazing and foraging was strong, as in France, landlords found it far more difficult to impose a new economic order. In France, also, a large peasantry owned small plots of land outright, adding up to approximately one-third of all agricultural land. These peasants had neither an interest in nor the financial capacity for change. In France, monarchs also tended to oppose enclosure, because the monarchy needed an economically stable peasantry to support its expanding tax programs. It therefore worked to secure peasants in the customary tenure of their farms. Thus defended, French peasants were better able to resist effectively attempts at enclosure launched by large landholders. English property owners were more fortunate, taking advantage of the absence of royal opposition during the Cromwellian period to enclose on a broad scale.

On the Continent, except for Holland, there was nothing comparable to the English advance in scientific farming. Nor, with the notable exception of Spain, was there a pronounced enclosure movement as in England and the Low Countries. Yet despite that fact, European food production became increasingly capitalistic in the seventeenth and eighteenth centuries. Landlords leased farms to tenants and reaped profits as rent. Often they allowed tenants to pay rent in the form of half their crops. This system of sharecropping was most prevalent in France, Italy, and Spain. Farther east, in Prussia, Poland, Hungary, and Russia, landowners continued to rely on unpaid serfs to till the land. But wherever the scale of production and marketing was altered to increase profits, it brought change in its wake.

NEW WORLD CROPS: MAIZE AND POTATOES

The eighteenth century saw the introduction of two crops from the New World, maize (Indian corn) and the potato, which eventually resulted in the provision of a more adequate diet for the poor. Since maize can be grown only in areas with substantial periods of sunny and dry weather, its cultivation spread through Italy and the southeastern part of the Continent. Whereas an average ear of grain would yield only about four seeds for every one planted, an ear of maize would yield about seventy or eighty. That made it a "miracle" crop, filling granaries that had been almost empty before. The potato was an equally miraculous innovation for the European north. Its advantages were numerous: potatoes could be grown on the poorest, sandiest, or wettest of lands where nothing else could be raised; they could be fitted into the smallest of patches. Raising potatoes even in small patches was profitable because the yield of potatoes was extraordinarily abundant. Finally, the potato provided an inexpensive means of improving the human diet. It is rich in calories and contains many vitamins and minerals. Northern European peasants initially resisted growing and eating potatoes. Clergymen taught them to fear the plant because it is not mentioned in the Bible. Some claimed that it transmitted leprosy. Still others insisted that it was a cause of flatulence, a property acknowledged by a French authority on diet in 1765, although the writer added, "What is a little wind to the vigorous organs of the peasants and workers?" Yet in the course of the eighteenth century the poor grew accustomed to the potato, although sometimes after considerable pressure. Frederick the Great compelled Prussian peasants to cultivate potatoes until the crop achieved acceptance and became a staple throughout much of northern Germany. By about 1800 the average north German peasant family ate potatoes as a main course at least once a day.

RURAL MANUFACTURING

Agriculture was not the only commercial enterprise in early modern rural Europe. Increasingly, manufactured goods—particularly textiles—were being produced in the countryside, as entrepreneurs battled to circumvent artisanal and guild restrictions that limited production in urban manufacturing centers. Unfettered rural industry was a response to the constantly growing demand of new markets created by the increase in regional, national, and international commerce. Entrepreneurs made use of the so-called putting-out system to address this demand and to reap large profits. Unhampered by guild regulations, which in medieval times had restricted the production and distribution of textiles to maintain price levels, merchants would buy up a stock of raw material, most often wool or flax, which they would then "put out," or supply, to rural workers for carding (combing the fibers) and spinning. Once spun, the merchant collected the yarn or thread and passed it to rural weavers, who wove it into cloth. Collected once more, the material was processed by other workers at bleaching or dyeing shops and collected a final time by the entrepreneur, who then sold it either to a wholesaler or directly to retail customers.

> Entrepreneurs made use of the so-called putting-out system to address the growing demand of new markets and to reap large profits.

"Rustic Courtship." This detail from an etching (1785) by the English satirist Thomas Rowlandson suggests the advantages of doorstep domestic industry: natural lighting, improved ventilation, and a chance to converse with visitors. Work under these self-paced conditions, though usually long and hard, was carried on to a personal rhythm.

Artisan and Family, by Gerard ter Borch. This seventeenth-century wheelwright, though a skilled artisan, is nevertheless depicted as living in a house whose condition suggests near-poverty. Sickness, a bad harvest, unemployment— any of these might easily drive him and his family over the edge.

Although the putting-out phenomenon—or, as it is often referred to, the process of protoindustrialization—occurred throughout Europe, it was usually concentrated regionally. Most industrial areas specialized in the production of particular commodities, depending on the availability of raw materials. Flanders was a producer of linens; Verviers (in present-day Belgium) of woolens; Silesia of linens. As markets—regional, national, and international—developed, these rural manufacturing areas grew accordingly. Industries employed home workers by the thousands. A major mid-eighteenth-century textile firm in Abbeville, France, provided work to eighteen hundred in central workshops but to ten thousand in their own homes. One of the largest woolen manufacturers in Linz, Austria, in 1786 was employing thirty-five thousand, of whom more than twenty-nine thousand were domestic spinners.

Rural workers accepted this system of manufacture as a means of staving off poverty or possible starvation in years of particularly bad harvests. Domestic textile production involved the entire family. Even the youngest children could participate in the process of cleaning the raw wool. Older children carded. Wives and husbands spun or wove. Spinning, until the invention of the jenny at the end of the eighteenth century (see p. 727), was a far more time-consuming process than weaving, which had been speeded considerably by the Englishman John Kay's early-eighteenth-century invention of the fly shuttle, a mechanical device that automatically returned the shuttle to its starting place after it had been "thrown" across the loom.

In addition to providing extra income, the putting-out system brought other advantages to rural home workers. They could regulate the pace of their labor to some degree, and could abandon it altogether when farm work was available during the planting and harvest seasons. Their ability to work at home was a mixed blessing, however, for conditions in cottages that were wretchedly built and poorly ventilated were often exceedingly cramped and unpleasant, especially when workers were compelled to accommodate a bulky loom within their already crowded living quarters. But domestic labor, however unpleasant, was preferable to working away from home in a shop, where conditions might be even more oppressive under the watchful eye of an unsympathetic master. There were also advantages for the merchant-entrepreneur, who benefited not only from the absence of guild restrictions, but from the fact that none of his capital was tied up in expensive equipment. (Spinners usually owned their spinning wheels; weavers either owned or rented their looms.) Governments appreciated the advantages of the system too, viewing it as one way to alleviate the ever-present problem of rural poverty. The French abolished the traditional privileges of urban manufacturers in 1762, acknowledging by law what economic demand had long since established: the widespread practice of unrestricted rural domestic production. By that time, proto-industrialization prevailed not only in northern France, but in the east and northeast of England, in Flanders, and in much of northern Germany—all areas where a mixed agricultural and manufacturing economy made economic sense to those engaged in it as entrepreneurs and producers.

Later generations, looking back nostalgically on the putting-out system, often compared it favorably to the factory system that displaced it. Life within the system's "family economy" was hard, however. Although workers could set their own pace to some extent, they remained subject to the demands of small, often inexperienced entrepreneurs who, misjudging their markets, might overload spinners and weavers with work at one moment, then abandon them for lack of orders the next. Though it often kept families from starvation, the system did little to mitigate the monotony and harshness of their lives. Its pressures are crudely if eloquently expressed in an English ballad in which the weaver husband responds to his wife's complaint that she has no time to sit at the "bobbin wheel," what with the washing and baking and milking she must do. No matter, the husband replies. She must "stir about and get things done. / For all things must aside be laid, / when we want help about our trade."

Textiles were not the only manufactured goods produced in the countryside. In France, for example, metalworking was as much a rural as an urban occupation, with migrant laborers providing a work force for small, self-contained shops. In various parts of Germany, the same sort of unregulated domestic manufacturing base prevailed: in the Black Forest for clock making, in Thuringia for toys. English production of iron grew fivefold from the mid-sixteenth to the late seventeenth century. The phenomenon of protoindustrialization

increased demand for raw materials. Pressure on timber reserves for fuel led to widespread deforestation, with a resulting exploitation of coal reserves, particularly in the Rhineland, England, and the south Netherlands. In 1550 the English mined two hundred thousand tons of coal. By 1800 that figure had risen to 3 million.

TRANSPORTATION

Rural industry flourished despite the fact that for most of the early modern period transportation systems remained rudimentary. In all but a very few cases, roads were little more than ill-defined tracks, full of holes as much as four feet deep, and all but impassable in the rain, when carts and carriages might stay mired in deep ruts for days. One of the few paved roads ran from Paris to Orléans, the main river port of France, but that was a notable exception. In general, no one could travel more than twelve miles an hour—"post haste" at a gallop on horseback—and speed such as that could be achieved only at the expense of fresh horses at each stage of the ride. In the late seventeenth century, a journey of sixty miles over good roads could be accomplished in twentyfour hours, provided that the weather was fair. To travel by coach from Paris to Lyons, a distance of approximately two hundred fifty miles, took ten days. Merchants ran great risks when they shipped perishable goods. Breakables were not expected to survive for more than fifteen miles. Transportation of goods by boat along coastal routes was far more reliable than shipment overland, though in both cases the obstacle of excessive tolls was frequently inhibiting. In 1675, English merchants calculated that it was cheaper to ship coal three hundred miles by water than to send it fifteen miles overland, so impassable were the roads to heavy transport. Madrid, without a river, relied upon mules and carts for its supplies. By the mid-eighteenth century, the city required the services of over half a million mules and one hundred fifty thousand carts, all forced to labor their way into town over rugged terrain. In 1698, a bronze statue of Louis XIV was sent on its way from the river port of Auxerre, southeast of Paris, to the town of Dijon. The cart in which it was dispatched was soon stuck in the mud, however, and the statue remained marooned in a wayside shed for twenty-one years, until the road was improved to the point that it could continue its belated journey.

Gradually during the eighteenth century transportation improved. The French established a Road and Bridge Corps of civil engineers, with its own training

Outside an Inn, by Thomas Rowlandson. Coaching inns brought the outside world into the lives of isolated villagers. Note the absence of any clearly defined roadway.

school, in 1747. Work began in the 1670s on a series of canals that eventually linked the English Channel to the Mediterranean. In England, private investors constructed a network of waterways and turnpikes tying provincial towns to each other and to London. With improved roads came stagecoaches, feared at first for their speed and recklessness much as automobiles were feared in the early twentieth century. People objected to being crowded into narrow carriages designed to reduce the load pulled by the team of horses. "If by chance a traveller with a big stomach or wide shoulders appears," an unhappy passenger lamented, "one has to groan or desert." But improvements such as stagecoaches and canals, much as they might increase the profits or change the pattern of life for the wealthy, meant little to the average European. Barges plied the waterways from the north to the south of France, but most men and women traveled no farther than the nearest market town, on footpaths or on rutted cart tracks eight feet wide, which had served their ancestors in much the same way.

URBAN MANUFACTURING

That industry flourished to the extent it did, despite the hazards and inefficiencies of transport, is a measure of the strength of Europe's ever-increasing commercial impulse. Rural protoindustrialization did not prevent the growth of important urban manufacturing centers. In northern France, many of the million or so men and women employed in the textile trade lived and worked in

cities such as Amiens, Lille, and Rheims. The eighteenth-century rulers of Prussia made it their policy to develop Berlin as a manufacturing center, taking advantage of an influx of French Protestants to establish the silk-weaving industry there. Even in cities, however, work was likely to be carried out in small shops, where anywhere from five to twenty journeymen labored under the supervision of a master to manufacture the particular products of their craft. Despite the fact that manufacturing was centered in homes and workshops, by 1700 these industries were increasing significantly in scale as many workshops grouped together to form a single manufacturing district. Textile industries led this trend, but it was true as well of brewing, distilling, soap and candle making, tanning, and the manufacturing of various chemical substances for the bleaching and dyeing of cloth. These and other industries might often employ several thousand men and women congregated together into towns—or larger communities of several towns—all dedicated to the same occupation and production.

Techniques in some crafts remained much as they had been for centuries. In others, however, inventions changed the pattern of work as well as the nature of the product. Knitting frames, simple devices to speed the manufacture of textile goods, made their appearance in England and Holland. Wire-drawing machines and slitting mills, the latter enabling nail makers to convert iron bars into rods, spread from Germany into England. Mechanically powered saws were introduced into shipyards and elsewhere across Europe in the seventeenth century. The technique of calico printing, the application of colored designs directly to textiles, was imported from the Far East. New and more efficient printing presses appeared, first in Holland and then elsewhere. The Dutch invented a machine called a "camel," by which the hulls of ships could be raised in the water so that they could be more easily repaired.

Innovations of this kind were not readily accepted by workers. Labor-saving machines such as mechanical saws threw men out of work. Artisans, especially those organized into guilds, were by nature conservative, anxious to protect not only their restrictive "rights" but also the secrets of their trade. Often, too, the state would intervene to block the widespread use of machines if they threatened to increase unemployment. The Dutch and some German states, for example, prohibited the use of what was described as a "devilish invention," a ribbon loom capable of weaving sixteen or more ribbons at the same time. Sometimes the spread of new techniques was curtailed by states in order to protect the livelihood of powerful commercial interest groups. On behalf of both domestic textile manufacturers and importers of Indian goods, calico printing was for a time outlawed in both France and England. The cities of Paris and Lyons and several German states banned the use of indigo dyes because they were manufactured abroad.

THE HUMAN IMPLICATIONS OF CHANGE

Changes that occurred in trade, commerce, agriculture, and industry, though large-scale phenomena, nevertheless touched individual men and women directly. Enclosure stripped away customary rights. A British cottager by 1780 might well have lost his family's age-old right to tether a cow on the common, which was now an enclosed and "scientifically" manured cornfield. Markets developed to receive and transmit goods from around the world altered the lives of those whose work now responded to their rhythms. A linen weaver in rural Holland in 1700, whose peasant father had eked out a meager living from his subsistence farm, now supplemented his income by working for an Amsterdam entrepreneur, and paid progressively less for his food as a result of the cheap grain imported to the Low Countries across the Baltic Sea from eastern Europe. A carpenter in an early eighteenth-century Toulon shipyard lost his job when his employer purchased a mechanical saw that did the work of five men. A sailor on one of the ships built in that Toulon shipyard died at sea off the French colony of Martinique, an island of which he had never heard, at a distance so far from home as to be inconceivable to those who mourned his death when they learned of it months later. Meanwhile, in vast areas of southern and eastern Europe, men and women led lives that followed the same patterns they had for centuries, all but untouched by the changes taking place elsewhere. They clung to the life they knew, a life that, if harsh, was at least predictable.

THE COMMERCIAL REVOLUTION

What factors facilitated the commercial revolution?

Hand in hand with changes in agriculture and industry came an alteration in the manner in which commerce was organized and trade conducted. So extensive were changes in these areas over the course of two hundred years that it is accurate to speak of them as comprising a commercial revolution.

CAPITALISM AND MERCANTILISM

The early modern world of commerce and industry grew increasingly to be governed by the assumptions of capitalism and mercantilism. Reduced to its simplest terms, capitalism is a system of production, distribution, and exchange, in which accumulated wealth is invested by private owners for the sake of gain. Its essential features are private enterprise, competition for markets, and business for profit. Generally it involves the wage system as a method of payment of workers—that is, a mode of payment based not on the amount of wealth workers create, but rather on their willingness to compete with each other for jobs. The capitalist system encouraged commercial expansion on a national and international scale. Activity on this wider scale demanded the resources and expertise of wealthy and experienced entrepreneurs. Capitalists studied patterns of international trade. They knew where markets were and how to manipulate them to their advantage.

The capitalist system was designed to reward the individual. In contrast, mercantilist doctrine emphasized direct governmental intervention in economic policy to enhance the general prosperity of the state and to increase political authority. Mercantilism was by no means a new idea. It was a variation on the medieval notion that the economic well-being of communities depended on the willingness of their populace to work at whatever task God or their rulers assigned them to benefit the community as a whole. The mercantilism of the seventeenth and eighteenth centuries translated this earlier concept of community as a privileged, but regimented, economic unit from the level of towns to the level of the entire state. The theory and practice of mercantilism reflected the expansion of state power. Responding to the needs of war, rulers enforced mercantilist policies, often by autocratic methods, certain that the needs of the state must take precedence over those of individuals.

Mercantilist theory held that a state's power depended on its actual, calculable wealth. The degree to which a state could remain self-sufficient, importing as little as necessary while exporting as much as possible, was the clearest gauge not only of its economic prosperity but of its power. This doctrine had profound effects on state policy. First, it led to the establishment and development of overseas colonies. Colonies, mercantilists reasoned, would, as part of the national community, provide it with raw materials, including precious metals in some instances, which would otherwise have to be obtained outside the community. Second, the doctrine of mercantilism inspired state governments to encourage industrial production and trade, both sources of revenue that would increase the state's income. Third, it led to the presumption that trade and industry were a "zero sum" game. Since the quantity of world trade and production was presumed to be fixed, the goal of a mercantilist state was to reduce the volume of trade and industrial production among its rivals, while increasing its own.

Although most western European statesmen were prepared to endorse mercantilist goals in principle, the degree to which their policies reflected those goals varied according to national circumstance. Spain, despite its insistence on closed colonial markets and its determination to amass a fortune in bullion, never succeeded in attaining the economic self-sufficiency that mercantilist theory demanded. But mercantilism, which appealed at least in theory to the rulers in Madrid, had little attraction for the merchants of Amsterdam. The Dutch recognized that the United Provinces were too small to permit them to achieve economic self-sufficiency. Throughout the seventeenth and eighteenth centuries the Dutch remained dedicated in principle and practice to free trade, often investing, contrary to mercantilist doctrine, in the commercial enterprises of other countries and promoting national prosperity by encouraging the rest of Europe to rely upon Amsterdam as a hub of international finance and trade.

Capitalism and mercantilism produced important consequences for individuals as well as for nations and regions. Laboring men and women frequently found themselves the victims of the policies and programs of those who managed and controlled dynamic, expan-

sionist national economies. For example, capitalists could afford to invest in large quantities of manufactured goods, and if necessary, hold them unsold until they could command a high price, favorable to them but damaging to the budget of humbler consumers. Mercantilism persuaded policy makers to discourage domestic consumption, since goods purchased on the home market reduced the goods available for export. Government policy was thus to keep wages low, so that laborers would not have more money to spend than it took to provide them with basic food and shelter.

THE GROWTH OF INTERNATIONAL TRADE AND BUSINESS

Together, governments and entrepreneurs designed new institutions that facilitated the expansion of global commerce during the seventeenth and eighteenth centuries to effect the commercial revolution of early modern Europe. While local and regional markets continued to flourish, international centers such as Antwerp, Amsterdam, and London became hubs for a flourishing and complex system of international trade. An increasing number of European men and women grew dependent on the commerce that brought both necessities and luxuries into their lives. The eighteenth-century essayist Joseph Addison sang the praises of beneficent merchant princes: "There are not more useful members in the Commonwealth," he wrote. "They distribute the gifts of nature, find work for the poor, and wealth to the rich, and magnificence to the great."

Enterprise on this new scale depended on the availability of capital for investment. And that capital was generated primarily by a long-term, gradual increase in agricultural prices throughout much of the period. Had that increase been sharp, it would probably have produced enough hunger and suffering to retard rather than stimulate economic growth. Had there been no increase, however, the resulting stagnation produced by marginal profits would have proved equally detrimental to expansion. Agricultural entrepreneurs had surplus capital to invest in trade; bankers put that surplus to use to expand their commercial enterprises. Together, capitalist investors and merchants profited.

Banks played a vital role in the history of this expansion. Strong religious and moral disapproval of lending money at interest meant that banking had enjoyed a dubious reputation during the Middle Ages. Because the church did come to allow profit making on com-

TWO VIEWS OF MERCANTILISM

Giovanni Botero (1544–1617) was a Jesuit educator and author, who is best known for his book entitled The Reason of State, *from which the following extract is taken. The connections Botero emphasizes between agriculture, industry and trade make it one of the most illuminating early expositions of mercantilist doctrines.*

The population and the power of the state are augmented in two ways: by increasing your own, and by attracting others' to you. You can increase your own through agriculture and the arts, by encouraging the education of children, and with colonies. You can attract others' by absorbing your enemies, destroying nearby cities, bestowing citizenship [on foreigners], concluding alliances, raising armies, establishing marriage bonds, and doing other similar things such as we will explain briefly one by one.

Agriculture is the foundation of population growth. . . .Thus the prince must favor and promote agriculture and show that he values people who improve the fertility of their lands and whose farms are exceptionally well cultivated. It will be his duty to initiate and direct everything that belongs to the public good of his land: drying up swamps, uprooting useless or excess forests and thus reducing the land to cultivation, and helping and encouraging those who undertake such works. . . .

It is up to the prince, then, to make provision for such inconveniences and, finally, to support all means for making sure that his country abounds and is fecund in all things he knows it to be capable of producing. If plants or seeds are not to be found in his state, it is his duty to see that they are brought in from elsewhere. . . .

Over and above these things, the prince must do his best to prevent money from leaving his state needlessly. Even if things that are needed are expensive within the state, the money spent on them will still remain within the country or return to the treasury in the long run in customs charges and taxes. Once the money leaves the state, however, both it and the profits it would have earned are lost. . . .

There is nothing more important for enlarging a state and for assuring it a multitude of population and of all kinds of goods than the industry of its people and the quantity of its trades. . . . They attract money, and they attract the people who make or traffic in manufactured goods, who provide materials to the workers, and who buy, sell, or transport the products of man's hands and ingenuity from one place to another. . . . Some may ask whether fertile soil or man's industry is more important for enlarging and populating an area. Industry, undoubtedly. . . . The things produced by a man's skilled hand are far superior in quantity and value than things generated by nature. . . . Moreover, many more people live from industry than from rents. Many cities in Italy can attest to this, but principally Venice, Florence, Genoa, and Milan, whose size and magnificence we need not dwell on, and where almost two thirds of the inhabitants live by the silk and the wool trades. . . .

Eric Cochrane and Julius Kirshner, eds. *The Renaissance: University of Chicago Readings in Western Civilization*, vol. 5. (Chicago: University of Chicago Press, 1985), pp. 244–247 (translated by Lydia Cochrane).

In the following selection, taken from a memorandum by King Louis XIV's great finance minister Jean Baptiste Colbert (1619–1683), we see clearly the mercantilist assumption that the total amount of trade is fixed and cannot be increased. Therefore, if France is to grow richer, this can only be at the expense of other countries, which must grow poorer.

The commerce of all Europe is carried on by ships of every size to the number of 20,000, and it is perfectly clear that this number cannot be increased, since the number of people in all the states remains the same and consumption likewise remains the same. . . .

It must be added that commerce causes a perpetual combat in peace and war among the nations of Europe, as to who shall win the most of it. . . . Each nation works incessantly to have its legitimate share of commerce or to gain an advantage over another nation. The Dutch fight at present, in this war with 15,000 to 16,000 ships, a government of merchants, all of whose maxims and power are directed solely toward the preservation and increase of their commerce, and much more care, energy, and thrift than any other nation.

The English with 3,000 to 4,000 ships, less energy and care, and more expenditures than the Dutch.

The French with 500 to 600.

Those two last cannot improve their commerce save by increasing the number of their vessels, and cannot increase this number save from the 20,000 which carry all the commerce and consequently by making inroads on the 15,000 to 16,000 of the Dutch.

J. H. Robinson. *Readings in European History,* vol. 2. (New York: Ginn and Company, 1934), pp. 279–280.

mercial risks, however, banks in Italy and Germany were organized during the fourteenth and fifteenth centuries, most notably by the Medici family in Florence and the Fugger family in Augsburg. The rise of these private financial houses was followed by the establishment of government banks, reflecting the mercantilist goal of serving the monetary needs of the state. The first such institution, the Bank of Sweden, was founded in 1657. The Bank of England was established in 1694, at a time when England's emergence as a world commercial power guaranteed that institution a leading role in international finance. The growth of banking was necessarily accompanied by the adoption of various aids to financial transactions on a large scale, further evidence of a commercial revolution. Credit facilities were extended and payment by check introduced, thereby encouraging an increase in the volume of trade, since the credit resources of the banks could now be expanded far beyond the actual amounts of cash in their vaults.

International commercial expansion called forth larger units of business organization. The prevailing unit of production and trade in the Middle Ages was the workshop or store owned by an individual or a family. Partnerships were also quite common, even though each partner was liable for the debts of the entire firm. Obviously neither the workshop or the partnership was well adapted to business involving heavy risks and a huge investment of capital. The attempt to devise a more suitable business organization resulted in the formation of regulated companies, which were associations of merchants banded together for a common venture. Members did not pool their resources but agreed merely to cooperate for their mutual advantage and to abide by certain definite regulations.

The commercial revolution was facilitated during the seventeenth century when regulated companies were largely superseded by a new type of organization at once more compact and broader in scope. This was the joint-stock company, formed through the issuance of shares of capital to a considerable number of investors. Those who purchased the shares might or might not take part in the work of the company. Whether they did or not, they were joint owners of the business and therefore entitled to share in its profits in proportion with the amount they had invested. The joint-stock company of the early modern period is best understood not so much as a conscious precursor of capitalist endeavor but as a pragmatic attempt at commercial expansion by both individuals and the state. A joint-stock company's structure was dictated by present opportunity and circumstance. Initially, for example, the Dutch United East India Company, one of the earliest joint-stock ventures, had expected to pay off its investors ten years after its founding in 1602, much as regulated companies had. Yet when that time came, the directors recognized the impossibility of the plan. By 1612, the company's assets were scattered—as ships, wharves,

A Square in Seventeenth-Century Amsterdam. This contemporary painting emphasizes the central role independent merchants, consumers, and trade played in Dutch city life.

The Lyons Stock Exchange. Built in 1749, the stylish and impressive facade of the structure bespeaks the prominent role of commerce in French society.

operation of their enterprise and, in the process, establishing a practice of continuous financing that was soon to become common.

Most of the early joint-stock companies were founded for commercial ventures, but later some were organized in industry. A number of the outstanding trading combinations were also chartered companies. They held charters from the government granting a monopoly of the trade in a certain locality and conferring extensive authority over the inhabitants, and were thus an example of the way capitalist and mercantilist interests might coincide. Through a charter of this kind, the British East India Company undertook the exploitation of vast territories on the Indian subcontinent, and remained the virtual ruler there until the end of the eighteenth century.

In most European countries, and particularly in France, government and commerce generally worked to promote each other's interests. The exception was the Netherlands. The Dutch almost exclusively put their capital to work not for the state but for the rest of Europe. In time of war, governments called upon commercial capitalists to assist in the financing of their campaigns. When England went to war against France in 1689, for example, the government had no long-range borrowing mechanism available to it; during the next quarter century the merchant community, through the Bank of England, assisted the government in raising over £170 million and in stabilizing the national debt at £40 million. In return, trading companies used the war to increase long-distance commercial traffic at the expense of their French enemy,

warehouses, and cargoes—around the globe. As a result, the directors urged those anxious to realize their profits to sell their shares on the Amsterdam exchange to other eager investors, thereby ensuring the sustained and exerted powerful pressure on the government to secure treaties that would work to their advantage.

A final important feature of the commercial revolution was the development of a more efficient money economy. Money had been used widely since the early Middle Ages, but the growth of trade and industry in the commercial revolution accentuated the need for more stable and uniform monetary systems at the national level. The problem was solved when every important state adopted a standard system of money to be used for all transactions within its borders. Much time elapsed, however, before the reform was complete.

The economic institutions just described never remained static, but rather existed in a continuously volatile state of development. This volatility, in turn, had a direct effect on the lives of individual men and women. One major result of overseas expansion, for example, was the severe inflation caused by the increase in the supply of silver that plagued Europe at the end of the sixteenth century. Price fluctuations, in turn, produced further economic instability. Businessmen were tempted to expand their enterprises too rapidly; bankers extended credit so liberally that their principal borrowers, especially noblemen, often defaulted on loans. In both Spain and Italy, wages failed to keep pace with rising prices, which brought severe and continuing hardships to the lower classes. Impoverishment was rife in the cities, and bandits flourished in the rural areas.

Speculative greed could, and sometimes did, threaten to bring a nation to its knees. Though feverish speculation characterized the early modern period as a whole, the most notorious bouts of that particular economic disease occurred in the early eighteenth century. The so-called South Sea Bubble was the result of deliberate inflation of the value of stock of the South Sea Company in Britain, whose offer to assume the national debt led to unwarranted confidence in the company's future. When buoyant hopes gave way to fears, investors made frantic attempts to dispose of their shares for whatever they would bring. The crash that came in 1720 was the inevitable result.

During the years when the South Sea Bubble was being inflated in Britain, the French were engaged in a similar wave of speculative madness. In 1715 a Scotsman by the name of John Law persuaded the regent of France to adopt his scheme for paying off the national debt through the issuance of paper money and to grant him the privilege of organizing the Mississippi Company for the colonization and exploitation of Louisiana. As happened in Britain, stock prices soared in response to this alluring but basically unrealistic scheme. Stories were told of butchers and tailors who made fortunes from their few initial shares. Ultimately, however, panic set in, and in 1720 the Mississippi Bubble burst in a wild panic.

COLONIZATION AND OVERSEAS TRADE

What was the "triangular trade"?

Despite the existence of increasingly profitable European commercial routes and centers, the most visible evidence of the economic expansionism of early modern Europe were the overseas colonies and trading posts developed and exploited during the seventeenth and eighteenth centuries.

SPANISH COLONIALISM

Following the exploits of the conquistadors, the Spanish established colonial governments in Peru and in Mexico, which they controlled from Madrid in proper mercantilist fashion by a Council of the Indies. The governments of Philip II and his successors were determined to defend their monopoly in the New World. They issued trading licenses only to Spanish merchants; exports and imports passed only through the port of Seville (later the more navigable port of Cadíz), where they were registered at the government-operated Casa de Contratación, or customs house. In their heyday, Spanish traders circled the globe. The lucrative market for silver in East Asia made it profitable even to establish an outpost in far-off Manila in the Philippines, where Asian silk was exchanged for South American bullion. The silk was then shipped back to Spain by way of the Mexican ports of Acapulco and Veracruz. The search for gold and silver was accompanied by the establishment of permanent colonies in Central and South America and on the east and west coasts of North America in what are now the states of Florida and California.

Spain's predominance did not deter other countries

The lucrative market for silver in East Asia made it profitable even to establish an outpost in the far-off Philippines, where Asian silk was exchanged for South American bullion.

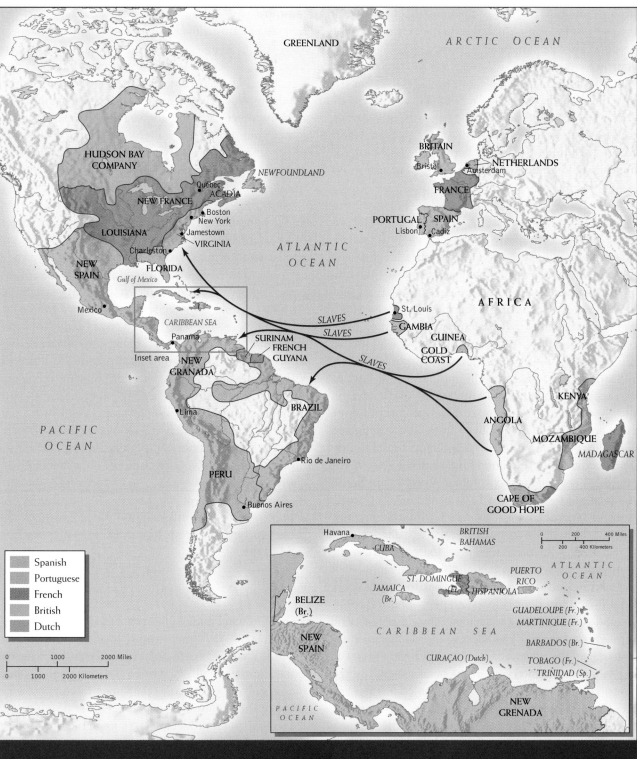

GREENLAND

ARCTIC OCEAN

HUDSON BAY COMPANY

NEWFOUNDLAND

Quebec
ACADIA
NEW FRANCE
Boston
New York
Jamestown
VIRGINIA
LOUISIANA
Charleston
NEW SPAIN
FLORIDA
Gulf of Mexico
Mexico

ATLANTIC OCEAN

BRITAIN
Bristol
NETHERLANDS
Amsterdam
FRANCE
PORTUGAL   SPAIN
Lisbon   Cadiz

AFRICA

St. Louis
SLAVES
SLAVES
GAMBIA
GUINEA
GOLD COAST

CARIBBEAN SEA
Panama
Inset area
NEW GRANADA
SURINAM
FRENCH GUYANA
SLAVES

Lima
BRAZIL

PACIFIC OCEAN

ANGOLA
KENYA
MOZAMBIQUE
MADAGASCAR

Rio de Janeiro

PERU

Buenos Aires

CAPE OF GOOD HOPE

Spanish
Portuguese
French
British
Dutch

0   1000   2000 Miles
0   1000   2000 Kilometers

Havana
CUBA
BRITISH BAHAMAS
0   200   400 Miles
0   200   400 Kilometers
ATLANTIC OCEAN
PUERTO RICO
ST. DOMINGUE (Fr.)
JAMAICA (Br.)
HISPANIOLA
BELIZE (Br.)
GUADELOUPE (Fr.)
MARTINIQUE (Fr.)
NEW SPAIN
CARIBBEAN SEA
BARBADOS (Br.)
CURAÇAO (Dutch)
TOBAGO (Fr.)
TRINIDAD (Sp.)
PACIFIC OCEAN
NEW GRANADA

THE ATLANTIC WORLD

Why were European governments so concerned with closely controlling the means by which certain products traveled from the colonies to European ports? How and why did the financial institutions of the late medieval period thrive on and encourage the economic policies of colonial powers? Why are the trade routes carrying slaves so prominently marked on this map? What does this suggest about the importance of unfree labor to the economic achievements of Europeans in the New World?

from attempting to win a share of the treasure for themselves. Probably the boldest challengers were the English. Their leading buccaneer was the "sea dog" Sir Francis Drake, who three times raided the east and west coasts of Spanish America. In 1587, the year before the Armada set sail on its ill-fated voyage north, Drake "singed the beard of the Spanish king" by attacking the Spanish fleet at its anchorage in Cadíz harbor. Yet despite dashing heroics of that sort, the English could do no more than dent the Spanish trade.

ENGLISH COLONIALISM

English colonists sought profits elsewhere by establishing agricultural settlements in North America and the Caribbean basin. Their first permanent (though ultimately unsuccessful) colony was Jamestown in Virginia, founded in 1607. Over the next forty years, eighty thousand English emigrants sailed to over twenty autonomous settlements in the New World. In this instance, however, religious freedom, as well as economic gain, was often the motive of the settlers. The renowned band of "Pilgrim fathers" that landed on the New England shores in 1620 was but one of a large number of dissident groups, both Protestant and Catholic, that sought to escape attempts to impose religious conformity. Religion also played a role in the efforts of the Spanish to colonize Central and South America, and of the French to penetrate the hinterlands of North America. Roman Catholic Jesuit missionaries, intent on converting Native Americans to Christianity, joined fur traders in journeys across the continent to the Great Lakes and the Mississippi.

Both England and France were quick to extract profit from their expanding colonial empires. England's agricultural colonies were producing crops in high demand throughout Europe. The success of colonial planters encouraged the governments of both Oliver Cromwell and Charles II to intervene in the management of their overseas economy. Navigation acts, passed in 1651 and 1660, and rigorously enforced thereafter, decreed that all exports from English colonies to the mother country be carried in English ships, and forbade the direct exporting of certain "enumerated" products directly from the colonies to Continental ports.

The most valuable of those products were sugar and tobacco. Sugar, virtually unknown in Christian Europe prior to the fifteenth century, became a popular luxury during the sixteenth century. Where once it had been considered a rarity or even a medicine, one observer now noted that the wealthy were "devouring it out of

gluttony." As we saw in Chapter 12, Europeans had first begun to produce sugar in their Mediterranean and African island colonies during the fifteenth century. Only in the New World, however, did sugar production reach such volumes as to create a mass market for the product. By the middle of the seventeenth century, however, demand for sugar had reached enormous proportions. In the eighteenth century, the value of the sugar that Britain imported from its small West Indian colonies exceeded the total value of its imports from the vast subcontinents of China and India.

Sugar, however, could only be grown in a fairly limited geographical and climatic area. Tobacco was much more adaptable. Although the tobacco plant was imported into Europe by the Spaniards about fifty years after the discovery of America, another half century passed before Europeans took up the habit of smoking. At first the plant was believed to possess miraculous healing powers and was referred to as "divine tobacco" and "our holy herb nicotian." (The word *nicotine* derives from the name of the French ambassador to Portugal, Jean Nicot, who brought the tobacco plant to France.) The practice of smoking was popularized by English explorers, especially by Sir Walter Raleigh, who had learned to smoke while living among the Native Americans of Virginia. It spread rapidly through all classes of European society. Governments at first joined the church in condemning the use of tobacco because of its socially and spiritually harmful effects, but by the end of the seventeenth century, having realized the profits to be made from its production, they encouraged its use.

FRENCH COLONIALISM

French colonial policy matured during the administration of Louis XIV's mercantilist finance minister, Jean Baptiste Colbert (1619–1683), who regarded overseas expansion as an integral part of state economic policy. He organized joint-stock companies to compete with those of the English. He encouraged the development of lucrative sugar-producing colonies in the West Indies, the largest of which was St. Domingue (present-day Haiti). France also dominated the interior of the North American continent. Frenchmen traded furs and preached Christianity to the native peoples in a vast territory that stretched from Acadia and the St. Lawrence River in the northeast to Louisiana in the west. Yet the financial returns from these lands were hardly commensurate with their size. Furs, fish, and tobacco were exported to home markets, but not in sufficient amounts to match the profits from the sugar colonies of the Caribbean or from the trading posts the French maintained in India.

DUTCH COLONIALISM

The Dutch were even more successful than the English and the French in establishing a flourishing commercial empire in the seventeenth century. They succeeded in establishing a colony on the southern tip of Africa at the Cape of Good Hope. Far more important, however, were their commercial adventurings in Southeast Asia. Their joint-stock East India Company, founded in 1602, rivaled its English counterpart in Asia, gaining firm control of Sumatra, Borneo, and the Moluccas, or Spice Islands, and driving Portuguese traders from an area where they had heretofore enjoyed an undisturbed commercial dominion. The result was a Dutch monopoly in pepper, cinnamon, nutmeg, mace, and cloves. The Dutch also secured an exclusive right to trade with the Japanese, and maintained outposts in China and India as well. In the Western Hemisphere, their achievements were less spectacular. Following a series of trade wars with England, they formally surrendered their North American colony of New Amsterdam (subsequently renamed New York) in 1667, retaining Surinam, off the northern coast of South America, as well as the islands of Curaçao and Tobago in the West Indies in compensation.

CONTRASTING PATTERNS OF COLONIAL SETTLEMENT

Differences in the commercial relationships European countries established with their New World colonies reflected important differences in settlement patterns between the colonies. In Central and South America, a relatively small number of Spaniards had conquered complex, highly populous Native American societies. To rule these new territories, the Spanish quickly replaced native elites with Spanish administrators and churchmen. But by and large they did not attempt to

The Dutch East India Company Warehouse and Timber Wharf at Amsterdam. The substantial warehouse, the stockpiles of lumber, and the company ship under construction in the foreground illustrate the degree to which overseas commerce could stimulate the economy of the mother country.

uproot or eliminate existing native cultures. Instead, Spain focused its efforts on controlling and exploiting native labor, so as to extract the maximum possible profit for the crown from the colonies' mineral resources. The native peoples of Spanish America already lived, for the most part, in large, well-organized villages and towns. Spanish colonial policy was to collect tribute from such communities and to convert them to Catholicism, but to do so without fundamentally disrupting their existing patterns of life.

The result was widespread cultural assimilation between the Spanish colonizers and the native populace, combined with a relatively high degree of intermarriage between them. Out of this reality emerged a complex and distinctive system of racial and social castes, with "pure-blooded" Spaniards at the top, peoples of mixed descent in the middle (native, Spanish, and African, in various combinations), and nontribal "Indians" at the bottom. In theory, these racial categories corresponded with class distinctions, but in practice race and class did not always coincide, and race itself was often a social fiction. Mixed race individuals who prospered economically often found ways to establish their "pure" Spanish ancestry by adopting the social practices that characterized elite (that is,

Spanish) status. Spaniards, however, always remained at the top of the social hierarchy of honor and status, even when they fell into poverty.

Like the Spanish colonies, the French colonies were established and administered as direct crown enterprises. The French colonies, however, were dependent almost entirely on the fur trade and on fishing; and the fur trade in particular depended in turn upon cooperative relationships with the native peoples of the New World. French colonial settlements were conceived mainly as military outposts and trading centers; as a result, they were overwhelmingly populated by men. The elite members of French colonial society were the military officers and administrators sent out from Paris. But below their narrow ranks, there was a broad community of interest among the fishermen, fur traders, small farmers, and common soldiers who constituted the bulk of the French settlers of North America. A mutual economic interdependence quickly grew up between these French colonies and the native peoples of the surrounding region, and intermarriage between French fur traders and native women was common. But most of these French colonies remained dependent upon the wages and supplies sent to them from the mother country. Only rarely did they become truly self-sustaining economic enterprises.

The English colonies along the Atlantic seaboard followed a very different model. English colonies did not begin as crown enterprises. Instead they were established either by joint-stock companies (as in Virginia and the Massachusetts Bay colony) or as private, proprietary colonies (such as Maryland and Pennsylvania). Building on their experience in Ireland, English colonists established planned settlements (known as plantations), in which they attempted to replicate as many features of English life as possible. Geography too contributed to the resulting concentration of English settlement patterns. The rivers and bays of eastern North America provided the first footholds for English colonists in the New World, and the Atlantic Ocean helped to tie these separated settlements together. But aside from the Hudson, there were no great rivers to lead colonists very far inland. Instead, the English colonies clung to the seacoast, and so to each other.

Like the French colonies, the early English colonies relied on fishing and the fur trade. But primarily, English colonies were agricultural communities, populated by small- and medium-scale landholders for whom control over land was the key to wealth. Partly this was a reflection of the kinds of people whom these privately owned colonial enterprises could persuade to immi-

grate to the New World. But this focus on agriculture was also the result of the demographic catastrophe that had struck the native populations of the Atlantic seaboard during the last half of the sixteenth century. European diseases, brought by the Spanish and by the French, English, and Portuguese fishermen who frequented the rich fishing banks off the New England coast, had already decimated the native peoples of eastern North America even before the first colonists set foot there. By the early seventeenth century, a great deal of rich agricultural land had been abandoned, simply because there were no longer enough native farmers to till it—one reason that many native groups initially welcomed the new arrivals.

Unlike the Spanish, English colonists along the Atlantic seaboard therefore had neither the need nor the opportunity to control a large native labor force. What they wanted, rather, was complete and exclusive control over native lands. To this end, the English colonists soon set out to eliminate, through expulsion and massacre, the native peoples of their colonies. To be sure, there were exceptions. In the Quaker colony of Pennsylvania, colonists and Native Americans maintained friendly relations for more than half a century. In the Carolinas, by contrast, enslavement of the native people was widespread, either for sale to the West Indies or, from the 1690s, to work on the rice plantations. Elsewhere, however, attempts to enslave native people failed. When English planters looked for bond laborers, they therefore either recruited indentured servants from England (who would be freed after a specified period of service) or else they purchased Africans (who by and large would be enslaved for life).

Social relations between the English colonists and native peoples also differed from the patterns we find elsewhere in the New World. In contrast to the Spanish and French colonies, intermarriage between English colonists and natives was rare. Instead, a rigid racial division emerged that distinguished all Europeans, regardless of class, from all Native Americans and Africans. Nor did the English make any significant effort to convert native peoples to Christianity. Intermarriage between natives and Africans was relatively common, but between the English and the non-European peoples of their colonies there remained an unbridgeable gulf.

COLONIAL RIVALRIES

The fortunes of these European colonial empires rose and fell over the course of the seventeenth and eigh-

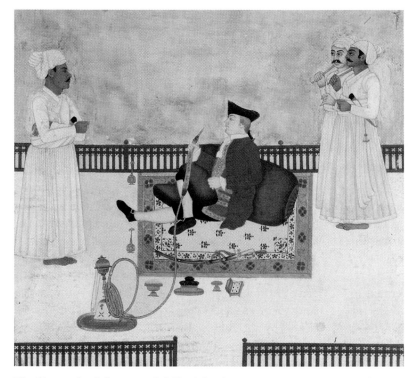

The Rewards of Commercial Exploitation. An English employee of the East India Company enjoying his ease and his opium, as depicted by an eighteenth-century Indian artist.

teenth centuries. The Spanish, mired in persistent economic stagnation and embroiled in a succession of expensive wars and domestic rebellions, were powerless to prevent losses to their empire. Their merchant marine, once a match for cunning pirate-admirals such as Drake, was by the middle of the seventeenth century unable to protect itself from attack by its commercial rivals. In a war with Spain in the 1650s, the English captured not only the island of Jamaica but treasure ships lying off the Spanish harbor of Cadíz. Further profit was obtained by bribing Spanish customs officials on a grand scale. During the second half of the century, two thirds of the imported goods sold in Spanish colonies were smuggled in by Dutch, English, and French traders. By 1700, though Spain still possessed a colonial empire, that empire now lay at the mercy of its more dynamic rivals. A brief revival of its fortunes under more enlightened leadership in the mid-eighteenth century did nothing to prevent its ultimate eclipse.

Portugal, too, found it impossible to prevent foreign penetration of its colonial economies. The British worked diligently and successfully to win commercial advantages. They obtained concessions to export woolens duty free into Portugal itself in return for sim-

ilar preferential treatment for Portuguese wines. (The notorious affection of the English upper class for port wine dates from the signing of the Treaty of 1703.) British trade with the mother country led in time to British trade with the Portuguese colony of Brazil, and indeed to the opening of commercial offices in Rio de Janeiro.

During the eighteenth century, however, a growing Anglo-French rivalry in India stole the commercial spotlight from the Dutch spice monopoly in the Far East. The French and British East India Companies employed mercenaries to establish and expand trading areas such as Madras, Bombay, and Pondichéry. By exploiting indigenous industries, European capitalists continued to increase the flow of fine cotton textiles, tea, and spices, which passed through these commercial depots on their way to Europe. The struggle for worldwide economic dominance reached a peak in the mid-eighteenth century (see pp. 623–24). At that time the Anglo-French rivalry in India was resolved in Britain's favor. As a sign of France's defeat, in 1769 the French East India Company was dissolved.

THE TRIANGULAR TRADE IN SUGAR AND SLAVES

Despite the commercial importance of India, however, patterns of world trade came increasingly to be dominated by western routes that had developed in response to the lucrative West Indian sugar industry, and to the demand for slaves from Africa to work the plantations in the Caribbean. Here Britain again eventually assumed the lead. Typically, a ship might begin its voyage from New England with a consignment of rum and sail to Africa, where the rum would be exchanged for a cargo of slaves. From the west coast of Africa the ship would then cross the South Atlantic to the sugar colonies of Jamaica or Barbados, where slaves would be traded for molasses, which would make the final leg of the journey to New England, where it would be made into rum. A variant triangle might see cheap manufactured goods move from Britain to Africa, where they would be traded for slaves. Those slaves would then be shipped to Virginia and exchanged for tobacco, which would be shipped to Britain and processed there for sale in Continental markets. Other eighteenth-century trade routes were more direct: the Spanish, French, Portuguese, and Dutch all engaged in the slave trade between Africa and Central and South America; the Spanish attempted, in vain, to retain a mercantilist monopoly on direct trade between Cadíz and their South American colonies; others sailed from Britain, France, or North America to the Caribbean and back again. And of course trade continued to flourish between Europe and the Near and Far East. But the triangular western routes, dictated by the grim economic symbiosis of sugar and slaves, remained dominant.

> The triangular western routes, dictated by the grim economic symbiosis of sugar and slaves, remained dominant.

The cultivation of sugar and tobacco depended on slave labor, and as demand for those products increased, so did the traffic in black slaves, without whose labor those products could not be raised or harvested. At the height of the Atlantic slave trade in the eighteenth century, somewhere between seventy-five thousand and ninety thousand Africans were shipped across the Atlantic yearly: at least 6 million during the eighteenth century, out of a total of over 11 million for the entire history of the trade. About 35 percent went to British and French Caribbean plantations, 5 percent (roughly five hundred thousand) to North America, and the rest to the Portuguese colony of Brazil and to Spanish colonies in South America. Although run as a monopoly by various governments in the sixteenth and early seventeenth centuries, in its heyday the slave trade was open to private entrepreneurs who operated ports on the West African coast. Traders exchanged cheap Indian cloth, metal goods, rum, and firearms with African slave merchants in return for their human cargo. Already disoriented and degraded by their capture at the hands of rival tribes, men, women, and children were packed by the hundreds into the holds of slave ships for the gruesome "middle passage" across the Atlantic (so called to distinguish it from the ship's voyage from Europe to Africa, and from the slave colony back to Europe again). Shackled to the decks, without sanitary

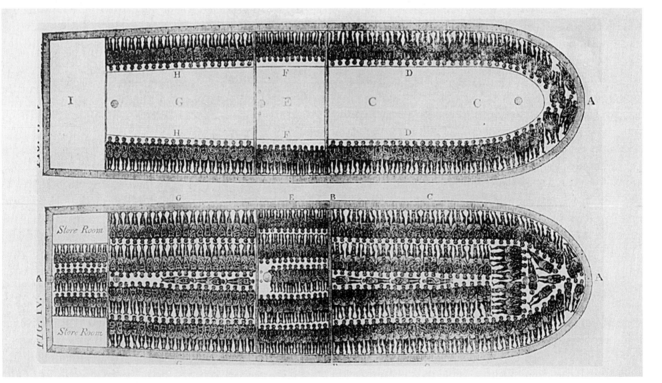

How Slaves Were Stowed Aboard Ship during the Middle Passage. Men were "housed" on the right; women on the left; children in the middle. The human cargo was jammed onto platforms six feet wide without sufficient headroom to permit an adult to sit up. This diagram is from evidence gathered by English abolitionists and depicts conditions on the Liverpool slave ship *Brookes.*

CONDITIONS ON BOARD A SLAVE SHIP

Olaudah Equiano (1745–1797) was born in West Africa. At the age of eleven, he was kidnapped by African slavers; after being bought and sold several times, he wound up on a slave ship to the West Indies. His account of conditions on the "middle passage" between Africa and the Americas is drawn from the memoir he wrote of his life many years later, after he was freed and had become a successful merchant in England.

When I looked round the ship too and saw a large furnace or copper boiling, and a multitude of black people of every description chained together, every one of their countenances expressing dejection and sorrow, I no longer doubted of my fate; and, quite overpowered with horror and anguish, I fell motionless on the deck and fainted. . . .

I was not long suffered to indulge my grief; I was soon put down under the decks, and there I received such a salutation in my nostrils as I had never experienced in my life: so that, with the loathsomeness of the stench, and crying together, I became so sick and low that I was not able to eat, nor had I the least desire to taste any thing. I now wished for the last friend, death, to relieve me; but soon, to my grief, two of the white men offered me eatables; and, on my refusing to eat . . . flogged me severely. . . .Could I have got over the nettings, I would have jumped over the side, but I could not. . . .

At last, when the ship we were in had got in all her cargo, they made ready with many fearful noises, and we were all put under deck. . . . The stench of the hold while we were on the coast was so intolerably loath-

some, that it was dangerous to remain there for any time, and some of us had been permitted to stay on the deck for the fresh air; but now that the whole ship's cargo were confined together, it became absolutely pestilential. The closeness of the place, and the heat of the climate, added to the number in the ship, which was so crowded that each had scarcely room to turn himself, almost suffocated us. This produced copious perspirations, so that the air soon became unfit for respiration . . . and brought on a sickness among the slaves, of which many died, thus falling victims to the improvident avarice, as I may call it, of their purchasers. This wretched situation was again aggravated by the galling of the chains, now become unsupportable; and the filth of the necessary tubs [latrines], into which the children often fell, and were almost suffocated. The shrieks of the women, and the groans of the dying, rendered the whole a scene of horror almost inconceivable.

Olaudah Equiano. *The Interesting Narrative of the Life of Olaudah Equiano, or Gustavus Vassa, The African, Written by Himself,* edited by Werner Sollors. (New York: W.W. Norton and Company, 2001), pp. 39–41.

facilities, the human "cargo" suffered horribly; the mortality rate, however, remained at about 10 or 11 percent, not much higher than the rate for a normal sea voyage of one hundred days or more. Since traders had to invest as much as £10 per slave in their enterprise, they ensured that their consignment would reach its destination in good enough shape to be sold for a profit.

The slave trade was risky, dependent on good wind and fair weather, and competition was increasing. Yet profits could run high, occasionally as much as 300 percent. Demand for slaves remained constant throughout the eighteenth century. By the 1780s, there were more than five hundred thousand slaves on the largest French plantation island, St.-Domingue, and two hundred thousand or more on the British counterpart, Jamaica. Those numbers reflected the expanding world market for slave-grown crops. As long as there was a market for the crops cultivated by slaves—as long as the economy relied to the extent it did on slave labor—governments would remain unwilling to halt the system that, as one Briton wrote in 1749, provided "an unexhaustible fund of wealth to this nation."

Apologists for the slave trade argued that though there was reason to rejoice that slavery had been banished from the continent of Europe (forgetting, apparently, the extent to which it continued to exist east of the Elbe in the form of serfdom), it remained a necessity in other parts of the world. Not until the very end of the eighteenth century did Europeans begin to protest the ghastly traffic. Public pressure, first from Quakers and then from others motivated by either religious or humanitarian zeal, helped put an end to the trade in Britain in 1807, and to slavery itself in British colonies in 1833. Slavery in French colonies was abolished in 1793, but only after slaves had risen in massive revolt on St.-Domingue. Elsewhere, in Latin and North America, slavery lasted well into the nineteenth century—in the United States, until the Civil War of 1861–1865. The racism it promoted has lasted until the present day.

Social ranks were demarcated by rights and privileges.

The slave trade was an integral part of the history of the dramatic rise of British and French commerce during the eighteenth century. French colonial trade, valued at 25 million livres in 1716, rose to 263 million livres in 1789. In Britain, during roughly the same period, foreign trade increased in value from £10 million to £40 million, the latter amount more than twice that for France. These figures suggest the degree to which statecraft and private enterprise were bound to each other. If merchants depended on their government to provide a navy to protect and defend their overseas investments, governments depended equally on entrepreneurship, not only to generate money to build ships, but to sustain the trade on which national power had come to rely so heavily.

LIFE WITHIN A SOCIETY OF ORDERS

How did the lives of eastern and western European peasants differ?

Despite the economic and demographic shifts that were occurring in early modern Europe, society remained divided into traditional orders, or ranks. The economic changes we have been describing occurred against the continuity of long-accepted social divisions based on birth and occupation. As circumstances altered, the fluid patterns of economic reorganization clashed with older, rigid assumptions about the place of men and women within a preordained—to many, a divinely ordained—social hierarchy. Jean Bodin, the French philosopher, wrote in 1570 that the division of the citizenry into "the three orders of nobles, clergy and people" was no more than natural. "There never was a commonwealth, real or imaginary, where citizens were in truth equal in all rights and privileges. Some always have more, some less than the rest." And some had none.

Most Europeans would have recognized subtle subdivisions among and between the three orders Bodin specified. Ranks were demarcated by rights and privileges. "Freedom" was understood as one such privilege, as a benefit, bestowed not on all men and women but on special groups whose position "freed" them to do certain things others could not do, or freed them from the burden of doing certain things that were required of others. A British landowner was, because of the position his property conferred upon him, privileged, and therefore "free" to participate directly in the election of his government. A French nobleman was privileged, and therefore "free" of the heavy burden of taxation levied upon the unprivileged orders. A German tailor who had served out his seven-year apprenticeship was free to set up his own shop for profit, something an unapprenticed man was not traditionally "at liberty" to do, no matter what his degree of skill with needle and thread. The master tailor's position conferred his freedom, just as the position of aristocrat and property owner conferred theirs.

HOW DID THE LIVES OF EASTERN AND WESTERN EUROPEAN PEASANTS DIFFER?

LIFE WITHIN A SOCIETY OF ORDERS   581

DISPLAYS OF RANK

The members of the higher orders attempted at all times to live their lives in a particular style that accorded with their rank. The nobility was taught from birth to consider itself above and apart from the rest of society. Merchants and manufacturers were just as insistent upon maintaining the traditional marks of privilege that separated them from artisans and peasants. Sumptuary laws decreed what could be worn and by whom. An edict promulgated in the German principality of Brunswick in 1738, for example, forbade servant girls to wear silk dresses, gold or silver ornaments, or anything but plain black shoes. A similar seventeenth-century law in the Polish city of Posen prohibited the wives of burghers from wearing capes or long hair. Style was not simply a matter of current whim. It was a badge of status, carefully adhered to. An aristocratic lady powdered her hair and rouged her cheeks as a sign that she was an aristocrat. Life within a society of orders demanded a certain degree of theatricality, especially from those at the top of the social hierarchy. Aristocrats "acted" their part in a calculatedly self-conscious way. Their manner of speech, their dress, the ceremonial swords noblemen were privileged to wear, the titles by which they were addressed—these were the props of a performance that constantly emphasized the distinctions between those above and those below. Noble families lived in castles, chateaux, or country houses whose size and antiquity were a fur-

ther proclamation of superiority. When they built new mansions, as did the *nouveau riche* capitalist British gentry during the eighteenth century, they made certain their elaborate houses and spacious private parks declared their newfound power. The English politician Robert Walpole had an entire village moved to improve the view from his grand new residence.

THE NOBILITY

The vast majority of men and women defined and understood social hierarchy in terms of the rural communities in which they lived. At the head of those communities, in all likelihood, stood a representative of the noble elite. The nobility probably numbered about 3 percent of the total population of Europe. The percentage was higher in Poland, Hungary, and Spain; lower in Russia, Germany, France, and Britain. Ownership of a landed estate was proof of one's elevated rank. Generally speaking, the more land one possessed, the higher one stood within the social hierarchy. In Hungary, five noble families owned about 14 percent of the entire country; the greatest of these nobles, Prince Esterházy, controlled the lives of more than half a million peasants. Most noblemen were not nearly so rich and powerful. Some, indeed, could rely on little more than inherited privilege to distinguish themselves from peasants.

Tradition had it that noble service meant military service; yet, as we shall see, that tradition was increasingly breached during the early modern period. Noble title was granted by a monarch, in theory for service to the state. But such service was more and more frequently defined as nonmilitary—as support, financial and political, for the expanding apparatus of local and central government. The pattern of noble life varied considerably from country to country. In Britain and Prussia, nobles tended to reside on their estates; in south and west Germany, and in France, they were more likely to leave the management of their estates to stewards and to live at the royal

Middle-Class Fashion. In this seventeenth-century portrait of a Dutch burgomaster and his family, the patriarch and his wife are wearing the costume of an earlier generation, while the children are clothed in the current style. All display the opulence characteristic of their prosperous class.

Gala Dinner at Schoenbrunn Palace in Vienna. Given on the occasion of Joseph II's wedding, this banquet was an example of the extravagance this Habsburg monarch believed suitable to the occasion.

through the purchase of expensive offices from the crown. Membership could be purchased in the legal nobility of the "robe," headed by members of the thirteen provincial parlements whose function it was to record, and thereby sanction, the laws of the kingdom, and to adjudicate cases appealed from lower courts.

THE PEASANTRY

Land ownership brought the nobility into direct relationship with the peasants and laborers who worked the land and over whose lives their masters exercised dominion. The status of the peasantry varied greatly across the face of rural Europe. In the east— Russia, Poland, Hungary, and in parts of Germany beyond

court or in cities. Despite the traditional assumption that noblemen should not soil their aristocratic reputation by commercial dealing, by the end of the eighteenth century they were involving themselves in increasing numbers in a variety of entrepreneurial enterprises. Some exploited mineral deposits on their estates; others invested in overseas trade. In France, two of the four largest coal mines were owned and operated by noblemen, while the duke of Orléans was an important investor in the newly established chemical dye industry. In eastern Europe, where there were few middle-class merchants, noblemen frequently undertook to market their agricultural produce themselves.

In no country was the nobility a completely closed order. Men who proved useful to the crown as administrators or lawyers, men who amassed large fortunes as a consequence of judicious—and often legally questionable—financial transactions, moved into the ranks of the nobility with increasing frequency during the late seventeenth and eighteenth centuries. Joseph II of Austria was making financiers into noblemen by the dozen during the late eighteenth century. In France, it was possible to attain nobility

> In no country was the nobility a completely closed order.

the Elbe—the desire for profit in agriculture and the collusion of the state with the nobility led to the growth of a "second serfdom," a serf system much stronger than that which had existed during the Middle Ages. In East Prussia, serfs often had to work from three to six days a week for their lord, and some had only late evening or night hours to cultivate their own lands.

Peasants throughout eastern Europe found their destinies controlled in almost all respects by their masters. Noble landlords dispensed justice in manorial courts and even ruled in cases to which they were themselves interested parties. These men were a combination of sheriff, chief magistrate, and police force in one, able to sentence their "subjects" to corporal punishment, imprisonment, exile, or even death, without right of appeal. Peasants could not leave their land, marry, or learn a trade unless permitted to do so by their lord. In Russia, where half the land was owned by the state, peasants were bound to work in mines or workshops if their masters so ordered, and could be sold to private owners. Although Russian peasant serfs were said to possess a "legal personality"

HOW DID THE LIVES OF EASTERN AND WESTERN EUROPEAN PEASANTS DIFFER?

LIFE WITHIN A SOCIETY OF ORDERS   583

that distinguished them from slaves, the distinction was obscured in practice. They lived as bound to their masters as had their great-grandfathers.

In western Europe, the position of the peasantry reflected the fact that serfdom had all but disappeared by the sixteenth century. Peasants might theoretically own land, although the vast majority were either tenants or laborers. Hereditary tenure was in general more secure than in the east; peasants could dispose of their land and had legal claim to farm buildings and implements. Although far freer than their eastern European counterparts, the peasants of western Europe still lived to a great degree under the domination of landowners. They were in many cases responsible for the payment of various dues and fees: an annual rent paid to landlords by those who might otherwise own their land outright; a special tax on recently cleared land; a fee, often as much as one sixth of the assessed value of the land, collected by the manorial lord whenever peasant property changed hands; and charges for the use of the lord's mill, bakery, or wine press. In France, peasants were compelled to submit to the corvée, a requirement that they labor for several weeks a year maintaining local roads. Even access to the often questionable justice meted out in the manorial courts, which endured throughout the early-modern period in almost all of western Europe, was encumbered with fees and commissions. To many peasants, however, the most galling badge of their inferiority was their inability to hunt within the jurisdiction of their landlord's manor. The slaughter of game was a privilege reserved to the nobility, a circumstance generating sustained resentment on the part of a population that looked on deer and pheasant not as a symbol of aristocratic status but as a necessary supplement to a meager diet. Noble landlords rarely missed an opportunity to extract all the money they could from their peasants while constantly reminding them of the degree to which their destiny was controlled by the lord of the manor.

> Although far freer than their eastern European counterparts, the peasants of western Europe still lived to a great degree under the domination of landowners.

Despite their traditional subservience, however, western European peasants found themselves caught up directly in the process of economic change. The growth of centralized monarchies intensified the states' need for income, with the result that peasants were more burdened than ever with taxes and required services. They responded by accepting a new role as wage earners in an expanding market economy, some as agricultural day laborers on enclosed estates, others as part of the work force in expanding rural industries. A few were genuinely independent, literate, influential members of the communities where they lived, owning not only land but considerable livestock. In France, some acted as intermediaries between their landlords, from whom they leased several large farms, and the sharecroppers who actually worked the land. Most, however, were far less fortunate. Those with claim to a small piece of property usually worked it into infertility in the course of one or two generations as they scrambled to make it produce as much as possible.

Poor peasants often lived, contrary to the biblical injunction, by bread alone—two pounds a day if they were lucky, the dark dough a mixture of wheat and rye flour. According to region, bread was supplemented by peas and beans, beer, wine, or, far less often, skimmed

A French Peasant. Tattered and overworked, this peasant farmer is shown feeding his livestock as the tax collector at his door relieves him of all of his profits.

milk. Peasant houses usually contained no more than one or two rooms, and were constructed of wood, plastered with mud or clay. Roofs were most often thatched with straw, which was used as fertilizer when replaced, and provided fodder for animals in times of scarcity. Furnishings seldom consisted of more than a table, benches, pallets for sleeping, a few earthenware plates, and simple tools—an axe, a wooden spade, a knife.

Peasant women tended livestock and vegetables and managed the dairy, if there was one. Women went out as field workers, or worked at home knitting, spinning, or weaving in order to augment the family income. A popular seventeenth-century poem has a laborer's wife lamenting her lot with a refrain that has echoed down the ages: "My labor is hard, / And all my pleasures are debarr'd; / Both morning, evening, night and noon, / I am sure a woman's work is never done."

URBAN SOCIETY

The spread of protoindustrialization broke down the demarcations between town and country, between the life lived inside a city's medieval walls and that lived outside. Suburbs merged urban and rural existence. In some suburbs, textile workers labored. In others, families of fashion took their ease, creating an environment "where the want of London smoke is supplied by the smoke of Virginia tobacco," as one Briton remarked wryly. Houses in areas inhabited by the wealthy were increasingly built of brick and stone, which replaced the wood, lath, and plaster of the Middle Ages. This change was a response to the constant danger of fire. The great fire of London in 1666, which destroyed three quarters of the town—twelve thousand houses—was the largest of the conflagrations that swept cities with devastating regularity. Urban dwellings of the laboring poor remained firetraps. Workers' quarters were badly overcrowded; entire families lived in one-room accommodations in basements and attics that were infested with bugs and fleas.

Urban society was, like its rural counterpart, a society of orders. In national capitals, noble families occupied the highest social position, as they did in the countryside, living a parasitic life of conspicuous consumption. The majority of cities and towns were dominated by a nonnoble bourgeoisie. That French term originally designated a burgher or townsman who was a long-term, resident property owner or leaseholder and taxpayer. By the eighteenth century it had come to mean a townsman of some means who aspired to be recognized as a person of local importance and evinced a willingness to work hard, whether at countinghouse or government office, and a desire to live a comfortable, if by no means extravagant, existence. A bourgeois might derive his income from rents; or he might be an industrialist, banker, merchant, lawyer, or physician. If he served in the central bureaucracy, he would consider himself the social superior of those provincials whose affairs he administered. Yet he would himself be looked down on by the aristocracy, many of whom enjoyed thinking of the bourgeoisie as a class of vulgar social climbers, often conveniently forgetting their own commercial origins a generation or two previously. The French playwright Molière's comedy *The Bourgeois Gentleman* (1670) reflected this attitude, ridiculing the manners of those who were trying to ape their betters. "Bourgeois," another French writer observed, "is the insult given by noblemen to anybody they deem slow-witted or out of touch with the court." The bourgeoisie usually constituted about 20 to 25 percent of a town's population. As its economic elite, these men were almost always its governing elite as well.

Throughout the early modern period, there was considerable movement into and out of the urban bourgeoisie. Prosperous tradesmen and successful small-time commercial entrepreneurs might see their offspring rise in station, particularly if they married well. At the same time, those who made their money in trade could purchase land, and by paying fees to their king, gain the right to an ennobling office. In seventeenth-century Amiens, a major French textile center, the upper bourgeoisie deserted trade and derived the majority of its income from land or bonds. Where the bourgeoisie thrived, it more often than not did so as the result of a burgeoning state or regional bureaucracy.

Next within the urban hierarchy was a vast middle range of shopkeepers and artisans. Many of the latter continued to learn and then to practice their crafts as members of guilds, which in turn contained their own particular ascending order of apprentice, journeyman, and master, thus preserving the pervasive principle of hierarchy. Throughout the early modern period, however, commercial expansion threatened the rigid hierar-

> In national capitals, noble families occupied the highest social position, as they did in the countryside, living a parasitic life of conspicuous consumption.

HOW DID THE LIVES OF EASTERN AND WESTERN EUROPEAN PEASANTS DIFFER?

LIFE WITHIN A SOCIETY OF ORDERS   585

The "Bon Ton." This English cartoon mocks the rage for French fashion and illustrates the affluence of a middle class able to afford the changing dictates of fashion.

chy of the guild structure. The expense and curtailed output resulting from restrictive guild practices met with serious opposition in big cities such as Paris and London, and in the industrial hinterlands of France and Germany, where expanding markets called for cheaper and more readily available goods. Journeymen tailors and shoemakers in increasing numbers set up shops without benefit of mastership and produced cheaper coats and shoes in defiance of guild regulations. In the silk workshops of Lyons, both masters and journeymen were compelled to labor without distinction of status for piece rates (wages paid per finished article, rather than per hour) set by merchandising middlemen and far below an equitable level in the opinion of the silk workers. Artisans like these, compelled to work for low wages at the behest of profiteering middlemen, grew increasingly restive. In France and Germany, journeymen's associations had originated as social and mutual-aid organizations for young men engaged in "tramping" the country to gain experience in their trade. In some instances, however, these associations fostered the development of a trade consciousness that led to strikes and boycotts against masters and middlemen over wages and working conditions. An imperial law passed in Germany in 1731 deprived the associations of their right to organize, and required journeymen to carry a certificate of identification as testimony of their respectability during their travels.

At the bottom of urban society was a mass of semi-skilled and unskilled workers: carters and porters; stevedores and dockers; water carriers and sweepers; seamstresses, laundresses, cleaners, and domestic servants. These men and women, like their rural counterparts, lived on the margins of life, constantly battling the trade cycles, seasonal unemployment, and epidemics that threatened their ability to survive. A number existed in shanties on the edges of towns and cities. In Genoa, the homeless poor were sold as galley slaves each winter. In Venice, the poor lived on decrepit barges under the city's bridges. A French ordinance of 1669 ordered the destruction of all houses "built on poles by vagabonds and useless members of society." Deprived of the certainty of steady work, these people were prey not only to economic fluctuations and malevolent "acts of God," but to a social system that left them without any "privilege" or "freedom" whatsoever.

THE PROBLEM OF POVERTY

Attitudes toward poverty varied from country to country. Most localities extended the concept of orders to include the poor: the "deserving"—usually orphans, the insane, the aged, the infirm; and the "undeserving"—able-bodied men and women who were out of work or who, even though employed, could not support themselves and their families. The authorities tended to assume in the latter case that poverty was the result of personal failings; few made a connection between general economic circumstances and the plight of the individual poor. For the deserving, private charitable organizations, such as those in France founded by the order of Saint Vincent de Paul and by the Sisters of Charity, provided assistance. For the undeserving, there was harsh treatment at the hands of the state whose concern to alleviate extreme deprivation arose more from a desire to avert public disorder than from motives of human charity. Food riots were common occurrences. In times of scarcity the French government frequently intervened to reduce the price of grain, hoping thereby to prevent an outbreak of rioting. Nevertheless, riots occurred. When property damage resulted, the ringleaders were generally severely punished, usually by hanging. The remainder of

Hanging Thieves. This seventeenth-century engraving is designed to teach a lesson. Troops stand by and priests bless the condemned criminals as they are executed by the dozen. "At last," the engraver's caption reads, "these infamous lost souls are hung like unhappy fruit."

the crowd was often left untouched by the law, a fact suggesting the degree to which governments were prepared to tolerate rioting itself as a means of dealing with the chronic consequences of poverty.

Poverty remained a central and intractable problem for the governments of all European countries. Poor vagrants were perceived as a serious threat to social tranquillity. They were therefore frequently rounded up at harvesttime to keep them from plundering the fields. Vagrants and other chronically unemployed persons were placed in poorhouses, where conditions were little better than those in prisons. Often the very young, the very old, the sick, and the insane were housed together with hardened criminals. Poor relief in England was administered parish by parish in accordance with a law passed in 1601. Relief was tied to a "law of settlement," which stipulated that paupers might receive aid only if still residing in the parish of their birth. An unemployed weaver who had migrated fifty miles in search of work could thus expect assistance only if he returned home again. In the late eighteenth century, several European countries established modest public works programs in an attempt to relieve poverty by reducing unemployment. France, for example, undertook road-building projects in the 1770s under the auspices of its progressive finance minister, Turgot. But generally speaking, indigence was perceived not as a social ill for which a remedy might be sought, but as an indelible stigma demarking those at the bottom of society.

EDUCATION AND LITERACY

European social institutions reflected the patterns of hierarchy. Nowhere was this more apparent than in the field of education. One barrier—a knowledge of Latin—separated nobles and a fair number of scholars and professionals from the commercial middle ranks; a second—the ability to read and write—separated the middle from the rest. Noblemen were generally educated by private tutors; though they might attend university for a time, they did so not in preparation for a profession but to receive further educational "finishing." Indeed, during the late seventeenth and eighteenth centuries, universities more or less surrendered intellectual leadership to various academies established with royal patronage by European monarchs to enhance their own reputations as well as to encourage the advancement of science and the arts: the Royal Society of London, founded by Charles II in 1660; the French Academy of Sciences, a project on which Louis XIV lavished a good deal of ostentatious attention; and the Berlin Royal Academy of Science and Letters, patronized by Frederick the Great of Prussia in the eighteenth century. Few noblemen had the interest or the education to participate in the activities of these august organizations, which were not, in any case, teaching institutions. Far better suited to their needs and inclinations was "the grand tour," often of many months' duration, which led the young nobleman through the capitals of Europe, and during which he

HOW DID THE LIVES OF EASTERN AND WESTERN EUROPEAN PEASANTS DIFFER?

LIFE WITHIN A SOCIETY OF ORDERS   587

was expected to acquire a kind of international politesse. One observer, commenting on the habits of young British noblemen abroad, remarked, "they game; purchase pictures, mutilated statues, and mistresses to the astonishment of all beholders."

Endowed, fee-charging institutions for the training of a governmental elite existed in France (the *collège*) and Spain (the *colegio mayor*) and in Germany and Austria (the *gymnasium*). Here the emphasis was by no means on "practical" subjects such as modern language or mathematics, but on the mastery of Greek and Latin translation and composition, the intellectual badge of the educated elite. An exception was the Prussian University of Halle, designed to teach a professional elite; a contemporary described that institution as teaching only what was "rational, useful, and practical."

Boys from the middle orders destined to enter the family business or profession as a rule attended small private academies where the curriculum included the sort of "useful" instruction ignored in the collèges and gymnasia. Girls, from both the upper and the middle orders, were almost invariably educated at home, receiving little more than rudimentary instruction in gentlewomanly subjects such as modern language, literature, and music, if from the noble ranks; and a similar, if slightly more practical training, if from the bourgeoisie.

No European country undertook the task of providing primary education to all its citizens until the middle of the eighteenth century, when Frederick the Great in Prussia and the Habsburg monarchs Maria Theresa and her son Joseph II in Austria instituted systems of compulsory attendance. Available evidence suggests that their results fell far short of expectation. An early nineteenth century survey from the relatively enlightened Prussian province of Cleves revealed dilapidated schools, poorly attended classes, and an incompetent corps of teachers. Educational conditions were undoubtedly worse in most other European communities.

Though modern scholars can make no more than educated guesses, it appears certain that literacy rates increased considerably in the seventeenth and eighteenth centuries; in England, from one in four males in 1600 to one in two by 1800; in France, from 29 percent of the male population in 1686 to 47 percent in 1786. Literacy among women grew as well, though their rate of increase generally lagged behind that of men: only 27 percent of the female population in France was literate in 1786. Naturally, such rates varied according to particular localities and circumstances, and from country to country. Literacy was higher in urban areas that contained a large proportion of artisans. In rural eastern Europe, literacy remained extremely low (20 to 30 percent) well into the nineteenth century. Notwithstanding state-directed efforts in Prussia and Austria, the rise in literacy was largely the result of a growing determination on the part of religiously minded reformers to teach the poor to read and write as a means of encouraging obedience to divine and secular authority. A Sunday-school movement in eighteenth-century Britain and similar activities among the Christian Brotherhood in France are clear evidence of this trend.

POPULAR CULTURE

Though the majority of the common people were probably no more than barely literate, they possessed a flourishing culture of their own. Village life, particularly in Roman Catholic countries, centered about the church, to which men and women would go on Sundays not only to worship but to socialize. Much of the remainder of their day of rest would be devoted to participation in village games. Religion provided the opportunity for association and for a welcome break from the daily work routines. Pilgrimages to a nearby shrine, for example, would include a procession of villagers led by one of their number carrying an image of the village's patron saint and accompanied by drinking, dancing, and picnicking. In towns, Catholics joined organizations called "confraternities" in France, Italy, Austria, and the Netherlands, which provided mutual aid and a set of common rituals and traditions centered around a patron saint. Religious community was expressed as well in popular Protestant movements that arose in the eighteenth century: Pietism on the Continent and Methodism in England. Both emphasized the importance of personal salvation through faith and the potential worth of every human soul regardless of station. Both therefore appealed particularly to people whose position within the community had heretofore been presumed to be without any value. Though Methodism's founder, John Wesley (1703–1791), preached obedience to earthly authority,

> The rise in literacy was largely the result of a growing determination on the part of religiously minded reformers to teach the poor to read and write as a means of encouraging obedience to divine and secular authority.

OPPOSITION TO THE EDUCATION OF THE LOWER CLASSES

During the eighteenth century, education began to appeal more and more to the laboring classes as a route to social advancement. Not everyone welcomed this development, however. Some, like the two authors cited here, argued that education would simply make such persons dissatisfied with their "natural" station in life.

L. R. CARADEUC DE LA CHALOTAIS, *Essay on National Education [France, 1763]*

Today, even the lower classes want to study. Laborers and artisans send their children to boarding schools in the small towns where living is cheap, and when they have received a wretched education, which has taught them merely to despise their fathers' trades, they fling themselves into the monasteries, become priests or officers of justice, and frequently turn out to be a danger to society. . . . The good of society requires that the lower classes' knowledge should go no further than their occupations. No man who can see beyond his depressing trade will ply it with patience and courage. The lower classes scarcely need to know how to read or write except for those members of it who live by these skills or are helped by them to make their living. . . . [France, 1763]

SARAH TRIMMER, *Reflections upon the Education of Children in Charity Schools [Britain, 1792]*

However desirable it may be to rescue the lower kinds of people from ignorance . . . it cannot be right to train them all in a way which will probably raise their ideas above the very lowest occupations of life and disqualify them for those servile offices which must be filled by some members of the community, and in which they may be equally happy with the highest, if they will do their duty. . . . The children of the poor should not be educated in such a manner as to set them above the occupations of humble life, or so as to make them uncomfortable among their equals. [Britain, 1792]

Julia O'Faolain and Lauro Martines, eds. *Not in God's Image: Women in History from the Greeks to the Victorians* (New York: Harper and Row, 1973), pp. 245–246.

---

his willingness to rely on working men and women as preachers and organizers gave them a new sense of personal importance.

Popular culture often combined in one event traditions that were part religious, part secular, and, indeed, part pagan. One such occasion was Carnival, that vibrant pre-Lenten celebration indigenous not only to Mediterranean Europe but to Germany and Austria as well. Carnival represented an opportunity for common folk to cast aside the burdens and restraints imposed upon their order by secular authority. Performances and processions celebrated a "world turned upside down." Popular throughout much of Europe since the later Middle Ages, this theme appealed to commoners for a variety of ambiguous psychological reasons, but in large part, certainly, as a way of avenging symbolically the economic and social oppression under which they lived. For a few days, the oppressed played the

HOW DID THE LIVES OF EASTERN AND WESTERN EUROPEAN PEASANTS DIFFER?

LIFE WITHIN A SOCIETY OF ORDERS   589

French Tavern. Often located outside the city limits so as to avoid the payment of municipal taxes, taverns such as this provided a gathering place for workers to drink, gossip, and relax after the day's labors. The tavern also served as a convenient place for public readings and for airing common grievances.

role of the oppressor and rulers were made to look like fools and knaves. In parades, men dressed as kings walked barefoot while peasants rode on horseback or in carriages; the poor threw pretend money to the rich. These occasions, although emphasizing social divisions, bound communities to a common cultural center, since, through most of the early modern period, both rich and poor celebrated together, as they did on major religious holidays. Annual harvest festivals, once sponsored by the church, became increasingly secular celebrations of release from backbreaking labor, punctuated by feasting, drinking, sporting, and lovemaking. Fairs and traveling circuses brought something of distant places and people into lives bound to one spot. The drudgery of everyday life was also relieved by horse races, cockfights, and bear baiting. Taverns played an even more constant role in the daily life of the village, providing a place for men to gather over tobacco and drink and indulge in gossip and gambling.

Laboring men and women depended on an oral tradition of myth, legend, and superstition to steady their lives and give them point and purpose. Stories in books sold at fairs by peddlers were passed on by those who could read. They told of heroes and saints, and of kings such as Charlemagne whose paternal concern for his common subjects led him into battle against his selfish nobility. Belief in villains matched belief in heroes. Witchcraft, as we have seen, was a reality for much of the period. So was Satan. So was any supernatural force, whether for good or evil, that could help people make sense of a world in which they, more than any, were victims of events beyond their control.

Though increasingly secularized, popular customs, celebrations, and beliefs remained a stabilizing force in early modern Europe. They were the cultural expression of that social order to which the vast majority of Europeans belonged. Popular culture in the main tended to reinforce the traditions and assumptions of order and hierarchy. Peasants and urban workers worshiped saints and venerated heroic rulers, thereby accepting the authority of the established, ordered society of which they were a part. They were seldom satisfied with their lot, yet they were as seldom willing to question the social structure they saw as a bulwark against the swift changes so often surrounding them. Popular culture helped to bind men and women to what civilization had been, as capitalism and mercantilism impelled them in the direction of what it would become.

Conclusion

Between 1600 and 1800, the European economy grew steadily larger and more complex. Powered by the profits of overseas colonial empires and fueled by enslaved African labor, European trade expanded enormously despite the efforts of mercantilist governments to restrict or channel it toward the direct support of political rulers. New institutions, including banks and joint stock companies, emerged to meet the capital needs of this expanding commercial economy. Industrial production also grew rapidly, in part as a result of investments in new, more efficient machines, but in part because wages for industrial workers remained low.

From the mid-eighteenth century on, economic growth was also driven by the rapidly increasing European population. Behind this population growth lay changes in agrarian organization and in crop rotation systems that vastly increased the productivity of European agriculture, albeit at the cost of considerable social and cultural dislocation among traditional peasant farmers. Throughout European society, the economic changes of the seventeenth and eighteenth centuries were undermining the rigidly hierarchical presumptions of a social order whose structures and categories had changed little since the Middle Ages. In western Europe, a new, urban-based middle class was emerging whose values and outlook differed both from the nobility and from the rural peasantry. In eastern Europe, by contrast, these same economic changes actually strengthened the traditional control that nobles exercised over their serfs. For the moment, Europeans in both east and west continued to believe that their social order was divinely ordained and immutable. But storm clouds were gathering that would soon wash away this entire early modern world in the tumult of the French Revolution.

Selected Readings

Berlin, Ira. *Many Thousands Gone: The First Two Centuries of Slavery in North America.* Cambridge, Mass., 1998. An excellent new synthesis, which tells the story from the perspective of the enslaved.

Burke, Peter. *Popular Culture in Early Modern Europe.* London, 1978. An influential account; somewhat dated, but colorful and full of interesting detail.

Bush, M. L., ed. *Social Orders and Social Classes in Europe since 1500.* New York, 1992. Essays on a broad range of subjects, including the church, tenant rights, and the concept of class.

Cameron, Euan, ed. *Early Modern Europe: An Oxford History.* Oxford and New York, 1999. A wide-ranging and stimulating multiauthor survey, topically arranged, that spans the entire period from the Renaissance to the French Revolution.

Canny, Nicholas, ed. *The Oxford History of the British Empire.* Volume I: *The Origins of Empire: British Overseas Enterprise to the Close of the Seventeenth Century.* Oxford and New York, 1998. A definitive, multiauthor account.

Cressy, David. *Birth, Marriage, and Death: Ritual, Religion, and the Life Cycle in Tudor and Stuart England.* Oxford and New York, 1997. A huge, wonderful book, full of arresting detail and riveting stories about daily life in early modern England.

Davis, Natalie Zemon. *Society and Culture in Early Modern France.* Stanford, 1975. Eight scintillating essays by a pioneer in the use of anthropological methods for the study of early modern European history.

———. *Women on the Margins: Three Seventeenth-Century Lives.* Cambridge, Mass., 1995. Artful biographical accounts by a master historian.

De Vries, Jan. *The Economy of Europe in an Age of Crisis, 1600–1750.* Cambridge and New York, 1976. Still the best survey of the economic history of the period.

Doyle, William. *The Old European Order, 1660–1800.* Oxford and New York, 1992. The best recent account of European society during the *ancien régime*, with chapters on population, trade, social orders, and public affairs.

Goubert, Pierre. *The Ancien Régime: French Society, 1600–1750.* London, 1973. A discussion with plentiful extracts from primary sources; particularly strong in its descriptions of rural life.

Hufton, Owen. *The Prospect Before Her: A History of Women in Western Europe, 1500–1800.* New York, 1996. A great book by an important social historian; extensive bibliographies.

Israel, Jonathan I. *Dutch Primacy in World Trade, 1585–1740.* Oxford and New York, 1989. An account of the rise and fall of the Dutch trading empire by the preeminent English-language authority.

———. *The Dutch Republic: Its Rise, Greatness, and Fall, 1477–1806.* Oxford and New York, 1995. The standard English-language account.

———. *European Jewry in the Age of Mercantilism, 1550–1750,* 3d ed. Portland, Ore., 1998. The best account of the economic and political context of early modern Jewish history.

Klein, Herbert S. *The Atlantic Slave Trade.* Cambridge and New York, 1999. An excellent and accessible introductory survey by a leading quantitative historian.

McManners, John. *Church and Society in Eighteenth-Century France.* 2 vols. Oxford and New York, 1998. A great book, both comprehensive and wise.

Ménétra, Jacques Louis. *Journal of My Life.* Translated by Arthur Goldhammer. Introduction by Daniel Roche. New York, 1986. The autobiography of a Parisian glazier who played checkers with Rousseau and was an eyewitness to the French Revolution.

Merrick, Jeffrey, and Bryant Ragan, eds. *Homosexuality in Early Modern France: A Documentary Collection.* Oxford and New York, 2000. An outstanding and scholarly collection of original sources, most previously unknown.

Mintz, Sidney. *Sweetness and Power.* New York, 1985. Anthropological investigation of the impact of sugar on Western societies.

Muir, Edward. *Ritual in Early Modern Europe.* Cambridge and New York, 1997. A sophisticated study of one of the central features of early modern life.

Northrup, David, ed. *The Atlantic Slave Trade.* Lexington, Mass., 1994. A judicious collection of primary and secondary sources that examines the entire sweep of the trade, from beginnings to the fight for abolition.

Overton, Mark. *Agricultural Revolution in England: The Transformation of the Agrarian Economy, 1500–1850.* Cambridge and New York, 1996. Authoritative and wide ranging.

Sabean, David. *Power in the Blood: Popular Culture and Village Discourse in Early Modern Germany.* New York, 1984. Anthropologically influenced investigation of peasant life in a single German village.

Schama, Simon. *The Embarrassment of Riches: An Interpretation of Dutch Culture in the Golden Age.* New York, 1988. A controversial account that describes the social and psychological tensions produced by the growing wealth of seventeenth-century Holland.

Thomas, Hugh. *The Slave Trade: The History of the Atlantic Slave Trade, 1440–1870.* London and New York, 1997. A survey notable for its breadth and depth of coverage, as well as for its attractive prose style.

Tracy, James D. *The Rise of Merchant Empires: Long-Distance Trade in the Early Modern World, 1350–1750.* Cambridge and New York, 1993. Important collection of essays by leading authorities.

Underdown, David. *Fire from Heaven: The Life of an English Town in the Seventeenth Century.* New York, 1992. A superb local study of the impact of Puritanism on an English town.

Wiesner, Merry E. *Women and Gender in Early Modern Europe,* 2d ed. Cambridge and New York, 2000. A thorough revision of a pathbreaking book

Wrigley, Edward Anthony. *People, Cities, and Wealth: The Transformation of Traditional Society.* Oxford and New York, 1987. Assesses the demographic impact of urbanization on European society since the sixteenth century.

———. *English Population History from Family Reconstitution, 1580–1837.* Cambridge and New York, 1997. The life's work of a pioneering historical demographer.

Young, Arthur. *Travels in France during the Years 1787, 1788, 1789.* London, various editions. Vivid observations by an English traveler.

CHAPTER SEVENTEEN

THE AGE
OF ABSOLUTISM,
1660–1789

T HE PERIOD FROM AROUND 1660 (when the English monarchy was restored, and Louis XIV of France began his personal rule) to 1789 (when the French Revolution erupted) is traditionally known as the age of absolutism. *Absolutism* was a political theory that encouraged rulers to claim complete sovereignty within their territories. To seventeenth- and eighteenth-century absolutists, complete sovereignty meant that a ruler could make law, do justice, direct a complex administrative bureaucracy, declare war, and levy taxation without needing the formal approval of churchmen, parliaments, assemblies, or local authorities for his or her policies. Absolutism therefore involved subordinating or eliminating the independence of all other governing authorities, such as towns, representative assemblies, or ecclesiastical councils, that might stand between the will of the sovereign ruler and the obedience of his or her subjects. Frequently, assertions of absolute authority were buttressed by claims that rulers exercised their authority over their kingdoms or territories by the same divine right that established a father's absolute authority over his household. After the chaos of the previous century, many Europeans came to believe that only by exalting the sovereignty of such absolute, "patriarchal" rulers over their families and their kingdoms could order be restored to European life.

Like all such labels, the "age of absolutism" is useful only so long as we acknowledge its limitations. In the first place, this label narrows our attention to politics, diplomacy, and economic policy. Although these are the primary subjects of this chapter, they are not the only important areas in which change was occuring during the age of absolutism. The social, demographic, agricultural, and economic developments of this period have already been described in Chapter 16. Intellectural, cultural, and religious changes will be discussed in Chapter 18. We have divided these changes in order to present them clearly; but we must remember that to the people of the later seventeenth and eighteenth centuries, they were a connected whole.

FOCUS QUESTIONS

- What were the aims of absolutist rulers?
- How did Louis XIV try to strengthen his control over France?
- What was the main challenge for most absolutist rulers?
- How was Russian absolutism unique?
- What was political power according to Locke?
- What was the "balance of power"?
- How did seventeenth- and eighteenth-century forms of absolutism differ?
- How did the balance of power shift in the eighteenth century?

Nor was absolutism the only political theory according to which European governments sought to rule during this period. In England, Scotland, the Dutch Republic, Switzerland, Venice, Sweden, and Poland-Lithuania, limited monarchies or republics continued to operate effectively; whereas in Russia, an autocratic tradition was emerging that envisioned the tsar as the absolute owner of his empire and as the unrestricted arbiter of his subjects' lives.

Finally, we must acknowledge the practical limitations of absolutism itself, even in such prototypically "abolutist" monarchies as that of King Louis XIV of France. Although absolutist rulers might claim the authority to make law by their own will, all acknowledged that they must nonetheless act in accordance with the rule of law. Law continued to have an authority independent of the will of any particular prince; and the traditional privileges of the social orders in European society (the nobility, the clergy, and even the common people) were still regarded as having a legal force that even an absolute monarch was obliged to acknowledge and respect. Nor, in fact, was the "intermediate" authority of representative assemblies, towns, and ecclesiastical councils so inconsequential as absolutist theory declared that it should be. In practice, even the most absolute rulers of seventeenth- and eighteenth-century western Europe could rule effectively only so long as their subjects were prepared, at least tacitly, to consent to their policies. When opposition erupted, even absolutists were forced to back down. And when, in 1789, an outright political revolution occurred, the entire structure of absolutism came crashing to the ground.

THE APPEAL AND JUSTIFICATION OF ABSOLUTISM

What were the aims of absolutist rulers?

Absolutism appealed to Europeans for the same reasons that mercantilism did. Just as mercantilists maintained that economic regimentation would produce prosperity, so absolutists contended that social and political harmony would result when subjects obeyed their divinely sanctioned rulers in all matters. Abso-

lutist monarchs insisted, in turn, on *their* duty to teach their subjects how to order their domestic affairs. As the eighteenth-century ruler of the German principality of Baden expressed it: "We must make them, whether they like it or not, into free, opulent and law-abiding citizens."

Absolutism's promise of stability, prosperity, and order was an appealing alternative to the disorder of the iron century that preceded it. This was especially the case for the quintessential absolutist monarch, Louis XIV of France. The political disturbances of his minority (known collectively as the *Fronde*) left a life-long impression on the young king. When marauding Parisians entered the bedchamber of the eight-year-old king one night in 1651, Louis saw the intrusion as a horrid affront not only to his own person, but to the majesty of the French state he personified. Squabbles among the nobility and criticisms of royal policy by the Paris *Parlement* during his minority convinced him that he must exercise his powers and prerogatives assertively and without limitation if France was to survive and prosper as a great European state.

To accomplish these objectives, such absolutist monarchs as Louis XIV sought to gather into their own hands command of the state's armed forces, control over its legal system, and the right to collect and spend the state's financial resources at will. These goals in turn required an efficient bureaucracy that owed its allegiance directly to the monarchy itself, and not to the towns, provinces, or privileged social groups over which that bureaucracy ruled. Creating such a centralized bureaucracy was expensive, but it was essential to the larger absolutist goal of restricting or even destroying the privileged "special interests" that had hindered the free exercise of royal power in the past. The legally privileged estates of nobility and clergy, the political authority of semi-autonomous regions, and the pretensions of independent-minded representative assemblies such as parliaments, diets, or estates general, were all obstacles in the eyes of absolutists to the achievement of strong, centralized monarchical government. The history of absolutism is, as much as anything, a history of attempts by aspiring absolutists to bring these institutions to heel.

In most Protestant countries, the independent power of the church had already been subordinated to the interests of the state when the age of absolutism began. In France, Spain, and Austria, by contrast, where Roman Catholicism remained the state religion, during the late seventeenth and eighteenth centuries monarchs devoted concerted attention to "nationaliz-

HOW DID LOUIS XIV TRY TO STRENGTHEN HIS CONTROL OVER FRANCE?

THE ABSOLUTISM OF LOUIS XIV   595

ing" the church and its clergy within their territories. These efforts built on the concordats that the French and Spanish monarchies had extracted from the papacy during the fifteenth and sixteenth centuries, but they went even further in consolidating authority over the church into the hands of the monarchy. Even Charles III, the devout Spanish king who ruled from 1759 to 1788, pressed successfully for a papal concordat granting the Spanish monarchy control over ecclesiastical appointments and establishing his right to sanction (or prevent) the proclamation of papal bulls affecting Spain.

The most important potential opponents of royal absolutism were not churchmen, however, but nobles. Monarchs dealt with this threat in various ways. Louis XIV attempted to control the French aristocrats by depriving them of political power while increasing their social prestige by associating them directly with his own lavish court at Versailles. Peter the Great, the talented but erratic tsar of early eighteenth-century Russia, required noblemen to enter government service. Later in the century, Catherine II struck a bargain whereby in return for vast estates and a variety of social and economic privileges including exemption from taxation, the Russian nobility virtually surrendered the administrative and political power of the state into the empress's hands. In Prussia, under Frederick the Great, the army was staffed by nobles, as was generally the case in Spain, France, and England. But in eighteenth-century Austria, the emperor Joseph II adopted a policy of confrontation rather than accommodation, denying the nobility exemption from taxation and deliberately blurring the distinctions between nobles and commoners.

Struggles between monarchs and nobles frequently had implications for the additional struggle between local and central government. Absolutists in France waged a constant but never entirely successful war against the autonomy of provincial institutions, often headed by nobles, just as the Spanish monarchy, centered in Castile, battled independent-minded nobles in Aragon and Catalunya. Prussian rulers intruded into the governance of formerly "free" cities, assuming policing and revenue powers over their inhabitants. And in Austria, the Habsburg emperors tried to suppress the largely autonomous nobility of Hungary. Rarely, however, was confrontation between crown and nobility successful in the long run. The most successful absolutist monarchies of the eighteenth century succeeded in establishing a political and social order in which nobles came to see their own interests as tied to

the those of the monarchy. For this reason, cooperation more often characterized the relations between kings and nobles during the eighteenth century than did conflict.

THE ABSOLUTISM OF LOUIS XIV

How did Louis XIV try to strengthen his control over France?

Examine a portrait of Louis XIV (1643–1715) in court robes; it is all but impossible to discern the human being behind the façade of the absolute monarch. That façade was carefully and artfully constructed by Louis,

Louis XIV, the Sun King. This portrait by Hyacinthe Rigaud illustrates the degree to which absolute monarchy was defined in terms of studied performance.

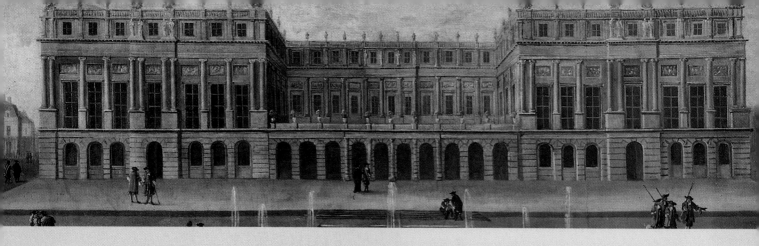

ABSOLUTISM AND PATRIARCHY

These selections show how two political theorists justified royal absolutism by deriving it from the absolute authority of a father over his household. Bishop Jacques-Benigne Bossuet (1627–1704) was a famous French preacher who served as tutor to the son of King Louis XIV of France before becoming bishop of Meaux. Sir Robert Filmer (1588–1653) was an English political theorist. Filmer's works attracted particular attention in the 1680s, when John Locke directed the first of his Two Treatises of Government to refuting Filmer's views on the patriarchal nature of royal authority.

BOSSUET ON THE NATURE OF MONARCHICAL AUTHORITY

There are four characteristics or qualities essential to royal authority. First, royal authority is sacred; Secondly, it is paternal; Thirdly, it is absolute; Fourthly, it is subject to reason. . . . All power comes from God. . . . Thus princes act as ministers of God, and his lieutenants on earth. It is through them that he exercises his empire. . . . In this way . . . the royal throne is not the throne of a man, but the throne of God himself. . . .

We have seen that kings hold the place of God, who is the true Father of the human race. We have also seen that the first idea of power that there was among men, is that of paternal power; and that kings were fashioned on the model of fathers. Moreover, all the world agrees that obedience, which is due to public power, is only found . . . in the precept which obliges one to honor his parents. From all this it appears that the name "king" is a father's name, and that goodness is the most natural quality in kings. . . .

Royal authority is absolute. In order to make this term odious and insupportable, many pretend to con-fuse absolute government and arbitrary government. But nothing is more distinct, as we shall make clear when we speak of justice. . . . The prince need account to no one for what he ordains. . . . Without this absolute authority, he can neither do good nor suppress evil: his power must be such that no one can hope to escape him. . . . [T]he sole defense of individuals against the public power must be their innocence. . . .

One must, then, obey princes as if they were justice itself, without which there is neither order nor justice in affairs. They are gods, and share in some way in divine independence. . . . It follows from this that he who does not want to obey the prince . . . is condemned irremissibly to death as an enemy of public peace and of human society. . . . The prince can correct himself when he knows that he has done badly; but against his authority there can be no remedy. . . .

Jacques-Benigne Bossuet. *Politics Drawn from the Very Words of Holy Scripture,* translated by Patrick Riley. (Cambridge: Cambridge University Press, 1990), pp. 46–69 and 81–83.

FILMER ON THE PATRIARCHAL ORIGINS OF ROYAL AUTHORITY

The first government in the world was monarchical, in the father of all flesh, Adam being commanded to multiply, and people the earth, and to subdue it, and having dominion given him over all creatures, was thereby the monarch of the whole world; none of his posterity had any right to possess anything, but by his grant or permission, or by succession from him. . . . Adam was the father, king and lord over his family: a son, a subject, and a servant or a slave were one and the same thing at first. . . .

I cannot find any one place or text in the Bible where any power . . . is given to a people either to govern themselves, or to choose themselves governors, or to alter the manner of government at their pleasure. The power of government is settled and fixed by the commandment of "honour thy father"; if there were a higher power than the fatherly, then this commandment could not stand and be observed. . . .

All power on earth is either derived or usurped from the fatherly power, there being no other original to be found of any power whatsoever. For if there should be granted two sorts of power without any subordination of one to the other, they would be in perpetual strife which should be the supreme, for two supremes cannot agree. If the fatherly power be supreme, then the power of the people must be subordinate and depend on it. If the power of the people be supreme, then the fatherly power must submit to it, and cannot be exercised without the licence of the people, which must quite destroy the frame and course of nature. Even the power which God himself exercises over mankind is by right of fatherhood: he is both the king and father of us all. As God has exalted the dignity of earthly kings . . . by saying they are gods, so . . . he has been pleased. . . . [t]o humble himself by assuming the title of a king to express his power, and not the title of any popular government.

Robert Filmer, *Observations upon Aristotle's Politiques* (1652) in *Divine Right and Democracy: An Anthology of Political Writing in Stuart England,* edited by David Wootton. (Harmondsworth: Penguin Books, 1986), pp. 110–118.

who recognized, perhaps more fully than any other early modern ruler, the importance of theater as a means of establishing his authority. Louis and his successors deliberately staged theatrical demonstrations of their sovereignty to enhance their position as rulers endowed with godlike powers and far removed from common humanity.

PERFORMING ROYALTY AT VERSAILLES

Louis's exhibitions of his sovereignty were performed most elaborately at his palace at Versailles, the town outside of Paris to which he moved his court. The palace and its grounds became a stage on which Louis attempted to mesmerize the aristocracy into obedience by his performance of the daily rituals and demonstrations of royalty. The main façade of the palace was a third of a mile in length. Inside, tapestries and paintings celebrated French military victories and royal triumphs, while mirrors reflected shimmering light throughout the building. In the vast gardens outside, statues of the Greek sun god Apollo recalled Louis's claim to be the "Sun King" of France. Noblemen vied to attend him when he arose from bed, ate his meals (usually stone cold, having traveled the distance of several city blocks from royal kitchen to royal table),

strolled in his gardens (even the way the king walked was choreographed by the royal dancing master), or rode to the hunt. As Louis called himself the Sun King, so his court was the epicenter of his glittering royal resplendence. Louis required France's leading nobles to reside with him at Versailles for a portion of the year; the splendor of Louis's court was deliberately calculated to blind them to the possibility of disobedience, while raising their prestige by associating them directly with the king. Instead of plotting some minor treason on his estate, a marquis enjoyed the pleasure of knowing that on the morrow he would be privileged to engage the king in two or three minutes of vapid conversation as the royal party made its stately progress through the vast palace halls, whose smells were evidence of the absence of sanitation facilities and of the seamy side of absolutist grandeur. At the same time, however, the elaborate, almost impossibly detailed rules of etiquette around the court left these same privileged nobles in a state of constant suspense, forever fearful of offending the king by committing some trivial violation of proper manners.

Louis understood such theatricality as part of his duty as sovereign, a duty that he took with utmost seriousness. Though far from brilliant, he was hardworking and conscientious. Whether or not he actually re-

The Château of Versailles. Dramatically expanded by Louis XIV in the 1660s from a hunting lodge to the principal royal residence and the seat of government, the château became a monument to the international power and prestige of the Grand Monarch.

marked *"L'état, c'est moi"* ("I am the State"), he clearly saw himself as serving the interests of the State. As such, he also saw himself as personally responsible for the well-being of his subjects. "The deference and the respect that we receive from our subjects," he wrote in a memoir he prepared for his son on the art of ruling, "are not a free gift from them but payment for the justice and the protection that they expect from us. Just as they must honor us, we must protect and defend them."

ADMINISTRATION AND CENTRALIZATION

Louis defined his responsibility in absolutist terms: to concentrate royal power so as to produce domestic tranquillity. While coopting the nobility into his own theater of royalty, he conciliated the upper bourgeoisie by enlisting its members to assist him in the task of administration. He appointed them as *intendants*, responsible for administering and taxing the thirty-six *generalités*

into which France was divided. Intendants usually served outside the region where they were born, and were thus unconnected with the local elites over which they exercised authority. They held office at the king's pleasure, and were clearly "his" men. Other administrators, often from families newly ennobled as a reward for their administrative service, assisted in directing affairs of state from Versailles. These men were not actors in the theater of Louis the Sun King; rather, they were the hardworking assistants of Louis the royal custodian of his country's welfare.

Louis's bureaucrats devoted much of their time and energy to collecting the taxes necessary to finance the large standing army on which the king's aggressive and highly personal foreign policy depended. These personal elements of early modern absolutism are important to remark. Despite its pretensions to represent a political theory, absolutism was fundamentally a mechanism designed to assist ambitious monarchs in their determination to increase their own power through conquest and display. As such, it was enormously ex-

HOW DID LOUIS XIV TRY TO STRENGTHEN HIS CONTROL OVER FRANCE?

THE ABSOLUTISM OF LOUIS XIV   599

pensive. In addition to the *taille*, or land tax, which increased throughout the seventeenth century and on which a surtax was levied as well, Louis's government introduced a *capitation* (head tax) payable by all, and pressed successfully for the collection of indirect taxes on salt (the *gabelle*), wine, tobacco, and other products. Since the nobility was exempt from the *taille*, its burden fell most heavily on the peasantry, whose periodic local revolts Louis easily crushed.

Regional opposition—indeed, regionalism generally—was curtailed, but by no means eliminated, during Louis's reign. Although intendants and lesser administrators came from afar, did not speak the local dialect, and ignored local custom, they were generally obeyed. The semi-autonomous outer provinces of Brittany, Languedoc, and Franche-Comté (several of the territories known collectively as the *pays d'états*) suffered the crippling of their provincial Estates. To put an end to the power of regional *parlements*, Louis decreed that members of those bodies that refused to register his laws would be summarily exiled. The Estates General, the national French representative assembly last summoned in 1614 during the troubled regency that followed the death of Henry IV, did not meet again until 1789.

LOUIS XIV'S RELIGIOUS POLICIES

Louis was equally determined, both for reasons of state and of personal conscience, to impose religious unity upon the French. That task proved to be difficult and time consuming. The Huguenots were not the only source of religious heterodoxy in France. Quietists and Jansenists—both claiming to represent the "true" Roman faith—battled for adherents to their particular brand of Catholicism. Quietists preached retreat into personal mysticism, emphasizing a direct relationship between God and the individual human heart. Such doctrine, dispensing as it did with the intermediary services of the church and of the orthodox authority those services represented, was suspect in the eyes of absolutists wedded to the doctrine of *un roi, une loi, une foi* (one king, one law, one faith). Jansenism—a movement named for its founder Cornelius Jansen, a seventeenth-century bishop of Yprés—challenged the authority of the state church with an unorthodox doctrine of predestination, proclaiming the salvation of no more than an elected few.

Louis vigorously persecuted Quietists and Jansenists, offering them the choice of recanting or prison and exile.

Against the Huguenots, however, he waged an even sterner war. Protestant churches and schools were destroyed; Protestant families were forced to convert. In 1685, Louis revoked the Edict of Nantes, the legal foundation of the toleration Huguenots had enjoyed since 1598. French Protestants were thereafter denied civil rights, and their clerics were exiled. As a result, two hundred thousand religious refugees fled France for England, Holland, the Protestant states of Germany, and America, where their professional and artisanal skills made a significant contribution to economic prosperity. Among many other examples, the silk industries of Berlin and of Spitalfields, an urban quarter of London, were established by Huguenots fleeing Louis XIV's persecution.

COLBERT AND ROYAL FINANCE

Louis's drive for unification and centralization was assisted by his ability to rely on increased revenues. These revenues were largely the result of policies and programs initiated by Jean Baptiste Colbert (1619–1683), the country's finance minister from 1664 until his death. Colbert was an energetic and committed mercantilist who believed that until France could put its fiscal house in order, it could not achieve economic or political greatness. He tightened the process of tax collection, and he eliminated wherever possible the practice of tax farming, whereby collection agents were permitted to withhold a certain percentage of what they gathered for themselves. When Colbert assumed office, only about 25 percent of the taxes collected throughout the kingdom reached the treasury. By the time he died, that figure had risen to 80 percent.

Colbert's efforts were not limited to managing the public debt and ridding the tax system of inefficiencies. Under his direction, the state also sold public offices, including judgeships and mayoralities, on an increasing scale. Guilds purchased the right to enforce trade regulations. The state extracted a profit from every office it created and from every privilege it controlled, demonstrating once again the way in which economy and politics were inextricably intertwined.

> The state extracted a profit from every office it created and from every privilege it controlled, demonstrating the way in which economy and politics were inextricably intertwined.

Jean Baptiste Colbert.

As a mercantilist, Colbert did all he could to increase the nation's income by means of protection and regimentation. Tariffs he imposed in 1667 and 1668 were designed to discourage the importation of foreign goods into France. He invested in the improvement of France's roads and waterways. And he used state money to promote the growth of national industry, in particular the manufacture of goods such as silk, lace, tapestries, and glass, which had long been imported.

Yet Colbert's efforts to achieve national economic stability and self-sufficiency could not withstand the insatiable demands of Louis XIV's wars. Indeed, by the end of Louis's reign, the limitations of his absolutist ambitions were strikingly evident. His aggressive foreign policy lay in ruins, and the country's finances had been shattered by the increasing costs of war. Colbert himself foresaw Louis's ultimate failure when he lectured him in 1680, "Trade is the source of public finance and public finance is the vital nerve of war. . . . I beg your Majesty to permit me only to say to him that in war as in peace he has never consulted the amount of money available in determining his expenditures."

ABSOLUTISM IN CENTRAL AND EASTERN EUROPE, 1660–1720

What was the main challenge for most absolutist rulers?

The success Louis XIV enjoyed as an absolute monarch was due in part to his own abilities, and in part to the efforts of his advisors and administrators. But it rested also on the fact that he could claim to stand as the supreme embodiment of the nation of France. Despite its internal divisions, France was already a unified kingdom with a sense of national identity long before Louis XIV ascended its throne. In this respect, France differed profoundly from the empires, kingdoms, and principalities to its east. In central and eastern Europe, rulers faced a much more formidable task than did Louis as they attempted to weld their disparately constructed monarchies into united, centralized, absolutist states.

THE HOLY ROMAN EMPIRE

The Thirty Years' War delivered a final, fatal blow to the power of the Holy Roman empire—memorably described by the eighteenth-century French philosopher Voltaire as being "neither holy, nor Roman, nor an empire." Instead, power now lay in the hands of over three hundred princes, bishops, and magistrates, who would continue to govern the assorted states of Germany until the nineteenth century.

Despite the small size of their territories, many of these local rulers attempted nonetheless to establish themselves as absolutists, building lesser versions of Louis XIV's Versailles and remodeling their capital cities to serve as explicit expressions of their authority. Broad avenues led to monumental squares and eventually to the grand palace of the ruler. Whereas the crowded, twisted streets and passageways of medieval cities had tended to mask the inequalities of the social order by forcing different social classes to live together in close physical proximity, absolutist capital cities celebrated inequality, their planning and architecture deliberately emphasizing the vast distance that separated their rulers from those over whom they ruled.

Aspiring German absolutists also followed the

MERCANTILISM AND WAR

Jean-Baptiste Colbert (1619–1683) served as Louis XIV's finance minister from 1664 until his death. He worked assiduously to promote commerce, build up French industry, and increase exports. However much Colbert himself may have seen his economic policies as ends in themselves, to Louis they were always means to the end of waging war. Ultimately, Louis's wars undermined the prosperity that Colbert tried so hard to create. This memorandum, written to Louis in 1670, illustrates clearly the mercantlist presumptions of self-sufficiency on which Colbert operated: every item needed to build up the French navy must ultimately be produced in France, even if it could be acquired at less cost from elsewhere.

And since Your Majesty has wanted to work diligently at reestablishing his naval forces, and since afore that it has been necessary to make very great expenditures, since all merchandise, munitions and manufactured items formerly came from Holland and the countries of the North, it has been absolutely necessary to be especially concerned with finding within the realm, or with establishing in it, everything which might be necessary for this great plan.

To this end, the manufacture of tar was established in Médoc, Auvergne, Dauphiné, and Provence; iron cannons, in Burgundy, Nivernois, Saintonge and Périgord; large anchors in Dauphiné, Nivernois, Brittany, and Rochefort; sailcloth for the Levant, in Dauphiné; coarse muslin, in Auvergne; all the implements for pilots and others, at Dieppe and La Rochelle; the cutting of wood suitable for vessels, in Burgundy, Dauphiné, Brittany, Normandy, Poitou, Saintonge, Provence, Guyenne, and the Pyrenees; masts, of a sort once unknown in this realm, have been found in Provence, Languedoc, Auvergne, Dauphiné,

and in the Pyrenees. Iron, which was obtained from Sweden and Biscay, is currently manufactured in the realm. Fine hemp for ropes, which came from Prussia and from Piedmont, is currently obtained in Burgundy, Mâconnais, Bresse, Dauphiné; and markets for it have since been established in Berry and in Auvergne, which always provides money in these provinces and keeps it within the realm.

In a word, everything serving for the construction of vessels is currently established in the realm, so that Your Majesty can get along without foreigners for the navy and will even, in a short time, be able to supply them and gain their money in this fashion. And it is with this same objective of having everything necessary to provide abundantly for his navy and that of his subjects that he is working at the general reform of all the forests in his realm, which, being as carefully preserved as they are at present, will abundantly produce all the wood necessary for this.

Charles W. Cole, *Colbert and a Century of French Mercantilism*, 2 vols. (New York: Columbia University Press, 1939), p. 320.

French example by maintaining standing armies and and imposing local tariffs and tolls that severely hampered economic development within the region as a whole. Such rulers often prided themselves on their in-

dependence from imperial control, but many were in fact the political clients of France. A sizable portion of the money Louis devoted to the conduct of foreign affairs went into the pockets of these German princelings, who were happy to form alliances against their own emperor.

BRANDENBURG-PRUSSIA

Most notable among these middle-sized German states was Brandenburg-Prussia, whose emergence as a power of consequence during this period was the result of the single-minded determination of its rulers. Foremost among these was Frederick William, elector of Brandenburg from 1640 to 1688, whose abilities have earned him the title of the "Great Elector." The rise of Brandenburg-Prussia from initial insignificance, poverty, and devastation in the wake of the Thirty Years' War resulted from three basic achievements that can be credited to the Great Elector. First, he pursued an adroit foreign policy that enabled him to establish effective sovereignty over the widely dispersed and underdeveloped territories under his rule: Brandenburg, a large but not particularly productive territory in north-central Germany; Prussia, a duchy to the east that was dangerously exposed on three sides to Poland; and a sprinkling of tiny states—Cleves, Mark, and Ravensberg—to the west. By siding with Poland in a war against Sweden in the late 1650s, the Great Elector obtained the Polish

king's surrender of nominal overlordship in East Prussia. And by some crafty diplomatic shuffling during the 1670s, he secured his western provinces from French interference by returning Pomerania, captured in a recent war, to France's Swedish allies.

Frederick William's second achievement was to create a large standing army, which became the primary instrument of his diplomatic successes. By 1688, Brandenburg-Prussia had thirty thousand troops permanently under arms. The Elector's ability to sustain an army of this size in a state with comparatively limited resources was a measure of the degree to which the army more than repaid its costs. Beyond its diplomatic and military value, the army ensured for the elector and his successors absolute political control by fostering obedience among the populace—an obedience they were prepared to observe if their lands might be spared the devastation of another Thirty Years' War.

The third factor contributing to the emergence of Brandenburg-Prussia as an international power was the Elector's imposition of an effective system of taxation and his creation of a bureaucracy to administer it. Here he struck an important bargain with the powerful and privileged landlords (*Junkers*) without whose cooperation his programs would have had no chance of success. In return for an agreement that allowed them to reduce their peasant underlings to the status of serfs, the Junkers gave away their right to oppose a permanent tax system—provided, of course, that they were made immune from the payment of taxes themselves. As in most European countries, taxes in absolutist Prussia thus fell most heavily on the peasantry.

Henceforth, the political privileges of the landlord class diminished. Secure in their right to manage their own estates as they wished, the Junkers were content to surrender management of the Prussian state to a centralized bureaucracy. Its most important department was a military commissariat, whose functions included not only the dispensing of army pay

Prussians Swearing Allegiance to the Great Elector at Königsberg, 1663. The occasion upon which the Prussian estates first acknowledged the overlordship of their ruler. This ceremony marked the beginning of the centralization of the Prussian state.

and matériel, but the development of industries to manufacture military equipment. Frederick William's success was due primarily to his ability to gain the active cooperation of the Junker class. Without their support, he could never have hammered together a state from the disparate territories that were his political raw material. To obtain that support, he used the army not only to maintain order, but as a way of enlisting Junker participation in the Prussian state. The highest honor that could befall a Brandenburg squire was a commission and promotion as a military officer in Frederick William's army.

THE AUSTRO-HUNGARIAN EMPIRE

Like the Prussian rulers, the Habsburg monarchs of Austria were confronted with the task of transforming four different regions into a cohesive state. In Austria, however, this effort was complicated by the ethnic and linguistic diversity of the empire's four main regions: the southern, German-speaking lands that roughly make up the present-day country of Austria; the northern Czech- (Slavic-) speaking provinces of Bohemia and Moravia; German-speaking Silesia, inherited in 1527; and Hungary (where the Magyar population spoke a non-Slavic, Finno-Ugric language), also acquired in 1527 but largely lost to Turkish invasion just a few years afterward. For the next one hundred fifty years the Habsburgs and the Ottoman Turks vied for control of Hungary. Until 1683 the Ottomans ruled three-fourths of the Magyar kingdom, extending their control to within eighty miles of the Habsburg capital of Vienna. In 1683 the Turks beseiged Vienna itself but were repulsed by the Austrians, assisted by a mixed German and Polish army under the command of King John Sobieski of Poland. This victory was a prelude to the Habsburg reconquest of virtually all of Hungary by the end of the century.

The task of constructing an absolutist state from these extraordinarily varied territories was tackled with limited success during the seventeenth century by the emperors Ferdinand III (1637–1657) and Leopold I (1658–1705). Most of their efforts were devoted to establishing productive agricultural estates in Bohemia and Moravia, and to dealing with the independent-minded nobility of these territories and of Hungary. Landlords were encouraged to farm for export and were supported in this effort by a government decree that compelled peasants to provide three days of unpaid work service per week to the lords. In return for this support, Bohemian and Moravian landed elites sur-

rendered the political independence that had in the past expressed itself in the activities of their territorial legislative Estates.

Habsburg rulers tried to strike this same sort of bargain in Hungary as well. But there the tradition of independence was stronger and died harder. Hungarian (or Magyar) nobles in the west claimed the right to elect their king, a right they eventually surrendered to Leopold in 1687. But the imperial government's attempts to reduce the country further by administering it through the army, by granting large tracts of land to German aristocrats and settlers, and by persecuting non-Catholics were an almost total failure. The result was a powerful nobility that remained fiercely determined to retain its traditional constitutional and religious "liberties." The Habsburg emperors could boast that they too, like absolutists elsewhere, possessed a large standing army and an educated (in this case, German-speaking) bureaucracy. But the exigencies imposed by geography and ethnicity prevented them from achieving the absolutist goal of a unified, centrally controlled and administered state.

AUTOCRACY IN RUSSIA

How was Russian absolutism unique?

Undoubtedly the most dramatic episode in the history of early modern absolutism was the dynamic reign of Tsar Peter I of Russia (1689–1725). Peter's accomplishments alone would have earned him his history-book title, Peter the Great. But his imposing height—he was nearly seven feet tall—as well as his mercurial personality—jesting one moment, raging the next—certainly added to the outsized impression he made on his contemporaries. Peter is best remembered as the tsar whose policies brought Russia into direct contact with the western European world. Previously the country's rulers had set their faces firmly against the West, disdaining a civilization at odds with the Eastern Orthodox culture that was their heritage, while laboring to keep the various ethnic groups that comprised their empire—Russians, Ukrainians, and a wide variety of nomadic tribes—from destroying not only each other but the tsarist state itself. As a young man, however, Peter traveled to several western European capitals, and returned to Russia determined to remodel his country's institutions along western lines.

Peter the Great. An eighteenth-century mosaic.

THE BACKGROUND OF PETER'S REIGN

Since 1613 Russia had been ruled by members of the Romanov dynasty, who had attempted with some success to restore political stability following the chaotic "time of troubles" that occurred after the death of the bloodthirsty, half-mad Tsar Ivan IV (the Terrible) in 1584. Tsar Alexis I (1645–1676) took a significant step toward unifying his empire in 1654 when he secured an agreement with the Ukrainians to incorporate that portion of Ukraine lying east of the Dneiper River into the Muscovite state. But the early Romanovs were faced with a severe threat to their rule between 1667 and 1671, when a Cossack leader (the Russian Cossacks were semi-autonomous bands of peasant cavalrymen) named Stenka Razin led much of southeastern Russia into rebellion. This uprising found widespread support, not only from serfs who had been oppressed by their masters, but also from non-Russian tribes in the lower Volga area who longed to cast off Muscovite domination. But ultimately Tsar Alexis and the Russian nobility were able to defeat Razin's zealous but disorganized bands of rebels. In crushing the rebellion, more than one hundred thousand rebels were slaughtered.

ABSOLUTISM AND AUTOCRACY

These campaigns were but a prelude to the deliberate and ruthless drive toward autocratic authority launched by the seventeen-year-old Peter after he overthrew the regency of his half-sister Sophia and assumed personal control of the state in 1689. Within ten years he had scandalized nobility and clergy alike by traveling to Holland and England to recruit highly skilled foreign workers and to study the craft of shipbuilding. Upon his return he distressed them still further by declaring his intention to westernize Russia, a process he began by cutting off the "eastern" beards and flowing sleeves worn by the leading noblemen at his court. Determined to "civilize" his nobility, he published a book of manners that forbade spitting on the floor and eating with one's fingers, and encouraged the cultivation of the art of polite conversation between the sexes. To promote this latter goal, he also ordered Russian women to appear, together with men, in western garb at weddings, banquets, and other public occasions.

Much as Peter wished to reshape his country in accordance with western models, his particular brand of absolutism differed from that of other European monarchs. Peter considered himself above the law and thus the absolute master of his empire to a degree that was alien even to the most thoroughgoing absolutist theories and traditions of western Europe. Autocrat of all the Russias, he ruled despotically, with a ferocious individual power that western European rulers did not possess. Armed with such arbitrary power in theory, and intent on realizing its full potential in practice, Peter brooked no opposition to his efforts to "modernize" the Russian state. When his son showed signs of resisting his father, Peter imprisoned him. Soon thereafter, the young man died in mysterious circumstances.

Peter's efforts quickly ran into opposition, however, particularly among the *streltsy*, the elite palace guard who sought to halt his innovations by restoring his half-sister Sophia to the throne. Their initial rebellion took place while Peter was touring western Europe. Peter quickly returned home from Vienna, and crushed the rebellion with a savagery that astonished even his contemporaries. Roughly twelve hundred suspected conspirators were summarily executed, many of them gibbeted outside the walls of the Kremlin, where their bodies rotted for months as a graphic reminder of the fate awaiting those who dared challenge the tsar's authority.

Peter then set out to create a large standing army, recruited from the ranks of the peasantry and scrupu-

PETER THE GREAT'S EXECUTIONS OF HIS PALACE GUARD

This graphic account of Peter's retribution against his rebellious palace guard (a group known as the streltsy*) was written by an Austrian diplomat living in Moscow in 1698, when these events took place. Peter's sister Sophia was widely believed to have been behind the uprising.*

How sharp was the pain, how great the indignation, to which the tsar's Majesty was mightily moved, when he knew of the rebellion of the Streltsy, betraying openly a mind panting for vengeance! He was still tarrying at Vienna, quite full of the desire of setting out for Italy; but . . . on the announcement of the troubles that had broken out in the bowels of his realm. . . . [h]e took the quick post, as his ambassador suggested, and in four weeks' time he had got over about three hundred miles [German miles, equivalent to about fifteen hundred English miles] without accident, and arrived the 4th of September, 1698—a monarch for the well disposed, but an avenger for the wicked.

His first anxiety after his arrival was about the rebellion—in what it consisted, what the insurgents meant, who dared to instigate such a crime. And as nobody could answer accurately upon all points, and some pleaded their own ignorance, others the obstinacy of the Streltsy, he began to have suspicions of everybody's loyalty. . . .

No day, holy or profane, were the inquisitors idle; every day was deemed fit and lawful for torturing. There were as many scourges as there were accused, and every inquisitor was a butcher. . . . The whole month of October was spent in lacerating the backs of culprits with the knout and with flames; no day were those that were left alive exempt from scourging or scorching; or else they were broken upon the wheel, or driven to the gibbet, or slain with the ax. . . .

To prove to people how holy and inviolable are those walls of the city which the Streltsy rashly meditated scaling in a sudden assault, beams were run out from all the embrasures in the walls near the gates, in each of which two rebels were hanged. This day beheld about two hundred and fifty die that death. There are few cities fortified with as many palisades as Moscow has given gibbets to her guardian Streltsy.

[In front of the nunnery where Peter's sister Sophia was confined] there were thirty gibbets erected in a quadrangle shape, from which there hung two hundred and thirty Streltsy; the three principal ringleaders, who tendered a petition to Sophia touching the administration of the realm, were hanged close to the windows of that princess, presenting, as it were, the petitions that were placed in their hands, so near that Sophia might with ease touch them.

J. H. Robinson. *Readings in European History*, vol. 2. (Boston: Ginn and Co., 1906), pp. 310–312.

Peter the Great's Execution of the Streltsy. This contemporary print shows scores of corpses gibbeted outside the walls of the Kremlin. Peter kept the rotting bodies on display for months to discourage his subjects from opposing his efforts to Westernize Russian society.

began his career as a cook and finished as a prince, a degree of social mobility that would have been impossible in any contemporary western European country. Instead, noble status became dependent upon governmental service, with all nobles expected to participate in Peter's army or administration. Peter was not entirely successful in enforcing this requirement upon all the *boyars*, but the administrative machinery he devised furnished Russia with its ruling class for the next two hundred years.

PETER'S FOREIGN POLICY

Peter the Great's Eurocentric world view also manifested itself in his foreign policy, as witnessed by his bold drive to gain a Russian outlet onto the Baltic Sea. Previous battles with the Turks to secure a port on the Black Sea, and thus a southern passage to the west, had failed. Now he engaged in a war with Sweden's meteoric soldier-king Charles XII (1697–1718), who devoted most of his reign to campaigns in the field against the Danes, the Poles, and the Russians. By defeating Charles decisively at the battle of Poltava in 1709, Peter was able to secure his outlet to the West. He promptly outdid his absolutist counterparts in Europe, who had moved their courts to the oustkirts of their capital cities, by moving the Russian capital from Moscow to an entirely new city he constructed on the Gulf of Finland. An army of serfs was employed to erect the baroque city of St. Petersburg around a palace intended to imitate and rival Louis XIV's Versailles.

Opposition to Peter's drastic reforms smoldered

lously loyal to the tsar. One of every twenty males was conscripted for lifelong service. He financed his army, as did other absolutists, by increasing taxes, with their burden falling most heavily on the peasantry. To equip his new military force, he fostered the growth of the iron and munitions industries. Factories were built and manned by peasant laborers whose position was little better than that of slaves. Serfs were also commandeered for other public works projects such as road and canal building.

To further consolidate his absolute power, Peter replaced the Duma—the nation's rudimentary national assembly—with a rubber-stamp senate, and appointed a procurator, or agent, dependent directly on him, to manage the affairs of the Russian Orthodox Church, which thus became an extension of the state's authority. At the same time, Peter was fashioning new, larger, and more efficient administrative machinery to cope with the demands of his modernization program. Although he preferred to draw into the bureaucracy "new" men, whose loyalty would be unswerving, he was compelled to rely on the services of the noble—or *boyar*—class as well, rewarding them by increasing their control over their serfs. Nevertheless, membership in his new bureaucracy did not depend on birth. One of his principal advisers, Alexander Menshikov,

C H R O N O L O G Y	
SEVENTEENTH-CENTURY ABSOLUTIST RULERS	
Louis XIV (France)	1643–1715
Frederick William (Brandenburg-Prussia)	1640–1688
Leopold I (Austria)	1658–1705
Peter the Great (Russia)	1689–1725

The St. Petersburg Palaces. This first of six versions of the Winter Palace (above) was erected in 1711. It quickly proved to be too modest for Peter's needs. Within a decade he had created a far more elaborate complex called the Peterhof (below), complete with fountains modeled on those in Versailles.

guard, under whom the resentful nobles reversed many of Peter's reforms. In 1762, however, the crown passed to Catherine II, a ruler whose ambitions and determination were equal to those of her great predecessor. We shall discuss her reign later in this chapter.

ALTERNATIVES TO ABSOLUTISM

What was political power according to Locke?

Peter the Great of Russia, Leopold I of Austria, Frederick William of Brandenburg-Prussia, and above all Louis XIV of France were the "great" seventeenth-century absolutists. Elsewhere in Europe, absolutism was far less successful. In Spain, the ineffectual, weak-minded Charles II found himself besieged by rebellions in Portugal and Sicily. In 1688, after years of fighting, he was forced to recognize Portuguese independence. In Sweden, Charles X and Charles XI managed to extend their territories at the expense of the Danes and to quell the independence of the aristocracy by confiscating their fiefdoms. During the reign of Charles XII, however, that legacy was dissipated by an adventurous but ultimately unproductive foreign policy, and Sweden returned to being a more obviously "limited" monarchy. In Poland, the opposition of the landed gentry—or *szlachta*—to any form of centralized government whatever produced a political stalemate that amounted to little more than anarchy. Foreign powers took advantage of this

under his imposing hand, and flared up into outright resistance in the succession struggle that followed his death, without direct heirs, in 1725. A series of ineffective tsars followed, mostly creatures of the palace situation to intervene in Polish affairs and, during the eighteenth century, to carve up the country and distribute it among themselves.

Although absolutism was the dominant model for

seventeenth-century European monarchs, it was by no means the only system by which Europeans governed themselves. In Venice, a republican oligarchy continued to rule the city; while in the Netherlands, the various provinces that had won their independence from Spain in the early seventeenth century combined to form a republic, the United Provinces, the only truly new country to take shape in Europe during the early modern era. Although Holland dominated the new republic economically and politically, the deep Dutch mistrust of monarchs that had been created by the Spanish wars prevented Holland's House of Orange (which had led the wars for independence) from transforming the republic into a monarchy. Even after 1688, when William of Orange became king of England in the "Glorious Revolution," the United Provinces remained a republic, despite the leading role William undertook in organizing a Europe-wide alliance against Louis XIV of France.

LIMITED MONARCHY: THE CASE OF ENGLAND

The political history of England in the late seventeenth century provides another alternative to absolutism as a foundation for effective government. England possessed in its Parliament the longest-surviving and most highly developed representative assembly in western Europe. English political theorists had for centuries seen their government as a "mixed" monarchy, composed of monarchical, noble, and common elements. During the seventeenth century, however, these traditions had come under threat, first through Charles I's attempts to rule without summoning Parliament, and then through Oliver Cromwell's dictatorial Protectorate. The restoration of the monarchy in 1660 resolved the question of whether England would in future be a republic or a monarchy; but the sort of monarchy England would become remained an open question as the reign of Charles II began.

THE REIGN OF CHARLES II

Despite the fact that he was the son of the beheaded and much-hated Charles I, Charles II was initially welcomed by most English men and women. Upon his accession, he declared a limited religious toleration for Protestants who were not members of the official Church of England, and he promised to observe Magna Carta and the Petition of Right, declaring that he was not anxious to "resume his travels." His delight in the unbuttoned moral atmosphere of his court, with its risqué plays, dancing, and sexual licentiousness, mirrored a public desire to forget the restraints of the Puritan past. The wits of the time suggested that Charles, "that known enemy to virginity and chastity," played his role as the father of his country to the fullest; but in fact he produced no legitimate heir and only a single illegitimate son to contest the succession to his father's throne. But as Charles's admiration of things French grew to include the absolutism of Louis XIV, he came to be regarded as a threat to more than English womanhood by a great many powerful Englishmen. Desirous though they were to preserve the restored monarchy, they were not about to surrender their traditional rights to another Stuart autocrat. By the late 1670s, the country thus found itself divided politically into those who supported the king (called by their opponents "Tories," a popular nickname for Irish Catholic bandits) and those opposed to him (called by their opponents "Whigs," a similar nickname for Scottish Presbyterian rebels).

As the new party labels suggest, religion remained an exceedingly divisive national issue. Charles was sympathetic to Roman Catholicism, even to the point of a deathbed conversion in 1685. He therefore opposed the Clarendon Code, which had reestablished the official Church of England and penalized Catholics and Protestant dissenters. In 1672, Charles suspended the Clarendon Code, asserting his prerogative to set aside Parliamentary legislation, but the resulting public outcry compelled him to retreat. This controversy, along with rising opposition to the expected succession of Charles's ardently Roman Catholic brother James, led to a series of Whig electoral victories between 1679 and 1681. But when a group of radical Whigs attempted to exclude Charles's brother James by law from succeeding him on the throne, Charles stared the opposition down in the so-called Exclusion Crisis. Thereafter, Charles found that his increased revenues, combined with a secret subsidy he was receiving from Louis XIV, enabled him to govern without relying on Parliament for money. Charles further infuriated and alarmed Whig politicians by arranging the execution of several of their most promi-

> English political theorists had for centuries seen their government as a "mixed" monarchy, composed of monarchical, noble, and common elements.

hanced, but he left behind a political and religious legacy that was to be the undoing of his less able and adroit successor.

KING JAMES II

James II was the very opposite of his worldly brother. A zealous Catholic convert, he alienated his Tory supporters, all of whom were members of the established Church of England, by dismissing them in favor of Roman Catholics, and by once again suspending the penal laws, approved by Parliament, that barred Catholics and Protestant dissenters from holding political office. James also flaunted his own Roman Catholicism, publicly declaring his wish that all his subjects might be converted, and parading papal legates through the streets of London. When, in June 1688, he ordered all Church of England clergymen to read his decree of religious toleration from their pulpits, seven bishops refused and were promptly thrown into prison on charges of seditious libel. At their trial, however, they were declared not guilty, to the enormous satisfaction of the overwhelmingly Protestant English populace.

The trial of the bishops was one event that brought matters to a head. The other was the unexpected birth of a son in 1688 to James and his second wife, the Roman Catholic Mary of Modena. This male infant, who was to be raised a Catholic, replaced James's much older Protestant daughter Mary as heir to the British throne. Despite a rumor that the baby boy was an imposter smuggled into the royal bedchamber in a warming pan, political leaders of both parties now began to take active steps to prevent the possibility of his succession to the throne. A delegation of Whigs and Tories crossed the Channel to Holland to invite Mary and her husband William of Orange, the *stadholder* or chief executive of the United Provinces and the great-grandson of William the Silent, to cross to England with an invading army to restore English religious and political freedom. As the leader of a Continental coalition determined to thwart Louis XIV's expansionist policies, William in particular welcomed the chance such a move represented to bring England into active opposition to the French (see p. 613).

THE GLORIOUS REVOLUTION

William's conquest was a bloodless coup. James fled the country, thereby allowing Parliament to declare the throne vacant and clearing the way for the acces-

Charles II.

James II.

nent leaders on charges of treason, and by remodeling local government so as to make it more dependent on royal favor. Charles died in 1685 with his power en-sion of William and Mary as joint sovereigns of England. A Bill of Rights, passed by Parliament and accepted by the new king and queen in 1689, reaffirmed English civil liberties such as trial by jury, habeas corpus (guaranteeing that individuals could not be imprisoned without being charged with a crime), and the right of subjects to petition their monarch through Parliament for redress of their grievances. The Bill of Rights also declared that the monarchy was subject to the law of the land. An Act of Toleration, passed in 1689, granted Protestants who were not members of the Church of England the right to worship, though not the right to hold political office. In 1701, with Queen Mary now dead and the son of the exiled James II reaching maturity in France, an Act of Succession ordained that the English throne was to pass first to Mary's childless sister Anne, who ruled from 1702 to 1714, and then to George, elector of the German principality of Hanover, who was the Protestant great-grandson of James I. The connection was a distant one, but the Hanoverians were the nearest Protestant dynasty with even a plausible claim to the English throne. Henceforth, Parliament required that all English monarchs be members of the Church of England. If foreign born, they could not engage England in the defense of their native land, or even leave the country without the prior consent of Parliament.

The English soon referred to the events of 1688 and 1689 as the "Glorious Revolution": glorious for the English in that it occurred without bloodshed (although James is reputed to have suffered a nosebleed at the moment of crisis); glorious, too, for defenders of Parliamentary prerogative. Although William and Mary and their successors continued to enjoy a large measure of executive power, after 1688 no king or queen attempted to govern without Parliament, which met annually from that time on. Parliament strengthened its control over the collection and expenditure of public funds. Future monarchs were therefore unable to conduct the country's business without seeking from the House of Commons the funds with which to do so. The revolution was glorious, finally, for advocates of the civil liberties now guaranteed within the Bill of Rights, and for defenders of the "Protestant cause," who saw nothing less than divine will as lying behind the favorable winds that blew William and Mary so speedily to England.

Yet 1688 was not all glory. It was a revolution that consolidated the position of large property holders, magnates whose local power base had been threatened by the interventions of Charles II and James II. If it was a revolution, it was one designed to restore the status quo on behalf of a wealthy social and economic order that would soon make itself even wealthier as it drank its fill of government patronage and war profits. And it was a revolution that brought nothing but misery to the Roman Catholic minority in Scotland, which joined with England and Wales in the union of Great Britain in 1707, and to the Catholic majority in Ireland where, following the Battle of the Boyne in 1690, repressive military forces imposed the exploitive will of a self-interested Protestant minority on the Catholic inhabitants of the island.

JOHN LOCKE AND THE CONTRACT THEORY OF GOVERNMENT

Although the Glorious Revolution was an expression of immediate political circumstances, it also reflected anti-absolutist theories that had taken shape in the late seventeenth century in response to the ideas of writers such as Bodin, Hobbes, Filmer, and Bossuet. Chief among these opponents of absolutism was the Englishman John Locke (1632–1704), whose *Two Treatises of Government*, written prior to the revolution but published for the first time in 1690, was used to justify the events of the previous two years. Locke maintained that humans had originally lived in a state of nature in which absolute freedom and equality prevailed, and in which there was no government of any kind. The only law was the law of nature (which Locke equated with the law of reason), by which individuals enforced for themselves their natural rights to life, liberty, and property.

It was not long, however, before humans began to perceive that the inconveniences of the state of nature greatly outweighed its advantages. With each individual attempting to enforce his own rights, confusion and insecurity were the unavoidable results. Accordingly, people agreed among themselves first to quit the state of nature and establish a civil society based on absolute equality, and then to set up a government to act as an impartial arbiter of disputes for the society they had already created. But they did not make that government absolute. The only power society conferred upon government was the executive power of the law

> The "Glorious Revolution" reflected anti-absolutist theories that had taken shape in the late seventeenth century in response to the ideas of writers such as Bodin, Hobbes, Filmer, and Bossuet.

THE AMERICAN DECLARATION OF INDEPENDENCE

The Declaration of Independence, issued from Philadelphia on July 4, 1776, is perhaps the most famous single document of American history. But its familiarity does not lesssen its interest as a piece of political philosophy. The indebtedness of the document's authors to the ideas of John Locke will be obvious from the selections below. But Locke, in turn, drew many of his ideas about the contractual and conditional nature of human government from the conciliarist thinkers of the fifteenth and early sixteenth centuries. The appeal of absolutism notwithstanding, the Declaration shows how vigorous the medieval tradition of contractual, limited government remained at the end of the eighteenth century.

When in the course of human events, it becomes necessary for one people to dissolve the political bonds which have connected them with another, and to assume among the powers of the earth the separate and equal station to which the Laws of Nature and of Nature's God entitle them, a decent respect to the opinions of mankind requires that they should declare the causes which impel them to the separation. . . . We hold these truths to be self-evident, that all men are created equal, that they are endowed by their Creator with certain unalienable rights, that among these are Life, Liberty and the pursuit of Happiness. . . . That to secure these rights, Governments are instituted among men, deriving their just powers from the consent of the governed. . . . That whenever any form of Government becomes destructive of these ends, it is the Right of the People to alter or to abolish it, and to institute new Government, laying its foundation upon such principles and organizing its power in such form, as to them shall seem most likely to effect their Safety and Happiness. Prudence, indeed, will dictate that Governments long established should not be changed for light and transient causes; and accordingly all experience has shown, that mankind are more disposed to suffer, while evils are sufferable, than to right themselves by abolishing the forms to which they are accustomed. But when a long train of abuses and usurpations, pursuing invariably the same Object, evinces a design to reduce them under absolute despotism, it is their right, it is their duty, to throw off such Government, and to provide new Guards for their future security. . . . Such has been the patient sufferance of these Colonies; and such is now the necessity which constrains them to alter their former Systems of Government. . . .

of nature. Since the state was nothing but the joint power of all the members of society, its authority could "be no more than those persons had in a state of nature before they entered into society, and gave it up to the community." All powers not expressly surrendered to the government were therefore reserved to the people themselves. All governmental authority was thus contractual and conditional. If, therefore, a government exceeded or abused the authority granted to it, it became tyrannical, and the society had the right to dissolve it and constitute another.

Locke condemned absolutism in every form. He

John Locke.

INTERNATIONAL RELATIONS AND THE EMERGENCE OF A EUROPEAN STATE SYSTEM

What was the "balance of power"?

As European states became more unified and centralized during the age of absolutism, contemporaries came more and more to think of them as entities with their own distinctive "interests," distinguishable, at least potentially, from the dynastic and religious interests of the monarchs who ruled over them. These were gradual developments, to be sure, but by the second quarter of the eighteenth century the abstract interests of "commerce" and "stability" were beginning to outweigh older modes of thought that had equated the interests of each state with the personal and familial interests of its ruler. The results were the emergence, for the first time, of a Europe-wide state system, and a significant redefinition of the aims and calculations of diplomacy and warfare.

DIPLOMACY AND WARFARE

The organization of diplomatic bureaucracies was one of the major accomplishments of the age of absolutism. The rationalization of diplomatic processes and the establishment of foreign ministries and embassies in European capitals, with their growing staffs of clerks and ministers, reflected a desire to bring order out of the international chaos that had gripped Europe during the early seventeenth century. To an unprecedented degree, the history of international relations from the late seventeenth century on therefore becomes a history of diplomatic coalitions, an indication of the extent to which negotiation was now a weapon in the armory of European states.

Warfare, however, continued to play an integral and almost constant role in the international arena. The armies of the period grew dramatically. When Louis XIV came of age in 1657, the French army numbered twenty thousand men; by 1688, it stood at two hundred ninety thousand; by 1694, four hundred thousand. These armies were increasingly professional organiza-

denounced despotic monarchy, but he was no less severe in his strictures against the absolute sovereignty of parliaments. Though he defended the supremacy of the law-making branch, with the executive primarily an agent of the legislature, he nevertheless refused to concede to the representatives of the people an unlimited power. Arguing that government was instituted among people for the preservation of property, he denied the authority of any political agency to invade the natural rights of a single individual. The law of nature, which embodied these rights, was thus an automatic and absolute limitation upon every branch of government.

Locke's theoretical defense of political liberty emerged in the late eighteenth century as an important element in the intellectual background of the American and French revolutions. Between 1688 and 1720, however, it served a far less radical purpose. The landed magnates responsible for replacing James II with William and Mary read Locke as a defense of their conservative revolution. James II, rather than protecting their property and liberties, had encroached upon them; hence the magnates had every right to overthrow the tyranny he had established and to replace it with a government that would, by ensuring their rights, defend their interests.

> Locke's theoretical defense of political liberty emerged as an important element in the intellectual background of the American and French revolutions.

tions, controlled directly by the state, and under the command of trained officers recruited from the nobility. In Prussia, common soldiers were mostly conscripts; in other European countries they were volunteers, either native or foreign, though often "volunteers" in no more than name, having been coerced or tricked into service. Increasingly, however, enlistment was perceived by common soldiers as an avenue to a career, one that included the possibility of promotion to corporal or sergeant, and in the case of France, the promise of a small pension at the end of one's service. However recruited, common soldiers became part of an increasingly elaborate and efficient fighting force. Above all, they were made to understand the dire consequences of disobedience, breaking ranks, or desertion. Soldiers were expected to obey instantly and unquestioningly. Failure to do so resulted in brutal punishment, often flogging, sometimes execution. Drill, not only on the battlefield but on the parade ground, in brilliant, elaborate uniforms and intricate formations, was designed to reduce individuals to automatonlike parts of an army whose regiments were moved across battlefields as a chess player moves pawns across the board.

THE FOREIGN POLICY OF LOUIS XIV

The patterns of international relations during the period from 1660 to 1715 show European monarchs making use of the new machinery of diplomacy and warfare to resolve the conflicting interests of dynasty, stability, and commerce. At the center of that pattern, as at the center of Europe, stood Louis XIV. From 1661 until 1688, in a quest for glory, empire, and even revenge, he waged war across his northern and eastern frontiers on the pretext that the lands in question belonged both to the Bourbons and to the French by tradition, by former treaty, or by dynastic inheritance. His aggressively expansionist policies, alarming to other European rulers, led William of Orange, in 1674, to form an anti-French coalition with Austria, Spain, and various smaller German states. Yet Louis continued to push his frontiers eastward, invading territories that had been Germanic for centuries, and capturing Strassburg in 1681 and Luxembourg in 1684. Louis's seizure of Strassburg (subsequently called Strasbourg by the French), completing the conquest of the German-speaking province of Alsace begun in 1634 by Richelieu, irreversibly incorporated the seeds of a Franco-German animosity centered on this region that would bear bitter fruit in the great wars of the nineteenth and twentieth centuries. A sec-

ond coalition, the so-called League of Augsburg (1686), which comprised Holland, Austria, Sweden, and further German allies, was only somewhat more successful than the first.

These allies were concerned above all to maintain some sort of European balance of power. They feared an expansionist France would prove insatiable, as it pressed its boundaries farther and farther into Germany and the Low Countries. Louis, mistakenly expecting that William would be forced to fight an English army under James to establish his right to his new throne and would therefore be too preoccupied to devote his full attention to developments on the Continent, kept up the pressure. In September 1688 he invaded the Palatinate and occupied the city of Cologne. The following year the French armies crossed the Rhine and continued their eastward drive, burning Heidelberg and committing numerous atrocities throughout the middle Rhine area. Aroused at last to effective action, the League of Augsburg, led by William and now including in addition to its original members both England and Spain, engaged Louis in a war that began in 1689 and was to last until 1697.

The major campaigns of this War of the League of Augsburg were fought in the Low Countries. William managed to drive an army under his predecessor, James II, from Ireland in 1690; from that point on, he took command of the allied forces on the Continent. By 1694 Louis was pressed hard, not only by his allied foes, but by a succession of disastrous harvests that crippled France. Fighting remained stalemated until a treaty was signed at Ryswick in Holland in 1697, which compelled Louis to return most of France's recent gains, except for Alsace, and to recognize William as the rightful king of England.

THE WAR OF THE SPANISH SUCCESSION

Ryswick did nothing, however, to resolve the dynastic tangle known as the Spanish succession. Since Charles II of Spain had no direct heirs, and since he appeared to be on his deathbed in 1699, European monarchs and diplomats were obsessed by the question of who would succeed to the vast domain of the Spanish Habsburgs: not only Spain itself, but also its overseas empire, as well as the Spanish Netherlands, Naples, Sicily, and other territories in Italy. Both Louis XIV and Leopold I of Austria were married to sisters of the decrepit, unstable Charles; and both, naturally, eyed the succession to the Spanish inheritance as an exceedingly tempting dynastic plum. Yet it is a measure of the degree to which even absolutists were willing to keep their ambitions within bounds that both Leopold and Louis agreed to William's suggestion that the lion's share of the Habsburg lands should go to six-year-old Joseph Ferdinand, the prince of Bavaria, who was Charles II's grandnephew. Unfortunately, in 1699 the child died. Though the chances of war increased, William and Louis were prepared to bargain further and arranged a second treaty that divided the Spanish empire between Louis's and Leopold's heirs. Yet at the same time, Louis's diplomatic agents in Madrid persuaded Charles to sign a will in which he stipulated that the entire Spanish Habsburg inheritance should pass to Louis's grandson Philip of Anjou. This option was welcomed by many influential Spaniards, willing to endure French hegemony in return for the protection France could provide to the Spanish empire. For a time, Louis contemplated an alternative agreement that would have given France direct control of much of Italy. When Charles finally died in November 1700, Louis decided to accept the will. As if this was not enough to drive his former enemies back to war, he sent troops into the Spanish Netherlands and traders to the Spanish colonial empire, while declaring the late James II's son—the child of the warming-pan myth—the legitimate king of England.

Once it was clear to the allies that Louis intended to treat Spain as if it were his own kingdom, they again united against him in the cause of balance and stability. William died in 1702, just as the War of the Spanish Succession was beginning. His position as first general of the coalition passed to two brilliant strategists, the Englishman John Churchill, duke of Marlborough, and his Austrian counterpart Prince Eugene of Savoy, an upper-class soldier of fortune who had been denied a commission by Louis. Under their command the allied forces engaged in fierce battles in the Low Countries and Germany, including an extraordinary march deep into Bavaria, where the combined forces under Marlborough and Eugene defeated the French and their Bavarian allies decisively at Blenheim (1704). While the allies pressed France's armies on land, the English navy captured Gibraltar and the island of Minorca, thus establishing a strategic and commercial foothold in the Mediterranean and helping to open a fourth major military theater in Spain itself.

The War of the Spanish Succession was a "professional" war that tested the highly trained armies of the combatants to the fullest. At the battle of Malplaquet in northeastern France in 1709, eighty thousand French soldiers faced one hundred ten thousand allied troops. Though Marlborough and Eugene could claim to have won that battle, in that they forced the French to retreat, they suffered twenty-four thousand casualties, twice those of the French. Neither Malplaquet nor other such victories brought the allies any closer to their final goal, which now appeared to be not the containment, but the complete destruction of the French military force. Queen Anne of England (Mary's sister and William's successor), once Marlborough's staunchest defender, grew disillusioned with the war and fired her general.

More than war weariness impelled the combatants toward negotiation, however. The War of the Spanish Succession had begun as a conflict about the balance of power in Europe and the world. Yet dynastic changes had by 1711 compelled a reappraisal of allied goals. Leopold I had died in 1705. When his elder son and successor Joseph I died in 1711, the Austrian monarchy fell to Leopold's youngest son, the archduke Charles, who had been the allies' candidate for the throne of Spain. With Charles now the Austrian and the Holy Roman emperor as Charles VI (1711–1740), the prospect of his accession to the Spanish inheritance conjured up the ghost of Charles V and threatened to give him far too much power. International stability therefore demanded an end to hostilities and diplomatic negotiation toward a solution that would reestablish some sort of general balance.

THE TREATY OF UTRECHT

The Treaty of Utrecht settled the conflict in 1713 by redistributing territory and power in equitable portions. No one emerged a major winner or loser. Philip, Louis's grandson, remained on the throne of Spain, but Louis agreed that France and Spain would never be united under the same ruler. Austria gained territories in the Netherlands and Italy. The Dutch, victims of French aggression during the war, were guaranteed protection of their borders against future invasion. The English retained Gibraltar and Minorca, as well as territory in America (Newfoundland, Acadia, Hudson Bay) and in the Caribbean (St. Kitts). Perhaps most valuable of all, the English extracted from Spain the right to supply Spanish America with African slaves. The settlement reflected the degree to which new interests had superseded old. Balance of power and stability among states were the major goals of the negotiations, goals that reflected a departure from the world of seventeenth-century turmoil when religion

HOW DID SEVENTEENTH- AND EIGHTEENTH-CENTURY FORMS OF ABSOLUTISM DIFFER?

ENLIGHTENED ABSOLUTISM AND LIMITED MONARCHY   615

had been a major factor in international conflict. The eventual "winners" were undoubtedly the English, whose dynastic concerns were limited to a general acceptance of the Hanoverian settlement, and who could therefore concentrate their efforts on amassing overseas territories that would contribute to the growth of their economic prosperity and hence their international power.

ENLIGHTENED ABSOLUTISM AND LIMITED MONARCHY IN THE EIGHTEENTH CENTURY

How did seventeenth- and eighteenth-century forms of absolutism differ?

Eighteenth-century absolutism was a series of variations on the dominant themes composed in the previous century by Louis XIV. Eighteenth-century rulers backed their sovereign claims not in the language of divine right, but in terms of their determination to act, as Frederick the Great of Prussia declared, as "first servant of the state." That phrase meant not so much service to the people as it did service to the goal of further strengthening the authority of the state over institutions that sought to challenge its corporate well-being. Enlightened rulers moved to curtail the privileges of old institutions. The Roman Catholic Church, for example, was compelled to suffer the expulsion of the Jesuits from most Catholic countries. Customary laws benefiting particular orders or interests were reformed. To strengthen the state community, innovative policies in the areas of taxation, economic development, and education were also instituted.

As we shall see in Chapter 18, rational schemes of this sort reflected the spread of Enlightenment ideals as manifested in the writings of thinkers such as Beccaria, Diderot, and Voltaire. (The last was, in fact, a guest at Frederick's court for several years.) Assisting enlightened "first servants" in the implementation of these charges was a growing cadre of lesser servants: bureaucrats, often recruited from the nobility, but once recruited, expected to declare primary allegiance to their new master, the state. Despite innovation, "enlightened" absolutists continued to insist, as their predecessors had, that state sovereignty rested with the monarchy. Authority remained their overriding concern, and to the extent that they combatted efforts by the estates of their realms to dilute that authority, they declared their descent from their seventeenth-century forebears.

CROWN AND *PARLEMENT* IN FRANCE

Louis XIV's successors, his great-grandson Louis XV (1715–1774) and that monarch's grandson Louis XVI (1774–1792), were unable to sustain the energetic drive toward centralization that had taken place under the Sun King. Indeed, during his last years, while fighting a desperate defensive war against his allied enemies, Louis XIV had seen his own accomplishments begin to crumble under the mounting pressure of military expenses. His heir was only five years old when he assumed the throne. As he grew up, Louis XV displayed less single-minded determination than had his great-grandfather to act the role of Sun King. The heroic, Baroque grandeur of the main palace at Versailles yielded to the Rococo grace of the Grand and Petit Trianons, pleasure pavillions built by Louis XV in the palace gardens.

During the minority of Louis XV, the French *parlements*, those courts of record responsible for registering royal decreees, enjoyed a resurgence of power which they retained throughout the century. No longer tame adjuncts of absolutist governmental machinery as they had been under Louis XIV, these bodies now proclaimed themselves the protectors of French "liberties." In 1770, encouraged by his chancellor René Maupeou, Louis XV issued an edict effectively ending the right of *parlements* to reject decrees. Protest on the part of the magistrates resulted in their imprisonment or banishment. The *parlements* themselves were replaced by new courts charged not only with the responsibility of rubber-stamping legislation but also with administering law more justly and less expensively. When Louis XVI ascended the throne in 1774, his ministers persuaded him to reestablish the *parlements* as a sign of his willingness to conciliate his trouble-making aristocracy. This he did, with the result that government—particularly the management of finances—developed into a stalemated battle.

THE RISE OF PRUSSIA

Stalemate was what the Prussian successors to Frederick William, the Great Elector, were determined to avoid. Frederick I (1688–1713), the Great Elector's im-

AGE OF ABSOLUTISM

What nations on this map were governed by "enlightened absolutists"? How did their competing claims to sovereignty differ from the absolutists who based their claim to rule on divine right? How did the conception of this new type of absolutism affect the relations between states and the construction of continental empires in the early eighteenth century?

mediate successor, enhanced the appearance and cultural life of Berlin. As the Roman numeral after his name attests, he also succeeded in bargaining his support to the Austrians during the War of the Spanish Succession in return for the coveted right to style himself king. (The Austrian monarch was the Holy Roman emperor and therefore had the right to create kings.)

Frederick William I (1713–1740), cared little for the embellishments his father had made to the capital city.

His overriding concern was the building of a first-rate army. So single-minded was his attention to the military that he came to be called "the sergeant king." Military display became an obsession. His private regiment of "Potsdam Giants" was composed exclusively of soldiers over six feet in height. The king traded musicians and prize stallions for such choice specimens and delighted in marching them about his palace grounds. Frederick William I's success as the builder of a military

HOW DID SEVENTEENTH- AND EIGHTEENTH-CENTURY FORMS OF ABSOLUTISM DIFFER?

ENLIGHTENED ABSOLUTISM AND LIMITED MONARCHY   617

machine can be measured in terms of numbers: thirty thousand men under arms when he came to the throne; eighty-three thousand when he died twenty-seven years later, commander of the fourth-largest army in Europe, after France, Russia, and Austria. Most of his soldiers were conscripts, drafted from the peasantry for a period of years and required to attend annual training exercises lasting three months. Conscription was supplemented by the kidnapping of forced recruits in neighboring German lands. To finance his army, Frederick William I increased taxes and streamlined their collection through the establishment of a General Directory of War, Finance, and Domains. In 1723, he instituted a system of administration by boards, hoping thereby to eliminate individual inefficiency through collective responsibility and surveillance. In addition, he created an inspectorate to uncover and report to him the mistakes and inefficiencies of his officialdom. Even then, he continued to supervise personally the implementation of state policy while shunning the luxuries of court life; for him, the "theater" of absolutism was not the palace but the office, which placed him at the helm of the state and the army. Perceiving the resources of the state to be too precious to waste, he pared costs at every turn to the point where, it was said, he had to invite himself to a nobleman's table in order to enjoy a good meal.

A hard, unimaginative man, Frederick William I had little use for his son, whose passion was not the battlefield but the flute, and who admired French culture as much as his father disdained it. Not surprisingly, young Frederick rebelled; in 1730, when he was eighteen, he ran away from court with a friend. Apprehended, the companions were returned to the king, who welcomed the fledgling prodigal with something other than a fatted calf. Before Frederick's eyes, he had the friend executed. The grisly lesson took. Thenceforward Frederick, though he never surrendered his love of music and literature, bound himself to his royal duties, living in accordance with his own image of himself as "first servant of the state," and earning himself history's title of Frederick the Great.

Frederick William I's zealous austerity and his compulsion to build an efficient army and administrative state made Prussia a strong state. Frederick the Great (1740–1786), building on the work of his father, raised his country to the status of a major power. As soon as he became king in 1740, Frederick mobilized the army his father had never taken into battle and occupied the poorly protected Austrian province of Silesia, to which Prussia had no legitimate claim. Although he had ear-

Frederick the Great and Voltaire. Although Frederick offered asylum to the French philosophe, this "enlightened despot" did not permit his own intellectual pursuits to interfere with matters of state.

lier vowed to make morality rather than expediency the hallmark of his reign, he seemingly had little difficulty in sacrificing his youthful idealism to the opportunity to make his Prussian state a leading power. The remaining forty-five years of his monarchy were devoted to the consolidation of this first bold stroke.

Such a daring course required some adjustments within the Prussian state. The army had to be kept at full strength, and to this end, Frederick staffed its officer corps with young noblemen. In expanding the bureaucracy, whose financial administration kept his army in the field, he relied on the nobility as well, reversing the policy of his father, who had recruited his civil servants according to merit rather than birth. But Frederick was not one to tolerate mediocrity; he fashioned the most highly professional and efficient bureaucracy in Europe. The degree to which both army and bureaucracy were staffed by the nobility is a measure of his determination to secure the unflagging support of the most privileged order in his realm, in order to ensure a united front against Prussia's external foes.

Frederick's domestic policies reflected that same strategy. In matters where he ran no risk of offending the nobility, he followed his own rationalist bent, prohibiting the torture of accused criminals, putting an end to the bribing of judges, and establishing a system of elementary schools. He encouraged religious toleration, declaring that he would happily build a mosque in Berlin if he could find enough Muslims to fill it. (Yet he was strongly anti-Semitic, levying special taxes on Jews and making efforts to close the professions and the civil service to them). On his own royal estates he was a model "enlightened" monarch. He abolished capital punishment, curtailed the forced labor services of his peasantry, and granted them long leases on the land they worked. He fostered scientific forestry and the cultivation of new crops. He opened new lands in Silesia and brought in thousands of immigrants to cultivate them. When wars ruined their farms, he supplied the peasants with new livestock and tools. Yet he never attempted to extend these reforms to the estates of the Junker elite, since to have done so would have alienated that social and economic group upon which Frederick was most dependent.

Maria Theresa of Austria. The empress was a formidable monarch and a match for Frederick the Great.

THE AUSTRO-HUNGARIAN EMPIRE

Although the monarchs of eighteenth-century Austria eventually proved themselves even more willing than Frederick the Great to undertake significant social reform, the energies of Emperor Charles VI (1711–1740) were concentrated on guaranteeing the future dynastic and territorial integrity of the Habsburg lineage and domain. Without a male heir, Charles worked to secure the right of his daughter Maria Theresa to succeed him as empress. By his death in 1740 Charles had managed to persuade not only his subjects but all the major European powers to accept his daughter as his royal heir—a feat known as the "pragmatic sanction." Yet his painstaking efforts were only partially successful. As we have seen, Frederick the Great used the occasion of Charles's death to seize Silesia. The French, unable to resist the temptation to grab what they could, joined the coalition against the new empress, Maria Theresa (1740–1780).

With most of her possessions already occupied by her enemies, Maria Theresa appealed successfully to the Hungarians for support. The empress was willing to play the role of the wronged woman when, as on this occasion, it suited her interests to do so. Hungary's vital troops combined with British financial assistance enabled her to battle Austria's enemies to a draw, although she never succeeded in regaining Silesia. The experience of those first few years of her reign persuaded Maria Theresa, who was both capable and tenacious, to reorganize her dominions along the tightly centralized lines characteristic of Prussia and France. Ten new administrative districts were established, each with its own "war commissar" appointed by and responsible to the central administration in Vienna—an Austrian equivalent of the French intendant. Property taxes were increased to finance an expanded army, which was modernized and professionalized so as to remain on a

HOW DID SEVENTEENTH- AND EIGHTEENTH-CENTURY FORMS OF ABSOLUTISM DIFFER?

ENLIGHTENED ABSOLUTISM AND LIMITED MONARCHY   619

Edict of Tolerance. An illustration from a pamphlet depicting Joseph II of Austria as an enlightened monarch.

par with the military establishments of the other great powers. Centralization, finances, army: once more those three crucial elements in the formula of absolute rule came into play.

Reform did not stop there, however. Together Maria Theresa and her son Joseph II, with whom she ruled jointly from 1765 to 1780, and who then succeeded her for another ten years, instituted a series of significant social reforms. Although both mother and son were devout Roman Catholics, they moved to assert their control over the church, abolishing the clergy's exemption from taxation and decreeing the state's ability to block the publication of papal bulls in Austria. In 1773, following the papal suppression of the Jesuits, they used the order's assets to finance a program of statewide primary education. Although the General Schools Ordinance of 1774 never achieved anything like a universally literate population, it did succeed in

educating hundreds of thousands, and in financing not only schools for children but schools as well for those who taught the children. Joseph followed these reforms with an "Edict on Idle Institutions" in 1780, which resulted in the closing of hundreds of monastic houses, whose property went to support charitable institutions now under state control. These reforms and others—liberalization of punishment for criminal offenses, a relaxation of censorship, the abolition of serfdom and feudal dues, and an attempt to eradicate superstition by curbing the practice of pilgrimages and celebration of saint's days—made Joseph more enemies than friends, among both the noble elite and the common people. "Enlightened" though Joseph II was, however, he nevertheless remained a staunch absolutist, as concerned with the maintenance of a strong army and an efficient bureaucracy as with the need to educate his peasantry. Joseph's brother Leopold II, who succeeded him in 1790, attempted to maintain the reformist momentum. His death two years later and the accession of his reactionary son Francis II (1792–1835) put an end to liberalizing experiments.

CATHERINE THE GREAT OF RUSSIA

Unlike Joseph II, Catherine the Great of Russia (1762–1796) felt herself compelled to curry the favor of her nobility by involving them directly in the structure of local administration, by exempting them from military service and taxation, and probably most important, by granting them absolute control over the serfs on their estates. Her policy grew out of her strong ties to powerful nobles and her involvement in the conspiracy that led to the assassination of her husband, Tsar Peter III, the last of a series of weak rulers who followed Peter the Great. Catherine was herself a German, and prided herself on her devotion to Western principles of government. Ambitious to establish a reputation as an intellectual and enlightened monarch, she corresponded with French philosophers, wrote plays, published a digest of William Blackstone's *Commentaries on the Laws of England*, and began a history of Russia. Her contributions to social reform did not extend much beyond the founding of hospitals and orphanages, and the expression of a pious hope that someday the serfs might be liberated. Although she did summon a commission in 1767 to codify Russian law, its achievements were modest: a minor extension of religious toleration, a slight restriction of the use of torture by the state. Catherine's interest in theories of reform did, however, stimulate the development of a social concience among certain gentry intellectuals, foreshadowing a more widespread movement in the nineteenth century.

Any plans Catherine may have had for improving the lot of the peasants, however, were abruptly cancelled after their frustration with St. Petersburg's centralization efforts erupted in a violent peasant-serf rebellion in 1773–1774. Free peasants in the Volga valley region found themselves compelled to provide labor services to nobles sent by the crown to control them, Cossacks were subjected to taxation and conscription for the first time, and factory workers and miners were pressed into service in the state's industrial enterprises. These and other disparate but dissatisfied groups, including serfs, united under the rebel banner of Emelyan Pugachev, an illiterate Cossack who claimed to be the late Tsar Peter III. The hapless Peter, who had spoken as a reformer in life, in death became a larger-than-life hero for those opposed to the determined absolutism of his successor. As Pugachev marched, he encouraged his followers to strike out not only against the empress but also against the nobility and the church. More than fifteen hundred landlords and priests were murdered, and the ruling classes were terrified as the revolt spread. Catherine's

CHRONOLOGY

EIGHTEENTH-CENTURY ABSOLUTIST RULERS

France	
Louis XV	1715–1774
Louis XVI	1774–1792
Brandenburg-Prussia	
Frederick I	1688–1713
Frederick William	1713–1740
Frederick the Great	1740–1786
Austria	
Charles VI	1711–1740
Maria Theresa	1740–1780
Joseph II	1765–1790
Russia	
Catherine the Great	1762–1796

forces initially had little success against the rebel army, but the threat of famine plagued Pugachev's advance and finally led to disarray among his troops. Betrayed in 1774, he was captured and taken in an iron cage to Moscow, where he was tortured and killed. Catherine responded to this uprising with further centralization and tightening of aristocratic authority over the peasantry.

The brutal suppression and punishment of the rebels reflected the ease with which the German-born Catherine took to the despotic authoritarianism that characterized Russian absolutism. At the same time, Catherine continued the work of Peter the Great in introducing Russia to Western ideas; she came to terms with the nobility in a way that brought stability to the state; and she made the country a formidable power in European affairs by extending its boundaries to include not only most of Poland but also lands on the Black Sea.

THE GROWTH OF PARLIAMENTARY GOVERNMENT IN ENGLAND

Eighteenth-century monarchs were determined to press ahead with the task, begun by their seventeenth-century predecessors, of building powerful, centralized states by continuing to attempt the elimination or harnessing of the ancient privileges of still-powerful noble

Catherine the Great.

HOW DID SEVENTEENTH- AND EIGHTEENTH-CENTURY FORMS OF ABSOLUTISM DIFFER?

ENLIGHTENED ABSOLUTISM AND LIMITED MONARCHY 621

orders and provincial estates. The notion of a limited monarchy, in which power was divided between local and central authorities and shared by monarchs, nobles, and legislative assemblies, struck them as a dangerous anachronism. Yet as the century progressed, they found that conviction challenged by the emergence of England, under limited monarchy, as the world's leading commercial and naval power.

England (or Britain, as the country was called after its union with Scotland in 1707) prospered as a state in which power was divided between the king and Parliament. This division of political power was guaranteed by a constitution which, though unwritten, was grounded in common law and strengthened by precedent and by particular legal settlements such as those that had followed the restoration of the Stuarts in 1660 and the overthrow of James II in 1688. The Hanoverians George I (1714–1727) and his son George II (1727–1760) were by no means political nonentities. Though George I could not speak English, he could converse comfortably enough with his ministers in French. The first two Georges made a conscientious and generally successful effort to govern within their adopted kingdom. They appointed chief ministers who remained responsible to them for the creation and direction of state policy. Yet because Parliament, after 1688, retained the right to legislate, tax, and spend, its powers were far greater than those of any European *parlement*, estate, or diet. During the reign of the first two Hanoverians, politics was on most occasions little more than a struggle between factions within the Whig party, composed of wealthy—and in many cases newly rich—landed magnates who were making fortunes in an expanding economy based on commercial and agricultural capitalism.

The Tories, because of their previous association with the Stuarts, remained political "outs" for most of the century. To the Whigs, national politics was no longer a matter of clashing principles. Those principles had been settled—to Whig satisfaction—in 1688. Nor was politics a matter of legislating in the national interest. Britain was governed locally, not from the center as in an absolutist state. Aristocrats and landed gentry administered the affairs

> Britain was governed locally, not from the center as in an absolutist state.

The House of Commons. Despite its architectural division into two "sides," the House was composed of men of property whose similar economic interests encouraged them to agree on political fundamentals.

of the particular counties and parishes in which their estates lay, as lords lieutenant, as justices of the peace, as overseers of the poor, unhampered, to a degree unknown on the Continent, by legislation imposed uniformly throughout the kingdom. The quality of local government varied greatly. Some squires were as "allworthy" as Henry Fielding's fictional character of that name in the novel *Tom Jones*. Others cared for little beyond the bottle and the hunt. A French traveler noted in 1747 that the country gentleman was "naturally a very dull animal" whose favorite after-dinner toast was "to all honest fox hunters in Great Britain." These men enforced those general laws that did exist—the Poor Law, game laws—which were drawn in such a way as to leave their administrators wide latitude, a latitude that they exercised in order to enhance the appearance of their own local omnipotence. Thus in Britain there was no attempt to pass a law establishing a statewide system of primary education. Centralizing legislation of that sort, the hallmark of absolutist states, was anathema to the British aristocracy and gentry. They argued that education, if it was to be provided, should be provided at their expense, in village schoolrooms by schoolmasters in their employ. Those instructors would make it their business to teach their pupils not only rudimentary reading, writing, and figuring, but the deferential behavior that bespoke the obligation of the poor to their rich benefactors. As the Church of England catechism had it, they were "to do their duty in that station of life unto which it shall please God to call them."

Politics, then, was neither first principles nor national legislation. It was "interest" and "influence," the weaving of a web of obligations into a political faction powerful enough to secure jobs and favors—a third secretaryship in the foreign office from a minister, an Act of Enclosure from Parliament. The greatest master of this game of politics was Robert Walpole (1676–1745), who was Britain's leading minister from the early 1720s until 1742. Walpole is sometimes called Britain's first prime minister, a not entirely accurate distinction, since officially that position did not exist until the nineteenth century. Prime minister or not, he wielded great political power. He took advantage of the king's frequent absences in Hanover to assert control over the day-to-day governance of the country. He ruled as chief officer of his cabinet, a small group of like-minded politicians whose collective name derived from the room in which they met. In time the cabinet evolved into the policymaking executive arm of the British political system; Britain is governed today by cabinet and Parliament,

the cabinet being composed of leading politicians from the majority party in Parliament.

Walpole was a member of a Norfolk gentry family who had risen to national prominence on the fortune he amassed while serving as paymaster-general to the armed forces during the War of the Spanish Succession. Adept at bribery and corruption, he used his ability to reward his supporters with appointments to ensure himself a loyal political following. By the end of his career, grossly fat and stuffed seemingly with the profits of his years in office, he was being depicted by cartoonists and balladeers as Britain's most accomplished robber. "Little villians must submit to Fate," lamented a typical lampoon, "while great ones do enjoy the world in state." Walpole was no more corrupt, however, than the political process over which he presided. Most seats in Parliament's lower House of Commons were filled by representatives from boroughs that often had no more than two or three dozen electors. Hence it was a relatively simple task to buy votes, either directly or with promises of future favors. Walpole cemented political factions together into an alliance that survived for about twenty years. During that time, he worked to ensure domestic tranquillity by refusing to press ahead with any legislation that might arouse national controversy. He withdrew what was perhaps his most innovative piece of legislation—a scheme that would increase excise taxes and reduce import duties as a means of curbing smugglers—in the face of widespread popular opposition.

Other Whig politicians succeeded Walpole in office in the 1740s and 1750s, but only one, William Pitt, later elevated to the House of Lords as the earl of Chatham, commanded public attention as Walpole had. George III (1760–1820), who came to the throne as a young man in 1760, resented the manner in which he believed his royal predecessors had been treated by the Whig oligarchy. Whether or not, as legend has it, his mother fired his determination with the constant injunction "George, be king!" he began his reign convinced that he must assert his rightful prerogatives. He dismissed Pitt and attempted to impose ministers of his own choosing on Parliament. King and Parliament battled this issue of prerogative throughout the 1760s. In 1770, Lord North, an aristocrat sastisfactory to the king and with a large enough following in the House of Commons to ensure some measure of stability, assumed the position of first minister. His downfall occured a decade later, as a result of his mismanagement of the overseas war that resulted in Britain's loss of its original thirteen North American colonies. A period of

HOW DID THE BALANCE OF POWER SHIFT IN THE EIGHTEENTH CENTURY?

WAR AND DIPLOMACY IN THE EIGHTEENTH CENTURY   623

political shuffling was followed by the king's appointment, at the age of twenty-three, of another William Pitt, Chatham's son, and this Pitt directed Britain's fortunes for the next twenty-five years—a political reign even longer than Walpole's. Although the period between 1760 and 1780 witnessed a struggle between crown (as the king and his political following were called) and Parliament, it was a very minor skirmish compared with the titanic constitutional struggles of the seventeenth century. Britain saw the last of absolutism in 1688. What followed was the mutual adjustment of the two formerly contending parties to a settlement both considered essentially sound.

WAR AND DIPLOMACY IN THE EIGHTEENTH CENTURY

How did the balance of power shift in the eighteenth century?

The history of European diplomacy and warfare after 1715 reveals that the twin goals of international stability and economic expansion remained paramount. The fact that those objectives often conflicted with one another set off further frequent wars, in which the ever-growing standing armies of absolutist Europe were matched against each other, and in which the deciding factor often turned out to be not Continental military strength but British naval power. The major conflict at mid-century, known as the Seven Years' War in Europe and the French and Indian War in North America, reflects the overlapping interests of power balance and commercial gain. In Europe, the primary concern was balance. Whereas in the past France had seemed the major threat, now Prussia loomed—at least in Austrian eyes—as a far more dangerous interloper. Under these circumstances, in 1756 the Austrian foreign minister, Prince Wenzel von Kaunitz, effected the so-called diplomatic revolution, which put an end to the enmity between France and Austria, and resulted in a formidable threat to the Prussia of Frederick the Great. Frederick, meanwhile, was taking steps to protect his flanks. Although anxious not to arouse his French ally, he nevertheless signed a neutrality treaty with the British, who were concerned with securing protection for their sovereign's Hanoverian domains. The French read Freder-

ick's act as a hostile one, and thus fell all the more readily for Kaunitz's offer of an alliance. The French indeed perceived a pressing need for trustworthy European allies, since they were already engaged in an undeclared war with Britain in North America. By mid-1756 Kaunitz could count France, Russia, Sweden, and several German states as likely allies against Prussia. Rather than await retribution from his enemies, Frederick invaded strategic but neutral Saxony and then Austria itself, thus once again playing the role of aggressor.

The configurations in this diplomatic gavotte are undoubtedly confusing. They are historically important, however, because they indicate the way in which the power balance was shifting, and the attempts of European states to respond to those shifts by means of new diplomatic alliances. Prussia and Britain were the volatile elements: Prussia on the Continent, Britain overseas. The war from 1756 to 1763 in Europe centered on Frederick's attempts to prevent the dismemberment of his domain at the hands of the French-Austrian-Russian alliance. Time and again the Prussian army's superiority and Frederick's own military genius frustrated his enemies' attacks. Ultimately, Prussia's survival against these overwhelming odds—"the miracle of the House of Brandenburg"—was ensured by the death of the Tsarina Elizabeth (1741–1762), daughter of Peter the Great, and by the accession of Peter III (1762), whose admiration for Frederick was as great as was his predecessor's hostility. Peter withdrew from the war, returning the conquered provinces of East Prussia and Pomerania to his country's erstwhile enemy. The peace that followed, though it compelled Frederick to relinquish Saxony, recognized his right to retain Silesia, and hence put an end to Austria's hope of one day recapturing that rich prize.

Overseas, battles occurred not only in North America but in the West Indies and in India, where Anglo-French commercial rivalry had resulted in sporadic, fierce fighting since the 1740s. Ultimate victory would go to that power possessing a navy strong enough to keep its supply routes open—that is, to Britain. Superior naval forces resulted in victories along the North American Great Lakes, climaxing in the battle of Québec in 1759 and the eventual surrender of all of Canada to the British. By 1762 the French sugar islands, including Martinique, Grenada, and St. Vincent, were in British hands. Around the globe in India, the defeat of the French in the Battle of Plassey in 1757 and the capture of Pondichéry four years later made Britain the dominant European presence on the subcontinent. In the Treaty of Paris in 1763, which

The Battle of Québec, 1759. Most often remembered for the fact that the British and French commanders, Generals Wolfe and Montcalm, were killed on the bluffs above the St. Lawrence River (the Plains of Abraham), this battle was even more notable for the success of the British amphibious assault, a measure of Britain's naval superiority.

brought the Seven Years' War to an end, France officially surrendered Canada and India to the British, thus affording them an extraordinary field for commercial exploitation.

THE AMERICAN REVOLUTION

The success of the British in North America in the Seven Years' War was itself a major cause of the war that broke out between the mother country and her thirteen North American colonies in 1775. To pay for the larger army the British now deemed necessary to protect their vastly expanded colonial possessions, they imposed unwelcome new taxes on the colonists. The North Americans protested that they were being taxed without representation. The home government responded that, like all British subjects, they were "virtually" if not actually represented by the present members of the House of Commons. Colonists thundered back that the present political system in Britain was so corrupt that no one but the Whig oligarchs could claim that their interests were being looked after.

Meanwhile the British were exacting retribution for rebellious acts on the part of colonists. East India Company tea, shipped to be sold in Boston at prices advantageous to the company, was dumped in Boston Harbor. The port of Boston was thereupon closed, and

representative government in the colony of Massachusetts curtailed. The British garrison clashed with colonial civilians. Colonial "minutemen" formed a counterforce. By the time war broke out in 1775, most Americans were prepared to sever ties with Britain and declare themselves an independent nation, which they did the following year. Fighting continued until 1781 when a British army surrendered to the colonists at Yorktown to the tune of a song entitled "The World Turned Upside Down." The French, followed by Spain and the Netherlands, determined to do everything possible to inhibit the further growth of Britain's colonial empire, had allied themselves with the newly independent United States in 1778. A peace treaty signed in Paris in 1783 recognized the sovereignty of the new state. Though the British lost direct control of their former colonies, they reestablished their transatlantic commercial ties with America in the 1780s. Indeed, the brisk trade in raw cotton between the slave-owning southern states and Britain made possible the industrial revolution in textiles that began in the north of England at this time, and that carried Britain to worldwide preeminence as an economic power in the first half of the nineteenth century. This ultimately profitable arrangement lay in the future. At the time, the victory of the American colonists seemed to contemporary observers to right the world

HOW DID THE BALANCE OF POWER SHIFT IN THE EIGHTEENTH CENTURY?

WAR AND DIPLOMACY IN THE EIGHTEENTH CENTURY   625

Dividing the Royal Spoils. A contemporary cartoon showing the monarchs of Europe at work carving up a hapless Poland.

balance of commercial power, which had swung so far to the side of the British. In this instance, independence seemed designed to restore stability.

THE PARTITIONING OF POLAND

In eastern Europe, however, the very precariousness of Poland's independence posed a threat to stability and to the balance of power. As an independent state, Poland functioned, at least in theory, as a buffer among the major central European powers—Russia, Austria, and Prussia. Poland was the one major central European territory whose landed elite had successfully opposed introduction of absolutist centralization and a consequent curtailment of its "liberties." The result, however, had not been anything like real independence for either the Polish nobility or the country as a whole. Aristocrats were quite prepared to accept bribes from foreign powers in return for their vote in elections for the Polish king. And their continued exercise of their constitutionally guaranteed individual veto

(the *liberum veto*) in the Polish Diet meant that the country remained in a perpetual state of weakness that made it fair game for the land-hungry absolutist potentates who surrounded it.

In 1764 Russia intervened to influence the election of King Stanislaus Poniatowski, an able enough nobleman who had been one of Catherine the Great's lovers. Thereafter Russia continued to meddle in the affairs of Poland—and of Turkey as well—often protecting both countries' Eastern Orthodox Christian minority. When war finally broke out with Turkey in 1769, resulting in large Russian gains in the Balkans, Austria made known its opposition to further Russian expansion, lest it upset the existing balance of power in eastern Europe. In the end Russia was persuaded to acquire territory in Poland instead, by joining Austria and Prussia in a general partition of that country's lands. Though Maria Theresa opposed the dismemberment of Poland, she reluctantly agreed to participate in the partition in order to maintain the balance of power, an attitude that prompted a scornful Frederick the Great to remark, "She weeps, but she takes her share." According to the agreement of 1772, Poland lost about 30 percent of its kingdom and about half of its population.

Following this first partition, the Russians continued to exercise virtual control of Poland. King Stanislaus, however, took advantage of a new Russo-Turkish war in 1788 to press for a more truly independent state with a far stronger executive than had existed previously. A constitution adopted in May 1791 established just that; but this rejuvenated Polish state was to be short lived. In January 1792, the Russo-Turkish war ended, and Catherine the Great pounced. Together the Russians and Prussians took two more enormous bites out of Poland in 1793, destroying the new constitution in the process. A rebellion under the leadership of Thaddeus Kosciuszko, who had fought in America,

CHRONOLOGY

SEVENTEENTH- AND EIGHTEENTH-CENTURY WARS

Glorious Revolution	1688–1689
War of the League of Augsburg	1689–1697
War of the Spanish Succession	1702–1713
Seven Years' War	1756–1763
American Revolution	1775–1783
The Russo-Turkish War	1787–1792

was crushed in 1794 and 1795. A final swallow by Russia, Austria, and Prussia in 1795 left nothing of Poland at all. After this series of partitions of Poland, each of the major powers was a good deal fatter; but on the international scales by which such things were measured, they continued to weigh proportionately the same.

The final devouring of Poland occurred at a time when the Continent was once again engaged in a general war. Yet this conflict was not just another military attempt to resolve customary disputes over commerce or problems of international stability. It was the result of violent revolution that had broken out in France in 1789, that had toppled the Bourbon dynasty there, and that threatened to do the same to other monarchs across Europe. The second and third partitions of Poland were a final bravura declaration of power by monarchs who already feared for their heads. Henceforth, neither foreign nor domestic policy would ever again be dictated as they had been in absolutist Europe by the convictions and determinations of kings and queens alone. Poland disappered as Europe fell to pieces, as customary practice gave way to new and desperate necessity.

CONCLUSION

Though absolutism met its death in the years immediately after 1789, the relevance of its history to that of the modern world is greater than it might appear. First, centralization provided useful precedents to nineteenth-century state builders. Modern standing armies —made up of soldiers or bureaucrats—are institutions whose origins rest in the age of absolutism. Second, absolutism's centripetal force contributed to an economic climate that gave birth to industrial revolution. Factories built to produce matériel, capitalist agricultural policies designed to provide food for burgeoning capital cities, increased taxes that drove peasants to seek work in rural industries: these and other programs pointed to the future. Third, in their constant struggle to curb the privileges of nobility and oligarchy, absolute monarchs played out one more act in a drama that would continue into the nineteenth century. French nobles, Prussian junkers, and Russian boyars all bargained successfully to retain their rights to property and its management while surrendering to some degree their role as governors. But as long as their property rights remained secure, their power was assured. The French Revolution would curb their power for a time, but they were survivors. Their adaptability, whether as agricultural entrepreneurs or as senior servants of the state, ensured their order an important place in the world that lay beyond absolutism.

SELECTED READINGS

Beales, Derek. *Joseph II.* New York, 1987. The standard biography of this "enlightened" Austrian despot.

Blanning, T. C. W., ed. *The Eighteenth Century: Europe 1688–1815.* Oxford and New York, 2000. Chapters by leading experts on political, economic, cultural, and religious developments.

Bossuet, Jacques-Benigne. *Politics Drawn from the Very Words of Holy Scripture.* Edited by Patrick Riley. Cambridge and New York, 1998. The standard English translation.

Brewer, John, and Eckhart Hellmuth, eds. *Rethinking Leviathan: The Eighteenth-Century State in Britain and Germany.* Oxford and New York, 1999. An innovative comparative history of state building in Britain and Prussia. All Brewer's works on eighteenth-century Britain are important.

Burke, Peter. *The Fabrication of Louis XIV.* New Haven, 1992. A study of how Louis XIV constructed a public image of himself through architecture.

Campbell, Peter R. *Louis XIV, 1661–1715.* London, 1993. A reliable recent biography; short, with primary source material and a good bibliography.

Colley, Linda. *In Defiance of Oligarchy: The Tory Party, 1714–1760.* Cambridge and New York, 1982. An influential examination of the political ideology of dissent in eighteenth-century Britain.

———. *Britons: Forging the Nation, 1707–1837.* New Haven, 1992. An illuminating study of the construction of a British (as opposed to English) national identity.

Dukes, Paul. *The Making of Russian Absolutism: 1613–1801,* 2d ed. New York, 1990. An authoritative account of the formation of the Russian state.

Finkelstein, Andrea. *Harmony and the Balance: An Intellectual History of Seventeenth-Century English Economic Thought.* Ann Arbor, 2000. A sophisticated study that traces the links between economic thought and the intellectual history of the period.

Grell, Ole Peter, Jonathan I. Israel, and Nicholas Tyacke. *From Persecution to Toleration: The Glorious Revolution and Religion in England.* Oxford and New York, 1991. An excellent collection of essays, reflecting recent research and approaches.

Harris, Ian. *The Mind of John Locke: A Study of Political Theory in its Intellectual Setting,* rev. ed. Cambridge and New York, 1998. A comprehensive, synthetic overview of Locke's thought that argues for a fundamental consistency between his philosophical and his political ideas.

Hobbes, Thomas. *Leviathan.* Edited by Richard Tuck, 2d ed. Cambridge and New York, 1996. The most recent edition, up-to-date and complete.

Hughes, Lindsey. *Russia in the Age of Peter the Great.* New Haven, 1998. An immensely detailed scholarly account by the leading British authority on Peter's reign.

Ingrao, Charles. *The Habsburg Monarchy, 1618–1815,* 2d ed. Cambridge and New York, 2000. A newly revised and updated edition of a standard work; authoritative and accessible.

Kennedy, Paul M. *The Rise and Fall of the Great Powers: Economic Change and Military Conflict from 1500 to 2000.* New York, 1987. A sweeping view of diplomatic and military history, with implications for the American military build-up during the 1980s.

Kenyon, John P. *Revolution Principles: The Politics of Party, 1689–1720.* Cambridge and New York, 1977. A study of the reception of Locke's ideas in the wake of the Glorious Revolution.

Kishlansky, Mark A. *A Monarchy Transformed: Britain, 1603–1714.* London, 1996. The best survey history of the seventeenth-century British Isles, which takes seriously its claims to be a "British" rather than merely an "English" history.

Koch, H. W. *A History of Prussia.* London, 1978. Still the best account of its subject, and especially of the Great Elector.

Ladurie, Emmanuel le Roy. *The Ancien Régime: A History of France, 1610–1774.* Oxford and Cambridge, Mass., 1996. A reliable survey by an eminent French historian.

Locke, John. *Two Treatises of Government,* rev. ed. Edited by Peter Laslett. Cambridge and New York, 1963. Laslett has revolutionized our understanding of the historical and ideological context of Locke's political writings.

Luvaas, Jay, ed. and trans. *Frederick the Great on the Art of War.* New York, 1966. A selection from the Prussian king's voluminous works on war and politics.

The Memoirs of Catherine the Great. Many editions. A fascinating autobiographical account.

Monod, Paul K. *The Power of Kings: Monarchy and Religion in Europe, 1589–1715.* New Haven, 1999. A wide-ranging study of the seventeenth century's declining confidence in the divinity of kings.

Quataert, Donald. *The Ottoman Empire, 1700–1922.* Cambridge and New York, 2000. Well balanced, up-to-date, and intended to be read by students.

Riasanovsky, Nicholas V. *A History of Russia,* 6th ed. Oxford and New York, 1999. Far and away the best single-volume textbook on Russian history: balanced, comprehensive, intelligent, and with full bibliographies.

Saint-Simon, Louis. *Historical Memoirs.* Many editions. The classic source for life at the court of Louis XIV.

Western, J. R. *Monarchy and Revolution: The English State in the 1680s.* London, 1972. Still in many ways the best account of the ideological significance of the Glorious Revolution as a check to the absolutist pretensions of Charles II and James II.

RULERS OF PRINCIPAL STATES

THE CAROLINGIAN DYNASTY

Pepin of Heristal, Mayor of the Palace, 687–714
Charles Martel, Mayor of the Palace, 715–741
Pepin III, Mayor of the Palace, 741–751; King, 751–768
Charlemagne, King, 768–814; Emperor, 800–814
Louis the Pious, Emperor, 814–840

MIDDLE KINGDOMS
Lothair, Emperor, 840–855
Louis (Italy), Emperor, 855–875
Charles (Provence), King, 855–863
Lothair II (Lorraine), King, 855–869

WEST FRANCIA
Charles the Bald, King, 840–877; Emperor, 875–877
Louis II, King, 877–879
Louis III, King, 879–882
Carloman, King, 879–884

EAST FRANCIA
Ludwig, King, 840–876
Carloman, King, 876–880
Ludwig, King, 876–882
Charles the Fat, Emperor, 876–887

HOLY ROMAN EMPERORS

SAXON DYNASTY
Otto I, 962–973
Otto II, 973–983
Otto III, 983–1002
Henry II, 1002–1024

FRANCONIAN DYNASTY
Conrad II, 1024–1039
Henry III, 1039–1056
Henry IV, 1056–1106
Henry V, 1106–1125
Lothair II (Saxony), 1125–1137

HOHENSTAUFEN DYNASTY
Conrad III, 1138–1152
Frederick I (Barbarossa), 1152–1190
Henry VI, 1190–1197
Philip of Swabia, 1198–1208 } Rivals
Otto IV (Welf), 1198–1215
Frederick II, 1220–1250
Conrad IV, 1250–1254

INTERREGNUM, 1254–1273

EMPERORS FROM VARIOUS DYNASTIES
Rudolf I (Habsburg), 1273–1291
Adolf (Nassau), 1292–1298
Albert I (Habsburg), 1298–1308
Henry VII (Luxemburg), 1308–1313
Ludwig IV (Wittelsbach), 1314–1347
Charles IV (Luxemburg), 1347–1378
Wenceslas (Luxemburg), 1378–1400
Rupert (Wittelsbach), 1400–1410
Sigismund (Luxemburg), 1410–1437

HABSBURG DYNASTY
Albert II, 1438–1439
Frederick III, 1440–1493
Maximilian I, 1493–1519
Charles V, 1519–1556
Ferdinand I, 1556–1564
Maximilian II, 1564–1576
Rudolf II, 1576–1612

Matthias, 1612–1619
Ferdinand II, 1619–1637
Ferdinand III, 1637–1657
Leopold I, 1658–1705
Joseph I, 1705–1711
Charles VI, 1711–1740

Charles VII (not a Habsburg), 1742–1745
Francis I, 1745–1765
Joseph II, 1765–1790
Leopold II, 1790–1792
Francis II, 1792–1806

RULERS OF FRANCE FROM HUGH CAPET

CAPETIAN DYNASTY
Hugh Capet, 987–996
Robert II, 996–1031
Henry I, 1031–1060
Philip I, 1060–1108
Louis VI, 1108–1137
Louis VII, 1137–1180
Philip II (Augustus), 1180–1223
Louis VIII, 1223–1226
Louis IX (St. Louis), 1226–1270
Philip III, 1270–1285
Philip IV, 1285–1314
Louis X, 1314–1316
Philip V, 1316–1322
Charles IV, 1322–1328

VALOIS DYNASTY
Philip VI, 1328–1350
John, 1350–1364
Charles V, 1364–1380
Charles VI, 1380–1422
Charles VII, 1422–1461
Louis XI, 1461–1483
Charles VIII, 1483–1498
Louis XII, 1498–1515
Francis I, 1515–1547

Henry II, 1547–1559
Francis II, 1559–1560
Charles IX, 1560–1574
Henry III, 1574–1589

BOURBON DYNASTY
Henry IV, 1589–1610
Louis XIII, 1610–1643
Louis XIV, 1643–1715
Louis XV, 1715–1774
Louis XVI, 1774–1792

AFTER 1792
First Republic, 1792–1799
Napoleon Bonaparte, First Consul, 1799–1804
Napoleon I, Emperor, 1804–1814
Louis XVIII (Bourbon dynasty), 1814–1824
Charles X (Bourbon dynasty), 1824–1830
Louis Philippe, 1830–1848
Second Republic, 1848–1852
Napoleon III, Emperor, 1852–1870
Third Republic, 1870–1940
Péain regime, 1940–1944
Provisional government, 1944–1946
Fourth Republic, 1946–1958
Fifth Republic, 1958–

RULERS OF ENGLAND

ANGLO-SAXON DYNASTY
Alfred the Great, 871–899
Edward the Elder, 899–924
Ethelstan, 924–939
Edmund I, 939–946
Edred, 946–955
Edwy, 955–959
Edgar, 959–975
Edward the Martyr, 975–978
Ethelred the Unready, 978–1016

Canute, 1016–1035 (Danish Nationality)
Harold I, 1035–1040
Hardicanute, 1040–1042
Edward the Confessor, 1042–1066
Harold II, 1066

HOUSE OF NORMANDY
William I (the Conqueror), 1066–1087
William II, 1087–1100

Henry I, 1100–1135
Stephen, 1135–1154

HOUSE OF PLANTAGENET
Henry II, 1154–1189
Richard I, 1189–1199
John, 1199–1216
Henry III, 1216–1272
Edward I, 1272–1307
Edward II, 1307–1327
Edward III, 1327–1377
Richard II, 1377–1399

HOUSE OF LANCASTER
Henry IV, 1399–1413
HenryV, 1413–1422
Henry VI, 1422–1461

HOUSE OF YORK
Edward IV, 1461–1483
Edward V, 1483
Richard III, 1483–1485

HOUSE OF TUDOR
Henry VII, 1485–1509
Henry VIII, 1509–1547
Edward VI, 1547–1553
Mary, 1553–1558
Elizabeth I, 1558–1603

HOUSE OF STUART
James I, 1603–1625
Charles I, 1625–1649

COMMONWEALTH AND PROTECTORATE, 1649–1659

HOUSE OF STUART RESTORED
Charles II, 1660–1685
James II, 1685–1688
William III and Mary II, 1689–1694
William III alone, 1694–1702
Anne, 1702–1714

HOUSE OF HANOVER
George I, 1714–1727
George II, 1727–1760
George III, 1760–1820
George IV, 1820–1830
William IV, 1830–1837
Victoria, 1837–1901

HOUSE OF SAXE-COBURG-GOTHA
Edward VII, 1901–1910
GeorgeV, 1910–1917

HOUSE OF WINDSOR
George V, 1917–1936
Edward VIII, 1936
George VI, 1936–1952
Elizabeth II, 1952–

RULERS OF AUSTRIA AND AUSTRIA-HUNGARY

*Maximilian I (Archduke), 1493–1519
*Charles V, 1519–1556
*Ferdinand I, 1556–1564
*Maximilian II, 1564–1576
*Rudolf II, 1576–1612
*Matthias, 1612–1619
*Ferdinand II, 1619–1637
*Ferdinand III, 1637–1657
*Leopold I, 1658–1705
*Joseph I, 1705–1711
*Charles VI, 1711–1740
Maria Theresa, 1740–1780

*also bore title of Holy Roman Emperor

*Joseph II, 1780–1790
*Leopold II, 1790–1792
*Francis II, 1792–1835 (Emperor of Austria as Francis I after 1804)
Ferdinand I, 1835–1848
Francis Joseph, 1848–1916 (after 1867 Emperor of Austria and King of Hungary)
Charles I, 1916–1918 (Emperor of Austria and King of Hungary)
Republic of Austria, 1918–1938 (dictatorship after 1934)
Republic restored, under Allied occupation, 1945–1956
Free Republic, 1956–

RULERS OF PRUSSIA AND GERMANY

*Frederick I, 1701–1713
*Frederick William I, 1713–1740
*Frederick II (the Great), 1740–1786
*Frederick William II, 1786–1797
*Frederick William III,1797–1840
*Frederick William IV, 1840–1861
*William I, 1861–1888 (German Emperor after 1871)
Frederick III, 1888

*Kings of Prussia

*William II, 1888–1918
Weimar Republic, 1918–1933
Third Reich (Nazi Dictatorship), 1933–1945
Allied occupation, 1945–1952
Division into Federal Republic of Germany in west and
    German Democratic Republic in east, 1949–1991
Federal Republic of Germany (united), 1991–

RULERS OF RUSSIA

Ivan III, 1462–1505
Vasily III, 1505–1533
Ivan IV, 1533–1584
Theodore I, 1534–1598
Boris Godunov, 1598–1605
Theodore II,1605
Vasily IV, 1606–1610
Michael, 1613–1645
Alexius, 1645–1676
Theodore III, 1676–1682
Ivan V and Peter I, 1682–1689
Peter I (the Great), 1689–1725
Catherine I, 1725–1727
Peter II, 1727–1730

Anna, 1730–1740
Ivan VI, 1740–1741
Ellzabeth, 1741–1762
Peter III, 1762
Catherine II (the Great), 1762–1796
Paul, 1796–1801
Alexander I,1801–1825
Nicholas I, 1825–1855
Alexander II,1855–1881
Alexander III, 1881–1894
Nicholas II, 1894–1917
Soviet Republic, 1917–1991
Russian Federation, 1991–

RULERS OF SPAIN

Ferdinand {
    and Isabella, 1479–1504
    and Philip I, 1504–1506
    and Charles I, 1506–1516
}
Charles I (Holy Roman Emperor Charles V), 1516–1556
Philip II, 1556–1598
Philip III, 1598–1621
Philip IV, 1621–1665
Charles II, 1665–1700
Philip V, 1700–1746
Ferdinand VI, 1746–1759
Charles III, 1759–1788
Charles IV, 1788–1808

Ferdinand VII, 1808
Joscph Bonapartc, 1808–1813
Ferdinand VII (restored), 1814–1833
Isabella II, 1833–1868
Republic, 1868–1870
Amadeo, 1870–1873
Republic, 1873–1874
Alfonso XII, 1874–1885
Alfonso XIII, 1886–1931
Republic, 1931–1939
Fascist Dictatorship, 1939–1975
Juan Carlos I, 1975–

RULERS OF ITALY

Victor Emmanuel II, 1861–1878
Humbert I, 1878–1900
Victor Emmanuel III, 1900–1946

Fascist Dictatorship, 1922-1943 (maintained in northern Italy until 1945)
Humbert II, May 9–June 13, 1946
Republic, 1946–

PROMINENT POPES

Silvester I, 314–335
Leo I, 440–461
Gelasius I, 492–496
Gregory I, 590–604
Nicholas I, 858–867
Silvester II, 999–1003
Leo IX, 1049–1054
Nicholas II, 1058–1061
Gregory VII, 1073–1085
Urban II, 1088–1099
Paschal II, 1099–1118
Alexander III, 1159–1181
Innocent III, 1198–1216
Gregory IX, 1227–1241
Innocent IV, 1243–1254
Boniface VIII, 1294–1303
John XXII, 1316–1334
Nicholas V, 1447–1455
Pius II, 1458–1464

Alexander VI, 1492–1503
Julius II, 1503–1513
Leo X, 1513–1521
Paul III, 1534–1549
Paul IV, 1555–1559
Sixtus V, 1585–1590
Urban VIII, 1623–1644
Gregory XVI, 1831–1846
Pius IX, 1846–1878
Leo XIII, 1878–1903
Pius X, 1903–1914
Benedict XV, 1914–1922
Pius XI, 1922–1939
Pius XII, 1939–1958
John XXIII, 1958–1963
Paul VI, 1963–1978
John Paul I, 1978
John Paul II, 1978–

TEXT CREDITS

Chapter 1: **23** (top): from *The Epic of Gilgamesh*. Copyright 1997, Bolchazy-Carducci Publishers. **35:** from *The Egyptian Book of the Dead*. Copyright 1967, Dover Books. **40:** from *Readings in Ancient History: Thought and Experience from Gilgamesh to St. Augustine*. Copyright 1995, Houghton Mifflin.

Chapter 2: **53:** from *Law: A Treasury of Art and Literature*. Copyright 1990, Beaux Arts Editions. **66:** from *History and the Homeric Iliad*. Copyright 1959, University of California Press. **76** (top): from *Ancient Near Eastern Texts Relating to the Bible* (3rd Edition). Copyright 1969, Princeton University Press.

Chapter 3: **87:** from *Ancient Near Eastern Texts Relating to the Bible* (3rd Edition). Copyright 1969, Princeton University Press. **99:** from *Ancient Records of Assyria and Babylonia*. Copyright 1926-1927, University of Chicago Press.

Chapter 4: **116:** from *Iliad*. Copyright 1990, Penguin Books. **124:** from *Herodotus*. Copyright 1987, University of Chicago Press. **145:** from *The Clouds*. Copyright 1973, Penguin Books. **146:** from *The Landmark Thucydides*. Copyright 1995, Landmark Press.

Chapter 5: **159** (top): from *Isocrates*. Copyright 1995, Harvard University Press. **159** (bottom): from *Demosthenes*. Copyright 1930, Harvard University Press. **171:** from *The Idylls of Theocritis*. Copyright 1988, Carcanet.

Chapter 6: **187:** from *The Early History of Rome*. Copyright 1960, Penguin Books. **197:** from *Life of Lucullus*. Copyright 1992, Modern Library. **204:** from *Roman Civilization, Sourcebook II: The Empire*. Copyright 1966, Harper and Row. **205:** from *Tacitus: The Annals of Imperial Rome*. Copyright 1989, Penguin Books. **209:** from *Juvenal: The Sixteen Satires*. Copyright 1974, Penguin Books.

Chapter 7: **238:** from *Didascalia Apostolorum Corpus Scriptorum Christianorum Orientalium*. Copyright 1979, Peters. **239:** from *Western Societies: A Documentary History*. Copyright 1984, Knopf **243:** from *Sidonius, Poems and Letters*. Copyright 1980, Harvard University Press.

Chapter 8: **274:** from *The Jews of Arab Lands: A History and Source Book*. Copyright 1979, Philadelphia Jewish Publication Society. **293:** from *The Reign of Charlemagne*. Copyright 1975, Edward Arnold.

Chapter 9: **315:** from *Byzantium: Church, Society, and Civilization Seen through Contemporary Eyes*. Copyright 1984, University of Chicago Press. **317:** from *Christianity, Social Tolerance, and Homosexuality*. Copyright 1980, University of Chicago Press. **320:** from *Chronicles of the Crusades*, Copyright 1963, Penguin Books. **340:** from *The Chronicle of Salimbene de Adam*. Copyright 1986, Medieval and Renaissance Texts and Studies.

Chapter 10: **348:** from *Readings in Medieval History*. Copyright 1997, Broadview Press. **360:** from *The Birth of Popular Heresy*. Copyright 1975, Edward Arnold Publishers. **373:** from *The Wandering Scholars*. Copyright 1934, Constable.

Chapter 11: **390:** from *Froissart: Chronicles*. Copyright 1968, Penguin Books. **397:** from *The Council of Constance*. Copyright 1962, Columbia University Press. **398:** from *Execrabilis: Defensorum Obedientae et alia Documenta*. Copyright 1968, Harvard University Press. **404:** from *Women and Writing in Medieval Europe*. Copyright 1995, Routledge.

Chapter 12: **431:** from *The Travels of Marco Polo*. Copyright 1926, Random House. **435:** from *Memoirs of a Janissary*. Copyright 1975, Michigan Slavic Publications. **443:** from *Mandeville's Travels*. Copyright 1967, Clarendon Press. **448:** from *The Compendium and Description of the West Indies*. Copyright 1968, Smithsonian Institution Press.

Chapter 13: **456** (middle): from *University of Chicago Readings in Western Civilizations*. Copyright 1986, University of Chicago Press. **460:** from *The Family in Renaissance Florence*. Copyright 1969, University of South Carolina Press. **463:** from *The Prince*. Copyright 1947, AHM Publishing Corporation.

Chapter 14: **495:** from *Selections from Conrad Celtis*. Copyright 1948, Cambridge University Press. **510:** from *What Luther Says*. Copyright 1959, Concordia Publishing House. **513:** from *Documents of the Christian Church*. Copyright 1967, Oxford University Press.

Chapter 15: **528:** from *Simplicissimus*. Copyright 1995, Daedalus. **532:** from *The Political Testament of Cardinal Richelieu*. Copyright 1961, University of Wisconsin Press. **539:** from *Montaigne: Selections from the Essays*. Copyright 1971, AHM Publishing Corporation. **541** (top): from *Divine Right and Democracy: An Anthology of Political Writing in Stuart England*. Copyright 1986, Viking Penguin. **541** (bottom): from *The English Civil War: A Fight for Lawful Government*. Copyright 1967, Random House.

Chapter 16: **559:** from *The Ancien Regime: French Society, 1600–1750*. Copyright 1973, Widenfeld and Nelson. **569:** from *The Renaissance: University of Chicago Readings in Western Civilization*. Copyright 1995,

ILLUSTRATION CREDITS

Maps on pp ii–iii and iv–v: National Geographic Society Image Collection

Part I

2–3: Giraudon/Art Resource

Chapter 1: 6: The Louvre, Paris. Photo: Giraudon/Art Resource, NY; 9 (**top right**): Courtesy Dept. of Library Services, American Museum of Natural History; 9 (**top left**): Ralph Morse, Life Magazine © Time Inc.; 9 (**bottom**): Courtesy Dept. of Library Services, American Museum of Natural History; 12: Courtesy of The Oriental Institute of the University of Chicago; 13: Hirmer Fotoarchiv; 22 (**top**): Hirmer Fotoarchiv; 22 (**bottom**): Courtesy of the Oriental Institute of The University of Chicago; 24: from *The Origins of War*, by Arthur Ferrill, published by Thames and Hudson, Inc., New York; 25 (**bottom right**): The British Museum; 26 (**bottom left**): Iraq Museum, Baghdad, Iraq. Photo: Scala/Art Resource, NY; 26 (**bottom right**): University of Pennsylvania Museum; 28: Hirmer Fotoarchiv; 23, 29, 35, 40: Bettman/Corbis; 33: from *The Origins of War*, by Arthur Ferrill, published by Thames and Hudson, Inc., New York; 34 (**top**): The Metropolitan Museum of Art, Rogers Fund, 1942. (42.2.3) Photograph © by The Metropolitan Museum of Art; 34 (**bottom**): Excavations of the Metropolitan Museum of Art, 1929; Rogers Fund, 1930. (30.3.31) Photograph © 1978 The Metropolitan Museum of Art; 38: The Louvre, Paris. Photo: Giraudon/Art Resource, NY; 39 (**top**): Roger Wood/Corbis; 39 (**bottom**): Charles & Josette Lenars/Corbis; 41: Harvard-Museum Expedition/Courtesy, Museum of Fine Arts, Boston

Chapter 2: 46: Egyptian expedition of The Metropolitan Museum of Art, Rogers Fund, 1930 (30.4.77); 51: The Nelson-Atkins Museum of Art, Kansas City, Missouri (Purchase: Nelson Trust); 52: Hirmer Fotoarchiv; 53, 67, 76: Giraudon/Art Resource; 54: The Louvre, Paris. Photo: Herve Lewandowski, Réunion des Musées Nationaux/Art Resource, NY; 58: British Museum, London, Great Britain; 60: The Nelson Gallery Foundation, The Nelson-Atkins Museum of Art; 63: Erich Lessing/Art Resource; 64 (**top**): Boltin Picture Library; 64 (**bottom**): Courtesy, Museum of Fine Arts, Boston; 65: Erich Lessing/Art Resource, NY; 66 (**top**): Staatliche Museen zu Berlin—Preußischer Kulturbesitz, Agyptisches Museum; 66 (**bottom**): Boltin Picture Library; 69: Wolfgang Kaehler/Corbis; 70: Gian Berto Vanni/Corbis; 71: National Museum of Greece; 72 (**top**): Scala/Art Resource, NY; 72 (**bottom**): Boltin Picture Library; 73 (**top**): Martin A. Ryerson Collection, 1922.4914. Photograph © 1997, The Art Institute of Chicago. All rights reserved; 73 (**bottom**): Alison Frantz

Chapter 3: 85: Courtesy of The Oriental Institute of The University of Chicago; 87, 90, 95, 99, 102: Courtesy of The Oriental In-

stitute of The University of Chicago; 96: British Museum, London, Great Britain photo: Erich Lessing/Art Resource, NY; 97 (**right**): Hirmer Fotoarchiv; 80, 100 (**top**): Gianni Dagli Orti/Corbis; 100 (**bottom**): Staatliche Museen zu Berlin—Preußischer Kulturbesitz, Vorderasiatisches Museum; 101: American Numismatic Society; 106: The Metropolitan Museum of Art, Fletcher Fund, 1954. (54.3.3) Photograph © 1982 The Metropolitan Museum of Art

Part II

112–113: Scala/Art Resource

Chapter 4: 116: Scala/Art Resource; 118: Art Resource, NY; 120, 125, 128, 148: Hirmer Fotoarchiv; 122: Acropolis Museum; 126: Réunion des Musées Nationaux/Art Resource, NY; 127: Staatliche Museen zu Berlin—Bildarchiv Preußisher Kulturbesitz: Antikensammlung; 130: American School of Classical Studies at Athens: Agora Excavations; 131: Naples National Museum, Photo: Gianni Dagli Orti/Corbis; 136: Museo Archeologico Nazionale, Naples, Italy. Photo: Scala/Art Resource, NY; 137: © Photo RMN, Paris; 138: Scala/Art Resource; 139: George Brockway/Warder Collection, NY; 140: The National Museum, Copenhagen, Dept. of Classical and Near Eastern Antiquities; 141 (**left**): Hartwig Koppermann; 141 (**center**): © Photo RMN, Paris; 141 (**right**): Nimatallah/Art Resource, NY; 142: Museo Nazionale Romano; 143: Réunion des Musées Nationaux/Art Resource, NY; 146: Photo: Paul Lipke/Trireme Trust, Montague, MA; 150: Erich Lessing/Art Resource, NY; 151: Deautschen Archaeologischen Instituts

Chapter 5: 154, 177 (**bottom**): Nimatallah/Art Resource, NY; 158 (**left**): The Metropolitan Museum of Art, Rogers Fund, 1923. (23.160.20) Photograph © by The Metropolitan Museum of Art; 158 (**right**): The Metropolitan Museum of Art, H. O. Havemeyer Collection, Bequest of Mrs. H. O. Havemeyer, 1929. (29.100.377) Photograph © by The Metropolitan Museum of Art; 159: Scala/Art Resource, NY; 160: Kunsthistorisches Museum, Vienna; 162: Gianni Dagli Orti/Corbis; 163, 169, 175, 177 (**top**): Scala/Art Resource, NY; 166: Hirmer Fotoarchiv; 168 (**top**): Hirmer Fotoarchiv; 168 (**bottom**): Gift of William F. Dunham, 1920.725. Photograph © 1997, The Art Institute of Chicago. All rights reserved; 174: Alinari/Art Resource, NY; 176 (**top left**): Erdmut Lerner; 176 (**top right**): The Metropolitan Museum of Art, Rogers Fund, 1909. (09.39) Photograph © 1977 The Metropolitan Museum of Art; 176 (**bottom**): University Prints; 177 (**center right**): Giraudon/Art Resource, NY

Chapter 6: 182: Scala/Art Resource; 185 (**top**): Villa Giulia Museum, Rome/The Warder Collection, NY; 185 (**bottom**): Musei Capitolini, Rome, Italy; Photo: Scala/Art Resource, NY; 187, 197,

501, 510, 513: The Royal Collection © Her Majesty Queen Elizabeth II; 496 (left): Museo del Prado, Madrid; 496 (right): Bayerische Staatsgemäldesammlungen/Alte Pinakothek, Munich; 497 (left): Staatliche Museen zu Berlin—Preußischer Kulturbesitz, Kupferstichkabinett; 497 (right): By permission of the British Library; 499: National Trust/Art Resource, NY; 502: John R. Freeman & Co.; 505: The Warder Collection, NY; 506 (top): Erich Lessing/Art Resource, NY; 506 (bottom): Inv. nr. HB 17566, Germanisches Nationalmuseum, Nürnberg; 507 (left): Giraudon/Art Resource, NY; 507 (right): The Warder Collection, NY; 512: Kunsthistorisches Museum, Vienna

Chapter 15: 518, 548 (top): Erich Lessing/Art Resource; 525: The New York Public Library: Astor, Lenox, and Tilden Foundations; 528, 532, 539, 541, 545: The Metropolitan Museum of Art, H. O. Havemeyer Collection, Bequest of Mrs. H. O. Havemeyer, 1929. (29.100.6) Photograph © 1992 The Metropolitan Museum of Art; 534 (top): By courtesy of the National Portrait Gallery, London; 534 (bottom): Photo Bulloz, Coll. Privée; 537: Bibliothèque Royale Albert I, Brussels; 544: The Metropolitan Museum of Art, The H. O. Havemeyer Collection, Bequest of Mrs. H. O. Havemeyer, 1929. (29.100.16) Photograph © 1990 The Metropolitan Museum of Art; 546 (top): Scala/Art Resource, NY; 546 (bottom): Museo del Prado, Madrid; 547: The Metropolitan Museum of Art, Rogers Fund, 1919. (19.164) Photograph © The Metropolitan Museum of Art; 548 (bottom): Nimatallah/Art Resource, NY; 548 (top left): Erich Lessing/Art Resource, NY; 549: The Metropolitan Museum of Art, Purchase, special contributions and funds given or bequeathed by friends of the Museum, 1961. (61.198) Photograph © The Metropolitan Museum of Art; 550 (left): © English Heritage Photo Library; 550 (right): Gift of Mr. and Mrs. Robert Woods Bliss, © 1997 Board of Trustees, National Gallery of Art, Washington, DC

Part V
552–553: Giraudon/Art Resource

Chapter 16: 556, 577: Victoria and Albert Museum, London/Art Resource, NY; 558 (left): Negativ aus dem Bildarchiv der Österreicheschen Nationalbibliothek, Wien; 558 (right): Inv. nr. HB 13157, Germanisches Nationalmuseum, Nürnberg; 559, 569, 579, 582, 588: Erich Lessing/Art Resource, NY; 560: Bridgeman Art Library; 564 (top): Bridgeman Art Library; 564 (bottom): Staatliche Museen zu Berlin—Preußischer Kulturbesitz, Gemäldgalerie; 566: Bridgeman Art Library; 571 (top): Giraudon/Art Resource, NY; 571 (bottom): cliché Bibliothèque Nationale de France, Paris; 575: John R. Freeman & Co; 578: The Warder Collection, NY; 581: Roger-Viollet; 583: Giraudon/Art Resource, NY; 585: Courtesy of the British Museum; 586: The New York Public Library: Astor, Lenox, and Tilden Foundations; 589: cliché Bibliothèque Nationale de France, Paris

Chapter 17: 592, 595: Erich Lessing/Art Resource, NY; 596, 601, 605, 611: Giraudon/Art Resource; 598: Giraudon/Art Resource, NY; 600: The Metropolitan Museum of Art, Gift of the Wildenstein Foundation, Inc., 1951. (51.34) Photograph © 1979 The Metropolitan Museum of Art; 602: by Friedrich Wilhelm Kurfürst von Brandenburg/Ullstein; 604: Erich Lessing/Art Resource, NY; 606: By permission of the British Library; 607: Society for Cultural Relations with the Soviet Union; 609: both: By courtesy of The National Portrait Gallery, London; 612: Bridgeman Art Library; 617: cliché Bibliothèque Nationale de France, Paris; 618: Erich Lessing/Art Resource, NY; 619: Erich Lessing/Art Resource, NY; 620: Giraudon/Art Resource, NY; 621: By courtesy of the National Portrait Gallery, London; 624: Courtesy of the Director, National Army Museum, London; 625: Giraudon/Art Resource, NY.

Every effort has been made to contact the copyright holders of the selections. Any corrections should be forwarded to W. W. Norton & Company, Inc., 500 Fifth Avenue, New York, NY 10110.

INDEX

The sounds represented by the diacritical marks used in this Index are illustrated by the following common words:

āle   ēve   īce   ōld   ūse

ăt   ĕnd   ĭll   ŏf   ŭs   fŏŏt

câre

ärm

Vowels that have no diacritical marks are to be "neutral," for example: Aegean = à-je'an, common = kŏm' on, Alcaeus = ăl-sē' us. The combinations *ou* and *oi* are pronounced as in "out" and "oil."